Summer Heat – Love on Fire
16 Romance novels by 16 award winning and best-selling authors

Caridad Pineiro

Nina Bruhns

Rebecca York

Jennifer Lowery

Taylor Lee

Traci Hall

Stephanie Queen

Kathy Ivan

Jackie Ivie

Michele Hauf

Rachelle Ayala

Katy Walters

Melissa Keir

Dani Haviland

Jacquie Biggar

Angelique Armae

Copyright 2016
Chill Out! Books
Individual copyrights by individual authors also apply

ISBN 978-0692702550

Table of Contents

UNDER THE BOARDWALK

Caridad Pineiro

NY Times and USA Today Bestseller

A passionate night under the boardwalk brought them together, but can Chase and Natalie rekindle that lost love in just one night?

Chapter 1

The brass key hung heavy in Chase Smith's pocket, the weight a reminder of what had been in the past and what still might be possible for the future.

Would Natalie remember that this was the place where it had all started? Chase wondered as he left the quaint inn in Ocean Grove.

Of course Natalie will remember, the little voice in his head reminded. She wasn't the one who forgot things like that or got so wrapped up in work that they'd let their personal life go to shit.

She wasn't the one who'd become a boring uptight prick who'd forgotten how to have fun, chastised the nasty little voice in his head.

Chase's gut clenched as reality sank its painful hooks deep. He took a deep breath and told himself to relax.

Tonight was supposed to be about having fun. Tonight was supposed to be about trying to recapture what it was that had brought him together with his wife.

Soon to be ex-wife if they couldn't find a way back to the couple they'd once been.

He rushed down Main Avenue, heading toward the Ocean Grove boardwalk. As he neared it, the scents and sounds of the Jersey Shore washed over him, cleansing some of the tension from his body.

It was always like that here, that sense of peace and calm and rebirth.

He hurried to the metal railing at the edge of the boardwalk and leaned against it, savoring the final remnants of the early fall day. The susurrus of the waves soothed as a refreshing ocean breeze blew inland.

The temperature had been in the high sixties earlier; the day sunny enough for some post-Labor Day beachgoers. Far less people than the crowds that packed the beaches during the height of summer, but as he glanced up and down the boardwalk, there was still a good amount of activity.

He lingered for a few minutes more, gathering his courage. Watching as dusk arrived and the last rays of the sun bathed the ocean with touches of gold.

Glancing at his watch, he realized he had to get going and do the half mile or so walk to Asbury Park to meet Natalie.

He turned and headed north toward the end of Ocean Grove, fingers jammed into the pockets of the black skinny jeans he'd bought earlier that day along with the T-shirt and hoodie. It wasn't what he'd originally planned to wear, but at the last minute, he'd decided that the button down shirt and khakis were a too visual reminder of the man he'd become instead of the man he used to be.

Luckily there was a surf and skate shop right on Main Avenue that had a nice selection of clothes that were just what he needed to discard his uptight self.

He quickened his pace, his long strides eating up the distance to the Casino along the boardwalk and the start of Asbury Park. Passing the Boardwalk Pavilion where Sunday services were held, he glanced at the Great Auditorium at the far end of Ocean Pathway. The bright white cross gleamed in the growing darkness and for a moment he felt a little guilty because what he hoped for tonight was far from pure or chaste.

What he hoped was that he and Natalie could rekindle the passion they'd once shared and find their way back to a marriage that had been filled with so much love and possibilities.

As he neared the Casino, the sounds of a lone guitar player echoed in the large metal shell of the building. The man stood playing as people strolled by, coming and going from one town to the other.

The man he had become would just pass the man by, but tonight was about being more like his old self. More open and accepting.

2

Chase reached into his jeans pocket, pulled out a dollar, and tossed it into the man's guitar case.

At the far entrance to the Casino, the start of the Asbury Park boardwalk loomed large and he knew that once he stepped out onto it, there was no turning back from tonight.

But he didn't want to turn back. He wanted Natalie back in his life. Back in his bed.

He pushed ahead, his gaze skipping from face-to-face in the crowd until it seemed to part before him like the Red Sea and there she was, standing by the railing.

After a month apart, he drank in her beauty like a thirsty man at a desert oasis.

Her cream-colored dress hugged her sexy curves, but the skirt was loose and billowing in the ocean breeze. Her shoulder length caramel-colored hair was loose and wafted around her face. As he watched, she tilted her head back, eyes closed, and a peaceful smile crept over her lush lips.

She was so lovely. So beautiful. Warmth pooled in his gut at the sight of her just as it had nearly a decade earlier, when he'd first seen her on this very same boardwalk.

He took a deep breath, fighting back desire and fear, and walked toward her.

***

Natalie sensed his presence and as she dipped her head and opened her eyes, she caught sight of him from the corner of her eye.

Or at least she thought it was him and resisted the urge to do a double take. When he reached her side, she finally allowed herself to face him and savored every inch of him.

Being a desk jockey hadn't added a pound to the long lean body she'd lusted over when she'd first seen him that fateful summer. And the tight black jeans and T-shirt accentuated every sculpted muscle far better than his usual button-down style.

"Chase. You look . . . different," she said, a hint of awkward in her tone as she leaned forward and skimmed a restrained kiss on his cheek.

"I'll take that as a compliment," Chase said, an uncertain smile on his lips, and took hold of her hand.

"You look stunning. Is this dress from your new line?" he asked and applied gentle pressure to guide her into a little twirl.

Natalie fought back the pleasure at his words and at the intensity in his cerulean gaze. "Actually, I made it just for tonight. I'm glad you like it."

The blue of his eyes darkened to almost midnight as he raked his gaze up and down her body hungrily.

"I like . . . *a lot*," he said, the tones of his voice low and strumming alive desire in her core. Maybe if they still shared passion, just maybe, they could find a way back to the couple they once had been.

Ignoring the heat flaring across her cheeks, she said, "Any thoughts on where to eat?"

He shrugged broad shoulders. "I was thinking we could decide together."

She appreciated the response that said he might be loosening up his got-to-be-in-control mindset. Looking down the boardwalk, she mentally ran through the various restaurants along the strip, finally settling for one that she thought Chase would like.

"How about Alex's?" she asked. The supper club had great food and music, and an upscale vibe.

He arched a dark brow. "Really? Is that where you'd *really* like to go?"

In truth, it wouldn't have been her first choice since she liked simpler and not as formal.

She shot another quick look along the boardwalk and hated the uncertainty between them, as if they were two strangers instead of husband and wife. But she knew the reason for his question: In the last year or so, as they'd drifted apart, she'd repeatedly deferred to him until she'd lost herself and had to leave to find her own footing again.

She decided to accept his peace offering. "I'd like to go to Porta. I know it might be a little crowded . . ."

"Porta it is, Nat. I love pizza," he said, twined his fingers with hers and gave a reassuring squeeze.

3

The weight of his hand was familiar and comforting, but it also brought back memories of his touch against her body. Of the way he knew just how to use that hand to either soothe or bring her pleasure. Lord, how he'd given her pleasure in the years they'd been married.

Fighting back the rise of desire, again, she smiled and playfully tugged on his hand. She led him in the direction of the restaurant, praying that her choice would be the correct one to get the night started in the right direction.

More than anything, she wanted for them to end the night together.

Chapter 2

Porta was a couple of blocks off the boardwalk in a part of Asbury Park that was in the throes of gentrification.

During the summer months, it was nearly impossible to get a seat on a Saturday night and Chase hoped it wouldn't be as difficult tonight. He worried that if they'd have to wait, he wouldn't know what to say to her. It was the reason he'd been mostly silent on the walk over.

Not a good start, he warned, but then reined himself in. Putting too much pressure on himself was part of the reason that their relationship was in the toilet.

At the door to the restaurant, the hostess greeted them and after scrutinizing the main dining room, grabbed two menus and led them to some free space at one of the long family-style tables.

They sat side-by-side on the bench, close together in deference to the other people around them. Not very private or romantic, he worried.

After a quick look at the menu, Natalie said, "Feeling adventurous?"

Not at all, not ever, he thought, but said, "Sure."

When the waiter came over, she ordered. "The grilled octopus to start and how about the carbonara pizza?"

Bold, he thought, much like Natalie.

As she gazed up at him, he smiled and nodded. "Sounds delicious. The house red also," he added to the order.

"I hope you'll like it," she said and to hear her better, he leaned close, which brought his side flush to hers. The round curves of her breast teased the flatness of his chest. Her fresh scent, something citrusy and flowery, filled his senses and brought memories of the first night they'd met. A night filled with anticipation and not hesitation like tonight.

He decided to banish that hesitation. "I will, Nat. No matter what, I like spending time with you."

Her half-glance was almost shy and a becoming hint of pink stained her cheeks. "I used to like being with you, too," she said so softly, he had to lean even closer to hear her.

Not that he minded, because it just brought their bodies flush all along one side. When she laid her hand on his thigh, his heartbeat kicked up a notch and the tight skinny jeans grew even tighter as he thought of her shifting that hand up and over just a little.

He wanted to ask her why if they both liked being together their marriage was falling apart, but the waiter arrived just then with their appetizer, killing the moment. Maybe a good thing because he wanted to keep the night fun and free of confrontation.

The sharp, but pleasant aroma of garlic and lemon wafted from the dish the waiter placed before them. The earthy scent of yeasty goodness followed as a busboy delivered a basket piled with slices of focaccia.

She motioned to the grilled octopus so he would take some, but he shook his head and said, "After you."

With a roll of her eyes, she said, "Being gallant or chicken?"

"Both," he admitted with a chuckle.

She speared a piece of the seafood and offered it up to him. He eyeballed it and then her, noting the challenge in her gaze. He suspected it was a test that was about more than the food and he didn't intend to fail.

After a deep inhale, he wrapped his lips around her fork and ate the morsel of octopus. A perfect blend of citrus and garlic filled his mouth, along with a hint of char from the grilling. The seafood was tender with no hint of fishiness. Not at all like what he had expected.

"Delicious," he said and reciprocated, forking up a piece for her and bringing it to her lips.

She accepted the offering and let out a little moan of pleasure as she licked her lips.

The husky sound and sight of her luscious wet lips sent a wave of need straight to his groin.

5

"Awesome," she said, grabbed a piece of focaccia, dunked it in the sauce for the octopus, and urged him to eat it.

He took hold of her wrist to hold her hand steady and accepted the piece of bread, but also licked along the edge of her thumb, where a little bit of sauce had dribbled down.

Their gazes locked with the action and he couldn't fail to notice how her hazel eyes darkened to molten gold.

When the waiter brought over their wine, he quickly poured them each a glass and raised his in a toast. "To finding our way together again."

She said nothing, but clinked her glass with his.

They each took a sip of the wine. Her hand trembled as she set the glass down and he laid his hand over hers as it rested on his thigh, wanting to ease her nervousness.

"If I'm pushing too hard – "

"Could we not talk about this and just let it happen?" she said, her tone a mix of annoyance and hopefulness. The tension in her body obvious against his.

Natalie had always been the one to live in the now, something he'd always found impossible to do.

Unlike Natalie, who'd grown up in an upscale family, he'd had to scrabble for everything he'd ever had. It was the reason he pushed himself so much: to avoid ever being in need again.

Only he did need now.

He needed Natalie in his life.

Forking up another piece of octopus, he ate it and said, "I like this. I'm glad I tried it."

Her body relaxed against him and she did a little half-smile. "Hopefully the pizza will be just as good."

She reached for another piece of seafood and bread, and as she did so, he asked, "What's new with you? Everything going okay at work?"

A little laugh escaped her. "If okay is the usual craziness, yeah, everything is good. The new line I'm working on is almost done, thank God. Cindy has been worried we wouldn't finish it on time for Spring Fashion Week, but it'll be ready."

"Cindy can be a handful." Natalie's boss was brilliant, but temperamental. More than once his wife had come home in tears after one of her boss's tirades.

A long pause followed his comment and some of the light left her eyes. "A nice opportunity has come up. It's risky, but could turn out to be great for my career."

Hearing "risky" from a risk-taker made his totally risk-averse gut tighten. He hesitated and a chill crept into her gaze.

***

Natalie knew why Chase was silent. Growing up with a father who was always chasing pipe dreams that kept his family in poverty had left him with a lasting fear of failure. But if they were going to make their marriage work, some things had to change.

But she had to change as well. She stroked her hand up and down his thigh to ease his anxiety.

"It's okay, Chase," she said at the same time that he asked, "What kind of opportunity?"

His tone was neutral and she could tell that he was really really trying to hold back his usual reluctance.

"I was approached by a television production company to be the costume designer for an upcoming series. They need original and trendy outfits for the actors and have seen my work. They think I would be perfect and there's a possibility of mass producing the outfits for sale through one of the retail stores."

He nodded and took hold of her hand. "It sounds like what you've always wanted. Your own line. Why the hesitation?"

The why was easy. In the many years of being together, she'd become more cautious and as she looked at him, it was obvious that he understood.

He cradled her cheek. "Nat. I never wanted to ground your dreams and hold you back. I'm sorry if that's what I've done."

There was no doubting the sincerity in his voice which gave her hope things could be different between them.

"What would you say if I said I was going to take the offer?"

Hesitation filled his features again and he said, "I'd say that I would worry about you being disappointed, because I don't want you to be hurt. But – "

"You always have a but, Chase," she said harshly.

He blew out a rough laugh and wagged his head, as if chastising himself. He cupped her cheek and tenderly swiped his thumb across her cheek. "But I know you can make this a success, Nat."

Her heart skipped a beat with joy and she fought back tears. "I'm sorry I lashed out."

"It hurt, I admit, but we need to be more open with each other, right? Isn't that what tonight is about?"

She nodded. "Yeah, it is and I like that."

She liked it so much that she leaned forward and kissed him.

He seemed surprised at first, but then gave himself over to the kiss, slanting his mouth across hers before taking a little nibble of her lower lip. That soft tug shot desire straight to her center.

She half-swiveled on the bench and pressed her body to his. Opened her mouth to accept the sweet slide of his tongue until an embarrassed cough reminded them of where they were.

They pulled apart, both of them breathing heavily as the waiter placed the pizza tray in front of them.

"Enjoy," he said a little facetiously and with a wink at Chase.

"Did he just wink at me?" Chase asked, surprise on his face.

"It's 'cause you're so cute when your embarrassed," she said and skimmed her thumb across the bright stain of color on his cheeks and the color deepened with her action.

He tried to hide his embarrassment by dishing up slices of the not-your-usual-pizza. Instead of the typical tomato sauce and cheese, it had a creamy carbonara sauce, roasted eggs, and slices of prosciutto. The rustic dough was thinner and bubbly in spots, and deliciously yeasty as she took the first bite.

"Mmm, delicious," she said.

"Yeah, delicious," he said, but his gaze was resting on her lips and as she licked away a bit of the sauce, the blue of his eyes deepened to the color of a stormy sea.

After he swallowed, he leaned close and whispered, "Do you know what that little sound of pleasure does to me? Or the way you lick your lips?"

She jumped, shocked by his openness and the desire evident in the roughness of his voice and the slight tremble of his muscles beneath her hand as it rested on his thigh.

The old Chase would have never revealed those emotions, too in control to be that open. But as they'd said just moments earlier, tonight was about being more accessible.

She moved her hand up his thigh until she could trace the ridge of his erection with her pinky. As she did so, she whispered in his ear, "Tell me what it does, Chase. I want to hear."

His low groan reverberated through her body and he shuddered against her.

"Nat, I'm not sure these jeans can get any tighter or they'll cut off circulation."

Chuckling, she took a quick look around the crowded restaurant. No one was paying any attention to them so she daringly ran her pinky along the edge of his dick and whispered, "Anticipation just makes the wait worthwhile."

He groaned again, a little louder, and someone across the way looked their way.

She dialed it back, but kept her hand close, occasionally teasing him with a delicate touch as they ate and talked.

***

Chase chewed slowly and swallowed, trying to curb the need raging in his body. But watching her eat, feeling her touch against him, had him aching to be inside her. To drive himself deep and feel the pleasure of her body. Bring her satisfaction with each stroke of his hips.

Lord, I'm going to lose it right here and now if I keep up such thoughts.

7

Luckily, they finished the pizza and wine quickly. The waiter came by and asked, "Anyone want to see the dessert menu?"

"No!" they both answered emphatically and in unison.

The young waiter barely contained a smirk. He hurried away and came back a few minutes later with the bill which Chase quickly settled.

Natalie popped off the bench, but he eased up more slowly, battling the pressure from his aroused state. Taking another deep breath to fight it, until Natalie glanced down and her gaze heated once more.

"Want to dance?" she asked as she slowly moved her gaze up to his.

"Nat, please," he said with almost a growl.

"Anticipation, remember."

Anticipation might kill me, but what a way to go, he thought.

"Okay. Where to?"

Chapter 3

As much as she had teased him about waiting, Natalie was close to giving in and going somewhere to explore the attraction that still existed between them.

Anticipation, she silently reminded herself.

With a quick look around the restaurant, she decided that she could only wait so long to be next to him.

"Come on," she said and tugged on his hand to lead him toward the front of the restaurant and the hallway that led to the club area.

***

It was dark, crowded, and loud, Chase thought, but didn't protest the conditions that had them moving together without an inch of space between them.

It was both torture and pleasure to have her that close, all her soft parts against his hardness. The tight nubs of her breasts rubbing along the cotton of his T-shirt.

God, how I want her.

He brought his hands down to the upper curve of her hips to draw her even closer against his erection.

He sucked in a breath as she did a sexy back and forth shimmy along his dick and he locked his gaze on her features, watching as she did a quick glance down to where they were plastered against one another before she raised her gaze to meet his.

She laid her hands over his and urged them upward until he was bracketing her back, his thumbs along the soft undersides of her breasts. She got up on tiptoes and whispered in his ear, "Touch me, Chase."

He groaned as she playfully bit his earlobe and shot a quick look around.

Between the darkness and their proximity, no one was likely to notice.

He shifted his hands just enough to skim his thumbs along her the fullness of her breasts and she mewled her pleasure and rotated her hips along his in time to the beat of the music.

The heavy lub dub of the bass guitar seemed to match the beat of his heart as it raced in his chest with his growing arousal.

He dropped one hand down to cup her sweet sweet ass while he did a quick swipe across her nipple and she let out a little gasp that had his cock nearly strangling in the tight denim.

Bending slightly, he licked the sensitive skin just behind her ear and whispered, "Nat, you're killing me. I need you so bad."

A seductress's husky chuckle filled his senses as she said, "The feeling is mutual, Chase."

He pulled away to see her face. Her eyes were glazed with desire and a becoming blush painted her cheeks with pink. She licked her dry lips and he couldn't resist taking her mouth with his, the kiss urgent and wild.

Over and over he plunged his tongue into her mouth as they danced and touched, lost in their desire and the heavy beats of the song that vibrated through their bodies.

As the song ended, the crowd cheered for the band and they broke apart, breathing heavily.

Dazed by his need, Chase didn't want to linger for another song, but he also didn't want to pressure her. But he was pleased that she seemed to want him as much as he wanted her.

As the band launched into another song, he pulled Natalie into his arms, but as she pressed against him, she rose on tiptoes once more and said, "Do you want to stay or go somewhere quieter?"

"I'd like to go," he said, but held back on mentioning the room at the inn, just in case he was either misreading her signals or it all went south after they left the club.

"I'd like that, too."

He grinned, grabbed hold of her hand, and led her outside, where a line of people waited to get into the restaurant.

9

They hurried past them and toward the boardwalk in silence. Every now and then he'd shoot her a quick glance, trying to gauge what she wanted, but couldn't.

It made him worry how they'd drifted so far apart that he wasn't able to read her until the little voice in his head told him to remember her touch during dinner and their dance.

That oh-so-sexy dance and the need that had vibrated between them and hadn't really been satisfied.

It had been like that the first night they'd met, the passion between them urgent and demanding.

As she looked up at him and smiled sexily, a mischievous glint in her eyes, he realized that maybe tonight was not much different.

When they reached the boardwalk, they strolled to the railing and leaned on it to watch the waves.

A sharp gust of breeze, cooler with night, kicked up and Natalie shivered beside him.

"Cold?" he asked and at her nod, he pulled off his hoodie, draped it around her shoulders, and moved behind her to hug her to the warmth of his body.

"Thanks. This feels nice," she said and looked at him over her shoulder.

He wasn't quite sure nice was the word for the way she fit against him perfectly, her beautiful ass soft against his hard. Her full breasts within reach of his hands if he only would shift them just a little.

Only there were a good number of people on the boardwalk since it was early, but just a sole couple down on the beach, close to the crumbling foundation of the section of the Casino building that had been torn down decades earlier.

The couple down on the beach certainly weren't letting the crowd stop them, he thought.

"Do you see that?" she said, threads of surprise and need tangled in her tones.

"Yeah, I do. It's . . ." Like Nat, he couldn't figure out what to feel, only it was starting to make him even hornier and a little guilty since he couldn't drag his eyes off the amorous couple.

"Chase," she said and let out a shaky sigh before plunging on. "Touch me, Chase."

He shot a worried look around at the crowd and warned, "Nat – "

"Please," she pleaded and butted her ass up against his hard cock.

"Fuck," he muttered beneath his breath, but did as she asked, reaching beneath the enveloping folds of the hoodie that hid his hand as he caressed her breast. Her nipple was tight again and he tweaked it between his thumb and forefinger. With each little tug, she did an enticing rub along his dick.

He was going to lose it and shot one hand down to her belly to keep her still. This time it was his turn to beg.

"Nat, please," he said.

She covered his hand with hers and twined her fingers through his. "Come on, Chase. They've left and we've got the beach to ourselves now."

He glanced toward the end of the Casino foundation and sure enough, the couple had finished their business and moved on.

They hurried down the boardwalk steps to the sand and nearly raced toward the water's edge. At the end of the decaying foundation, they slipped around to the wooden pilings and the safety and privacy they provided.

No one on the boardwalk could see them here.

There was no one else on the beach.

Chase couldn't wait any longer and judging from the look on Natalie's face, neither could she.

10

Chapter 4

Natalie laid her hands on his broad shoulders as he pressed her back against the wooden piling, his hands bracketing her back to protect her.

She met his gaze for only the briefest of moments, but there was no denying the need in his gaze. His blue eyes had darkened to almost midnight and glittered in the moonlight, alive with emotion.

She trailed her hands down to his chest and cupped his pecs. His nipples were hard beneath her hands and she teased them with her fingers, dragging a rough groan from him and the rock of his hips against her belly.

"I want you," she said and moved her hands across his lean abs, tracing the ridges with her fingers before she reached the snap on his jeans.

"I want you, too," he said and brought one hand around to cup her breast and play with her nipple, tugging and rotating it the way she liked. Sending sharp shots of pleasure to her clit, which was throbbing for his touch.

She fumbled with the snap on his jeans, but then quickly worked down the zipper and freed him from his briefs and the jeans.

His dick was long, smooth, and hard in her hand and she stroked him roughly, knowing how he liked it. Loving the long loud groan as she worked him and he tweaked her nipple even harder, making her gasp with pleasure.

She couldn't wait any more.

She took hold of his hand and urged it beneath her skirt. He shook as he found her center and shifted aside the small scrap of lace that was her panty to ease a finger into her.

His cock jerked in her hand as he said, "Fuck, you're so wet. So hot, Nat."

"Come inside, Chase," she urged and he dipped down to ease beneath the hem of her dress.

She guided him to her center, where he paused and met her gaze. "Are you sure, Nat?"

"I'm sure, Chase. I want you. Now. Inside me."

With one sure stroke, he plunged deep, driving her up against the piling with the force of his possession.

They both gasped as he held still, keeping her pinned there for long moments before he finally withdrew and then plunged into her again.

Oh God, it had been so long since they'd been together. Months between their separation and the time before that, when they'd both gone their separate ways in their too busy lives.

With each sure move of his hips, she remembered how good it had been between them before. How he filled her body so perfectly and could bring her such pleasure. How they'd once been so in tune with each other, both physically and emotionally.

She dug her hands into his shoulders, urging him on and he cupped her buttocks to drive ever harder, his hips grinding into her until she was almost there. Almost at the peak and ready to go.

**

Her body contracted around him, increasing the friction against his dick as he stroked in and out of her, savoring the feel of her. Enjoying the perfection of her body moving in time to his.

She was close to her climax. Her body on edge and trembling.

He was almost there as well.

Just another stroke. Just a little more to feel all of her.

Chase groaned as he buried himself deep and she arched her back and dug her nails into his flesh.

That little bite of pleasure/pain pushed him to the edge, but he wanted her to fall over with him.

11

He reached between them and found her clit, caressed it as he drove in again and again and she met him with each thrust until with one final surge, she cried out her release and pulled him into ecstasy with her.

He lingered inside her, savoring the aftershocks of her climax until the last little waves of it ebbed and he reluctantly retreated, but he didn't leave her side.

Gathering her into his arms, he reversed their positions and lowered them to the sand, Natalie tucked against him on his lap. They were both breathing heavily until little by little, some calm returned.

Her head was tucked just beneath his chin and she rested her hand on his chest. Stroked her hand back and forth lovingly above his heart which still raced from the passion they'd shared.

"That was . . . nice," she said, a little too hesitantly.

"Just nice?" he asked in a semi-teasing tone, because he'd call it a lot of things – earth shattering, amazing, unbelievable – but not just nice.

She chuckled and looked up at him. "If I said anything else, you might get a little too cocky."

Considering that his cock was still tucked against her warm moist center beneath the privacy of her dress skirt, he was just fine with anything involving his cock. In response to her and those thoughts, his balls tightened and his dick jerked to life again.

Arching an eyebrow and glancing down toward his lap, she said, "Really? So soon?"

"You know how I like to please," he kidded, although that was maybe part of the problem in their relationship. He'd been so busy trying to please at work that he'd forgotten about trying to please her. He intended to change that for the future.

She eyeballed him, as if trying to make sure that he was serious, and as if realizing that he truly meant it, she said, "Is that a key in your pocket because I can tell you're happy to see me."

He grinned at her jest. "That other hard thing down there is most certainly a key. To a room in our inn. That is if you'd like to come and spend some more time with me."

***

Normally Natalie would have been a little pissed that he'd made such a presumption and reserved the room, but then again, at one time she'd liked his Boy Scout-always-be-prepared ways. She had known she could always rely on him which was a good thing.

And just like he was obviously trying to change, she had to as well. Making this marriage work wasn't a one-way street and she'd gotten too uptight about him always taking the lead. Sometimes it was nice, like tonight.

"I do and I'm glad you got the room. That place has a lot of special memories for us."

"It does," he said and cupped her cheek lovingly, applying gentle pressure to tilt her head up so he could kiss her.

Unlike their earlier wild and impassioned kisses, this was one filled with tenderness and caring. With optimism and expectation.

She freed herself to those emotions and to his kiss, relishing the lightness filling her heart. Praying that the night would breathe life back into their foundering marriage.

Over and over she met his kiss until with a shaky breath, he pulled away and said, "I've missed you so."

She remembered her earlier anger and fought it back, accepting his statement for what it was and not any kind of pressure. "I've missed you, too."

He hesitated for a second and she hated that she was a big part of the reason for his uncertainty. To ease the moment, she skimmed her fingers across his jaw and to his lips, where she silenced him with her index finger.

"I'd like to go to the room now. I hope you'd like to also."

Beneath her finger his smile grew bright. It was that sexy boyish smile she remembered from the night they'd first met right on this boardwalk.

They rose as one and she stayed close to give him some privacy as he carefully covered up his semi-erect cock beneath the restrictive fabric of the jeans.

When he was decent, they strolled hand-in-hand away from Asbury Park and onto the Ocean Grove beachfront.

Without the many restaurants and shops along the boardwalk, it was quieter here. More peaceful and that serenity slipped into her soul, bringing a tranquility she hadn't felt in a long time.

It had used to be like that with him during simpler times. Before so many other things got in the way of their love.

She tightened her hold on his hand and he glanced down at her, smiled that delicious smile again.

She grinned back, happy for these moments together. Not wanting them to end. Not wanting to rush them which gave her an idea.

With a quick look to see where they were, she said, "How about some ice cream?"

Surprise registered on his features before he teased, "Think I need to cool down?"

Chuckling, she playfully swung their hands. "*Everything* is always better with ice cream."

Chapter 5

It was impossible for Chase to miss the sexy innuendo in her statement.

"Everything?" He raised his eyebrows and scrutinized her to make sure that she understood the one treat he was looking forward to.

She leaned into him and laughed huskily. *"Everything."*

"Who am I to say 'no' then?"

With a swing of their joined hands, he led her away from the sand and to the boardwalk. Past the Pavilion and up Ocean Pathway toward the auditorium with that bright white cross, only he wasn't feeling quite as guilty.

There was no reason to feel shame about loving his wife and wanting to show her just how much in any way he could.

A last quick look at the Great Auditorium and they were headed toward Days, their favorite ice cream parlor. Since discovering it years earlier, they'd always stop by the quaint shop with its old-time counters, rapid fire servers, and amazing ice creams.

There was a small line thanks to the unseasonably warm night, but Chase wasn't going to complain. It gave him more time to spend with Natalie and of course, created that delicious anticipation which had his palms sweating and his heart pounding in his chest.

Within minutes they were inside the ice cream parlor and ordering, only this time Chase wasn't going to play it safe since tonight was about being different and taking chances.

"Caramel waffle cone, please," he said, earning a sidelong glance and small smile from Natalie.

"Triple scoop of vanilla in a dish, please."

Shaking his head, he said, "You're killing me."

She scooted up on tiptoes and whispered in his ear, "Not yet."

His hand trembled as he accepted the cone from the server and his heart skipped a beat before settling down into an insistent rhythm.

Easing her hand from his to grab her dish, he wondered how she'd ever finish the mound of vanilla since she usually wasn't a big eater. But as their gazes collided, he nearly crushed his sugar cone at the look in her gaze that said she had very special plans for that ice cream.

He paid and they hurried out of the store and around the corner, heading in the direction of the inn two blocks over. As they walked, shoulders brushing, he ate his cone and watched from the corner of his eye as she spooned up a bit at a time and licked it off the spoon.

His cock, which seemed to have a mind of his own, jumped and swelled at the sight of her perfect little tongue moving across the spoon and the way she licked away a smidgen of ice cream off her lips.

Fuck, how he wanted to taste those lips. Find out if they were cold from the confection or as warm as they had been on the beach earlier that night.

"You okay?" she asked and heat raced across his cheeks at the realization he'd let out a little moan in connection with his thoughts.

"I'll be better when we're somewhere private," he admitted, anxious to reach the inn and their room.

That sexy smile crept across her lips again. "Me, too."

He stopped and faced her, let himself experience what he wanted . . . for starters.

Bending, he kissed her. Her lips were cool from the ice cream and he warmed them with his kiss until she was up on tiptoes and leaning into him. They kissed for long moments until something wet and cold slipped down over his knuckles.

He moved away, but she licked the melted ice cream off his hand before she shifted back and they continued the walk, their pace slightly faster.

Inside the lobby, the innkeeper called out a greeting and smiled. "Good evening, Mr. Smith. Mrs. Smith."

"Have a good night," Natalie said without hesitation which was a relief. She was still Mrs. Smith, but for how long, no one knew.

***

Mrs. Smith.

It had always felt a little weird to her to go from her ethnic Ramirez surname to the very vanilla Smith. In some ways, those names and ethnicities had been a big part of the differences between them, although in unexpected ways.

He'd been the one from the wrong side of the tracks. The bad boy that her *mami* had warned her to avoid. A very sexy bad boy in faded ripped blue jeans and a tight T-shirt that showed off every muscle of a body hard from years of manual labor.

Just like he looked tonight, although those muscles were from the gym now, she thought as he held out his hand and invited her to go up the stairs.

She nodded and started up the steps, putting an extra seductive wiggle in her hips. Loving the little moan she heard from behind her and his strangled whisper as he said, "One more flight. Room 201."

One more flight. Just another ten or so steps and then . . . .

At the door, she moved to the side to let him open the door, the dish of ice cream in her hand, almost untouched. Melty, but still mostly frozen.

Perfect.

He dug the key out of his pocket and fumbled to stick it into the lock. She steadied his hand and smiled in encouragement. Walked in without hesitation as he threw the door open.

The room was bigger than the one they'd shared on their first anniversary when they'd been just getting started and money had been scarcer. This room was bigger and more luxurious because they were successful now.

Successful, but apart.

But not tonight. Tonight was about being together.

The snick of the lock sounded loud behind her and she faced him.

He had jammed his fingers into the pockets of the jeans and stood there, rocking back and forth on his heels. Hesitant again, but she wanted to get him past all that.

She walked to the bed and sat on the edge. Patted the space beside her. "Why don't you come here and help me finish this ice cream?"

In the blink of an eye he was next to her, grinning.

She spooned up some of the ice cream and held it to his lips, but as he went to eat it, she yanked it away and said, "Why don't you take off your shirt? You know how clumsy I can be and I wouldn't want it to get dirty."

***

Fuck, fuck, fuck, Chase thought.

He tore off the shirt and tossed it to the floor. Loved the way her gaze heated and dipped down his body before shifting upward again.

She went back to the dish and scooped up a very messy spoonful that she brought to his lips. But as he leaned forward to eat it, she tilted the spoon just enough to let a big drop of cold vanilla creaminess plop onto his chest.

"Oh my, so sorry," she said, but obviously didn't mean it.

He ate the ice cream and she spooned up another big glob. Lost another dollop of it onto his chest.

He licked the spoon clean and after, leaned back on his elbows. "What are you going to do about the mess you made?" he said, because the pressure in his pants was growing almost too hard to bear.

She set the dish of ice cream onto the bedspread and scooted until her thigh was pressed to his. Leaning on one hand, she bent and licked off the first blob of ice cream which by now had melted and trailed down to his nipple. She licked all around that hard nub before swiping her tongue across it.

God, her mouth was so warm, so perfect, he thought as she skimmed it across his chest to the other splotch of ice cream. She cleaned off his chest quickly and moved to his other nipple, drawing it deep into her mouth and yanking a rough groan from him.

"Nat, please," he said and dug his hands into the soft strands of her hair to keep her close.

"Please, what, Chase? Tell me what you want."

He wanted so so much, but for starters . . .

"I want your mouth on me. All over me . . . and more ice cream," he said and grinned.

She laughed, warm and loud and with abandon.

Reaching back, she snagged the dish and dribbled drops of ice cream in a line down toward the waistband of his jeans. She set the dish down next to him and undid the snap with eager fingers. Just as quickly, she unzipped the pants and he flexed his hips so she could drag his jeans off.

Tossing them aside, she urged his thighs apart so she could kneel between them. Rising up on her knees, she licked him clean, but paused by his erection, teasing him with the softness of her cheek along his cock.

He tangled his fingers in her hair and silently pleaded with her, but she held her ground.

"Say it, Chase. You always hold back. Don't hold back tonight."

He sucked in a ragged breath and slowly nodded. "Your mouth. I want your mouth on me, Nat. I love the way you suck me. Lick me."

Her vagina clenched with his words and a wave of heat and damp exploded between her legs.

She would do as he asked, but first . . .

She grabbed the dish of ice cream and gobbled down a few spoonfuls. Then she did as she had before and plopped a big glob right on the tip of his penis.

He jumped from the cold and gently pushed against her head to urge her forward. As he'd asked, she licked the tip of his dick the way she would a cone, a swipe across the tip. A long swirl all around the sensitive edge of his cock that made his fingers tighten on her skull and the muscles of his thighs shake with need.

"Do you like?" she asked, needing to know. Needing him to bare himself the way she would later lay open all that she wanted.

"I like. A lot, Nat. Please. More," he said and she covered the head of his penis with her mouth and worked him, sucking him. Tonguing the sensitive tip while she wrapped her hand around him and stroked. Soft and hard. Slow and fast as he showed her with the movements of his body and his soft moans just how much she was pleasing him.

Chase watched her going down on him and it took all his willpower not to come.

The dollop of ice cream and her mouth had been cold at first, but there was nothing chilly about her mouth now and every sure stroke of her hand dragged him closer and closer to the edge.

But he remembered her words. Her plea. He wanted to do as she'd asked.

"More, Nat. Touch me down there," he begged.

She cupped his balls, massaged him, and he shook with the pleasure of her caress.

Flexing his hips, he pushed into her mouth and she took him in deeper. Stroked him with her hands and played him with her tongue until he came undone with her loving.

With one final jerk of his hips, he lost it and called out her name.

Chapter 6

Natalie worked her way up his body, trailing kisses along his heated damp skin until she reached his mouth.

She paused there to search out his features. His gaze was dark with passion. That boyish grin graced his mouth and she traced the edges of it with her index finger.

"Nat, that was . . . " He shrugged and wagged his head a second. "I'm not good with words. You know that."

"Yeah, I know." She hesitated because she was aware that this discussion could go in a lot of ways, but she wanted to keep it light. She wanted to spend easy time with him, exploring all that had brought them together in the past before dealing with all that was separating them in the present.

She circled his lips with her finger and smiled as she said, "But I remember what good things you can do with your mouth."

The grin blossomed beneath her finger and his blue eyes glittered with humor. "You remember, do you?"

She nodded and replaced her finger with her lips, brushing them all around the edges of his mouth. "I do, but maybe you can refresh my memory?"

He laughed and in one smooth move, laid her against the bed and pinned her beneath his body. He swept her arms upward and trapped them above her head with his hands.

"Let me think. Where should I start?" he said while his gaze swept across her face, neck, shoulders, and breasts.

Heat erupted across her body as his gaze settled on her breasts and her nipples tightened beneath the soft fabric of her bodice.

He didn't fail to notice.

He cupped her breast and tweaked the tip. Heat zapped from there down to her core.

"Maybe here?" he said and continued his caress, but then surprised her by bringing his lips to the sensitive skin beneath her ear.

A lick and a nibble had her trembling. When he kissed her and bit gently, she arched her body, pressing her hips to his.

He opened his mouth on the soft skin of her neck and sucked a little harder, the force of it creating an enticing tingle that traveled to her breasts as she imagined his mouth on them.

Moving his mouth downward, he nipped at the junction of her neck and shoulder and then bit more intensely, dragging a gasp from her. Making her beg for that bite elsewhere.

"Please, Chase."

His chuckle vibrated against that delicate skin and yanked a sympathetic one from her.

"Don't tease me, Chase." She playfully tugged at his hair to urge him downward.

"Impatient, are we?" he said, but licked and bit his way down to the swells of her breasts where he continued his teasing seduction.

She cradled his head in her hands and he relented, caressing her nipples with his fingers until that wasn't enough.

"Help me get this off," she said and together they worked quickly to undo the zipper on her dress and drag it up and over her head, leaving her in nothing but a lacy sand-colored bra and the matching thong.

"Beautiful," he said as he eyed her, but she undid the bra with one quick twist and tossed it away.

"Even more beautiful," he said, urged her onto the mattress, and followed her down, covering her with his body. Lovely heat and strength greeting every inch of her skin.

He kissed her, exploring every inch of her mouth with his lips and tongue until she was arching up against him, needing more.

He answered her plea, trailing kisses along the side of her face. Down her neck where with a quick lick, he awakened the love bite he'd left earlier.

17

She closed her eyes, moaned and tugged at his hair, wanting his mouth on her breasts. Needing that heat and wet.

A dribble of cold assaulted her senses and she looked down to her breast where he had spooned some of the melting vanilla ice cream. He plopped another spoonful on her other breast and her nipples tightened even more with the cold.

As he leaned over and placed the cup with the ice cream on the nightstand, he whispered in her ear, "Turnabout is fair play, don't you think?"

But as he licked and sucked the chill sweetness from her breasts, all she could think about was the feel of his mouth on her flesh and the long hard ridge of his cock trapped between their bodies.

She spread her legs and he eased between her thighs, but made no move to enter her and she protested his restraint with a soft mewl which earned a rough chuckle from him.

"You make me so hard with that sound, babe, but not yet. I want you to come for me first."

She was already close to that, her insides clenching on emptiness and drenched with her arousal.

When he eased aside her thong and found her clit with his sure fingers, she nearly did come, keening with pleasure at the insistent feel of him caressing that tender nub.

He let out his own little moan and said, "So wet. So hot. I can't wait to taste."

Shuddering with his words, she moved with him as he wrapped his arms around her thighs and urged her to the edge of the bed. He sank to his knees on the floor and buried his head between her thighs, tasting her. Gifting her with kiss after kiss along her center as he played her with his hands, easing his fingers inside and stroking. Applying subtle pressure against her clit with his thumb.

She rocked against his mouth and hands. Cradled his head in her hands, urging him on with her body and the soft cries spilling from her lips until with one sure stroke of his fingers, she came.

Chase savored the sweetness of her release against his mouth and hands and slowly brought her back, but just as the final spasms registered, he rose up and guided his cock to her center.

He locked his gaze with hers, so dark now with desire, her hazel-gold eyes warm like hot chocolate. The flush of desire stained her cheeks and down her throat to her breasts, the tips still hard from his caresses.

"Chase," she said, her voice husky with desire.

Slowly he eased inside her and watched as her eyes drifted closed and she lifted her hips, drawing him ever deeper into her body.

He grasped her buttocks and held her still, afraid that with the slightest move he'd lose it and he didn't want that just yet. He wanted to feel all of her surrounding him. The ebbing aftershocks of her climax. The warmth of her, so inviting.

The peacefulness of being one with her.

He realized that now. With her he could be a different man. A better man.

It had taken her absence from his life to show him that.

"Nat, this feels so right. So special," he said.

She slowly opened her eyes and he took heart from the joy he saw there.

"Love me, Chase."

He moved, a leisurely stroke that kindled the embers of her desire. Another retreat and thrust and her body came alive again, drawing him in. Caressing him as he moved once more and guided the rhythm of her hips with his hands.

Shooting a quick glance at her, he realized she was watching him. Watching where they were joined as he drove in again and then withdrew, a little slower to keep from losing it too quickly.

"Hard, Chase. Love me hard," she said.

He freed what little restraint was left in him, rocking into her again and again until his legs were trembling from the effort.

Inside him, the climax built, tightening his balls and as she let out a long sibilant moan and her release burst around him, he buried himself in her welcoming warmth and let himself come.

Leaning down, he took her mouth in a gentle kiss, soothing her as little by little they both came back down to earth, still joined.

Long moments passed and she cradled his cheek and offered him a warm smile. "That was amazing."

"It could be even better, Nat."

She narrowed her gaze and scrutinized him. "How?"

"Stay the night."

Chapter 7

Natalie hadn't thought much past going with him to his room and she hadn't really prepared to stay the entire night with him.

Plus, as he looked at her so seriously, she knew that what he really wanted was for her to stay with him and not just for the night.

The little voice inside her head asked, "Would that be so bad? Chase is a hard-working, intelligent, funny and sexy man and most women would jump at the chance to have a man like that in their lives."

Only he'd also become too driven and too serious, she reminded the annoying voice.

"Nat?" he pressed at her prolonged silence.

"I'll stay," she said despite her doubts because in the short time they'd spent together, he'd shown her that he was trying to find the man he'd once been and recapture what it was that had brought them together.

Besides great sex.

Passion had never been a problem between them until the very end when he'd been either too tired or too busy to share that part of himself with her.

He finally slipped out of her and together they drew back the bedspread and eased beneath the soft sheets. Meeting in the middle of the bed, they faced each other and she pillowed her head on his arm and twined her legs with his. He flung his other arm over her waist to keep her close and she laid her hand on his chest, right over his heart.

"This feels nice," he said as he lazily stroked his hand up and down her side.

"It does." She'd always loved sleeping with him like this, all tangled together. Hearts beating against one another until they seemed to synchronize and become one.

In the month since she'd moved out she'd missed this horribly and hadn't slept well because of it.

Now she tucked her head beneath his chin and inhaled deeply, loving the smell of him, masculine flesh with the faintest hint of the cologne he wore. The scent always struck her as a mix of ocean breeze and clean cotton and reminded her of times like this. Long days on the beach and sensuous nights along the boardwalk.

She inhaled deeply again, wanting to take in that smell and hold it inside forever much like she hoped she could keep him with her forever.

"You can," the little voice chastised, but she shut it down.

The morning would come soon enough and with it the moment of deciding what they would do next.

For this moment, she was going to enjoy the now and being with him. Savor every second because she didn't know what the future might bring for them.

The slight tension in her body communicated her mixed feelings to Chase and he understood.

While he thought he'd made some headway tonight in showing her that he could be the man she'd met and married, it would take time to show her that he was serious about being that man again.

So he didn't press. He just stroked her back and relished the feel of that creamy skin beneath his palm. Enjoyed the muscled strength of her legs interwoven with his, bringing the hardness of his abs tight to the flatness of her belly. The soft curves of her breasts brushing along his chest.

Lord, how he missed having her near like this. Missed the warmth of her body and the way her breath spilled across his chest.

She let out a barely noticeable snore and he smiled, glad that she was so comfortable that she could fall asleep.

He knew sleep wouldn't come so easily to him. Not when there was still so much unsettled between them.

If it wasn't meant to be, he wanted to cherish every second of this night to keep him warm on the lonely nights to come.

He tightened his embrace, a tender squeeze that didn't wake her, but brought her a smidgen closer. The warmth of her body bathed his front and her scent, that clean citrusy scent, enveloped him.

Smiling, he stared up at the ceiling and the play of lights from outside, and remembered their first time together, weeks after they'd met on the boardwalk. They'd been hesitant to start until something had clicked and it had all seemed so right.

Just like tonight, he thought and finally closed his eyes.

***

He must have dozed off because when he woke, it was to the heat and wet of her mouth on him, sucking him to hardness.

"Natalie, you don't have to do this," he nearly groaned and clenched his gut to fight the rise of desire.

She raised her head, her gaze glittering in the dim light spilling in from a streetlamp outside.

"I want to. I *need* to," she said and encircled his hardening cock in her hands, stroking him before she put her mouth on him again.

He shut his eyes against the sight of her going down on him because if he didn't, he was sure he'd lose it. As it was, he was close to release when she straddled him with her body and guided him to her center.

"Watch me, Chase. I know you like to watch," she said.

His eyes snapped open and fixed on her as she slowly lowered herself onto his erection and cupped her breasts, playing with the tight tips. Tweaking and rotating them as she ground her hips against him.

He reached up and covered her hands with his, urging hers away so he could touch and play. So he could sit up and taste.

Natalie moaned as he sucked hard, the pull of his mouth at the perfect edge of pleasure/pain. His hard cock stretching her and filling her with his heat.

She pushed down on him harder, wanting to feel every inch of him buried inside her. But then the urge came to move and feel the friction of their bodies building the rise of passion.

Raising her hips, she withdrew from him before plunging back down and sighing at the feel of him, so perfect. She repeated the motion, more urgently as the tug of his mouth on her breasts made her insides twist with need.

Over and over she rode him, ever faster and stronger until her release shimmered along the edges of her consciousness, but eluded her.

"Chase, I need . . .." she said, but didn't quite know what she needed until he reached between their bodies and found her clit. Urgently caressed it with his fingers and her body shattered against his.

She arched her back, roughly pushing onto him, and cried out his name as her release washed over her.

The force of it had barely ebbed when he rolled her over and pinned her to the mattress, his still-erect dick buried inside her.

Her gaze locked with his and he said, "I want to watch you come again. I want to watch everything while we make love."

He stroked in and out of her roughly and a ragged sigh escaped her at the pleasure of it.

"That's it, Nat. Tell me how you like it," he said and moved again, jerking another moan of pleasure from her as he propelled her toward another climax.

She licked her dry lips and said, "I love the way you fill me, Chase. The way it feels . . . so right."

He drove in forcefully and held still for a moment. "This is right, Nat. This is perfect."

With a sexy wiggle of his hips, he pushed in just a little more and she cradled his body with her knees.

Her movement rubbed her clit against his body and when he stroked in and out again, teasing that sensitized nub, she lost it, calling out his name and wrapping her legs around his buttocks to keep him close.

A second later, his body shook with his release and he murmured her name almost reverently.

She stroked her hands up and down his back and urged him down, wanting to feel every inch of him on her. Inside her.

He came willingly, resting against her for a few minutes before rolling them to their sides, still joined, and tucking her against him.

She sighed and relaxed, loving the feel of him. The heat of his body and his smell. So masculine. So Chase.

As his breath lengthened and became regular, she realized he had fallen asleep.

Smiling, she closed her eyes and laid her head next to his chest. The lub-dub of his heart was strong beneath her ear. Constant, like Chase.

She had always known she could count on him, she thought.

But was that enough? The little voice in her head asked as she drifted off to sleep.

Chapter 8

The enticing smells of coffee, eggs, and bacon roused her from a deep deep sleep.

She rolled over to find Chase juggling a shopping bag, two foam take-out containers, and a beverage carrier with two cups. He was freshly showered judging from the damp strands of his dark hair and he looked just too sexy again in those black jeans, another form-fitting T-shirt, and the hoodie.

When she gave him a puzzled look, he said, "You were asleep so deep, I didn't want to wake you. I went to the surf and skate shop to get you something to wear and to Nagle's for some breakfast."

He plopped the shopping bag with the OG store logo on the floor and laid the containers and cups on the nightstand. Standing by the bed a little hesitantly, he said, "We could go out to eat if you want or you could go home, but it looks like it's going to be a beautiful day. I thought you might want to stay for a while."

She sat up in bed, drew some errant locks from her face, and pulled the sheet up to hide her nakedness.

"First I'd like for you to sit down and get comfortable and then, coffee. Please please please some coffee."

He grinned, toed off his shoes, and sat cross-legged on the bed opposite her. Reaching back, he snared the two cups and handed her one.

She tore back a piece of the plastic lid and took a sip. It was done just like she liked it. Creamy, light, and sweet.

"Thank you," she said and a second later, her stomach growled noisily.

"Hungry?" he asked and arched a brow.

After last night, she was starving and not just for food. But that had to wait until some things were more settled between them.

"Famished," she said and he laid the two foam containers before her and opened the tops to reveal the two different breakfast sandwiches inside.

"Pork roll or bacon?" he asked.

"How about we share?" she said, knowing how much he liked both the breakfast meats.

He grinned and grabbed half of the egg and pork roll sandwich. She did the same and they sat there, satisfying one hunger while another grew steadily, especially as he occasionally looked at her, his gaze the deep blue of desire.

She chewed thoughtfully and finally said, "I like this. . . ."

Her voice trailed off as she struggled to find the right words for their current situation.

He lowered a dark brow and grinned sexily. "This? Like breakfast or something else?"

"Breakfast is always good," she said and popped the last bit of her sandwich into her mouth.

"So is sex, like last night," he said and she nearly choked as she swallowed while fighting back a laugh.

She couldn't deny it had been good, but there had been lots more that had been good the night before.

"I liked that we talked," she said.

"During sex?" he teased, dragging intense heat to her face and a protest.

"Chase. . . ."

"You wanted me to be more open, so I'm being more open. I liked telling you what I like. Hearing what you like, especially – "

She leaned forward and laid her index finger on his lips. "Stop, please. Be serious."

He playfully bit the tip of her finger and said, "I *am* being serious, Natalie. I liked sharing with you. Talking with you. Sleeping with you. Making love *with you.*"

The heat across her cheeks deepened and traveled downward. Beneath the protection of the sheet, her nipples puckered into tight nubs.

23

She wanted him again, but it was just too soon.

Sitting back, she grabbed her half of the second sandwich and took a bite. He followed suit, grabbing the remaining half and devouring it in just a few bites. She ate a little more slowly, needing the time to consider his offer to stay.

She hadn't planned on it and didn't have any clothes, but then again, he had gotten her some judging from the full bag sitting by the bed. At a minimum, she wouldn't have to do the walk of shame in last night's dress.

But if she stayed. . . .

She didn't want to think about what might happen again, as much as she wanted him physically.

She wanted to see what the day would be like with this new old Chase. Was he truly serious about spending a lazy day down on the beach or would he be itching to pick up his phone to check his messages? Would he be willing to stay the night again at the inn and be late for work tomorrow or would he want to rush home so he could be at work at the crack of dawn?

There was only one way to find out.

Swallowing her last bite of the sandwich, she said, "Were you serious about spending the day together?"

***

Chase had never been more serious about anything . . . except maybe marrying Natalie.

"Totally serious," he said and motioned to the shopping bag. "If you don't like what I got for you, we could go back to the store and get something else."

"I'm sure it'll be fine. Let me just take a quick shower," she said.

"Do you need help washing your back?" he teased.

"Not if you want to get to the beach any time today," she said, dropped a quick kiss on his lips, and hopped off the bed.

Snagging the bag with the clothes, she rushed into the bathroom, but not before shooting him a sexy grin. "Maybe later, Chase."

He grinned and sat back against the headboard, imagining just how he could help her in the shower later. As the sound of the running water stopped and he heard her moving around in the bathroom, a thought came to him.

He grabbed his smartphone and was checking out the surf and skate shop's website when she popped out of the bathroom, smiling. The smile faded quickly as she saw him on the phone.

"It's not what you're thinking," he said, a little disappointed at her lack of trust. He held up the phone so she could see the screen and explained. "The shop rents surfboards. It's been a long time since we went surfing and I was just checking the conditions."

She walked over and snared the phone from his hand, swiped up and down and said, "Bummer. It's kind of flat. I guess we'll just have to lie on the beach and soak up the sun."

"Such a hardship," he kidded, thankful that the awkward moment had passed.

"Thank you for the thought and the clothes. They're perfect," she said, motioning to the boardshorts, T-shirt, and swimsuit top visible beneath the shirt. He skimmed his gaze down her long lovely legs to the sandals he'd bought and the bright pink nail polish on her toes.

"You look beautiful."

"Thanks. Now it's your turn," she said and held up a pair of men's boardshorts. "I'm assuming these are for you?"

He grinned. "For sure," he said, walked to her and grabbed the shorts.

"See you in a second," he said and dropped a kiss on her cheek before heading into the bathroom to change.

Once inside, he sucked in a long inhale, fighting back the rise of desire once again. The sight of her, even in something as simple as the casual wear, had him hard and aching to be with her again. But he knew that today demanded patience and restraint after the night they'd shared.

Today had to be about more than just the physical.

He changed into the boardshorts and luckily they were loose enough to hide his aroused state. With a few more deep breaths and a splash of cold water on his face, he had tamed his need enough to be able to grab some towels and head back out to the bedroom.

She was waiting for him, hair pulled back into some kind of knot that made her look years younger, much like the teenager who had captured his heart on that long ago summer night.

She held out her hand to him and said, "Ready?"

He slipped his hand into hers and said, "Totally."

Smiling, she swung their hands playfully and they walked out of the room and down the stairs. In the lobby, the innkeeper greeted them again with a friendly smile and said, "Have a nice day."

Out on the street, they did the short two block walk to the boardwalk and onto the beach. Luckily it was past twelve since the town normally wouldn't open up the beach until Sunday services were over. With the summer season over, there weren't any beach badge checkers which meant a good number of people were out on the sand, taking advantage of that and a gorgeous September day.

"So nice," Natalie said as they neared the water's edge and laid out the towels.

"It's one of my favorite times of year to come to the beach," he said. He sat down beside her and pulled off his shirt, eager to feel the warm kiss of the sun on his body. Appreciating the subtle once over she gave him that kindled another kind of heat in him.

Natalie sighed at the sight of him, so beautifully male. All lean muscle and smooth skin except for the smattering of hair across his chest that trailed down to . . . .

No, don't think about that, she warned herself. There would be time enough for that later, or at least she hoped there would be.

They hadn't talked about tonight or tomorrow. Neither was guaranteed to them given the current state of their marriage, but they were still husband and wife despite the separation.

And he was trying hard and so would she.

She slipped off the T-shirt he'd bought her to reveal the bikini top with the colorful almost tribal print. The tropical hues of the top perfectly matched the boardshorts he'd bought and she liked that the shorts were cut a little longer than some. She'd never been a fan of exposed butt cheeks and judging from the way Chase slowly swept his gaze up and down her body, he wasn't complaining about her outfit.

Easing down onto the towel, she closed her eyes against the bright sun and sucked in a deep breath of ocean-kissed air. There were few waves today, but there was still that sussurus of the sea coming and going. Seagulls squawked nearby and melded with the excited shouts of some young children playing at the water's edge.

She smiled, content with the peace of the day and peeked out of the corner of her eye toward Chase.

He was lying beside her, a content grin on his features. His arm outstretched with his hand palm up on the sand not far from her.

She slipped her hand into his and he started, surprised, and shot a half glance in her direction, but said nothing. His smile grew stronger though, bringing out a boyish dimple on one side of his face.

Twining her fingers with his, she smiled back and closed her eyes again to savor the peace of the morning.

An hour or so passed and the heat of the day grew stronger and heat built as the ocean breeze stilled.

She was starting to feel the burn of the sun on her skin and as she sat up and gazed at the water, Chase did the same.

"Time for a dip?" he asked.

She nodded and together they rose from the sand and ambled to the water's edge.

It had been a warm summer and September's temperatures hadn't cooled off all that much so the water was still really pleasant.

Chase tugged her into calf-deep water and then released her hand to dive into the waves.

As pleasant as it was, the water was cold enough to bring goosebumps to her sun-heated skin.

"Chicken?" Chase called out from a few feet away as he rose from the ocean and slicked back damp strands of his dark hair. The drops of water on his chest glistened with the touch of the sun, making her itch to wipe them off.

But first she had to brave the chill of the water and there was just one way to do that.

Sucking in a breath, she dove in and with a few strokes, came up beside Chase, shivering.

"Shit, shit, shit, it's cold," she said and wrapped her arms around herself.

Chase laughed and embraced her. Drew her close to the warmth of his body. "You always were a wuss in the water, Ramirez."

She grinned, thinking, "I might be a wuss, but I'm right where I want to be right now."

Tucked close together, they floated in the water, enjoying the lazy ebb and flow of the ocean. Their bodies warm at every spot they connected, but soon the cool water started to rob that heat and she shivered roughly against him.

"Time to dry off," he said and she wasn't about to argue.

They hurried out of the ocean and back to their towels. He'd grabbed a third one and gallantly offered it to her to dry off first.

She quickly wiped off the water and handed it to him. Appreciated the sight of him and the play of muscles as he rubbed the towel across his body and then lay back down for some more sun.

Resting on her side, she watched him for long minutes until he turned to face her.

"You okay?" he asked.

"This is nice," she said, unable to recall the last time they'd just spend the day together, without worries or interruptions.

He grinned and cradled her cheek. "It is nice. I'm glad we decided to do it."

She was glad as well and flipped onto her back to savor the heat of the sun on her skin.

She pushed all negative thoughts from her mind, wanting to just enjoy a glorious day and time with her husband.

Her husband.

She liked the sound of that. She liked the time they had spent together this weekend.

She hoped they could spend more time together.

Smiling, her eyes closed, she eased her hand into his again and just appreciated being in the now. Appreciated being with him.

The day would end soon enough and she wasn't sure she was ready for that.

Chapter 9

The sun was beginning to sting and Chase wished he had picked up some suntan lotion as well at the shop in town. He sat up and gazed down at the flush all along his chest and down his abs.

He glanced at Natalie and realized that his wife's skin had a faint trace of pink also.

Tracing a finger along her flat midsection, he roused her gently and said, "I think we need to get out of the sun for a little bit."

She leaned up on her elbows, shot a quick look at herself and him. "Yeah, we're looking toasty."

"How about a shower and an early dinner?" he said, hopeful about her response.

"I'd like that," she said and in a flurry of movement, she was up on her feet and picking up her towel from the sand.

He smiled, stood, and followed her, his hand resting on the small of her back as they walked off the sand and up the two blocks to their inn.

Trying to be respectful of her wishes, he kept his emotions neutral once they entered the room and she said, "Did you want to shower first?"

He wanted to shower together, but her question seemed to have foreclosed that possibility. He motioned to the bathroom and said, "Ladies first."

She grinned sexily and sauntered the few feet to where he stood. Taking hold of his hand, she said, "You know, we could be environmentally conscious and try to conserve some water by sharing that shower."

"I'm all for saving the environment," he said and his words freed the restraints they both seemed to have had in place.

In a rush, clothes flew off and across the room and they hurried to the bathroom with its large shower stall.

Chase was thankful the hot water came up quickly because he didn't know how long he could wait to have her inside the stall and beneath the jets, her skin all soapy and warm.

They stepped inside the shower and came together, kissing and touching. Eager to share their bodies and loving.

He squirted a gob of body wash into a washcloth and worked into a lather. Turning, he urged her away from the stream of water and smoothed the lather all across her shoulders and arms. Moved the washcloth down to skim it across the puckered tips of her breasts.

She moaned as he passed the washcloth across her again and he tossed it aside and cupped her breasts, playing with the soapy tips. Tweaking them before shifting back a little to let a stream of water fly over his shoulder and onto her body to wash away the suds.

Natalie shivered with need as Chase bent and sucked her nipple into his mouth, the feel of it even hotter than the warm water sluicing across his body and onto hers. Her insides clenched with want as his dick brushed her belly, but she didn't want to rush. She loved the way he touched her. Licked and teethed her nipples.

She needed to touch him and reached down, encircled him. His cock was slick from the water and soap, and she stroked him hard, wanting to bring him the same kind of pleasure he was giving her.

Over and over she shifted her hand along the hard length of him, drawing a jagged breath from him and a rougher nip on her breast that had her shuddering and on the edge.

"Nat, I want to be inside you. I want to come with you."

She wanted it, too.

Shifting, she leaned against the wall of the stall and guided him to her center.

He bent and nudged her legs apart, and slowly eased his dick inside her, filling her. Filling her heart with the gentle way he embraced her and said, "I can never get enough of you, Natalie. I need you so much."

She shattered with his words and he kissed her, swallowing her cries of release and as her climax ebbed, he finally moved, drawing her up and over into another. Kissing her and urging her on as he rocked in and out of her, reaching for his own release until with one final hard thrust, he came with her name on his lips.

He held her in his arms while the water washed over them, his breath ragged until little by little, peace returned.

They separated, but were never apart for long. A soapy caress across smooth skin and strong muscles. A lazy swipe to wipe away the last of the suds as they finished washing. An embrace as he wrapped a towel around her and briskly rubbed her dry.

Hand-in-hand they walked to the bed and climbed in. Became another tangle of arms and legs as they embraced and kissed. Desire roused and they made love yet again before slipping off to sleep for an afternoon nap.

When Chase woke, the room was growing dark as dusk settled in. He sighed heavily, knowing their time together was growing shorter with every passing minute.

Beside him Natalie roused as well and sat up. Her hair was sleep-tousled, cheeks pinkened from the warmth of cuddling together. Lips slightly swollen from the intense kisses they had shared.

She had never looked lovelier to him and he hoped he would be able to see her like this every day of his life, but he knew he had to be patient.

Their problems hadn't taken a day to develop and a solution wouldn't just take a day or two either.

"Would you like to go to dinner? Moonstruck?" he asked, naming one of their favorite local restaurants. They hadn't eaten a thing since breakfast that morning.

"I'd like that," she said.

He nodded and they rose from bed and dressed. Since Moonstruck was a little more upscale, Natalie slipped back into the dress she'd worn the night before.

"I'll have to be a little bit more prepared to stay next time," she said, so easily and without hesitation that his heart swelled with joy. And yet he held back again, afraid to push too soon and ruin the magic of their time together.

He offered her his hand and they walked together out of the inn and toward Pilgrim's Pathway. That street would take them past the Great Auditorium and the tents for which Ocean Grove was famous. Many of the tents were still up and inhabited, but it wouldn't be long before the tents would be closed up for the winter season and emptied until summer came again.

Natalie glanced at Chase as they walked past the tents, wondering if when summer came they'd still be together.

He'd shown her a taste of the old Chase this weekend. The fun, considerate, loving man she had fallen in love with.

Dare she dream that he was back for good and that they could make their marriage work again?

As they walked past the Great Auditorium, she glanced up at the cross and reminded herself to have faith.

Faith and love made all things possible.

At the end of Pilgrim's Pathway, they crossed the foot bridge into Asbury Park and strolled across the street to the restaurant. It was in a big Victorian style building with wraparound porches on each floor where patrons could eat during the summer months. Inside the ambiance was understated elegance and a coziness that just made you feel at home.

They were quickly seated near the corner windows on the second floor where they had a clear view of Wesley Lake and the Casino farther down along the beachfront. Lights were coming on as it grew dark, but muted blues and pinks still mingled in the dusky sky, creating an almost magical feel.

She smiled and reached over to caress Chase's jaw. Stroked her thumb across his lips in a touch more intimate than a kiss. "I had a lovely weekend. Thank you."

"The weekend isn't over yet," he said with a grin, but then grew a little more serious. "I never asked, but did you drive down?"

She shook her head. "I took the train from the city. Figured that was easier than driving."

"I can drive you back tonight if you'd like."

It was impossible for her to miss the uncertainty in his tones and the tension that had crept into his body, so she tried to ease past the moment. "If it won't make you too late for work in the morning, you can drop me off then."

There was a very visible wave of relief that washed over him and brought a smile to his face. "I can definitely do that."

She was grateful for the response that said that maybe, just maybe, he was going to make their relationship a priority.

The waiter came over at that moment with the menus and told them about the specials for the day.

Chase ordered a bottle of wine for them and the waiter stepped away to get their wine.

They quickly perused the menu and placed their orders when the waiter came back with wine glasses and the bottle they had ordered.

After the young man had poured their wine, Chase raised his glass in a toast and said, "To this wonderful weekend."

Her hand trembled as she held her glass and brought it to clink against his. "To this wonderful weekend," she said, but wished for more.

Chase narrowed his gaze and scrutinized her as she took a sip of her wine. Unnerved by his perusal, she looked away.

He cupped her cheek and gently urged her to face him again. "What's wrong, Nat?"

"Nothing," she lied and hated the choked sound of her voice as she battled back the emotions swamping her.

He let out a rough breath and shook his head. "Bullshit. I know you too well not to know something's wrong."

It wasn't that something was wrong more than so much had been so right. The whole weekend had been so right and she didn't want it to end, but she couldn't find the words to say it.

The waiter came over with the appetizers they had ordered, forestalling additional conversation, but just as Chase knew her too well, she understood him also. He wasn't going to leave it alone and for once, she was glad for that.

She ate her beet and goat cheese salad woodenly, not really tasting it thanks to her upset. A shame since the food at the restaurant was always exceptional.

When the busboy came by to whisk away their plates, Chase picked up his glass of wine, took a big sip and swallowed before facing her again. "Back in the room you said that you had to be better prepared for next time. Did you mean that? Do you want there to be a next time?"

Bam and there it was. The question that had been hanging over their heads not only all weekend, but in the two weeks since they'd agreed to give themselves this weekend in the hopes of making their marriage work again.

Her throat was so tight with emotion that all she could do was nod and eke out a whispery, "I do."

Chase shakily placed the glass back down on the table, reached over, and took hold of her hand. "I do, too. I want this to work."

"I want that, too, Chase," she admitted, grateful that the weekend had gone as well as it had.

He smiled tenderly and said, "I guess I should reserve our room for next weekend as well?"

"I'd like that, but on one condition," she said.

He gave her a puzzled look. "What condition?"

She grinned and playfully said, "You meet me under the boardwalk first."

He laughed and leaned forward to kiss her, stopping a hair's breadth from her lips. "I love you, Natalie."

"I love you, too, Chase," she said and gave herself over to his kiss, more certain than ever that their weekend rendezvous was a first step toward a lifetime together.

About the Author

NY Times and USA Today Bestseller Caridad Pineiro is a Jersey Girl who just wants to write, travel, and spend more time with family and friends. Caridad is the author of nearly 50 novels/novellas and loves romance novels, super heroes, TV and cooking. Caridad writes dark and sexy romantic suspense, erotic military romance, and paranormal romances for those who live to love on the edge. Her sweet, but still naughty side, Charity Pineiro, writes contemporary romances packed with emotion and humor. For more information on Caridad/Charity, please visit

http://www.caridad.com

_Or

http://www.rebornvampirenovels.com.

You can also find Caridad/Charity on:

Twitter at **https://twitter.com/caridadpineiro**
Facebook at **https://www.facebook.com/Caridad.Author**
Pinterest at **http://pinterest.com/caridadpineiro/**
Tsu at **https://www.tsu.co/CaridadPineiro**
Goodreads at **https://www.goodreads.com/Caridad_Pineiro**

Caridad also sends out a **newsletter** to her friends! To subscribe, please visit **www.caridad.com**.

If you liked UNDER THE BOARDWALK,
check out these other sexy and emotional stories by Caridad:

Take a Chance Military Romances
Rookie of the Year
Gambling for Love Romantic Suspense Box Set

FAST AND FLIRTY

A SHORT-LENGTH
CONTEMPORARY ROMANCE NOVELLA

NINA BRUHNS

NEW YORK TIMES & USA TODAY
BEST SELLING AUTHOR
With over 35 award-winning novels
More than 2 Million copies sold worldwide

The top-secret package STORM Corps transporter Kade Maddox is hired to deliver turns out to be way more trouble—and a whole lot sexier—than he ever anticipated.

Cajun Hot Press
May 2016
Published by Cajun Hot Press
Copyright © May 2016 by Nina Bruhns

The west coast of Italy

Nikki Phoenix whistled softly as the black and red sports car she'd been expecting to pass by topped the crest of the next rise and whipped around the road's hairpin turn toward her. *Holy mole.* Kade Maddox had one sweet ride, that was for damned sure. One of the new Lotus Evora Roadsters, if she wasn't mistaken. Wow. This was going to be even more fun than she'd thought.

She gave her tight sweater and miniskirt a quick zhuzh and leaned under the open hood of her BMW, bending over to give Maddox a good view of her backside and her long, bare legs. After a second, she reached in and loosened the alternator cable. Just in case.

The meticulous research she'd done after getting this assignment had revealed that STORM Corps transporter Kade Maddox always followed a firm set of self-imposed rules when he drove. He never broke them. Never. And one of his top rules was: *No passengers.*

Yeah, they'd just see about that.

Nikki stayed bent over and curled one designer high heel around the opposite ankle, doing her best to look cute and helpless as the Lotus took the nearest curve and sped toward the cutout where she'd parked the Beemer.

"Come on, baby. You don't need no stinkin' rules," she murmured to the engine block, deliberately not looking up. Any former Marine intelligence operator worth his salt would smell a setup a mile away.

She smiled at the air filter as her target slowed. "Oh, yeah. Who's your mama," she whispered, satisfaction swirling through her. Hell, she might actually pull this off. She wiggled her butt. Just a little.

From the corner of her eye, she watched the Lotus approach. The highly-polished black and red convertible shone in the bright Italian sunshine, sleek and elegant, backdropped against the sparkling azure blue of the sea beyond the twisty ribbon of road that clung to the cliffs. The car's top was down and she could clearly see it was Maddox behind the wheel wearing his usual STORM transporter uniform—a meticulously tailored charcoal-grey suit over a white button-down shirt and tie. His attractive dark hair was just long enough to be tousled by the wind, making him look deceptively casual and easygoing.

She knew better. From what she'd learned, the man was focused as a laser.

The Lotus slowed to a crawl. She held her breath and pretended not to notice as the man studied her through his mirrored sunglasses. Then the engine gunned and the convertible sped away without stopping.

Damn.

She straightened up and stared after him with a puff of frustration, hands on her hips. *Well, hell.*

Okay, yeah, she'd suspected it wouldn't be that easy. In fact, she might have been suspicious if it *had* been. Maddox wasn't the only one concerned with falling into a trap. But for some strange reason, she'd been looking forward to sharing a ride with a somewhat legendary—and surprisingly handsome—STORM operator. Why? She had no idea. By all accounts this particular man was her polar opposite—stiff, stolid, predictable. A rule-follower to the Nth degree. Nothing like her.

Maybe a fascination of opposites?

Or maybe she was just horny. The guy was a looker, and he had a killer body, too, if the photos of him she'd managed to find online were anywhere near reality. And it had been a good, long while since she'd allowed herself the indulgence of a fling.

Not that *he* would indulge, she had a feeling. Rule number 7, no doubt: *No monkey sex with strangers.*

Whatever. She wasn't interested in him, anyway—other than as a means to complete her assignment for Interpol. A freelance investigator specializing in art theft, Nikki had been hired to acquire the package he was transporting, and turn it over to Interpol.

Preferably without breaking any laws.

Yeah, yeah. But sometimes a girl had to do what a girl had to do.

Which was probably why they'd come to her in the first place, as opposed to any of the other investigators on the Interpol roster. Nikki Phoenix had been breaking rules since well before being unceremoniously tossed out of her career-diplomat father's house at seventeen, and she had no intention of stopping anytime soon.

So, *caveat Maddox.*

With an extra spurt of anticipation spinning through her, she rehooked the alternator and slammed her car's hood closed, climbed into the Beemer, and fired the engine to life.

Time to capture the eye of a STORM.

It didn't take Nikki long to catch up to Maddox. In less than half an hour she was easing the Beemer up behind him on the road.

She glanced down at the speedometer with a frown. He was actually doing the speed limit.

Really? The man was driving one of the most powerful sports cars in the universe, and he was going at minivan speed? Another one of his stupid rules?

She rolled her eyes, waited for a snippet of straightaway, stepped on it, and slingshotted around him. As she passed, she glanced over and gave him a little finger wave.

"Hi," she mouthed with a flirty smile.

Nothing.

Not even a crack in that hard expression.

Gawd. Rule number 28, she assumed: *Absolutely no smiling.*

The man needed a major lesson in lightening up. She might not be a Paris runway model, but she wasn't all *that* bad looking. What kind of guy didn't flirt with a pretty girl in a Beemer?

Good thing she loved a challenge.

She pulled ahead, far enough that she had glimpses of the Lotus in the rear-view mirror, and gradually increased her speed. To her satisfaction, he sped up and kept pace with her. Herd mentality—it worked every time.

But she didn't want to be driving point. She didn't know where he was heading to make his delivery—his final destination could be anywhere from Tuscany to Finland. If he made a turn and she lost him, it would be all over.

She wouldn't lose her job—she worked for herself. But she would tarnish her perfect record on her assignments from Interpol. They used her because she was the best. She wanted to keep it that way.

When she spotted a village up ahead, she decided to put Plan B into action.

After sending a quick text message, she pulled into a petrol station and pretended to fill gas in the car. Two minutes later, the Lotus drove in and stopped on the other side of the same pump. Yes! He *had* noticed her flirting.

Elation shot through her. She could almost hear the sweet sound of rules breaking into a million pieces as Maddox climbed from his vehicle.

She studiously ignored him.

"I see you got your car going," he said, punching buttons on the pump.

She slowly turned to look at him. "Yes," she said with a bland smile, "No thanks to you," and turned away again.

"What was wrong with it?" he asked to the sound of the nozzle sliding into the tank.

She waited a beat, then turned back, taking the opportunity to look him over from head to foot. His body was tall and muscular, and his suit fit perfectly. His face wasn't movie star handsome, but hard and rugged, his calm, patient blue eyes gazing through a wealth of experience. Nothing would scare this guy.

A coil of attraction tightened in her center. The man was frikkin' sexy as hell. Just her type. *Not good.*

She recovered her wits enough to ask, "Do you really care?"

One broad shoulder lifted. Still no smile. "Just curious." He leaned back against a fender in a negligent pose. "You seemed to have things under control."

She lifted a brow. "You think?"

He tipped his head. "Figured you knew what you were doing. If you'd needed help you would have flagged me down, not buried your head under the hood."

She mirrored the angle of his head. "Would you have stopped?"

The ghost of a smile flickered, then he turned to remove the nozzle from the gas tank and replace it on the pump.

"Anyway," she said with a wave of a hand. "I don't really want to deal with breaking down again. Can I catch a ride with you?"

He gave her a quick glance. "No. I don't accept passengers."

"Oh, stop," she teased. "I promise I'm not an ax murderer." She smiled broadly, grabbed her oversized purse from the front seat, and walked toward the Lotus as if she fully expected him to capitulate.

His face took on a politely stubborn edge. "Sorry. Not possible."

God, he was cute when he got all rigid and stubborn. She watched, inwardly amused, as he climbed in, doing his best to ignore her as she stepped up to the convertible's passenger side.

"Don't be silly," she said cheerfully, and in a smooth, practiced move, she slid her butt over the door and plopped onto the buttery leather seat. She tucked her bag onto her lap and grinned over at him. "Okay, let's go!"

He just stared, a multitude of reactions streaking across his face.

"I'd make it quick," she said, giving him a mischievous wink.

He frowned at that. "You need to get out of the car."

"Sorry, no can do. I really need a ride."

Right on cue, a police siren sounded in the distance. She smiled innocently. His frown deepened. "What have you done?"

She happened to know another of his stupid rules was: *Always be on time*. A run-in with the *carabinieri* would cost him precious time. *Oooh*, which rule would win out? She was betting on the last.

"I'll tell you all about it on the way," she said.

His eyes narrowed dangerously. "To where?"

"Wherever you're heading. But seriously. I'd go. Now."

He gave her the evil eye for a brief moment. Then, to her relief, he put the car in gear and took off. "I'll let you out at the next village."

Yeah. She beamed inwardly. She didn't think so.

Kade Maddox had seen a lot of pushy women in his day. But never anything quite like the cheeky little thing currently batting her eyelashes at him as if there was nothing at all unusual in hopping into a guy's ride without so much as a by-your-leave, practically shocking him into a damned heart attack. But the sirens—and the smug look in those pretty green eyes—made him think twice about refusing.

At his reluctant command, the Lotus leapt to life and peeled out onto the road.

Well. Maybe she wasn't so little. She was tall and curvy. And to be honest, those long-lashed eyes were damn attractive...along with the rest of her. Had he mentioned she was tall and curvy? With a fall of beautiful golden hair that made a man's fingers itch and his mind go right to where the nearest pillow might be to spread it out on and—

Shit.

This was not in the plan. He had a job to do. A package to deliver. *That* was where his mind needed to be. Not on—

Focus, Maddox.

He clamped his jaw and ground out, "I don't appreciate you involving me in your bullshit."

She chuckled. "Sorry." She shifted around in her seat to look at him, her expression not the least bit contrite. "Where are you headed, anyway?"

Like he'd actually tell her. "What are the cops after you for?" he demanded.

"The Beemer," she said, and nibbled her lip. With a twinkle in those expressive eyes, she added, "It may have been borrowed."

The audacity of the woman shouldn't surprise him, all things considered, but it did. What kind of game was she playing? Clearly, she took him for a damned fool. Which...okay, was possibly not so far from the mark at the moment.

He let out a silent groan. He'd *knew* he shouldn't have agreed to this stupid assignment. Already she had made him violate more rules than he had since joining STORM a year ago to work for his former Marine commander, Major Llowell. What else did she have up her sleeve? He really didn't want to find out.

"I should stop at the next police station and turn you in," he said. It would serve her right. If not the mission.

She just laughed. "I wouldn't, if I were you."

He snorted. "No? Give me one good reason."

She leaned toward him and ran her finger down his arm. Even the substantial layers of his suit jacket and shirt didn't stop the zing that went through his flesh at her unexpected touch.

She leaned in closer. "I'll tell them you're my boyfriend who runs a chop shop and you made me steal it." The fearless glint in her eyes said she'd do it, too.

Spending time in an Italian jail was not on his agenda. And it could be days before the cops straightened everything out and let him go, unless he called the major to intervene. In which case, Kade would fail his assignment.

Not an option.

Well, hell.

He took a calming breath, and eased it out as he steered the car around a serpentine curve bordered by bright magenta flowering vines. This was ridiculous. He knew the annoying woman had been sent by Interpol to intercept the small but priceless antique music box he was transporting, and take possession of it. No doubt using any means necessary.

At least he assumed she was the one. She resembled the photo he'd been given. Though, God knew, in every other way this woman was just about the opposite of who he'd expected them to send. In reality, she could be anyone.

Stolen during the war by the Nazis, the music box had recently been unearthed during a STORM operation in Tunisia, and was now on its way back to its rightful owner—albeit via a somewhat circuitous route. There were those who didn't appreciate the delay—including Interpol—and he'd been warned to be on the alert for possible hijackings.

That fake car breakdown had been all too obvious a ploy. When he'd first spotted her, his plan had been simply not to let her get her mitts on the music box, and just continue driving to his final destination. She'd no doubt tail him, but after delivery, whatever happened would be out of his hands. The client could do what he wished with the music box, and with her. None of his business.

But that had been before she'd so rudely landed in his passenger seat.

He reminded himself of Rule #1: *Do the job.*

That was not just his own rule, but the whole STORM Transporter Division's. Completing the mission was the one thing Major Llowell expected of all his transporters. No way was Kade letting him down.

Even if it meant putting up with a little bullshit along the way.

"You do realize blackmail is illegal?" he muttered over a rush of sea air as the road skimmed the edge of a steep cliff that bottomed into a churning froth of blue waves.

"Now you're just being melodramatic," she scolded with a curve of her lips.

His gaze snagged on those lips. They were very nice. Plump and shiny with a slick of dark pink that made them stand out nicely against her smooth, fair skin.

Kissable lips.

He dragged his gaze away and focused on the road ahead. *Dangerous lips.* Damn, he was in such big trouble.

"Look," he said, steeling his resolve, "I don't know who you are or—"

"I'm Nikki," she interrupted cheerfully. "Nikki Phoenix. And you are...?"

He didn't want to tell her. Which was totally irrational. If she knew he was a transporter, she sure as hell already knew his name.

"Maddox," he said grumpily. "Lance Corporal Maddox." Why he'd given his former rank, he had no idea. It just bugged him that Ms. Nikki Phoenix was so cavalier about...well, everything. Maybe she'd think twice about outright theft if she knew he was a former military man who could bring her down with one arm tied behind his back.

She looked over at him curiously. "Army?"

"Marines. Ex."

"*Ah.* Once a Marine, always a Marine," she murmured, then hiked a brow. "*Hmm.* A Lotus on a military salary? Interesting."

He returned her look levelly. "What are you implying?"

Again, if she knew he was a transporter, she had to know this was a company car. Which meant she was deliberately trying to rile him into revealing more than he should.

Her mistake.

She just smiled. "So. Where are we heading?"

He had to admit, she was persistent. With a very unique brand of torture.

"Fine, never mind," she said at his silence, settling back in her seat and shoving her huge purse down to the floor. "Surprise me."

Oh, he'd surprise her, all right.

"What's this?" she asked, fingering the special custom tablet that STORM installed in all their vehicles.

Positioned in front of the glove box, the tablet was attached via a flexible goose-neck so the driver could easily move it around to see better. Along with awesome computing power, the unit was equipped with a sophisticated GPS along with satellite cell service and wifi, so the driver always had instant access to the internet...and the STORM Command supercomputers.

Not that she needed to know that.

"GPS," he said, and noted a passing road sign that stated the next village was just two kilometers ahead. Thank God.

"Doesn't look like a GPS." She poked a finger along the row of front buttons. "What else does it do?"

"Hey! Don't touch th— *Shit*," he said as the monitor sprang to life. "Tabby, turn off," he instructed it loudly.

"Tabby? *Ooh*, voice command," Nikki exclaimed gleefully. "Awesome. Tabby, turn on. Show me your menu."

"What the hell do you think you're doing?" he sputtered. "Tabby, turn off and lock."

But it was too late. The monitor didn't even flicker. Somehow, Nikki had pulled up the physical keyboard from beneath the dash and was typing like crazy, locking him out.

"*Wow*, this is amazing!" she exclaimed. "Look at all this—"

His pulse took off like a rocket. *Jesus.* Had he misread the situation? Was she after something vastly different than Nazi treasure? STORM Corps—Strategic Technical Operations and Rescue Missions Corporation—was a nongovernmental spec-ops outfit whose main business was hiring out to private companies and individuals, most often to recover and defend hostages and other valuable assets—or in the case of the Transporter Division, to transport the same. But STORM was also hired to carry out sensitive or controversial covert ops all over the world, in situations where official government agencies couldn't or wouldn't go. As a result, the company was in possession of a whole lot of top secret intel. Much of which was accessible through that tablet.

"Turn it off," he ordered in a voice that conveyed he meant business.

"*Whoops.* I think I—"

Suddenly, there was a metallic *snap* and a small panel flipped open behind the seats. The familiar soft whir of propellers sounded as the 34-B—a miniature traffic drone—took off from its hiding place and pelted up into the sky.

"God *damn* it!"

"Holy crap. What was that?" she cried, her eyes widening in astonishment as she twisted in her seat and focused on the little mechanical wonder zipping above them. Her attention whipped down again as the steep mountain road and the bordering ocean snapped onto the tablet screen in full living color. "My God. A drone. This is so freaking insane."

And so freaking classified. The tablet also held the software for the 34-B—STORM's newest secret weapon—recently designed by the fiancée of one of the other transporters. When launched, the baseball-sized drone was an eye-in-the-sky of infinite usefulness, sending down invaluable data on road, traffic, and weather conditions, along with views of the surrounding countryside, as seen through a whole host of possible lenses and filters.

He was going to have to report this breach.

"What else does it do?" she asked, her gaze glued to the screen.

Thankfully, a jumble of white stucco buildings loomed up next to the road. He stomped on the brake and pulled over in front of a small hotel. *Time to put an end to this farce.* The damned woman had knocked him so far off kilter from the first second he saw her that, ever since, all he'd been doing was reacting.

Marines didn't react to situations. They controlled them.

He stopped the car. "I need you to get out now." He calmly reached for the shoulder holster hidden under his suit jacket.

She grinned as she glanced up at him. The grin faltered somewhat when she saw the Glock 19 he was now holding—pointing at her—but only for a split second. "Or what?" she asked dryly. "You'll shoot me? Like Jason Stratham in that stupid Transporter movie? Because of your stupid rules?"

He ground his teeth. "The rules are not stupid," he said. "And for your information, Jason Stratham did not shoot the fourth guy. The client did."

Her grin widened.

He slammed his eyes shut in a real effort not to do anything rash. Like shoot himself. And counted to ten.

Make that twenty.

"How many times have you seen that movie?" she teased.

He opened his eyes and gave her a withering glare. "Out."

"So..." A slight frown creased her forehead as her eyes flicked downward for a brief moment. "I take it your mini-drone is programmed to collect all sorts of interesting data. And spot potential hazards. Like, say, armed bad guys."

He let out a derisive noise. "Nice try. You're stalling. I'll give you till—"

"So, you're saying it's not? And those aren't?"

He was honestly starting to get a headache. "Those aren't what?"

"Bad guys. With guns. Hiding behind the next building up."

He blinked. And sliced his focus to the tablet. Sure enough, the 34-B was hovering far enough above three suspicious-looking men that they couldn't hear it, but the video stream plainly showed their drawn weapons. Jericho 941s, he noted.

Fuck.

He had been *that close* to jettisoning the menace.

But he only wanted her at arm's length, not dead. Who knew how far those tangos would go to acquire their target—which was probably the music box. But he'd worked in the intelligence biz long enough not to rely on assumptions. They could be after anything.

Him.

The Lotus.

STORM intel via the tablet.

Or maybe even Nikki Phoenix.

Just great.

With a frustrated exhale, he growled, "Scoot down on the floor. It's about to get ugly."

Surprisingly, Nikki obeyed and ducked down to the floor.

Kade felt a quick spurt of satisfaction as he holstered his Glock, then swung the tablet's keyboard close and started typing with one hand while working the trackball with the other.

But his relief was short-lived. She bolted up again almost immediately—holding a Sig P220. He wasn't exactly surprised...but damn.

Thankfully, she didn't aim it at him, but just held it at the ready, her attention swinging back to the tablet. "Who are they?" she asked, eyes narrowed.

"You tell me," he suggested as the video stream showed the tiny drone buzzing straight toward the tangos.

"What the hell is that thing doing?" Alarm threaded through her voice.

"Creating a diversion."

As he'd hoped, the two bad guys spun around to scowl up at the spy drone, then raised their weapons and started shooting at it. The echoes of their gunshots bounced off the white-stuccoed buildings of the village.

"Holy crap," she squeaked, instinctively ducking from the digital bullets on the screen.

So did the drone. It was programmed to avoid being hit by pretty much anything incoming. It zipped back and forth at lightning speed, confusing the bads even more.

"It's like a damned quidditch ball," Nikki said, clearly awed by the performance.

"Way better," Kade assured her, swung the keyboard away again, threw the car into gear, and sped out of the parking lot. "Hang on," he ordered. "And don't shoot anybody," he added with a quick frown at her Sig.

Naturally, this time she *didn't* do as she was told. Instead, she lowered the weapon, reached for the keyboard, and started moving the trackball back and forth. The drone followed right along. "Ha!" she exclaimed, and proceeded to lead the tangos on a merry chase with it. Damn, she was a quick learner.

In the ensuing chaos, Kade was able to pass the tangos before they noticed the vehicle streaking by. Instantly, they gave chase. Luckily, they were driving a normal Fiat which was no match for a Lotus. But even so, between traffic and the crazy curvy road, Kade was unable to shake them completely. The shooters clung determinedly to their tail, if losing a bit of ground for every kilometer. The 34-B kept pace high above the Lotus, sending video of the road below so they always knew where their pursuers were, along with all the other traffic.

"That is one amazing gadget," Nikki remarked, studying the control buttons on the monitor. "It's got macro, telephoto, night vision, and infrared? Jeez. Does it cook and do windows, too?"

He chuckled. "I wish."

"So, those guys," she said conversationally. "Did you notice their guns?"

"Hard to miss," he drawled.

"I mean the type."

He had. They'd been carrying Jericho 941s. A bit unusual. But why had *she* noticed? He looked over at her with growing suspicion. "What about it?"

"Why would Mossad be chasing you?" she asked, as if she hadn't noticed his mistrust.

All right. That clinched it. Only someone in the military or the spy biz would know the Jericho 941 was Mossad's weapon of choice. But he had to know for sure if she was who he thought she was. Or someone completely different.

"Who the hell do you work for?" he demanded, and added, though there was little doubt about this part, at least, "And what do you want with me?"

"I think that's a longer conversation than we have time for right now," she said with a grimace. "Those guys looked serious. We should probably put as much space between us and them as we can."

He clamped his jaw. "There is no we," he reminded her.

Nevertheless, he stepped on it, even as his imagination ran wild, casting her as everything from a Russian spy to that serial killer ax murderer she'd denied being.

Though he tended to believe her about that.

What he didn't want to believe was that this was the woman he'd been told to expect. The one he, somehow, had to deal with. A sinking feeling settled in the pit of his stomach as he wrestled with what to do. He wanted her gone. Out of his car. She was too unpredictable. Too dangerous.

And too fucking attractive by far.

She was messing with his mission. Messing with his mind. And if he wasn't careful, she'd be messing with his body. Big-time. One unguarded look at her smoking figure and he'd be a gonner. Hell, his body was already quickening just thinking about those luscious curves.

He did not need a woman like her in his car. Or in his life. A woman with skewed priorities, who skipped along her merry way with no thought for others, or for the consequences of her actions.

A woman just like his parents.

At the thought, a shudder went through him. *God.* Just what he wanted. *Not.* He loved his parents dearly, but if you looked up the phrase "flakey, space-cadet hippies," their picture would be right there on top. His entire childhood had been one long gypsy van ride after another. *Ugh.*

Though, seriously, why he was even thinking along these lines, he had no idea. Want her in his life? *Hell,* no. He had no personal interest in Nikki Phoenix. Was he freaking kidding?

"I need to make a phone call," he muttered, and at her glance of agreement, he said, "Tabby, call home."

Seconds later a voice came through the satcom. "Dispatch."

"This is Maddox. Tell the major I've got shooters on my tail carrying Jericho 941s."

"Mossad?" came the incredulous reply.

"That would be my guess. Check the drone footage for confirmation. Any help would be appreciated."

There was a brief pause with muffled conversation in the background. Then, "The package?"

"I picked it up. It's safe," he said, giving Nikki a short glance. He frowned when he noticed she'd pulled out her cell phone and her thumbs were flying over the keyboard. "For now."

He listened with one ear to admonitions to stick to the plan and call in when he lost the tangos.

"Will do." After he hung up, he demanded, "Who were you texting?"

She gave him an enigmatic smile. "You phoned home. So did I."

"Where? Jerusalem?"

She choked out a laugh. "Yeah. Because, you know, my fellow agents are always shooting at me on the job."

"Wouldn't be surprised," he mumbled.

She stuck out her tongue at him. "Now you're just being rude."

Despite everything, he cracked a grin. Okay, maybe she had a certain bad girl charm. He had to admit, he liked a woman with a little sass.

His mind raced, trying to decide what to do, until they hit the outskirts of Rome. When the first of the seven famous hills came into view, he returned his focus to figuring out a plan to evade their ever-persistent pursuers. He was fairly familiar with the layout of the city since the European STORM headquarters was located just down the road in Naples. He and the guys drove up to Rome pretty often for a night or weekend. But he had a feeling these tangos probably knew the city a whole lot better than he did. Mossad generally didn't skimp on the details. If that's who they really were. Which sort of made sense, considering the history of the music box. This was just an unanticipated complication.

Time to get serious and shake these trigger-happy bastards. Getting shot was definitely not on his agenda.

"Tabby, calculate the optimum route to lose our tail," he ordered the computer. Less than half a minute later, a map popped onto the screen, enhanced by drone video, showing a glowing pink line snaking through a complicated network of streets. Instantly, the robotic voice started telling him where and when to turn. Nikki chimed in with a few observations not immediately apparent to the computer, and even typed in a couple of midstream course corrections. Within fifteen minutes, they had lost their pursuers.

"Pull in here," Nikki said a few moments later, pointing to an obscure alley between two ancient brick apartment buildings.

Running on autopilot, Kade did as she instructed without thinking. Which he instantly regretted. The alley was a dead end, dark and dirty, filled with overflowing trash cans. The perfect place for an ambush.

He slammed on the brakes and started to grind into reverse. He couldn't be*lieve* he'd let his guard down so badly. "God damn it! What the hell? A *trap?*"

His gut twisted. He was so fucking screwed.

Wow. He really didn't trust her.

"No. It's a safe house," Nikki answered Kade evenly, batting back more than a twinge of annoyance. A trap? Seriously? The man really had a one-track mind.

Which, okay, could be an advantage at times. Like, say, when you were in the middle of a shoot-out. Or, you know, making out with a guy. Or better yet, making love. But at times like now, with all that suspicion in Kade's eyes—even after she'd helped him evade those Mossad agents trying to appropriate his shipment—not so much.

He might be sexy as hell, but talk about flat-out paranoid.

Even if it was somewhat justified.

"I thought it would be nice to have that conversation you've been wanting, uninterrupted by gunfire," she said.

He looked over at her doubtfully. "What kind of safe house?"

She didn't stop to debate the wisdom of what she was about to do. She'd already made the decision to come clean with him. It was easy to see that Kade Maddox was a just-the-facts-ma'am kind of operator who would not be swayed by games, or lies, or even sex. He would see through all of that and toss her out on her butt in a nanosecond. She sensed he would only respond favorably to the truth.

Well. Maybe sex would work. She'd seen the way he looked at her when he didn't think she was watching. But that strategy wasn't a certainty. He'd probably just enjoy the sex and not give in about a single other thing.

Not helpful.

Besides, despite his drool-worthy body, he was not her type. Far too stiff. And not in a good way.

So, she told him the truth. "It's an official Interpol safe house."

His brows went up skeptically. "You want me to believe you're with Interpol?"

Even more annoyance flared, and she balled her hand into a fist against the urge to smack him. "You want me to believe you're not an asshole?" she shot back.

Unexpectedly, the corner of his lips curved up slightly. "No. I am definitely an asshole. My friends are always telling me so."

"Some friends," she observed.

"But you didn't answer the question."

She pushed out a breath. "I'm a freelance investigator, but I've done a lot of work for Interpol."

"Are you working for them now?"

She nodded.

He frowned.

"Pull in after me," she said, hopped out of the car, and strode as best she could in high heels over the uneven cobblestones to an old, dilapidated-looking garage door that was set into the apartment building's ground floor, facing the alley. She typed the entry code into a hidden panel in the molding, and the door silently went up. The garage might look rundown, but everything was actually high-tech and very secure. She waved Kade in as the lights snapped on.

He parked, carefully recalled the drone to its hiding place behind the seats, then reluctantly followed her up the sagging stairs to the top-floor apartment that was the safe house.

"You've been here before?" he asked, glancing around and taking stock.

"Yep. It's small but cozy, and it's kept well-stocked with food and fresh linens."

Once inside, she tossed her shoulder bag down on the sofa and headed for the narrow galley kitchen. "I'll make us something to eat. Why don't you open a bottle of wine?"

He stared at her incredulously. "Are you for real?"

"What? Not hungry?" She glanced at the wall clock. It was well past noon—almost three, in fact. "Well, I am, so I hope you don't mind if I eat."

"What about that conversation?"

"I talk better on a full stomach."

He pushed out a breath. "Fine. We'll eat first. But then you'll tell me exactly what this is all about."

Reaching for the refrigerator door, she smiled. "Not worried about meeting your deadline?"

A muscle ticked below his left eye as he regarded her.

She smiled wider. "Why, yes, Lance Corporal Kade Maddox. I do know pretty much everything there is to know about you. Including your unholy penchant for sticking to your damned rules."

"Something you're clearly unfamiliar with," he muttered. But at least he seemed less skeptical about her credentials. "Can you prove any of what you're saying?"

Or maybe not.

She sighed. "I think I'm going to need that wine now."

He must have agreed—and believed her, at least a little bit—because he just nodded, went to the wine rack in the eating nook next to the kitchen, and picked out a bottle. "Red okay?"

"Perfect."

She threw together a quick meal of spaghetti Bolognese and salad, with fixings she found in the fridge. As she cooked, she sipped on the wine he'd poured, and he watched her from the small kitchen table with an inscrutable look on his face.

"So, you're a private investigator," he said when they'd finished their salads and were waiting for the pasta to finish cooking.

"Not exactly. A freelance investigator. I don't find missing dogs or straying spouses. My specialty is art. I generally work for wealthy private individuals around the world, or for law enforcement agencies when they don't have jurisdiction."

He was back to looking dubious. "I thought Interpol has jurisdiction worldwide."

She took another sip of wine. "Interpol isn't an enforcement agency. They're a facilitator. No guns, no powers to arrest anyone. Therefore, as I'm sure you're aware, jurisdiction is a moot issue."

"And what does any of all that have to do with me?" In spite of the words, his expression said he knew exactly what it had to do with him. She got the distinct feeling this whole conversation was just monkeys clicking on a typewriter.

Before she answered, she got up and drained the spaghetti. Steam arose, filling her senses and making her stomach growl. She dished up plates and ladled sauce over them. "Hey, want to eat out on the balcony? There's a nice little bistro table with a sweet view of the rooftops of Rome."

Again with the raised brow. "You mean, so it's easier for those Mossad agents to shoot at us?"

Oops. "Right. Good point." She set their plates on the kitchen table and took the seat across from him, reaching for the freshly grated parmesan.

He refilled her wine glass, which was nearly empty. His, she noted, had hardly been touched.

"Okay," he said. "Enough stalling. Let's hear it. I want to get out of here and back on the road asap."

"So, you *are* worried about your deadline."

He shook his head. "No. I have three days to get there."

"Where?"

He took a deliberate bite of spaghetti. "This is great."

God, he was obnoxious.

"In that case," she said, "I think we should spend the night here."

He stared at her for a long moment, his expression bouncing between dismissive and intrigued.

Inwardly, she winced. At the mention of spending the night, his mind had obviously gone places she hadn't intended. It just struck her that it might be a good idea to lay low to let the dust settle.

However...now that he mentioned it...

"Not a chance," he said.

She tipped her head flirtatiously. "Why not? Scared?"

His lips curled. "Of what? You? Hardly."

"*Oooh*," she purred, and leaned toward him. "Big tough Marine, *huh?*"

"You bet."

She leaned a bit closer and murmured, "Incorruptible. Undistractible." She wet her lower lip with her tongue suggestively. "Unseducible."

He surprised her by leaning forward, too, almost touching her nose to nose. "Oh, but you're wrong. I'm imminently seducible. Wanna give it a try?"

Her body seemed to be suddenly taken over by aliens. Before she knew what she was doing, she closed in, brushed her lips over his, and whispered, "Oh, yeah. I'd like that."

She didn't know who was more shocked—him or herself. For an instant, neither moved. They hovered so close together, she tasted the tang of wine and sauce on his warm breath, and could smell a masculine note of cologne under the spicy, tomatoey aroma wafting from their plates. Almost unconsciously, her eyes closed, and she lifted her parted mouth a fraction of an inch, pressing it lightly to his. The taste of him, musky and toe-curlingly sexy, teased the tip of her tongue.

A coil of arousal, strong and insistent, tightened in her center.

Ho-boy.

This was totally not in the plan.

She started to pull away, but his fingers drilled through her hair and caught her around the back of her neck. "No," he said. And deepened the kiss.

She made a sound. It was supposed to be a protest, but it sounded more like a plea. And it was. After that, the only sounds she made were soft moans of pleasure.

He kissed her and kissed her. Until the table between them was too much of a barrier, and he pulled her up and around it, and into his arms.

A shiver of electric need zinged through her whole body. It had been a long, long time since she'd felt anything like it. If ever.

God, she wanted him.

She grasped his lapels and gripped them in her fists, trying like hell to get hold of herself. "This," she managed, "is not a good idea."

"Don't worry," Kade murmured, caught up in the searing pleasure spilling from Nikki's lips down through his whole body. Holy *fuck*, the woman could kiss. "We can reheat the spaghetti later."

Nikki choked out a laugh, and pulled away a little. "Not exactly what I meant."

He tugged her back to him. "What's wrong? You're the one seducing me, remember?" He kissed her again, long and thorough. Being seduced had not been part of his careful mission agenda, but hey, a man had to be flexible.

"But..." she murmured against his lips. "Isn't this breaking, like, ten of your rules?"

No shit.

Rule #1: *Do the damn job.*

The reminder brought him painfully back to reality. Or rather, it should have. But his inner caveman rebelled.

Against his better judgment, he adjusted the press of their bodies. Closer. Firmer. Their curves and hollows fit together perfectly, center to center, her breasts pillowing up against his chest like succulent fruit. He literally ached to bend down and taste them. It was torture not to.

"Trust me," he assured her hoarsely. "I have no rules against having sex with a beautiful woman."

Except this particular woman. Because he had a job to do, he reminded himself, groping desperately for his badly failing willpower. Having sex could screw up this assignment in all sorts of unpredictable ways. And there was nothing he hated more than unpredictable.

Even so, his hands had a mind of their own. They wandered up her body, delighting in exploring every sensuous inch of warm flesh.

She stopped them before they reached really interesting territory. "So," she said, her tone carrying more than a hint of acerbity, "I guess, then, you make a habit of this sort of thing."

He was on the verge of saying, "Hell, no," but stopped himself just in time.

Right. *Reality check.*

"Sex?" He forced a shrug. "Define 'habit.' I'm a guy, yeah?"

Predictably, she stepped well back from him. "You are *such* an asshole."

Sometimes doing the damn job could be a real bitch. "I believe we've been over that already."

He saw exactly when cold realization dawned in her passion-hazed eyes. "Wait. This was—" They snapped to a clear, icy green. "You *played* me? *On purpose?*"

He smiled at her, all the while berating himself inwardly. He forced another shrug. "I figured kissing you would be a lot more fun than agreeing I'm unseducible and insisting on sticking to business. I knew you'd see the light."

She just stared at him, her pretty, kissable mouth agape.

And there it was. The biggest reason he should never let his guard slip and bend the damn rules.

He'd hurt her.

Sure, she'd willingly set herself up for the fall, but that didn't make him feel any less of a jerk for taking advantage. Regret avalanched through him, but he drove his point home before he did something *really* stupid. Like kiss her again. "Sometimes, men are not the hormone-driven, idiot lunkheads you seem to think they are," he murmured.

Liar.

Her eyes narrowed. "No. Sometimes, they're just plain idiots." She huffed, and marched back to the table, sat down with an angry *plunk*, and grabbed up her fork.

No argument there.

Guilt cooled the arousal that had heated his body just moments before. He knew what it felt like to be rejected sexually. It sucked. And the truth was, he'd do almost anything to be able to *not* reject her offer.

Almost.

"For what it's worth," he said, joining her again at the table, "I *don't* make this a habit. And it's just about killing me to turn you down." She stabbed her fork viciously into her spaghetti, and he added with a wince, "Not that us having sex would've gained you anything. It just would have been"—he swallowed back the burning frustration—"fucking amazing."

An unreadable emotion steamrolled through her eyes, but she kept her gaze firmly on her meal. "You'll never know, will you," she ground out.

The sizeable devil dancing in his cock made him volley back, "I have a policy never to say never."

She actually snorted.

Oh, yeah. Life well and truly sucked.

"Anyway," he muttered. "You never told me what Interpol wants with me."

She finally looked up. Her cool gaze held no trace of the woman who'd so recently been practically melting in his arms. "They don't want you. They want the music box."

All righty, then.

The news itself was no shock. STORM had carefully leaked word of the transport last week, along with certain misinformation, specifically to attract Interpol's attention—and hers. But Nikki's ready admission that she was after the music box surprised the hell out of him. He'd definitely expected her to continue to try and con him out of it. Instead, she'd been honest with him.

Okay. His planning might have gotten turned around backwards and upside down, tangling him hopelessly in threads of deception, but...the mission plan was actually working.

Unfortunately.

He gave a mental sigh. Because never in a million years had it occurred to him that his personal feelings would get involved in a job.

But they had on this one.

In a very big way.

This was not the usual kind of mission. Far from it. And he was seriously doubting the wisdom of taking it on, at all. Not for himself—that was already a given—but for STORM Corps. He was starting to question the motives of the client.

Nikki Phoenix believed she knew exactly what she was doing. What *he* was doing. She'd been told he was transporting a package. Which was true enough.

She believed the package was the beautiful music box that had been recovered in Tunisia. The precious object stolen by the Nazis so long ago, which STORM had put out they were selling to a collector rather than returning to its rightful owner.

But she was wrong.

STORM had every intention of restoring the antique to the descendants of those unlucky victims whose lives and possessions had been so cruelly stolen from them.

But the music box was not his true job.

It was not the real package.

She had no way of knowing the actual package he was delivering to this client was something vastly different.

That the package was...

Her.

Kade took so long to respond to Nikki's terse comment about what Interpol wanted that she didn't think he intended to speak to her ever again. Which would have been, you know, totally logical since *she* had been the injured party in his charade.

Men.

At length, he did look up. His expression was scrupulously neutral...as though he was fighting some inner battle he didn't want her to see. Or maybe his emotions really were just that uninvolved.

"I'm sorry you went to all this trouble," he said levelly. "Interpol can ask us for the music box all they want, but they have no legal right to take it. Our client has hired us to deliver a package to him, and as long as I'm not breaking the law, that's what I intend to do."

A stab of frustration hit her. "But you *are* breaking the law. You're transporting stolen property."

"Can you prove it's stolen?"

Reluctantly, she shook her head. "No, not formally. Yet. But there's plenty of anecdotal evidence. We were counting on you doing the right thing."

His head gave a little shake. "I don't have that authority. I'm just the transporter. Bring me a court order and I'll be happy to turn over the music box. Until then, there's nothing I can do."

She felt a spike of scorn. "Just following orders, *eh?*"

He bristled. "Both of my grandfathers and three of their brothers fought in that war," he said through clamped teeth. "One of whom died fighting the Nazis. In case you've forgotten, a big part of what we were fighting for over here was the right to the due process of law."

She blinked as a brush of shame went through her. Good point. She hadn't ever looked at this retrieval from the other side of the coin. She'd only seen the gross injustice of what had happened in the past—in terms of reparation, the very *least* the victims deserved was to have their stolen property returned.

But Kade was right. STORM Corps hadn't broken any laws in obtaining the music box—not even in Tunisia. Everything was aboveboard, paperwork in order. Interpol had checked. If he was not willing to give it up voluntarily, she couldn't force him. Not that she ever would. Returning the property should be done legally, through a court of law, if need be. Otherwise, she was no better than the Nazis.

"Okay," she reluctantly said. "I can respect that."

He looked vaguely surprised. "Oh. Okay. Good." After a brief hesitation, he picked up his fork and began twirling spaghetti. "It's not that I disagree with you, in principle. It's just—"

She held up a hand. "I know. You'd lose your job if you just handed it over to some random person who says they work for Interpol. I get it."

He shifted slightly in his seat. "Yeah. Something like that."

She took a bite of her pasta and grimaced. "This is cold. I'll heat it up again."

She reached for his plate and her hand collided with his. Their eyes met, and held. And just like that, a shot of warmth spread through her like a jigger of bourbon. Erotic memories of their long, hot kiss enveloped her, sending a wave of goose bumps cascading over her skin.

Ho-boy.

She'd thought they'd gotten over their highly inconvenient sexual attraction.

Apparently not.

"Thanks," he said, his voice sounding as rough as her nerves.

She grabbed the plates and stuffed them into the microwave. No way was she going there again. He'd rejected her once, and she was a very quick learner.

"I suppose you'll be leaving as soon as we've eaten," she said, desperate to change the channel on her thoughts.

Again, he was silent for a few moments. Then he really shocked her by saying, "Look. I can't tell you who the client is, but I won't stop you from following me to the delivery. Once we get there, you could ask him if he'd be willing to give Interpol the music box, or let them arrange its rightful return."

"Really?" she asked hopefully. His suggestion was pretty much her Plan B, anyway.

"I mean"—his lips curved up slightly—"somehow, I can't see you giving up quite so easily. I assume you're planning to follow me whether I give you permission or not."

She smiled. *Smart man.* "Just three hours, and you know me so well."

He smiled back. But below the amusement lurked a shadow of something more...carnal. Something that wordlessly said, "Hell, no. Not nearly well enough."

Another shiver of arousal stole through her.

Then the microwave gave a loud *ding*, startling the daylights out of her. She jumped, and spun to retrieve their plates before he could see how badly he'd flustered her without even trying.

At least...she assumed he wasn't trying. After all, he was the one who'd stopped things earlier. If he hadn't, they'd be in bed right now, naked and sweaty, and having "fucking amazing" sex.

She swallowed. Oh, yeah. He'd said that, hadn't he.

Okay, maybe he *was* trying.

How on earth was she supposed to deal with this explosive, ridiculously confusing situation?

The man was frustrating as hell!

She put their plates down on the table with a clatter. "That would be great," she managed to say. "But I don't actually have a car to follow you in."

His brows lifted. "And this stopped you before?"

She made a face. "Right. About that. The Beemer wasn't really stolen. I just said that to— Anyway. I texted someone to pick it up, so it's back in Naples by now."

He dug into the spaghetti, seemingly unconcerned. "*Ah.* Too bad."

She tilted her head. "Of course...you could keep giving me a ride."

Their eyes met again, and he chewed slowly. Consideringly. She had the uneasy feeling he was looking right into her soul, reading her very deepest thoughts.

Forbidden thoughts.

Arousing thoughts.

Naked and sweaty thoughts.

Her nipples twirled into tight buds, sending jolts of need down to her center. *Heaven help her.* Could she really still want him this much?

She swallowed again.

"Maybe," he said in a deep, suggestive voice, "we could leave tomorrow morning?"

Nikki's fork halted halfway to her mouth.

"Sound like a plan?" Kade gave her a transparently innocent look. "What do you think?"

Oh, God.

He really didn't want to know what she was thinking. Or maybe he already did... Was that sinfully wicked look in his eyes for real? Or just in her hopeful imagination..?

Again, the memory of their kiss shivered through her whole body, followed closely by an epic wave of lust.

"Sure," she managed. "Sounds good."

They both knew exactly what they were talking about, and it didn't have anything to do with cars or music boxes. The idea of a whole night of unbridled, no-strings sex with this incredibly hunky man was...intoxicating.

Now that her identity and her objective were both out in the open, and no other secrets lingered between them to spoil things, well, there was no reason not to indulge herself. And him.

Or was she not thinking straight...?

***

Two—or maybe three—glasses of red wine later, they were sitting out on the balcony enjoying the awesome late afternoon view of blue sky and puffy clouds floating over the panorama of Rome. The sun was dipping toward the horizon, the burnt-orange of clay roof tiles deepening to red atop ancient brick walls that were splashed with the thousand colors of flowering vines, peeling painted advertisements, and rows of flapping laundry. The summer scents of honeysuckle and sundrenched detergent lingered on the soft, warm breeze, along with the smell of simmering sauce wafting up from an apartment below them.

It was a sensory delight that made Nikki relax in a way she hadn't done in ages. Maybe ever. Relax...and yearn for the sensual touch of the man sitting on the other side of the tiny wrought iron balcony bistro table. Kade looked super sexy. He had long since taken off his suit jacket and tie, and rolled up the sleeves on his button-down white shirt. Oh, yeah. Good enough to eat. His knees were tucked up right against hers in an intimate embrace. They would barely need to lean forward to touch their lips together and kiss.

But they hadn't.

Anticipation was highly underrated. It made her pulse thrum in an ever-increasing primitive beat and her blood slowly heat to an electric sizzle.

They had been flirting with their eyes and their body language for the past few hours as they chatted about their jobs and their lives, and a million other things. Her whole being savored the slow torture of knowing exactly where they would end up...but the tantalizing journey of getting there was far too pleasurable to make a move to end it yet.

Besides, it was his turn. This time she wanted him to pursue her. She wanted him to take control. She wanted to be the one who was tempted and seduced.

Which...there was little doubt in her mind he was doing. His technique was subtle and slow, but masterful.

"Tell me about your family," she said, leaning back in her chair, needing to be distracted, but also curious to know more about him. Her research had turned up virtually nothing about his background. Which wasn't too surprising, considering his job.

He grimaced. Not in an unkind way, more in a disapproving but indulgent sort of way. "My parents are..." He let out a resigned laugh. "Into vintage travel trailers."

She blinked. *Oka-ay.* Of all the things he could have said, that was pretty much the last thing she'd have expected. "You mean, like, those old silver ones that look like cigars?"

His grimace deepened. "Airstreams. Yeah. And Shastas. And canned hams."

She stared at him incomprehensively. "Canned hams?"

"Yeah. But they're more into the home-builts. They make their living rehabbing old units they find in salvage yards or abandoned out in the desert."

Abandoned hams? The man was speaking Greek.

He must have realized he'd lost her. He closed his eyes for a moment, then opened them again, and a smile dashed over his lips as he shook his head. "Never mind. Let's just say they've been wandering gypsies all my life."

She smiled at the picture. That, she could relate to. "It sounds heavenly." Colorful and free. So different from her own rigid, constricted childhood.

And so different from the person Kade Maddox was today—firmly welded to his job and the tightknit brotherhood he'd become part of in the Marines. Anchored to his concrete set of rules to live by.

How had such a radical change happened?

"Trust me," he drawled. "Growing up like that was the furthest thing from heavenly." His expression left no room for doubt. "Anyway." He tipped his head. "What about you? What's your family like?"

It was her turn to grimace. "No family."

He looked briefly taken aback. "Really? None?"

She waved her hand. "No siblings. My mom died when I was eight. And my dad, well..." She took a fortifying breath. "He kicked me out when I was seventeen. We haven't spoken since."

Dismay flooded Kade's face. "Jesus. I had no idea. Sorry, I—"

She gave him a sincere smile. "It's okay. Really. Ancient history."

He searched her face. "Why would a father do something like that?" He looked genuinely upset.

Her heart totally melted. Especially because he hadn't asked her what she'd done to deserve it.

Was it possible to fall in love in a split second?

"My father needs to be in complete control of everything at all times," she said, and shrugged. "I hate being controlled."

In Kade's eyes she saw a world of dawning compassion and empathy. And something much more compelling.

Understanding.

He might be her opposite in nearly every respect, but he clearly understood her and the forces that had shaped her. A light bulb went off in her mind. *Because those exact same forces had shaped him, too*—just going in the reverse direction.

Control. She rejected it. Kade craved it.

A rush of warm emotion flooded through her. Who'd have thought they'd have something so fundamental in common, in a bizarre sort of way?

"Yeah," he said, his lips curving. "I kinda got you like being in charge."

She gazed at him intently, and instantly her physical awareness of him roared back to life.

The man was deeply attractive. Handsome as sin, killer sexy. But more than that, under all the hunkiness, he was a seriously good person. Which only made him all the more attractive.

Okay. Maybe, under certain circumstances, letting someone else call the shots wouldn't be so bad.

Depending on who was in control...

What was she waiting for?

Slowly, she smiled. "Unless, of course," she qualified, "I give a man permission."

Her body throbbed with the need to be with him. With an urge to explore this unfamiliar desire to be controlled by him. To do his bidding. Willingly. Eagerly. And find out what she'd been missing.

Her skin flushed warm, then cold, then warm again. Her breasts tingled, her nipples hardened, aching for his touch.

The air shifted as he smiled back, slowly and deliberately. "Do I have your permission, then? To do as I wish?"

His dark bedroom eyes lured her to erotic thoughts of sinful pleasures. His knowing smile made her fantasize about all the toe-curling things he could do to her with those masculine lips. All the things that devilish smile was telling her he had every intention of doing to her.

Oh. My. God.

How could a woman get so lucky?

"Convince me," she murmured, "to trust you."

Her center went hot and slippery with the desire to be filled.

When he finally, finally, *finally* stood up and casually leaned a hip against the balcony railing, her heart just about jumped out of her chest.

Those sensual eyes told her she didn't stand a chance of resisting his every whim. He reached over and drew her out of her chair, running strong fingers down her arm. For a moment they just stood there, taking each other in. Anticipating. Wanting.

She loved the way he smelled. All woodsy and spicy, like a man's man. Being this close to him and his heavenly scent, her hormones were going crazy, jumping up and down and shouting at her to get on with it—*kiss* the man, already!

She resisted the overwhelming temptation. "This is still probably not a good idea," she murmured, a last ditch at sanity.

"Oh, I thoroughly disagree," he returned, intent shining in his gaze.

Then his mouth was on hers, and she couldn't turn him away if her life depended on it. *Thank God, it didn't.*

She moaned, opening to him, and wound her arms around his neck. *This was such a good idea.* He lifted her off her feet and her legs instinctively wrapped around his waist. She could feel the restrained power in his muscles as his arms caged her. She found she liked it. A lot. Who knew it could be such a turn-on to be held captive by a strong and powerful man?

They kissed madly, unsteadily, on the balcony until he pushed her up against the building wall. He held her tight against it and devoured her mouth. The kiss was hot and shivery and deep, and everything she craved.

The sound of a zipper was followed by a whoosh of cool air on her back. She gave a mewl of pleasure and dropped her feet, letting her short dress slide off and float to the floor. He groaned, pulling away to give the breasts spilling out of her bra a predatory look. In a swift movement he removed the bit of lace and tossed it aside, then his hands found her bare flesh, lifting her up into his arms once more.

His tongue ravaged her mouth as he touched her everywhere. He pressed his body hard against hers and they both groaned in a torrent of need. His fingers slid between her legs and parted her wet folds. She cried out as he found her desire and touched her there.

"That's right, give it to me," he whispered into her mouth. His fingers circled, dragging a ragged moan from her. "I want it all."

"Kade," she cried. "Please, I— *Nhh...*"

It was no use. He was too skilled, too perfect, and she was too aroused to stop the tidal wave of pleasure that crashed over her. She arched, her body shuddering over the edge, and she surrendered to the awesome sensation.

He drew it out as long as it would go, playing her climax like a fine instrument.

By the time he let her slide to her feet, she was trembling so hard she could hardly see straight.

Then he ordered huskily, "Bedroom."

Nikki squirmed, moaning softly in pleasure as Kade fell back on the bed and tugged her down on top of him. He cupped her breasts, flicking her nipples with his thumbs.

How did he seem to know instinctively how to make her want to beg for more?

"No need to beg," he whispered.

Surely, she hadn't said that aloud?

He pulled her closer, taking her aching flesh into his mouth, using his teeth and his tongue to drive her mad with want. She let her body melt over his, straddling his hips, catching his arousal in the juncture of her thighs.

He laved and sucked her breasts. She writhed and ground into him. They both panted and moaned.

And suddenly she was on her back, and he was on top.

He gazed down at her with half-lidded eyes spilling over with desire. He leaned down and whispered in her ear, "I'm going to fuck you now. Long and hard. I want you screaming in pleasure."

Then he told her how he intended do that. Filling her mind with sensual fantasies. Erotic fantasies. Fantasies that made her blush with embarrassment. Fantasies that made her even wetter with anticipation.

She closed her eyes and let his low, gravelly voice stroke over her body like strong, masculine fingers. Or maybe it really was his fingers. *Yes, it was.* They touched her, driving her need higher, ridding her of her panties, coaxing her to surrender to him, fully and completely.

She was already naked, already trembling with need for him. She could do surrender.

"Open your eyes," he ordered. "Look at me."

She suddenly realized he was still fully dressed. Heat ripped through her at the contrast of her pale, nude skin to his dark trousers and formal shirt. At the contrast of male to female.

His body was bigger than hers. Taller. More powerful. *More dominant.* He lay above her, pinning her to the bed with a wall of solid muscle. A ripple of excitement trilled down her spine.

"Take off your clothes," she said on a shiver of need, unwilling to wait another minute to see him. To feel him, skin to skin.

He whisked his shirt over his head, then held himself above her. "Are you sure about this?"

"You're kidding, right?" she whispered. But respected him all the more for asking.

His gaze swept down the length of her body. He looked like a predator trying to decide what morsel of his prey to eat first. She swallowed, feeling at once vulnerable, lying naked under this dangerous man she'd met mere hours ago.

Was she making a huge mistake?

A corner of his mouth curved up, as if he sensed her shift in awareness and found it amusing. "Nervous?"

"Should I be?" she asked, trying to wriggle free.

He didn't let her. The other corner curved up. "Only if you don't like screaming in ecstasy."

Oh, but she did. At least she thought she would. No man had ever managed that feat in bed. It sounded...delicious.

She licked her lips, and his eyes followed the movement hungrily. "I dare you," she whispered.

"You'll lose," he warned, his voice like ripped silk.

She undulated her body under him and whispered "Promise?"

"Hell, yeah."

He levered down and captured her mouth with his. His broad, bare chest brushed her breasts, tickling them with his springy chest hair. His cock felt long and thick between her thighs. She arched up, wrapping her legs around his waist and her arms about his neck.

Her pulse thrummed. She loved the feel of him on top of her. Loved the weight of his body pressing into hers. Loved the brush of his corded muscles holding her fast, and his masculine hair rubbing against her sensitive skin. Especially loved the hard length of him straining toward her.

In the morning, she'd probably regret sleeping with him. He was, after all, the opposition. And she was already crushing on him far too much for her own good. But she'd regret it a whole lot more if she didn't.

Just one night. Was that too much to ask? Just one night of being with a man who rocked her world to the core. A man who was already burrowing deep in her heart.

Talk about dangerous.

But there was time enough tomorrow to worry about possible fallout. And the potential damage to her heart.

Tonight she wanted to be his.

All his. Only his.

Oh, yeah. Tonight she wanted to forget her own name.

And to scream.

Kade had never experienced lovemaking this intense.

In fact, he wasn't sure he'd ever really made love before tonight with Nikki.

Sex? Plenty of times. But making love...? Not so much.

God, she was beautiful. So willingly vulnerable. So responsive. So everything he'd ever wanted in a lover.

And so everything he should stay a thousand miles away from. Because he knew damned well, in the long term, Nikki Phoenix was so everything exactly wrong for him.

Nothing had made that plainer than that brief, painful description of her relationship with her father.

Her father...the client.

This whole situation was one giant powder keg ready to explode. And explode, it would. Of that, he was certain. Right in his face.

But he hadn't been able to help himself. He'd wanted her too much. *Still* wanted her too much. And he'd be damned if he'd let himself develop a conscience about grabbing what was freely offered. Maybe tomorrow he'd agree they'd probably made a big mistake.

Maybe.

But not tonight. Not with her sweet, soft body tucked under his, open for his taking. Not on his life.

He brought her to climax twice with his mouth before plunging into her, deep and hard, and pumping her over the edge one more time. He could still feel her nails on his back from that one, the sweet pleasure-pain of her passion.

God, she did it for him. On every level. He couldn't get enough of her. He wanted to bury himself in her and not pull out until he'd made her hoarse from calling his name, until they were both breathless, boneless puddles of quivering, sated flesh, unable to tell her body from his. Until he'd claimed her so compellingly and so thoroughly she'd never want to be with another man, ever again.

So, he did just that.

And when the first light of dawn was creeping over the windowsill, he held her in his arms and eased out a breath of troubled contentment.

So *this* was what his parents had experienced every morning of their marriage. No wonder they were still so crazy in love with each other, not caring which way the wind blew them...as long as it blew them together.

He kissed Nikki's lips and closed his eyes, and told himself he was thinking like a fool. Amazing sex did *not* make up for being rootless. Homeless. Without plans and without rules. He couldn't live like that again. It would drive him slowly insane.

But he had to admit, it sure would feel good along the way...

No.

No, no, no.

Just sex, Maddox, he silently chanted as sleep washed over him at last.

This was just sex. Nothing more.

And tomorrow, he would deliver her to the client—to the father who'd so cruelly rejected her—as ordered. Because this was his job and he didn't have a choice.

And she would be so furious with him she would, without doubt, never want to set eyes on him ever again in this lifetime.

There. His whole dilemma neatly and tidily solved.

Despite his inner turmoil, Kade managed to beat back the acute attack of guilt, and awoke the next morning feeling pretty damn awesome. His relative lack of sleep was more than made up for by the warmth of Nikki's soft, supple body snuggled up against his under the light, fluffy comforter. Sunshine streamed in through the open French balcony doors, birds twittering happily in the brightly blossoming vines surrounding them. It was like a goddamn Disney movie.

Even if he felt a bit more like the villain of the story than the hero...

Well. Except for the long hours of skin-slicking, bone-rattling, mind-bending sex he'd shared with the heroine last night. Definitely not a Disney flick.

Hell, no one even *made* movies with sex that good.

He let out a low, satisfied hum at the memory, and turned to reach for her again.

And instantly froze, his pulse launching like a rocket.

There was a man sitting in the easy chair across the room. His foot rested casually on one knee, and there was an amused look on his scruffy face as he surveyed the scene on the bed— Kade with his pants down, gorgeous naked woman next to him, rumpled sheets. Scattered condom wrappers.

"I gotta say, Maddox, you are one hella fast worker," the jerk drawled.

"Dane. What the fuck are you doing here?" Kade demanded in a low voice, not wanting to wake Nikki. He glanced at her, then eased himself out from under the covers.

"You're the one who sent out the distress call last night," Dane said cheekily. "But it looks like you've taken things well in hand."

Kade grabbed the top sheet from the floor to keep from decking his friend, and wrapped it around his waist. "You're a fucking riot, asshole," he muttered, leading him out onto the balcony, where—*shockeroo*—another STORM operator lounged at the bistro table. He was actually sipping a latte. And naturally, it *had* to be Jake Warner. The boss's best friend.

Kade clamped his jaw and quietly pulled the French doors closed. This time, he legitimately *was* so fucking screwed.

Which, oddly, didn't bother him nearly as much as it should have. He was feeling too good this morning to be upset by a minor detail like being suddenly unemployed. Besides, ever since last night, he'd had an overwhelming urge to call the major and tell him exactly what he thought of this goatfuck of a mission. Which would definitely get him fired anyway.

So, what the hell.

Jake tipped his chin toward the sleeping woman beyond the French doors. "Does she know?"

Kade ground his teeth. "I'm not a total idiot."

Jake's brow hiked.

Kade clamped his jaw harder. All right, fine. He was an idiot. But not for that reason. "No. I didn't tell her. That would be breaching confidentiality." Not that he hadn't thought about it. A lot.

Dane gave him a pitying look, and murmured, "Hell. Wouldn't want to be you when she finds out."

Join the fucking club. "I'll live. Besides, this"—he twirled a finger between her and himself— "isn't what you think. Now, tell me why the hell you're here." He ignored their incredulous looks, and didn't bother to ask how they'd found him—a tracker was standard on all vehicles—or how they'd gotten inside—they'd all been in the same field intelligence unit under Major Llowell, and a little B&E was child's play. The fact that Kade hadn't woken up when they entered was a bit more worrisome...but not really, all things considered.

"Just wanted to let you know the major got hold of his contact inside Mossad," Dane said. "They denied those guys shooting at you yesterday were theirs."

"I'm stunned," Kade drawled. Denial was SOP. But Llowell undoubtedly reassured them about the mission objective, and because of STORM's stellar rep out there in the world, the agents would be pulled back as courtesy. They'd still be watching, but from a distance, no guns involved. That worked for Kade. But he could feel there was still something these bozos weren't telling him. "You could have texted that. Why are you *really* here?"

Jake gave him a lazy smile. "Just checking up on our boy." He rose easily to his feet and gave Kade a wink. "Wouldn't want you getting into any trouble, now, would we?"

Kade scowled. Was he kidding? "Thanks, but I can take care of myself."

Dane gave another cheeky grin. "Clearly."

Jake's shoulder lifted. "It's not so much you we're worried about."

From behind them came a low, feminine snicker. "Wow. I'm flattered. I think."

They all turned to see the French door was now open, and Nikki was leaning against the doorframe. Her golden hair was mussed as if she'd just awoken from a night of amazing sex. Kade's breath caught in his chest. *Yeah, that happened.* And she was dressed—if you could call it that—in nothing but his white button-down shirt.

His shirt.

"But I assure you," she continued as if they weren't all staring with jaws hanging down to their knees, "your *boy*, here, has been a perfect gentleman." She smiled at him like a woman who'd just awoken from a night of amazing sex. *With him.* "All. Night. Long."

Hell, yeah. That had definitely happened.

"Leave," he said to the other men. "Now."

Chuckling, Dane slapped him on the back on his way out.

Jake dipped his head to Nikki—"Ma'am."—then sauntered out after him.

When the bedroom door closed behind them, Kade dropped the sheet from around his waist. His erection was already thick and at full height.

He leveled her a gaze, and murmured, "Who're you calling boy?"

A little over an hour later, Nikki rolled off Kade and sprawled across the bed, panting, sweaty, and delightfully exhausted. She felt well and truly fucked.

In the best possible way.

"Oh, my God, Kade. That was..." She had no words. Seriously. None.

He grunted. "Un-fucking-believable," he helpfully supplied between gulps of breath.

Yeah. That. Exactly.

She managed to moan in agreement.

"I'm pretty sure you've killed me," he said on a groan several minutes later.

She shuddered a breathy smile and let out another moan. "Ditto."

Never. Ever. *Ever.* Had sex felt this incredible. Her whole body tingled and pulsed. The electric pleasure that still zinged around her veins felt like a pinball machine gone wild.

If he hadn't killed her, he had certainly ruined her for life, for any other man. For any other lips. *For any other cock.*

Holy crap. This was...

Terrifying.

She heard a soft snore and realized he'd fallen back asleep. Somehow, she dredged up a chuckle. *So fucking typical.* But for some unfathomable reason, the irritation and snippiness she usually felt when a man just turned over and fell asleep after sex never materialized. Instead, she just felt warm and content.

And *that* was even *more* terrifying.

What the hell was happening here?

She thought about the myriad emotions this man had caused her to feel in the ridiculously few hours since they met. Emotions she'd never before felt in her life. Or...at least not since her mother had died. Emotions that made her feel safe. And sheltered.

And loved.

Which was, you know, completely and totally insane.

Because how could you love someone after knowing them less than twenty-four hours? During most of which time you'd both felt completely and totally opposite and wrong for each other?

Could their bodies possibly know something their logical minds failed to grasp?

She stared up at the ceiling for a good, long while, debating with herself.

Nah, she concluded. That was just plain nuts.

Love at first sight only happened in books and movies. Stuff like that didn't happen in real life.

Even if the sex was seriously epic.

***

Nikki awoke with a start and sat straight up in bed. The whole place smelled like... *Wow.* Coffee and fresh bread. *Yum.*

It took her several seconds to remember where she was...and with whom. And what they'd done. Though, the screamingly sore muscles in places she'd never known she had, that should have been a big clue.

Ho-boy.

This could get awkward.

Kade swept into the bedroom with a huge smile on his face and an overloaded tray in his hands. "Hey, baby. I got breakfast."

Or not.

On the tray she spotted two of those metal Italian coffee pots and a carafe of steaming milk, cups, sugar bowl, jam, and a large plate filled with scrumptious-looking pastries and breads.

"Oh, man, does that look good. I'm starving," she admitted with a grateful smile and a kiss for him as he set the tray on the bed. "I'll be right back."

She did a quick run to the bathroom to wash up, then happily hopped back into bed.

Kade had already poured her coffee, and was digging into a pastry. A reverent look crossed his face as he bit into it. "Pure heaven," he murmured. "God, I love this country."

"Me, too." She took a bracing sip of espresso. And suddenly wondered, "Do you live here in Italy?"

He chewed and swallowed. "For the time being. The unit's based in Naples. But eventually we'll be spread out all over the world."

Right. The STORM Transporter Division was fairly new. Established just three or four years ago, according to his file.

She perked up. "*Ooh.* So cool. You could go anywhere you like? That's awesome."

He peered at her over the rim of his coffee cup as though she'd grown horns. "That's a matter of opinion."

She peered back. "You're kidding, right?"

"I like it here. I like living close to my friends. The thought of breaking up the unit..." A muscle jerked in his cheek. "Anyway. I'd miss the food."

Uh-huh.

She thought about their oh-so-brief conversation last night about family. He'd said something incomprehensible about canned hams or some such, but the thing that had really stuck with her was the way he'd said growing up with wandering gypsies was the furthest thing from heavenly.

Miss the food? More like, miss the stability. And his buddies.

Her heart softened. Maddox might look like a big, tough Marine, but inside he was a marshmallow. A handsome, sexy, sexual-dynamo of a marshmallow.

God, could a man get more perfect?

Well. Other than the whole inflexibility and rules thing. Too bad about those—a real deal-breaker.

Of course...

"Tell me," she said. "How many of your rules have you broken since yesterday?"

He halted briefly at the abrupt change of topic, stared at her, then cleared his throat. "Way too many."

"How does that feel?"

He picked up another pastry with a chuckle. "Talk about a loaded question."

She smiled, but didn't comment. Just waited.

He winked at her. "Obviously, last night felt incredible."

He didn't go on, so after a moment she asked, "And this morning?"

He put down the pastry, lifted his coffee cup, sipped, and then studied it. Almost as if he was avoiding her gaze. Trying to figure out what to say. To let her down.

Feathers of disappointment fluttered in her stomach. Really? They were going to do this already?

All righty, then.

"Never mind," she said with forced cheer, tossed back her espresso, and jumped off the bed. "We should get going. Bad guys to avoid. Deadlines to meet. Music boxes to return."

He watched her, his expression going concerned. "Nikki—"

"Nope," she cut him off. "It's okay. It was what it was, and now it's over, and we move on."

For some reason, her cool analysis seemed to surprise him. He appeared torn.

Yeah. As if they'd ever had a prayer of working. They both knew better.

She grabbed her bag and strode into the bathroom for a shower, careful to close the door behind her. No sense prolonging the inevitable. She set her things down, made sure there was a fresh towel waiting on the counter, then turned on the taps in the glass enclosure full blast.

Every logical, rational bone in her body said he was all wrong for her.

Wrong, wrong, *wrong.*

But when she stepped in and the steaming hot water cascaded over her passion-sensitized body—the body he'd woken to life as no man before him—she didn't even try to stop the tears from sliding down her cheeks.

Because every single cell in her aching heart told her he was...oh, so right.

Kade had blown it.

That was a pure, damned certainty.

The evidence was plain as day in Nikki's jovial, meaningless banter and her pleasant, emotionless facial expressions as they made the four-hour drive to the client's home in Switzerland.

The client. Ambassador Charles Mayfield Gibson, retired.

Nikki's father.

Kade had assumed the different last name was because of a marriage. Now he knew that wasn't the case. She'd changed it. Super easy these days. He didn't even need to wonder why she'd chosen the name Phoenix. The metaphor was all too obvious.

It was also simple to guess what her reaction would be to the coming meeting. She'd be angry—understandably—to be manipulated into a confrontation with the father who'd thrown her out of his house with the garbage. The father she'd deliberately evaded all these long years.

Kade wished like hell he could ask her about it. About what had happened. Whether she or her father had ever reached out to the other, tried to reconcile. It didn't matter what had prompted such a resolute break. No child deserved that kind of coldness from the one person on earth who was supposed to love and nurture them. Say what he might about his own parents, but Kade had never doubted their love for him. No, they didn't listen. They never listened to him, nor heard his needs. But they'd never had a problem saying "I love you." They said it all the time. Even to this day.

He couldn't even imagine growing up without that solid foundation of love.

It made him realize for the very first time how truly lucky he was, despite everything, for his crazy, peripatetic, agonizingly uncomfortable, but very loving childhood.

He glanced over at the woman in the passenger seat of the Lotus—so cool and confident and gorgeous and mouthwateringly sexy that it hurt his balls just looking at her. And he was simply unable to stop the words that came out of his mouth.

"What the hell happened with your father?"

The flow of her words—some inane comparison between skiing in St. Moritz versus skiing in Vail—halted abruptly. "Excuse me?"

"When you were seventeen. What the fuck happened?"

Her expression stiffened, and it took her a moment to respond. "That," she said, "is none of your damned business."

She had no idea how wrong she was. It was *all about* his business.

He'd questioned this assignment before now, but ultimately he'd trusted that Major Llowell knew what he was doing when he'd taken it on. If a father wanted to bring his daughter home, even if it was via an elaborate subterfuge, could that be a bad thing? Kade hadn't wondered why the client found it necessary to lie to his own child. Naïvely, Kade had just assumed it was some sort of ongoing family game. Until now, he hadn't considered he might be taking an innocent victim somewhere she fervently didn't want to go. Or that actual harm might come to her because of it. Which, it wouldn't. Of that much, he was confident. The major would never in a million years accept a job that might result in harm to an innocent, physical or otherwise. He would have asked the right questions, and gotten the right answers.

STORM were the good guys.

Kade was the good guy.

He reminded himself firmly of that when he saw the betrayed look on her face as she peered over at him now.

He shouldn't have asked that. It was none of his business.

Rule #3: *Mind your own business.*

But he just couldn't let it go.

"I'm sorry if—" He shook his head. "I'm just trying to understand. It was so..."

"Reprehensible?" she suggested calmly. "Heartless? Inhuman? No shit. Thus, my reasons for never speaking to him again."

Kade couldn't help asking again, "Has he never tried to get in touch with you? To apologize, or—"

"I don't know, and I don't care. I changed my name. Never gave out my address to anyone except employers. As far as I'm concerned, he died that day."

Kade swallowed. He could certainly understand her feelings of betrayal. But... "What if he has regretted his actions? What about forgiveness? Wouldn't it feel good to forgive and put it all behind you? If he reached out and tried to make it right?" Kade silently prayed that's what was going on here, with this job.

She stared evenly at him for a good, long moment, a hundred different emotions chasing through her eyes. At length, she said, "I'll never know, will I?"

Kade's stomach sank like an anchor.

Yeah. She would.

And he would be right there in the middle of it. Taking the brunt of her fury.

He could hardly wait.

No.

He had to tell her the truth.

She'd despise him, and demand to get out of the car, and he'd fail to complete his assignment, and probably lose his job for stepping over the line in so fucking many ways…but it was the right thing to do.

She didn't deserve to be blindsided.

He had to tell her.

And soon. Like, now.

Because they'd just passed the Wilkommen sign for the small Swiss village where her father now worked as a consultant to multi-national companies, using the many contacts and favors he'd racked up over a long, illustrious career as a diplomat with the US State Department. In less than ten minutes, Kade would be turning the Lotus into the beautifully landscaped and gated drive of Ambassador Gibson's luxurious lakeside chateau, and it would be too late.

For Nikki.

For Kade.

Taking a fortifying breath, he pulled into the parking lot of a small, lakeside *biergarten* and shut off the engine. A big stein of beer might help after he'd endured the ass-chewing he was about to receive. Or two. Or three.

Nikki glanced over at the quaint outdoor tables filled with laughing tourists, then back at him. "Thirsty?"

He shook his head. "There's something I need to tell you."

Her expression went wary. "Yeah?"

"Yeah."

He closed his eyes and was hit by a solid wall of regret. Regret over being so clueless and not questioning things sooner. Regret over having to cause this amazing woman even a moment of pain. Regret over losing any possibility of a future with her in it. A future he hadn't realized until this moment that he desperately wanted a chance at having.

It might not work between them. It probably wouldn't work. But he would really have liked to give it a try. Because she was the most incredible woman he'd ever met. And he really, really liked her. And the thought of letting her walk away… Yeah, it fucking killed him.

"And?" she prompted when he remained silent for several long moments.

"And… I need to tell you this job is—"

All at once, three cars careened into the parking lot and squealed to a halt surrounding the Lotus, boxing them in.

Shit!

"What the—"

He didn't even have time to react before four muscular men leaped from two of the vehicles and blocked the convertible's doors. They hadn't drawn weapons, but conspicuous under their jackets and sweatshirts were the telltale bulges of shoulder holsters. Carrying Jericho 941s, no doubt.

"Lance Corporal Maddox, I presume," said the man who appeared to be the gang's leader, leaning a hand against the Lotus's driver-side door.

Kade froze in shock. They knew his name?

The man glanced over at Nikki. "And Ms. Phoenix. So nice to see you again."

Wait. *What?*

Kade whipped his head around to scowl at her. She didn't look the least bit surprised by this development. He gripped the steering wheel hard, so he wouldn't reach for his own weapon as he grappled with the reality that *he* was the one who'd been set up.

"What the hell is going on?" he growled.

"Kade," she said without a trace of guilt, "this is Ben Rosen. We've...occasionally worked in tandem. Art recoveries, mostly. And his team—David, Ari, and Lev." She smiled at them. "Hi, guys."

The men all smiled back and nodded greetings.

They'd occasionally worked together.

Ah. So this *was* a hijacking. Obviously orchestrated by Nikki.

He had to hand it to her. She'd been masterful. She'd had him hoodwinked from word one. Played him like a fiddle.

And, here, he'd been about to tank his entire career for her. Outstanding. A sucker was born every day.

As if she could hear the self-recriminating thoughts catapulting through his mind, she shook her head at him. "No. Not what you're thinking."

Sure, it wasn't.

"Look," he ground out, "I'm not going to—"

Ben Rosen held up a hand. "Hang on." He extended his other hand, which held a cell phone. "Here. This should explain everything."

After a brief hesitation—during which Kade forced himself to count to ten in order to calm down enough to think clearly...not that it actually helped—he reluctantly reached for the phone. A call was already engaged, and to his shock, he saw a familiar number on the screen.

What the fuck...

"This is Kade," he said, feeling doubly betrayed.

"Hey, man," Major Llowell said, "don't worry. This is not an ambush. Jake filled me in on your...updated circumstances...so when Interpol contacted me this morning, I figured it would be okay to agree to change the plan on you."

Interpol? Not Mossad? Or some art heist gang?

Kade had no idea how to even begin to respond to that, so he just mumbled, "Sir," and kept his mouth shut.

"Interpol requested that we cooperate with Commander Rosen. He's brought someone to look at the music box. We're officially relinquishing control over it to you and Ms. Phoenix. Listen to what the person has to say, and decide how to proceed from there."

Kade didn't like this. Not one bit.

"Whatever you say, sir," he bit out.

He stared at Nikki, whose expression lay somewhere between pleased and apologetic. So, she already knew exactly what was going down. It got better and better.

"About the real mission," Llowell continued, and cleared his throat. "That's not going to be a problem, is it?"

"No problem at all, sir," Kade assured the major coolly. Not anymore.

"Good. Keep me updated. And report to my office first thing in the morning."

"Roger that." Kade hung up, and handed the phone back to Rosen.

Rosen waved a hand toward the third vehicle, a black limousine which Kade had totally forgotten about. He unbuckled and started to climb out of the Lotus, when a hand on his arm stopped him.

"Kade," Nikki said. He glanced back at her, determined to keep his emotions firmly in check. Her eyes looked troubled. Uncertain. "Are we okay?"

Was she serious?

He gave her a bland smile. "Just peachy. Excuse me."

He got out of the car, leaned over the side to reach the cargo hold behind the driver's seat, and popped a well-hidden latch that opened a shoebox-sized smuggler's compartment. From inside, he extracted a small waterproof container that held the very carefully wrapped and secured antique music box.

When he straightened, he saw that another muscular man, presumably the driver, was helping someone out of the limo. Someone small, and frail, and birdlike.

It was an old woman. She had to be at least ninety.

Kade's heart stalled, and he was suddenly flushed with overwhelming emotion.

Good God. This must be the original owner of the music box. The innocent woman who'd been ripped from her home, and everything she'd known and loved taken by the Nazis.

He stood stock still and held the package in unsteady hands.

Leaning on the guiding arm of the driver, the old woman walked slowly up to him, an indescribable expression on her face. She looked...radiantly happy.

"Hello, young man," she said in a wispy, lightly accented voice. "I understand you may have my music box. The one my father gave to me on my sixth birthday."

Kade met her gaze, clear and bright and guileless. He gathered himself and smiled down at her.

"Yes. I sure hope so. Here. Let me open it for you."

Carefully, he peeled away the protective layers of bubble wrap and tissue from the delicate porcelain, and gingerly extracted it from the container. Cradling it gently in both palms, he held it out to her.

It was as if her whole body sighed in happiness and delight. She lifted her wizened hand and reverently touched it with adoring fingertips. "Yes," she whispered. "This is the one."

She didn't take the music box from him, but gently lifted the lid. Whoever packed it must have left the mechanism partially wound, because sweet, tinkling musical notes began to play, filling the air with an elusive, intricate melody that brought a spill of goosebumps to Kade's arms.

Tears glistened in the old woman's eyes. "Thank you for finding it," she whispered, and tenderly closed the lid again. "Thank you from the bottom of my heart."

Kade swallowed. "My pleasure, ma'am. I hope it brings you much joy," he managed softly. He returned it gently to its wrappings and container, then handed it to the driver, who smiled kindly down at the old woman and helped her back to the limousine.

Kade watched until it pulled away, as did the other two cars that held the four Mossad agents. If he lived to be a hundred, he didn't think he would ever forget the overwhelming feelings that filled his heart witnessing that touching reunion.

He shuddered out a breath, then turned back to the Lotus.

And instantly, the situation with Nikki slammed him in the gut.

Nikki sat in the passenger seat of the Lotus, wiping her watery eyes with a ragged tissue.

"Wow," she whispered. "That was a once-in-a-lifetime."

She glanced up as Kade jerked open the car door. Her heart squeezed painfully at the look he gave her.

Cold.

Hurt.

Betrayed.

All the warm fuzzy feelings at a brilliantly successful conclusion to her assignment dissolved in the acid of that look.

He thought she'd planned all this from the start.

Okay, maybe she had. But what about *his* secrets? What about *her* hurt and betrayal over his clear rejection this morning?

"Kade," she began.

He held up a hand. "Don't. I can't talk to you right now."

Normally, she wouldn't let that stop her from speaking her mind. But his expression was so closed-off, so unyielding, she knew she'd be wasting her breath trying for a meaningful conversation.

So, she held her tongue as he started the car and drove through the quaint Swiss village, then stopped at the entrance to a long driveway guarded by a massive gate. He punched in a code, and the gate silently began to glide open.

She drew in a deep breath, steeling herself for what lay ahead as tears pricked her eyes over what lay behind them.

Maybe having rules wasn't such a bad idea, after all. If they'd followed his stupid rules, they would never have made love, and she wouldn't be feeling like her heart was being torn from her body right now.

He pulled the Lotus up in front of a stately mansion at the end of the long, tree-lined drive. There was a man standing in the doorway watching their approach. His face and hair had greyed with age, but even after all these years, she recognized him instantly. Though, instead of his usual ramrod-straight stance, his shoulders were rounded, his hands in his slacks pockets. He looked...nervous.

She swallowed heavily, grabbed her shoulder bag, and reached for the car door handle. "This should be fun," she muttered, her stomach in knots.

Kade peered over at her. To his credit, his expression held concern. "You know who that is?"

"Of course I do."

He stared at her. "You knew all along where I was taking you? That you were the job?"

She met his gaze evenly. "No. Not until we got here to the village."

"You know where he lives. You've kept track of him."

She smiled humorlessly. "How else would I know what places to avoid? What postmarks on letters to shred?"

Kade looked away and pushed out a breath. "I'm sorry. I was going to tell you. Earlier, when—"

"I know." She glanced up at the man in the doorway. "It's okay. Watching that old woman and her music box...all I could see in her face was joy. Even after the horrible things done to her in the past, she was only seeing the good in the present. It takes a strong person to be able to do that." She shouldered her bag and swung open the car door. "You were right. It's time for forgiveness."

"Nikki. Wait."

She halted, but didn't turn back to him. She didn't think she would survive another look at the face of the man she had fallen for so hard and so fast...but couldn't ever have.

He cleared his throat. "You called it when you said I'm an asshole. Please. I can't let you go like this. We need to talk."

A trickle of hope seeped through her. "Talk about what?"

"Baby, look at me."

At the endearment, the tears that had been threatening sprang to her eyes. Slowly, she turned to face him.

"On second thought, fuck talking." He pulled her into his arms.

And then he kissed her. A kiss so full of passion and need and...promise...that her heart was flooded with elated certainty. Certainty that he was feeling the same things about her that she was feeling for him.

He broke the kiss. "I know on paper we're all wrong for each other. But here"—he laid a hand over his heart— "we feel so right. I know you hate my rules, and I swear I'll try to be better, if you'd just—"

"No," she cut him off, and his face fell. She smiled. "I don't hate your rules. In fact, I was just lecturing myself how much smoother things might have gone for both our assignments if we'd followed some of them."

He blinked. "Our assignments."

"Yeah." She fingered the top button of his shirt. "Of course...then we probably wouldn't have had amazing, earth-shattering sex last night."

Slowly, his lips curved up. "As I said, we don't need no stinkin' rules."

"Just one," she said, and gave him a soft kiss. "No more secrets between us."

He kissed her back. "That's a deal."

She glanced back up at the mansion where her father was still waiting patiently for her at the door. Wow. He really had changed. Maybe there was hope for that relationship, too.

"You should go to him," Kade said. He pulled a card and pen from his jacket pocket and scribbled a phone number on the back. He handed it to her. "When you're done here, call me. I'll come pick you up."

She kissed him and shook her head. "It's going to take a while. I'll find you. Naples, right?"

He searched her eyes. "Promise?"

The whole idea terrified her. Being with him would mean a relationship. Compromise. Emotions. Commitment. Trust. All those scary things she'd been avoiding most of her life...because of the painful actions of the father waiting for her at the top of the mansion steps. Actions she was about to forgive, and move past. Which meant those scary things should no longer terrify her.

And they wouldn't.

Not with this man who held her so tenderly in his arms.

She kissed him again, and whispered, "I promise."

•• Epilogue ••

"We've set a date for the wedding. August fifth."

At the announcement, everyone at the party on the pretty terrace cheered and whooped. Kade clapped, too, trying his best to put his heart into it. He was genuinely happy for good friend and fellow transporter, Darryl, and his fiancée Linnea. They'd met last year and had been living together in this cozy little cottage ever since—getting to know each other, they always joked, since it had taken them all of five seconds to fall in love, and five days to get engaged.

Kade just wished Nikki were here to share the moment with him, as she'd promised. It had been two long weeks of waiting. Would she ever come? He was beginning to think she'd changed her mind.

Dane shoved a flute of champagne into his hand and slapped him on the back. "Smile, dude. It's a wedding, not a funeral."

Kade punched him back, and toasted the happy couple along with everyone else. "A funeral could be arranged, *dude*."

Dane grinned. "You and what— Hello. What do we have here?"

Kade took another gulp of champagne and turned to see what Dane was looking at.

His heart stopped, then took off like a dragster.

Nikki!

She was standing at the top of the terrace steps holding a small suitcase and looking around uncertainly. Suddenly, all chatter stopped. Everyone at the party turned as one to look at her.

"Um. Hi. Am I in the right place? I'm looking for—"

Their gazes met and he stepped forward, shoving the champagne flute at Dane. For a split second, he just stood there and took her in, every dream he'd ever had come true.

She was really here. This wasn't a dream.

In two strides he was with her, reaching for her suitcase and tossing it aside, trusting someone would catch it. He scooped her up in his arms and kissed her. And kissed her. And kissed her.

He vaguely heard more cheering, and hoots and hollers, and then nothing but the sound of his heart beating madly in his chest.

"You made it," he murmured. Touching her. Holding her.

She gave him another kiss. "Did you doubt me?"

"For a minute or two. Or three. How'd it go with your father?"

She smiled. "Good. We made amends. Talked a lot. Still a way to go, but a good start."

"I'm glad. I'd like to meet him."

"I'm sure he'll come to the housewarming."

"Housewarming?"

Her shoulder lifted. "Thought I'd stay in Italy for a while. I hear the food is amazing. And the men."

He hiked his brows. "Men?"

She gazed up at him. "Well, man. One man in particular."

"Oh?"

"Yeah." Her green eyes went dark and soft. "Amazing. And sexy. And willing to overlook a woman's...less desirable traits."

"Impossible. Everything about you is desirable," he assured her with another kiss.

"See? That's what I mean. He's kind of perfect."

"Far from it. But together, I think we could be. Really perfect."

Her smile was a brilliant as the Italian sunshine. "I think so, too. Should we give it a try? Being together?"

He hugged her close, the woman who'd broken all his rules. The beautiful woman he loved with all his heart. "There's nothing I want more, my love, than to be with you forever."

THE END ••

THANK YOU!

I HOPE YOU HAD FUN reading about the beginning of Kade and Nikki's adventure of falling in love! FAST AND FLIRTY is book 2 in my new STORM Transporter series of novellas. Book 1 is DANGEROUS CURVES.

If you have a moment, please help others enjoy this book!

Review it! Help others choose what to read—tell them why you loved this book!

If you do write a review, drop me an email at **NinaBruhns@aol.com** and include a link to it, and if you like, request that I put you on my list of beta readers. You'll receive an invitation to review my next book ahead of the crowd. ☺

Want to know when my next book comes out? Visit **www.NinaBruhns.com** and sign up for my **New Releases** email list, and I'll let you know when each new book is published.

NEW YORK TIMES AND USA TODAY *Best Selling* author Nina Bruhns (also writing as Nikita Black) pens adventurous romantic thrillers that contain a unique blend of interesting characters and settings, twisty suspense, and sizzling romance. To date, she has published over 35 award-winning novels (many also available in German):

3-time Daphne du Maurier Award winner
National Readers Choice Award winner
3-time RITA Award nominee
4-time RT BookReviews Reviewers Choice Award
#1 Amazon Bestseller in Romantic Suspense, Police Procedurals, Anthologies, and Movers & Shakers
Top 30 Amazon Most Popular Romance Authors
Top 50 Amazon Bestseller in Thrillers, Romance, Action & Adventure, Mystery, Contemporary Romance, Thriller & Suspense, Detective, Anthologies, and Women's Fiction
Amazon Germany Top 10 in Krimis & Thriller and Polizeiromane
Amazon Japan Top 100 in Police Procedurals and Romantic Suspense
Amazon UK #1 Bestselling author in Anthologies & Collections

Read more about Nina Bruhns and her books at **www.NinaBruhns.com** Sign up for her **New Releases** email list, and she'll let you know when each new book is published.

Facebook: **facebook.com/Nina.Bruhns.author**
Twitter: **@NinaBruhns twitter.com/NinaBruhns**
Pinterest: **pinterest.com/ninabruhns**
Email: **NinaBruhns@aol.com**
Website: **NinaBruhns.com**
Goodreads: **goodreads.com/author/show/50896.Nina_Bruhns**

OUTLAW JUSTICE

Rebecca York

(A Decorah Security Series Novella, Book #13)
A Paranormal Romantic Suspense Novella
Ruth Glick writing as Rebecca York

I want to particularly thank my long-time critique group, The Columbia Writer's Workshop, and my husband. Not only does he suffer the ups and downs of living with a full-time writer, he is also the best copy editor in the world and my travel director who plans the trips that are so important to my research. And, of course, I must thank my fans who have made my long writing career possible.

- *New York Times* and *USA Today* best-selling Author Two-time Rita finalist in the prestigious RWA writing contest
- Recipient of two *RT Book Reviews* Career Achievement Awards
- Recipient of the RWA Centennial Award
- Prism Award winner
- *Affaire de Coeur* Critics Choice Award for Contemporary Novel

"Rebecca York delivers page-turning suspense." ~ Nora Roberts

"(Her) books ...deliver what they promise: excitement, mystery, romance."
~ Michael Dirda, Washington Post Book World

Published by Light Street Press

CHAPTER ONE

"Just great," Steve Outlaw muttered as he took in the beer bottles, pizza boxes, and other debris littering the floor of his mom's old house on the Eastern Shore of Maryland. Obviously, the last tenants had trashed the place.

The mess was bad enough, but something else made his senses tingle. The scent was wrong for a dwelling that had been closed up for weeks.

It smelled like someone was in here. Or maybe burglars had recently broken in, then cleared out.

He stifled a curse. If he'd still been on the job with the Baltimore PD, he would have been carrying his service revolver. But he'd quit six months ago after recovering from a nasty gunshot wound to the leg. Medical had wanted to keep him on desk duty, and he'd been too restless to sit on the sidelines.

Now he looked around the room, hoping to see something he could use as a weapon. When he spotted a broom leaning against the sagging couch, he picked it up and held it in front of him as he turned toward the closet near the door. The bad leg ached from the effort to move quietly. He ignored it and kept going.

The closet was clear and so were the dining room and the kitchen, except for a couple of folding chairs lying on their sides. But the smell of humanity was stronger near the pantry, and when he threw open the door, a figure leaped out, trying to knock him down in a frantic rush to escape. Since he wasn't entirely steady on his feet, the tactic almost worked. Dropping the broom, he spun to the side, grabbing a slender arm and wrenching the intruder toward him.

The light was dim, but the breath froze in his lungs when he saw her face. Was he making it up? Or was the woman standing in front of him really Leah?

For a moment he was transported back to the last steamy afternoon they'd spent here, her naked body pressed to his, her fingernails digging into his shoulders, her lips moving urgently over his. In his teenager's bed, the blue of her eyes had deepened with need, and her chestnut-colored hair had been a tangle around her elegant face.

Not now. His mind snapped back to reality as he saw her breath quicken and her hand tremble—not with passion but with fear.

"Leah?" he asked, struggling with his own roiling emotions as past and present collided.

Her head bobbed in answer to the sound of her name.

Trying to cope with this out-of-kilter meeting, he asked, "What in the name of God are you doing here?"

She glanced at him, then down at the tips of her running shoes, as though she could avoid confrontation by looking away. Although he didn't want to break the physical contact, he could feel the tension radiating through her. To give both of them a little space, he let his hand drop away from her arm, but he kept his gaze fixed on her, hoping she wasn't going to make another run for the door.

In a voice he had to strain to hear, she answered, "I couldn't think of anywhere else to go."

Again his mind zinged back to the intimate weeks they'd spent together in this very house—before she'd gone off to Boston University. He'd thought they'd resume their hot and heavy sexual relationship when she came home for Thanksgiving vacation. Instead, she stayed in Boston for the holiday because she'd met a guy named Warren Pendelton.

After reading her carefully worded letter, he'd snatched a beer mug off his desk and thrown it across the room, where it shattered against the wall. As the weeks dragged on, he'd gone from anger to resignation, yet he couldn't let go of a tiny spark of hope—until she'd married the bastard the next year and dropped out of school.

He'd known he had to get over her, and he thought he'd succeeded. But as they stood facing each other, all the unfinished business simmering between them seemed to explode inside his head.

Struggling for some perspective, he tried to focus on the immediate problem—whatever it was.

"You can't go home?"

He wasn't prepared for her explosive laugh—or the way she sobered immediately—as though she'd allowed herself a few seconds of emotion that she was fighting to keep under strict control.

Raising her head, she met his questioning gaze. Her voice turned edgy as she said, "Sorry to intrude. I'll get out of your way now.

CHAPTER TWO

No way was Steve going to take the brush-off, not when she'd brought the past slamming back into him like a wrecking ball. And not when she'd already aroused all his protective instincts.

In response to her sharp tone, he made his own voice gentle. "Just tell me what's wrong, and I'll try to help you."

"You can't."

As he heard the flat statement, he felt a tearing inside his chest. At the same time, he was coping with a moral dilemma. He wouldn't hold her here by force. But he wasn't going to simply let her walk away when he could see she needed help.

How had she even gotten to his mother's house? He hadn't seen a car outside, but she could have put it in the garage out back.

"You're making me nervous, and I need to use the bathroom," she suddenly said, perhaps scrambling for a way to break off the close contact with him.

"Sure."

When he stepped aside, she scuttled past him down the hall. He figured she was buying herself some breathing room, but she didn't know about the psychic ability that was going to give him an unfair advantage in this sparring match.

He watched her hurry away. When the door closed behind her, he scanned the pantry, seeing only the crumpled junk food bags and boxes the tenant had left on the shelves. None of them was what he needed.

Striding from the room, he walked into the first bedroom on the right and glanced around. Nothing.

In the second bedroom, he found what he was looking for. She'd been sleeping here, and she'd left a small overnight bag beside the bare mattress on the floor.

Before he could change his mind, he crossed to the bag, knelt down, and pulled it closer to the wall. He had a special talent that could give him the information he needed. But at the same time, it would make himself vulnerable as hell now. After sparing a quick glance toward the hallway, he reaching inside the bag and shuffled through the tee shirts and jeans she'd brought—searching for something that was important to her. He had no idea what that might be, but he'd know it when he found it. The moment his hands touched the cold metal of a small heart-shaped locket Leah had worn back in high school, he felt a jolt of electricity zing through his body. At the same time his vision blurred. In a swirl of mist, reality around him faded. Physically, he stayed where he was, but his consciousness traveled somewhere else.

He might have fought the feeling of disorientation that swept over him, but he'd learned that it was best to simply go with the flow and see where the current carried him. This time it was to another bedroom, far different from the one at his mom's modest house. Leah was there, with a sandy-haired man—probably her husband. And the scene between them must have taken place in the recent past because she looked pretty much the way she did now, only she was a little better dressed—in cream-colored slacks and a pale blue knit top instead of scruffy jeans and a long-sleeved tee shirt.

The bedroom where they stood was probably twenty feet long and almost as wide, with dark wood furniture and a king-sized bed adorned with a brocade sea-green spread. Elaborate valances and curtains framed the windows. It was a beautiful room, but the action taking place was far from pretty. The man's expression was fierce as he stepped menacingly toward Leah who backed up quickly. But he closed the distance between them and raised his large hands to push her against a carved chest of drawers.

Steve heard her make a whimpering sound as he raised his hand and slapped her across the face. She screamed and tried to duck around him, the way she'd tried to duck around Steve. But the guy's arm snaked out and caught her, slamming her backwards.

He was speaking, but Steve couldn't hear what the guy was saying above the roaring in his ears. And Leah's answer was lost in the same wash of sound. As often happened, Steve withdrew abruptly from the scene. He was suddenly back in his mom's house, feeling sick and shaky. Eyes closed, he leaned his head against the wall, struggling for breath and fighting to ground himself in reality.

A sound made his head jerk up. Leah was in front of him, staring from his face to the place where his hand disappeared inside her bag.

"What are you doing?" she demanded.

"I had to find out why you were in trouble."

"If I'd wanted you to know, I would have told you."

Yeah, that was obvious.

Feeling at a disadvantage with her looming over him, hands on her denim-clad hips, he let go of the locket and heaved in a breath before pushing himself up to a standing position and pressing his back to the wall. At least he had some height on her now, but with his bad leg, he didn't trust himself to take a step forward.

She stood glaring at him, her arms folded across her chest, which pulled up the sleeves of her shirt, exposing a nasty looking bruise on her left arm. When he saw it, he drew in a quick breath.

Ignoring his reaction, she demanded, "How does pawing through my things tell you anything about me?"

"I thought I might find something."

"Like what? Were you looking for drugs—or anything else illegal?"

"No."

"Then what?"

When he didn't answer, she snatched up the bag. "I'm leaving."

"Your husband hurt you," he heard himself say. "That's why you left home. That's why you can't go back."

Her eyes widened in shock. "What—did he hire you to find me, and I made the stupid mistake of coming here?"

"No, of course not."

"You think because I have a bruise that he did it?"

"No," he said again.

His words had no effect. As she headed for the door, he wanted to reach out and grab her arm, but he knew that was the worst thing he could do after what he'd seen.

"Wait!"

"Why should I?" she demanded.

At least she was willing to listen.

He swallowed hard, knowing he'd trapped himself into going down a road he'd rather not travel. But now he had to do it if he wanted her to trust him.

"You know I was a cop?"

She nodded.

"Last year, I left the Baltimore PD and joined a detective agency—Decorah Security."

"And what does that have to do with . . . this situation?

"They wanted me for a reason. They hire agents with unusual talents."

She waited for him to elaborate. Only desperation made him willing to reveal the secret he'd kept from her and everyone else in town when he'd still lived here.

"You remember how the kids accused me of spying on them—because I knew stuff?"

She nodded.

"I didn't exactly spy." He dragged in a breath and let it out before saying, "Since I was ten, I've been able to touch things that are important to other people, and I see scenes from their lives."

She laughed again. "Nice try."

"It's true."

"Oh come on. You expect me to believe a fairy tale like that?"

"Not without evidence." He dragged in a breath and let it out. "I've never been to your house, but when I wrapped my finger around the locket in the bag—I saw you in a bedroom—with dark furniture, a green spread on the bed and matching drapes." He swallowed hard. "I watched . . . a guy slam you against a chest of drawers and slap you."

"You couldn't."

"Then how do I know about it?"

The words hung in the air between them. Then her shoulders sagged, and he figured she'd caved. When the impossible is the only explanation, you gotta go with it.

"Nobody was supposed to know about that."

"It was your husband, right?"

She answered with a small nod.

A mixture of emotions flared inside him. He wanted to help her, but it had been a devastating blow when she'd walked away from him eight years ago. Now he couldn't stop himself from grabbing at the confirmation that she'd married the wrong man.

He pushed that self-serving thought away. Whatever happened between them from this moment forward, the first order of business was to make sure the bastard never got another crack at her.

CHAPTER THREE

Steve waited for a response. When it didn't come, he heard himself say, "Off and on, I'd see your old high school friend Candy, and she'd tell me you and Warren were happy."

"Because that's what I wanted people to think. I didn't even come clean with *her* that anything was wrong. I mean, what would you do if you realized you'd made the worst mistake of your life? Would you tell everyone about it?"

"I'm sorry."

"It's obviously not your fault."

"Maybe you'd better fill me in on the real story."

She looked defiant—then resigned. Perhaps as a signal that she wasn't going to run away, she dropped her bag and sat down on the floor with her back against the wall. The wounded look on her face made him want to pull her close and rock her in his arms. Instead, he left a few feet of space between them when he joined her.

Her voice went flat as she said, "Warren was charming and exciting when I first met him—and he was very focused on me. He came from an old, established family. He had a lot of money, and he could take me to restaurants and concerts. I couldn't help being thrilled that he'd chosen me over a lot of the other girls in my class." She looked down at her hands. "You remember how my parents didn't pay much attention to me?"

"Uh huh."

"My dad must have worked sixty hours a week, and my mom spent a lot of time at the country club."

He was tempted to say, "Yeah, and they didn't know you were running around with the town bad boy," but he kept the observation to himself as she continued.

"It meant a lot that Warren put me first."

Steve couldn't stop himself from thinking that Warren had been a direct contrast to the hometown boy who'd had to work at a dead-end job for enough cash to take Leah to a hamburger joint. And while he kept himself from bringing up their shared past, he was thankful that this was the place she'd chosen to hide out—and that he'd come here at the right time. Had fate sent her to him—or what?

No, it was his boss, Frank Decorah, who'd told him to take some time off and settle the problems with the property. Sometimes Frank did things like that out of the blue. It was like he had access to information nobody else possessed. But why was that so strange when he'd hired a staff of agents who all had psychic abilities?

Leah was still speaking. "But after I agreed to marry him, he acted like he had the right to make decisions for me. Maybe that should have been a warning sign, but I was still too caught up in the relationship to object.

"It was his idea for me to drop out of school so I could make a home for him. He still spent money on me—on us, I guess—but I gradually realized that he was taking over more and more of my life—and separating me from my friends. I mean, Candy was the only one left." She looked down at the hands clasped in front of her. "And then he started getting angry—and lashing out at me when he was upset.

"I felt like I was walking around on ice that was melting under my feet, trying to make sure I didn't do anything that would make him flare up."

"Didn't you have new friends?"

"Sort of." She made a snorting sound. "I hung out with women in the Junior League. I went to lunch with them and did some charity projects like working at their thrift shop so I wouldn't feel useless, but I wasn't close to any of them—nobody I could confide in about my, . ." She stopped and swallowed. "About my marital problems."

Steve nodded, then probed for more information while she was in the mood to open up. "When did he start hitting you?"

For a moment he thought she wasn't going to answer. Then she grimaced and said, "A couple of years ago. But it was mild at first. Like a slap on the arm or something. Then it got worse. Anything that didn't go right in his life, he acted like it was my fault."

Steve clenched and unclenched his hands.

"A few nights ago, I knew I had to get away."

"After that scene I saw?"

"Yes," she answered.

"But I couldn't use my credit cards. And I had hardly any money."

"Couldn't you go to your parents?"

"Dad died of a heart attack five years ago. It turns out they blew through all of their money. Mom is in a nursing home—that Warren pays for."

"I didn't know any of that."

"How would you?" she asked, then went back to her recent circumstances. "I had started saving money from the cash he gave me every week. It wasn't much, because we mostly used credit. But I took that and ran."

"You drove here?"

"Yes. I didn't want to spend the little money I had on a motel, and I knew the house was empty."

"How?"

"Candy fills me in on stuff about people in town. I knew you'd moved your mom to a senior community in Baltimore County—and that you'd been renting out the house. But the last tenants had made a mess and left without paying the rent."

"That's a lot of information for her to know."

"She still comes back to town to see her parents—and high school friends. She married Dave Markham, then divorced him a couple of years ago. You remember him from school?"

"Yes. He was going to build high-end yachts for the people who have vacation homes down here."

"He does."

"Would Candy tell Warren if she knew where you were hiding out?"

Leah looked shocked. "No."

"She might think she was helping to patch up your marriage."

Leah closed her eyes and opened them again. "I guess that could be right, but I was careful not to be seen here. I hid the car in the garage," she confirmed what he had suspected. "And I didn't use any lights after dark."

"How did you get in?"

She lifted one shoulder. "The key was under the same rock where it always was."

"I'd forgotten about it."

"And you didn't know I was in here, right?"

"Not until I got inside," he conceded. "Then the house didn't smell empty."

Once she'd started talking, she had given him a lot of information in a short amount of time. Now she looked drained.

The slump of her shoulders made him ache to comfort her, and when he stretched out his arm, she came into his arms.

He stroked her back, then reached to run his fingers through her hair, feeling her tremble in his embrace. He'd found her here by accident, and she'd tried to come across like she didn't need his help, but he knew that was all an act.

She lifted her head, searching his face, and what he saw in her eyes made him go very still. Probably she'd been frightened for a long time, and now she had finally found a champion.

It had been forever since he'd held her in his arms, and he'd resigned himself to the emptiness of living without her. But here she was, putting her trust in him. More than trust. She was silently acknowledging that she hadn't forgotten how good they'd been together.

Without giving himself time to consider the consequences, he lowered his head. The touch of his lips against hers was like a homecoming.

She murmured his name against his mouth, then opened for him, telling him that she wanted this as much as he did. Angling his head, he moved his lips against hers, absorbing the pleasure of the intimate contact. She made a small sound in her throat as she slipped her hands around his shoulder, holding him to her.

He had resigned himself to never holding her again—kissing her again. Now he felt dizzy with the intimate contact, drunk with the intoxication of enjoying what he had dreamed of for years. Her taste was familiar, transporting him back to the time they'd been together. And her body felt so right in his arms.

He wanted to keep kissing her forever—taking everything she was willing to offer and giving back in return. In his heated imagination, he pictured shifting his body, stretching out on the mattress and taking her with him. He'd undress her slowly. Do all the things that he knew she liked, and when she was aroused to a fever pitch of need, he'd join their bodies. He could feel it. Taste it. See it. But a small voice in the back of his mind told him that pushing the two of them over the edge was wrong—for a lot of reasons.

When he'd been a kid, he hadn't known how to handle his gift of second sight. Even when he was on the job with the Baltimore PD, he'd been uncertain about using his special talent to solve crimes. It had taken Frank Decorah to show him effective ways to utilize his unique sense of touch that gave him a window into another person's life.

Since joining Decorah Security, he'd realized that his psychic power carried an obligation to help people—not take advantage of them—the way he he'd be doing if he made love with Leah. And he wouldn't let himself take advantage of Leah now—no matter how much he ached for her.

Fighting for self-control, he lifted his head. Leah's eyes blinked open, and she stared at him with a mixture of confusion and hurt that made him feel like the air had turned to ash in his lungs.

"Steve?" she asked in a low voice.

He moved back, putting a few feet of space between his heated body and hers. "Sorry."

"About what?"

"Things were heating up pretty fast."

She had lowered her head. Now she raised it again. "Don't you think I would have stopped you if that was what I wanted?"

"Sure, but you're in fragile shape right now. You're not in any condition to make sexual decisions. Plus, you're a married woman."

"A married woman," she repeated, her voice as dry as parched earth. "Yeah, that might signify something if the marriage still meant anything."

This time she was the one who moved farther away along the wall, and he ached to reach for her and pull her close again, but he kept his arms at his sides.

"We need to figure out how to help you—not ignore the problem."

She raised one shoulder. "Like how?"

"I saw that scene where he pushed you against the chest and hurt you. But I couldn't hear what he was saying. What was he angry about?"

She kept her gaze steady. "I answered the phone."

"Huh?"

"I'd forgotten he'd told me not to answer if it rang."

"Why not?"

"He didn't say. It was just something that he'd decided to require."

Steve winced at the way she said it. "And your answering was enough to make him go batshit?"

She kept her gaze steady. "Yes."

He repressed a curse. There was no use getting angry. Instead he glanced out the window. When he saw it was getting dark, he asked, "Are you hungry?"

"Complete change of subject?"

"Yeah."

"There was some junk food here, not much. And I was afraid to have people see me at the grocery."

"I'll go out and pick something up. What do you want?"

She shrugged. "Whatever."

"Why don't we go with carryout from the Crab Depot? I always liked their stuff."

"Fine."

He used his cell phone to put in an order, then looked at her. "Will you be okay here alone?"

"I was here alone before you arrived."

"True."

Outside in the spring night, he called Decorah and apprised Frank of the situation.

"I kind of thought you might run into trouble down there."

"Why?"

"Just a feeling I had."

"One of your hunches?"

"Right. Let me switch you to Teddy."

That was Teddy Granada, one of the Decorah IT guys, who promised to do some research on Warren Pendelton. "If you come up with anything interesting, send it to my phone."

"Will do."

<h1 style="text-align:center">oOo</h1>

As Leah watched Steve walk to his car and drive away, she felt her chest tighten. She couldn't stop herself from thinking that it might be better if she were gone when he came back. She hadn't expected him to show up, and it wasn't fair to drag him into her problems. But if there was anyone who could help her, it was probably him.

She thought about what he'd revealed—about his talent for touching people's things and getting information about them. He'd hidden that well. What she'd seen all those years ago was a darkly appealing tough guy. He still had the same dark good looks, although he was older and a lot worldlier.

But when they'd been teenagers, there was also the rebellion factor. If there was anyone who her parents would have considered unsuitable for her—it was Steve Outlaw. Which made him deliciously forbidden fruit.

She remembered their heated encounters—especially the one when they'd said good-bye. She'd thought she'd get together with him when she came back from school for Thanksgiving. That was before she'd met Warren, and he'd started monopolizing her time.

She muttered an unladylike curse under her breath. She hadn't seen it back then, but Warren had picked her *because* he thought he could control her. That was the kind of relationship he was looking for. And if she hadn't been so eager to fall in with his plans, he would have dropped her for someone else. She would have been crushed by the rejection, but she would have escaped a lot of emotional and physical pain.

What if she'd come home for Thanksgiving and gotten back with Steve? It was nice to think that she would have picked up their relationship. But it would have been too complicated. It was one thing to sneak around for a few delicious weeks without her parents knowing what she was doing. It was quite another to bring the town bad boy home to dinner.

From bad boy to cop to PI. All in a very appealing package. He'd looked lean and hungry when they'd said good-bye eight years ago, clasping each other so tightly that she'd thought he wasn't going to let her go. He was still lean, but it was with an athlete's toned body. And he had a startlingly firm moral compass. How many guys would have stopped themselves from making love to her a few minutes ago when she was practically throwing herself at them?

When she'd met Warren, she'd told herself that she was getting into a normal relationship, not some furtive tryst with a guy who was too much of a loner to settle down. Now she knew she'd gotten it exactly backwards.

Her thoughts were interrupted when she heard a car door slam outside and tensed.

"It's me," Steve called as soon as he'd opened the door, obviously aware that she was going to be anxious.

He switched on a flashlight, sweeping it around the room and directing the light away from where she still sat on the floor with her back propped against a wall.

"Are you okay?" he asked.

"Yes." It might not be true, but it was the only answer she could give.

CHAPTER FOUR

Scrambling for something else to say, Leah whispered, "I'm sorry it's so dark."

"That's the way it should be if you wanted the house to look like nobody's here."

He laid the flashlight down, aiming it against the far wall where it gave enough light to see the bags of food he'd brought.

He spread several napkins on the floor, then opened the bags, setting a wrapped sandwich in front of each of them, plus small cartons of coleslaw and paper dishes of deep fried onion rings.

"I didn't ask what you wanted to drink. Coffee okay?"

"Fine."

When he joined her with his back against the wall, she unwrapped her sandwich.

"I got them to put several of the mini crab cakes into each bun," he said.

She took a bite. "I'd forgotten how good this was."

"Eastern Shore comfort food," he said. For generations, many of the men in town had made their living on the water—fishing, crabbing or tending oyster beds. Or like Candy's former husband, shipbuilding.

Leah took another appreciative bite. "I tried making crab cakes for Warren. He never got into them."

"Where is he from?"

"New Jersey."

"And that's where the two of you live?"

"No we moved to the northern part of Baltimore."

"Why?"

She lifted one shoulder. "I think he wanted to establish his own outpost."

"It's an upscale part of town."

"Yes, but I'm not going back."

He answered with a tight nod. "Good."

She wanted to touch him, maybe to thank him for not suggesting she should return to a bad marriage because that was what a wife was supposed to do. Instead she spooned up some of the coleslaw. It was also good—with that down-home tang she remembered.

"So you came here. What were you planning to do after that?" he asked.

"Maybe drive out West, get a low-wage job where I could work 'off the books,' save enough money to get a new identity." She dragged in a breath and let it out. "Of course, a new identity is probably pretty expensive."

"You said you didn't have girlfriends who would help you. Why didn't you come to me?" he asked suddenly.

She kept her gaze focused on the food. "I knew I'd made a mistake getting mixed up with Warren. And I was ashamed to have you know about it."

He answered immediately—with no hesitation. "You didn't have to feel that way."

"I should have known better."

"Don't say that. He knew how to fool you."

"You mean manipulate."

Ignoring the interjection, he went on, "Plenty of women end up in that situation. It takes guts to get yourself out—when he'd cut you off from any reasonable avenue of help."

"I waited long enough."

"But you did it. On your own."

"Yeah," she answered, thinking about the course of her life. It had gradually deteriorated. But the realization that she was in serious trouble had only gradually crept up on her.

"Do you know why he got violent?"

"I thought it had something to do with his business."

"Which is what?"

"Basically, retail. He has several furniture . . . galleries, he calls them. And in the past few years, he acquired a couple of electronics stores. But I think he was worried about money, or something. Or maybe someone was putting pressure on him."

"You're not sure what?"

She shrugged. "He didn't discuss business with me. And if he didn't want me to answer the phone, I guess he didn't want me to know his business."

"Yeah."

"Thank God I didn't have a baby."

"What?"

The room was dark, and she hoped he couldn't see her flush. "Did I say that out loud?"

"Yeah."

"I didn't mean to." She heaved in a breath and let it out. "At first I wanted children. Then I figured out that Warren was too wound up with having me take care of his every need to share me with anyone else."

oOo

Steve winced, wondering how he would feel if he were forced into a bunch of revelations he'd rather not share. Well, he'd been forced into one, and it seemed to have worked out okay.

Leah looked down at the remaining food. "I don't think I can eat any more."

"Okay." He waited a moment before asking. "Is there any chance he would think you'd come here?"

"I hope not."

"I'd take you to a motel, but we'd need two rooms, and I don't want to leave you alone."

"Okay."

"You've been sleeping on a mattress on the floor?"

"Yes. I don't mind."

He hesitated again, thinking he could drag another mattress in here. Then he decided it was better to avoid temptation and stay down the hall. If someone came to the house, he'd only be a few yards from her.

He stood up, and after sitting on the floor for so long, his bad leg threatened to crumple.

"What's wrong?" she asked, seeing him falter.

"I was shot—during a drug bust gone bad."

"I'm sorry."

"It doesn't get in the way much," he answered, thinking he had less of a problem than his boss, Frank Decorah, who had come home from Vietnam with half a leg missing.

He made a stop in the bathroom, then went into the smaller bedroom—where he'd slept when he was a kid, glad that all trace of his living there had been erased. He didn't want to bring up any more memories. Except there were some he couldn't banish. As he lay down on the mattress, still fully dressed, he was thinking that this was where he had made love with Leah when his mom had been at work.

It was strange how they'd gotten together. He'd been aware of her in some of the classes he took—and he knew she was aware of him. Because he'd considered her way out of his league socially, he hadn't tried to get anything going with her until one afternoon when school was out for the summer. He'd been cruising around town on his motorcycle when he'd seen her outside the local ice cream shop—one of those places where you ordered at a window and ate at a picnic table out front. She was walking toward the window, and one of the town losers, a guy with greasy hair and a week's worth of beard stubble, stepped into her path. When she tried to move around him, he kept up the sideways dance, a smirk on his face.

Steve cut his engine, pushed down his kickstand, and walked over.

"Leave the lady alone."

The jerk turned to face him, the smirk replaced by anger. "You gonna make me?"

"If that's what it takes."

When Steve took a step closer, the other guy ended up backing away—and finally left. After making sure he wasn't in danger of a sneak attack, Steve turned to Leah. "You want to get out of here?"

He'd had no expectation that she'd agree, but after a moment's hesitation, she said, "Yes."

He inclined his head toward the bike.

She was game to climb in back of him and circle his waist with her arms. He took her to a local park, where they watched ducks gliding across the water as they got to know each other a little better.

She flipped her long hair over her shoulder. "Thank you for getting that guy off my back."

"It seemed like the right thing to do," he allowed.

"Are you enjoying your summer?"

"When I'm not working at Smith's Hardware."

"Are you earning money for college?"

"We'll see," he answered, thinking that would be a stretch. Maybe he could take a few courses at the community college, but would that make any difference in his life?

He took her to a burger joint for dinner, then back to the park for a more up close and personal encounter. When she agreed to see him again, he was riding a high that would last the rest of the summer.

They started going to his house when Mom was at work, and it was a slow but steady process to get her to go all the way with him—starting with more and more intimate make-out sessions in the privacy of his bedroom. Really, they were both learning about sex. But he wasn't shy about experimenting and discovering what gave her pleasure. And perhaps because he was so open about wanting to fulfil her needs, she went along, doing the same for him.

He grew hard as he remembered the first time he'd made her come, his finger stroking into her hot, wet folds as she rocked her hips to increase the friction. After that, she'd asked how to do the same for him. He'd wrapped her hand around his cock, showing her how to pump up and down to bring him off. They'd pleasured each other like that for a few weeks, until she'd let him take her virginity. His mind leaped from the past to the present. From the way she'd responded to his kiss earlier this evening, he was pretty sure that she'd let him do what he wanted now. Did it really make a difference that this was eight years later, and she was a married woman?

"Cut it out," he muttered to himself. Making himself hot with thoughts about Leah in the next room wasn't doing him any good, and he sure as hell wasn't going to bring himself off with her practically lying next to him. He closed his eyes, willing himself to catch some sleep so he'd be ready to get her out of here in the morning. And then what? He still wasn't sure.

He must have drifted off because the next thing he knew, every cell in his body was on alert. He'd heard a scream from down the hall—from the room where Leah was sleeping.

Still angry with himself for not coming armed, he leaped out of bed and pounded down the hall. The door to her room was open, and he rushed in without stopping to see if he might be barreling into a trap.

CHAPTER FIVE

Steve saw Leah lying on the mattress. Like him, she was wearing the clothes she'd had on earlier. Her head was whipping back and forth on a pillow. She was sleeping, and he was sure that she was caught in a nightmare.

A muffled moan escaped her lips as he moved closer, then came down beside her on the mattress, calling her name.

When she didn't respond, he laid a hand on her shoulder trying to gently wake her.

"Leah, it's okay," he soothed. "It's Steve. You're having a nightmare."

But the effort to calm her was wasted. Her eyes were still closed when she lashed out an arm and flailed at him, slapping him across the face.

He reared back, and she came after him, still swinging.

His only option to protect himself without hurting her was to fold her close, clamping her arms to her side as he held her down.

"Leah, it's Steve," he repeated, trying to get through to her. "You're with me. You're safe."

For long moments she kept fighting him, kicking him, making his bad leg throb. Then she finally went still.

"Steve?"

"Yeah." He rolled to his side so that his weight was no longer on top of her.

"Oh God, did I hurt you?" she asked, the question coming out on a sob.

"No. I'm fine," he answered, stifling the impulse to make sure he hadn't cut his mouth when she hit his teeth.

"I'm sorry."

"No problem."

He could feel her struggling for control and heard the tears in her voice as she continued.

"I was back at home. He was coming at me again, but I ducked around him. I was running. Down a long hall. I was trying to get to the door, but the hall was endless. The farther I ran, the farther I had to go. I was trapped.

He reached to soothe his hand across her shoulders, feeling the knots of tension.

"It's okay. He can't get you here."

"I wish I knew that for sure."

He stayed where he was, cradling her in his arms. She rolled to her side, burying her face against his chest.

"I should let you get back to sleep," he whispered.

She grasped his arms, her fingers digging painfully into his flesh. "I don't want to be alone."

There was only one answer he could give. "Okay."

He eased to his back, and she came with him, reversing their original positions.

"You remember when we used to come here?" she asked in a low voice.

"You were thinking about that?"

"Yes. Before I went to sleep. Were you?"

He wanted to lie. Instead, he said, "Yes."

"You taught me about making love."

"This is going in the wrong direction." When he tried to shift away, her hand tightened on his arm.

"Is it?"

She moved up so that she could press her lips over his, and he was instantly transported back in time.

As her mouth stroked persuasively against his, he opened for her, enjoying the hot invasion of her tongue and the pressure of her breasts against his chest when she molded herself to him.

He knew he should disentangle himself before things got out of control, but he couldn't do it. Then she shifted fully on top of him, positioning his erection in the cleft between her upper thighs, making heat shoot through him.

The rocking of her hips against him was like striking a match against tinder. His cock swelled painfully inside his jeans. And when she raised up so that he could reach her breasts, he accepted the invitation, cupping the soft mounds in his hands as he glided his thumbs across the hardened tips.

"Do what you used to do," she whispered against his mouth. "Squeeze my nipples between your thumbs and fingers. Lord, that used to feel so good."

He heard desperation in her voice and felt his own desperation rising.

"Leah, we can't," he managed to say as he dropped his hands to his sides.

"Why not?" she asked, emphasizing the question by torturing him some more with her lower body.

"You're married to someone else."

She raised her head, staring down at him. "It hasn't been a real marriage for a long time."

"It's a legal marriage," he said, still struggling with the meaning of right and wrong. Gently he lifted her off of himself, and they both lay on the mattress, dragging in air.

"You're too much of a gentleman," she whispered.

"And you're trying to forget the nightmare."

"I'm trying to forget a lot of things."

He reached for her hand and clasped her fingers with his. "We'll get you out of this."

"Maybe you can't. Maybe nobody can," she answered, her tone bleak.

Words of reassurance leaped to his lips, but he stopped himself from making promises he might not be able to keep.

"Stay here," she murmured.

He wanted to agree immediately. Instead he asked, "Is that a good idea?"

"I'll behave myself."

"Okay," he answered in the darkness.

"I married the wrong guy," she whispered.

The simple statement tingled against his nerve endings. "Don't say that."

"Teenagers have stupid values."

"Yeah. And I didn't look like marriage material."

"Are you now?" she asked, and he wished she wasn't being so direct.

"I don't know." He gave the only answer he should. He'd wondered for years what would have happened if she'd come back that fall. By then he'd gotten into a program at the local community college for disadvantaged youths who wanted to study criminal justice. If you did well, you could finish at the University of Maryland. He wanted one of those slots, and he was loving the challenge of getting good grades.

Now he said, "Go to sleep, and we'll figure things out in the morning."

"If I can."

He had the same thought. Sexual need still zinged through him, and he knew what would make him relaxed enough to sleep. Instead he tried to focus on his breathing.

oOo

A sound from outside woke him early in the morning. When he got up to investigate, Leah stirred beside him.

"What?"

"I hear someone out there."

He saw her whole body go rigid. "It's Warren."

"We don't know that. Stay out of sight." He walked toward the front of the house. Before he got to the living room, someone pounded on the door and shouted, "Police. Open up."

Steve ran his fingers through his hair, then walked to the front door and looked out. Two uniformed state troopers stood on the front porch. They were both young guys, and Steve didn't recognize either one of them. They wore brass nametags on their uniform shirts. One said Winston and the other said Campbell.

When they saw him through the window, the one named Campbell shouted, "Open up."

He put the chain on the door and opened it the few inches that the security device would allow.

"What's this about?" he asked.

"We're looking for Leah Pendelton."

"Why?"

"She's wanted for robbing and assaulting her husband."

CHAPTER SIX

Clever move, Steve though. If you wanted the cops to help find your runaway wife, accuse her of a crime. Hoping he was keeping any emotion out of his face. "What makes you think she's here?"

"Her husband thought she might be."

"Why?"

"You used to know her, right?"

"Yeah, but I haven't seen her in years."

Campbell, who was doing all the talking asked, "What are you doing here?"

"The last tenant who rented the house trashed the place. Before I put the property on the market, I have to evaluate the damage."

"Mind if we come in?"

"Yes, I do mind."

"You're not being cooperative."

"I'm a former Baltimore City cop and now work for Decorah Security. I know when I have to cooperate and when I don't."

Both men looked disgruntled when they realized their status wasn't enough of an intimidation tactic, but they knew Steve was within his rights to deny them access to the interior.

Campbell gave him a curt nod and backed away. Steve shut the door and watched them through the window. As soon as they'd stepped off the porch, he started for the back of the house.

Leah was already in the hall, looking scared.

"Did you hear that?" he asked.

"Yes. It's a lie. I never assaulted Warren. But I guess he made it sound plausible." She gulped. "What am I going to do now?"

"We're getting the hell out of here. Grab your stuff."

"I don't have much."

She zipped up her bag and he took it from her. When he glanced out the window again, he saw the two officers heading for the garage—where they were going to find a car with a license plate that belonged to Warren Pendelton.

Outside, Steve pulled his keys from his pocket and reached for Leah with his free hand.

"Hurry."

He hustled her across the weedy lawn toward his SUV, which was parked at the curb—thankfully in front of the police cruiser.

Leah slid into the front seat and closed her door. He had just closed the driver's side door when Campbell shouted, "Hold up."

Were they going to shoot, he wondered as he jammed the car into gear and took off.

In the rearview mirror, he saw the two officers pelting for their cruiser. Too bad he hadn't had time to let the air out of their tires.

He drove straight down the street, then took the second right, hoping he remembered his way around the area.

Beside him, Leah was hunched down with her arms wrapped around her shoulders.

"Tell me how far behind they are."

She swiveled in her seat. "They haven't taken the turn yet."

"Good."

He made a left, just missing a car at the next cross street.

"Warren's lying," Leah repeated what she'd said in the house.

"I know."

"How?"

"Because I know you're trustworthy."

"I could have changed."

"Are you trying to get me to stop and wait for the cops to catch up?"

"It would be better for you. This way you're—what do they call it—an accessory after the fact."

"We'll prove you didn't do anything besides escape from an abusive marriage."

"How?"

"I don't know yet."

He made it out of town and slowed down a little after turning onto one of the country roads that crisscrossed the area. Hopefully the state cops would have a much less intimate knowledge of the immediate surroundings.

Leah gave him a doubtful look. "You're getting yourself in trouble."

He shrugged and kept driving, taking a twisting route through the corn and alfalfa fields, making sure that the patrol car hadn't picked up his trail. When he got to a familiar section of the county, he drove off the blacktop onto a dirt road.

"Where are we going?"

"Out of here."

He pulled up in back of a gray weathered house that was next to one of the many rivers in the area.

A stoop-shouldered gray-haired man wearing faded jeans and a tee shirt that said Rehoboth Beach came out when he heard the vehicle. He was holding a shotgun.

"He's armed," Leah gasped.

"He's cautious. Wait here," Steve answered.

He got out, watching the old guy watch him as he approached.

"Jerry," he called out.

"Steve Outlaw?"

"The same."

"What you doin' back here?" he asked, shifting the barrel of the weapon downward.

"I need to rent a boat, and I need to stow my car," he said, gesturing toward the SUV.

"You in trouble?"

"You could say that. I'll pay cash for the rental."

He pulled out his wallet and extracted two fifties. "Will this do?"

"Yeah."

Turning back to the SUV, Steve motioned to Leah, who got out of the vehicle and waited while he drove it into a barn out back and closed the doors.

"Jerry, this is my friend Leah," he said. "Leah, Jerry."

"Nice to meet you," they both said, each of them eyeing the other with curiosity.

"Leah ran into a little trouble. If two state cops come looking for her, it's better if you never saw us."

The old man didn't ask what kind of trouble. He simply led them down to a small but well-kept wooden boat dock where several craft were moored.

"Where are you goin'?"

"Better if I don't say."

"How do I get my boat back?"

"I'll phone you after we tie up."

Jerry considered the arrangement, then said, "Only for you."

"Appreciate it."

The old man led them to a sleek model with an inboard motor, a long back deck and a small enclosed area at the front. Steve helped Leah onto the deck, then directed her under the canopy. Jerry and Steve talked for a few minutes about the craft's operation before he started the engine. Then the older man climbed back onto the dock and cast off the line.

Steve motored slowly down river until they were well clear of the dock, then throttled up the engine.

"Where are we going?" Leah asked.

"Baltimore. Decorah Security has a couple of slips in Fells Point," he said, naming an older part of the city on the Inner Harbor. It was where the police station in the TV show, *Homicide*, had been filmed.

"How do you know Jerry?"

"He and my father used to fish crab together. After dad passed, Jerry kept in touch with me. He'd take me out fishing, and sometimes we'd spend the night on one of his boats."

"I never met your father."

"He died of lung cancer when I was ten. I figure he got it from the asbestos floating around where he worked in a shipbuilding factory."

"Oh, I'm sorry."

"He was a good dad. I always wonder if I would have turned out differently if he'd lived." He turned toward her. "I never met your parents, either."

"I kept you away from them because they would have considered you way below their social level—and hanging out with the right people was important to them."

"And they approved of Warren."

"Yes, but after his initial charm campaign, he kept us away from them. I think now that he didn't want me running back home if I needed help."

"Nice."

"And like I told you, Dad's dead now, and Mom's in a nursing home."

"Yeah."

"I didn't say thanks for getting me out of there."

"I wasn't going to turn you over to those guys, and of course, they might not even *be* cops."

She gave him a startled look. "How could they not be cops?"

"Well, either Warren lied to the police, or he hired actors to play the parts."

"And put them in a cop car?"

"Or one from a movie company. I don't really know which."

"You said you trusted me. I want everything out in the open. I told you I was squirreling away some money." She closed her eyes for a moment. "And before I left, I did take some money from his wallet—but since I was married to him, I think it's my money, too."

"Yeah."

She dragged in a breath and let it out. "But I didn't assault him. It was the other way around. And I didn't steal anything from the house—which is how I think he was making it sound."

"Right."

"I mean what would I do with any of his stuff?"

"Sell it?"

She laughed. "Don't you have to give ID at a pawn shop?"

"Uh huh."

"Well, that leaves me to sell on a street corner."

He nodded, believing her and thinking that Pendelton had made her departure seem as bad as possible.

As they approached the Baltimore Harbor, Steve said, "Go below. It's better if people only see a guy on this boat—not a couple."

"Right."

Leah went down to the lower level, and Steve motored toward one of the Fells Point piers. After one of the nearby boat owners attached the line for him, Steve went down and called Decorah Security on the company's secure line.

Frank answered, and before Steve could say anything, his boss warned, "The cops came here. They'll looking for you and Leah."

"Shit."

"Don't stay on the line. We see your location from your phone. Turn it off. You can pick up the car that's parked near the Visionary Arts Museum."

"Thanks."

When he clicked off, he saw Leah staring at him.

"It looks like you got some bad news."

"Yeah. That was Frank Decorah, my boss. He says the cops came there looking for us, which means that we can't go to a Decorah safe house because I can't implicate them in this."

"I understand," she said in a thin voice. "Warren was pretty clever—the way he cut me off from help."

"Yeah. But you have me. And there's a Decorah car in the area."

"Why?"

"One of Frank's contingency plans. It's across the harbor. But before we go over there, you probably want to buy a hat and maybe a different shirt from one of the shops on Broadway." He thought for a moment. "Actually, I could use a change of clothes and a toothbrush."

"You think the cops know we're here?" she asked.

"I hope not, but I'm not taking any chances."

Steve made a quick call to Jerry to tell him where the boat was moored. From the dock, they walked over to a funky apparel shop where Leah bought a loose-fitting gauze shirt and a wide-brimmed sun hat and Steve picked up an Orioles cap and a dark tee shirt. There was a dollar store a few doors down where he bought a cheap carry bag, underwear, and a toothbrush. After changing in the rest rooms, they took the water taxi across the harbor to the street below Federal Hill where the Decorah car was parked.

Steve stooped down to get the keys from the right front wheel well. Once he'd opened the car, he reached into the glove compartment where he found an envelope with a thousand dollars in small bills.

Leah eyed the money

"Decorah leaves that kind of cash lying around?"

"Yeah, they figure that if you need to pick up a car, you might not be able to use your credit card either."

"What would we have done without a car?"

"Maybe stolen one."

"Seriously?"

"If it was my only option."

"And the money? Were you going to rob someone?"

He laughed. "I don't think I'd go that far."

"But you're not sure?"

"Let's be glad Decorah came through for us."

"It sounds like you hooked up with an interesting outfit."

"I thank my lucky stars that Frank Decorah found me."

"How?"

He laughed. "In a bar. He started a conversation with me, and I realized it wasn't just a coincidence."

"Are you going to tell me more about that?"

"When we've got the time."

As he drove away from the parking spot, she asked, "What now?"

"We need to get off the street."

Steve had been a cop in this city, much of the time patrolling Pig Town, a working class area in the southwest section of the city. It had gotten its name in the second half of the nineteenth century when it was filled with butcher shops and slaughterhouses.

Now it was a mixed neighborhood of condos, apartments and typical Baltimore row houses, some with original brick facades and others modernized with the artificial mica-specked stone that was popular in the fifties and sixties.

Steve headed for the older section of town and cruised slowly down a street of row houses. He slowed when he saw The Hot Spot bar.

"It's a little rough in there," he told Leah. "But they have rooms upstairs for rent."

As he spoke, the door of the Hot Spot opened and two guys came out, swinging at each other. One turned and fled. The other took off after him.

CHAPTER SEVEN

"You're sure this is where you want to stay?" Leah asked.

"Yeah. The high-class atmosphere makes it less likely that anyone would look for us here."

"High class. Right."

When she started to get out of the car, Steve put a hand on her arm. "Stay here until I set things up. And pull your hat down so nobody can see your face."

"Okay."

He walked toward the door of the bar and turned back to her. She looked like she'd rather be somewhere else, but this was the better choice. He gave her a reassuring smile before disappearing inside, where he stood taking in the familiar atmosphere. He hadn't told Leah that most of the upstairs rooms were rented to prostitutes. He could see some of the women sitting at a couple of tables. Most of the establishment's clientele were working-class men, though.

A guy he didn't recognize was behind the bar, which was good. The man wasn't going to ask why Steve Outlaw was back in town and needing a cheap flop.

He made his way through wooden tables.

"I understand you rent rooms," he said to the bartender.

"Yeah."

"Me and my girl would like one."

"We charge by the hour."

"I heard. I want to pay for the night."

The guy looked him up and down, probably deciding what he was willing to pay. "That will be a hundred bucks. In advance."

An outrageous fee, Steve thought, but he quickly agreed and forked over the money.

The guy ducked in the back and returned with a room key attached to a wooden paddle with the number three stamped into the surface. "Where's your date?"

"My gal's kind of shy. She's waiting in the car."

"Married?"

He shrugged. "I'll get her."

"Sure."

He went out, returned to the car and motioned to Leah. "All set."

After he'd retrieved their carry bags from the backseat, he slung his arm around her shoulder. "I told him you were shy."

"Under these circumstances, yeah."

In the vestibule, there was a set of stairs that they climbed to a dimly lit hallway on the second floor.

Steve found room three and inserted the key in the lock. Behind the door was a space about eleven by twelve with a fake brass bed, a wooden chair in one corner, a scarred dresser, and a small private bath with a metal shower in the corner.

Leah sat down on the chair, her arms hugging her shoulders.

"It could be worse," Steve said.

"How?"

"You might have to go down the hall to the bathroom."

"True." She swallowed hard. "Do . . . prostitutes use these rooms?"

"Sometimes."

She went to the window and he followed, looking out on an alley lined with backyard fences. The bar had a one-story extension at the rear. If they had to make a strategic getaway from the room, they could climb out the window to the lower roof—then to the ground.

Leah kept her gaze fixed on the view. "I should get out of here."

"Because working girls come here?"

"No. Because I've already caused you enough trouble."

"I don't want to hear any more of that."

"The cops are looking for you."

"Like I said, maybe that's a ruse."

When he'd brought her here, he'd been thinking they had to hide out. Now he was pretty sure it hadn't been his only consideration.

His gaze locked with hers, and he could feel electricity crackling in the small room. He'd told himself all the reasons why he shouldn't make love with her. But when she stood, crossed the worn floorboards, and circled his shoulders with her arms, he surrendered to the heat that had been simmering between them and covered her lips with his.

Yet he was still struggling for restraint—until she sighed. That small sound was like a jolt of arousal. He went from gentle to hot and hungry in a heartbeat, and she responded as she had the night before.

When he lifted his mouth a fraction, her heated gaze questioned his.

"We shouldn't be doing this," he forced himself to say.

"Why?"

"For all the same reasons as the last time I kissed you."

"Let's forget about reason and logic," she answered.

Maybe she was right. Discarding sanity and caution, he gathered her close.

He had craved more of her all night. Now he opened his mouth to savor her taste more completely. And in his mind, she tasted of all the sweet and female things that had been missing from his life since forever.

His hands moved restlessly up and down her back, pressing her against the hard wall of his chest, so that she could feel the pounding of his heart. He wanted to be with this woman— more than he had wanted anything in a long long time.

And it wasn't just last night that reminded him of what had been missing in his life. All the old memories of her surged to the fore while his mouth sipped and nibbled at hers. It felt like a homecoming as his tongue played with the serrated line of her teeth before teasing more sensitive tissue beyond.

Her tongue met his, stroking and inciting until they were both breathing in jagged gasps.

He angled her body away from his so that his hand could slip between them and cup one of her breasts. She murmured her approval, then made a low sound of pleasure as he found her hardened nipple and brushed back and forth.

He reversed their positions, leaning back against the wall, splaying his legs to equalize their height and bringing her center against his. When she felt the hard shaft of his erection, she moved against it.

He dragged in a sharp breath before his mouth came down greedily on hers again.

The bed was only a few feet away, yet he had to make himself say, "You want to do this?"

"Yes. Stop trying to do the honorable thing," she murmured as she traced the line of his cheekbone, scraping against the sandpaper of his day's growth of beard.

Her finger returned to his lips, retracing territory she had claimed with her mouth.

He bent to kiss her brows, the tender place where her hair met her cheek. His lips brushed her eyelashes before coming gently back to her mouth.

Slowly, then more quickly, she pulled his tee shirt up and off, then bent to press her cheek against his chest before giving him an openmouthed kiss there.

He heard his own gasp.

His hands came up to tenderly clasp her, marveling that she was with him like this again. He had dreamed of making love to her so many times. Now she was in his arms.

He reached for the buttons of her shirt, easing them open before freeing her arms from the sleeves and reaching to unhook her bra.

She stood before him, naked to the waist, and her body was as he remembered it, perfect with her high breasts, creamy skin and coral crests, beaded to tight points.

He reached to cup one soft mound in his hand before doing what she'd asked, squeezing and twisting her hardened nipples.

Her back arched. "That's so good."

"Oh yeah."

Desperate for the feel of her breasts against his chest, he pulled her close, unable to hold back a shuddering sigh.

The only thought in his mind was that he needed to get closer to her—as close as he could get. When he eased away so that he could reach for the button at the top of her slacks, she let him do what he wanted—and followed his example, her hands fumbling with his belt.

As she slid his zipper down, he went very still, the sensation of her palm pressing against his cock taking his breath away.

She kicked away her slacks. He did the same.

Before he lost the ability to stand, he swept back the bedspread, blanket and top sheet, then brought her down to the horizontal surface.

She clasped the back of his head as he swirled his tongue around one tight nipple, lapping up the taste of her, then sucking strongly. When she cried out, he felt a wave of gratification that almost overwhelmed him.

He slid his hand down her body, stroking over her abdomen and lower—into the hot, wet folds of her sex. She responded with a breathy sound of pleasure.

She rocked against him, then took his hand away. 'You'll make me come."

"That's the idea."

"But I want you inside me for that. I want to feel my muscles clamp around your cock."

He groaned. "God, yes."

She lay on her back, completely open to him. Shifting above her, he moved between her legs—then took her in one sure, possessive stroke, burying himself in her tight, wet warmth.

She clasped her arms around his shoulders, holding him tightly as she tilted her hips and took him deeper inside her.

In the long years since they had been together, he had remembered the physical pleasure, but now the power of the moment stunned him.

He raised his head, looking down at her, seeing the passion and the wonder on her face. When he pulled back and then surged forward in a deep, claiming stroke, she smiled up at him.

He wanted this physical reunion to last. But the need of his body was too great. Quickly the pace became more urgent, more demanding.

An overwhelming tide of pleasure flowed through him, and he called her name.

"I'm . . . with you. . . all the way," she gasped out between broken breaths, meeting each thrust and retreat with the motion of her hips.

He felt himself spin out of control as the tide carried him beyond urgent need. A crest of fulfilment slammed through him. At the same time, he felt her nails digging into the slick flesh of his shoulders, felt her body convulsing under him, around him.

When the storm had swept past, he shifted his weight off of her, taking her with him, holding her in his arms.

"Thank you," he said, his voice hoarse with emotion.

"Thank *you*."

He held on to her, unable to break the connection.

And when she snuggled down against him, he felt himself drifting off to sleep, still inside her.

CHAPTER EIGHT

An hour later, when Leah eased away and slipped out of bed, she felt Steve tense.

"Bathroom," she murmured.

He nodded, and she found her underwear and blouse on the floor. Snatching them up, she exited the bedroom, feeling his eyes on her. Quietly she closed the door, used the facilities, washed and dressed again.

It was mind-blowing to think she and Steve had made love again. He was on the other side of the door, lying in the bed where they'd renewed their passion.

She'd never forgotten him, and as things had gotten worse with Warren, she wished she'd had her head screwed on straight all those years ago. Back when they'd been teenagers, sex with Steve had been wonderful, and she hadn't realized it would be any different with someone else. She'd found out with Warren that wasn't true. He was always focused on what would be best for him. But today she'd gotten a glimpse into what a good relationship would be like. It was a long time since she'd made love rather than had sex. But this was definitely the former. She'd known that Steve wanted her badly, but he'd been as concerned about her pleasure as his own. Still, she couldn't discount the circumstances or the surroundings. She'd gotten him in bad trouble just by showing up at his mom's house, and she hadn't even realized how bad until those cops had woken them up in the morning. Suppose she got him arrested?

She glanced toward the little bathroom window, thinking it would be best for Steve if she could walk away from him. But then what?

A knock on the door made her jump. "What?"

"What are you doing in there?"

"Um . . ."

"Are you thinking about running out on me?" he asked in a taut voice.

She opened the door and saw that he'd pulled his clothing back on. "You're a mind reader, too?"

"Not in the psychic sense. But I do remember how your thought processes work."

Well, at least he wasn't focusing on the usual conversation two people might have after making love—when they hadn't been together in years and one of them was married.

She raised her chin. "I've put you in a difficult situation."

"We'll get out of it." To punctuate the statement, he reached for her and folded her close. She clung to him, wishing they could have gotten back together some more normal way. But what would that have been? If they'd bumped into each other in a restaurant or something, would they have just made polite small talk before going their separate ways? Maybe it had taken something dramatic like this for them to admit how they really felt. Or at any rate, she knew how she felt. She was afraid to probe his emotions too deeply.

That uncertainty made her catch a shaky breath.

"What?"

Scrambling for a reason for her reaction, she said, "You're cut off from the people who usually help you."

He shrugged. "They can still help me do some research."

"It flitted through my mind to sneak out, but I know that would be dumb. I've got a better idea."

He tipped his head to the side, waiting.

"You remember I told you that Candy and I stayed friends?"

"And?"

"I think she'd help us."

"Like how."

"Starting with a better place to stay. She's got a beach house on the Jersey shore."

"But if Warren knows you and she are friends, he might look there—like he sent the cops to my mom's house."

"She's got a lot of connections. We wouldn't have to stay at her place. She could ask around."

He nodded slowly, and she could see he was at least considering the idea. Finally he said, "You can call her. Tell her you've run away from Warren, and you need help. Don't let her know that you're with me."

"Why not?"

"I want to keep our options open. We should call from a pay phone. That will make it look more authentic."

She nodded and exited the bathroom.

"Are we coming back here?"

"I don't know. But to be on the safe side, we'll put our stuff in the car."

When she finished dressing, Steve led her back down the stairs, where she was glad she wasn't right in the line of sight of bar patrons. Probably guys who glanced their way thought Steve had paid for a few hours of her time, but perhaps that was better. If anyone asked, they'd say the couple were simple normal patrons of the upstairs rooms.

They returned to the car and drove a few blocks.

"There used to be more pay phones," she murmured.

"Yeah, before everyone had one in their pocket or purse."

They finally found what they were looking for in the parking lot of a gas station, and Steve pulled in.

"Is there some way you can come up with a meeting place that only the two of you will know about?"

"Why?"

"In case her phone is tapped."

Her head jerked toward him. "You think it would be?"

"I think we have to be prepared for something like that. I mean, why not if Warren sent cops to my mom's?"

Leah closed her eyes and thought for a moment. "She and I came to a restaurant in Greek town for my birthday. I mean, we were with my parents. It was an unusual treat. She should remember that."

"Okay."

When she pressed between the plastic shields on either side of the phone, Steve came up right in back her. As she held the receiver to her ear, he brought his head close to hers and clasped his arm around her shoulder.

Her hand was shaking as she pushed the buttons on the keypad, then waited with her nerves jangling while the phone rang. Finally her friend picked up.

"Candy, this is Leah," she said quickly, hearing the strained quality of her own voice.

"Leah, what's wrong? You sound . . . strange."

"Long story. I left Warren."

"I know. He called looking for you."

"What did you say?"

"That I hadn't seen you, of course. Thank God you contacted me. What can I do to help?"

She fought tears when she heard the concerned tone of her friend's voice. "I always acted like everything was okay with me and Warren, but things have been getting—bad."

"Like how?"

"He started getting abusive."

On the other end of the line, Candy drew in a quick breath. "Oh you poor thing. I'm so sorry."

"He seems to be under a lot of pressure. I was hoping to lie low while I figured out my next move."

"Are you with anyone?"

Leah glanced at Steve, and he shook his head. "No. There was nobody I could call. Then I got scared, and I was hoping you could help me."

"Of course. You should come to my house."

"No. I don't think that's safe. I think he has people looking for me."

"Leah."

"I know I sound paranoid, but I can't help it," she answered, considering telling Candy about the police showing up. But she knew that would only lead to a bunch of questions she wasn't prepared to answer. "Do you remember my seventeenth birthday—with my parents?"

"Yes, of course it was . . ."

Leah cut her off before she could name the restaurant. "Don't say it. I can meet you there."

"Okay, good."

"How soon can you get there?" Leah asked.

"I'm at the DC house. I can be there in a couple of hours."

"Okay. I can't tell you how grateful I am."

She hung up and looked at Steve. "Was that okay?"

"Perfect, and we have time to get over there and make sure you're not gonna get trapped."

"It's Candy."

"I'm not taking any chances."

She took in the set of his jaw and wondered what he was planning, and wondered even more when they drove to an area that was more run down than Pig Town. As she looked around, she saw men standing on street corners making furtive transactions.

"They're selling drugs?"

"Yeah."

When Steve turned onto a narrow street that was little more than an alley, she gave him a questioning look.

"I need to make a stop."

"For what?"

"A weapon."

He pulled up in front of a shop with three gold balls painted over the door and a wide variety of merchandise displayed on shelves in the window—everything from what looked like diamond rings to Crock-pots and power tools.

"A pawn shop?"

"Yeah." He hesitated, "I'd like to leave you in the car again, but this isn't the greatest neighborhood."

"I noticed."

They both got out and walked quickly into the shop, which was packed with more of the items displayed in the window.

A short dark man with a fringe of hair at the sides of his head and a shiny bald scalp covering the rest looked up and focused on Steve.

"Outlaw?"

"Uh huh."

"What you doin' back in town? You come over to the dark side?"

"I'm in private security now, Davie, and I need a piece."

The guy cocked his head to the side. "You ain't got one?"

"I do, but it's at home. Long story."

"You want something that can't be traced?"

"Right," Steve agreed. The two men walked over to a case against the wall and entered into a complex negotiation that Leah couldn't follow. But fifteen minutes later Steve had a handgun, a box of ammunition, and a light jacket.

"Aren't you supposed to have a background check and a license?"

"Yup."

"But you didn't."

Steve shrugged as he tossed the jacket in the backseat. "In for a penny, in for a pound."

She kept her gaze on him. "What was that business about a piece that couldn't be traced?"

"Davie thinks I'm into something illegal."

"And you are."

"We're going to come out smelling like orange blossoms."

"Oh sure. Now you've got the cops after you—and you're carrying an illegal gun. How much did it cost?"

"You don't want to know."

He used the GPS to navigate to the vicinity of the restaurant and drove around the area. It was much like what she remembered from the birthday visit, with Baltimore row houses plus restaurants, bakeries, coffee shops and small retail stores. But now there seemed to be as many Latino businesses as Greek. There was also a lot of new residential construction.

"Looks like a thriving neighborhood," Steve commented.

"Yes. It's hard to imagine you're going to need a gun here."

"Better safe than sorry."

He drove past the restaurant, which was on a corner, then found a parking place a few doors down.

"Unfortunately, you have to go in alone," he said.

"I'll be fine."

"I'll go around the back to the kitchen entrance. Once we're both inside, I'll keep you in sight."

"Okay."

"Try to get a table where you can have your back to the wall."

"Like a Mafia don?"

"Yeah."

Despite that last exchange, Leah told herself there was nothing to worry about when she got out of the car. However, as she walked back to the restaurant, she felt a shiver of apprehension.

But it was too late to back out now. When she stepped inside, she saw that the interior was much as she remembered it. The walls were painted to resemble the exterior of buildings on the Greek isles with white stucco and blue trim. The tablecloths were white, and the chairs were light-colored bentwood.

There were few diners in the middle of the afternoon. When a fifty-something waiter wearing a white shirt and black slacks approached, she said, "I'm meeting a friend. Could I have a cup of tea and a piece of baklava?" The sweet pastry of honey and ground nuts layered between leaves of phyllo dough was one of her favorites, but she wondered if she could choke any down this afternoon.

"Certainly."

Following Steve's directions, she found a table along the wall and glanced toward the back of the restaurant. When she saw the corridor was empty, she felt a dart of panic. Had something happened to Steve out on the street? Then she heard a door open at the back of the restaurant, and he came striding down the hall, stopping just before the dining room.

She nodded at him in relief before he took several steps back, turning a corner where he couldn't be seen from the eating area.

She thanked the waiter when he brought her order, then stirred milk and sugar into her tea.

Was Candy going to stand her up, she wondered as she broke off a piece of the baklava and forked it into her mouth, but she could hardly taste the familiar confection.

Leah had just taken a sip of tea when Candy came in, looking her preppy put-together best.

The petite brunette glanced around the dining room, spotted Leah and hurried across the room, her high heels clicking on the tile floor.

Wearing a slim sleeveless dress, she could have been on her way to a garden party—making Leah conscious that she was dressed in a rumpled shirt and slacks.

"There you are."

Leah stood, and they hugged.

Candy gave her a critical inspection. "Are you okay?"

"Yes."

"You really scared me with that call."

"I scared myself. I mean, I had to take off. Then I didn't know where to go from there."

"What happened?" her friend asked in a sympathetic voice as she joined Leah at the table.

"Life with Warren has been getting—rough. He hit me a couple of times."

The other woman shifted in her seat. "Why?"

"I'm not even sure. I didn't have to do much to set him off."

Candy reached over and laid a comforting hand on Leah. "Oh you poor thing. What are you going to do?"

Leah closed her eyes for a moment, fighting tears. Her friend's support meant a lot. "I thought I could stay with you while I figured it out."

"Of course. That's a good idea. Let's get out of here now."

Leah glanced toward the back of the restaurant, but Steve had vanished. Should she get up and go out front without him?

"Come on," Candy urged, standing up.

Leah pushed back her chair uncertainly. This wasn't going exactly the way she'd expected. Candy was rushing her, but maybe she was thinking it was best for Leah to get out of sight quickly.

"Probably you're short of cash."

"Uh huh."

Her friend put some money on the table, then took her arm and led her toward the door. Again she glanced back to where Steve had been but didn't see him.

Candy propelled her toward the entrance. Taken by surprise, she followed along.

As they stepped outside, two large, rough men converged on them, one from either side of the door. Leah didn't recognize them, but she knew the type—men Warren hired for guard duty.

CHAPTER NINE

A look of triumph on her face, Candy ducked out of the way as the men closed in on Leah.

"Candy?"

"Warren's been frantic. Thanks for letting me know where you were."

Leah fought the sick feeling rising in her throat. She'd been so willing to trust her oldest friend. Now that looked like a bad miscalculation. "What are you doing?"

The woman who was supposed to be her friend raised her chin. "Bringing you back where you belong."

"Why?"

"Because it was naughty of you to run away like that," she said in a voice that reminded her of the honey in the baklava—with flies stuck in the syrup.

One of the men stepped forward, hooked his arm around Leah's and tugged. She looked wildly up and down the sunlit street. At this time in the afternoon, she saw no one nearby. Would anyone hear if she screamed?

Knowing she was in a world of trouble if these guys brought her back to Warren, she pressed her feet against the sidewalk. For all the good that did. She could only slow her forward momentum as the man with his hand on her arm pulled her toward a car that stood at the curb.

"Come on," the guy growled.

Leah stamped on his foot, and she was rewarded with a grunt of surprise. Too bad Leah wasn't wearing Candy's high heels so she could have done more damage.

"You little bitch," he muttered as he shifted her in front of him where she had less chance of mounting another attack. The other guy opened the car door, and Leah reached for the metal frame, bracing her outstretched arms.

"Hold it right there," a voice rang out.

Steve had come around the corner, the gun in his hand.

The two men and Candy froze.

Leah let go of the car, ducked under her captor's arm and started toward Steve.

"Get her purse," he said.

"What?"

"Candy's purse."

Leah pulled it from the brunette's hand, resisting the impulse to kick her so-called friend in the butt, then moved to Steve's side. "Walk back toward our car," he said.

With her heart almost blocking her windpipe, she did as he asked, walking rapidly down the street, looking back to see that he was following, but walking backwards.

When they reached the car, he handed her the keys. "You drive. I'll keep them covered."

She slid behind the wheel and turned on the ignition, then waited for him to get into the passenger seat. When he was beside her, he rolled down the window, pointing the gun back toward the trio on the sidewalk.

"Go."

She pulled away from the curb and headed down the block.

"Take the first right, then the next right, then a left."

She did as he asked, gripping the wheel to keep her hands from shaking.

"How, how did you get there so fast?" she asked.

"I slipped out and came around to the front entrance. I saw Candy come in and those guys take up positions near the door.

"Thank God." She kept driving. "Now what should I do?"

He looked around the residential neighborhood of row houses. "Pull over."

When she did, he waited a moment to make sure the bad guys weren't in sight, then asked her to switch places with him.

oOo

Behind the wheel again, Steve glanced at Leah, who looked pale and shaken. He wanted to take her in his arms and reassure her that she was safe, but this was no time to let down his guard. Instead, he drove back to the bar where they'd been hiding out.

After collecting their luggage from the trunk, he led her up the stairs to their room. As soon as the door closed behind them, she reached for him, and he felt her shaking as he folded her close.

"I thought Candy was my friend," she said in a broken voice. "My last real friend."

"Obviously, that's what she wanted you to think. Or it could be that Warren has some hold on her."

"Maybe," she whispered.

Steve ached to keep holding her, but he knew that they didn't have a lot of time to figure out their next moves. Which meant he had to take the shortcut route.

"I think I can find out," he said, hating that he had only one option if he wanted information quickly. When she gave him a questioning look, he went on. "You remember the way I saw that Warren was abusing you?"

"Because you wrapped your hand around something of mine that was important to me. My locket."

"Yeah." He clenched his teeth, then fought to relax his jaw. "I'm sure there's something in Candy's purse that will be similar. But . . ."

"What?"

"I don't usually do this in front of anyone else. Well, I never do it in front of anyone else," he amended.

"Why not?"

"You saw the tail end of it when you came back from the bathroom. I'm probably going to look like I'm having a seizure."

She kept her gaze steady. "I could leave."

"No," he answered immediately. "I don't want you on your own—especially when I'm out of commission."

Without getting into further discussion, he went into the bathroom and returned with a towel, which he wrapped around the purse. Then he straightened the covers, plumped up one of the limp pillows and lay down on the bed.

Leah sat down beside him. He glanced at her, then at the little package he'd set on his stomach. Anticipation mixed with trepidation as he pushed aside the towel and reached inside the purse.

At first nothing happened as he moved his fingers through the objects inside—feeling a lipstick, an emery board, a comb. Then his hand brushed against a folded rectangle, her wallet. As he made contact with the leather, he was instantly somewhere else—somewhere he'd rather not be. Like the last time he'd done this, he was in an upscale bedroom, but this time it looked like a hotel room. Candy and Warren were standing beside a bed, passionately kissing while he lowered the zipper at the back of her dress, and she kneaded her fingers into his butt.

It was like watching a scene from a porn movie, a parody of a warm and loving relationship.

Disgusted, Steve tried to pull away. For a few seconds the ugly scene kept its claws in him, and he was forced to watch the torrid action until he could wrench himself away. When his eyes blinked open, he was back in the downscale bedroom, breathing hard. Leah was leaning over him, her eyes filled with concern and her hand on his arm.

"Are you all right?" she asked.

"Yeah. What did I look like?"

"Like you were seeing something that made you sick, and you were trying to get away."

"That's a good description."

She waited for him to continue, and he knew there was no easy way to tell her what he'd seen, so he simply blurted out, "Candy and Warren are having an affair."

She caught her breath. "How do you know?"

"I saw them in a bedroom."

"Not my bedroom," she said immediately. "I mean, how could they? I never get out of the house."

"Maybe a hotel."

"What was she wearing?"

"A long green dress."

"What was he wearing?"

"Khaki slacks. A light blue knit shirt."

Her gaze turned inward. "I remember when he put on that outfit. He said he was going to a business meeting."

Steve reached out and laid a hand on her arm. "I'm sorry."

"I'm not sure whether I'm angrier at him—or her. She kept pretending to be my friend, and all the time she was sneaking around behind my back." She grimaced. "Lately, Warren was much less interested in me . . . sexually. I figured he was . . . fucking someone else," she added, putting it in the crudest possible terms. Still, the wounded look on her face tore at him.

He dropped the purse on the floor and pulled her into his arms, holding her tightly as he ran his hands up and down her back.

He could feel her struggling for control.

"It's okay," he soothed.

"Yeah," she muttered. "Now I really can get on with my life." She raised her head. "If he doesn't have me killed first."

Steve felt his features harden. "You said you thought he was into something that was stressing him out. But it wasn't the affair. He knew he had that under control. I'm going over to his house and get something on him."

"Like what?"

"I'll know it when I find it."

Her hand tightened on his arm. "No! That's too dangerous."

"I'm not going to just lie here and let him keep messing with you."

She sat up and slicked her hair back with her hand. "If you're going, then I'm going with you."

"No," he said automatically.

"You said you didn't want to leave me here."

"Going over there is dangerous."

"But I can help you. In the first place, I can tell you the layout of the house. And what if I go up to the front door and tell him I've come home—that I know I made a mistake and I'm sorry. I mean, there's no way he can know you saw him with Candy."

Steve sat up, too, thinking it over before nodding.

"So you agree that's a good plan?"

"I was agreeing about the affair. But Warren's thugs saw me at the restaurant."

"I could say I decided you're too dangerous."

He didn't like it. Instead of arguing, he said, "Tell me about the house. If you go to the front door, where would be the best place for me to get in?"

"There's a sunroom built across the back. It's only one story high. Do you think you could get to the roof and in a second-story window?"

"Maybe. Are they locked?"

"I leave one in the bedroom unlocked because sometimes I open it for fresh air. As you face the back of the house, the bedroom is on the right."

"How would I climb up?"

"There's a storage shed at one side of the family room. If you move a patio chair over, you should be able to get to the shed roof, then to the next roof. His office is up there."

"I don't like putting you in danger. What happens when I finish searching upstairs?"

"I say I want to go up to the bedroom, then I meet you in the office."

"There are too many things that could go wrong."

"You're bringing your gun, right?"

He nodded, still not liking it.

"Then we should go before you over think this."

"Will Warren be alone?"

"Unfortunately not. He's always got a couple of tough guys in the house." She laughed. "Unlike his wife, they have the option of quitting. So they change pretty frequently."

"The guys who came to Greektown with Candy?"

"No, that would have been a dead giveaway. I guess he hired someone else for that."

"Uh huh."

She pictured his current security men. "The ones he's got now are both bodybuilder types, but Carlton has long blond hair he wears tied at the back of his neck. Jimmy is dark, a little shorter, and he's got a scar running down one side of his face."

"Okay."

She stood up "Enough talk. Coming?"

He gave her a hard look, aware that she wasn't going to back down, probably because she had to prove to herself that she wasn't afraid of Pendelton. Or at least too afraid to confront him.

He followed her to the door, then down the steps to the car. He knew the approximate location of the house, but he asked Leah for the address and punched it into the GPS.

"What are you waiting for?" she asked as he sat without moving.

"I might need backup."

He put in a call to Decorah Security.

"The situation hasn't changed," Frank told him.

"Actually it has," he answered, telling his boss about the attempted abduction in the afternoon.

"I see what you mean," Frank said, then made a few suggestions. When Steve hung up, he was feeling somewhat better about the evening's activities.

They headed for the northern suburbs of the city, where the houses were large and set on spacious lots. The sun had set before they arrived in the upscale area.

When they were within a few blocks of their destination, Steve slowed, taking a look at the neighborhood. Every house had a two- or three-car garage, and there were no vehicles parked at the curbs.

"We're going to stand out like zombie invaders from a horror movie."

She made a clucking sound. "I told you I was friends with some of the Junior League ladies. I know Nita Martin, is on vacation with her husband—in the Bahamas. We can park in her driveway."

He nodded. "Okay."

First they drove past Pendelton's, where almost every window blazed with lights.

"You're sure he's not having a party?"

"He likes it bright at night."

After drifting past, Steve let Leah direct him to the Martin house. It wasn't anywhere as bright as Pendelton's, but it wasn't totally dark, either.

"You're sure they're gone?"

"Pull in the driveway, and I'll ring the bell and see."

"What if she's home?"

"She won't be."

He kept the engine running while Leah rang the bell. When no one answered, he cut the engine and they both got out.

As they walked down the block, Steve hated the exposure, but he didn't see any alternative unless they were going to drop out of the sky with a parachute.

They reached Leah's block, and she pointed toward her house.

"There's a gravel and stepping stone path on the left side as you face the front. You open the garden gate by reaching inside for the latch."

"Okay. Give me ten minutes to get to the second floor. Then you ring the bell."

"How did I get here?" she suddenly asked.

"In a cab, but you had them let you off around the corner."

"Why?"

"Because you felt funny showing up without your car," he answered.

"And where is the car?"

"In a lot downtown."

"Why?"

"You bashed the fender."

She laughed. "Yeah, he won't want to hear *that*."

They were standing in the shadows under a maple tree. He reached for Leah and hugged her tightly, and she clung to him fiercely. Finally he forced himself to ease away, hoping this wasn't going to turn into a disaster.

She gave him a determined look before he turned and walked down the block like he belonged in the neighborhood. Really, he'd felt more at home in Pig Town, but he didn't see anyone watching from the windows as he stopped at the edge of Pendelton's lot, then took the path to the backyard, being careful to walk on the stepping stones and not the gravel.

There was a high fence at the back, but he reached over the gate and found the latch, then slipped inside, stopping to listen. As far as he could tell, no one had heard him enter the yard.

Behind the one-story addition was a patio and swimming pool. The storage shed was to the side.

So far, so good.

After making sure no one was watching, he picked up one of the patio chairs, carried it to the back of the shed, and used it to boost himself up to the low roof. From there he climbed to the top of the addition and moved quietly along the roof until he reached what must be the bedroom. He began pushing at window sashes and found one that was open. While he eased it up, he was thinking that if he could get in this way, so could a burglar.

After making sure the room was empty, he climbed inside. As he came down on the floor, he heard the doorbell ring.

CHAPTER TEN

Leah's heart was pounding as she rang the doorbell at the house she had shared with her husband. When she'd moved here, she'd tried to convince herself her life was on the right track. Warren had given her a beautiful home and an upscale lifestyle. But she'd secretly had some doubts about the marriage.

She shook her head, cursing her inability to make the right decision. She should have left years ago, but there had been too many reasons to hang on. Her husband had made sure she didn't have any good way to support herself. And then there was the fear. What would Warren do to her if she left and he found out where she'd gone?

She had the answer now, and it wasn't pretty. As far as Warren was concerned, she belonged to him—whether or not he actually wanted to make a life with her.

And what would he do now?

She steeled herself as she heard footsteps approaching the door. Someone looked out through the translucent curtains screening the side light. When the door flew open, she was facing her worst nightmare—her husband.

Unprepared for the burning fury in his eyes, she struggled to catch her breath as he grabbed her arm and pulled her inside.

"Why did you leave?"

"I knew I made a mistake. Now I'm back."

"You're answering the wrong question—why did you leave?"

"I was scared," she said in a voice filled with genuine fear.

"Of what?"

"You were so angry. You hurt me."

oOo

Upstairs, Steve gritted his teeth as he stood looking around the small but nicely appointed office with wooden file cabinets and a top-of-the-line computer on the wide desk.

Probably the computer was password protected. Instead, he pulled on rubber gloves and began opening drawers and looking through papers and folders. He found a lot of stuff here, including bank and credit card statements, but nothing that looked like a red flag. He glanced toward the door, knowing he had limited time. With a sigh he peeled off the gloves, sat down, and started searching again, not through papers, but touching the objects on the desk and in the office.

He hit pay dirt when he cupped a hand around an ornate globe of the world, smaller than the usual model but apparently made out of semiprecious gemstones.

As he grasped the object, he was seized by a wave of dizziness.

Then he felt the familiar sensation of disorientation as his gift transported him from the present to a scene in this very office. A man a few years older than Steve was sitting in the desk chair. It was the same man he'd seen hit Leah—and grope Candy.

Steve took in details he hadn't focused on earlier. Dressed casually in jeans and a white polo shirt, Pendelton wore a heavy gold chain around his neck. He had a diamond ring on the middle finger of his right hand, and he was playing with the globe while he spoke on the phone.

"Listen, Malcolm, I know we have a deal, but it's getting harder to funnel cash through my legit businesses."

He listened for a minute and said. "Half a mill is a hell of a lot. I want more of a cut."

Again he listened, then said, "Yeah, okay," but he didn't look very happy with the answer.

The conversation and Steve's Baltimore PD background had given him what he needed, and he struggled to pull away. Before he could come back to present reality, he heard a sharp voice that seemed to come from out of thin air.

"Put your hands flat on the desk."

The command filtered through Steve's consciousness. He blinked and looked up to see a man holding a gun. Not Pendelton. One of his goons that Leah had described. The blond guy with the ponytail. Carlton. The other one, Jimmy, was behind him. Although both of them looked like they could snap a normal man in half without breaking a sweat, Carlton was holding an automatic pistol pointed at Steve's chest.

He shook his head to clear it, silently cursing the talent that had given him the answer to an important question but at the same time had made him as vulnerable as a puppy in a tiger's cage.

"Keep your hands where I can see them. Stand up."

Steve stood.

The other guy frisked him, found the gun tucked into the back of his waistband, and removed it.

"Get moving. We're going down."

With no other choice, Steve walked out of the office and toward the stairs, his mind scrambling for a way to save Leah.

oOo

This ruse had been Leah's idea. Now she knew she might never leave this house alive. The sound of footsteps on the stairs made her head jerk up and wonder why Steve was coming down. Then she saw he was followed by the two bodyguards—one holding a gun at Steve's back.

"He was in the office," Carlton said.

Warren looked up in satisfaction. "Got ya." Swinging back to Leah he said, "I thought you might be with this guy all along."

Explanations danced through her head, but she knew none of them was going to do her any good.

"Take him into the sunroom," Warren said, clamping his hand painfully on Leah's arm. When the trio had passed, he led her down the hall after them.

She fought a sick feeling as Warren pushed her onto the couch beside Steve.

"Sorry," she whispered.

"Shut the fuck up," her husband ordered. "I know you were poking into my business. Your boyfriend in my office proves it. But there's nothing for him to find up there. I don't keep records on paper, and he can't get into my computer."

"He's not my boyfriend."

"Then what's he doing here?"

She didn't answer, because anything she said would be wrong—as far as Warren was concerned.

He must have caught the sick expression on her face.

"Yes, I know what you're up to. After you didn't find anything, you hired this guy." He jerked his head toward Steve. "But you don't have any money, so you must have been paying him with sex."

Leah's face flamed. She couldn't deny that she was sleeping with Steve, but it was nothing like what Warren had said. It hadn't been for any kind of payment.

oOo

Steve interjected himself into the conversation, keeping his voice hard and even. "I do know something about your work ethic, actually. You're laundering drug and prostitution money for Malcolm Herman—Malcolm the Hammer—through your retail businesses. And now you're afraid the IRS is going to figure it out."

Warren's eyes bugged as though he'd turned into a bullfrog. The reaction told Steve he'd hit the mark with his educated guess about the guy on the other end of the line. Malcolm the Hammer was a well-known Baltimore crime figure.

Though Warren blanched, he kept his voice even. "You're lying. There's no way you could get to that."

108

"But I did. And I know that you're also in trouble with his organization because you're not getting the job done fast enough."

"Jesus. How did you figure any of that?"

Without hearing the other end of the conversation, Steve had done a lot of guessing—partly based on Leah's description of Warren's behavior. He'd been nervous about something—and was taking it out on her.

Reaching for another bluff, he added, "Candy told me."

"What?" Pendelton spat out, the syllable sharp as a steel blade.

"I got it from Candy," Steve said again. "You're fucking her, but she's not the loyal little girl you thought she'd be. In fact, she's probably about to go to the Feds on her own because rats always desert a sinking ship."

Warren's eyes blazed. "I'll take care of you in a minute." Stepping to the door, he shouted, "Get in here."

When there was no response, he shouted again, "Get your ass in here before I kick it around the block."

Candy appeared in the doorway. She'd changed from the dress she'd been wearing that afternoon into jeans and a pale yellow knit top. But the most conspicuous thing about her was the way her face had drained of color.

"So you've betrayed me too," Warren bellowed.

If possible her skin went a couple of shades paler. "No. I would never. I did just what you asked me to do. I went down and tried to bring Leah home. And here she is," she added, stretching out her arm as though she was a magician who had just pulled off a seemingly impossible trick.

Pendelton laughed. "Nice try. No thanks to you. And when did you clue him in to my business dealings?" he asked, jerking his head toward Steve.

"I didn't. He's lying."

"Then how the hell would he know anything?"

All she could do was give Pendelton a blank stare.

The two bodyguards had turned toward the couple exchanging angry words. With no time to warn Leah what he was doing, Steve stood, braced his bad leg, and picked up the heavy wooden coffee table in front of the sofa. Putting all his weight into the throw, he hurled it at the men. Taken by surprise by the flying furniture, they were pushed backward, into Warren, who stumbled against Candy. While all of them were wavering on their feet, Steve grabbed a cut glass bowl from the side table and hurled it at Carlton's head.

He went down, and Steve grabbed the gun from his limp hand. In the space of heartbeats, the whole scene had changed. But unlike one of his visions, this was the here and now, and he had to get Leah away from danger.

While the bad guys were trying to sort themselves out, he picked up the table again, grasping it by one end, then whirled and hurled it through the large window in back of the sofa. The twist sent a sharp stab through his leg, but he fought to ignore the pain as he listened to the sounds behind him.

At least one of the guys was scrabbling up. Gritting his teeth, Steve snatched up Leah and carried her through the massive hole in the glass, coming down hard on the patio. The unyielding surface was a shock to his bones, and glass dug into his hands. Ignoring the pain, he pulled himself up and started toward the gate.

But the leg had already taken a beating. As he tried to run across the patio, he stumbled. Leah grabbed him, giving him support as they fled. Before they reached the gate, shots peppered the area near the exit.

They were trapped inside the high fence, but Leah led him into to the shrubbery beyond the pool deck, heading toward a large planted area at the back of the property. They crashed through a bed of azalea bushes and into a small stand of pine trees.

As they hunkered down on the ground, floods snapped on in the yard, and lights began to pour from the windows of other houses. He could hear voices of people asking what was going on.

"Is there another way out?" Steve whispered.

"That's the only gate, but maybe we can get over the fence."

He looked in back of them, seeing that the barrier was not uniform where it was screened from the house. Perhaps part of it had been put up by the people who owned the property behind the Pendelton's.

Bullets crashed into the bushes, but it was clear that Warren's crew couldn't see Steve and Leah's location. Not yet. And Steve wasn't going to fire and give it away. He crawled toward the fence, every move sending fire through his leg. At the back of the yard, he found a place where two different sections joined—one board on board and one stockade.

When he pulled on the stockade section, it gave a little, but he knew he couldn't pull it apart from the bottom. As he started to stand, Leah grabbed his arm.

"No."

"I need leverage. You stay down."

He stood and began to pull the section back and forth, making a larger and larger gap.

Ignoring his orders to keep under cover, she stood and began to help. But the noise must have alerted Warren and his goons to their location, because the shots began hitting closer.

"We got 'em trapped," Warren called out. "Spread out."

CHAPTER ELEVEN

Steve cursed under his breath and pulled Leah down. He considered tossing her over the damn fence, but that would make her too much of a target when she was in the air.

Putting her behind him, he returned fire. He didn't think he would hit anyone, but at least he'd remind them that he was armed.

As he'd hoped, the opposition stopped shooting and regrouped. In the lull, he led Leah along the fence several yards away, positioning them in back of a large pine tree.

He was preparing for an assault, when a bullhorn rang out.

"This is the police. Drop your weapons and come out with your hands in the air."

In his anger, Warren had long since passed beyond rationality. Instead of obeying, the man charged across the patio toward Steve and Leah, still shooting, determined to take them down before anyone could stop him.

Two police bullets felled him, and he flopped to the patio.

"Come out with your hands up," the booming voice repeated.

The two bodyguards followed directions.

"His mistress is still in the house," Steve shouted.

"Hands up. Show yourself," the bullhorn ordered.

"Raise your hands," Steve told Leah. He put his weapon on the ground and raised his own hands.

"We're coming out of the bushes at the back of the yard. We're unarmed," he called out. "Don't shoot."

Still this was a dangerous moment, and Steve steeled himself as they stepped from cover with their hands in the air.

Beside him, Leah gasped as she saw Warren lying on the patio. But then the view was blocked as a SWAT team swarmed from the house and through the gate into the yard.

"It's okay," Steve whispered as the cops patted them down. Steve was glad that Warren's goons had taken away his illegal weapon. That was one less thing he had to explain.

A man in a suit stepped through the gate and walked toward them.

"Outlaw?"

"Yes."

"I'm Lieutenant DuBois. You were with the BPD, right?"

"Yes. I took a medical discharge rather than get stuck behind a desk."

DuBois looked from the smashed window to the bullet-riddled yard. "You wouldn't have gotten into trouble behind a desk."

Steve shrugged.

"Your boss, Frank Decorah, gave us a heads up. We were still blocks away when we heard the shooting start.

Steve wanted to say better late than never, but he kept the observation to himself.

"They're okay," the detective said to the SWAT team leader.

Steve squeezed Leah's hand tightly. "Pendelton was laundering money for Malcolm the Hammer. When his wife figured that out, she ran away. He sent his mistress, Candy Markham, to kidnap her and haul her back."

Some of that was true. Some of it wasn't, but Leah didn't correct his story, and he hoped she would stick to his account during questioning, because he didn't want to explain how he'd figured out Pendelton's illegal activities.

When he looked at Leah, she gave him a small nod before they were separated and taken to the closest police station. After being interviewed in separate rooms, they were allowed to leave.

Out on the sidewalk, he said, "Thanks for not saying anything about my . . . talent."

"I knew you wanted me to keep quiet about it." She scuffed her shoe against the ground. "I don't want to go back to my house."

"I figured," he said as he led her toward the Decorah car which an officer had driven over for them.

"Then where are we going?" she asked as she got into the vehicle.

He slid into the driver's seat and said, "To a Decorah safe house."

"We're not safe now?"

"Yeah, we are, but I thought I'd give you some time to decompress."

"From being married to a psychopath?"

"Yeah. And from almost getting killed out in the backyard."

"Will Candy be charged with anything?"

"Attempted kidnapping, if you want to pursue that."

"I'll have to think about it."

He nodded. "And think about us."

She turned to him. "I shouldn't have walked away from you years ago."

"Like I said, I didn't have much going for me. Plus Warren was good at manipulating you—and everyone else." He laughed. "But not Malcolm the Hammer. I think old Malcolm had him sweating bullets. And he was taking out the stress on you."

She opened her mouth, then closed it again.

"You don't have to make any decisions about us now," he said, wishing he could press her.

"Everything's changed," she said in a small voice.

"For the better."

"Well, it would be, if I had a job—or some skills. I didn't even get my degree."

"I think Decorah Security can help you with that."

Her head jerked up. "How?"

"Frank Decorah has a victim assistance fund. For education, job training, even housing."

"Why?"

"Because he knows that people who have been in trouble can't necessarily dig themselves out."

While she thought about that, he reached over and wrapped his hand around hers.

"Leah, I want you in my life. But I'm not going to push you into anything. I mean, a relationship with me probably seems scary."

"Why do you think so?"

"You'd be getting mixed up with a guy who's got a strange talent—and feels compelled to use it to help people. It's an obligation I accepted when I joined Decorah Security."

"I like that. It's kind of the opposite of Warren." Then her expression became questioning "What?"

"Is that how you feel about me? Compelled to help?"

"Lord no." He gathered her close, his lips coming down on hers for a long, hot kiss. When it broke, they were both breathing hard.

"That's how I feel about you," he answered. "I love you." He hadn't meant to say that yet, but it had been too close to the surface to hold back.

She looked stunned. "You do?"

"I never stopped."

"Oh, Steve. I would dream about what my life would have been like if I'd stayed with you."

"We were pretty young."

"And now I don't want to waste any more time."

He wasn't sure how far he could have driven. He'd told her they were going to a safe house. Instead, he pulled in at the first hotel he saw. Luckily, in this part of town it was pretty upscale.

"Is this pushing you too fast," he asked as he pulled up under the marque.

She glanced from him to the hotel entrance and back again. "No."

Still, she looked a bit dazed as he left the car with a valet parking attendant and took her to the registration desk where he got a room with a king-sized bed.

As soon as he closed the door behind them, he reached for her, and she came into his arms.

They clung together, as though each of them needed the other for an anchor. When she raised her face, he bent toward her, covering her mouth with his for a kiss that was hot and sweet, desperate and measured all at the same time.

When they finally came up for air, his pulse was pounding.

She looked around the room. "This is a lot nicer than the last place you took me to."

"This time we're not hiding out. Or maybe we are. Maybe I'll hold you captive here for a few days."

She grinned, and he saw that the fear had disappeared from her eyes. "And do what?"

"Anything you want," he said, hearing the thick quality of his voice.

He saw her consider the offer, then give the room a closer inspection. "Okay. Sit down over there," she said, pointing to the antique-style chair at the desk.

He pulled it out and sat down, wondering what she was going to do now.

"Stay there," she ordered as she began to slowly unbutton her shirt, her sensual movements making him instantly hard.

"I see you want to get up," she whispered. "I think we'll have more fun if you stay put."

His mouth was so dry that he wasn't sure he could answer. Instead he nodded as she tossed the shirt on the floor, then unhooked her bra and sent it to follow the shirt, all the while softly singing "Sometimes When We Touch," an old song by Don Hill that they'd both liked. When he recognized it, his eyes misted.

Naked from the waist up, she lifted her breasts toward him, then played with the nipples, tugging and twisting them.

He saw the passion on her face and gripped the edges of the chair to anchor himself. As he watched, she unzipped her pants, slicked them down her legs and kicked them away. Then she hooked her thumbs in the elastic at the top of her panties and slowly slid them down, until she was standing naked in front of him.

"Keep your hands where they are," she said.

Slowly she came toward him, stopping close enough to lean over and roll up his shirt, lightly dragging her nails across his skin as she did it. She pulled the shirt over his head and threw it on the floor before reaching for his chest, gliding her hands over him, making trails of heat. Finding his nipples, she tugged and twisted them the way she had done with her own, and he had to dig his hands into the chair bottom to keep them in place.

One hand glided down to his belt buckle, which she quickly opened, then unzipped his jeans. Reaching inside and into his shorts, she pulled his aching cock free. It was full and red and very ready for action, but he stayed where he was, still letting her have her way with him.

"Nice," she whispered, catching the bead of moisture at the tip and stroking it over the head and down the shaft.

"Leah," he moaned.

"Right here."

She straddled his lap, driving his cock into herself.

"Can I use my hands?" he gasped out.

"God, yes."

He reached for her breasts, playing with the nipples as she rode him, her movements rapidly becoming frantic.

She had brought him to the peak of need without his being able to touch her. There was no way to slow down now. He shouted his pleasure as he came, and he felt her convulse around him as she followed him over the edge.

She collapsed against him, gasping for breath, clinging to him as he stroked her back and shoulders.

"In case you're wondering, I never did anything like that before," she whispered. "I wanted to make up for all the time we lost." He heard her swallow. "And I wanted to prove to myself that I could be a different person. Not the wet-behind-the-ears girl you used to know—or the scared woman I turned into."

"And you wanted to find out if I'd let you be in charge," he added.

"Uh huh. It felt good to call the shots."

He laughed. "On this end, too."

After hugging him to herself, she stood. He followed her up, walked to the bed and pulled back the covers.

She disappeared into the bathroom for a moment then came back to join him in the bed, snuggling against him.

Closing his eyes, he hugged her close. He knew she needed time to get back to normal, and he'd give her that time, as long as she understood that the two of them belonged together.

Right now they were going to have some quality private time. But he wanted her to realize she had more skills than she thought.

"You said you did charity work for the Junior League," he said.

"Uh huh."

"Like what?"

"I helped manage their thrift shop."

"Which means you know retail."

"And I managing the accounts, but it was only charity work."

"But it's real work experience."

"I guess."

"Don't sell it short," he advised, thinking he would love watching her grow and bloom and become the person he knew she could be. He'd be there to help her in every way. Well, he was going to try not to hover over her.

"Something you should know," he said. "I never got into a serious relationship because I never forgot you."

"I'm sorry if I screwed up your life."

"When I touch objects, I see the past—not the future. But maybe I always knew we'd get back together. Or I hoped, anyway."

"Now you have me—for as long as you want me."

"Forever will be a good start."

THE END

Rebecca York loves to hear from readers!

Web site: **http://www.rebeccayork.com**

Email: **rebecca@rebeccayork.com**

Twitter: **@rebeccayork43**

Facebook: **http://www.facebook.com/ruthglick**

Blog: **http://www.rebeccayork.blogspot.com**

Sign up for Rebecca York's **Newsletter** to get all the scoop on Rebecca's SEXY ROMANTIC SUSPENSE at **http://rebeccayork.com**

The Fall

an ATCOM novella

Jennifer Lowery

ATCOM agent, Brendan Devayne loves his adventurous lifestyle. A family isn't in the cards until he rescues a boy then falls for the mom. When Mia Lawrence's son brings home a stranger, her world's shaken. He's like her ex and Mia refuses to repeat that mistake. Can Brendan change her mind?

This book is dedicated to my Street Team—Jennifer's Tactical Team—or my JTTs. Without them, writing would be a lonely business. All their help, support and generosity keeps me going. Love ya, JTTs

Editing by Piper Denna

Chapter One

Brendan soared along the slope of the mountain, shifting his weight in the paraglider away from the ridge. Riding the updraft created by the formation, he drew in a deep breath. In the air he felt free. Always had. Either in the pilot's seat or under an inflatable wing made of nylon like the one above him.

The open sky, no boundaries, no destination. Simply a man one with nature where a strong wind could end him. The walk with danger exhilarated him, made him feel alive. Right now he needed that more than ever.

Before guilt had time to set in, he pulled on the lines to direct the glider toward the open sky. The Pacific sparkled beneath him, broken up by the Hawaiian Islands. The midday sun beat down on him, partially shaded by the wing of his glider.

His destination, one of the many waterfalls on the island where he'd set up camp, lay a quarter mile away. No hotels or resorts for him. He much preferred to camp out in a deserted area where no one would bother him.

Glancing across the hill he'd just crested, his gaze tripped on something near one of the waterfalls. Narrowing his gaze, he saw a figure standing on a rocky ledge above the fall of water. On closer inspection he saw it was a teenager. Only one that he could see, but the kid was awfully close to the edge.

Brendan steered in that direction, a knot forming in his stomach. He'd cliff-dived off a few dangerous places himself, but this particular waterfall wasn't the place to do it. The water fell too close to the slick rocks for a safe jump. The risk of hitting them outweighed the thrill of the sport. Or it should.

He watched the boy take a few steps back, lean forward and take off. When he reached the edge the kid faltered, sliding to a stop, arms wind-milling.

Brendan cursed as momentum forced the boy over the edge in a panicked fall. Arms and legs flailing, the kid hit the wall and freefell into the pool below.

Sonofabitch.

Stupid. Cliff jumping required commitment.

Cutting his ride short, he turned into the wind to slow his speed and began his descent. Wouldn't be an ideal landing, but he had to get to that kid.

Pulling the brakes as he approached the ground, he trimmed his speed around ten feet. The glider continued to descend toward the cliff where the kid had jumped from so he adjusted his speed for the second half of the flare.

His feet touched the ground and he ran a couple steps before coming to a stop just inches from the ledge. His wing floated to the ground behind him. Wasting no time, Brendan stripped out of his equipment, leaving it lay on the ground.

Spinning around, he took a running jump over the cliff. The freefall didn't exhilarate him like usual. All he could think about was that kid and he prayed he hadn't drowned.

Feet first, he plunged into the pool of crystal blue water. Surfacing, he spun in a circle, searching for the kid. He saw him flailing in the water a few feet away. With strong strokes, Brendan swam over to him, put an arm around his chest and began swimming toward shore. The kid fought him at first until he realized Brendan was helping him, then he went limp.

At the edge of the pool he climbed out, dragging the kid with him. Safely on the grassy slope he rolled the kid over. Wide, brown eyes met his. Blood dripped down his hairline.

"Who are you?"

"I'm the one who just saved your life, kid. What the hell were you thinking?"

That snapped him out of his haze. Eyes flashing with defiance, the kid sat up. "I don't need your help."

Brendan tore a strip off the bottom of his t-shirt. "Wrap this around your head. Tight. It will help stop the bleeding."

Wary, the kid accepted the torn strip and did as told. After knotting it he asked, "How did you see me?"

"I was paragliding. Did you really think you could chicken out of that jump once you'd started?"

"I didn't chicken out."

Brendan cocked a brow.

The kid dipped his head and muttered something beneath his breath, reminding Brendan of himself at that age. Defiant, rebellious, looking for the next adventure to feel alive.

"Are you hurt anywhere else?"

The teen shook his head and pushed unsteadily to his feet. He tried to hide it, but Brendan recognized the aftereffects of a near-death experience. Hell, he'd had a few himself. Had felt the weak knees, the tremble in your body that didn't seem to go away, the pit in your stomach.

Brendan rose to his feet, towering over the kid by at least six inches. "What's your name?"

"Why?"

"So I know what to put on your tombstone if you try anything stupid like that again."

The kid sent him a scathing look. Brendan grinned. Yeah, this kid could be him twenty years ago. "Relax. I just want to know what to call you besides kid."

"I'm not a kid."

Major chip on this kid's shoulder. "Just give me your name."

"Are you going to turn me in?"

"No. You didn't do anything wrong except bow out of your commitment to jump that cliff."

The kid studied him, wary. "What commitment? I was out here having fun. Nothing more."

"Yeah, but cliff jumping isn't something you do for fun. It's a sport. And when you commit to doing it there is no turning back. Unless you want to end up dead like you almost did today."

Properly chastised, the kid drew himself up to his full five-foot-ten height. "How do you know so much about it?"

"Let's just say we have a few things in common. Name?"

Reluctant, he said, "Jason."

Brendan held out a hand. "Brendan."

They shook hands.

"You're really not going to turn me in to the cops?"

"Nope. But, I am going to take you to the hospital to have that head looked at."

Jason's eyes widened. "No. Look, my mom's a nurse."

Suspecting Jason wouldn't tell his mom what he'd done today, Brendan said, "I'll take you home. Did you drive here?"

"Our rental is parked over there. I don't need a chauffeur."

"Too bad. You got one. Until we know if you have a concussion or not I'm not letting you get behind the wheel and endanger yourself or others."

"Seriously?"

"Afraid so."

"What if I refuse?"

Amused, Brendan crossed his arms over his chest.

The kid's eyes flashed. "Whatever." He walked away.

Brendan followed, shaking his head. And that was why he never wanted kids. They were a pain in the ass.

They reached the rental car, a small, economy sized hybrid. Looked more like a toy car than one you would drive.

"Keys?"

Jason sent him an odd look. "It's a keyless start, man."

Of course. Damn, he much preferred his four-wheel drive truck back home. Only a few years old, but without all the fancy bells and whistles the new cars had. And it still required a key to start. Pushing a button just felt wrong.

"What century are you from?" Jason muttered, climbing in the passenger seat.

He was only thirty-six. What the hell? Kid looked at him like he was a hundred. With a scowl, he slid into the driver's seat, sliding it all the way back to accommodate his height. Jesus, he felt like a giant in this damn toy.

Jason chuckled beside him. Brendan sent him a warning look and the kid held up his hands, remaining silent. Wise choice.

"Where to?" he asked after starting the car.

Jason gave him directions, grudgingly. Only took a few minutes to reach the foothills and one of the older neighborhoods on the island. Older didn't mean run-down or shabby by any means. The houses here were worth more than he'd want to pay.

"Right there. With the privacy fence and carport," Jason said, pointing to the left.

Brendan parked beneath the carport and turned off the engine, relieved to be out of that little golf cart.

"I got it from here," Jason said.

Brendan strode past him. "Not getting off that easy, kid."

He heard the kid mutter beneath his breath as he pushed past him. The front door opened before they reached it...and a pretty brunette with the most incredible eyes he'd ever seen stepped out. His steps faltered when her gaze met his. Deep brown, intelligent and mesmerizing. Tall, slender, with a hint of curves beneath her white cropped pants and mint-colored blouse. This couldn't be Jason's mom. She looked much too young to have a teenager.

Concern pulled her brows down as her gaze bounced to her son. "Jason?" She rushed forward and reached up to touch the bloody strip of shirt wrapped around his head, but he dodged her hand. "What happened?"

"I'm fine. It's no big deal."

"You're bleeding."

The look she sent the kid made Brendan want to take a step back to avoid being burned. He'd lost his parents at a young age, but he still remembered 'the look'.

"God, Mom. I said I'm fine. Can I go change, please?"

Although he said please, he didn't sound respectful. That pissed Brendan off. Puberty, hormones, whatever, he wasn't going to stand here and let the kid disrespect his mom. He stepped forward, but the kid let out a disgusted sniff and stormed inside, slamming the door behind him.

The brunette turned to him with a pinched smile. "I'm sorry. He likes to push my buttons."

Not what he expected. Most moms would make excuses for their child's behavior. Maybe she had the mettle to handle a kid like Jason.

She stuck out a hand. "I'm Mia Lawrence."

He accepted her soft hand. "Brendan Devayne."

Her hand slipped out of his. "I assume you're the one who got my Jason out of trouble."

"Caught him attempting to cliff jump. Let's just say it didn't go as planned."

She drew in a breath. "Cliff jumping. Sounds dangerous."

"It is if you aren't fully committed to the jump."

Her gaze met his. "You saw it?"

Brendan nodded. "He changed his mind at the last minute and ended up freefalling down the waterfall. That's how he hit his head."

"Damn it." She held up a hand. "Sorry. I should be thanking you."

"Not necessary. I was in the right place at the right time."

"Thank goodness for that. God knows what would have happened if you hadn't been there. Thank you for bringing my son home safe." She ran a hand through her long, dark hair, smoothing it behind her ear. "Let me at least show my thanks by getting you a towel to dry off with."

He probably should have refused and high-tailed it out of there, run as fast as he could to his campsite, but something made him say, "That'd be great."

Chapter Two

Mia mentally berated herself as she led the tall, dark stranger into the house. What was she thinking? She didn't invite strangers into her home. Well, her aunt's home. Soon to be someone else's.

"You'll have to excuse the boxes."

"Packing or unpacking?"

"Packing. This is actually my aunt's house. She passed a couple months ago."

"Sorry."

Good Lord, his voice slid over her like rich, dark chocolate. Shaking it off, she led him into the kitchen. "Thank you." She motioned toward the table. "Have a seat. I'll get you a towel."

"I don't want to ruin your furniture. I'll stand."

Mia turned to face him. He towered over her with a presence so strong it filled the room. His dark hair had begun to wave where it touched his collar. She wanted to reach out and run her fingers through it.

"Be right back."

She went to retrieve a towel, detouring to Jason's room. As usual, he had the door closed. Knocking lightly, she opened the door and popped her head in. Her son sat on the bed, earbuds in his ears, a sullen look on his face.

He ripped one of them out of his ear and sent her a what-do-you-want-now look.

"As soon as our guest leaves you and I are going to have a talk while I take a look at that wound."

"Leaves? He's still here?"

"I offered him a towel."

Jason stared at her like she'd grown a second head.

"What?"

He shook his head and put the tiny headphone back in his ear. "Nothing."

Conversation over. She backed out of the room and closed the door, a small, triumphant smile on her lips because her son hadn't argued with her about the talk. Lately, everything had been a battle with him. Especially since his father had tried to contact him a few months ago. After ten years of no communication, which she was glad for, he suddenly wanted to see his son again.

Jason was sixteen, nearly a man. He could make his own decision if he wanted to see his father or not, but that didn't mean she wouldn't do everything in her power to keep the bastard away from them both. She'd never hid the truth from Jason about who his father was, but she also didn't let her anger and resentment sway her opinions. She knew one day Ray would contact his son and she wouldn't risk Jason hating her for making him hate his father.

Pushing those thoughts away, she continued on to the bathroom, where she grabbed a thick, aqua-colored towel.

Brendan stood right where she'd left him. His green eyes met hers as she handed him the towel.

"Thanks." He used it to scrub his hair, making the waves more prominent.

Fascinated, she watched him run a hand through the thick curls, slicking them away from his face. He then blotted his very broad chest and muscular arms. When he did the same to his midsection her gaze froze on the washboard abs peeking through his t-shirt where it clung to his skin. Good God, the man was a solid wall of gorgeous.

With an amused glint in his eye he handed her the towel. She draped it over the back of one of the chairs. "So, where can I drive you?"

"Not necessary. I can walk."

"You saved my son's life. I am not letting you walk home."

The corner of his mouth tilted in a sexy half-smile. "I'll look both ways before I cross the street. Cross my heart."

Realizing she sounded more like a mom than a single woman, she laughed. "That came out wrong, didn't it?"

"I appreciate the offer, but I'm not far away."

She really didn't want him to leave yet. Not only because he'd saved her son's life and brought him home safely, but because she wanted to spend a few more minutes with him. Ridiculous, because she didn't live here and he probably did. She'd only come down to pack up her aunt's house, put it on the market, and meet with the lawyer to accept her inheritance. Her aunt hadn't been rich, but she'd managed her money well and had left Mia a nice chunk. Enough to buy her own house and put Jason through college. They had moved around a lot, mostly to keep Ray from finding them, and it had taken a toll on her and her son. They didn't have a place of their own to call home and she regretted that now. As soon as the check cleared she planned to change that. Settle down.

She glanced at Brendan. What would he think if he knew of her dream to move to the mountains and live a peaceful life in a cozy log cabin with a fireplace and a loft bedroom? She could become a virtual teacher and never have to leave home.

A sigh escaped her lips. It might be her idea of heaven but Jason would hate it. He loved the city. Loved to do parkour with his friends. She'd bandaged him up more than once. Her son wanted to be agile and adventurous, but he took after her and spent more time falling than achieving. Today being a perfect example.

"Jason's head is going to need a couple stitches. He said you were a nurse."

She lifted an eyebrow in surprise. "He told you I was a nurse?"

"Yeah. That's why I didn't take him to the hospital."

Amused, Mia shook her head. "I may as well be, considering how many bumps and bruises I've tended over the years. No, I'm not a nurse. I'm a teacher."

The surprised look on his handsome face had her rushing to explain. "Jason hates hospitals. Has ever since he was little. Maybe because he spent so much time there. He's always been adventurous, but clumsy."

"He lied to me." Disbelief colored his tone.

"He did and I'll have a talk with him about it."

"Can I?"

Not expecting that, she hedged. Her son didn't do well with authority figures. Typical teenager, but his mistrust ran deeper. Her fault for trying to pick up the slack from an absent father. In her desire to provide everything for him and fill the void she'd caused by divorcing Ray, she'd caused Jason to rebel. Hard.

Since she didn't know this man, she decided against letting him have a go at her son. If she did, Jason wouldn't forgive her. With all the tension between them lately she didn't want to add to it.

"I'd rather—"

Jason came into the kitchen, cutting her off. His gaze bounced from her to Brendan. "You're still here?"

"I was talking to your mom. She tells me she's a teacher."

Jason opened the fridge, peering inside. Mia tensed, prepared to intervene. "Yeah, she is."

"Why'd you tell me she was a nurse?"

Closing the fridge, Jason shrugged.

"The lie wasn't necessary. I would have honored your request, regardless what it was."

Her gaze jumped to Brendan. He told the truth. Nothing on his face said otherwise.

"Thanks, man," Jason said.

Shock didn't even begin to explain her feelings right now. Her son wasn't angry about being confronted or called out on his lie.

"You still need that wound looked at," Brendan said. "Head wounds can be tricky. I have some medic experience. I could take a look. If your mom approves."

Both sets of eyes turned to her, Jason's hopeful and Brendan's seeking approval. How could she say no? She'd never get Jason to a hospital and it would save her bandaging another wound on her child.

"You have medical experience?" she asked him.

"In the Air Force."

A military man. Somehow she just didn't see him as a rigid, take-orders kind of guy. Not with his cocky half-smile and devil-may-care aura. All of which she found very intriguing. "Oh. You're enlisted now?"

"No. Retired a few years ago."

"Mom. God. Stop with the third degree. He's qualified enough."

"Don't speak to your mother that way. She's your mom and she deserves respect."

The reprimand caught them both off guard. Mia gaped; Jason pulled himself up. No one had ever stuck up for her before. Even if she were still married to Ray she doubted he would. He'd never been that kind of stand-up guy.

"Yes, sir."

What just happened? Her son remembered his manners and called Brendan "sir". Joy filled her, making her want to hug her son, and Brendan for bringing out the boy she remembered.

"Do you have a first aid kit?"

It took a moment for her to realize Brendan was asking her. Snapped out of her happy stupor, Mia nodded. "I'll get it."

She hurried out of the room to retrieve the kit, taking a second to let today's events sink in. When she'd woken up this morning, she had no idea her day would go from packing up her aunt's things to meeting a hot former military man who saved her son's life.

The shock of almost losing her son set in hard and fast, about knocking her to her knees. She gripped the edge of the sink to remain standing.

She'd. Almost. Lost. Her. Son.

Drawing in a shaky breath, she forced her fears back. Living with a child who sought dangerous exploits on pretty much a daily basis gave her palpitations every time he left the house. Worse, she had to see him bruised and broken when he failed. Part of her knew Jason did it because of his father, somehow trying to gain his approval, even though his father would never know how hard his son tried.

A point of anger for her. Ray had screwed up all their lives and she hated the impact it had on her son.

She put a hand to her forehead. God, so many mistakes. When would she get it right?

Chapter Three

Turned out the kid didn't need stitches after all. Brendan put a butterfly bandage over the wound and covered it with gauze and tape in case it bled.

Leaning back in his chair, he said, "Change that bandage daily. If it gets wet, change it." He turned his gaze to Mia, who watched his every move. "Keep an eye on him overnight. Can't rule out a concussion. Watch for things like blurred vision, nausea and vomiting, loss of short term memory or repeating things."

Mia nodded. "How do I know if I should take him to the emergency room?"

"If he loses consciousness, extreme drowsiness or inability to walk, slurred speech. Go with your gut. If it tells you to take him, then do it."

"Hello, I'm right here," Jason said, waving his hand. "I'm fine. Can I go now?"

Mia looked at him and Brendan scooted his chair back to let the kid pass. There wasn't anything else he could do for now. The rest would be up to Mia and Jason. Not that he trusted the kid to tell his mother anything. He seemed closed off where his mom was concerned. Typical teenager. Maybe. All he knew was he didn't like the way Jason talked to Mia. Disrespect he wouldn't tolerate. In anyone.

His initial impression indicated Mia was a good mom. Patient, caring, and willing to do anything for her son. He particularly liked the fact she didn't make excuses for his bad behavior like a lot of parents did. Mia didn't wear rose-colored glasses. That alone made her a good mom in his book.

But, a mom could only do so much. A boy like Jason needed a strong hand. She wore no wedding ring, but that didn't mean she was single. And he wasn't about to ask. Hell no. Single, married, didn't matter. He didn't do kids. Or marriage. Or anything that went along with it.

The thought of settling down with only one woman, raising a family, being tied down, gave him palpitations. He liked his lifestyle just the way it was. His. He could come and go as he pleased. Didn't have to worry about anyone worrying about him while on a mission or away trying a new extreme sport.

Extreme sports were more than a hobby. They were a calling. Something he had to do. Needed to do. He'd never been one to sit still for long. Too much energy coursed through him. Being tied down to a family would suffocate him.

Why was he thinking about this anyway? He had no intentions of getting involved with a married woman, or a single mom.

No matter how freaking beautiful she was.

Fighting a scowl, Brendan rose and started cleaning up his mess.

"You don't have to do that," Mia said, helping him.

A knock on the door snapped her head up. "Excuse me." She tossed the bandage wrappers in the trash on her way to the door.

Brendan continued to put stuff away. When he heard Mia's voice rise, he dropped everything and strode to where she stood blocking the door from whoever stood on the other side. Her posture told him everything he needed to know. The visitor wasn't welcome.

"Everything all right here?" he asked, coming to stand behind her.

A fit man with dark eyes had his hand on the door, preventing her from closing it. Neither looked happy.

"Who's this?" the man asked Mia.

"No one. Please leave, Ray."

"Not until we talk."

Mia's body language spoke volumes so Brendan stepped in. "The lady asked you to leave."

"Stay the hell out of this. It's between me and my wife."

"Ex-wife," Mia snapped. "Don't treat my guest like that."

"He's your guest? Did you sleep with him too?" Ray challenged.

Brendan shifted in front of Mia, putting himself between her and her ex. "Time to go." His tone leaving no room for argument.

"Stay out of this."

The warning didn't faze him one bit. He'd dealt with worse men than this. This guy had the hard edge of a criminal, but Brendan wasn't bothered. He liked a challenge.

Since the guy didn't seem willing to go, Brendan jerked the door from his hands and pushed through, knocking the guy back a step. The door closed behind him.

"I told you to leave."

Ray didn't back down. He pulled himself up and tried to stare Brendan down. That made him laugh. Who the hell did this guy think he was?

Rage flared in Ray's eyes.

Brendan quirked a challenging brow. *What ya gonna do about it, buddy?*

"Stop this." Mia's voice stopped her ex from doing whatever he'd planned next. "Ray, leave. Brendan, back off."

Ray tried to stare him down. Brendan advanced a step.

The door opened behind him. Mia positioned herself between the two of them, facing her ex. "Do I need to call the police?"

Ray took a couple steps backward. He cast a hard glare at Brendan. "This isn't over. I'll be seeing you, Mia."

With that he turned and walked down the driveway, disappearing around the bushes. Mia's shoulders slumped. She turned to him, brows furrowed.

"Do you have any idea what you've done?"

Helped, he thought.

"You can't taunt men like Ray. It always ends badly."

Not angry. Defeated. He didn't like seeing her that way. "I can handle myself."

"I can see that. What you don't realize is that by provoking him you've made my life harder."

He hadn't thought of that. All he'd been thinking about was protecting her. "That wasn't my intention."

She rubbed her forehead. "I know."

"What kind of hold does he have on you?"

"He doesn't. Well, he thinks he does, but I will never give him what he wants."

"Which is?"

Her lips pressed together. "Nothing. It's not your problem. It's mine." She moved past him to the door. "Thank you for saving my son." With that, she went inside, closing the door behind her. Effectively shutting him out.

Damn if it didn't sting. What the hell? He'd done his duty by bringing her son home safely. He owed her nothing. She owed him nothing.

So why did he want to go back inside and fix her problems?

Maybe because her ex left with a threat and looked like a hardened criminal. The ink on his neck looked like a prison tat. How did a woman like Mia get twisted up with a man like that? He couldn't see it. Or he didn't want to.

Brendan cursed and raked a hand through his hair. Like she'd said, this was her problem. He had no business here.

Shaking the unease from his shoulders, he started down the driveway. When he got to the empty street he headed toward the mountains to his campsite near the waterfall and to his solitude.

Absently, he rubbed a palm over the scars on his chest. Healed, but a physical reminder of a screw-up that had almost cost his sister her life. And his.

Attie forgave him. He couldn't forgive himself. He'd fallen hook, line and sinker for the ploy that got him kidnapped and used as bait for his sister. His weakness for women had played right into Santiago's hand and he'd almost lost everything because of it.

Never again. He'd sworn off picking up women in bars, airports, hotels, and anywhere else they temped him. Hardest thing he'd ever had to do, but damn if he'd make the same mistake twice.

A sound behind him made him turn. Straight into a closed fist. The blow landed solid on his chin, snapping his head back. Reacting on instinct, he struck back, busting his attacker's nose with a resounding crunch.

They guy stumbled back, his hands going to his nose. Brendan advanced, prepared to defend himself. When he saw Ray glaring back at him he hesitated.

"Seriously?" he muttered, lowering his fist. "What the fuck?"

Ray tilted his head back to stem the blood flow. "That was your first warning. Stay away from my wife."

"She's not your wife anymore."

Ray lowered his head, eyes narrowed. "Just stay away from her. Or next time I'll do more than break your jaw."

Brendan scoffed. That punch would leave a bruise, but it sure as hell didn't break his jaw.

"I don't take kindly to threats," he said in a low, lethal tone. "Unless you want an ass-kicking you'll never forget, you better move along."

"What's going on here?"

At the sound of Mia's voice both men took a step back. Mia hurried over, her brows drawn in an angry frown. She looked at Ray, then to him.

"Why is he bleeding?" she demanded, propping her hands on her hips.

"I punched him in the nose."

Her lips thinned. "I put that together already. *Why* did you punch him?"

He wasn't about to get into this with Mia. Her plate seemed a bit full. Adding Ray's threats to it wasn't something he would do. Besides, he could handle a fool like Ray.

"Bastard attacked me," Ray said, pinching his nose.

Brendan shot him a look.

"Why would you do that?" Mia accused. "And in the middle of the street. What if Jason had seen you?"

Jesus. He didn't need this. Exactly the reason he steered clear of relationships. Jason was a teenager; no doubt he already knew what kind of man his father was.

"Brendan? Aren't you going to say anything?" Mia persisted.

"Yeah. I have to go. Later." He turned and started walking away.

"Wait—"

"Let him go."

Ray's voice grated down his spine. Lying bastard. Mia had saved him from an ass-kicking. Right now Brendan really wanted to pound him into the ground.

Something made him stop and turn back around. Just in time to see Mia try and yank her arm free of Ray's hand.

Dammit.

Gritting his teeth, Brendan strode toward the couple, something deep in his gut telling him this would be a mistake he'd never recover from.

Chapter Three

Brendan lengthened his stride, gaze narrowed on Ray, whose knuckles were turning white where he held Mia's arm. He saw Mia wince, heard her demand to be let go and saw Ray's other arm pull back.

Seeing red, Brendan grabbed Ray's arm right before it connected with Mia's face. He twisted, forcing Ray to let go of Mia. "Go inside," he said to Mia without taking his eyes off her ex.

He heard Mia's footsteps fade and bore down on Ray, dangerously close to breaking his wrist. To his credit, Ray didn't balk.

"You're lucky I don't break every bone in your body," Brendan threatened. "Take my advice. Get the fuck off this island and don't ever bother Mia again."

Ray tried to jerk his arm free. Brendan held tight. He got in Ray's face. "Are we clear?" With that he released Mia's ex and waited until the bastard had climbed in his car and sped off.

Adrenaline still coursing through his veins, he drew in a deep breath. He needed a release. A free climb or a base jump. Maybe both.

Instead, he went to check on Mia. She opened the door before he could knock. "Come in."

He stepped inside, not liking the waver he heard in her voice. "Are you all right?"

"I don't know. Ray has never lifted a hand against me." Absently, she rubbed her wrist.

"Let me see." Brendan moved forward, gently pulling her wrist toward him. Angry bruises circled the soft flesh. He rubbed his thumb lightly over the marks, wanting to rub them away. "Can you move it?"

"Yes," Mia said, breathless.

Anger and regret filled him. "I shouldn't have walked away."

"This isn't your fault. Ray...he's different. I've never seen him so aggressive."

The hell it wasn't. He'd read Ray right. Knew the guy was trouble. Yet, his issues had made him turn his back on a woman in need.

The last time he helped a woman in need he'd ended up with a needle in his neck and woke up to a nightmare.

That had been about sex. He'd just returned from a mission and needed to release excess energy. This was about protecting a woman from her ex. Not sex. Not adrenaline.

"What does he want from you?"

"Something I'll never give him."

"His son."

Mia scoffed. "Ray has never wanted to be part of Jason's life."

"Then what?"

She pulled her arm free and turned away. "He wants to steal my dreams."

Brendan frowned. "How can he do that?"

"By taking the money my aunt left me." Her shoulders lifted in a sigh. "I planned to buy my own house. A home for me and Jason. And use the rest to put him through college."

"I don't see how Ray could take that from you. The money is yours. He'd have to steal it to get it."

"Or threaten me."

Brendan went rigid. "What is he threatening you with?"

A pause. "To tell Jason that I was the one who turned his father into the police and put him in prison." She turned to face him. "Why am I telling you this? It's not your problem."

He put his hands on her shoulders. "Would it be so bad if Jason knew the truth?"

Her shoulders sagged. "In case you haven't noticed, I'm not my son's favorite person right now."

"Sounds like a normal teenager to me."

"It's more than that. Jason blames me for divorcing Ray and taking away his father."

"Jason knows Ray has been in prison, right?"

"Yes, but he doesn't know I put him there. He'd never forgive me." She met his gaze. "I can't lose my son. He's all I have."

He stared down into her pretty face. What kind of man would want to hurt a woman as kind as Mia?

"Let me help you," he heard himself say.

"How? Ray wants me to pay—literally—for what I did. The past can't be undone. Besides, why would you help us? You don't even know us."

"Let's just say I'm good at taking care of this kind of problem."

She leaned back. "What exactly do you do?"

"Told you, I'm a retired Air Force pilot."

"Yes, but what do you do now?"

Distracted by her soft lips, he said, "I work for an organization called ATCOM. We specialize in criminals."

"Sounds dangerous."

If she only knew. "Nah. We're pretty good at what we do."

"Well, I can't ask you to fix my problems. I married the jerk—I'll find a way to handle this."

He cupped her chin, gently lifting so their gazes locked. "You didn't ask. I'm offering."

Her gaze wavered. "What do you plan on doing? Moving in?"

"If that's what it takes."

Did he really just say that?

Her brown eyes widened. "Are you for real?" she whispered. "I've never met a man like you."

He grinned. "Maybe you've been looking in the wrong places."

"I guess so. I…I don't know what to say."

"Say yes. All I need is a place to lay my head and I promise your ex won't bother you again."

"So you save damsels in distress and perform miracles, too?"

Her teasing tone made him grin. "Something tells me you've never been a damsel in distress. You seem to handle yourself pretty well."

"Well, I have taken a couple self-defense classes. Every woman should."

He couldn't agree more. Women needed to be able to handle themselves. "Is that a yes?"

She drew in a deep breath. "Yes."

Without thought he planted a kiss on the tip of her nose. "I'll go get my stuff and then we'll talk to Jason."

She nodded. "He seems to respond to you better than anyone. Or, this could blow up in my face."

"He's got to grow up someday, Mia. Realize some things are out of his control. Becoming a man isn't easy."

She patted his chest. "I know. This is just happening so fast. How do I know I'm doing the right thing?"

"Your ex wants something from you and he isn't going to stop until he gets it. I've dealt with men like him. They're desperate. Consumed by whatever bad stuff they've gotten into. He already raised a fist to you. I won't let him do it again."

"You really think Ray would hurt me?"

"He already did."

The tiny frown lines on her forehead showed her struggles with this. Not that he blamed her. His mind reeled from what he'd offered to do. They were virtual strangers and he asked her to trust him with her life. To let him protect her from harm. Not knowing if he was dangerous or not. To allow him to stay in her home until Ray was no longer a threat. Risking her son going ballistic over the changes.

He wouldn't walk away and leave her to her own defenses. It wasn't who he was. As much as he knew he should, he couldn't.

She drew in a long breath and let it out slowly. "I've never done anything like this before."

"Nothing to worry about. Just go about your life as normal and I'll take care of the rest."

She scoffed. "Nothing about this is normal."

"Agreed. But, you have a problem and I'm the one to fix it."

Squaring her shoulders, she stepped out of his grasp. "All right. I can do this. I don't like relying on others for help, but I've never seen Ray like that. I really do think he would hurt me to get what he wants."

Brendan remained silent while she came to terms with everything. Hell, it was a lot to take in. Even for him. Although he didn't expect Mia to stab a needle in his neck and set him up for a fall, that part of him still remained gun-shy.

Mia gave a final nod. "Okay. Take my car to go get your stuff and I'll set up the guest bedroom. Hopefully, this is all for nothing and you can return to your vacation without incident."

He doubted that, but didn't say anything. Ray wanted something Mia had and Brendan was just the person to keep him from getting it.

****

Brendan parked Mia's car under the carport and stared at the pale yellow house. So serene. What the hell had he been thinking?

Girding himself to do something he'd sworn he'd never do, he climbed out of the car and grabbed his bags. Definitely a first for him. He'd never moved in with a woman. For any reason. No matter how temporary.

It went against everything in him. Already his skin began to feel too tight for his body. Energy surged though him, seeking an outlet. This was how it began whenever he thought of settling down. The edginess, the restlessness. And he hadn't even set foot in the house yet.

The light at the end of the tunnel was that this was a temporary arrangement. He would take care of Mia's problem and be on his way.

That didn't help settle the blood racing through his veins as he strode to the front door. Did he knock? Jesus, he hated this. With extreme sports, his career, and flying there were set rules. A certain way of doing things. Often, those rules changed, but they were always there. He liked that. This situation had no rules. He didn't like that. Made him feel out of sorts and his skin itch.

He rapped his knuckles on the door, fighting the instinct to get the hell out of there and go back to his camp. Seconds later, Mia opened the door. She looked as uncomfortable as he felt.

"You don't have to knock." She pushed the door open.

He stepped inside.

"I'll show you to your room. Jason hasn't come out of his room yet so I haven't talked to him about this."

Brendan followed her down the hall to a good-sized bedroom. A queen-size bed sat against the middle wall amongst boxes and bubble wrap.

"The bed is freshly made. You'll be all right with walking around a few boxes?"

"I don't mind." He set his bags on the floor next to the door. "We need to discuss how much you want Jason to know."

A cloud fell over her face. "I've never lied to my son, so the truth. Except the part where I turned his father in."

"He's bound to find out eventually. Would you rather he hears it from you or your ex?"

"I'd rather he not hear it at all." She let out a small laugh. "I know what you're saying. I just don't know if I'm ready to tell him."

"Tell me what?"

They both looked up to see Jason standing in the doorway, glaring at them. "What's he still doing here?"

Mia put a hand out in attempt to console her son. "There are some things we need to talk about."

"I'd say so. Like why the hell his bags are in the spare bedroom."

"Language," Mia cautioned. "If you'll let me explain—"

"Explain that you're shacking up with some stranger? God, Mom. You don't even know him."

The anger and hurt in his voice didn't escape Brendan. He stepped forward. "It's not what you think. Let's go sit down and talk about this."

Jason sent Mia a wounded look. "Dad's back and you're moving this guy in? Whatever." With that he darted out of the doorway.

Mia ran after him, Brendan following. But Jason had already slammed through the front door and taken off on his bike.

"Want me to go get him?"

Mia shook her head. "No. Give him time to cool off. He'll come back. He always does." She let the screen door close. "How does he know Ray is here?"

"Two options: Either he saw him today in the street or Ray has been in contact with him."

Mia's face paled. "I never gave Ray our information. I don't even know how found out we were here."

"Not hard to find someone in this day and age."

"That doesn't make me feel any safer."

Forgetting she didn't live in his world, he put his hands on her shoulders. "Your safety is something I can guarantee. Your son's response to my being here, not so much."

"No kids of your own, huh?"

He choked out a laugh. "No. Definitely not. Not in the cards for me."

Her smile didn't quite meet her eyes. "That's too bad. Nothing in the world compares to the love of your own child."

"Until they become teenagers, right?"

This time her laugh was genuine. Music to his ears.

"I wouldn't trade it for anything."

He believed her. She was one of those moms. The kind that put her kid first and loved him unconditionally, no matter what he did. His mom had been like that. She never stopped loving him, even with all the trouble he gave her.

Being around Mia made him miss his parents. Although they'd passed a long time ago, they were always in his thoughts. More so lately after what happened to his sister. He'd always been there to protect her. Until Carlos Santiago decided to make Brendan a pawn in his revenge against Attie.

"If you're having second thoughts I won't make you stay. I can handle my ex."

Mia's voice snapped him out of his thoughts. She had mistaken his remorse for hesitation, which couldn't be further from the truth.

"I'm all in," he said, pushing the thoughts to the back of his mind.

Relief shone briefly in her eyes before she stepped back. Not fast enough to hide it from him.

"Are you hungry? I have leftovers in the fridge. Or we could grill some steaks. I haven't packed the kitchen yet."

"Leftovers are fine." He wouldn't burden her with having to cook. Certainly not for him.

"All right. I'll go heat them up while you get settled." With a small smile she left the room.

Brendan watched her go, unable to keep his eyes off her. She was a beautiful woman. Soft curves made for a man's hands.

Tearing his eyes away, he silently cursed himself. Normally, he'd be sleeping in the master bedroom. Getting his fill of this woman and leaving when he finished. Mia wasn't the type of woman you had casual sex with. She was the kind of woman you kept.

Alarm trickled down his spine. He didn't keep women. That would be like having a noose around his neck.

Since he didn't plan on staying longer than necessary, he kept his things packed. The day he unpacked at a woman's house would be the day he surrendered his lifestyle. So, never.

He did a quick inspection of the house before finding Mia in the kitchen. The table had been set with three place settings. His steps faltered only for a second. Uncle Jed, the man who had raised him and Attie after their parents passed, always insisted they eat as a family. Didn't happen often with his and Attie's career with ATCOM, but when they were home, they sat down to dinner. Uncle Jed was a terrible cook, but they ate every last bite because they owed him so much.

For the first time since his offer, he had reservations. Mia and Jason were a family. And him? A stranger who didn't belong at their dinner table.

Uncertainty rushed through him. Made him want to grab his gear and go do something dangerous.

Mia glanced over her shoulder at him from where she stood in front of the stove, stirring something in a pot that smelled heavenly. "Would you get the iced tea from the refrigerator, please, and fill our glasses? Do you like tea?"

Chest tight, he nodded.

Mia smiled. "Thanks. Dinner will be ready soon."

Through lungs that wanted to seize, Brendan strode to the fridge to do as asked. God help him, what had he done?

Chapter Four

Mia stirred the chicken and wild rice soup, trying to ignore the tingle of awareness that made every hair on her body stand up to attention. What was it about Brendan that made her heart race in her chest? She'd seen handsome, rugged men before. Dated a few, but never brought them home. Before now, she'd never invited a man into their home. She refused to be that kind of mother. Bringing home a different man each time she thought he was the one. That would do nothing but traumatize and confuse her son. Something she wouldn't do. They had enough issues without her adding to them.

This whole Brendan thing still had her spinning. It had been so easy to say yes to him. Too easy. She'd been on her own since Jason was six. Leaning on a man hadn't been in the cards for her. Then or now. Ray had been anything but a stellar husband. The fact he'd fooled her for as long as he had still made her angry. Usually a good judge of character, she blamed herself for not seeing him for what he was. He'd hid his criminal tendencies from her exceptionally well.

The signs were there; she'd refused to see them. Or, didn't want to believe the man who made love to her almost every night led a double life. That mistake she would never make again. She'd never fall for a man who craved danger again. Been there, done that. Not doing it again.

Behind her she heard Brendan pouring tea into glasses. Why was she so nervous about feeding him leftovers? The soup recipe had been one of her mom's. Even Jason had liked it. And soup reheated very well.

Ridiculous. She wasn't a teenager with a crush. They were both adults and his purpose here wasn't to break her sexual dry spell.

The front door slammed, startling her. Snapped out of her thoughts, she put the spoon on the spoon rest and turned to see Jason bound into the room. He looked at her then Brendan and rolled his eyes.

"Can we sit down and talk about this?" Mia asked. "It's not what you think."

"I doubt that."

A chair scraped on the floor. "Have a seat," Brendan said, his tone leaving no room for argument. To her surprise Jason did as told and sat without a word. "Your mom is trying to talk to you. I suggest you listen."

"How about we eat first?" She turned off the stove and carried the pot to the table where she dished out three servings.

"I'd rather hear this first." Jason crossed his arms.

Setting the pot back on the burner, she sat next to her son. Brendan took the seat at the head of the table. How long had it been since a man sat to dinner with them? Not since her divorce. It felt oddly surreal. And somehow right.

"As you know, your father is here."

"Yeah, he emailed me when he was released."

Ray had been emailing her son? For how long? And why hadn't Jason said anything? "Have you been talking to him for long?"

"About a year now."

She straightened her shoulders, ready to accept the fact Ray may have told Jason what she'd done. "I see. I wish you'd told me."

Jason shrugged.

"I've never lied to you and I won't do it now. Brendan is staying with us because your father threatened me."

Jason sat up in his chair. "What? How?"

Time to pay the piper. "You know we came down here to pack up Aunt Ginny's house and collect the inheritance she left me?"

Jason nodded.

"Well, between the sale of the house and the inheritance, we'll have enough to finally buy the home of our dreams." She put her hand over his, happy when he didn't pull away. "Remember how we used to talk about moving to the mountains and living in a rustic log cabin? You even picked a name for the dog we'd get. Rover. Remember? Those things can happen now. We have the money to do it."

For a moment, her little boy who used to dream about owning a dog flashed across her son's face. "That's great, Mom. You know I'm going to college in a couple of years."

Not ready to think about her son leaving her, she said, "Now you can go to any school you choose. I'll have enough left over for tuition."

"Really? We can afford for me to go to school?"

"Yep."

A glimmer of hope shone in his eyes, making her heart melt. She wanted to give him everything, and now she could. Well, except a father figure and someone he could look up to.

"What did Dad do?"

"He wants the inheritance money. That's why he followed us to Hawaii."

Jason's face reddened. "He said that?"

Damn her ex. She'd give anything not to have to do this. "Yes."

"How did he hurt you?"

She shook her head. "He didn't because Brendan was there to stop him."

"I would never let anyone hurt your mother," Brendan said.

She glanced at Brendan, then back to Jason. "That's why he's here. He's going to help me find a way to put an end to this."

"You don't even know him." Jason's voice rose. "You're fine with letting a complete stranger in the house, but not my own father."

How could she explain to him that she trusted Brendan more than she trusted her ex? She couldn't explain it to herself. Somehow, she just knew Brendan was a good guy.

"Sweetie, it's not like that. You know who your father is. I never hid that from you." But, she hadn't told him all of Ray's dark secrets. Jason didn't need to know her ex had gone to prison for more than robbing a few houses.

"All I know is my dad just got out of prison and now he's here. You say he threatened you. The man I met doesn't fit that profile."

They had met? Good God, how many secrets did her son have from her? She began to speak, but Brendan spoke first.

"See this bruise on my jaw?" He tilted his head. "Your dad attacked me when I left today. Warned me to stay out of this. I broke his nose for it."

Shock showed on Jason's face. "*You* broke his nose?"

Mia stared at her son. "You've met with him recently?"

"Yeah, that's where I went on my bike," he answered, distracted, his gaze pinned on Brendan. "He said you attacked him. That you wanted him out of the way so you could get to Mom."

She had learned long ago not to let Ray's lies get to her. It took a while to see through them, but eventually she did.

"Believe what you will," Brendan said. "Just know that I'm not here to *get* your mom. I'm here to protect her. And you."

Jason bolted out of his chair, sending it skidding across the floor. "I'm the man in this family. We don't need you."

Mia stood. "Jason—"

He stepped out of her reach. "No. Just leave me alone. You guys are making my dad out to be a monster and I won't stand for it. God, Mom, why can't you just let me be happy?" Sending her a wounded look that broke her heart, he ran out of the room. His bedroom door slammed a few seconds later.

Exhausted, emotionally and physically, Mia dropped down into her chair and propped her head in her hands. Jason's words hurt more than she cared to admit. Happiness was the only thing she'd ever wanted for her child. To give him the best life she could. On a teacher's salary it hadn't been easy, but they'd done all right. Could have been worse.

A pair of hands landed on her shoulders, startling her. Definitely not used to having a man around. Brendan must think her a jumpy flake.

His fingers dug gently into the tight muscles. She let out a low moan.

"Are teenagers always this difficult and unreasonable?" Brendan asked.

The feel of his hands on her skin made talking impossible. Felt so good. Too good. She shouldn't be doing this. If Jason walked in and saw them...

Forcing her head up, she shifted so his hands fell away. Immediately missing his touch. "We may as well eat. Jason can heat his later."

Brendan returned to his seat and picked up his spoon. She picked hers up, too, but her appetite had fled.

"I can camp out in the backyard if my being here will cause too much trouble for you. I don't need to be in the house to protect you."

Sounded reasonable, but if she were to be honest with herself, she didn't want him to leave. She felt safe with him in the house.

That wasn't the only reason, but she wasn't ready to go there.

"I don't know." She sighed. "Maybe I'm being over-dramatic."

"I know men like your ex and he's desperate. If he needs that money he's going to get it. No matter what it takes."

Mia rubbed her forehead. "I don't want to believe that, but I know Ray's history and if he's back in the game he'll stop at nothing."

"What was he involved in that sent him to prison?"

Setting her spoon back down on the table, she met his gaze. "Home invasion and attempted murder."

Brendan didn't react. Not like she'd expected when he heard her ex had almost killed someone. That gave her courage to go on. "He shot one of the homeowners on his last job. Wounded the man, but didn't kill him. I had no idea he was involved with criminals like that. I guess I refused to see the truth. When I put the pieces together—his absence during the robberies, the reports I saw on the news about break-ins—the way he lavishly spent money that I knew his job as a bartender didn't afford us." The high he'd been on when he came home. Made for great sex, wild and a little rough, but didn't quiet the voices in her head telling her he'd changed. That he wasn't the man she'd married. That something was wrong with this picture.

None of that she spoke aloud. It only served to show what a blind fool she'd been. Thank God her parents weren't alive to see how much she'd screwed up her marriage. Theirs had been a marriage made in heaven. They married young, loved long, and died happy. Mia always thought she'd have the same kind of marriage as them. Thought Ray was the man to give it to her. In the beginning, he had. Then he started disappearing more. Staying out all night. Meeting with friends he never introduced her to.

"You confronted him about it?"

She nodded, remembering that night. He'd come home, riding that high he always got after a job, wanting sex, but she denied him. Said they needed to talk. That set off his temper. Since he'd never raised a hand to her, she'd pushed forward, asking him where he'd been, about the blood staining his shirt sleeve. When she brought up the robberies he got angry and stormed out. That's when she knew for sure. She'd gone straight to the police. Ray was arrested the very next day. They found him in a hotel room with a hooker, stolen goods and the weapon he'd used to shoot the home owner. He'd been offered a reduced sentence if he rolled on his cohorts, but Ray was no snitch. He served his time, protecting the ones who helped him with his criminal activities. The man he'd shot declined to press charges so his sentence was reduced to assault with a weapon and home invasion. She assumed his partners had gotten to the victim and somehow got him to back down from charging Ray. The less she knew the better, she figured.

Out of fear they would find out she had turned Ray in, she'd packed up Jason and moved without telling anyone. Every few years she'd move again, telling Jason she'd found another job instead of the truth that she worried Ray's partners would retaliate for her snitching. It didn't help her relationship with her son any, but she had to protect him. He was her world and it would end her if she lost him.

"Then I went to the police," she said. "And, the rest, as they say, is history."

"History but not freedom."

No, she was anything but free. That, she could never change. As long as Ray walked the earth he would always have a hold on her through their son.

"Once I'm finished with him he won't bother you again."

Mia lifted her gaze to meet his. She thought she'd had her fill of alpha-type males. Brendan's declaration made butterflies set flight low in her belly and her heartrate speed up.

Someone pounded on the door, breaking the moment.

"I'll get that," Brendan said, already on his way.

She followed. Ray burst in before Brendan had a chance to open the door. He glared between them. "Where's my son?"

"In his room. What are you doing here?" Mia stepped up beside Brendan, his presence solid and strong.

"Jason called me and said you had some guy living here."

Hurt that her son had run to Ray instead of talking to her, Mia pointed to the door. "That's none of your business. Please leave."

"I'm not going anywhere until I know my son is safe."

Now her temper had risen. Where did he get off calling Jason his son when he hadn't seen him in ten years? He'd never been a father to him. He didn't have the right to worry. "Jason is fine. He's been fine since the day you were arrested."

Ray's face tightened into angry lines. "I wouldn't have been arrested if you hadn't snitched. Does our son know that his mother was the reason he lost his dad?"

Outraged, she stepped forward. "You bastard."

Ray laughed without mirth. "Priceless. You tell him everything except the most important detail. No wonder he grew up hating me."

Brendan opened the door and held it open. "I'll walk you out."

"Why, so you can sleep with my wife?"

"For the last time, I'm not your wife any longer." Did he keep calling her that just to get at her? Sounded like Ray. And she'd stepped in it with both feet.

Ray pointed a finger at her. "Next time I come over, he better not be here."

On impulse, she pressed herself against Brendan and slipped her arm around his waist. Good Lord, the man was a solid wall of muscle. "This is my house. I'll have whomever I choose stay here. And, if that happens to be in my bed then that's none of your business."

Face red, Ray stormed out of the house. Brendan let the door close without slamming, muscles shifting beneath his t-shirt. He smelled like the outdoors, clean and rugged. Felt like more man than she'd ever been with. To say her body stood up and took notice was an understatement.

Feeling his eyes on her she glanced up. Mistake number one. The lazy, sensual look in his green eyes mesmerized her.

"In your bed?" He quirked a brow.

It took a moment for her to realize he wasn't making an offer, but repeating her words. Disappointment filled her, much to her distress.

Finding her voice, she said, "I said that for Ray's sake."

His head dipped so that their lips were inches apart. His warm breath mingled with hers. Her belly flip-flopped.

"Are you sure?" he asked, low and sexy.

No. No, she sure as heck wasn't. At the time she'd done it to get back at her ex. Retaliate for his hurtful words. Now, she wondered if her subconscious had been speaking, knowing things she didn't. Or, did, but refused to acknowledge.

The way he looked at her, the husky tone. Very seductive. The man practically oozed sensuality. A woman knew, instinctively, how good certain men would be in bed. This man would be off the charts.

"Yes," she breathed. Only because she had to. As much as she wanted to explore that darkly sexual side of him, she knew she couldn't. It would push Jason back to his father. Possibly for good.

The corner of his mouth lifted. "Then maybe you should let me go."

"Oh." Reluctantly she stepped out of his arms. Why did his words haunt her so? Maybe because she didn't want to let him go.

Chapter Five

Brendan tugged a t-shirt over his head, grabbed his running shoes and strode out of the guest bedroom. The warm morning air drifting through the open windows called to him. Great time for a run to release the energy zinging through his veins. He'd had a sleepless night. The house too quiet. The bed too small.

Not to mention, knowing an incredibly beautiful woman slept in the next room. Alone. Probably naked. No, Mia wasn't the sleep-in-the-buff kind of person. Something more practical, but just as sexy.

Giving himself a mental shake, he sat on the couch and slipped on his shoes. Would he never learn? Didn't almost losing his sister teach him a lesson? He wasn't here to take Mia to bed. No matter how much his body desired her.

Damn if he didn't want to.

"Where ya going?"

At the sound of Jason's voice his head snapped up. The kid stood in loose pajama pants and a t-shirt, eyes heavy-lidded like he hadn't slept that well either.

"For a run."

"Is that how you stay in shape?"

The curious, slightly awkward question made him return to tying his laces, as if it were no big deal. "Partly. Running is great for cardio. I like to add some pushups and sit-ups to my workout."

"How many can you do?"

"Around one hundred in two minutes."

Jason's eyes widened. "Seriously?"

Brendan chuckled. "Seriously." He rose from the chair. Jason seemed uncomfortable, as if something occupied his thoughts. Sensing the kid wanted to ask him something, he busied himself stretching out.

After a moment, Jason asked, "Could you teach me?"

Straightening from his quad stretch, he answered. "I won't be here long, but I can teach you the basics so you can continue your workouts after I'm gone."

"Okay."

"Go get changed. We'll start now."

Eyes now wide open, the kid nodded and jogged to his room. Brendan had grown up without his father, but Uncle Jed had done a damn good job keeping him out of trouble. He'd always been there for him and Attie. Where would he have ended up if they'd been put in foster care? Raised without parents. Having no one to teach him how to be a man. Moms were essential, but a boy needed his father. There were just some things a mom couldn't teach her son.

Only took the kid a few minutes to change.

"Is your mom still sleeping?"

"Yeah. She'd have coffee going if she wasn't."

"Should we leave a note in case she gets up?"

Jason shrugged.

Brendan strode to the fridge, picked up the dry erase marker and scribbled a note to Mia, letting her know where they were. Then he turned to the kid and said, "Let's go."

Outside they went through a series of stretches before hitting the road. To Jason's credit, he kept up fairly well. He had the lean body of a runner, just had to get his breathing synchronized and build some muscle. Then he'd be a force to be reckoned with. He certainly had the tenacity.

Brendan may not be around long, but he would teach this kid everything he knew before he left. Give him a leg up for next school year. Maybe, make life a little less difficult on the kid.

"Come on," he said, picking up the pace. "One more mile and you earn a break."

Face red, Jason matched his stride.

With a touch of pride he hadn't felt before, Brendan pushed forward.

****

Mia stared at the note scrawled on the white board hanging on the fridge. Broad stroke, confident, incredibly manly. Her hand hovered over the writing. Something wouldn't let her erase it. Silly, but she left it.

Last night had been a long one. Knowing Brendan slept in the room next to hers kept her awake. When she did sleep her dreams were filled with images of that hot body and what it would feel like to have his hands on her. She'd come as close to a wet dream as one could get without actually having one, resulting in restless sleep and unsatisfied sexual desire.

"Geesh," she said to the empty kitchen, wandering over to the coffee pot. As she made a fresh pot her thoughts were on her son and Brendan. Out for a run? Together? How had that happened? Jason had always been an active kid, but his activities tended to run more along the lines of parkour and biking.

For a moment, she let her thoughts drift to what it would be like if Brendan were Jason's father and they were out sharing their morning run while she woke up and made coffee and breakfast. Happy. Content. A family.

The coffee pot hissed signaling the end of the cycle, drawing her out of her dreams. Maybe someday she'd have the family she'd always wanted.

Finding a mug, she poured a cup. With an appreciative sip, she closed her eyes and let it work its magic. Voices in the back yard drew her attention. Walking to the sliding doors and out onto the deck she saw Brendan in a push up position, arms extended, biceps popping, head turned away from her, talking to Jason.

A wave of awareness tingled from her head to her toes. After last night's dreams she really should turn right around and go back inside. Work on packing. Did she do that? Nope. She leaned against the porch railing and enjoyed the view.

She watched Brendan show Jason the proper way to do a push up, lowering himself slowly, holding it only inches from the ground to instruct her son about keeping his back straight and elbows tucked.

Mia got a hot flash just watching the pure strength in Brendan's big body. The power it took to hold himself in that position wreaked havoc on her hormones.

He pushed up into a starting position, checked Jason's posture, and began pumping out a series of pushups so fast her head spun. Her son couldn't keep up with the pace, but he gave his all; she could see the determination on his face. He collapsed after about a minute. Brendan kept going for at least another minute. She lost count at seventy.

When Brendan finished he clapped a hand on Jason's shoulder. "You did great. Tomorrow, we'll work on some chin-ups."

Pride shone in Jason's eyes, making her heart break. All he wanted was approval. Aware of it or not, Brendan was giving him exactly what he needed. She wasn't sure how to take that. Yes, she wanted a father for her son, but, she wasn't ready for a relationship. Not with things up in the air like they were. She and Jason would be moving into a new home soon. Starting over. Or, getting the start they deserved. Brendan had his own life and it didn't include an already-made family.

Jason spotted her and she waved. He grinned from ear to ear as he crossed the yard next to Brendan, who towered over him. She loved seeing him so happy. Smiling. And she had this gorgeous man to thank for that. He gave her son something she couldn't and Ray wouldn't.

Oh, boy. She was in trouble. In a short time, she had begun to fall for this man. A man who'd all but said he didn't want kids.

"Hey, Mom," Jason said. "Ran a seven-minute mile this morning. And, did fifty pushups in less than one minute."

He seemed so proud she couldn't help but rush over and give him a hug. For a brief second he let her hold him then he pulled back. "I'm all sweaty. Gonna go shower." Over his shoulder he said to Brendan, "Thanks, man," and disappeared inside the house.

Mia turned her gaze to Brendan. "Thank you." She wanted to say more, but her throat closed. It had been a long time since she'd been able to hug her son.

"Kid's got potential. With the right training he could go far."

Forcing her emotions down, she said, "He's always been active. Loves the outdoors."

"Has he ever joined any sports teams?"

"No. He prefers things that are more dangerous."

Brendan nodded. "I can relate. He would be a good candidate for the organization I work for."

Distracted by the way his damp t-shirt clung to his chest and abs, Mia said, "What organization is that?"

His mouth tilted in an amused grin. "A group called ATCOM, remember? We specialize in anti-terrorism."

She nodded absently. "Right. Military?"

"No. Private sector. Would be beneficial if Jason went into the military then applied for ATCOM, but not necessary."

"Sounds dangerous."

He shrugged, reminding her of Jason.

"Jason has plans to go to college and become a personal trainer."

"He'd be good at it."

Mia smiled. "I think so, too. I think you helped him realize that today. You'll make a good dad someday."

He sobered, making her regret the words. In fact, he looked ready to bolt, which went against everything she knew and expected of this man. How could kids scare him so much when he was such a natural around them?

"I better shower, too."

She nodded. "Of course. There's a second bathroom at the end of the hall. Towels are in the cupboard."

He disappeared inside the house as if his heels were on fire. Part of her berated herself for spooking him. The other part wanted to go jump in the shower with him.

Better to make a grocery list and run to the store so they could have dinner tonight. Brendan seemed the kind of man who would enjoy a thick, grilled steak covered with her homemade Montreal Seasoning. And her banana dessert.

Energy renewed, she went inside to pour another cup of coffee and make a list.

Chapter Six

Brendan slapped a hand on the shower wall and lowered his head beneath the jet spray. He'd never run from anything in his life. Yet, a slender woman with a teenage son spooked him like never before. The sooner he took care of Mia's ex and got out of here, the better.

A knock on the door brought up his head.

"Brendan? I'm going to run to the grocery store and pick up a few things for dinner."

Turning off the water he pushed the curtain back and reached for a towel. "Give me five minutes and I'll go with you."

A pause. "All right. I'll be in the kitchen."

He dried off, toweled his hair and slicked it back out of his eyes before putting on the clothes he'd brought in with him. Cargo shorts and t-shirt. After tossing his towel in the hamper he met Mia in the kitchen. His steps faltered briefly when he saw her. A red sundress with white flowers flattered her curves, falling just above her knees. There wasn't anything overtly sexy about the dress, but damn if it didn't make his blood race.

"There's coffee if you'd like a cup to go." She motioned toward the coffee maker.

"I'm good, thanks." He rarely drank coffee or caffeine. Didn't need it. He had enough energy zinging through his veins most days, he didn't need the boost. Today, Mia served as an entire pot of coffee, the way she got his engine going.

"I told Jason we'd be right back."

They walked out the door into the bright sunlight. Mia reached into her purse for a pair of sunglasses and slipped them on.

"I'll drive," he offered. Without hesitation she rounded the car and got in the passenger seat.

Dreading getting back into the compact car, he made sure the seat was pushed back before sliding behind the wheel. When he glanced at Mia he saw her fighting a smile.

"What?" He brought the quiet engine to life.

"Oh, nothing."

Amused, he said, "Nothing, my ass. You think I look hot and sexy in this thing, don't you? Especially how my head nearly touches the roof."

Her laughter escaped, filling his senses with the musical sound. Open and free, like the person he suspected lay beneath the persona. He backed out of the drive, grinning, knowing exactly how he looked in the toy car.

"I don't know about that, but you are certainly drawing attention," she said on another chuckle.

He glanced out the side window to see people staring and pointing as they drove past. "What, they've never seen a man drive a golf cart before?"

Her laughter bubbled over. "I guess the car is a bit small."

He chuckled. "You think?"

Mood light, they parked in front of the grocery store and walked in. Mia pulled a list out of her purse while he grabbed a cart. While he pushed she gathered the items she needed. When she stopped at the meat section to peruse steaks, he stepped in.

"Let me," he said, scanning the packages. "What did you have in mind?"

"Grilled steaks. As long as you run the grill?"

He grinned. "Grills are man's domain. I got this."

"I need two pounds."

"You got it." He picked up a New York Strip.

"I'm going to go grab a couple more things. Be right back."

Not liking her wandering off by herself, even though they were in a public place, he did a quick scan of the customers before nodding. He doubted her ex would be hiding behind the cereal display.

Mia walked away, his gaze tracking her. More like watching the sway of her hips, the way her dark hair fell loosely down her back in soft waves. When she turned down one of the aisles he lost sight of her and went back to choosing steaks. Without knowing it, the woman had spoken to his heart. Grilled steak was his favorite dinner.

Finding suitable cuts, he put them in the cart and went to find Mia. He didn't miss the appreciative smiles he received from the women as he passed. Grocery stores were known to be meat markets—literally. And he was guilty of picking up a woman or two along with his groceries.

Sending them a nod and a smile he turned down the aisle Mia had taken. He found her standing in front of a row of spices, talking on her phone. As he approached he saw a big smile on her face. She disconnected and dropped her cell in her purse, then turned to him, eyes dancing with joy. Before he could ask what had made her so happy she ran into him, hugging him tight. He instinctively wrapped his arms around her, inhaled the scent of her coconut shampoo. Damn, she felt good in his arms. Almost like she belonged.

Whoa. He took a mental step backward because she still hugged him. This woman came with strings. A sixteen-year-old and an ex-husband.

"Guess what?" She leaned her head back to look up at him.

"What?" He stared into her brown eyes.

"The inheritance was transferred to my bank this morning."

"That's great."

"It is, isn't it? Now, I can make my dreams come true."

Should he tell her he lived in a rustic log cabin in the mountains of Montana? Exactly where she dreamed of being.

What the hell was he thinking? Asking her to move in with him? Or worse, marry him?

Stunned by his thoughts, he forced a smile. "I'm happy for you."

"Thanks. As long as Ray doesn't find out, everything should be fine." She glanced around them and stepped out of his arms. "Sorry. That was inappropriate of me."

He wanted her back in his arms. Instead he grabbed the cart. "Do you have everything you need?"

"I do."

Those words hit him in the gut with the force of a punch. He liked the way she said them. Even if they did remind him of vows.

Thunderstruck by his thoughts, Brendan started unloading items onto the belt. What the hell happened to his vacation? He'd come here to clear his mind, try and erase some of the guilt that still nagged him over what happened to his sister. Attie had never blamed him. He did that himself. How could he not? He'd almost gotten his sister killed because of his weakness for women.

Falling for this woman wasn't an option.

The cashier gave him the total and he paid it, sending Mia a look when she protested. She raised her hands in surrender and started putting paper sacks in the cart. He accepted the receipt and took over putting the bags in the cart.

Together they walked out of the store and unloaded them in the back of the car. The drive home took only minutes. A smile lurked on Mia's lips when she looked at him scrunched behind the wheel.

When he pulled into the drive, Jason came out to meet them. By the anxious look on his face something was wrong.

"What's wrong?" Mia asked him, already out of the car.

Jason shifted from one foot to the other. "Dad's here."

Mia went rigid. "Where is he?"

"Inside. I swear I didn't call him, Mom."

"I know, honey. It's okay. Help Brendan unload the car, will you, please?"

Brendan motioned toward the back of the car and followed Mia inside. They found Ray sitting at the kitchen table drinking a cup of coffee. He didn't look happy to see him walking in with Mia.

"What are you doing here, Ray?" Mia asked.

"I came to visit my son. I see you've still got your boy toy around."

Brendan let that one go. He'd been called much worse and it never bothered him.

"You can't keep showing up here. It's confusing to Jason."

Ray rose to his feet. "Don't worry, I'm leaving."

He left without confrontation. Brendan followed him outside, passing Jason with his arms full of bags. "Are you leaving?" he asked his dad.

"Yep. Got what I came for. I'll be in touch."

What the hell? Ray had been nothing but confrontational every time they saw him. Why the change? Not trusting the man, Brendan escorted him off the property, not liking the fact Ray never parked in the driveway, but on the side of the road.

Returning back inside, he joined Mia and Jason in the kitchen, keeping his unease to himself.

"Why don't you guys go make sure the grill works while I prepare the steaks," Mia suggested.

Jason glanced at him. "You know anything about grills?"

Brendan grinned. "Man's domain. Come on, I'll teach you everything you need to know about grilling meat."

****

Mia watched the two disappear outside, an uneasy feeling in her stomach. Jason really responded to Brendan and seemed to like him. What if he got too attached? He was at an impressionable age. Brendan would leave the same as Ray had. How would that affect her son?

How would it affect her?

Unwilling to think about it, she got to work mixing her homemade seasoning blend. Then she mixed it with olive oil and coated the steaks in a baking dish, setting them aside to marinate. She wrapped baked potatoes in foil after sprinkling them with salt, pepper and seasoning salt. She added a slice of onion to each packet and a few sprinkles of water, then sealed them up tight. A trick she'd learned from her dad, who had made the best baked potatoes in the world.

She went to work on the banana dessert, making the shortbread/macadamia nut crust first. Try as she might she couldn't get Ray out of her head. He'd been too nice. Too accommodating. She wasn't fool enough to believe he'd come to terms with everything. That she'd moved on and wasn't giving up her dreams. The money should be safely in her account by now.

A smile touched her lips. Her inheritance. She'd already done a little browsing for the perfect house. Last night when she couldn't sleep.

Not going there.

Maybe, just maybe, Ray had come to his senses and wouldn't bother them anymore. She knew better than to believe he wanted a relationship with his son. In the ten years he'd been incarcerated he hadn't contacted Jason once, except for the past year when he started emailing him. As much as it hurt to admit, she suspected he was using Jason as an excuse to get what he wanted from her. He didn't have any real interest in being a father or getting to know his son. If he did he wouldn't be threatening her.

Putting the crust in the oven to bake, she prepared the pudding layer and sliced bananas. Then tossed together a salad.

Jason came in. "Have those steaks ready?"

She motioned toward the baking dish. "Yep, all set to go. Grab those potatoes, too."

"Do I smell banana?"

She smiled. "You do."

Jason groaned. "Oh, man, you made your banana dessert, didn't you?"

"I did."

"I'm gonna miss your home-cooked meals when I go off to college." He picked up the dishes and carried them outside.

Off to college. Less than two years away, but felt like tomorrow. Time moved much too fast for her liking. How did a mother come to terms with her child leaving her?

Squelching the sadness that seeped into her soul, Mia gathered plates and glasses and set the table. Already the scent of grilled steaks drifted through the open windows. It had been awhile since she'd had a man-grilled steak. Her attempts to use the grill back home resulted in epic failures. Jason wasn't too bad with it, but they'd decided to give up on it because char-burned meat wasn't very appetizing.

As she put silverware by each plate she allowed herself to dream for a second that the three plates belonged to her happy family. That she was happily married to Brendan and their house exploded with joy. She'd always wanted that. A man who loved her. A good man. One who loved her son as much as she did.

Pushing the thoughts out of her mind, she poured lemonade into the glasses and went to put the dessert together now that the crust had cooled.

By time she had everything cleaned up the boys came in bearing meat and potatoes. Jason proudly set them on the table.

"Those smell delicious," she said. "And they aren't burned."

Her teasing tone drew a smile from her son, making this day perfect.

"Yeah, seems turning the heat all the way up on the grill is the wrong thing to do," Jason said.

She laughed. "I'll remember that."

"Oh, no, you won't," Brendan cut in. "Grilling is a man's domain. No women allowed."

"Yeah, Mom, no women allowed."

Instead of feeling like an outsider to their man club, she was filled with happiness. This was what she'd always wanted.

"All right, all right, you win. I'll stay away from any and all grilling. You guys sit down while I get the salad."

Her men sat down while she tossed the salad, grabbed two kinds of dressing and set them on the table. She took her seat and motioned for them to get started. "Dig in."

They chatted lightly as they ate, Jason asking Brendan questions about free climbing and sports. She didn't like the sound of free climbing but kept it to herself. Jason had an interest and Brendan had the answers so she let it go.

"Whatever you put on these steaks is incredible," Brendan said, reaching for another.

Mia preened. "Thank you. It's a homemade seasoning blend."

"Well, it's the best I've ever had. And I thought I knew everything about grilled steaks."

A man who could admit he was wrong. Yep, the inevitable had happened. She'd fallen for this man.

"Thank you." She took a drink of her lemonade to hide her epiphany. How had this happened? They hadn't known each other long enough for her to fall for him. She didn't even know that much about him except what he'd proven so far. That he was a standup guy. One who didn't want to be a father, but would make an excellent one. A man who put himself in danger to protect others.

"Wait until you taste the dessert," Jason said, bringing her out of her thoughts. "It's one of my favorites. Do you like bananas?"

Brendan nodded. "I do."

"Then you're going to love this dessert."

"I can't wait to try it."

The comment was directed toward her and her stomach flip-flopped. She met his gaze, captured by the allure in his. Did he feel it too? The chemistry between them.

Was she prepared if he did?

Yes. She'd been a long time without a man in her bed and right now she wanted this man next to her, making love to her, showing her the passionate side of herself. Because sex with this man would be anything except mediocre.

Something sparked in his eyes and she knew for certain he felt it, too.

She better be ready because tonight just might be a turning point in her life.

Chapter Seven

Brendan did one last perimeter check of the house, making sure all the doors and windows were locked. Restless energy zinged through him. Dinner had been amazing. Good conversation, comfortable, the best steaks and dessert he'd ever tasted. It felt like home, as much as that thought bothered him. Home for him was anywhere the wind took him.

Jason retired to his room soon after dinner. His door was closed, but Brendan heard the television. Mia had opted for a shower. Twenty minutes ago. What did women do that took so long?

He wanted to talk to her about Ray. Something wasn't right there. A man like that wouldn't give up so easily. They needed to be on their toes until he found out what the man was up to.

"Want a glass of wine?"

Mia stood in the doorway leading to the kitchen, wearing a pair of sleep shorts and spaghetti strap tank that hugged her curves and showed her silky-smooth skin. Skin he longed to run his hands over. After the look they'd shared over dinner he should be running out the door instead of saying yes to a glass of wine.

"You sit. I'll get the glasses."

While she disappeared into the kitchen, he dropped down on the sofa. She walked in a few minutes later with a bottle of red wine and two glasses. The glasses she set on the coffee table, the bottle and opener she handed to him before sitting next to him.

He popped the cork and poured the rich red liquid into the glasses. Mia accepted one, taking a long sip. Nervous? That wasn't like her.

"Thanks for teaching Jason to use the grill," she said.

Small talk. All right. "No problem."

She took another sip, then let out a tense laugh. "What are we doing?"

"Unwinding with a glass of wine."

"Is that all?"

Her low tone made him set his glass down and gently take hers from her hand and put it on the table next to his. Leaning in, he pressed his lips against hers. Something he'd wanted to do since the moment he saw her. At first she didn't kiss him back, then, as if the flood gates on a dam opened, she opened her mouth and let him deepen the kiss.

God, she tasted like wine and honey. Sweet and incredible. Like no other woman he'd ever tasted.

A low moan escaped her mouth as she climbed on his lap, circling her legs around him. The feel of her rubbing against him set his blood on fire. He grabbed a handful of her hair and pulled her head back, allowing him access to her neck where he kissed a fiery trail down to the neckline of her tank. Her nipples budded through the thin fabric.

A gasp escaped her lips when he nipped the delicate spot on her throat where her pulse pounded.

"Bedroom," she breathed, grinding against him.

Brendan rose with her still wrapped around him and carried her into the master bedroom, trying to focus on putting one foot in front of the other. Not easy, with the way her tongue licked his earlobe. Damn erotic.

Once inside, he tossed her on the bed and went to close the door, hearing her soft laughter. He could listen to that carefree sound all day long. After locking the door in case Jason got curious, he shucked his clothes. Mia had already slipped out of hers and lay naked and beautiful on the bed. For a moment he could only stare. God, she was the most beautiful woman he'd ever laid eyes on. Soft curves, silky skin, incredible breasts.

And a smile that melted his heart. Unable to withstand any longer, he lowered himself on the bed and claimed her lips. This time her response was instant, her tongue melding with his. Her hands were everywhere, as if she couldn't get enough of touching him. That only fueled his need for her.

He traced a path down her neck to her breasts. Drawing a nipple into his mouth, he circled it with his tongue, causing her back to arch. Turned on by her uninhibited response, he moved lower, aching to taste her.

"Yes," she whispered when he ran his tongue over her sweet center. Her hips raised, inviting him in. He didn't hesitate to taste all of her.

Her hands kneaded his shoulders, nails digging into his flesh. He gripped her hips, hearing her breath come in pants as she neared climax. Sliding a finger inside her wet heat he urged her to the edge. Her body convulsed, a stifled cry escaping her lips as she clenched around his hand. After tasting every last drop of her he climbed over her.

Breathing still labored, she clutched his shoulders, drawing him closer. He was so hard he could barely move. Never had he wanted a woman this badly. Felt like he would die if he wasn't inside her soon.

"Condom," she panted, rubbing against him.

Shit. He'd been so caught up in her he'd forgotten to put one on. What kind of spell had this woman put on him?

Forcing himself off her, he tore through his wallet, grabbed a condom and rolled it on. Then he was inside her, surging deep, letting out a feral growl when she took him in. For a second he couldn't move, couldn't breathe. She felt…right. Like coming home.

Her hips moved, urging him on. Unable to hold back any longer, he thrust, his fingers digging into the soft flesh of her hips. She buried her head in his shoulder to hide her moans as she rose to orgasm.

His own orgasm came in a wave of heat, so strong he clutched the headboard to hold on. He stifled the shout of pure ecstasy as he came. She moved with him, clutching around him, milking him until there was nothing left.

Brendan collapsed on top of her, bracing his weight on elbows that shook. As he stared down into her soft brown eyes he felt himself falling. And knew he'd never done anything as dangerous as making love to this woman.

****

Mia let out a contented sigh and stretched, her eyes tracking Brendan as he took care of the condom. Making love to him had been everything she expected and so much more. She'd never come twice like that. And never with a man. Ray had been a good lover, but he had nothing on Brendan. He made her feel things she'd been afraid to feel. Made her feelings for him grow stronger than she'd imagined possible.

Her body felt thoroughly and utterly sated. Her mind at ease. Could she stay here forever?

When Brendan returned to the bed and pulled her into his chest she fought her emotions. Honestly, she'd expected him to leave her and go back to his own room. He didn't seem the staying type.

Happier than she'd ever been, she ran her fingers over the three parallel scars on his chest. She'd noticed them when they made love, but had been too distracted to mention them.

"How did you get these?" she asked softly.

For a moment she didn't think he was going to answer, but then he spoke in a low voice. "Tiger. Swiped me with her claws."

"Oh my God. How did you get that close to a tiger?"

She sensed his hesitation, but urged him on by kissing his chest.

"I was kidnapped a little over a year ago. By a man who wanted my sister to pay for betraying him. She'd been undercover as his mistress until he discovered who she really was. He…"

He trailed off, swallowing hard. Mia's heart ached for him. She didn't want to dredge up the past, but did she want to know? She tightened her arms around him.

"Santiago, that's the drug lord Attie went undercover for, built a maze of deadly games my sister had to survive in order to find me. Bastard used me as bait. Knew my weakness and I played right into his hand."

"What weakness?"

"Women. I used them to satiate my needs after a mission. Or, for whatever. And it almost got my sister killed."

A stab of jealousy shot through her but she forced it down. "How did he use women against you?"

"He sent a stacked blonde to the airport bar where I was waiting for a connecting flight home. She said all the right things—I went back to her hotel. Before I could get there she'd stuck a needle in my neck. I woke up tied to a chair in the middle of a nightmare."

The bitterness in his voice made her lift up on an elbow to look at him. "You couldn't have known what she was up to. You can't blame yourself."

"The hell I can't. I was a bastard who used women for my own needs. And almost lost my family because of it."

"But you didn't, right? Attie is okay now?"

Ghosts filled his eyes. "Yeah, she's doing much better now."

"Then you have to let go of the past. What's done is done, you can't change it. Don't let this ruin you. Believe me, I know what guilt can do to you."

His arm tightened around her, letting her know he understood. She laid her head on his chest, listening to the steady, strong beat of his heart. "Forgiving others is easy. Forgiving yourself, not so much. I forgave Ray for all the crap he'd done to me and for not being a father to Jason. It's harder to forgive myself for letting my son grow up without a father."

"You've done a great job with him."

"Thanks. Doesn't feel like it most days."

He kissed her forehead. "Trust me, you're a good mom."

She nipped his shoulder. "How about we stop talking and make use of the last few hours of nighttime?"

Brendan rolled her beneath him in one smooth move, making her laugh. She clamped a hand over her mouth to stifle the noise. Sex with this man was fun. Exciting. Unpredictable. Yep, she was in trouble.

In her ear he whispered, "I like that idea."

Chapter Seven

Brendan wrapped a vase in newspaper and put it in a box along with a few other things he'd packed for Mia. He'd slipped back to the guest room at daybreak, in time to change and meet Jason in the kitchen for their daily workout. If the kid suspected anything he didn't show it. He'd had to cover Mia's mouth more than once to quiet her. Little vixen had liked it.

For a schoolteacher she'd been more fun and adventurous in the sack than he'd expected. Every time he looked at her his thoughts flew south. Picking her up and carrying her into the bedroom seemed to be the only thing he really wanted to do today. A dangerous thought. He'd never spent the night with a woman. Always had his fun and left. Staying the night meant commitment. Something he didn't do. So why in the hell had he stayed with Mia? And why didn't it bother him as much as it should?

An outraged gasp came from the kitchen. Dropping the candle he'd just picked up, Brendan sprinted into the kitchen. Mia sat at the table, laptop open in front of her, face pale. She looked up when he entered.

"What's wrong?" He scanned the room for signs of Ray, only to find it empty.

A tear trickled down her cheek. "It's gone. All of it. Gone."

He frowned and walked over to her. "What's gone?"

She turned the laptop toward him. Her bank account sat open on the screen. With a zero balance.

"Did you call the bank?"

"Yes. They're looking into it for me. Seems my money was transferred out of my account this morning."

"Transferred by who?"

Mia wiped away her tears. "By me."

"Do they have the account number of the bank it was transferred to?"

"They're looking into it. That's all they would tell me."

Pieces were already falling into place in his mind. Ray's odd behavior yesterday. His comment about getting what he'd come for. If Ray had connections at all he'd have no trouble finding a hacker to do the transfer. Happened all the time, sadly.

"Let me call my team. We have resources to find out things the banks can't."

Mia looked up at him, hope in her eyes. "You can help me?"

He would anything for her. Denying it would only make him a fool. He'd fallen for this woman and her son and nothing could change that. Not the past, not his mistakes.

"I'll make a call." He pulled out his cell phone.

He passed Jason on his way into the living room so he could speak privately. As he punched in Noah's number he heard Mia explaining to Jason what had happened. He knew she wouldn't blame Ray until they knew for sure. That's who she was. Fair, forgiving.

His brother-in-law picked up on the second ring. "You're supposed to be on vacation."

Brendan grinned at the gruff note in Noah's voice. "I'm still in Hawaii. I need Rogan's help."

"What happened?"

Brendan explained Mia and her son, the ex, and the missing inheritance. Noah listened patiently until he'd finished.

"I'll have St. Klare in the air within the hour."

"Thanks. How's that sister and niece of mine?"

"Attie is as stubborn as ever and our daughter is taking after her."

Brendan laughed. "Sounds about right."

"Let me know if you need anything else. More backup?"

"Won't be necessary. Ray is no threat."

"Let's keep it that way. Attie would kill me if anything happened to you."

His sister loved fiercely. God help anyone who hurt one of her loved ones. "Tell her everything is fine. I'll keep in touch."

They disconnected and he turned to see Jason standing there, looking upset. "Is it true? Did someone really steal all the money my aunt left us?"

"I don't have much information yet, but it looks like it."

The kid cursed under his breath. "Who would do that?"

Brendan decided to keep his suspicions to himself. "Someone without morals. I have a friend coming over to help figure all this out."

"That's who you were talking to just now?"

"That was a member of the organization I work for. And a friend. But, he's not coming. Another operative is."

"Operative. This is the group you told me about? ATCOM?"

"Yes." They had talked about the military and ATCOM during their run this morning. Jason had seemed genuinely interested in both.

"I'm glad you're here to help my mom," Jason said quietly.

"I wouldn't let anyone hurt her."

"You think my dad did this?"

Brendan met the kid's troubled gaze. "We'll find out soon enough."

****

Rogan St. Klare was not what Mia expected when he arrived a couple hours later. Not as tall as Brendan, but still at least six-foot, with a deep tan, shaggy, surfer dark blond hair, bold Hawaiian print shirt, board shorts and flip-flops. In truth, probably the most beautiful man she'd ever seen. Brendan had told her ATCOM resided in Montana. This guy looked like he'd just stepped off the beach. Instead of a surfboard, he carried a high-tech looking laptop and some other equipment.

Brendan grinned when he let Rogan in, clapping him on the back. "Thanks for coming, man."

"Anything for you, Indiana."

Mia stepped closer. "Indiana?"

Rogan turned a pair of ocean blue eyes on her. Good Lord, the man was too gorgeous for his own good. But, he did nothing for her. He didn't get her blood racing like Brendan did. "Well, hello, there. You must be Mia." He extended a hand and she accepted. Nope, no zing of energy like when Brendan touched her. "Indiana is just a nickname we gave Devayne here."

"Really? Why?"

Rogan grinned. "Because he gets himself into sticky situations like Indiana Jones. Not to mention his daredevil antics."

Unease snaked down her spine. Daredevil. Indiana Jones. She'd watched every one of Harrison Ford's movies, and of all of them she found Temple of Doom and Raiders the hardest to watch. Too many daredevil stunts and dangerous situations. Reminded her too much of the kind of life Ray led.

"Let go of her hand, St. Klare," Brendan warned half-heartedly.

Rogan turned her hand over and kissed her palm before letting go. Oh, this man was a player. Too bad her heart had already been stolen by his coworker.

A coworker that lived a life of danger and apparently liked it. She couldn't do that again. Couldn't go through the long nights wondering where he was and what he was doing.

"You can set up in the living room," she said. "There's a desk and internet access in there."

They went to get started and she went to make a pot of coffee. Something to occupy her hands because she sure as heck couldn't occupy her thoughts with anything except the fact Brendan resembled her ex in all the wrong ways. He may not be a criminal, but he lived the life of a thrill-seeker and that was enough.

Confused, disappointed, saddened, she poured water into the pot. She'd done it again. Fallen for the wrong man. Only this time it hurt. Like never before. Losing Ray had hurt after the bitterness wore away, but not like this. This time her heart tore in half. She wasn't sure she'd recover from this one.

148

"Mom? You okay?"

Pulled out of her thoughts she looked at her son, grabbing a bottle of water out of the fridge.

"I'm fine. Why?"

"You look upset. Is it the money?"

She wished. Somehow the loss of her inheritance hurt less than finding out Brendan was the kind of man she'd vowed to steer clear of. "I'm sure it will work out."

"Brendan and his friend seem confident."

"Yes."

Jason took a swig of water. "You think Dad did this?"

Some of the fight went out of her. "I don't know. It's kind of odd that he showed up at the same time my money disappeared."

"Can I tell you something?"

"Of course. You can always be honest with me, you know that."

Jason shifted uneasily. "That day you came home from the grocery store to find Dad here."

He paused and she moved to his side, put a hand on his arm. "What did he do?"

"He asked me to brew a pot of coffee so I did. I thought he would wait in the living room, but when I came out…"

"It's all right. Nothing you say will make me upset with you."

Jason averted his eyes. "I found him going through your laptop."

Mia squeezed his arm. "What did he say when you caught him?"

"Just that he was leaving you a note."

"You believed him?"

Jason nodded.

She hugged him. "Honey, you didn't do anything wrong. This is on your father."

Jason hugged her back and her heart soared.

"He really is a bad man, isn't he?"

She'd never wanted him to think that of his father, but Ray's actions made it impossible to see him as anything else. Damn him for using her son to get her account information. "I'm sorry, Jason. All that is on your father and me. You've done nothing wrong. I love you and that will never change."

His head bobbed against her shoulder. "I'm sorry, Mom. I blamed you for taking away my father. Now, I realize why you did."

She'd never wanted him to see the true Ray. Not fully. It would only hurt him and she'd do anything to prevent that.

"Don't hate him. He just made some bad choices."

"I don't want to see him if we find out he stole the inheritance."

She leaned back. "You don't have to. It's completely your decision and I will stand by you, whatever you decide."

"Mia? We found something."

Brendan's voice ended the mother/son bonding. Jason looked at her then led the way into the living room where Brendan and Rogan were hunched over Rogan's computer screen.

"What is it?" Jason asked.

"Rogan tracked the bank transfer to an account in the Cayman Islands. Looks like your ex is using an alias. Ever heard of Joey Lane?"

Her stomach clenched. Joey Lane. The name of the bar Ray had taken her to on their third date. Said a friend of his owned it. Now, she wondered if the bar had been a front for Ray and his cohorts' illegal activities.

"Mia? Does that sound familiar?"

"Yes. It's the name of a bar Ray and his friends hung in."

Brendan studied her so intensely she wanted to bristle. He already knew all of her secrets. Even the one that could drive her son away forever.

"So this proves it? My dad stole the money?" Jason asked.

"Too many coincidences to think otherwise," Brendan answered.

Jason dropped down on the sofa, looking stunned. Mia went to him and sat beside him, putting her arm around his shoulders. To Brendan, she asked, "What do we do?"

"We've already contacted the police. No doubt it'll go Federal. We have enough evidence to prove it was Ray."

Some of the color drained from her face, she felt it go. If Ray got convicted of this, he would go back to prison. And probably never make it out. As much as she knew he deserved it and had done this himself, didn't make it any easier to accept. Her son truly would grow up and live the rest of his life without a father.

"The hacker he hired was sloppy," Rogan said, tapping keys on his laptop. "Didn't cover their tracks good enough. Pretty damn nice try though."

Mia didn't hear the rest of what they said. The cops showed up, invading her home, the same as they had ten years ago. Déjà vu hit her like a wrecking ball. Except this time Jason was a teenager and not an innocent six-year-old. He stayed by her side as things swirled around her. People coming at her with questions, then at Jason. Brendan by her side, fielding the attacks. Rogan printing page after page of proof, sealing her ex-husband's fate forever.

Finally, when the whirlwind settled, she wrapped her arms around her middle and shuddered. Jason had disappeared into his room to process in his own way. Rogan packed up his equipment, preparing to leave. He'd done what he'd come for. Found enough evidence for the Feds to convict Ray.

A glass appeared in front of her face. Blinking, she looked up to see Brendan standing there. "Drink this."

Numb, she accepted the amber liquid and took a swallow. When it burned down her throat she coughed, but welcomed the way it warmed her insides.

"I'm going to walk Rogan out. Be right back."

As if in a dream she nodded, waving to the shaggy-haired Adonis, listening, but not hearing what he said to her. When Brendan returned a few minutes later he sat next to her, took the glass out of her hand and pulled her into his chest. She went willingly, needing his strength right now. The rug had been pulled out from beneath her so many times today she couldn't process it all. Ray stole from her, proving he hadn't changed. Her son would never know his father. And, she'd fallen for a man who walked a razor thin line between danger and safety. Somehow, that hurt worse than the rest.

Maybe because she would also spend the rest of her life alone. Soon, Jason would go off to college and she would be by herself. Worse, she thought she'd finally found a man she could spend the rest of her life with and he turned out to be just like her ex.

"Is everyone gone?" she asked.

"Yes."

"Good."

"What can I do?"

She snuggled closer, taking refuge in his strength. "Exactly what you're doing." Right now she needed him. Later, she would worry about letting him go.

His hand stroked her hair, helping release the tension in her body. How could something so wrong feel so right?

"I suppose you'll be leaving now?" she asked, stomach clenching at the thought. "You did what you promised."

"Is that what you want?"

Sadness filled her heart. It had to be. She couldn't take that risk again. "The house is almost packed up and the money should be back in my account soon so there isn't any reason for Jason and me to stick around. My realtor is taking care of the sale of the house. My work is done here."

Silence stole the air from the room. They both knew she'd just broken off whatever they'd had. As much as it pained her. Her heart felt like it was being torn out of her chest.

"I'll pack my things and be out in the morning," Brendan said, putting distance between them.

She wanted to tell him how sorry she was that they hadn't worked out. How she couldn't get involved with a man that cared more about his thrill-seeking adventures than his family. But no words came. Instead, she slipped out of his arms, said goodnight and went to her room, knowing she'd really said goodbye.

Chapter Eight

Brendan packed his things, a heaviness in his chest he couldn't place. Hell, he knew what it was, he just didn't want to face it. Something had happened in the few short days he'd known Mia. It made him want things he'd sworn he never would. Not only had he fallen for the pretty schoolteacher, he liked her son. The kid had potential. With the right guidance he could make something of his future.

And he was the right guidance? Him? The one who ran in the opposite direction at the mention of a family and settling down. That life wasn't for him. He couldn't give up the things he loved. And a woman like Mia deserved someone who would be home every night and not worry her like her ex had. He couldn't ask her to accept his lifestyle. Even if the extreme sports he sought out suddenly didn't hold that much appeal when it meant losing Mia.

Could they find common ground? Was he ready to slow down? Settle down. Expecting the usual restless energy to zing through him, he zipped his pack closed. Only, it didn't come. The urge to jump off a cliff or climb Everest wasn't there.

What the hell had happened to him?

Grabbing his pack, he exited the room, stopping short when he saw Jason waiting for him by the door, running clothes on. When the kid saw his bag and regular clothes he frowned. "What's going on?"

"Time for me to go. Your mom's problem has been taken care of."

Hurt flashed in the kids eyes. "You're leaving?"

Feeling like a bastard, Brendan nodded.

"But I thought you and my mom had something. Now you're running out on her?"

"It's complicated."

"Do you love her?"

Caught off guard by the question, he clenched his jaw. How to answer that? His insides were twisted up like downed wire; he couldn't get Mia out of his head. If he were completely honest he'd admit he didn't want to leave. Ever. And that the thought of coming home to Mia after a mission instead of burying himself in some stranger sounded better than anything had in a long time. His sister and Noah were making it work. Why couldn't he? Attie had told him someday he would meet the right woman and everything would change in a heartbeat. He'd laughed it off, saying not him.

"Look, kid, I gotta go. Take care of your mom."

He didn't expect the right hook that caught him on the cheek.

"You bastard," Jason railed. "You're a coward, just like my dad. You both take, take, take but when it comes to taking responsibility you run away."

Stunned, Brendan touched his sore cheek. He wasn't Ray. He'd been good to this kid. Taught him his workout routine, gave him something to focus on besides trouble. Hell, he'd been a better father than his actual father.

The thought brought him up short. He stared at the kid with the wounded eyes and saw himself at that age. And he'd had Uncle Jed to help him through the tough times. Suddenly everything fell into place. He loved this kid. Wanted to be a father figure to him. Put him on the right path of life like Uncle Jed had done for him.

"I love her," he said in shock. He met Jason's equally stunned gaze. "I love your mom."

Jason stepped closer, eyes narrowed. "Did you hear what you just said?"

He nodded, dazed. "I want to be your father."

Jason clapped him on the shoulder. "You did it, dude. You admitted you love my mom. And I'd be okay with you teaching me more workouts."

Knowing that was the kid's way of saying he approved, Brendan could only nod.

A sound near the doorway made them both turn to look. Mia stood there, a befuddled look on her face. Her hair fell over her shoulders in sexy waves, tousled from sleep, her pajamas hugging her curves and making him want to tear them off her. He'd never seen a more beautiful sight in his life.

"I'll let you two talk," Jason said, bouncing out of the room.

Brendan set his bag down. "How much of that did you hear?"

"All of it."

Damn.

"Did you mean it?"

He met her gaze. "Yes."

She took slow steps toward him. "I don't know if I can go through another thrill-seeking marriage."

"I can't give up my hobbies, but I can promise to scale them back to where you're comfortable."

Her eyes lit up. "And your job?"

"Nothing I can do there, but I'll do everything in my power to make it home to you."

"Promise?"

"Yes."

She had reached him and now stood in front of him. It was all he could do not to kiss her.

"I think I can live with that."

"Can you live with a rustic log cabin in the mountains of Montana?"

A smile spread across her lips and he fell.

"I think I can."

Unable to stand it any longer, he wrapped his arms around her and claimed her lips in a kiss that made all of his promises a deal. She kissed him back with fervor, her hands everywhere. God, he couldn't wait to spend a lifetime with this woman.

The front door slammed, tearing them apart. Ray stormed in, eyes locked on him, face red. He charged. Brendan pushed Mia out of the way and met Ray's attack with an uppercut to the jaw that sent Ray sprawling.

"You're going to pay for that," Ray raged. "You stole everything from me."

Only he wasn't talking to Brendan. He aimed the darts at Mia, who stood wide-eyed behind the sofa.

"You got everything you deserved, Ray. That money was mine. You had no right to take it."

"You bitch—"

"Don't you call her that." Jason ran at Ray, fist pulled back. Brendan didn't stop him. This was something the kid needed to do.

Ray ducked Jason's blow, shoving him away. "You dare turn on me, son? I'm your father."

"You may be my sperm donor, but you're not my dad. You never will be."

Seeing the shift in Ray's demeanor, Brendan moved between them just as Ray struck out at his son. Mia cried out when the blow landed on Brendan's ribs. He spun Ray into a chokehold and said to Mia, "Call the cops."

Ray wasn't done. He fought, but Brendan didn't let go. To his son, Ray shouted, "You're siding with *her*? Did she tell you that she was the one who turned me in ten years ago? That she's the reason I went to prison? Is that the kind of mother you're going to side with?"

Seeing the hurt in Jason's eyes, Brendan dragged Ray out of the house and forced him to the ground. He kept a foot on the back of his neck so he wouldn't move.

The cops showed up minutes later, handcuffed Ray and took him away. When they were out of sight he went back inside to find Mia crying and Jason looking ready to join her.

"It's true," she told her son. "I turned your father in when I found out he and some of his friends were responsible for the break-ins I'd seen on T.V. He almost killed a man and that's what pushed me over the edge. I couldn't let him get away with his evil deeds. I'm sorry. I had to do it."

Brendan waited for Jason's response to the final truth.

When the kid's shoulders slumped and he said, "I get it, Mom," Brendan knew all had been forgiven and Mia's biggest fear had just been alleviated.

Now, and only now, could they be a family.

The End

About this Series: *The Fall* is the second book in my ATCOM series. *The Maze* was the first and featured Brendan's sister, Attie and navy SEAL, Noah. I hope you enjoy their stories as much as I enjoyed writing them! Look for Book #3 coming in the near future.

Meet Jennifer:

NY Times & USA Today bestselling author, Jennifer Lowery grew up reading romance novels in the back of her math book and on the bus to school, and never wanted to be anything but a writer. Her summers were spent sitting at the kitchen table with her sisters spinning tales of romance and intrigue and always with a tall glass of ice tea at their side.

Today, Jennifer is living that dream and she couldn't be happier to share her passion with her readers. She loves everything there is about romance. Her stories feature alpha heroes who meet their match with strong, independent heroines. She believes that happily ever after is only the beginning of her stories. And the road to that happy ending is paved with action, adventure, and romance. As her characters find out when they face danger, overcome fears, and are forced to look deep within themselves to discover love.

Jennifer lives in Michigan with her husband and two children. When she isn't writing she enjoys reading and spending time with her family.

Connect with Jennifer:

Read more about her books on her website: **http://jenniferloweryauthor.com/**

Join her on Pinterest: **https://www.pinterest.com/jenniferlowery/**

And on Twitter: https://twitter.com/JLoweryauthor

Please "like" her Facebook author page!

  https://www.facebook.com/AuthorJenniferLowery/

Sign up for Jennifer's Newsletter and get a FREE book:

http://jenniferloweryauthor.com/join-my-newsletter/

Join Jennifer's Street Team: **http://jenniferloweryauthor.com/join-my-street-team/**

JARED

Book 1: The Justice Brothers Series

Taylor Lee

"**USA Today best-selling author Taylor Lee** does it again! *Jared,* **Book 1** kicks off Lee's provocative new series, *The Justice Brothers*.

- On her first mission, Officer Hailey Michels confronts the leader of a dangerous Cartel.
- Her chance to become a hero evaporates when the powerful Cartel member turns out to an undercover agent.
- It was bad enough to blow his cover but when she discovers who he really is, Hailey's budding career, along with her heart, takes a decided nose dive.
- The rookie cop learns the hard way that when tangling with the Justice Brothers, Justice—like Love-- isn't always fair <u>or</u> easy.

Any inquiries can be made to: www.taylorleebooks.com or
taylorlee@taylorleewrites.com

Prologue

Hailey Michels snagged a gasping breath, praying the sharp intake wasn't audible. It was bad enough that her heart was a staccato drumstick beating against a tightly strung snare drum. Surely he could hear it; but the tall shadowy figure standing less than twenty yards in front of her didn't look her way. She could only hope the misty hangover from the pelting rain that had drenched her and the woods around them gave her cover. Hailey cautiously leaned back against the towering Norway pine. Grateful for the huge trunk that was nearly as wide as she was, Hailey dug her boot heels into the wet ground, praying for purchase on the slippery leaf-strewn path.

It took her a full second that felt like a lifetime to come to grips with the fact that the man less than half a basketball court length away was one of the bangers they were chasing. Hailey knew that if she had the sense of a mindless mosquito facing a can of Raid she would be terrified--but her racing heart, spitless dry mouth, and blood rushing in her ears spoke to exhilaration not fear. Not even the badass tats decorating what she could see of the gangbanger's corded neck above the collar of his leather jacket sounded a warning bell. Heck no. Her excitement flared realizing that she, Officer H. C. Michels, a rookie cop on her first honest-to-God mission, had a chance to bring down a member of the feared Dragon's Curse gang. Inching her hand behind herself, Hailey reached for the 9mm Glock tucked in her back holster. Cautiously drawing the weapon, she silently racked the slide, grasped the leather grip with both hands, and pointed it at the hardened criminal in front of her.

Steadying her grip on the lethal weapon, Hailey promised herself that if necessary she absolutely would shoot to kill. A tiny shiver of doubt tricked up her spine but she immediately squashed it. Admittedly, she'd never killed a man. To be completely honest, she'd never shot a gun outside of the CQ tactical gun range. But by God, she'd put her ballistic scores up against the best recruits in her academy class. Okay, so she wasn't at a Friday night GSSF Match at the local range, and the man in front of her wasn't a paper target silhouette. No, to the contrary. The tats on his neck and fierce dragon insignia decorating the back of his jacket confirmed his membership in the Dragon's Curse gang, an offshoot of the Balkan Organized Crime network.

From a crash course on Cartels for new police officers, Hailey knew that the BOC was one of the world's most vicious Cartels, trafficking in cocaine, heroin and MDMA. They gave the South American Cartels a run for their money in sheer violence and fervent devotion to spreading their vile empire worldwide. The Croatian-based syndicate had invaded the unsuspecting upper Midwest in the guise of the Dragon's Curse. In addition to their poisonous products courtesy of the BOC, the fierce motorcycle gang had aligned with the Aryan Brotherhood, America's largest prison-based white supremacist alliance. The combination of the finest shit the DEA had seen to date and a fanatical adherence to the principles of "white-might" hate made the rag tag crotch rocketeers the most dangerous gang ever to set up shop in the normally placid Northern Lake Country. Sucking in another surreptitious breath and with a clamoring heart, Hailey acknowledged that a member of the vicious gang was standing mere yards away from her.

Hailey had been thrilled when Lieutenant Justice included her in the raid. Not believing her luck, she'd quickly agreed when he admonished her that she was back-up only and was to stick to Sergeant "Solly" Solberg like 'ugly on an orangutan.' Shaking with excitement, Hailey had huddled by the big Swede with the ruddy cheeks and ample gut who'd always treated her respectfully. Hailey didn't kid herself; she knew that behind her back Solly likely joined in the chauvinistic trash talk that the guys usually managed to squash when she entered the room. But Hailey wasn't deaf *or* blind. More than once, hearing the smothered chortling, she'd whirled in time to see one of her randier teammates mimicking wanking himself off at the sight of her backside.

Hailey's sisters in blue warned her when she arrived that the old prejudices against women recruits were alive and well. Even in the supposedly enlightened, politically correct Duluth PD, it was assumed that an *attractive* women got to where she was by spending a good bit of time on her back—or her knees. Over beer and harder booze, her sarcastic female colleagues scoffed at her surprise, asking what the hell she'd expected. As Mitsi, the longest serving and most outspoken of the female detectives had snorted, "Look, Goldilocks, given your blonde hair and showgirl gams, you may as well accept the fact that that righteous rack of yours is the 'go to' jerk off trigger for every one-pump-chump in the locker room." According to Hailey's cynical friends, the only redeeming factor in this particular police department was that Commander Justice came down hard on the adolescent-testosteroned perpetrators and more than once had relegated a particularly outrageous chauvinist to an enervating stint on traffic duty.

Focusing on the sinister man in front of her and acutely aware of her solitary vulnerability, Hailey wondered how she could have lost her squad. One minute she was joined at the hip with Solly, a mountain of a man, the next she was struggling to find the team. It was clearly her fault. Admittedly she was a city girl, unaccustomed to traipsing around a dense forest on a moonless night. When the storm hit and the skies opened up pouring sheets of icy rain on their squad, Hailey lost her bearings. Huddling under an outcropping of brush, she'd frantically scanned for a sight of her team, trying to determine how she'd lost them. In fairness, she comforted herself, it wasn't hard to do. The sleeting rain, thick branches, and virtually identical trees along the myriad paths in the thick woods distorted her sense of direction. She had been about to give up and simply try to find a hiding place when the rain abruptly stopped. It was as though a giant hand had reached up into the sky and shut off a gushing fire hydrant. Miraculously, at the same moment a break in the overhanging cloud cover allowed a stream of moonlight to pierce the bleak night. Not daring to believe her luck, Hailey was about to go find her squad--or die trying--when she saw *him*.

Marshalling her courage, Hailey took a deep breath and raised her Glock in outstretched hands. To help steady her shaky knees she gingerly pressed back against the sturdy pine; but when she did, the root securing her foot gave way. Before she could brace herself her leg shot forward across the slippery ground. Careening down an embankment she hadn't known was there, only her frantically flailing arms and smashing against a broken tree stump kept her from landing flat on her face. Her cheek hit the ground at the same time that she painfully wrenched her ankle. Unable to stifle the cry that fled her lips, Hailey managed to hold on to her Glock.

The stabbing agony shooting up her ankle signaled a likely sprain, maybe even a break. The pain vanished into the dark night when she saw the yawningly empty space in front of her where seconds before the gangbanger had stood. The hard steel muzzle against the base of her skull underscored the obvious. In case she'd missed it, his deep voice expelled a warning she didn't need to hear to know that she was doomed. His guttural threat said it all.

"Move an inch, asshole, and it's the last thing you'll ever do."

Hailey froze, then cried out in surprise when he hit her wrist with a sharp knifehand strike, sending her Glock skittering across the ground and well out of her reach.

At the pained shriek, the assailant grabbed the DPD cap off Hailey's head, jerking her long blonde ponytail free. Kneeling over her back, his strong thighs straddling her hips, his surprised grunt and muttered expletive, "What the Fuck" confirmed that he saw that she was a woman. Certain that he would rape her then kill her, Hailey desperately fought back. With a frantic cry she arched up her hips trying to buck him off. Her attack caught him by surprise and she managed to free herself enough to scoot forward; but he caught her boot and yanked her back across the rough ground. Stretching his full length on top of her, he pressed the muzzle of his pistol harder against her neck. His raspy voice was layered with menace.

"Goddamn it, I told you not to move."

Knowing that she had nothing to lose, Hailey fought to jerk free but she was pinned so tightly between the hard ground and an even harder man that moving wasn't an option. In fact, she could barely breathe.

Still pressing the steel muzzle against the base of Hailey's skull, he grabbed her ponytail and yanked her head back with his free hand. Pressing his lips against her cheek, he growled, "Jesus Christ, woman. Do you have any idea what one false move on your part could do? Christ, this extended Sig of mine would blow your head clear across the fucking lake and they'd never find enough pieces to identify you. Hell, there wouldn't be enough left to attract the goddamned minnows, much less a decent sized walleye."

Driving her harder against the damp ground, he added, a note of incredulity striping his harsh tones, "Which brings me to the bigger question of this fiasco. What the *hell* is a Barbie Doll doing playing Big Bad Policeman all by *herfuckingself* in the deep, dark National Forest in the middle of the night? Didn't anyone ever tell you, Sweetheart, that Ken, not Barbie, gets to play the badass cop?"

Hailey violently shook her head, determined to free herself from his fierce grip. Righteous anger at his chauvinistic taunts spurred her on. Thrashing from side to side, she didn't care how inane her angry order sounded.

"Damn you! This is…unacceptable! I demand that you let me up! Now!"

Obviously not impressed with her impassioned command, the big man snorted.

"Not fucking likely, Sweetheart." Tightening his grip even further, he added, his voice dropping dangerously low, "And for the last time, Sugar, *don't* move."

When Hailey ignored his order and raised her hips, trying valiantly to free herself, to her surprise he laughed. If she didn't know better she would've thought that he was actually amused. The rasp of his beard brushing against the sensitive curve of her neck, and a deep insinuating chuckle confirmed it was unlikely that she would share his amusement. His hard thighs pressed against her bottom, she was startled at the flagrantly sexual intimation in his voice.

"On second thought, Sugar, maybe you *should* move. Especially if you keep moving like *that!*"

He ran his tongue across her ear, and then bit down on the tender lobe, sending a shockwave of sensation streaking across her thighs. Stunned at his audacious action, and even more so at her untoward response, Hailey gasped when he traced his hand over her butt and wrapped his huge hand around her thigh. Running his fingers along the inside of her upper thigh, he let the searching digits lie suggestively close to the apex between her legs.

At her shocked shriek and fierce attempt to break free, he chuckled mockingly.

"Hmm. Hell yeah, Honey, keep it up. You can move that hot little ass of yours all you want. *Any* way that makes you feel as good as it's making me feel." He added with a derisive chuckle, "I have to admit, Sugar, it's been a while since I've had a receptive woman squirming on the ground beneath me."

Shocked that he had felt her reaction to his overtly sexual overture, Hailey tried again to break free. But he merely used her raised hips to draw her closer to his strong body. To her horror she felt his arousal pressing against her upraised bottom. As if that wasn't enough, he grasped her thigh several critical inches higher, his strong fingers probing the tightly stretched crotch of her regulation trousers. Hailey prayed that he didn't hear the soft moan that escaped unbidden from her lips--but his throaty chuckle confirmed that she'd prayed in vain. To her dismay, he slid his hand across her belly then reached up and dragged his roving fingers across her breasts. Halting at the full curves, he whistled appreciatively.

"Daaamn, don't tell me that the little fighter not only has a great ass, but has tits that would make any Barbie Doll blush."

He laughed aloud at her outraged shriek, but before Hailey could try to deal with the challenging mix of rage and unwanted arousal sweeping over her, a deep voice shattered their clearly erotic grappling.

"Is it asking too much, Agent, to request that you get the hell off my rookie cop?"

Too shocked to do more than gape at the imposing man standing in the shadows at the side of the clearing, Hailey was stunned to see her boss, Lieutenant Jake Justice. His mouth was set in a stern line that competed with the obvious amusement lighting his slate gray eyes.

158

The man on top of her rose up on his knees. Still straddling her backside, he gazed up at the formidable commander, a slight grin twisting his full lips. Keeping one big hand on Hailey's back, he tossed his head and snorted derisively.

"I'll consider it--when you tell me when and why the big, bad Duluth Puhleeze Department decided to send a Barbie Doll look-a-like who thinks she can fight her way out of a Sig Sauer in her skull on a solo midnight mission. Or did Miss Sweden convince you that a perp would be so bowled over by her baby blues and righteous tits that he'd just beg her to take him in?"

Commander Justice laughed and shook his head. Holding out his hand, he pulled Hailey's audacious attacker to his feet and clapped a big arm around his shoulders in a bear hug. When the dark-haired man stood next to him, it was clear that her assaulter was as tall and as muscular as her commander. Lt. Justice reached down to help Hailey up, but to her surprise her assailant brushed Lt. Justice's hand aside. Instead, he leaned over and grasped her under her arms, lifting her up next to him. Too shocked at the unexpected turn of events and shaking too hard to stand alone, Hailey allowed herself to sink against the strong man holding her protectively against his side.

Lt. Justice shook his head and raising his hands in mock surrender, he flashed Hailey an apologetic grin.

"While I can see that you have already...ahem...*met* him, let me formally introduce the man who was shamelessly accosting you."

Her commander stepped back and held up his hands with a rueful shrug. "Officer Michels, meet my baby brother, Jared Justice."

At Hailey's startled gasp, Lt. Justice added with a grimace, "Which makes you, my somewhat clueless rookie, one of a very small group of insiders who knows that my outrageous brother, aka DEA Agent Jared Justice, is *also* my crack undercover agent in the Dragon's Curse Cartel."

Chapter 2

Jared raked his eyes over the pale young woman clinging to him, then turned on his brother with a sneer.

"*Somewhat* clueless? Damn, Bro, that's like saying the kid who just took the training wheels off his trike is ready to fire up the streets with his V-Rod Harley. Hey, don't smile. This ain't funny, Jake. Where did you get this little prom queen? Off a California beach after you tracked her down from the Sports Illustrated Swimsuit Edition? Jesus, man, what the hell were you thinking? Letting an inexperienced rookie roam the woods alone? With a gun for God's sake!" He added caustically, "Christ, Lieutenant, she could have killed someone. Like *me*, for instance—totally by accident of course. But I prefer DEA to DOA, thank you very fucking much."

Lt. Justice grimaced, pinning Hailey with a frown, and nodded at his brother in apparent agreement.

"Without calling her out, which I will do later, let's just say that as her commanding officer, *I'm* responsible for the fact that Officer Michels, fresh out of the Academy, was on this mission." He emitted a heavy sigh. "I'll grant it may not have been my wisest decision. However, I'm still not sure how Officer Michels managed to lose the squad in the middle of an exceedingly dangerous operation and ended up facing a supposed DC Cartel member all by her lonesome." Turning from Hailey to Jared, the beginning of a smile tugged at Jake's lips, "But you are correct, Agent Justice. Officer Michels does indeed hail from California. Which may help explain her inability to navigate our Superior National Forest in a torrential rainstorm in the middle of the night." Winking at his brother, Jake grinned, "Although I plead innocent to the unfounded charge that I discovered her on the cover of SI."

"Humph!" Glancing at the young woman standing beside him, her cheeks flaming hot with what he assumed was a mix of anger and embarrassment, Jared was disinclined to let his brother off the hook--or miss the chance to further embarrass the rookie. "I dunno, Bro, she sure as hell looks like cover girl material to me." Seeing what looked like angry tears puddling in Hailey's azure eyes, Jared took pity on the new recruit. After all, not five minutes earlier and sporting an impressive hard-on, he'd been firmly ensconced on her curvy backside. Not exactly by-the-book behavior for an officer of the law, he admitted, even if he *was* undercover.

Hell, he thought to himself, if he had any class at all he'd be as embarrassed as she seemed to be. Fortunately class wasn't something Jared aspired to. And Christ, knowing his cover was likely blown, combined with happening upon one of the sexiest chicks he'd seen in a lifetime of memorable hook-ups, who the hell could blame him for indulging. Plus this little rookie needed to know that playing cops and robbers didn't cut it in the real world of violent Cartels and unscrupulous men.

Acknowledging the way he'd manhandled her reminded him that the Valley Girl had cried out when she'd hit the ground, and again when he'd Karate chopped her wrist to knock loose her Glock. Christ, the least he could do now was to see if she was hurt. Facing her head on and seeing for the first time the nasty scrape on her soft cheek, Jared huffed a harsh grunt. Sure as hell, she'd have a rockin' bruise on that alabaster skin by daylight. He also didn't miss the flash of pain flooding her eyes, or the way she clutched his sleeve to keep her balance when he pulled her toward him.

"Okay, Valley Girl, out with it. Where are you hurt?" Jared reached over and stroked the mark the tree stump had left on the side of her face. "Besides this nasty-ass scrape on your cheek, that is."

Hailey shoved at his hand and snapped, "Nowhere. I...I'm not hurt...anywhere." Jerking up her chin, she added, "And even if I was, what's it to you?"

As she angrily spun away from him, Hailey stumbled and grabbed Jared's arm to keep from falling.

Jared glared at her as he caught her. Ignoring her rudeness, he focused on the pain radiating in her eyes. He nodded and said carefully, "Well, Sugar, since I feel as though I already know your bodacious body better than I should, and given that I might have played a role in any injuries you sustained, how about you be a good girl and answer my question?"

Putting his hands on her shoulders, Jared tipped up her chin with his thumbs and held her agonized gaze.

"Last time, rookie. Besides your wrist, which I'll look at in a minute, where does it hurt? Your ankle or your knee?"

Hailey hesitated and pressed her lips together. As if seeing from his implacable frown that he wouldn't let her go, she stammered, "My…my ankle…hurts."

Ignoring her surprised yelp, Jared scooped her up in his arms and deposited her on top of a knee high stump. Dropping to a crouch in front of her, he said, "Right or left, rookie?"

Closing her eyes but not quickly enough to keep a tear from escaping, Hailey whispered, "The…the right one."

Jared studied her for a long minute through narrowed eyes, then reached for her foot.

"Okay, Sugar, let's see what we've got."

Even before he got her boot off, her anguished wail confirmed that the little rookie had sustained at least a sprained ankle, and from the looks of the way it was swelling over the top of her boot, it was a bad one. Carefully removing the stiff boot, Jared was shocked to see that Hailey's ankle was swollen at least three times bigger than it should be and already mottled with ugly bruises. Gently exploring the taut skin with his expert fingers, he turned to his brother and telegraphed his conclusion with a nonchalance he was far from feeling.

"Hey, Bro, seems our little Valley Girl has a bitchin' sprained ankle. How about you make yourself useful and rustle up some of those cold rocks from the lakeshore and a passel of damp leaves to wrap them in."

Meeting Hailey's teary gaze and pale, strained expression, Jared did his best to tamp down his rising anger at himself. Holy fuck, he couldn't begin to imagine how much pain she had been suffering. And he and Jake--make that especially him--had been taunting her about her incompetence in the unfamiliar woods. Christ, he wasn't sure how he could feel like any more of an insensitive asshole. Fighting to keep from projecting his anger onto her, he asked in as calm a voice as he could muster, "Gotta ask, rookie. Any reason you didn't tell me, or your commander, if you weren't speaking to me, that you were in a shitload of pain? Holy hell, Sweetheart, my ankle throbs just looking at this."

When she shook her head and didn't answer, Jared carefully secured her trouser leg above her knee, and then elevated her foot on a nearby stump. Taking handfuls of the cold wet leaves that Jake piled beside them, Jared shrouded Hailey's ankle in nature's version of an ice pack. Stripping off his jacket, he hauled his long sleeved t-shirt over his head, ignoring the damp cold that hit his bare chest. Ripping the t-shirt into long strips, he chuckled at Hailey's wide-eyed expression as he shrugged his jacket back on over his naked torso. Acknowledging her surprise, he said with a cocky grin, "You'd be amazed sweetheart, the practical wisdom you acquire when you're raised in the boonies. These woods have taught my brothers and me more about surviving and thriving than we learned in six years of college plus another six in the military."

Hoping that his explanation didn't make her feel more inadequate than his earlier taunts had, Jared focused on bandaging her wounded ankle. With the improvised bindings he'd made from his shirt, he wrapped her swollen foot as tightly as he could to reduce the swelling without stopping the circulation. With the last of the t-shirt strips, to further support her ankle he splinted it between two branches that Jake had whittled to size with his K-Bar. As he ministered to her, Jared kept a careful eye on Hailey's physical and emotional reactions, knowing from her stoic responses that her searing pain had to be taking a toll. Sharing a glance with his brother confirmed that they both knew the little rookie was close to losing it. To shock, if not to pain.

Rising to his feet, he held up his hand to stop Jake when his older brother reached down to pick up his wounded officer.

Shaking his head, Jared said, "Not so fast, Bro. You're the big bad commander here. You lead the way. I'll pull up the rear and be the packhorse transporting this delectable cargo."

Jake frowned, then seeing that Jared wouldn't be deterred, nodded in agreement.

Jared squatted beside Hailey and stroked her porcelain cheek, trying to ignore the pain that had darkened her sky blue eyes to a troubled cobalt color.

"Listen up, Sweetheart. The *last* thing you should do with a sprain like the one you have is put weight on it. For that reason, that medical reason, I am going to carry you back to the road."

Hailey frowned and shook her head "No, please, I don't want you to carry me. Now that you put a splint on my leg, I can walk. I...I'm sure I can."

Jared forced himself to smile rather than yell at her the way he was tempted to. For Christ's sake, between him and Jake, they could have reduced the swelling in her ankle dramatically if the little rookie had bothered to tell them that she was hurt. Huffing a sigh, he admitted that his lusty and abrasive actions to date hadn't exactly been conducive to convince the rookie to ask for help. Choking back a harsh response, he said instead, "C'mon, Cover Girl. How about I kneel down here in front of you and you climb up on my back and hold on tight?"

When it looked like she would continue to resist, Jared's patience snapped. Trying to squash the edge in his voice he said with a grim smile, "The alternative, Sugar, is that I toss you over my shoulder like a duffel bag and carry you with your head hanging down my back and your ass in the air." He added with a grating laugh, "Come to think of it, that's one hell of an alternative. Hmmm. I'm thinking access to that curvy butt of yours could make our trek back to the road a hell of a lot more interesting—at least for me."

Hailey's pale cheeks flushed bright red and she bit down on her bottom lip. A second later she tipped up her chin and glared at him, her cerulean eyes flashing with anger. With a dismissive snort she tossed her head and prepared to climb up on his back.

Jared covered his amusement at her irritation and nodded tersely.

"Good decision, rookie. Although I have a feeling that at some point in the near future I'm gonna be paddling that classy ass of yours, if for no other reason than to teach you how to ask for help when you need it."

Ignoring her shocked gasp, Jared knelt in front of Hailey to allow his brother to lift her onto his back. He wrapped her good leg around his waist and hooked her splinted leg over his elbow to support her ankle. Five minutes into their journey Jared admitted the last thing he needed was more access to her ass than he already had. What with her curvy bottom securely resting in his large interlaced hands, her arms hugging his neck and her full breasts pressing against his back, it was all he could do to contain the iron-hard erection straining his jeans. His simmering anger at her refusal to ask for help only served to raise the temperature on his libido from hot to scalding. It didn't help that Hailey's occasional whispery moan and what Jared could swear was tell-tale dampness between her legs, and her unmistakably erect nipples palpable through his leather jacket, confirmed that the little rookie was as involuntarily turned on as he was. He shook his head. Damn, adrenalin was a bitch. Especially the way it played havoc with hormones.

As they carefully picked their way down the murky path, Jared decided it was a damn good thing the moon had chosen to bury itself behind the impenetrable clouds. He knew from long experience that Jake wouldn't be able to keep from remarking on Jared's obviously aroused state. As it was, his brother's occasional snicker confirmed that the random slivers of moonlight strafing the path were more than adequate to publicly reveal Jared's prominent reaction to the little blonde rookie who'd turned his night and potentially his life upside down.

Chapter 3

Jared waited while Solly raised the cargo door of the police van then rested Hailey's backside on the edge of the loading deck. Keeping her injured leg extended in front of her he carefully slid her into the back of the van. Scrambling up beside her he grabbed a stored tarp and wrapped it around her legs and hips. Elevating her injured foot on a weapons kit, he folded a smaller tarp into a makeshift pillow and tucked it behind her head.

Grunting softly, he stroked her cheek. "That should keep you warm and as comfortable as I can make you until they get you into some dry clothes. *And* shove a few dozen ibuprofens down your throat." He slid out of the van and met her questioning gaze. Flicking his fingers in a careless salute he said with an impudent grin, "Catch you later, Valley Girl."

He added with a mock frown as he prepared to close the cargo door, "And stay out of trouble, little rookie, you hear?"

Hailey leaned against the backseat of the van and listened to the men's voices through the open window, struggling to come to grips with her impossible situation. Except for the agonizing pain in her ankle she wouldn't have believed the events of the last three hours were real. How could she? They were truly unbelievable as well as inconceivably embarrassing. To recap, on her first mission with the Duluth PD she'd managed to: lose her squad; blow the cover of her commander's undercover agent; possibly irreparably destroying the overall mission; be assaulted by said agent who happened to be her commander's brother; and not incidentally--to *respond* to said undercover agent's sexual advances. It was that last component that had Hailey squirming with mortification and praying that the vivid memories tormenting her were her amped up brain's idea of a hideous joke.

Unfortunately the sound of Jared's deep voice and earthy chuckle confirmed that her humiliation was real. No, there was nothing imaginary about the tall, dark-haired man standing scant feet away. Saved by the barrier of the van between them, Hailey allowed herself to remember her assaulter grinning at her before he shut the cargo door. God, was it possible that he truly was that gorgeous? Ruggedly handsome didn't begin to describe him. She slammed her eyes shut trying to erase the image of the powerful man--but there was no way her sex-sodden brain would allow her to dismiss the brilliant picture ravaging her psyche.

She shouldn't have been surprised that he was beyond gorgeous. Look at his brother for God's sake. All of the women at the DPD, from the hardened female homicide detectives to the starry eyed interns in accounting, lusted after Lt. Jake Justice, their commander. How could they not? The top cop in the biggest police department in Minnesota, except for the ones in the Twin Cities, was every woman's fantasy he-man. If that fantasy happened to include a muscular, six foot plus frame, black curly hair, slate gray eyes and a 1,000 watt smile. Hailey admitted that she hadn't been immune to her commander's many charms. But given Lt. Justice's professional bearing and the respectful distance he maintained between himself and his admiring flock of breathless females, Hailey kept her fantasies where they belonged--in her imagination.

But not even in her imagination, active as it was, could Hailey have conceived of the fantasy come to life—in the form of the commander's "baby" brother, Agent Jared Justice. Nope, the outrageous man who had spent at least ten minutes assaulting her in the most insulting yet tantalizing ways imaginable was the equivalent of his older brother, only more so. He was as tall as the Lieutenant and definitely as muscular, and he shared his brother's drop dead good looks. But, Agent Justice went one better. In short, the devilishly handsome, emerald-eyed charmer was every woman's wicked dream and her mother's worst nightmare, the bad-boy come to life.

It wasn't until Jared had put his hands on her shoulders and forced her to look at him, insisting that she tell him where she was hurt, that Hailey had done more than glance at the man. How could she given that most of their short acquaintance took place with her lying on the ground with the powerful man stretched out on top of her? Until he insisted she look at him the most that Hailey knew was that the scary stranger was exceedingly strong, had a compelling voice, wickedly roving hands, and without a doubt, an erection the likes of which she had never felt. *And* that in their brief encounter he'd aroused her more than she'd ever been aroused in her life.

Even now the memory of what he had done and said to her *and* the way that *she* had responded to him, shocked and exhilarated her. Feeling her cheeks heat and her stomach clench she acknowledged that the worst part was that he'd known how she'd responded to his sexy overtures. How could he not, considering that she hadn't been able to keep from moaning! Good God, it was bad enough that she'd never be able to look him in the eyes again without blushing. She could only hope that he hadn't known that his advances had made her nipples harden and her panties wet. But given where he'd put his fingers....

Hailey had been so caught up in her machinations that she wasn't aware that the van had left what she was now calling the 'scene of the crime' and arrived at their destination. To her surprise and relief, it was Sgt. Solberg, accompanied by her boss, Lt. Justice, who opened the cargo door. Peering into the streetlight lit night Hailey saw that they had parked in front of the Justice family home. When she first arrived in Duluth, a pleasant woman from the HR department had given her the newcomer's city tour. Betty Zigmanski insisted that one of the "must see" attractions in the charming city located on the shores of Lake Superior, one of the five Great Lakes, was the historic mansion on the hill, known simply as the Justice Mansion.

"We decided that it was best to bring you here, Hailey, rather than to the station. We need to debrief Agent Justice and now that you know his identity, you need to be in that briefing."

From the frown on Lt. Justice's face and his curt tone, Hailey knew that her escapade had not done her any favors in her commander's eyes. Rather his unusually somber expression and tense body language confirmed that she had gone down in his estimation, likely irreparably. When she started to haul herself out of the van, Lt. Justice put up his hand and stopped her. Ignoring her insistence that she could walk, Lt. Justice nodded to Sgt. Solberg.

"Take her upstairs, Solly, to the lounge. I called ahead and instructed Margarite to dig up some dry clothes for her. When she's changed, bring her back down to the library."

"Copy that, Lieutenant."

The big man scooped her up in his arms and headed toward the extraordinary house at the end of the cobblestone path. Once inside, Solly trotted up a winding staircase. From her helpless perch in Solly's enveloping grip, Hailey forced herself to pay attention to the remarkable architecture of the famous turn-of-the-century Queen Anne mansion. Awed by the impressive art and architectural features, Hailey forgot for a brief moment why she was here and allowed herself to marvel at the historic masterpiece.

Sgt. Solberg entered what looked like a large sitting room, then walked across the carpeted expanse to a door that opened to a bathroom. Once inside the surprisingly modern bathroom, Hailey saw a stack of clothes on the counter. Solly carefully stood her on her feet and pointed to the clothes.

"How about it, Officer, you think you can get out of those wet duds into these dry ones? Although from the looks of 'em they will be at least five sizes too big."

The embarrassed expression on his flushed face as he looked her up and down, confirmed that the last thing he wanted to do was to help her undress.

Hailey managed a short laugh. "Don't worry, Solly. I'm glad to get out of these clothes and I definitely can dress myself."

After he assured her that he would be right outside the door, Hailey desperately eyed the toilet across the marble floor. Clinging to the edge of the counter she gingerly made her way to the commode. When she reached it she shoved her damp trousers to her knees and gratefully sunk onto the toilet seat. After she relieved herself she began the arduous task of getting rid of the rest of her wet clothes. Grateful for the stack of fluffy towels on the edge of the sink, Hailey dried her shaking body. She didn't have to look in the mirror to know that her chilled body was covered with goose bumps, but she wasn't prepared for how pale she was. Staring at her stark white reflection marred by ugly scrapes and bruises, it was no wonder Solly thought she couldn't dress herself. Good God she looked like a survivor of a desperate mission gone bad, which considering what had happened tonight, she was.

In a crazy way it helped that the sweat shirt and sweat pants some kind person had laid out for her *were* at least five sizes too big. She managed to get the pants over her swollen ankle and finished dressing. Shrugging at her reflection, she acknowledged that only a hot bath and a soft bed would begin to relieve the tension that was rampant on her pale face. Hopping carefully to the door she called out to let Solly know she was ready. In seconds he was at the door reaching for her. When she wasn't able to stifle her pained cry when he scooped her up in his arms, he was aghast.

"Damn, Hailey, I'm sorry. It's just that with dry clothes I thought you would be feeling better. I almost forgot about your ankle."

Trying to reassure him, Hailey said bravely, "I...I'm really okay, Sergeant Solberg. I...I think I might be able to walk..."

Solly snorted as he marched toward the ornate staircase.

"Sorry Hailey, I value my family jewels too much to risk the wrath of the Justice Brothers. No Sirree. The commander told me to carry you to the library and, Officer Michels, that's precisely what I'm going to do."

Settling back against his massive chest, Hailey tried to relax, convinced that the night couldn't get any worse. She revised her hopeful conclusion when Solly kicked open the library door with his massive boot. Standing with his back to the door, at what appeared to be a lavishly stocked bar, was none other than her nemesis, Agent Justice. Glancing over his shoulder, Jared's dark green eyes lit with amusement. Confirming that her imagination had not been exaggerating, Hailey acknowledged that her attacker was even more compelling than she'd thought. She'd forgotten the dark beard that made him look like a pirate although she'd certainly felt it rasping against her cheek and neck. And how could she have forgotten his powerful thighs that his lazy pose emphasized when he turned and leaned back against the bar? His lip quirked up with a sly smile as he turned to his brother who'd joined him at the bar.

Nodding at her and Solly, Jared said, "Well, well, look who the big bad commander brought with him. I'm glad you agreed that we should include the little rookie in our discussion, Jake, *and* that you got her out of those wet clothes." A grin kicked up the corner of Jared's mouth. "I'm just sorry, Sgt. Solberg, that you didn't wait for me. I would have been pleased to ahh *help* you with the dressing and undressing process."

Chapter 4

Not hiding his displeasure, Jake grunted. "That'll do, Jared. The situation is bad enough without you adding sexual harassment of one of my officers to your offenses. And, Dude, much as I would like to think that tonight never happened, since Officer Michels is now one of only six people who know that you're working undercover with the DC, whether I like it or not, we need to include her in our discussion. If for no other reason than to keep her from endangering, you and the op more than she already has."

Jared chuckled. "Yeah, Bro, if the little rookie is anything, she's dangerous. I'll definitely have to be on guard."

Lt. Justice snorted as he poured himself a healthy portion from the bottle of Maker's Mark on the bar and quaffed half of it. Glaring at his brother, he said, "How about you be on your best behavior instead, little brother? We have some serious shit to deal with, Jared, and I do not like having a rookie officer involved in it."

Hailey hated that her usually pleasant commander was clearly annoyed with her--but she had expected that. God knows she deserved his anger. What she hadn't expected was that Agent Justice would continue to taunt her with overt overtures. Obviously he saw her as a bungling woman with long blonde hair, big tits, and a nice ass; certainly not as a respected fellow officer of the law. But then most of her colleagues couldn't seem to get past her appearance either. The problem with the amused man grinning at her was that her actions had *earned his* disrespect. She could almost handle that. What she couldn't handle was the knowledge that her commanding officer had relegated her to the same unprofessional camp. Ducking her head against Solly's shoulder, to keep from looking at either of the Justice Brothers, Hailey promised herself that she would slit her wrists and bleed to death right there on the Justice's imported carpet if a single drop of the waterfall burning her eyelids dared to fall.

From the shelter of Solly's massive chest, Hailey didn't see Jared coming toward her. She could only let out a startled squeak when he wrested her from the gigantic sergeant. As if she weighed nothing, Jared carried her over to the brocaded divan and set her down. He propped her up against one of the large rolled arms then put several throw pillows under her injured foot. When she managed to meet Jared's gaze, Hailey was startled to see that he looked serious, the way that he had in the forest when he realized that she was hurt. She didn't know which was more challenging, his open derisiveness or this grim, narrow-eyed focus on her. Both made her feel insignificant and helpless in the face of his overwhelming presence.

His voice was crisp, authoritative.

"Hailey, before we get started, we need to get some serious drugs into you. I wouldn't want that pained expression on your face to take hold. Don't want to be responsible for spoiling perfection. Which makes me think that whatever drugs my big brother comes up with will be better washed down with a glassful of booze. Tell me, Sugar, which best suits your taste, expensive whisky or even more expensive scotch?"

Before she could answer, Jared added, "And don't you dare tell me you prefer wussy white wine."

Hailey managed a small laugh. She paused for a moment, realizing that for the first time Jared had called her by her real name rather than one of his disparaging nicknames. And considering what he'd said about her face, he might actually have paid her a compliment. Of course, it was all about her looks rather than her actions, but given his stream of seemingly never ending put-downs, she'd take a compliment no matter how lukewarm it was.

Hailey acknowledged that Jared was right. He'd pegged her as a clueless California beach bunny and before she'd started training for the Academy, that's pretty much what she was. And, yes, she *did* prefer white wine over hard liquor. It was disconcerting that just having met her, he knew her so well. But when she saw the handful of pills Lt. Justice put in front of her, Hailey decided she better man up.

166

With a determined sigh, she said, "Since I've never had either one, I guess I'll start with the scotch."

Jared laughed. "Good choice, Angel Face. What with your first acquaintance with the hard stuff combined with some righteous drugs, we'll have you toughened up in no time. Besides, if the Glenmorangie Scotch doesn't float your boat, you can always hit the Maker's Mark."

When both he and Jake had piled on, Jared knew he'd gone too far with his relentless teasing. Hell, given that Hailey was a newbie, and a fucking clueless one at that, the least he *and* his brother should do was cut her a little slack. Looking as shattered as she must feel, when the little rookie had buried herself in Sgt. Solberg's big comforting chest, Jared had an overwhelming need to get control of the situation *and* of her. Ashamed of himself, and desperately wanting to wipe the misery off of Hailey's face, he'd yanked her out of Solly's big bear grasp and taken her in his arms.

Parking her on the sofa, Jared knew enough about field medicine to know that Hailey was in severe pain, hence his chosen remedy of drugs and booze. Knowing she couldn't tolerate much of either, he'd ordered Solly to hit the freezer in the massive kitchen and bring him a supply of ice packs. Now after 20 minutes, her elevated ankle was encased in legitimate ice packs and she'd swallowed several ibuprofens and a half glass of Glenmorangie. A minute ago she'd actually shot him a shy smile when he raised his glass to her in a silent toast.

Jared watched her carefully for the next several minutes as she sipped on the amber liquid. He was relieved when a slight flush pinked Hailey's pale face with the righteous bruise marking her alabaster white cheeks. Thank God for the healing properties of expensive liquor. Of course the ibuprofen went a long way to boost the power of the booze. Whatever the reason, Jared was glad to see the little rookie actually smile at one of his tasteless jokes rather than looking as though she would burst into tears.

Staring at the young woman, Jared admitted that he was stunned by how lovely she was. Everything had been so crazy in the woods, including the fact he'd barely seen her face-- although he sure as hell had felt her body. He knew he should be ashamed of the way he had come on to her. She was clearly under duress and frightened as hell. But his fury at being outed, and six fucking months working his way into the DC possibly down the drain, had short-circuited the distance between his big head and his small one. It didn't help that she'd responded to him, which had only egged his dick on more. Remembering her soft breathless moans and shivering tremors, he had a sneaking feeling that Hailey was about as experienced sexually as she was a cop.

All of his recriminations hit the trash can as he studied her. What he hadn't seen in the darkness was how truly beautiful she was. Christ, he wasn't far off with his Miss Sweden taunt. Her honey-blonde hair tied up in a high ponytail with distracting tendrils falling around her face and neck made him wonder what it would take to weave those waves of sunshine in his expert fingers. His dick jerked at the thought, confirming that once again his little head was asserting its power. He'd felt enough of her sensational body to hazard a guess that if she hadn't won at least three beauty crowns and a fitness contest or two, it was only because the judges had been blind. Dark feathery lashes and arched brows framed the wide–spaced, summer sky blue eyes that dominated her lovely face. Dragging his gaze from Hailey's eyes to her mouth, Jared fought a surge of lust and promised himself that the next time he was on top of her, he'd insist that it be face to face. How else could he enjoy probing those full, luscious lips that begged to be kissed?

Jake's pensive observation jerked him out of his lusty contemplation.

"Okay, Bro, looking on the bright side, tonight could have been an even bigger disaster. Fortunately, Officer Michels is the only one of our team who now knows that you were meeting me in the woods."

Casting Hailey an intimidating glance, Jake said curtly, "I'm confident we can impress upon my rookie cop how important it is that she not disclose your undercover role."

When Hailey started to interject, Jake shook his head and held up his hand, his frown deepening. "Hold up, Officer Michels. Both Agent Justice and I agree that it was a stroke of bad luck that you ended up in the wrong place at the wrong time. As I said earlier, I take responsibility for the fact that you were on the mission." Again, he raised his hand stopping her objection. "If I'd paid more attention to the weather report and knowing our thick forests are challenging to navigate--especially for a newbie--I wouldn't have included you on the op."

Seeing Hailey's flushed cheeks and downcast eyes that were no doubt brimming with moisture, Jared broke in.

"C'mon, Bro, lighten up. Yeah, we're going to have to realign our strategy. Getting outed by the rookie has just forced us to speed up our timeline. Hell, if you think about it, if anyone was going to see me, it's lucky the Valley Girl did. If I'm reading her expression right, all you have to do to keep her quiet is continue looking at her the way you are now. Shit, man, I've seen cornered baby fawns facing a Ten Point Carbon Xtra CLS crossbow who look less scared than the rookie does."

As if seeing Hailey's strained expression and obvious fear for the first time, Jake relented. Huffing a hard sigh, he nodded to his brother.

"You're right, Jared." Turning to Hailey, he said apologetically, "Look, Hailey, Agent Justice is correct. In truth, nothing that you did tonight has caused *irreparable* harm. Either to the operation or to your standing in my eyes. You're a good cop, and you will be even better. And yes, you need seasoning, but for Christ's sake, you've only been here for a month." He snorted, and shot his brother a reproachful glare. "Hell, Officer Michels, you did what half the female population of our fair city has been unable to do: you bowled over my infamously elusive baby brother. Damn, you actually brought him to ground." He shrugged and flashed Jared a grin. "Although I did notice that the 'grounding' appeared to be mutual."

Chapter 5

Jared chuckled and gave his brother a mock salute as he walked over to the bar and replenished his drink. Turning to Hailey, he raised his glass.

"Yeah, rookie, I gotta tell you, as if you didn't know, you surprised the hell out of me tonight." Eyeing her outstretched body he flashed a cocky grin, "In more ways than one. It's not every night that a bodacious babe tumbles down a hill into my arms." He added with a dismissive snort, "But as good as that roll down the hill was, it's got repercussions that we need to deal with."

Jake agreed with a hard sigh. "The understatement of the year, Bro." Yanking his phone from its holster, Jake checked the i.d. then nodded to Jared and Sully.

"I need to take this." He pinned a hard frown on Jared and said. "As for you, Bro, behave yourself. I think Officer Michels has had enough excitement for one night."

Jared chuckled then turned to see Hailey studying the photograph on the fireplace mantel. He nodded at the picture with a grin.

"Believe it or not, that's me at the ripe old age of eighteen. The Judge insisted that we get a picture of all four brothers before I went off to college. Guess he thought once I fled the nest I might not come back."

He added with a rueful grin, "At the time that wasn't unthinkable. Although I confess that as I grew out of my rebellious teens, my appreciation for my family has grown exponentially. I never realized how close my brothers and I were until they weren't harassing my ass on a daily basis."

Hailey studied the picture of the four Hollywood handsome young men clowning for the camera. She was stunned at how gorgeous they were. Trying to hide her amazement, she said, "Obviously I know Lt. Justice, and I met your brother Jude, the District Attorney, the first time I testified in court." Glancing at the man next to Jared she said, "I knew you had three brothers but I've never met him." She studied the dark haired, green eyed man then met Jared's gaze. "He almost looks like your twin."

"So we've been told for years. That's Josh. He's two years older than I am and as you can see, is the better looking one."

Hailey huffed a soft snort. As if anyone could be better looking than the arrogant man beside her. Wanting to continue the casual almost normal conversation she pointed to the laughing man with his arm around Jared. "Where does Josh live? I know I've never seen him here."

"He's overseas."

Surprised at his curt response, Hailey asked cautiously, "Is he in the military?"

His eyes narrowing, Jared hesitated then said with a quizzical smile, "Let's just say, he's at an undisclosed location."

At that moment, Jake strode into the room, a frown darkening his usually pleasant expression. He pulled up a chair in front of the sofa and nodded to the overstuffed armchairs, indicating that Jared and Solly should sit. Taking a hefty swallow of the amber liquid in his glass, Jake said. "Okay, team, let's get started. Jared, how about you fill Officer Michels in on the op and then we'll map out our plan?"

Jared sat in the chair across from his stern bother and put his glass on the end table. Not wanting to scare the rookie any more than she already was, Jared needed to impress upon her the assholes they were chasing and what could have happened if he had been one of them.

"Look, Sugar. I know you probably have a *Cartels for Dummies* understanding of the Dragon's Curse, but let me tell you, take everything you've heard about them and add several hundred layers of viciousness, and know that you aren't even close to knowing how bad these bad-asses are. Sweetheart, if I *had* been one of the DC gang, you wouldn't be lying here sipping on Glenmorangie Signet."

Jared closed his eyes to shutter the horrific image assaulting his all-too-knowing brain. He couldn't hold back a harsh grunt as he glared at her. "No, Officer Michels, at this moment you would have known at least four of the assholes up close and personal. And, Honey, rape would only be the beginning of getting to *know* the motherfuckers. *If* you survived the night, Boris Jankosky, or Janko as he's known, would decide if you were in good enough shape for another round. If you were, and you still looked halfway decent, Janko might make you his woman for a week or so. After that he'd pass you off to the gang in order of their seniority—and how open they were to sloppy seconds, thirds or tenths, whatever you were at that moment."

Jared watched Hailey's expression change from fear to horror. Deciding he'd made his warning gruesome enough to shock her, he continued.

"Rookie, I'm telling you this not to upset you, but to make you understand the kind of men we are up against. These guys are as bad as any I've faced. And that includes the murderous haji sons of bitches I tangled with in Afghanistan. Six months ago, I went undercover for my brother and the DEA. I've shown up in these parts only occasionally since I left active duty. The most the locals know is that I do off the grid government work. That alias allowed me to worm my way into the DC's. I am well known in these parts as the youngest Justice Brother and as big a hell raiser as this staid city of ours has known. Janko and I hung out together as kids. I don't know who was a bigger jagoff, Janko or me. I had what I considered at the time to be a disadvantage, three tyrannical big brothers and a grandfather who could scare the bad out of Attila the Hun. The four of them kept me on a leash so tight that not even Janko and the lure of the dark side could capture me."

Lt. Justice shared an aggrieved glance with Sgt. Solberg then turned his stern gaze on Hailey. "Don't think it was an easy job, Officer Michels. More times than I can count, my brothers and I nearly lost Jared to the bad guys." He frowned at Jared and added with a grunt, "Although it took all of us hauling your ass back, I'm still not sure how we kept you from going over, Bro. Guess it was worth it, given that your badass rep made it a slam dunk to work you into the DC."

Jake's frown deepened and he huffed a gloomy sigh. "But I gotta tell you, as much as we needed an inside guy in that rabid pack of rats, I still hate the idea of my baby brother working side by side with those despicable animals."

Jared snorted and chugged on his scotch. "Yeah, sure you do, Bro. That's what you and Jude, not to mention Josh and Grandpops, get for beating the crap out of me to turn me around." Glancing at Hailey he said with a sneer, "Don't misunderstand, rookie. They never actually beat me, they just set up a training regimen so arduous, I was lucky to make it through the day. Let me tell you, no undeserving fucker on a 19th century slave gang got worked harder than my loving family worked me. And I was only fifteen years old. Christ, in comparison, Ranger training was a slam dunk. Hell, just two days into it, when half the guys had vomited their guts up and were heading for the hills with their shriveled up dicks hiding in their asses, I was doing an extra 250 pushups morning and night to keep from going soft."

Jake laughed. "Yeah, I'll say that for you, Bro. You were and are the toughest fucker I've ever known. But, we were lucky. The whole MMA craze came along just when we were trying to figure out how to keep you tethered." He nodded to Hailey and said with an admiring shake of his head, "Just so you know, this cocky guy took to that vicious sport like Rocky did to the ring. When he was eighteen years old he placed in the top tier of the UMMAF Midwest Division. Won every match he fought."

Jared put up his hands with a disparaging frown. "Enough, big brother. Yeah, I won a few dozen tournaments, and more than anything my passion for the sport pulled me back from the abyss. Meantime I went off to college and then spent six years in the Ranger Corps. When I left active duty I joined the DEA on the down low. I'd discovered from my Special Forces days that I was a natural at subterfuge and the DEA was thrilled to exploit my talents. When the DEA told me they wanted to plant a UC in the Dragon's Curse--right here in my neck of the woods, I managed to convince my reluctant brother that the mission had my name on it. My connection to Janko and my rep as a hell raiser made it as quick 'n easy for me to hook up with the Dragon's Curse as shit through a goose.

"The DEA cooked up a credible cover story that left questions about my exit from the military. As far as the Dragons and anyone without top level clearance knows the reasons for my leaving active duty are in a sealed file. That subterfuge allowed me to worm my way into the DC. Janko was suspicious, but the DEA info I fed them was too sweet for him to pass up. Besides, he'd always believed that I was as corrupt as he was, which I gotta admit at least for a time in my life was true."

Jared grinned at his brother and said with a chuckle, "Janko believed that if it hadn't been for Grandpop's connections and the Justice name, I never would have made it into the military. It was easy to play on his paranoia that the only reason I achieved anything was because I was a Justice. In his mind my off the books 'dishonorable discharge' was just one more example of JM&M--Justice Money and Manipulation rigging the system."

Jared glanced at his brother and seeing his agreement pinned Hailey with a hard frown.

"So, little rookie, here's where we are in the op. Big Picture. The Dragon's Curse is small potatoes in the world-wide illegal drug industry, but with the impressive shit they're getting via the BOC, the Dragons are on their way to becoming a gen-u-ine player. The last thing we want is for the BOC to gain a foothold in the upper Midwest, especially through a homegrown organization like the Dragons. Trust me, those Balkan assholes have been eyeing our strategically located Twin Port cities for years now. Not only are we close to the Canadian border but we're also at the tail end of the St. Lawrence Seaway, which connects the Atlantic Ocean to the Great Lakes. Our goal is to cut the Dragons off at the knees, sending a clear message to the BOC that the North Country isn't open for their despicable business."

Jake stepped in to add to the tale. "Playing on his connection to Janko, my outrageous brother's managed to insinuate himself into the Dragon's Curse. He convinced Janko that he has a wealthy off-the-market Asian buyer looking for a reliable access to prime product and lots of it. Janko has been working his ass off trying to convince the BOC that he should be their go-to guy in the Upper Midwest. No fool he, Janko knows that if he can pull off a deal the size of the one Jared is offering, the BOC will have to take him seriously."

Jared lifted a cocky brow and interjected. "Of course if anything goes wrong.... For example, if the DEA turns out to be the buyer and makes off with a mountain of BOC prime product... that would be 'unsettling' for the DC." He added with a satisfied snort, "Those Balkan assassins don't tolerate fuckups."

Reaching for the Glenmorangie, Jared refilled his glass and topped off Hailey's. He could see that the booze was having a salubrious effect on the little rookie. The pained expression she'd been wearing since their tryst in the woods had softened. Hell, she looked almost relaxed. The tears that had been hovering in her stunning indigo eyes had been replaced by an attentive interest in the operation he and Jake were describing. Jared had to give the rookie credit. She'd never once complained about her ankle, and moreover had done everything he told her to do, from swallowing the drugs to looking as though she was enjoying the scotch. Thinking about the items he still had on his agenda for the night, Jared wondered if she would continue to be as...amenable. He smothered a soft chuckle deciding it was time to wrap up the briefing. The rookie had to be tired. What she needed now was a comfortable bed. And ever the solicitous host, Jared intended to find her one.

Speaking directly to Hailey, Jared said, "To date, all of my communications with the Dragon's Curse foot soldiers have been from a distance, via Janko. But his rabid freakos were getting antsy. Wanted to see me in the flesh, confirm that I'm as bad as they are. Plus they think that having one of the Justice Brothers in their racist ranks will add credibility to their sick organization. Give them a cachet--of sorts. Jake and I agreed. We've spread the word that Grandpops is ill and that I'm coming back to the Zenith City to check up on him. Jake and I have been meeting surreptitiously and planned to have me return soon. But tonight's escapade, which could have been a disaster if it had been anyone but you who saw me with Jake and Solly, confirms that we need to speed up our timing."

With that, Jared rose to his feet, and eyed his brother.

"Don't know if you noticed, Bro, but the little rookie looks like she's about to nod off. Seems with all the beds we have in this house, the least we could do is tuck her in one."

Before Jake could respond, Jared reached down and picked up Hailey. Ignoring her surprised squeal, Jared held her close to his chest and pinned his brother with a narrow gaze.

"Given that I'm the reason the Valley Girl hurt her ankle, and being the gentleman that I always and ever am, I'm obligated to offer her my old bedroom, don't you agree?"

Not waiting for Jake to answer and ignoring the warning frown on his brother's face, Jared sauntered to the door and said over his shoulder, "Tell you what, after I get Officer Michels safely tucked in my comfortable bed, you and Sgt. Solberg and I can finish planning my reentry into our fair city."

Glancing at his watch, Jake barked, "You're pushing, Jared. And, you're right. We do have an op to plan. Sgt. Solberg and I will be waiting right here for you, buddy. Don't dally. You hear me, Agent Justice?"

Jared laughed a hearty laugh. "Hey, Lieutenant, I'm nothing if not a quick worker. You of all people should know that, Jake."

Jake's disgruntled sigh sounded heartfelt. "Yeah, little brother, I agree. Along with all of your other skills, you've always been able to get to the heart of the matter quicker than anyone I know."

Jared was still chuckling as he walked out into the hallway and over to the staircase, holding Hailey snugly in his arms.

Chapter 6

Knowing that Jared wouldn't put her down even if she insisted, Hailey burrowed against his muscular chest. She clung to him realizing that for the last five hours, one big man after another had carried her in his strong arms. While Sgt. Solberg was one of the men, and she'd appreciated his caring solicitousness, the strong arms that had her gasping for air were the ones holding her now. As he mounted the stairs, Hailey didn't dare to think what would happen when Agent Justice got her up to his bedroom, much less *into* his *bed*, as he'd cavalierly informed his brother he intended to do. God, he had to feel her heart pounding against her chest. Hailey wasn't sure if it was from fear or excitement, or, she admitted, more likely from both.

Reaching the top of the stairs, Jared entered the room at the end of the hallway.

"Okay, little rookie, we're here. Just so you know, I spent my teenage years in this room, but I'm confident my Gramps had it fumigated at least twice after I left for college. I promise you it is now safe—at least from unhealthy transmittable diseases."

With a soft laugh, Jared firmly kicked the door closed behind him. Trying not to be alarmed that they were alone, in his bedroom, no less, Hailey peeked up and surveyed the room. It was huge, more like a suite than a bedroom. Hailey sniffed dismissively. If anything epitomized a man-cave, or at least a spoiled rich kid's idea of a man-cave, this was it. The apartment-sized haven had a lounging area, a study den, and every kind of video and audio equipment that a privileged kid could desire. From the bank of computer equipment to a ten foot wide television screen to the wall of cd's, dvd's and video game paraphernalia, it was clear that the boy who'd lived in this jam-packed room had wanted for nothing in the way of adolescent diversions.

Unfortunately, the expected boy toys didn't hold her interest for more than a minute. What had Hailey's heart beating impossibly faster was the bed--if you could call the three foot high platform replete with banked cushions and multiple pillows a bed. To call it king-sized didn't do it justice. No, giant-sized, or maybe, party-sized, would better describe the mattress topped playground that stretched yawningly along one wall.

Jared must have felt her startle because he chuckled.

"Yeah, Valley Girl, I gotta confess, that bed was my declaration that if my family refused to let me be a bad-ass gangbanger, they couldn't stop me from being a hound dog." He added with a self-deprecating laugh, "It took me a lot of years to admit that what makes a bed exciting was less about the furniture, and more about the man and the woman in it."

When Hailey stiffened at his obvious reference to his sexual escapades, Jared relented.

"Relax, rookie. I'm too old to be a hound dog and you're too exhausted for me to tease you anymore. How about you make use of the john, and then I'll tuck you into bed like the gentleman I occasionally am?"

The adjoining bathroom had an enormous shower with shower heads on all four walls. The hot tub next to it could've hosted a party of eight. Hailey didn't want to imagine the group extravaganzas that had made use of this bathroom. Thinking back on her sheltered teenage years, Hailey huffed a hard sigh. California girls and guys were supposed to be the party animals, not small-town, Northern Minnesota hicks. Although Duluth was more like a small city, it was still decidedly Midwestern without California's 'anything goes' reputation. So much for stereotypes.

Jarring Hailey back to the present, Jared stood her on the floor next to the commode then tipped up her chin and winked at her.

"Need any help taking those sweat pants off, rookie? Remember, we gotta be careful of your ankle."

Horrified at the idea of him taking her pants down, and not a little embarrassed that he seemed to think she didn't need privacy to pee, Hailey shoved at his hand.

"No, Agent Justice, I don't need your help. But I *do* need my privacy. If you don't mind, I'd like to be alone."

Jared's voice was rich with amusement as he gave her a sharp salute, "Eye eye, Officer Michels. But, know that I'm right outside the door. As James Taylor says 'if you need me, just call my name and I'll come running…You've got a friend…"

Hailey couldn't keep from smiling as he left the room singing one of her favorite songs. She realized with a guilty start, that unlike the song, a "friend" wasn't what she wanted from the arrogant man. She wasn't sure *what* she wanted. But whatever it was, and whether or not she was brave enough to ask for it, one thing was certain. The accomplished man humming outside the door could give it to her. Hailey was washing her face, and trying to ignore the fact that in a couple of minutes she would have to face Jared again, when a sharp knock on the door startled her.

"Promise I'm not coming in, Angel Face. Just thought this t-shirt would be more comfy than those sweats Solly dressed you in."

Hailey looked at the door to see Jared drop a t-shirt on the floor. Admitting that the five sizes too large sweatshirt and pants she was wearing would be less than comfortable pajamas she reached for the colorful Harley Davidson t-shirt. She smiled when she read the warning slogan on the front: *Ever been shot from a moving motorcycle? Keep riding my ass!*

Her laughter stuck in her throat when she saw that Jared's t-shirt hit her mid-thigh, revealing a good bit of bare skin. It was one of the challenges of her long legs and what she was sure Jared would derisively label her 'Barbie bod.' Hailey sniffed. She was aware that the embattled Mattel Co. was trying to reengineer what the politically correct mavens called Barbie's *unrealistic* image and were creating more "normal" varieties of girl-shaped dolls. For better or worse, Hailey was stuck with the long legged, big busted original Barbie shape. It was a figure that had brought her no end of male attention since her body chose to add some distinctive 'swells' to her gangly pre-teen figure. She looked back on her pre-adolescent years with a regretful sigh. Life definitely had been simpler when she had a stick-like figure and her nickname was Icha-bod.

Remembering the appreciative way that Agent Justice had been openly assessing her, Hailey admitted that big boobs had their benefits. At least she got noticed. The problem was that most of the men she met assumed that her breasts, and maybe her ass, were the only things she had going for her. The thought that she might have a brain in addition to her dick magnet body never seemed to occur to the men slobbering over her. Not that Agent Justice slobbered. He was much too knowledgeable about the effect his righteous body had on women to sink to slobbering. Rather, he leered knowingly; assuming any woman was his for the taking--if he chose to imbibe.

Preparing to hobble out to meet him, Hailey reassured herself. It wasn't as though she hadn't met men who were almost as compelling as the bad boy waiting for her on the other side of the door. And it wasn't as though she didn't know how to handle horny men, either. She'd had years of practice saying no to the hordes who'd come on to her. Unfortunately she didn't know if she would know how to say no when her aroused body was screaming yes!

Jared laughed when the little rookie came hopping out of the bathroom. With her pony-tail in arrears and the flush on her face, she looked like a ten-year old Pippi Longstocking rather than Anna Kournikova's twin sister. Ignoring her protesting squeal, he scooped her up in his arms and headed toward the bed. Any thoughts of a rosy-cheeked little kid vanished when he held her voluptuous body against him. It didn't help that when he laid her on the bed his hand skimmed her bare butt. He choked back a groan, barely. When she tried to free herself from his grip, he shook his head. Sitting beside her, he firmly clasped her hip and said gruffly, "Uh uh, Valley Girl. I've got you now."

At her wide-eyed cry, he blew out a harsh sigh. "The question is now that I have you, what the hell do I do with you?"

Not waiting for her to answer, Jared carefully put a pillow under her ankle, then crawled alongside her. He tried unsuccessfully to ignore the heady fragrance emanating from her sumptuous body. It was an intoxicating mix of spice and musk, the latter betraying that the shapely rookie was as excited as he was. Given that she was essentially naked and his cock was about to break through his pants, Jared concluded that subtlety was neither necessary nor possible. Reaching to clasp Hailey's bare thigh in one hand, he tipped up her chin with the other. Her eyes were shining with a mix of anxiety and desire. He knew that the next few seconds would determine if he took this gorgeous creature the way that his rock hard cock was begging him to or if he'd actually behave himself. The fact that his big brother was one floor below and no doubt counting the seconds until he returned didn't discourage his randy dick, but was a potent deterrent nevertheless.

Jared huffed a hard sigh and pulled back, leaving scant inches of breathing room between them. Holding Hailey's chin he gazed into the molten cobalt pools of her astonishing eyes and shook his head.

"Look, Valley Girl, there's no use pretending that you aren't as hot for me as I am for you." When she frowned and tried to push him away he tightened his grip on her leg, eliciting a soft moan that hardened his dick to nail-pounding status.

"Admit it, rookie. You are as turned on by me as I am by you. That little moan was a giveaway, as if I fucking needed one." He chuckled when the bright pink splotches on her cheeks flamed a deep scarlet. "Oh yeah, Angel Face, I know when a woman is hot for me. And in the event you don't think what's between us is mutual, you might want to see the evidence." He placed her hand on his hard erection and grinned, "Or at least *feel* it."

Pressing Hailey's hand against his throbbing staff, Jared barked a harsh laugh at her surprised gasp. Christ, she should be impressed. He sure as hell was! Knowing he was making a mistake, Jared admitted he couldn't leave her without tasting her enticing lips. He held her chin tighter. Promising himself that a taste was all he would take, he bent down to kiss her. At the touch of her lips on his, the sparks of electricity that shot through his groin confirmed the enormity of his misjudgment. It was clear that tasting Hailey's moist mouth would never be enough. Before he could stop himself, he roughly pressed against her lips forcing them open. In seconds, he was devouring her mouth. He actually might have been able to stop but Hailey stunned him by kissing him back. To his surprise, she wove her eager fingers in his hair and tugged on the roots, sending a riot of sensations to his already burgeoning cock. When Hailey cried out, a deep passionate sound, and frantically began tangling with his tongue, Jared knew they'd crossed the Rubicon.

Later Jared would marvel that he'd been the one to pull back. But before he did, and knowing that he was minutes away from flat out taking her, he allowed himself a few seconds of blissful exploration. Groaning, he ran his greedy hands across her taut stomach and reached for her full breasts. Cupping them, he groaned in delight at their lush softness. It didn't take her sobbing shriek to know that her nipples were hard aroused nubbins begging to be sucked. And God, was he willing to suck them! Instead he somehow pulled back, unwinding her fingers from his hair, fighting against his need to attack her breasts, suckle them, and when he'd brought her to a screaming orgasm, move on to her weeping pussy.

Standing next to the bed, Jared shook his head and expelled a deep sigh, shoving his hands into his jeans' pocket. He held her gaze with a fierce glare.

"We're not done with this, Valley Girl. Not by a long shot, little rookie. You deserve to experience a guy who wears boots--not tasseled loafers or worse flip flops. A guy who knows how to make love to a woman, not a Barbie doll. Soon, little rookie, you and I are going to tangle. And, Honey, when we do, I'm going to take you places you and your beach bum buddies never knew existed."

Jared stared at her for a long moment knowing that he was the cause of the confused dismay streaking her beautiful face. He sucked in a deep breath and said. "Best you know, Angel Face. As the youngest of four arrogant brothers I learned from the best. I've made a life-long habit of getting what I want." He added with a gruff snort, "And, Sugar. I want *you."*

He reached down, and gently pinched Hailey's cheek, then headed for the door.

Chapter 7

The warm sunshine streaking through the latched windows above her bed nudged Hailey from a deep slumber. For a minute, she struggled to remember where she was. The jolt of pain she felt when she moved her ankle made last night's unbelievable events brain shatteringly real. Gingerly lifting her foot she acknowledged that her sprained ankle was the least of her worries. Struggling to drag herself up to a sitting position, Hailey glanced around the room then slammed her eyes shut as if she could reorder the overwhelming sight. But it was not to be. There was simply no way she could change her location *or* her predicament.

She groaned remembering the damning sequence of events. It was bad enough that she'd compromised her very first op with Lt. Justice by getting injured and outing his undercover sibling. Her carelessness had forced her boss to sequester her overnight in the Justice's family home--where to her horror, she'd slept in the bed of her commander's brother. It didn't take the blanket rasping across her sensitive nipples or the tell-tale scent of arousal suffusing the tangled sheets to remember the man who'd laid her in this amazing bed and then crawled in beside her. When he'd kissed her in a way that she had never been kissed, he did what she never could have done: He stopped.

Remembering Jared standing beside the bed, naked lust gleaming in his emerald hard eyes, Hailey was shocked at the surge of electricity that sparked through her groin. Dear God, the least she should be was embarrassed. But, knowing she'd have the rest of her life to regret what she'd done, for a stolen moment Hailey gloried in the memory of the sexiest man she'd ever known coolly telling her that he always got what he wanted. *And* that he wanted *her*.

Glancing at her phone, Hailey saw to her dismay that it was after nine o'clock. Hoisting herself to her feet, relieved that she could put weight on her injured ankle, Hailey hobbled into the bathroom. A quick glance in the mirror confirmed that she looked as disheveled as she felt. Gazing longingly at the mammoth designer shower Hailey admonished herself. No matter how much she needed it, a shower was not on the agenda this morning. No, her mission was to get as far away as fast as she could from this overwhelming house. Her narrow hope was she could avoid meeting anyone as she fled.

On the bathroom counter, Hailey saw the clothes she'd worn in last night's torrential rainstorm. Her uniform had been cleaned and pressed. Even her underwear was folded neatly on top. Next to her clothes, Hailey was surprised to see designer jeans and a classy vintage t-shirt that seemed to be precisely her size. For a moment she wondered how the hell Jared could know her sizes, then shrugged. Of course, he would. Why not? She was hardly the first woman who'd sneaked out of his bedroom in the morning who needed fresh clothes. She snorted in disgust. Undoubtedly her arrogant caretaker had a closet full of women's clothing in various sizes.

Knowing that she had to get to her apartment, and not wanting anyone to recognize her as a cop, Hailey yanked on the jeans and t-shirt. Taking advantage of the toiletries on the vanity, she brushed her teeth, washed her face, and worked her tangled blonde hair into a respectable ponytail. Shoving her swollen ankle into her regulation work boots wasn't gonna happen. Instead she carried her boots and uniform and headed to the doorway in her stocking feet, praying that she could find a back exit somewhere in the daunting mansion.

A deep voice from the bottom of the stairwell shot her prayer to hell.

"Well, well, I wondered when Sleeping Beauty was going to wake up."

Hailey looked down the stairs to see a tall, white-haired man peering up at her. His pressed trousers, tailored shirt and vest revealed his ramrod frame, confirming that the elderly man had maintained his military bearing. Introductions weren't necessary. Clearly the ruggedly handsome, green-eyed man was Jared's grandfather, James Justice, the patriarch of the Justice family. From the abbreviated history she knew of the Justice family tragedy, the octogenarian eyeing her with a frown was the man who'd raised his grandsons after his son and daughter-in-law died in a tragic boating accident. Swallowing hard, Hailey prepared to tell the imposing man who she was and why the hell she was creeping down his stairs when he continued.

"Hmm, you must be Officer Michels. I understand you were hurt in the mission last evening. I'm glad to see that you can walk." He added unnecessarily. "I'm James Justice. You may call me Judge. Everyone else does."

Before she could protest, the big man took her uniform and boots in one big hand and offered his other to her. Helping her down the last steps, he studied her thoughtfully then shot her an appreciative smile.

"Hmm, I can see now why that arrogant grandson of mine left a list of orders this morning for Margarite and Gregory. Not only were they to clean and press your uniform, but to provide an alternative outfit as well." Sweeping his approving gaze over her, he nodded. "Apparently our overworked staff followed his orders explicitly."

Hailey tried to hide her distress but couldn't keep from stammering. "I…I don't know what to say, Sir. I would have worn my uniform…I…I didn't ask him to--"

Judge Justice put up his hand, stopping her protest. "First, please call me Judge. I stopped allowing people to call me Sir when my ill-mannered grandsons started saluting every time they said it." He added, "One thing you should know, Officer Michels, when that incorrigible grandson of mine gives an order, we all jump. Especially, Gregory and Margarite, who have been caring for him for nearly thirty years. Moreover, they are so thrilled that he has returned they would crawl over glass on their hands and knees to do his bidding."

Mortified, Hailey glanced longingly at the front entrance, wishing that she could sprout wings and fly away. The astute man confirmed that he understood her beleaguered expression when he winked at her and smiled.

"Unlike the servants, I don't always follow Jared's orders. For example, I'm *not* going to encourage you to stay here through lunch, or even insist that you have breakfast. Instead, I've asked Gregory to bring the car around and take you to your apartment where I'm sure you will be more comfortable." He hesitated then added carefully, "I understand from Jared and Jake that you are aware of Jared's undercover status?" His expression hardened when she nodded in affirmation. His voice was soft, but the underlying threat was clear. "I trust you know how important it is that no one else knows this. We have planted the rumor that I have serious health issues which is the reason Jared has returned to our fair city."

Hailey was stunned that he thought for even a second that she might expose Jared. How stupid did they think she was? "I understand, Sir, I…I mean Mr. Justice. I promise you, I would never reveal Jared's undercover role." Realizing that he thought she couldn't be trusted, that she was just a blonde ditz, she added coolly, "I'm a police officer, Sir. And…and I would never do anything to hurt Jared."

Judge Justice eyed her narrowly as if considering, then nodded in agreement.

"Yes, Officer Michels, you are a police officer and according to Commander Justice, you are a damn good one."

As he walked her out to the town car in the driveway, the solemn man concluded, "Do know that in addition to Jared's list of commands, Lt. Justice, your boss, ordered you to take the day off and keep your ankle elevated. He indicated that one of his sergeants would be stopping by to see that you have everything you need, or want."

Hailey breathed a grateful sigh of relief when she was safely inside the luxurious town car. When she started to thank Judge Justice, he shook his head. "No need, Officer Michels. It was a pleasure to meet you. I hope I see more of you, and that your ankle heals quickly."

Judge reached into his vest pocket and took out an envelope. Handing it to her, he said, "I almost forgot. Among his litany of orders, Jared indicated that I should give this to you."

As he closed the door he smiled at her and nodded as if in agreement.

"Yes, Officer Michels, I do hope to see you—often."

Bolstered by his gentlemanly and seemingly sincere wish, Hailey waited until Gregory had maneuvered the impressive automobile onto the street before opening the envelope.

Willing her hands to stop shaking, she removed the single sheet. Neither the bold handwriting nor the crisp, authoritative warning surprised her.

"Just to confirm what I said last night, rookie. We're not through. No, Angel Face, you and I have barely begun. J."

****

Hailey put the bottle of white wine and three glasses on the coffee table and said apologetically to the stern woman sitting on her sofa, "Sorry, Mitzi. This is all the alcohol I have."

Remembering what she'd done the night before after she'd had her first glass of hard liquor, Hailey figured it was just as well that she only had white wine. At the memory Hailey felt her cheeks flame. Fortunately Sgt. Olson and her fellow officer, Tara Peterson, didn't seem to notice. They were too eager to hear about her last evening's escapade. Hailey went over the details one more time wondering what the two veteran cops would think if they knew what actually happened. Retelling the story that she and Lt. Justice had agreed to, she explained that she'd gotten lost in the rainstorm and that Sgt. Solberg and Lt. Justice had found her and brought her home.

After taking a big swig of the Sauvignon Blanc, Mitzi shook her head in disgust. "Jesus, girl. You need to get yourself some real booze. And while we're discussing the ridiculous, how the hell can anyone get lost in the rain?" The hefty woman snorted, "Nothing like acting like the blonde bimbo you look like."

Tara jumped to Hailey's defense.

"Jeepers, Mitzi. Can't you see how bad she feels? Look at her ankle?! You think she tried to get hurt? And just so you know, not all of us grew up in the woods like you and the Justice family. Some of us grew up in towns and cities where they have streetlights and don't depend on the moon to see at night."

Mitzi put up her hands and agreed. "My apologies, rookie. I forget how green you are. And I'm sorry you got hurt. That *is* one righteous sprain you have."

Emptying her glass in one large swallow, Sgt. Olson poured herself another full glass and turned to Hailey her eyes bright with excitement.

"But, girl, you are hardly the news around here. The big news, and I do mean *big* news is that Lt. Justice's brother, Jared, is back in town."

Tara eagerly picked up the tale. "You don't know him, Hailey, but Jared Justice, the youngest of the Justice Brothers, hasn't been back to town since he left the military."

Mitzi glowered. "You mean since he got *booted* out of the Army for God knows what outrageous things he did!" She added conspiratorially, "Which is why we shouldn't be surprised that now the Justice bad boy has up and declared himself to be a member of the Dragon's Curse. Can you fucking believe it? He's even sporting their ugly tats. Word is that he and his brothers aren't speaking." She shook her head and quaffed another hearty swallow of the wine. "He always was the badass of the bunch, but this is unbelievable. Looks and brains, but no character. It must break the Judge's heart, him being sick and all."

Tara nodded but couldn't hide her excitement. "You're right, Mitzi. Jared really *is* the black sheep of the family. But…."

Turning to Hailey, her bright eyes gleamed. "You know how gorgeous Commander Justice is, right, Hailey? Wait until you see his baby brother. I'm telling you, there isn't a woman who grew up in this town who isn't spilling her juices knowing that Jared Justice is back. If anything the tats will make him even more dangerously handsome." At Mitzi's outraged shout, Tara flushed then tossed her head and giggled. "C'mon, Mitzi, admit it. The women he's screwed can hardly wait to be done again and the few who haven't are lining up like at Disneyworld."

Hailey swallowed hard and filled her wine glass to the brim. She decided that as soon as her friends left, she was heading to the liquor store. It was time that she invested in some real alcohol--the kind that could get her drunk enough to forget what a fool she was.

Chapter 8

Jared yanked a chair from the table and parked himself next to Janko. Ignoring Brittany, the tatted Goth babe who'd fought her friend for the chair on the other side of him, he nodded to the wide-eyed waitress.

"A bottle of Jamesons, sweetheart. Glancing around the table at the glowering DC members and their hangers on, Jared qualified. "On second thought, honey, make that two bottles. My friends and I are celebrating."

Janko grunted in agreement. "Yeah, man. It's about time you showed your ugly mug." He snorted a harsh laugh. "Fuck, Jared, you'd think Jesus fucking Christ had climbed down from the cross." He surveyed the room and snorted. "Look at 'em. There isn't a cock sucking motherfucker in the room who isn't pretending they don't see one of the righteous Justice Brothers sittin' at the DC table. Fuckin' A. Makes me right proud to be with such a celebrity."

Jared laughed. "C'mon, Janko. You always were a celebrity. Of sorts. The bad sort, that is. Hell, there wasn't a father in this town who didn't lock up his virgin daughters when you sauntered in."

Janko ripped the cap off the bottle the frightened server carefully placed in front of him, and grinned at Jared as he handed him a full glass of the odiferous liquid.

"C'mon, bro. Admit it. After you turned fifteen there wasn't a virgin left in this town worth fucking. Hell, if I remember right, even the nuns at St. Mary's kept a light on for the youngest Justice Brother. It was only when I got as big balls as you had that I gave you a run for your money." Wrapping a big arm around Jared's shoulder, he said, "But seriously, Bro, I'm glad you're here." Janko's expression darkened and he lowered his voice. "We have some shit-kicking business to discuss."

Jared glanced at the men who were studying him then turned back to their leader and said quietly, "That we do, Janko. That we do."

One hour and three bottles of Jamesons later, Jared allowed himself to look over at the table where Hailey was sitting with a group of women. He'd seen her the minute he'd walked into the packed bar. Make that, he'd *felt* her. Hell, like a fucking animal in heat he could swear he'd actually smelled her. His cock had reacted to the presence of the gorgeous woman as though it was heat-seeking missile securing its target. He looked up, noting that Janko saw him looking at Hailey. Jared pointed his chin in her direction and shrugged.

"I admit, Janko, that I know most of the babes in this rowdy place." He added with a smirk, "Like you, Bro, I know more than a few of them in the biblical sense."

He joined in the raucous laughter, then nodded to Hailey shaking his head.

"But I sure as hell don't remember that *particular* piece of ass. Who is she? And which centerfold did she star in?"

Janko guffawed. "Yeah, man, given her 'assets' she coulda been in all of them. Don't want to shock you buddy, but that *particular* piece of ass as you rightly called her is a member of the Duluth PD."

Jared frowned. "What? You mean she works for the City--"

Janko interrupted him with a snort. "No, Dude. Believe it or not that babe with the righteous rack works for your fucking brother. She's a pig, Jared."

Jared reared up in mock surprise and whistled. "Well, I'll be goddamned. Leave it to Jake, the politically correct asshole, to hire Miss Sweden to fill out his ranks." He shook his head and frowned. "I wonder if he's doing her. I'll admit that's not his M.O. But holy Christ, if anyone could tempt him to break his 'nobody fucks with the help' rule it would be that sweet young thing."

"Tell me something we don't all know." Including the other men at the table in his threatening glare, Janko grunted, "I got a few rules of my own. I've warned my guys that they'll be chomping on their peckers for breakfast if they ever dare to fuck a cop, even one with tits like that one has." Janko sniffed in disbelief. "Believe it or not, the word around town from

179

the assholes who went after her, and anyone with a dick and two eyes has tried, she's as innocent as she is hot."

He leaned in and spoke softly for Jared's ears only. "I dunno, Bro, after we consummate our deal how 'bout we celebrate with a little 'barely touched' meat? Hell, we could do her together like we used to do the St. Mary's cunts. Dammit Jared, remember those little plaid skirts and the white cotton panties they wore under them?" Staring at Hailey, Janko shook his head thoughtfully then smacked his lips and grinned.

"Yeah, Bro, after we fuck over your self-righteous brother, let's you and me celebrate with a sweet piece of police pussy."

Swallowing the bile threatening to choke him, Jared congratulated himself for his restraint. Instead of knocking Janko's teeth down his throat, Jared drained his glass and poured himself another Jamesons. Smiling at his one-time friend, he spoke evenly, "That sounds like an interesting plan, Janko. Only with a woman that sweet, I may not want to share."

Janko barked a harsh laugh and raised his glass. "Tell you what, you arrogant bastard. How about we flip a coin—to see who gets her *first*."

Jared rose to his feet and grinned at Janko. "Before we start letting a woman come between us, Dude, I think I better see if she's as hot up close as she is from across the room."

Like everyone else in the room, Hailey kept her head down pretending to ignore the ominous group at the table in the corner. She'd been shocked when Jared strolled in with the leather-clad members of the D.C. The hush that settled over the noisy bar at their entrance spoke volumes. If danger came in pairs, the five members of the DC gang with Jared bringing up the rear signaled that Armageddon had arrived.

Hailey jumped when Tara jabbed her in the side and said in an excited stage whisper, "Don't look up, but *he's* coming this way. OMG, I don't *believe* it, Jared Justice is coming to *our* table!"

Keeping her head down, refusing to meet his gaze, Hailey focused on her drink.

Mitzi growled. "For God's sake, Tara, act your age. Just because you were hot for him when you were fifteen years old…" Mitzi's disparaging warning died when a deep voice rumbled.

"Good evening, Ladies. Don't tell me that your overbearing commander allows his harem to frequent the bars? Doesn't he know that dangerous men are likely to accost them?"

"Beat it, Jared. My friends and I are enjoying each other's company. We get enough testosterone on the job. Besides, don't you and your gangbanger buddies have some heroin or crystal to hawk?"

Jared laughed a deep, sultry sound that sent a shower of sensation sparking across Hailey's overwrought nerves.

"Now, now, Mitzi, is that any way to greet an old friend? Hell, woman, don't tell me wild, wicked Mitzi Olson has changed her stripes. C'mon girl, you're not too old to remember the nights we spent at Finnegan's Field--"

Before he could finish his sentence, Mitzi growled. "I'm serious, Jared. Get lost. My fellow officers and I spend enough work time with pond scum to deal with the likes of you on our nights off."

"Hmm. That may be true of you, Officer Olson, and potentially, the lovely Tara, but the *least* you can do is introduce me to the Barbie Doll. What's Miss Sweden doing hanging out with cops? She need protection from all the badasses tripping over their tongues to get close to her?"

Knowing that her face was flaming, Hailey stared at her drink and refused to acknowledge him.

Mitzi answered for her. "For your information, hotshot, Officer Michels is a *cop* and happens to work for your brother. You remember him, one of the Justice Brothers who is a credit to his family and community, not a blight on the family name?"

A shrill voice prevented Jared from answering.

"Hallelujah, girls! You're right! It *is* Jared Justice. Damn, big guy, where've you been keeping that sexy ass of yours? I'm telling you half of the women in this town have forgotten what it's like not to have to fake a climax. Thank God, the prodigal son has returned!"

Hailey looked up to see Chloe Reynolds and two other women who topped the vice squad's list of known prostitutes crowding around Jared. To her surprise three women wearing DC tats on their virtually naked bodies, left their gang table and stomped over to join the crowd of lusty women surrounding Jared. Hailey stood it as long as she could watching the women make fools of themselves fighting to be the next one to dance with the grinning Lothario who was clearly the "Chris Brown" figure of this northern woods capital. When Brittany, one of the Goth girls, smacked Chloe across the face, starting what looked like it would become a brawl, Hailey'd had enough.

Ignoring the raucous laughter from the envious men watching the superstar in the middle of the circle of drunken women all fighting for his attention, Hailey shoved back her chair and battled her way through the crowd to the exit. Stumbling down the alleyway, she bent over to catch her breath and block the ugly sight of the women pawing Jared. Fighting back hot angry tears, she admonished herself for being such an idiot. How could she have thought that Jared was interested in her?

His sultry query startled her. "Where you going, Valley Girl? Scene too hot for your beach bunny bod?"

In seconds he was beside her, a dark, dangerous wall of muscle. He grabbed her arm and pulled her toward him. Pressing her against the wall, he growled in her ear, a low, lusty sound. "That's too bad, Sugar, because it is about to get a hell of a lot hotter."

At her mangled cry, Jared grabbed her hands in one of his and dragged them up above her head. He drove his strong thigh between her legs, pinning her against the wall. Hailey struggled against him, fighting both Jared and the fiery heat now flooding her body. With his free hand he lifted her chin forcing her to look at him. His jaw was rigid, his emerald eyes blazing with lust.

"Damn, woman, I haven't been able to think of anything but you for the last week. Especially that hot mouth of yours and how I'm going to take it *and* take you." He pressed her harder against the wall and huffed a raspy command. "Open to me, rookie, the way you did that crazy night. You didn't want to stop then did you, baby? *Did you?*"

At her soft breathy moan, Jared couldn't squelch his groan.

"Oh *yeah*, baby. That's the way. Climb up on my thigh. Ride me, rookie, ride me hard! Christ, yeah, darlin', like that!"

Hailey cried out a shaken plea tormented with desire. "Oh God, Jared. I...I...can't..."

Running his hand over her chest, he crooned, "You can't what, rookie? You can't keep your heart from pounding? Can't keep your nipples from hardening, begging me to suck them?" At her whimpering cry, he slipped his hand between her legs and groaned a deep male sound. "Can't keep those sweet juices from soaking my fingers?"

He grabbed her ass in his big hands and jerked her against his rock hard erection. He pressed his lips against hers and murmured, "Tell you what, Angel Face. How about you don't say another word? Just let your hot sexy body speak for you. The way mine is speaking for me."

Jared rubbed his hand across her chest reaching unerringly for her throbbing nipple. Just when Hailey was sure that she would faint if he didn't release her aching breast, a taunting voice reverberated across the alley.

"Hey, Bro, ain't you jumping the gun a little, Buddy? Thought we were saving *her* for later. You know, for some of that...mmmm...two-on-one action we both like?"

At the ugly question, Hailey lurched around to see Janko and three of his forbidding men approaching.

Jared jerked Hailey up against himself, sheltering her with his strong body. His harsh laugh sliced across the ominous silence.

"C'mon, Dude. You know I never did follow the rules."

Jared looked down at her with a grin but Hailey didn't miss the iron in his eyes or his tight, protective grip. She felt rather than saw him punch his phone. His voice was lazy, but riddled with an undercurrent of danger.

"But I gotta admit she doesn't seem all that willing."

Janko snorted as he and his men slinked closer, surrounding them in a menacing circle. "Since when was *that* a problem for *any* of us, *Bro?* The only question now is whether my boys get to flip a coin for their place in the circle jerk."

Just then the squealing tires and flashing lights of a trio of squads pulled alongside the gangbangers, stopping their foreboding advance. Hailey breathed a sigh of relief when Lt. Justice leaped out of one of the cop cars.

He ambled toward her, one hand resting on his hip inches away from his holstered Glock. His voice was laced with irony. "I know you're off duty, Officer Michels, but how about I give you a ride home? I wouldn't want you to tempt these fine upstanding citizens. We'd hate to have to detain them for loitering in alleyways."

Chapter 9

"Jesus Christ, Jared, are you insane? What the hell were you doing, Dude? Christ, you *both* coulda been killed. Thank God, we were tailing you and I got your alarm."

Jake's voice was harsh with anger. Jared didn't need to see him to know that his brother was furious. He'd waited until he got to his rented apartment before he flipped on his phone. He held the phone away from his ear, allowing his brother to rail at a distance. Sucking in a deep breath, he shook his head then spoke into the phone.

"I don't know, man, maybe I *am* insane." Jared snorted a hard sigh. "I have to admit it, Jake. I've got it bad for the little rookie. Christ, man, you know me. I never fall for a woman, not like this. But since last week, I can't stop thinking about her. Somehow I've managed to stay away, kept from going after her, but seeing her sitting there tonight all flushed and upset while those horny babes were assaulting me--"

"Yeah, Dude, I heard about the stampede in the *Shipwreck*. I can just imagine how hard it was to tear yourself away from the throng of hungry women after your ass. But did you have to go out in the alley and jump one of my officers!?"

"Like I said, Jake, I can't explain it. Fuck, man, I can't remember when if *ever* a woman has gotten to me the way that the rookie has." He blew out a hard breath. "But before you crawl any further up my ass, I do have news, big news. The exchange is set for tomorrow night at an as yet undisclosed location."

Jared was quiet for a moment as he considered the enormity of what they were about to do. He couldn't hide his excitement when he added, "I gotta tell you, Jake, if we pull this off it will be one for the history books. Janko is wetting his jeans he's so charged. Convinced he's about to become the BOC's go to guy in Northern Minnesota and will soon rule the entire St. Lawrence Seaway. If he wasn't such a disreputable prick, I might feel bad for the way he's going down."

"Don't waste a second of pity on that asshole, Jared. He's been bad from birth and we've got him at the scene of at least a hundred drug deals, and not a few murders. But he's smart as hell and slippery as a goddamned eel. Now that he's into that 'white might' shit he's even more dangerous. We haven't been able to get enough evidence but it's a 99% certainty that the rash of fires on the rez is the work of his moronic racist followers. Given the shit he's been shilling, the bodies we can pin directly on him, and his asshole followers, Janko's earned his inner circle of hell."

"You're right, Bro. From the time Janko set cats on fire for fun and beat up homeless drunks to add excitement to a boring Saturday night, he's been bad to the bone. Even as a snotty teenager I knew that and was secretly relieved when you and Jude yanked me back. Plus, if Janko gets the full force backing of the BOC like he's damn close to getting, he'll become more powerful, more dangerous than his wildest dreams *and* our worst nightmares. But that's not going to happen, Bro. We're gonna take him down in the slickest way possible."

Jake's low whistle over the ether was admiring. "You're sure as hell right about that, baby brother! Those international compadres of yours have changed the way an op goes down. In the old days—a year or so ago, we would have been exchanging suitcases of marked bills and bags of crystal. Now we're doing it over the internet? Amazing!"

"Yeah Jake, if all goes as planned, when I give the signal and my 'client' in Thailand confirms that he's received the crystal, I'll hit the code on my IPhone and $30 million will race over the internet to the BOC's numbered account. Neat, clean, very high tech. Only the money that electronically goes into their account is marked just like the counterfeit bills in the old days. But the crystal our Thailand guys receive will be as real and valuable as ever. As will the BOC team who hands them the dope and then shuffles off to prison."

"Beautiful, buddy. Soon as you know where you and the gang are meeting, contact me. I need to get all of our men in place. The best part of this whole operation will be seeing those assholes' faces when they get taken down by the local boys."

"I agree, Jake. Those motherfuckers need to know that as always, *Justice* rules our fair forests. As for the exact location, I'll send you the coordinates as soon as I get them. Just know it will be somewhere with access to an international financial exchange." He added with a laugh, "Which in this crazy new world of ours is as close as the phone in my hand."

"Sweet, man. Almost unbelievable for a backwoods cop like me. But you gotta know, Jared, the only part of this gig that makes me nervous is that at least in the beginning you'll be alone with Janko and his animals."

"Yeah, but you'll be there in the shadows, Jake, rushing in to 'save' me. Like you always have, big brother. I can see it all now: Just as our DEA team sweeps in and captures the BOC guys in Thailand, the Duluth PD--led by their indomitable Commander Jake Justice--will saunter in and take down the Dragon's Curse. Like a flock of mallards a half hour before sunrise on opening day of duck hunting season, the sorry bastards won't know what hit them!"

***

Jared was confirming the final details of the exchange with his team in Thailand when there was a knock on his door.

"I have to sign off. Someone's at my door. But, everything is copacetic, correct, Agent Thomas?"

Jared's point man in Thailand responded in his usual outrageous manner.

"Absofuckinglutely, Big Guy. We're in the back of the sluttiest titty bar you've ever seen. Our UC confirms that the BOC marks are half a block away. They'll deliver the stash to us when they confirm that the money has been sent. Now if I can just keep these randy guys of mine sober, with their hands off the bar girls and their dicks in their pants for the next four hours, we'll be ready to rumble."

Jared laughed. "Are the rest of you as ready as your scandalous commander is?"

At the chorus of "Copy that, Agent Justice" from the members of the Thai-based team, Jared said, "Thanks, men. I'll check back at 2300 hours for a final sit rep."

At the second sharp knock, Jared closed his phone and walked to the door. To his surprise, he saw Janko and five of his goons standing on the balcony. Striving for nonchalance, he stepped back and frowned at Janko.

"What the hell, man. What's up?"

Shoving past Jared, Janko and his glowering men entered. Turning to Jared with a sly grin, Janko said, "Not much, Bro. It's just that me and my boys decided we couldn't wait to get this rodeo started. We want to do it *now*."

Jared managed to mask his surprise.

"What's that supposed to mean?" He added threateningly, "Don't tell me your BOC pricks are pulling back?"

Janko shook his head. "No way. They're in place and ready to hand over the crystal when I give the word. But I wanna move up the timeline." His frown tightened. "We're gonna do the exchange now."

Jared started. "Now? What the hell, Janko?! I arranged for the exchange at midnight our time."

"Change it."

Seeing Janko's fierce expression and wondering what the hell was going on, although the snakes crawling up the back of his neck confirmed that he was in deep shit, Jared said carefully, "I don't know that we can, buddy."

Janko sneered. "What? You saying that you, a *Justice Brother*, can't make somethin' happen? Fuck it, man. You know goddamned well that in 'Justice land' the sun doesn't rise or set without permission from one of the golden boys."

Jared glared at him, assuming an aggrieved tone. "What's going on, Janko? Has something happened on your end? Christ, man, we're four hours away from closing the biggest deal of a lifetime. This isn't the time to start fucking around. My buyer doesn't tolerate 'problems.'"

Janko shook his head. "Relax, Jared. It's just that, like you, I prefer to be in control. You know I trust you. Or as much as I can trust a Justice Brother. Humor me, Dude. I wanna be sure you don't have nothin' up your sleeve." He nodded at the surly men surrounding them. "As do my boys." He added with a foreboding smirk, "C'mon, Jared, how about you pull strings the way you always do? We've alerted our team in Thailand that the timing has changed. I told them to meet your boys in ten minutes and deliver the stash. I also assured them that the money will be there when they arrive. As you've said, all you need before you wire the money is confirmation that your men have the drugs."

He pinned Jared with a hard glare.

"So whadda you say, Buddy? How 'bout we saddle up and get this rodeo started?"

Holding Janko's gaze with a frown of his own, Jared took out his phone but before he could open it Janko snatched it out of his hand.

"Uh uh, Jared. If you don't mind, I'll place the call."

Jared shrugged. "You really are a paranoid son-of-a-bitch, Janko. Go for it, asshole. Put the damn thing on speaker and hit redial. I just hung up from my head guy in Bangkok."

Jared breathed a sigh of relief when Agent Thomas merely responded, "Yes?"

"Mr. Thomas, the schedule has changed. The exchange will take place at the designated location in ten minutes. Initiate Scorpio now."

Jared decided he might survive after all when Agent Thomas simply answered, "Yes, Sir," and hung up.

"You better not be fucking me, Jared." Janko frowned betraying his distrust. "What does Scorpio mean?"

Jared snorted, "First off, *you* better not be fucking *me*, old pal. Second, it means that when I type in the code and hit send, $30 million dollars will scamper across the internet into your BOC buddies' offshore account."

Janko glared at him. "Alright. Then how about you hit that button?"

Retrieving his phone from Janko, Jared punched in the code and shrugged.

"Consider it sent!"

Chapter 10

Preparing to meet Mitzi and Tara at the *Shipwreck*, Hailey studied herself in the mirror. She was surprised that she looked like she always did. Except that she seemed to have developed a permanent flush on her usually pale cheeks and her eyes were darker, more mysterious. You'd think that she would look like the wrath of god considering what she'd been through. It was scary enough that a gang of hardened drug dealers had threatened to attack her. But even the vile lowlifes were nowhere near as intimidating to her body and spirit as Jared Justice. Remembering him pressing her against the wall describing all the things he intended to do to her and how she made him feel, fierce sensations rioted through her core, stealing her breath. The fiery sparks were a potent reminder of the man who'd invaded her mind and her body in ways she'd never known were possible. The memory alone made her cheeks flame brighter.

"You look different, girlfriend. What's going on with you, Goldilocks?" Mitzi sucked a noisy slurp of Guinness through her teeth and studied Hailey with a frown. "You worried that badass jackass Jared Justice and his ganger buddies will show up again?" She grunted. "I wouldn't be surprised if he did. Nuthin' like the banty rooster strutting through the barnyard to make sure his hot little hens are waiting for him."

Mitzi glanced at the corner table where five of the female DC gang members were sitting.

"Whadda you know? Looks like the DC hoes are on their own. Must have been abandoned by their big bad drug-dealing masters." She sneered at the table of women huddling together and added with a snort, "You better watch your back, Goldilocks. From the daggers those bitches are throwing your way, like everyone else in this town, you can bet that they know all about Jared Justice accosting you. Particularly that tatted up bitch Brittany Kramer, who Jared dropped on her ass when he chased after you last night."

Before Hailey could stammer out a response, Tara piled on, her eyes dancing with glee.

"Yeah, girlfriend. Why do you think Mitzi and I dragged you here tonight? Nothing like the hottest guy that's ever tramped through this boring town of ours hitting on one of *us*. Jeepers, Hailey, do you have any idea how jealous we are? Let's hear it, sister--*all* of the deets. No holding back!"

Hailey shuddered. She wasn't surprised that her teammates had heard the gossip. After all, she'd been with them when Jared and his gang entered the *Shipwreck* and they saw her race out of the bar. They had to have heard what had happened next—or at least a version of it. Every time she'd walked into a room at the precinct today, the whispered conversations stopped. She knew that Lt. Justice had read the riot act to the guys who'd been with him in the alley. Warned them that if they valued their family jewels they wouldn't discuss what they'd seen. But the news of Jared Justice hitting on a cop in a back alley while a bunch of DC members waited their turn was a secret too hot to keep.

Seeing the eager expressions on Mitzi's and Tara's faces, Hailey knew she'd have to say something. She took a deep breath and prepared to recite her well-rehearsed version when she saw another of the DC women rush in and join her friends. Their excited whispers and shocked expressions made it clear something was up. When all of the Goth girls jumped up and headed for the bathroom, Hailey was afraid their news might concern Jared. Excusing herself from her companions, she headed for the side door of the ladies room and ducked unseen into one of the stalls. The heated conversation she overheard confirmed that her instincts were on target.

"Listen up, bitches, I don't give a flying fuck what Janko will do if we crash the party."

Hailey recognized the angry voice. It was Brittany Kramer, the woman that according to Mitzi, Jared had "dropped on her ass" when he chased Hailey out of the bar.

Brittany's voice was contorted with anger laced with anticipation. "If you think for one minute I'm going to stay here and wait for Janko to show up, when he and the men are taking down that arrogant cocksucker Jared Justice, you're crazy. I just hope they don't finish beating him to death before we get there. I want to hear that conceited motherfucker scream." She confirmed gleefully, "I'm telling you, bitches, between Janko and Dinks, I don't know who is better at inflicting pain."

Hailey waited until she was sure the women had left then snuck out of the bathroom and dashed to the parking lot. Hiding in the shadows, Hailey watched the women pile into a white van with tinted windows. Darting between parked cars she got close enough to slap a patch onto the rear bumper of the van as it peeled out of the lot. Running to her trusty Corolla, Hailey jumped in and prepared to follow them.

***

Sgt. Solberg rushed into Jake's office, his ruddy face dangerously flushed. "Fucking Christ, Commander. Something's way wrong. Agent Thomas just called. Jared called for the exchange, told Agent Thomas to activate Scorpio NOW. Thomas said they had no choice."

At that moment Jake's personal line squawked. Agent Thomas's voice was taut, his message curt. "Jake, it's done. On Jared's order, we made the exchange. Our guys have the shipment and Jared just wired the funds."

Jake stepped back in shock. "Holy mother of God, what happened?"

"Not sure I know, Lieutenant, but for some reason your DC bad boys got antsy. Jared didn't have a choice. And neither did we. Someone or something put a bomb up Janko's ass to make him change the timing. My Bangkok team confirmed that the DEA has the drugs and have captured the BOC criminals. That's the good news. But I don't have to tell you that in a matter of minutes Janko and his DC guys will know that they've been had. I sure hope you have a bead on that brother of yours. This can't bode well for him."

His heart pounding, Jake turned to Solly. "Get hold of Jared. Find out what the hell happened *and* where the hell he is."

Solly's red face had paled considerably.

"I tried, Jake, while you were talking to Agent Thomas. Jared's phone is dead." He added, his voice tight with fear, "Which means that we don't have his GPS, Jake. Fuckin' Christ, how the hell are we going to find Jared?"

Before Jake could answer, Carrie Seagraves, his desk sergeant entered. Her worried expression confirmed she expected his grim response.

"Lieutenant, I'm sorry to interrupt but Officer Michels says it's urgent. She says she *has* to talk to you now."

Reaching in his weapons cabinet and yanking out a Glock 42 and a Salient Arms AR 15, Jake punched on his speaker.

"Officer Michels, I can't talk now."

Hailey's shrill response sent a wave of fear riveting up his spine.

"Commander, it…it's Jared. They have him."

"What the hell, Hailey?"

"Lt. Justice, I heard Brittany Kramer…and the others. They said Janko is going to kill Jared, beat him to death!'

"Jesus, Hailey, we know they have him. We just don't know *where*."

"I'm following the women, Jake. Brittany said she wanted to watch Janko kill him."

Jake exploded. "What the fuck, Hailey, how are you *following*--?"

She interrupted him. "I…I slapped a tag on their bumper. It's a white paneled van, tinted windows, no plates. They just pulled off HWY 2 on a dirt road. I'm right behind them. You've got my coordinates…. Hurry, Jake!"

Jake shouted to Solly, "Sound the alarm! I want every available man on the road, now!"

He spoke into the speaker, "We're on the way, Hailey. Great work. Thanks to you, I know they've got him at Finnegan's Field." He added hoarsely, "You stay put, you hear me? Stay where you are and wait for us."

187

"I can't, Jake. I...I don't think you can get here in time." Her voice rose shrilly, "They're going to kill him. I have to stop them!"

As he and his fellow officers charged out to the waiting squads, Jake roared, "Goddammit, Hailey. Stand down. That's an order, Officer Michels! Do. You. Copy?"

Her refusal was barely audible. "I can't, Commander Justice. I have to stop them."

***

It took every ounce of strength Jared had not to scream at the double sucker-punch, followed by another crushing blow to his ribs. Who would have thought that this homegrown bunch of sadists could out-torture the best of the Afghani freakos? At least Jared had managed to do serious injury to the gonads of more than a few of the Dragons when they hauled him out of the car. It helped that most of them were hopped up on crystal, but outnumbered twenty to one, he was fighting a losing battle. Now hanging from his bound wrists from the overarching limb of a large Maple, his arms blessedly numb from the strain, he could only hope that the unconsciousness gods would get their asses on site soon. He didn't want to imagine what Janko and his animals intended to do with the red hot pokers resting in the blazing bonfire lighting the dark field.

For a distorted moment he'd thought that the van he heard was Jake to the rescue. Jared knew that if anyone might intuit that Janko would head for Finnegan's Field, it was Jake. More times than Jared could count, Jake and Jude had tracked his inebriated teenaged gang to the FF. But the shrill laughter signified that it was Brittany and her slutty pals who'd come to revel in Jared's demise—not Jake and his officers.

With the arrival of the women, Janko stopped kicking Jared's ribs long enough to preen for the ecstatic spectators. Prancing back and forth like the drama whore he was, Janko crowed.

"All I can say is I shouldda known. Fuck me for the sentimental trusting asshole that I am. My men warned me. Did I listen? Hell no! I did something I never should have done. I trusted a Justice Brother. Fuck you, Jared."

Janko slammed his fist into Jared's gut. "Goddamn you to hell, you murderous, double-dealing traitor! After they saw the picture I sent of us high-fiving it, it wasn't three minutes before my BOC contact called to say that his boss knew you—met you at a high level DEA function no less. It took them less than six minutes more to confirm that the 'money' you sent was studded with tags."

Pacing across the field, Janko jerked out his phone, his voice thick with anger. "You need to hear this, Jared, hear what you've done."

A silky accented voice echoed across the warm night air.

"Unfortunately, Mr. Jankosky, you have cost the Balkan Organized Cartel $30 million of the finest heroin available today. Worse, you've led the DEA to our offshore accounts. Not to mention that six of our top men are headed for a high security prison." There was a dramatic pause then the soft voice concluded, "You may expect to hear from us, Mr. Jankosky. Soon."

Janko stopped pacing and strode to the raging fire. He yanked a leather glove out of his back pocket then reached down and extracted one of the glowing pokers from the fire. Moving slowly toward Jared, his eyes blazing with demonic hatred, Janko said, "Look around, Bro, while you can. I'm going to start with your eyes, and then stick this poker into every orifice you have, ending with your fucking traitorous mouth. I want to hear you scream as long and loud as possible. And then, Buddy, like I used to do with the neighbors' cats, I'm going to gut you with my trusty Bowie."

"Not with a 9mm slug in your brain, you're not."

The only thing that shocked Jared more than the unexpected threat was its origin. Horrified, he acknowledged that the apparition emerging from the dense forest was Hailey. A formidable Athena, but terribly alone, she stood tall, her arms stretched out in front of her, pointing her Glock at Janko's forehead. For a split second Jared reveled in her daring arrival; then seeing Dinks skulking up behind her, he screamed a tortured warning. But it was too late.

In seconds the massive brute had knocked Jared's avenger to the ground, her Glock skittering uselessly across the field.

Janko's surprised shout was triumphant. "Fuckin' A, I must be living right. Hell, to think all I intended to do, Buddy, was to blind you then burn you to death piece by piece. How much better that the last sight you'll see is the little cop cunt being gang raped."

Dropping the poker, he yelled at Dinks. "Bring the bitch here! Next to the fire. I want Jared to get a good look at her before we take her on." Surveying his men, he chortled with anticipation as the burly muscled man dragged Hailey by her hair across the rough field and threw her at Janko's feet.

Grabbing her by the arm, Janko yanked Hailey up before Jared. His expression was twisted with hate, his eyes gleaming blood red in the light of the fire.

"Whadda you know, Buddy? Looks like I'm going to get the cop cunt first after all." Janko roared a hideous laugh. "And we didn't even have to flip a coin. Fuck no. The only coins that'll be flipped are by my men to see in what order they get to fuck the blonde bitch. Hot damn! For once the gods of blood and pussy have abandoned a Justice Brother." At the seconding roar from his men, Janko crowed manically, "Who says the devil never wins?"

The excited shouts from the crowd of agitated men and women were shattered by a volley of gunfire.

"I do, for one."

Jake stepped forward, his heavily armed men rapidly closing in around the shocked DC circle. His voice was as calm as his glare was fierce.

"Drop your guns, assholes, or the next bullet will be in Janko's brain. *Or* don't drop 'em. Nothing would please me more than making good on Officer Michels' warning."

Epilogue

Hailey wished she could make herself invisible. At least long enough to sneak by the formidable group of men in the center of St Vincent's Emergency Room. Not just one Justice Brother, but both of Jared's brothers--plus the patriarch himself, Judge Justice--were holding forth in the crowded anteroom. Hailey thought with a groan that the Earp brothers and Doc Holiday striding through the OK Corral had nothing on the three impressive men filling the room with their powerful aura. As much as she wanted news of Jared, Hailey didn't dare invade the tight circle of concerned Justice men and the cordon of uniformed officers surrounding them.

In the melee at Finnegan's Field, Hailey had hovered on the side as four SWAT members freed Jared from his hideous bonds. The most Hailey could tell from her distance was that Jared was conscious. A team of medics had him strapped to a gurney and hustled into an ambulance within moments. The wailing siren sounded through the dark night as they raced away to the hospital. Lt. Justice was commanding the arrest of the cowering DC gang members when he saw Hailey standing forlornly to the side. He shouted to Sgt. Solberg to get Hailey to the emergency room and see that a doctor checked her for injuries. When she got the all clear from the chief resident, Hailey returned to the waiting room, startled to see the crowd that had gathered.

Intending to slip by them unnoticed, Hailey was horrified when a brusque voice called her name.

"*There* she is, our heroine. Officer Michels, don't think for a minute you're getting out of here without our thanks."

Looking up to see Judge Justice striding toward her, Hailey knew there was no escaping the crowd who'd all turned to stare at her.

"Ladies and Gentlemen, please show your appreciation to this courageous young woman who is responsible for my grandson being alive!"

A voice from the back of the cheering crowd called out, "Not only alive, your honor, but with all my body parts intact!"

The crowd turned as one to see a nurse pushing a grinning Jared down the hallway in a wheelchair. In the free-for-all that followed, Hailey joined the amazed crowd marveling that except for heavy duty bandages on one shoulder and a sling on the other, plus myriad bruises decorating his face and neck, Jared looked reasonably well. When he got to the center of the crowd he insisted that his oldest brother Jude help him from the wheelchair.

"C'mon, Brother, help me stand. I don't give a damn about rules that say a patient has to leave the hospital in a wheelchair. Hell, anyone who knows me knows there ain't a rule I haven't broken."

Leaning now against his grandfather whose face was damp with tears, Jared grinned at his brothers.

"Damn, men, did you ever think you'd be tracking me down to Finnegan's Field when I'm thirty years old? Wouldn't you think that Janko and I had left that shit behind at eighteen, not fuckin' thirty!!"

The crowd roared with delight as his brothers clasped Jared in a bear hug and whispered grateful thanks.

Jared surveyed the uniformed cadre of men and women crowding excitedly around him and shook his head in wonder.

"I gotta tell you, fellows, if I'd done something to get all of you coming after me when I was in my teens, I don't think even my Gramps coulda busted me out of that one." He paused for the laughter. "Okay, okay. But lemme tell you. I've never been happier than I was tonight to have my brother Jake and half the frickin' DPD on my ass."

When he spotted Hailey hanging back in the crowd, Jared's voice dropped and tears welled up in his eyes. Motioning her forward, he murmured "C'mere, you."

Hailey walked unsteadily toward him, knowing her face was firehouse red. When he pulled her up next to him she buried her face against his chest to hide her tears.

Stroking Hailey's back, Jared held her close and said with a groan, "But nothing will give me more nightmares and more lusty dreams than the sight of this woman striding out of the forest with her gun raised, threatening to put a bullet in Janko's pea brain."

Hailey's colleagues roared their approval and laughed when Jared added, "Damn, Valkyrie, the Avenger's blonde goddess, couldn't have made a better or more timely entrance. Especially since Janko was about to put out my eyes with a burning poker, and then move on to other critical body parts."

The groans and angry murmurs confirmed that the hardened police force knew they had been within minutes of seeing their hero die a hideously painful death.

Jake stepped forward and put a big arm around Jared and Hailey. His stern jaw and glittering eyes spoke to his banked anger.

"I don't have to tell any of you how close we came to losing Jared. The Judge is right. If Officer Michels hadn't realized something was up with the DC women--and tagged their van then followed them--there is no way we could have gotten there in time. When Hailey called and told me where they were and that she was right behind them, I gave her a direct order to stand down and wait for us to arrive. To my everlasting gratitude the 'little rookie' as Jared calls her, disobeyed my order and singlehandedly confronted a gang of twenty armed men."

Jake took a moment to deal with his obvious emotion, then added, his voice quavering, "Brave and smart and insubordinate, a real triple threat. Hailey's distraction saved my brother. But they...they both could have been killed...."

A heavy silence fell over the room, underscoring the emotional tsunami swamping the hushed crowd.

Jake turned to Hailey. Making an effort to lighten the tension, he said with a mock frown, "At some point, say a hundred years from now, Officer Michels, I will let you know what happens to rookies, or any officers of mine, who disobey a direct order from their commander."

Jared broke into the relieved laughter and challenged his brother.

"How about you let me handle punishing the little rookie, Jake? I plan to take her to our family cabin for a week...or so. As long as it takes me to teach her the error of her ways and show her how the Justice Brothers keep their women in line."

In the raucous hoots that followed his provocative assertion, Jared tipped up Hailey's chin and swiped at the tear on her cheek. Gazing into her eyes, his voice was gruff.

"And while we're at it, Bro, I think it's time that we find a different name for this outrageous *and* courageous young woman. 'Little Rookie' doesn't cut it. How about Jared's Avenger instead?"

#########

The Justice Brothers Series has everything you've come to expect from Taylor Lee. Memorable characters, high octane action, and Lee's special brand of sizzling hot romance. The four Justice Brothers are powerful men. They are as well known for heating up the sheets as they are for keeping the peace. Take a deep breath and prepare for some powerfully provocative reading.

Jared: Book 1: The Justice Brothers Series
Jude: Book 2: The Justice Brothers Series
Jake: Book 3: The Justice Brothers Series
Josh: Book 4: The Justice Brothers Series
The Judge: Finale: The Justice Brothers Series

USA Today Best Selling author Taylor Lee writes Suspenseful Mystery Thrillers – with a heavy dose of Sexy to Sizzling HOT Romance.

In the four years that she has been writing, Taylor has written more than thirty books. Her seven, soon to be eight, series track her Special Operatives, Covert Agents, Cops, Firefighters and other iconic heroes and heroines, through the harrowing situations that make up their lives. From human trafficking rings to corrupt politicians, Taylor investigates the underbelly of society and the criminals who flourish there.

Taylor says: "From the residue in my personal blender of mixed races, cultures and world views, my characters emerge. It comforts me to know that while evil slinks in the shadows, the "good guys and gals" of the world sniff it out – and snuff it out. My characters are arrogant alpha males and the feisty women who bring them to their knees – and vice versa… They fight hard, love hard and don't mince words. They are dangerous men and women in dangerous times. Love, passion and ridding the world of evil? What's not to like?

Contact Information
Taylor Lee loves to hear from readers!
Email: **taylorleewrites@gmail.com**
Twitter: **@taylorleewrites**
Facebook: **taylorleewrites**
Blog: **www.taylorleebooks.com**

Sign up for Taylor Lee's **Newsletter** to get all the scoop on Taylor Lee's SIZZLING ROMANTIC SUSPENSE at www.taylorleebooks.com.

Festival by the Sea

Traci Hall

Al Cooper's too bad to be a cop and too good to be a crook forcing old
friend Darcy Smith to see him in a new light.

*With an impressive bibliography in an array of genres, USA Today bestselling
author Traci Hall has garnered a notable fan base. She pens stories guaranteed to touch the
heart while transporting the reader to another time and place. Her belief in happily ever after
shines through, whether it's a romantic glimpse into history or a love affair for today.*

Chapter One

Darcy Smith leaned out over the rail on the pier, searching the pale turquoise water for loose nets or tickle sticks. Folks were practicing for mini-lobster season—everybody *and* their mothers wanted a fresh lobster dinner, times twelve, the local limit.

Bugfest was a three day festival that brought in revenue for the whole seaside town. The Dive Shop, which she owned with her brother, Dax, offered off-shore diving and lobster equipment rental, including snorkels and fins. For an extra twenty bucks, they cleaned the spiny underwater delicacies and stuck the tails in a cooler for the customer to enjoy at their leisure.

A deep bark preceded a long, wet tongue up her calf. Forcing a stern expression, Darcy turned around, one hand on her hip as she faced Al Cooper. The late afternoon sun created a shadow behind his broad, linebacker shoulders. He took off his sunglasses and stuck them in the pocket of his khaki cargo shorts.

"You're not supposed to have dogs on the pier." She reached down and scratched behind Buster's ears. The chocolate brown Pit Bull mix wagged his cropped tail and nuzzled her fingers. "Watch out for hooks in his paw."

Al had the audacity to wink. "Ah, sugar. It's okay. I know the owners." He kissed her cheek. "Buster just wanted to say hi."

"How'd *Buster* know I was here?" Darcy ambled toward a bench that gave a broad view of the open water along with a welcome breeze and sat, patting the space next to her in invitation. Typical of Al to pick and choose the rules he followed.

"Buster spotted your white braids." Al joined her, his hairy calf tickling hers. Summer in South Florida meant wearing as little as possible with lots of sunscreen. "They make you look like you're sixteen."

"I wish." Sixteen had been a simpler time. She'd wanted to marry Phillipe Cousteau Jr. and travel the ocean by submarine. "I can't believe I was ever that innocent." An older couple in designer beachwear walked in front of them, the woman's floral perfume battling the smell of bait fish and losing.

"You were sweet—sometimes." Al nudged her with his leg. His muscular thigh was twice the size of hers. "The baby of the family."

Darcy eyed his bulky frame, then gripped his bicep—her fingers couldn't go all the way around. "I can't imagine you as a baby. Your poor mother."

He rubbed his tanned, smooth-shaven head and grinned. "A ten-pounder. If Mom was alive, she'd tell you I was the reason she didn't have more kids. I was perfect. Why bother to do it again?"

"Ten pounds? The woman was a saint." Darcy shuddered as she pictured *that* coming out of her body. She folded her hands over her knee and scooted over for Buster to sit by her feet. "I'm sorry, about your mom."

His grin faded. "It's been five years. How are you doing?" He tugged on the tip of her braid. "Your dad was a good guy."

Darcy blinked back tears, smoothing a tuft of fur over Buster's collar. "I miss him, of course."

"Yeah." Al rested against the back of the bench and Buster dropped his muzzle on the wood plank between them, his black nose twitching.

Most of the fishermen were done for the day, but still, Darcy looked around to ensure they were alone before she said in a low voice, "I'm a little pissed off at Dad. For lying about how sick he was." It felt like a betrayal to say what she'd been thinking out loud. To Al. But he'd been a friend for so long, she knew he'd understand. "I would've come home sooner. Dax didn't have to do it all." And now being here again felt like squeezing into a t-shirt two sizes too small.

"Darcy, he wanted to tell you." Al leaned forward, his forearms on his knees.

She massaged her knee cap, her temper rising. "I know." It had been months but the rancid emotions wouldn't settle. It was easier to fixate on her anger rather than the train wreck she'd left behind in Melbourne. "I want to let it go, but I can't."

As if sensing the direction her thoughts had gone, Al asked, "How's school? Got that fancy degree done yet?"

"Yeah. I'm a marine biologist." The title was too wrapped up in painful memories. "Just need to finish my thesis for my master's degree." A pelican flew at eye level across the water, landing in the calm waves.

"What are you waiting for?"

She closed her eyes. That was the fifty-million dollar question. "I don't know what to write about."

"What happened to the internship?"

Al, an ex-cop, had the instincts of an FBI interrogator, which made him the perfect private investigator. "Nothing," she said smoothly. "I completed the assignment." *And should have gotten extra credit for all of the extracurricular activities.*

"Write about that."

Her professor would get fired if she did. No, she wanted nothing to do with Professor Petrovsky and his coral studies. "Not interested in the reefs anymore."

"Pick something else then."

"Don't bug me, Al." She lifted her face to catch the salty sea breeze.

"I'm a pain in the ass. Part of my charm." He scowled. "It'll come to you."

"I've been waiting for the lightbulb to go off, but so far, it's dark in here." She tapped the side of her head. She used to be smart, used to care, used to, used to. How could she be washed out at twenty-seven?

"A lot has happened in the last few months. Give yourself some time. It's okay to just *be*, Darce."

His words soothed her bristly mood. She was tired of hurting, of lashing out. "Sorry. Don't mean to be a bitch about it."

He put his hand on her leg, just above her knee. "You can vent. I'm always here for you."

Darcy squirmed as a surprising warmth spread up her thigh from his touch—the squeeze so gentle it was almost a caress. Al's hands were huge. Tanned, workman's hands with golden hair across his rough knuckles. He wasn't afraid to get dirty in an honest day's work. The complete opposite of her prissy professor. God, what had she been thinking?

"You've been massaging that muscle. Did you hurt yourself running? You shouldn't push with an injury."

"I'd go totally insane if I couldn't run." If she thought about it, she'd started running when her mom died fifteen years ago and hadn't stopped.

"I get it. I hit the gym after a tough case. Sweat therapy."

Al worked out, and his trim, solid body was the proof. How old was he, anyway? She thought of him as an older brother. A cousin, maybe. The way he'd made her stomach jump just now? Better be a step-cousin, twice-removed. "Are you working on a job?"

"Just finished one. I don't know why people bother getting married if they don't plan on being faithful." He looked out at the water, his jaw tight. The pelican had been joined by another so that now two bobbed in the aqua waves. "It goes with the vows."

"Agreed." She thought back to his girlfriends over the years. He and Dax always had dates when they wanted but nothing serious—neither of them were players. And now Dax loved Celia, owner of Ambrosia by the Sea. *Where do I fit in?*

"Are you dating?" She studied his sharp profile. Slim nose, dark coffee-colored brows. A full mouth with a dimple on the left when he bothered to use it.

"Too much work." Al averted his gaze and rubbed the back of his head.

"How so?" She rolled her eyes and snorted, the noise waking Buster from his doze. "And what else are you doing?"

"My P.I. business is full time."

"You work out of your condo when and if you want. Nice, by the way." She bumped her elbow into his arm. "How'd you get to be rich again?"

"I'm not rich." His cheeks flushed and he coughed into his fist. "You don't have to win the lottery if you know how to invest."

Darcy looked him in the eyes, noting that they were the greenish-blue-gray of the ocean. Sometimes less blue, sometimes more gray, they changed with his surroundings. Gruff Al, investing money. Probably a secret millionaire, driving a beat-up old Ford. "Will you show me?"

"Sure. But it'll cost you."

"Cost me what?" She crossed her arms and Buster growled, looking from her to Al and back.

"Weell..." He stopped. Seemed to consider his words before saying, "Lobster."

She laughed, sensing there was more. "Lucky for you, they're in season."

He took his sunglasses from his shorts pocket and slid them on against the glare of the sun. "What do you want out of life?"

Her skin prickled at the deep timber of his tone and she scooted away from him. "Whoa, how'd we get from trading dinner for stock tips to life questions?"

"It makes a difference in how you invest." Al faced her, his eyes now shielded behind shiny blue lenses. "Do you want to pay off school loans, or are you saving for retirement?"

"I got scholarships for school. No debt. When Dad died, we inherited a little money along with the shop. I don't know what I want to do with it." She wished she had her sunglasses to hide behind but they were back at the shop. Al seemed different today, more intense somehow. "Investing sounds safer than spending it on fast cars and loose women," she joked.

Al chuckled. "I knew you were smart. Loose women will get you, every time." He cleared his throat. "Actually, I *do* have a favor."

"I knew it!" Al was wound way too tight to just hang out for no reason. A massage and, well, *a girlfriend*, could help with that. She balanced her palms on the edge of the bench and leaned forward, her braids swinging down over her collarbone. "What do you *really* want?"

Al gestured toward the end of the pier where a giant plastic lobster statue was being erected as local businesses geared up for Bugfest. The square would have live music, crafts and food for three days straight. "My regular surveillance guy is on vacation."

Darcy kept her expression neutral. Surveillance? Like, spying on the neighbors?

"I asked Dax, but this is the worst time to leave the Dive Shop—as you know."

"We're busy, true." Dax had hired extra help, though, so things were under control. He managed everything perfectly, leaving Darcy uncertain as to where she fit. Since she lived in the studio above the shop, she was always around to work the register or answer the phone. *Was it enough?* He wanted to talk, but she couldn't. Not yet.

Al pulled her back into the present by settling his hand over her knee, which brought a stab of awareness. Skin on skin. "I've been hired to drive down to Cudjoe Key, check out some property." He lifted his hand.

She rubbed at the lingering tingle of his handprint but the warmth didn't go away. *What's the matter with me?*

"Dax reminded me that you spent a lot of time with the Girl Scouts around there."

"Islamorada," she clarified. Kayaking and camping. Ghost stories. "Over ten years ago."

"Point is, I could use another set of eyes." Al lifted his shades to the top of his head, his blue-gray orbs boring into hers and doing funny things to her body temperature. "My client wants to know why their choice property isn't selling. You might see some changes in the area that I wouldn't pick up on." His voice lowered. "I'll make it worth your time."

From anybody else, that might be a sexual innuendo. *From Al?* No way. Darcy shifted, the backs of her shorts sliding across the painted wood. "When do you want to leave?"

"In the morning. First thing."

She noticed the burnished gold hair on his forearm. Would it be as soft as it looked? Had it always been such a golden color? "Sure." She focused on his mouth. *Mistake.* "But you're buying lunch."

"I bill for expenses." His dimple appeared as he granted her his killer smile.

"Maybe I should learn to be a P.I.," she said, her throat dry. "Seems like the benefits are good."

"You're a scientist," he reminded her in a cool tone. "Don't need a weapon's permit for that." Al's dark eyebrow lifted in consideration.

If she'd had a gun, she might have used it on the professor. "Probably just as well." Darcy stood up, hoping some distance from Al cleared her mind. "We've got to be back by tomorrow night or Dax will have a fit. He hired extra guys to help with the dives, but I promised I'd drive the boat all day."

"I got roped into boat duty Saturday morning, and I'm helping in the office on Friday— checking out the property won't take more than a few hours." Al also rose. "Saturday afternoon, I'm manning the grill for Celia, since Ambrosia's part of the festivities."

"That's great, Al." He really was an awesome friend. *Family friend*. Good ole Al.

He patted his trim stomach and picked up Buster's leash, heading toward the entrance of the pier. "I tried some of Celia's lobster recipes. I get to eat whatever I want."

"So, you'll do anything for a free meal?" They stepped off the pier to the sand. The dive shop was to the left, and Al and Buster were poised to go right.

"Free," he said with another wink that made her stomach knot with confusion. He slid on his shades. "Ain't nothing free, sugar."

"Don't I know it?" She flung her braids over her shoulder and left with a smile. Al should have a wife and kids already. Then again, though big, he wasn't exactly teddy bear material. He had a dangerous edge that dared her to come closer even though she knew better. He was off limits. Darcy put some sass in her walk, suddenly conscious of Al as a man. A very *sexy* man.

***

Al was glad to see that smile—Darcy'd been a mess *before* her dad passed away and time hadn't helped her get better. He watched her go, appreciating the slight sway of her hips. Darcy had captured his heart long before she got braces, affection that had turned into unrequited love somewhere along the way.

He'd assumed she be gone by now, following her dreams with a fellow scientist, sailing the seas in search of answers on how to save the ocean and its inhabitants. Yet, she was home instead. Quieter than usual and not as quick to smile. *Why?*

His phone rang and he answered as he walked Buster toward his condo on the north side of town. "Hey, Dax."

"Well? What'd she say?"

"Like she'd turn down a favor," Al said. He'd been in the Dive Shop going over the boat schedule with Dax when his surveillance guy called and declined the job. A thousand bucks was a thousand bucks, so Al knew he'd go himself. Dax, overhearing the conversation, immediately volunteered Darcy—with the caveat that Al find out what was bugging her during the two hour road trip. "We'll leave in the morning."

"What did you tell her?"

Buster sniffed his way down the sidewalk, pausing at the small green areas the size of a sandbox the town called parks. "That I needed a second pair of eyes and that you were busy."

"Good. Darcy used to confide in you," Dax said, his voice heavy with emotion. "She won't talk to me; she shuts down when I bring up Dad. She won't move home."

Al remembered her worries over boys and grades before she left for college. He had an idea that whatever was bothering her now was bigger than that. "I'll try."

"Bring her back with a smile, okay? Gotta run, she just walked in."

With a smile? *Shit, Dax*. His best friend had no clue how he felt about Darcy.

Al dropped his phone into his pocket, imagining Darcy cooking a lobster dinner in his kitchen as he shared his investment secrets. Shorts, bikini top, a frilly apron and bare feet. Nah, skip the clothes. Apron only.

As much as he wished differently, Darcy had him glued strictly in the "friend" zone. Five years older than her, he'd kept his distance as his feelings changed. The last few months of her being home had brought his suppressed emotions to the surface.

And now, at Dax's insistence, they'd be going on a road trip together. If he wasn't a chicken-shit, he just might confess his feelings over beers and shrimp tacos.

She'd probably laugh, not realizing that he was serious. He'd pick up the pieces of his idiotic heart and suffer in silence on the long drive home. No way would Darcy be interested in a burned-out cop, if she managed to get past him being a friend. After the jolt he'd gotten from touching her knee, he knew it was time to man up once and for all—even at the risk of his friendship with Dax.

Chapter Two

Darcy dressed casually in denim shorts and a powder blue t-shirt over her swimsuit, stuffing a cloth backpack with a dress made out of material you could wad and wear without wrinkles. You never knew what might happen in the Keys, and she liked to be prepared. If they were near water, there was a good chance she was going in it, so she added a blue beach towel.

She twisted her hair into a messy bun at her nape and grabbed her sunglasses. Last night she'd done some research on the houses around Cudjoe Key. Al hadn't given her specific information, but there were less than a thousand homes so it hadn't taken long. Pockets of neighborhoods ranged from old-school vacation homes to newer construction in the million-dollar range.

It had been nice to have a purpose instead of numbing her brain with cheese popcorn and Netflix before trying to sleep, only to stare at the ceiling.

Taking the stairs down from the studio apartment to the shop below, she met Dax by the long counter that held the cash register and phone. His blond, rumpled curls needed a brush, his blue eyes sleepy and at half-mast. She'd already done her morning run and showered.

"Mornin'," she said. "You sure you don't mind me going with Al? Last chance to change your mind and put me to work here."

Dax barely looked up at her, sipping from a chipped Dive Shop mug. "Al's great, but a second pair of eyes comes in handy."

"That's what he said." Practically word for word. "But he wanted *you* to go."

"I'm sending you, that's almost as good," he teased.

"Maybe the place is haunted," she said, reaching over to steal his mug and take a drink of his coffee. "Indian Key is a ghost town, and not far from Starfish Bay." She made a face. "This needs sugar."

"Get your own." He gestured to the old coffee pot on the back counter. "Ghosts don't wander." Dax spoke with authority. "They're impressions of something that happened—they don't travel. Don't you remember Paranormal Investigations? Give me my cup."

"Gladly." She took another sip before sliding it back. They used to watch those shows together, eons ago. Crashing on the couch after swimming, eating turkey and cheese sandwiches off paper plates so they didn't have to do the dishes before their dad got home. "I feel guilty, leaving."

"Don't." He stared at the schedule he'd printed out and tapped her name on the spreadsheet. "You've been working every day for months now."

"Fine for you to say—you've been going non-stop since Dad got sick."

He'd taken on the role effortlessly. Where did that leave her? She'd never imagined living here again, at least not until she was a hundred and retired or something. Now she didn't know where to go, or if she had to stay. Did she *want* to stay?

"You've been a part of the shop like you never left," Dax said. "It's been great having you here." He eyed her, biting the corner of his lower lip.

She decided to wait outside before Dax asked any questions—like what she planned on doing with her life. Al's innocent question on the pier yesterday had kept her tossing and turning all night. The warm interest in his blue-gray eyes hadn't helped.

"I think I hear Al's truck."

"Have fun. But not too much fun. Hanging with Al can get crazy." He picked up the schedule then dropped it. "Maybe you shouldn't go."

She smiled and leaned on the counter. "What kind of crazy? Strippers and tequila? Should I bring bail money?"

Her big brother frowned. "Nah. He knows I'd kill him if anything happened to you." Dax shrugged his shoulders like he was shaking off a chill and then pointed at her. "Don't be late. Friday is an important day, and you're both working, got it?"

"Got it. We'll be back this afternoon. I still don't know what help I'm going to be—he's the professional. I used to roast marshmallows around a campfire."

Dax tilted his head, his expression hard for her to read. "Al's family, Darce. We gotta help him out."

Family. Al's touch on her knee yesterday made her wish he wasn't. She left with a wave, hiking her bag up her shoulder. She remembered Al skirting the law as a teen; she'd been surprised when he'd chosen police work after college. No amount of badgering over the last few years got him to tell her why he'd left.

Darcy reached the sidewalk as Al rounded the corner. Buster, tongue lolling, sat in the passenger side of the truck. The black Ford was about twelve years old and retained a shiny luster. She remembered when Al'd bought it, right after joining the police force. Pure machismo. All it needed was a roaring muffler to go with its silver rims. Then again, a loud vehicle wouldn't be so good undercover while the old truck blended.

She hopped into the cab, forcing Buster to scoot over on the long bench seat. "Morning," she said, waving away dog breath. "Whatever happened to your boat?"

Al took her backpack and put it behind the cab seat. "Sold it a few years back. Why?"

"It was the reason, you said, you bought a truck in Florida." She'd teased him about being a redneck in a seaside town.

"Someone gave me a decent offer and I never replaced it. I brought bagels. I figured we'd get real breakfast closer to Cudjoe, at this little place called The Shack. Awesome hash browns."

She pushed Buster to the side so she could see Al's face. Smooth-shaven, tanned. Full lips and a square jaw. Familiar. Two cups of coffee steamed from the cup-holder below the radio. "Thanks. Do you miss the boat?"

He lifted a shoulder and scowled under her scrutiny. "I'll get another one someday. You're gonna have to sit in the middle," Al said. "Buster likes the window."

"I don't think so." Darcy forced the hundred-pound mutt to the center of the truck bench. "Stay."

Buster woofed and licked her cheek. Al laughed at her expression. "Good morning kisses."

She plugged her nose. "You need to brush his teeth or something." Darcy noticed a white paper bag the size of a lunch sack on the dash and her stomach growled.

Al gave her a slow smile and headed toward the interstate. "Dig in. As I recall, you pack a wicked tongue until you're fed." At her questioning look he added, "Not aimed at me, no, but your brother's been flayed alive a couple times."

Darcy scratched behind Buster's ears and the dog leaned against her, content for the moment to let her sit by the passenger window. "That's different."

"Siblings. I get it. Made me glad I didn't have a sister."

Ouch. "What about the benefits? Like, you and Dax coming home after a few too many? Who made you breakfast at midnight?" She patted her chest. "Me, that's who."

"We probably would have burned the house down if we'd tried to cook for ourselves," Al agreed as he drove down Commercial. They managed to hit all green lights and made good time toward I95. "You make a mean omelet."

"It was self-preservation." As the younger sibling, she'd slept lightly on the couch until they stumbled noisily in, then got up to cook so they didn't have hang-overs in the morning. It was her part of their weekend ritual. "But I liked feeding you guys."

She snuck a peek at him as he drove, super-imposing her memory of him as a younger man, back when he'd had golden-brown hair, over this image of Al, the cop, private investigator, reluctant do-gooder. Handsome with hard lines and rough edges. She had difficulty catching her breath.

Buster kept a large paw on her leg as she reached for her the white bag. "Scoot, Buster. Want one, Al?"

"We already ate. Down, boy."

Buster obeyed, immediately curling his body between them. They listened to the radio, comfortable together. *Friends.*

Once Darcy finished her bagel, she took a sip of coffee and sighed. Running gave her peace, but it also made her very hungry. "Now I can think."

"You'll notice I didn't interrupt."

She hefted her chin and sat back, admiring his confident handling of the truck. Al made her feel safe—always had. Out on the ocean, the weather sometimes got rough but he and Dax knew how to control a boat even better than a car, which was saying something. "Smart man. So, last night I did a little research around Cudjoe Key, which is close to Indian Key. Any chance the property could be haunted?"

His brows sunk into a vee above the black rims of his sunglasses. "Are you freaking serious?"

"What?" She hid her grin in her coffee cup, altering her voice to make it ghostly. "There are things we can't explain in this world."

"A bunch of crap."

She allowed a partial smile to show. He had *never* believed in ghosts. "Such a detective. Aren't you supposed to have an open mind?"

"Every scary thing I've run across can be traced right back to a real man—or woman."

"You've never witnessed something you can't explain?" She wasn't a big believer in spirits, but she didn't rule them out, either. There were times when she'd felt her mother's presence when she was younger that she couldn't dismiss. A loving whisper after a bad dream. A soothing touch on her fevered brow.

"And all this time I thought you were the practical one."

"I am." She pointed at him with her coffee cup. "You shouldn't be so black and white." Buster swiveled his gaze between them. "People have captured orbs in their pictures. Especially around Key West."

"Key West is a hotbed of the strange, all right. Humans. Alive. Obnoxious." He got onto 595 and headed toward Homestead. "But they bleed. Ghosts don't. I'd appreciate it if you'd be on the look-out for something real."

Darcy couldn't hold her laughter inside a second longer and she let it go, tossing her head back and pressing a hand to her stomach. "Got it. You're so *stuffy* sometimes, Al."

***

Al loosened his tense, one-handed grip on the wheel. She'd been teasing, of course. Now he had no choice but to stick to his hard-ass position. "Stuffy? Logical."

"Whatever." Her laughter wound down but her smile remained. She slipped her sandals off and tucked one bare foot under her butt on the seat, giving him a view of her long legs. For the life of him, he couldn't figure out why bench seats had gone out of style. Darcy reached into her bag and drew out her smart phone. "Is there something I should look for, specifically?"

He liked her jokes and knew he was just defensive because he was nervous. Today could be the best day of his life, or end up as the worst in history. Al reeled off the address of the property. "I did the standard checks. My clients have sold this place three times in the past two years only to have it fall through." He shifted to get more comfortable. "No mention of ghosts."

"Haha. And it's the same realtor?"

Al glanced at Darcy and pushed his sunglasses up the bridge of his nose. "Lori Ferguson. Owns the company. I did a preliminary search, but nothing popped."

"Well, maybe she's having some bad luck. It must suck to keep putting that same place on the market. I mean, it costs her every time."

Feeling sorry for a realtor? Darcy's heart was way too big. Far as Al was concerned, they were slick salespeople with one thing on their mind: the bottom dollar. "Realtors just want their commission, that's what I think." He turned his attention back to the road. Miami traffic was a bitch but they were almost on the south side.

"I'm sure that's true, too."

Practical. That was more like the Darcy he knew.

"The owner is in Greece," Al said. "Doesn't live here, so the realtor is doing all the work. Greece's economy is in the tank, which is probably why they need to unload the property." Willing to part with an extra grand just to have him rush down and put a stop to the bleeding.

"So why *are* the sales falling through? Does the bank pull out, or is it the buyer?" She hummed then swiped a few more pages. "It's a cute place. Why don't I call and make an appointment to see it this afternoon?"

His original plan had been to have his guy take some pictures of the property and send those to his client. Why not use Darcy to his advantage, since she was here? "Good idea. We should get in around 10, which gives us plenty of time to eat and then scout the area before meeting the realtor."

She looked up from the small screen, brown eyes sparkling. "So, what's the plan?"

Al switched lanes. His objective was to make Darcy see him outside the friend zone but if he thought about his idea long enough, he'd change his mind. He spoke quickly. "I say we go in, act like a married couple looking for a house to buy."

She flinched. "Married?"

Not the reaction he'd hoped for, but he brazened through. "Playing a part."

"If my brother had come, would you have worn matching polos and tennis shorts?" Her leg bounced on the seat.

"Darcy, don't be ridiculous."

"I'm just saying." Her chin jutted forward stubbornly.

"You said you'd help. The best way to gain someone's trust is to have the appearance of being trustworthy. A young couple and their dog, looking for their first home."

"Young?" She snorted and Buster barked.

Al tapped his thumb against the wheel. "I'm thirty-two, Darcy, which is young in the scheme of things. Just because you're a baby..."

"Twenty-seven is not even close to being a child. I've got crow's feet."

He thought she was beautiful. Her pretty blue shirt complemented her blonde hair, which she'd pulled back from her face in a loose bun. "You're being silly."

Darcy tugged at Buster's ears and his dog settled his nose on Darcy's thigh. "How many bedrooms does this place have again?"

"Two."

She hummed. "Kind of small. Some day we might want kids."

His gut knotted like he'd been sucker punched. "Nope." Kids with Darcy's eyes? Her smile? Oh, yeah. "Kids are a pain in the ass."

"Why not?" She made a *tsking* noise. "Men are supposed to be focused on procreation for recreation. I read that somewhere."

Al wanted to be anywhere but in the truck. "Sounds romantic."

"Since when do you care about romance?" She brushed blonde wisps away from her forehead.

He'd imagined romancing Darcy with rose petals and champagne, dancing on the beach under a starlit sky. But he couldn't tell her that—not yet. "This is pretend."

Darcy stared out the window at the passing traffic on the freeway. "Whatever. You and Dax can grow old together."

"He's got Celia." *I've got nobody. I want you.* "I'm fine on my own."

Buster barked "bullshit" in his ear. Darcy was right—the dog needed his teeth brushed.

Chapter Three

Darcy made sure to keep the conversation away from emotions, babies and procreating. What might have been a throw-away comment in the past, when she viewed Al as only a family friend, now fell between them with an awkward *thunk*.

She'd taken Al's solid presence as something stable in her life. She understood change was part of the cycle. But Al, like Dax, was always there in the background.

Now she couldn't keep from glancing at how he filled the cab of the truck, his strong hands against the wheel, the way the sun caught the golden hair along his thumb, his long, muscled legs. She was on the tall side, but Al was taller.

Her professor had been a short man. Should've been the first clue, when they were nose to nose while kissing, that he wasn't worth her starry-eyed dreams.

She finished her coffee, the grounds at the bottom of her cup catching in her closed throat. Swallowing hard, she stared out the window, determined to enjoy the day in the Keys without letting the memory of that asshole ruin it.

Darcy called Lori Ferguson, listening to the phone ring until finally an answering machine clicked on. "Hi, this is Darcy, er, Cooper, calling about a listing you have on Starfish Bay? My husband and I would love to see the place today, while we're in town." She left her number.

Al nodded. "Thanks, Darcy."

"Sure." Darcy switched the station on the truck radio, searching until she found a song they both knew. "You and Dax used to love the Red Hot Chili Peppers."

"Haven't heard this song in ages."

"You'd crank it on the boat." She laughed. "Remember the first dive we ever went on together?" She'd been ten, and he'd been fifteen. A giant her brother had befriended at school and brought home.

"Your dad had that old twenty-foot Cruiser, the Sea Maid." Al rubbed the top of his head, the corner of his mouth lifting in a smile.

"Saving to buy a new one!" A year later, they'd given the Sea Maid an honorable burial at sea. "And you thought you were going to tell me what to do?"

His cheeks darkened beneath his tan. "I was older."

Self-confidant now, he'd been filled with unbridled male cockiness then. "But not wiser." Darcy shook her finger. "You screamed like a girl."

"I was a kid from Jersey." His broad shoulders rose in defense. "Never saw a shark before. You shouldn't have been in the water with one."

"Baby nurse shark." She grinned at the memory. At ten, she hadn't thought tall, practically grown-up Al could be afraid of anything. But he'd been scared for her.

Al snapped his teeth, strong and white, as if to bite her. His black tee fit snug around his muscular arms. He'd been a scrawny teen once. *Sure wasn't one now.* They'd lived in their swimsuits, on the water every free moment. If they weren't working for the Dive Shop, then they'd fished for pleasure, or hunted the Gold Coast for treasure. Never did find any, she thought.

Darcy sang along with the songs she knew as they got onto the only road leading into the chain of small islands. Al added back-up, thumping his thumb against the wheel, or using his palm against the dashboard for a particularly awesome drum solo.

Comfortable. Friends. *Stop looking at his hands!*

They reached an outside diner on the right side of the road just after ten a.m. The dirt lot had five other vehicles parked before an unpainted square building with a stacked tin chimney. He'd called it the Shack, but she didn't see a sign.

"This okay?" Al asked.

Darcy's stomach rumbled. "I could eat." She hopped out of the truck as Al clipped Buster's leash to his collar.

Al walked the dog over to a stand of trees to take care of business while Darcy went inside. The interior was dimly lit and about the size of a service station, minus the pumps. Instead of gas, steam rose behind a high counter as the smells of bacon and onion drifted over. She counted ten square tables, all packed with people eating breakfast.

"In or out?" The hostess, a woman in her mid-forties, grabbed a menu and looked to see if she was alone.

Darcy held up two fingers. "Out, please." The air conditioning didn't seem to be working, or maybe it just couldn't keep up with the stove. A trickle of sweat tickled her lower back and she gratefully followed the woman outside. "We've got a dog."

"Fine. Follow me."

The outside seating area was made of gravel and sectioned off with palm trees. There were six picnic tables, four of which were occupied. She brought Darcy to the table on the edge of the gravel closest to the murky green canal. An egret stared at her with unblinking beady black eyes from the shelter of a mangrove.

The hostess dropped the menu. "I'll bring a bowl of water for the pup. Coffee?"

"Just water for us too, please."

"I'll be back." She went inside the unpainted, slatted wood building.

Al sat down opposite her and Darcy whispered, "Are you sure about this place? If I get sick, you're paying me double."

Al chuckled. "Best hash browns in the state of Florida, guaranteed."

Darcy sniffed the air, picking out savory grilled onions over the oily scent of fish on the water that led to the Gulf. "How'd you find it? There's no sign or anything."

"A buddy brought me when I was still working with the police department. The guys all know. It's word of mouth and great food that keeps the Shack in business."

"I'm literally putting my life into your hands." God, she shouldn't have said hands. Now she had to look at his again. Why were they such a turn-on? A dusting of golden hair along his forearms. Long, thick fingers with short nails. She knew from experience that his palms were rough, his grip strong, from the time they spent on the boat together.

She crossed her legs, bumping her knee on the underside of the wooden table. Buster noticed the egret and barked in greeting to what looked like the perfect chew toy.

Al patted the dog's head. "Quiet."

The order, given in a firm tone, made Buster snap his teeth together and shiver with excitement but he sat still. "Impressive," Darcy said. "How long have you had Buster?"

"A year, now. Got him from Pet Rescue."

"I know the place." The woman who owned it ran a no-kill shelter and made designer dog treats. "Lucky dog."

The hostess, who as it turned out was also the waitress, brought two cups of water for the humans in one hand and a bowl for Buster in the other.

"What's the special?" Al asked.

"Bud caught grouper this morning. Can fry that up with some mango salsa."

"Hash browns?"

"Yeah." The woman nodded, her mouth pursed.

"I'll take it." Al looked at her. "Darce?"

"Is there a point to trying anything other than the special?" She posed the question to Al, who shrugged.

"We got eggs, bacon." The woman tilted her head, her expression unamused. "Can make pancakes if you'd rather have something else."

Now Darcy felt like a jerk. "I was just joking," she quickly explained. "He's been talking about this place the whole way here from Ft. Lauderdale."

The hostess/waitress cracked a smile. "Hmm. Two specials then?"

Al and Darcy nodded in unison and the woman walked up the dirt path to the restaurant. Just then a breeze came off the canal, cooling her neck.

"It's going to be hot today," Al said.

Darcy nodded. "I don't mind." The subtropics were in her blood. Maybe that's why she'd ended up back here, despite her dreams of grandeur. "You ever think about leaving Florida?"

Al blinked slowly, as if searching for hidden meanings in the question. "Nope." He paused and took a drink of his water. "You?"

She sighed. "I wanted to see the world."

"It's not too late, Darce. Christ, you're not even thirty."

That once was considered old, in her book. "I thought I would change things. Make a difference. You see that egret? I used to care about brackish water conditions. People dumping garbage illegally into the canals or bays. Now?"

She propped her elbow on the table and leaned her chin into her palm. "I'm just not that fired up about it. I used to be the loudest advocate." Blinking back tears, she sniffed and dropped her hands to the wooden bench. Her professor had revealed the dirty secrets behind the show curtain. Pay-offs exchanged for specific "scientific" results. When she'd questioned his findings, Professor Petrovsky had told her to grow up.

"Nobody can save the world. You just have to take care of your part of it. Is that what's been bothering you lately?"

She bit her trembling lower lip and studied the rough planks of the table. Someone had carved a heart in the wood.

"You graduate college and realize life's a crap-shoot?"

Al was so straightforward that Darcy doubted he'd ever get lost in ideals. "Florida is supposed to be underwater in a hundred years," she said. "Nothing we can do about it."

Al burst out laughing. "Darcy, sugar, I don't know what's going on inside that super-smart brain of yours, but I think you need to quit thinking so much."

Darcy took off her sunglasses and set them on the table next to his. "Stop thinking? That's your solution to water pollution? Lame, Al."

"Not what I said." His mouth tightened and his eyes narrowed. "But maybe my Greek clients are right—it's a good time to sell if you've got waterfront."

"Funny."

"All jokes aside, Darcy, you know that you can tell me anything. I'll even talk water filtration if that will bring a smile back to your beautiful face."

"Thanks." Could she tell him about the professor? God knew she couldn't talk to her brother about it. He wanted to sue the college and the professor, when it was her mistake. Her parents were dead. But the ugly truth had to come out, before the wound festered anymore. She couldn't sleep, couldn't run fast enough. Al used to listen to her, back when she'd had boy troubles in high school.

"Darce?"

She picked at a splinter in the worn wood of the table. "I'm glad I have my degree in marine biology. I'm trying to say that I miss the sense of purpose I used to feel."

"You're still recovering from your dad's death. That's going to take time to heal." Al cleared his throat, his tones strong. Inviting. "Unless you tell me what happened in Melbourne, I can't give you advice on how to get past it."

Of course he knew something was wrong. Al was a smart man. Had Dax told him, anyway? She shivered. "You probably already know," she hedged. God, he'd think less of her. She couldn't lose his respect.

"I wouldn't ask if I did." He held her gaze.

"I," she moistened her lower lip and swallowed, gathering her thoughts. "I was lucky to get an internship right out of college."

"They were lucky to have you." Al spoke with surety, leaving no room for argument.

"Yeah." As it turned out, her brown eyes and blonde hair had probably gotten her into the elite group just as much as her grades. "Well, Professor Petrovsky was doing his study on the coral reefs. I thought I would do my thesis on that."

"You changed your mind..."

The splinter came loose and she lifted her head, her eyes unblinking.

It was now or never. Trusting Al with the truth, she said, "I slept with my professor."

The hostess, having arrived in stealth mode, loudly cleared her throat, her cheeks bright red as she set two plates of the grouper special on the table. "Anything else?"

Darcy's breath caught and she wished she could dive into the canal and swim far, far away. *Shit.*

***

Al, stunned into silence at Darcy's blatant confession, shook his head at the waitress who quickly turned tail and ran back inside. He didn't blame her.

Darcy, her poor face the color of a ripe beet, held herself still.

Months ago, Dax had hinted that something was wrong, but hadn't told him what. Al had assumed that she was having a hard time with the studies, or maybe just needed a break from her ever-active mind. When Dax had arranged this outing so that Al could get Darcy to talk, had he suspected this?

It never occurred to him that she'd have an affair with her professor. Darcy was smarter than that. *Right?*

Al unwrapped his knife and fork from the napkin they were rolled in, and then did the same for hers. "Eat."

Darcy accepted the silverware with trembling fingers.

He cut into the grouper. White, flaky center, with a thin, crisp breading. He speared a piece onto the tines of his fork, but couldn't put it in his mouth. An affair with her professor? What kind of jackass would take advantage of a young woman looking to save the world?

"I'm sorry," she whispered, her eyes downcast. "I shouldn't have said anything."

Al dropped the fork to the center of his plate and got up, walking around the table to where Darcy sat with her head bowed. He pulled her up from the bench seat so that they stood face to face. He knew from experience that if you kept that kind of crap inside, it ate at you. "I'm glad you told me." Lifting her chin, he forced her to look at him. "He's an asshole."

Her body tensed. "You don't know the story."

"I know he's an asshole."

She searched his steady gaze. Her eyes watered. "I'm so ashamed of myself." One tear slid down her cheek. "I know better." A second and third tear followed, breaking Al's heart. "I thought I was special."

He pulled her close and let her cry against his shoulder, rubbing her back as he murmured into her hair, "You are, Darcy. You are."

Al couldn't imagine anyone more special and it took all of his hard-earned self-control to keep his hold on her gentle when he wanted to drive up to Sebastian and shoot himself a professor.

Chapter Four

Cherished. That's how Darcy felt in Al's embrace. Was this wrong, too? Her head fit perfectly against his solid shoulder, his hands cradling her as if to protect her from further harm.

"You probably think I'm a stupid twit," she mumbled against his neck. He smelled like Al, part Banana Boat sunscreen, part ocean.

"Nope."

She slowly pulled back from his arms, reluctant to leave. Darcy stared into his eyes, wondering if he would kiss her, if she should kiss him, if she was being a bigger twit for even thinking about his mouth against hers. She couldn't help it.

Friends hooking up was a bad idea. Darcy hooking up with *Al* was a terrible idea. He'd always been larger than life to her. Al, dancing on the Sea Maid II in a summer storm, sheltering her with his body when the lightning flashed too close as her brother captained them back to the marina. She'd been seventeen, then. Noticing Al while pretending indifference.

Last night she'd dreamed about him, in her bed. Was it right? *No.* She needed to start showing some solid decision-making skills before she really screwed up her life.

If Dax found out? He'd kill them both.

Darcy wiped her eyes with the back of her hand. "I'm going to clean up," she said, leaving him there with an expression she didn't understand. *Disappointment?*

Would he have kissed her if she'd stayed? His interest had been obvious in his embrace, jutting against her hipbone.

She hurried to the outdoor restroom and washed her hands. The blurry silver sheet that served as a mirror showed her hair loose in half waves around her face and shoulders. "You're a mess. Don't drag Al into your shit, got it?"

With those words of wisdom, she rejoined him and Buster at the table.

"You should have eaten," she said, sliding onto the wooden bench as if nothing had changed.

"It's okay."

She dug in, surprised by the rich flavor in the fish. "This is even good cold."

"It's not cold," Al said, taking a bite. As if he created reality with his words. "Taste the mango? Get some of those hash browns on there."

Darcy nodded, grateful that Al was willing to play along. To let her off her own hook. She knew he must have a million questions but they finished the tasty meal with small talk. The hostess left the bill, not looking at Darcy.

"Awkward?"

Al grinned. "She walked into a bombshell."

Darcy wrinkled her nose. "It was stupid." *I was stupid.*

"Learn from it and it won't be a wasted experience. Then let it go."

She sipped her water. The breeze fluttered an occasional feather which was the only thing that gave the white egret away. *Let it go.* "Excellent advice."

"Do you still," Al's voice hitched, "love him?"

"I didn't love the professor," she explained quickly. It had felt like love, and hurt like love but at some level she hadn't let him all the way into her heart. "It's been almost a year since I broke things off." She swirled her finger in the condensation from her water glass. "I was infatuated. He was my Philippe Cousteau Jr. We were going to save the reefs and be famous."

"I remember your crush on Philippe. He was all you talked about." Al's eyes darkened. "Other girls had crushes on rock stars, but you went for the grandson of the great French underwater explorer."

"What do I care about rock stars? Protecting the ocean is what matters."

"Glad to hear it." His expression was so sincere it made her uncomfortable.

"Can we talk about something else, please?"

"You promise you aren't suffering a broken heart?" He asked the question in his serious way, which wouldn't let her get away with a joke in return.

Darcy had raked through her feelings so many times that she knew there was nothing left for the professor. "I'm worried that I can't find my passion for the ocean when it used to be so strong. Somehow it's all gotten knotted together with what happened." Her professor had sapped her enthusiastic naiveté, drying her out like coral in the sun.

Reaching across the table, Al took her hands, rubbing his thumbs across her fingers. "Then let's get you untangled so you can get on with your life, huh?"

She smiled, feeling lighter than she had in a while, her burden shared. "Okay."

He handed her Buster's leash, leaving a pile of cash under the plate so it wouldn't get blown away. "My treat."

"Thank you." Grateful they wouldn't have to go inside, she and Buster followed Al to the truck. Now, if she never had to talk about the professor again, she'd be happy.

Al started the truck and punched the address of the property into his GPS. "Looks like there's just one road into the neighborhood. Five houses total. Starfish Bay."

"How far are we?" She looked at the map but it all seemed like squiggles.

"Fifteen minutes."

From Overseas Highway they turned left onto an unpaved side road lined with palmetto brush and tall palm trees. Darcy sat on the edge of the seat, one arm slung around Buster.

"Want me to record anything?" She gestured to her phone on the dashboard. "For the owners?"

"This is our first look. Let's just see what's there."

"When I came here with the Girl Scouts, we stayed on the Gulf side. We camped and told ghost stories—like I said, Indian Island's haunted."

Al winced as they hit a pothole and the front tire dipped. He slowed down. The map showed them taking a right, which led them deeper into a forested area.

"I saw online that this area was rural," Al said. "I figured it was all resorts. Marinas maybe. But this is pretty rustic."

Darcy's phone rang, and she recognized the number as the one she'd called for the realtor.

"Hello?" She put the phone on speaker so that Al could hear too.

"Hi. May I speak to Darcy Cooper?"

Darcy's breath hitched and her belly tightened. "That's me."

"You'd like to see the property in Starfish Bay?"

Al put a finger to his lips and nodded. She assumed that meant the less shared with the realtor the better. "Yes."

"Today, you said?"

"Yes." Darcy bit her tongue to keep from adding more information.

"The soonest I can be there is three o'clock." Lori Ferguson's voice was high-pitched and fussy. "I'll have no time to get the place cleaned up."

"That's fine. My husband and I will see you then."

Darcy hung up, feeling Al's searching gaze on the side of her face. "Good job."

"Thanks," she said. They drove for about half a mile and gradually turned toward the Atlantic. A huge canopy of mangrove trees shaded the dirt road. Light filtered through, but despite it being the middle of a summer day, the cover made it seem like dusk.

"Creepy." She peered into the trees and bushes, half expecting to see glowing yellow eyes staring back at her.

Al hunched over the steering wheel. The truck lights clicked on, triggered by the shade of the trees. "What?"

She forced herself to sit back, but kept an arm around Buster. "Why would someone want so much privacy in the middle of nowhere?" Every scary movie worth its salt took place in the middle of nowhere.

"People like privacy. So long as they aren't hurting anyone, nothing wrong with that. But I think I'd want better roads."

Al was a man who thought for himself, and she liked that. No way would he do the wrong thing for personal gain. She touched her lower lip, remembering his arousal against her body when he'd hugged her earlier. She'd liked that, too. A lot.

"Shouldn't we be turning toward the ocean?"

She squinted and found the red dot that was the truck on the screen of the GPS. "There's a left coming up."

Al slowed the truck and made the sharp turn. The sun did its best to filter through the thinning trees, making the way into the neighborhood somewhat easier to navigate as they drove out of the forest of pines and palms.

The dirt road led to pavement now that they were inside the development. She breathed a sigh of relief and counted three houses, each a mile or so off the road. "I thought there were five homes?"

Al studied the map he'd printed from the computer. "These three, and one to the very right of that. It's not visible yet. And there," he pointed to a lone house in the center of the neighborhood on a half-acre lot.

"It sticks out like it doesn't belong. Why bother without water access?"

"I wouldn't want it."

Buster barked and wagged his tail, stepping on Darcy's lap to look out the passenger window. His nails dug into her bare skin, so she gave up her choice spot and scooted across the bench seat closer to Al. Aware of him in a new way, her body prickled, tensing as she carefully kept her leg from touching his. *Friends.*

"These don't look like half a million dollar homes, Al." Sure, they had views of the water, but they were older with overgrown yards. "Maybe they have a home owner's association that forbids maintenance."

"Cute." He drove forward under a large, overgrown mangrove.

They came out the other side and Darcy sucked in a surprised breath. "Oh. The website said it had old Florida character. This is, it's a..." She searched for the right words as she turned to Al. "It's a hot mess."

***

Al tightened both hands on the steering wheel, acutely aware of Darcy sitting next to him. Her leg against his, her arm brushing his thigh. *Thank you, Buster.*

"You're right." He pulled his gaze from her slender finger and followed where she pointed. The "character" was piles of driftwood against the wooden frame of the single-story home, faded to pale blue. Buoys and old lobster traps hung from a clothes line. Chimes made of shells interspersed between them.

He rolled the truck forward.

"Wait." Darcy clutched his arm as she pointed to some house numbers attached to the side of the house in mosaic tile. "Wrong house. This is 420, we're looking for 415."

He'd never been so grateful to be at the wrong place in his life. His clients had led him to believe they had a choice piece of real estate. This wasn't it.

"Good." He backed out of the dirt drive onto the road, then coasted along until the next turn.

415. It wasn't marked, but according to the GPS and map of the area, it was the only other possibility.

His client had asked for a report of the property. They hadn't been to see it in two years. The sale of the place would alleviate their financial burden. Al had some tough questions for the realtor, Lori Ferguson.

Next door the neighbors had decorated their yard with crap they found floating in the bay. Not a good selling point. And you seriously needed a map to find the place. Strike two.

Al went slowly down the driveway. The overgrown brush on either side had once been landscaped. Florida's tropical atmosphere made everything lush and green. Paradise became a jungle if you didn't stay on top of it.

He turned onto the circular drive in front of the house. Darcy sat forward on the cab seat. "Beautiful," she said. The wide expanse of turquoise bay glittered with the sun's rays. "Now we're talking. Look at that dock!"

The wooden dock attached to the white sandy beach extended into the bay about twelve feet. He nodded and turned his attention to the house. Cement block, painted light coral, with deep green hurricane shutters. Steel roof, courtesy of a past hurricane remodel, according to the spec sheet.

"Are we getting out?" Darcy looked up at him, her eyes shaded by her sunglasses, her mouth painted with soft pink gloss that smelled faintly of strawberry. *Kissable.*

"Yeah." Al parked and grabbed hold of Buster's leash. What would it be like to really look at a place together? She hadn't loved her professor.

"I can't believe what a difference a single lot can make." Darcy slid out his side. "Look at that water. The view is gorgeous. This property should've sold for the original asking price."

He agreed. "Let's not jump to conclusions."

"P. I. lesson number one?" She pulled away and walked ahead, adjusting her sunglasses. "It's okay to say you like the property, Al."

"I did." Buster followed her and Al lost his hold on the leash.

"With a caveat." Darcy breathed in and coughed. "What is that smell? It's like something died."

Al instinctively patted his hip where his gun was normally holstered—he'd locked it in the truck for the day—and sniffed the air. "God, dead fish?" He eyed the bay and the dock leading from the beach to the water. Two faded yellow kayaks were chained to the side piling. Maybe something had gotten caught?

He turned his attention to Darcy, who had wandered toward the house as if actually interested in buying.

"Somebody put some money into this place once upon a time." Buster stayed at her heels since she'd picked up the leash he'd dropped. Darcy nosed up to the window shutters and scraped the paint with her thumbnail. "It just needs a little love." She pulled at the over-grown hibiscus bush at her feet, the pink flowers bright against the dark green foliage. "You could hire some landscapers."

Al held up his hand. "Whoa. I'm not here to spruce the place up." Just to figure out why it's not selling.

She peered between the slats on the windows, standing on her tiptoes in her sandals. "Maybe it sucks inside."

"The website said character." He supposed the tropical colors counted as local flavor. "And that a total remodel had been done of the bathroom and kitchen."

She looked cute, he thought, trying to sneak a peek inside. Her hair was down around her shoulders, wavy from the earlier bun. "I wonder what color they painted?"

"We'll see at three. Right now, we're supposed to be doing recon."

"Right. Under the radar." Grinning, she brushed her hands together and settled back on her heels, nodding at him before heading toward the dock. "Finding that stench should be top priority."

Al looked around, seeing nothing out of the ordinary. Ceramic planters with dead plants. Neglected. Two years without care explained that. The overgrown walkway wouldn't stop a buyer if they were interested in making a lower offer. The stink?

He plugged his nose and breathed through his mouth. That could be strike number three.

Chapter Five

Darcy walked down a slight incline to the small beach on the property. Half shaded by mangroves, it was perfect for sun bathing or cooling off. "What size is this lot?"

Al answered, "Half an acre."

"That's nice." She nodded and he noticed that she was breathing through her mouth, too. "I really hope this stench isn't permanent. That would be a deal-breaker."

He joined her at the three wooden steps leading up to the dock and pulled on one of the kayaks. "How do you feel about taking these out?"

She tilted her head. "They're chained."

Al cracked his knuckles. "I can jimmy a lock. The owners wanted me to check the place out. I think we should see the bay." He looked at his watch. "It's 12:30 now. We've got plenty of time."

Darcy's smile went from hesitant to excited. "Don't have to ask me twice. This is beautiful. Look at the grouping of mangroves—who knows what kind of treasure could be trapped in the roots?"

"Crabs and turtles, maybe." Al took a penknife from his side pocket and flipped open a long, thin strip of metal that was perfect for picking combo locks. Buster's tongue dripped saliva as he raced between him and Darcy.

Al jiggled the metal pick until the lock clicked open, freeing the chains that held the kayaks to the pilings. He looked inside. Sniffed. *All clear.* "Good. Paddles are here, too."

"Great work." Darcy fastened her hair in a ponytail. "You could've been a thief."

"No money in it," he said with a straight face.

"So that's why you became a cop?" Her tone droll, she added, "I wondered."

"No money in that either." Boy, wasn't that the truth?

"Which is why you..."

"Don't go there." He refused to talk about why he left the force. He had a thing against men who were supposed to wear the white hats but didn't. A crook was a crook and didn't try to act any differently—that he could respect.

Darcy took one end of the kayak and pulled it toward the small area of white sand, obviously imported for ascetic value as it was too refined to be local. She brushed away spider webs without any squealing, which Al appreciated.

"There's room for Buster on my kayak. Do you think he'd stay?"

Al shrugged. "One way to find out—I've got a doggy vest in the back of the truck. We'll stay in sight of the shore, just in case." He tossed Darcy the keys and she ran up the sand to the mostly dirt yard and the trunk of supplies in the back of his rig. He never got tired of watching her move, lean and graceful.

He hoped that the smell would fade once they got out to the wind on the bay. No way would anyone buy a place that stank, but it sure looked nice. Quiet and secluded.

Darcy returned with her backpack over her shoulder, which she set on the dock, and the blue dog vest, which she tossed to Al. Then she proceeded to pull out all kinds of stuff from that bag, like Mary Poppins.

Towels, sunscreen, water bottles, granola bars. Buster let him put the vest on then gave his body a massive shake. It wasn't going anywhere, so Buster trotted over to Darcy and sniffed at the granola bars.

"How about some water instead?" She filled a pop up water bowl from a bottle then she drank the rest. "Want some?" she asked Al.

Why couldn't everyday be like this? Him, Darcy and Buster hanging out by the bay. A family. He'd loved her from afar for so long. This was better.

He nodded and she sent a water bottle sailing toward him, underhand. He caught it and looked away before he said something stupid. Like, hey, wanna marry me? Have a dozen kids? She'd make a joke, not realizing he was serious. Break his heart.

He wiped his mouth with the back of his hand and gestured to his dog. "Are you sure you want to take Buster?"

"Yeah. He'll fit in the space for carrying a bag. He's a good boy and won't jump. Right?" She scratched Buster's ears and he thumped his stumpy tail against the sand. "It's hot and smelly here. Let's go. Oh, wait." She pointed at him. "Shirt on or off?"

He gulped, then realized what she wanted. He slid his shirt over his head and tossed it next to her bag on the dock.

She squirted Al with sunscreen, her touch swift and her strokes sure as she rubbed the lotion into his shoulders. Down his back, her fingers following the line of his shorts. When she stood in front of him to do his chest, he noticed her breaths catching as she swirled sunscreen across his abdomen.

Torture. He hated it to be over. "Your turn?"

She shimmied out of her light blue top. Al, tongue-tied, should have realized she'd be wearing a bikini underneath. He used to tease her about being part mermaid. He slathered lotion across her shoulders, trying not to stare at the perfect bronze of her soft skin, the curve of her breast, the fragile arc of her neck. The slight feminine flair of her hips accentuated by her trim torso disappearing into denim shorts.

It was a painful relief to put the cap on and settle Buster into the kayak, pushing it into the water. He grabbed the end to steady it as she got in, then handed her a paddle. "Fun times." He barely recognized his own voice. "Don't drown my dog."

"Whatever. Catch us if you can!" She quickly paddled away from him, her strong arms using efficient strokes through the calm water.

He jumped in his own kayak to follow. God, what he wouldn't give to make this his real life. "Loser pays for drinks!"

***

Darcy darted ahead, chuckling at the look of challenge accepted on Al's face. His abs were drool-worthy, not that she should be noticing, just as she shouldn't give two hoots about his hands, but it was too late.

She'd noticed and now she couldn't stop.

Buster sat in front of her, his ears pointed high, his mostly Pit Bull body solid as a masthead. Darcy knew he was good on boats and trusted he'd be all right in the kayak. No way could the single man kayak hold both Al, at 240 pounds of solid muscle, and the 100 pound dog. It made more sense for Buster to be with her.

What would it be like to live so close to the calm bay? No ocean waves, no aqua of the Intracoastal she'd grown up on, but navy blue water surrounded by lush tropical green plants. Anhinga roosted in the mangrove roots and she kept watch for manatee just below the surface.

Al joined her as she paddled toward the grouping of mangroves about fifty yards out from the dock. The other side of the bay was closed off with trees, making the enclave private.

"Paradise?" Al asked with a sexy grin.

No, not a *sexy* grin. *No, no.* No.

She cleared her throat. "Yes. It's really nice. Peaceful." She pointed to the opposite side. "Is that the preserve?"

Al nodded. "Protected by the government, which means nobody would be able to build."

"We'd have to add that to the plus side." Buster, still as a statue, watched Al but stayed on the kayak.

"Yeah." Al's slick, tanned body shone in the sun. "And the stench is gone out here, which means it's not the bay itself. What do you think?"

Her brain was scrambled, so she looked away from Al in order to speak clearly. "I like what I see."

"Could you live here?"

"Definitely."

"Even though it's far away from your brother? The Dive Shop?"

"As a vacation home?"

"I don't know. It might be nice all year."

She lifted her paddle and glanced at Al. "Aren't we supposed to be in character or something?"

He flipped bay water at her, splashing her and Buster before taking off toward the other side.

They paddled around the area and followed the outlet to the Atlantic Ocean. Bright aquamarine water for as far as they could see. Dolphins jumped in the distance which made her smile. Her dad said they were her spirit animal. God, she missed him. Were he and her mom together again, at last? He'd claimed to love her mom so much there couldn't be another woman in his life after she'd died.

I miss you, Dad. I'm sorry I wasn't there.

Everything is fine, baby girl. Peace descended on Darcy and she lifted her face with surprise. A soft wind crossed her cheek like a kiss on the air.

She blinked, her spirit light. All right, so she might not know what was on the other side, but there had to be something. Her parent's love was eternal—their love for her always there.

"You okay, Darce?"

She reached for Al's hand, her fingers clasping his across the expanse of water. "Better than okay."

They sat together, kayaks bobbing, watching the dolphins for a while longer. She didn't hear her dad's voice again, but the feeling of rightness stayed in her heart. Al had given her this, and she wouldn't forget it. It was time to uphold her part of the job—be Mrs. Al Cooper, possible future home buyer.

"Let's go back." She nudged his kayak with her paddle and turned around with a giggle. "First one to the mangrove wins!"

He couldn't refuse a challenge, she knew this, and so she put her back into it as they raced from the ocean to the bay. Buster's ears went flat, as if that would help their speed.

Al, his kayak right next to hers, laughed out loud, a beautiful man against the elements— she almost paused to watch him in motion before digging her paddle deep.

The mangrove was two kayak lengths ahead when a fish jumped from the water in front of them, returning with a splash to the murky depths below. Buster barked sharply and strained forward.

In that second, she knew he was going to jump. She had to choose between stopping Buster or winning.

It was close, but she grabbed Buster's leash, somehow managing to keep her paddle as the kayak rocked and the dog leaned against her hold.

"I win!" Al, tanned and broad-chested, raised his paddle in both hands, his arm muscles flexing. His grin revealed white teeth, his triumph hidden behind the gloss of sunglasses.

He gave one extra air-pump before settling back in the boat.

Darcy's kayak nosed into the mangrove roots with a small thump and crabs scurried out of the way. Her precarious grip on the paddle loosened and it fell into the water between her and Al.

Buster, seeing the paddle float by, leapt from the kayak, his heavy body upsetting the balance as he landed with a splash in the clear blue water. In an instant a sinking feeling knotted in Darcy's stomach and the plastic kayak flipped, dunking her in.

The cool water wasn't bad in the heat of the day, but it came as a shock. She kicked her legs and bobbed to the surface. She couldn't touch the bottom, but her bare feet touched rock. Spluttering water as her head cleared the surface, she said, "Grab my sandals, would you?"

Al, laughing, reached out for the paddle, the sandal and Buster's leash. The dog was happily swimming with her other sandal in his mouth. "Got it. How's the water?"

She splashed him with a sweeping arc of her hand over the surface, barely missing his sculpted figure. "Wet."

Balancing on the rocks, she felt something against her bare foot and snatched it upward. "Ooh. Something's down there."

Al, maneuvering his kayak toward shore, looked over his shoulder. The sun beamed down and glinted off his devilish smile. "Hopefully nothing hungry."

Nice guy. "We should've brought the snorkel gear. Could be treasure!"

"Dreamer. Come on, you've wasted enough time taking a swim break. Need help getting back in?"

She flipped him the bird. "I got this." Using the roots as leverage, she braved her foot down on the rocks. "You know what else likes rocks? Lobsters."

"Lobsters. Bugfest has you obsessed."

Darcy steadied the kayak, and, with the grace of a water buffalo, poured herself into the boat. It teetered, but she grabbed onto the mangrove roots to stay upright.

Al clapped. "I wish I had that on video. Dax could put it up at the Dive Shop. Training on what *not* to do."

Her teeth chattered and she held out her hand for the paddle. "We can just forget this ever happened."

"Not a chance, Darcy." Al's wide grin took her breath away. "Not a chance."

Buster started swimming toward shore, the life vest keeping him afloat. "Is Buster okay on his own?"

"The dog's a machine."

Al sounded like a proud parent as he followed behind his pet. She shook her head, letting the hot sun soak into her skin and dry the droplets as she balanced on the kayak. It was a good thing she'd brought a change of clothes, or else she'd meet the realtor looking like something the cat yakked up.

Mrs. Al Cooper.

Thinking of herself that way brought a flurry of mutiny to her stomach. But if being attracted to him was wrong, why was she so mesmerized by him? Was she just attracted to doing the wrong thing?

She'd seen him near naked a million times, yet watching him row, his body as much of a machine as Buster's, didn't make her feel anything close to sisterly.

Darcy wanted him to hold her again. To smell his skin. To feel his arousal against her hip. Against her...

Buster reached shore at the same time as Al coasted his kayak up on the white sand. The owners must have brought it in to create their "beach" area, about the length of three kayaks, nose to nose. And about the same distance back, which was plenty of room for some lounge chairs, a grill and an umbrella.

The property had her sold, and they hadn't even gone inside. She was even getting used to the smell.

Al got out and pulled the boat back to the dock piling. Buster ran back and forth barking for her to hurry and join the party.

"I'm coming," she said.

Hand out, Al waited for her to hit the shore before pulling her in. She stumbled to her feet and he caught her against his chest. Hot skin, safe. But so...forbidden.

Darcy bit the inside of her cheek. "Thanks." She pushed gently away, peeking at him through her lashes.

His gaze was heated, his eyes stormy gray. He kept his hand on her hip, steadying her as her knees buckled.

He blinked once, a droplet of water on his lashes.

She swallowed, parted her lips.

Waited, her breath in her chest.

Would he? Kiss her?

Yes, please.

The sound of a gun cocking made her forget about Al's kiss.

Chapter Six

Darcy spun away from Al, though he had already stepped in front of her, blocking her with his body. Al called Buster to his side. She had the water at her back, and 340 pounds of combined muscle between her and danger.

All done within a second.

She peeked around Al's shoulder, hearing Buster's low growl. The animal's alert ears twitched, but he stayed put.

Al gave nothing away as he stared ahead.

Darcy swallowed and dared a glance at the gun-holder. Then she let her shoulders drop. The man had to be about 143 years old, the long rifle a relic from the Civil War. His scrawny arms shook with the weight of the gun.

His bare chest, sunken in by time, his prominent ribcage showing quite a few forgotten meals, wasn't made any prettier by the leather-tan skin.

"Whatchya doin' on this property?" His voice was a crackle of indignation. "Get on, now. Afore I shoot ya."

Al snapped his fingers and Buster relaxed, though he stayed at Al's side. Clearly, Al was not worried that this was your run-of-the-mill murderer. The gun kept dipping forward as the man's arms trembled with fatigue.

Darcy quickly surmised he had to be the homeowner to the left, if she were facing the water. Not the one that owned the house with all the "character".

"Hello there," Al said. Calm, soothing.

"Get out." The old man's voice cracked.

Al put his hand up. "I'm Al Cooper, this is my wife, Darcy. We're here to look at the property."

Darcy loved the sound of that, even if it wasn't real.

The man let the point of the rifle hit the dirt with a relieved sigh. "Thought it sold already."

"Fell through." Al took a single step forward, as did Buster.

Darcy kept her position behind Al.

"Again?" The old man's wavering tones caught after a coughing fit. He shuffled his feet, bare, with thick soles and gnarly nails that suggested a loathing for footwear or pedicures.

She looked away, focusing on his face instead. "What was your name?"

"Parker." Cough, cough. "Parker Watson."

Darcy came around Al's solid body, her hands tucked in her front pockets. "Nice to meet you. How long have you lived here?"

He eyed her with suspicion. "Forty years. Don't plan on leaving anytime soon, either."

"Oh?" Al asked. Though he spoke casually, she sensed his underlying interest in the man's words.

"Folks keep wantin' to buy me out. I don't care if it is a quarter-million dollars. Where else am I going to find all this? Usually quiet too."

He thought it was only worth a quarter million?

"You notice the smell?" Al asked.

"What smell?" Parker turned to the right and spat.

Could be coming off of him, Darcy thought, keeping her smile in place. "You said it was usually quiet?"

"You two disturbed my nap, swimming and shouting out there. Hope you won't be so noisy if you move in."

Darcy shrugged apologetically.

"Course, it ain't the first time somebody was s'posed to buy, after those foreign folks left." His eyes narrowed.

"Why do you suppose this place hasn't sold?" Al moved closer, keeping the question conspiratorial.

Darcy gave Al points for going in. She was standing downwind and Parker's body odor made her eyes water.

"Well," he said, thoughtfully scratching at his stubbly chin. "Could be asking too much money for the place."

"You think so?" Al asked.

The old man shifted his bony hips, the denim jeans held up by a black belt and his hip bones. "Could be 'cause the place is cursed."

Darcy ducked her head to hide her smile. Buster had followed at Al's heels and when she looked up, she saw that Al was now scratching his chin, too.

Instead of showing impatience, Al, as if he had a long-standing belief in the paranormal, added a nod. "Makes sense. Indian's buried around here?"

The man looked affronted. "No, sir. Pirates."

"Pirates," Al repeated, dead-pan.

Leaning against the rifle, the gun's nose deep in the dirt, Parker drawled, "I was a chile when my pop told me that about Captain Corker and his pirate scavengers. Sank a ship apurpose for the gold and jewels, killing Spanish sailors down to a man. Buried treasure right around these islands."

The old guy glanced to the side to see how Al was taking the story.

So did Darcy.

Al, a pro, a chameleon, looked so interested that Darcy forgot what a non-believer he was and inched forward herself.

"My pop said the pirates buried that treasure somewhere on this bay." Parker leaned against the rifle. "Captain Corker, he laid a curse on anyone who touched it. He and his greedy crew went back to scavenging, wantin' more gold to add to their horde. But...the Spanish queen sent out another ship, filled with soldiers, to get her treasure back."

Darcy nodded. She *knew* it.

"The pirates were attacked by the Spanish ship!" Parker pointed toward the water. "The men fought hard," he paused, "but in the end, only Captain Corker was left of his crew, and he just narrowly escaped with his life." Parker pinched two gnarly fingers together. "The captain returned to Starfish Bay, a wantin' his treasure, vowing to give up his pirating ways and live quietly in the Bahamas."

The old man moved his weight to his other hip, leaning against the rifle, his watering gaze holding Darcy's.

"He made it to the bay, alright, a worried he was too late. What if one of his scurvy pirates had gotten to the stash before him?" He inhaled, his jeans falling below one hipbone. "But he found his treasure undisturbed. Dug it up, he did. Dreamin' of sipping rum from a coconut, surrounded by beautiful women." He eyed Darcy. Heaved a sorrowful sigh. "Alas, when he placed the curse on the treasure, he'd neglected to name himself safe." He wheezed a dry laugh. "The instant he touched the treasure, his heart seized up." Parker made a bony fist. "Fell down. Dead."

"What happened to the treasure?" Darcy asked, having come close enough to see the tobacco staining the old man's teeth.

Al rolled his eyes.

"Nobody knows, aye?" He winked, his mouth quivering with repressed merriment.

Busted. Darcy laughed at herself. "You're a great story teller," she said, shaking her head. "I believed you, right until the bitter end."

Al put his hand on her lower back, caressing her skin softly.

The old man snickered and picked up the gun. "I'm off, then. Good luck buyin' the place. You might be okay neighbors." He paused and jerked his thumb toward the house on the other side of the Greek's house. "You meet them whackos over yonder?"

"You're the first one we've met," Al said with a straight face.

Darcy elbowed him.

"Talk to them afore you put any money down. They're crazy." The man dragged his gun behind him and disappeared into the bushes between their homes.

"Well?" Darcy looked at Al, hardly able to control her laughter. She took his hand and squeezed. "Shall we go meet the *crazy* neighbors, honey?"

***

Al's heart jumped as Darcy looked up at him and flirted. Her hand fit in his palm as if it belonged there. His other hand settled on her lower back, where he imagined an ice cube melting in the curve as he licked its cool trail against her warm skin. That old man with his pirate stories had ruined his chance at a kiss.

"He seemed sane," she said, jokingly.

"Right. Probably not the best judge of character. Still, it's a good idea to meet them."

"Recon. I know." Her fingers curled around his and he led the way through the palms at the back of the house, looking for a trail to cut through like the old man had done on the other side of the property.

He didn't see one. In fact, as he pulled at some ivy, he found a concrete fence meant to keep people out. "There's no short-cut." Tugging Darcy behind him, he said, "We'll have to drive."

"Can I grab my shirt?" She pulled free with an awkward smile as if remembering who they really were. "Crank the air conditioning so the truck will be nice and cool." Jogging to the dock, she gathered their things and tugged on her top.

He turned on the truck, then joined her at the dock. He shrugged into his own shirt, wishing they could go back to where they'd stood before Parker interrupted them. He'd been so close to kissing her. Twice now. Would he get a third chance?

"That old geezer had you going," he said, recalling how she'd leaned in to listen.

They got into the truck and she slid all the way over to the passenger side door. Buster took the middle. Dang dog. Blockin' his moves.

"Yeah. I've always been a sucker for a pirate story. Can you imagine?" Her voice lifted with excitement. "Treasure?"

"Aye," he said in a pretty impressive pirate growl. "Plunder and pillage, that's me motto."

Darcy shook her head and laughed. "Al, you'd be Captain of the Guard, protecting the jewels. And the queen. You act like a pirate, but you're one of the good guys."

He cursed. "Show's what you know."

She shifted on the seat, her shorts still damp. "It'd be nice to change before we meet the realtor."

"You can change in the truck—nobody's around."

Darcy flipped her hair back. "Was I born yesterday, Al?"

He grinned. "Can't blame a guy for trying."

Her brown eyes flashed with humor. "We can ask if I can change in their house."

Smart. "Check it out, see if you notice anything odd?"

"Okay, but I have a feeling everything will be, er, interesting."

He drove out of the driveway of the Greek's property and, on purpose this time, down to the house covered in sea junk. Was that seat in front of the house part of an old boat? There was water access, but no dock.

He parked the truck and a couple, about sixty, both with long gray hair, tanned skin and quick smiles, hurried from the house. Al and Darcy got out, Buster on Al's heels.

"Hey!" The woman was twice the size of the man and wore a bright pink muumuu. "Are you lost?"

"We saw you drive in earlier." The man yanked his denim cut-offs up to his faded wife beater as he walked.

"Actually," Al moved closer to Darcy and put his hand on her shoulder, "We're thinking about buying the place next door. Can you tell us about it?"

"Why sure! That would be nice, wouldn't it hon?" The woman studied Darcy with shrewd eyes and edged closer to her man.

He nodded. "Care for some iced tea?"

Darcy looked to Al and Al gave a quick yes motion with his hand.

"Bring your pup in, too." The woman leaned down to pat Buster, who wagged his stumpy tail, his tongue out to the side. "He's a cutie. I'm Lola. This is Brian."

"Thanks," Al said. He made the introductions, watching Brian check out Darcy when Lola wasn't looking.

Old pervert.

"You're all wet," he observed.

"I, er, fell off the dock," Darcy explained.

"You're welcome to change," Lola told Darcy. "Or dry your hair."

"No business of ours what yer doing." Brian smiled. "Right, neighbor?"

"Darcy, honey, want me to get your bag?" Al joined her by the passenger side of the truck. "You said you brought extra clothes."

Darcy took her hair from the tie and let it fall, wet, to her shoulders. "That would be heaven. Sticky clothes are miserable."

When he'd brought Darcy with him, he hadn't expected to meet the neighbors. Or to meet the realtor. He noticed that people were way friendlier to him as part of a couple than if he'd come snooping alone with his dog. She was a real asset.

He handed her the backpack and they went inside Lola and Brian's house. The dim interior was just as eclectic as the outside, with blown glass vases and bowls of broken shells. Hookahs. *Huh.* There was a saggy couch covered with a floral sheet and a coffee table piled with dog-eared magazines.

Darcy followed Lola into the kitchen. Linoleum from when the house was built in the 70's graced the uneven floor. A square beige Formica table with steel legs, four chairs from the same era, and variegated plants in brown macramé hangers took up all the space.

They could've been in a damn time capsule. "Are you the original owners?"

"Oh, we've been here, what honey, since—" Lola trailed off without answering.

Funny that they hadn't given their last name.

Brian poured them each iced teas and put sliced lemon and sugar cubes in the center of the table. "We don't have visitors much. No cause to stop by; there's just three of us that live here on the bay."

"We liked the Greeks. They invited us all for a barbecue when they first moved in." Lola stirred a sugar cube into her glass and sipped.

Darcy took a drink of her tea, then reached for the sugar.

Buster sat at Al's feet, leaning against his leg. He even let Brian scratch his ears. These people might be weird, but they weren't killers. So what were they hiding behind the thick concrete fence?

"I was surprised to find Starfish Bay practically vacant." Darcy rubbed at a droplet of condensation on her glass. "I mean, this is going to be our vacation home so we won't be here all the time, either, but I suppose I thought it would be more..."

"Populated?" Brian coughed into his fist. "We like it quiet."

"I don't know, sugar," Al said, the endearment coming naturally to his lips. "That bay is something else. How's the fishing?"

"It's great off their dock." Brian flushed, probably remembering that it was private property. "I imagine."

"I hate fishing," Darcy said with bright eyes as she fluttered her lashes. "I just can't get past the bones."

He thought of how adept she was with a gutting knife and bit the inside of his cheek. "We're meeting the realtor later," Al said. "It's nice of you, offering Darcy a chance to freshen up. Can't keep her out of the water." He caressed Darcy's shoulder.

"The bay is lovely," Darcy said. "But what is that smell?"

"Smell?" Brian looked to Lola, who blinked quickly.

Lola tapped Darcy's arm. "Come on darlin', the bathroom is this way."

Chapter Seven

Darcy grabbed her backpack and followed Lola toward the bathroom. The place hadn't been remodeled since it was built with pink tile, a single sink, and a stand-up shower.

She wondered how Lola even fit in the tiny room. "Thanks."

"Sure. Help yourself to whatever," Lola waved her hand.

Darcy shut the door. She turned the sink water on to cover the squeak of the mirrored door hinges. Who wasn't curious about the hidden contents in a stranger's medicine cabinet?

Darcy did a quick perusal. Hemorrhoid cream, suppositories, KY jelly, antifungal cream. *Ew.* Serves me right for looking, she thought.

Next, she checked beneath the sink. Giant rolls of single-ply toilet paper. Stacks of bar soap, industrial sized. As if they came from a business. Clog remover for the drains. Nothing suspicious.

These people were guilty of living in an old house and having bad taste. Possibly fishing off of their dock. No, not my dock, she reminded herself. The Greek's dock.

She slipped the silky rayon dress down her body, adjusting the thick spaghetti straps. The hem flounced at her knees, the color a vibrant purple. Towel drying her hair took a few minutes and she added a slick line of gloss across her lips, blowing herself a kiss in the mirror. Recon, done.

Catching sight of something brown and shiny on the window sill behind the bottle of lotion, Darcy turned to inspect the object.

She chuckled at the round bowl with the three-inch long pipe stem. Not so curious an object, and after meeting Brian and Lola, no surprise either. She sniffed, getting a hit of the remains of good old-fashioned Mary Jane. Probably home-grown, which would explain the privacy fence.

Darcy packed her damp swimsuit and clothes in the bag, swung it on her shoulder and left the bathroom. Joining the others in the kitchen, Darcy slipped by Al to sit at the table. He caught her hand and kissed her fingers. "You look great," he said.

Blushing, Darcy sat down. "Thanks, hon."

"We were just talking about real estate taxes around here," Al said casually. "They haven't been adjusted since the Greeks bought their place."

"Just a few years ago, then?" Darcy repeated.

"Brought property values up. But ain't nothin' around here to support it." Brian scowled. "A man's gotta be a millionaire just to get by."

Lola nodded in commiseration.

"We aren't millionaires," Al said. "What do you both do?"

"Bit of this and that," Brian answered, his gaze slipping from Al's.

"I work at the elementary school in Islamorada during the year," Lola said. "Got the summer's off."

A school. That explained the super-sized soap and toilet paper, Darcy thought.

"How about you?" Brian asked, scratching at his scraggly beard.

Al lowered his tone, his hands folded around his tea glass. "I'm retired from the police force." His gruff voice sent chills up and down her spine. What would it be like to live with Al? Wake up to that voice, those hands? She swallowed, her mouth dry. Wait a minute—had he just told them he was an ex-cop?

Lola suddenly pushed back from the table and stood, her girth making the floor shake. "Well, we'll be happy to have ya as neighbors, won't we, Brian?" She narrowed suspicious eyes at Darcy. "If it works out. Won't be the first time the sale on that place has fallen through."

Darcy got the hint—it was time for them to go. Why had he done that? She rose, picking up her backpack. "Come on, guys. Hate to be pests before we even move in."

"You're no bother," Lola said quickly, her smile strained as she and Brian escorted them from the house. Had the woman remembered what was in her bathroom for Darcy to see? To tell Al?

They waved from the truck, backing out of the drive. Darcy sat in the middle, letting Buster have the passenger window for the two-minute ride. It was no hardship to sit thigh to thigh on the bench seat. Al returned to the Greek's house and parked in front in front.

"Two vacant houses, hippies and a crazy old man," Darcy summarized. One woman, in lust with the wrong man. *Again.*

"People are strange." Al looked at his watch, the sunshine turning the hair on his wrist dark gold. "Ten minutes to two. Should we try for Robbie's now, or wait until after we visit with the realtor?"

Darcy shrugged. "I have a granola bar in the bag. If you're nice, I'll share."

He turned to her, his eyes a dark blue, the color of the bay. "Let's wait. That way we don't have to rush through our meal." His breath smelled like lemon from the tea, close enough to warm her face as he spoke.

"I've got a towel we can sit on." She had to get away from him, before she launched herself at his broad chest. "On our private beach. I brought water and snacks. It's not wine and caviar, but it'll tide us over."

He took the keys from the ignition and opened the truck door. "You're so practical."

"Just what a girl loves to hear." She followed and got out of the truck, the heat shocking after the chill of the air conditioning.

He flashed her that dimple and her belly whirled. "Don't be that way, *honey.*"

Darcy, unable to keep from touching him, gave his arm a light punch and stepped back. "You owe me. I'm doing you a favor."

Al grabbed her wrist before she jumped out of reach and curled her into his chest, her body shivered with awareness as he dipped her low, his large hand supporting her head. "You're being well paid for your time."

Not for one second did she feel as if he might drop her, and her blood heated with anticipation as his eyes searched her face.

He watched her. Searched her soul. Was he waiting to make sure his kiss would be welcome? Their mouths, so close but not touching, his fingers splayed in her hair.

Darcy moistened her mouth, craving the feel of his lips against hers.

She flashed back to when she'd been a young teen and Al telling her best friends did not flirt with little sisters.

That was then.

Al had his own rules, and who was she to stop him from breaking them?

***

As Darcy's arms went around his neck, as her mouth parted slightly, as her eyes darkened with desire, Al forgot about crazy neighbors, about Dax, about the realtor—about everything except the woman in his arms.

He'd watched her grow up, at a safe distance. When had he fallen in love with her? It had been so seamless that he couldn't pick a time when he hadn't loved her in one way or another.

He gently cradled the back of her head, the funny dip he'd been planning up in a puff of smoke as he held her in his arms, her mouth ripe for kissing.

She wanted to kiss him, he sensed it. He softly pressed his mouth to hers, getting to know the tender bow of her lips, her sweet taste. He pressed harder as she opened herself to him, then slowly brought her upright so they were standing, their chest's heaving, mouths an inch apart.

She blinked, her eyes dilated. "Oh."

Al swallowed, instantly aching for her. "Shit."

Darcy tilted her head, her pink mouth rosy. "Is that what you say to all the girls?"

Scuffing the back of his shaved head with his palm, Al walked to the truck and grabbed her backpack. "You have *never* been one of the girls."

She followed on his heels and spun him around by his elbow so that he had his back to the open driver's side of the truck. "What does that mean?"

"Skip it, Darce." Now that the time had come to share his feelings, his heart, he was too scared. Him, fearless Al, afraid of a blonde chick with braids.

"Fat chance!"

Al headed down to the small beach area with Darcy a breath away as he spread out her blue beach towel. He gestured for her to sit, and she did, with a frustrated scowl. He got her water bottles and a granola bar, motioning for Buster to settle down near the dock.

They faced the dark blue bay, their legs stretched in front of them. Damn, she had great legs. Long, tanned. The dress she wore was nice and short, perfect for the summer. Perfect for dancing, or making out on the beach.

But he had a feeling she wouldn't be into any more kissing until he offered an explanation.

"Any time you're ready, Al," she drawled angrily.

He tossed the granola bar he'd been about to eat to the towel. "What do *you* have to be mad about?"

She reached for the bar and broke it in half, took one for her and handed him the rest. He noticed her fingers shaking.

"What could I be mad about? Well," she said, loading the word with sarcasm. "How about Mr. 'Best Friends Don't Do Sisters'?"

"You were a kid," he said. Darcy, maybe thirteen, practicing her flirting. He eyed her figure now. "You've grown up."

They ate in silence. After about fifteen minutes she finally asked, "How long ago did you change your mind?"

He drank his water. "It's been a while."

Darcy turned toward him, getting to her knees, her pretty dress covering her prettier legs. "I don't understand. How could you have feelings for me? I'm a mess."

Al faced her and scooted closer. He put his hand to her chin and stared into her sweet, open face. "Confused, maybe, but Darcy, you've always been steady as a rock. You hold things in too often, trying to outrun your feelings. Sometimes you need to talk."

"I do. To you." Her brown eyes glittered with uncertainty.

"Not often, Darce."

"I'm confused *now*. You, I—when?" She touched his face with soft fingertips, as if she could read the answer on his cheekbone like braille.

He gently kissed her, her fingers, her mouth. "I don't know when my feelings changed into something deeper. They just did."

"Why didn't you tell me?" She spread her arms to her sides.

Why? *Why?* This was too hard. "There was never a good time."

She bowed her head, inching closer to him so that he could put his arm around her bare shoulder. Her weight settled against his body. Nothing had ever been so right.

"Your dad died, your professor sounds like a dick, and you need to finish your thesis so you can move on."

She lifted up from where she'd rested her head with a laugh that made her eyes bright. "Well. I guess that's it, in a nutshell, as they say."

"Too simple?"

"Nah. You got the highlights."

In a move he never saw coming, Darcy shifted her body so that she was sitting on his lap, facing him, with her arms around his neck. He couldn't hide his arousal, just as she couldn't hide the tight points of her breasts against his chest.

His breath caught, his entire body ached. *Needing.*

"What are you doing, Darcy?" He didn't recognize his own husky voice.

"Making sure that you really do kiss as well as you did back there by the truck." She cupped his face in her hands.

He'd dreamed this so many times but the reality was so much better. She licked his lower lip, kissing him with a tenderness that surprised him. Her passion was sweet. Hot. Burnt sugar melting over his tongue as she pressed her mouth against his, her body a welcome heat in the shade of the secluded bay.

Al dug his hands in the waves of hair at her scalp, holding her close, not sure where to touch first now that he'd been given permission.

Keeping one palm anchored in her hair, he traced her silky skin with the other. Her toned arms, her smooth legs, her thighs braced wide on either side of his legs, her purple dress covering her secrets.

Their mouths melded together in a blast of need, want—going from tentative and exploratory to demanding, searching, tasting.

He couldn't get close enough; she clung as if she could be a part of him.

His core strength kept them in a sitting position, though he was tempted to lay her back.

They had to slow down. One more kiss, one more stroke, one more shared breath.

God, their first time together couldn't be a quickie on a beach towel in the sand in broad daylight.

He nuzzled her neck, lightly biting her earlobe and she moaned, tilting her head so he could reach the other side of her throat. She clasped his shoulders, kneading his muscles, her eyes closed as she let herself just feel.

Al couldn't stop now, not when she was freely enjoying his touch. He took his tongue and licked the base of her throat, the dip and hollow, before nuzzling her neck up to her waiting mouth.

Slipping one strap of her dress down her shoulder, Al kissed his way across her collarbone, his palm cupping the underside of her breast. The firm curve with its tight peak. *Heaven.* He lightly pinched and she surged forward with pleasure, the juncture of her legs hitting the hard length between his.

She opened her eyes and looked down with surprise. "Oh…" Her breaths came quickly, her thoughts pulled into the here and now. She straightened and blinked, her small pink tongue touching her lower lip, her fingers to her breastbone.

He watched as she realized what they were doing, where they were.

Would she jump up? Tell him to stop?

He didn't want to, but if she did…

She tensed, her breaths heavy.

Al brought the pad of his finger slowly, teasingly, up her bare thigh. He would remember the sleek texture for the rest of his damn life.

They both watched as his finger dipped under the hem of her dress. She held her breath. Al waited, watching her.

Would she pull away?

Run?

No. This was Darcy. She met his gaze and accepted his challenge, her eyes flashing as she dared him to go too far.

He grinned, his dick throbbing against the rough feel of his shorts. So close to Darcy, but separated by layers of clothing.

The silky fabric covered his finger, but he felt the heat coming from her core. So freaking sexy, with her hair in waves around her face, her breasts thrust upward as she leaned back, one strap of her dress sliding down her shoulder in abandon.

Al swallowed, hurting. *Wanting.* Damn it.

How had things progressed so fast?

He didn't give a shit, he just knew that he'd bared his heart to Darcy and here she was—in his lap like a gift from the gods.

With all this talk of treasure, she was all the treasure he would ever need.

Her hips lifted in anticipation, her body slick with perspiration despite the shade. His finger edged beneath the lace of her panties and she jerked forward, her body wanting, her eyes on his.

But he had to look, he had to see the beauty of her. As if she read his mind, she slowly shimmied the dress up her thighs, higher, to the scrap of black lace covering her blonde mound. His finger edged beneath the lace and stroked her damp curls.

She inched up and scooted forward, hovering over the ridge of his shorts. He touched her tender skin as she moved on top of him, grinding down against him. Pleasure, yes, it felt good but he wanted her naked, he wanted candle light and a freaking bed, but they were here.

On a blue beach towel.

With clothes on.

He fell back and she rode against him, her eyes closed, her hand splayed against his chest as she moved her hips rhythmically, faster and faster and he watched the flesh above her breast turn rosy, her mouth parted as she hit her peak.

For the first time since he was a teenager, Al came in his pants.

***

Darcy fell forward, her breaths heaving, her breasts against Al's chest. "What was that?" she asked, dazed. "I couldn't think straight, I just had to keep kissing you." She stroked his jaw. "It's your hands, Al. Sexy. I've never done that before."

Al shook his head. "This was not how I wanted to do this."

She was thrilled that he'd thought about it. About her. "You just had an orgasm and you're complaining? Al, that's crabby even for you."

Darcy kissed his temple, watching his pulse jump. She'd had no idea that he'd make her feel so...wanted.

He got up and slipped his shorts off, keeping his boxers on, wading into the bay before diving under. God, he was gorgeous. Slim-hipped with broad shoulders and a wicked mouth that knew how to kiss.

She stood and lifted her dress to her belly as she was going to dive in after him when Buster gave a series of sharp barks.

Darcy froze, smoothing her dress back down as she pulled her strap up. Did she look like she'd just been seduced on the beach? Probably the old man again, getting a look. Maybe the weird neighbors.

Al grumbled as he trudged from water, shaking like a dog as he reached for his dry shorts. "The damn realtor."

Darcy pulled Al close, kissing his cheek. "Oh honey. Are you the kind that needs a nap after sex?" She patted his butt and watched the flush rise up the back of his scalp. "You are too cute. Now, let's go buy a house."

Chapter Eight

Darcy climbed over the rise of the beach area, Buster on one side and Al on the other. A silver BMW gave two beeps as a tall woman in a light pink fitted skirt and summer short-sleeved jacket locked the car with her remote.

"Hello!" She waved a folder toward them and patted a pink wallet-purse before pulling out a key. "You must be Darcy Cooper and..."

"I'm Darcy, this is Al Cooper, my husband." He'd wanted to pretend they were married. Maybe things had gone a little too far, but she wouldn't hold it against him. However, for the moment, she planned on playing her part to the hilt. "So pleased to meet you..."

"Lori Ferguson." The realtor, her hair sprayed in a smooth, brunette bob, glanced at them. "Did I get the appointment time wrong?"

"No." Al spoke crisply.

Darcy smiled. "My husband likes to be early." She heard Al's choked laugh and followed the realtor to the door.

Without further comment, Lori stuck the key in the lock and opened the door. "Come on in."

Darcy thought it odd that the realtor hadn't come early herself to spruce the place up. Maybe open a window or two. Then again, it was a last-minute appointment.

She froze on the threshold and covered her mouth with her hand. The stink was coming from inside the house. Al stepped between Darcy and the realtor, his body alert. Lori Ferguson gave a delicate cough.

"What is that smell?" Darcy asked. Buster whined and scratched at the floor. She tightened the hold she had on his leash.

Al paced the small living room, checking in corners. There was no furniture, and the flooring was amber tile.

Lori Ferguson shook her head and lifted her cell phone. "I've called the city—I think there must be a raccoon or something." She met Darcy's eyes and whispered, "Under the house."

"How long has it been like this?" Darcy looked at Al, but he gave nothing away.

Patting her helmet-hair, Lori shrugged. "They've been here once already."

Darcy didn't back down from a challenge. Al's clients needed to know what was going on with their property, so they had to check out everything. "Honey, we came all this way. Can we see the kitchen?"

Al winced, but nodded and took her hand. "Sure."

Lori Ferguson waved them forward, her nostrils flared. "It's been redone."

They turned a corner into a kitchen that could've been cute if there weren't mice droppings all over the floor. Grimy white cabinets, possibly turquoise counters—it was hard to tell.

Darcy stared at the realtor, who had the grace to back up a step as she said, "It'll just need a little elbow grease."

"Really?" Darcy kicked at something stuck to the floor.

"Why didn't you hire a service?" Al asked, anger simmering in his tone. "How can you sell the property like this?"

Lori looked offended and held her cell phone to her chest. "I've put enough money into this place. It's up to the owners to make it shine."

Darcy blinked. The smell inside the kitchen was overwhelming and brought tears to her eyes. Buster pulled her toward the refrigerator, her sandals sliding on the dirty ceramic tile.

Al jumped in front of her and gestured her to stop.

He put his hand on the refrigerator door.

The realtor took a step back. "I don't think," she said, then let her words trail off as Al opened it wide.

Darcy gagged and turned around, breathing in through the crook of her elbow. "What *is* that?"

Al, stoic and calm, didn't overreact at the moldy interior. He narrowed his eyes and studied the contents before turning back to the realtor. "Limburger cheese."

Lori Ferguson paled. "Disgusting."

"You didn't bother to clean the refrigerator?" Al asked.

Backing from the kitchen, the realtor covered her mouth with her little pink purse. "Let's go outside for some fresh air," she suggested.

Darcy stole sips of air through her open mouth. Buster growled at the refrigerator while Al stared as if cataloguing every last mold spore.

"Al? Is that really cheese?"

He nodded then slammed the refrigerator door shut. "Yeah. We used it as a prank for a guy on the force that just got married. Nasty shit. Lingers forever."

Remaining in character, she took his hand, enjoying the tingle that came from their joined skin. "We should definitely lower our asking price."

Al's dark brows shot upward and he flashed a surprised smile. "Yeah?"

"We have to cover the cost of a new fridge and fumigating this house." If they were really married, she'd help him paint. They'd take a swim in the bay after a hard day's work. Cool off with wine. Heat back up again by making love on the beach.

Al kissed her knuckles and followed her down the hall, peeking in at the two bedrooms. "Look," he said, pointing to the master. "A full view of the bay."

"It's beautiful," she agreed, taking in the lush preserve across the sparkling blue water. The mangroves and wildlife they could see from the window. *Their bed.*

"You're beautiful." He looked away from the window and smoothed her hair back from her cheek. She smiled at him, wishing this could be for real. But no, they'd gotten caught up in the moment, in pretending they were different people. That had to explain what happened on the bay. Would his mouth be as addicting if she kissed him now? Her body temperature rose. "Let's go put in an offer."

Al gently pushed her forward, whispering, "I got this—but let's get outside first, before we both pass out from the fumes."

***

The realtor was on the phone when they escaped the house, but she hung up when she saw them. "I just reamed the cleaning service a new one. I can't apologize enough."

Cleaning service? It hadn't been touched since his clients had gone back to Greece two years ago. He'd bet his P.I. license on it. But he had to figure out what game the realtor was playing. And were the inhabitants of the bay in on the joke?

"We need to talk about it." He caressed his thumb over Darcy's palm and watched her pulse jump at the wrist.

Lori slipped her phone into her purse. "All right. You have my number."

No trying to do the hard sell? Odd. Maybe she realized she had to do a lot to get past that stench. His dog wanted desperately to go back inside and smell it some more. The police force had trained him to get past those things, but it was nasty. Darcy's fortitude impressed him.

Al snapped his fingers and Buster heeled. "Do you mind going down to the bay to get our towel, hon?" He looked at Darcy, who nodded with a love-sick look in her eyes. He wished. What if she'd just gotten caught up, playing a role?

"Sure, babe." She walked over the small decline of dirt yard to the secluded bay and the dock.

He looked at the realtor. "My wife wants this house. What's it going to take to make it ready?"

Lori blinked in surprise. "Oh? Uh…well."

Al wondered where his client had found this woman. Realtors R Us?

Darcy walked slowly toward them, her backpack over her shoulder, looking care-free and gorgeous in her short purple dress. He'd remember the look of pleasure in her eyes forever. Hoped like hell he could go there again.

He took the bag and put his arm around Darcy's shoulder to face the realtor. "Get back to me with some amazing numbers and we might make a deal. But I want a new paint job to get the stench out of the walls. A new refrigerator, too."

"But I can't, I mean, there are no promises." Lori clamped her mouth tightly together. "I'll call the owners, Mr. Cooper. See what I can do."

That was more like it.

Darcy looked up at him with a sappy smile. "You mean it, honey?"

"We'll see." Al leaned down to kiss her soft cheek. "Ready? We've got a long drive."

"Nice to meet you," Darcy said, getting in the passenger side. Buster jumped into her lap, leaving her no choice but to slide over to the middle. She waved to the realtor as Al got in behind the wheel.

She kept smiling as they pulled out of the drive, patting Buster and humming under her breath.

Al drove slowly around the curved dirt road of Starfish Bay. Old man Parker was out by his mailbox, leaning against his rifle, staring at them as if they'd never met.

"Old coot," Al muttered.

"Yeah?" Darcy's smile didn't slip. "Check out the rearview." She looked in the side mirror. "The hippies are in the road, watching us drive off too."

"This place is strange." Strange wasn't always bad, but something was going on under the surface that he'd have to figure out. Not just for his clients—this was personal.

"I don't know," she said. "Parker's old and crotchety. The hippies? Bet they're hiding weed in the mangrove roots around their house. They had a pipe in the bathroom, which is probably why Lola wanted us out so fast. They don't want nosy neighbors, especially an ex-cop," she said with a side-glance his way. "Why did you tell them that?"

"A lot of P.I. work is going with your gut. Shake things up—we were asked out pretty quick, confirming that they're doing something illegal. I saw a small boat by their water access, right across from the preserve. Makes me wonder *where* they might be growing whatever they're growing—but I don't care, personally, about that crap." Al shrugged and checked his mirrors. Lori Ferguson was in her car, but hadn't left the property. "They can smoke their brains out so long as they aren't hurting anyone else."

"I love that you follow your own road. I wish I was more like that."

One hand on the wheel, he rested his other arm behind Darcy on the cab seat. "How so?"

"I mean, I tried to live my own life but I got off track completely." She shrugged and wouldn't look at him. Her voice trembled.

Al scrubbed his forehead with a rough palm. No wonder Dax hadn't pressed the issue with her; she slayed them with her sadness. "Drama, drama. Not like you, Darcy."

Annoyance replaced tears as she snapped, "I'm too practical for drama?"

"Yeah." He scooted over, very slightly, so that his leg touched hers. Accidentally, of course. He wasn't sure she was sold on the *Al loves Darcy* show. "Obviously not, if I was willing to sleep with my professor." Her nose lifted with defiance.

His gut knotted. "I'd bet my license that it wasn't for a grade."

She sighed and relaxed her body. "No."

"So, you got hurt." Al wanted to help her over that hurdle. For selfish reasons, but he had to have her in his life. In his bed. Not on a towel for Christ's sake. "What else did you learn?"

She rubbed the soft fur between Buster's ears as the big dog looked out the window. "I don't condone taking money to skew test results. I don't have a passion for coral?"

"What do you have a passion for?" He hoped she'd say him.

"What's in my life? The Dive Shop. Bugfest. God, Al, I never thought I'd end up back home again."

Al put his hand on her thigh and her cool skin heated. "What do you want?"

Her eyes welled as she stared straight ahead. "Time to focus on my master's. That bay was gorgeous. And the dolphins?" She glanced at him. "Don't laugh, Al, but I swear I heard my dad tell me that things were fine."

Al kept his opinion to himself. If it made Darcy feel better, then what did it hurt if she believed that? "Not laughing."

"Thank you."

They hit Overseas Highway, leaving Starfish Bay behind. Darcy slid her fingers through his as she covered his hand. "So, now that we aren't playing Mr. and Mrs. Cooper anymore, care to explain to me what is going on with that realtor? She needs to be fired!"

Chapter Nine

"I'll call my clients," Al said, letting go of Darcy's leg to hook up his phone to the speaker. Then he hit the disconnect button. "Wait a sec. You still up for Robbie's shrimp tacos? We can hash out a plan over late lunch."

"Yeah!" Darcy casually moved across the bench seat as if to reach for her purse and phone, scooting Buster to the middle of the bench. Being so close to Al flustered her senses. The man exuded testosterone and for some reason, she was soaking it up like a sea sponge. His palm on her skin was so hot it should have left an imprint.

She checked her phone. "Two texts from Dax, wondering how things are going." God, if he knew what she and Al had done on that towel he'd shoot them. She shook her head, refusing to think of where his hands had been. *So good.*

Al scowled and looked away from her. "I'll call him from the restaurant."

"He's probably nervous," she said, keeping her tone chatty. "Tomorrow's the first day of Bugfest. It gets crazy."

"I'm in the office, while you guys dive," Al said. "I traded time for your help today. You played the part of Mrs. Cooper very nicely."

Her skin flushed. "Just an act."

His brow lifted. "Some things you can't fake."

Squirming, she cleared her throat and stared out the window. Could she die now, please? "That realtor was awful."

"I'm going to recommend they find another realtor. Their home was a pit."

"Great view from that master bedroom though."

"Worth a half-million?"

"Maybe once the cheese smell is gone," she said, keeping her tone light.

He didn't have to call her practical, she felt him think it. Within five minutes, they pulled into Robbie's Marina. The place was packed, but they got a small table by the water.

She ordered a South Florida brew, Monk in the Trunk, while Al went for a Sam Adams draft. Buster was between them on the ground, alert for any food that might fall while he people-watched from under the table.

"Shall we have a toast?" Darcy lifted her beer. "To my first P.I. case."

"You'd do it again? It's not that glamorous." He clinked his glass to hers. "You did great, though." Al drank. "What was your first instinct about the realtor?"

Darcy considered how Lori Ferguson hadn't come early to air out the property, or mark the turn-off. "She didn't do her job."

"Exactly." Al tapped the table with his thick finger. "She *overtly* didn't do her job."

Darcy leaned forward. "You think she put the cheese in the fridge?"

Al snapped his fingers. "I do."

She frowned. "That doesn't make sense. If the house doesn't sell, she is out a major commission."

"Maybe." He sat back. "This is where P.I. work gets really tedious—loads of paper trails to follow that usually lead nowhere. Until you find that golden thread and voila! The lies come crashing down."

"That sounds terrible!"

"Nine out of ten times, if it smells rotten, it's rotten. You can help me research tonight, if you want."

"Sure." At his condo? After what happened in broad daylight today, being alone in his private space might not be a smart tactical move on her part. What if he'd been telling the truth about how he felt about her?

Fear rushed through her. She'd been through so much change already that more seemed overwhelming, even if their experience earlier had been freaking awesome. Lovers were intimate. "Friends" was safe. Friends meant they could work together at the Dive Shop tomorrow without it being awkward.

What would Dax think?

His baby sister and his best friend?

"You okay, Darce?"

Al pinioned her with his blue-gray gaze.

"Yes. Thanks." If he *truly* cared for her, when she wasn't sure how she felt—other than turned on—it wouldn't be fair to take their physical relationship further.

He jerked his chin as if he wanted to say more, but the waiter brought out two steaming platters of shrimp tacos with sweet potato fries.

They each concentrated on the food. She let the chili pepper settle on her tongue, cooling the heat with a dollop of sour cream. Angel-hair cabbage and red onion all wrapped together in a fluffy flour tortilla.

"I dream about these," she said. Watching Al take his in four bites. Big hands, big…

She took a large drink of her amber beer.

"They're good." He wiped his mouth with the paper napkin and sat back. "Worth the drive." His phone rang and he looked at Darcy, then narrowed his eyes. "Big brother." He answered with one hand, setting the phone on the napkin holder between them. "Yo. Got you on speaker."

Her brother's voice shouted, "Hey! How's it going? Me and Celia have been wondering what's up with you two?"

"The house stinks," Darcy said, exchanging a smile with Al.

"Too bad," Dax said, not getting the joke. "You get paid no matter what, though, right, Al?"

Al scratched his chin. "Up front."

"You on the road?"

"Nope. Tacos at Robbie's."

"Jealous!" Dax paused. "I bet Celia could make them better."

Darcy nodded with enthusiasm. "She should try, for sure."

Al chuckled. "It's all about the food with you people."

"So you're coming home…when?"

Darcy gave the phone, and her brother, a look. "When we get there. We're fine."

"Hey, I'm just worried about tomorrow. You're both on the schedule. Are you all right, Darce?"

"Fine." She finished her last bite, chasing it with her beer. *What was his problem?* "We'll be there." It was on the tip of her tongue to call him dad, but that memory was too fresh so she held back.

"Will you be coming to the house? We can watch a movie or something."

Darcy shook her head. Since when had her big bro decided she needed a keeper? "Nope. I'll be staying above the shop, like I have been."

"Okay, okay." He cleared his throat. "Your old room is waiting for you."

"Thanks, Dax." She was confused about going home. Her dad's memory, her anger at her brother for keeping Dad's illness from her. So where did she belong? Nowhere. "Love you. See you in the morning."

"Bye." Al ended the call and dropped the phone in his pocket. He studied her over his empty beer glass.

"What?" Darcy sat back, sated.

"You tell me."

Al was good at that, waiting longer until the other person felt compelled to speak. "I don't think I fit at home."

"The Dive Shop?"

"I love that place; you know I do. It's in my blood. But I can't move back into my old bedroom and live there forever. I'm not that person anymore. I still have a Violent Femmes poster over my bed."

Al smirked.

"I love South Florida." She looked around. "Think I could get a job bartending at Robbie's? Will work for food." She smiled, but stopped before it spread too wide.

"Maybe you need your own apartment. One away from the shop."

She rubbed her arms and dug deeper. "It's not the shop. It's me."

"How?"

She struggled for the words. "I went to college with the idea that I'd make important discoveries. Save the ocean. Doing that internship, well, I realized that it's all politics. When we were out on the kayaks this afternoon, it was peaceful. That fills my heart, connects me. I like that you were there with me."

His nodded, listening.

"I need to finish my thesis. Which means I need to be at the shop, working, until I get it done." She formed the plan as it came to her lips. "I've got to tell Dax, so he knows what to expect. He wants to ask, without prying."

"He loves you."

She bowed her head and gave Buster a sweet potato fry. "Love is like a lobster trap."

Al snorted. "I don't think Hallmark will go for that."

She chuckled. "When somebody loves you, you're obligated to be a decent person to them. Like, I can't be an asshole to Dax because I know he loves me. I love him; we are all we've got left in the world."

Al reached out and took her hand. "You've got me. No matter what happens later, you will still always have me."

She met his gaze, terrified by what she read there.

"I love you, Darcy."

Swallowing hard past the lump in her throat, she nodded. God, that took guts for him to share. She owed him honesty. "Thank you." Mustering courage, she said, "The bitch of it is, I don't know what to do with that."

His jaw clenched and he rubbed his thumb over her palm. "We've established that you can't be an asshole."

She laughed.

"That's enough for now. We'll take things slow."

"What if..." Her brother's smiling face loomed in her thoughts.

"If you and I decide to take this friendship in another direction, Dax will understand."

She shook her head. "I'm not so sure. It's a bad risk—I'm not good with relationships."

Al inched his empty glass forward. "I don't believe that."

Darcy sipped from her iced water. "Haven't you listened to a word I've been saying?" She tried to keep her words light, the emotion too heavy for her to embrace. "I am obviously incapable of making life decisions."

"Bullshit." Of course, Al called her on it.

The waiter dropped their bill on the table. Al paid with cash, leaving a good tip. He was a great guy. Friend. Lover? She wasn't sure they could be both.

He tugged at Buster's leash and they walked out of the marina to the gravel parking lot. "You made a mistake, Darce. But until you forgive yourself, you won't get over it."

"What do you know about guilt?" She could write a book, she thought, scuffing her sandals along the gravel toward the black Ford. The evening sky turned the colors of rainbow sherbet, the weather cooled by the breeze off of the Gulf.

"I know plenty."

His clipped speech told her to pay attention. "Yeah?"

"Do you want to know why I left the force?" He wouldn't look at her as he unlocked the truck.

She'd asked over the years and been shut down. He'd been angry in those days, determined to do things his way. "I'd assumed it was because you wanted to work for yourself."

"Yeah." He climbed in, his body stiff. "That was part of it."

Once inside, she closed the passenger door and he started the vehicle. Buster, in the middle, whined to be in her lap. "Stay," she told the dog as she checked the time. Just after seven, they'd be home before ten.

"Al, you don't have to tell me, not if you don't want to." She understood that sometimes it was better to keep things buried.

"I owe you."

"What?" She clicked her seatbelt. What could he mean by that?

"Yeah." He hesitated, adjusting the mirrors as if stalling for time. "You've been honest with me all day. I don't want any misunderstandings between us."

"Uh, you've been pretty honest yourself." Saying he loved her. Like, love-loved her.

"You've been a great help with the realtor, and meeting the neighbors. The best company I could ask for."

Her heart hammered in her chest as she waited for him to get to the damn point.

Al rolled his shoulders. Drove out of the lot and onto the highway. Pinks and oranges turned magenta and gold as the sun set behind them.

"Your brother wanted me to bring you along today. To find out what was bothering you." He smacked his fist against his thigh, glancing quickly at her before retuning his attention to the highway. "I've been trying to talk to you for months, but you shut down faster than a poked sea anemone. This was a chance to get you alone."

No P.I. work? Her chest constricted. "Dax set me up?"

"It's not like that."

"It feels pretty shitty." She rubbed her aching throat.

Al, her champion, coerced into talking with her? And she'd spewed like a geyser.

"We've all been so worried about you."

"So my big brother asked his best friend to help out his little sister. Tell me," she snapped, seeing red. "Does Dax know your secret? That you've got feelings for me?"

"No. He doesn't. But I'm going to tell him, Darcy."

Her eyes welled with bitter tears. She'd trusted him. It had felt so good to confide in Al. To hold his hand. To consider the possibility of more. "Don't bother."

"Why? I am not ashamed that I love you."

"It's not going anywhere, so don't risk your friendship with my brother." God, all she wanted to do was to run but she was trapped in this truck for two hours.

Buster licked her hand and she buried her face in his soft fur. Was love supposed to hurt?

Al, his voice thick, said, "Whatever you tell me? It's between us, Darcy. I have never betrayed your confidences. I won't. I never thought I'd have the opportunity to tell you how I felt, so I didn't see the point in sharing my feelings. But, now you know. I'll tell your brother. What Dax does with that information is up to him."

Darcy heard the truth in Al's words, though they stung like an open cut doused in salt water. They drove in silence, Darcy's emotions on overload.

"I left the force because I got a guy killed."

Sniffing, Darcy lifted her head. "Al, you don't have to tell me. You don't owe me a thing."

"Following supervisor's orders. I knew the call was bunk, but I had to follow the rules. Be a cop." His grip on the wheel shone white along the knuckles. "I should have said screw procedure. I didn't." He gritted his teeth. "I have to live with that for the rest of my life."

A man was dead. No wonder Al didn't talk about it. "A criminal?"

"A fellow officer."

Damn. Her heart went out to him—he'd been following orders. The rules. They'd gone wrong. She knew he was a good man, and that must have been torture.

"I wasn't even thirty, and I had blood on my hands." Al spoke in a monotone.

"It was your job, Al. Not your fault."

"It was." His jaw clenched. "I could have said forget it."

"And been *fired*." He'd been between a rock and a hard place.

"Officer Gary Lane would be alive. What's more important?"

She contemplated that in the near dark, her thoughts flickering like the oncoming headlights. He'd told her something private. A painful secret in exchange for hers. Were they even? Did that matter? Their relationship had crossed into something new.

Finally she concluded, "If you don't follow rules while you're a cop that could get *you* killed too." Darcy reached across the seat to touch his shoulder—not because she forgave him, but because she cared. "I'm glad you chose your own road."

He shifted and glanced at her. "Thank you. I don't talk about it. Time doesn't make you forget, but the memories get easier to live with." Al put his hand on the seat between them, palm up. "Don't let that asshole take something you've earned away. The ocean is your life."

She thought of all the time she'd spent documenting reefs and sniffed. The professor could keep his coral. There was a big blue sea for her to make her own, somehow. Darcy put her hand in Al's.

***

Al dropped her off at the Dive Shop, not pressing when she asked him to take her there instead of his condo. He was just glad she was still talking to him. Sort of. Clipped sentences instead of chatty conversation, but that was better than two hours of silent recrimination.

"See you in the morning," she said, leaning across Buster, who spread out between them, drowsy. She kissed Al on the mouth, sensually, but not in invitation. Just…saying good night. "I'm serious. Don't talk to Dax about anything, all right? Not until after Bugfest. Talk with me first."

He nodded, owing her that.

"Don't work too late. I emailed you the notes we discussed in the car. I think you should check what that area is zoned for, first."

"Agreed. You did good, Darce. I'd hire you."

She backed up, her hand on the passenger door. "Yeah? It's good to have options."

"In case the marine biology thing doesn't work out?" She questioned, poked and prodded, which is what made her a great scientist. Turned out those same qualities were needed in his line of work.

Shrugging, she dragged her backpack out behind her. "Thanks Al, for everything. It means a lot."

She shut the door before he could answer back.

He'd confessed his feelings. She hadn't professed feeling the same, but she hadn't laughed at him, either. And damn, being with her—holding her—had been the stuff of dreams.

He drove home, parking his truck in the gated garage below the building. Buster did his business, then they went upstairs. His condo, done in deep browns and grays, reflected his minimalistic style. Comfy, though, he thought, sinking into the deep-cushioned leather couch. Instead of flipping on the television, he powered up his laptop.

Darcy had brought up some good questions on the ride home. What would make a realtor turn her back on a hefty commission? South Florida was paradise, so why was Starfish Bay so rural? Given the residents, a commune wasn't far off the mark.

He checked public records for zoning laws. Starfish Bay was residential only.

A guy he'd used while on the force had shown him how to hack into just about any website. His mind had a talent for figuring code. Darcy was right—he could've been a criminal. He'd decided on a white hat instead and then, tossing it to the side, no hat at all. If shit went bad, he knew who to blame.

It took him thirty minutes to get into Lori Ferguson's realty website. He ran another program to break into other files on the server including a restricted folder titled: Starfish Bay. Within twenty minutes, he sat back and cracked open a beer. There had been ten offers for the property, some of them *over* the original asking price.

His clients were hurting for cash and this crooked realtor was screwing them over. He clicked on a separate file in that same folder called, Big Deal. "Hmm. Big deal."

Al straightened so fast he startled Buster on the floor at his feet. "Holy shit. There's an offer for the entire bay for over ten million dollars." He immediately checked the county's permit office. Sure enough, a request had been made to change the zoning, making it open for a hotel and casino. *Decision pending.*

He stayed up way too late researching how to change zoning, and what happened to the people who already had homes. He remembered the two vacant homes and ran a quick search.

Lori Ferguson was the mortgaged-to-the-hilt owner of both.

Chapter Ten

Channel surfing at midnight didn't help quiet her mind. Al's declaration aside, his kisses aside, her brother's meddling aside, Darcy was determined to untangle at least one emotional thread so that she could move forward.

The studio apartment didn't seem like *home*. But since her dad's death, being in their family house was bitter sweet.

It was Dax's place. He and Celia hung out there a lot. He'd asked her what she wanted to do with it, since they'd inherited the house together. He'd offered to sell it, or share it, or buy out her half.

The garage was full of old, broken memories that she'd put behind her when she'd gone to college—with the idea that they would be there for her to bring out whenever she was nostalgic. Her stuffed bear from her first carnival win, her skateboard with the missing wheel. The idea of a stranger living there freaked her out. She'd rather Dax had the house, so she could visit when she wanted. *Selfish, Darcy.*

Was it right for him to pay her for it? She didn't want his money. Maybe *he* needed to move on? The small inheritance from their dad was enough to give her a head start wherever she wanted to go. She put peanut butter on a saltine cracker and chewed in contemplation.

Which was where, exactly?

God. She'd been better grounded as a teenager.

Darcy turned off the television and pretended to sleep. She smothered mistakes and regret in her pillow, counting lobster tails instead of sheep.

Up before dawn, she went for a morning run. She dressed in the dark, crossing the studio apartment to the door leading down into the shop below. Confident of where to put each step—having grown up here equal time as their house—she didn't bother to light the stairs and exited from the back entrance of the shop.

Inhaling deeply, the familiar smells of the ocean, fish oil and salt, instantly soothed her troubled mind.

She loved the cool sand between her toes, the pound of the waves as she fell into a rhythm. Running allowed her brain to turn off. Something about the stretch of muscle, the pull of tendon, the challenge to push a little bit harder, satisfied the part of her head that wouldn't shut up.

No room for the professor, or her mistakes. Al was right, and she had to let it go. He'd done it in his own life, not dwelling on the past and pain. No wonder he chose not to believe in ghosts.

A thought occurred so suddenly that she stopped and fell to her knees in the surf. Salty water landed on her upper lip, tasting like tears. She wiped her cheeks. *Tears.*

Her poisonous anger came from realizing that if Dax had called her home to be with her dying father, a noble, loving action, then she wouldn't have stayed with Professor Petrovsky and had her dreams of saving the world disillusioned. A cramp seized her side and she pressed down.

And here she was, ready to add more blame to poor Dax, who loved her.

Enough. Own it, Darcy Smith. Shit happens. She got to her feet and dug into the sand, head down, balls-out for home. *Just me. Releasing the professor, forgiving myself. Let it go.*

She finished her run and burst into the back door of the shop. Al was at the register with two coffees when she arrived, drenched in sweat. "We have to talk," he said. His shaved head gave him a sexy, pirate-look, aided by the Vin Diesel half-snarl he'd perfected.

"Sure." She took a paper towel from the roll by the empty coffee pot and ran it under cool water in the sink before wiping her face. "You stopped at the gas station?"

"It seemed simpler," Al said. "Khanti says hi."

Darcy nodded and took the cup, lifted the lid and inhaled. "You remembered. French vanilla creamer."

"So, want to hear what I found out last night while digging around on the Internet?"

She blew on the hot brew, grateful that he hadn't started in about his feelings. They weren't going away, and she didn't want them to, but she needed more time. "I do."

Al grinned. "You were right, about the zoning."

"Yeah?"

"Starfish Bay is residential." He clicked his Styrofoam cup to hers. "Lori owns two of the five houses and has a request in to change the zoning laws. She wants to build a five-star resort and casino. As unethical as your professor, only against the law, too."

"Well, if you're going to dream, dream big," she said. "Did you turn her in?

"I've got a call in to my clients. We'll see how they want to play it."

Sweat from her run was drying on her neck. "That's great news, Al. But for the record, I don't have a professor." She flicked her fingers into the air. "Released, this morning. Now, I'm headed for the shower."

"Good to know. That means I can do this..." He came around the cash register and took her by the chin, kissing her so tenderly that her eyes closed.

"You have to stop that." She pulled away, a smile dancing around her mouth.

"Why?"

"You know why. You kiss me and I..." Darcy started for the stairs leading up to the studio, but Al was quicker.

"Wait. I love you."

She hadn't wanted to go there. "Stop, Al. Don't say another word." Darcy put her coffee between them, keeping her face set. Hiding her emotions, while his were plain to see across his beloved face. "I need to think about this. Make sure it's not a mistake."

His blue-gray eyes turned charcoal in the dim interior of the shop. "Give me a chance. We need to talk, Darcy."

"No, Al. We need to pretend that we," she gestured between them, "are just friends. Just like always."

Chapter Eleven

Saturday afternoon, Darcy slid her sharp silver knife up the back of the lobster, separating the head from the tail while getting as much of the meat as possible, then putting the tail in a briny salt bath with ice in a cooler.

"Did you ever see such a big one?"

She bit the inside of her cheek, knowing that the innuendo was innocent. The man with the Canadian accent was totally focused on the size of his lobster. He and his wife, dark-haired, sunburned and beaming, stood shoulder to shoulder as they watched her prepare their catch. Just another service that came with the diving package.

"You can come back in an hour, if you'd like. They'll be perfectly chilled. Ready for cooking tonight." Darcy's gloves protected her from the lobster's sharp spines.

The wife smiled and put her hand through the crook in her husband's arm. "We could have a glass of wine while we wait." She gestured toward Anglin's bar, a covered outdoor seating area attached to the pier.

"They've got a decent selection of craft beers, too." Darcy knew the owners well and mini lobster season added a nice bump for business in a hot summer for everybody.

The husband reluctantly allowed his wife to pull him away. "I don't know..."

Darcy pointed to the bucket with six lobsters left to clean, and the white cooler that had their name on it. "These will go directly in there. Nobody will get yours, I'll make sure of it. You got terrific tails here."

He sighed and followed his wife.

There was a party atmosphere with the grills and outside booths in the center of town. A two-man band played Caribbean style music and kids ran between the fountains to stay cool. Plastic lobsters were everywhere.

She'd missed this, being away for college. Her parents had raised her and Dax on the beach. Always in the ocean, snorkeling, free-diving, offshore diving. She'd manned the cash register in the Dive Shop from the time she was twelve. She'd give just about anything to go back to those days.

But she couldn't. Starting today, there would be no more regrets. She and her brother needed a heart to heart, first thing Monday morning. She adored him, and there was no being an asshole to someone you loved.

Dax, bleached-white curls around his face, joined her, holding a giant squirming lobster in his gloved hand.

"Holy shit!" Darcy said, dropping hers in the Canadian's bucket. "That's got to be fifteen pounds!"

Average size was around eight pounds. Anything too small was illegal to harvest.

"I know!" Dax grinned. "The boys from England got this one."

The boys were literally teenage twins whose parents got them the lobster hunting experience as a pre-college present.

Pale and fair-haired, Darcy had insisted on extra sunscreen for them before they'd gone out this morning.

She looked up as they shouted for Dax to wait. They carried a bucket between them, filled with lobsters. Shoulders red, noses red, grins wide.

"Well done!" Darcy waved.

Dax set the lobster on the scale they'd brought to the cleaning area by the pier. "Sixteen. You boys should be proud."

"Let me get a picture for the website," Darcy said, taking off her gloves and pulling her phone from her back pocket. "Travis, Trevor, get on either side of the lobster. Don't let go, Dax."

The giant "bug" was still alive and wasn't happy about being caught. Its long thin legs reached out, the antennas sweeping the air for something to grab onto.

"Yeah," Travis said. "Don't let go."

"You already caught it, Trav!" Trevor slung his arm around Dax. "Our mates will be jealous."

"Gotta post it on Instagram." Travis held up two fingers, the equivalent of the American middle finger.

Darcy shook her head. *Boys.* "One, two, three, smile!" She took a couple, one without the fingers. "I'll send them to you. And hey, get some aloe on your faces."

"Darcy?"

She turned toward Al, who walked Buster on a braided leather leash. "Hey, great job on the boat this morning. The customers are very happy. Where did you go? Some of these lobsters are monsters!" Buster sniffed the coolers and the basket of lobster heads.

"I found a little alcove up toward Pompano. Big rocks, big lobsters."

Tapping her chin, she noted that most of the bigger lobsters had come from that area this year. An ember that she'd worried had died flared to life. "I have got to be the slowest marine biologist in the world."

Al frowned. "What?"

"I know what I'm doing my thesis on." She grabbed his arm, smiling wide, so glad that he was part of her revelation. It felt good—it fit.

"Tell me." Al rubbed her bare shoulder, his eyes searching her face as he smiled in response to her widening grin.

She wanted him to kiss her. She wanted him to hold her. His thumb caressed her skin. She lifted on tip-toe, her mouth raised...

Buster barked, breaking their locked gaze. *Probably for the better.* Darcy leaned down and hooked her fingers under his collar for a scratch. "Hello, baby."

Al held out his hand, palm up. "I'm dying here, Darce. What's your plan?"

She shuffled her feet in a little dance. "*Panulirus argus*...lobster. South Florida spiny lobster."

Al looked around at all of the plastic lobsters and Bugfest paraphernalia. "Freaking awesome. Love it—your research *will* make a difference." He put his hand on her shoulder.

The new direction brought a rush of adrenalin. "Maybe. I'll have to do some research first. Tag them. Follow them from this year to next." Lists of things to do came at her in a flood and she couldn't keep still. "All because of your excellent advice, Al."

Tossing caution aside, Darcy threw her arms around Al's neck and hugged him tight. She lifted her face for a kiss as Dax's voice cut across the cleaning area. "Hey. What's wrong? Darcy, are you all right?"

Reluctantly, Darcy pulled away, giving her brother a pointed look. "Nothing's wrong." Monday couldn't come fast enough.

He eyed her with suspicion.

Al stayed at her side. She casually moved away. Would it always be a tug of war? "Al just helped me figure out what I'm doing my thesis on. Lobster."

"That's brilliant, Darce. Can't believe we never thought of that before." Dax turned to Al. "Celia's asking for you. She's getting the grill fired up."

"No problem. I'll run Buster home and be right back." Al looked at Darcy, his expression unreadable. "Congratulations."

***

Al found Celia by the large silver barbecue grill and a wooden sign that read, Ambrosia by the Sea.

"Looks good," he said. "Any regrets, moving to the beach?"

Celia, a pretty blonde with a perky ponytail and wide blue eyes, tied an apron around her waist. A crimson lobster sprawled across the front, holding an ear of corn in one claw. "None. I'm doing what I love, cooking, with people I care about." She pointed to Dax and the Dive Shop station before focusing on him. "I've made great friends. When are you going to find someone special, Al?"

"All you couples think everybody should be coupled. I'm happy on my own. Hell, I got Buster to watch the sunset with."

"I like dogs as much as the next person," she said, moving to the cooler behind the grill. "But it's not the same." She smiled, a pair of barbecue tongs in her hand. "I have a friend..."

Al groaned and took the tongs. "I'm here to cook, Celia. Don't fix me up. Please."

She quirked a brow. "Is your heart already spoken for? Say, a tall blonde scientist-type?"

He clenched his jaw.

"Being the new kid on the block, I see things differently. She looks at you, too, you know."

"Yeah?"

"She knows you're there for her, and that means a lot."

Changing the subject, he looked inside the cooler at the different containers. "All right, what do we have here?"

"The usual—potato salad, tomato and cucumbers, coleslaw."

"You don't do anything in the usual way." Al rubbed his stomach. Celia had a way of taking a dish and making it her own. Watermelon and chives? Freaking delicious.

She brushed loose strands of blonde hair from her eyes. "I think we're just about set. Can I bring you a beer?"

"Not yet. Later, after I've worked up a thirst."

"I'll be back in a few minutes with Dax. He's giving me a good deal on lobster."

"I bet."

Celia flipped her ponytail and smiled. "There are some benefits for the café owner dating the local lobster catcher. I won't deny it."

Al chuckled as Celia walked across the square toward the pier and Dax, who saw her approaching and wiped his hands before hugging her tight and kissing her cheek.

They made a good team.

He and Darcy made a good team, too. But she'd pulled away from him once Dax called out to her. She'd come a long way, but would she be brave enough to choose him, and possibly anger her brother? She'd lost so much already that maybe it wasn't fair to ask her to put that relationship at risk.

Damn feelings. Al fired up the grill, putting his on hold.

Dax brought over a small cooler of lobster tails. "Start with these, big guy—there's plenty more where that came from. Ten bucks a skewer."

Al tested the heat on the grill, skewered a lobster tail, squeezed lemon over the meat and set it on the silver rack. The aroma was slightly sweet with a kick of citrus.

Dax leaned over the skewer and sniffed. "You could always be a chef. It's not like you have a real job. Damn, that's good."

"I have a real job, thanks." Odd hours, always something different. Best of all, he was his own boss. "You're just jealous because I don't punch a time clock."

"Nope. I love my job. I get to go swim all day."

"Sounds good to me." Darcy joined their group around Ambrosia's grill. "Can I get one of those?"

"Ten bucks, little sister," Dax said.

"Ignore him." Celia smiled at Darcy. "You can have as many as you want. On the house."

"Get the watermelon, Darce," Al advised. She looked beautiful, her hair long and loose around her tanned, bare shoulders instead of braided or up in a bun. She wore a halter dress the pinkish color of a Key West sunset. Delicately strapped sandals adorned her long feet. Nice dress, but he liked the purple one best.

Did she regret what happened?

He put three more tails on the grill, forcing himself to keep his mind off of her pretty legs.

"Okay. Let me eat, and then put me to work. I'm happy to help."

"You've been working all day," Celia chided. "Sit behind Al, there, on the cooler. It's shaded. Dax, get your sis a beer."

"Hey, I've been working all day too." Dax uncapped a local brew and poured it into a plastic cup. "Ready for a drink, Al?"

"Yeah." The heat this close to the barbecue was amping up. The fact that Darcy was going to be sitting next to him, her tan legs a mile long, didn't help cool him down. "I'm ready."

***

Darcy took the beer and set it by her feet before accepting the paper plate of succulent lobster meat, watermelon salad and coleslaw with a piece of cornbread.

She took a bite and moaned. "This is what I'm talking about. You're a genius on the grill, Al. Celia. God, this is terrific. Can't get it in a restaurant like this. Me and Al have a shrimp taco recipe we want you to figure out, okay?"

Celia's face lit up, a sure sign she was doing what she loved.

Al turned to Darcy. "She'll nail it. But we should take another road trip and bring her back one of the tacos, so she can taste it."

Another road trip? Darcy hoped her cheeks weren't red as she recalled how close they'd gotten on the last one.

"Sounds good." She had no idea what to do about Al. Wasn't sure if she could trust her own judgment enough to take a chance. There was so much to be lost if things between them failed. And her track record wasn't so hot.

"I got a message from Lori, the realtor? She says she can't get ahold of the Greeks. Which I don't believe, being as I've been on the phone with them multiple times today."

"Why don't they fire her?"

"They're going to have her arrested instead," Al said, giving her a searching look as she wiped her mouth with the paper napkin.

She immediately imagined his mouth on hers, licking up melted butter. His eyes darkened but then he turned back to the grill before saying anything else.

As the delicious aromas from Ambrosia's grill hit the square, a line formed. Darcy did her best to stay out of the way, watching to see where she could jump in and help. Celia piled plates with a choice of salad, cornbread and a skewered lobster tail with a choice of butter sauce.

"You should be charging more," Dax said as he brought back another cooler of tails from the shop.

"We'll know for next year," Celia answered pertly, never breaking her routine.

Darcy noticed the sweat beading down Al's back as he turned corn over lapping flames. She got up and poured him a cold beer. "Drink?"

His mouth, firm and rosy, met the edge of the plastic cup. She watched him swallow, mesmerized by his Adam's apple. Her stomach knotted.

He met her gaze, his eyes dilating. She took the cup and cleared her throat, backing up so quickly her calves hit the cooler behind her. *Jesus.*

"Thanks." Al returned to slapping skewers on the racks, flirting with the women customers, acting like every guy's friend. He had a witty comment for everybody.

When had he gotten charming? *I'm already in it, if I think Al Cooper is charming. Blinded by lust—or love?*

"I've got to run back to Ambrosia for more watermelon salad," Celia said.

"I'll go." Darcy stepped toward her. Celia handed her the stack of plates with instructions instead.

"I know where it is. You load 'em up, Al will finish with the lobster tail. I can't believe how well we're doing. Dax, could you help me bring back the food? You two can handle this." Celia pulled Dax away.

"Potato salad and cornbread, please." A woman in rhinestone glasses and a pink sundress came up to the counter and handed over a ten-dollar bill.

"Coming up." Darcy took the cash and handed the plate to Al, who added a skewered lobster tail. She knew they worked well together, they'd been friends for so long. Could friends become lovers, without ruining the friendship?

His lower lip pressed against the beer cup made her think of his mouth on hers, his touch, sensual, gentle, demanding. She stole glances at his profile even as she accepted money, plated salad.

There was no break to talk, especially since Al was so busy schmoozing everybody. Salad, bread, napkin, skewer. The later it got, the longer the line and soon Celia was taking the cash while Darcy filled plates, rubbing arms with Al, while Dax helped wherever he was needed.

After the last customer was served, Celia gave a nervous giggle and plunked down on a cooler. "I owe you guys! I've never seen downtown so crazy."

Darcy laughed. "This is your first Bugfest. Our little town's biggest summer festival."

Randall Wallace had mandated that the outdoor food stop being served at ten, though music still played and you could find a seat, if you were lucky, in one of the restaurant's patios.

"I'm ready for a real drink," Al said, cleaning the grill. "After I run home to let Buster out."

"Go do that," Celia said. "And bring him back. We can bring our own seats for the music. I've got chilled wine. Cheese and crackers. Let's relax."

Darcy tied a garbage bag. "Sounds great to me."

Dax pulled Celia close. "We've got dives in the morning, first thing, so it can't be too late."

Darcy tossed a wadded up paper plate at her brother. "Old man! Staying up until ten."

"Midnight!" Dax gave an exaggerated yawn. "Me and Al are the old farts."

"Speak for yourself, Dax. I can stay up all night."

Darcy caught the way Al didn't look at her and blushed.

Dax winked at Celia. "That's what I'm saying hon. I think we should go home and reeeest."

Darcy gathered the trash together. "You know what? Forget it. I'll go home and watch a movie."

Al chuckled. "I'll buy you a drink, Darce."

Now, why did that seem like a really terrible and yet terrific idea?

Celia looked right at her, her hand on Dax's shoulder. "I think you guys *should* go get a drink or two together. The night is young."

Dax narrowed his eyes, his gaze going from Darcy, who swallowed hard, to Al. This time, Darcy refused to back down. If she wanted to pursue a relationship with Al, then she would, she decided. It was not for Dax to choose. She wouldn't rub it in his face, but she wouldn't give up on a chance at love to avoid conflict.

Decision made, she turned to Al and took his hand, gently caressing his thumb with hers. "I'll go with you to let Buster out."

Celia piled Dax's arms with trash bags and pointed him toward the Dumpster. "I'm right behind you, honey," she said.

"Is there something going on?" Dax's voice hitched.

Celia cradled his back with her hand. "We can talk about it later."

"But…"

"*Later.* Move it." Celia nudged him on.

Al twirled her around, bringing her face to face. "You mean it?"

"I want to try," Darcy said, holding his gaze.

His eyes brimmed with love, for her, and she accepted his precious gift.

"I was running this morning. Releasing guilt. With each step I took, I felt like you were there. When I imagine my life, you are always in it." She took a deep breath. "I love you, Al. As uncertain as I am, I know *that* for sure."

Al tugged her close, so they were nose to nose, his eyes closed. His arms wrapped her tight and she rested her head against his strong chest. "Good," he whispered against the top of her head. "That's really great." He pulled an inch back and tipped up her chin. "So, I bought this property today…"

Her stomach clenched. "You're kidding…"

"It has a private beach."

"A lingering cheese odor?"

"Maybe. Great view from the master bedroom." He said the words seductively against her mouth. Speaking just for her. "Want to go see it?"

Her heart was so full she knew if Al wasn't holding her she'd fly away.

"Let's wait until after the cleaning crew leaves. I hope you bargained for a new refrigerator?"

"Just as the missus ordered."

"I love you, Al." She ran her finger along his taut jaw. "Nothing's settled. Nothing's perfect. But I can't wait to see how our journey unfolds."

"I've loved you for so long that I can't even tell you when it began. If you want to tag lobsters off the Australian Reef, I'd go." He kissed her thoroughly, leaving her breathless.

"Let's start a little closer to home."

She wrapped her arms around his neck and pressed as close as possible, her mouth clinging to his. His embrace was so filled with love that Darcy knew she was cherished with a love to last forever.

The End

Thank you so much for reading Festival by the Sea!

As you probably know, word of mouth is how stories are discovered so if you could leave a review on your favorite reading forum, I would really appreciate it. You can find a list of my books on http:www//tracihall.com--if you sign up for my newsletter, you can download a free short story. I don't share emails and I promise not to overwhelm you with posts.

Next up in this series: **Forever by the Sea** and **Sand Dollars by the Sea**.

Sign up for my newsletter and a free short story:

http://www.tracihall.com/bythesea

Other books in the **By the Sea** series:

> **Ambrosia by the Sea**
>
> **Karma by the Sea**
>
> **Puppy Love by the Sea**
>
> **Masquerade by the Sea**
>
> **Holiday by the Sea**
>
> **Festival by the Sea**
>
> **Dancing by the Sea**

USA Today Best-selling Author, Traci Hall. 'Still Believing in Happily Ever.'

http://facebook.com/traciella

http://twitter.com/tracihallauthor

http://enovelauthorsatwork.com/traci-hall/

Beachcomber Heat

Stephanie Queen

This summer's heat wave on Martha's Vineyard is breaking records, but so is the crime wave. The combination is causing a wave of red-hot dangerous desire between Dane and Shana.

Praise for Stephanie Queen's Books

The Throwbacks: "Boston comes vividly alive in the first of Queen's Scotland Yard Exchange Program series. Grace is an engaging heroine with charm, humor and sass. Resplendent in rich detail, laugh-out-loud moments, a fast-paced plot and spellbinding characters, *The Throwbacks* is a stellar not-to-be-missed standout!" —*Romantic Times Book Review*

oOo

With gratitude to the Name That Character contest winners, Jean Patton and Sharolynne Barth—thank you for your assistance and support. Most of all, thank you for naming the mysterious jewel thief in *Beachcomber Heat*, Angelique Dubois.

Chapter 1

Dane watched Shana reach back with both hands and lift the heavy mane of hair off her neck, arching her breasts forward, exposing the glistening pale column of her neck. Her head was thrown back, supported by her long bare arms gleaming with a film of perspiration. He stared and held himself as still as a mountain—with an effort. He wished they were anywhere else on the planet besides Captain Colin Lynch's office at State Police Headquarters on Martha's Vineyard.

Cap—the name his inner circle gave him—cleared his throat. Dane turned to him.

"Get on with it. What'd you call us in for—an overdue parking ticket?" Dane said.

Cap raised a brow and said, "No, but I'll be looking into that." Cap shifted his gaze to Shana. Dane held his jealousy muscles in check.

"I got a request for your services."

That got Shana's attention. "Do tell." She dropped her hair and leaned forward, all business now. A rotten shame. But a relief to Dane's too tense man parts.

"You want us to fix your air conditioning?" Dane said. He didn't mind disrupting Cap and annoying Shana. But this time she didn't even bother to glare at him with her Shana the Destroyer look.

"We've had a rash of missing jewelry—likely thefts. The first report came from an insurance company, but by the time we got the third report of high-end jewels missing, we figured they were stolen. And all by the same person or team." Cap paused.

"And?" Dane said.

Shana glared at him. He smiled.

"Someone wants to hire us to get their jewels back?" Shana said.

"Not exactly."

"Security?"

"Partly. I think they want you to prevent a theft. We think they're being targeted. When we looked into the matter and found each of the reports of missing, presumed-stolen jewelry had one thing in common—the owners had recently hosted parties."

"You think someone from a backyard barbeque ran inside and lifted the family jewels?" Dane said.

"These were no backyard barbeques—these were lavish affairs in the most expensive oceanfront neighborhood on the island. Their family jewels were worth millions. The parties' guest lists overlap substantially and they include anyone who's anyone on the island—and some from off-island. Wealthy or famous—"

"Or apparently notorious—they've got a jewel thief on their list," Dane said.

"Will you please take this seriously?" Shana said. "We need a case and these people have money to pay us."

"She's right—you should charge double your normal rates," Cap said.

"We don't have normal rates. We don't have any rates."

"That's the problem," Shana sighed. "You don't take the business seriously. We need to try making more money."

The instant tensing of muscles across his back and the tightening of his chest reminded Dane of a mild tazing—either that or he was having a heart attack. But in truth, the tension was all too familiar—it was his *what happens if Shana leaves the island* tension. He couldn't bring himself to figure out the answer. That would only lead to gut wrenching misery. And then he might have a heart attack for real.

"Okay. Fine. We'll charge them whatever you want, girlie. You can be in charge—"

"Oh no you don't. You're not bailing out of doing the work. We're in this together, aren't we?"

A warmth like he'd just downed a mug of hot cocoa ran through him, easing the previous tension down to a background annoyance—one he could operate with. One he had been operating with. All in the name of pursuing those flashes of warmth. Of pursuing the normal pleasures in life that he'd missed since he was a kid.

"We are. We're partners."

She frowned and turned back to Cap. Dane noticed Cap was enjoying their exchange. As usual. He shook his head and then continued giving them the background on the jewel heists.

"That's the theory—that someone from the parties is a jewel thief, but they have no idea who. These parties are outfitted with security, all the homes have alarms and state-of-the art safes. All the caterers and staff have been vetted and all have been working for at least three summers on the island. The guest lists are large and we're going through them. It's possible someone brought a guest who the hosts didn't know. If an invited guest brought someone, none of the hosts turned them away."

Dane said, "That'll teach them to be gracious."

Shana swatted a hand at him. He caught it and held on. She tugged but he didn't let go. She stopped tugging and let him hold onto her hand. There was no point in her resisting him. They both knew he'd win. It was like that.

He wondered what it would be like if he didn't have to struggle with her. Would the magic disappear—or is that when the magic would start?

"The next party is scheduled for tomorrow night. William Gable is the host."

"Gable? The movie producer?"

"That's him. He wants to meet with you today. He wants more than his usual security and more than the state and local police can do." Cap pulled his drawer out and took something from it. "Here's his card."

Shana freed her hand from his, reached out and snatched the card from Cap before Dane finished reacting to losing his hold.

"We'll call him, but I don't know what we can do for him," Dane said.

Cap shrugged.

Shana said, "I'll find something to do for him."

Her words sent a frisson through him. "You? I thought we were partners."

She turned and gave him a no-nonsense look. "Then start acting like it."

Chapter 2

The day was at its hottest by 4 p.m.—or at least Shana hoped it wouldn't get any hotter. Dane drove—as usual—and they sped by the ocean on the right toward the exclusive neighborhood in West Tisbury where the rash of jewel thefts and parties had taken place. Sweat trickled between her breasts. The windows were open because the Jeep had no air conditioning. It had broken long ago, according to Dane, and he'd never bothered to get it fixed. If she had any money, she'd get it fixed herself. She hadn't adjusted to the wild weather here. It was too unpredictable compared to home in Sydney. How could she possibly adjust when the roller coaster was always about to take a plunge or turn a corner. Her mind had shifted from weather to Dane and she sighed.

"How about if you let me do the talking?" she said.

"Go for it, girlie." He didn't take his eyes off the road. Just as well. She didn't need one of his unnerving looks right now. She'd dressed up for their meeting with Mr. Gable in her best business suit. Pale gray silk with a pink blouse and tasteful fake pearl choker. Dane had scoffed at her and compared her to a Barbie doll. It was probably the spike heels. But she left them on. She was hot now and regretted not wearing her usual cotton sundress.

They got through the gated drive past a stern-looking guard and pulled to the front door behind a Jaguar in the circular drive.

"That looks a lot like your car," Shana said after they got out and walked to the door.

"It's a later model."

"Where is your Jag? We could probably use it right now—"

"Never mind that. Ring the bell."

In the next moment Shana found herself stepping into a different world—as if through the looking glass. This place felt more like something out of The Great Gatsby than reality. It wasn't the opulence, but the throwback style of the place with the black and white marble checkerboard entry foyer, the art deco furnishings and the man who answered the door—an actual butler.

"This is disorienting," she whispered to Dane as they walked after the man who'd said, "Follow me this way."

"What's the matter? A little too retro for you?" Dane smiled and added, "At least there wasn't a Duisenberg parked out front."

He'd read her mind. As always. They stepped through heavy double wooden doors into a light, airy parlor of sorts done in the same art deco style with plush rugs and a chandelier. Standing in the middle of the room, facing away from them and looking out the window was Mr. Gable, she presumed. He didn't turn to greet them until after the butler left. *They were in for some drama.*

"Mr. Blaise and Ms. George—thank you for agreeing to meet with me on such short notice. We do have a bit of an emergency. Very distressing business. Please sit." He pointed to the seating arrangement opposite the windows, complete with a coffee table holding a pitcher of something cold and several glasses. She'd bet her left pinky the crystal was Baccarat.

Dane said nothing. Then she remembered she'd promised to do all the talking. She took a breath. She was a professional investigator and this was the twenty-first century on Martha's Vineyard and they weren't looking for a Grace-Kelly-type cat burglar.

"No problem, Mr. Gable. It's our specialty to respond to emergency situations."

"Of course—you're famous for it." Mr. Gable paused and looked them over. She and Dane stood in front of the small sofa. Dane remained silent.

"Famous?" she said. She sat. Dane sat.

"Yes—surely you're aware—the video?" He paused. "At the Lucky Parrot. I've seen the video of your recent takedown of a notorious cartel boss from South America. Amazing." He looked at Dane. "I hope your arm has healed well?" Mr. Gable sounded like a fan in the presence of a movie star. His eyes glittered and she could picture bursts of stars popping from his head if this were a cartoon.

Dane lifted his arm. He wore a short-sleeved linen shirt and the scar from the knife wound still looked raw. "It's functional." Dane looked at her. His face was like a picture etched in stone, void of expression. But she knew him and knew he was expressing impatience by the mere fact that he looked at her instead of their client.

"Mr. Gable, can you tell us specifically what service you would like us to provide?"

"Yes of course—this business. I'm sure you know by now about the rash of jewel thefts at our parties in this area. We love our parties—gala events, actually. It's the reason we're here for the summer. Vacationing and gathering with friends and celebrating life and our ... success."

In her mind, Shana substituted the word *excess*. But she said, "Of course. And you have a ... gala planned for tomorrow night?"

"Yes. I have security—the usual—motion sensors, alarms, security personnel and even dogs. But since none of this seemed to stop the thefts from some of my best friends, I find I must take further steps. That's where you come in—after seeing that video—and checking up on your credentials, I think you two will be perfect to go undercover at the gala tomorrow evening—as guests—to catch the thief red-handed, as it were."

"To catch the thief?" Dane said. His voice was casual, but Shana knew he was mocking Mr. Gable and even if Mr. Gable were star struck, he wasn't an idiot. She moved her spike-heel-clad foot over her knee and stabbed Dane in the calf. He didn't move and didn't make a sound. But she knew he felt it. He smiled.

"Yes, ironic, isn't it? The reminiscence to a Cary Grant movie did enter my mind. But it's all too real, I'm afraid. The insurance company—the same one insures everyone in the area—is pressuring us to step up security or stop hosting parties. But I'm not going to stop living my life over a jewel thief."

"Of course not," Shana said.

"So you'll do it then?"

"Yes."

"I'm not sure how payment for your services works, but I've prepared a check for your retainer." Gable reached inside his sports jacket pocket, pulled out an envelope and handed it to Dane. Shana smiled and kicked Dane's leg again. Dane took the envelope and grinned.

"Thank you, Mr. Gable. I'm sure this will be fine, but Shana will send you our contract later. Can we have a look around?"

Mr. Gable popped up to stand and reverted to fan-man as he led them back to the foyer. Shana followed the two men, caught up and said, "We'll need a copy of your guest list as soon—"

"Of course. I'll have Frank—our personal assistant—you met him at the door—send that to you along with the blueprint of the estate, schematics for our security system and details on our security personnel. Anything else?"

*****

"Yes—can we meet Mrs. Gable?" Dane said. He didn't like the way Mr. Gable was looking at Shana at that moment—as if she were a piece of art he might collect. It was a good thing she was wearing the stodgy business suit and not one of her usual sundresses. Or maybe Gable was being polite.

"Yes—she'll be joining us out at the ballroom terrace."

They walked through the multi-chandelier-lit space of the ballroom—it took a few minutes to cover the expanse of tile—and Dane thought he'd need to clone himself and Shana three times to cover this room at the party. When they made their way in time with the clicking of Shana's heels to the furthest terrace doors, which swung wide and overlooked the ocean in a stunning high vista, an equally stunning woman joined them and smiled at Dane without looking at Shana. He smiled back—his polite no no-nnsense smile. Mrs. Gable reminded him of a forties-era movie star with her shiny waves of brown hair framing her face and her cinch-waisted dress falling to mid-calf. She was painfully thin but elegant-looking in a Kathryn Hepburn way.

"You must be the famous—or should I say notorious—Dane Blaise." She reached out a hand and he took it, giving her delicate hand a shake though he felt like he was supposed to kiss it.

"This is my partner—"

She turned to Shana and said, "Yes, the lovely Shana George—equally famous." She did the obligatory handshake. Dane recognized the icy smile Shana wore and silently willed his girl to keep herself in check. Not that he cared about the assignment, but he knew Shana would somehow blame him if they lost the gig.

"I have the guest list for you, and the guest lists from the last three parties which were all robbed. We're all concerned about this jewel thief. What is the likelihood that he might turn violent?"

"Unlikely," Shana said.

"What makes you think the thief is a man?" Dane said.

Mrs. Gable raised her brow and Mr. Gable laughed. "Touché."

They took a tour of the perimeter, then pointed out the balcony and French doors to their bedroom where the safe was kept, inside, in a closet. Very predictable.

"You should consider moving the safe to your kitchen—no one ever looks there," Dane said.

"Hmm... Yes, I see your point. I'll consider it," Mr. Gable said. It was obvious he'd do no such thing. Dane got the idea the man enjoyed being a cliché.

Shana had her mobile phone out in camera mode and was busy taking pictures.

"Where are the motion sensors tripped?" she asked.

"I have no idea—it's all in the plans we'll provide." Gable watched Shana and followed along with her.

"Would you like a cold drink, Mr. Blaise—to take the edge off the heat?"

He did want one—desperately. "No thank you. I think we're about finished here. We have some background work to do."

Shana slipped her phone back into her purse and joined him. She was a good girl. She knew a hint when she heard one. Plus she looked hotter than he did—sweatier too. And her hair. Others might have called it unruly, but Dane thought it looked sexy as hell—like she'd just got out of bed after making wild love. The perspiration-touched tendrils framing her face gave her an irresistible—

"Ms. George—may I call you Shana? Please have a cold drink before you go—"

"We can't stay," Dane said and stepped to her side. He resisted throwing an arm around her because then he'd have dragged her out of there and—

"What will you do next?" Mrs. Gable asked.

"We'll study the security plans and—" Shana began.

"For one thing we'll need to go shopping. The attire for your soirée is formal, I take it?" Dane said, his expression back to his polite, meaningless smile.

"Yes—oh most definitely. May I suggest a dress shop—"

"Please be sure to include the cost in your expenses," Mr. Gable said. His smile for Shana looked far from meaningless. Dane decided they ought to get out of there before Mr. Gable suggested she buy jewelry for herself too—at his expense—like a gift from a potential lover.

Mrs. Gable lead them back out to the checkerboard foyer. Dane paid a lot of attention to the surroundings, noting the dramatic stairs. No way their thief had taken those to the second floor—it would have been like being on stage. The butler showed them the door and they got in the Jeep.

"This car is like a furnace," Shana said.

"I don't mind. I like seeing you sweat."

She punched his arm. "I can't go dress shopping until I take a shower."

"No time. We're on a tight schedule. I'm going to need to come back here in the morning and install cameras."

"They already have security cameras—I saw them—"

"On the outside. I'm talking about inside."

"Fine. Take me to the dress shop."

As they pulled up along the curb at the store, Shana's phone rang.

"It's probably Mr. Gable telling you don't forget to buy some jewels—at his expense, of course."

Shana scowled at him and looked at the phone before answering it.

"It's my brother." She pressed it on and then pressed it to her ear.

Dane got out of the Jeep partly to give Shana privacy for her call, but mostly because it was so stiflingly hot in the Jeep. He was human. He went to the dress shop door—the boutique where they'd shopped before—and saw the clerk, Emma, inside. He wanted to go in the air-conditioned shop, but he waited for Shana. He was a sap.

As she got out of the car she tossed the phone back into her bag and frowned at him. But this wasn't her usual frown of general disapproval or annoyance, it was worry.

"What did he want?"

"Mum wants to come for a visit—here—at the end of the summer."

"Cool. Problem?"

"Yes. They already booked the flight and I'll have to find somewhere for them to stay."

At least that meant Shana was staying until September.

"What's the problem?"

"I'm not sure where they got the money for the flight—he gave me some story about winning a sweepstakes. Sounded fishy."

It *was* a fishy story. Dane knew this because he was the one in charge of the sweepstakes and her mother had been the only entrant.

"Don't look a gift horse—"

"I'll have to find a place of my own in the fall—something bigger than Mrs. Jones's studio where I stayed last year—"

"Don't go starting with that again. Your mother and brothers can all stay at the shack. Plenty of room. We'll double up and—"

"Now don't you go starting that again."

"Let's not have this discussion in the street."

She pushed past him, inside. The whoosh of cold air was a relief, but not as much as ending that line of discussion. Dane had until September to convince her to stay with him. He had until September to make sure he wanted her to stay with him.

Emma assaulted them, sweeping Shana into a French hug and kiss—distant and for show—and they disappeared into the recesses of the shop. Dane wandered in the direction of the dressing room to have a seat and watch *his* favorite show—Shana parading for him in sexy dresses—when he bumped into a petite, dark-haired woman.

He was not a klutz and not unaware of his surroundings, which meant that the woman had purposely taken him by surprise and run into him with a goal in mind. She looked up and he saw brown eyes swimming in mirth.

With a flirty French accent, she said, "I was wondering when I might run into you."

Chapter 3

Dane nodded. "I don't know you, but you bring to mind the only French person I know."

"Let me guess. Jean Luc Ruse?"

Dane didn't even bother with a nod. Deep down he wasn't surprised. Jean Luc had been part nemesis and part ally the previous summer when he ran a scam surfing competition as a front for a Brazilian human trafficking operation. Jean Luc had cooperated with the Brazilians under duress and had helped him and Shana tag the notorious Tavares brothers. It seemed a lifetime ago—his first case with Shana—but now seeing this young lady, who was obviously related, it got his heart rate up a beat with some kind of excitement.

"He sends his regards."

"And you are?"

"Angelique Dubois."

From the corner of his eye he saw Shana emerge from the dressing room. He stifled a wolf whistle. But his pounding heartbeat gained speed and his nerves went to full alert from his chest down to his toes and especially certain parts in between. The turquoise dress shimmered like the sun reflecting off the ocean, but as he turned his full attention to her, his eyes were naturally drawn to the places the gown didn't cover. The plunging halter front might have reached her naval and the slit up her right leg went far too high for panties. She swirled in a circle on her way to him and he saw that there was no back to her gown—only Shana's golden, glistening skin. She stopped in between him and Angelique, making a circle and looked at the young woman, towering over her.

"Are you related to Jean Luc Ruse?" Shana asked.

"I am his niece."

Dane laughed. "That's what they all say."

"No, I see what you think, but I am his niece. Really. *Vérité*." She put out her hand, a delicate porcelain perfect hand tipped in frivolous pink polished nails. He took it and squelched his urge to kiss it. He gave a light squeeze and she caressed his hand as he let go.

*****

Shana watched and felt hot and bothered by this smooth, dark-haired, dark-eyed, pale-skinned petite beauty. Shana felt like a giant next to her. A clumsy giant. But she was not.

Shana said, "Don't pay attention to Dane. The family resemblance is obvious." She smiled and hoped it looked friendlier than she felt. "I'm Shana George."

"I knew you must be. Uncle speaks fondly of you."

"Are you in the family business?"

Angelique was not taken aback, but laughed a graceful musical laugh and shook her head and said, "*Non, non.*" Her French accent was annoying but Shana could see it might charm a weak-minded man. She glanced at Dane.

It was a good thing he was not weak minded. Of course, he did have other weaknesses that Shana should be more concerned about.

"Nice to have met you, Ms. Dubois. We have some shopping to do." Shana looped her arm through Dane's.

Before she could draw him away he said, "What's wrong with the dress you have on? Why don't we buy that one and be done with it?"

Resisting her temptation to punch him in the ribs—and if she were honest, her temptation to take his face in her hands and devour his lips—she gave a small shake to her head.

"He is right. That dress becomes you." Angelique smiled in such a sincere way that it made Shana feel mean.

Angelique said to Dane, "I'm glad to have met you. I hope we meet again during my stay."

"How long will that be?" Dane asked.

"We'll see..." Angelique glided toward the door with a wave and a mysteriously provocative look. Shana didn't trust her no matter how sincere she might sound. Angelique was cut from the same cloth as Jean Luc.

"Let her go. We'll look into her later," she said. She knew Dane would want to follow the woman. He had to be suspicious too. Waving her hand in the direction of some silky, expensive-looking dresses that looked like they were made more for someone like Frenchie than Shana, she said, "I'm sure Mr. Gable wouldn't mind if I purchased a second dress as a backup."

Shana was proud of her athletic strong body. She had a generous share of curves along with the muscle. She looked toward another rack with a hot pink tube dress made of Lycra and something more expensive, if the price tag was any indication.

"'I'll try on that one." She reached for the one in her size and eyed it skeptically.

Dane growled in a voice for her ears only. "Damn. I should take you shopping more often. I can't wait for you to try that on. Of course, I'm not so sure you ought to wear it in public—especially not on assignment. I'd be too distracted."

"I'm sure you could keep your eyes off me and on your work."

"That's not the problem. The problem is I'd have to fight the men off you. You will definitely need protection if you wear that dress out."

"Lucky thing I for you I know how to take care of myself."

He smiled and nodded.

She took the dress off the rack and purposefully sashayed back into the dressing room. Emma came over and offered Dane a drink.

"Something cold. Lots of ice."

Shana heard Dane before she closed the dressing room door and didn't feel guilty about being so girlish.

*****

"Yes, of course. This heat wave has been terrible," Emma said.

It wasn't the heat wave Dane needed cooling off from, but he didn't bother explaining.

Later that evening Cap, Shana and Dane sat on the cement patio out in back of the beach shack. Three tall glasses of cold beer sat on the metal table. Cap sat back, relaxed. Shana sat, leaning forward on her elbows and Dane stood. He swiped the back of his hand across his forehead. It still felt like someone had put the entire island of Martha's Vineyard inside a giant sauna and cranked up the heat. He picked up his glass and took a long swallow, then touched the frosty glass to his cheek.

"Acer looked at the security schematics at the Gables' place and confirmed my evaluation. I checked with the neighbors and they all have the same system. It's state of the art. It would need to be disabled from the inside. The safe was top notch and would take some time and skill to crack, but he figured it could be done."

There's no way we'd have missed the thief on the surveillance videos if they'd been outside intruders."

"I reviewed the surveillance videos," Shana said. "Everything from early afternoon—well before the parties started—until the next morning for each of the three homes. Nothing. The thefts were inside jobs."

"Of course they could have disabled one of the cameras and then fixed it again on their way out, but they'd have to know where the cameras were and that would take some doing without close inspection," Dane said.

"You checked the cameras at the neighbors' too?" Cap said.

"We're very thorough." Shana said.

"I could have saved you the trouble—we already looked at their systems and checked all the videos."

"Sure, but you weren't getting paid two hundred bucks an hour," Shana said. She winked. Cap laughed.

"We didn't get to the good part yet," Shana said.

"Don't jump to a quick conclusion, girlie—if you do that you'll cut your opportunity for more fees," Dane said. "And you might miss catching the real thief."

"Dane is kidding, but I'm not when I say we already have a suspect and you'll never guess who it is."

"Angelique Dubois—niece of Jean Luc Ruse," Cap said.

Shana stared at him, mute. "You knew she was here?" She sounded like she was accusing him of being a baby murderer.

"I suspect Cap didn't know long before we found out. Which was exactly when she wanted us to know."

"We finished up interviewing guests from the last soirée today and she was one of the last. The detective who interviewed her popped into my office just before I came over to give me a message from her—from Jean Luc, actually. Apparently he says hello," Cap said.

"She's a piece of work. She probably figured if she pretended to know you the detective questioning her would get distracted from his task," Shana said. She stood and started pacing around like a restless tiger. Normally Dane enjoyed her restless tiger mood, but this time he didn't think he was the one making her restless.

"What's bothering you?" Cap asked.

"She's arrogant." Shana stopped her pacing and picked up her glass of beer. "It's that obnoxious brand of elitist arrogance that I especially hate. She's a flaunter." She knocked back half the glass.

Dane didn't know if he wanted her to chug the whole thing down so he could convince her to work out her agitation on him, or to grab the drink away from her and make her calm down. Either way, it was a challenge not to be distracted by the trickles of perspiration sliding down her neck over her collarbone and disappearing into the shadowy dip between her breasts and beneath her tank top.

"You think Dubois is your thief?" Cap said. He sounded skeptical.

"You don't think it's coincidence that she shows up—with her grand hello from Jean Luc—and we just happen to have a rash of jewel thefts at the same time?" Shana said.

Dane said. "The safe was top notch and would take some time and skill to crack, but I figure it could be done if you were a guest wandering upstairs—or maybe a security guard."

"So we agree—she looks good for an inside job."

"Possibly," Dane said.

"I think we have our prime suspect," Shana said.

Dane held his patience and repeated himself. "Don't jump to conclusions because you might miss something."

Cap said, "She could have a partner."

"Like that," Dane said.

Shana shot a look at him and smiled.

"What?" he said.

"I knew you'd see it my way."

"I didn't say it was Angelique parading around as a guest and sneaking up to the safe—it could just as easily be someone from the catering staff or more likely the security staff. Like Cap said—we need to look for a partner."

"We haven't completed our background checks on all the staff for the last three parties—they used almost the identical list of employees—but I'll let you know if I spot anything," Cap said.

"Why are you skeptical?" Shana asked Cap.

"I'm suspicious of the obvious. Angelique is worse than obvious—"

"Like I said—she's a flaunter," Shana said. "She's taunting us. It's like she has some kind of grudge. She probably also has an ace up her sleeve. Jean Luc must have told her something to make her hate us—and to give her an advantage."

"Or he told her something to make her relish the challenge," Dane said.

"So you do think it's her," Shana said. She folded her arms across her chest, hiding the trickle of sweat and the rest of what was distracting him.

"I'm not as certain as you. I'm with Cap. Hard to believe she'd be that obvious—knowing her motive would be key. We need to know more about her. Get her story."

"I agree—there's something missing," Shana said.

"I enjoy a taunt as much as the next guy—probably more," said Dane, "But if Angelique Dubois is the thief and she is putting herself purposely in our path to stick her tongue out at us, so to speak, then she's either crazy, or she has some kind of serious agenda."

"Or both," Shana said. She unfolded her arms and leaned down to pick up her half empty glass. "It was no coincidence that she showed up at the dress shop. Jean Luc knew that dress shop."

Dane stepped closer. She said under her breath, "Stop staring. Even if I were in the mood, and even if you were the last man on earth, it's far too hot."

Dane flashed a glance at Cap to see if he'd heard her. Probably not.

"What the hell?" Dane breathed close to her ear, taking in her scent intensified by the heat.

"You heard me." She said this out loud so that Cap heard her. He'd witnessed the exchange anyway. He was shaking his head.

"Did I miss something?" Cap said. He stood. "I'm not staying around to watch you two and your endless sparring."

"Don't leave yet," Shana said.

"Let the man go. Maybe I'll go too." He left the words *I know when I'm not wanted* unspoken.

"Don't pretend to be hurt," she said.

He didn't move. He downed the rest of his beer. He didn't get it. He'd thought they were on good terms. His heart thudded hard and slow as if his blood were made of molasses. He pushed his hand through his hair. His palms were sweaty. Probably from the heavy heat. Looking toward the harbor, he thought of jumping in for a swim. It wouldn't be the first time.

"I'll call you if I come up with anything—you do the same." Cap saluted and disappeared around the corner of the house.

Shana stood with her empty glass in hand. He reached out and grabbed her hand and yanked her with him across the short expanse of grass to the pier.

"What are you doing? You planning to throw me in?" She stumbled along, not exactly resisting, not going easy either.

"Don't tempt me. I just want to put my feet in the water and cool off and—" He stopped. He didn't know what. He wanted to talk? Not really. He wanted her to talk, to tell him what was wrong—to tell him she was his for as long as he wanted with no strings? Not damn likely. Her arm was hot and slimy with sweat where he'd grabbed her. Her skin felt like it did after a bout of lovemaking. It had been too long and he'd thought that might change now. *Wrong.*

They stopped at the end of the narrow wood pier and he sat, pulling her down with him. Twilight was falling and the mosquitoes were out, but Dane didn't care. The house was too hot and stifling.

"Okay—we're here—what do you want, Dane?" she sighed heavily as if breathing were hard. As if everything was difficult and she was weary.

A hot burst suddenly shot through in his chest like electric paddles that stimulated his heart to a racing beat from the mild trot where it had been. *She was tired of him.*

"You want to leave, Shana?" He asked against his own will, sounding calm. He stopped breathing and watched her.

"Do I—I don't know. I never know. My mother, my brothers..." She stopped talking and looked out at the water. It was just as well. He wouldn't hear whatever she said now because his blood pulsed so loudly, pounding at his temples. He breathed in deep. The sea air was still and heavy. It didn't have the usual calming effect. Or maybe he was too far gone.

"I wish this weather would break," she said.

"You're making no sense."

She shrugged. Not a good sign. There should be a spark of anger at his insult.

He lifted himself off the edge of the pier, pulled his shirt over his head, emptied his pockets and dove into the water.

*****

What the hell was he doing? What the hell was *she* doing? Shana scrambled to her feet and stepped back from the edge of the dock as if the water might suck her in after him. Was it her fault he jumped into the harbor? More likely it was the heat.

She needed to make a decision about Dane—before her mother and brother came for their visit. Before she was lost forever to a self-destructive commitment. She needed to move out into a real place of her own and get some distance from him. She couldn't make a decision about him when she was with him all the time, enticing her with his scent and his power and his charm and his boldness.

He belonged with someone like Angelique Dubois. Someone who enjoyed taunting and playing games with people. Shana didn't like that.

Or did she? What was it that kept her here?

She watched the water. He'd been under for almost five minutes already. She heard him splash to the surface and turned. He was to the left and walking toward the stone wall at the shoreline along his property. She walked off the pier to join him as he stepped over the short wall and onto the grass. Night was falling fast now. Her heartbeat picked up as if the darkness signified danger. But it was her approach to Dane that signified danger.

She reached him where he lay in the grass, wet and glistening under the twinkling stars and harbor lights. She stopped and he grabbed onto her ankle. She knew what he would do next and she let him. She went down gracefully, considering, and ended up half lying across his chest, propped on her elbows.

"What do you want, Shana? What if you could have anything in the world? What would your life be?"

She tried to laugh his question off, tried to think of it as silly, but her heart beat faster against her ribs and against his. There was no way to hide her agitation from him.

"I never pegged you for the fanciful type—"

"Answer me."

"There is no answer. Why don't you answer it—what would your perfect life be?"

He stared at her. His eyelashes glistened with water, his stare intense. She had a heartbreaking glimpse inside his battered soul. She closed her eyes. She didn't expect him to answer—that was her point. That was the message in his eyes. There was no answer to such a question. But he spoke and caused a stutter to her heart and she opened her eyes again as if he had commanded her.

"I don't know what my perfect life would be, but I do know one thing." She waited. His eyes had lost their vulnerable look. Her heart thudded again, pounding in her ears and against his chest. She strained to feel his heartbeat, needed to know if his beat as wildly as hers. He seemed implacable. And silent. She wanted to prompt him but didn't. He finally spoke again.

"It would include you." He rasped the words. She grasped at them and wanted to hear them again, wanted to capture them and hold them and to hold him. She moved more fully on top of him now and held his face in her hands as he moved his hands to hold her waist. She felt a tremor but it might have been her own.

"Why are you telling me this? What does it mean?"

He shook his head. Then he raked his hands up her back and through her hair and pushed her face toward his until he caught her lips with his mouth and latched on, nibbling and kissing and pulling her tightly to him. She wanted to be devoured by him, wanted to devour him, to revel in the taste of him, the salty harbor water mixed with sweat and that special flavor of Dane, strong and bitter and bold.

The feel of his strong deft hands slipping inside her shorts and pressing into the flesh of her buttocks, cool and wet and maddeningly sensual. She moaned as her hips ground into his and the aching press of his cock found that sweet center between her thighs, spiraling her need and driving everything.

When he pushed her shorts and panties from her hips, a surge of panic combined with the heart-pounding thrill. Her chest bubbled with excitement and she moved her hands over him, pulling at his clothes, reaching between them to find his zipper in the crush between their bodies.

All the while, he never let go of her mouth, nipping and catching her bottom lip with his teeth and plunging his tongue to claim every corner in possessive strokes. When she freed his cock from his pants, he lifted her hips to fit himself between her legs. The shock of his bold move and the sudden quick separation followed by the intimate joining of his pulsing cock sliding deep and alive and penetrating shocked her senses so that she called out his name.

He dragged her face back down to his and nuzzled her neck and whispered in her ear like a caress, endearments of every kind, words of love and promise and forever and never. His hard breathing and soft words and thundering heart and pulsing cock inside her filled her mind and became the entire world. The vibrating of her entire being surged until she could stand it no more and he pulled her hips close and moved in that way he had that made her scream at the agonizing jolt of pleasure and release in wave after wave of seemingly endless searing mind-melting ecstasy.

He moved her hips with his strong hands in unrelenting rhythm against his, hard and fast until her world exploded again and he exploded inside her and she felt more searing heat and the swelling of pleasure went through her entire body, filling her chest and her mind like a white light, suspending her in time for a moment like a stop-motion picture.

After what seemed like forever and as though she were returning from a different world from far away, from an imaginary universe without dimension, she came back. She felt the hard surface of his chest beneath hers as the heaving breaths slowed. She felt the tight hold of his arms around her relax. She became aware of the heat and sweat and the earthy scent of their lovemaking mingling with the heavy summer night air surrounding them. And then he whispered in her ear as he brought a hand up to touch and caress her hair as he always did.

"You know I adore you."

The words sent a surge of warmth and a spasm of pleasure around his cock still inside her. He chuckled softly into her hair and nibbled her earlobe. She wanted the moment to last, but she already felt it slipping away.

As happened on these rare occasions where they stole some intimacy, pretending they were a real couple, the lovemaking glow didn't last and left them more distant. It was as if the lovemaking exposed the gap, making it seem wider when it was over. But Shana knew that wasn't true. It was the fear filling the gap—the fear of exposure of what was there in their hearts and souls, the longing. They both needed to hide that from each other and from themselves too.

So each time they made love, threatening to reveal their deep down heart's desire, they doubled down on closing up, hiding and armoring themselves against the exposure.

Dane rolled to his side so that she lay next to him, separate, and he zipped his pants. He looked over at her saying nothing, expressionless. He'd already shut down the tenderness, removed any trace of intimacy or vulnerability.

Shana rose from the grass to a stand and left him. She shuddered from the chill of losing his warmth, of losing the tender moment. It terrified her. She pushed it all aside and ignored the scared pounding of her heart as she went inside the back door to the stifling heat of the beach shack. She walked straight to the shower, turned the cold water on full blast and stepped under the bracing chill of the spray.

Chapter 4

Shana avoided him the next day. He let her. He rose early, abandoning her warmth, but leaving a pot of coffee and a note for her. When he got to the end of the note, the compulsion to sign it struck him and he struck back. He dropped the pen without writing his name—or any closing—like "affectionately" or "yours truly." Or "*love.*"

It wasn't that he was a coward. It was that he didn't have it in him. He'd been there once—maybe twice. He'd lost whatever ability he had to trust that kind of bond. He knew it was poison. He knew his limits. *He'd been a fool to tell her he adored her.*

He'd rather face down an ambush in a remote mountain village—again—than head into another romantic commitment. He told himself he was no fool.

Somehow, he didn't believe himself.

That was the mood he'd left the house in and drove around town in, ran the beach in, ran down records in and returned home in. He had all the information he needed to go to the damn party and catch their damn thief. He'd half hoped he might run into the French pretender in town so he could drag her sweet ass into Cap's police station and wring a confession from her, then call it a day. How hard would it be?

Sweaty and not caring if he was the world's biggest meanest bastard, he headed home. Shana hadn't called him once. She was angry. Or maybe he imagined she was. She'd been avoiding him.

Or maybe he'd been avoiding her.

He flung open the screen door to the beach shack and then swore loud enough to scare the neighbors into hiding when he paced through the house to find Shana not there. That's when he became aware of his raging need for her, to be with her, for her touch and for her loving and her barbs, for every scrap of her—good and bad—everything she had in her. The empty feeling surprised him. And reminded him—

The door opened behind him as he stood in the kitchen and he spun around. His senses shot to awareness of her all at once. When her eyes met his, she stopped and backed up an almost imperceptible step. Hers looked startled and frightened and then worried. His chest tightened and that pit in his stomach pushed him forward. She stood her ground. Because she was Shana.

"Where the hell have you been?" He wanted to yell the words, needed to feel the anger, but the relief overtook him before he could gain control and he let it as he pulled her into his sweat-soaked embrace. And she let him.

"I was..." She never finished her sentence. She wrapped her arms around him.

A phone rang. She moved to pull away and he clamped down, hard, holding her to him, spreading his hands along her spine and over her ass, her beautiful perfect round ass. She moved again. He clamped down again pulling her hips against his cock. It was diamond-cutter hard. She sighed and leaned into him, arching and fitting herself to him.

They were back to playing house.

The phone stopped ringing and when the answering machine came on, Dane realized it had been the house phone—the secure line—that had been ringing. They both came to attention then and he let go.

"Give me a rain check on that," he said. His voice sounded raw, like someone sawing lumber with a dull blade. He went to his living room-turned-office, checked the message and cleared his throat before he picked up the phone and punched in the number. He wasn't too surprised, but the caller ID made him smile.

"Who was it?" Shana asked from close behind him. Dane drew a ragged breath and thought maybe they needed to take a shower. Together.

"Jean Luc Ruse."

Chapter 5

"I won't bore you with preamble," Jean Luc said in his perfectly charming French accent—or so women seemed to think, although Dane couldn't see why. Refused to see why. Shana hovered over his shoulder, leaning on him, making him hot. So he forgave her the smile she wore for Jean Luc.

"I suppose you're calling to ask me to look after your niece while she's visiting—you really should have called ahead, Jean Luc. Then we could have prevented all those jewels from going missing and your little niece wouldn't have to get thrown in jail."

"*Non.* You have it all wrong. I am calling to tell you there is someone else. He has followed her to Martha's Vineyard and he uses her entrée—"

"Who?"

"He has many aliases."

"Pick one."

"I'm not sure what he goes by. He is French, but one would never know it. He speaks many languages and can have either an American or British accent. He is middle aged—like yourself."

"Watch it—"

"And he is dangerous. But don't worry, Dane. He is not a womanizer. He is overweight and bald and not attractive. He may wear a toupée, he may have a moustache and glasses or he may not. He is short—"

"So you're telling me to watch out for a short, fat, middle-aged man and you have no other information on what he looks like or his nationality or name—that it?"

A beat of silence followed. Dane wanted to sound dismissive, but he was not. Either Jean Luc was trying to throw them off his niece's trail or he was concerned. Either way, Dane was paying attention.

"I am sorry I don't know more. She has felt like she's being followed but has not been able to identify her tail. I will work on finding out more. Until then, I ask you something I know I have no right to ask you—for your help. I would like you to protect my niece."

Dane was about to respond when Jean Luc added, "I will pay you."

He slid his eyes to Shana's to catch the jolt of pleasure he knew would be in her face and it sent a familiar sizzle through him.

"You're on. Does she know about it?"

"*Non.* Do not tell her—she will never forgive me."

Dane didn't waste an eye roll, but he wasn't impressed with the charade.

"Okay Jean Luc. I'll watch out for her—and for this dangerous, fat, middle-aged man. I'll see that he doesn't go near her. Shana will work with me. But there's one caveat."

"Yes? Of course."

"If she steals anything, all bets are off."

No response. Dane thought the line went dead after a few ticks, but then Jean Luc spoke up again.

"All bets? You would have her arrested?"

"Yes."

"So you say. Then that is the deal."

Dane was about to ask Jean Luc what he meant by his comment—but the line went dead and he wouldn't have gotten a straight answer anyway. He put the receiver into its old-fashioned cradle and turned his attention back to Shana. She was vibrating with excitement and it didn't matter to Dane that it was the case that had her in this state. He meant to take advantage.

*****

They made it to the party at the appointed time—before the other guests arrived—to check out and meet the staff. But it had been tight. Shana was anxious about the close call.

"If we were late, that would have been unforgivably unprofessional."

"Almost doesn't count, girlie." Dane smiled and he tossed the keys to the valet, giving him a close look and committing his face to memory.

They were driving his Jag tonight. The fact that he'd had it delivered from storage bought him all kinds of brownie points with Shana. He wasn't sure how he felt about that, but for now, they were a couple. Not much of an undercover couple since everyone on the island knew who they were, but they were dressed to the nines and out at a posh soirée for the night—probably all night, if reports were correct.

Shana had arranged for Ronnie Ryan, a twenty-something kid they knew who delivered food on the island and had proved trustworthy even if he was a goofball, to work the party as a server and wear an earpiece. She'd also arranged for Sassy, a twenty-something young lady they'd hired to help them with a baby they'd been protecting—and who also happened to be an excellent pie baker—to work in the kitchen with an earpiece. They figured they'd need extras to spot their fat middle-aged man whether he was a danger to Angelique or her accomplice. They weren't sure which.

Cap was told to keep uniforms clear since they wanted to catch the thief. Dane didn't bother telling Mr. Gable they knew who the thief was. Shana would have killed him since she wanted to maximize their fees—or rather, *do a thorough job.*

Mr. and Mrs. Gable, dressed in their finery, met them in the foyer after Shana rang the bell and waited a few beats. Mr. Gable whistled at Shana. Dane wondered what Mr. Gable would do if Dane whistled at Mrs. Gable. Shana read Dane's mind and elbowed him in the ribs.

"So you are an undercover couple?"

"I don't think that'll work, Gable. You know everyone on this island knows who we are."

"Yes—that's true—in fact my guests are very excited that you'll be at the party. I'm afraid they're hoping for some... action."

Dane thought they might need to triple their fee, whatever it was.

"I will be playing an undercover role of sorts. We have a suspect—a very likely suspect. A woman. I'll seduce her—"

"Your role is to seduce a jewel thief?" Gable's voice raised a couple octaves, but he checked it and returned to normal quickly. Gable's eyes slid to Shana and back to Dane. Dane folded his arms across his chest, stood straighter and looked down at the man.

"Nothing wrong with that," Gable said. "It's brilliant, in fact—an undercover agent seduces a lady jewel thief—it's great—"

"We're not shooting a movie," Dane said. Shana shifted closer to him—within elbowing distance. She caught him in the ribs with a move no one but he would notice.

"Of course not. I understand this is serious business, but you have to admit there is potential for drama."

"Just stay out of the way and no one will get hurt," Dane said. It was a completely unnecessary and irrelevant thing to say except to calm the guy down. Dane would have to ask him for the surveillance tapes later, or he had a feeling he and Shana might be the stars in another home movie highlight reel at cocktail parties around the globe or wherever this guy went. It occurred to him that he'd done his homework on everyone involved except their own client. Shana had taken care of that. Dane knew Gable made his money making films. But it didn't matter what he did as long as he wasn't a drug lord running a cartel.

"Dane and I will do a check of the systems now and let you get to your own obligations. We'll be in the main room—"

"The ballroom," he said.

"Yes—when the guests begin arriving."

*****

Dane and Shana stood shoulder to shoulder, almost like co-hosts of the party, inside the ballroom door with the Gables. The room remained cool in spite of the growing crowd.

"Time for us to start circulating and keeping watch," Dane said.

"Angelique didn't arrive yet—we need to keep our eye on her most of all."

"We split up. We can both keep our eye on the entry. Don't forget—she likely has a partner. We need to spot the guy."

"You think the old fat guy—"

"Middle-aged."

"You think he's the accomplice?"

"Yes. It's classic. They're setting him up to take the fall."

Shana nodded and leaned in. "Don't wander too far. Remember—you're mine at the end of the night." Her green eyes sparkled under the perfect lighting of the chandeliers. The room was lively but not too bright. Her words jolted his blood to raging through his veins and he fisted his hands to keep from grabbing her by the hair and dragging her up the stairs in the main entryway. The thought of everyone seeing him drag her off excited him even more and he turned away as she left his side. He couldn't afford to watch her bare back retreat into the crowd. He'd end up being drawn after her. Like the shutting of a rusty door, he put the thought of making love to Shana from his mind and focused on the room.

The party—or soirée —was in full swing. Keeping one eye on the entry, Dane wandered toward the terrace doors past people in dinner jackets and tuxes and gowns and shimmering mini dresses and all kinds of sparkling jewelry on ears, necks, wrists, hands, and even ankles. They were drinking, eating and dancing to the swing band. He could imagine himself in a different era, but he wasn't sure which one this party tried to emulate. It seemed like a mix of 20s, 40s and 60s. It felt like he was in a Best of Partying eras mash-up. He smiled as he reached the doors to the terrace and swung them open. The heat had abated some, but the air was still heavy. He looked out at late-night lights shimmering off the water and left the terrace doors open to let the AC drift out to the sultry night. It had cooled off just enough to be bearable. Most people had stayed inside. He could barely see the entrance from here. He pressed the control to his earpiece and spoke to Ronnie Ryan.

"Cover for me—get your eyes on the front entry and look for our mark."

"Copy. Over and out. Roger dodger."

Shaking his head, Dane clicked the earpiece to mute. He took a turn around the area and was about to go back inside when he spied her. How the hell had she got in without them noticing?

Angelique Dubois stood at the stone wall lining the terrace and looked out at the water. Without turning toward him, she spoke.

"It's so gorgeous here. Reminds me of the south of France—the less crowded seaside towns. Not the wild and tourist-filled Monte Carlo."

He approached and stood next to her. "I hadn't pegged you for the country bumpkin type."

Angelique laughed a musical laugh and looked up at him. She had to lean her head back to meet his eyes, exposing the delicate line of her neck—and the plunging neckline of her dress leaving a considerable portion of curving flesh showing. She had an outstanding body. Petite well proportioned and gracefully sculpted. He stared at her eyes a beat to see if she had the kind of heart and soul to match. It would take some study.

"I didn't see you arrive."

"I didn't—not yet," she said. "I came around the terrace after we parked. It's too beautiful out here not to stop and ..." She sighed.

"We? You have a date?"

"If I didn't know better, I'd say you sound disappointed, Mr. Blaise."

"If I wanted to be honest, I'd admit I would be. But whoever you're with isn't a date, is he?"

She shook her head and kept her eyes on his, drifting closer so that he could breathe her exotic scent. It sent a message to his libido before he could shut it down. It was only one of those automatic male reactions, but it annoyed the hell out of him. His so-called seduction of her was to be a professional exercise and nothing more. He wanted to catch her in the act of thievery—or catch her with the jewels. He only needed to stick close, charm her and gain her trust. Real seduction would be overkill.

But then he realized seduction was her plan for him, so he'd play the game.

"*Non*—no date. An escort—a friend who invited me to the party. That's all." She smiled up at him.

"His name?"

She tilted her head at him and drew a brow up in question.

"I'm in charge of security—I want to make sure he's on the guest list."

"His name is Baylor Bellarine. Satisfied?"

He nodded. He'd seen the name on the guest list. He'd bet the man was fat and middle-aged, but he didn't ask. He'd pay deference to Jean Luc's request for secrecy for now. Until he figured out who needed protecting from whom.

"Shall we go inside?" Dane didn't wait for an answer.

*****

Shana had kept one eye on Dane until he disappeared outside to the terrace. Even if it was irrational, she didn't like him disappearing from view. It was a leftover effect from their harrowing case in Brazil when she thought he might be dead. She turned away to keep her eyes on the rest of the room. She didn't spot anyone meeting the description Jean Luc gave them. She kept as vigilant as possible in between begging off invitations to dance, endless questions about the recent shootout and how they'd taken down a notorious criminal at the Lucky Parrot, comments about the intrigue of a jewel thief in their midst and conspiratorial winks. This was the least 'under' undercover assignment she'd ever worked. She could be wearing a sign saying 'I'm undercover looking for a jewel thief and she'd be less conspicuous.'

After an interminable fifteen minutes, she spotted Dane laughing with Miss Dubois as he walked back inside from the terrace. God help her for breathing easier. Shana headed for the kitchen to check out the staff. It was the one place she hadn't been yet.

She pushed inside the swinging door to the full commercial kitchen off the ballroom and could have sworn she was in a hotel. Spotting Sassy, she motioned the girl over as she scanned the chefs and kitchen help. None of them looked like what she'd call fat, though a couple could be counted as middle-aged.

The girl scurried over to her with surreptitious looks around, stood too close and whispered, "How's it going out there? Anyone look suspicious?"

"No one except me and Dane," Shana said. Sassy looked puzzled. "Never mind—who's the short plump-ish man over there? Is he American? French?"

Sassy turned and took an obvious look before responding. "That's Chef Goody. He came over from Hyannis. He does all the parties in the neighborhood. He has a restaurant and catering business in—"

"Gotcha. Never mind. How about the short stocky man at the sink?"

"Manny?"

"You tell me?"

"He's my mother's cousin. He helps out Chef Goody on all his local catering events—"

"Okay. We're good in here then." Shana took a last look around. Everyone else was either too young, too skinny or female. She hoped to hell Jean Luc's bad guy hadn't gone on a diet recently. "Keep up the good work and keep your eyes and ears open."

Sassy saluted and scurried back to her station prepping plates of veggies.

Shana turned to go back outside but before she pushed through the door she caught a glimpse of none other than a fat middle-aged man—and he was bald. Bingo. He stood no more than two feet from her on the other side of the door and he had a phone to his ear. She couldn't quite hear him, so she pushed the door open a crack.

What she heard then caused her gut to turn to lead and drop. At the same time her heart jumped into piston pumping mode. The man was speaking Portuguese. It was unmistakable—the unforgettable language of the Brazilians from their last case. Hearing it again now raised goose bumps on her flesh in spite of the heat in the kitchen. She forced herself to concentrate and listen, but she couldn't make out what he was saying, nothing distinct.

Then pushing aside the lump of fear, she pushed through the door and walked by him for a closer look from her peripheral vision. She didn't walk far. He stopped talking. She took a deep breath. It had to be a coincidence. The Tavares family cartel had been shut down. All the major players were dead or in jail. Thanks to her and Dane. The man slipped his phone in his jacket and without looking around, walked through the middle of the dancers, and disappeared from view.

Shana automatically searched for Dane and flipped her earpiece on talk. She took another breath to calm herself, following the man as best she could. He had to be their man.

He was Angelique's predator or her accomplice, but he didn't have to be connected to the Tavares clan. The odds were against that. It was coincidental that he spoke Portuguese. There was only one person left of the Tavares family that she knew of—who had a grudge. That would be Gabriele Tavares—if she weren't locked up in a Brazilian insane asylum by then. The woman had been mad.

"Dane? I spotted him. We're headed toward the foyer. Meet me there." Shana spoke and walked. "Ronnie—you there? Look for a short fat bald man wearing a plain black tux meant to blend in. I lost my visual. See if you can pick him up."

"Got it—Roger—Over," the kid answered.

She fought her way through the partygoers to the entry foyer hoping to find her mark there. She hadn't gotten a response from Dane, but she expected to find him ready to pick up their mark, waiting for her in the foyer.

*****

After coming inside Dane looked for Shana and saw her go inside the kitchen. He needed to watch the ballroom for Jean Luc's idea of a dangerous man and he decided the best way to do that would be to dance with Angelique. After all, he had promised Jean Luc he'd look out for his niece.

Her fluid black silk sheath felt cool under his hands. Dane held her close, taking in her delicate scent, and said, "It's remarkable that a jewel thief such as yourself is wearing no jewels."

"You jest. I am not interested in jewels. That is why I do not wear them."

"If you're not a jewel thief, then what are you?"

"I am a museum curator." She smiled up at him. The music stopped but he continued to hold her.

"What is a museum curator from France doing on Martha's Vineyard?"

"So many questions, Mr. Blaise. Are you a policeman after all?"

"What are you doing here, Angelique?"

"Very well, I will answer your interrogation. I am here partly on business and partly on vacation."

The answer meant nothing, but he led her from the dance floor and looked around for Shana. It was automatic, like a reflex. He needed to know where she was at all times and it had nothing to do with the case. This case was nothing like the last one—a chase to Brazil to tangle with the Tavares cartel. He spotted Shana across the room headed toward the foyer. She was talking and tapping her earpiece. He tapped his, made sure it was clicked on and heard nothing. The sight of her walking away was like an irritant, like he was missing something, but he kept a surreptitious eye on her. The band had started another song. Angelique clutched his arm.

"Is there something wrong?"

"No." He wasn't going to tell Angelique his earpiece wasn't working.

She took a glass of champagne from a waiter—from Ronnie Ryan, who winked as he passed by. She said, "Jean Luc was right—you and Shana are lovers. He warned me that you would still be together."

"Why did you come here? Are you carrying out some vendetta for your uncle?"

"No, it is coincidental, pure chance these jewel thefts." She said no more, but lead him back to the dance floor. He went along with her. He decided he ought to stick with her since they hadn't spotted anyone else suspicious. But he'd need to check in with Shana soon. He brought Angelique around to Ronnie again.

"I'll have another champagne."

"Yes, sir,"

261

Dane spoke under his breath." Tell Shana my earpiece isn't working, Have her meet me outside in fifteen minutes."

Ronnie's eyes took on that twinkle like he'd just shared an inside joke. Dane hoped the joke wasn't on him.

"It's crowded inside—let's go back outside." Angelique took his arm again.

"Do you have a partner in crime?" Dane walked Angelique out to the terrace, to where they met.

"You're incorrigible. I'm not a criminal. I'm not your jewel thief. Do you think I would be crazy enough to try and get away with it with you here?"

He watched her eyes twinkle and he knew he was being played. He needed to play back and come on hard and strong if he was going to win this one. If he were doing his job right, doing it professionally, he would be going home with Angelique tonight.

But he couldn't tonight. His mind slipped to Shana. They had to stay and talk to their client and check on the jewels. Then he would go home with his girl.

Angelique brought him back when she raised a hand to his cheek and caressed it. An oddly intimate gesture.

"What are you thinking, Dane? About her?"

"Who?"

"Don't pretend. You are with her. She's a lucky one."

"That's sweet of you to say." He drew a breath for drama and plunged into his role. "But it's not true. We're platonic partners these days—spending too much time together sometimes dampens the romance. We weren't meant to be a couple, Shana and I. We were meant to be partners."

"Partners? That is all?" She laughed that musical laugh. He regretted for a blink of time that she was a jewel thief and he was there to catch her.

"I don't know, Dane. I don't think I believe you." She drew her hand down from his face and laid it on his chest over his heart. He had a flash of her conducting her own little version of a lie-detector test.

"What can I do to prove it to you?"

That wiped the smile from her face. He shifted closer and pressed his advantage. She was small and he towered over her and enveloped her in his arms until she was lost, tight against him. The warmth of her body and the softness of her small breasts had their effect on him. He held her chin in his hand. She looked innocent. He could feel the rapid-fire excitement of the pulse in her neck. He pressed his mouth to her lips. They felt foreign. They weren't Shana's lips.

But Angelique kissed back, a sweet kiss and he responded, falling into his role more comfortably.

*****

Shana rushed around the corner and stopped short before she ran into a couple.

She backed up a step and realized the couple in a heated embrace was none other than Dane and Angelique. They broke apart. Shana's heart stuttered and the air seemed to get sucked from her lungs.

"Excuse me." She hadn't meant to sound breathless.

Angelique smiled. Sweetly. Shana's judgment of the woman snapped into place. No matter what Angelique Dubois did or didn't do, no matter what she was or was not, Shana would detest her from that moment forward.

Dane gave Shana a look. One that she had no idea how to read, but she knew there was no apology in it.

"We need to talk." Shana paused a beat, flicking a glance at Angelique. "When you have a minute."

She went back inside to do her job and hoped to hell Dane was doing his job. *Of course he was doing his job. What else could it have been?*

She stopped herself from answering that question. It didn't bear answering.

262

In the meantime, she went upstairs to check on the safe—to make sure the Portuguese speaking man hadn't lifted the jewels while she'd lost track of him. Spotting Bill Gable, she took him by the arm and led him to the entry hall.

"Come with me to check on the safe." She turned to go up the stairs.

"So that's what you're calling it?"

"Pardon?" Shana looked at him and stopped herself in the nick of time from slapping the wolfish smile off his face.

"I'm here to protect your jewels, remember? We're really going to check the safe."

"Too bad. You know we've had security at the top of the stairs all night—no way anyone got past them—"

"Unless someone bought them off or—"

They stopped at the top of the stairs and she could see the security guard leaning against the wall texting or doing something on his phone.

"See—all is well."

"Let's check now that we're here."

"I'm with you. I like that you're being extra cautious."

They approached the guard and he slipped the phone in his pocket.

"Have you seen anyone come up stairs—maybe ten minutes ago?" she asked.

"No—but I might have been on break."

"Who covered for you?" She asked.

"Covered for me?"

She didn't say what she was thinking. None of her thoughts were fit for her client to hear.

Bill said, "No one covered for you—you went on a break and left the hall—the master bedroom—unguarded?" He sounded calm but she knew his voice was not normally so high.

The guard shrugged. He was twenty-something years old.

"You can take a break now. Permanently."

Shana went past the open-mouthed guard into the master bedroom to the closet where the safe took up the bottom third.

"Nothing looks out of place—but that doesn't necessarily mean anything. Will you open it?" She said.

Gable bent and took thirty seconds to open the door, then he took an audible breath. Shana glanced inside.

The jewels were there.

"That's a relief."

"Now we need to make sure no one else comes up here." At least not from the inside. Shana walked over to the French doors leading to a balcony. It was a long way down and nothing was out of place. She let her breath out.

"I'll have someone else re-assigned—I'll make sure they put their best man up here this time," Gable said.

"How many security people do you have here tonight?"

"You mean besides you and Dane? We have six. That's standard for a party this size."

Shana nodded. Crowd control was a far cry from dealing with a jewel thief.

"I need to consult with Dane. We think our suspect has a partner, but we won't know unless we can catch him. Maybe we should leave the guard off the upstairs duty."

"And then what? Are you going to hide in my bedroom and surprise the thief? Because I'd—"

"No. No theatrics, Mr. Gable."

"Call me Bill."

"We'll need to catch them red-handed—with the jewels after they leave the premises."

"That's very risky."

"It's your call."

"Let's see what Dane thinks."

As they walked down the stairs to go back to the party, the looks people gave them were not lost on Shana. She'd better have a chat with Mrs. Gable before her friends did.

Now to find Dane. Her chest tightened. He'd be with his new girlfriend. She walked with her client back into the ballroom.

"There he is—."

He stood on the perimeter, alone, entertaining a group of guests and sipping a drink she'd bet was tequila over ice. Shana headed in Dane's direction with Gable.

Ronnie emerged from the crowd and she stopped and took a glass of champagne from his tray. He said, "This party is too cool for anyone to leave—you'd have to be crazy," He looked around and held his tray high at his shoulder. Shana hoped he didn't get it knocked off his hand.

"What do you mean? People are leaving?" Gable asked.

"Yes sir. Only a few."

"I'll be a minute," Shana said and pulled Ronnie aside. "Did you see the fat middle-aged bald man I told you about?"

"I think so. He just left."

"Damn—when?"

"A few minutes ago."

"Double-damn." She saw Gable pulling Dane aside. "Good work, Ronnie. I have to talk to Dane."

She caught up with Gable and Dane as they headed her way and met at the kitchen door. She said, "Where's Dubois?"

"Powder room. Why?"

"Didn't Gable tell you?"

"That the jewels are still in the safe?"

"Yes. But I've been trying to get you on the earpiece—I spotted the suspected accomplice—then lost him. Ronnie said he left about five minutes ago."

"Then he left without the jewels."

"And that means Angelique is—"

"Right behind you." Angelique said. "Is there a problem?"

"No, nothing at all," Gable said. "You all enjoy the party. I'm going to arrange for that second floor thing," he added to Shana. She nodded. She didn't blame him. She and Dane weren't exactly hitting it out of the park with their attempt to trap the thief.

She looked at Dane. Angelique stood next to him making her feel like the third wheel. But that was ridiculous—she was no third wheel.

"Dane, we need to talk business for a minute." She reached out and took his arm—the one next to Angelique and practically ripped him from her grasp. She said over her shoulder, "Business."

They walked in the direction of the terrace. Shana felt hot. She really did need some air.

*****

"Someone needs to keep an eye on Angelique you know," he said. But he didn't mind being dragged to the terrace by a hot and bothered Shana.

"Shut up. I want her to steal the jewels. It's the only way we'll catch her. In the act."

"Then let's go up to the bedroom—"

"I'm serious."

"So am I—"

"You're as bad as Gable—"

Those are not words he wanted to hear. "What do you mean?"

"Oh nothing. We can't hide in the bedroom to catch her. She would know and she wouldn't steal anything. She's not an idiot."

"That leaves the balcony. It would be tricky," he said. But the more he thought about it, the more it made sense.

"What about the cameras?"

"They're not night vision cameras. If the thief dressed in black, they could stay fairly invisible."

"So you think the Portuguese speaking man—"

264

"Portuguese speaking? What the hell are you talking about?" He hoped the hell she wasn't saying what he thought she was saying.

"I heard the suspected accomplice speaking Portuguese."

He took a beat to calm his pulse. They both knew it couldn't be the Tavares family.

"It's a coincidence, Shana."

She nodded. "Has to be."

"Yes, I think he left early because he was going to climb up the balcony and break into the open doors." He looked in the direction of the master bedroom window. He saw nothing, but too much time had gone by. He was long gone if he'd done it.

"It's probably futile, but let's take a walk around back."

Chapter 6

By the time the party was over it was almost morning. Dane shut the door of Angelique's taxi and watched the car pull away. Then he went back inside the house to find the Gables and Shana waiting.

"I think the night was a roaring success," Bill Gable said.

"And no robberies," Mrs. Gable smiled. "Would you like some coffee?"

"Hold that thought. Let's go up and check the safe—to be safe," Dane said. He took Shana's arm and squeezed it to prevent her frown from getting any further. They'd spotted the area below the balcony where the accomplice likely climbed up, but they had nothing solid. Cap could send his team to check for prints and evidence but they wouldn't find anything. He and Shana had checked the surveillance tapes but they saw nothing. They weren't sure who the hell he was but they were fairly certain he got the jewels. One thing Dane was certain about was that Angelique Dubois had not stolen any jewels that evening.

"Of course. Let's go confirm our defeat of the great Martha's Vineyard Jewel Thief," Bill Gable took his wife's hand and they led Dane and Shana up the stairs. Laura Gable giggled.

"What are we going to tell them?" Shana whispered.

"We'll get the jewels back. I'll get her to talk."

"You'll get her to talk?" Shana's whisper rose in pitch, but the Gables weren't paying attention to them as they stumbled ahead into their master bedroom down the hall at the top of the stairs.

"Don't worry. I won't hurt her."

She whispered, barely, "It's not her I'm worried about. While her accomplice was busy stealing jewels, she kept you busy." She glared at him. He smiled at the sparks in her eyes. He loved those sparks. He felt the jolt of desire then and this was the worst possible time. He tamped down and took her arm, turning his attention to their clients.

The Gables were in the room and Bill was deftly spinning the lock on the safe door when he and Shana walked in. He felt Shana's nerves.

"Mr. Gable—" she said.

Dane tugged on her arm and leaned his head to whisper in her ear. She tugged away from him, but he tugged back, ignoring the stab between his shoulders paining him at her resistance. He should be used to it.

He said, "Don't worry."

Mrs. Gable hovered to one side and Mr. Gable stepped to the other, looked over his shoulder at Dane and Shana and the swung the door open with a flourish.

"Voilà —the jewels."

Mrs. Gable sucked in a swift breath and brought her hands to her mouth. Mr. Gable frowned and turned to look into the safe.

Dane made no reaction and held Shana's arm. Shana, to her credit, held herself stoically in check while she no doubt calculated the loss in fees in her head that they would suffer when the Gables fired them.

The safe was empty. No jewels.

No one spoke.

Dane said, "We'll get your jewels back."

Mr. Gable turned to him and folded his arms, speechless for a moment.

Then he said, "You'd better get them back—if you want to get paid."

Dane nodded, grabbed Shana and they took off as the sun was coming up. But they didn't drive back to the beach shack, they drove to the airport.

"What are you thinking?" Shana said.

"She's taking off because there's no way she can—"

"You don't even know if she has the jewels,"

"Oh yes I do."

"Now who's jumping to conclusions?"

266

"Her or her accomplice. Same difference. I did my homework and came to a well-considered and well-reasoned conclusion. She's here on behalf of her uncle. She's here as a taunt."

"What makes you say that?"

"She had no jewelry on. She came in the back door and spoke to no one but me."

"So? Her accomplice came separately."

"She knew we were coming here tonight so she made it a point to be at this soiree. And she sabotaged my earpiece tonight so we couldn't communicate."

Shana's mouth was open but it took her moment to speak.

"When were you going to tell me about the earpiece?"

"And ruin the surprise?"

"You should have—"

"Ditched her to talk to you and prevented the robbery? Like you said. We needed to catch them red-handed. You are not at your best when you have an ax to grind."

She shut up. He could tell she knew he was right. He could feel her anger rising, could see the perspiration glisten on her bronze skin and the dawn light gleam off her blond-streaked hair.

*****

At the airport they talked to security and called Cap to get them access to surveillance films. Shana talked to the tower people and found out that there were no charters or private jets or helicopters or small planes that had taken off in the last two hours. There had been no commercial flights for the past four hours.

"If she left the island, she did it by private boat," Shana said as they walked back to the Jag.

"Maybe she's still on the island," he said.

"Where is she staying?"

"I don't know—somewhere in Edgartown."

Shana scowled at him. He sighed. He had not found out where she was staying—hadn't done his job. He hadn't taken it seriously enough.

"Who was seducing whom tonight?" she said, but there was no heat in her words.

"Let's go."

They drove to Edgartown and Dane called Cap again to see if he had any intel on where Angelique was staying. He didn't.

"What now, Sherlock?" Shana raised a brow at him. He couldn't tell if she was angry or happy to be gloating at his rare screw-up.

"I have an idea."

They stopped at the exclusive dress shop where they'd run into her and Dane convinced Emma to tell them where they had delivered Angelique's purchase from the day before.

*****

Dane and Shana banged on Angelique's door at the Admiral's Inn. Shana wasn't so sure this was a good idea, but she didn't have any better alternatives. Angelique answered the door all sleepy and in a white filmy robe, but she let them in. Shana watched Dane stalk around the room, searching the drawers and bags.

"What the hell are you doing? *Mon dieu,* are you mad?"

Angelique swore at him in French and Shana jumped in to keep her away from Dane as best she could as he finished his search.

"Where are they?"

"What are you talking about? You're insane."

"You stole the jewels from the Gables' house during the party tonight. I don't know what you did with them or what you're planning next, but I'll figure it out. I'll find the jewels and I'll catch you cold."

"Impossible. I don't have any jewels. I know nothing about what you—"

"Oh shut up," Shana said. She took Dane's arm and pulled him toward the door. He'd done the same to her more times than she should forgive him for. He went along.

Shana had hardly ever seen Dane blow his cool. It was one of the most unsettling things she'd experienced when it had happened before. But this time, it was surprising and unsettling in a different way.

*****

"You're slipping." Cap said. Shana had been thinking it. Dane nodded agreement.

"You shouldn't agree. Where's your pride?"

"Don't you worry, girlie. It was a one-time-only slip. The kind that makes me more determined. You didn't think I'd let it defeat me, did you? Didn't think I'd let her defeat me?"

"No." She hoped he couldn't read her uncertainty. But of course he could. He stared at her for a few beats in silence with his cool granite face—or what passed for it in the sweaty heat of Cap's office.

She turned away from Dane and said, "When the hell are you going to get your AC fixed?"

"As soon as the heat wave breaks, I expect. We're low on the list for the technicians. We don't pay a premium for special treatment. Besides, enduring the heat is good for building character."

"Shana needs some character building. She's got some things to learn. Like having faith in her partner, for one." Dane spoke to Cap and his voice was light, but she felt the hurt underneath. It might be her guilty conscience, but what if she had hurt his feelings by doubting him? She couldn't wrap her head around it, so she shook it off.

She scoffed and gave him the finger.

Dane smiled. "There's my girlie."

Red-hot warmth spread through her. He could see right through her, down to the guilty conscience, she could swear.

"Now what? We track her? We wait till the next party and set a trap?"

"We won't have to wait long," Dane said. "I got a text from our client. His friend and neighbor has a party scheduled for tonight and we're on—in spite of the theft. I've convinced them I have a lead."

"Who's watching Angelique at the Inn?"

"Pie girl."

"Sassy?"

"She'll do. But there's a change of plans for tonight's party. You'll need to get another date," Dane said and tilted his head toward Cap. "You own a tux?"

"Of course. It might still fit."

"What is it? Left over from the prom?" Dane asked.

Cap laughed and held up his middle finger.

Shana stood. "Do I have a say in this plan?"

"No." Dane stood, fronting her, convincing her. "We need to flush out her accomplice—or whoever the hell he is. There's something about this story that doesn't fit together."

"You're going to invite Angelique on a date to a party after you've just accused her of being a thief?" Shana said.

Dane stared. Didn't speak.

"To what end? You expect her bring the stolen jewels with her?" Cap said.

"Exactly. I need her to trust me and confess to having the jewels."

"And you think she has the jewels?"

" I think it's personal with her—something about the story—both hers and Jean Luc's—doesn't fit together. I made some calls to verify the background story and to double-check on Baylor Bellarine, " Dane said.

"You think Bellarine is the Portuguese speaking man?"

Dane didn't answer. He didn't bother trying to explain his instinct that something was out of focus—he had no explanation. He walked to the door and called over his shoulder.

"See you tonight, Cap." He turned at the door and said, "Let's go, girlie. We have more shopping to do, unless you want to wear the same dress two nights in a row."

"I already have a dress. You have some work to do on your mark." She sat on the edge of Cap's desk and crossed her legs.

268

He studied her. She was inscrutable and that wasn't a good sign.

She was giving him permission to seduce Angelique—his mark. That rankled him to a ridiculous degree. It made him want to shake her. He kept his hands at his sides and forced himself to remain in the door, to not go to her, to not drag her from the office. Away from Cap. He turned to Cap, feeling his chest tighten. Cap would never betray Dane. But Shana... he wasn't sure if Shana knew that.

"Don't let me stop either of you," Cap said.

Dane gave Cap the finger before he strode out the door.

*****

"Do you want to know why I came here to Martha's Vineyard?" Angelique walked into her room at Admirals Inn ahead of Dane. "Not that I should be speaking to you after your horrible accusations." Her pure white skin glowed in the dim light. The shades were down and the air conditioning was cranked up, but a slight sheen covered her skin like dew on flower petals.

He closed the door behind him and leaned on it, offering her a half smile. He watched the playful twinkle in her eyes. She was young. She couldn't be more than twenty-five—younger even than Shana—in more ways than one in spite of her sophistication and her pretense at being hardened.

"Why?" He stood watching her. He reached out and touched her hair. It was soft and fine like baby hair. He tamped down on the churn of guilt. He had nothing to be guilty about. He reached out and turned on the light switch.

"I came because the Dane Blaise who Jean Luc spoke of was the kind of man I was looking for. You were like that fairytale hero I'd always dreamed of as a girl—only you were real—or supposed to be real. I had to find out for myself if you were." She leaned forward resting against his chest. Then she tiled her face to kiss his mouth with her soft cool lips, so different from Shana's. He closed his eyes and commanded himself to stop comparing, to reinforce his professional mantle. This was all part of the job, doing what he needed to do. *Shana had given him her damn permission.*

He scoffed at himself—this was about some missing jewels of a few rich people and at least partly for their amusement. This wasn't about the kinds of things he usually put aside his soul and his heart for—like life and death and the misery of human trafficking or torture by warlords or tyrannical governments. This case hardly justified him lifting a finger, let alone pretending at romance with the likes of Angelique Dubois. There was no cause for him to risk his integrity. Assuming he had any when it came to romantic entanglements. He pushed all the thoughts aside and pushed her.

"I know you're young, but you didn't come here because of some girlish notions put in your head by Jean Luc."

"He also told me he couldn't believe that you were the kind of man that would settle on this small island for long. He said there was a rogue in your heart, that you were a renegade, not a true law-enforcement soul." She paused for a moment and then asked him with her brown eyes impossibly wide and innocent looking. Even though he knew it was an act for his benefit, his body responded.

"Is it true that you were once a gun for hire?"

"What if I said yes?"

"I would believe you. You have that delicious need to 'save the damsel in distress' and I can see you being drawn into all kinds of such missions." She sighed. He raised one brow.

"You can see how I was drawn into this venture to meet you in the flesh, to see for myself," she continued.

"Not really. What I see is that you're *not* telling me far more than you *are* telling me."

She laughed and stroked his face in that way she had. It was a compelling habit. He waited for her to continue. He had time. If there was an agenda in her back pocket, he doubted he was in any danger. There were no kidnap victims and no mad cartel members after him. And Shana was getting her coveted serious money case. He shouldn't feel this uncomfortable.

But the nagging thought that there was something he was missing never left him, whether from the well-learned habits of self-preservation or some immediate need, he didn't know. He took a long deep breath, too big to be called a sigh.

Looking over her shoulder, he spotted a guitar in the corner of the room. She turned and said, "You play?"

"You?"

She laughed. She went and took the acoustic guitar from its perch and sat on the bed. Then she sang. Something French and sweet as she strummed the cords. When she finished he clapped.

Then she held out the guitar to him. He told himself to forget about it, but the excitement of temptation, of a moment out of time, a time that didn't count in his life, buzzed and built until he stepped forward and sat next to her on the bed. She watched him and said nothing. No cajoling. She knew. Somehow she knew it was a hard choice, and a mindless leap at the same time.

Because she didn't force it, he took the guitar from her, putting aside the years of abstinence, pain and longing in the flick of a switch. The instant he felt the weight and curve of the wood in his hands, skimmed his fingers down the strings, he felt the trench of loss. All the lost songs, the lost time. The loss of his father who shared his music with Dane who gave Dane his first and only guitar. He took a deep shaky breath and played. And sang.

"Yesterday..."

She listened and leaned into him and slipped her arms around him when he finished.

And it was all wrong. He put the guitar aside, took her arms from him and stood.

"So beautiful. Everything about you I learned was right," she said. "You were painted as an exciting man by my uncle, but I did my homework on you also. I went far beyond what Jean Luc told me. I know why you choose to sing this song about lost love." She paused until he returned his attention to her. "I found out about Elena." She studied his face for a few beats.

He gave nothing away. None of the churning in his gut showed on his face or in his body, not even one drop of perspiration popped. He'd been steeling himself for many years against this assault weapon.

"I found out about her betrayal," Angelique continued in her musical voice. "About how you left the Chicago police department after losing her. I know you must feel bitter. Whether or not Elena had been a bad cop and whether or not you'd been a bad cop—I don't judge either of you."

Hearing that left a bitter taste in his mouth and he turned from her as she went to him and attempted a kiss. He said, "Don't talk about Elena." He meant he didn't want to hear anymore from Angelique, that she knew nothing and had no right to talk about his private world. But he knew she'd take it to mean that he didn't want to think about bad times.

"We're here now. Let's make the most of it," she said. She took his hand and skimmed it along her rib cage, placing it on her small taut breast, so that it cupped the tender curve.

"It's late in the day." He moved away from her.

"You have somewhere to go? We have a date tonight."

"What about your accomplice?"

She sighed. "I've dismissed him." She turned her face away from him.

A chill hit his gut. "Dismissed him?" In three words, she'd not only confirmed that she'd had an accomplice, but she implied that she got rid of him. Dane wasn't often taken by surprise, but this was one of those bad surprises—the kind that made him rethink everything and dread what he would find.

"Yes. Dismissed. He's gone. Enough said." She pushed away from him, still not meeting his eyes, pulling her dress off as she walked to the bathroom. "Let's get ready. I have a plan."

Once she was in the bathroom, Dane looked around for her phone. Once he found it, he checked it and didn't like what he saw in her text history, but it didn't surprise him. He put her phone back exactly where he'd found it, then he quietly left the room. Schooling his voice against the bubbling dread, he called Cap.

"Look for a missing middle-aged, fat, bald man. I believe he'd been registered here at the inn. Using the name Baylor Bellarine. Presumed dead."

"Dead?" Are you sure? Murder is a big leap—"

"No. I'm not sure—we'll see what the evidence says. It could have been self-defense." He took a breath and spoke from his gut. "She's in over her head. She's working with someone else—besides Bellarine—I'll explain when I do more checking. I think she trusts me—thinks she's seducing me—she may be counting on my help to stay out of prison."

"Watch your back," Cap said. "I'll let you know what I find."

Dane ended the call and wrote a note to tell Angelique that he'd be back later to pick her up.

He needed to confirm that their fat, middle-aged man and Bellarine were one and the same. Pronto. He left the room behind with one backward glance at the guitar and one spiral of regret through his gut to his chest. The pain settled between his shoulder blades and he felt the searing sting as he pulled the door closed behind him.

The words to the song *Yesterday* haunted him as he walked to his car and he thought of Shana. The song was wrong. Love was never an easy game to play.

What the hell was it that he had with Shana? Was it a commitment? He knew there was no explicit commitment, but he wasn't too much of an idiot to know that it felt like one. Even when they pushed each other away, some kind of hold kept them in each other's orbit—and not just as partners.

Whatever it was—it was messing him up—coloring his ability to read people. He never should have started with her, never should have let it get physical no matter how much he wanted it. He knew it was bad for him—for both of them.

And it made his job too damn difficult.

He got into his Jag, wishing it were the Jeep. He wanted to find and search the dead man's room, but he'd have to do it later when Angelique wasn't so close by. Or maybe have Shana do it. He drove to Cap's office at State Police Headquarters. He hoped to hell Shana wasn't there.

Chapter 7

Shana strolled into Cap's office without knocking. She realized she should have called, but his company soothed her. He was on the phone, but he gave her a welcoming smile and gestured for her to sit, so she did as he hung up.

Before he said anything she jumped in.

"I need to make a decision about Dane by summer's end. My ma and brothers are coming for a visit and—" She couldn't continue. She didn't need to. Cap rose from his chair and came around to her. She stood and stepped into his arms. He was warm and she shivered at the contrast to the ice-cold air. He'd finally gotten the AC fixed.

"You'll figure it out," he said over her head. She gave him a squeeze and backed up.

"The problem is that it's not up to me—"

"Yes it is. He'll—"

"No he won't. He'll fight it. If I throw myself into it, if I go all in—he'll fight it or he'll take advantage of it."

Cap frowned. "What makes you so sure? He's had relationships before. He knows how to…"

"That's the problem, Cap. He's too afraid to do it again. Especially with me."

"Because you're too good for him."

She laughed. It sounded bitter. It felt bitter.

"On the other hand," she said, "he won't let me go."

"On that you can sure as hell defeat him." Cap's mouth was flat and grim and determined. She smiled at him.

"All I need to do is pull the trigger."

"So to speak."

"You'll be there for him." She whispered the words, sounding desperate she knew, but she was desperate. He was with Angelique that moment. He'd felt no compunction about seducing the young woman. And for what?

Because she'd said it was okay?

Cap sighed. They both knew it would be a hard thing all the way around.

"Then that's my decision, isn't it?" she paused and let the searing sweep of pain settle in her chest. She took a few breaths to make sure she still could with the constriction so tight. "I wonder if we could still work—"

"Don't even think about it," Cap said. "If you decide to leave Dane, you go with your ma and brothers and get as far away from here as possible."

She was about to tell him she had no intentions of going back to Sydney when his phone rang. He leaned over his desk and answered it. She took more deep breaths and squeezed her eyes shut. Everything in her screamed at the thought of leaving Dane, rebelling in waves of bile in her gut as if the notion were poisonous.

Had she decided to leave Dane?

How much of their relationship's dysfunction was her own fault? *Why hadn't she told him what she really felt about him seducing Angelique—or rather allowing her to seduce him?* Why hadn't she screamed *don't you dare* or *I'll kill you and then I'll kill her*—because that's what her insides had screamed at her?

She turned to the door. Every nerve in her wanted to run through it and find him and shake him to make him understand. But first she had to come to an understanding with herself.

Cap said, "That was one of my men over at State Beach. We have a lead—want to come?"

She cleared her head as best she could. Returning to business mode, she turned to Cap. He smiled at her and she felt her spirits buoyed by his easygoing manner. The complete lack of stress or conflict between them refreshed her, calmed her jittering insides enough for her to function. She felt her mind easing back to the rational world. To the case and their client and the fee.

"What do you have? Did you find the accomplice?"

"Yes."

They talked and walked toward the front door of the building that had become like a second home to her.

"Did he have the jewels? Is he going to give up Angelique Dubois?" She hoped to hell the answer was yes to that. She'd love to hang a grand larceny conviction around Angelique's delicate little neck.

"Not exactly." Cap stopped when they stepped outside the building and into the sauna of late day heat and heavy still air. If her relationship with Dane weren't already killing her with the hot and cold antics between them, this heat wave would surely do it.

"What?" she sighed and fanned her face.

"Let's get in the air-conditioned cruiser and on our way I'll fill you in."

She didn't argue with that, but she did realize that Cap was stalling. That wasn't a good sign. "Dane's—"

"Fine," he said as he opened her door. Cap was polite to a fault. She slid in and he followed and fired up the AC. After a minute they were on their way to State Beach and she couldn't stand his silence. She prompted.

"What the hell is this about, Cap?"

"Her accomplice is dead."

Boom. Her hand went to her chest as if she could stop her heart from jumping through, or stop it from stopping altogether.

"No—" And what about Dane? Was he in danger after all?

"It's either murder or possibly self-defense."

"What does he know?" Her heart sped up more now and no amount of AC could keep her from sweating.

"He doesn't know anything. I'm—we're going to check out the body and the scene and then call him." She didn't ask where he was, why he couldn't check it out himself. The thought pinched her mind shut and she forced herself to stay in the moment.

They got to the scene and two staties with a handful of local police had the area surrounded, along with a horde of flies. No buzzards overhead—yet. The body was fresh.

One of the state police officers greeted them and filled them in.

"No identification. No wallet. But he does have a gun that had recently been fired. Looks like it was fired by him. There was a struggle of some kind. He has bruises. But I'd bet the cause of death was the stab to his chest."

They stepped closer and Shana shut her mouth tight and tried not to breathe. She smelled the blood and decay hastened by the steamy weather. The body didn't look as bad as some she'd seen during her time on the beat in Sydney.

"Is this the man you spotted at the party last night?"

She examined his face. It was him. The Portuguese speaking man. She noted that the stab was expertly placed. Then she looked closer at his face—there was something odd about him.

"Yes—but have the medical examiner do me a favor and check inside his mouth. Look at his left cheek—it's unnaturally large, like he has a walnut in his mouth." Or something. She had an idea of what.

The medical examiner arrived a minute later and they had their answer.

"I'll be damned—congratulations, Shana. Your client will be thrilled," Cap said.

She checked the small pile of jewels held on a tray by the ME and accounted for every single piece of jewelry that had been in the Gable's safe.

"It's too easy, Cap. We're missing something."

He nodded. "Looks that way—like what about the jewels from the other three parties?"

"And what about Angelique? What's going on with her? If she was in a fight with this guy, why and how did the jewels end up in his mouth?"

"We'll need to figure out who he is."

Cap took out his phone and placed a call. She knew he was calling Dane and couldn't help the tightening of every muscle in her body in anticipation of him, of even hearing his voice from Cap's phone, and especially the anticipation of seeing him again later. It was damn unhealthy. To be so compelled and repelled by a man at the same time couldn't be good.

But how much of that was Dane—and how much of it was her—and her own fear?

Cap said into the phone, "Meet us at my office."

*****

Dane stood in the door. He hadn't had a chance to shower after he left Angelique's bed. He was too well aware of her lingering aroma and didn't want to share it with either Shana or Cap. But especially not Shana.

"Thank the lord you got the air conditioning fixed," he said.

Shana sat in her usual chair in front of Cap's desk. She didn't look at him. She busied herself looking through the ME's file. He was sure she'd already memorized every word.

Cap said, "You figure Angelique was framing this guy—Baylor Bellarine?"

"You sure that's his real name and not an alias?" Shana said.

"According to Interpol," Cap said. "That's his only name. And his job is international jewel thief."

Dane straightened from leaning against the doorjamb and took a step inside the room, but no further. "She wasn't framing him. I did some checking myself." He paused a beat and waited for Shana to look at him. When she did, he noticed her nostrils flare. Otherwise her face was inscrutable. Damn.

He walked all the way inside and sat down next to her in the chair facing Cap.

"What the hell, Dane? You wearing perfume now?" Cap smiled and waved his hand.

Dane hesitated a beat and then said, "It's French." He noticed Shana's almost imperceptible flinch from the periphery of his vision. "I did my own checking and it looks like Angelique lied to us about who she is—"

"No kidding." Shana said.

"She's an investigator for an insurance company. For the Gables' insurance company to be exact—and the same company who insures everyone in the neighborhood. Seems they all know the same agent who works with Lloyd's of London."

"You're shitting me." Cap said. "Why would she lie to us about that?"

"I'll find out."

"Are you sure?" Shana said. She sounded disappointed and he reached out a hand and patted her knee—more to test the waters than to comfort her. She didn't flinch or pull away or bat his hand away. She didn't react at all except to scowl at him. She gave him that gorgeous Shana the Beautiful scowl. He winked at her. She rolled her eyes.

"I'm sure, girlie. Sorry to disappoint you."

"So we have our thief and he's dead. Now all we need to do is find the rest of the jewels."

"Why? They don't belong to your client." Cap said. "That's my job—and I suspect it's Angelique's job as well."

"Which once again begs the question about why the jewels were found in his mouth." Shana said "I know you need them for evidence in the murder case, but can we bring the jewels to the Gables to confirm they're the missing ones?"

"Sure," Cap said. "I'll go with you." He turned to Dane. "I'll also need to bring Angelique in for questioning on the murder of Mr. Bellarine. Maybe she'll know something about the missing jewels from the other three thefts."

Dane thought about it. He knew there was something wrong with all the pieces to the puzzle. They didn't quite all fit together. His phone buzzed—it was his friend Acer. "I have to take this call—it's important to the case." He stepped to the side and listened. Cap and Shana watched him and waited in silence.

After he finished his call, he came back to them and said, "I have a better plan."

"Yes?" Shana prompted. He dreaded sharing the intel with her.

"Angelique may be working as an insurance investigator, theoretically on the right side of the law, but I had a bad feeling about her. While you two were at State Beach after I found out about Angelique's real identity, I also did some checking into the provenance of the missing jewelry. Most of it was unremarkable—except for one piece. This piece—owned by a neighbor of the Gables—the second house to be robbed—had been obtained from an estate sale in France twenty years ago.

"It had belonged to the Ruse family for several generations and was last owned by Angelique's maternal grandmother, Marguerite Ruse." He stopped and gauged their reaction—mostly Shana's reaction. She nodded and scowled.

"And Acer tracked Bellarine's bank account. The money came from Rio—the name on the account is Gabriele Tavares. " He paused to let Cap and Shana take this in. The air was still.

"Should we be thanking Angelique for killing him then?" Shana said quietly.

"No—there's more. I called Jean Luc and we had another chat. I asked him if Angelique had any friends by the name of Gabriele Tavares."

"Don't tell me—"

"They went to private school together."

"Interesting," Cap said. "Things make more sense now. Angelique is working with her old friend Gabriele to carry out a revenge plot."

"Jean Luc insists that Angelique doesn't know how crazy Gabriele is—they hadn't seen each other for a while."

Shana lifted her chin and said, "And what do you say? You think she's innocent?"

"No. I think she's trying to set me up. And I think she murdered Bellarine. I had a chance to check her phone before she disposed of it."

"And?"

"She communicated with someone—it must have been Gabriele. She said she killed Bellarine—the hired assassin. She said she'd agree to set me up and see me thrown in jail, but that was all. That would be enough punishment for my partner because she—"

"I get the picture," Shana said. She put a hand up as if to stop him. She knew what he was going to say. That she was hopelessly in love with him. He'd wanted to say it. To test the truth. But not with Cap in the room.

Cap said, "This case is now a horse of a different color. So what's your plan?"

"My guess is that you won't find the missing heirloom anywhere except in Angelique's hot hands." He took a breath. "I want to catch her with it."

Shana said, "How do you propose to do that—sleep with her again? Only this time do your job—"

"Let him tell his plan, Shana," Cap said.

A thudding shock at Shana's reaction went through Dane and left him with a stuttering heartbeat in his tight chest. He wanted to shout at her that she was all wrong, that he didn't sleep with Angelique, but she should know that. He took a long slow breath and said nothing to her. Beyond the shock was pleasure. And guilt and sorrow. He numbed himself, turning to his granite persona before it overwhelmed him.

Stick with the plan to nail damn Angelique Dubois.

"Cap, when you bring her in for questioning, we stage a disagreement and I'll be on her side—like good cop/bad cop except it'll be clear I'm no cop. I'll have a big fight with Shana…"

"Just like always."

He ignored her, ignored the sharp stab through his shoulder blades as if she were wielding a real knife.

"You act suspicious and I'll tip her off that there's a search warrant and offer to help her hide the jewels."

"Why not just search her place and find the jewels and bring her in?" Shana said. "We don't need an elaborate scheme—"

"You're obviously not thinking straight, girlie. You know she would never keep the jewels in her room for that very reason." He licked his lips and looked straight into Shana's eyes. "Besides, I want to gain her trust so that she confesses everything—including the murder." He paused and lowered his voice, "I want to know exactly how dirty or innocent she is from the one person who knows—herself." *And he wanted to make Angelique pay for playing him.*

"What makes you think she'll confide all this in you? No, never mind—" Shana turned away, but not before Dane saw it. He saw the sparkle of unshed tears in her eyes, felt the emotion erupting from her like she could no longer hold it in. She vibrated with it. Shards of disgust, disappointment, sadness, anger, longing and need hit him.

Dane turned to Cap, who had gone still. He watched Shana with concern and Dane with a question in his eyes.

"I'll gain her confidence and suggest it's about time for me to get away from the confines of the island. She'll invite me with her. I know she'll take me into her confidence." He paused. There was no response from either Cap or Shana. No affirmation, no argument, not even an acknowledgment. They didn't like it. They didn't defy him. They knew it would work.

Dane stood, his knees straightening with that now familiar ache like an old door reluctantly opening. Like everything else in him, his knees needed attention, needed fixing.

"Keep your book open on the self-defense charge—could be more like manslaughter. I don't doubt he tried to shoot her and she had to kill him in self-defense—but I bet she instigated it. I bet she taunted him. She has a habit of taunting."

Shana turned to him with a gaze that looked like she saw him from a great distance. He felt the coldness go through him and was helpless against it. Then he knew—this was not about him or something he did or didn't do. This distance, her new attitude was about her and her own mind. Something he could do nothing about.

"Okay," Cap stood too. "Let's put the plan into place."

*****

Dane left the office and went to the beach shack to dress before going to pick up Angelique at the Inn.

She opened the door and said, "You're early." She smiled and reached her hand to caress his cheek, but he caught it and stopped her.

"The police are coming to search your place." He pushed past her to step inside the room. "They found the body of your fat middle-aged man with some of the jewels and they're looking for the rest of them."

"Let them look."

"Smart girl. Problem is they're going to take you in for questioning for the murder."

She said nothing.

"I know you didn't murder him. I know it was self-defense."

"How do you know?"

"I know you're no murderer." That much was true.

"Thank you, Dane." She kissed him and said, "Then there is a chance for us?"

"More than a chance." That was not true.

"I'll dress for the party anyway—maybe we will convince the police and still be able to go later."

Dane didn't bother to talk her out of it. He knew she was dressing up to show off, to taunt. She'd have an audience of him, Cap and Shana—and she knew it.

The police arrived within twenty minutes and turned the place upside down. Angelique took it well—as if it hadn't been the first time she'd suffered a police search. They found nothing, but they insisted she come in for questioning and Dane insisted on going with her. All part of the plan. All making him damned uncomfortable. He did not look forward to playing his role with Shana and Angelique in the same room.

****

Dane looked at his watch. He sat at the table in the interrogation room at State Police Headquarters in Vineyard Haven. It was a place he'd been many times. But he'd never been the one cooling his heels waiting for the interrogators. He looked around. Angelique sat silently next to him. She was a pro. She knew the police would hear everything that was said and see everything Angelique and Dane did in this room. They remained silent and still.

It was close to eight p.m. He'd warned the Gables that neither he nor Angelique would be making the neighbors' party. Bill Gable knew they had a plan and had seemed more excited than worried about not getting his jewels back until the suspicious death of Bellarine was resolved.

After only twenty minutes, Shana and Cap walked into the room. Shana was dressed to kill in white and Cap wore a tux that fit him fine. Apparently they had no intentions of missing the party. They sat across the table from Dane and Angelique. It felt very odd being on the wrong side of the table from his girl. Shana played her role of estranged lover well. Too well.

Angelique explained that she'd been hired by the insurance company to follow this Baylor Bellarine and then to recover the jewels.

"I took the assignment when I discovered Bellarine was going to Martha's Vineyard and I'd have a chance to meet the legendary Dane Blaise."

Shana scoffed. It was part of the act, he assumed. And part real.

"Where are the rest of the jewels?" Shana leaned forward and stared at Angelique. Dane kept his smile to himself. Angelique remained unflustered.

"I have no idea where the jewels are. Bellarine didn't share that information with me before he aimed his gun and took a shot."

Cap said, "Lucky for you he was a lousy shot."

"Not so much luck—I was prepared. I evaded the shot."

"How did you end up on the beach?"

Angelique shrugged her bare shoulders. She was dressed for the party. She had hoped they would be released from their interrogation in time to arrive fashionably late. Dane knew better but didn't enlighten her. He wore a black dinner jacket with an open-collar white shirt and black jeans with boots. Angelique had liked the look, had laughed when she saw what he wore. A wave of sadness that she was so misguided went through him, but it was quickly followed by anger. At Jean Luc. At himself. At the unjust world at large. He calmed himself by turning his attention to Shana. Her green eyes sparked and she scowled, but her gorgeousness still gave him a jolt.

Now she waited patiently for Angelique to answer, staring the French woman down.

"I followed him. He got out of his car and I assumed he was going to where he hid the jewels. So I followed. When I stumbled in the sand—I made the mistake of wearing heels because I had no notion of sandy beaches or that Bellarine," she waved her hand, "would go there."

"Then what happened?" Cap said.

She turned to Dane and smiled at him.

"After I successfully defended my life, I found the jewels on him and realized they were the Gables' jewels." She eyed Dane again from under a flicker of her lashes. "I left them for you—to return to your client. I thought you could redeem yourself."

"That's another thing," Shana said. "How did he get into the room and rob the safe without being seen or detected?"

"He is skilled at being invisible, that Bellarine," she said. "He is also an expert in *électroniques*. For him it is child's play to.... fix the security program... to show what he wants. To hide what he wants."

"You mean *wanted*, don't you? Because he's dead now," Shana leaned forward again. "Conveniently—"

"Wait a minute," Dane decided it was time he jumped in to rescue the damsel in distress— as she expected. "It was self-defense. You know he shot at her. What more do you want?"

"Lots—" Shana glared at him. He reminded himself it was a role, but he felt the chill all the same.

Cap spread his hands and said, "Wait a minute—calm down everyone. We're conducting an investigation—that's all. We know it was self-defense, Ms. Dubois—ninety-nine percent sure. But we need all the facts. So you say you don't know where the rest of the jewels were stashed?"

"No. But it is my current assignment to find them, so you can be sure I will continue looking."

"She won't be leaving the island any time soon," Dane said.

Cap nodded. "Good. Because we may need to bring you in again, Ms. Dubois, for further questioning." He stood. Shana stood. Cap said, "While you're searching for the missing jewels, don't interfere with our investigation. It's also my job to find them."

"Then we can go?"

"After you write everything down." Shana slid a notepad and pen across the table toward her. Shana followed Cap to the door to leave and then turned before she walked out of the room and said, "For the record, Angelique, I think you're a lying murderer."

Dane stood and said, "You're way out of line—" But Shana slammed the door behind her. He'd felt silly saying the line but needed to do something. He'd be lying to himself if he didn't admit to being a little shaken by the fact that Shana's anger was real.

Angelique touched his arm, caressed it. He turned and found her smiling at him. Then she started writing.

Chapter 8

When Dane left the police station with Angelique, she took him to the stash of jewels, including the one key piece that had belonged to her family. It was as if she had a copy of the script he'd planned and was following along. They'd been hidden in the trunk of a rental car that she had parked at the airport. He hadn't even thought to check rental records. Stupid mistake. He drove her back to the Inn.

"I think you're going to need a new room."

"*Non.* They have already taken care of it."

He opened the door to see that she was right. The room was all put back together after the police search.

She invited him to leave the island with her the next morning. He said he wanted to go with her, but it would look too suspicious if they left together. He'd follow and meet her.

She said, "How do I know if you're telling the truth?"

He said, "You'll have to trust me."

She gave him a long look. And then nodded. It was too easy. She was too trusting. Guilt felt like sludge in his gut, accumulating and clogging his soul and heart. What was supposed to be an easy case, a lark, had taken on too much weight. It had been a test of his character of his resolve to be a real person, capable of leading a real life.

The weight of failure loomed like a raised sledgehammer about to drop.

*****

He spent the night with Angelique, but he kept her at arm's length and she remained quiet and pensive.

"I know you are troubled, my Dane. But I will let you wind your way to peace with your decisions. You must come to know that it's the right one in your own time." She smiled, caressing his face and kissing his cheeks.

He envied her serenity. Even knowing it would be short-lived. He hated and admired her at once. He'd do his job—or help Cap do his—get the jewels back for his client and the insurance company and move on. Jean Luc would forever be his enemy and Angelique Dubois would go to jail for a stint. When she got out, she would be another bitter enemy he'd need to watch for over his shoulder.

Was it all worth it? Why the hell was he doing this?

For Shana. He realized everything he did now was for Shana.

She did it for a sense of justice defined by the law. Same with Cap—their jobs were clear.

But Dane—his missions were not defined by laws and other people. He was called by his soul. And now it seemed, he was called by his bond—whatever the hell it was made of—with Shana. That was loyalty of a kind he hadn't known before.

In the past, his comrades had shared the mission and their belief in the mission and had each other's back for matters of life and death. He'd had that with Shana too.

But this—this was another thing. He had her back even though he didn't share her sense of mission and even though it was not a matter of life and death. He was following her lead blindly. The feeling and the concept were foreign to him and, no matter if it fit or not, he couldn't change it.

These were the things that kept him up through the longest night of his life. And he'd had some long ones in his time, including sitting up listening to gunfire and in jungles under monsoons. Tonight, underneath the soul searching, his mind kept spinning back to Shana's new distance and anger.

He resolved to find out what was behind it. And to fix it. Whatever it was. Knowing what that might mean. Knowing it might mean a real commitment. He put it aside. He didn't want to test his heart with the danger of going down that deadly road again, the one that lead to certain hell.

He knew he'd reached the point with Shana that meant hell was certain no matter which road he took.

In the morning, Dane needed to call Cap about the plan to leave the island. But Angelique expected Dane to join her in the shower.

If he didn't, he had to face the possibility of derailing the plan. Then he'd have to use force to take her in. Remembering the fact that she'd killed the last man who used force against her, he went along with the shower. It should have been no big deal. A minor tactical decision. But the prospect of showering with her made him feel like he'd end up more dirty than clean. He didn't want to be so weak that he responded as any man would. He was weak now. Weakened by the dread he felt surrounding his relationship with Shana. But he couldn't do it.

"You go ahead." He separated himself from her embrace. She was naked and warm and inviting. She scrutinized his eyes.

"It's the girl—Shana—isn't it?"

He said nothing. Angelique nodded with a knowing look.

"You were together a while—a year?"

"Yes." His voice was a growl. He did not want to discuss Shana with this woman. He stepped back. "I need air."

"Are you leaving me?" she asked matter-of-factly, hugging her arms around her body to keep herself warm. He saw the chill go through her. He felt sorry for her. He knew at least part of her problem was the influence of men in her life like Jean Luc. *But she was smart. Too smart to be falling for his act.*

"What's this all about, Angelique? You have a good career on the right side of the law. You could get your family's jewel back—you could probably buy it off the owner."

"This is what you ask? Now? I thought you understood. I thought you shared my excitement of challenges in life. I thought you were the same as me, as Jean Luc in understanding our own moral code of right and wrong—"

He grabbed her shoulders and shook her.

"Stop. I am my own man. Don't ever think you know everything there is to know about me."

She smiled then. He'd turned himself into the exact kind of enigma that she found enticing. A challenge. A prize.

"All right. You taunt me to take a risk. It is fair. I've taunted you with pretense. I will let you play your game. I will gamble that you measure me the same way I measure you." She turned and went into the shower alone.

Determination gripped him as he slipped the phone from his pocket. He knew with more certainty than he could remember having which road to hell he would take. It would be the one with Shana by his side. He wouldn't let her go.

While Angelique was in the shower alone, he called Cap to meet them at the airport with full force.

"She'll be wearing the family jewel around her neck. It means a lot to her."

"You're not having second thoughts about nailing her—I mean having her arrested, are you?"

Dane let the waves of self-loathing pass. He did this for Shana, but he'd done more than he needed to. He didn't know if he deserved Shana. Maybe he was right to keep him at arm's length, to rebuff his advances ninety percent of the time. But he knew he needed her more than ever.

"No second thoughts."

Chapter 9

Dane drove Angelique to the airport and parked in the private hangar area. He walked her to the waiting corporate jet in silence, with his hand lightly touching her lower back. He noted the absence of possessive sizzle.

She turned, leaning into him, and said, "It's the last time I'll ask. Are you sure you don't want to come with me now?"

"What's the matter—don't you trust me?"

She laughed softly—her usual musical laugh. He took that as a no.

"I'll join you later." He wrapped an arm around her for reassurance and put his hand on her chin. He lowered his mouth for a kiss and figured he deserved an Oscar and special compensation for this role, but he didn't want to lose her now.

"You have everything?" he asked.

She laughed again. "You mean the jewels? Of course." She pulled an old metal chain from inside her blouse—the kind he'd used for dog tags back in the day—but in this case it held a shiny platinum ring filled with a glinting icy diamond as big as a walnut. She waggled the chain, taunting. It was a bad habit of hers. She watched him watch the prisms of light. He drew the moment out wondering what the hell was taking so long.

In the next beat, the sound of heavy boots storming down the metal steps of the small jet boomed.

Cap shouted, "Stand where you are, hands in the air."

Angelique had no time to do more than spin around in surprise before no less than three state troopers accosted her with Cap barking orders. They had her trussed in cuffs in moments; her mouth open and eyes round in disbelief.

Cap stood at Dane's side and she was thrust around to stand in front of them.

She stared at Dane with accusation pinching her face, now closed and angry, creased in a frown. Cap reached a hand out and pulled the chain from its hiding place, checked the bauble and lifted the chain from around her neck and over her head. He didn't tear it or break it or yank at it roughly—that wasn't Cap's style and Dane admired that. If it were Dane, he'd have made sure he tore the chain from her along with a hank of her silky hair. Angelique was no less than a viper, unworthy of his concern. He hated her for tempting even the most base and normal flicker of desire in him. More likely he hated himself for that, but hating her was easier, more convenient.

In Dane's periphery he caught a glimpse of blond tresses billowing and heading their way across the blacktop from the nearby hangar.

He stepped back while he let Cap read Angelique her rights and seal the bauble into an evidence bag.

Walking slowly toward her, he tried reading Shana's face. It usually spoke to him. Or her heat, her energy, her essence spoke to him. Something. Right now she was closed up tight. He didn't bother resisting his compulsion to open himself up to her. She stopped four feet from him and he stopped. He let his face show how he felt. Apology, sorrow, self-loathing, and most of all his longing for her. He put that into his best smile and hoped he didn't look like a forlorn fourteen-year-old. She didn't change her expression or move, just stared him down with icy green cat eyes, looking wise and superior. Right now she was and he felt that like an icy sting of reprimand as if she'd lashed him with a whip.

In spite of that, and maybe because of it, because he was a sick one he supposed—something was wrong with him—he went to her, closing the gap entirely. He came to rest in front of her, wrapping his arms around her so that they touched from head to toe. If she hadn't been stiff, if not resisting, he would have tightened and squeezed, but he'd wait.

"I'm sorry, girlie." He whispered the words in her hair, breathing in the scent and taking in the softness. He hoped she'd heard the words. He didn't know if he would say them again—if he could say them again.

He took another deep breath. She stirred in his arms. He tightened them but she stiffened more. He hoped she hadn't heard him.

But he didn't let her go.

And she didn't push him away.

###

*Look for news about the full novel edition of **Beachcomber Heat** coming this summer and sign up for the newsletter (and receive all the latest on new books, contests, prizes and an exclusive FREE book: **Dane Blaise: Once Upon a Time**) at www.StephanieQueen.com.*

Stephanie Queen Books

Beachcomber Investigations Series:
The Beachcombers – Prequel Edition
Beachcomber Investigations – Book 1
Beachcomber Santa – Novella – Book 2
Beachcomber Valentine – Novella – Book 3
Beachcomber Baby – Book 4
Beachcomber Trouble – Book 5
Beachcomber Heat – Novella – Book 6

Scotland Yard Exchange Series:
Between a Rock and a Mad Woman – Prequel
The Throwbacks – Book 1
The Hot Shots – Book 2
The Romantics – Book 3
The Beachcombers – Book 4

Small Town Romance Series:
Small Town Glamour Girl Christmas
Small Town Glamour Girl Wedding: a novella
Small Town Hot Shot Bride

Other Stephanie Queen books:
Playing the Game

SEX, LIES
AND
APPLE PIES

Kathy Ivan

A televised baking competition brings them together. But deceit, intrigue and revenge are on this menu. Can their love survive?

This book is dedicated to the wonderful ladies of the Summer Heat box set, who invited me to join them in the adventure. It's been a blast working with you and getting to know you all.

It's also dedicated to my sister, Mary Sullivan, who's the driving force behind my writing and keeps me motivated. She lets me go on and on about story lines and plots and lends a hand when I'm stuck. Sister, you're the best!

CHAPTER ONE

It took a lot of finagling, arm twisting, and calling in of favors, but Slade Coleman was finally in paradise. Or more precisely, South Beach at the height of summer.

Florida. Sunny skies, white sandy beaches, and glorious bikini-clad women as far as the eye could see.

He'd put down the top on his rented convertible and drove along the beach. Felt the warm winds whip through his hair as he sped past the shimmering sands loaded with tourists.

Summertime in Miami was smoking. Hot nightclubs. Hot food. Hot beaches. And most importantly, hot women. He planned to immerse himself to the fullest in all of them, but first he had a job to do.

With practiced ease, he pulled the convertible up to the front entrance of the condo complex where he'd be staying for this gig, handed his keys to the uniformed valet, and gave the information for the unit he'd be staying in for the duration. Just another of the perks he'd enjoy while in this town overflowing with decadence were all the high end benefits that came along with his friend's place.

He looked around the sleek lines of the building's front entrance. The place looked more like a five star hotel than a condominium complex, but who was he to complain—he'd only be here a short time. And he didn't kid himself. Though his life had changed over the last five years, he still wasn't used to the excesses that wealth brought.

He was a simple country guy at heart, and always would be. While living like this from time to time when he was on the job was a nice perk, it wasn't the life he'd want long term. No, he needed lots of wide open space and fresh air. Maybe a couple of horses and a dog. That was more his style, though he'd need to be within driving distance of a big city if his dream of opening his own restaurant was to come to fruition.

His friend, a professional football player, had been more than happy to loan him his vacation condo along with all the amenities that came along with it, including twenty-four hour concierge service, valet parking, two pools, a high-end gym, and private beach access. What more could he ask?

Within minutes, he walked through the front door of the twenty-second floor condo, dropped his bag in the foyer, and headed straight to the wall of windows overlooking the Atlantic Ocean. Clear blue skies and glistening azure waters as far as the eye could see. Bright sunlight reflecting off the ocean was a wicked invitation to plunge beneath its watery depths. One he wished he could indulge in immediately.

Instead, with a flick of his hand, he slid open the patio door and strolled out onto the balcony, inhaling the salty tang of the ocean. Oh, yeah, this was exactly what he needed, a couple of weeks of rest and relaxation in paradise. It was a crying shame most of his time would be spent working.

But not all of it, he reminded himself. He planned to get in a little R and R while he got the job done. His last off-the-official books job had strained him to the brink, and he sorely needed a break. He stretched, feeling the stiffness in his muscles from sitting on a plane for several excruciatingly long hours.

Damn, he was tired. It was the kind of bone-weary, aching tiredness resulting from lack of sleep and a lack of faith in humanity. He was sick of dealing with people who cared so little about others and the toll their capricious whims caused.

He shook his head, cleared his thoughts. Walking back into the condo, he dropped onto the leather armchair and dug his cellphone from his pocket. With the slide of his finger across the screen, he dialed his longtime friend, Max Lamoreaux.

"I'm here." He leaned back against the pillowy depths of the chair, resting his head against the back cushion. "I've got a meeting with the TV show's producers in a little while, to get the rundown on exactly what I'm supposed to be doing."

"Any problems?" Max's voice sounded a bit distracted, and Slade heard another muffled voice in the background. His friend and sometimes boss was still at the office. Damn, he hated government work, and all the secretive B.S. that went along with it, but his buddy's private investigative business thrived on it lately.

Max had the whole mom, Uncle Sam, and apple pie mentality and it worked for him. Slade was more of a live-and-let-live kind of guy.

"No. The flight went smoothly. All the contract details have been ironed out by my agent and he assured me they were practically drooling at the chance for me to star in their show." He scrubbed a hand against his face, felt the five o'clock shadow roughening his cheek. "Tell me again why you need me to work on this piece of dreck?"

Max sighed. "I'm stuck here in New Orleans under subpoena to testify in the Trejo case and can't get down there. I need a set of eyes and ears around the television studio. They've got things locked down as tight as Fort Knox."

"Couldn't you have hired a tech to work behind the scenes? It would make more sense. I don't have a damned clue what you expect me to find."

"There's not a whole lot I can tell you at this point that you don't already know. The client hired us to look into threats she's been getting. It's your run-of-the-mill basic blackmail stuff. Pictures and demands for money to buy their silence."

"Why me? Anybody could handle this."

"Hang on." Max whispered to somebody, his voice muffled, and then he was back. "You're good at spotting things that don't smell right."

Slade rolled his eyes at his friend's comments. If he listened to Max, his friend would try to convince him he had some kind of ESP or psychic woo-woo going on. Though if anybody would know about all that woo-woo stuff, it would be Max. After all, he was married to a bona fide psychic. But him, Slade Coleman? Hell, no. He was just observant. And most people were idiots.

"Bro, I'm still trying to wrap my head around this. I mean, it's a *baking* show. What am I going to do, protect someone from flying cupcakes?"

His friend laughed. "I'm really hoping it's nothing but a disgruntled fan and we catch them right away. Until then, I'm following where the evidence leads. Besides, this might be good for you."

Slade pulled the phone away from his ear and stared at the screen, before putting it back to his ear.

"Don't you think I'm a little overqualified for this gig?"

Max snorted a laugh. "You're qualified for cooking, sure. You can outcook anybody in the country, but..."

"Baking? Pastries and cakes and cookies? Not really my speciality." Slade knew his limitations when it came to making sweets. He might be able to handle a boxed cake mix, but that would be stretching it. Cooking he understood. Cooking didn't have the same rules as baking. Cooking made sense because he got to add his own spin on taste and make it uniquely his.

"You don't fool me, bro. Your Michelin star says you're one of the best. Your previous boss stated in The New Yorker you had the best palate he'd ever taught. You've apprenticed under some of the biggest names in the industry."

Slade grimaced, uncomfortable with his buddy's praise. He loved his job—most of the time. Put him in the kitchen with a six burner gas range and a handful of ingredients and he could whip up a meal fit for the President. He just didn't like all the other stuff that went along with being a *celebrity chef.* Truth be told, he hated that part. Especially the nickname the paparazzi had given him. Seriously, who wanted to go around being known as *The Culinary Cowboy?*

"Again, that's cooking. Not baking. Two totally different skill sets."

"All kidding aside, man, do you think you can't judge a baking competition? Seriously?"

As much as he wanted to lie, two things kept Slade from arguing. One, he knew he *could* judge the blasted contest fairly. And, two, if he wanted to open his own restaurant, be his own boss and forget all this *Culinary Cowboy* nonsense, he needed the media exposure along with the hefty fee the show dangled in front of him. And thirdly, and probably the most important reason—Max asked for his help.

"I already said I'd do it. But why do I have the feeling you're hiding something from me? I hate walking into this blind."

The silence on the other end went on for so long Slade knew there was more to this job than what he'd been told.

"Spill it, Max, or the deal's off."

Max sighed, and Slade could hear the weariness underlying the sound. "Okay, but you're not gonna like it. I swear, I didn't make the connection when I read her name, but then I saw her picture—"

"Who?" Slade found himself leaning forward in the chair until he was perched on the edge, a tingling sense of anticipation crawling across his skin.

"Gwendolyn Cunningham." The words were rushed and half-muffled, enough Slade almost didn't understand them. *Almost.*

"Gwendolyn...do you mean Wendy?"

"She goes by Gwendolyn now. Gwendolyn Cunningham. Not sure what's up with the last name change—unless she got married or something."

Slade pinched the bridge of his nose, and squeezed his eyes tightly closed. "Damn, I haven't thought about her in a long time."

Liar.

"I thought you'd have run into her by now, since you're both in the same field. She's opened some fancy-pants bakery in New York and is making quite a name for herself."

"Hard to believe. That girl couldn't stand being in a kitchen for longer than five minutes. Now you're telling me she makes her living in one?"

"Apparently. I've sent you Intel on everybody associated with the show. Production staff, contestants, and the other judges. It should be in your e-mail now. That'll give you a chance to read up on their backgrounds, everything I've got."

"Well, it'll have to wait. I'm on my way to meet one of the producers. I'm actually heading out the door in about ten minutes to meet him at his hotel. Wish me luck."

"You've got it. Keep me posted. You know the drill, call me if you dig up anything, and I'll keep you up-to-date on everything I learn on my end. If I can get out of this court case early, I'll head down to Florida and help out. Say hello to Wendy for me."

"Hell, bro, she probably doesn't remember us, but I'll tell her. Call you later."

With a sigh, he stood and stretched, heard the audible crack and pop of his joint when he reached toward the ceiling. With a grimace, he picked up the black Stetson, part of his stock-in-trade, a well-known and identifiable part of his public persona, and headed out the door with a grin tugging his lips upward.

He couldn't wait to see Wendy's face when she saw him, and wondered if she'd thought about him at all.

Because he'd never forgotten her—or the way she'd tossed aside their future together and walked straight out of his life.

Who knows, maybe this job might turn out to be more fun than he'd anticipated.

CHAPTER TWO

"I think we've got a real hit on our hands." Wendy watched the television show's producer rub his hands together, a huge crocodile grin spreading across his lips. "The focus groups went nuts for the concept. Sweetheart, this project could launch you and your bakery into the stratosphere."

She made a little moue of distaste and, with a deliberate movement, lifted his hand off her knee with her thumb and index finger. She didn't want to touch the smarmy jackass, but if he didn't keep his hands to himself, she was going to knock him ass over teakettle before she walked away from this project for good.

Why can't these television people keep their hands to themselves?

"I'm sure my agent told you I already agreed to do the National Bake-Off Championship." Ugh, she hated the show's name, but figured it was better than some attempt at humor like Bake Your Butt Off or something equally lame.

She couldn't help wondering why the production company had pursued her so ferociously. Well, other than the fact the Wall Street Journal hailed her as the *Princess of Pastries* when she opened her high-end bakery-chic boutique eatery.

Baking had been very good to her and she was in negotiations to open a second and possibly a third store, one in Los Angeles and one in Dallas. Not bad for the girl who'd grown up on the wrong side of the tracks in a blink-and-you'll-miss-it town in rural Louisiana. A fact she kept well hidden. It had taken a lot of hard work losing the patois in her speech. She'd changed her name and created an entirely new persona when she'd walked away from her old life and set out on a course of discovering who she really was.

Appearance was everything. Nobody wanted to buy expensive, though high quality baked goods, from an unknown upstart. Forget about getting a business loan. The old saying was true—you needed money to make money. But with a little clever marketing, a legal name change, and strategic branding, Gwendolyn Cunningham was born.

"Well, there have been a few changes since the last time we talked with your agent, Ms. Cunningham."

She'd been so lost in thought she hadn't realized Jack started talking again. Not until he almost beaned her with one of his hands. The guy talked with flamboyant gestures, arms swinging, and had narrowly missed bopping her on the noggin a couple of times already.

Wendy didn't like last minute changes. No, she was all about organization and control. Her shop assistant claimed Wendy was more than a little OCD. Maybe she was, but being organized and prepared got things done. And she'd learned the hard way exactly what spontaneity got her—nothing but trouble.

When she'd first been approached to do the baking show, she'd considered it for about a minute and then politely declined. Still, they kept coming back, upping their ante until she'd agreed to be one of two judges on the fledgling program.

The publicity garnered from being on national television, especially if the show turned out to be as big a hit as predictions showed, would do wonders for her expanding bakeries. To say nothing of cementing her in the forefront of consumers' minds and pocketbooks when it came to gourmet baked goods.

Did her motives sound selfish? Yes, but in the long run she didn't have anybody she could depend on except herself—another lesson she'd learned the hard way.

"I thought everything was settled. Aunt Suzy and I are supposed to judge a group of eight home bakers over a series of six episodes. After the finale, the winner will be named the Bake-Off Champion. What's changed?"

The sinking feeling in the pit of her stomach intensified at the gleeful look in the producer's dark brown eyes. The scraggly mustache above his upper lip still held crumbs from the cookies he'd been munching throughout their interview, and she bit back the words that longed to spring forth, instead silently handing him a napkin from the tabletop.

"Oh, thanks." He scrubbed it across his mouth, getting most of the crumbs. "Here's the thing. When we showed the pilot episode to the focus group, they loved the concept of the Bake-Off, but the overall consensus was two judges wouldn't work. They suggested three."

She slid her palms along her thighs, smoothing down her skirt. "Why three?"

"The participants felt there needed to be another voice, another vote, in case of a tie."

Wendy closed her eyes and counted to ten. She needed this TV gig, and telling the executive producer he was full of crap probably wouldn't endear her or gain her any brownie points. Instead she pasted on a serene smile.

"I don't anticipate there being any problems with Aunt Suzy and me making an educated decision, though if you feel it's necessary, I certainly understand adding an additional judge. I can work with that."

He nodded vigorously, a huge grin spreading across his lips. "Good, good. I knew you'd understand. You're a professional. Aunt Suzy on the other hand, well, she didn't take the news nearly as well. She threw quite a conniption fit when I told her about bringing on another celebrity judge."

That didn't make any sense. Aunt Suzy was a nice, mild-mannered older woman. Wendy had met her a couple of times during the negotiations, and she'd seemed pleasant enough.

"Why in the world would she have a problem with it? It's not that big a change."

"Well, I think it was more she didn't like the identity of the third judge, if you ask me." Jack gave her a conspiratorial wink.

Uh oh. There was that sinking feeling in the pit of her stomach again. If Aunt Suzy from Aunt Suzy's Sweets was objecting to the choice for the third judge—

Jack droned on without pausing. "Now, you've got to understand, when we realized we had a shot at getting him, corporate was over the moon. I mean, he's the hottest thing to hit the foodie community in—I can't remember how long. Everybody wants a piece of him."

Ah, hell. Wendy squeezed her eyes shut.

Please don't say it. I promise I'll be good. I'll be the perfect judge. No more complaining about anything. Just don't say his name.

"It's a major coup. Think of the publicity we'll get the minute his name is attached to this project. We've got the perfect trifecta. We're shooting the show in an exotic locale, with the contestants baking up a storm in a South Florida paradise. We've got a coveted time slot on network television. Add Slade Coleman to the mix and we are golden."

Wendy swallowed past the lump in the back of her throat. She'd been getting excited about taking this job. *Right up until this moment.* Now everything had dissolved into a smoldering pile of ashes at her feet.

If Jack and the rest of the production team got their way, she'd be sharing television time with the last man on the planet she ever wanted to see again.

Slade Coleman was the seductive serpent in her paradise. She hadn't been strong enough to resist him before, and she wasn't sure if she had the strength to resist him now.

Reaching into the small handbag clutched in one trembling hand, she pulled out her cellphone. Maybe if she acted fast, her agent could get her out of this contract.

Her finger hovered over the call button, some sixth sense making her hesitate. A frisson of awareness tingled along her spine and she squeezed the phone hard enough her hand hurt.

"Hello, darlin'."

She knew that voice, recognized it on a gut deep level. Because she heard it in her dreams almost every night. She shook her head, not wanting to turn around and see the last person she ever wanted to run into again.

There was no question about it—she was doomed.

CHAPTER THREE

"Hello, Slade. Jack was just telling me you're joining the judging panel."

Lame, Wendy, really lame.

Slade's gaze met hers directly before his eyes slid downward, and it felt like a physical caress along her skin, the faint sensation akin to an invisible touch, and goosebumps spread along her forearms.

"It's been a while. You've definitely changed."

True. She'd made a conscious choice and changed everything about herself after she'd picked up and raced away from the tiny Louisiana town where she'd been born and raised, looking for a better life. She didn't regret a single choice she'd made since.

Well, that wasn't entirely true. She had one regret, and all six foot three inches of it was standing face-to-face in front of her right now.

Slade Coleman being part of her life had been a blessing and a curse. Slade and his twin brother, Shane, had been pretty much the only friends she'd had back then and she still felt a twinge of remorse at leaving without saying goodbye.

Hindsight was twenty-twenty, and while she might like to amend the way she'd left things with the brothers, there wasn't another damn thing she'd fix. She'd managed to land on her feet and have the kind of career she'd only dreamed of, and things were on the upswing more than ever.

"I've seen the press coverage about you recently. You've become quite the mover and shaker in the world of foodies. Congratulations."

A wash of color spread into his cheeks. "Don't believe everything you read. Some PR guru decided to stick me with that ridiculous moniker, and it's taken on a life of its own."

She grinned because she'd so rarely seen him uncomfortable in his own skin, but apparently his new nickname didn't sit well—though it fit. He was most definitely a cowboy at heart, even if he wasn't living deep in the heart of the Lone Star State.

"You don't like being *The Culinary Cowboy*?"

"Hell, no. Makes me sound like an uneducated buffoon. I'm damn proud of my cooking skills. It's hard for people to see past the cowboy hat and boots."

Her eyes slid along his denim-covered legs down to a well-worn pair of black Tony Llama's. "If the boot fits, cowboy."

His strongly muscled arms crossed over his chest, and he looked at her from beneath his Stetson. "You've done pretty well for yourself, sugar. Or should I call you The Princess of Pastries?"

"Please don't."

He chuckled. "Looks like we both got stuck with labels trying to define us. Though I have to admit, I'm curious." She waited, quirking her brows. "Back in Louisiana, you despised being in the kitchen for more than a minute. What changed your mind?"

She stared down at her hands, unsure what to say. It had been several years since they'd seen each other, and a whole lot of experiences, both good and bad, happened in between. For now, it was better to keep her mouth shut.

"It's a long story. But I've learned to love everything about baking. It's become my passion. I still can't cook worth a damn, though."

A clearing throat beside them reminded her they weren't alone.

"I've got a list here," Jack stated before handing them each a manila folder, "for tomorrow's shoot. You'll need to go over it tonight, and give me a call if you've got any questions."

She rifled through the pages, not really seeing them. With any luck, this meeting would be over soon and she'd look at them back at the hotel. She needed to put some distance between her and Slade. Otherwise, there was a distinct possibility she'd jump his bones here in the middle of Jack's room.

"No problem. If that's everything, I'm going to head back to the hotel."

"I think we've covered everything, Ms. Cunningham. I'll see you bright and early, and introduce you to the contestants."

Slade's hand on her elbow froze her in place. The touch of his hand on her bare skin shot a quiver of awareness straight through her. Damn, she'd forgotten how potent the simplest touch of his hand felt. How she'd get weak in the knees whenever he smiled her way.

"I'll walk out with you. Have a good evening, Jack."

His grip was solid. Unless she wanted to make a scene in front of the show's producer, she needed to smile and walk out the door. He sidetracked to snag her purse, and with measured steps led her to the hallway.

"I think it would be a good idea to talk."

"I disagree." She frowned. "I don't have anything to say that hasn't already been said." At his sarcastic chuckle, she stopped, digging her heels into the carpet.

"Sugar, we've got unfinished business. Now we can be pleasant and professional, or it can be down and dirty. How about some dinner? I'll cook."

His crooked grin was more than she could resist. Even after all the years apart, that slightly lopsided grin caused the butterflies in her stomach to dance.

"Slade, this isn't a good idea."

"On the contrary, it's a brilliant idea."

They walked through the glass double doors, and the heat rolling off the cement struck her like a physical blow. South Florida in the middle of summer might be a gorgeous place, but the humidity was a killer if you weren't prepared for the slap in the face it dealt you.

"Did you drive or take a cab?" His quietly voiced question brought her mind screeching back to the here and now. She was intimately aware of his hand still holding a firm grip on her arm.

"I…a cab."

"Perfect. I'll drive."

He started forward again, and she practically had to jog to keep up with his pace. Thank goodness she'd worn comfortable flat sandals for this meeting or he'd be hauling her into the emergency room for a broken ankle.

As he sped into the sunset glow, she wondered if taking this job might turn out to be the biggest mistake of her life.

She gazed toward the man seated beside her, and felt a quiver ripple deep in her core again.

Yep, it was going to be a long night.

CHAPTER FOUR

The elevator doors opened onto an elegant hallway, the thick carpet beneath her feet displaying a swirling pattern of blues and greens and beiges, a subtle understatement of elegance and wealth.

Slade's hand rested on the small of her back, the touch light and barely there, though she felt it like a hot brand against her skin.

Had she lost her mind? What demonic imp coerced her into agreeing to come back to his condo for dinner? The idea of catching up after so much time had passed, finding out about all of the people back home, had been a strong temptation. But the bigger temptation? Being in the same space with Slade, spending more time with him.

They stopped in front of a nondescript door, no different than any other along the corridor. He paused long enough to give her an encouraging smile and opened it, ushering her inside. Directly across the room, the enticing view whispered to her, and she could no more ignore its splendor than she could stop breathing. The majesty of the Atlantic Ocean sprawled before her in all its panoramic glory, vast and daunting. The sky had begun darkening, as dusk held silent sway, refusing to lose itself in the oblivion of night.

No buildings obstructed her gaze, and she watched as starlight began peppering the darkening sky, and she wrapped her arms around her middle, awed by the wonders of creation.

"It's gorgeous, isn't it? I think waking up to that view every morning might be enough to persuade me to move to Miami."

"Aren't you used to it? I mean, having a place like this…"

"This isn't mine." He chuckled. "A friend let me borrow it for a couple of weeks, while I'm here filming. It's a great condo, but not really my style."

She turned and glanced around at the lush furnishings, the dark brown leather sofa, all sleek lines of chrome and steel. It really wasn't his style. Or not the Slade she remembered. He'd been more down to earth, liking comfort and nothing frou-frou. She smiled, thinking about her own tiny apartment in Manhattan, and knew he'd hate the cramped quarters, and the girly décor. Good thing he'd never get the chance to see it.

"Would you like a drink?" He walked into the kitchen, flicking on the overhead lights. "We've got wine," he held up a couple of bottles, "either red or white. I know there's beer. Or I can make coffee."

"White wine, please." She moved further into the room, and perched on one of the bar stools lined up in front of the kitchen peninsula. Topped with dark gray quartz peppered with golden flecks, it gleamed and sparkled beneath the lights, and she ran her hand across its shining surface.

He poured two glasses and handed her one with a grin. "A bit different from the stuff we used to sneak out in my dad's shed."

Wendy chuckled at the memory. "Oh, I remember that stuff. One drink and Shane was down for the count. Does he still have a problem handling his liquor?"

"He's okay with a beer or two, but more than that and he's sleeping like a baby."

He spun, opened the refrigerator, and peered inside. The shelves were stocked with packages and bottles as well as assorted vegetables. He pulled out a white wrapped package and set it on the countertop. Reaching down, he pulled out a skillet and a cutting board. With efficient movements, he placed the skillet on the burner, and turned up the heat.

Fascinated, she watched his every movement. There was a contained sensual grace inherent in the man. When he reached up into an overhead cabinet, the muscles grew taut beneath his shirt, and she nearly sighed out loud. Lifting her glass, she took a sip, hoping she'd covered the awkward sound.

His movements were like a magician, and she found herself watching him in fascinated wonder. The speed and accuracy of the knife blade made quick work of the herbs and garlic. He moved so fast it seemed almost invisible, yet there was a restrained efficiency as he diced the sweet potatoes. He had amazing knife skills, far and above anything she'd be capable of—she'd have lost a finger or two if she tried.

Within minutes, tantalizing aromas filled the kitchen, making her mouth water. Sweet potatoes were roasting in the oven, coated with a layer of salt, cinnamon, nutmeg, paprika, and olive oil.

Thick pork chops went into the skillet, the sizzling hot pan searing the meat and creating a caramelized outer crust. In a separate sauce pan, he whipped up a mixture for the pork, what he called an apricot, pineapple, soy glaze. When he zested an orange into the sauce, the fresh citrus scent perfumed the air, mixed with the smell of the sizzling pork and her stomach rumbled.

"It'll be ready in just a few minutes." He grinned as he stirred the pan. "I figured something quick and easy would be the best thing for tonight."

"You call this quick and easy? My definition and yours are light years apart. To me, quick and easy is microwaving a frozen meal, leftovers, or take out."

He quirked a brow. "So you really can't cook?"

"I *bake*. There's a huge difference. Baking is more of a science. You follow a recipe, measure ingredients precisely, set the temperature, and you get an edible finished product. Cooking is more a pinch of this and a dash of that. Whenever I try, it usually results in something not even the rats in New York would fine palatable."

With an efficiency she secretly envied, he poured the apricot glaze mixture over the pork chops in the skillet and placed them in the oven alongside the roasting sweet potatoes.

He straightened to lean against a bank of cabinets, relaxed and confident. He looked like he was in his element—which apparently he was, since every culinary magazine she'd seen in the last six months stated he ruled in the kitchen. The gossip rags insinuated he ruled in the bedroom too.

"What got you into baking? Back in Louisiana, you couldn't stand being anywhere near a kitchen."

Wendy debated how much to tell him. Things had been rough the first year after she left. When she'd packed up her meager belongings at seventeen and fled Louisiana, she'd had big dreams. Dreams she'd never shared with anybody—not even Slade. Reality could be a real bitch though, and she'd soon learned what she thought she wanted didn't mesh with the reality of what life was really like. Fortunately, she'd met a wonderful woman who'd given her a home, and mentored her, teaching her that not all people were cruel monsters, and that reality was whatever you wanted to make it, good or bad.

"I met a wonderful woman who showed me everything I was missing." That was true. "She shared her recipes with me, ones passed down from her grandmother, to her mother, and then to her. Minnie didn't have any children of her own, so she started teaching me a little at a time."

"Minnie?" He sounded curious, but she didn't want him digging too deep. The pain of her loss was still fresh, and her heart squeezed tighter within her chest, remembering the dear woman who'd taught her about life and what true love really felt like.

"I met Minnie not long after I moved to New York." *Another truth*. "She helped me find my feet when I felt overwhelmed, a stranger in a strange place. At first, she tried to teach me how to cook, but that didn't work out very well."

What an understatement. On her very first attempt, Wendy had set fire to the stove in Minnie's walkup apartment. After that, Minnie only assigned her the non-cooking duties, like chopping vegetables, and peeling potatoes.

"Cooking will never be something I'm good at. I accept that. But there's something about baking. I can remember the formulas. The measurements. Baking makes a kind of sense cooking never does. It's not spontaneous. It's controlled and you know exactly what to expect when you're finished."

Slade watched her closely, his gaze never leaving her face while she spoke. She didn't feel uncomfortable, because she knew he was really interested in what she was saying. He wanted to know what happened after she'd left Louisiana.

There were things she'd never tell him, but talking about Minnie—she didn't mind sharing her love for the older African-American woman with him.

"Let me ask you the same thing. I don't remember you being into cooking. What changed?"

He pulled the skillet out of the oven, checking the pork chops and adding another layer of glaze, spooning it over the top. The aroma had her peering over the edge of the counter, trying to get a look at the contents of the pan causing her stomach to growl.

"After you left, things got a little rocky. I moved to New Orleans, and kinda got lost in the big city for a while." He stuck a fork into one of the cubes of sweet potato and pulled it out and angled the fork at her, with the golden tasty bite still attached.

"Here, try this."

She glanced between the proffered bite and him, saw the curve of his lips as if daring her to say no to the intimate exchange. Like she was going to turn down good food? She blew softly on the offered tidbit, before opening her mouth and letting him slide the forked bit of goodness inside.

Her eyes closed at the explosion of taste against her tongue. A myriad of flavors spun together in that one bite. Who would have thought something so tiny could pack such a wallop of flavor?

"It's delicious."

His smile grew at her words. "Good. Do you want to eat at the table, or would you be more comfortable here at the counter?"

"Here's fine."

All too soon he'd plated up a meal worthy of the nicest restaurant, with the perfectly browned and sauced pork and sweet potatoes and sauteed asparagus.

"It's almost too pretty to eat."

"Well, if you're not hungry…" he teased, reaching for her plate.

"Mine," she growled, hunching over her meal protectively. "Don't touch." She gave a playful wink before digging in to another bite of the sweet potatoes. Damn, she really needed to figure out how to cook these. He'd made it look so easy.

There was none of the nervousness she'd expected after being apart for so long. They'd fallen back into a comfortable repartee without too much difficulty. Slade and his twin brother, Shane, had been her best friends all through her teenage years.

They'd moved to her little town in Louisiana when she'd been a freshman in high school and they'd both been juniors. From a little town in West Texas, when their parents divorced, they'd moved with their mother back to her home state. Though they'd been two years older than her, the age difference didn't matter, and they'd become friends.

Until she'd decided to hightail it out of Louisiana as fast and as far as her frugally hoarded funds could take her.

"You're a million miles away. What's going on in that pretty little head of yours?"

When she looked up, Slade held his fork out with a piece of the apricot glazed pork on the end. Like a baby bird, she opened her mouth and he slid the tines inside, and she closed her lips over them, her gaze never leaving his.

She chewed slowly, wanting to savor every nuance. Obviously his reputation as one of America's foremost culinary experts was well-deserved, if this meal was any indication. Nobody else she knew could have made such simple ingredients tastes like five star cuisine.

"Mmm. So good."

He grinned and raised his napkin to her lips, carefully teasing away the drop of glaze that lingered. Her eyes met his, and she was caught in the maze of desire reflected back.

"Glad you like it. I like things quick and simple when I'm not at work."

Needing to break his sensual spell, she reached for her wine glass, taking a healthy drink. A smooth warmth filled her.

"If I cooked like this, I'd end up as big as a house." With a sigh, she pushed away her now empty plate. "Maybe I can return the favor, and bake something for you—though not tonight. I think you're going to have to roll me home."

"Trust me, sweetheart, there's not a damned thing wrong with the way you look." The heat in his gaze confirmed his words. She savored them, letting them sink deep. It felt good to know he still found her attractive. Because she most definitely loved the way he looked.

"Dinner was nice, but I've got to get some sleep. We've got a long day tomorrow." It was definitely a good idea to call it a night, before she did something really stupid.

Slade reached out and snagged her hand between his, running his thumb gently along the back of it in small movements and she drew in a deep breath. This was not a good idea. Yes, the sparks were still there between them. If anything, she wanted him now more than ever.

Wanted to feel his lips pressed against hers. Wanted to feel his naked skin as he sprawled above her and she ran her hands across his muscular chest. Wanted to feel him sink within her body—and see if reality could live up to her fantasies.

"I'd rather you stayed."

He was offering her a choice. Run like the scared rabbit she'd always been. Or stay and take a shot at something momentous.

It could never last—she knew better than to believe in happily ever after. But maybe she could take this short moment out of time in paradise and make it into something to remember. If she went into things with her eyes wide open, no expectations of forever—

Her mouth opened, ready to decline, to turn down a second shot at making love with Slade Coleman, her fantasy man. Yet the words that spilled forth weren't the ones she intended. Instead of following her head, for once her heart overrode her brain.

"I'll stay."

CHAPTER FIVE

Her arms twined around his neck as his mouth devoured hers. Devoured felt like the right word, because it was so much more than just a kiss. A kiss was a mere meeting of lips, but Slade was an undisputed master at making love to her mouth.

Her lips parted beneath his, allowing Slade complete and total access, while his hands pulled her closer against him. She felt the rock hard erection he sported rubbing against her belly. Her knees trembled with the knowledge he wanted her—almost as much as she wanted him.

"Damn, I've missed you, baby." The whispered words caused her insides to clench in response. How long had it been since anybody had called her baby with so much desire in their voice? Need swirled like an eddying river, coursing through her swift and sure flowing toward its ultimate destination.

Was she a fool for giving in to her needs, her wants? More than anything she longed to be lost in the vortex of desire. Not worry about anybody or anything except feeling.

With a sigh, she relaxed in his arms, her hand sliding into his hair. This was what she wanted. She was honest enough to admit she'd secretly hoped for this to happen when she'd heard Slade was going to be part of the show. To have one chance to relive her youthful infatuation with the young boy who'd become such a strong and forceful man. A chance to change fantasy into reality for one glorious night.

"Make love to me." Without waiting for a response, her lips melded with his and she kissed him as if there were no tomorrow, no yesterday, just this one moment out of time. If this was all she could ever have, she'd take it, hoard it and bring out the memories for those nights when life became overwhelming.

"Sweetheart, nothing would give me greater pleasure." Wendy suddenly felt weightless, as Slade's arms slid beneath her thighs and swept her up into his embrace and strode down the hall to the bedroom.

A single bedside lamp burned, bathing the room in a warm golden glow. His lips brushed against her ear as he whispered, "I want you." She shivered at the touch, his warm moist breath a visceral caress. A frisson of electricity shot through her when his hand eased upward from her waist to her breast, and cupped the mound gently before squeezing the distended nipple covered by only the filmy bra.

"Want you too," she murmured, arching into his touch. Her hands clutched at his shoulders as he gently lowered her to her feet, never releasing his hold on her. Leaning forward, she nuzzled against the nape of his neck, inhaling deeply the masculine scent clinging to his skin. Beneath the soap and aftershave was the familiar tang of the man she'd never forgotten, as achingly fresh and heady as she remembered from her dreams.

Her hands clutched at his shirt, feverishly working the buttons free. Taking a deep calming breath, she forced herself to slow. Fisting the material in her hands, she rested her forehead against his chest. She was tempted, oh so tempted, to rip it open, uncaring if it got destroyed in the process, anxious to get to the bared skin beneath.

"Darlin', we've got all night." His hands cupped her face, angling it for another soul-searing kiss. Damn, the man kissed better than anybody she'd ever known. A heady intoxication seemed to sink into her skin and seep into her pores with each brush of his lips against hers. Her mouth blossomed beneath his, opening like a flower to the sun, and he plundered deeper within, his hot mouth covering hers, as his tongue swept in, staking his claim.

Fingers dug into her ass and she arched up, moaning as sensation coiled deep in her belly. It had been so long since she'd felt this driving aching need. It built higher and she closed her eyes, moaning against his mouth, her hands still clenched in the fabric of his shirt.

Her body sang with arousal, and a fire of need spiraled deep in her core. His answering groan caused her to smile. At least she wasn't alone in this overwhelming coil of want.

She needed more.

Pulling back, she gasped a harsh breath, and stared into his blue eyes, wanting to drown in their sensual glow. With a muttered curse, his hand grabbed the back of her head, and her scalp tingled at the slight tug; felt the roughness of his fingers against her scalp.

Angling her head just right, his mouth brushed her throat, and his teeth scraped lightly against the exposed skin. Her entire body arched into him, grinding against his in ruthless abandon. Breaking the kiss, her hands cupped his head, tugging him down to her breast. Heat bathed her skin when his open mouth pressed against her areola. Teeth tugged at the nipple still covered by her blouse and bra. That wouldn't do—she wanted to feel him against her bared flesh.

Pushing against his chest to give her room, she frantically tugged at her clothing, anxious to feel him against her with nothing separating them. Slade mimicked her actions, pulling his shirt free and tossing it to the floor in a heap. Within seconds his pants followed until there was nothing covering that gorgeous masculine body except the warm glow of lamplight.

Her eyes raked him from head to toe, drinking in the corded muscle, the dips and valleys honed from years of hard work. Reaching out, her fingertips grazed his abdomen, followed the notches on his hips downward.

His hand grabbed hers before she could go further. "Don't." His voice was a deep growl, raspy with need. "If you touch me, I'll never last. I need to be inside you. And I want to make it good for you, baby."

His hands cupped the mounds of her breasts, his thumbs rubbing across the distended nubbins, and she felt a shock of electricity shoot straight to her core.

She sucked in a breath when his hand was replaced by his mouth, his tongue again lashing around the puckered, sensitized flesh and she bit back a moan. Arousal clawed at her, and she whimpered. Heat burned up her spine, and she arched forward, pressing her breast deeper between his lips. He tweaked the opposite nipple between his thumb and finger, and the dueling sensations had her legs trembling, her knees nearly unable to hold her upright.

With a gasp she pulled back and stared into his heated gaze. His eyes shone bright with passion, an electric blue darkened with emotion, and his breath sawed out in a harsh, jagged sound.

"Damn, woman, why is it always like this with you?"

She laughed. "Stop teasing and make love to me, Slade."

"As you wish, sugar." He tossed her onto the bed, the mattress sinking beneath her weight before he sprawled atop her. A warm familiar scent curled around her. Arousal, need, and…him.

Wendy blinked up at Slade, saw his eyes widen when his knee slid between her thighs and felt the dampness there. A grin creased his lips.

With a gentle touch, he brushed the hair from her face and placed a chaste kiss against her lips. His hand slid along her cheek and she turned into his palm, nuzzling against the rough skin.

His knee rubbed against the tender flesh between her legs, and she whimpered and writhed as fire began to engulf her, arousal and need coiling deep in her belly.

"I want you so much." The whispered words sounded abnormally loud in the silence of the room. She closed her eyes, and arched upward, wanting—needing the close contact of her skin against his. She didn't want to think about anything but how he made her feel.

"Sweetheart…" he broke off, shaking his head. "Be right back." He levered himself off her body and practically sprinted across the room to his suitcase, tossing things on the floor in his hasty search.

She bit her lip to keep from laughing, because she was pretty sure she knew exactly what he was looking for. And thank goodness somebody was thinking straight, because it had been a very long time since she'd needed to be concerned about that.

"Yes!" A huge grin creased his face, and he held up his foil-wrapped treasure. Tossing it onto the mattress by her head, he angled his body next to hers, a serious expression across his face.

"I know we kinda let things get out of hand for a minute, but if you want to change your mind, now's the time."

He was giving her an out. While she appreciated it, she had no intention of taking him up on his gallant gesture. What she did want was the man lying less than a foot away.

"Shut up and kiss me."

The slow smile across his lips made her teasing response worthwhile. He ripped the foil packet open and quickly sheathed himself, then rolled until he was sprawled atop her.

Lowering his head, he pressed his mouth to hers in a blinding kiss filled with need and want. When he lifted his head, breaking the kiss, his eyes met hers. Wendy had a momentary twinge of guilt, because she knew this interlude would be forgotten by Slade in the morning, while to her it meant something. Yet she couldn't give him the satisfaction of knowing she'd never forgotten him or that he was the only man who could make her feel this way.

"Stop overthinking things. I want you. You want me—unless you've changed your mind?" He voiced the question softly, and paused as if waiting for her response.

One word. She could stop everything now with one word. Hell, she didn't even have to say anything. A simple shake of her head and everything would cease. There wasn't a doubt in her mind Slade wouldn't force things. He'd never had to, not when he lit her up like the Fourth of July with a simple glance.

No matter what happened later, she would have this. She wouldn't let her insecurities ruin what would be another memory to add to the few she clung to like the greediest miser.

"I'm sure. Make love to me."

Without a word, his body pressed forward. Though it had been a long time, she was wet and ready for him. Sliding into her oh so slowly, he paused, allowing her to become accustomed to the sensation of him filling her, her body stretching to accommodate him.

She stared at his face poised above her, taking in the tightly clenched jaw. A muscle ticked in his cheek at the strain to remain still and give her time to adjust. At her nod, he moved forward another inch before pulling back and gliding forward again.

She felt her body stretching and opening to meet his thrust. Tears threatened to spill because it felt perfect. There was no pain, just a sense of fullness she'd missed. Her hands clung to his shoulders even as her legs rode along his hips, her heels locked around him.

She stopped thinking and let herself feel. If she wasn't careful, she'd fall for the big man from her past. But at least she'd feel something, anything beyond the aching numbness she'd endured for the last several years.

Ever since she'd left him behind.

"You feel so good, sweetheart." He whispered the words against the side of her throat, tickling the skin at her nape. She could feel the rumble of the deep timbre of his voice sliding along her, evoking an arousal she couldn't deny. The feel of his tongue along the tender flesh beneath her ear, his teeth nipping at the lobe all evoked sensations that centered directly in her core.

With each breath he plunged deeper. Making love with Slade was like waking after the longest sleep. The feel of his body atop hers did something to her. He was big—all over—in the best way.

He pressed her into the mattress, his hips spreading her legs apart, making a place for himself between her spread thighs. When his chest pressed lightly against hers, the fine hairs rasped against already sensitive nipples.

"Slade, I...please." Her voice came out in a keening wail.

His lips hovered over hers. "That's right, baby." She could feel him buried deep within her, his hips pumping. He pressed his thumb against her clit, circling the sensitive bundle of nerves, and the heat in her core built higher and higher.

Want and need coursed through her. Without thinking, her hands buried in his hair, tugging him down for a mind-numbing kiss. "Please," she whispered against his lips. She practically begged, as her body coiled tight, sensations flooding through her each time he moved.

She offered herself to him, giving him everything she had to give. His mouth fused to hers with a command unlike anything she'd ever felt. When he surged forward, she grasped his biceps, holding on tightly. A gasp escaped, but he'd made sure she was ready for him, and her body accommodated him easily.

He stilled, his entire body frozen and he rested his forehead against hers. "I wanted to make this last. You feel so good around me."

He pulled back and then surged forward again. His mouth captured the little cry she made when he shifted his thumb once again, rubbing at the top of her clit.

She felt so full. He seemed to take up every inch of space, and she held on tight to the feeling of connection, of one heart to another.

"Yes, darlin'. That's it. Hold on to me." He pulled out and stroked back again deeper, his movements measured and strong, grinding his pelvis against hers. His forehead was covered with beads of sweat, and she felt his control, saw the muscles in his forearms bulge under the act of holding his upper body off hers.

Stroking her hand down his back, she let her hands slide downward across sweat-slicked skin until they cupped his wonderfully round backside, squeezing.

She wanted him to lose control. Because she knew she was close—so close—and needed to take him with her when she flew into the sun. He arched up onto his arms and slammed into her, and she felt him grind down on her, stimulating her engorged pearl, stroking the deep place inside that made her fly.

She couldn't fight it—didn't want to because this was right. Perfect. Orgasm slammed across her body as wave after wave of unending pleasure swamped her. She held onto Slade, felt the moment his control broke as he plunged into her body over and over again.

His eyes closed and he threw his head back, and he shouted her name as he exploded in his own release. Though she'd just had the most amazing orgasm of her life, she felt sparks igniting again as her body quivered back to life from the tsunami of sensation and she spun out of control again.

He collapsed on top her, his face next to hers. The warmth of his body caused her to sigh, and she was swamped by the myriad of feelings playing out in her head.

She wasn't sure what she'd expected. Maybe for him to jump off the moment they finished, say he'd had a great time and rush her out the door. Instead, Slade cuddled her body against his, his head lying against her breast.

With the softest touch, she ran her fingertips through his hair, marveling at the silkiness. With a muffled grunt, he rolled over and off her still tingling body. He settled onto his side, and pulled her against him, and flung one leg across her thighs, spooning her willing body. Instead of feeling trapped, she snuggled against him, breathing in deeply and catching the scent of shared sex and the muscular fragrance that was all Slade.

"You okay?" His thumb brushed lightly against her bottom lip with the gentlest touch.

"Better than okay." She felt tears prickle her eyes and snuggled her head against his solid chest. She wasn't willing to let this feeling end—not yet. With a wiggle, she moved upward and placed her lips against his.

His mouth covered hers, gentle this time. "Stay with me." Staring up into his eyes, she knew he meant for the night, and a small part of her couldn't help wishing he meant for a lifetime.

With her tiny nod, he smiled before leaning over and kissing her again. She snuggled into his embrace, and prayed she wasn't making the biggest mistake of her life.

CHAPTER SIX

"There's been another blackmail note."

Max Lamoreaux's voice rang in Slade's ear. Though he was almost nine hundred miles away, his clipped tones bespoke his barely contained anger. Slade got it. Max took any threats to his clients personally, and he was still stuck in New Orleans, unable to be hands on and relying on somebody else for information.

"Son of a—when did it arrive? I've kept my eye on her as much as I could, and I didn't catch anything out of the ordinary. At least, not around the Bake-Off set."

Slade sipped on his second cup of coffee of the morning. It was strong and black, just the way he liked it. He needed the jolt of the extra strong brew, since he'd been up since the butt-crack of dawn. Ever since Wendy snuck out the door without a word. Without saying good-bye—again.

Just like before.

"She called this morning. Found the note under her hotel room door. It had to have been slipped there some time during the night. I've looked at the security cameras in the lobby and hallway, but they didn't catch anything."

Slade didn't have any problem reading between the lines. Max had somebody hack into the hotel's closed circuit TV system because there was no way in hell he'd gotten a court order that fast. Hey, sometimes you had to bend the rules. They were trying to identify anybody who might be the blackmailer, and thus far nobody stood out on their suspect list. *A very long suspect list.*

"What did this one say?"

"Same as all the rest, demands for money or they'd expose information to the national press on our client that would destroy her reputation and her career."

Slade rubbed the base of his skull, before rolling his neck, heard the pops and cracks. Damn, he was getting too old for this.

"Bro, you need to let me talk to her. Let her know I've got her back. Maybe she'll open up to me, and we can catch this son of a bitch and this will all be over."

Max sighed and he sounded as tired at Slade felt. "She's scared, and I'm stuck between a rock and a hard place. It's already stretching things that I revealed her identity to you, so you could keep your eyes peeled."

"Dude, I've gotta admit, there's more to Aunt Suzy than meets the eye. Have you met her?"

"Once, which was more than enough. If she wasn't a friend of a friend, I'd have turned down the case, if you want the truth."

Slade understood. The woman was like Doctor Jekyll and Mrs. Hyde. One minute she'd be the ice queen, berating and ordering her assistant around, and the next she was sweet Aunt Suzy, the kindly older lady who peddled her sweets and was the patron saint to babies and puppies.

"Can you send me a copy of the note?"

"It's already in your e-mail."

Slade set down the coffee cup and fired up his laptop, pulling up his e-mail and clicking on the attachment from Max. The note wasn't different from the previous two he'd read.

I'm getting tired of your stalling. I mean business. Don't mess with me, bitch. I know all your secrets—even the ones you thought so carefully buried. Unless you want those photos sent to every major paper and gossip rag in the country, I want my five million dollars. You have forty-eight hours.

The entire e-mail was printed in large block letters on the kind of plain white paper and ink sold in any office supply store. Nothing that would narrow down identifying it.

"I don't suppose she'll let me take it in for fingerprints?" Slade tossed out the idea, already knowing the answer.

"No more than she would the previous two." Max answered. "There's something else going on here, but I can't put my finger on it. This feels like it's about more than money. It's—"

"Personal." Slade thought the same thing. "I keep going back to the line *I know all your secrets—even the ones you thought so carefully buried.* I'm focused on the word secrets."

"Yeah, I felt that too. Aw, screw it. I'll call Suzan and tell her you're my eyes and ears there and to talk to you." Frustration laced Max's words and Slade knew it went against everything Max believed to not accede to the client's wishes, but it was more important to find and catch this person, because something about the tone of this letter was off, and he had a bad feeling in the pit of his stomach things were going to get a whole lot worse before they got better.

"I'll talk to her today. Maybe she'll open up and I can find out more about what the blackmailer really wants. By the way, it talks about photos. Has Aunt Suzy mentioned anything about those? That might point us in a better direction."

"Damned if I know. When I brought up the question of photos, she turned pale, but said she had no clue what they were talking about."

"That's bull. She wouldn't be willing to pay a blackmailer if she didn't know what they held over her head. She knows—and I'll get her to talk." If there was one thing everybody who'd ever met Slade knew, it was he didn't back down from a challenge and he didn't take no for an answer.

"Do what you've got to do, but we need to find this person. Theresa's got a bad feeling about this, and I trust her instincts." Theresa, Max's wife, was a psychic, the real deal, and Slade knew her well enough to know if she felt something was off, you damned well better take her seriously.

"I'm on it. I'll call you later with an update."

"Thanks. By the way, how's Wendy?" Slade heard the humor in Max's voice, knew he was grinning that *I've-got-you* grin he always wore when he was teasing Slade.

"Jackass."

There was a long pause before Max spoke. "Son of a gun! You slept with her, didn't you?" *How the hell did he know that?*

"I owe Theresa a hundred bucks. She woke me at five o'clock this morning and told me you'd had sex with Wendy."

Slade shook his head. "Tell Theresa to mind her own business."

Max laughed, long and loud. "Bro, that's like telling Theresa to stop breathing. When she cares about a person—and she cares about you—she's gonna meddle. It's part of why I love her."

"Well, let her know my love life is off limits. And give her a big hug for me. Talk to you later."

Ending the call, he stood and stretched, then glanced toward the bedroom. The one he'd shared with Wendy the night before. She was a mass of contradictions, and he meant to unravel every single one of them before their short time together ended.

But right now, he needed to get dressed and head over to the television studio. Scope things out before he talked to Aunt Suzy about honesty—and blackmail.

CHAPTER SEVEN

Wendy strolled across the parking lot and out onto the grassy area where the huge white tents had been set up for filming the National Bake-Off. The morning breezes stirred the palm fronds, the gentle whistling noise a reminder of her feeling like a fish out of water in this exotic locale. The whole tropical paradise theme was a great hook for the television viewers, and the producers were playing that angle to the hilt.

Her jaws were clenched so hard her teeth ached. They'd been that way from the moment she'd woken up in Slade's bed at the crack of dawn. Calling herself every kind of a fool, she'd silently dressed and crept out without waking him.

How had she let her traitorous body overrule her head? Sleeping with him was one gigantic mistake, one she didn't intend to make again. At best, they were professional colleagues and would have minimal contact during filming. At worse—oh, who was she trying to kid?

She'd gone willingly, even eagerly, to his bed, and if she was totally honest, she'd end up back there again if she had the chance. Because her heart refused to lie even if her head wouldn't admit the truth. She still loved him. She'd never stopped. Neither time nor distance changed how she felt.

The best thing, the safest thing, would be to walk away with her pride intact—except she couldn't leave the show in the lurch. It was too late to find another judge. No, she was stuck in close proximity with Slade for the next few weeks.

A fist of anguish tightened around her heart. Guilt stabbed at her, because the whole fiasco was her fault. She'd instigated their shared night of passion, and she fully took the blame, and she'd been the one to sneak away in the semi-darkness.

Closing her eyes, she took a deep cleansing breath. Somehow, she had to make it through filming the competition, and keep things easy-breezy.

Definitely no hanky-panky. No more nights filled with sweat-soaked bodies rolling around on silky sheets. No more intimate dinners filled with talk of remembered pasts. No more wanting what I can't have—a future with the man I want more than I want my next bakery opening.

And there lay the crux of the matter. If there was a snowball's chance in hell of making things work with Slade, she'd find herself sliding back into that frightened teenager who'd run away from Louisiana without a backward glance. Give up everything that made her feel worthwhile, if it meant she'd have Slade's love. But that wasn't a chance she was willing to take—the cost would be too high.

"Good morning, Gwendolyn. Ready to begin the first round of judging?" Aunt Suzy stood slightly to her right, a large to-go cup clenched in her white-knuckled fist. She was pristine from head to toe, though Wendy couldn't help noticing the tightness around Aunt Suzy's mouth that belied her cool and relaxed demeanor. And no amount of makeup could disguise the dark shadows beneath her eyes.

"Hi, Suzan. I'll be ready as soon as I get one of those." She pointed to the other woman's cup. "I need the extra caffeine this morning."

Suzan gave a nonchalant shrug and smiled. "Me too. Have you seen Slade?"

Wendy felt heat blossom in her cheeks and wondered if she looked as guilty as she felt. Surely the other woman couldn't tell they'd spent the night together? Suzan peered at her over the top of her coffee cup, and there was a decided twinkle in her eyes. *Great.* She might not know for certain, but she definitely suspected. This needed to be nipped in the bud now, before anybody else caught wind of it.

"No, I haven't seen him." Her voice was cool and aloof, or at least she hoped so. "Excuse me, but I need to ask Jack something." With a quick wave, she walked away, needing to put a little distance between her and her nosy co-judge. The knot in the pit of her stomach seemed to multiply in size at the thought of facing Slade this morning.

The murmur of voices just beyond her line of sight had her turning toward them, and she spotted Slade talking with one of the stage hands. He gestured toward a kitchen setup, and the crewman nodded enthusiastically before rushing away. When Slade looked up, his gaze met hers, his blue eyes flashing in the morning sunlight.

Okay, he doesn't look angry. Just play it cool, and pretend nothing's different. Right, you can do this.

Her hand moved in a jerky wave and she turned to the break table, loaded down with an assortment of coffee dispensers, tea pots on portable electric burners, and a vast variety of snacks. Filling one of the tall paper cups with coffee, she added a ton of creamer and sugar before putting on the lid. A good caffeine kick was definitely in order this morning, especially before she faced Slade one-on-one.

"Morning, darlin'."

Damn, I didn't even get my first sip.

"Good morning, Slade."

"I'd kinda planned on fixing you breakfast, but you disappeared." He reached past her and poured his own cup of coffee, ignored the lids and drank straight from the foam cup. "Anything wrong?"

"Of course not. I needed to get back to the hotel and shower and change before this morning's contest."

His intense gaze studied her over the rim of his cup, seemed to bore beneath the surface and she struggled to erect an invisible barrier between them. Standing this close, after their shared night of lovemaking, her body wanted nothing more than to find a deserted corner, shove him up against the wall and have her wicked way with him. Or maybe she didn't need a deserted corner, he looked so good in his button-down shirt and dark jeans she might just jump him right where he stood.

Snap out of it, damn it.

A smug smile was quickly hidden by his coffee cup, but not before she saw it. Her eyes narrowed, but she didn't utter a word, simply quirked her brow and took a sip from her own cup. She had no problem letting him make the first move and cutting him off at the knees, stopping any flirtation in its tracks. It kind of felt like closing the barn door after the horse got out, but she couldn't let herself be lured back into his arms. Or his bed. That would lead to disaster.

"Have you seen Suzan?"

"Yeah, I spoke to her a few minutes ago." Wendy pointed toward the side of the tent, where the woman stood, almost obscured by one of the large pillars. "She's over there."

He lifted his cup in salute. "Thanks." With that he walked away, leaving her wondering what the hell just happened. Other than his brief comment about making her breakfast, he hadn't mentioned anything else about their night together. Had it meant so little to him?

The coffee she swallowed sat like burning acid in the pit of her stomach. Even more so when she watched Slade lean in close to Suzan, whispering something in her ear. A look of surprise crossed her face before she gave a jerky nod and walked away, Slade following closely behind.

What the hell?

A burst of laughter distracted her, and when she glanced back, both Suzan and Slade were out of sight. Wendy drew in a deep breath. She couldn't afford to let what Slade did bother her. They'd had a fling, a one night stand, and now she had a job to do, and a contest to judge.

The contestants milled around the coffee tables, sipping their morning drinks and discussing the upcoming opening day's competition. There were eight contestants. All home bakers, they'd been selected from video entries from amongst thousands of applicants. She really was looking forward to seeing what they could produce, since she'd kind of started out the same way.

This was the part of the show she looked forward to—helping others get some much-deserved recognition of their talent and be rewarded for their diligence—and their skills.

"Okay, people, ten minutes. Contestants, follow me." Jack motioned for everyone to move to the outside of the huge white tent, and the area became a hive of activity, with voices shouting and people running around. A couple of cameramen worked their hand-held equipment, and one stationary camera was set in position to capture the majority of the actual baking area.

Still, she couldn't help wondering where Slade and Suzan had disappeared to. Suzan's assistant and general behind-the-scenes right hand, Becky Armstrong, stood beside one of the columns, almost blending into the background. The woman reminded Wendy of a little field mouse. Pale brown hair and brown eyes, she was nondescript and timid, yet inquisitive in a bashful, not-wanting-to-intrude kind of fashion. She barely uttered a word, and Suzan treated her like she was her own personal Cinderella. Yet Becky meekly followed along behind Aunt Suzy with a worshipful look on her face, like every scathing comment that dripped from Suzan's lips was rarest gold.

Yet, when Suzan left with Slade, Becky had remained behind. She couldn't help wondering if Suzan ordered her to give them some privacy.

Stop thinking like that. You don't own him or have any claim on him or his time. Or who he spends time with. It was a one night stand, not a lifetime commitment.

Jack brought all the contestants back under the tent and each took their place behind their individualized stations. One of the contestant's she'd met earlier, Mary Beth, gave her a tentative smile, and Wendy returned it, trying to ease the other woman's nerves.

"Three minutes people. Get to your places." Jack's voice rang through the tent, and she moved over to the small area set up for the judges. Earlier, she'd been shown the long counter-style table with three chairs behind it, covered with a solid peach-colored cloth and trimmed out with tropical flowers. Hibiscus, gardenias, and pale pink roses were attached to the corners and draped along the front.

She rubbed her hands along her upper arms as a chill slid across her skin. Once filming started, there was no turning back. No changing her mind. The publicity from this show could make or break her fledgling business.

"One minute." Jack glanced toward her and frowned, obviously noting his other two guest judges weren't in their appointed places.

Wendy huffed out a breath she hadn't realized she'd been holding when Slade strode over and stood beside her, Suzan hot on his heels. She pasted on a big smile, because the cameras were ready to start filming, even if she wasn't.

Butterflies rioted in her stomach in anticipation. She'd done interviews before, right after the Wall Street Journal proclaimed her the *Princess of Pastries*. But nothing prepared her for the thought of spending days in the spotlight, talking in front of a camera, and doling out fatalistic blows to other people's dreams, their once in a lifetime chance at fame and fortune.

"I'm going to be sick." The whispered words sounded loud in her ears. Slade's hand slid into hers, squeezing gently.

"You'll be fine. Just breathe, honey."

"Easy for you to say, you're a natural in front of the camera," Wendy shot back.

Jack raised a hand, and pointed to the show's host, a regular on several of the food channel's shows, and hugely popular with their key demographic. He counted down and pointed to the host, who began the on-camera introduction.

"Welcome to the very first National Bake-Off Championship. We've brought together some of the best home bakers from across the United States, and they'll be competing against their fellow bakers and the clock for some wickedly good prizes which include a full page spread in Easy Baking For Today magazine, their own baking webisode on our YouTube channel, and the grand prize of one hundred thousand dollars."

Jack pointed toward the judges, and the camera swung in their direction, and she pasted a smile on her face, swallowing down the bile which threatened to make an appearance. Wouldn't that be the icing on the cake—throwing up on national TV?

The host strolled over to join them. "Let's introduce you to our elite panel of judges. Owner of Aunt Suzy's Sweet Shops and one of the most recognized bakery owners in the country, the wonderfully talented Suzan McDonald." He gave a dramatic pause before continuing the introductions.

"Next we're lucky to have one of the hottest pastry chefs to hit the food scene in years. Her bakery has garnered a reputation for serving elegant and decadently delicious confections, earning her the nickname *The Princess of Pastries*, Ms. Gwendolyn Cunningham."

A smattering of applause from the contestants filled the awkward silence following the introduction, and Wendy gave a brief nod to the camera, trying to keep what she hoped was a pleasant smile plastered on her face.

"And last, but certainly not least, we're honored to have one of the biggest names in the culinary industry here to help judge our baking competition. Celebrity chef *extraordinaire*, Slade Coleman, *The Culinary Cowboy*."

The camera then panned away from them, while the host introduced the contestants, and she blew out a sigh. There were going to be days like this, and she'd darn well better get used to it. Especially since she needed the extra publicity to help bolster her expanding business, and get her new store open.

It was time to get this party started, and she smiled at Slade before tapping Suzan on the arm and nodding toward the contestants.

"Let's do this."

CHAPTER EIGHT

Wendy fumbled with the catch on her purse, cursing under her breath when the stupid thing refused to open. Why she had brought the useless piece of crap with her on this trip was a mystery, except it looked nice with her blue dress. Vanity in the name of fashion.

Finally working it open, she dug through the side pocket, unearthing her key card. Fortunately, shooting for the show had wrapped for the day and all she wanted was to slide into a hot bath and forget about Jack, with his incessant questions, the nosy production crew, and lounge neck deep in bubbles with a nice glass of wine.

The elevator doors whooshed opened, and she stepped through, automatically glancing to the right and the left before heading down the narrow hall toward her room. With her head lowered, she didn't notice the person standing in front of her door until she practically ran over them.

"Suzan!"

Her eyes were red-rimmed and it looked like she'd been crying. The paleness of her face worried Wendy too. So did the way the older woman kept glancing over her shoulder toward the bank of elevators, practically jumping out of her skin at every sound.

"What's wrong?" Wendy reached out, placing her hand on the woman's forearm. Whatever the cause, Aunt Suzy was terrified.

"Do you know where Slade is?"

She was looking for Slade?

Though she didn't want to jump to conclusions, she couldn't stop the clenching of her stomach at Aunt Suzy's words. For a split second she wondered if Slade was playing fast and loose with her feelings, seeing Suzan while he'd been sleeping with her.

"Not since I left the set. Have you tried calling him?"

Suzan frowned, wrinkles marring her forehead and she gave Wendy a bemused stare. "I don't have his number—why would I? You seemed close; I was hoping you'd have it." Suzan ran a shaky hand through her hair, which wasn't up in its usual chignon. Instead it tumbled around her shoulders, making her look younger. If she hadn't looked so ashen and shaky, Wendy probably wouldn't have recognized her as the same sweet older lady from her ads. "I mean...I thought you..."

She took a long look at the other woman's face, noting the fact her whole body trembled like a frostbite victim, and Wendy shoved the key card into the lock and opened her door.

"Come in and tell me what's wrong."

She watched Suzan stiffen her spine and walk through the open doorway. Wendy's instincts kicked into high gear. And she'd learned to trust her instincts. They rarely let her down.

She wasn't a sucker for every sob story she heard, but watching Suzan, there was something that refused to let go, some indefinable urge to gather her close and offer comfort. She couldn't turn her back on the woman. Looking at her now, without all the hustle and bustle of the television show and the public persona Suzan assumed for the camera, she appeared younger than her years. And scared half to death.

Gone was the floral print dress, the frilly apron and the carefully coifed hair, part of her unique trademark. The woman standing in front of her appeared out of breath, and visibly shaken to her core.

"Let me see if I can get hold of Slade." She dug out her cellphone, ready to dial when Suzan's hand covered hers.

"No, wait. I'm sorry. This was a mistake. I shouldn't have come here. You don't need to be involved in my mess. I just panicked when I got to my room and—"

"Suzan, something has you terrified. Please—it's obvious you need somebody to talk to. How about me?"

Suzan's whole body seemed to deflate and she lowered herself onto the corner of the bed. Rubbing a hand across her eyes, heedless of the carefully applied makeup, she drew in a deep shuddering breath.

"My life is a disaster."

Wendy tossed her purse on the dresser and rushed to sit beside Suzan. She reached out and squeezed her hand, noting the other woman's fingers were ice cold.

"Problems don't seem nearly so bad when you share them." Suzan gave a strangled laugh, and Wendy smiled. "See, you're looking better already. Talk to me."

"It's this whole television thing. I thought it was a great idea and so did everybody with my company. Did you know I've been offered the chance to host a show on The Cooking Channel?"

"That's wonderful! I'm sure you'll do great."

Suzan shook her head. "It's never going to happen. Not after people find out what I did."

Something about the way she said the words had the tiny hairs on the back of Wendy's neck standing straight up. *What could she have done that was so terrible?*

"There's nothing so bad that it can't be fixed, Suzan."

The other woman jumped up and paced several steps away. "You don't understand. When the news gets out, I'll be ruined. My career. My friendships. Everything I've spent the last half of my life building—it'll all be gone."

Whoa. This sounded way bigger than she could deal with—but she had to try. She measured her words carefully, because Suzan obviously needed somebody she could confide in.

"When what comes out?"

The look in the other woman's eyes nearly broke Wendy's heart. Anguish and despair shone plainly in her brown eyes. Whatever her secret was went soul deep, because it was tearing her apart from the inside.

"My whole life is based on a lie. Aunt Suzy is the sweet little lady next door. The Sunday School teacher and president of the garden club kind of woman who never set a foot wrong in her entire life. Once people find out about the real me, Aunt Suzy's Sweet Shops will be ruined."

Wendy's brain immediately went on high alert. What could be momentous enough to make Suzan think her career would be destroyed? This wasn't the normal panic you'd see with low ratings or a bad business decision. No, she was scared, wringing her hands and pacing back and forth, a wild glint in her eyes.

She spun around, staring at Wendy before wrapping her arms around her body. "Maybe you'd better call Slade. If I'm going to spill my guts, I only want to tell it one time."

"Okay." She moved to the dresser and picked up her phone, quickly dialing Slade's number. Thank goodness, he'd given it to her the night she'd spent at his condo, or she wouldn't have any way to contact him. Thinking back on that night, heat flooded her cheeks.

"Hey, darlin'. What's up?" His deep masculine voice immediately soothed her, despite Suzan's frenetic pacing beside the queen-sized bed. If she kept that up, she'd wear a rut in the carpet.

"Slade, I'm in my hotel room with Suzan. Can you come? She wants to talk to both of us."

"Dammit. I'll be right there." The line went silent before she could say another word. It rang again almost immediately. "What the hell is your room number?"

She laughed despite the tension filling the space. "Seven eighteen. We'll be waiting."

"I'm on my way. Ten minutes, babe."

She pressed the button to end the call.

Suzan stopped pacing, her gaze looking past Wendy, unfocused. She was still paler than Wendy liked, but at least most of the trembling had stopped.

"Slade will be here in ten minutes. Can I get you anything?"

The laugh she gave was ugly and bitter. "Don't suppose you've got any whiskey?"

Seriously?

"No, but I can call down and get a bottle sent up."

Suzan gave a brisk shake of her head. "No, I probably...oh, what the hell. We'll probably need a stiff drink anyway."

Wendy made the call to room service, who assured her they'd be up momentarily with her order. Goosebumps rose along her skin and she noted the distinct chill in the room. Housekeeping must have cranked up the air conditioner when they'd cleaned, because she'd set the temperature to seventy-four earlier that morning before leaving for the shoot.

"I can't believe this is happening. So much time has passed, I thought..."

Her words trailed off at the knock on the door. Walking over, Wendy quickly swung it open, and signed the room service slip, snatching the bottle from the server's hand.

"Thanks."

Setting it down on the dresser, she grabbed two glasses out of the bathroom and poured a small amount of the amber liquid in each. Handing one to Suzan, she watched the other woman toss the drink back without blinking and hold the glass out for another. Wendy poured a smaller amount into the glass before capping the bottle.

"Slade should be here any minute, and we'll figure out what to do."

She watched a shudder pass through the other woman's body before she collapsed onto the end of the bed, her head in her hand. Easing forward, she plucked the empty glass from Suzan's fingers and put it beside the whiskey bottle, unsure what to do next.

Fortunately, a knock on the door saved her from the uncomfortable silence. When it swung open, Slade stalked through, going directly to Suzan's side. He spared Wendy a glance before sitting on the edge of the bed beside Suzan and taking her hand in his.

"Wanna tell me what happened?"

Suzan inhaled a deep breath and closed her eyes for a second before straightening, squaring her shoulders as if readying for battle. Wendy watched her closely, realizing the woman was mentally girding herself. Suzan's back stiffened until it looked like she could balance her whiskey glass on the top of her head without spilling a drop.

"I got another note."

Note? What kind of note?

"Same as the others?"

Wait, Slade knew about Suzan getting notes—plural—as in more than one?

The other woman shook her head. The little bit of color that had washed into her cheeks with the whiskey drained away, leaving her ashen once again. She reached into the pocket of her rumpled jacket and pulled out a hunk of wadded up paper.

"Here." She shoved it at him.

Slade smoothed out the wrinkled page and started reading. The corners of his mouth tightened with each word, and his eyes grew cold. Whatever was in the letter pissed him off, and made Wendy more curious than ever to know what was going on.

"Slade?"

"Gimme a minute, babe." He started to hand the letter back to Suzan, but Wendy grabbed it out of his hand. He frowned but didn't try to get it back. Not that he could. No way was he keeping her out of this. Suzan came to *her* for help. Okay, maybe she'd come looking for Slade's help, but she was in the middle of this now, and wasn't going to let his misplaced sense of machismo keep her out of the loop.

The breath caught in her throat at the virulent hatred contained in the words she'd read. Her eyes scanned the page a second time, trying to take it all in.

Bitch, I'm tired of waiting. Do you think I'm joking? The secrets from your past weren't hidden well enough. All it will take is sending those photos to the press and sweet Aunt Suzy's whole business empire goes down the drain. You won't be good for anything except fodder for the tabloids.

I'm not bluffing. I WANT MY MONEY! YOU OWE ME!

Don't think hiring that private dick is gonna help you either. Nobody and nothing will stop me from destroying you—so you'd better pay up.

Wendy handed the letter back to Slade, the unasked question rising between them like fog in the San Francisco Bay. He slowly shook his head and mouthed the word "later."

"Did you call Max?" Slade addressed the question in a soft voice to Suzan. She didn't seem surprised at the mention of Max's name.

Wendy straightened though when she heard it. He'd mentioned Max and Remy when they'd talked the night before, filling her in about Remy becoming a police detective and Max opening a private investigator business after he'd left the force. Ah, that explained the wisecrack about the private dick in the letter.

Suzan's hands smoothed the paper over and over, flattening the creases before folding it into a small square.

"No," Suzan whispered. "When I saw this," she waved the square of paper in front of her face, "I panicked and came looking for you. When we talked this morning, I didn't get your number, and..."

"You thought Wendy would have it."

Suzan's eyes widened at Slade's use of her nickname. Guess the cat was out of the bag anyway.

"Wendy? I thought your name was Gwendolyn."

She sighed. "My legal name is Gwendolyn. This big dummy," she jerked a thumb in Slade's direction, "has always called me Wendy."

"I knew it! You knew each other before you came down here for the show, didn't you? There was something between you. I couldn't put my finger on it, but..."

"Wendy and I go way back, though we haven't seen each other in a while. But we need to get back to this." His hand touched the note. "When did you get it?"

Suzan closed her eyes, and Wendy knew she was going through the steps of what led up to her finding the blackmail letter. It didn't take a rocket scientist to figure out that's what the letter meant. Threats and demands for money usually only meant one thing.

"We left the set. I took a cab back here and changed for dinner. There wasn't anything in my room when I got here. I went downstairs to the restaurant, had a bite and came back up. When I opened the door, it was sitting on the floor."

"Do you think somebody shoved it under the door?" Wendy asked, playing out the scene in her mind.

"That's the only thing I could figure. I looked around but didn't see anybody. Whoever did it was long gone."

Slade stood and pulled out his phone and sent a quick text. Within seconds it beeped in response. He scanned the answer and frowned before typing back a quick message and putting away his phone.

"We're going to check a few things out, and Max will get back to me soon. In the meantime, I think we should move you."

"Why? Whoever this is knows where I live. They've obviously followed me to Florida. Changing hotels won't keep them from carrying out their plans. Chances are good it will just make them mad, and they won't wait for the money." Suzan stared down at her hands, still tightly gripping the letter. "Money I don't have."

"I don't want you staying alone. The threats are escalating, and time is running out." Slade ran a hand through his dark hair, before crossing his arms across his chest.

"She can stay with me." The words popped out of Wendy's mouth before she could stop them.

"What?" Both Slade and Suzan asked at the same time.

"Look, it makes perfect sense. It's a big room. There are two queen beds here. And maybe whoever this is won't mess with her if she's staying with somebody else. Or at least it will make them think twice before they act."

"Gwendolyn..."

"Call me Wendy." She smirked at Slade before turning back to Suzan. "It'll cut down on the confusion."

Suzan gave a tentative smile. "Wendy, you don't have to do this. You barely know me. I can't ask you to put yourself in the middle of my problems."

She stepped forward and wrapped her hands around Suzan's upper arms in a firm grip. "You didn't ask me, I'm volunteering. We've all made mistakes in the past." She couldn't stop herself from glancing at Slade, before she continued. "Nobody has the right to extort money from you because of it. Max Lamoreaux is a good man and he'll figure out who's behind this. Plus, if he dragged this big guy into the mix," she jerked her head toward Slade, "you're doubly protected. They won't let you down."

Suzan slumped back onto the edge of the bed. "I don't know what to say. Neither of you know me, yet you're willing to turn your lives upside down to help me. Why?"

Slade moved to kneel in front of her. "Suzan, nobody has the right to threaten you. Max asked me to keep an eye on things and keep him posted until he can get here."

"*We'll* keep an eye on you." Wendy added moving to stand behind Slade, her hand resting on his shoulder. "We've got your back."

Tears spilled down Suzan's cheeks, before she looked at them. "Thank you."

Slade stood and extended his hand to the older woman. "Okay, let's go grab your stuff and get you settled here with Wendy."

They headed for the door and Wendy placed a hand tentatively on Slade's forearm. He stopped walking but refused to look her way. "I'll explain everything, but let's get this done first. Then we'll talk."

The gentle snick of the door closing left her standing there with a ton of questions, and not a single answer. But the big guy better realize, he had a lot of explaining to do, and she wasn't going to let things rest until she got answers.

CHAPTER NINE
Two days later

Holding the unlit flashlight in her left hand, Wendy turned the doorknob and pushed the door open the smallest amount, praying it didn't squeak. Because that would be the icing on the cake, wouldn't it? Have the haunted house creaky door announce to the villains intrepid Nancy Drew was hot on their heels.

Fortunately, only silence greeted her and she swung the door open far enough to squeeze through. Outside the grounds were bathed in blackness, a small shaft of moonlight spearing across the damp grass. Already soaked with sweat from South Florida's infernal heat, she paused long enough to pull up the hood on her black sweatshirt and headed into the backstage area of the studio space. The actual baking part of the show was filmed outdoors, across the open parking lot separating the studio from the grassy area where the tents were set up. But tonight, she needed to be inside the actual studio.

She wasn't sure what she was looking for, but time was running out. Tomorrow was the final day of filming, and the grand champion would be crowned amidst a metric ton of publicity, including their family, friends, and as much of the public as they could safely squeeze into the park.

Tonight was her last chance to figure out who was sabotaging the show.

There were too many problems to chalk it up to coincidence. The first couple of contestants had been eliminated fairly—at least she thought so. She'd gotten suspicious when it came time for the third elimination.

Mary Beth mistaking salt for sugar could be overlooked as a careless error. Except Wendy remembered looking at the canisters on Mary Beth's station during their talk-to-the-contestant segment during filming, and they were clearly marked on the front with bold black letters on a white label. And the sizes of the canisters were distinctly different. The sugar was in a much bigger container than the salt. Any experienced baker would know the difference. And Mary Beth was an experienced baker. Wendy had figured her as a shoe-in for the finale.

Jerry's lavender and honey scones, though, had been a real shocker. Too much lavender added to a recipe and the end product ended up tasting like soap. She'd watched Jerry chop the lavender and add in what looked like the correct amount. She shuddered, remembering the taste of those scones. The lavender had been right at the edge of being too much. Coupled with the scorched bottoms from an overly hot oven, they'd had no choice but to eliminate him.

The temperature dial on the oven was set at the correct temperature, according to the electrical technician when Jerry had lodged a complaint, but with his signature item inedible, the judges had no choice but to eliminate him from the competition.

So they had two contestants expelled over technical errors which didn't make sense. One mistake she could buy. But at this level of competition, two was more than a coincidence.

The studio and the grounds were guarded by roaming security guards, keeping watch over the expensive state-of-the-art equipment. They did a walkthrough every fifteen minutes, alternating between the studio and the outside tent areas with all the baking paraphernalia.

The grassy expanse was completely fenced in, keeping out unwanted and unauthorized people. As long as she kept her eyes open and listened for the guards, she figured she had enough time to take a quick look around.

The beam of the flashlight swept across the backs of the refrigerators lining the outer rim of the backstage area. All the baking supplies resided in a walk-in pantry, their large quantities kept fresher indoors. The refrigerators contained all the dairy products needed throughout the competition.

They were down to the final three contestants. She knew the outside tent area was switched around every day at the end of the competition, the eliminated baker's station being dismantled and removed to make more room in the oversized outdoor tents. At this point, only three baking stations remained. Gleaming cooktops and stainless steel, state-of-the-art convection ovens provided by the show's sponsors still held pride of place under the huge white canopy.

Her eyes swept across the indoor area, or as much of it she could see by flashlight, but she couldn't spot tampering of any kind. She huffed out an exasperated breath. *What did you expect, Sherlock? The guilty party hiding backstage, waiting to be caught? Maybe throw in an evil laugh to complete the scenario?*

"You're an idiot," she murmured as she spun around, and ran smack into a wall of solid muscle.

"I have to agree, sweetheart. You are an idiot."

Wendy slapped her hand against Slade's chest. "Damn it, you scared me half to death, sneaking up on me like that."

"You're lucky it was me. Are you out of your mind? You could have gotten yourself killed."

The gleam from the flashlight lit his face, and she noted his clenched jaw. Oops, the big guy was pissed. Too bad. Nobody else seemed to want to listen when she said something fishy was going on. Well, besides Suzan's blackmail stuff.

If she couldn't figure out not only who was knocking the others out of the contest, but why, the wrong person could be crowned the winner. The problem was she couldn't figure out a plausible motive. It was a baking show, for goodness sake, not a breach in national security.

"You didn't believe me, so I figured I'd look around. I'm not hurting anybody."

His grip tightened on her upper arms and he shook her, not enough to hurt, but it definitely got her attention riveted on him.

"Damn it, you're sticking your nose into something that isn't any of your business, darlin'. Stirring up a hornet's nest of trouble with you smack dab in the middle."

Fear clenched deep in her gut. Did he know more about what was going on than he'd let on? She jerked her arms free and took a hasty step back, her hip bumping against one of the refrigerators. The hand holding the flashlight clamped tight around its base.

"Great. Now you don't trust me. Wendy, we need to get out of here. Right this minute. The guards will be back any second and they can't find us here."

"Why?"

The sound of approaching footsteps echoed in the silence. Furtively she glanced around, wondering if there was a place they could hide. Because he was right, they couldn't afford to get caught here without a good excuse. While they could probably talk their way around the security guard since they were on the show, chances were good they'd be reported to the producers and all kinds of uncomfortable questions might arise.

"Fine, let's go." Her voice puffed out in a husky whisper.

Slade raised a finger to his lips and pointed to his right, and then motioned for her to follow. Great, now she was taking orders from him. She huffed out a sigh, but followed along in his wake, shining the flashlight on the ground.

"Turn that off." His whispered words were barely audible, but she clicked the light off, plunging them into darkness. There was the slightest illumination of the long hall from an overhead skylight, with just enough light to keep her from tripping over her own two feet.

He turned and his forearm slid across her breasts as he pushed her gently against the wall, her back resting against the drywall. She sucked in a breath, feeling the strength in his forearm where it rested against her. Her breasts pebbled beneath her bra.

Idiot. This isn't exactly the time or the place to let his touch affect you like this. Start thinking with your brain, not your traitorous body.

He stood rigid as a statue, staring into her eyes while listening intently.

"Okay, let's go." His voice sounded calm and assured, as though his touching her had no effect. Too bad she didn't feel the same. Every single cell of her body clamored with need. Damn it, how could just a simple touch make her want to strip him bare and smother him in chocolate sauce? Lick it up slowly, inch by incredible, delicious inch.

"Fine." Arguing wouldn't have done any good. Knowing Slade, he'd have slung her over his shoulder caveman style and hauled her out if she'd protested. She'd let him think he'd won and then—

"Don't even think about it. You are not coming back here tonight. I'm taking you back to your room and you're staying put. Got it?"

The more he talked, the more she became convinced he knew more about what was going on than he'd said. Within minutes, he had her stowed in the passenger seat of his sports car, strapped in tight, and speeding away from the studio.

"Are you completely insane?" His words echoed, loud in the car's interior, and his hands were white-knuckled on the wheel.

"There is something going on."

He exhaled a heavy sigh. "Yeah, there is and I can't tell you about it."

"I knew it!" She swiveled in the seat as much as her seatbelt would allow. "Somebody's sabotaging the contestants, right?"

He shook his head. "Not exactly—well, yes, but...

"We can't let whoever is doing it get away with cheating. It's unethical and totally unfair to the people they've gotten kicked off the show."

"Sweetheart, people being booted off the show is low priority, trust me."

She narrowed her eyes at Slade. The muscle in his jaw looked carved out of solid rock. Whatever was going on, it was big.

"Is the cheating behind the scenes related to what's going on with Aunt Suzy?"

"Damn, I always said you were smart. Yeah, but I can't say anything more until I've got proof."

She slapped her palm against the dash hard. Harder than she'd meant to when pain lanced up her arm.

"Damn it, Slade, I already know about the blackmail. Remember, Suzan came to me too."

"You weren't meant to be involved in this. It's better if..."

"Don't you dare! I'm not the little woman to be shunted into the background so you can keep me in the dark. What the hell is going on?"

Slade pulled into a fast food restaurant, swerving into the drive-through lane. "It's a long story. Sometimes, when the situation calls for it, I do the odd job or two for Max." If she hadn't been watching his face closely, she'd have missed the almost imperceptible wince as he told the half-truth. He'd always had that tell, even when they'd been younger. A little grimace movement when he wanted to tell the truth but instead circled all around it without ever outright lying.

"Slade, are you a cop?" She whispered, keeping an intense gaze on his face.

"Hell, no. I'm exactly what I said I was. What the public sees. I'm a professional chef. I managed to catch the eye of a few important people, who've helped move me into the national spotlight." He glanced her way before focusing back on the car in front of him in the drive-through. "Do you think I like being referred to as *The Culinary Cowboy*? It makes me sound like some sissified dweeb. No, this gig is on the up-and-up."

Again with the wince. Which meant he skirted the truth without outright lying.

"So why did Max Lamoreaux pull you into this case?" Her gaze wandering downward, over the sculpted muscles of his biceps and along his muscular forearms to strong hands. Callused hands he used to stroke intimately against her skin. To play along the nerve endings, spending sparks of desire spilling through her body.

She squirmed against the leather upholstery, her body responding to the proximity of his. *Stop it. Think about where you are, what's going on. Don't think about how good it felt to have him pressed up against you. How it felt when his mouth spread kisses along your exposed skin. How he sank deep inside, showering your body with pleasure.*

Heat blossomed in her cheeks. Focus, find out what Max has to do with a baking show in South Florida.

She watched the play of emotions across Slade's face, knew the exact moment he decided to answer her question honestly.

"You already know about what's going on with Suzan. She started getting threatening letters a couple of weeks ago. Apparently, she has a mutual friend who used Max's services before and concluded if anybody could find the blackmailer and maintain Suzan's anonymity, Max could."

Rolling down his window, he ordered two coffees and pulled forward, paying for them and handing both to her. He then drove around the side of the building and pulled into a parking spot.

"I want your word you won't mention anything I tell you—not to anybody—especially not to Suzan." The rough timbre of his voice caused the little hairs on her arms to stand at attention.

"I promise."

Slade paused, weighing his words carefully, and she bit her lip to keep from screaming at him to get on with it. The anticipation along with the adrenaline shooting through her system, not to mention the healthy chug of caffeine she'd just taken, had her practically bouncing in her seat.

"Yes, we think somebody is sabotaging the competition. Max and I have narrowed it down to a handful of people, but I can't waltz up and confront them. Not without proof."

"Who are they? The show hasn't even been on the air yet—why would somebody want to see it fail?"

Slade reached forward and ran his fingers along the side of her neck, and she felt a shiver of excitement course through her. Tingles of awareness peppered her skin and she leaned into his touch, her eyes half closed.

"Darlin', you need to take a step back. Whoever is behind this could be dangerous, and I'm not letting you get into the line of fire."

With each word he spoke, she felt her body stiffening, unable to believe he was trying to shut her out. She'd been keeping an eye on Suzan, down to sharing a room with her, and had even started to like the woman, once she got to know her better. Heck, she even put up with her assistant, Becky, traipsing through their room at all hours of the day and night, taking care of all the details that kept Suzan's Aunt Suzy Sweets thriving.

Suzan was a holy terror to those who worked for her. She kept them on a tight leash and demanded perfection. The woman was downright scary when things didn't go according to her plans.

"I can't."

"Sweetheart, Max and I agree, there's a connection between the sabotage and the blackmail, and we're working to pin it down, but there's a thread eluding us."

He raised his hand and pulled the clasp from her hair, allowing the waves to spill across her shoulders. Lifting a curl, he twisted it around a finger and tugged lightly, and a zing of desire zipped through her.

Dang, but she needed to keep his hands off her if she wanted to think straight. The second he touched her, all rational thought flew straight out the window.

"Explain it to me. Maybe I can see a pattern, look at it with a fresh set of eyes."

"I don't want you getting dragged into this any deeper. Things are spinning out of control, coming to a head, and I'm worried that it's going to get dangerous. I've advised Max to call in the police. Suzan's adamantly opposed. She's still afraid of whatever information the blackmailer has, and won't tell me squat."

"Slade, the competition ends tomorrow afternoon. If we can't figure out who the blackmailer is before then, everything's going to blow up in her face anyway."

He took a sip of coffee, his face contemplative and she knew she'd gotten her way when he thumped his head against the headrest, his eyes squeezed shut.

"Fine. Max is checking but he's narrowed it down to four people. They all seem to have gaps in their backgrounds or an ax to grind with Aunt Suzy."

"Who?" Her fingers tightened around the coffee cup. She couldn't take her eyes off Slade. With each breath, the black T-shirt molded against his skin, outlining the sculpted muscles beneath. Always a sucker for muscular forearms, she almost sighed aloud when the muscles flexed and shifted beneath his skin. He was grace and power personified, and she knew firsthand the man knew how to use his body to its best, having been on the receiving end of his sensual attention.

He ran through a list of names but only one made her sit up straighter. "Becky? Suzan's assistant? Slade, the woman is afraid of her own shadow. I can't see her sending threatening letters or trying to blackmail Suzan."

"I know it doesn't seem likely, but according to Max she's on the short list. The woman has access to most of Suzan's life, public and private. Who's to say she didn't do a little digging and come up with something big enough to take the chance at a big payout?" He shrugged before finishing his coffee and crumpling the cup in his hand. "People will risk a lot for millions of dollars."

"Yeah, you're right. Okay, I'll keep an eye on her."

His glare could have melted steel and he pointed straight at her. "No, you won't. You'll keep your pretty little nose out of things and do the job you were hired to do, which is a television show."

"But…"

"No. That's final, sweetheart. Your little stunt tonight could have gotten you into serious trouble. If anybody caught you and called the cops, not only would you be spending some time in the slammer, but your career would be toast."

Her shoulders slumped against the seat. "Crap. I didn't think of that. It's not just the Suzan thing, though. The thought of somebody sabotaging the contestants pisses me off."

He reached forward and ran his fingers through her hair, and she shuddered at the slight touch. "Me too. It'll get straightened out and the right person will be awarded the prize. In the meantime, let's focus on making sure nobody gets to Suzan. Okay?"

"Yeah."

He leaned across the console and brushed his lips against hers. "I can't tell you how scared I was that I wouldn't get there in time and somebody was going to catch you snooping. The thought of you behind bars, even for a second, tears me up. Promise me you won't do anything stupid."

Her hands pressed against his chest and she leaned against the passenger door. "It wasn't stupid. I was trying to help."

"Okay, maybe that's the wrong word. You're very smart—I know that. Keep your eyes and ears open, that's all I ask. If you see something…hear something…come get me. We'll handle it together. How's that?"

She smirked before letting out a chuckle. "Better. I guess I should get back to the room. I kinda snuck out without telling Suzan where I was going."

His hand cupped her cheek and she leaned into his touch, savoring the warmth and the slightly abrasive roughness of his fingertips. Work worn hands with a strength of purpose.

"I'd like nothing more than to take you back home with me and make love all night long. One taste definitely wasn't enough, babe."

She sucked in a breath. Did he mean he wanted more than the one night they'd shared? Her heartbeat sped up and the butterflies quivering in her stomach were doing somersaults.

"I—no, it wasn't nearly enough."

"Let's get through tomorrow. It's the finale. Once all the hoopla dies down, we can slip away and pick up where we left off."

Afraid to say anything, she simply nodded. At her acquiescence, he leaned forward once again and took her mouth in a demanding, all-consuming kiss. She opened her lips beneath his and allowed his tongue to surge forward, tangling with her own.

Damn, but the man knew how to kiss. Even in the confines of the front seats of a sports car, he made her melt into a puddle of shivering need.

He pulled back with an audible sigh. "Right. Back to the hotel."

He drove in silence, which was a good thing, because her mind was a jumbled mess. Could they have a chance beyond the duration of the show? Was this more than just a casual fling, another notch in his bedpost?

She'd find out tomorrow night, once the finale was finished. If she was honest, she found herself looking forward to after the show a whole lot more than the actual competition finale.

CHAPTER TEN

The noise from the crowd was deafening as the three finalists paraded their finished baked goods to the podium set up in the center of the grassy area outside the baking tent. Their families, friends, and even the press were assembled to find out which home baker would be named the national champion.

Wendy wiped her hands along the sides of her skirt, wishing everything was already over and done. One of the three finalists would be crowned, the filming finished, and she couldn't wait. Under normal circumstances, she'd probably have had a blast here at the final day, yet all she could think about was later—with Slade.

"Ladies and gentleman, for this final round of judging, we've invited the finalists' families and friends to witness exactly what's been happening every day, and give you a little *taste* of what they've gone through to get to this point."

Wendy stood shoulder to shoulder with Suzan and Slade, and looked at the pies prominently displayed on each elaborately decorated stand. The final baking challenge seemed innocuously simple yet was decidedly not as easy as it sounded.

Apple pie.

America's favorite dessert, it was challenging in its simplicity. A badly done crust could ruin a pie, no matter how good the filling. And the same was true for what went inside. Too much cinnamon and your pie was no good. Pick the wrong apples and your filling would become mushy or not have the right quality or consistency.

The host made a showy production of introducing the judges, noting this would be their last time judging together. Unless, of course, the show was picked up for a second season, which she wasn't sure would happen once the behind-the-scenes sabotaging came to light.

"Our first contestant in the finale is Mitzi Flynn from Sacramento, California. Ms. Flynn, tell us about your pie."

While the contestant explained about how she'd concocted her recipe, Wendy clutched at Slade's hand. "What are we going to do? We have to stop this before…"

"It's been handled, sweetheart. Trust me." Slade squeezed her hand before turning it loose. Suzan glanced around Slade's broad shoulders and gave her a reassuring smile.

"Our next finalist is Stephen Smith from Tyler, Texas. Mr. Smith, tell us about your pie." As the only male contestant left, Smith had made a good showing with a beautiful lattice-topped apple pie. He explained how he'd made it, but Wendy barely heard a word he said, instead watching the faces in the crowd. Was one of them the blackmailer?

"And finally, we have Anne Marie Burton from Cheyenne, Wyoming. Ms. Burton, tell us about your entry."

The final tasting was ready to take place and she was scared to death. With only three contestants left, who knew if there'd been another sabotage? The whole competition had been tainted, but the decision was out of her hands. She'd complained and nobody listened except Slade—who assured her everything would be okay. It better be, she was trusting him.

"Judges, now it's your turn to taste the entries and make the final decision on who will be the National Bake-Off Champion."

As one, they moved to the first station. Suzan picked up the knife and cut into the apple pie, placing a large slice onto a plain white plate. Each judge took their time, examining the presentation, with its golden brown crust. Mitzi had chosen to do a two crust pie, which meant the top and the bottom were both completely covered with crust, as opposed to a different style.

Reaching for a fork, Wendy scooped up a large portion of pie, as did the other judges. The taste burst across her tongue, sweet and spicy and absolutely delicious. The crust was perfection, with flaky golden layers, which proved the baker knew her way around a pie crust.

With a polite nod, they moved on to Stephen Smith's offering. He'd made the lattice top pie, which meant he'd created a woven pattern of strips of pie crust across the top, in an intricate design, leaving bits of filling bubbling through the openings.

They proceeded in the same manner, with Suzan cutting off a large slice and placing it on a white plate. Unfortunately, the filling of the pie had overflowed several areas of the latticework, detracting from the attractiveness of the entry. Wendy knew immediately it knocked him out of the running for the top prize.

Still she tasted his offering. The filling was superb, better than the first pie. It was a shame about the overflow, but it happened to the best baker. Sometimes no matter how good a baker, when it's not your day, it's just not your day.

She gave him a bittersweet smile, and he nodded, though from the look on his face, he knew it wasn't his best effort. That only left one more entry to be judged.

Anne Marie had chosen a Dutch apple pie, with a crumble topping. It was nice to see, Wendy decided, that each contestant had done a different interpretation of an apple pie.

Cutting into the third offering, Suzan placed the wedge onto another white plate, and they examined the crust. The outer edge color was excellent, a beautiful golden brown. The filling held its shape, the apples firm and evenly coated with brown sugar and spices.

Wendy dug her fork in, anxious for a taste. Raising it toward her mouth, she paused when she saw something in the pie pan. Her stomach dropped.

In the bottom of the pan were lumps of uncooked flour and butter mixture the crust raw in the very center. Being a baker herself, she knew it was probably caused by the glass baking dish the pie had cooked in. Baking with a glass dish was risky because it took longer to brown and cook the bottom crust and she always adjusted her time accordingly—when she was the baker. The other two contestants had elected to use metal pie pans.

Glancing at Slade, he quirked his brow, and she knew he'd spotted the flaw too. Suzan's lips turned down in a slight frown.

Really? In the finale of the biggest baking show to hit the airways, what were the chances of two of the final three having these kinds of mistakes?

"Our judges will now take a few moments to confer and decide on who will be the new National Bake-Off Champion. Stay tuned for our exciting finale."

"And cut." Jack walked over and put his hand on Slade's shoulder. "Okay people, who's our big winner here?"

"Nobody."

"What!" Jack's voice was loud enough the people closest to the podium stopped talking and stared. He immediately lowered his tone. "What do you mean nobody? You have to choose a winner. Award the grand prize. Look, man, the press is here. I'm not going to let you three ruin the best show to come along in years." He ran a hand through his hair, dislodging his headset.

"Only one contestant delivered something we'd consider edible. The other two had flaws."

"I tried to tell you…" Wendy stated, but Jack cut her off.

"I don't want to hear about your stupid sabotage theory again. Nobody is ruining their baking." He paced back and forth in front of them. "If only one is good, then that's your winner. I need a name—now."

"Mitzi Flynn." Slade growled out the name, his voice laced with disgust. "If you want to continue with this farce, then she's your winner."

"Excellent. Do your part and when the host asks, announce the winner. Do your job, Coleman."

Jack strode away, heading for the show's host, and Wendy shook her head. "This fiasco keeps getting better and better."

"It's not our fault." Pulling on her Aunt Suzy persona, Suzan patted Wendy's hand. "We've done our jobs, the best we can. The production company will have to sort out the problems after we wrap shooting. I'm sure they don't want to cause a scene in front of all these people and the press."

"Places people. Ten seconds." Jack's bellow could be heard over all the noise. He counted down to three and then pointed again toward their host.

"We're back and now we come to the best part of the show—announcing the grand prize winner of the National Bake-Off Championship. Judges, have you made a decision?"

After waiting for a dramatically long pause, Slade answered. "Yes, we have."

Suppressed excitement spread through the space, as the crowd edged closer, waiting to hear the final name called.

"The winner of the National Bake-Off Championship..." Wendy started.

"And the recipient of one-hundred thousand dollars is..." Suzan continued.

"Mitzi Flynn." Slade finished.

The applause and cheers from the crowd was deafening. The camera panned past the judges to Mitzi's face as she was handed a trophy along with an over-sized check. The other two contestants stood off to the sides, clapping like good sports.

A few minutes later, everyone mingled on the grassy area outside the tent, among their family and friends, and Wendy shook her head. She'd make sure and send a letter to the president of the network expressing her outrage at being part of something that was so mishandled from beginning to end.

"Don't worry about it, sugar. It'll all work out in the end." Slade slid his arm around her waist. "I've gotta go call Max and update him, find out how we're going to handle things with Suzan now that filming has wrapped."

"Go, I'm going to mingle a bit and maybe get a glass of champagne. Meet you back here in about half an hour, okay?"

He leaned forward and whispered in her ear, "Don't drink too much champagne. I've got a bottle cooling at the condo for us—later."

Tilting her head back, she looked up into his blue eyes and smiled. "That sounds like the best offer I've had all day."

He kissed the tip of her nose. "Be back soon."

She took a glass from the table, and sipped. Filming was done, but she still had an antsy, unsettled feeling in her gut. Her instincts said nothing was over and she needed to be sharp, vigilant.

Her eyes scanned the crowd, finally landing on Suzan talking with her assistant, Becky. She watched Suzan shake her head vehemently at whatever Becky said, the other woman pleading with her. When Suzan turned and started to walk away, Becky marched up behind her, snagged her elbow and whipped her around.

Whatever she said to Suzan had the woman falter back a step. Her eyes widened before she slowly nodded at whatever Becky stated.

Together the women headed toward the door leading into the indoor studio space. She looked around for Slade, but he was nowhere in sight. Damn, he'd have baby kittens if she went haring off after them, but something about the look on Suzan's face, a combination of fear and resignation, had her feet moving before she realized.

Patting her pocket, she felt her cellphone and wondered if she could call Slade. It could be a disagreement between an employer and employee and she'd feel like an idiot for calling in the cavalry for something trivial. No, she'd figure out what was going on and then she'd call.

Pulling the door open enough to squeeze through, she took a second to let her eyes adjust to the darker interior.

"I really was hoping you'd mind your own business, Ms. Cunningham. You might as well join us."

Becky stood in front of her, a hand wrapped around Suzan's elbow. That didn't bother her. No, the part that alarmed her, had her frozen in place, was what Becky held in her other hand.

"Dang, did I mention I hate guns?" Feeling like a fool, Wendy raised her hands, waiting to see what Becky would do next.

Yep, she should have called Slade.

CHAPTER ELEVEN

The barrel of the gun pointed at her head didn't waver a centimeter. Becky's hand held it firm and steady, even though her gaze never left Suzan. Wendy felt like an idiot. Why hadn't she listened when Slade said Becky might be the villain of this little drama?

It should have been obvious. Suzan treated the girl like dirt, ordering her around. Treated her basically like an indentured servant instead of a trusted assistant. Though on second thought, the trust might have been pushing things, seeing she now held them both at gunpoint.

Becky wheeled around, getting right up in Suzan's face. "You stupid cow. All you needed to do was pay the money and this would all be over. You'd have kept your precious career alive and thriving. Instead, you brought in Nancy Drew," Becky waved the gun at Wendy, "and let her screw everything up."

"Becky, let her go. This is between us. Wendy has no part in this."

Becky's eyes widened, the gleam in them almost maniacal. "Are you kidding me? We had everything planned, down to the last detail, and she had to stick her nose in where it didn't belong."

We? Oh, hell, she's not working alone. Who else was part of Becky's foolish blackmail scheme?

The overhead lights in the studio streamed downward, illuminating Becky, her light brown hair unkempt and spilling from her usual ponytail, to fall around her shoulders. Hard lines bracketed her mouth and made her look years older and hardened beyond those years. Wendy took a step backward, and instantly the gun pointed straight at her. If she didn't miss her guess, the barrel was centered right between her eyes.

Her breath caught in her chest. What the hell was she going to do? She was pretty sure Slade hadn't seen Suzan slip away with Becky and disappear through the studio's door. There hadn't been time to hunt him down either, which would have been the smart thing to do.

No, she'd decided the only shot they'd get at keeping Suzan safe from the blackmailers was to follow. But sometimes first impressions were solid impressions, and her gut told her to follow them. Maybe it had been the look on Suzan's face, or something in the way she'd stood facing Becky. Or the expression in her eyes, as if confronting the inevitable.

Whatever the case, she'd screwed up and there was no way to get word to Slade. He'd never know the person responsible for the blackmail—or judging by the look on Becky's face, the killer's identity.

"Becky, Ms. Cunningham has nothing to do with any of this. Let her go and I'll give you everything you asked for. You have my word."

"I can't do that, Suzan. She knows too much."

Suzan shook her head. "I didn't tell her everything. I swear. The only thing she knows about for certain is the photos. Please..."

"I don't believe you." Becky moved, shifting her weight from one foot to the other, and the gun barrel dropped a tad lower. Wendy took a deep breath, her muscles tightening in anticipation. Her hands were trembling, and she balled them into fists, hoping nobody noticed.

She needed to be ready, because she'd only get one shot at trying to subdue Becky. If she screwed this up, the crazy woman might shoot both her and Suzan.

She eased to her right a few inches, and immediately Becky lifted the gun again. The black metal didn't shine in the overhead light like she'd seen on TV and in the movies. Instead, the black matte finish made it appear even more dangerous. Deadly and lethal in its simplicity.

"Don't move again or I will shoot you, I swear." Becky's voice got higher with each word, cracking on the last one. She ran a hand through her hair, then raised the hand holding the gun toward her head, resting it against her cheek.

"Becky, I've got the money ready. One phone call, and it'll be transferred anywhere you want. That's all it will take. One call." Suzan pleaded with the other woman, though Wendy knew Suzan's words to be a lie. She'd confessed to her and Slade she didn't have the kind of money the blackmailer demanded. Even if she sold everything she owned, including her business, there wouldn't be enough to cover the five million dollars.

"No calls. You'll wire the money directly. We've set up an offshore account in the Cayman's." She pointed to a backpack sitting on the studio floor, propped against the wall. Its inconspicuous appearance sent a chill down Wendy's spine. This wasn't an unplanned accidental meeting spot. When Becky led Suzan away, she'd intended to bring her here.

The knot in her stomach expanded with each breath. Her brain raced, trying to come up with a way to get Becky's focus shifted off Suzan. The longer she could keep the other woman talking, the better chance she had of finding out who else was part of this plot—because there was no way Becky was smart enough to do this on her own. And she kept slipping and saying we, which meant she had a silent partner in her blackmail scheme. But who? And why?

"Becky?"

The woman's head whipped around at Wendy's voice. Her face was red, whether from anxiety or anger Wendy couldn't tell, but she needed to try and diffuse the situation, because an agitated Becky was a dangerous Becky—well, more dangerous than she already was with a loaded gun in her hand.

"What?"

"I know about the photos of Suzan when she was younger. If those nudes ever surfaced, they would tarnish her reputation, but there's more, isn't there? Because this seems like it's personal."

As soon as she said it, Wendy realized it was the truth. This was about more than money. Some underlying fact was still undisclosed. There was a secret with farther reaching implications than just a set of thirty year old nude photos. Heck, the public would probably take one look at them and make Suzan more famous than she already was—after all, look what happened to the Kardashian girl when she did a sex tape.

"You're a very bright woman, Ms. Cunningham. Or can I still call you Wendy?" The deep masculine voice asked from behind her, and she recognized it instantly.

Jack O'Hara, the show's producer stood inches away, close enough she could feel his breath on the back of her neck. He took a final step closer, until his body was pressed intimately against her back, and he rested his chin on her shoulder.

"Jack. You're Becky's partner."

"Smart lady." His arm slid around her waist, and she felt something cold and metallic rest against the skin of her stomach. The bottom edge of her blouse had pulled free from the skirt, exposing a narrow band of skin, and he rested the muzzle against her abdomen. Looking down, she noted the shiny metal, the firm grip with which he held the weapon, an innate familiarity with it.

"Jack, why are you doing this?" Suzan stood frozen in place, staring at the man, tears rolling down her cheeks. The carefully applied makeup from earlier was nothing more than a blotched, ugly mess, but the other woman couldn't seem to take her eyes away from the man pressed against Wendy's spine.

She gave a wiggle, trying to put space between them, and he ground his pelvis against her backside. Feeling his erection through their clothing, she froze, not wanting to incite him further.

"Oh, Aunt Suzy, you don't understand anything. But you will, I promise." He rubbed his face along Wendy's cheek, his five o'clock shadow scratchy against her skin, and she winced, yanking her head to the side, not wanting his touch.

"Darling, she says she has the money ready to go." Becky's face lit up, her eyes on Jack. She reminded Wendy of a worshipful puppy looking at its master, eager to be petted for performing its trick.

"Excellent. Go ahead and set up the laptop, love, so we can be finished with all this unpleasantness and start our lives together."

Wendy nearly retched at the look of adoration crossing Becky's face, and watched her snatch up the backpack and pull out the laptop. She set it on top of a table propped against a wall and booted it up.

"You're going to kill us once the money's transferred, aren't you?" Wendy kept her voice low, not wanting Suzan to panic. There was no way Jack could leave them alive, not after extortion and blackmailing five million dollars from Suzan.

"I'm truly sorry, Wendy, but you're right. I can't afford to let any of you live. I'm not going to spend the rest of my life in prison or on the run. Not for the likes of her." He jerked his head toward Suzan.

"What did she do to make you so angry?"

Jack licked the side of her neck from chin to cheek, and Wendy fought to hide her shudder of revulsion. This guy was one sick freak, but she needed to keep him talking. The longer she delayed, the better the chance Slade or somebody else would notice two of the judges were missing from the finale party. Where were the damn paparazzi when you needed them?

"You think I'm a monster, but let me tell you, she's the real monster. Do you know what she did?"

Wendy shook her head. "But I'd like you to tell me. I want to understand."

Keep him talking. Keep him distracted. Please, please, Slade, notice I'm missing.

"You know about the pictures, right? The photos she's so desperate to keep away from the public?"

"Yes." Wendy's eyes met Suzan's, and she tried to silently communicate with the woman to focus on Becky, who was tapping away at the keyboard.

"See, a little over thirty years ago, sweet Suzy fell in love. Isn't that precious?"

Wendy's heart squeezed in her chest. There was an edge in his voice that she didn't like. This wasn't just personal. Instead it smelled like a vendetta, which scared the crap out of her.

"There's no law against falling in love."

"Of course not, sweet thing. Love is wonderful, when it's with the right person. Only Suzy didn't fall in love with the right guy, did you?" He addressed the question to Suzan, whose face grew even more ashen.

"We can't always pick who we love," she whispered.

"So very true. But let's get back to our story. Suzy was a beautiful young lady. Have you seen the photos? Truly exquisite. So much in love with the man who took them, weren't you, Suzan?"

"Yes. He was my whole world." Pain laced each word.

"But he shouldn't have been your world. He was married, very happily, until you came into the picture. Once he met you, everything changed. You spread your legs like a good little whore and seduced him away from his wife and his family."

The hand resting on her stomach, the one holding the gun, swung outward, and pointed at Suzan. She straightened to her full height, looking more like the woman Wendy was used to seeing and less like the timid cowering mess she'd been ever since Becky dragged her into the studio.

Becky's gun.

Becky had put it down in order to type on the computer. Suzan was closer. How could she let the other woman know to make a move?

"That's sad, Jack, but it's not a crime."

His left hand raked through the hair at the back of her head, yanking it backward. "No, it's not against the law, but she knew better. I've researched dear Aunt Suzy very carefully. Raised in a nice home, attended catholic school, she was taught to be a proper lady. Yet the second she's out on her own, she steals another woman's husband." The gun still clenched tight in his hand, he turned toward Becky. "Aren't you ready yet?"

"Just another minute, my love. The connection is so damned slow in here. The Wi-Fi is a piece of crap."

"Becky, how'd you get dragged into Jack's scheme? It's not too late to—"

Jack's hand dug tighter into her hair, wrapping it around his fist and pulling hard. Tears welled in her eyes at the sting on her scalp. Damn, that hurt.

Becky glanced toward Wendy with a grin. "Oh, this wasn't Jack's idea. It was mine, right sweetie?" She blew him a kiss and turned back to the keyboard.

"And it's a brilliant plan, my darling. I'd been tracking down Suzan for a long time. She's been very good at staying behind the scenes everywhere she went. I lost her trail for years. Honestly, I nearly gave up searching for her. Then she opened Aunt Suzy's Sweet Shops. It brought her into the public spotlight, and I found her again."

Wendy's head was reeling from all the information she'd heard in the last few minutes. But one thing was abundantly clear—this wasn't going to end well.

For a brief second, she thought she saw movement out of the corner of her eye, but when she surreptitiously glanced that way, she couldn't spot anything. The slight glimmer of hope she'd had plummeted to her toes. Rescue wasn't coming. Nobody knew they were gone, and nobody would find them until it was too late. It looked like Jack and Becky would get away with murder, even if they didn't get the five million dollars.

"You look like your mother." Suzan's voice interrupted her thoughts, and doused over her like a bucket of ice water. "I wouldn't have recognized you. Obviously I didn't. But now, knowing—you look like her. Except for your eyes. You have your father's eyes."

Jack's whole body stiffened, the hand holding her hair loosening the smallest amount. Looks like she surprised him, Wendy thought. Keep it up, Suzan, keep him off balance.

"Shut up, bitch. Don't talk about my mother or him." He spat the last word like a curse. "He left everything behind to be with you. My mother. Me. He walked away without a backward glance because he was dazzled by a young whore who seduced him away with her looks and eagerness to spread her legs."

"It wasn't like that, Jack. I loved Henry with my whole heart. I didn't mean for it to happen. I'd gone to him to have some pictures taken for my portfolio. Head shots. But he was sweet and charming and I fell in love—we both did. It wasn't planned, but it was real."

Suzan's head lowered as her eyes closed and when she looked back up, they were filled with a glittering determination Wendy had never seen the older woman show. "He was the only man I've ever loved, and I'm never going to apologize again for what I felt. Do you hear me? Am I sorry he left you behind? Yes, and he regretted it to his dying breath. But I don't think he would have changed a single minute we had together, as short as it was, and I wouldn't either."

"He'd still be alive if he'd stayed away from you, you lying cow. If he'd stayed, he wouldn't have died in that crash. He'd have been home when I needed him, when Mom needed him. But he wasn't because he'd gone sniffing after you, and tossed us away like garbage."

Suzan shook her head. "That's not how it happened, Jack. You're not remembering things the way they really were."

There it was again. Movement right beyond Suzan's shoulder. Wendy's eyes widened when she spotted the dark hair and broad shoulders. She'd recognize them anywhere.

Slade!

"Sugar, we're ready." Becky stood, taking a step back from the computer. "Get over here, boss lady, and let's finish this." Her finger latched onto Suzan's arm so tight, Wendy could see the indentions in the older woman's skin.

"What's your part in this, Becky? You're obviously in cahoots with Jack. What are you getting besides money? Or is money the only thing of interest?" Wendy watched Slade's dark head slip out of view, and braced both feet solidly against the floor. She needed to be ready to make a move the second she could, but she'd wait for his sign. She knew he'd let her know somehow.

Becky laughed like she'd heard the best joke ever. "Do you have any idea what it's been like working for this monster? Being treated like you don't exist unless she needs something? I was the person Jack talked to when he first started checking into Aunt Suzy's background." She waved at her sweetie with one hand, while the other dangled by her side, grasping the pistol she'd picked up.

"Becky's been a wonder, getting me all kinds of information. Once you know where to start looking, it's rather easy. Plus I had all my father's old records and photographs from when he abandoned his business." Jack's hand finally released from her hair and wrapped around her waist once again. She gave a sigh of relief. Dang, who knew having your hair pulled for so long hurt like a son of a gun.

"Once I found out Jack intended to extend a little payback to our favorite Aunt Suzy here, well I just had to be front and center." Becky shoved Suzan to her knees in front of the computer, placing her at an odd angle for typing, with her head just barely above the edge of the tabletop.

"I must admit, it was a surprise finding such a kindred spirit working side-by-side with the whore. When we compared agendas, things just clicked into place. My dear Becky has been most helpful. And now, Suzan, if you'd be so kind as to transfer the funds, we'll end this farce and be on our way." He pointed the gun at Wendy's head. "Of course, if you stall, I'll blow this one's brains all over the floor."

A sob escaped Suzan, and her hands reached for the keyboard. "I'll do it. Don't hurt her. She's innocent in all this."

"Nobody's innocent. She stuck her nose in where it didn't belong. And you, calling in a private detective. Smart. With Becky's help, he's been kept off track since the beginning. We fed him misinformation and downright false facts, kept the waters muddied. You really made things easy. Until this busybody poked her nose into things."

Wendy stiffened as a thought took root. "You were behind the sabotages, weren't you?"

Jack grinned. "Took you long enough to figure that out. Sweet Becky helped with that. She's really clever with her hands, and it was surprisingly easy for her to slip into the stations and cause a little mischief."

"Why?"

"The Cooking Channel offered that bitch a job hosting her own show. Can you believe it? I couldn't have that happen, and what better way than to discredit her in the eyes of the public on a corrupt baking competition. Our show will never make it on the air, but the scandal alone will bring her down. Too bad you and Coleman are getting caught in the crossfire, but things happen."

The gun barrel stroked against the side of Wendy's cheek and she winced at the feel of the cool steel. What was taking Slade so long? Or had she been wrong? Maybe she hadn't seen him at all and it had been a figment of her imagination.

Suzan's fingers paused on the keyboard and she sucked in a choking sob. Wendy knew the second she hit send, their lives were over.

"Jack, think for a second. Somebody's bound to find us. If you and Becky are missing, you'll both be the prime suspects. There won't be any place you can hide." Her heartbeat raced so fast she was afraid she was going to hyperventilate and pass out. If that happened, he'd have no problem putting a bullet in her brain and walking away.

"By the time the cops start looking for me, I'll be in a non-extradition country with enough money to live comfortably for the rest of my life."

"Wait! Don't you mean us? We're a team. You love me." An edge of hysteria colored Becky's words and her eyes widened. "Jack, please. You promised."

"Of course I promised, sweetie. Except...I lied." In a single movement, he raised the gun and fired. Wendy's body jerked in his grasp, but he held tight. She watched the shocked expression on Becky's face. Saw the blood splatter across her chest where the bullet struck.

"Jack..." Her voice trailed off as her body slumped to the floor, eyes wide open. Bright red blood pooled beneath her body, a thin line trailing across the concrete floor in a scarlet path.

Suzan's screams filled the space, echoing off the walls.

"Shut up! Finish sending the money, or she's next."

The gun pressed against Wendy's temple, no longer cool steel but warm from being fired. Adrenaline coursed through her blood, her heartbeat pounding. A rushing sound filled her ears before an eerie calm enfolded her.

She was going to die. Nobody was coming to the rescue. Everything slowed. Sounds became muffled and indistinct. Every movement seemed exaggerated and distorted, as if she were submerged deep in the ocean, buoyant and floating.

This is the end.

Suzan's hands wiped frantically at the blood splatter coating her face and arms, hiccuping sobs erupting from her in almost silent screams. Still on her knees, she crawled toward Becky's sprawled body in a vain attempt to help her.

It was no use. Wendy could see Becky's vacant and lifeless eyes staring straight ahead.

"Suzan! Finish wiring the money now." Jack's voice had changed, a more frantic edge lacing his words. Though his arm was still wrapped tight around her waist, the hand with the gun now hung at his side. He drew in a shuddering breath, trying to get things back under control.

Wendy knew she only had one chance. One shot at stopping the insanity. Curling her hands into claws, she reached for his eyes, digging deep and hard.

"Run, Suzan!" She gouged at his face, her nails scraping across his eyelids and cheeks. His yell bounced off the walls and he started to raise the hand holding the gun.

A dark blur appeared from out of nowhere, barreling into them with such force Wendy was knocked free of Jack's hold onto the hard concrete floor. The sound of flesh striking flesh reverberated in her ears.

The gun dropped from Jack's hand as he tried to protect himself from the blows raining down on him. Slade's fist connected with his face, pounding brutally over and over again.

Jack stopped struggling after the last blow, and Wendy grabbed Slade's arm, stopping him from raining more blows on the now helpless man.

"Stop. He can't fight back, he's unconscious." The wildness that had consumed Slade faded before her eyes and he rose over the slumped body of the man who'd caused them such anguish, sucking in lungsful of air.

He pulled her into his arms and she went willingly, pressed against him with her head against his chest. The reassuring heartbeat beneath her ear soothed her.

They were safe. Alive. Except for Becky, who'd paid the ultimate price for misplaced love in a twisted act of vengeance.

"Is he dead?" Suzan walked over and stared down at the man who'd been responsible for weeks of torment.

"No, he's alive. We need to call the cops, though." Slade's arms tightened around Wendy, squeezing her closer. Not that she minded. She'd been so sure nobody was coming to rescue them. Yet, Slade had been there, waiting for the right moment.

"Maybe we shouldn't wait for the cops." Wendy's breath caught in her throat when she spotted the gun in Suzan's hand. The same gun Becky held right up until Jack put a bullet in her chest.

"Suzan, no! You can't kill him."

"Why not? If he lives, he'll go to trial and everything will come out. I'm ruined no matter what. He's made sure of that."

Wendy tugged free from Slade's arms and moved to stand beside Suzan, standing over Jack's prone body. "It's all going to come out anyway. How you handle things when it does is more important. Don't let him win, Suzan. You talk to the press—tell them the truth. The whole story. Yes, it might tarnish your image, maybe even hurt your business. But you're strong. You'll get through this with the help of your friends." She pointed to herself and Slade. "We'll help you."

Suzan looked between them, seeming to mentally shut down right before Wendy's eyes. With a last glance down at Jack, she turned the gun around and handed it to Slade.

"Take this and call the cops. Let him rot." She turned and started toward the door but stopped. "All the press outside—I don't think I can face them."

"Not today." Slade walked up and put his arm around the older woman. "Let's deal with one thing at a time. Cops first. Then we'll call a press conference and lay everything out. Put a positive spin on things, and salvage as much as we can from this fiasco. Okay?"

Wendy could almost see Suzan pulling herself together before her eyes. The stiffening of her spine. Brushing her hair back from her face, she tugged at her floral dress and pulled her trademark apron back in place.

Slade turned to Wendy and whispered, "See if you can find something to secure him with, while I call the police."

Within minutes the wail of sirens filled the air, and she knew everything was over. The show. The blackmail scheme.

But one question ran through her head, one she desperately wanted the answer to—was this the end for her and Slade? Or had they found something here in South Florida to build a life together with?

She only hoped she got the answer she prayed for, because she wasn't sure she could take losing him again.

CHAPTER TWELVE

He stared at the closed condo door, ready to head home. The suitcase at his feet was packed and he knew he should head to the airport. There was nothing keeping him in South Florida.

Filming was over, and he wasn't sure the show would ever make it to the airwaves. Though knowing the way television feasted on the carcasses of scandal, he'd be willing to bet they'd find a way to capitalize on all the sensationalism surrounding Becky's murder and the subsequent arrest of the show's producer.

It was time to head back to Louisiana. Debrief with Max about the case, and take a good long look at what he wanted out of life. One thing was certain—he still wanted to open his restaurant. He also wanted to step back from the publicity machine of traveling and celebrity endorsements and the whole *Culinary Cowboy* persona. More than anything he wanted to get back to his passion—cooking.

It had been fun for a while, but it was past time to go for what he wanted most. He gave a sarcastic laugh. Funny how the one thing he wanted most had changed ever since Wendy resurfaced in his life.

Deep in his gut he knew he'd give up everything to be with her. The restaurant. The power and prestige he'd garnered in the culinary world. Hell, he'd even give up New Orleans and move to New York if that's what she wanted—if she'd have him.

Things had been chaotic since Jack's arrest. They'd spent hours at the police station, being questioned ad nauseam about Becky's death, the blackmail, and hostage situation. Finally the cops and the district attorney were satisfied. All the evidence had been turned over, including the blackmail notes and the incriminating photos.

It was going to be hard on Suzan, but she was a strong woman and she'd pull through this one way or another. Hell, the way the American people ate up salacious gossip and scandal, she'd probably become even more famous.

But in all the chaos, he hadn't had a chance to talk to Wendy. They'd spent a couple of wild nights together, but was that all it was to her? A brief fling, easily forgotten when she went home? It had meant more to him, but then he'd always wanted her, and no amount of time or distance had dulled his feelings.

The knock on the door startled him from his musings. He swung it open to find Wendy standing there looking as beautiful as ever, with her long hair tumbled about her shoulders.

Her curves were encased in a pink sundress with a darker pink belt cinched around her waist, her purse clutched in her hands. She looked calm and cool, and he'd never have suspected she was nervous at seeing him, except for the white-knuckled grip she had on her purse.

"Hi." She gave a tentative smile.

"Hi, yourself. Come in." He ushered her through and closed the door. "I thought you'd already left."

"No, my flight's not until this afternoon. I wanted to say goodbye." She tossed her purse onto the end table beside the big leather sofa and walked across the condo's living room, facing away from him and he couldn't read her.

"You could have called."

"I know." She whispered. "I nearly chickened out and left without a word. But I didn't want to run away like I did last time."

He wished she'd turn around, let him see what hid in the depths of her hazel eyes. The way they changed colors helped him gauge her moods, but she kept her back to him. Damn, he wanted to pull her close, drag her body against his and tell her all the things he wanted to share with her.

But he didn't. Because the last time he'd spilled his guts to her, exposed his heart and soul, she'd headed for the hills and never looked back.

"But this is still goodbye, right?" He walked up behind her, and placed his hands on her shoulders, felt her stiffen almost imperceptibly before relaxing beneath his touch.

"Yes…no…that's why I'm here. I don't want it to be goodbye." She spun around to face him, her hazel eyes showing a hint of golden brown behind a sheen of tears. "I second-guessed myself all the way over here, half of me hoping you'd already left, and the other half praying you'd open the door."

"I'm still here." There was a lightening in his heart, though he tried to maintain a grip on his emotions. Maybe she wasn't sure how to tell him they didn't have a shot.

She chuckled. "Yeah. I need to ask you—"

"Anything, sweetheart. You can ask me anything." Damn, he hoped he wasn't being a fool, but he couldn't help hoping, wishing, she wanted the same things he did—a second chance to get things right.

"I've done a lot of thinking since I've been here. Soul searching really, something I should have done a long time ago." She stepped back and his hands dropped to his sides, and he fought the urge to pull her close, wrap her in his arms and never let go.

"I've been thinking too."

"Damn, I don't know why I'm so nervous. We're friends."

Her words stabbed at him like a knife blade straight to his heart. "Is that all we are, sweetheart? If that's all you have to give, well—"

"No! I mean, yes, we're friends. You were my best friend. The one person I could be myself with. That I didn't have to hide away who I was or what I wanted. Then things changed."

"When I told you I loved you." *Hold it together, don't let her know you're falling apart inside.*

"I know I hurt you when I ran, Slade, but at the time it seemed like my only choice. My life was a living nightmare, and I needed to go, as far away as I could get, even if it meant leaving you behind. If I'd stayed, I'd have lost a part of myself I'd never get back."

"I remember how bad things got at your place. But you could have turned to me."

She shook her head. "That's part of it. I didn't want to be dependent on anybody but myself. If I'd stayed, we've had been just like the rest of the people in our town. Stuck in a never-ending rut we couldn't escape. I wanted more than that for you—for us." She reached forward and cupped his cheek. "I loved you so much. But we were both young and foolish, and it never would have lasted. I couldn't bear the thought of you growing to hate me."

"Honey, I could never hate you."

She raised her brow and opened her mouth, but he pressed a finger to her lips. "The past is the past. I'd rather know how you feel now."

Her eyes explored his face, something deep in her gaze giving him hope. Because what he saw shining in the depths of those beautiful hazel eyes, the light green flecked with gold, was love.

"I want to be with you. The time we've spent together here has made me see no matter how far or fast I run, I can't run from how I feel." Her hands cupped his cheeks, and she stepped into his open arms. "I love you. I always have and I always will."

"I love you too." He let his forehead rest against hers and groaned. "I was going to give you a couple of days and then I was coming after you."

His hand curled around the back of her head and he kissed her, his mouth plundering hers with all the pent up longing he'd buried. All he knew was he needed her in his life, in his arms, and in his bed.

She pulled free of his kiss and grinned. "Bedroom?"

"Nope. Too far away." His head jerked toward the leather sofa. "Best I can do."

She giggled and the sound shot straight to his groin and instantly he was rock hard. He lifted her in his arms, carried her to the sofa and placed her gently against the cushions. She leaned back with a happy sigh, and her fingers began working her belt free and dropped it onto the floor. With a crook of her finger, she invited him closer.

"Be sure, because I'm never letting you go again, darlin'. Once you're mine, you'll stay mine until the day I die."

"I've never been surer of anything in my life, Slade Coleman. Now shut up and kiss me."

He took a deep breath and let himself be still for a second, staring at the vision before him. He wanted to memorize everything—the way she looked. The sounds and scents and textures of this moment. It was like coming home. He'd been numb inside, refusing to feel anything more than mild friendship with anybody once Wendy left, and he'd finally healed a grievous wound.

His mouth met hers in a soul-deep, curl-your-toes melding of lips and tongue. When her arms slid around his neck, he eased to his knees before her, settling between her spread thighs. Never breaking the kiss, he pulled her closer against his chest. Felt her nipples harden against him.

One hand moved upward to cup her breast, his thumb strumming over the distended bud and she moaned into his mouth.

Her hands unwound from around his neck and moved to the buttons on his shirt, opening the first and moving to the next. Slade gave a grunt of impatience, moved her hands aside, gripped the front and tore it open. Buttons flew across the room and hit the floor. He couldn't wait to have her hands on him, feel her touching his skin. The urge to rip the dress from her delectable body nearly overwhelmed him.

"Off. This needs to come off now." His fingertip slid beneath the shoulder strap. With a sexy little shimmy, she tugged the dress up and over her head in one smooth movement, leaving her clad only in pink lace.

His breath caught at the sight. "Gorgeous." Impulsively he leaned forward and placed a kiss along the side of her throat. She jumped, smiled, and caught his hand, bringing it to the front clasp of the bra. Slade leaned closer, his gaze fixed on her breasts as they spilled free, filling his hands.

"So beautiful, my love."

Her head was thrown back against the cushions, and she gasped when he flicked her nipple before taking it into his mouth and sucking hard. The gasp quickly morphed into a sexy moan when his hand slid along her stomach and rested atop her mound, still covered by the lacy boy shorts.

"Oh, Slade, that's so good." Her hips bucked against his hand and his fingers skimmed lightly along the waistband of the panties before dipping beneath the elastic edge. Felt the heat and moisture pooling at her core.

"Need you." The words barely left his mouth before she wrapped her legs around his hips, rubbing her cleft against the rock hard erection behind his zipper. He needed her with an urgency he couldn't explain.

With a yank, her panties were free and tossed over his shoulder. Wendy released his mouth to gasp and arch against him. His arms closed around her, pinning her against his chest, as an overwhelming ache to be inside her roared through his veins. A deep-seated urge to be joined fully and completely with the woman he loved.

Inhaling a ragged breath, he stood and toed off his sneakers, while his hands made quick work of the button on his jeans. The rasp of the zipper sounded loud and he sucked in another breath when it finally opened all the way.

Shucking his jeans, he reached for Wendy, but stopped abruptly.

"Damn it, I don't have a condom. They're in my suitcase."

"You love me, right? We're going to find a way to make this work, so it's okay. Make love to me." The glow in her eyes nearly brought him to tears. He'd been such a fool to let her get away. At least, that was one mistake he'd never make again.

She shrieked when he plucked her from the sofa and seated himself where she'd been in one smooth move, repositioning her until her thighs straddled his lap. Her glorious hair spilled across her shoulders as she leaned forward to kiss him, her hands gripping his biceps.

He could feel her wetness, knew she was more than ready for him. Grasping her hips, he eased forward an inch and stopped, watching her eyes widen in surprise. He slowly arched his hips and sank another inch within her warm yielding body.

Gripping her hips, he urged her down slowly on his rigid length, his eyes glued to her face. He watched her, fascinated with the array of emotions crossing her face, until he was fully sheathed within her.

She leaned forward, arching her back. Her breasts rubbed against his chest, and he sucked in air like a starving man. He'd wanted to make this last, but he was hanging on by a thread.

Pressing forward, he stroked within her. Her whole body undulated in a sensuous rhythm, and she lifted up and slammed back down, creating an excruciatingly delightful friction. When her inner muscles clamped down on him, he groaned.

"Sweetheart, you're killing me."

"But what a way to go, babe." She smiled and gave a little twist and ground her pelvis against him. Two could play that game, and he slid his hand between their joined bodies, unerringly finding the little nub of flesh and rubbing small circles around it.

She gasped, her head flung back, and he watched her breasts rise and fall. With every catch of her breath, he knew she grew closer to coming. His body tightened, and he knew he wouldn't be far behind.

Squeezing her clit, he watched her eyes close and she cried out, the sounds of her pleasure like the finest symphony. Her muscles bunched and clenched around him and he plunged deep inside. Faster and faster he bucked against her until he joined her in a mind blowing climax.

His hand glided along her back, down to her ass and up along her spine again, while her body continued spasming around him. Her head snuggled into the crook of his neck and she placed a series of kisses along his nape.

"You know, I'm planning on opening a second store, right?" Her words whispered against his skin.

"I'd heard that."

"I was considering Los Angeles or Dallas. But, how would you feel if I decided on New Orleans instead?"

He clasped her face between his hands and shifted her until he could look into her eyes. Read the tentativeness along with what he thought was hope.

"You'd do that?"

"I'll be turning over the running of my New York shop to my assistant manager, and making her the full time manager. I'd need to focus all my attention on the second location if I want it to be a success."

He pulled her face toward him and placed a gentle kiss against her lips. Brushed another kiss across each eyelid, soft as a butterfly's wings.

"You know I'm opening my restaurant in New Orleans."

The corner of her lips quirked up. "I might have heard a rumor to that effect."

"We can make this work. I know it's a lot, asking you to relocate..."

"You didn't ask. It's my choice. It's a sound business decision, and the only reason I didn't pick New Orleans in the first place was because I was afraid if I saw you again, well, I guess I thought we'd end up exactly like this."

He chuckled. "I'd say we were meant to be together. No matter what tricks of fate conspired to reunite us, I'm never letting you go again."

"I'm not running anymore. I've found exactly what I was searching for, here in your arms."

He pulled her back against his chest. "I think we missed our flights. That means we'll have to spend one more night in paradise."

She wrapped her arms around his neck. "Sounds like a great idea to me, cowboy. As long as we're together, anywhere is paradise."

NEWSLETTER
Want to stay informed and up-to-date with all my new releases, sales, giveaways and contests? Sign up for my newsletter.
http://kathyivan.com/contact.html#newsletter

ABOUT THE NEW ORLEANS CONNECTION SERIES
Sex, Lies and Apple Pies is part of the New Orleans Connection series, romantic suspense books that take place in and around New Orleans. These are stand-alone stories, although recurring characters appear in each book.

READING ORDER FOR THE NEW ORLEANS CONNECTION SERIES
Desperate Choices
Connor's Gamble
Relentless Pursuit
Ultimate Betrayal
Keeping Secrets
Sex, Lies and Apple Pies
FOR FULL A LIST OF KATHY IVAN'S BOOKS, GO TO
http://www.kathyivan.com/books.html

MEET KATHY IVAN
USA TODAY Bestselling author Kathy Ivan spent most of her life with her nose between the pages of a book. It didn't matter if the book was a paranormal romance, romantic suspense, or action and adventure thrillers, sweet & spicy or sexy novella. Kathy turned her obsession with reading into the next logical step, writing. Her books transport you from a paranormal lodge in the Colorado Mountains in her Destiny's Desire Series, to the sultry splendor of the French Quarter in New Orleans in her award winning romantic suspense and mysteries, to Las Vegas in her contemporary romantic comedies. Kathy tells stories people can't get enough of; reuniting old loves, betrayal of trust, finding kidnapped children, psychics and even a ghost or two. But one thing they all have in common - love (and some pretty steamy sex scenes too). You can find more on Kathy at:

WEBSITE: www.kathyivan.com
FACEBOOK: https://www.facebook.com/kathyivanauthor
TWITTER: https://www.twitter.com/@kathyivan

The Hunted

Jackie Ivie

*"...THE HUNTED is an exciting suspense/romance that will keep readers
at the edge of their seats till the very last page."*
K. Roma

The Hunted is dedicated to my great friend and fellow writer, Miriam
Matthews. Your help and guidance is invaluable to me. Thank you. I
couldn't have written LeeAnn and Kane's adventure without you.

CHAPTER ONE

4:57 a.m.
Exactly.

LeeAnn glanced at the digital read-out on the desk clock. Excellent. Her inner clock was working perfectly. The wake-up call was scheduled for 5:00. Her back-up alarm on her phone for 5:03. She looked toward the window next. She hadn't drawn the room-darkening drapes. That was probably stupid, but she loved things open. Transparent. Open windows. Clear minds. What she didn't like was subterfuge. Cheating. Shady dealings. That's why she'd gone into accounting in the first place. Numbers weren't negotiable. Figures didn't lie. Unless liars did the figuring.

A groan slid past her lips. She glanced toward the clock again. 4:58 now. She was not looking forward to the breakfast meeting with Chad. The man was charming. Good-looking. Single. Smart. But he had a huge problem with integrity. Thank goodness she'd gone with her gut instinct and never had sex with the guy! Talk about adding complication. Then again, LeeAnn wasn't an easy type, like he favored. Nor was she the kind of accountant to overlook accounts that ran through millions of dollars without any source of income. Regardless of how handsome, charming, and debonair her business partner happened to be.

The window drew her gaze next. Again. As if it called to her. Pre-dawn was just starting outside, highlighting wisps of clouds. Nothing that would bring rain. Not this week. This was just another hot night in a hot week. She was going to be inundated with sunlight. Miami had a lot of that. Especially in the summer. The city was sexy. Sultry. Sticky. She shouldn't have turned the air conditioning down last night. Bed linens clung to her legs as she rolled onto her back.

"Don't. Move."

The words were distinct. Separated. Spoken in a hissed whisper. Carried a lot of threat in a definite bass tone, and resonant with all kinds of masculine vibes. They were accompanied by a long cylindrical item that looked like a rifle barrel. Right above her ribcage.

LeeAnn's heart jumped into her throat, choking her. Her breath caught. Shivers flew down her limbs. Everything went immobile. Deer caught in the headlights. Prey sighted. Spotlighted. Frozen in fear.

Staying still was not going to be a problem.

The rifle shifted farther, elongated. Became a long barrel. Equipped with a large scope. Steadied with his left hand. His other one was on the trigger mechanism. It was attached to a large arm. A really large arm. With a lot of muscle.

Her heart started beating again. Shallow bits of breath were right behind it, followed by mental acuity. She slanted a glance toward him and instantly wished she hadn't. The guy was hooded. His upper face in shadow. But that didn't stop her gasp. Nor the series of shivers that started up.

This was beyond interesting. She must be dreaming here. Nothing else made sense. Bad guys weren't this good-looking. Nor were they sexy as hell. Or ripped. They really weren't supposed to smell nice, either. This was a really great dream.

But what if it wasn't...?

The analyst portion of her psyche kicked in. If this was real, she'd have to file a police report. She needed details. Specifics. LeeAnn licked her lips. Concentrated.

She couldn't see as much as she wanted. It wasn't light enough yet. He was little more than an amorphous mass in the midst of a lot of black. She could barely make out the tip of his nose down to his shirt collar. A scruff of dark whiskers delineated his jaw. They might match his hair color. He'd dressed in fabric that sucked up light. Everything looked black. No reflection. Not even his gun. The scope was another match. LeeAnn didn't know a lot about rifles, but he wasn't going to hit anything vital in that position. Not on her, anyway.

"You want to live?"

The words were hissed in another whisper. His right arm tensed, putting a lot more forearm definition in her line of sight. She wondered how to describe that to a sketch artist.

"Yes."

"Then, quit moving."

He called this moving? She made a face before replying. "Look. You're in my hotel room. I'm not screaming. I think I'm doing pretty good here. Okay?"

He sighed, sending a slight touch of air across her throat. It lifted all kinds of goose bumps on her skin. She'd selected a peach-colored nightgown last night. It wasn't covering her shoulder area. In fact, it wasn't in evidence at all. The satin felt tangled around her, along with the sheet.

"You should have closed your drapes," he told her.

"Why?"

"Issues."

"With who? Window-washers? I'm on the 29th floor."

"Your levity is out of place."

Levity? What the heck? Who talks like that?

"See that light?"

He gestured with a slight nod. It wasn't necessary. The moment he'd spoken, a long slice of red came through the window, reaching her approximate ankle area. It started moving up from there. She was guessing on its proximity. She didn't check. She'd seen too many suspense movies and crime dramas to be innocent. It looked exactly like she'd seen on a screen.

"Is that a—? No. It can't be. A...*laser sight?*"

The last words were choked. The frozen feeling came back with a vengeance. The guy was completely unaffected. His reply was in the same modulated, calm, deep voice. For some reason, that was even more frightening.

"Yes."

"Well...do something!"

"Have to find him first."

His finger moved, the gun pulsed, giving a slight whisper sound, and the phone rang. Simultaneously. What a time for a perfectly timed wake-up call.

Mister Big-and-Bad had as much strength as it looked. He snagged her about the waist, yanking her and her bedding onto the floor between the bed and wall. That hurt. A thump accompanied her hip hitting the floor, followed by her exclamation. He didn't note it. All kinds of male moved as he reached up and swatted the phone off the nightstand. It landed near her head, sending off a bell tone. A pre-recorded message followed. He settled the handset back onto the phone stopping the noise. LeeAnn wasn't paying much attention. The guy had as much mass as it looked. She was getting squashed. Things were actually going dim.

"I missed."

He sounded surprised. She shoved. He grunted and actually got heavier somehow.

"I can't believe it. I never—"

"You're heavy!" LeeAnn interrupted him.

"Oh."

His rifle made a slight sound as he set it beside her. He pushed up. And nothing had ever felt so sweet! LeeAnn sucked a solid lungful of air, let it out, and grabbed another.

"You hear that?" he asked.

Was he joking? She'd almost suffocated. Loud heartbeats filled her ears along with the sound of her own breathing. LeeAnn inhaled deeply, held the breath, and listened. Heard what sounded like little puffs of air. They were accompanied by smacking sounds as something hit the wall beside him.

She nodded.

"That is the sound of failure."

LeeAnn rolled her head. There was a line of dark spots in the wall that hadn't been there before. Her eyes were wide as she returned them to his face. Or what she could see of it.

"Failure?"

"I never miss."

"Please don't tell me those are bullet holes, okay? Just don't."

"Those are bullet holes."

"I just asked you not to say that."

"Somebody wants you dead. I failed to stop them."

"Oh, come on. This isn't happening."

"You ever been hunted?"

"Hunted? Are you crazy? I'm here to meet with—no. Chad might be laundering money, but—no. He wouldn't hire someone to kill me! This kind of thing does not happen in real life. Okay? It just doesn't."

"We have about three minutes."

"Before what? A room explosion?"

He lowered his chin. She had to imagine the look he was giving her. It was too dark to see in the well of space they occupied, and he was still hooded.

"You said you wanted to live."

"I do."

"Then, follow me. Do exactly as I say. Don't argue. Don't question."

"No way. Do I really look that stupid? And I've got news for you, mister. I'm not leaving without my purse and ID."

"Dead people don't need ID."

"Excuse me?"

"Weren't you listening? I never miss. This is new territory for me, too."

"New territory? Okay. Enough is enough. Who *are* you? Exactly?"

"Guardian angel."

LeeAnn would have laughed, except he was serious as he said it. And everything was just too weird at the moment. As if his occupation was a real possibility. That decided it. She was definitely dreaming.

"I thought guardian angels were old guys...with white beards...you know. Like skinny Santa's. Or, they're beautiful young women. Mostly blondes. And they have wings. Big ones. And...I don't know. This is insane. They don't even exist."

"You ready to try the door?"

"I'm still asleep. That's it, isn't it?"

He might have sighed if the amount of breath touching her neck was an indicator.

"This could be dangerous, LeeAnn."

"How...do you know my name?" Her heart stuttered.

"Later. We have to leave. Now. Right now."

"So, what's stopping us?"

"The door."

"Guardian angels can't get through doors?"

She tried to say it without snickering, but failed. He lowered his chin more, dropping the hood farther, sending a shadow to his mouth. He didn't look remotely angelic. His appearance was pretty damned sinister. And frightening. And he expected her to leave with him?

"Hotels keep their halls brightly lit. Your room is dark. You failed to shut your drapes last night. The moment the door opens, he'll know it."

"You think he's still watching?"

His lips twitched. Her heart leapt. And that was just more weirdness.

"Won't know until we try," he finally replied.

"Give me one good reason why I should trust you. Just one."

"I saved your life."

LeeAnn reached over and ran her finger over one of the holes on the wall. It looked real. It sure felt real. This was starting to get scary.

"We don't have time for this. Hang on."

"To what?"

He didn't give her any time! And the bedding made it easy for him. LeeAnn found herself wrapped in wads of cloth and atop a shoulder, but at least she had a peephole for air. He acted like her bulk was nothing as he squatted at the side of her door.

"We're going to be exposed for a few seconds. You ready?"

"Do I have a choice?"

"Nope," he replied.

A whir of gear noise started up. He swiveled in a sickeningly quick motion. LeeAnn rocked atop his shoulder. Swallowed. A couple of moments later, the noise halted.

"That's my phone!"

He opened the door and slid to the other side, shutting it behind him. She shifted as he resettled her, banging her legs against what was probably his rifle.

"You're not going to let me take it?"

"Dead people don't need phones, either," he informed her and then he started jogging.

CHAPTER TWO

Kane had a complication. A big one. It grew larger with each passing moment. The rules were clear. Complete the assignment. Clear out. Stay hidden. Whatever happens, do not engage.

Well.

He was pretty engaged now.

The woman watched him unblinkingly from the back passenger seat. She hadn't said anything as he took twenty-nine flights of stairs at a jog – stopping once as a hotel maid entered below them and walked up a flight before exiting. Kane had stepped into the shadows and waited. Watched. Listened. The maid hadn't even looked up. The moment the door closed behind her, he'd continued, taking stair-chewing strides. It hadn't been difficult. A walk in the park compared to ground training and survival skill tests.

The underground parking garage had been deserted. *Good thing.* A hooded man dressed in black, carrying a body-sized bundle over his shoulder, while packing a rifle, would get noticed. Kane crouched down and scanned the area. Nobody was around. No shout rang out as he reached his SUV. Nothing moved. His weapon took some misuse. He dropped the 308 *Lapua* over the backseat into the luggage compartment. The gun gave a slight thud as it landed on the carpet, but it shouldn't be harmed. His sniper rifle should be secured in a case, but he'd had to leave that behind.

He'd left a lot of things behind.

Like his sanity.

His rifle case was now collateral damage. It shouldn't be an issue. That case didn't have any distinguishing marks. It was common back-pack style, PVC construction. Hard to get fingerprints off that material. If any forensic lab managed to pull prints, they'd be smudged. Indistinct. All of that aside, he'd worry about it later.

When they were safe.

Kane had taken a deep breath, lifting her with it, and held it for a full minute. Spent the time scanning the garage again, but he'd mainly used the time to calm down. After-incident jitters could derail any assignment. Aside from the mistake of engaging LeeAnn in the first place, he'd already screwed-up. He hadn't dangled the 'DO NOT DISTURB' sign from her door handle. That would have gained him all kinds of time.

For a man who avoided attention, he was certainly engendering a bunch of it. His mind snapped through scenarios. He had a few hours before a maid would spot the bullet holes in the wall. She'd report it. The authorities would be called. It should be a 'Missing Person' case. There wasn't any blood. No signs of injury. No dead body. But any investigation would probably lead to the room he'd confiscated – unless he was lucky. The room had been unoccupied. They might not use it for days yet.

Kane exhaled slowly. Handled LeeAnn's bulk next. She resembled a mummy bundle, strapped as she was into a lap belt and shoulder harness. He didn't know where her arms were. She hadn't wriggled. She hadn't spoken. She might be in shock. He didn't know and he didn't have time to find out.

Time was passing. Each second upped the risk factor. Kane hadn't gotten a good look at her hunter. It could be anyone. Coming from anywhere. Anytime. If this had been his botched hit, he wouldn't waste time. He'd be right on his flushed quarry's ass.

Black leather sucked him into place in the driver seat. A thumb touch started the engine. His next move shifted gears. Each move was automatic. A well-oiled machine. Auto-piloted. Fastening his safety belt with one hand, he eased the vehicle out of the parking spot, checking constantly for anything that moved, snagged his attention, or looked out-of-place. The place was a mass of polished concrete, lots of lighting, and rows of expensive, well-cared-for vehicles.

Nothing else.

Dawn was progressing, the sun rising, daylight just brushing the tops of buildings. Kane reached for his sunglasses with one hand, while he maneuvered the SUV up the ramp and through the pay lane. He had the glasses in place before he shoved his hood off, settling it on his shoulders. Big, black SUVs like this one caught attention. An anonymous-looking driver wearing a big black hood would collect more of it. He had dark windows throughout the back, but up front, the glass was smoke-tinted. Easy to see through.

That usually kept entanglements to a minimum.

He sent a glance through the rearview mirror toward his passenger. She had one eyebrow lifted, making a slight line on her forehead above it. That was cute. And something more. The expression highlighted her riveting light blue eyes. He was snagged momentarily by her gaze. Caught.

Shit.

That nuance hadn't been in the file. Kane looked back to the street. Even at this hour, Miami was awake. The place was alive with vehicles, noise, and humanity. He cleared his throat.

"You okay back there?" he asked.

She didn't answer. He brought the vehicle to a stop at an intersection and watched pedestrians for a moment. Must be too early for tourists. He scanned the conglomeration of humanity crossing in front of his bumper. Looked like a mix of inebriated ex-party-goers, homeless citizens, city workers, and street vendors. Nothing looked odd. Nobody paid particular attention to him. He looked at her through the mirror again. She had her other eyebrow up now. *Man!* He had to adjust his earlier assessment. She didn't just have riveting light blue eyes. She had really beautiful ones. Clear. Stunning.

He looked back out the front window. Swallowed. Debated donning driving gloves.

"LeeAnn?"

"How do you know my name?"

He flashed another glance at her before the light turned green. She'd narrowed her eyes. Driving claimed his attention for a moment. She waited.

"It came with the assignment."

"I'm an assignment?"

"You want to listen to music?"

The vehicle had a fully equipped stereo, usually set to a special frequency scanning mode. He fiddled with the control switch. Bach's *Suite No 1 in G major* started emanating from the speakers, filling the cabin with mellow strands of a master musician playing the cello.

"I don't want music. I want answers. Okay with you?"

"Yes. And no."

Kane wiped his hand down his thigh before turning the stereo down. He didn't turn it off. Background music helped with a lot of things. Like nervousness.

"No?"

"Didn't you hear me earlier? This is new territory for me."

"Tell me about it," she inserted.

"I'm unsure what to tell you. And how much."

"I'm just supposed to be docile and uninformed?"

"You're alive, aren't you?"

She didn't answer for a bit. Kane checked. She was frowning again. He looked back at the road.

"I want to know how you know my name."

"I'm not...a guardian angel. Exactly."

"Really? Well. I did have that suspicion," she replied.

Kane choked on a chuckle. That was another oddity. He was known as the humorless type. "You could say I'm more of a hunter."

"What do you hunt?"

He sucked in his cheeks, tipped his head, and debated options. When that didn't work, he settled with a shrug that lifted the hood to his ears before it dropped back.

"That's not an answer."

"I know. I'm working on it."

Kane checked her reflection in his rearview mirror again. Her lips twitched. She acted like she caught his glance before turning away, looking out her window. Sunlight was making a dent on the world. Dawn touched her face, highlighting all kinds of things. A slight pout to her full bottom lip. The shadow of long eyelashes. A rose shade that tinted her cheeks.

LeeAnn Schultz was a stunning woman.

Not good.

The complication of keeping her with him multiplied. Kane turned his attention back to the road. They'd reached the Overseas Highway. The freeway merge claimed his attention for a span. Even at this time of morning, there was traffic.

"You're a very careful driver."

"Bad driving can be a deciding factor in any situation. That's how they caught the serial killer, Ted Bundy. And Berkowitz. Nobody caught them with detective work. You sure you don't want to listen to music?"

The opening strains of Chopin's *Nocturne in B-flat minor* had just started up. Kane considered turning it up a little. Chopin was considered an operatic composer. A poet of the piano. This piece was one of his best. It might soothe the dismayed expression she'd just assumed as she'd jerked her head back to look at his reflection. And then she started wriggling about.

"Calm down back there. You're safe with me. I swear it."

"You just compared yourself to...serial killers!"

Her voice was shaking. At a slightly higher pitch than before. For some reason, that affected him.

"See? I have to watch what I tell you. And how much. I bring out that driving issues can change everything and look what happens? You react."

The leather continued to creak as she moved about.

"LeeAnn, listen! I was trying to explain that getting pulled over with a woman strapped into the back seat of my car would not be a good thing at the moment. It would create attention we don't need. Now, stop that. Or, I'll pull over and handle it."

She stilled instantly. Her eyes were huge. Kane cursed silently before looking back to the road. He was doing poorly already, and they had a long drive ahead.

"You need to calm down. Please. You're safe."

"I don't...feel safe."

Her voice shuddered. He sighed heavily. "I belong to an elite group. I can't tell you much, but trust me. I'm one of the good guys."

"Good guys don't break into hotel rooms. Nor do they kidnap people."

"They do if it will save lives. Or are you forgetting that?"

"How can I believe anything you say?"

"My...group monitors chatter. Somebody put out a hit on a LeeAnn Schultz. Arriving on Tuesday. 6 pm. I was given the assignment."

"I arrived on Wednesday morning."

"I know. Your flight was overbooked. You gave up your seat. I've been tracking you since before you landed at Miami/Dade International. I know every place you've been, everything you purchased, and what hotel you were staying at. And when they coded your room key, I even got your room number."

"No way."

"You know that little chip on your credit card? That isn't just for security. It collects and sends data every time you use it."

"You can hack that?"

"Pretty much. Especially since you kept using free Wi-Fi service."

"That's...unnerving. Is that how you got in my room? With a spare room key?"

"Nope. The rooms above yours were vacant. Told you it was a mistake to leave your drapes open."

"You climbed down from a balcony?"

"Three of them."

"At thirty-plus stories above the ground? I can't—no. This is too unbelievable."

"It gets worse."

"How?"

He sent a glance into the mirror toward her. She had her lips pursed. She didn't look frightened anymore. She looked young. Unsure. And cuter than—

He didn't dare quantify it. He could have sworn his heart just skipped a beat. That was illogical and ill-timed.

"Since I missed your would-be assassin, we got problems. I don't know who he is. What he looks like. Or when he'll strike again. All I know for sure is, he will."

The Chopin selection finished. Beethoven's *Symphony No 5* started up. That was a little too lively. Kane reached over and turned the stereo system off. Music hadn't worked at calming him, anyway. That was another oddity. He was unsettled. On edge. Extremely wary.

"Will what?"

"Strike again."

She gasped. He didn't have to see it. He heard it.

"Don't worry. First, he has to find you."

"So...I'm going into hiding?"

"That's the plan."

"Where?"

"The Keys. Safe house."

"Key West?"

"Close."

"Hmm. I've never been to Key West. Is it nice?"

"Yeah."

She was silent for so long, he had to check to see why. The sunlight had moved to his side of the vehicle, putting her in a shadow-land back there. She looked sleepy. She even yawned. His heart skipped another beat.

Uh oh.

This was bad. First he was engaging? And now getting interested?

She looked toward him and caught his glance. Kane immediately shifted it back to the road before realizing that idiocy. He wore dark glasses. She couldn't possibly see through them.

"What's your name?"

Kane sucked in his cheeks and tilted his head. That was a big one. He twisted his lips next. He had his orders. No entanglements. No names. No history. No trail.

"What? Is it a secret?"

"Yes. And no," he answered.

She yawned again. He had a hard time stopping the smile.

"Fine. I'll name you. You look like a Kane."

He wasn't prepared. He jerked slightly and sent a quick glance at her again. She was smiling. Sunlight was just touching her left side. She looked angelic. And wide awake.

"Is that it? Your name is Kane?"

He didn't answer. He'd thought she was sleepy. Another mistake. He was making way too many of those, in a very short time. Kane shrugged again. Toyed with turning the stereo back on. Shifted. His seat creaked in accompaniment. He reached for the climate control switch.

"You okay back there? Not too hot? Cold?"

"I'm fine."

"You thirsty?" he asked.

"Not unless you have coffee."

"Never touch the stuff."

"That figures."

"I've got cold water. Bottled."

"Thanks, but I can't get my hands free to drink it. You know what, Kane? I think I'll just try and take a little snooze back here. Maybe when I wake up, I'll be back in my hotel room, and this will have been a very strange dream. That okay with you?"

"Dream on, baby."

Oh.

Hell.

He did *not* just say that. Not in a thousand years. He wasn't just exhibiting slow wits. They appeared to be missing entirely. Kane's fingers tightened on the steering wheel, making the leather wrap rotate under his palm. Luckily, she didn't respond. A milepost passed. Another one. He sent a peek in the rearview mirror toward her.

She had her head tilted to the side. She looked asleep.

And she was smiling.

CHAPTER THREE

LeeAnn wasn't sleeping. Only stupid, insipid individuals would actually sleep at a time like this. She was vulnerable. With a complete stranger. And, even if it did appear as if he'd saved her, she was still at his mercy. Wearing little more than a nightgown. Sans her phone. Identification. Cash. Credit cards. She couldn't even prove who she was. The last thing she needed was to be unaware of her surroundings and how she got there. She'd read this plot too many times. She needed to keep her wits about her. Gain an accurate account of time. Distance. Check when the vehicle changed speeds. Make certain of turns. How many. Which direction.

The rising sun was mostly on the driver side now, so they were definitely heading south. She could just make out the dash clock. His arm blocked it for a moment, as he turned on his stereo again. Classical music surrounded her. She didn't know composers or tunes, but it was strangely soothing. Oddly comforting.

All bad.

And counterintuitive.

She didn't need or want comfort. She was in way over her head here, and didn't like the feeling. Her mind kept sending possible scenarios. Potential plans of action. A lot of truly frightening endings. She really could use some caffeine. She'd even take it cold. With carbonation. And a day's supply of sugar. She peeked occasionally out the window, checking for anything that could be a potential landmark. Looked like a lot of clear blue sky. A lot more ocean. And tons of sunlight. It was going to be a gorgeous hot, sunny day.

The sun sent a lot of warmth with its rays. The heat was like another layer of comfort. Soothing. Reassuring even as it cocooned. LeeAnn mentally shook herself. Slanted a glance toward Kane. She could just make out the back of his neck. She instantly had to stanch a whisper of reaction through her belly.

This wasn't good.

Then again, it couldn't just be her. The guy was beyond good looking...even if a tad overly alpha, a bit too masculine, and entirely too close-lipped and predatory. He was still gorgeous. He had the tall, dark, and handsome monikers covered.

In spades.

Really, LeeAnn. Stop. Just stop.

His jaw was really chiseled. The line was apparent beneath the slight shadow of black whiskers. She knew now that it matched his hair color. She'd been right with that assessment. His hair was definitely dark. More...coal black. Looked straight, but he wore it pulled back, which might exaggerate that quality. She couldn't tell the length. It wasn't short. The start of his queue was just visible before it disappeared beneath his clothing. A few strands slid down his neck.

He had a really thick neck, too.

Another shiver of something unbidden sliced through her, sending a layer of reaction in its wake. Entirely pleasant. And uncalled for. She didn't even like big, muscled guys. Now, that she thought of it, she didn't really know any. Kane looked wrestling-superstar fit. She'd never seen a guy as ripped. He had wide shoulders. Massive arms. The rest of him was probably a match. She didn't know why she even pondered that. He'd jogged down so many flights of stairs, carrying her hundred and thirty pounds that her head had grown dizzy. He hadn't even been breathing hard.

One thing was certain. She wasn't going to be able to fight him. Or outrun him. She'd have to rely on cunning.

Palm trees started showing up in her view. They'd left the highway? When had that happened? The vehicle geared down as he slowed. She heard him flip the turn signal lever.

What?

No.

It couldn't be. She'd actually slept? LeeAnn checked the dash clock. Blinked on the proof before her eyes. Sagged back into her seat with disgust. He made a couple of right turns. Sped up slightly.

Crap.

She was a complete failure at this covert stuff. She didn't know where they were. All she knew was over two hours had elapsed, and that only because of the dash clock. The palm trees gave way to privacy fencing – mostly white stone. Or stucco. She wasn't in the construction business so she didn't know. She'd had construction company clients. She knew their debits and credits. She didn't know a thing about their operations. They'd had a lot of them, actually. Her partner, Chad, was like a magnet when it came to businesses predominantly owned by guys. *Wait.* She needed to call him her ex-partner. It was probably his hand behind her assassination attempt. *Really, LeeAnn...who else could it be?* She didn't even know that much about him...except he was handsome, single, and charming. The background check had been clean. She should have dug deeper. Taken self-defense classes. Joined a gym. Bought a gun and learned how to use it.

All of which was not going to help a thing now.

The fence was connected intermittently with stacks of cemented stones. Very artistic. They were mostly light shades. A few gray ones here and there. Some pinkish toned. The vehicle slowed. Kane signaled. Turned. And stopped before a two-story arched gate. She heard the window retract.

"Leon," he said.

"Kane."

The man's reply sent a flush of pleasure through her. She'd been right on his name! Knowing she'd tagged him correctly almost offset her failure at everything else.

Almost.

They passed beneath a portico. The vehicle darkened. Bright sun flooded in as they came out the other side. And then it grew really dark as the vehicle drove into a cavernous space that might be a garage. They passed vehicle after vehicle, answering that question, before pulling into a spot. Her hands turned into icicles against the sides of her thighs. Alarm bells hit both ears.

He spent a lot of time putting the vehicle into park before turning it off. Unhooking his safety belt. Rearranging the rearview mirror. And then he turned swiftly toward her, surprising her. That wasn't fair. He didn't even take off his sunglasses.

"We're here," he told her.

Her eyes widened. Any words got caught in a ball at her throat.

"You ready?"

"For...what?"

That little, hesitant voice couldn't possibly be hers! *Ugh.* LeeAnn looked away. Checked out the roof of the classy-looking limo just outside her window. She used the time to collect herself mentally, but it was mostly a berating. She didn't have to just be a victim? She had to sound like one, too?

"I'm taking you inside now."

"Inside?" she asked the window glass.

"And you're not going to give me any trouble. We clear on that?"

What a farce. *Trouble?*

Her?

"I know you faked sleeping. You probably think you know exactly where we are. You may already have a plan of escape. I'm not amused. Okay? I'm the good guy here."

She caught the instant smile before looking back at him. He hadn't known she slept? Maybe she wasn't such a failure, after all.

"I've never brought anyone here...especially a woman. It may create some interest."

She choked.

"Actually, it will engender a lot of interest. Conjecture. Nothing I want to address. So, no screaming. No yelling. And no fighting me."

"I'm just supposed to be docile?"

"Would you rather be unconscious?"

One of his brows lifted above the sunglass frame as he asked it. Nothing else moved. On him. Her reaction was the opposite. Her eyes widened. Every limb went ice-cold, her belly dropped nauseatingly. Her heart stopped. And her breathing was right behind it, as if on cue, making an audible gasp.

He smiled. It didn't make him look more approachable.

"That's what I thought."

LeeAnn forced a breath as he just sat there, watching her. There wasn't a descriptor for how these shivers felt as they coursed her skin.

"We good, then?"

He waited for her nod before exiting. The vehicle rocked as he released it from the burden of his weight. Shut his door. It seemed like a moment later her side door opened. He reached across her lap, unfastened her belts, and wrapped an arm about her middle. She was hefted atop his shoulder again. Got a narrow view of polished floor. She didn't fight. She didn't struggle. She didn't make a sound.

He walked through the garage. A whir sounded as a door must have opened. Kane passed through it and she squinted as her vision got overwhelmed with artificial light. The floor turned into a span of light shaded tiles that matched the fence stones outside. Light gray. Off-white. Some pink. The room echoed with his steps. LeeAnn turned her head. Caught a glimpse of stainless steel. A lot of big kettles. Rows of what looked like marine gear. Lifejackets. SCUBA tanks. Spear guns. She couldn't see it all. They entered another space, this one dark. Carpeted. Muted. His steps didn't make much noise. He crossed another portal, and entered a space ablaze with sunlight. LeeAnn narrowed her eyes and tipped her head toward the source, and her jaw dropped. The wall was a solid span of big windows. At least two stories high. They showcased an outside swimming pool that was larger than her entire apartment. It was framed with lounge furniture. Palm trees. Rimmed by more of the privacy wall. And beyond that was a solid horizon of ocean.

Holy crap.

This wasn't a safe house. It was a mansion. The kind featured in stories about the rich and famous. Overpaid celebrities. Rock stars. Billionaires.

He entered an area with a cream colored floor. The walls matched. It was a rotunda. Round. Could be the entranceway. Kane didn't give her any time to decipher it. He was moving so rapidly, she felt queasy. Her head was starting to pound, too. And her abs hurt from contact with his shoulder. They reached a staircase. He began climbing, two steps at a time. Then a voice hailed him, stopping his progress.

"Kane! You're back."

"Rafael."

Kane spun. LeeAnn got a quick panorama of more sunlit windows attached to what looked like a second floor landing, leading to a lot more space. But the way she viewed it was sickening. She wasn't the motion-sick type, but this method of transportation was definitely testing it.

"What you got there?"

"Complication."

"Need any help?"

"No."

He turned back around. LeeAnn's head dropped to the middle of his back. *Leon? And now Rafael?* They had very interesting and unique names in this house. That was one thing she could list for the authorities.

"Wait." Kane spun back as he said it. His back vibrated with the word. LeeAnn swallowed.

"I need women's clothing."

"Any particular size? Type?"

"Just send Jezzie. She'll know."

Jezzie? The relief was palpable. Like a wash of cool water. It didn't help the pounding in LeeAnn's head, but it relieved the anxiety. She wasn't the lone woman here. But then the unseen Rafael had to go and ruin it.

"You sure you want her?"

"Yeah."

Kane spun and started mounting steps again. LeeAnn tried to focus and peek, checking for the man beneath them. It was useless. He was in the shadow thrown by the balustrade and Kane moved too quickly.

"Hope you know what you're doing, big guy."

Kane answered beneath his breath, altering the new-found relief with worry again. LeeAnn's eyes went wide and he probably felt her gasp.

"Me, too."

CHAPTER FOUR

Kane stepped out of the shower, grabbed a towel and ruffled his hair with an efficiency that nearly sent sparks. Dried the rest of his body with the same quick, almost-angered motions. Wrapped the towel about his hips, tying it with a bit more strength than he needed. His movements matched how he felt.

Exactly.

He was in what the others referred to as his black mood. Fighting inner demons. The kind that kept everyone away until it passed. Nobody knew what brought them on. He hadn't either. Before.

This time, he knew the cause.

LeeAnn Schultz.

He was suffering something very close to lust. LeeAnn was at the center of it. Causing heated sensations that sent fire licking at his thighs. Groin. Its heat stirred primal needs. Animalistic wants. His body acted as if a bellows were at work on it, sending oxygen to an already hot fire. Fueling a constant state of arousal. The erection distorting his towel was the proof. Impossible to hide. Readily apparent. The situation was really starting to anger. Frustrate.

Kane slicked his hair back with his hands, finger-combed it back into a tail again, and spent a couple of seconds looking for a strap before letting it go. Steam gradually dissipated, leaving him with a focused view of the room. Him. And his problem.

He snarled at his mirrored image before tipping his head to one side. He concentrated. The bathroom was like a space vacuum. Deathly quiet. No sound came from outside the door, though. No screams. No yelling. No alarms being sounded. LeeAnn must be behaving.

And Jezzie.

The woman's real name was Jezebel. In Hebrew it meant "not exalted." That pretty much explained Jezzie. She wasn't the type to go out of her way for anyone or anything. She liked causing trouble. She'd looked at him with a calculated gaze as he'd explained what he wanted. As if she sensed an attraction he didn't dare acknowledge. Seeing LeeAnn into attractive garments should be right up Jezzie's alley. She could set up a doomed situation and see what developed.

Kane's expression turned into a frown. In retrospect, he should have kept LeeAnn with him, despite how her proximity unsettled, and then challenged. He could have waited to shower. Shave. Change clothes.

Shit.

He was turning into a class-A dimwit here.

One with a testosterone problem.

He really shouldn't have sent for Jezebel, but the tall brunette looked the same size as LeeAnn. She should have something the girl could wear. Kane was guessing on LeeAnn's exact dimensions, but he figured she was about five-and-a-half feet tall. She weighed an easily-portable one-hundred, thirty-five. Maybe less. She was slim. She didn't make an unwieldy bundle even swathed in bedding.

The frown cleared slightly. He was overanalyzing this. Adding issues that might not even happen. Moreover, he wasn't a babysitter. Jezebel might be a manipulative and spite-filled woman, but LeeAnn had proven capable. She dealt with traumatic situations well, followed instructions, and had a quick mind. She could handle Jezzie.

Besides...they were only two doors away. Same floor. Kane leaned toward the mirror. Studied his eyes for several long moments before giving it up. Nothing had changed. And time was wasting. He needed to check on LeeAnn. Make sure she was clothed. Had eaten breakfast.

Kane smirked at his reflection before opening the door. He sure felt like a babysitter.

Air-conditioned air cooled the space immediately. The chill raised goose bumps on his skin and helped with his groin problem. Good thing. He'd set out above-the-knee swim trunks. Jammers. Spandex and PBT construction. They were fit exactly to his proportions. Created less drag...but they had other issues. They were going to show off a lot. He should've chosen loose-fit trunks. Then again...this misguided arousal was one-sided. LeeAnn hadn't acted remotely interested in him.

Kane cinched the waist with more strength than required, and then had to let some of the nylon cord out before stepping into wet-shoes. What the hell was he doing? Thinking? He didn't *want* LeeAnn interested in him! That was just more craziness this situation didn't need.

He grabbed his t-shirt as the phone rang. Land line. Kane yanked the receiver off the cradle with more strength than that required, too. He tightened his hand about it for a second or two before moving it to his ear.

"Kane? You there? It's Leon."

"Yeah."

"We have company."

"Description?"

"Police officers. Two. Unmarked car."

"Anybody have a warrant?"

"No."

"They say what they want?"

"They're saying you dinged a vehicle in a parking garage in Miami this morning. They have a picture of your front bumper. Mainly the license plate area. From the exit area. Pay stall. It's time stamped at...yep. This morning. A little after five. It's your vehicle, all right."

Oh, shit.

Hindsight was a real bitch. He wasn't just in unfamiliar territory. He was mucking everything up while there. He hadn't hit anything. LeeAnn had some major players on her ass. Moneyed. Connected. Fast. And smart. He should have waited in the parking garage! *Not* been the first vehicle to leave after a botched hit. Talk about painting a target on his back.

"Hit the silent alarm, Leon. Red alert."

"You'll be right down, then? Excellent, my man. We'll just break out the coffee while we wait," Leon replied. "Hey! I hope you two police officers won't mind if I turn my tunes back on, will you?"

Loud strains of rock music came clearly through the telephone receiver. The lights went out, diverting electricity to the perimeter. A humming sound started emanating from deep within the structure as gates went up. Spikes lifted next along the back perimeter walls. Kane tossed the phone onto the bed, along with the t-shirt. Snagged his 9mm from the nightstand drawer. Shoved it into the back of his trunks. Pushed a pair of sunglasses onto his face next. He didn't open his door. He slammed through it. Two doors down looked like a very long way. He smacked into her door with a shoulder, knocking it off hinges, as well. For nothing.

The space was empty.

Just like his head must be.

CHAPTER FIVE

Wow.

This was the life.

Too bad it wasn't hers.

LeeAnn closed her eyes. Soaked up rays. Floated aimlessly. She was out at the pool. She wasn't poolside. She was floating on it, atop an inflated lounger-thing. Sucking up this decadent lifestyle, even it if wasn't hers.

Then again, she could pretend that she belonged. Who would care? Not that Jezzie person. *Oh. Wait.* The woman preferred to be called Jezebel. That was the first thing she'd said after Kane set LeeAnn onto her feet, started unwrapping the sheet from about her, and then left the women together.

Oddly enough, LeeAnn had immediately missed him. Felt vulnerable. Unsure. And really leery. Jezebel wasn't much help. The woman didn't appear to have a bone in her body devoted to altruism or charity. The vibes coming off her had been positively chilly. She hadn't appeared pleased with the summons. Or LeeAnn. It felt weird being around someone who disliked her on sight. Then again, everything about this morning's events had that problem.

Complete weirdness.

Jezebel had the strangest eyes, too. So dark, they were almost black. Soulless-looking. LeeAnn had glanced at her once and then avoided it. Besides, somebody had ordered up a breakfast tray with all kinds of great-smelling and tasty-looking selections. She didn't know who. She didn't even know who'd brought it. And, wonder of wonders! They'd even included a carafe of coffee.

She could definitely get used to this lifestyle.

Some time ago, she and Chad had discussed what it would be like to live in the same manner as some of their clients. Surrounded by luxury. Not having to worry. Someone else around to handle everything. Mortgage issues. Utility payments. Student loan debt. Insurance. Chad had been the instigator of the conversations. He'd done spreadsheets and tacked them onto the office walls, each one devoted to a different strategy toward his goal. There was one for playing the stock market. Another for real estate investment. Another for the pricing structure with their clients. It had been his idea to use a sliding scale. If the client had big bucks, they got charged more.

LeeAnn had ceased arguing over it. Chad had control issues with women. It wasn't worth a blood pressure spike to argue with him. He charmed the socks off everyone he met. Nobody complained about their bill. And – she had to admit – the extra income was useful. She just wished they'd raised rates across the board. Made it fair. She'd thought of discussing that, but Chad was hard to pin down anymore. Come to think of it...they hadn't spoken for some time. She'd had to set up this morning's meeting via email. He'd moved out of Fall River. Given her a PO Box number to use for any business correspondence. She wasn't even sure *where* he lived.

She'd been so naïve!

She should have gone to the authorities the moment she noted the odd account fluctuations. That would have been the intelligent thing to do. But what had she done? Set up a breakfast meeting to discuss the problem. With a man who had this much to lose?

She might have to adjust her thinking here. Naivety was too nice of a word.

LeeAnn paddled slightly. The pool was immense. Shaped like a big, fat snake, wending its way about the backyard, or whatever they called this area. There was a shallow zone. The rest of the pool was pretty deep. She didn't know how deep, for certain. It wasn't marked on the sides or anything. Beautiful blue water. Perfect temperature. Just cool enough to soothe a sun-warmed body if she dove in. That might prove too much for the bikini Jezebel had brought her, however. LeeAnn might as well be wearing elastic bands. The top was so tight it restricted her breathing.

All of which was her fault.

Jezebel had asked her size while LeeAnn was shoving big bites of ham and cheese omelet into her mouth. The woman sounded snide as she'd correctly pegged LeeAnn as an eight. Stupidity had kicked in. LeeAnn had instantly stated that she wore a size six, thank you very much. This is what she'd reaped: A neon yellow bikini bound to make her skin look sallow, and bonus! Nothing came with a string tie she could let out. Or even a range of adjustments with clasps. She'd never shown off this much skin. But she wasn't letting Jezebel know that it bothered her.

Oh.

No way.

LeeAnn had just gone to the bathroom, tugged the suit on, made a face at her reflection, and then returned. Jezebel hadn't said a word as LeeAnn picked at the rest of her omelet, foregoing even a bite from the display of frosting-covered cinnamon rolls, or the strawberry-glazed crepes, the stack of sausage links. She hadn't touched the mouthwatering pile of bacon. She'd even passed on the perfectly toasted wheat bread.

She probably should have eaten more. Her belly rumbled as she thought it. Breakfast felt like hours ago, but it couldn't be.

This lazy lifestyle altered time or something. Slowed it to a crawl. Then again, she couldn't be sure. She didn't wear a watch. That's one thing she used her phone for. It couldn't be noon yet. The sun hadn't reached its highest point. Last check of the area revealed small shadows around the lounge furniture and the areas that contained foliage. Heat radiated from the ground, distorting the view slightly. She should probably go sit beside the pool. Find some shade.

And she would.

In a minute.

This just felt so damned sinful. Decadent. She yawned, and then shook herself. She daren't fall asleep! A slight bit of tan was one thing. A full-fledged sunburn something else. Her fingers trailed through the water as if she did this every day. And then an odd buzzing sound caught her attention. LeeAnn looked up, lifted a hand to shade her eyes, and checked. There were two small airborne things just above the palm-tree line. They flew side-by-side. Like little helicopters. And that was just cute.

Somebody played with remote-controlled toys around here?

"LeeAnn! Dive!"

What might be Kane came sprinting from the house. LeeAnn's jaw dropped. He was wearing sunglasses. His hair wasn't bound. It was straight and glossy and black. About mid-back length. She'd guessed he was fit, but she'd been way off. The guy was unbelievably ripped. And wearing way too little. She didn't even know the names of some of the muscles rippling beneath his tanned skin as he raced toward her.

"Get in the water!"

If he wanted to make sense, he needed to put some clothing on. She couldn't think. She couldn't even take it all in. LeeAnn sat up, drenching her butt and thighs as the raft thing bowed in the center. Kane wasn't paying any attention to her. He had a gun in one hand and was shooting toward the toy-things. While running?

The water started jumping as it got pebbled with projectiles. The float took a hit. Started whistling as air escaped. And that's when she knew what was happening. Someone was shooting at her!

With real bullets!

Shock made her clumsy. Shaky. None of which helped in a life-or-death situation. LeeAnn rolled off the deflating float while the water continually erupted about her. One of the helicopters exploded overhead. And then she watched, with wide, unblinking eyes, as Kane launched through the air in a distance-spanning dive.

LeeAnn sucked in a breath just before he slammed into her. His arrival shoved her several feet under the water, beneath the burst of bubbles at his entrance, down to where all kinds of white lines of foam were splicing through water. They were the bullet paths as they lost momentum in the water. For the span of a heartbeat, she watched the scene, recognizing that this looked exactly like what she'd seen in movies.

And then adrenaline kicked in.

She'd been above a deep section. It didn't feel deep enough. LeeAnn dove, steadily swimming down, not stopping until she reached the pool bottom. Kane hadn't followed. His legs were kicking from what looked like a long way above her as he maintained a position. What was he? Returning fire? That was ridiculous. Guns didn't fire underwater.

Did they?

The white foam lines stopped. Disappeared. LeeAnn let an air bubble out. Another followed. She swallowed next, holding air in, trying for time. Her ears popped. Her lungs were starting to burn. She knew she couldn't stay here much longer. And then Kane loomed out of the space at one side, grabbed her, and shot upward. Toward the surface.

And air. Sunlight. Life.

He lifted her above the waterline, and held her there so she could pull in air. As adrenaline waned, weakness took its place. Her arms and legs felt like limp spinach, and emotion sapped what was left of her strength. *Oh. Crap.* She refused to cry. There had to be a better emotion available. Easily grabbed. And there was. Red hot. Heated. Completely illogical.

Anger.

Kane surfaced beside her, sending a wake of water. Wet. Big. Black hair framed his face and shoulders. He was actually still wearing his sunglasses. And that was just full-out ridiculous.

"You okay?"

"No! I am not okay!"

He swam to the side, hauling her along. He might have been gentle. It didn't feel it. Her waist felt like a vise was around it. And then he pivoted, put both hands about her midriff and set her on her butt atop tile so sun-heated, the water off her bottom sizzled. But her only other option was the soles of her feet. LeeAnn jumped up, and started hopping about, trying like hell not to cry. One of the helicopter things had disintegrated, making a trail of blackened pieces about what had been pristine tile. She couldn't spot the other one.

"Now what?"

Kane loomed out of the water, and rose beside her. He didn't have any trouble with hot tile. Because he had wet-shoes on.

"I told you I'm not okay! Didn't you hear me?"

"You're yelling at me," he replied without inflection.

"Yeah? So?"

"You sound like you're fine."

Something exploded behind her, sending a palm frond onto a table. And when that collapsed, the entire thing hit the patio. LeeAnn squealed, leapt, and latched onto Kane's middle with both arms. And just stayed there, hugging him. She hadn't planned it, but her feet ended up atop his, and that was one really nice bonus to this embrace. He also felt pretty good. Stable. Warm. Muscled. Alive.

Correction.

He felt a lot better than just pretty good. Her entire front half was getting a full dose of hard male. Contact with him sent something major. Almost electrical. Her belly constricted. Her thighs tightened. Even her nipples got in on the act. She only hoped he couldn't feel them through this stupid bra top against his chest.

Kane cleared his throat. The sound echoed through his chest. "It's all right, LeeAnn. It's dead."

"What...were those things?"

"Drones."

"Someone is trying to kill me!"

"I know. I told you as much."

She shook her head. Lanky, wet strands of hair slid along her back and arms. "No, Kane! You don't understand! They're really trying to kill me!"

Crap. Crying was going to win the emotion battle after all.

"LeeAnn?"

His voice was low-toned. Softer than she'd ever heard it. Her eyes stung. She blinked rapidly, silently cursing tears that threatened. She held back a sniff, but her voice trembled when she answered.

"Y-yes?"

"You're not going to die. Not on my watch."

Oh, double crap. She'd sniffed.

"We have to leave. You ready?"

She nodded. And sniffed again.

"Oh. Hell."

His curse preceded hauling her atop one shoulder, before he started running. She sent a silent prayer of gratitude that she didn't have to face him! His actions said far more than words. She might be totally turned on by him, but it was obvious the feeling wasn't mutual.

Not by a long shot.

They reached the house, entered the rotunda/foyer area. A strange buzz was radiating throughout the rooms, all of them unoccupied. And every window had a bank of bars on the outside of it now. Those, she knew hadn't been there before. LeeAnn hung from his shoulder and tried to be invisible. Weightless. And if she could wish herself anywhere else, she would have.

It wasn't remotely as comfortable as holding to him, but at least he wouldn't feel the wayward tear she failed to prevent.

CHAPTER SIX

They reached the equipment room. It was just off the garage, past the kitchens, where a day's catch could be cleaned and packed. A row of generator-fueled, small blue lights delineated the ceiling. Walls. The door leading to the boat ramp. The lights were the extent of visibility. It was more than Kane needed. He bent forward and eased LeeAnn off his shoulder. Set her on her feet. Held her upper arm with one hand while she wobbled. And tried like hell not to notice how little she looked.

Little. Lost. Afraid.

And – heaven help him – she also looked womanly. Really, dream-worthy feminine. Curvy. Soft. Fascinating.

Damn that Jezzie.

No. Wait. This was his fault. He'd sent for the woman so she could clothe LeeAnn. He'd suspected what would happen. But how could he have known how torturous the reality would be? The bathing suit selected for LeeAnn was useless. Absolutely and completely. Especially when wet and under blue lights. He *did not* need the image of her form etched onto his eyeballs. Not right now.

What was he thinking?

This view wasn't ever on his list of needs. He needed to get her into a wetsuit. Covered. Neck-to-ankle.

"You okay?"

He grumbled the phrase. It was the best he could manage. LeeAnn nodded. She was squinting as she looked up at him. He lifted his hand away and stepped back, watching her waver momentarily. He forced another step away from her.

The woman was industrial-grade magnet.

And he was steel.

Kane snarled before whipping around. Grabbed the handle on a suit locker with a bit too much power. It broke in his hand, but the door had opened a slit. He stuck his fingers in and pulled, bending the metal open. She gasped behind him. Good thing she couldn't see what he did, but the sound was a good indicator. She probably ranked him a step above a Neanderthal. He told himself it didn't matter and reached inside, shuffled through a pile of suits, and chucked several into the room behind him.

"K-Kane?"

If her voice was any gauge, she was still shaky.

"Yeah, babe?"

Shit.

He really needed to cease calling her that.

"Um. How...can you see?" she asked.

"Don't need to. I'm familiar with the room."

The entire house rumbled warningly. The blue lights turned red. Steel doors started slamming into place throughout the home, moving with bone-crunching efficiency. Metallic sounds echoed about them for a moment. Kane's shoulders sagged slightly.

He was out of time. Covering her with a wetsuit just became a waste of precious seconds. He'd have to ignore the fact that she was so womanly and desirable. And then endure it. What a joke. His body was giving him trouble again. He sucked in his abs. Tightened the rest of his frame. Shuddered for a moment.

"What...was that?"

"Lock down."

There were two sets of tanks left in place on the bench, his and Leon's. The tanks were already connected to hoses, and nestled within Integrated Buoyancy Compensator vests. The gear was fitted to his exact specifications. Ready at a moment's notice.

Like now.

Kane sat and donned flippers with angered motions before sliding his arms through the armholes of his vest. A seam ripped somewhere. He stood, grunting slightly at the weight and bulk. His movements were quick. Effective. And harsh. Calming just slightly as he fitted his crotch straps. He maneuvered them between his legs gingerly, going around both sides of his problem, as if framing the area.

He scowled before standing fully upright. He had to stop and physically force a few seconds to pass before securing his gear. Get his emotion in check. His desire for LeeAnn was misplaced. Misguided. Supremely annoying. It messed with his abilities. Made him look and act slow-witted. And had a real impact on his movements. He needed to calm down. Project a certain demeanor. Experienced. Competent. Capable. Even if the situation was dire, he had a novice diver on his hands. The last thing they needed was panic.

The chest fastener pressed into his abs with each breath. The straps were like a caress to his groin. This wasn't normal. Everything felt erotic. He groaned softly. He needed to get into the water and hope the chill put a damper on this. Something needed to.

He took off his sunglasses. Secured them in the little pocket sewn into the waist of the jammers. Grabbed a defogger rag and swiped the inside of his facemask before pulling it on. And then he glanced in her direction. He could swear the floor rocked beneath them as he did so. He moved his gaze before something worse happened.

"I can hardly see you. What are you doing?"

"Getting into SCUBA gear."

"What? Oh, no. You're not—? We're not—? You can't possibly—? No."

"You still want to live, don't you?"

"Well, yes, but—"

"Then quit arguing."

"Please say you're joking."

"There is only one way out of here, LeeAnn."

"Why can't we take a vehicle?"

"Because we've been flushed."

"What?"

"Haven't you ever hunted?"

"No."

"Well. First you track your prey. And when you find them, you flush them out of hiding. Anything that moves is targeted. We can't take a vehicle. Or a boat."

"But, Kane—?"

"Look. Hon."

Damn his mouth! Another endearment?

He cleared his throat. Spoke at a lower octave. "Uh. The house was already on lock-down. The light change means the perimeter has been breached. Four guesses who it is. And the first three don't count."

"The guy after me?"

"Exactly. And he's good. I've got to give him that."

She moved back from him. What looked like fear stained her expression. He nearly swore aloud.

"I can't do this, Kane."

He took a deep breath. Selected a facemask from the spare rack. Swiped it with the defog rag before pocketing it, too. "Sure, you can."

"No, Kane. Please?"

"LeeAnn. You have somebody with major skills on your ass. He even used a diversionary tactic at the front gate to gain access. The guy is good. I mean, *really* good. That means I have to be a lot better than I have been. Starting now."

"But...this is insane! I didn't do anything. I'm a certified public accountant. I add and subtract numbers! Balance accounts! I live a boring life. In a landlocked state. I've never even been near the ocean until now!"

"You may be a paper-pusher, but you're also really good in a crunch. Calm and focused when you need to be. Extremely level-headed."

"I am?"

"Don't tell me nobody noticed before."

"Um. No." She shook her head.

"You were surrounded by morons. Come on. We're out of time. I'll help you."

Stupid idea, Kane. Really stupid.

He grabbed a set of tanks and approached her, working the IBC vest open as he neared. He stood above her. Inhaled. Then he looked down, trying not to notice she had some really sweet cleavage. The red-toned wash of light caressed one hell of a bosom. And it was right in his line of sight.

"Here." He placed the mask into one of her hands. Waited for her fingers to grasp it. "Put this on. I'll adjust it to your face."

He watched her hands flutter as she took it from him. "But, Kane! You don't know me! I am not calm and focused! I'm going to drown! I'll suck air in the wrong way, and—!"

"You'll be fine. I'll make sure of it. Okay? Now, listen up. The mask covers your nose. The only way to get air is through your mouth. You won't drown, babe."

Damn his mouth. He'd called her an endearment again. Failure made him tense. Edgy. And angered again. None of which helped. He was dealing with real desire here. He'd just have to accept that his body craved hers. Massively. And continually.

Then, he'd have to ignore it.

And not fail at that.

She was shaking. Kane sighed before bending down, leaning the tanks against his leg on the floor. He stood back up. Reached and took the mask from her fingers, and jerked away as the contact zapped. Sent sparks. And singed. He wondered if his hair was smoking. He looked up toward the ceiling, pulled in another deep breath, and dropped his vision back to the top of her head. She didn't balk as he worked the mask over her. Settled it into place. Cinched it tighter. Bent down to check her eyes through the goggles. She was squinting at him.

"Now. Just remember to let the air out completely before pulling another breath in."

"Do what?"

She sounded really cute with her nose pinched. He couldn't help smiling, but sobered almost instantly as her eyes widened. She had some really gorgeous light blue eyes. And he really needed to keep his mind clear. He moved his glance to a wall. Cleared his throat again. It didn't help. Nothing much did.

"We need to focus on the objective here. We're going underwater. It's a whole different realm. You'll need to breathe slowly. Make sure you exhale completely before inhaling again. Your regulator will handle it. I'm putting your tanks on now. You ready?"

"No," she replied.

He smirked, bent to pick her gear up, and got a very good view of her legs while down there. And damn! The woman had some shapely legs, too.

It figured.

Kane stayed bent over for longer than necessary, his hands gripped about the tanks while he struggled with all kinds of things. He was making way too many mistakes already, starting with letting her would-be assassin get this close in the first place. And here he was wasting what precious time they had. But, everything in his body was working against him! He was up against a red-hot feeling of need he'd never felt before. He hadn't even known it existed. Ignoring the sensation wasn't working. Fighting against it was useless. And she was wearing such a tiny, provocative bikini!

The jammers swim trunks weren't going to hide this.

"Um. Kane?"

Her voice was added torment. He tensed. The tanks clanked together in his hands. She sounded more scared than before. That was probably his fault.

What was he thinking?

It *was* his fault.

"Yeah?" Now, he sounded like he was talking around a mouthful of pebbles. This couldn't get much worse. "Just checking the oxygen level." He fiddled with the knob as though adjusting it.

"Is everything...okay?"

"Yeah," he lied.

He stood. Stepped behind her and assisted her into the gear. And had to hold her upright as the weight made her sway.

"K-Kane?"

Great.

She sounded scared. He was going to have to do this in the missionary position.

Worse and worse.

He moved around to face her, holding her upright as he did so. He debated trying to get flippers on her, but she'd probably fall over if he let go. He shook his head. Frowned.

"Looks like we're going to have to do this buddy-style, LeeAnn. You okay with that?"

"How is that?"

Dang! She sounded so cute with her nose pinched! "I'll swim. You hold my vest. It's just like sky-diving the first time."

Her eyes went enormous.

"Don't tell me you never did that, either. Well. You lived a really adventurous life, didn't you?"

She straightened. "I read! A lot. Okay?"

He almost smiled. Not only at the words, but how they sounded with her nasally voice. A large bang against steel came from somewhere in the home. Kane sobered instantly.

"Put your regulator on, sweets. It's time to go!"

"My what?"

He adjusted the hose at her mouth. Waited for her to take a breath. He put his regulator into place. Then he picked her up. She immediately wrapped her legs about his hips, which was perfect for stability and balance, but wreaked hell on concentration. Kane yanked every muscle tight, held her against him with one arm, and started moving, lifting each leg high due to his flippers.

Sunlight bombarded his eyes before they reached the dock. Walked past two speedboats, and a trawler. Nothing with a lot of draft. The big boats were out in deep water. Just out of sight. Within easy underwater swim distance...if he was solo.

He started down the ramp doing his best to ignore the signals firing from his loins. They pulsed down his legs. Through his belly. Into his chest. Down his arms. Existence had become a living hell. Fire. Brimstone. There was too much contact happening. He could swear he felt skin. His every pore was alert. Primed.

And he had to swim this way?

Kane tightened his jaw. Clenched his teeth together. He didn't look down. He didn't dare. He was using every muscle he had to keep from lunging against her.

They were waist deep in ocean water before she reached for his vest.

CHAPTER SEVEN

An assassin's bullet wasn't going to be the death of her. Embarrassment had first shot. Mortification. LeeAnn tried to keep from looking and acting like they were in a lover's embrace. She did her absolute damnedest. But her body wasn't listening. She had her legs hooked about his waist. His groin pressed to hers. They weren't wearing enough to counteract the sensations as he walked.

And worse.

Or better.

Kane was very well-endowed.

The bright Florida sunshine made her squint. It was exceptionally invasive when coming from a darkened windowless room. Rays caressed and bounced off the span of ocean visible over his shoulder. She kept her gaze glued to that vista. Tried ignoring things. Mentally shifted her focus. Concentrated. Hard.

Harder.

Why...if she was home right now she'd be at the office. Waiting for the coffee to finish brewing another pot. Or, she'd be inputting all kinds of receipts into spreadsheets for clients. She might be scanning the physical receipts Mister Peterson had sent via courier. And that, only *after* he made a photocopy for his records. Martin Peterson wasn't just set in his ways. He was a dinosaur. He refused to scan anything into a program that would send digitally to her. So, she did it for him, without telling him. She didn't even charge him extra...

Cool water lapped at her thighs, taking her back to the present. The chill should have altered things. Stopped this predicament. Helped alleviate things. And...*damn everything!* Her first thought wasn't of an assassin and the threat of death looming over her.

Oh, no.

That would be too sane.

Sensations engulfed her, every one of them linked to the man carrying her. This embrace. How amazing it felt. Thoughts of numbers and coffee and querulous old clients were outgunned. Instantly obliterated. And there wasn't anything she could do to stop it.

Kane wielded massive doses of stimulation. They fired at her with each step he took. She'd never been up against anything like this. It trumped everything she tried. She already had her thigh muscles so taut, the muscles were starting to burn. And that almost didn't work. Every impulse was to move against his hard-on. Rub where she needed it most.

And here she'd thought him cold. Curt.

Completely uninterested.

Water closed over her head. Her initial gasp brought a blast of oxygen. Kane's arm tightened and he moved his head as if to check on her. LeeAnn forced her mind to work again. She wasn't going to be a problem. She refused. She detested people who needed help all the time. What had the instructions been again? Exhale completely before inhaling?

He went deeper. Sunlight glinted on all kinds of things as it diffused. Her ears popped. The water was incredibly blue. Clear. She caught a flash as yards in the distance something moved. Like a fish.

Oh. Sweet.

She was underwater!

She felt faint for a moment. He must have known, for he'd stopped. Bubbles obscured her vision and her hearing. They didn't come from her. LeeAnn watched them dissipate before she exhaled, listening to the sound of bubbles gurgling. She made certain to empty her lungs before taking another breath. That sound was a hiss. She watched and listened to his bubbles again as he exhaled. Then she heard all kinds of other sounds. Pings. Clicks. Long, drawn-out notes that were almost musical. All kinds of humming sounds that might be from motorized craft. Or pumps. And the occasional splashing of waves.

What was this?

She'd thought the only audible things might be her breathing. Maybe her heartbeat. That was wrong. The ocean was alive with sounds. Sights. Another flash of something occurred in the distance. LeeAnn watched it, wondered at its origin, and didn't even concentrate on exhaling completely. Her next breath was almost natural. She was very proud of herself.

Kane must have sensed it because he started moving again. He stretched out. Released his arm from about her, and then – heaven help her – he started swimming!

Oh.

My.

LeeAnn's eyes widened. Each arm lunge shoved his chest into hers, while his kicking motion did all kinds of destruction everywhere else. His groin grazed against hers repeatedly. Rubbed. All kinds of things happened. No amount of mental concentration worked. His kicks grew stronger. So did his arm motions. LeeAnn eased her ankles apart. Maybe she'd be better off dangling from him, rather than hooked in place, barely suppressing an orgasm.

She let go of him with her legs, and immediately felt the pull on her fingers as water tried to suck them apart. He grabbed her again, handling swimming motions with just one arm. That was her fault. She was already a burden. She needn't handicap him, too. LeeAnn slid her arms into his vest, bringing her a lot closer to his chest, where her nipples got all kinds of stimulation.

Worse and worse.

Or better.

Depended on her viewpoint, but her move must have been the correct one, for he let go of her. Checked his watch, turned slightly to the left, and then started swimming again. Her ears popped again. She looked up, through the water. They must not be deep. Not that she had any clue, but she could easily spot the sun. Looked like it was noon. The sun was directly overhead. She chanced a glance to Kane. He had his cheeks sucked in, but nothing else looked different.

This position was actually manageable. It didn't require much effort on her part, other than ignoring how her nipples itched and irritated. But that was legions better than the full-on male-to-female contact she'd initiated originally.

Besides...

Kane might not be human.

The thought was fantastical. Unbelievable. Insane. But maybe – just maybe – Kane was something like he'd said. He really could be a guardian angel. And they actually came as gorgeous guys. Big. Muscled. Beyond masculine, if there was such a category. All kinds of capable. Why...if Kane hadn't been at her side, she'd have died hours ago. Her life would have been snuffed out. *Finis.* Nothing ahead but a dirt nap.

But...if he was her guardian angel...?

Oh. No. She wasn't really thinking that. *No, LeeAnn.* Impossible.

LeeAnn had no grasp of time, but it felt like they'd been swimming hours, the sun had definitely moved from its zenith, and Kane never seemed to tire. He never even slowed except to check his wristwatch. Kane couldn't possibly be an angelic entity. The man was a machine.

Oh. Wait.

Maybe he was human. He was slowing down. She tipped her head back and looked at why. A span of darkness loomed before them. Any sandy bottom had disappeared. The bottom looked like a big dark abyss. It didn't look like they'd gone much deeper. Her ears hadn't popped but once more, but they were definitely offshore. In really deep water. In the midst of all that darkness was a flashing light. Kane headed for it. As they neared, she got a better view. It was a thick line, dangling down from what looked like the bottom of a large ship. Right above them. Kane had found a ship in the middle of the ocean?

How was that even possible?

Kane grabbed the rope, did something that stopped the flashes and then started climbing. His legs bumped into hers more than once. LeeAnn went with nature and wrapped her legs about him again, only this time it was even more intimate. She didn't pull her forearms out of his vest. She cinched her legs and held on. She couldn't help noticing that any hint of an erection was missing. And she mentally chided herself for even checking. She wasn't just being a burden and a victim here...she had to be a voyeur, too?

Ugh.

She was just adjusting to that bit of embarrassment when he reached a ladder, grabbed the bottom rung and started hauling them up it. His weight. Hers. And their combined SCUBA gear. She didn't know what all of that weighed, but his display of strength was mind-boggling especially when they came out from the water. All kinds of heat, light, and noise assailed her senses. But above all that was the sensation of being attached to Kane as he moved. Muscles rippled beneath skin. Water ran down him in rivulets that glistened. Locks of shiny black hair framed his shoulders. They reached the top of the ladder. Kane flung a leg out and straddled a ledge. It was wooden. Sun-heated. Her butt got a full dose of both as she settled atop it as well. She should let him go. Move back. She knew she should. He plucked his regulator from his mouth with one hand, while the other messed about at his waist. His knuckles touched her inner thigh more than once. More erotic sensations hit her. And with those came the embarrassment again.

He had to be human.

He sure felt it.

He pushed a cheek out with his tongue as he looked down at his hand, unfolded what he'd been after, and then turned away. She watched silently as he pulled the facemask off and put sunglasses on. He'd been after those?

Well.

Maybe he was feeling some of this, too.

Kane turned and caught her looking. Her heart swooped to the pit of her belly. It started pounding from there, sending all kinds of tingling to just about everywhere. He lifted his eyebrows above the lens frame.

"You can take the regulator off now," he said.

CHAPTER EIGHT

Kane watched LeeAnn remove her mouthpiece. She was quaking. Visibly. He frowned. Reached for the clasp at his chest.

"We have to get out of the open," he informed her.

"O-o-okay."

She was definitely shaking. Despite the sun pumping heat onto the deck. He ripped the fastener open, loosening the crotch straps. The instant release of pressure from between his legs was a welcome change. She didn't move.

"We'll need to get out of our gear first."

She nodded.

Kane unzipped his BCD vest, and would have shrugged everything off except her forearms were still latched in place at his upper abdomen.

"LeeAnn. You're going to have to release me."

"Oh."

She flashed a glance up at him. Sunlight touched the light blue of her eyes for the barest instant. That was enough. The testosterone overload he'd experienced earlier came back with a surge. Intent. Powerful. And visual. It brought something else with it this time. Something that lanced his throat. Speared his chest. Grabbed his heart. Made everything in his chest tight. Pressurized. It was almost painful. His ears even hummed. This was massive. Incredibly special. He'd never felt anything like it.

Ever.

This couldn't possibly be...?

Oh. No way, Kane. Fall back, man. Regroup.

This couldn't be...love? There was no such thing. Love was a fictitious emotion. A wayward fantasy dreamed up by poets. A bit of fluff that marketers used to get advertising dollars. It was an ephemeral spark to passionate encounters.

Nothing more.

If this was love, it wasn't anything like he'd envisioned. Or heard described. He actually felt like he'd been fused to the spot, instantly alert and aware and afire. Fine-tuned to her every nuance. It was too unbelievable.

And wrong.

Love was *not* on the agenda.

Kane watched with wide eyes as she looked away from him, squinting out at the waves. Two spots of color appeared on the tops of her cheeks. She pulled her cheeks in next, which put her lips in a kissable-looking pout. She was pretty damned adorable. He shook his head slightly. He needed to put his gears in neutral. Clear his head. Regain equilibrium.

Nothing worked. If anything, she just looked more endearing. He nearly grinned. *Oh, man.* This was insane. The timing was horrible.

"Um. Sorry."

The mumbled word accompanied her movements. She pulled her arms out first before releasing her legs from about his hips. She probably would have scooted back if she'd had any way to get her feet between them.

"LeeAnn?"

His voice was a croak. He was surprised it worked. He pushed back from her enough he could shrug his tanks and vest off. He slung the bundle down to the deck, making a thud as it settled. Then he reached out to snag her zipper-pull. It slid open down her belly, revealing an itsy-bitsy bikini top and perfect cleavage that looked a little pink, like it might have had a touch too much sun. The vest opened with an erotic gesture. His dick immediately got involved. Kane lifted one leg, shielding his lack of control. And then she glanced up toward him again.

Oh. Man.

Eye contact sent another electrocution-level surge through him. Kane sucked in a big gulp of air, held it for long moments as his heart pounded in heavy beats. His cheeks puffed out as he released the air slowly. He probably glowed. Well. That made it official.

He was hooked.

Caught.

And reeled in.

"Kane?"

"Pull your arms out, babe."

The endearment slid off his tongue automatically. It was instinctive. Perfect. He no longer chided himself. She was his babe. And so much more. And he really needed to get her out of here.

"LeeAnn. Focus, hon. We gotta move. It would normally be safer for you out here. In the sunlight."

"Normally?"

She pulled her arms out. He slung her gear over his shoulder and dropped it beside his. And then he swiveled. Sideways. Her legs fell away. That felt odd. Almost bereft. Kane yanked a flipper off. Then, the other.

"I don't know what kind of resources we're dealing with."

"What?"

He slanted a look toward her. "Hunters do several things if their prey escapes. They hunt it down. Widen the circle. Get it?"

She shook her head.

"We didn't leave any tracks. So...we're either hiding in the house somewhere...or we went underwater. Option two means we'll surface somewhere. Within a certain radius. We already know he has access to drone technology. He might have satellite capability, too. Come on." He stood, shielded his crotch as if adjusting his jammers with one hand, while holding the other out to her.

"Where are we going?"

"Showers. Inside. Salt water dries the skin. It also itches. Come on. Give me your hand, babe."

She gave him her hand. He pulled her to her feet and she instantly hopped atop his discarded flippers. *Oh. Man.* He was lousy at this. He wore wet-shoes. The deck radiated heat. Sun-hot. Burning level. That meant he had to carry her. Again. And why on earth was that bothersome?

She must have sensed his reticence. And misdiagnosed it.

"I...can run. I think. Which way?"

He had her in his arms before she finished. The stupidity of it amazed him. He should have slung her over his shoulder. Like before. Because this move placed her way too close. Right against his abs. Chest. Shoulders. Everything was getting blasted with a series of charges. Carrying heat. Electricity. All kinds of energy. Power.

Kane gritted his teeth. Tightened every muscle. The move lifted her as his arms responded. And then she tucked her nose into the juncture between his shoulder and neck.

Oh. Hell.

Kane moved, charging with swift steps along the bulkhead. Ducked beneath an overhead. Found a hatch. He jostled LeeAnn's knees, using his left hand to lift the handle. Then he spun, bent forward slightly, and hit the hatch with his backside. The door flew open, smacking against an inner bulkhead with a thud that reverberated.

He needed to ease off the throttle here. Get a grip on his emotions rather than just her body.

Oh, man. Bad time to bring that up.

Kane stepped in, turned, and closed the watertight hatch by dogging it down. Everything was secure again. Except his emotions. LeeAnn didn't seem to be breathing. He made up for it. Kane took another deep breath. Held it for a long moment. And then he started moving again.

They'd entered a large cabin, lined with all kinds of aquatic equipment. Life vests. SCUBA tanks. Buoyancy control devices. Flippers. All of it a reminder. He needed to get their gear off the deck. Out of sight.

"Um. Kane?"

The whisper of her breath was an instant dart heading right for his heart. It affected his balance. Kane stumbled. Caught it before he banged into something. He almost cursed. And finally managed to answer. It was a guttural sound.

"Yeah?"

"I'm not—? I mean, we're not—?"

He entered a passageway. It got lighter. The air grew moist. Warmer. Almost muggy. Dual doors of etched frosted glass came into view. They led to the showers. The doors opened automatically. *Good thing.* He didn't know if he could adjust her weight again to open a door. Not without doing something stupid.

Like kissing her.

A wall of cool air surrounded them. Nothing noticeable. The lights came on next. Motion activated. They were set to a dim level. Cast a muted yellow glow about the area. Everything in this environment was serene. Peaceful. Tranquil. When he needed something intense. Something viciously cold and massively bright. So it could temper some of the nuclear-level fission. Cool things down. He only wished he could set the shower temperature to full-out, icy cold.

But, not here. All he'd get was a pleasantly warm spray of water. Nothing below 79 degrees Fahrenheit. Just like always.

"I mean...um."

Her voice dribbled off. She pushed her forehead farther into his shoulder, and shook her head, adding to her assault. *It figured.* Maybe she didn't suspect the trouble he had dealing with the touch of breath that accompanied her every word, and that's why she closed in. Not much else made sense.

"You gonna finish that, or leave me guessing?"

He asked it as he smacked the door switch, cancelling power to the portal. It was better than a lock. It would cause delay and give advance warning. They neared the communal showers. Four bays. Separated by frosted glass. Equipped with white painted, wooden stools. They matched the color of pristine cotton towels folded and ready in stacks at the stall edges, as if framing the spaces. Each shower stall held dispensers of potions. Soaps for cleaning. Gels for conditioning. Lotions for lubricating...

Oh. No.

He did *not* just think that! He didn't need images like that in his head! Wasn't the physical reality of holding her enough?

"Am I...showering with you?"

Kane stopped with such a quick motion they rocked forward before he could prevent it. His wet-shoes stuck in place on the tiles, keeping him upright. But nothing stopped the swell of sensation that overtook him. A solid wave of it hit his chest. Belly. And then his groin. He looked down at her head. Back at the shower stalls. And wondered when – exactly – he'd lost control of the situation so completely. He wasn't just dealing with massive lust. Want. Need. And gut-clenching desire.

He was orchestrating it.

In hindsight, he realized he should have set her down already. Ceased physical contact. The moment they'd reached shade. The soles of her feet would've been safe.

So would he.

"Yes. And no," he finally answered.

She lifted her head. She might have glanced toward him. He didn't check. He was in a realm of suspended motion, while pretending to regard the row of stalls facing them. She craned her neck, turning away to look over exactly what he was. And that just put her perfect bosom on display! Despite the idiocy of it, Kane glanced down. One breast was getting smashed and lifted by contact with him. The other was barely held in check by her little bikini bra. As he watched, the pink tone of her skin went darker. She turned back to him, but didn't look up. She was focused on the approximate area of his upper chest.

"Oh. Geez. I am so sorry," she whispered.

"You have to do something for me, LeeAnn. Okay?"

"I don't know what got into me."

"Don't move. Okay? Don't even twitch."

"Kane. Um—."

"I'm about to do something really stupid. Ill-advised. And dangerous."

She lifted her gaze to his. Making eye contact with her was a huge mistake. Even through his dark lenses. The connection sent a swell of sound through his ears while a bolt of electricity shot through him, singeing skin the entire way.

'What?'

Her mouth made the gesture. She may have said it. He didn't hear anything except a long, drawn-out, perfectly pitched note. He couldn't think. He just stood there, vibrating with the effort of keeping everything checked. Held in place. Locked.

Her eyebrow lifted as she waited. And Kane replied with something his mind hadn't cleared.

"I am going to kiss you."

She gasped. Her lips curved slightly in a smile. Despite the hold he exerted everywhere, he almost returned it.

"You are?" she asked.

He licked his lips. "Yeah."

Oh. Shit.

She moved.

CHAPTER NINE

LeeAnn leaned upward while her thighs tensed against his arm. She'd had one arm about his shoulders. She used it now with debilitating effect. Her fingers tightened on his skin. Her other hand reached up, and, before he could stop her, she pulled his sunglasses off.

That was beyond risky. Kane immediately squinted against the barrage of light.

"Well. That answers *that* question."

She carried TNT with the words. The level of peril was beyond what she'd wielded with every breath. Kane's knees wavered warningly. He wrenched his thigh muscles tighter. Pulled in a breath that shuddered. Prepared an explanation.

"Lee...Ann?"

He said her name. He knew he did. The vibration went through his throat. He didn't hear a damn bit of it.

"You are beyond gorgeous."

Oh.

He heard that.

The awe in her voice triggered all kinds of reaction. As if someone had lit a fuse. He could sense it sizzling somewhere near. He could almost smell the black powder wrapped around the inner string as it burned...nearing combustion.

"I suppose you already know it. That's why you wear these all the time."

She gestured with his glasses and then dropped them. He didn't notice or care. She was too close! Her mouth near his. The last of her words were whispered against his lips, cursing him with another hint of breath. Kane held his. Her lips touched...

And a shaft of brilliance went through his chest. Sheer blissful pleasure.

And absolute wonder.

If he hadn't recognized what emotion he felt for her already, the kiss would have done it. Kane slammed his eyes shut, barely catching an arc of light that flashed through the showers. He could still see it behind closed lids, though. He could swear he watched it intensify, before spewing a blizzard of sparks that flared and then dissipated.

She moaned. Moved her lips. Each touch carried life. Passionate regeneration. And every kind of intensity. He couldn't get enough, despite trying. Groans erupted from him as he plundered her mouth. Met each and every caress she sent. Throbs of baritone filled the room accompanying her higher-pitched moans. The sounds blended. Became a physical force.

It overwhelmed.

And then it shattered.

There was little means of controlling anything, despite his strength. Not against this much power. Energy. Voracious hunger. And an insatiable level of need.

The shower stalls were cool to the touch. Or he was on fire. Kane's back slammed into one. He heard it crack. It didn't matter, either. Nothing did, except her lips. This kiss. And the amazement of sensation that came with it.

The automatic shower turned on.

The water temperature should be pleasantly warm. It felt anything but. It was hot enough to cause steam and alter reality. Rivulets streamed over his head, across his shoulders, down his back, affecting his ability to breathe. He didn't much miss it. Her kiss was too precious. This connection beyond value. He'd never dealt with anything so wondrous. It was light. Power. Paradise.

It was her move that broke their kiss. LeeAnn pushed from him, arching back to pull in a long breath. That just put her perfect breasts beneath the water. Kane watched, fascinated as the yellow bikini got saturated again. Little nipples from each breast tip puckered the fabric. He turned the spigot toward the wall, and when that didn't feel sufficient, turned sideways in order to block the water with his back. All so he could lift her. Bend forward. Shove material out of his way. Nuzzle her nubs. Lick. And then suckle.

Her flurry of gasps filled his ears. They became cries. Almost screams. Each one sent a flash of something roaring through his veins. It was huge. Heated. And as necessary as air. It was nearly uncontainable. Every limb trembled warningly. Kane lifted away from her bosom and locked his arms before he dropped her. Narrowed his eyes as she looked down at him. Met her gaze. Got struck by something electrifying. And that did it.

He fell.

The stool took the brunt of it, wood creaking ominously as his rear smacked onto the flat surface. His swim trunks flexed, but not enough. His balls got pinched. His erection smashed. Pain got mixed with pleasure as she jolted to a stop atop his bent thighs. And then her breasts *bounced.*

Kane shoved his head back, knocked it against the stall, and sent a roar into the space. He didn't stop until he ran out of air. And then he sucked in another breath and did it again. It didn't help. If anything, it made things worse. He brought his head back down. Glared across at her. Sent harsh breath after harsh breath her way. Her eyes were wide. So was her mouth. He was still blocking most of the water, although some of it splashed off his shoulders and neck and onto her skin. It gathered in little pools so it could drizzle down her perfection. Drip off her nipples. Reach him. And each one felt like it carried fire. Especially when they touched his groin.

'Wow.'

She mouthed the word, and then she ran her hands down her torso. To her hips. She linked her thumbs under the sides of her bikini bottoms and ran her hands backward and then forward, reaching the little triangle of fabric covering her front. Her motion sent things from pleasure/pain to an excruciating level. And then made it hover there.

"What do you think? Like what you see?"

Kane's answer was a growl that grew in volume. She flicked her tongue out onto her upper lip. Lifted her eyebrow. And flashed a glance down to where the jammers were contorted and stretched. Back up to his eyes. And then she smiled.

"Want to see more?" she asked.

"*Yeah.*"

He should have growled that reply, too. The guttural word sounded like a beast being tortured. It sent shivers through him. His tone affected her, as well. He watched little bumps form on her skin. Race her body. They tightened her nipples into even tighter, smaller peaks. A tremor shook him next, rattling the stool, and sending all kinds of clacking sounds through the shower stall.

She pushed off him. Stood. He watched with baited breath as she slid the bikini bottoms down her legs, bending forward to free her ankles. Her golden hair was saturated with water, making it an indeterminate dark shade. She didn't wear it much longer than her shoulders. That was way too long at the moment. Kane bit back any reaction at being momentarily blocked from the view. And then she bent her head enough to look across at him. Locked gazes. And winked.

Kane jerked. The stool tipped before re-righting beneath him. And she smiled as if it was funny.

"Well...I want to see more, too," she told him.

His ears got an instantaneous buzzing noise. He shook his head to clear it. She mistook the move. And him. And sounded especially hesitant.

"N-no?"

He shoved upward, sliding his shoulders along the wall, leaning back just enough to get his thumbs beneath his waistband. The move gained shower spray onto his chest and belly that splashed outward, misting the scene. The jammers were doing their job a bit too well. They were supposed to stay in place. Keep drag from slowing him down when he swam. Now, that asset was beyond irritating. It was enraging. He ripped the fly apart. Yanked the waistband open. The damn trunks might as well be glued into place. The material went inside-out as he peeled it down.

And.

Finally.

His erection sprang free.

The relief was palpable. She made a sound. He sent a glance her way. Her hands covered her mouth, and her eyes were especially wide. Intensely blue, even through the haze of vapor between them. He didn't know what her expression meant. She could be awed and impressed.

Or frightened.

Kane looked down to finish disrobing. He shoved the trunks down his thighs with brutal moves. Shimmied them off his knees. They fell to his ankles. A kick sent the garment sailing out into the shower room. And then, he steeled himself. Wrenched every muscle. Shook in place as his body obeyed. All so he could look toward her again. Withstand something beyond containment. Somehow be gentle and lover-like. When everything wanted to pounce. Grab.

Maul.

He probably resembled an enraged beast.

Exactly like he felt.

The shower wall vibrated along with him. He leaned farther into it, making the frosted glass support him. The move put everything on prominent display. As if he did it purposely. And he wasn't a small man. Anywhere.

"Are you...for real?"

The words were barely audible. Kane glanced at her again. Then down.

"Last I checked."

"Oh. Wow."

A portion of him registered that she didn't sound frightened. She sounded pretty damned impressed. He would have grinned, if he wasn't holding so tightly to everything, his body pulled taut like a finely tuned bowstring. Armed and ready to fire.

"Oh. My."

He watched her reach for him. Felt the connection of her fingers with his abs, and despite the impossibility of it, he pulled them tighter. Bowed backward even more. Launched a low-pitched, agonized-sounding reply into the space.

"Sit."

He dropped. It wasn't graceful. It probably should have hurt. The stool shuddered beneath his ass, but held. But he didn't care. Or feel anything attached to his drop. His eyes widened and his mouth followed. Because she lifted a perfectly curved leg and put it over him. Straddling him. Her fingers wrapped about his dick. Positioned him. And then she lowered her body onto his. All while cooing the sweetest sound in existence.

Kane arched backward, lifting to meet her move. Steam-laden water misted the scene. It upped the moist pleasure that belonged just to this. Her body sucked him in. Caressing. Melding. Massaging every inch as she slowly lowered into place. And then she was there! She gave a soft cry as she engulfed him. Joining her body with his. Fully. Completely.

LeeAnn looked toward him. Her eyelids lowered seductively. That look sent a tremor in its wake. The stool shuddered in concert.

And then she started back up.

Kane grabbed her waist before she got very far. His hands shook as his fingers clamped tight about her. And, he didn't know how he managed it, but somehow he got his fingers to ease up. Changed his grip to one of guidance, rather than direction. Assistance-giving, not control oriented. Helping her strokes...rather than dictating them.

Again.

And again.

Hot, tight coils of pleasure surrounded him. They gripped so tightly, squeezed so pleasurably, held him in a grasp of wet satin. Every move she made toyed and prolonged. And added. No. It multiplied. Her movements sped up. Her breathing became more strident. Kane tightened his grip and used it to pump her. Up. Back down. Each thrust going deeper. Harder. Carrying more power, his efforts assisted and enhanced by the continual shower of water that hit his head and shoulders, and sent droplets spraying from there. Turning the scene into a fantastical vista of glistening perfection.

He helped her lift again.

Thrust back down.

Again.

And again.

And so many times! Her gasps for breath grew heavy with moans. Her skin rosier. The temperature hotter. Steamier. And then she went into a tight series of piston-quick motions atop him. Her breasts bounced in accompaniment. Her screams filled the enclosure.

And Kane lost control of everything.

The stool wasn't constructed for this kind of use. He felt it crack beneath him. An instant later he was on his feet, had her back pressed against the opposite shower wall, his hands cradling her buttocks, and he was thrusting in a non-rhythmic fashion that sent pounding sounds throughout the shower area. Sensation fueled every move. The quest for fulfillment grew fiery hot. Lightning-charged.

Any hint of gentleness got obliterated, overwritten by the need to dominate. Totally. Grunts accompanied each shove, adding to the cacophony of sounds they were making. LeeAnn was at the center of it. She had her legs linked behind him again, and was using the position with vicious efficiency, alternately pushing him away and yanking him back.

Pressure built in his lower back. Slithered through his legs. Grabbed his core. Fused with it. Hovered there, poised in place for an infinitesimal amount of time while his breath caught. His heart lurched. His throat closed off.

And then it detonated.

Kane launched upward, gripping LeeAnn to him as the world exploded, and took him along for the ride. Wonder obliterated reality. Incredulity filled any gap. And absolute bliss permeated everything. His chest took a series of hammer-like blows as his heart tried absorbing this. His eyes watered. His legs locked up. His belly erupted. And his throat tore as a long, agonized-sounding cry burst from him.

And through it all, LeeAnn held on, her limbs locked tightly around him. Her arms hugging him to her. Meshed with him. Linked. Completely and totally.

His cry ended on a sobbed note. He bent his head. Sucked in another breath. Started trembling. The world began reassembling. It wasn't going to be good. His muscles had gone on hiatus somewhere without permission. Or warning. The sounds of water intruded next. It was no longer hot. It wasn't even pleasantly warm. The shower now felt cool. Making his trembling worsen.

"Kane?"

LeeAnn's whisper added to this unbelievable weakness. She put a hand to his forehead to push a lock of dark hair out of his eyes. Kane squinted as she regarded him. He'd never seen anything as beautiful as the look on her face.

Ever.

"That was pretty...um. Unbelievable."

"Uh..."

His throat was raw. The word sounded like he'd been smoking three packs of cigarettes a day for a half-century.

"What on earth do you do for an encore?"

"Uh..."

He tried again. Got the same result. Her lips curved and that's when Kane started laughing. He couldn't remember the last time he'd laughed. And never with this much abandonment. He should have known what would happen, too. He collapsed into a corner of the shower, and forced the walls to hold them.

CHAPTER TEN

His silence was bothersome. As was the way he shied away from eye contact. She was having trouble getting her arms and legs to work properly, too. She could really use a nap about now. LeeAnn stifled a yawn and went back to drying off. These were really nice towels. Thick. Moisture-sucking. Wet skin didn't have a chance. She bent forward and ruffled one about her hair a few times before wrapping her head, making a large, unwieldy turban the size of a small laundry basket. The weight wasn't balanced properly, either. She tilted her head to one side to keep from toppling. Then, she tipped it the other way. She should probably start over. Do a re-wrap.

Kane was way ahead of her. But he'd cheated. He didn't exactly dry off before moving onto other things. He was already covered and cinching the belt on a thick white, terrycloth robe. It was a match to the one he'd brought out for her.

After he'd quit laughing.

Back in the shower.

LeeAnn looked over at the rather forlorn-looking shower stall. The stool was upside down, one leg a little crooked. There was a big bulls-eye of broken glass in one wall. Cracks radiated outward from it, sending sparkles of color if she moved her head far enough. She sighed softly. It still looked heavenly.

What was she thinking?

It *had* been absolute heaven.

She'd never felt anything like making love with Kane. It wasn't just her body adrift in a perfect blend of satiation and sense of well-being. Her soul felt like it radiated happiness, as well. His laughter had seemed the perfect accompaniment. It had sounded carefree. Infectious. She'd almost joined him. But then he'd just stopped. Without any slow-down of mirth and zero warning. His laughter had ceased. He'd lowered his chin. Narrowed his eyes. Regarded her for long, heart-stopping moments.

And then he'd disengaged her legs from about him and set her onto her feet.

She'd been shaky. Perhaps he'd known. That could have been why he'd taken her arm. Guided her from the shower stall. Grabbed a towel from the stack of them. His gestures had seemed a little brusque. Almost angry. It matched how he'd unfurled the towel and held it out for her.

He'd wrapped the next one about his hips. These towels were large. She still wore the first one. It covered from armpit to knee. Not his. *Oh, no.* On Kane, these towels didn't look remotely bland and innocuous. Or he needed to wear it higher. Chest level. Not low about his hips.

She'd watched him walk from her. Open a tall cupboard. She hadn't noticed it before because it was painted white. LeeAnn had looked about as she realized it. The lighting was really dim. It cast the slightest shade of pale yellow into the area. That didn't do much to alter the impression. Everything was in the same white color. Walls. Floor. Ceiling. Furnishings...

The color was spotless.

Pristine.

Weird.

He'd walked back to her. She watched that, too. It wasn't hard. She could look at him for hours. She didn't want to delve into why. Not just yet. Maybe not ever. It was enough that he was gorgeous. A fantastic lover. His body beyond ripped. And with that white towel barely doing its job, he was showing off a lot of those assets.

That's when he'd brought the white robes. Probably would have handed one to her, except she had her hands full with her hair towel. The garments got set on the floor. And then he'd stood back up and worked his hair into a loose braid of sorts. He had really nice hair. Coal-black. Long. Thick. Shiny. LeeAnn was envious. If she had hair like that, she'd wear it long, too. There was a bonus to watching him. The movements rippled and flexed all kinds of interesting muscles throughout his torso.

Until he'd caught her at it, anyway.

LeeAnn snickered softly at the memory of his expression. It looked like he'd flushed. Been a little self-conscious. But that was just fanciful thinking. Any man that looked like him and had the skills he exhibited, along with the package to back it up...? Well. That man probably had an entire army of women on speed dial.

She'd been easy.

Now, it was her turn to blush. A little late in the day for that. Stupid, besides. So...she'd gone a little sex-starved crazy and practically attacked him. She couldn't be the first woman.

Big fib, LeeAnn.

There was no 'practically' to it. She *had* attacked him. But he'd been a willing participant. She hadn't heard any complaints, anyway.

The lights inset somewhere in the ceiling flickered.

She looked upward. Back down.

"LeeAnn? We need to go. This room...isn't private."

"It's...not?"

Oh. Crap.

She'd been beyond easy. Her voice displayed the mortification. She pegged the emotion easily. Her blush rapidly receded, leaving her feeling a little dizzy.

"Wait. When I muck things up, I sure do it well. I misspoke. This place *was* very private...but that flash is a signal. We've got a new arrival. He'll head for the showers. We need to be gone before that happens."

"Oh."

"You need to don the robe."

"Robe. Yeah. Good plan."

She bent to pick it up and the towel unwound, pulling her hair down as it dropped off her head.

Great.

Now she was clumsy, too. A stab of tears hit her eyes. She was going to cry? Oh. *No. Please, no.* That was too horrid to consider. She blinked rapidly.

"Babe. Please. You are really adorable. But we need to go."

His words sent something sweet flashing through her. It erased everything in its wake. The span of white tile came back into focus. She couldn't do a thing about how her heart seized up. Or the tremor that ran down her back before entering her legs.

"W-what?" she replied.

"Uh...I'd rather not explain the condition of that shower stall. Leon is not stupid."

"Leon?"

"The last hunter. We've been waiting for him."

"We have?"

"I'll explain everything. Well. I'll try to, anyway. The moment we're safe. But, for now, we gotta go. Fair?"

Her answer was halfway between a sniff and a giggle. And then the robe disappeared as he grabbed it up.

"Here. I'll help."

He lifted her to her feet. Stood looking down at her. His eyes were still narrowed. He still looked angered.

"Kane?"

"You need to shed that towel. It's damp. Probably cold."

He shook the proffered robe out. Held it open. The muscles of his jaw clenched. LeeAnn pulled the end of her cover open and dropped it. The robe shook in his hands.

"Oh. *Hell.* You are so beautiful. I am either extremely lucky...or especially cursed. Here. Put this on. Please?"

He was right. The towel had been chilled. The robe's thickness was nice. But it didn't warm her near as much as his words. Or the tone.

"Where are we going?"

She asked it as he stopped at a door, cracked it open, and peered outside. There wasn't much to see. The lighting system out there looked even dimmer than what was in the shower room. But it couldn't be. Or Kane had some real light-sensitive issues. He held her hand with one of his, while the other fished a pair of sunglasses out of his robe pocket. He opened and positioned them onto his face with the same hand. Easily. Almost automatically. The accessory made him look unapproachable. And pretty damned scary.

He looked down at her solemnly for a moment. And then sighed heavily, sending a blast of air that ruffled the dried hairs along her forehead.

"The only place I can think of."

"Is it...private?"

"It's safe."

"But not private? Well. Darn."

She had to hide the smile as he jerked slightly. His fingers tightened about hers.

"LeeAnn—?"

He said her name with an undertone of anxiety. LeeAnn scrunched up her nose and watched her reflection in his black lenses. "Oh, come on, Kane. I was kidding."

"It is not amusing."

She tried to match his attitude. What she could see of his expression. The set look of his shoulders. But she had to factor in the tiredness that dogged her, turning her into the consistency of a leftover limp spaghetti noodle sitting in a cauldron of tepid water. The best she could manage was an eyebrow lift.

"You sure are a serious guy," she remarked finally.

"I have to be."

"I'm beginning to think you're a cyborg, Kane, and I'm not that imaginative. Oh. Wait. I must be. I mean, look at the evidence here. In one day's time I've been shot at. Kidnapped. Almost drowned in a pool. Gone SCUBA diving – without *one* lesson, mind you." Her voice grew louder as she continued. The words came quicker, too. "And then I just had the best um...uh. Well. Sex is not the right word for what happened, is it? I can't even call it a romantic encounter. That was the most amazing session of lovemaking I have ever experienced! Okay? I am still wiped out. And—. Damn it! I can't believe I just said that. This is so not me."

"You're doing fine, babe."

"Fine? Me? Aren't you listening? This is spy stuff! I rarely played video games when I was a kid! I'm a numbers person! I'm considered constant and reliable, not risky and dangerous. You know what I consider adventurous? Adding flavored creamer to my coffee! You wouldn't believe the calories involved!"

His lips twitched. Then, the smile evaporated.

"I've gone from being a successful businesswoman to one without clothing, money, or even identification! I have a deranged killer after me! I'm in the clutches of a sinfully sexy stranger who could be a bad guy for all I know, and oh! You better add in that I have absolutely no idea where I am, either!"

"North, two four. Three zero. Zero seven. West, eight one—"

"What are you doing?"

"Giving you numbers."

"To what?"

"Our location."

"You're giving me longitude and latitude?"

He nodded.

"I was right before. You are not real. Nobody goes around spouting those. Confess. You're a robot. Right?"

He shook his head.

"Then what?"

"I told you. I'll explain later. When we're safe."

"We're on some ship in the Atlantic Ocean somewhere. How can that not be safe?"

He stepped closer. Pushed away an errant lock of hair from where it had fallen across his lenses, making him even more shiver-inducing. "Babe. Please? I lost my head for...a span there. As well as my objective. My focus. And a good chunk of time. I need to check things. Assess. Evaluate."

LeeAnn regarded him for a long moment. Tried not to react. It was really difficult to stay annoyed. "Lost your head, eh? That's what you're calling it?" she finally asked.

"Lee. Ann."

He separated her name into two separate chunks. He might have been trying to sound stern. It didn't work. The man had a voice that matched the view.

"Yes?"

The lights flickered again. That was followed by the sound of the automatic doors opening. Kane pulled her to him. The contact was instantly incendiary. She wondered if he felt any of that.

"We're leaving right now. You ready?"

"Um. Sure. I guess."

"Stay close to the bulkheads."

"What's a bulkhead?"

He swiveled his head, the move cracking something in his neck. And then he looked down at her again.

"Just..." He grunted mid-sentence before finishing it. "Stay close."

He opened the door wide enough to ease through. Pulled her with him. The door shut behind them with a hissing sound that sent a huff of air with it. Any lighting was a joke. She could hardly see. It took several seconds for her eyes to adjust. The halls were beige-toned. The lighting had the same dun quality. The only reason Kane stuck out was his attire. The white of his robe was just a bit lighter than the wall he was flattened against. His arm was crooked about her chest, just above her breasts, sticking her in place alongside him. She didn't have much choice.

But she wouldn't have moved if given one.

CHAPTER ELEVEN

His idea of a safe place turned out to be his rooms. Or, what he called a cabin. It was located in the middle of a long hallway, above the shower room by at least two floors. Only he called them decks. The flights of stairs were termed ladders. Halls were called passageways. Bulkhead was the name for wall. She knew all that now, because he'd informed her in whispers. Despite telling him she wasn't interested in a career at sea.

Especially not on this vessel.

The entire ship exuded luxury, but it hadn't been put to good use with the color scheme. From the hall of beige-ness, he'd led her up a ladder to a passageway of barely-colored sage green. Then they'd traversed a bluish span of hall that made his skin look sallow. That's when he'd gotten hyper-vigilant. Spent all kinds of time checking the path before proceeding. Continually glanced behind. Always keeping her in his shadow, like an extension of himself. They finally reached these rooms located in a passageway with such a pale pink tone it probably rated 'distinct pallor' in any mime's face-painting box.

And she was lost.

Kane had stopped beside a nondescript pinkish-toned door. Lifted his hand. Placed it flat on the wall at his shoulder level. That was interesting. She could just make out framework around a panel. Her eyebrows rose as a pale light emitted about his hand, apparently scanning his palm. After a distinct click, the door opened inward an inch or so.

Okay, LeeAnn.

This was the stuff of movies.

And pretty darn cool.

Kane pushed against the door, slit it open enough to slither through. Brought her with him. The door closed automatically, barely missing her heels. He turned back, leaned his forehead against the door, and sucked in a large breath. She heard another distinct click of the locking mechanism.

He exhaled. Spine-tingling words came with it. "Oh. Thank heaven. We made it."

"Kane?"

He pulled her into an embrace that sent massive warmth. An unbelievable sense of joy. Exhilaration. His heartbeat was heavy. Full. Easily heard with one ear pressed to his chest. LeeAnn tried to move even closer, loving every second. Being in Kane's arms was paradise. Heaven. Nirvana. All rolled into one. Her earlier claim of tiredness evaporated, leaving awareness. An itch of interest. All kinds of heart-pounding emotion. And Kane just stood there. Looking down at her. He still wore dark glasses. She watched her reflection while the silence grew.

And grew.

She licked her lips. He groaned.

"I broke every rule bringing you here, love. But I didn't know what else to do. I couldn't leave you."

Love?

Her knees quivered and she would have fallen if he hadn't been supporting her. His mouth neared hers. His breath meshed with hers. LeeAnn leaned upward, connected their lips, and held the cry inside. Ecstasy slammed through her. Joy. Happiness. And then he lifted his head. Nuzzled her nose. And sent a shaft of light right through her with his words.

"I love you."

LeeAnn gasped.

He shook his head slowly, back and forth. Several times. "I know it's too soon. I know it's impossible. I know it's a huge mistake. I know all that, and yet it doesn't change anything. I didn't expect this. Don't deserve it. And still can't stop it. I love you. I do. I don't know how it happened...or why. I only know I love you."

This time, his kiss stole her breath. Her sanity. And her heart. They were both shaking when he lifted his head away, and sent a groan so raw it brought tears to her eyes. She held to him until it ended.

"Kane?"

"I just wish love was enough."

She lost her breath. Her heart felt like someone had it in a big fist and was squeezing their fingers about it. "You're joking. Right?"

"I need to set you down."

"Why?"

"And I need you to walk away from me. Understand?"

"No."

"You will."

"But...why, Kane? Why?"

He didn't answer. He set her down with a lurch. His arms fell away. LeeAnn didn't move for long moments while her heart absorbed something heavy. Painful.

He put his hands on her shoulders and turned her around, placing her back against him. And then she lost that contact as he moved away. It took a few moments to see anything. More time passed as she used her sleeve to dab at her eyes, sopping up moisture that shouldn't even be there. She hadn't even known him before 4:58 this morning! She couldn't possibly feel love for him, too. And yet, she knew what he spoke of. It was a physical ache to watch him move farther and farther away from her, until he almost disappeared in the dimly lit, grayish color scheme. The tone seemed appropriate somehow. It matched how she felt.

Exactly.

LeeAnn faced a sea of grayness. There wasn't one window to break it up. Nothing contrasted. It was difficult to decipher what was furniture and what was floor. There was an old-school phone on a table beside a same-shade gray couch. Kane picked it up. Despite his request, she followed as if there was a rubber-band around them and it had flexed too far. He lifted the receiver.

"Yes. Kane. Yes. One." He hung up. Looked down at where she hovered about six inches away. "LeeAnn, this is too close."

"Give me one good reason why."

He looked over her head as if debating something. She had to guess since he still wore his glasses. And then he looked back down at her.

"I must go. Get dressed."

"You're leaving me?"

"I will return. I promise."

"Look. Kane. Come on. Please? I'm in way over my head here. You can't just announce that you love me and then leave me!"

He'd untied his belt. Walked from her toward a gray-toned door at the back of the room. He pulled an arm free from the robe before turning to face her, and that just made him look like a Grecian statue with a toga draped on it.

"Don't move," he said.

The door shut behind him. Silence descended. It was an eerie silence that lifted goose bumps along her skin. LeeAnn sat on a sofa. What she wouldn't give for a book right now! Something to take her mind off the image of him. Shedding his robe completely. A magazine would even work. Heck, she'd even go for a pamphlet from a doctor's waiting room. Graphic and gory. Anything to take her mind off—

"I'm back."

LeeAnn was slack-jawed as Kane dropped onto the couch opposite her, denting it with his bulk. He'd been gone mere moments. Or she'd lost all concept of time. He was dressed in black again. Black denim. Black t-shirt. Black sunglasses. He had his hair pulled back tightly and secured this time. She'd never seen anything as perfect.

"What?" he asked.

"You."

"What about me?"

"You're...um. Beyond gorgeous. I can't help noticing."

He colored and looked away for a moment. That was cute.

LeeAnn considered him. "Oh, come on, Kane. I can't be the first woman to tell you that. I refuse to believe it. I mean, really. Do I look that gullible?"

"Yes."

"Oh. Great. I look gullible? But that should come as no surprise. I'm here, aren't I?"

She stood. Shoved one side of her robe farther across the other. Yanked her belt tight. Did her best to glare down at him. It didn't help that he was almost her height when sitting. Nor, that he truly was the most handsome thing she'd ever seen. It really didn't help to remember their lovemaking session. And especially his follow-up declaration of love. That alone was guaranteed to soften her glaring ability. LeeAnn sighed.

"Sit down, baby. Please? I am going...to try to explain things. I don't think I can do it with you glowering at me. Please?"

LeeAnn sat. Folded her arms. Did her best to look like a certified public accountant facing an agent from the IRS. At an official audit. "Okay. I'm listening."

"I don't know where to start."

He ran his hands down his thighs. Hugged his knees for a fraction. Slid his fingers back up his legs. It might be a nervous gesture, but it caught her glance. And that sent sparks shooting through her lower belly. She shifted slightly.

"The beginning."

"Which one?" he asked.

"Which one? The first one. How about birthplace. Where were you born?"

"South Carolina."

"Raised?"

"Same."

"Really? I would never have guessed."

"You wouldn't?"

"You haven't got a trace of a southern accent."

"That's because I haven't been there...for a long time. A powerfully long time."

"Okay."

He folded his arms, matching her stance. His move sent all kinds of muscle definition bulging into view. The guy had immense arms. LeeAnn looked there. Suffered a distinct tremor. And somehow managed to move her gaze back to his sunglass lenses.

He uncrossed his arms. Put his hands back atop his thighs. That just moved her attention. He had such massive thighs. And a really nice bulge at his groin. LeeAnn tried her best not to move or act like she'd noticed. She felt the blush burn her cheeks, but otherwise thought it worked.

"I...was the outdoors type. Water sports. Mud-bogging. Hunting. Fishing. Camping. You name it. I was into it."

"Sounds fairly normal so far. I mean, I've never been to South Carolina, but I've seen the ads. Watched documentaries. Been to movies."

LeeAnn slipped a lock of hair over her shoulder. Adjusted the collar of her robe where it had gapped. Decided against re-tying the belt.

"This isn't working. Perhaps you'd better get dressed, too. I can't concentrate."

She looked down at her robe. She was concealed from her throat almost to her ankles. She looked back up. "How much more do you want me to wear?" she asked.

"A lot."

"Do you have anything in my size?"

"Probably not."

"Well. If you want me to wear one of your shirts...you just let me know. But I have to warn you. That's gonna be very revealing without a bra."

He gulped audibly. LeeAnn nearly laughed. Hearing his declaration of love had altered things considerably. Made this a lot more potent than it might otherwise have been.

"I really wanted to be a SEAL," he blurted out, changing the subject completely.

LeeAnn lifted an eyebrow. "The Navy Special Forces kind of SEAL?"

He nodded.

"Well. That couldn't have been hard. You were probably top man on the recruitment list."

"Took me six years to qualify."

"Six years? You? No way."

"It was a new program. I was young."

"Okay. So. You're a SEAL. That explains a lot."

"No. I'm not a SEAL. I *was* a SEAL."

"Was?"

He nodded.

"Okay. So...what happened? You had an injury that forced your retirement? After which, you joined a group of mercenaries? And now you spend your time hunting bad guys?"

He shook his head.

"You don't look like the kind of guy who'd go psycho and get booted out of the service."

"I'm not."

"I give. Tell me. Why aren't you a SEAL any longer? You're fit. Young. Extremely capable. And you're...um. Really skilled."

She actually got the words out without stammering. That was a surprise. He took a deep breath. It expanded his t-shirt. LeeAnn's gaze dropped to his chest. She sucked on her bottom lip. She couldn't tell his expression due to the stupid dark lenses, but she definitely heard his groan.

"You need to stop that," he informed her.

"Stop what?" LeeAnn gave him her best innocent look before tipping her head down and adjusting the terrycloth covering her lap. She picked at an imaginary speck as she waited.

"This is not working, either."

"You really know how to beat around a bush, Kane. You know that? Your parents must have pulled their hair out trying to pin down where you'd been when you came home after curfew."

"Did you ever study names?" he asked.

"What?" LeeAnn's head came back up. He looked serious.

"Your birth name. LeeAnn. Do you know what it means?"

She gave him her 'CPA-listening-to-a-lie-from-a-client' smile before replying. "Yes. It means my grand-mother was named LeeAnn. As was her mother before her."

"Lee means 'dweller by the wood'."

"I'll take your word for it. But how do you know?"

"I've had...a lot of time. I met someone named Lee. He has a few strange quirks. I wondered why, so I did some checking. Grew interested. Wondered if a name had any significance. And consequence."

"You have a bookish side? That's—um. Wow. I'm almost speechless here."

He pulled his head back a little. "Are you making fun of me?"

"Oh. Never," she replied.

"I think the name Ann means 'graceful.' Or perhaps it would be better phrased as 'full of grace'."

"So, my name means I'm a graceful being from the woods. I sound like a fairy. Nice. But not remotely accurate. Look, Kane. You and I are opposites. I'm the indoors-type. Basic hermit version. I've been called a workaholic. And when I'm not working, I'm usually reading. I have a hard time even getting to the gym. That is the farthest thing from a fairy I can imagine."

He sighed heavily. "Can you guess what my name means?"

"Sure. I'll take a stab at it. If it's spelled with a 'C', I'm going to say you were named after the Biblical bad boy, Cain. The slayer of Abel. That Cain. You're not going to tell me you're a descendant, are you? Because I'm not the religious type. I quit going to church in my teens."

"That's the Hebrew origin. It actually means 'spear'."

"Spear. Okay."

"But my name is spelled with a 'K'."

"And that means something different, right?"

"Kane is an Irish name. Celtic. It means 'fighter'."

"Good name. I don't know where we're going with this, but the name definitely fits. Your parents are to be applauded."

"This is not working, either."

"Perhaps you could just give me straight answers?"

"I'm trying, but it's not easy! I told you. This is new territory for me. I've been called cold. Curt. Emotionless. Heartless. Mean. I can go on."

"No? Really?"

"But I've never loved anyone before. I didn't know anything about love. Or how it felt."

Her heart stuttered. Swelled. She didn't know what to reply. Or how.

"I keep thinking of some way to soften this. So you...won't turn from me."

Oh.

She knew how to reply to that.

"Turn from you? Look. Mister. I'm not that faint-hearted. Try just spitting it out. But before you do, I have a confession to make. I'm already...yeah. Let's just say I'm not immune to you, either."

"You aren't?"

"It can't be that big of a surprise. You are extremely easy to fall for. Especially once you dropped the heartless, mean, cold, etcetera veneer."

"Oh. LeeAnn. Love. This is not making it easier."

He had a definite frown now. It sent a line across his forehead.

"Anything I can do to help?"

He lowered his chin. She wasn't certain, but he looked like he was regarding his hands atop his thighs. And that just drew her attention there again. He looked back over at her. She wasn't prepared. He caught her ogling. And that just heightened his color again.

"Do you know where you are?" he finally asked.

"Um. With you?"

"Lee. Ann."

He separated her name like he had before. Probably trying to sound stern again.

"Okay. Yes. As a matter-of-fact, I do. You gave me coordinates. Remember? I am on a boat in the Atlantic Ocean somewhere around the north twenty-fourth parallel. Something like that."

"It's not a boat. It's a ship."

"Oh, brother. Fine. I'm on a *ship* in the Atlantic Ocean somewhere around the north twenty-fourth parallel. You are such a stickler for mariner terms. Must be the SEAL thing."

He slid to the edge of his seat, closing in on the available space and sucking up more than his share of oxygen. It was hard to get a breath. He instantly looked alert. Intense. The hairs on the back of LeeAnn's neck lifted.

"This ship is named *Abaddon*."

"Okay. Interesting name."

"Do you know what it means?"

"I think we've already proved I don't know the meaning behind names. So...no. I don't."

"It means...purgatory."

LeeAnn blinked several times. He looked serious as all get-out. While saying something preposterous. She regarded him for several long moments. "Is that supposed to be funny, Kane? Because...I have to tell you. It's not."

Kane leaned even closer in response. And then he pulled his sunglasses off.

CHAPTER TWELVE

The light was excruciatingly bright. At first.

Kane refrained from narrowing his eyes and just accepted the discomfort. LeeAnn had asked about light-sensitivity issues. What he suffered was much worse. It was a mark. And curse. All of them carried it. His eyes were full black, as if the pupils had been medically enlarged and couldn't contract. It was a dull black shade. Light didn't reflect. They appeared bottomless. Empty. Nothing behind them. He knew. He'd studied his reflection often enough over the years.

He thought he'd kept the affliction hidden from her because most light sources were painful. Now, he knew the reason. He loved her. The more that feeling had grown, the longer he'd held back. He hadn't shown her, because he was terrified of her reaction. Literally terrified. His knees shook for the barest instant. His gut churned. The blood in his veins froze. Kane had experienced fear. Every soldier in Vietnam had. He'd always met it head-on. And then conquered it.

Just like he now tried.

But he'd never felt so vulnerable or exposed.

He locked eyes with her, watching for a reaction, even as he tensed in order to withstand it. He didn't blink. She matched that, too, despite her need. He watched her light blue eyes glisten as tears formed atop the surface. His chest felt like a vise had seized him and was clamped in place, winding tighter with each heartbeat. His throat went dry. He tried swallowing anyway. That was stupid. The move scraped and burned. And that was before he tried speaking.

"Lee...Ann?"

"Your eyes are really dark, Kane."

"I know."

"I mean...really dark."

She broke their gaze, and looked down. Hiding from him. He watched her dab at her eyes with the cuffs of material at each wrist. She stood. Kane jerked back so they wouldn't touch, despite how he craved that very thing. She cinched her belt robe tighter about her waist. She was trembling. Her voice reflected how badly.

"I think...I could use a bathroom about now," she informed him.

"Sorry, love. That's a negative."

"Excuse me?"

"There isn't one."

"It's through here. Right?"

She walked to the door to his other room. Pushed it open. He heard her walking about the space. She'd find a closet that held his clothing. A bureau and mirrored dresser that did the same. A platform for him to rest atop. Nothing more.

She came back.

"You don't have a bathroom in there," she informed him.

"I know."

"So...this is like a hostel? The facilities are shared? And out in the hall somewhere?"

"No."

"I mean passageway. Is that the problem here? I'm not speaking mariner lingo? Should I call it a passageway, and the bathroom a 'head'?"

"That's not it, LeeAnn."

This was harder than Vietnam. Worse than when his SEAL Team had hit the wrong village. Killed innocents. And four of his teammates had slaughtered witnesses before Kane could stop the carnage with more of it. That action was what got him sent into this limbo rather than the real hell. Once it was over. And everyone was either dead. Or dying. He still remembered it. Vividly. He'd never forget. He still suffered visions of how every moan from the blood-soaked scene had faded...

And then gone silent.

"Then, what is it, Kane?"

Her voice brought him back to the present with a jolt. It was followed by the sound of the cabin door handle getting joggled. He snapped his head toward the sound. LeeAnn was at the door, working the door handle up and down.

"Babe. Stop. Please."

"Why won't this door open?"

"You don't have my palm marks."

"You have to do that on the inside, too? Well? Come over here and open it for me."

"Why?"

"So I can search out a bathroom!"

"There are no bathrooms out there, either."

"Okay. So where are they located? Near the shower room?"

"No."

"Then where?"

"You are in purgatory, LeeAnn. No one needs them here."

She opened her mouth. Shut it. Put her hands on her hips. Looked really small. Slightly obstinate. Disbelieving. And eternally beloved. If his heart wasn't sending solid shards of pain with every beat, he'd have smiled. The vise about his chest squeezed tighter, nearing crippling capacity. He leaned forward to absorb it.

"Okay. Cut the bullshit, Kane. I wasn't going to do anything other than splash water on my face. Maybe take a sip of water. But now, I'm going to start getting pissed. I don't believe in purgatory. Or—or vampires. Or zombies. Or...any of that crap! Now, get off your ass and help me!"

He sucked in a breath. Stood. It took an act of will to straighten to his full height. And it sent a lot more than pain. He looked down at his chest. Odd. Nothing showed. He should be hemorrhaging from a gaping wound.

Exactly like it felt.

"Now. Get over here and open this door."

"That's not...a good plan."

"It's better than yours."

He walked toward her slowly, wincing once before he caught it. He'd never been in love, so he'd never dealt with rejection of it. He hadn't known it sent physical trauma. And that love, too, had a dark side.

"I've got to get this door open. Find a phone. Or...maybe the lifeboats. That's it! There's got to be a lifeboat station. I can figure out how to lower one. It can't be that hard. There are probably placards. There are signs for everything."

He neared. Each step was agony. She was everything that was light. Warmth. Wonder. He loved her with every fiber of his being. And what had he done?

Brought her into the darkness with him.

The full extent of what he'd done overwhelmed him for a moment. He felt ill. Completely shaken. Tremors ran his frame. Tears stung his eyes. He'd been sent here to earn a place in heaven. Maybe another chance at life. Not blow it this badly.

Kane looked away. Blinked rapidly. Watched a bulkhead blur and mesh into a wash of gray tones. And then he closed his eyes and silently begged for help. Because he had to rectify this. She didn't have anyone else.

"LeeAnn. I'll get you...off the ship. I promise. LeeAnn?"

"What?" She spun, planted her back against the door and looked up at him.

"I can't...let you out there. Not yet."

"Why not?"

"It's...too dangerous."

"That's it! I refuse to believe that there is a hitman out there with the resources to track me underwater to this nightmare, and that he is, right now, hunkered down around a corner, waiting for the perfect shot at me! I refuse! You hear me?"

She was yelling, but the space around them easily absorbed the sound.

"He's not the problem, love."

"Don't call me that! Not right now! Please?"

Her voice broke. And he'd been wrong. The vise-like pain had merely been a prelude. Kane sucked air in so rapidly his teeth iced. Agony roared through him, sending everything to an excruciating level. Fire-hot. Flesh-burning. It didn't seem possible he could absorb it and continue functioning. He slammed his palm onto the wall in order to remain standing.

"Are you all right?"

She sounded truly worried. Her hesitant step toward him matched the impression. As did the touch of her hand where she placed it on his upper arm.

"It's not...your would-be...assassin. It's the...others."

He couldn't even get through a sentence without pausing. That was bad. Her eyes went huge. They drew him, and despite knowing she'd see the emptiness of his soul, he locked gazes with her. She had such beautiful eyes. Perfectly formed. Clear. So full of life. The connection lasted mere seconds. But it sent absolute rapture. Complete bliss. Wonderment beyond imagining. Things he'd never experience again.

And he knew it.

Kane set his jaw and broke away from her gaze. But he couldn't prevent the moan that escaped his lips.

"Kane?"

Her voice was soft as she said his name! So incredibly beautiful. He wondered if he'd get to keep the memory when he ended up where he was going.

"I have to keep you from...Jezzie. Leon. Rafael. Dozens...more."

"I'm in danger from them?"

He nodded.

"Why?"

"We're in purgatory."

"Give it a rest, Kane. Okay? You're starting to sound crazy."

"Dark angels...normally blend in with humanity. Co-existence is not...a problem. But in purgatory, we revert. Crave...what we do not have. The...human spirit. Light. Life force—"

"Dark *what?*"

"Angels. We're all dark angels."

Her mouth opened. Closed. Opened again. Kane started talking. And it actually got easier. "We're stuck here, hovering between heaven and hell. Purgatory has different names. Different locations. This ship is just one of them."

"What? How?"

"I was pulled from death in 1969, LeeAnn. I've spent the years since trying for redemption. Because the alternative is hell. Literally."

"No way."

"Sometimes...I've heard we can get another chance at life. But I don't know how to—"

She interrupted his explanation. She started gesturing. She got louder and faster as she spoke. As if he wasn't less than a foot from her. Unable to cease listening.

"You know, I always dreamed of meeting a man like you, Kane! Strong. Handsome. Uber-sexy. I'd fall in love! We'd have great sex. A nice wedding. Get a house in the suburbs. Have two-point-eight kids. A family car. We'd live the dream! I wanted to find my soul-mate! Is that so bad?"

She stopped and pulled in a breath.

"I wanted to find the man I could grow old with! But does any of that happen? Oh, *no*. Not to me. I can't be normal! Not LeeAnn Schultz. I have to fall for a guy who says he's already dead! That's what I do!"

"What...did you just say?"

He didn't notice the light outlining his palm, even as it warmed her face. Lit her features. Gave her an ethereal glow.

"You heard me!"

She said it militantly, but then she launched at him, flung her arms about his neck and gave him heaven. Her kiss was pure magic. Filled with healing light. Kane wrapped both arms about her and rocked backward, his fall stopped by the bulkhead.

And then the cabin door clicked open.

CHAPTER THIRTEEN

Leon came through the portal, pushing the door wide. He had a gun held to his head. It was attached to an arm that turned out to belong to a fellow in black. Approximately Kane's height, but a lot thinner. He pushed Leon into the room. His other hand held another 9mm. He immediately aimed it at toward LeeAnn. Kane shoved her behind him, and held her there with an arm.

"Hi, cupcake," the guy said. "Surprised to see me?"

"What's going on, Leon?" Kane asked.

"Address me, asshole. He's a patsy."

The man shoved Leon away from him. Leon stumbled and caught the door, holding it open as he lurched to a stop. His move kept the door from automatically closing. Kane met Leon's gaze for a moment. Leon smiled. Kane didn't return it.

"You got a name, buddy?" Kane asked conversationally.

"Yeah. Victor. As in...winner. Champion."

"I knew that already, Victor, but thanks for the lesson. So. What can we do for you?"

"You are a hard man to track, pretty boy. Not impossible, but hard. Took every nano-tracker I had."

"You used a nano-tracker?" Kane nodded as if impressed.

"Cute little units. Send a strong signal. Easy to hide anywhere. Real easy to hide in SCUBA gear. You thought you lost me with that little underwater stunt back in the Keys, didn't you?"

"Well. It was a hope."

"Lame. And here I thought you'd be a challenge."

"Likewise," Kane replied.

"So. You know what I want. I suggest you just hand her over."

"That's a negative."

"I'm really not interested in you, bub. Or the little patsy. And I'd really hate to put bullet holes in this ship of yours. But don't tempt me."

"How did you get here, Victor?"

"You had a couple of speedboats at your place. Forget those, did you?"

"Smart. So. You planted a tracking device on Leon's gear, and then you used one of our boats to follow him. And you didn't even get wet. The boat must be close."

"Starboard side. Bottom of the ladder. Enough shit talk. You gonna move, or do you want a bullet?"

"I think you already know the answer, Victor."

"Fair enough."

LeeAnn's hitman was less than a yard away. He lifted the barrel to Kane's chest. Kane narrowed his eyes. Tightened his chest for the impact. Instantly canceled his heartbeat, respiratory functions...determined to live long enough to fulfill his promise to LeeAnn.

"Wait!"

LeeAnn's screech was loud and surprising. Kane embarrassed himself by flinching. Victor's gun didn't even waver.

"Can't we negotiate or something?" she asked from behind him. "I mean, how much is Chad paying you anyway?"

"Chad? I don't know any Chad, lady. And I'm really getting tired of pointless chit-chat."

LeeAnn answered, talking exceptionally fast. "He's my business partner! I'd discovered some high dollar money transfers he needed to explain! I was supposed to meet him over it!"

"Oh. That guy. Shit, lady. He was my first target this morning. Just before I went after you."

"Chad...didn't pay you?"

"He couldn't afford me. Few people can. I work for a family organization. They don't like it when people call them with problems...like a meeting with a suspicious partner. Sounds like

Chad didn't have a head for high finance. Well. He won't have to worry about that anymore. And if pretty boy here doesn't move, he's going to have basically the same problem."

Kane caught the vaguest hint of sound out in the passageway. The slightest rumbling noise came through the door. Leon heard it, too. He straightened, making the door waver. Victor didn't seem to notice.

"So. Where do you want it, pretty boy?"

"No!"

LeeAnn stuck her head around his shoulder. Kane swiveled. Victor got off two rounds. One bullet grazed Kane's arm, leaving a gash across his bicep. The wound burned. Immediately started bleeding. LeeAnn screamed. Kane smashed her against his back, preventing her from watching the mass of arms and hands that reached through the open door, grabbed anywhere they could on Victor, and yanked him back out the portal.

Leon surged after him. Kane didn't wait.

He swung LeeAnn to his front, flung her over his shoulder, and leapt the mass of bodies swarming the passageway. He didn't need to see. He knew what they were doing. Victor's screams were bloodcurdling. Loud. And then diminished into strangled-sounding as he got overwhelmed. His life force drained.

And then consumed.

LeeAnn hyperventilated. At least she wasn't screaming. Kane took the ladder with churning steps that echoed. The next one with even more haste. He didn't check for pursuit. He didn't waste the time. The upper deck had never felt so far away. And then they were there.

Kane shoved the handle down and smacked through the hatch, hearing it slam behind him. It didn't immediately reopen. That might mean he'd had a good enough head start. It could also mean they were coming a different way. His luck still held. It was twilight. Millions of stars littered the sky. Nothing bright enough to hamper him. But Victor had been a little off. He hadn't left the boat on the starboard side. Kane couldn't find a mooring ladder anywhere.

"What's the matter?"

Damn everything!

"I can't find the boat."

"What...are we going to do?"

Kane stopped. Approached the side. They were five decks above water. It was going to be a hard landing. But, at least he could see. He pulled LeeAnn into his arms. Hugged her close.

"I'll get you to safety, love. I promise."

"H-h-how?"

"We're not that far from shore. I'll swim it."

"You can't swim that far. Not...with me!"

"I'm going to have to throw you overboard."

"You're coming too, though. Yes?"

"LeeAnn. I didn't know what love meant until now. Right now. I will do whatever it takes to save you. It doesn't matter what happens to me anymore! I give up my hope of heaven! That's how much you mean to me. Don't you get it? I love you!"

Kane caught a glimpse of movement to one side. A second later he was atop the railing. Crouched. Ready to jump.

"Kane! If you're not coming. I don't want to go. You hear me!"

"Quick breath, love."

That was all the warning he had time for. Kane gripped her to his belly and sprang as far away from the ship's side as he could. A long keening cry split the night behind them. From a hunter. Who'd barely missed its prey.

And then they smacked into the water.

CHAPTER FOURTEEN

The sun was already peeking above the horizon when LeeAnn awoke, signaling another gloriously hot, sunny, Florida day ahead. She nuzzled her nose against Kane's neck. Snuggled closer. They'd run out of gas some time ago. The boat was swaying back and forth as it drifted. Good thing she wasn't the seasick type.

She lifted her head to look up at him. "Kane?"

He grunted a reply. It echoed through where they touched.

"It's...morning."

"Yeah."

"Did you ever find sunglasses?"

"No."

"What are we going to do?"

"It's not a problem, LeeAnn. I know where we are. It's a short swim to the coast."

LeeAnn lifted her head higher and looked over the boat's edge opposite the sunrise. Saw nothing but water. "What coast?"

"Key West. Yonder."

If she squinted, she could just make out a shadow at the edge of the horizon. "I thought you said it was a short swim."

"I'm an ex-SEAL, babe. Give me an hour."

"Better wrap another sock around your arm first. You don't want to tempt any sharks."

He lifted his arm with the bloody sock wrapped about his bicep. Frowned at it.

"What is it?"

"I usually heal quicker than this."

"Why didn't you go while it was still dark?"

"You slept in my arms, LeeAnn. All night long. I...won't get that particular joy again. I wanted to memorize it."

"Don't say that. Please?"

"All right. Then I'll blame it on your attire. Or, lack thereof."

"That's not my fault. The robe weighed me down too much."

"I know. It's not your fault that Victor apparently had the same grasp of nautical terms as you, either. Jerk didn't know starboard from portside. But I did most of the swimming. Admit it."

"True."

"My shirt fits you like a micro-mini-dress, sweetheart. Who could leave? I mean, I may be dead, but I'm not that dead. I think we proved that yesterday. In the showers."

"I love you," she said.

He didn't answer. A glance revealed he was looking out at the waves and blinking rapidly. Each of his breaths shuddered.

"Kane?" she whispered.

"Right with you, love. Just...give me a minute. Fair?"

"Ahoy there! You need help?"

The words carried across the waves. Kane sat up, taking LeeAnn with him. There was a large yacht bearing down on them, the rising sun right behind it. Nicely trimmed. Fancy. Three men and a woman were standing at the foredeck, all waving. The name of the boat was emblazoned on the bow.

Halo Annie.

LeeAnn waved back.

"Well. I guess that settles that."

Kane remarked it when she settled back onto his lap.

"Why so glum? It'll save you a swim."

"We are about to be rescued. That means...my time is up. The assignment over. Consequences await. You are an amazing woman, LeeAnn. Capable of handling anything that life throws your way. It was an honor...knowing you."

He flashed a glance at her, and then looked away. LeeAnn grabbed his chin and yanked him back to face her. Her eyes were wide at what she'd glimpsed. He had his eyes narrowed to mere slits.

"Open your eyes, Kane."

He shook his head.

"Kane!"

"We did this maneuver already, LeeAnn. I don't think...I can handle a repeat. Not at the moment." His voice broke.

She ran a thumb along his eyelashes. They came away damp.

"Kane! If you don't open your eyes, I'm going to—! Please? I'm begging here. Please?"

He cracked an eye open. Her heart kicked up a notch. She'd been right. Where there had been nothing but black, it was now a warm, golden brown. And his pupils were tiny.

"Your eyes are brown."

His lips thinned. He lifted his brows next. But then he opened his eyes. The longer she looked, the wider his eyes went. His mouth dropped open next. Until he was staring with a wide-eyed shocked expression.

"LeeAnn?"

"Yes?"

"Oh, dearest God. I can see! Do ya' know what this means?" His voice got more excited. And he had a definite drawl starting to come out.

"You don't have to wear sunglasses all the time anymore?"

"I've earned another chance!"

"You mean...you aren't going to leave me?"

"Oh, babe. Oh, joyous morn! You just try to lose me!"

He started laughing. The next moment, he was on his feet, with her in his arms, rocking the boat worse as he twirled. And then he sobered. The boat was still swaying wildly beneath them. He didn't have any trouble compensating for it. He looked at her with beautiful warm brown eyes. She wouldn't have moved her gaze for anything.

"I got a question for you, Miss LeeAnn Schultz."

"Yes?"

"Will you marry me?"

"What?"

LeeAnn was stunned.

"I love you. You say you love me. Sounds like we got that part covered. I'm following the list you gave me. Wedding is next. Right?"

"I think we should try out some more of the great sex part first."

She ran a tongue along her upper lip. Raised her eyebrow a couple of times suggestively. Really loved how he stumbled and clumsily dropped onto his backside. The boat rocked wildly several times.

"Lee. Ann. You need to cool your jets. We are about to be rescued."

In answer, she ran a finger along the collar of his shirt, pulling the t-shirt material away from her skin slightly. He growled.

"All right. You asked for it."

And then he rolled backwards and dove into the water with her.

~ ~ ~

THE HUNTED is the debut in my new series *Chronicles of the Hunter* featuring dark angels with a mission! Because I just love a good story where light and dark collide, and humans get in the way...

About the Author

Jackie Ivie lives in the enormous state of Alaska with her husband and three very spoiled pets. She started her writing career writing hot highland historical romances for Kensington Publishing. There are now ten "Clans series" books, available in seven languages. Keeping her head in the clouds most of the time, Jackie now spends her time researching, developing, and writing her paranormal series – the **Vampire Assassin League**, the NEW **Chronicles of the Hunters**, as well as her other historical line – the **Brocade Collection**.

Jackie loves hearing from fans, who can contact her at
www.jackieivie.com or **www.VampireAssassinLeague.com**

Want to keep up with the assassins of the Vampire Assassin League and the dark angels of the Chronicles of the Hunters? Sign up for Jackie's newsletter at **http://jackieivie.com/para/news.htm.**

Want to know and discuss all things VAL? Consider joining the Assassin Street Team at **http://www.facebook.com/groups/379151425455048/**

THE GEEK GETS THE GIRL

Michele Hauf

Mistaken for the IT geek? This sexy CEO is about to learn the intimate operations of his company—up close, and personal.

For questions and comments about the quality of this book, or review inquiries, please contact **swellcatpress@gmail.com**

Chapter 1

According to the wrinkled strip of paper taped over the original brass placard on the office door, Rachel Parker was the manager of the Paris Haute Heels office. Zac assumed Miss Parker was the woman who strode down the parquet-floored aisle between cubicles with the air of a confident runway model, red heels clicking smartly. Not even the weight of the office supplies she carried could lower her proud jaw. Juggling a coffee cup in one hand, file folders, binders, purse and briefcase in the crook of an elbow—not to mention a mouthful of pink phone messages—she shrugged by Zac where he stood in the doorway to her office, and lunged toward the glass-topped desk to release her burden.

The sleek bend of her body sprawling over the desktop begged attention. A clingy, dark blue dress hugged her from shoulders to mid-thigh, and he visually caressed the taut curve of her ass. Hmm, what did the French call it? Derriere. Nice. And when in France... His fingers cruised an imaginary stroll over the dangerous curves. Shifting into high gear, he hugged the corner and stepped on the accelerator, moving down around her thigh. Breathy pants encouraged his actions until—

Those breathy pants ceased, and the woman whose curves he'd just mastered in a matter of three fantasy seconds stood staring at him, green eyes narrowed in stern summation.

Conjuring a save to cover the distraction that had almost netted him the yellow flag, he tapped the paper taped over the door's nameplate. "Snazzy décor you've got here, Miss Parker."

"Cutbacks. Tightening the proverbial office belt. It works for me." Long coils of chestnut hair danced over the spill of office ephemera as she nestled the paper coffee cup into a nook amidst the scatter. "And you have finally arrived."

She caught his surprise and reacted, propping a manicured hand on her hip. "Seriously? How long does it take for IT to process a call for help? I know all eight private offices in this building share one tech department, but you must have more than one guy to handle service calls."

"IT?" Nowadays, he generally put his fingers on sales figures, outlook charts, and the butter-soft leather in the company jet. Zachary Cosgrove had moved up from humble IT guy. Way up. "Oh, you assume—"

"Yes, I assume." The woman whose curves he could still imagine warming his palms gestured absently toward his face. "Serious glasses. Skinny tie. And you have the air of...of..." She snapped her fingers, searching her mental stores.

He tugged at the tie he'd purchased at a supermarket on the dash from the airport after arriving in Paris less than two hours earlier. The airline had lost his luggage, and he'd needed a change of clothing. Far from the Ermenegildo Zegna he was accustomed to, but he could work the budget look with the best of them.

Miss Parker swept her hand to take in his attire, still trying to decide about him.

Want to take me for a spin, Mademoiselle Derriere? I'll handle your curves like a pro.

Curious green eyes held his gaze a bit longer than was socially acceptable. He nudged up the black-rimmed glasses—emergency pair—the ones he'd been forced to wear because his contacts were tucked in with his luggage.

He liked this woman for her daring assessment of him, as incorrect as it was. He also liked the way she made him feel. Confident and—most unexpectedly—horny with a side of let me lick those curves until you moan.

"The air of..." she continued. A violet fingernail tapped her pretty pink lip. "...geekery," she decided. And then an admonishing finger marked the air between them. "I've waited two weeks for you to resurrect the relics this company likes to call computers. So! Under my desk."

"Wha...?"

She didn't catch his dismay at her invitation to kneel before her. Instead, she rapped the desktop. "You'll find my computer is eager for your attention."

Right. Her computer. Unfortunately, not her curves.

Subtle beauty claimed Rachel Parker. She wasn't overdone with cosmetics and overpowering perfume. De rigueur for most office managers he'd the opportunity to meet. Yet if he looked at her too long, he'd begin mentally detailing where on that soft, peach-toned skin he'd first like to lick. At her chin where the slightest dent inspired a slow, curious perusal? Or maybe at her neck where a long, silver chain glinted as if distant headlamps from an oncoming Lamborghini? And she smelled like oranges. A cheery scent that didn't match her confident stance.

"Right, then." With that, she sailed out of the office as quickly as she'd drifted in, leaving him sniffing for the barest hint of citrus, and thinking this introduction to the Paris branch of Haute Heels could not have gone better.

IT guy? Perfect. He now had a cover identity for what he'd hoped to keep a low-key fact-finding mission. According to the Haute Heels' Operations Director, Joel Stinson, this office had been in the red for six months. Joel hadn't bothered to hire a new manager because he'd not wanted to fund what he'd termed a dead zone. The Paris office hadn't produced a marketable design or campaign in over a year. By the end of the week, the Operations Director intended to either fire everyone and start fresh, or close the office.

An office that had been Madeline Cosgrove's dream. Zac's mother had founded Haute Heels, and this had been the flagship location. There was a touch of her in every detail that fashioned this office.

While not one for hands-on relations with the Haute Heels branches, Zac wanted to make sure this office was performing as poorly as the reports detailed before such a drastic move as shutting it down. He'd already had a ticket to Paris: his mother's apartment, sitting empty for ten years since her death, needed to go up for sale.

So he'd told Joel he would stop into the office and have a look around. Joel had suggested he send him a list of any salvageable assets, including employees. They were scheduled to make a sales meeting with Le Grand Chaussures on Friday, but Joel predicted it would fall flat.

Joel had also suggested Zac go incognito. If the employees knew the boss was peering over their shoulders, they'd freak. Zac had agreed. He didn't want to cause panic amongst the employees should they learn the big guy had come for a final look around. If the smallest hope of resurrecting the office existed, Zac would put in a good word to Joel.

Right now, he bent to look under the desk, assuming the IT role with ease. Holy hell.

"Relic, indeed. I guess I'll be getting on my knees after all."

*

Two hours later, the intrepid Miss Parker floated in for another brief docking. Zac had listened to her heels click to and fro about the office all morning as if background music. Harried control defined her mental state, but her appearance still landed firmly in the nonchalant sensuality column.

Still on his back and beneath the desk, his focus on the ancient motherboard he'd excavated from the computer, Zac almost took a pointed leather shoe-tip to the cheek as she slid her feet under the glass-topped desk. He noted the steel heel. The design was Haute Heels. Last season, if he wasn't mistaken. And those ankles. Sleek, lightly tanned, and stretching down to a glide of foot that revealed a peek of high arch above the shoe's red leather shank.

The woman attached to the killer heels took no note of the guy she'd almost skewered, so through the glass desktop, he observed the sweep of her hand as it sorted paperwork. Her wrist was slender and attractive, as well. He could easily imagine wrapping a hand about both, pinning the gorgeous limbs to clean, white sheets and holding her at his command.

Snacking on some kind of power bar, her eyes affixed to her cell phone screen.

Compelled beyond mere fantasy, Zac reached for her sexy gam, sliding his fingers along the smooth, warm skin. Felt like summer. And with a warm July rain spattering the office windows, he was eager for the vacation. Cruising slowly over her anklebone, he closed his eyes, thumbing the rise as if it were a more intimate part of a woman's body, yes, that sweet spot between her legs that was like an intricate puzzle a man must learn, lick, and master.

With his schedule keeping him in the City of Light for the week, he wasn't sure his libido could handle five days without a hookup. Another body lying next to him through the night would make the hotel room feel less empty, and—a man could not survive on spreadsheets and frequent flyer miles alone.

Inhaling, he drew in the sweet flavor of orange and...leather, from the shoe. He loosened his tie. He imagined the steel heel pressing into his chest as she stood over him, exerting her dominance in a way that he would gladly succumb to...

A surprised chirp alerted him that he'd been successful in diverting her attention from the phone. Miss Parker tugged her foot away and skirted toward the door.

"Uh..." she started.

An apology didn't feel necessary, so, tilting his head out from under the desk and offering a non-threatening smile, he waited for her to speak.

"Right. I forgot. The guy under my desk," she gasped out.

"Zachary," he offered, realizing he'd not the opportunity to introduce himself earlier.

"Of course. Zachary, the IT guy. I completely forgot you were there." She slid the toe of her shoe along the back of her opposite ankle. "I, uh, have work to do. Uh... Out there. In the office. Away from...you—uh, here!"

She spun out of the office and down the hallway.

Zac chuckled softly. She'd be back. And so would those slender ankles and that tight little derriere. Before the day was over, he intended to learn a lot more about Miss Parker's software.

Chapter 2

Seated in LeTrec's chair before the mangled stack of papers he deemed to call order, Rachel excavated her way through the accounts payable bills and attempted to do the work LeTrec should have finished days earlier. Out with the flu in the middle of summer? She hoped he was miserable.

Accounts payable was not her forte. She didn't do numbers. Well, she could, she just didn't like exercising that particular zone in her frontal cortex. Numbers made her brain hurt. Promotion and marketing was her calling, and she made it her religion to know what it was consumers wanted. The makeshift sign on her door named her Rachel Parker, Office Manager. It was a lie. She had been hired into Marketing as Director, and had only agreed to look over the office when the last manager had abruptly quit. Something about evading a tax issue when he'd left the States three years earlier.

Rachel had been waiting for Haute Heels' new manager to arrive for two months. She wasn't complaining. Too much. When the chips were down, she rallied. And she had the ability to juggle three, four, a dozen tasks, if necessary. Her motto: I am woman; hear my fingernails scratching up the corporate wall to gain recognition. The path to her goal didn't have to be straight. She just had to stay on it, no matter the curves and sudden dips or rises. She was all about making the challenge a learning experience. And she was learning about past-due bills today.

She had almost begun to think the wait for assistance from IT would go on as endlessly as the wait for a new manager. Which reminded her of the sexy computer geek she'd left sprawled beneath her desk.

Young, lean, and attractive. At least, from what she could tell with those severe, black-rimmed glasses detracting from his face. Yet behind the spectacles, blinked dark brown irises that had seemed to clutch at her and pull her in closer for an embrace that could only end in lusty kisses and tingling body parts. And he'd spoken English as if a native of the States. She was so over French men and their inflated sexual egos. A few sweet nothings whispered with an American accent would really get her steaming.

Really, Rachel?

Er, no, the guy was not sexy. He was an IT nerd, for heaven's sake. And double no to her straying thoughts.

Back to accounts payable.

Yet as her eyes sorted through the columns of figures and dollar signs, her hand strayed down past her Anne Klein skirt to her ankle. He had touched her there. Stroked her skin with such agonizing leisure she had almost moaned right there in the office, be damned what the cubicle gophers might think. She had let the contact continue much longer than propriety allowed. Because what woman could resist a caress like that? The man's touch had curled up through her calves, thighs, and stomach, and had tickled at her nipples as if he'd actually stroked them.

"Mmm..." So good. She could really use some boldly blatant touching. When had she last had sex with someone other than herself? Two weeks? A month?

What was she thinking? If she didn't get this accounts payable mess sorted out, she would not be able to move on to the next mess. Sophie LaPierre was out having her baby. Which meant sorting through shipping documents was also on today's roster. And when she'd walked in this morning, Amelie, her secretary, had reminded her to read—something. Surely it had been in that stack of messages she'd abandoned on her desk.

No time to wonder what she was missing. If it were good news, it would avoid her like the plague. If it were bad news, it would find her and infect her like no plague ever had.

She sorted the invoices into alphabetical order and logged into LeTrec's accounts payable program. This insufferable computer was so slow. Almost as slow as that IT guy's touch had been.

Rachel couldn't seem to steer her thoughts from the man whom she knew was still in her office, touching her things, gliding his fingers into the deepest recesses of her computer...

His appeal had to be the spicy cologne she'd noted as she'd slipped between him and the door. Because it certainly wasn't the pencil-thin black slacks that revealed bargain bin shoes, or those studious black-rimmed glasses. And toss in a skinny tie? She'd known he was from tech support without an introduction. Those guys never seemed to have a sense of style.

And yet she'd lingered on his mouth for a few seconds too long. That mouth had been intricately formed, with the bottom lip slightly thicker than the top. And stubble had darkened his jaw, framing those pouty lips. Lips that had absolutely demanded a kiss. She could have kissed them. But had not. Because?

Just because.

Or, no! She knew the answer to that one. She was at work, and office managers did not kiss the tech help.

"Right," she whispered, and focused on the folders popping up on the computer screen. "You are the manager, Rachel. Act like it."

Yet that lusty little vixen that lived inside her shivered with anticipation, shook her hips in a sexy boogie, and whispered, "Come and get me, geek boy."

Oh, mercy, but she needed sex.

Shaking her head and repressing a smile, Rachel noticed that the monitor prompted her for LeTrec's password. She shoved the vixen into her red-velvet-walled closet and clicked on LeTrec's employee profile where the company passwords were stored. Another wait as the little spinning ball taunted her.

She wondered if the geek liked to be called Zac? Hmm...

Then she wondered what it would feel like as his dark stubble brushed her skin and made her nipples tighten and knees soften. And if the vixen were prodding at her, then she had been ignoring her lately.

Her last hookup had been...well before Bastille Day. And it was July 28th today. Rachel, you so need to get laid.

No, she needed to be the manager the paper sign on her door stated she was. Because in assuming the role, perhaps she could win the role. It was a possibility that she didn't want to slip through her fingers.

With all the work to be done, she hadn't a moment to think about her sex-starved vixen, or the man sprawled under her desk, not two doors down; his cheap shoes tapping rhythmically as he hummed some random tune she'd heard before but couldn't quite place. His deep tones resonated in her bones, setting her at the edge of the seat. She squeezed her thighs together, focusing a flash of wanting sexual energy.

"Mercy."

No. He was not distracting her. She would not allow it—

Ah! Saved by the password.

But really? The red velvet door hung open, and the vixen stuck her head out, hungry for attention.

Chapter 3

The office always cleared out at five, on the dot. Despite the workload piling up on her desk—and everyone else's desks—because she'd skipped lunch and her stomach was not happy, Rachel decided to leave early tonight. Early, being an hour after closing time. Normal departure time for her? Well after eight or nine.

Lately, she hadn't much of a life beyond the office. Dating was out of the question. Thank God for girls' night out on Saturdays. It was hookup night, and no one went home alone. And if they did, it was because the idea of a late-night movie while snuggled up in a warm blanket and nursing the Pamprin was the better choice.

It had been a long day. She needed carbs and red wine.

Something crinkled in her skirt pocket. Right. The note Amelie had suggested she read immediately this morning. She tugged it out and read it while gathering her purse and slipping on her shoes.

"Oh, no."

The plague she'd anticipated had descended upon Haute Heels.

"Headquarters is sending in a bigwig to assess the Paris office this week?"

Her breaths ceased for a full six seconds. She pounded her chest to kick her lungs back into action. Purse in hand, she staggered out from LeTrec's office toward one of the beige cubicle walls, she clutched the edge as if it were a life raft bobbing in the ocean.

She'd heard rumors the company wasn't doing well financially because a couple of their branches were underperforming. And if a company exec were arriving to assess this office? That meant she had to make him believe they were worth saving. Because they were. They just needed a little tender loving care at the moment.

Rachel was trying to hold it all together. Juggling. That was her strength. She loved working for Haute Heels. Small town girl from the States snags a job at a ritzy Paris shoe company? Hell, yeah. Two months earlier, she never would have thought she'd be managing an office instead of working in Marketing where her real strengths could shine. But still. She was a trooper. She didn't do stress. Stress was not a word in her vocabulary. Instead, she confronted challenges.

Stretching back her shoulders, she inhaled then exhaled long and deep.

"I can do this. I need to do this. I am the best person for the job," she said in a confident tone. "This company needs me."

Turning around, she braced her elbows upon the cubicle wall. One more deep breath for good measure. Poised for action, her feet remained planted. But seriously? What to do? She had to get her head together, assess the situation, and rally the troops.

The troops had all left for the evening.

"Chill, Rachel."

She exhaled again, finding a calm that had seen her through many a crazy office storm lately. There was nothing she could do until morning. And a good night's sleep would put her brain back on track.

With a decisive nod, she shut off the lights in the office, and headed down the hallway toward the elevator bay. When she saw the doors closing, she picked up speed, her steel heels clicking on the marble floor.

"Hold it!"

A foot jammed between the doors and they buffered open to allow her in. The bespectacled tech guy winked and flashed a grin. Oh, that stubble. Something so masculine about it. Very un-nerdlike.

"Car park," she said.

The button was already lighted, but the doors remained open. This old elevator took its time with everything.

Rachel had deftly avoided Zac throughout the day in an attempt to keep the red velvet door from bursting wide open. Because she knew one sniff of his spicy scent would lure her closer, making her forget her name and beg for his touch.

And what was with that tie? She wanted to touch it. Or was it that she wanted to touch him?

Tugging at the skinny black tie that should have been vanquished to the 80s hall of fashion shame, he then offered his hand. "Rachel."

She was about to correct him that Miss Parker was appropriate—or even, Mademoiselle Parker—but the sound of her name coming from those kissable lips made her silently offer blessings to some random Goddess of Self Control. Because she wielded it now to keep from gripping that tie and pulling him in for a kiss.

He quirked his brows together in consternation. Thick, black brows that looked so...touchable.

"Uh, right. That's me. Rachel."

"Whew! I was worried you'd had a stroke for a second there."

Seriously? She was so off her game. And why was that? The guy was not even remotely of interest to her. She preferred hooking her men in the executive pool.

The elevator doors slowly shut.

"So tell me, Rachel, I'm having trouble understanding how an office in this day and age can exist with such old equipment. Personally, I'd brick your computer."

"Brick it? I'm sorry, nerd terminology is beyond me."

Zac lifted a finger between them. "I prefer the term geek. Nerds wear their pants to their armpits and belong in the eighties."

"Oh. Uh, sure." But she caught his smirk and sensed he was playing with her. "Geek it is."

"And a brick means a fried computer. Best thing to do with a brick? Toss it or use it to erect a shelter."

"But my computer isn't fried."

"In theory, no. But it could happen any day now. Your office should have desktop monitors with LED displays for the designers. Not to mention the entire network should be in a virtualized private cloud."

"I have absolutely no idea what any of that means." But the tech-speak sounded so sexy, her nipples instantly hardened. "Trust me, I've submitted requisitions for updated equipment. The home office keeps telling me I don't exist and thus have no grounds for such a request."

"You seem very real to me."

His eyes tripped down the front of her silk dress and strolled along her hips. A blatant assessment. But instead of offending, it reminded her how delicious his touch had felt.

Please, sir, can I have some more?

Rachel mentally slammed the red velvet door shut, and quickly offered, "I was hired into Marketing. When the manager quit a few months ago, he asked me to look after the office until his replacement arrived. I'm still waiting."

"That's rough. Abandoned dreams?"

"No, just delayed a bit, is all. And there's nothing whatsoever wrong with management." The control she'd been given these past few months was heady. Even if it felt as if she were a captain going down with a sinking ship more than sailing into shore. "Promise you won't leave until you get our computers in tiptop shape? I've waited too long for IT to notice us. I don't want to lose you now."

Oh, Rachel, the innuendo in that statement. No, she was not waiting for a man. She was perfectly happy without a boyfriend. She'd been raised by an independent woman who'd divorced when Rachel was three. Mom had taught her to be smart, use common sense, and never believe a man was required to 'complete' her. Go, girl power!

But, like breathing, a girl did require sex. Orgasms tended to fuel her creativity. Seriously. A good sex life made for a happy, relaxed, and well-fueled brain. There had been studies to prove it.

"You've got me for the week," Zac said. "Though, like I said, bricks."

"Well, if you've some magical means to get the office new computers, then, by all means, brick mine."

His smile, though straight, arched up a thick eyebrow. The man was all spiky black hair, bushy brows and stern glasses. Severe. Yet his kiss-me-if-you-dare lips softened everything. Her knees felt bendy and supple. The velvet door popped open once more.

A whole week to ogle this curious specimen of man who challenged her sensual restraint? Joy!

No. Not joy. With a secret visit from a company exec on the roster, she would be too busy to notice the IT nerd—oops, make that geek. Which was a good thing.

Seriously, she was not interested in this man.

Maybe a little.

If a little meant a lot.

She inhaled a waft of spicy cologne and closed her eyes—until she realized he was waiting for her to speak.

"Yes, uh…whatever you need this week, just ask. I may be very busy, though. So many tasks on my plate. Everyone from marketing is out sick or having a baby so I'm handling that, as well. There's so much to do! The Paris market is a bitch."

"How so?"

"Haute Heels needs to sex up their image. They're a bit old-fashioned."

"Really? I thought shoes were innately sexy?"

Rachel's eyes landed on that alluring stubble. Mmm, rub that against my skin. Send shivers over my body. Sexy? Oh. Right. The company's image.

"Their ads are too focused on not offending. This is Europe. The French are all about the sensual. Flirtation and sex is in their blood. I wish I had more time to work on ad copy. We've a meeting at the end of the week with Le Grand Chaussures, an elite shoe store. I'm not prepared. Sorry. You don't need me to dump on you."

"You're obviously a very busy woman. Dump all you like. I enjoy listening to you talk."

He did? Hmm… Rachel reached for his skinny tie and gave it an adjustment. Finally! She'd touched the tie. Brazen points for her. "You're coming undone."

He caught her hand before she could tighten the knot further. "Leave it. This is how I relax at the end of the day."

He didn't let go of her fingers. The fire in his touch moved up her wrist and arm as if fast-moving lava. Inexplicably compelled, she stepped forward—too close for an office discussion. He smelled like cloves and something darker. Licorice? Nummy.

The red door jittered on its hinges.

Of a sudden, the elevator lurched—and stopped. The door didn't open.

"Does this happen a lot?" he asked in a husky voice that was markedly tinged with want.

His eyes traveled across her face and down her neck. The intensity in the air hung between them like an unspoken scream of desire. Rachel pressed her thighs together, the pressure teasing at her tingling apex.

"Never," she said dreamily. She shook her head out of the fog, a result of standing in his intoxicating scent. "Oh, you mean the elevator?"

The man's smile was small, but oh, that mouth. Kissable.

"Yes, it does," she said. "It's much like our computers—aged and in need of repair. I get stuck at least every other week. Ten minutes max. Guess we'll have some time to chat."

He leaned against the elevator wall. The slant of his body was easy and even made the line of his cheap suit look stylish. "What do you like to do after hours, Rachel?"

"Uh…" Was he coming on to her?

Of course, he was. And she was no slouch when it came to the pickup. Much as he enjoyed listening, Rachel decided it was time for action not words.

She gripped his tie again and planted her mouth on his soft, yet firm lips. He mumbled something that may have started as a protest, but he quickly got over that. Their bodies touched at breast, hips, and toes. The outline of a pen nestled in his breast pocket rubbed her nipple, making it diamond hard. Or was that the incredibly hot kiss that was currently being returned as good as she gave?

His wide, strong hand wrapped about her waist and eased her closer. She didn't resist; instead, melting against the hard frame of his chest and hips. When had office geeks transformed from ninety-eight-pound weaklings to…this? Beneath the linen shirt, his pecs were solid as stone, and with every movement, the muscles flexed deliciously.

"Mmm, you work out," she muttered into his mouth. "I like that."

"And you are aggressive."

"Assertive."

"Same thing."

"Very different. You have a problem with confident women?"

"I…don't think I do," he said, as if deciding he'd go with whatever the crazy woman tossed his way.

She preferred the term assertive. And he would soon learn the difference between the two.

An office romance? Never. But a little mixing it up in the elevator with the sexy IT geek who wasn't an official employee of Haute Heels? She had never been attracted to the studious type. Too introverted, too closed off, too mental as opposed to physical.

On the other hand, she did like to try new things. And she so needed to feed her creativity with an orgasm to get her through this week.

Pulling from the kiss, she focused on Zac's parted mouth. A hush of warm breath brushed her chin. She hugged her breasts against his chest, loving that he must feel her hard nipples, and offering him a teasing smile. He acknowledged the tease with a glide of his tongue over that thick bottom lip, and his hand journeyed up her spine, claiming, as he pulled her to him.

Another kiss took away all thought. Answering the sudden, wanting crush of his mouth to hers, she slid a leg up and over his hip, pressing her palms to the elevator wall behind him. His hands skated up her sides until his thumbs hooked under her breasts and toyed with the underside of the lacy La Perla bra concealed by the silk dress.

Rachel's skin warmed as if she were lying nude beneath the noonday sun. She sighed into the kiss and deepened it. He tasted like espresso, and not the cheap brand Amelie stocked in the office breakroom. He must have stopped in at the café across the street that served freshly ground blends with a rich swirl of farm-fresh cream. Mmm. His tongue danced a shiver over her inhibitions.

Seeking as much as she could take, she did not relent.

He lifted her from the floor and she slapped a hand to his chest, gripping his unloosened tie to secure her hold. And then she didn't want to secure too good a hold, because falling was exciting. Turning her to land her shoulders firmly against the wall, he held her along the thighs and she wrapped her legs about him. Her steel heels clicked together behind his hips. He undid the top buttons on her dress and licked a path down to the curves of her breasts. The demi-bra allowed his tongue to lash the crest of a nipple.

Mercy.

And she had been prepared to give this Monday a check in the Disaster column? This man could explore her software as much as he liked.

"I don't do this," she felt compelled to say.

"Hook up with a random stranger?"

"You're not exactly a stranger. I've known you half the day."

"True. So what is it you don't do? Have sex in elevators?"

"The office romance thing. I wouldn't think of it—I shouldn't." She pressed the heel of a palm against his shoulder, but not with any conviction.

"I'm not heading toward happily ever after here, Miss Parker. And you did start this."

"So I did. Call me Rachel. There's something about your mouth. I had to feel it on mine. But we don't have much time."

He slipped his hand up her skirt and discovered that she had not been in a mind to put on panties this morning. Hey, some days a girl honors her inner vixen. "Rachel, you are assertive and naughty."

As he nuzzled, gently biting kisses against her breasts, she spread her legs wider to allow him access. No password required. Because she needed right now. And he gave.

Her core stirred, humming with anticipation. She'd grown wet for his touch. He groaned with pleasure as he slipped a finger inside her. Rachel clutched his hair, knocking his glasses lopsided on his face. With his free hand, he tucked the specs in his pocket, while his other found her swollen clit and rubbed over it with a slick thumb. She gasped at the mind-altering sensation of hot-wet-tingle-glee.

Pressed tightly against the wall, she felt he anchored her there. Wishing the elevator would never whirr back to life, she knew their time was limited. Normally, she needed to focus and allow herself to let go in order to come, yet she was surprised by the sudden and insistent spinning in her core. Every part of her focused on the imminent big bang. It was so close. Zac played her expertly. As if he'd been there before and knew exactly how to speed up his touch, then slow it down, then a bit harder, then a little softer.

"Oh…" She dug her fingernails in at his shoulder and the back of his neck. "Yes, need this. More than you know."

"Come for me, Rachel," he whispered in her ear.

And as softly as he'd commanded, she sighed out a lingering moan. Her body shuddered against his, falling into orgasm. The press of his lips beneath her ear electrified the sensations and prickled across her skin in the best feels-so-good-never-stop-yes-yes-yes way.

"You come on strong," he whispered. "But you end so sweetly. Good girl."

And the elevator jerked into motion. It descended the remaining two floors while Rachel's heartbeats remained high in her throat, her body succumbing to the pulse-thundering release. The skirt of her dress fluttered down into place. Her fingers glided down the front of Zac's shirt as he set her on the floor and kissed her mouth. A testing kiss. A sealing the envelope and sending it off kiss. She was too caught up in the moment to reach for that skinny tie and hold him there.

The elevator doors opened to the carport, and with one last quick kiss, Zac said against her mouth, "See you tomorrow." Before she could reply, he turned and strode off.

Rachel wanted to call out, Wait, let me get you off. Turn around is fair play, and all that.

Instead, with a grin on her face, she sank to a squat. Her cheeks flushed and breaths panted. She reached up and pushed the hold door button. Whew! She was no interior decorator, but she would say the inside of the elevator was definitely in need of some red velvet.

Zac didn't get into a car, instead walking up to street level. Must be catching a cab. Didn't he work in the building? Or maybe he walked home.

So much she didn't know about the man who had just worked her body as if he had known it forever. And yet, it wouldn't have happened if she hadn't made the first move. She had the control. She needed the control. Without it, she would never survive this rat race called life or succeed in the cutthroat business realm.

So why did that small, swirling aftershock of orgasm toggling her core giggle right now and make her think she'd just relinquished some of her staunch need to be the one in command?

Chapter 4

Just as she was pouring a hot cup of chamomile tea—her pre-bed ritual—two raps pattered Rachel's apartment door. She didn't bother to call out or move out of the kitchen to answer it. She knew who it was.

"Hey, sweetie!" Melissa called as she snuck inside and closed the door behind her. "Got some treats for you."

Melissa and Rachel had both moved into the building within weeks of one another, were former residents of the Midwest, founders of the Saturday Girl's Nights Out, and were passionate observers of the masculine species.

Already in her cotton pajama bottoms with hot pink skulls on a black background and a tank top that hugged her petite figure, Melissa curled up on the sofa and waited for Rachel to hand her a cup of tea.

Melissa, in turn, offered her a plate of freshly made macarons as Rachel nestled on the couch beside her. Melissa worked at Paul, a popular patisserie chain, but spent her off-hours crafting her own concoctions. She wanted to open her own shop some day.

"What flavor?" Rachel asked, palming a crisp-shelled treat that she knew would melt in her mouth with the first bite.

"Just taste." Melissa's bright blue eyes twinkled and she sipped the tea. "I think it's the one I'm going to use to enter the bake-off competition."

Rachel had never tasted macarons until Melissa introduced her to them. Heaven sandwiched by even more heaven was the best way to describe the little cookies that were two soft yet crisp outside layers caressing creamy yet firm ganache innards.

She couldn't prevent a lingering moan as the sweetness coated her tongue and she recognized the flavor that made her instantly homesick. "Rootbeer," she said with a sigh. "Oh, Melissa, this is amazing. This is the one."

"You think so?"

"I know so. Mmm." She devoured the next two macarons.

"You're not the usual uptight and not right tonight," Melissa commented as she clanked her teacup against Rachel's. "Good day at the office?"

"The IT guy finally showed to fix our computers."

"Score! You've been waiting awhile for him."

"He worked on me, too."

"He—" Melanie turned on the couch to study Rachel closely. Her eyes widened with glee. "Seriously? You got it on? You did?"

Rachel nodded and covered her not-so-shameful smile with the teacup.

"Touchdown!" Melissa met Rachel's hand in a fist bump. "But really? The IT nerd?"

"He's a geek, not a nerd," she corrected. "It was the stubble. Or maybe the thick black glasses."

"Oh, kill me now," Melissa said, sprawling back against the couch arm and mocking death with a fake blade to her heart. "Rachel does the office geek. I don't know whether to laugh or—"

"All I'll say—" She stood and fingered up the last few crumbs of macaron from the plate. "—is that men who work with computers all day? Really know how to use their fingers."

With a wink, she strode off into the kitchen with the empty plate. Melissa's sigh gave her a smile of triumph.

*

Rachel slid her legs under the desk, not expecting the 'ouch!' that echoed up from below. She'd been so busy checking emails on her phone that she hadn't noticed the long, lean man sprawled on her office floor, his head beneath her desk. Yet the computer tower sat on the table before the window, which overlooked the lime trees queuing down the avenue below.

She bent to peer under the desk and found Zac's big brown eyes, surrounded by those impossibly geeky black glasses staring up at her. "What is it beneath my desk that you find so infinitely fascinating?"

He crossed his arms and delivered an upside-down grin. "Do I really have to spell it out for you?" He slid a hand up her ankle.

She used all her powers of resistance to tug away and twist her legs out from under the desk. Really. Amelie was sitting right outside the office door. And if he touched her too long, her skin would turn molten and the lust she'd felt in the elevator last evening would re-ignite.

Who was she kidding? The yearning lust was already there, anticipating the explosion.

"Someone attached the hard drive to the underside of your desk," he said, sitting up and waving the small black box and a screwdriver.

"Huh. And here I'd always thought that was the classic black box and Haute Heels was spying on me."

"We'd be sneakier than that," he muttered as he stood. "Uh, I mean— I'm sure the company would do it through emails and apps."

"Really? You think the company is keeping track of my every move?"

Zac shrugged. "You should always assume emails sent from a company computer are not private."

"I know. But there's not a little camera somewhere, watching me, is there?" She cast her gaze about the upper lines of the walls, papered in gold-flocked rococo stuff that would be better suited in Versailles. So tired. But classic Parisian. "That would just be creepy."

"As creepy as being watched in the elevator?"

"There are cameras in the elevator?" Her heart thudded. Great. Just what she needed. Not the best evidence to have floating around when a girl wanted to move up the corporate ladder. "Uh, can you do something about that?"

"What? You mean like go through the security footage and erase our hot and heavy tête-à-tête? You watch too many spy movies, Rachel."

"Doesn't it bother you that we were recorded?"

His boyish grin told her that was a stupid question. Men and their need to flaunt—well, everything. Something about macho points. And, certainly, the geek wanted all the points he could rack up, right?

"I don't think it wise to advertise public displays of affection," she said firmly.

"Of course not. I was teasing about the elevator cameras. There were none in that one," he offered. "What happened was a one-time thing, yes?"

"No. I mean…" She gauged the flicker in his eyes as he waited for her to walk her way out of that impulsive reply. It was the curve at the corner of his lips that clued her in that he was playing with her. "You never know what another day will bring," she offered airily, picking up a file to fake like she had work to do.

She did have work to do. But seriously? She watched Zac place the hard drive on the table next to the computer tower and all she could think about was how those fingers really knew how to play her. But she'd only gotten warmed up. And anticipating the big finale could set her off course from her business trajectory.

"So, you'll be working in my office again today?" she asked.

"For a bit. Then I'm going to take a look at the rest of the equipment throughout the office. If you don't mind."

"Mind? I expect a thorough job."

"You are the last person I would ever disappoint, Miss Parker."

He turned away and tugged out his iPhone, tapping notes into it. His profile was all stubble shadow and slicked-back hair. 50s rocker with the cool élan of office studiousness. The look was growing on her. So different from the muscled blondes whose arms she generally melted into. But even more, she wondered about running her fingers through his black hair. So thick and soft. And then she'd clutch it, and kiss him roughly—

"Rachel? What are these?"

Shaking herself from a fantasy re-do of the elevator scene, she eyed the boxes he pointed to stacked on the table beside the computer hardware. "Shoes for the new line."

"Can I move them over to make some room to work?"

"Sure. Shove them wherever. I plan to sort through them later." She winced inwardly. She'd never find the time today. The ad meeting was this Friday. She needed an entire ad campaign within four days. God, help her. "Tomorrow for sure. I'll have Amelie remind me."

"Sounds like you've a plan. So, uh…since you're all about keeping it all business in the office and…er, avoiding hidden cameras—"

"Don't ask me out on a date," she rushed out before he could continue. "I don't do the commitment thing. At least not at this point in my life."

"Is a date a commitment?"

"No. But it's too…expected."

"Oh. Uh…okay. Wouldn't want to do what was expected of me. But really? You expected me to ask you out?"

"No, I just…" Had weird imminent date radar that she tried to avoid like bargain-basement flip-flops. "This is not appropriate conversation for a business office."

"Right. So how does one go about arranging time to, uh…see you again? Should I have Amelie set up an appointment?"

He wanted to see her again? He was standing right there. He could look all he liked. But she knew he wanted to see her privately. Which would then allow him to touch as well as look. And she did anticipate seeing just how hot he could make her. Because after hours? She could do as she pleased.

"We could go Dutch," she suggested. "There's a great little restaurant not far from where I live in the 7th. Sans tourists. We could meet there around eight this evening?"

Zac's brows furrowed and his mouth pursed in thought. "Sounds suspiciously like a date."

"Oh, it's not. Because I say it's not."

"Your logic is astoundingly refreshing, Rachel. To a non-date at eight, then. Could I possibly pick you up?"

"It's not far from my place. I'll text you the address. I can walk there."

"It's supposed to rain later. The sky is already darkening."

She studied the gray sky through the window. Paris had been pouting for days. "I suppose a ride would not construe a date."

"Because you say so?"

"Exactly." Oh, Rachel, what art thy strange rules of which you speak?

After entering his number into her phone, she texted him her address, then left him alone in the office, thinking when she returned it would smell like cloves with a touch of masculine leather. That gave her the initiative to work swiftly so she could get back before the scent disappeared.

*

Thank you, weatherman. It was pouring outside. Zac's plan to keep Rachel Parker in her home—and all to himself—would prove a success. Balancing the bouquet of white freesia and the takeout bag in one hand, he knocked on her door with the other.

She answered with a bright smile and enthusiasm. Then her eyes averted to the takeout bag, and the smile wobbled. "I thought we were going Dutch?"

"I took the liberty of picking something up."

"But I…" Her palm smoothed over the red dress that hugged her curves and stopped high on her thighs. Gray gladiator knee-high sandals emphasized her slender legs. The sexy vibe continued in her loosely pulled-up hair. She'd dressed to seduce, but also, to be appreciated.

"I can't imagine you skipping out into the rain and getting that pretty dress wet. Or your hair."

She twirled a finger into a tendril that spilled from the upsweep and tickled at her neck. "I'm not one of those women who complain about a little wet."

Oh, the comeback he could give to that comment.

"Indulge me," he entreated, wondering if he'd judged her incorrectly. She was into him, wasn't she? The suggestion they get together for a non-date had been hookup code. Or had she been serious about the elevator being a one-time thing?

The woman sucked in her lower lip and gave his suggestion too much thought. Zac was almost ready to call defeat and suggest he hand her the takeout and leave, when she nodded and tugged him inside by the tie.

His luggage had arrived early this morning and he felt much more comfortable in Zegna from head to toe, but at the last minute, he'd gone with the cheap shirt and shoes. He couldn't blow his cover this early in the game.

"You're not wearing your glasses," she commented as she took the takeout bag and the flowers.

"Sorry. I wasn't aware I needed to fulfill some sort of geek fantasy for you."

"You don't. I mean, you are fantasy material. Uh—" She slipped around the corner into the kitchen. "I said that wrong," she called. He heard her fuss with the plastic wrapped about the flowers.

She'd said it exactly as she'd meant it. Fantasy material, eh? Was it the stolen office liaison, or indeed, the geek she'd pegged him as? Either suited him fine. Because neither was a stretch. Not that he was an expert on office liaisons by any means, but he was willing to give anything a try once. Twice, if it felt good.

Last evening in the elevator had only stoked his desires. No one was getting out without an orgasm—or two—tonight.

Zac strolled to the table beside the low, red velvet couch and picked up a Mason jar half-filled with buttons of all sorts, colors, and sizes. He gave it a shake, and the sound of plastic bits clattering against the glass made him smile.

"I pick them up when I see them on the ground," Rachel called from around the corner. "Find them everywhere when I'm walking in the city. I love to wonder over whom the button might have belonged to. Does he or she miss it? Are they aware? Or is she on a date and, at that moment, revealing bra from across the dinner table? I'd like to return one some day. Just so I could get my questions answered."

He smiled and set the jar down. Interesting chick. A collector of lost security devices, a makeshift office manager, and a sexy temptress all rolled into one incredible package. Thank you, Paris.

He wasn't going to give one moment's thought to the fact that he shouldn't even be standing in this apartment, admiring the distant view of some famous monument he didn't have a name for. That he was the boss and should keep this search and destroy visit to Haute Heels strictly business. No fooling around with the employees in order to learn company secrets.

He wasn't here tonight to learn any secrets but those that might be whispered as Rachel gasped and came beneath his exploring touch. And he could handle playing the role of geek. She didn't need to know he was the boss. He'd leave Paris with the facts, and great memories of an intriguing and sexy woman.

"Dinner is officially plated," she announced, peering around the corner and beckoning him with a finger.

Zac wanted that finger to loosen his tie all the way tonight.

Chapter 5

"Once the computer system is virtualized, the entire office will function more smoothly." Zac finished the red wine and wandered into the living room from the tiny kitchenette wedged between the windowed wall and the fridge.

Rachel hastily tossed the dishes in the sink and grabbed the opened wine bottle, following him like some kind of puppy to heel. She still didn't understand his geek speak, but it absolutely turned her on. Or possibly, it was everything about him. He relaxed on the couch, holding up his goblet so she could fill it. The suit looked nicer than yesterday's offering. More expensive? She could usually spot a designer label from across the room, but those shoes—the poor man.

"If you can make it happen," she said. "Then I don't care what you're talking about. Just make my life and that of the rest of the office easier. I want the Paris branch of Haute Heels to succeed. I just wish they hadn't decided to send in a spy this week, especially when half my staff is either out with the flu or having babies."

"Seriously? How many are having babies?"

"Well, only the one. But three have the flu or nasty spring allergies, and we don't have a large staff to begin with. I almost forgot. I have dessert." She rushed into the kitchen for the plate of macarons Melissa had dropped off earlier.

Smoothing her hands over her dress, she was secretly thankful they had spent the evening inside. Sharing Zac with the ambient noises of a restaurant didn't feel right, and she had been saved from having the world observe her silly infatuation with the man.

Not silly. There was nothing wrong with being interested in a sexy guy. It was just the different kind of man that she found herself attracted to that induced a sort of inner battle. To do him or not to do him? Sure, he was sexy, but did she really want the challenges that accompanied an office romance?

"Did you say something about a spy?" Zac called.

On the other hand, he wasn't on the office payroll. He worked in the building, not specifically for Haute Heels, so it wouldn't be that difficult to keep the two separated. And damn it, she deserved whatever good vibes he wanted to send her way.

"Yes. I got a memo that some bigwig is stopping by. I suspect it will be a clandestine visit. Our office hasn't been performing well."

Before she could turn to go back into the living room, a hand glided over her hip and his nose nuzzled against her hair.

"I just hope…" she started.

"You hope?"

"No, forget that conversation thread. I don't want to talk about work. Let's keep business and pleasure separate."

"Agreed." Wine-scented breath heated her neck, sending a good shiver up the back of her scalp. "Dessert?" he wondered.

She turned to pull him up against her. "What are you in the mood for?"

He eyed the macarons that sat a hands-reach away on the counter. She picked one up and offered it to him. His bite crumbled the cookie's light, airy shell and crumbs fell onto her dress.

"Rootbeer? That's awesome." He swept his fingers over the crumbs, ever-so-slyly running the back of his hand over her nipple. He opened his mouth, and she stuck in the remaining half of the macaron. The man even chewed sexy.

"My neighbor is a pastry chef. And a sugar dealer. She feeds my habit." She slid her hand along his and beckoned it back to her nipple. "Another?" she asked.

He tugged aside the neckline of the dress to expose red lace (always matching underthings). "Yes."

He lifted her against the counter and she wrapped her legs around his hips. The man's lips firmly landed on hers and she sighed into his breaths. He tasted savory, like wine with a top note of rootbeer and sugar.

He glided a hand up her spine and she arched against his chest. He held her securely, breasts to chest, as he peppered kisses down her chin and over her jaw to lash his tongue along her neck.

"Not another elevator quickie," he said against her skin. "I need more of you, Rachel, longer this time."

"Are you kidding? You're not getting away from me that easily. Oooh. Yes, right there."

His kisses landed on the top of her breast. The demi bra barely covered her nipple, and his serious attention to her curves vanquished any lingering vacillation she had regarding whether or not to engage in an affair. The vixen had pushed the door wide open.

"Bedroom?" he asked.

"Around the corner."

"Wine," he said, as he lifted her from the counter, his kisses landing at her collarbone, her breast, and deeper, between her cleavage.

She swept up the half bottle of wine, and he carried her down the short hallway into the bedroom's pink depths. Pink, because she kept a red scarf over the low-wattage lamp near the bed. She liked the soft color playing across the white walls and sheets. And no, it was not bordello chic as Melissa liked to tease. The rest of the room was clean pine furnishings with spare, brushed steel hardware, and not a decorative pillow or silly wall hanging in sight.

Zac didn't comment on the lush atmosphere as he crawled onto the bed with her in his arms. He was strong, and again she had to wonder when geeks had started to work out, because his biceps were solid and bulging under her exploratory fingers. Did it matter?

With one shoulder of her dress in each hand, he pulled the clingy red rayon down to expose her bra. "I like red." He nibbled the lacy edge and tugged it down with his teeth to reveal her nipple. "But I like this rosy color even better."

She moaned as he painted his hot tongue around her nipple. Rachel clutched the bed sheets in utter pleasure and dug her heels into the mattress.

"Is this all right?" he muttered between tongue lashes to her skin. "Away from the office?"

"Yes," she gasped, as he began to peel the dress down her stomach. "Just don't kiss and tell, okay?"

"So we're doing the secret sex?"

"No, I mean…" She lifted his head with a hank of his hair. "You do work in the same building. I don't want to walk down the hall to the chorus of snickers from the other IT guys."

He clasped his hands over her stomach and assumed a serious moue. She didn't want a conversation right now but sensed one coming.

"Is there something wrong with me being from IT?" he asked. "I sense a certain discrimination in your tone every time you mention it. Not good enough for the high fashion office chick?"

"No, that's not it at all. Hell, you're smart. Probably much smarter than I am. I've just never, well…"

"So I'm a fascination to you?" He rested his chin gently on her panting stomach.

The view between her breasts and down her stomach was all brows and dark eyes and oh, that soft hair. She ran her fingers through it. "You are a fascination. And I like to indulge my adventurous whims. Got a problem with that?"

He thought about it. And she squeezed her thigh muscles to contain the waning flutters of desire. His shirt collar tickled her mons through the dress, and she was thankful she hadn't worn panties.

When his hand glided up her leg, over her knee, and between her thighs to land at the heat of her pussy, she didn't need to hear his response. Nor did he give one. Instead, he bowed his head and put his tongue to better use. Slicking, gliding, sucking, and teasing her into a panting, wanting girl on fire.

"But really." All exquisite goodness focused on her clit suddenly ceased. Zac looked up again, a dash of dark hair had fallen across his forehead. "I'm not good enough for you, is that it? That's why you didn't want to do the date thing."

"You are thinking far too much, and veering down dangerous paths. I just want to have sex with you and not discuss the social implications of our hookup. Can you deal?"

"Yes. I…right. I'm overthinking this. I have a tendency to organize and view from all angles…" He bowed his head, lush dark hair tickling her bared skin. "Sorry."

And Rachel sighed, falling down from the high of what had promised to be a sudden and explosive orgasm. He'd said sorry. That was the last word a girl wanted to hear in bed. Even if they weren't officially in bed, just more sprawled on it in a furious race to the finish line. This time, the trace of his tongue over her folds didn't quite stir the flame.

They should have never talked. Damn it!

She shuffled away from his tongue and sat up, bending her legs to sit and pushing the hair from her face. He was still fully dressed, and she… Sometimes, she was so brazen. And, normally, she was okay with that. But right now, she pulled a pillow across her lap and leaned her breasts against it. A form of protection from the weird emotions jittering around inside her.

"What did I do wrong?" he asked in the sweetest, little boy manner that made her want to pat him on the head—but she didn't.

"You asked questions," she said plainly.

He rolled to his back and blew out a breath, stretching out one arm to run down her leg and clasp the ankle. "Right. Too deep for a hookup. I get it. Sorry, normally I'm much better at this."

Another sorry. Aggh!

"Stop apologizing for something that doesn't require the sentiment." Rachel raked her fingers through her long curls. "Maybe we should have left this in the elevator."

"No," he said with conviction. "This is not an office hierarchy fascination thing for me, Rachel. I wanted you tonight because…" He rolled over onto his elbows and kissed her thigh. "I haven't been able to get oranges out of my brain."

"What?"

"You smell so good. I entirely expect to taste the tang of citrus when I lick your skin."

She used bergamot oil from a jar of preserved oranges. A drop behind each ear, at her elbows, and behind her knees—every morning and night. It was something her grandmother had taught her. She liked the fresh scent and being a little different than all the Chanel No. 5 fans.

"Oranges and spice," she said absently, feeling as though the conversation might blossom into an official, get-to-know-one-another talk, and so not wanting that. Too soon. Too intimate. Too much.

Especially for a hookup.

Zac's cell phone rang. Rachel sighed, dropping her shoulders. "I'll let you get that. The mood is spoiled."

"It is—sorry."

And yet another sorry. Twisting her legs off the bed, she pulled up her dress top and strolled out. "I'll give you some privacy."

*

Zac answered the late call, doing the math as he did so. It was four p.m. in New York. "Joel." He looked down the hall and didn't spy Rachel, but decided to sneak into the bathroom behind the closed door anyway.

"How's it going in Paris?"

"What's this about a memo to the branch stating a bigwig was on the way? I thought this was a covert mission?"

"It is. Shit. The office knows? I might as well just pull the plug right now, then."

"No! I haven't had a proper look around yet."

Was he saying that because he needed to delve further into the office activities, or because he still hadn't fucked Rachel? And while that wasn't the goal, it was the desire. Mixing business with pleasure? He could handle it.

He could.

"It would be a mercy to the employees if we closed up shop before the scheduled ad meeting on Friday," Joel insisted.

"I don't believe so. Just don't do anything. I still have my cover. Give me until Friday morning." And he hung up, not waiting for approval. Because he was the CEO. He told people what to do. Not the other way around.

And yet… Was it the very fact that he'd been mistaken for a low man in the office hierarchy that he was enjoying this whole experience so much? Since arriving, he hadn't been expected to command and conquer. Rather, he'd been ordered to his knees and asked to do his best. He kind of liked the freeing feeling of not being the big man on top that everyone feared.

Now. To command and conquer the woman? Or to stand back and assess, allowing her to show him how she wanted this to go?

Zac nodded. Allowing Rachel to lead the way was becoming more and more pleasurable.

Chapter 6

Rachel turned on the arm of the couch where she sat, straining to hear Zac's phone conversation. Impossible. Which was just as well. She didn't want to know his secrets. And yet… She'd come to a conclusion in the few minutes she'd been sitting here.

Zac wandered out of the bedroom, fixing his tie and smoothing a hand through his hair.

"I've thought about it. Us," she corrected as she stood and grabbed his tie, tugging him closer. "I'm not one to play games. I expected certain things when you invited me to dinner tonight, and I'm not going to wimp out just because you haven't caught up with the program. So get on board." She slid a hand down and gripped his crotch, satisfied to find that his erection was hard. "Fast."

"Oui, mademoiselle."

"You speak French?"

He slid a hand up to her breast and squeezed the nipple. "Oui. Non. S'il vous plait. Merci. You have now heard my entire French oeuvre."

"I wish I knew how to say on your knees in French."

His eyebrow quirked and a smile lit in his eyes. "That's the second time you've requested as much from me. Do you call this manner of yours aggressive or assertive?"

She tugged his tie, and he bent at the knees, keeping eye contact as he went down. "Most definitely assertive."

He kissed her thigh and nudged her skirt hem with his nose, raising it slightly, then glided his fingers up under the fabric and pulled her in close to kiss her bared mons. His tongue lashed out, tasting her wetness.

Rachel clung to his hair, clutching and moaning every time his tongue touched her sensitive clit.

"I've always favored software studies over hardware," he commented with a wink up toward her. "Let's see how long it takes to get your system online."

And despite his corny metaphors, Rachel couldn't find a protest as his fingers slid inside her to tease, coax, and explore, working in tandem with his tongue. She bobbled backward and let her body fall onto the couch. Zac followed, lifting her leg by the ankle to direct it over his shoulder. Gladiator sandal pointing in the air, she lifted her hips, seeking his delicious ministrations.

Zac's hand slid under her thigh and squeezed her ass, pushing her up as he greedily fed on her. Sucking in the corner of her lip, she fell into the shimmery, jittery sensations that caressed her body from head to toes. He worked an indescribable magic on her. Fueling her desire, her pleasure, and, at her very core, her creativity in ways he couldn't even imagine. But more than that? He was completely focused on her, and that kind of attention never got old.

"Yes, right there," she whispered as his fingertip glided along her outer labia, putting delicious pressure on her clitoris. "Oh…" She clutched Zac's hair and the couch beside her, tightening her muscles and then… "Yes!"

Having brought her to orgasm swiftly and with flare, Zac knelt over her, hastily tugging off his tie. He shed his shirt, and she heard the distinctive tick of his zipper as he set free his hard and ready cock. As Rachel rode the waning orgasm, she gestured that he glide his erection inside her. And he filled her with an exquisite hardness that reignited the orgasm and again pushed her over the edge. Gripping him by the shoulders as he thrust into her, she cried out in joy at the tremendous release.

It didn't take him long to reach the same pinnacle, and with a satisfied chuckle and a kiss to her breast, he then lifted her into his arms, destination, the bedroom.

*

Zac glanced at the bedside digital clock. 12:40 a.m. He wasn't tired. But he was deliciously exhausted.

Rachel nudged him even as she burrowed her face into the pillow and managed a deft sheet cover with her knee. "You should leave."

He rolled over and gaped at her, but she didn't notice his astonishment. Hair tousled and a smile on her face, she was toeing the doorway to Nod.

She was kicking him out of her bed?

"I can't do the sharing a ride to the office thing," she murmured. "Not wise. See you in eight hours, lover. Mm, that was so good."

He couldn't even find anger. There was no need. She was right. He needed to return to the hotel and leave for work from his base, not hers. They were not a couple. They didn't share rides, or even showers.

Though he wouldn't refuse a shower with her if she offered. Sucking her wet nipples into his mouth? His cock pulsed.

Sitting up, he reluctantly gathered his clothes and tugged the pants on over an erection he knew he'd have until he finally did shower. After four orgasms, he hardly felt it was fair to seek another quickie before leaving. Rachel was exhausted. And he was blissfully satiated, as well.

He leaned over and clicked off the soft pink light that colored Rachel's skin as if it were a rosy fruit. The room went dark gray. A slash of gold from a streetlight beamed through the curtains. He kissed her on the head, drew in the scent of her... Oranges and spice? Ah, she'd been referencing his cologne with the spice. A nice combination.

"Until later."

Locking her front door behind him, he took the stairs down to the lobby. Zac couldn't help but replay his thoughts about Rachel being in control. Her confidence was a key sexual attraction. He bet she was a force, delivering a presentation or arguing the benefits of one marketing campaign over another. Even if she did harbor some reluctance about pulling off the managerial position, he sensed it was because of her work overload. Talk about taking over a shitload.

But the control. He smoothed a hand down his tie. Normally, he preferred to be the one who directed a relationship, whether it was a one-night stand or a multiple-month fling. Yet with a job as demanding as his had been lately, he felt a grateful relaxation fall over him to know that someone else had taken the reins.

He could relinquish control around Rachel. He'd never felt so relaxed around a woman. Or unthreatened. Except that part where he'd almost blown it by asking her about the IT fascination thing.

Rachel Parker didn't need a man. She just wanted to have fun. And that was incredibly sexy to him. And also, a challenge. Because, truthfully? He'd like her to need him.

Just a little bit.

*

For some reason, work seemed to grow easier. Rachel couldn't be sure why the computer apps she normally found confusing suddenly seemed to remind her of meetings or due projects. Nor could she figure why she could actually find the design files for which she'd been searching days.

She'd mark it off as getting her groove on and finally tapping into her creativity.

Because, seriously? Zac had stoked her fire last night. Call it orgasm mojo. This morning she'd flown out of bed, showered, and sang at the top of her lungs. She was surprised birds hadn't helped her dress while squirrels bounced down the sidewalk accompanying her on the walk to the metro.

She sipped coffee and blushed. Yes, Rachel Parker was sitting alone in her office, getting all hot and bothered as she considered the intensity of Zac's tongue tracing her skin and arriving at the sweet spot that he had known how to control. Was it because the man was already a master of various other kinds of buttons? He was certainly snapping the office computer system back into shape.

Amelie popped her head into the office and waved a stack of pink messages. Her bouncy ponytail thwapped her cheek. "You look pleased," she said, though voiced as an uncertain question.

"I am pleased." Rachel indicated her nearly clean desk. "LeTrec's accounts are balanced, thanks to my clear head this morning. Now, I've just a few shipping invoices to approve and when I'm finished—"

"You'll work on the design ideas for Friday's meeting?"

"Crap." She set the coffee mug down sharply on the glass desktop. "I forgot about that." No, she hadn't, she'd simply set it aside mentally until her coffee could be enjoyed. "Have you heard from the home office? When is that guy supposed to be here?"

"No idea. The person who sent me the memo heard it from another person who heard it from another person, who thinks they overheard a phone conversation."

"Seriously? So this is all hearsay?"

Amelie winced. "I do trust my source."

Rachel splayed out her fingers on the glass desktop, seeking calm. "Fine. I'll deal with that disaster if and when it crosses my path. Now. The ad."

"If you need some ideas for the meeting…"

She tilted her head at Amelie. "What do you mean?"

Amelie shrugged that sheepish little girl movement that always angered Rachel. Women should stand up for themselves and not shrink into the wallpaper at the mere opportunity to stand out.

"Spit it out, Amelie. Do you have ideas?"

"Actually, I have a few sketches. I like to doodle when I have downtime. They're nothing really."

How many times had Rachel used that phrase 'nothing really,' when inside, her soul had been beaming, waiting to break free and show the world what she could do?

"Show me."

Amelie nodded and bounced out.

Curious, Rachel strolled out to her secretary's desk, and when Amelie handed her a sketchbook, she poked her at the base of her spine, a move her mother had made many a time to make her stand up straight.

"Your voice is stronger when you stand up straight. And you look better when you hold your shoulders back. Work it like you mean it."

"I try. I just…what do you think?"

Rachel paged through the spiral-bound book, which featured sketches of shoes, and even a few pages of ad ideas. It was remarkable. "You've got the storyboard process mastered. This one is interesting. The couple on the couch, talking about her shoes. But not sexy enough."

"I have trouble with the sex," Amelie confessed. "I never know how far is too far."

Rachel handed her the sketchbook. "I know what this pitiful office has to do to survive getting axed. We need to sex up the company's campaign."

"I'm afraid I'm not very sexy."

"Nonsense." She took in Amelie's proper black slacks and white dress shirt. Office attire. "You just…need to let your mind wander. When you think about shoes and sex, what comes up?"

Amelie winced. "Incompatible?"

"Really?" Rachel rather enjoyed wearing shoes to bed with a lover. "What comes up are long, sexy legs ending in fuck-me pumps, kicking the air as her lover licks her skin, mapping out her erogenous zones."

"Wow," Amelie said on a gasp.

Right. Wow. She was still flying high from last night. Did it show? She didn't care. For the first time in months, confidence had returned to soar through her veins.

"I need to get back to work." To focus the high she was feeling on business before it got her in trouble. "Hold my calls. And, I'll be working late to hash out the campaign. I'd…like to incorporate your ideas, Amelie. Would you mind?"

"Mind?" Amelie squealed, pressing the sketchbook to her chest. "I'd be honored!"

"Excellent. And do see if you can get solid information from headquarters about our visiting bigwig."

"Will do."

"Oh, and Amelie?"

"Yes, Miss Parker?"

"Keep sketching." Rachel winked at her and strode down the hallway, smiling to herself when she heard the quietest 'yes' of triumph echo out from her secretary's cubicle.

*

Zac stood before the window that ended the long entry hallway in the eleventh arrondissement apartment his mother had once occupied. Dusty and bare of linens and curtains, he'd opted for the hotel instead of fighting dust bunnies. His mother had lived here nine months out of the year. The other three months had been devoted to travel and visiting him in New York. The top-floor apartment had roof access that led to a neat collection of beehives that were still serviced by a local apiarist. Zac's mother had loved bees, and one of Haute Heels' first shoes had been 'bumblebee yellow.'

He sighed now, remembering the funeral ten years earlier. His mother had died young but had lived a good life. Ever traveling, learning, and always the first with hugs and the question, 'What makes you happy?'

So what made him happy lately? The prospect of having to close the one office his mother had coddled through the decades certainly didn't; it killed him. She lived in every piece of dated wallpaper, chipped-painted cornices, and even the scooped-shell marble basins in the bathrooms. He didn't want to close the office.

But he wasn't stupid. And if his trusted Operations Director said the office needed to go, it would go. The bottom line always mattered. Though, he wondered now... If Rachel could actually manage to throw together a campaign that would wow the clients on Friday, he'd hold off on pronouncing the office closed.

He wanted to see her succeed. She deserved success. She'd done a remarkable job holding the office together since the previous manager's exit. And working with little funds—corporate had to assume some responsibility for that.

His mother would have never allowed such neglect from corporate. And as Zac pressed his fingers to the window now, and thought to still smell a lingering wisp of Channel No. 5—his mother's signature scent—he mentally promised her he'd do what he could to see this office resurrected.

And he wasn't going to sell this apartment. Not yet. Not until...

He did travel. And Paris was a stop at least once a year. If he hired a maid to come in every few months, it would be nice to have a landing place. And if he had reason to stay longer, perhaps because there was someone special who lived in the same city...

Zac shook his head. What the hell was he doing? He'd just met Rachel, and they'd had no-strings sex. That did not a relationship make. Besides, he wasn't the guy who did relationships. He was the corporate raider who kept a different woman in every city and generally wore arm candy to events. But to get to know those pretty and mindless props?

Ugh. He'd just considered women as props. Rachel was no man's prop. What an amazing woman! Could he hope to earn her respect and admiration?

"You've gone about things the wrong way," he muttered. "You need to tell her who you are."

Chapter 7

The office was quiet, the overhead fluorescent lights out. The soft glow of floor lights that lined the walls gave off enough illumination to see around the cubicles. Zac had arrived just as the employees were leaving. Excellent. Now he had opportunity to really look around.

Much as the Paris office was failing spectacularly, Zac couldn't force himself to hit the fire 'em all button. And it wasn't because he'd slept with the office manager and had developed a sweet spot for her gorgeous set of gams.

It was because Rachel Parker possessed a vitality and determination that he believed could pull this office up from the depths, and maybe—just maybe—breathe new life into it.

But she couldn't do that without an excellent support team. And did she really enjoy her position as office manager? Or did she prefer to be back in marketing? He'd had a glimpse into her creative mind—it needed feeding. But he also felt strongly about her supervisory skills.

Pausing in the supply room doorway, he gave his thin Zegna tie a tug and loosened the tight knot. Since arriving at this office, he'd felt more relaxed, not so inclined to support the stern corporate raider image he'd mastered over the years.

But he was lying to Rachel every day he did not confess who he really was. The lie hadn't bothered him two days ago. Even yesterday, when he'd learned she might have a clue about the secret visit. Who at the New York office had alerted Paris to his presence?

Such secrecy was…stupid. It had initially felt necessary, to not alarm the employees. But now? Zac was rethinking that plan. The employees were people. People who had families and mouths to feed. They had a right to know what was going on.

As did Rachel. Something had developed between them beyond the personal relationship. A sort of business trust. And while not revealing his position in the company wasn't going to kill anyone, it would definitely drive a wedge between him and Rachel.

Was that a problem? It shouldn't be. He'd flown to Paris for the week. After today, two business days remained. He'd fly home. Life would move on. Whether or not he decided to keep this office intact.

It was this no-strings thing they had started. Hell, if he was muddling over it so much, it must mean he wanted to take it to the next level. The I'll call you, you call me level. The I'll see you exclusively level. The can I keep a change of clothing in your apartment? level.

"Really?" he muttered.

No woman had ever gotten under his skin so quickly. And if he pursued the taking it to the next level idea, then he wasn't sure how it would work for them on the business side of things. He couldn't have both relationships. Could he? Why else had he decided to keep the apartment if not because he had hope for the two of them?

He shook his head.

A moan from down the hallway alerted Zac that he wasn't the only one in the office. He spied the dim light coming out of the office manager's doorway. Of course, she would still be here. The woman was dedicated.

And yet, she had moaned. Had that been a good moan or a bad moan? And if it had been good, why was he still standing there?

Wandering down the aisle, he arrived at her door, smirked at the paper sign—she deserved a nice bronze plate—and pushed it inward. Shoes in open boxes were scattered over the floor, the black leather couch, and the desk. Shoes in every color, style, and heel height. He didn't immediately notice a human occupant until a box toppled from a stack and another moan echoed out.

"That bad, huh?"

"Who's there?" echoed out from around the corner of her desk. "Zac? I thought everyone had left for the day. I didn't even see you come in."

"I was finishing up some last minute—er, stuff." Like vacillating on whether or not to shut down the office. "Thought I was the only one here. What's up with the shoe deluge?"

Rachel's head popped around the corner of the desk and she thrust out a fuchsia satin heel. "What do you find sexy about this shoe?"

Zac tapped a finger against his lower lip and eyed the shoe, which he knew was part of the new fall line. Haute Heels had gone with deep, jewel tones to emulate a rich, decadent lushness. But if he revealed he knew that the shank had been engineered to expose the arch of the foot because men found that sexy, she'd know he knew too much.

"The pointed shape of the toe," he decided. "It's wicked."

She tilted her head, assessing the shoe. "It is wicked. You nailed it in less than three seconds. I've been sitting here all afternoon, racking my brain over ideas for the campaign meeting on Friday, and you nail it like that."

"All afternoon? You need a break."

"No. Nope. Nada. I will not leave this office until I've something to present to the Le Grand Chaussures in two days. I've got some notes from Amelie. She's very talented. I like this idea she's sketched, but not sure how to execute it."

He waded through the sea of footwear and plucked the fuchsia shoe from Rachel's hand, while grabbing her hand with the other and pulling her to her feet. He handed her the shoe. "Put it on."

"What?"

"Have you worn any of them?" He splayed his hands to take in the scattered boxes of shoes. "The best way to get a feel for the product is to wear it, isn't it?"

Her mouth dropped open and her eyelashes fluttered. She'd not considered that, but he was going to chalk it up to overworked and under-assisted.

"Put them on, and give them a go down the catwalk." He gestured out the door. "Let's see what you've got."

The smile that curled her mouth was too quickly hidden as she twisted down to slip on the shoes. Her derriere wiggled in the snug gray skirt she wore. He exhaled, recalling the feel of that gorgeous bottom in his hands. When she walked past him, he inhaled oranges. Perfect way to end a long day—breathing in summer.

She walked down the hallway, emulating a model's confidence and swagger. The thing about high heels? They gave every woman a sexy swagger, a hip-shifting swing, an innate confidence that made them carry their bodies straight, shoulders back and head high. It was enough to make any man hard.

And Zac was any man.

She pulled a runway turn at the end of the aisle by the Accounts Receivable desk and swung back toward him, exaggerating her strides as she assumed a model's pony-like prance. Zac recalled his mother always camping it up by modeling the season's newest shoes in just such a manner at holiday dinners and before friends.

"Modeling Haute Heels' fall line is the lovely Rachel Parker," he narrated as she neared him. "The shoes are fuchsia. The model is gorgeous."

"The narrator has a hard-on," she commented with another swing that took her down the aisle.

"Indeed, he does," he muttered on her return. "I don't suppose we can use the ad slogan 'Gives men a woody,' eh?"

"We? Remember, you're just IT." She tapped him on the nose admonishingly. "Next pair. I'm not feeling these." She ducked into the office to forage through the boxes. "These!"

Moments later, she again strode the makeshift catwalk, a pair of impossibly sexy black lace-ups hugging her ankles. The big black satin bows tied at the back of her narrow calves, crisscrossing once in front and in back, made him want to crisscross her with his arms and pull her in to crush against his erection. Which demanded some attention.

He needed a drink.

Spying a bottle of water sitting on her glass desktop, Zac twisted it open. Rachel strolled in and gave his chest a shove. Toppling over a stack of shoeboxes behind him, he landed on the couch. A nudge of her foot cleared the boxes between them. She put a foot on the cushion between his legs and leaned over. "What do you think of this pair?"

Zac's eyes were level with her breasts, which were neatly covered by her button-up lavender silk shirt, but those nipples were dangerously hard.

She tapped his chin. "I'm talking about the shoes, lover boy."

He set the water bottle on the floor beside an open shoebox. "Let me take a closer look."

Chapter 8

Computer geek that he was, the man had the right idea by suggesting Rachel put on the shoes and walk in them. Haute Heels were not the kind of shoes a woman slipped into at the last minute and slipped out of as soon as her feet were beneath a table or desk because they were so damned painful. These shoes were a dream to wear. Almost like walking on clouds. The owner's mother—the company's founder—had one stipulation for every pair of shoes sold: they must be comfortable.

And the pair Rachel wore right now caressed her soles. The silk ties that wrapped about her ankles made her feel like a cross between a ballet dancer and something more daring and sensual, like maybe a stripper.

Nothing wrong with feeling like an angel who also grips the pole. And thinking about poles...

Zac's hard-on was obvious as she drew her foot along his thigh to give him a closer look at the shoe. He gripped her ankle firmly and growled as the heel dug into his thigh. His hand glided over the silk ties and then he danced a fingertip along the inner curve of her arch. Oooh, that felt as good as if he were stroking her nipple.

"This shoe is sex tied up in black silk," he commented.

"I like that. More," she encouraged, leaning in to dash her tongue over his lower lip. Again, he tasted like the expensive coffee the barista across the street sold. Discerning geek. "Does the shoe turn you on?"

"The shoe on the woman turns me on."

"So the woman is an integral part of the seduction?"

"Hell, yes. You think I'm going to get off on the shoe? Just a shoe?"

She smiled against his lips and kissed him quickly. Meeting his soulful brown eyes, she said, "I've been told there are some who prefer just the shoe."

"Not me. I like what's inside them. And these satin ties definitely make me think about tying you up."

"Is that so?"

He slid his hands up her thighs, nudging up the skirt until she felt the air on her pantiless crotch. She straddled him, kneeling on the couch. The idea of a little kink appealed, but when her brain started to sort out how that could happen in an office—no restraints, no silk handkerchiefs or ties—her business logic struggled to take charge and resisted. Besides, she had to stay in the creative moment.

Zac leaned forward and bit the button on her silk shirt just between her breasts. He tugged, button in mouth. Once it had pulled free from the buttonhole, he released the other three buttons as quickly and glided his hands up to cup her lace-hugged breasts.

It was dinnertime, the office was empty, and the lights were low, but the shades were not pulled. Rachel briefly considered leaping up to draw the shades, then decided against it. If the man wanted a little kink, what could be more adventurous than the risk of being seen?

Gripping his skinny, gray tie, she loosened it and tugged it free, tossing it to the shoe-littered floor. His jacket slid off next, followed by his shirt as she unbuttoned it in tandem with him unsnapping the clasp in the front of her bra. She sat on his lap, grinding her mons against his impressive erection.

As his warm palm cupped her breast, he leaned in to gently bite her nipple, causing a heady sensation to zing from chest, to core, to her wet, wanting insides. "You sure this is safe?"

"You want it to be?" she asked.

"Only thinking of you and the office gossip mill."

"None of our employees are so dedicated you'll catch them here after hours."

"You're here." He lashed his tongue over the other nipple. Rachel felt the heat all the way to her core, and her skin prickled sweetly. Big, brown eyes smiled up at her.

"And so are you," she said. "Let's get back to the shoe research, shall we? You think the shoe is only as attractive as the woman wearing it?"

411

His sigh echoed what must be his growing frustration. But Rachel wouldn't tease much longer. Still. She did have work to do.

"The woman doesn't have to be a certain kind of attractive," he said, "it's all in how she carries herself while wearing the shoe."

"That's perfect," Rachel gasped as he leaned back and unzipped his pants. "The shoe makes a woman carry herself with more confidence. Gives her more power. Makes her feel sexual. Sensual. But that's been overdone." She exhaled, sighing futilely, then realized she was pouting.

Not on her watch.

With a tilt of her hips, she dragged a strappy, sexy shoe over the front of Zac's pants and toggled the head of his emerging cock with the hard, black stiletto heel. He ground her name out through a tense jaw and gripped her ankle.

"You've confidence in spades, Rachel. I don't think you need the shoes for that. But you can keep them on."

He groaned and shoved down his pants to his ankles then quickly made work of her clingy jersey skirt. She stepped out of it and straddled his lap, lowering, her heels clicking together above his knees.

"Come on," he dared her. "Ride me. I've heard sex is good for creativity."

"Oh, trust me, it is. And I will take all the creative mojo you're willing to give me."

She lowered onto his erection, humming deep in her throat as the hot, molten steel of him filled her, pierced her. Bowing to receive his kiss, Rachel rocked her hips, riding him. Taking exactly what she wanted, and giving in return.

The man groaned and leaned back, his palms sliding along her ribs and up to her breasts until his thumbs found her nipples. He pinched both, and the electric but sexy pain ramped up her rhythm.

"Yes, faster," he murmured.

His head tilted back and his eyes closed. He'd surrendered to the sensations, the moment, the dive into the creative well. For, truly, Rachel felt every part of her come alive, hum and tingle with energy. Oxygen infused her brain. Perspiration bejeweled her breasts, slickening Zac's pulling and tweaking of her nipples. Everything felt right. The challenges of work slipped away. This man filled her with all that she needed and could ever want.

Rachel felt his hips begin to shake as orgasm taunted him, urging him to release. So she gripped the base of his penis and squeezed, hoping it would prolong his release while she got off on the pistoning pleasure of riding him. Slipping him out, she then rubbed his hard, wet erection against her clit, causing Zac to moan even louder.

And when he tilted his head forward and met her gaze, she recognized the want and need, combined with unrelenting desire there. Taking him inside her again, she gasped as all parts of her hummed and soared toward the same precipice he balanced upon. And when he gripped her hips and slammed up into her, holding tight, they both came, shouting, gasping. Rachel even laughed a little as the tremendous release relaxed her muscles and she collapsed against his chest.

They sat there for long minutes, breathing in oranges and spice, listening to the heartbeats of one another. He was perfect. Handsome, smart, talented, and incredibly well-built. And attentive to her needs in a way she'd never before experienced from a man. He was everything a woman could ever want.

Did she want him? For more than just a few hot and heavy hookups?

"I want you," he singsonged as he stroked the hair spilling down her back, "I need you…"

Rachel sat up a little and met his heavy-lidded gaze. "I heard you humming that tune when you were under my desk. What is it?"

"Elvis."

"Oh, yes, now I recognize it. Hmm, you've got a little Elvis in you." She slicked her fingers through his hair to give him a bit of a ducktail coif in the front. His dark, harsh features smirked. "I want you."

He responded with a thrust of his hips against her lusciously aching mons. "I need you," he sang out boldly. "I love you."

"Wait!" Rachel's brain flashed like some kind of nuclear cloud going off. "That's it!"

Tugging out of the man's grasp, she toppled backward and almost fell over a stack of boxes, but managed to catch herself against the desk. Picking up her skirt, she swung around the side of the desk to land on her chair. Shirt open and breasts exposed, she grabbed a pen and paper and started sketching.

"Inspiration?" the sated man on the couch wondered.

She glanced up, and in those brief seconds, saw his perspiring chest strapped with gorgeous muscle, his satisfied grin that never grew too big, and that sneaky hard-on that was ready for round two. Oh, sex on a stick, how he served her creativity.

"He's singing to her," she announced with creative glee. "He's seducing her. And she's mirroring him." She tapped the pen against her lips. "Singing back!"

"You're leaving me high and dry here, Rachel."

She swished the pen in the air before her in a conductor's move. "Sing it again."

"Sing? Really?"

"Please?"

He broke into the lines from the Elvis song, ending with a crooning, "I love you."

"But you don't really love me," she felt the need to interject curtly. "That's just lyrics, right?"

He nodded. But did he wince at the end?

"Good." Some things a woman needed clarified. Love was not on the table. It couldn't be. Could it? "He's singing, and she is, too…" She drew an empty thought bubble above the sketch of the woman Amelie had drawn. "But she's thinking about the shoes!"

She had it. The ad campaign. And she had Zac to thank for it.

Chapter 9

The hotel room felt a little less vacant this morning, despite the fact that Rachel was not lying in the bed all sex-tousled and content. She'd wanted to go home alone last night after their office tryst, and Zac hadn't argued. Too much. She'd said something about keeping him at bay.

Really? Was she playing hard to get?

It was working.

Of course, she'd also mentioned the campaign and didn't think she'd sleep a wink. He had been the one to spur her creative epiphany, and he patted himself on the back for that. His cock had never served a more useful purpose.

He leaned forward, inspecting his fresh shave job in the bathroom mirror. He always nicked his earlobe, but today not a speck of blood. Interesting. Must be due to how relaxed he was feeling. Almost as if the world had suddenly fallen into order.

But not completely.

He wanted to look good when he walked into Rachel's office today. Because he intended to confess all. It had to be done.

"Just like ripping off a Band-Aid," he muttered.

Hell, the smart move would be to break it off and let her stand tall and grant her the promotion she deserved. A promotion befitting her talents. He'd walk away. And when given all the necessary support, the Paris Haute Heels office would thrive under Rachel's control.

But he didn't like that version because it meant he'd have to walk away from the girl.

So, after his confession, he'd try to make it work. Because he was falling for the woman. Hell, he'd tripped and landed in her arms, and didn't want to struggle free. He just had to cross his fingers she could hear him after he told her who he really was.

*

Amelie followed Rachel down the aisle toward the office with her usual armload of files and message slips. She kept starting to tell Rachel something, but Rachel continued to shush her. She needed to get to her coffee and then she could settle in and listen to the days' forthcoming scheduled disasters.

"It's urgent," Amelie tried.

Rachel rounded her desk, wading through the shoeboxes she hadn't cleaned up after last night's planning session, and sat, placing the coffee cup before her. In a grand ritual, she placed both palms to the warm cup, closed her eyes, inhaled the roasted aroma, and allowed herself two seconds of bliss.

She peeled open one eyelid. Amelie fairly vibrated, her ponytail swishing back and forth behind her skull.

Ripping off the plastic lid, Rachel conceded, "Give it to me. But please—" She put up a staying finger. "— let me enjoy one sip before the deluge."

The coffee was hot, and she lingered on the creamy brew. Zac had converted her to the expensive stuff. Or was it that the coffee reminded her of him and anything lesser wouldn't do? Her vision averted to the leather couch. A space was cleared of boxes and shoes where Zac and she had fucked. A broad smile grew behind the coffee cup.

"My contact in the home office emailed," Amelie blurted out. "She was wondering how it was going with the visiting bigwig. When I replied that he hadn't arrived yet, she told me his name."

Amelie ceremoniously placed a pink message slip on the desk, face down, no pre-printed fill-in-the-blanks showing. On the back was written a name in bright red. Rachel leaned forward to read it.

She choked on the coffee. It burned the back of her throat. Amelie squealed and rushed out of the office. Rachel felt her lungs seal up and struggled to breathe.

Her secretary flew back in with a bottle of water and cracked the plastic seal, thrusting it toward Rachel like a pro emergency worker. Rachel drank half the water before sitting back and staring at her secretary in utter horror.

She read Rachel's terror. "I know. What a sneak, eh? And I kind of thought you had your eye on him."

Her eye? More like her hands, thighs, breasts—oh, bloody hell!

"Well, I've seen how you look at him," Amelie continued, oblivious to Rachel's inner breakdown. "Behind those nerd glasses lives sex on a stick."

"They're geek glasses," Rachel whispered, feeling all her confidence slush out at her toes. "Big difference between a nerd and a geek." Her shoulders hit the chair and she slumped down against the fake leather, feeling oh so used. "He lied to me."

"It was a good cover, you have to admit. If anyone in the office would have known the big guy was coming to assess us with plans to shut us down?"

"Shut us down?" The initial memo hadn't mentioned anything like that. Seriously? Amelie was just telling her that now? "Leave me, Amelie."

"Do you want me to pick up the shoes lying on the floor first?"

Rachel shook her head. "Hold my calls, and when Monsieur Cosgrove arrives—"

A lush bouquet of deep red roses appeared in the doorway. Behind them popped up a pair of thick, black-rimmed glasses and that devastatingly sexy smirk that Rachel now wanted to crush with those flowers—and pray for thorns.

"Did someone say my name?"

Amelie popped upright from collecting a few pairs of shoes, her gaze flashing from Rachel to Zac, then back to Rachel. "I'll hold your calls," she said, and clutching the shoes to her chest as if they were life preservers, she slipped out as Zac stepped into the office. Amelie closed the door behind her.

The sensation of tears tugged at Rachel's eyes. But no. She wasn't a crybaby. Instead, she straightened her spine and channeled her inner...aggression. Yeah, she would now show the man the meaning of aggressive.

Shooting upright behind the desk, she strode around it, kicking aside empty shoeboxes. Crossing her arms over her chest, she was surprised that Zac didn't flinch from the death vibes shooting out from her pupils.

"I thought red would complement your gorgeous skin," he said. He offered the roses, bound with a black satin ribbon.

Just like the shoes that sat on the couch right now. Last night's catalyst to an amazing evening of sex. And an ever more amazing campaign idea. And now Rachel realized it had all been a lie. He had been using her in the most horrible, underhanded way. He was going to shut down the office?

She grabbed the roses then shoved them back at him. Hard. The man toppled backward, tripped over a shoebox, and caught himself against the wall. "Rachel?"

He had the audacity to look shocked! "How dare you?"

He looked at the crushed bouquet. "You don't like red? I'm sorry—"

"You're the bloody bigwig!"

"Oh." He tossed the roses to the couch, where they landed on top of the shoes. A symbol of her disastrous love life, those untied shoes and crushed roses. "I don't understand how you found out. There must be a mole in the home office?"

"Seriously? You intended to keep it a secret? Who are you? No." She thrust up a palm to stop his explanation. "I know who you are. The CEO of Haute Heels. Or are you the IT guy from downstairs? Clever disguise. Do you even wear glasses?"

He pushed up the glasses on his nose but remained silent. Smart man.

"I can't believe I let you use me like you did."

"Rachel, I had no intention of using you. Do you think I did?"

"What do you call sleeping with the office manager? Because I'm really interested in those sneaky tactics. I don't understand how fucking me was going to make closing the office—oh.

Wait. Did you think to get me on your side, let me down gently? Sleep with the girl and send her off with a smile?"

"Rachel, please. What happened between you and me was not what I'd intended. The sex just happened. It has nothing to do with Haute Heels and my being here to assess the office."

"Undercover! As some nerdy IT guy."

"You mean geek."

"You ass!"

He silently put up his palms to placate her. With a tilt of his head and a suppressed wince, he said, "I came here today with the intention of telling you all. When you mistook me for IT that first day, I thought to go with it. The Operations Director and I had agreed to keep this visit low-key. I didn't want to upset any of the employees. Thought it would make my looking around easier and no one would have reason to be nervous around me or—"

"Or maybe the office manager would just fall into bed with you? I can't believe you. I can't believe myself. I'm smarter than this!"

Rachel pressed her knuckles to her forehead. What a way to go. Fucked by the boss, and then kicked to the curb. And she had been so close to perfecting the ad campaign for tomorrow's meeting. Her creative mojo was top form. Things had been looking up since Zac's arrival.

Or she had just been too blind to the truth. That the man standing before her intended to fire the employees and send them packing. Oh, how she had failed this office. She didn't even deserve the paper sign on the door.

"Rachel, there's no way to make this better. I considered breaking it off between us and stepping back but—"

"You don't think lying to me is grounds for breaking things off?" She checked her volume, flashing a glance through the window. No one was looking toward the office. But she knew better. This old building had been solidly built, but the cubicle gophers could hear a high-pitched dog whistle if given the right impetus.

In a quiet but firm tone, she said. "We are through. I don't ever want to see you again. In fact, I'll make things easy for you. I know you're going to shut down the office. You don't have to worry about firing me because I quit."

She grabbed the coffee on her desk and looked about for her purse. There it sat, on the couch next to the shoes and roses. Remnants of an affair she'd had just as much a hand in encouraging as Zac.

Heaving in a big inhale, Rachel suddenly had a switch in temperament. No. This wasn't the way to do it. She had obligations to Haute Heels. Granted, they were ones she'd taken on in the wake of the former manager's departure—she wasn't even manager material. But she would not step down from what she had started.

Rachel Parker was not a quitter.

"Tomorrow," she corrected. "After the meeting with Le Grand Chaussures. I'll deliver the campaign, and then it's all yours. Sweep the blade. Ax everyone in the office and strip the walls down to the ugly, flocked paper."

"I'll have you know my mother chose that wallpaper. I rather like it."

"Your mother?" Right. She'd known an eccentric French woman with a passion for comfort and shoes had founded the company. So Zac was her son? Mercy, this just got better and better.

But not really.

And she wasn't in the mood to deal with the fallout of her stupid mistake.

"Leave," she stated firmly. "I have a lot of work to do before tomorrow."

She had just told her boss to take a hike. And he was standing there like a wrinkle-browed puppy dog that had been denied a treat. She would not crumble. She wouldn't allow herself to retract a single hateful thought at the sight of his thick black brows and his pouty brown eyes.

"Haute Heels needs Rachel Parker," Zac said softly. "That's why I've put in a requisition for your official promotion to office manager. I intend to keep the Paris branch open. This office was my mother's brainchild. But the only way that dream can succeed is if you are heading operations. With an excellent staff to support you. We'll be pushing funds through for more hires and updated equipment. I hope you'll accept the promotion."

Rachel inhaled and breathed through her nose, seeking calm. A promotion? To the job she'd already been filling? Would he also give her the pay raise she deserved?

Hell, what was she thinking? It was all tainted now. And she had had a hand in making it wrong. Inside, she was shaking, raging. But outside, she pulled on calm. "I don't sleep my way to the top, Monsieur Cosgrove."

"You did not do that."

"Are you sure about that? Because I'll never really know if I did or did not get that promotion because we shared a bed. And I can't live with that. My resignation remains. I'll take my marketing skills elsewhere. Somewhere they don't use underhanded tactics to spy on their employees."

Zac bowed his headed and nodded. "Whoever is fortunate enough to gain your talents will be a very lucky company indeed. You will excel no matter where you go, Rachel. I wish you luck. It's my fault we're losing you. I'll have to go back to corporate and tell them the truth."

"That you tricked me."

"It wasn't intentional. Just a really stupid decision on my part. Rachel…" He sighed and shoved his hands in his pockets. "All right. Resignation accepted. Business discussion complete. But can we have the us discussion now?"

"Are you—" The word crazy wouldn't rattle off her tongue. But her heartbeats raced so quickly she wanted to push against her chest to still them. And it took all her courage not to let her voice shake when she said, "There is no us."

"For a few amazing days there was an us. Admit it. You were into me."

"I was into the geek beneath my desk who I mistakenly trusted was telling me the truth."

"Yeah, about that geek." He rubbed a hand at the back of his neck. "That really was me about a decade ago. I started out in IT at Haute Heels. Never thought I'd follow in my mother's footsteps as head of the company, that's for sure. Being an executive is…well, it's weird. It still doesn't feel right to me some days. Hell, you mistaking me for the geek was refreshing. I admit, you made me want to be that guy again. The regular guy. The one no one makes demands of. Everyone always wants something from the CEO. And I'm expected to be some kind of ruthless raider. That's not me. You, Rachel, demanded nothing but my presence, and a little computer magic."

Rachel swallowed. She would not succumb to the guy's feel-good rising-through-the-ranks story. Everyone had one of those. And besides, he was the company founder's son. How hard had he really had to struggle to become the owner?

"I got to enjoy the remarkable experience of learning you." He smiled to himself and glanced at the flowers. "I like what we have going, Rachel."

"Had going," she corrected.

"We can make this work. I want to make this work. Don't you, even a tiny part of you? Don't you want that, too?"

She crossed her arms tighter, resisting the mutinous scream that wanted to leap from her mouth and agree with the man. It was her heart, vying to be heard, wanting to rise up from the mundane of the nine-to-five (but really nine-to-eight) and grasp on to something wonderful. Something she hadn't realized she'd needed until she'd met Zachary Cosgrove.

She had enjoyed the us.

Even now, knowing it had been a lie.

If she could believe Zac, the us part hadn't been a lie. And he had only been using the cover she'd mistakenly given him that morning when she'd assessed him as the office geek. But seriously, what CEO wears a pocket protector?

A glance over Zac's impressive Italian suit revealed a peek of white vinyl beneath the jacket. He did. Guess you could promote the guy to head of the company, but you couldn't erase all the geek from the CEO.

"Rachel?"

But she couldn't concede. Such floundering after she'd announced her resignation was unacceptable. And he had accepted her resignation. Just like that. Not even a lackluster argument over him wanting her to stay.

"I'm sorry." She picked up a random manila folder from the glass desktop and walked around Zac to the door. "I have work to do. If you could find a way to stay out of my office, I'd appreciate it. As I've said, I'll finish what I started before officially leaving. I'll see you tomorrow morning at the client meeting."

"Rachel."

She turned the doorknob. Her heart pounded. Her feet wanted to turn her body around. Her arms wanted to pull him to her. Her soul screamed for more of what they'd given one another.

"Thanks," he said to her back. "For your honesty. And for an amazing few days. I wish it could have been different, but I'm unsure how to make things right for you."

Without a word, she left the man standing in her office. Rachel spied a cubicle gopher's head bob down, and she beelined for the ladies' room. She'd never cried at work before.

There was a first time for everything.

Chapter 10

Today was the morning of Rachel's last day at Haute Heels. She had given Zac—Monsieur Cosgrove—her resignation. She hadn't seen him since the angry tossed roses scene in her office. And well he should avoid her. The asshole had lied to her.

Very well. He'd perpetuated a mistruth she'd believed about him. Same thing.

Right?

She picked up a velvety rose petal. The bouquet still sat on the couch and the flowers hadn't faded nor had the petals wilted overnight without water. It was as if they were desperately holding on, a symbol of the hope for the relationship between her and Zac.

"Relationship. Yeah, right," she muttered. "It was sex. We both took advantage of the other. I fueled my creativity with the sex. He…"

He'd said the sex had nothing to do with the business. That he wanted them to continue to be an us. What was that about? How could that even work? He lived in New York. And even after she walked away from her job today, Rachel would remain in Paris.

"Hopefully, it won't be too difficult to find another job."

She had to admit, she was beginning to feel comfortable in the management chair. And as Zac had said, had she the proper funds to hire more employees and do the job right, she may have just shone in the position. But it was too late for that dream now.

"You ready?"

Curling her fingers over the rose petal, she nodded at Amelie's entreaty.

"The meeting is in five minutes," Amelie said. "I've just seated the marketing team for Le Grand Chaussures, and we're waiting on Monsieur Cosgrove."

Rachel's heart double-stepped. Oh, Zac. It had been she who labeled him the IT guy, setting this whole lie in motion.

No. She wasn't going to blame herself for this.

"I'll head down there right now," Rachel said. "You're sitting in, Amelie."

"To take notes?"

"No, silly." Rachel picked up the sketches from her desk. Amelie's sketches that she had revised and worked up on the whiteboard that she'd set up in the conference room an hour earlier. "I told you I wanted to incorporate some of your ideas, and I did. This is as much your project as it is mine."

The woman beamed.

"Let's do this," Rachel said.

*

Zac thought Rachel Parker had felt something for him. A purely physical and sexual attraction, sure. The same need for no-strings sex he'd felt. But beyond the surface stuff, he'd thought they had begun to connect. It had been but a few days, and—yes, he knew—romance took longer than that.

But did it really? What about all that love at first sight stuff? Couldn't a man have sex with a woman and then allow his heart to catch up to the excitement and genuinely want to continue the relationship?

Or was he making up a fiction that worked for his need to fill the emptiness in his life?

It wasn't empty. He had a great job, an amazing cadre of friends, and a bank account that would keep him and his future family comfortable for many generations to follow. Zachary Cosgrove had everything.

Except the one woman who appealed to his sense of desire, uniqueness, and wanting to simply enjoy life with someone who made him feel alive. And who didn't ask anything of him save to be in the moment when he was with her.

Refreshing. And whether or not their relationship could survive a long-distance stint, he wanted the chance to give it a go.

But he couldn't blurt that out right now. So he shoved a hand into his pocket and palmed the item he'd picked up from the floor of Rachel's office. She'd gotten under his skin, and he didn't want to rub her away.

Rachel stood before the whiteboard—a red, tailored dress hugging her body and flaring flirtatiously at her knees. She wore the black ribbon shoes she had worn the other night when they'd fucked on the couch. She flipped through the campaign design sheets on the Powerpoint display, knocking the socks off both the clients and him. Her ad campaign was seriously sexy and right on point to capture the consumer's attention.

It was also very familiar.

The storyboard featured a sexy couple making out on a couch in a shoe store dressing room, the man stroking his hand along the woman's leg. She wore the black satin tieups. And as Rachel narrated the man's thoughts—which echoed the Elvis song Zac had sung to her—the clients' heads bobbed. They loved it.

And when she revealed the twist, that the woman was thinking the same thing—I want you, I need you, I love you—only about the shoes, the clients burst out in applause.

The head of Le Grand Chaussures' marketing team shook Rachel's hand and confirmed their interest in going ahead with the campaign. She paused when the client asked how soon the preliminaries could be delivered, and looked to Zac. He had been introduced as Zachary Cosgrove, the CEO of Haute Heels. Here on a routine visit, and just sitting in on the conference.

Zac cleared my throat. "Timeline? I'm not sure. The Paris office just made an offer for a new office manager but we're not sure she'll accept."

Rachel flashed him the evil eye. Hey, he had one last chance to win her for his team. And that was the Haute Heels team, not the Zac Needs a Girlfriend team. He was pulling out the big guns.

The marketing director expressed concern.

"We'll make it happen," Rachel said. "I'll head the campaign myself. I'm, uh…not going anywhere as long as this project needs attention."

Handshakes were exchanged. Everyone was happy. Even Zac could concede happiness in the wake of his failed personal life. Amelie led the clients out, and Rachel stayed behind to gather the abandoned files and pens.

Zac stood and paced to the other side of the conference table, watching her. He sensed her annoyance at him standing there, eyeballing her. He could feel her need to give him the evil eye. Points to her for repressing that need. But he didn't want to leave her orange-scented atmosphere. Because to leave would surely mean the end.

When the folders had been stacked, Rachel strolled around the table to where he stood. He held the final file folder. Without saying a word, she held out her hand. So Zac dug into his suit pocket and placed something small on her palm.

Rachel gaped at the white button. It had fallen off her shirt the evening they'd had sex in her office, and Zac had picked it up off the floor before leaving. He'd immediately recalled her button jar, and how she always wondered about those who had lost the tiny treasures.

"I know you like to collect buttons and wonder about the owner. Let me tell you about this one," he said. "I know its owner is young, female, and very smart. She's got confidence in spades, and isn't afraid to take charge even in the most dire circumstances. She takes what she wants without being aggressive, and has no regrets. I believe that's called being assertive. And she's pretty damn gorgeous, too."

"I didn't even realize it was missing." She curled her fingers over the button. "From the other night?"

"Yes. I'm glad you've decided to stay on," he said.

"Only until the ad is complete. I started this campaign; I'll see it through. And if I can do something about improving the office's output in that interim, I'll certainly do it. I've decided that I can't let personal feelings distract from professional goals. I'll prove to you that our branch deserves a second chance."

"You've already done that. You'll notice your HR budget has been increased. You can start hiring your dream design team as soon as you wish. I'd suggest promoting your secretary to Design."

"Will do. Amelie has some great ideas. I couldn't have managed this campaign without her sketches."

"I know you're intent on leaving Haute Heels, but I'd like to see you officially accept the position of office manager. Rachel, this office needs you. I know it can thrive with you at the helm."

"Can I have the weekend to think it over?"

"Of course."

"Do you fly out tonight?"

"Sunday. I gave myself an extra day to do the tourist thing. Can you believe I've never been to the Eiffel Tower?"

"You should go tonight. It's gorgeous after the sun sets. They light it up at the top of every hour for ten minutes."

"It would be more interesting if I had a date to accompany me."

"Zac."

He took her hand, and remarkably, she didn't pull from his grip. So he leaned back and closed the meeting room door. There were no windows out to the office. And no security cameras.

Turning around, Zac pulled Rachel into his arms and kissed her. Deeply. Lingering. Pulling her hips against his to secure her, to hold her. To keep from doing something crazy like rushing away from that which scared him the most—committing to a crazy long-distance relationship. And she didn't pull away, which flooded him with hope.

"Just give me tonight and the Eiffel Tower?" he asked. "I don't want to walk away from you, Rachel."

"You can kiss me all you like. I still don't sleep with my boss."

"Technically…" He lifted a finger between them. "…I'm not your boss. I'm the owner of the company. You answer to Joel Stinson, the Operations Director."

Her smile widened. "I never thought of it that way."

"Well, you should. And if you ever think about sleeping with that guy—"

"I hear he's an old man. And he's married."

"Good to know you have morals."

"Coming from the man who lied to me about who he was."

Another kiss silenced her nicely. He'd wronged her. Professionally. And he should have never mixed business with pleasure, despite both of them insisting they were not. They had. No denying it.

On the other hand, if he had not done just that, he may have never lost his heart to this incredible woman.

"We started out wrong, and because I liked it so much, I perpetuated the lie. I'm sorry, Rachel."

She stroked his cheek and then ruffled her fingers through his hair. "I know you are. It was as much my fault for allowing it to happen."

"You harbor no blame in this. Can we give it one more day?"

"And what happens after that?"

"Maybe we can figure something out. Maybe not. But another day is all I ask."

"I'll give you a night and a day. Dinner at the Eiffel Tower tonight. And tomorrow? We'll discuss that in the morning."

"I'll pick you up at seven?"

"I'll be waiting."

Zac grabbed the office door pull and opened it, but turned back. "Uh, there's one more thing that I know about the owner of that button."

"That she's abandoned all rational thinking?"

"Not at all. It's that she's stolen my heart."

Rachel's mouth fell open. Zac winked at her, then strolled off down the hallway.

Epilogue

One month later...

Palm pressed to the glass, Rachel couldn't even worry that she stood before the living room window, naked, her head tilted back because Zac's fingers clutched at her hair while he thrust his cock deep inside her. So the neighbors would get a show. She was pretty certain that, standing in the dark room, and with the streetlights hidden around the corner, no one would see too much. Shadowplay, perhaps?

Let them ogle.

Zac had left Paris a month earlier, handing her the key to his mother's former apartment and telling her she could visit it, fix it up, do whatever she liked to it. He hadn't suggested she move into it, which she appreciated. She did not like to think of herself as a kept woman.

But she did consider herself Zac's girlfriend. His lover. His confidante and friend. And he promised to make a point of visiting Paris at least every other month. In between those visits, Skype served them well. She'd never gotten so much use out of her vibrator as she had in the last few weeks while Skyping Zac.

Now he slipped his palm down from her breasts, over her stomach, and fingered her slippery clitoris. He was in town for five days, and she was using some vacation days to make the most of them. As he landed on the perfect spot and her core exploded with sensation, she felt his teeth gently dig into her shoulder. That erotic touch released her orgasm and she shuddered, falling back into his arms, tilting her head onto his shoulder.

"This geek got the girl," he murmured.

And together they laughed.

∞OO∞

The End

I really appreciate the time you took to read **The Geek Gets The Girl**! If you liked the story, I would love it if you'd take a few minutes to leave a review at Goodreads. Reviews help authors who are self-publishing their work to get advertising! The book page for the SUMMER HEAT anthology, which this story appears in is:

https://www.goodreads.com/book/show/28966094-summer-heat

Follow me in Twitter: **http://twitter.com/michelehauf**
Visit my Website: **http://michelehauf.com**
Visit my Tumblr page: **http://haufsbeautifulcreatures/tumblr.com**
Visit my Pinterest page: **http://pinterest.com/toastfaery**

BAD BOYS FOR HIRE: KEN

Bad Boys for Hire Series - Book Two

Rachelle Ayala

After Jolie Becker is left at the altar, her friends secretly hire a handsome

beach bum to cheer her up.

To Joëlle Beebe, you fill my life with beautiful pictures and stories. Thanks for bringing your sparkle to my fan club.

Amiga Books
© 2016 by Rachelle Ayala
All rights reserved.

Chapter One

"Bad Boys for Hire, how may I help you?" Rex Carter fumbled with his phone and dropped it on the gym mat next to a pile of weights. He'd been bulking up lest his girlfriend think of hiring one of his new line of male stripper bad boys.

"Hello, anyone there?" a female voice chirped. "I'm in need of a bad boy, right away."

Bad Boys for Hire was an entertainment service putting clients together with role-playing actors, and Rex was always getting emergency requests, most of the time for fake boyfriends and party dates.

"Rex Carter here, just a minute while I find a quieter place." He ambled from the weight room to the deck in back of the club. It overlooked a parking lot bordered by a trickling creek.

"Mr. Carter," the female said. "I'm Nikki Chu, but I'm not calling for myself."

Uh oh, one of those. Rex leaned over the balcony and sucked in a breath of fresh air, preparing himself for the comforting hems and haws to assure the potential client of confidentiality.

"Go ahead, let me know what your friend needs."

"This is an emergency," Nikki said. "We have a wedding in progress—a wedding without a groom."

Rex moved the phone from his ear and stared at it. Over the years, he'd gotten some strange requests for his escort service, but this one took the wedding cake.

"You're looking for a substitute groom?"

"Yes. All the guests are sitting in the ballroom. The bride and her bridesmaids are assembled. The father of the bride is pacing the hallway. Everything is a go, but we need a groom."

"How much time do we have?"

"The mother of the bride is singing a special to hold the guests, but with the way her voice wobbles, I'm afraid people will be leaving soon. By the way, the bride doesn't know her fiancé is missing."

"That's horrible. How do you know he won't show up?"

"We have him hogtied in one of the suites. He was caught with his pants down. There's no freaking way we're letting our best friend marry a cheating imposter who's only after her for her family's money."

"You want her to marry a stranger instead?" Rex leaned further over the balcony.

A brunette swished her fine ass out of the gym and walked toward her car.

"Of course not. It's only for the ceremony. They don't have to sign the marriage certificate. Oh, please, hurry. Here she comes, asking me for something borrowed."

"Great, I'll order a groom to go," Rex said, holding back a whistle at the sexy lady who was getting into her convertible.

"I'll text you the address. Send a blond man to match the groom, but please hurry." Nikki's voice lowered. "The flower girl's already starting down the aisle."

"Caught you, jerk." A fist walloped Rex, sending the phone spinning from his hand.

It landed smack in the backseat of the convertible as it drove below him.

"Hey, stop. Stop!" he yelled at the brunette. "My phone. You have my phone."

The car stopped and backed up.

"What did you say?" the brunette lowered her sunglasses.

Before Rex could answer, his girlfriend, the one who'd punched him, picked up his legs and flipped him over the balcony.

His arms and legs spiraling, Rex belly-flopped into the backseat of the car. Pain exploded over his body, but at least he had his phone.

Chapter Two

Jolie Becker felt like puking. Yes, puking. She was trussed up in her tight wedding gown, strangled with beads, and tottering on stilts—er, stiletto pumps.

And she was left all alone in the hotel room while her good for nothing bridesmaids went in search for wedding essentials—something old, something new, something borrowed, and something blue.

Shouldn't all of these precious things have been planned beforehand? What happened to making a list and checking it twice, thrice, and more? This was her day, and everyone was supposed to be on hand to pamper her and help her settle her jittery nerves, not have her stress out over details.

Not that she trusted anyone to do her makeup. She was, after all, a makeup artist, and she was very particular about the quality and purity of her cosmetics. She also did her own hair—not easy without the three way mirrors she had at her salon, but then again, no one knew the exact sequence of product application to make her hair shine.

To top it off, she didn't even have a bouquet!

Her maid-of-honor, or actually newlywed matron of honor, bestie Terri Martin Slade, had delivered her flowers to another wedding party, and if what she heard in the hallways could be believed, her other bridesmaids were faring no better.

Nikki Chu was in charge of the wedding photography, but instead of setting up the cameras, she was dealing with a scheduling problem. Leanna Rivera, the baker, was busily patching cracks in the wedding cake, and Sherelle Edwards, who owned the catering company, had to roll back the finger foods for the reception, because she forgot Jolie and half of her family were allergic to shellfish.

Which was why Jolie Becker, the bride, was left all alone minutes before her impending wedding.

"Stay put," they'd said, as one by one, her mother, her auntie, and four best girlfriends in the whole wide world, had disappeared.

That had been at least an hour ago.

Jolie blinked at herself in the mirror, wondering how her groom, Warren Wayne, was faring. He would be at the front of the assembly, shaking hands and joking around with the groomsmen. He, at least, would know what the hold up was about. Maybe they were missing a preacher, or her father had spilled punch on his tux, or the ring bearer had lost the pillow with the rings.

It was terribly unfair for the bride to be in the dark. Why wasn't anyone coming back for her? For all they knew, she could be slitting her wrists or puking her guts out.

She swallowed bile and rushed to the door. It opened with a crash, and her matron of honor, Terri, barged in with a trailing bouquet of bright blue forget-me-nots.

"This was the best I could do," Terri said. "The concierge screwed everything up when they directed my delivery man to the Booker-Wang wedding instead of the Becker-Wayne wedding. Seems his accent is hard to understand."

"Blue? Blue?" Jolie stomped her foot, wincing as she turned her ankle. Drat these heels. "My wedding theme is pink. Fifty Shades of Pink!"

"There's not a pink flower left in the shop, or within the entire fifty mile radius. You ordered all available shades of pink." Terri jiggled the blue forget-me-nots. "Believe me, Booker and Wang were unhappy about the pink, but they went ahead and used the flowers already—unless you want me to ask if Mae Wang has tossed the bouquet yet."

"I hate blue." Jolie grabbed the bouquet.

Behind Terri, her other three bridesmaids filed into the room, looking harried and dejected.

"At least we covered two bases here." Smart-mouthed Sherelle pushed her glasses up across the bridge of her nose. "You've got your something blue and something new. I was able to scare up an assortment of meatballs for the reception. Fresh from the slaughterhouse."

"Meatballs?" Jolie shrieked. "Whoever heard of meatballs for a reception?"

"There's lamb, beef, chicken, and even vegan ones," Sherelle said. "Not a shellfish in sight. Entirely kosher, too."

"Okay, okay, fine," Jolie turned to her other two bridesmaids. "Are we ready?"

"Cake's patched up." Leanna strutted by, shaking a spatula. "I filled in all the paw prints. No one will notice."

"She was brilliant," Nikki said. "She even put a doggie biscuit on top of the biggest crack, so if anyone sees the paw print indentations, they'd think it was part of the design. And don't worry, I can Photoshop everything else."

"Yep, yep, yep." Leanna preened her dark, luscious hair and jutted her triple-D bosom toward the mirror. "I'll say, I do look good in ruffles, like frosting on a cake and just as lickable."

Nikki groaned and Sherelle rolled her eyes. Terri, who was a plus size gave Leanna the finger. "Nikki, can you Photoshop the ruffles from my dress?"

"Remember, change the color of my dress to rose," Sherelle said.

"I want slimmer hips," Terri added. "And don't make me too pale or washed out."

"Seriously, girls." Jolie snapped her fingers. "Rather than worrying about the Photoshopping, we need to get going."

She, of course, had no need to be Photoshopped. She was a slim size six, had lustrous multihued red hair with blond highlights, and being a makeup artist, she'd blended her colors perfectly—all except for the blue flowers she had in her hands.

"Actually I take that back, Nikki." Jolie shook the bouquet as if it were her fist. "Make these pink forget-me-nots, and I'll toss the bouquet your way."

"Okie doke," her roommate chirped. "I can do wonders with Photoshop."

"Including Photoshopping the groom," Sherelle gave her a thumbs up. "Nikki's a wiz."

"Yes, please, give him a tan and make sure to whiten his teeth." Jolie's spirits lifted. The wedding was about to happen. Everything was okay now that her best friends were here. "You all are the best friends a girl could ever have. Bumblebees sting!"

The five fast friends, all members of their preschool Bumblebee dance troupe, turned their behinds toward each other and bumped.

Chapter Three

"But soft! What light through yonder window breaks?" Ken Cassidy held the script with one hand while puffing out his chest to project his voice. "It is the east, and Juliet is the sun! … Arise, fair sun, and, and, kill—"

His landline phone rang, and Ken held his breath. These days, no one called except for telemarketers, robocallers, and bill collectors. They could all wait.

He walked into his bedroom and shut the door. The summer theatre season was starting soon, and he needed to get his lines down if he were to play the role of Romeo. Problem was, he couldn't focus or concentrate without getting a headache.

After glancing at the script, he threw it on the bed and stood in front of the mirror. He was handsome enough to be a Romeo, objectively speaking. Blue-gray eyes, sandy blond hair, and a year round tan thanks to his professional surfing career—one which ended when he suffered a concussion after being pummeled by a fifty-foot El Niño-spurred wave at an extreme surfing competition.

Here he was, washed up at twenty-nine. His balance was off, and he suffered dizzy spells, which meant he couldn't even wait tables while trying to land an acting role.

Ken opened the window, took a breath of fresh air, and recited the lines from the beginning of the scene. The morning sunlight filtered through the majestic redwoods lining the creek behind the complex. Tiny saplings peeked from beneath the thick trunks of the old growth, oblivious to their bleak prospects, given the lack of sunlight and space to grow. What choice did they have?

The wipeout was one of the worst in surfing history and Ken had been damn lucky to survive. All it meant was that one door had closed, and therefore another one had to open. During high school, he'd balanced his time between surfing and theatre. He'd had his day in the surf, now it was time for drama and playacting—if only he could remember his lines.

"Arise, fair sun, and kill the envious moon, who is already sick and pale—"

The phone rang, clanging like an electronic bell.

"Aren't you going to answer it?" his sister's voice sounded from the hallway. "Could be someone important."

He opened the door and stepped around Carol's wheelchair. "I haven't even auditioned yet, so it's not anyone offering me a role."

"You never know," Carol said, wagging her head. "You're more talented than you think."

"Said by my lovely sister." He bent and gave her a kiss on the temple, then jogged toward the phone.

Carol was two years older than he and a brilliant software developer at one of the hottest internet startups in Silicon Valley. While he was getting his head banged up, she'd broken her back in a hiking accident when she fell off an icy trail on Mt. Baldy.

There was no question he would come to live with her and help her get around. She worked from home, and with Ken around to do the grocery shopping, cooking, and handyman stuff, the two of them fared not too badly.

Ken grabbed the handset before voicemail kicked in.

"Hello, Ken Cassidy here." He always identified himself so Carol's coworkers wouldn't think she was living with a guy—well, a guy who wasn't her brother.

"Rex Carter," the man on the line said. "I've got a job for you. I need you right now."

"Okay." Ken looked at the Fitbit health monitor he wore. "What's the emergency?"

"A bride needs a groom. You have to get to the Rose Hill Hotel right away."

Ken wiped his hand through his hair, shaking his head. "Won't she know I'm not the real groom?"

"It doesn't matter. Her parents are bigwigs. Movers and shakers. Head surgeons at Stanford. You get the picture. The guests won't know. One thousand dollars if you pull this off. A bridesmaid will meet you with further instructions. I'll text you her name and number."

The dial tone droned through the vacant line. Rex had hung up.

"What was that all about?" Carol creased her forehead. Her blue-green eyes were wide and curious.

"Looks like I'm about to get married."

Chapter Four

Ken parked his sister's van in the visitor's parking area of the posh hotel. Tall spires of Italian cypress lined the marble driveway leading to an artificial waterfall which cascaded over a series of rock ledges.

Bellhops and doormen clustered around the entrance, waiting for the well-heeled guests who would arrive in limos filled with designer luggage.

Ken and his sister definitely looked out of place.

Carefully, he extracted her wheelchair and rolled it to the passenger side, then helped her get seated.

"Where's the lady you're supposed to meet?" Carol asked. "Do you think this is a practical joke?"

Ken scratched his head and pushed the wheelchair toward the entrance. "We'll walk in like we belong. These days, no one can tell if we're not eccentric dot com millionaires."

They sauntered up to the doorway, and one of the doormen opened the door, welcoming them to the hotel.

"Is there any particular party you're looking for?" he asked.

"Yeah, a wedding," Ken replied.

"At any given time, we have four to five weddings," the doorman explained. "Name of the bride and groom?"

Ken glanced at the white board easels directing guests to the different venues: Garden Patio, Courtyard, Ballroom, Forest Area, with the names of the parties.

Before he could make a guess, the double doors to the ballroom swung open, and a large man with a black beard trampled out. He ripped off his tuxedo jacket to expose a biker's leather vest and stormed toward the exit.

Ken pulled Carol's wheelchair back, but he wasn't fast enough. The black bearded man slammed into the wheelchair and toppled it.

"Carol!" Ken reached for his sister, but the large man was faster.

He scooped Carol off the floor with one arm and righted her wheelchair with the other. "Miss, are you okay?"

"Don't you watch where you're going?" Carol snapped.

"Not when there's someone as pretty as you in my way." The man dropped Carol back into the wheelchair. Grabbing the handlebars, he twirled her around. "My name's Drake, and I'll take you wherever you're going."

"Wait a minute." Ken wrestled the wheelchair from Drake. "My sister and I are on our way to a wedding."

"A wedding without a groom," Carol added. "Might you know which one?"

"That's the one I'm leaving," Drake said. "I was the best man, but I'm not taking the place of the groom."

"I'm Carol." His sister smiled sweetly at Drake. "My brother's supposed to be the groom."

"You're kidding," Drake said. "Did Warren put you up to this? Because when I find him, I'm going to wring his neck. You don't leave a woman at the altar and embarrass her in front of three hundred guests."

"You mean the wedding's over?" Ken's head swirled and he palmed his hand over his temple.

"You're too late." An Asian woman wearing a perfusion of pink ruffles strode toward them. "I'm Nikki Chu. You're Ken Cassidy, right? The guy from Bad Boys for Hire?"

"Yes, I am, but you didn't give me much time, and you didn't answer your cell phone," Ken said. "Since I and my sister came here for nothing, it's only fair if you give me a tip to compensate me for my time."

"A tip?" Drake hovered over them with his huge bearlike frame. "Let me get this right. The groom skips out, and you're getting paid to marry the bride?"

"It was only to stop the embarrassment," Ken said. "Not to truly marry her. You know, the three hundred guests."

"Where are they all now?" Carol asked.

Nikki waved her hand toward the garden. "After the bride came down the aisle only to find this lug head"—she glared at Drake—"standing in for Warren, her groom, she told everyone to go ahead and enjoy the reception, eat the meatballs, and cut the cake. They're all at the garden right now, and if you hurry, you can still be in time for the bouquet toss. She can't wait to get rid of those blue forget-me-nots."

Carol clapped and looked at Ken. "I love blue forget-me-nots. Can we go? It's not like we have any place else to be."

"I'll be glad to escort you, fair maiden," Drake said. He pried Ken's hands off the handlebars of the wheelchair. "Allow me to steer your chariot."

Carol giggled and fluttered her eyelids, clearly pleased with the knucklehead's attention, leaving Ken no choice but to follow them.

Nikki trailed at his side. "Do you still want to earn some money?"

"Well, yeah, money would help," Ken said. He hated being between jobs, occupations, or open doors. "I was a professional surfer but had to retire, so I'm taking up acting."

"Acting? That's great, because the bride could use some cheering up. I'm amazed how composed she is and taking everything in stride. She ordered an open bar, and she's insisting on shaking everyone's hand even as she returns their wedding gifts. Deep inside, she's got to be hurting, and I know just the thing to lift her spirits."

"What's that?" Ken was already admiring the unnamed bride for her bravery. Anyone else would have collapsed in a mess of tears or gone into hiding never to appear again. This one sounded like a tower of strength.

"A honeymoon romance, that's what," the Asian woman said. "How would you like an all expense paid trip to Hawaii?"

"That sounds tempting, but I can't leave her." Ken pointed toward his sister who was annoyingly flirting with Mr. Black Beard. Maybe a refresher on Blackbeard the Pirate was in order.

"I'm not sure me and my friends can come up with enough money to pay both of your airfares," Nikki said.

"What exactly is the job?" Ken stopped at the trellis and spotted the bride. Her flaming red hair piled over a sparkly dress of shining beads and wispy gauze. Tall, slender and fiery, she stood in the gazebo with her parents on both sides, smiling and chatting with the guests. Beside her was a layered cake, listing slightly to one side. The groom figurine was stuck upside down on the top of the cake, and a dog biscuit stood in place of the bride figurine.

It wasn't the cake that held his attention.

"I know her," Ken said. "She was supposed to play Cinderella back in fifth grade, instead she got sick. I was in the cast as the pumpkin."

"You were the pumpkin boy?" Nikki stared at him with a furrow in her brow.

"Yes, and I'll take the job," Ken said. "Instead of paying me, buy my sister's plane ticket and we're all yours."

Chapter Five

The airplane approached Honolulu Harbor, giving Jolie a stunning view of Diamond Head, a saucer-shaped crater from the island's volcanic past. Down below lay a crescent of beaches, hotels, and resorts glittering off the blue-green waters frosted white with surf.

"Isn't it beautiful?" Nikki leaned against Jolie to get her share of the view. Usually, she insisted on taking the window seat, but because of Jolie's emotional heartache, she'd made a supremely friendly sacrifice on this trip.

"It is," Jolie said, trying to keep her voice steady. She'd been tearing up off and on during the entire flight. This view should have been shared with Warren Wayne, her groom up until the hour they were supposed to be married.

"I'd ordinarily try to get a few shots, but didn't want your big nose in the way," Nikki said, angling her jumbo super fancy digital SLR camera.

Jolie leaned back as far as she could. "Sorry to inconvenience you, but seeing as how you're using Warren's ticket, and I just had the absolute worst day in my life …"

Nikki craned her lens across Jolie's boobs. "You'll get over it. I'd say it was a lucky escape." Snap. Snap. Snap.

"Do you always have to be so heartless?" Jolie gave her roommate a shove. They'd been classmates and friends ever since preschool when she, Nikki, Terri, Sherelle, and Leanna were in the same Bumblebee dance class.

They'd beaten out the Ladybugs, the Fireflies, and the Hummingbirds team for first place the year they graduated from Montessori and had been best friends since.

"Only because I, of all people, know Warren wasn't your true love," Nikki said. "That's why you picked sentimental Terri to be your maid of honor. She bought the faux romance hook, line and sinker. Can you believe she was the one crying at your busted wedding? If I hadn't spied on Warren …" Nikki gave an exaggerated shudder.

"Please, spare me the details. I don't get men. I seriously don't. As if that last minute was so important—because believe me, it had to have been with less than a minute to go."

"I was suspicious when Leanna told me they smuggled a giant cakebox into the guys' hotel room."

"Guess the bachelor party ran all night, and he couldn't get it up until morning." Jolie took her eyes from the approach to Honolulu International Airport.

"Yep, and I knew something was wrong when Terri's husband, Ryker, told her the guys were too drunk to get into their tuxes." Nikki snapped a shot of the condos and palm trees rearing up right before the airplane touched down on the runway.

Jolie bit back another bout of tears. "I don't even know why I'm so sad. You're right. It was a lucky escape. Except right now, I should be kissing my husband on landing at our honeymoon destination. Instead, I get to spend it with you."

"Oh, I think you'll get luckier than hanging out with me," Nikki said. "I'm going to be busy blogging for that travel website I've a contract with."

"You can't leave me alone." Jolie jutted out her lower lip. "Or I might slit my wrists."

"You're way stronger than that." Nikki put her camera into the bag. "You did so well at the reception."

"Ha, fooled you. My smile was as caked on as my makeup. Now, just leave me on the beach to burn to a crisp. Maybe I'll disappear into the sand and never be seen again."

"Spare the drama." Nikki unbuckled her seatbelt as they prepared to deplane. "There's a hot guy who's been checking you out the entire flight."

"Where?" Jolie scanned the passengers in line to deplane.

"Aisle seat across from us."

"Oh, he must be jealous of our view. Right hand side of the plane gets the best scenery flying into Honolulu. Besides, he's with that woman." Jolie spotted the man who was solicitously helping a pretty brown-haired woman get her bags together. "I'm not a home

432

wrecker. Not even a relationship wrecker. And I'm definitely not going on the rebound with a cheater."

"Wow, that's an assload of assumptions you just made," Nikki said. "As for rebounding, didn't you tell me Warren's screw-up screwed up your timetable? College by twenty-two. Check. Business by twenty-five. Check. Engaged by twenty-eight. Check. Marriage by twenty-nine, baby by thirty, second baby and minivan by thirty-three …"

"Stop!" Jolie pressed her hands over her abdomen. "If you're not going to allow me to be perfectly miserable on my non-honeymoon, you can stay on the plane and turn around."

Nikki did her annoying whistle—the one she always used to preface a particularly snotty remark.

"And miss Prince Charming with a glass slipper? I think not." She pointed her finger at Jolie as if she were a fairy godmother.

Right. As if anyone still believed in fairy tales.

Chapter Six

"I am not wearing makeup." Jolie pressed her lips together and grimaced at Nikki. "I'm on my bittermoon and I'm not doing a thing. No leg shaving. No moisturizing. No exfoliating, no nothing."

After all, wearing makeup her usual way hadn't kept her from being dumped at her wedding.

"Okay …" Nikki held up a flowery wrap she'd bought at the hotel's souvenir shop. "You should at least wear aloha clothes for the luau we're due at."

"Why? As pale as I am, there's no way anyone will mistake me for a hula girl." Jolie nevertheless grabbed the skimpy wrap and tied it over her bikini. Even if she wanted to be grumpy, she couldn't spoil Nikki's assignment to find the most romantic things to do in Waikiki, as if hanging around with a jilted girlfriend qualified.

"Fine, have it your way. No makeup," Nikki said. "It's not like I care if handsome, single, available, men swarm around you like bumblebees buzzing a hibiscus. And don't pretend to be brokenhearted. You and Warren hardly ever talked when you were dating."

"That's because he was always undercover." Jolie had no clue why she had to defend the dastardly dickhead. He'd been undercover all right, with anyone but her. "Then it turns out he's not even a real FBI agent."

"Just a Bad Boy for Hire posing as one," Nikki said. "I always was suspicious about him. Remember when I told you—"

"Please, enough." Jolie held her hand up to cut off her friend and her detailed, meticulous memory. "Let's go to the luau. Might as well enjoy the half-naked male dancers. At least Warren's not here to gawk at the hula girls."

"That's the spirit!" Nikki held up her hand for a high five.

Jolie ignored it and opened the door of their hotel room. Fifteen minutes later, they were in line at the luau, holding their tickets and waiting to get to the buffet table.

"This feels like a cafeteria back in school," Jolie complained. "Line them up with their meal cards, hurry them through and seat them all in a row."

"They do have the system down," Nikki said, as a woman looped a purple and white lei over her neck.

"Oh look, that man's cutting the line." Jolie pointed to the backside of a well-built man wearing a tank top, board shorts and flip-flops. His sandy hair glinted with blond highlights and his even, smooth tan showed he was a guy who spent time outdoors. Too bad he was pushing a woman in a wheelchair.

"It's that guy who was checking you out," Nikki exclaimed. "Ah … look how sweet he is. He's getting food for that woman. I wonder if she's his sister."

"Sister, humph," Jolie said. "Guys aren't so nice to their sisters. Trust me, I know."

Her dearest brother had not only been in the room with the stripper when Warren was caught, but had complained that he hadn't had his turn yet.

Disgusting.

"They do look very similar," Nikki said "Her hair is a little darker than his, but look at the facial shape and bone structure. They're good looking enough to be movie stars."

Jolie's eyes rolled. Nikki obviously had a crush on Mr. Nurse Maid, although to be honest, he was pretty hot. Tanned, tall, not too muscular, but well-defined, he was a man who'd have every female drooling—if he wasn't one hundred percent devoted to the woman Nikki *wished* was his sister.

"If you like him so much, why don't you ask them to sit at our table? Unless the seats are reserved." Jolie glanced at the ticket to see if a seat number was printed on it.

Nikki was off like a shot, parting her way through the crowd. People glared at her, sniffing indignantly at the brazenness of her line-jumping.

"Excuse me, this isn't China," one haughty old lady said. "The line starts back there."

"No speak-ah, no speak-ah," Nikki said in a god-awful imitation accent.

"That's what I hate about tourists," a man wearing a loud aloha shirt huffed. "So rude."

Jolie giggled and followed her girlfriend. "Excuse me. That's my exchange student. I have to keep an eye on her. Excuse me."

Now that she and Nikki were standing directly in back of the godlicious hunk, now what?

The line of people grumbled louder. "Line cutters. Can you believe it? I ought to complain."

"We paid for premium seating and now this?"

Nikki tapped the hunky man's arm and whispered in his ear. Wow. Jolie had no idea her roomie was so fast!

Mr. Hunk of Tan smiled with teeth so white they dazzled, and suddenly, Jolie wished she had dabbed a little makeup on her face—actually make that a full makeover. Her heart did that pitter-patter flip-flop dance step she learned in preschool, and just like she'd fallen off the stage in her starring role in the Crippled Lamb play, she felt her knees weaken and buckle as a worrisome flare of heat sent her pulse skyrocketing.

"I'm so sorry," the tan godman announced. "These two ladies are with me. I was holding their spot. But if you'd like, we can all go to the back."

The woman in the wheelchair agreed, nodding emphatically, but of course, everyone relented. Jolie's cheeks flushed hot at how they'd taken advantage of the crippled lady, but then again, it was Nikki's fault. She was the one who had the hots for the Slab of Abs standing so close to them.

Jolie turned her back, but it was hopeless. She was enveloped in the scent of his aftershave, body wash, and the cascade of pheromones flooding from the Barbie doll's boyfriend's pores.

For a moment, she was glad she wasn't married, but the thought of being back on square one in the marriage game threw her into a tizzy of panic. All the good ones were taken.

# # #

Ken couldn't stop feasting his eyes on Jolie Becker, the girl he'd rehearsed with in fifth grade. She'd probably forgotten him by now since he'd had to transfer schools when his father passed away, but he could never forget the flaming red hair, the determination, and the fierce competitiveness that young lady had.

She'd beaten out girls with more drama experience for the part. She might not have been the best dancer either, but she'd practiced her heart and soul out. Many afternoons, Ken had spied on her as she went through the routine over and over again in the back of the gym while her friends sat around gossiping.

Too bad Jolie wasn't returning the googly eyes, at least not for him. Instead, she'd turned all her attention to Carol. Rather than get her own food, she pushed Carol to a table near the front of the stage, and moved the plates from Carol's lap to the table.

"Don't expect me to do all the work," Nikki said, holding her plate to the server for slices of kalua pig. "And yes, I'd like a large scoop of poi."

"I've got this," Ken replied to Nikki while waving off the poi. "After all, you're not hiring me. I'm volunteering."

"Semantics, semantics," Nikki said. "I don't know how you're going to sweep her off her feet with your sister hanging around. I can't think of anything less romantic."

Ken bristled at Nikki's cold-hearted assessment of his romantic quotient.

"I have no trouble in the romance department, I assure you." He picked up a slice of pineapple cake with coconut frosting. "Your friend doesn't look like she wants to have a good time."

"Would you? After the most horrible thing that could ever happen to you?"

"No, I guess not." He well remembered the funk he'd been in after his concussion put him out of surfing competitions. "Maybe this is too soon. It takes time when you lose the love of your life."

"That's just the point," Nikki said. "He wasn't the love of her life. Jolie was on a timetable to get things done. She's very obsessive—OCD, you'll see. Once she sets her mind to doing something, she'll accomplish it, no matter what."

"Marriage isn't an accomplishment," Ken said, wondering where that had slipped out from. "But I understand. I lost my first love, surfing, to an accident, so I'm pursuing my second love, acting."

"Why don't you concentrate on pursuing Jolie? It'll hone your acting skills and help her have a happy honeymoon." Nikki checked the box for her drink order and handed it to the attendant. "I'll distract your sister and let you go in for the kill."

"Sure, but you have to tell me what she likes. I noticed she's so busy helping my sister, she hasn't gotten a morsel of food for herself."

"You'll find out soon enough," Nikki said. "Oh, look, I see a group of Chinese tourists I want to go interview. Talk later."

With that, she sauntered off without looking back.

Ken puffed out his chest and tried to look confident. He could do it. He didn't need Miss Busybody Blogger to help him charm the jilted Jolie. Oh no, if he wanted to get the role of Romeo, he would have to put on the charm himself.

Chapter Seven

Jolie craned her neck to see where Nikki was off to. That woman never sat still. Neither could she keep her mind on the same man, flitting to and fro like a bumblebee.

"Looks like your friend found people to talk to," Carol said. "Thanks for helping me with the food. I'm still not used to life in a wheelchair."

"I'm sorry. It happened not long ago?" Jolie didn't want to pry, but it was a heck of a lot easier talking to Carol than standing around wondering why Nikki was flirting with a man who was so obviously with another woman.

"I was one of the hikers who fell off Mt. Baldy. My bad. I used to be a very accomplished hiker and rock climber."

Jolie put her hand on Carol's and rubbed it. There was no ring on her finger.

"It must be hard," she mumbled. What was wrong with her? Checking a stranger's finger for a ring. But then, she was only protecting Nikki, should she get involved with this attentive man who seemed so perfect.

"I can't pretend it's not," Carol said. "Not that I'm fishing for sympathy."

"Oh, no, I'm sure it's a big adjustment. I can't even imagine." Jolie glanced at the direction of the buffet table, unable to keep her eyes off the man who was off-limits.

His eyes locked with hers and even though he was walking toward them—correction, walking toward Carol, Jolie's heart rate kicked up a notch.

What would it feel like to have a man like that take care of her needs?

"Is he your boyfriend or husband?" Jolie couldn't help asking. "He seems so devoted to you."

Carol's eyes narrowed and she grinned. "He *is* very devoted to me. Best brother ever."

"Buh-brother?" Jolie's jaw dropped and all sorts of wild and crazy ideas jostled in her mind. Had Nikki tagged him first? Would it be too dirty if she swiped him? Or should she wait for her friend to take the first pass?

"Let me introduce you properly," Carol said, as her brother set the laden tray down. "Jolie, meet my devoted brother, Ken. He's quite single, in case you were wondering."

"Oh, well, I wasn't wondering." Jolie gave Ken a nervous smile. "I mean, I'm kind of on my honeymoon. Not wondering at all."

"It's nice to meet you," Ken said, his smile gleaming sexy and sweet. "I've brought you a sample of each item on the buffet table."

"Kind of on your honeymoon?" Carol asked. "What exactly does that mean?"

"It means, I'm taking my honeymoon with Nikki, my friend."

"You mean your friend who's over there flirting with the entire Chinese men's gymnastics team?" Carol quirked an eyebrow Nikki's direction.

"Oh, is that who they are?" Sweat prickled the back of Jolie's neck at being so close to Ken. Now that she knew he was single, all sorts of possibilities opened.

But wait. What kind of woman would she be if she could get involved or even think to get involved with someone so soon after being ready to marry another man?

She tamped down her irrational thoughts and kept her attention on Carol. "Go ahead, eat. Don't worry about me and my quasi-honeymoon."

"Aren't you going to have anything?" Ken asked. "Try the lomi-lomi."

He pushed a plate filled with pink chunks of raw fish mixed with chopped tomatoes, jalapeños, and scallions.

"I can't have seafood," Jolie said. "I'm also allergic to all shellfish."

"Oh, then, how about some kalua pork?" He pointed to another heaping plate.

"I don't eat pork," Jolie said. "And no dairy either."

"Then try the potato salad."

"Does it have mayonnaise? I'm allergic to eggs."

"How about Hawaiian sweet rolls?"

"They need to be gluten-free."

"Spinach salad with blood orange and macadamia nuts?"

"Can't have nuts," Jolie replied. "Not any citrus."

"Okay ..." Ken rearranged the plates. "Banana and papaya fruit salad?"

"Ugh, no bananas either, sorry." Jolie wrinkled her nose.

"Can I ask a question?" Carol said, her mouth half full of food. "Why did you come to a luau if not to eat?"

"Warren booked the luau," Jolie said as her eyes threatened to tear up. "I should go and find my friend. You two carry on. Have fun. I don't want to ruin your evening."

"Wait, don't go." Ken placed his hand on her arm. "Tell me what you can eat, and I'll see if I can scare some of it up for you."

"I can't let you go to the trouble," Jolie said. "I'll eat some of the watermelon or the chicken. Although I can't have soy sauce. I can have broccoli and cucumbers. Lots of things. Avocados, too. But no yogurt or dairy products."

"Would you like a steak? Baked potato?"

"Yes, yes, I'd love that. And broccoli, too."

Ken stood. "I'll get some food you can eat."

"It might not be part of the luau," Jolie said, hating her dietary restrictions. What a way to ruin anyone's parade. Maybe that was why Warren decided to bail. Life with her would be full of food restrictions and watching out for allergic reactions.

"Don't worry about it," Ken said. "I'll put a special request to the kitchen. You're a guest, and they need to accommodate you."

He leaned over, and for a moment, Jolie wondered if he would kiss her. It seemed so natural. Her man taking care of her.

Ugh. She ought to slap herself. Ken definitely did not belong to her. He had his hands full with Carol, and once Nikki returned from interviewing the Chinese men's gymnastics team, she was sure to claim him as her find of the day.

She pried her eyes from his tantalizing backside and turned to Carol, shrugging apologetically. "I didn't mean to waylay your brother. He seemed upset I couldn't eat anything."

"He gets like that when there's no wheelchair ramp, or people park in handicapped spots. I'm guessing he's pissed your Warren booked a luau knowing you can't eat half the things here."

"I was going to enjoy the show and let him eat," Jolie admitted. "He planned the entire honeymoon. The only reason Nikki and I came was to laugh at him for not getting to go to any of the things he paid for."

"Ha, ha, ha," Carol laughed and pounded the table. "Serves him right that you two are enjoying his poi, lomi-lomi, huli-huli, and mahi-mahi."

"It's about the only joy I can take out of this crummy situation," Jolie said.

That and the fact handsome Ken had gone to the kitchen on her behalf. Maybe, her honeymoon wouldn't be so bitter after all.

# # #

Ken walked back into the luau with a waiter in tow. He picked up all of the uneaten dishes and piled them to the side as the waiter set a silver platter in front of Jolie.

"Aloha," Ken said, bending over her. "I believe you didn't get a lei."

"Excuse me?" Her eyes tracked him, widening, and a hint of a smile tickled her cheeks, giving him all the reward he needed—for now.

"You skipped the lei line, remember?" With a flourish, he produced a large and lush orange and white lei made of fiery orchids and pristine tuberoses. "This one matches your gorgeous hair."

"Oh, my. Thanks." Jolie let him slip the lei over her head. "But this isn't the free one they gave out. You didn't have to."

"It's your honeymoon, remember?" Ken grinned and took the opportunity to move her long, radiant hair from under the lei. "There's nothing too good for the newly-freed bride."

"Newly-freed, ha, ha, I like that." Jolie's smile widened, but she looked down, seemingly embarrassed at her pleasure.

"My lady." The waiter opened the silver platter. "Enjoy your Steak Diane, roasted asparagus and portabella mushrooms with a baked potato. And a salad of broccoli, cranberries, and sunflower seeds—no mayonnaise, I used dill pickle juice and balsamic vinegar. Your friend was very specific."

"Ah, thanks. This is all too much." Jolie clasped her hands in front of her chest.

"Actually, there's more." Ken pulled a chair to sit close to her. "A bottle of Bordeaux. I took the liberty of choosing one for you."

"You sure know how to spoil a girl," Jolie said, her face brightening. She wasn't wearing makeup, and despite the circles under her eyes, probably from crying, she looked sweet and wholesome.

He liked that about her. A woman who wasn't vain, but was brave enough to come on the honeymoon she should have enjoyed with a new husband, was quite a rare bird.

Courage. That was the ingredient he'd been missing. His surfing accident and Carol's hiking accident had squelched his "you only live once" spirit. But here with Jolie, a woman who'd been emotionally crushed, Ken saw a light at the end of that dark tunnel he'd been trapped in.

He might not ever surf competitively again, but he could be happy for the small things in life—finding a meal for a woman plagued by allergies, helping his sister enjoy a vacation without dwelling on her legs, and doing good deeds. That was something a man suffering from a traumatic brain injury could do.

Ken allowed the waiter to uncork the bottle and pour two glasses of wine. After the waiter departed, he picked up one of the wine glasses and proposed a toast.

"To the most beautiful newly-freed bride. May aloha dwell in your heart."

She clinked her glass with his. "And yours, too. You kindhearted knight in shining armor."

"More like a tank and board shorts, but always your knight." Heat rushed to his face. He was blatantly flirting with a woman who until a day ago, was someone else's bride. Not that the jerk who ditched her deserved her, but still, he should slow down before he made her uncomfortable.

They toasted and sipped the wine. After pouring a half glass for his sister, Ken dug in to enjoy some of the luau food. Beside him, Jolie bowed her head. Her lips moved with a silent prayer before digging into her steak.

She cut the meat and broccoli into tiny pieces, and then lined them up, one alternating with the other. When she popped a piece into her mouth, she chewed twenty times before swallowing.

She must have noticed him staring, because her cheeks pinked a moment later and she raised her head. "Thanks, Ken. You're so kind."

"It's the least I could do," he started.

"Please, I'm not a charity case. I'd like to think you did this to impress me."

"He did want to impress you," Carol said from across the table. "My brother feels sorry he didn't meet you before that douchebag you were supposed to marry did."

"Really?" Jolie twirled the piece of broccoli on her fork and looked at him sideways. "Maybe I'm happy I'm not married after all. I'm newly-freed, not newlywed."

"Ooh, la, la," Carol said, fanning herself. "I better turn around and let you two get it on. The show's about to start."

She turned her wheelchair to face the stage. The steady roll of drumbeats grew louder as women in grass skirts wiggled their way on stage in a frenzy of shaking and slapping.

The lights dimmed and the announcer, a man wearing a circle of green leaves around his head and nothing else but a decorated cloth wrapped around his waist, welcomed the crowd.

Ken took the opportunity to scoot closer to Jolie and put his arm over her shoulder. "I'm not feeling very sorry for myself right now. I hope you enjoy the show."

"Don't feel sorry for me, either." She tilted her face toward him. She was so close he could feel her breath run across his lips. Her flowery scent and the perfume of the lei, the tang of wine across her lips, and the softness of her skin brought him back to a time when he was fearless, perched on the crest of fifty foot waves, riding down the trough with the crash of white surf pouring over his head.

Her lips met his in a perfect fit, and they were kissing, softly at first, then more eagerly—breathless and slippery. He covered her mouth possessively as she opened for him. Their tongues wrapped in an intimate embrace, dancing and swaying to the slow ballad of the welcome hula.

He felt her smile as she wrapped a hand around his neck. Her tongue darted along his, and the tiny sounds she made were sexy as all get out. Lust and longing slammed him as hard as a rogue wave, and he slanted his head to drink in more of her sweet nectar.

She made a strangled sound and froze, stiffening in his arms. Great. He'd moved too fast and ruined everything. What a douche he'd turned out to be.

Ken instinctively broke the kiss and cupped Jolie's face. "What's wrong?"

The whites of her eyes turned over, and she clutched her throat, gasping for air. All he could hear was a tiny wheeze as she fell backward, shuddering and trying to cough.

"My purse," she managed to say. "EpiPen. Shot."

"Did she eat peanuts?" Carol asked, turning her chair toward them. By now, a crowd of people gathered, and all Ken could do was hold onto Jolie, supporting her on his lap.

"Get her EpiPen," Nikki said, barging through the crowd. She swiped Jolie's purse and in a flash, she uncapped the medical device and plunged the needle into Jolie's thigh.

A lady sitting at their table hurried to his side. "I'm a doctor. We have to get her to the emergency room. Is she allergic to peanuts?"

"Yes," Nikki said. "But she never eats them. I don't see how she got any into her system."

"It's my fault," Ken admitted, still holding onto Jolie who was coughing and wheezing. "I munched on a few cocktail peanuts when I went to get her food."

"And then what? You gave her the kiss of death?" Nikki stared at him, wide-eyed and angry. "How could you be so careless? You're supposed to wine her and dine her, not kill her."

Chapter Eight

"It wasn't Ken's fault," Jolie said to Nikki back in their high rise hotel room. "He didn't know."

She'd been doped up with antihistamines and had been checked out at the Emergency Room. Thankfully, the EpiPen had done the job, and other than a rash and residual swelling of her lips and tongue, she was good to retire for the night.

"Didn't you taste peanuts on his breath?" Her friend knit her eyebrows and narrowed her eyes. "What were you thinking, kissing a guy you just met?"

Jolie hesitated. Nikki looked so angry. She had probably marked Ken for herself. But then, she was an incessant flirt without seeming like it. Yep, that innocent line about interviewing for her blog always worked.

"He kissed me. I was sitting there eating my steak and potatoes, watching the show." Jolie shrugged. "I'm sorry. I know you had your eye on him, but no one told you to run after the entire Chinese Olympic team."

"Well … if you really like him, I'm sure I'll recover," Nikki said, patting Jolie's hand. "So tell me, how was the kiss? Is he as hot and luscious as he looks?"

"You sure you want to know?" Jolie could never figure out where Nikki stood with the flirtations of her life.

"Of course, I want you to be happy, and it seemed like you two were getting into it before you started choking. I mean, my body temperature rose to heatstroke levels, and well, sorry, but the entire Chinese Olympic team, as you put it, were taking pictures and videos. You two could audition for America's Hottest Couple. Whew."

There she went again, putting her journalistic spin on everything. Jolie changed the subject, not wanting to make more of the kiss than she had to, at least before she had time to think about it. "We have to get up early if we want to hike Diamond Head tomorrow before it gets too hot."

"You sure you want to retrace Warren's plan? Why don't we do our own thing?"

"I'm sticking to the itinerary," Jolie said firmly.

"Why? He's not even here." Nikki checked her cell phone. "Besides, Ken and Carol might want to do something else."

"Wait, I didn't know we were hanging out with them." Jolie wasn't sure whether to feel excited or afraid. "I don't want things to get funny between you and me, about Ken, you know."

"Don't worry. He's all yours." Nikki waved her hand. "Let me text him. I'm sure I can find something for Carol to do. We can drive around and sightsee the caves and coves."

Jolie yawned and rubbed her eyes. Something didn't make sense. Nikki was usually so competitive about men—always making sure she had all the attention. She was a petite and bubbly Asian woman who made averaged-sized guys feel big and brave. Her eyes were another alluring feature, slanted at the corners and so dark they shone like polished onyx.

Yet Ken had obviously chosen Jolie, the jilted bride with all of the food allergies, over her attractive friend. He'd insisted on accompanying her to the ER, but Jolie had just as firmly insisted he and Carol stay for the show. There was no way she'd ruin their vacation, especially since it was the first one after Carol's accident.

"I'm going to turn in," Jolie said, entering the bathroom to brush her teeth. "I'm half asleep as it is. Hopefully, all the hives will go away by tomorrow."

Besides, she had to process the kiss. How had she allowed a complete stranger to kiss her when she was supposed to be married to Warren? He still hadn't contacted her and no one seemed to know what had happened to him after he was caught with the stripper.

How could it be that he preferred a stripper to her? Maybe he hadn't wanted to marry her, and the stripper was a convenient excuse to get out of it. Then why didn't he just say so?

As she looked in the mirror at her puffy lips and skin pink with rash, she couldn't help wondering about Ken. The kiss had tingled throughout her body. It could have been an allergic reaction, but it was definitely hot, and something she'd never felt before. Warmth had bloomed in her heart, and a hunger she'd never had was awakened. Her skin prickled and her face was flushed, and the itch to crawl out of her skin and rub herself against Ken was overwhelming.

When she came out of the bathroom, Nikki was no where in sight. Someone knocked on the door.

"Room service," a male voice called.

"Nikki?" Jolie scanned the empty room. Her stomach growled at the memory of the uneaten steak. She crossed the room and opened the door.

Ken stood there, all blond, tanned, and smiling with a bouquet of fresh flowers and a silver platter. "I came to see if you're okay. I'm so sorry."

"Sorry about the kiss?" She let him in. "Or that we didn't finish."

"Definitely the latter, if you're all right." His blue-gray eyes twinkled. "But first, my lady. Flowers and food."

"You didn't have to," Jolie said, even as her heart swelled with joy. She took the flowers, a fiery orange collection of orchids and lilies. "Where's Carol? Did you leave her alone?"

"She's playing gin rummy with Nikki. Seems they have a lot in common." He moved into the room and set the platter on the table. "Sorry, no wine. I figured they gave you medicine for your allergies."

"You're really too kind." Jolie rubbed her hands which still itched. "Why are you being so nice to me?"

"Other than the obvious reason?" Ken feathered his fingers over her shoulders. "You're not only gorgeous, but you're strong and brave, and I want to get to know you better. Will you let me be your honeymoon date?"

Jolie giggled and her heart did a cartwheel. "You make me sound like a cheater. Whoever heard of a honeymoon date?"

"Fine, then, honeymoon hunk, but that would be too arrogant, wouldn't it?"

"Honeymoon honey." She tapped his nose. "Sure beats the bittermoon I was on before I met you."

He closed in, slanting his head. "Don't worry, I washed the peanuts out of my mouth."

"Then what are you waiting for, honeymoon honey?"

"Hunk," he muttered right before their lips touched.

Jolie closed her eyes and leaned into the kiss. She carefully wrapped her hands around his broad shoulders and inhaled his sweet, minty breath. Even after her brush with death, she felt safe and protected in his arms.

As soon as their lips were pressed together, heat rushed through her like the gas jets in a hot air balloon. Lazily, she swept her tongue across the seam of his lips and sighed into his mouth. Kissing him was like a fairy tale dream, where colors brightened and music chimed. She, who had been numb, picture perfect, plastic, was now alive and awake, in the embrace of her delicious prince.

Somewhere in the fuzzy parts of her mind, a voice told her she was behaving badly—that she was Warren's fiancée and that she wasn't fast—not at all. She never threw herself at men, especially a stranger she met at a hotel. How sleazy did that sound?

But the tender way Ken kissed her, as if he cherished her, the way he moved slowly, savoring her like fine wine, drew tears like raindrops from a sunny sky. She should be floating with happiness. She was still desirable, wanted, and even admired.

It wasn't just how hot he was physically, but the way he cared for her and her welfare. She didn't deserve how considerate he was. She was a woman men left at the altar, and if he really knew how obsessive she was with her schedules, lists, and restrictions, he'd be gone too.

Wetness flowed down her cheeks and she hoped Ken wouldn't notice, that he'd keep the sweet nibbles going—that he'd overlook the things she lacked compared to other women—qualities no amount of makeup, which she wasn't wearing, could cover.

"What's wrong?" He kissed a tear from her cheek. "Are you feeling blue?"

"It's those blue memories. I'm sorry, it's not you." Jolie hastily wiped a tear. What was wrong with her? She could spoil a romantic evening, not once, but twice. "Did you and Carol see the end of the show?"

"I stayed because you made me promise to stay, but I wanted to be with you." He wiped the corner of her eye. "Am I making you uncomfortable by coming on so fast?"

"No, I love kissing you. I don't want this to stop. Bet you think I'm this crazy, needy chick who got dumped at the altar."

"That's not what I'm seeing." He twisted a strand of her hair around his finger and swept it over her ear. "You don't know how grateful I am you're not married. That was a close call, I'd say."

"One door closes and another one opens?"

"Exactly. Are you okay with hanging around with me and Carol? How long are you staying?"

"Five days, four nights. Warren went all out for the honeymoon. It's the only thing he spent money on. I'm lucky he used my account to set everything up."

"Then I'm in luck, because Carol and I are also staying the same time. All here in Honolulu?"

"Yes, with day trips to the other side of the island."

"Great. Let's enjoy our open door." He caressed her cheek. "No more tears."

"I can't promise that. I'm the tearing type. I even cry when I'm happy."

"Then I'll kiss them all away, every last drop." He feathered his lips over her eyes.

Jolie shuddered. It was no use tamping down her feelings. Everything was raw, an open wound, pain and pleasure heightened, extra sensitive. After the way Warren hurt her in front of three hundred guests, what did it matter if sweet talking Ken hurt her at the end of her bitter honeymoon?

She'd go with the flow, but no way was she getting her heart knotted up over Ken in Shining Armor, no matter how perfect he seemed.

She tilted her lips up to his and dissolved in the gentle rainfall of his kisses, until drowsiness overtook her, and she ruined a romantic evening for the third time, thanks to the antihistamines in her blood putting her to sleep.

Chapter Nine

The next morning, Ken, Jolie, Nikki, and Carol were assembled at the entrance to the Diamond Head National Monument. Even though they'd come early, the trail was half-full of hikers.

"There's only a tiny section of walkway before you have to turn back with that wheelchair," a park ranger said at the kiosk.

"It's okay, we can enjoy the views however far we get," Carol said. "I used to be an avid hiker. Mt. Whitney, Mt. Fuji, I even made it up Half Dome once."

Someone behind them snickered, so Ken said, "You'll make it to the top of this hike, too. No worries."

Laughter burst out and Jolie whipped around. "Laugh all you want, douche canoes. You're seriously tempting God by making fun of the disabled."

Wow. She was a spitfire, and pride rose in Ken's breast at how tigress Jolie became, sticking up for his sister. He could really fall for her, if he wasn't already halfway there. It wasn't easy finding a woman who wasn't jealous of his devotion to Carol, and so far, he liked everything he saw about Jolie, even her strange little habits of wiping door handles with alcohol wipes.

"Can you believe we're inside the volcano's crater?" Nikki asked, taking pictures of the switchbacks in front of them. "It's like a death march. Look at those rows and rows of people. I'll stay with Carol and interview the hikers coming back."

"You won't have to. Carol's going to the top," Ken said. "There's more than one way to climb a peak."

"You're going to carry her?" Jolie's face flushed as her eyes widened.

"I'm going to try, and to make it easier for me, I want you to tell me something interesting about yourself." Ken puffed out his chest, feeling like a schoolboy telling tall tales to the girls. Too bad, Jolie showed no signs of remembering him from fifth grade, or maybe that was for the better, considering how unpopular he'd been.

"You mean you two didn't talk last night?" Nikki sniffed, rolling her eyes. "Carol and I wore out the card deck, didn't we?"

"I was half asleep from the antihistamines," Jolie said. "Ken brought over a nice safe dinner, and well, I fell asleep."

"Yes, she snores, too," Ken joked. "Sleeping Beauty missed the good parts."

"Too much information," his sister said, plugging her ears. "I don't want to know what you did to put her to sleep."

Ken looked at Jolie and she stuck her tongue out at him.

Had she any idea what that did to him?

"I'll take Carol while there's still sidewalk," Nikki said. She took over pushing the wheelchair and drove forward.

Ken took the chance and clasped Jolie's hand. "Now we get to talk. I'll tell you something about myself first, then it's your turn."

"Is this speed dating?"

"Yes, I like to move fast. Here goes. I used to be a professional surfer. Hit the big fifty feet waves at Mavericks and wiped out."

"You're a surfer?" She turned her greenish blue eyes on him. "Is it hard? I don't think I could ever balance well enough to do it."

"Sure you can. Waikiki is perfect for beginners."

"I've always thought it would be cool to surf, but I'm a redhead. Me and beaches don't mix."

"A tube of sunscreen would fix that. Want me to teach you?"

"I'd love it, except it's not on the list of activities Warren bought tickets to."

The small bushes and trees became sparser the further up they walked. Ken swallowed and cleared his throat, not sure how to respond. Nikki had told him Jolie insisted on following her fiancé's itinerary. Was she still pining after him, and trying to live as if it were her real honeymoon? Or, she could be going through a ritual of happiness, because in her mind, her carefully planned wedding and honeymoon had to be perfect. No wonder Nikki had tried to order a groom substitute. It was all about an orchestrated appearance, not reality.

Maybe even now, he was only a stand in for Warren.

Should that matter? This was his chance for the girl he'd crushed on since fifth grade. He'd hated it when they had to move to San Diego after his father died.

He squeezed Jolie's hand and brought it to his lips. "The offer to surf is still open. We can rent some long boards. If Agatha Christie could do it, so can you."

"Seriously? Agatha Christie, the great mystery writer, surfed?"

They were approaching the end of the concrete sidewalk. A pitted and rocky dirt path lay beyond.

"You'll be surprised what you learn hanging around the theatre crowd. My second obsession is acting and drama. Now, that's two for me, and zero for you."

"I'm a makeup artist," Jolie said. "Except I'm on strike, so I didn't bring anything but lip gloss, sunscreen, and mascara."

"Do you do stage makeup?"

"I love doing that. I'm part of the backstage crew for the Evergreen Theater back home."

Ken's ears perked with that news. "You must know the director. I'm trying out for Romeo. Can you put a good word in for me?"

"Maybe." Jolie gave him a sideways wink. "Depends on how well you play with me."

His heart skipped a beat, and a grin widened across his face. "We might play at being honeymoon honeys, but one thing I'll never do is play with your heart."

"I'll hold you to it, Ken in Shining Armor," Jolie said. "Looks like the sidewalk's ending."

They caught up to his sister and Nikki. Ken reached for the wheelchair and put on the brakes. "Okay, Carol, up you go."

He squatted in front of the chair and lifted his sister onto his back while she put her arms around his shoulders. The hardest part of the hike was still in front of them. There were the switchbacks and the killer steps, tunnels and more steps, but he was ready to prove to Jolie he was a man of his word.

# # #

"This is torture," Nikki said, barely able to catch her breath. "We're at the bottom of the longest flight of stairs I've ever seen."

"I don't know if I can make it." Jolie peered up the long narrow stairway walled on both sides. Metal handrails were provided, but so many hands had touched them and they were definitely not clean.

"You can do it. Go ahead, I'll bring up the rear." Ken nudged her as Carol gave her a thumbs up. Of course she was getting a piggyback ride on the back of Sir Hunk-a-Lot.

Nikki went first, and then Jolie, although she wasn't sure about having Ken directly in back of her. He could be checking out her butt cheeks. She'd worn shorts and a thin tank, because the trip would be hot. Passing out from kissing was embarrassing enough after the anaphylactic shock. What more memorable moments would she experience?

"Have fun going up the ninety-nine steps," a tourist on his way down said. "The view's totally worth it."

After what felt like hours later, they completed the grueling set of stairs, went through a dank tunnel, climbed a spiral staircase and emerged, bathed with sweat, onto an observation deck with a three-hundred-sixty degree view.

Nikki's camera went crazy, snapping away, and the breeze at the top was refreshing after the humidity of the tunnels and staircases. Jolie dabbed herself dry with a tissue and cleaned her hands with a wet wipe. That felt great.

"This is the reward," Ken said, resting against the rails. "Carol, can you see?"

"Yes, it's breathtaking," Carol agreed. "Turn around so I can see everything."

Jolie spotted the famed Waikiki Beach below, as well as airplanes traveling by and landing at the airport. The mountain ranges to the north and west were green and lush, and the ocean below was a patchwork of blues, ranging from turquoise to aqua to cerulean and the darker azure. Definitely better than the disastrous shades of pink wedding she almost had. Maybe next time, she'd go with blue. That color was lucky for Terri, and Leanna had leapt in front of Nikki at the bouquet toss and snagged the blue forget-me-nots. Besides, Ken's eyes were blue too. Maybe blue should be her go-to color from now on.

"I want to remember this special honeymoon moment," Jolie said, her hair whipping in the breeze. "I always dreamed of standing here, and here we are. We made the climb."

"We sure did." Ken leaned toward her, pursing his lips.

It was so natural to kiss him, so she did. She'd take what she could get, and she closed her eyes and savored the salty taste of his mouth, dipping her tongue with his, and letting the feels wash over her.

Warren had never kissed her just to kiss, but always as a prelude for the next step—something to check off, but with Ken, he never rushed, and each peck and caress drew shivers of delight up and down her spine.

"Enough, you two." Nikki pointed her camera at them. "Or I'm taking pictures."

"Go ahead," Carol said. "I think my brother's finally found his missing half."

Jolie dropped back and stared at her feet. Did they think she was desperate or on the rebound? She'd better cool her heels or she'd be in for another broken heart.

Casting for something to do, she fished a tissue from her purse and dabbed Ken's face. "You're sweaty, and I bet you hadn't had a drink the entire way."

"You noticed." He grinned and drank from the water bottle Jolie held. "Carol's thirsty, too."

"I didn't do any work," Carol said."

"But you shouldn't get dehydrated," Ken argued. "Go ahead and drink."

Jolie held the water for his sister, too. After she finished, they lined up for the pictures. Ken offered his elbow and she leaned close to him. As Nikki snapped them against the mountains on one side and the bright blue sky over the ocean on the other, Jolie wished she didn't come with so much baggage, that this was the beginning of something new and exciting.

All she had to do was finish Warren's plan, and she could check honeymoon off her list of things she had to do with her life. Then maybe, she would finally be free of him.

Chapter Ten

"We are not going to Big John's Famous Shrimp Truck," Nikki said, ripping the printed itinerary from Jolie's hand. "You're allergic to shrimp."

They had finished the hike, and Ken was busy putting Carol back on her wheelchair. Everyone was sweaty, and Jolie was about to collapse.

Her pulse jittered, and her palms itched. Changing plans was scary and uncertain. "But this Shrimp Truck is famous and people sign their names on it. Of course, I can't put a heart around my name and Warren's anymore."

"See? That means plans have changed," Nikki said, looking at the piece of paper. "I can't believe the rest of this. Marlin fishing for ten hours when you're prone to motion sickness. Another killer hike. What? Sneaking up the Stairway to Heaven. Oh, and the Dole Pineapple plantation, so romantic."

"Give that back." The itching spread onto Jolie's arms. She had forgotten her sunscreen, something she was usually meticulous about. "We already paid for the charter."

"I'm sure I can scalp the charter to someone who didn't plan months in advance," Nikki said. "Maybe those guys from the gymnastics team want to go. The question is, what do you want to do?"

Jolie caught Ken's eye as he raised an eyebrow. Carol, also, gave her a questioning look.

"Why are you all grilling me? This is my honeymoon."

"Without a groom," Nikki most unhelpfully reminded. "You should figure out what you want to do for the rest of your vacation."

"My vacation?" Jolie threw up her hands. "I'm only here to finish what I started. The wedding and honeymoon. I can't let anything go to waste."

"Your time's a wasting," Nikki said. "I've an idea. Carol and I have some investigations to do. This hike was decidedly not handicap friendly. I'm going to put together a wheelchair access guide to touring the island of Oahu."

"Sounds like fun," Carol quickly agreed.

"Which means we're splitting up." Nikki grabbed the wheelchair handlebars. "You and Ken can reenact the honeymoon to your heart's content."

She pushed the wheelchair down the path.

"I don't believe this," Jolie said. "I always finish what I start."

Ken put his arm around her shoulder. "Shouldn't you enjoy yourself instead of checking things off a list?"

"Yes and no. I hate how I have to make a list and do everything on it. It's just that we planned everything already."

"Plans change. It might be fun to be surprised, don't you think?"

It felt so comfortable walking with him, side by side down the trail toward the parking lot. Meeting Ken and Carol were good surprises, too.

He turned his face toward her, and she kissed him without thinking.

"Did you plan that?" he asked. "The kiss you just gave me?"

"No, I didn't. It felt right," she stammered, unable to take her gaze off his.

"Then let's do whatever feels right from now on. Take a chance, and let me surprise you."

Jolie's breath caught in her throat. She'd never allowed herself to let things happen.

"I like to be prepared," she said. "You're not going to surprise me with anything dangerous, are you?"

"The only preparation you need is sunscreen, a hat, a bikini, and your smile." He dipped for another peck on the lips. "Think you can do it?"

"Can I trust you? I have to give you a list of things I can't do and foods I can't eat."

"I'll take your list into consideration, but I'm still going to surprise you." Ken pulled her closer and stepped off the trail behind a tree with lush foliage. "Since we're pretending to be on our honeymoon, you're going to have to let me take the lead and pay for everything. That's tradition."

"Yes, tradition." She barely breathed as he crushed her lips with a deep, aggressive kiss— nothing sweet or nice, but oh so very hot.

Chapter Eleven

That evening, Jolie held hands with Ken as they sat inside a small community theater. The air conditioning was perfect, and she was neither too hot or too cold.

They'd had dinner at a healthy farm-to-table restaurant, or as the locals called it, "locovore," serving gluten-free menus with locally grown, organic fruits and vegetables with range-fed beef and foraging chickens.

"The set design is so tropical. I love the mixture of colors," Jolie said, leaning her head on Ken's shoulder.

"You'll love the story, too. It's Hawaii's version of Romeo and Juliet."

"Seriously? Why is true love always forbidden?"

"In this case, they caused their own problems," Ken explained. "Fire and water don't mix, do they? Anyway, I won't tell you the entire story, other than the hero is a man who shapeshifts to a pig."

"A pig man?" Jolie pinched Ken's tight belly. "Are you talking about yourself?"

"Only if you're the fiery one." He brushed his fingers through her hair. "You're a strong woman, Jolie. And very determined. I'm glad you're letting me refresh you. Think of me as balm over your burns, water over your sparks, a safe haven of rest."

"You're so romantic." Jolie shivered with a frisson of delighted chills. She snuggled closer and was rewarded by him stroking her arm. The little, subtle touches and the way he would look at her, as if there were no others present, tempted her to jump in, as if he were her personal swimming hole.

"I'm a surfer who loves stories." He kissed her, a simple peck on the lips. "And I want to retell your story and give you a happy ending."

Happiness suffused Jolie and she closed her eyes, taking a deep breath scented with his sporty cologne and the heat coming off his body. Why couldn't Warren have been so romantic and sweet? Could it be the spark was long gone, if it had ever existed?

She'd met Warren three years ago right after she'd started her business. He'd stepped into her beauty salon while investigating the business next door for insurance fraud. After warning her about business scams, he'd asked her out. They'd slept together after the third date, progressed to exclusivity after six months and were engaged within two years with the schedule allowing for a full year of wedding planning. Everything had been mapped out perfectly, or so she'd thought.

The play started, and Jolie was drawn in by the majestic costumes of the Hawaiian gods and goddesses. She caressed the lei Ken gave her, full of fresh flowers with sweet scents. If he was a storyteller aimed at fixing her sad song, she would enjoy all the pampering while their "honeymoon" lasted.

Onstage, Pele and Kamapua'a were fighting for dominion. She was the goddess of volcanoes, heat, and fire, and he was a demi-god, a trickster, whose rainfall made the harsh lava rock fertile and green.

His gentle, persistent rainfall wooed Pele. She tried to fight him off, her fire turning his water to steam, consuming him as he flooded her with love.

Tears watered Jolie's cheek when Pele finally succumbed to one glorious night of love. The tough, prickly woman had turned tender, yielding to the fierce looking pig-man covered with sharp-edged tattoos.

"Could this work?" Jolie asked Ken during intermission. "I'm afraid something's going to happen."

He put a finger to her lips and grinned. "Fire and water should rule together, don't you think?"

"Depends on if they cancel each other. I'm afraid Pele doesn't want to drown in his love and lose her identity."

"Is that what you're afraid of, if you lose your lists and plans?" He led her to the refreshment stand. "Let me surprise you with a drink."

"It can't have—"

"I've got it." He turned to the bartender and ordered a passion fruit mimosa, no grenadine, and no orange slice.

Jolie's heart was as light as a helium-filled balloon. Ken really did get it. He didn't seem to mind that he couldn't have a beer or snack with nuts, and he'd even wiped the seat handles with alcohol wipes before she sat down.

"Wow, you do have my restrictions memorized." Jolie took a sip of the cocktail. "Mmm … this is awesome."

"Told you, I have to butter you up before the second half of the play."

"Where it falls apart, I bet." She twirled a finger around her red hair.

"Maybe for them, but not for us." He took her hand and she clasped it tight. She hadn't told him she was afraid of water—of being dragged down and held under by a big wave.

They stared at each other, eyes always returning contact, as they made their way back to the auditorium. Being on a date with Ken was easy. He didn't let her worry about a thing, whether it was getting good seats, or having a reservation for dinner.

Except, he seemed too perfect—as if he were playing a part. Jolie finished the mimosa and handed him her champagne glass. She'd go with it for now, but there was definitely something off with how much care he showered on her, the same way Kamapua'a deluged Pele with gifts of flowers, fruits, pigs, fish, wood, shells, and a giant outrigger canoe.

What was in it for him?

Chapter Twelve

"That was such a sad story." Jolie wiped tears from her eyes. "Why wouldn't she relent?"

"Pele wanted to rule her own domain." Ken caressed Jolie's hand. "She didn't want to share."

"And that's why each island has its dry side and wet side." Jolie intertwined her fingers with Ken's. "They'll never be together again."

In the play, Pele regretted giving into the weakness of love and losing control. To keep Kamuapua'a away, she spewed lava at him and caused an underground earthquake. She didn't realize his deep love would cause him to rush into a lava tunnel to find her, fearing she'd been buried beneath the molten stone.

The heat evaporated him, turning him into the hissing steam over the lava vents. When Pele saw him disappear into the wind, she was so distraught she hurled herself off a cliff and was dragged under by the treacherous surf.

"That was the interpretation played here," Ken explained. "In other versions, they're both alive—some even say they're husband and wife. He soothes her after each eruption, and she allows beautiful flowers and trees to grow from her soil."

"I like that much better." Jolie strolled alongside Ken as they exited the theatre. The weather was tropical, and there was no evening chill, although the moist breeze soothed her sunburned shoulders.

They browsed gift shops and wandered around various touristy monuments. The city was filled with obvious honeymooners, and several store owners assumed Jolie and Ken were newlyweds, complimenting her on the lei she wore and the happiness on her face.

"Don't you feel guilty, impersonating honeymooners?" Jolie sipped the free ice tea she got for being a supposed blushing bride.

"Nope, as long as we're enjoying ourselves," Ken said. "Shall we head back to the hotel, my bride? I have a surprise for you."

"Another one?" Her heart was stirred by this wonderful man. "Do you think Carol and Nikki are okay? Should we check on them?"

"They're fine," he replied with a sweet kiss. "Honeymooners aren't supposed to worry about anything besides enjoying their new love."

Our new love? His words had her melting; every bone and muscle softening. Looking at him, feeling his lips on hers, and being surrounded by his warmth—it was hard to believe she wasn't on her real honeymoon. If only ...

"Okay, then, I'm ready for your next surprise," Jolie said, regathering her composure. "So far, nothing's gone wrong. I'm not choking, it's not raining, and the play was awesome."

"You're allowed to surprise me, too," he said as he took her hand. "I have no limitations, none whatsoever."

"Okay, then, let me think of something for you." She kicked off her sandals when they got to the sand. It was still warm even though the sun had already set. The lights of the skyline blinked behind them as the peaceful sound of surf and the scent of the sea beckoned her toward the water.

They walked leisurely, kissing every few steps, until she was up to her knees in the gentle surf. She let her hands wander under his shirt, warming them on the planes of his muscles.

When he brushed her breasts, she sighed into his mouth with relief. It was about time he started acting like a honeymooner and not a boy scout. She'd ignored the fact that leading up to the wedding, she'd been too stressed out to have sex, not that the quickie wham-bam-not-even-a-thank-you-I-got-what-I-wanted qualified for any form of lovemaking. But still, her body had needs.

Correction. She had needs—to be wanted, loved, and cherished.

If the hard rod in Ken's board shorts was any indication, he, at least, wanted her right now. Molten heat simmered in her belly, and she rubbed up against his giant erection.

He moaned and broke the kiss. "I want you so badly, I'm going to take you right here."

"Is that what honeymooners say?" She teased him by wiggling against him, but before he could reply, she drew his head down between her breasts.

"You're killing me," he said right before mouthing her through her clothes. "If we don't get indoors, we're going to be arrested."

She heard the catcalls around them, so she complied when he dragged her from the surf. They picked up their sandals and ran, hand in hand.

As soon as the elevator doors closed, they locked lips again, touching and tangling their hands and body parts. Her knees weakened, and she felt her skin glow with a scintillating expectation.

If the way he kissed were any indication of the rest of his lovemaking, she was in for an experience she'd never forget.

She sealed her lips against his and kissed him greedily. This hunk of man was hers for the duration of her honeymoon, and one of the things people did on their honeymoon was have sex.

The elevator doors opened with a well-greased slide, forcing them apart. Taking her hand, Ken led her down the hallway toward her room.

Fingers of anxiety crept up her neck, and she glanced quickly left and right. "Your room or mine? What if Nikki's there?"

"She's not. She texted me earlier. She and my sister checked out. They're going on an around-the-island car tour. Ready for your surprise?" He swooped her off her feet and raced toward her door.

"You're my surprise." Jolie latched onto him, hugging him with both her arms and legs and smothering his face with kisses. "This is going to be my best honeymoon ever."

"Mmmm …" His tongue mated with hers, now unrestrained as he plundered her mouth. He set her down and trapped her against her door, rocked his arousal against her hips and gazed at her with half-closed bedroom eyes—darkened with passion. "Do you want this, Jolie?"

His rough voice sent tingles of pleasure down her spine, especially the way he said her name, all rough and rumbling.

She stared him straight in the eye. No flinching. Not a hesitation in sight and nodded. "Yes, I want this. I want the perfect honeymoon."

"So do I, with you." He lowered his head to her neck. His long, slow sucking kiss had her knees ready to give out as she fumbled for her keycard in her purse.

He palmed her breasts and teased, pinching her nipples through her clothes, and she dropped her purse. Why was he torturing her so much? Couldn't he wait until they were safely in the room?

"Wait. Let me get the door," she mumbled weakly.

She bent to pick up her purse and the door opened behind her. She half fell into the room and hit something hard—well, not quite as hard as Ken.

"Jolie, what the hell?" Warren grabbed her wrists and turned on Ken. "Who the fuck are you?"

Chapter Thirteen

Jolie blinked, once, twice, three times, but Warren didn't disappear. Hot and cold sweat fought to exit her pores, and she reeled as if she'd been slammed by a monster wave and trolled on the bottom of the sea.

From the corner of her eye, she saw Ken slink away. Apparently, he hadn't cared enough to stand by her. But then he was only an actor, and this was her groom, Warren Wayne, the man she was supposed to marry.

Warren slammed the door and dragged her to the bed. His mean green eyes were fierce with anger, and his sandy blond hair hung over his eyebrows.

"How dare you change the tickets on me?" He glared at her. "You should have waited for me."

"Waited for you? You dumped me at the wedding." The words tumbled from her mouth. "You embarrassed me in front of all our guests. Your parents didn't know where you were. You didn't answer any of our text messages. We thought you took off with the stripper."

"Took off with her? Are you out of your mind? She was the hired help."

"Hired help?" Jolie pushed off the bed and jutted her chin at him. "As in whore? I can't believe that was the last thing on your mind before marrying me."

"You had your bachelorette party. I'm sure you had male strippers."

"To look at, not to touch. There's a big difference."

"Whoever that beach bum was, you certainly weren't just looking at him. You were all over him. Ready to fuck him."

"I went on a date, that's all." Jolie crossed her arms and pinched her upper arms to tamp down her rising anger. "Seeing as you decided not to marry me, I'm entitled to a little fun."

"I was tied up by your friends, Terri, Nikki, and Ryker. While you were out there tossing the bouquet and cutting into our cake, I was gagged and bound on a hotel bed. Why did you believe them and not come looking for me?" He grabbed Jolie by the shoulders.

She shuddered at the ick factor crawling up her skin at being touched by Warren's clammy hands. Anger roiled in her belly and she snorted. "Did you have sex with the stripper? And don't lie. My brother said he hadn't gotten his turn yet, so it looks like you were first in line."

"Your brother's a fink."

"Oh, please, come up with something better." Jolie sneered and wiped his hands from her. "If you had sex with the stripper, I don't want you to touch me."

"I wasn't married to you yet. I can do what I want."

Jolie was too pissed to roll her eyes. Did the man not get commitment? True love? Security and family?

She pointed to the door. "Get out. Go. You never cared about me. I almost died at the luau you wanted to go to because they had peanuts there. As for Big John's Shrimp truck, they don't serve anything but shrimp, something I'm deathly allergic to."

"You agreed to all the plans. All of it." He swept his hands across the paperwork on the table. "And why the hell did you cancel the marlin boat? I called and they said you transferred the tickets to a blogger and a lady in a wheelchair. You know how much I wanted to catch a marlin."

Jolie's hands turned into fists, and red hot lava rose inside of her. Her ginger was about to snap—full force.

"You came all the way from California for the fishing trip? No apologies, no explanations. No 'let's see if we can fix this,' but 'where's my fishing charter?'"

"Hey, I'm not the one with my legs wrapped around a male prostitute."

"Male prostitute? How dare you. Ken's a friend. Someone I happened to meet on the trip."

"Oh, really? Is that what he told you?" Warren put his hands on his hips and knocked his head back, laughing hard. "It might have taken me a while, but once I got a good look at his slinking behind, I finally figured out what kind of scum he is."

"Are you saying I hired him from an escort service? Do you think I'm that desperate? I'm not like you. I never pay for sex."

"Maybe you didn't, but Ken works for Bad Boys for Hire. Last time I saw him, he was sitting on a barstool pretending to be your friend Terri's groom, telling a tall tale about her death to trick Ryker's brothers."

Jolie had heard about the ruse, but didn't know Ken was the actor hired to play the part.

"So? That doesn't mean a thing. He and his sister are on vacation. I didn't pay him a dime."

Except a couple of times, she saw Nikki whispering to Ken, as if she were instructing him. Blood rushed to Jolie's face and her cheeks burned. Could it be true?

"You didn't, but I bet he was paid to squire you around. Think about it, Jol, why else would a guy like that want to put up with your list of allergies and restrictions?" Warren slumped himself on the bed and picked up the TV remote. "Since this is my room, too, I'll be staying."

"But, we're not married."

"Welcome to the obvious," Warren said. "Never stopped you from sleeping with me before."

Jolie's tongue was numb, her sunburn flared, and nerves prickled her stomach. She narrowed her eyes at Warren. On the outside, he was a hunk—tattooed, muscular, a former football player who'd played a few years in the pros before being cut from the team. Now, he tooled around with a motorcycle club and claimed he did undercover work.

"I'm not sleeping with you. Not tonight. Not tomorrow. Not ever."

"You're pissed because you wanted to get laid by the hired hand." He waved her off as if she were no consequence. "Suit yourself. I'm not moving. This is my room, under my name."

He switched the TV to the pay-per-view porn station.

"Wait a second," Jolie said. "All the reservations were made by my credit card. You haven't paid me yet."

"Pay you? Honey, once we're married it's all joint property." He leaned back on the body pillow and raised the volume, filling the room with moans and grunts.

Jolie rushed to the closet and grabbed her suitcase. The past day or two had shown her how little Warren cared about her allergies and making sure she was comfortable. If she'd stayed tethered to his honeymoon plans, she wouldn't have enjoyed the Kamuapua'a and Pele play she saw this evening. Instead, she could have ended up in the emergency room from her shrimp allergy.

She emptied the bathroom of her things and snagged her laptop from the table. The bouquet of orange flowers Ken had given her were missing.

"What did you do with my flowers?" Jolie marched to block Warren's view of the TV.

"Why? Did you pay him to give them to you?" Warren made motions for her to get out of the way while craning his neck. "I tossed them. They give you allergies."

She switched off the TV. "I have food allergies, not flower allergies. I'm leaving, and checking out of this room, so you better be packed, unless you put the bill on your credit card."

"Suit yourself." Warren leaned over the bed and pulled a bag of peanuts from a shopping bag. "You were always more trouble than it was worth. Good luck with your certified Beach Bum Bad Boy. Don't believe me? Look it up on the website."

#

Ken went for a long run on the sand, both to cool off and to clear his mind. No matter how attracted he was to Jolie, she didn't belong to him.

Her groom had shown up, and what could he do but back away? Except, a part of his heart shriveled, and he missed Jolie already. What had started as a lark, seeing if he could get his childhood crush to recognize him and like him back, now felt like being pounded by a Mack-sized wave.

He clutched his chest, fighting the ache deep inside. Warren was here, and Jolie could go back to her list of things to do with her groom. They could run down to city hall and get hitched, and there was nothing he could do about it.

He pumped his arms and ran faster until his legs turned into ribbons of pain. Somehow, Jolie and her strawberry red hair, her chameleon eyes changing from blue-green to blue-gray had him hooked, mesmerized, unable to picture a life without her.

How had this happened? Was there truly magic on these Hawaiian islands that made people fall in love? Fire and water, like two halves of the island, windward and leeward, east and west. Both sides of the jeweled island paradise.

He jumped into the surf to cool off and swam out into the bay. The breakers were gentle, with swells just right for beginners. If he were ever to get a chance with Jolie again, he would show her that waves weren't to be feared, but to be ridden. That love can be as gentle as the rain, and as sweet as a garland of lilies and daisies.

Ken swam until his arm muscles felt like noodles. It was peaceful so far from land, looking back at the glittering skyline of Honolulu, the beautiful lights, the pinpoints of stars, and the water rising and falling, embracing him like a woman's arms.

He lay on his back and stared at the moon, reciting his lines, wondering if he were worth anything to his dear, beloved Jolie.

Ah, Juliet, if the measure of thy joy
Be heap'd like mine, and that thy skill be more
To blazon it, then sweeten with thy breath
This neighbour air, and let rich music's tongue
Unfold the imagin'd happiness that both
Receive in either by this dear encounter.

These lines were spoken by Romeo to Juliet before their secret wedding at the friar's cell. Would he get a chance to hear Jolie's reply?

A star twinkled, winking its answer, and Ken shook the water from his head. He'd wasted enough time on self-pity. He swam for shore with powerful strokes. It was time to make his plea, time to act and fight, not only for himself, but for dear Jolie.

Whatever happened, she didn't deserve to be put underfoot by a man like Warren. It was time for Ken to show Jolie what true love's hand could do.

Chapter Fourteen

Jolie dragged her luggage into the elevator and punched the button for the lobby. She was going home. She should face the facts. She had been dumped by her groom, duped by her honeymoon hunk, and betrayed by her best friends.

Instead of tying Warren up, they should have escorted her to his hotel room so she could question him directly. Did they not trust her? Did they truly think she would have married him to keep up appearances? That her OCD would force her to complete everything she started, exactly as planned?

Fury blazed through her veins, and her hands shook as she texted Nikki. *Did you hire Ken to come on to me?*

She wouldn't put it past her friend. Nikki always had this smug, superior, know-it-all attitude when it came to relationships. She prided herself as being immune to notions of infatuation, passion, and the types of emotions that caused rational, logical adults to act like lovesick teens—Jolie being a prime example of an irrational woman bent on self-destructive relationships, at least in Nikki's opinion.

Jolie hated that her friend was proven right in the Warrengate disaster. She wanted to kick the walls of the elevator, stomp her feet and punch the buttons, but she held it together when the doors opened. A pair of honeymooners stepped in, their lips conjoined in heated passion.

Sheesh, hadn't these people heard of closed doors and privacy?

The presumed bride cooed, and the groom was tender and endearing as he whispered sweet words into her lips.

Gag. Jolie wanted to hurl her head against the wall.

The elevator stopped again, and more couples joined them, crowding the kissing couple to the corner. They held hands, made eye contact only with each other, smiled, laughed, and touched frequently—just like she and Ken—in their own little world.

Ugh. Where had that thought come from? Ken, if Warren could be believed, was the hired hand.

The elevator stopped at the lobby, and all of the honeymoon lovers strolled off, each in their own bubble of happiness.

Jolie's phone rang and Nikki said, "What's going on? And no, I didn't hire Ken. Why would you think that?"

"Because Warren showed up and said Ken works for Bad Boys for Hire."

"So? And that makes him guilty?" Nikki voice smacked like she was chewing gum. "If you're so insecure, why don't you try and hire Ken yourself and see if he'll take the job?"

"What do you mean?" Jolie stood in line to check out.

"Offer him money to take you places, teach you to surf, even charge per kiss."

"I'm not hiring a male prostitute," Jolie yelped, before noticing faces turning toward her with varying expressions of surprise and curiosity.

"Carol and I have to go to sleep because we have to meet the skipper at the marina at five in the morning."

"You're going on the marlin trip. Warren's pissed it got changed."

"And you care?" Nikki smacked her bubblegum again. "Tell me something I can believe."

"I'm hurt, okay? Hurt that he never cared about me—only seeing my limitations. I get seasick. I have allergies. I'm obsessive compulsive. I'm afraid of the unexpected."

"And? What about Ken? Did you like his surprises?"

Even though she was shaking with nerves, the mention of Ken's consideration flooded her with an unexpected yearning. "Yes, I did, except the last one. He claimed he had a surprise in my room, but it turned out to be Warren."

"Ken wouldn't do that to you," Nikki said. "I bet Warren sweet talked himself into the room and threw out Ken's surprise."

"You're probably right. He tossed the flowers Ken gave me. You know he said someone paid Ken to give—"

"Wait, hold on," Nikki cut her off.

Jolie fingered the lei she was still wearing. If Nikki said she hadn't hired him, then he'd given her everything with his own money—either that, or Nikki was lying.

Bringing up the browser, Jolie searched for Bad Boys for Hire. Her phone was slow in serving the pages, so she put Nikki on hold and hit the call button. Oh, heck, they were asleep in California already.

She left a brief message. "I'm interested in hiring a certified Beach Bum Bad Boy for hire. Must be able to surf. I prefer a blond, since I'm having a Barbie and Ken beach party. Call me."

She hung up and returned to the held call with Nikki.

"Where were you?" her friend asked. "Carol says Ken is falling for you. She claims he's usually not so sweet. All he cared about was surfing and spending hours in the sea. A slob too, he never picked up after himself, and he doesn't date much, at least from what she could see."

Nikki was way too eager to have her believe Ken was above board. How could Ken fall for her when she was technically another man's bride? Not to mention how difficult she was to live with, as Warren reminded her.

"You seem to protest too much," she said to Nikki. "Now that I think about it, you pointed out Ken on the airplane, and you set up these coincidences for us to get together. If I find out you're lying to me …"

Beep, beep, beep. The call ended.

Jolie shook the phone and threw it into her purse. She was next in line to check out, so she squared her bill and dragged her suitcase to the shuttle bus stop where passengers were embarking.

She took one last look at the darkness beyond the lights where the surf swished onto the beach. She inhaled the faintly scented tropical air, and gazed at the twinkling stars above. So, this was it. The end of paradise. The entire trip had been a lie anyway—one to fool herself into thinking things would be okay if only she followed the plan.

What had they said about the best laid plans?

"Let me take your bag, Miss," the driver said.

"Wait, wait!" Ken ran toward her, dripping wet. "Don't go, my bride. We're not finished with our honeymoon."

He wrapped his wet arms around her and swept her off her feet as his lips descended on hers. Swinging her around in circles, he kissed her over and over again, as the waiting passengers clapped and cheered.

Chapter Fifteen

"I'll take her bag," Ken said to the shuttle bus driver after they'd held up the line with their marathon kiss.

The departing crowd wished them well, and Jolie walked hand in hand with her Prince Charming. Okay, fine, he was as wet as a guppy, but the thrill of having total strangers believe she was one of those treasured brides was more than enough compensation.

Swinging their hands, they sauntered back into the lobby, kissing every few steps. By the time they got to the elevator, Jolie went on the rampage and cornered Ken, plastering herself against him. She inhaled his salty taste, nipping and sucking on him while her hands snuck beneath his wet shirt.

Forget propriety and doing the right thing. Forget the fact her ex was upstairs watching porn by himself. Forget the accusations of Ken being bought and paid for. She was on fire, consumed by flames, and for once in her restrictive life, she wanted no boundaries, no lists, no checkpoints, nothing.

"Since I checked out already, we better go back to your room," she gasped between kisses.

"I reckon you're right, sweet bride." He licked a line down her neck. Her nipples tightened and tingled with shivers of arousal, and she wondered if she could last the rest of the floors without tearing his clothes off.

The elevator stopped and the doors opened as people stepped on. Now it was her turn to pretend they didn't care if she was groping her man, hands roaming all over that perfect manly body.

He nipped her ear and she giggled. He tickled her, brushing over her breasts and she wiggled in his embrace. Her eyes never left his, and what she saw rocked her to the core. If this wasn't love, it was surely a credible imitation. His pupils were dilated and his expression was adoring, indulgent, and slightly cocky, as if she belonged to him and he knew it.

She rather liked that. No man had ever found her irresistible. But then, she'd always been stiff and proper, a real stick in the mud, insisting on hand cleaner and checking the mattresses for bedbugs instead of throwing herself to the throes of passion.

"How many fricking floors does this thing have?" Ken growled into her ear as the elevator stopped at each floor.

His hot breath and impatient tone made her quiver with delight. He'd found her, probably been thinking about her the entire time after he left her room. She'd never had such passion before, nor the piercing blue eyes focused on her—only her.

Since they couldn't get any hotter without combusting, she asked, "What was the surprise you had for me? I'm not thinking it was my ex."

"Oh, so he's now the ex." Ken lifted an eyebrow, looking entirely too pleased. "You're right, it wasn't him, but if I tell you now, I can't surprise you tomorrow night."

There was going to be a tomorrow! He was already thinking ahead.

"I can't wait," she squealed. "But I'm also supposed to surprise you, too."

"Sure, but can it wait a day or two? When you left, I went for a swim and thought of all the things I wanted to do with you if I got the chance, and now, I'm looking at my chance." He dipped his lips and massaged hers for a bit.

That was fine. Her surprise could wait. She'd have to think of something spectacular—something he'd never forget, and those types of adventures took planning.

The elevator rocked to a stop at their floor.

As calmly as she could, not easy given her panting breath and the dampening between her legs, she and Ken exited the elevator. As soon as the door closed, they dashed to his room.

Ken whipped out the keycard and before she was aware, he lifted her over the threshold. Turning, he kicked the door shut with a slam. In two steps they plunged onto the large, king-sized bed. She peeled his wet shirt off, and he lifted her sundress over her head, then replaced the lei.

"So beautiful, like the flowers, like paradise." He ran a knuckle over her cheek. "Let me make you my bride tonight, dear Jolie."

His deep drawl, and the way he drew out her name made her quiver with anticipation. She would finally be a man's bride—tonight.

Wow.

She nodded, and a smile licked her lips. "And, you, Ken, tonight you're my groom. I want it all, so don't you stop. Not now, not ever."

His grin widened and he made a motion of tipping a hat. "Yes, ma'am."

"Come to me, babe." Reaching up, she pulled his body over hers. His skin was still cool from the dip in the ocean, and his board shorts were wet. She shuddered from the mixture of cold and heat when he slipped his hot tongue into her mouth. She took it all in, wanting more, and need mounted in her veins.

She grappled with the waistband of his shorts and closed her hand around his heavily loaded cock. A growly moan escaped his lips as she stroked up and down, cupping her palm over the tip, slick with pre-cum.

"Sugar, you're going to have to stop that." He took her hand away from his erection. "I'm a believer of ladies first."

Jolie stared up at Ken and swallowed a boatload of drool as he lifted himself and shucked off his shorts. The man was perfect, with no tan lines on his sculpted body. His cock was so thick and long, it looked positively scary.

She was fit to die and go to heaven when Ken lowered his lips to the line between her breasts. Skillful fingers untied the bikini top, and the second his tongue encircled one nipple, Jolie almost shot off the bed. He palmed her other breast and suckled slowly, deep and full, drawing out her nipple and rolling his tongue around the tip.

Jolie's eyes closed and she arched her head back at the pleasure assaulting her with his heavy cock resting on her thigh, twitching for attention, full of luscious promise.

Could she handle it? She wasn't that experienced. What if she was a dud in bed? She swallowed hard and stiffened as anxiety flooded her and the pleasure of his fondling diminished.

"Hey, you okay?" Ken lifted his head, his caring eyes blinking softly. "Did I do something wrong?"

"No, I'm not that experienced. I'm not a virgin, but I've only ever been with you know, the douche canoe."

"That makes two of us." He nuzzled her earlobe.

"You mean, you've been with the douchebag, too?" she joked.

"No, I chased tubular waves over women. Surfing is exhausting, and when your balls are freezing in cold water for hours at a time, you're not in the mood to do more than warm up and sleep."

"You warm them up with a woman?"

"I wish." He shook his head, his blond hair dipping into his eyes. "The places I surfed, no sane woman would hang at. I venture to places no one else dares to surf, which means camping on windswept beaches with no amenities or creature comforts."

"No high rise hotels, paved roads, and facilities."

"Exactly. There's no way you're going to be outshined by anyone. But if I suck, well, guess you can kick me out of the bed."

"Oh, you can keep sucking," Jolie said, heartened at Ken's humbleness when it came to sex. Too many men were arrogant, as if they were God's gift in that department. Usually those types thought all they needed were a set of biceps and a hammering penis. Warren sure didn't work for her fulfillment, quitting after a few pathetic attempts and blaming her for being unresponsive, before falling asleep.

"I'll suck until you're screaming for me to stop." He nosed his way from her breasts to her belly button, kissing and licking, blowing softly. Goosebumps raised over her as he approached her bikini line. She was fully waxed in preparation for her wedding night, and even though this was a few nights later, she was still bare as a baby's bottom.

Instead of lowering her bikini bottom, he rubbed his face back and forth, kissing her mound and nipping her thighs. She held her breath, waiting as he ran his sturdy fingers up and down her legs, lazily.

Her body strained, crying for more, for him to center on the nub of pleasure throbbing for his attention. Why was he such a tease?

"Stop holding your breath, my bride." He whispered to her lips below. The vibrations of his voice were enough to make her squirm.

If she were only bold enough to remove her own bikini bottom as casually as he took off his shorts. She looked down at him, at his sculpted perfection and the cock pointed proudly at her and the heavy balls behind it. How she wanted to palm them, to touch, and fondle, to make him lose control and brand her with his love.

Stop being a pussy, she chided herself. If she wanted him to lose control, she had to make the first leap.

Decision made, she lifted her hips and kicked off her bikini bottom, watching for his reaction at her waxed bareness.

He sucked in a breath, licked his lips and instantly plunged his face between her legs.

Ah ... sweet pleasure. She spread her legs, no longer caring whether he liked what he saw or not. His tongue flicked the length of her slit, teasing open her lips, before settling on her clit. He flicked it gently, shooting sparks over her body. She gasped as electricity arced over her, blinding her with feral need.

She grabbed ahold of his shoulders, barely aware of his bobbing head between her legs. His mouth and tongue dipped and sucked, firing her up to blast point. Wanton with passion, she jerked her hips up and down in a frenzy as she rode his tongue with a wildness she'd never experienced.

Intense sensations flooded her with ecstasy and all she sought was that rush of climax as she clamped her legs around his head and wiggled her crotch against his face. When he inserted a finger, rubbing it over her inner walls, she practically flew off the bed.

"Ken, Ken," she panted, close to the edge of her universe.

He kissed her hard around her clit and shoved a second finger in. She liquefied, pulsing and pulsing around the fingers he pumped in and out of her white hot core. Rocked by the most exquisite orgasm, only a single thought went through her mind.

Surprises were awesome.

# # #

Ken licked the hot lava juices Jolie spewed with volcanic force, smiling to himself. He'd never made a woman come with such ease. Jolie was so responsive, she was made for him.

He lifted himself and marveled at the flush reddening her skin from head to toe. "You're so beautiful, so pink and perfect."

She reached up for him, and his heart expanded, loving the way she beckoned. Her face was sweetness and satiation, her eyes glazed and focused intently on him, taking in his every move.

Her lips, half pouting and half smiling made his balls ache and his cock twitch. Reaching over to the nightstand, he found a wrapped condom and handed it to her.

His gaze smothering her, he lowered his face to her, forehead to forehead. "I want you, Jolie, to be my bride, not only for tonight, but on our own real honeymoon."

"Real honeymoon?"

He nodded. He shouldn't take advantage of her while still in the afterglow of an orgasm, but before he made love to her, he had to know she was into him, too.

She blinked, those beautiful eyes of hers changing from blue-gray to blue-green, and dangled the condom in his face. "You want an answer? Now?"

"It would make the difference between me fucking you or making love to you." His voice rasped in his tightening throat. He hadn't thought she would say no. After all, he had her where he wanted her.

"If you're my groom, then you can do both." She tore the wrapper.

460

When she touched his cock and stretched the condom over it, he closed his eyes at the raging inferno heating up inside his veins.

Catching her in his arms, he turned on his back and placed her slick entrance above him.

Her mouth gaped as she stared down at his upright cock. "I'm not sure I know what to do."

"Ride it, sweetie. Ease yourself down. I'm putting you in control."

Her breasts jiggled, and her chest heaved. She sucked in a breath as he picked up his cock and held it against her. He wasn't making it easy for her, but he knew she'd appreciate the control.

Besides, it was a heck of a lot sexier to watch her lower herself.

"Kiss me, bride." He pursed his lips, inviting her to press herself against him.

She did, closing her eyes, and when she moved forward, she took in the tip. A low groan escaped his throat. She was so tight.

He wrapped his fingers around her hair and pulled her closer, jerking his hips so that she opened another inch or so. Sweet paradise, her movement sent shock waves radiating from his cock to his heart.

"Ride me, bride. Ride me until we come apart. Let me love you, Jolie, go, go, go," he urged her until he was fully inside her heated channel.

Her eyes opened with wonder, and her hair tangled over her shoulders and breasts, cascading onto his chest. He held her hips, grinding his pubic bone against her clit while bolts of electric pleasure coursed through his body.

Moaning low and throaty, she threw her head back and rode, rubbing herself faster, up and down as her tits jiggled and bounced, and her butt cheeks slapped his balls. Looking down, he was treated to the sight of him piercing her bare pussy, over and over again as she rode harder and faster, a fire goddess bent on another volcanic eruption.

Her walls clenched him, rubbing him with a burning friction. His eyes rolled to the back of his head and he was losing it, unable to to control the inferno blazing inside him. He was hurtling toward the edge, too fast, too hot, but he was lost, too lost in passion and everything Jolie.

He grabbed her breasts and flicked his thumbs over her nipples, pinching them and driving her so crazy she howled a series of guttural cries before shattering. Her walls tightened, pulsing around his exploding cock.

He shoved himself up hard, shuddering from spurt after spurt of a natural high so high he burst apart into thousands of shards, each piercing his heart with a drug so potent and addicting that only his bride, Jolie Becker Cassidy, could satisfy.

She collapsed over him, breathing raggedly, her sweat mingled with his. She kissed him, her lips moving languidly.

Ken kissed her back, lazily, loving the afterglow. He was still half hard when she lifted off him and then immediately lay on top of him, gifting him the sweetest after sex cocktail he'd ever tasted.

It was only when drowsiness washed over him, that he remembered she hadn't answered his proposal, because that was what it was, wasn't it? A real honeymoon meant real bride and groom, joined in marriage, which meant a real wedding and a real life afterward.

Chapter Sixteen

Jolie locked herself in the bathroom. She stared at herself in the mirror. What had she done?

In the other room, Ken lay, still naked, asleep. Of course, she'd purposely put him to sleep with her kisses. She hadn't wanted to talk, didn't want to answer his question.

Had he really meant for this to be their real honeymoon? Was that a proposal? Or just a way to get between her legs?

She'd never been with a man who unsettled her more than Ken. And to think she had come all over his face and then again while riding him like a screaming banshee? Sheesh, what was this world coming to?

This wild woman wasn't her. She was the careful one. The one who dotted her I's and crossed her T's. Had she even checked if the condom hadn't ripped?

Her usual climaxes were measured and self-administered, controlled by the level she allowed, oftentimes no more than a polite sneeze, not the internal combustion that had just rocked her world.

Her body still humming with the throes of what Ken did to her, she texted Nikki.

Hey, I might have made the biggest mistake in my life. Can you help?

If they were planning on going marlin fishing, it meant they were still in the area. Maybe she could bunk with them tonight, and let things cool off between her and Ken.

She'd been dumped by one groom; neither her heart nor her soul could take another dousing. If Ken was playacting, she didn't want to know. Better to cut her losses before he woke up and denied everything.

A text from Nikki came in. *Are you saying you slept with him?*

Jolie's face heated and prickles fried her sunburned skin. That wasn't what she'd meant to say. She placed a voice call to clarify.

"You know what time it is?" Nikki answered the phone. "Carol and I have to wake up early."

"Let me go with you. Where are you staying? What room are you in?"

"You did sleep with him." Nikki giggled. "I bet it was so awesome, you lost control. He finally got you out of your box."

"Shhh …" Jolie hissed. "Don't say anymore."

"Why? You're going to deny it? You're scared shitless and you're going to run, even go fishing with us when all you'll do is barf your insides out."

Nikki's all-knowing tone grated over Jolie's eardrum. She shifted the phone to her other ear. "I'm not running. In fact, I'm supposed to plan a surprise for him. I can't think of a thing to do. Could you ask Carol what Ken likes to do besides surf?"

"Quit changing the subject and go back to your man," Nikki said. "Sounds like you're hooked on surprises."

"Can you just get Carol?" Jolie had no comment for her dastardly friend who, for all she knew, had orchestrated the entire honeymoon charade. She might as well grin and bear it, go through with her end of the bargain to surprise Ken and rescue the remaining dregs of her honeymoon. At least she was doing something and not sitting around moping over her failed wedding.

"Hello?" It was Carol. "Nikki says you need advice on an activity to surprise my brother with."

"I haven't thought of anything yet," Jolie said.

"Good. I bet he hasn't told you he has restrictions."

"Restrictions? You mean there are things he can't do?" Now, Jolie's curiosity was spiked. "He told me anything is good."

"I figured he would," Carol said. "He never wants to inconvenience anyone, and he wants to seem brave and courageous."

"Go ahead." What could Ken be afraid of? And why hadn't he told her?

"He's afraid of heights. Don't take him rock climbing or hiking where there aren't any guard rails. The Diamond Head hike was relatively tame with rails and stairs, so he was okay there. But if he's on a steep trail with no guardrail, he'll freak out."

"Like that Stairway to Heaven hike I had on my list?" Somehow the thought that Ken wasn't invincible calmed her.

"That hike is illegal anyway. A lot of places are not maintained, and the way is treacherous. Don't even think about it." Carol's voice tightened, probably remembering her own fall on Mt. Baldy.

"Don't worry," Jolie said. "I'm not a rule breaker."

"That's good," Carol said. "You have a good time, you hear?"

The bathroom door rattled, and Ken called, "Jolie, are you okay?"

Shit. Carol would hear the banging on the door and think they'd had a fight. She had to get her off the phone.

"Sorry about waking you guys up," Jolie said. "Text me where you're staying and we can meet for lunch."

"Sure thing. Good luck with my brother."

Jolie said goodbye and slipped the phone back in her purse.

Ken knocked on the door. "Jolie, honey, what's the matter?"

"Everything's fine. I had to use the bathroom. Go back to bed."

"Come back and cuddle with me. I'm not finished with you." His deep, rough voice made her tingle in all the right and wrong places.

She threw open the door. Why not? Whatever predicament she was in, another round of sex wasn't going to make anything worse.

His heated presence filled the bathroom as his grin spurred her lust to rise.

"Want to try another position, my bride?" He tilted his head in the direction of the bed.

"Sure, groom, let's do it some more." She leaped into his arms and licked his neck as he carted her back to the bed. As long as she kept him too busy to talk about serious things, she could handle the rest of the honeymoon.

Maybe.

Chapter Seventeen

Many positions later, Jolie lay satiated in Ken's arms, listening to the steady thumping of his heart. If he was half as exhausted as she, they'd need to take an easy day to recover from all the loving.

"What do you say we lounge at the beach tomorrow?" He nuzzled her earlobe. It was amazing how he was always in tune with her thoughts, almost like he could read her mind. "We can rent a couple of longboards and I can teach you how to paddle and ride the waves."

"Sounds heavenly." She stretched in his arms and hummed. "I didn't tell you before, but I'm afraid of being dragged out to sea. Being held underwater scares me."

"I'm glad you told me." He kissed her temple and stroked her hair. "You have nothing to worry about. The beach I'm taking you to is so shallow you can walk all the way out to where the waves break."

"Wouldn't that be boring for you, Mr. Champion Surfer?"

"Not at all. Watching the expression on your face when you get up and ride a wave will be worth it." He kissed her again, fingers caressing her.

He acted the part of devoted groom with aplomb. Always kissing and touching, he made her feel cherished and loved. But this was now, while everything was fresh and new. He'd tire of her dietary restrictions, her obsessions, fears, and uptightness. She had to see just how much he'd put up with, and now would be the time, while still in the honeymoon stage.

"Ken?" she asked as his breathing steadied and his eyes closed.

"Uhmmm …" he mumbled, a smile still on his lips.

"What happens after this honeymoon's over?" It was just like her to not be able to relax and let things flow.

"We go home and keep doing this." He grinned, cupping her breast and caressing it.

"Is this just sex for you?" *Or even worse, a paid career.*

"Is it for you?" He touched her cheek with the tip of his finger.

"I'm not that kind of girl."

"I know you're not," he said. "I've a confession to make."

Jolie's heart jumped to attention and her stomach cringed. If he had been paid and admitted it, then she was not precious in his eyes, nor did he really consider her limitations—he was only putting up with them for money.

"Don't look so nervous." He gave her a peck on the temple and rubbed her arm with a calming motion. "You might think I'm moving fast with you, making love to you and asking you to make this our real honeymoon."

"Well, yeah, that is pretty speedy," she admitted. "We barely know each other."

"Maybe you've forgotten me, but I'm the boy in your Cinderella play, the fat one who played the pumpkin."

Whatever Jolie had expected, this was not it. She was pillow-talking with a pumpkin?

She squinted to get a better look at the hunk in front of her. No way was he that chubby kid with the buck teeth and double chin. But then, the eyes, almost teal blue like the sea, seemed familiar. Her skin flushed as she recalled the bullies chasing him through the schoolyard.

"You were Ken Dog?"

He winced at the nickname. "Hey, I tried for Prince Charming, but all I got was the pumpkin part."

"Oh, I remember that pumpkin, but forgot it was you." Jolie twisted her lips. He wore an orange costume and pushed a wheelbarrow that stood in for the carriage. Hey, it was an elementary school play, and they had to improvise.

"I'm rather forgettable." He blinked and flattened his lips. "Except when people made fun of me. I was fat, wore old-fashioned clothes, never had a haircut and I stunk."

"You didn't stink," Jolie said. "But look at you now. You're in great shape. What happened?"

"We moved to San Diego after my dad died, and my mother married a surfing instructor. He took me under his armpit."

"As opposed to his wing?" Jolie licked her lips. She couldn't argue with the results. This new Ken was a chiseled hunk, and not only that, he didn't parade around as if he were God's gift to women.

"The truth is, I've been liking you a long time, Jolie, and when I realized how close you came to being married, I had to make my move. Getting back to your question about what happens after the honeymoon's over …" He smoothed his fingers through her hair. "I'd like to keep seeing you."

"How many times a week?" *What's your hourly rate?* Gah. She sounded like she was interviewing a sex therapist.

"As many times as you can fit me into your schedule." He lowered his lips toward her and kissed her.

And budget.

"Isn't your time valuable? Do you work a job or anything regular?"

"Not regular, but I do get called away on business some evenings." Ken winked. "When I'm not working, I'm all yours."

She would probably be his most lucrative client.

"What kind of work?"

"Odd jobs, here and there." He pulled her on top of him. "Shall we try another position?"

Even though he hadn't answered her question, Jolie nodded. Heck, if he were giving her a freebie to hook her into paying for his services, she might as well take advantage of it, but once the honeymoon was over, she'd have to go cold turkey. As if being a jilted bride wasn't enough, she wasn't so desperate that she had to hire escorts for sex.

Chapter Eighteen

The beaches at Waikiki were crowded, as expected, but Ken rented a longboard and waded with Jolie into the gently rolling water. She was wearing a hot pink bikini which had him hankering to tear it off her, not that he hadn't gotten enough sex the night before. Correction. He could never get enough of her. It wasn't only her delectable body, her great tits, and awesome shape, but also the way she challenged him, holding him accountable, and making sure he had honorable motives. She wasn't a woman to be toyed with, not after what Warren had done to her, and tonight, he'd go ahead with the surprise he'd tried to improvise the night before.

He scanned the hordes of beachgoers, wondering where her ex had gone. Everywhere he looked, men were ogling his fire goddess, but he wasn't the jealous kind. After all, when one grew up being mocked and laughed at, it was pretty cool to be seen as the lucky bastard with the red hot bride.

"Let's get you used to the board first," Ken said once they were in waist-deep water. "You can lie on it, and I'll push you out there."

"How many feet are the waves?" Jolie asked, biting her lower lip and squinting toward the ocean.

"Does it matter?" Ken asked. "Hawaiians measure waves different from mainlanders who stretch and exaggerate wave height. When Hawaiians say three to five, everyone else says six to ten."

"Oh, but how high do you think they are?"

Ken smirked, nodding. "One to two feet, baby waves."

"You're kidding," Jolie said. "Then I'll tell everyone they're two to four feet."

He held the board for Jolie, and walked her out beyond the breaking waves. He explained how she had to get the rhythm of the wave, knowing when they were about to break and anticipating it, so she could paddle into position to ride it.

Once she got onto the board, belly down, he gave it a push. "Paddle, now."

She missed the wave, while several kids next to her caught it and rode off.

"Next time, paddle faster. You don't have to stand just yet, but I want you to get the feel."

She paddled as fast as she could, but if Ken didn't push her, she missed the wave. Meanwhile, the people around her were all catching waves, even the little kids.

"This board's too big," she complained. "Why don't we get one of the smaller ones?"

Ken threw his head back and laughed. "The waves are too gentle for shorter boards. Besides, longboards are more stable."

Jolie slid off the board. "Then let's see you do it."

"Seriously? You're challenging me?" He roped her around the waist and burned her with a deep, searching kiss.

Jolie groped the muscles bordering Ken's waist while her lips did a slow tango before breaking off and pouting. "I've never seen you surf. You say you're a big wave surfer, these ankle biters should be no problem."

"They aren't. Get on the board. We're surfing together."

"What? How?"

"You'll see. Get in front and lie down, then I'll mount you." His breath sizzled with a mischievous grin.

"Sure we won't get arrested for indecency?" Jolie took the surfboard by the rails and crawled back on.

In a single motion, Ken was in back of her, his chest over her legs, and his face right above her butt crack.

"Now, start paddling. We're going further out to the bigger break."

Jolie stared at the horizon where the sailboats and catamarans were flitting about. A large outrigger canoe paddled by them, bouncing up and over the waves without flipping.

Together, they paddled beyond where the children were and joined the lineup at a long, rolling wave.

"I'm going to turn us and get in position," Ken said. "You stay on the board, and then paddle as hard as you can."

"Then what?" She held onto the board, bobbing up and down in the water. "How deep is it out here?"

"Not over your head. Ready? Paddle. It's a beautiful right hander, I hope you put your left foot forward."

"What? I'm standing? But …" Jolie hadn't gotten the words out when Ken tugged her up, and she was surfing.

Wow! She held her hands out to the side and her hair fluttered in the wave. Best of all, she was safe with Ken's steady hands on her waist.

Could this honeymoon get more perfect?

She leaned back and relaxed, letting Ken guide the surfboard. Maybe she could stay out in the surf forever and let him steer and guide her entire life.

The way he treated her, always touching, considering, and gazing at her as if she were precious, was something no woman was immune to. Except she had to know whether he'd really put up with her for the long haul, or was this honeymoon soon to be over?

Chapter Nineteen

"Will you still have my surprise?" Jolie asked Ken as soon as they stepped onto the elevator that evening. They'd had dinner at another organic, gluten-free, no eggs, no diary, no nuts, bar and grill, and were ready to watch a movie and chill out in the hotel room.

Ken tapped Jolie's pert and freckled nose. "You've been bugging me about your surprise all day. What about my surprise?"

She tipped her head to the side and narrowed her eyes. "You'll get yours, don't worry."

"I can't imagine what you'll come up with. But if we need to go to the grocery store, let me know."

She poked his hard abdominals and giggled. "Is it you or your stomach I'm surprising?"

"The way to a man's heart is his stomach." He grasped her around the waist and pulled her close.

"It's not your stomach that's hard right now," Jolie said as the elevator arrived at their floor. "I bet you have no clue what the way to my heart is."

"You'll see." Ken took her hand and together, they sauntered to his door.

He opened the door and watched Jolie's jaw drop and her eyes pop wide. The entire room was decorated with pink streamers and pink balloons. Pink rose petals were spread all over the white bedspread, and a pink champagne bucket was sitting on the table.

"What is this?" Jolie tugged his arm. "Why's everything pink?"

"To hide the clues." He picked up a card on the table and handed it to her. "Let's see if you can find your surprise. I'm going down to the bar. Text me when you're ready."

"When did you have time to set all this up?" Jolie blinked at the decorations.

"You didn't really think I fell asleep on the beach that long, did you?" He pecked her cheek.

"You snuck off and left me on the beach alone?" She stretched, still relaxed from her post-surfing nap.

"Alone on Waikiki? Not a chance."

"Sure, there were people around, but they were strangers. I can't believe you didn't tell me."

"Because then it wouldn't be a surprise." He wiggled his eyebrows and gave her a nudge. "Go ahead, open the card. But first, let me get out of the way."

He swung himself out the door and closed it before Jolie had a chance to question him. She started after him, but stopped herself.

Her heartbeat tripled in speed and she patted her chest. Why didn't he want to see her unveil her surprises—unless he was pulling pranks on her? She'd better be careful about sitting on the bed. He could have filled it with tiny cups of water. As for the toilet, there could be Saran wrap across the bowl. Ha, she knew every trick in the book, thanks to her Bumblebee besties.

Slipping her finger under the envelope flap, she extracted the note.

To my dearest bride, every minute I'm with you is like flying high. You're a real treat for a lucky guy. Peel back the sheet for your first sweet.

The corners of Jolie's mouth crinkled up and warmth rushed over her chest. So, this was a scavenger hunt.

She was still prepared for a jumping snake or spider toy to spring from the sheets, so she carefully peeled back the sheet, scattering some of the rose petals, and found a box of her favorite vegan chocolates: no nuts, no diary, no gluten, no eggs. A pink ribbon was tied around the box.

"Oh, Ken, you're unbelievable," she whispered as she untied the ribbon to reveal the smooth round globes of truffles. She took one and bit in, unable to stop humming her pleasure.

A note was tucked underneath the paper.

My bride, you're one sweet cookie, especially for this rookie. For your next clue, look for something not borrowed, but blue.

Something blue? Jolie peeked around the room. Every decoration was pink from the banners to the streamers to the balloons. She walked around the hotel room. The artwork on the wall was of paradise, with hula girls, outrigger canoes, and of course, the deep blue ocean.

One picture showed a surfer tearing down a giant wave. A pair of earrings were taped to the glass over the picture.

Silver wire was wrapped around aqua blue sea glass. A card attached to the earrings called them mermaid tears.

"They're beautiful," Jolie said. "Ken, why aren't you here to watch me put these on?"

She removed the earrings she wore and replaced them with the blue sea glass. A note was attached to the back of the earring card.

Dearest bride, looking at you never makes me blue. I get such a cheer when I touch your hair. My next favor for you to savor is full of rubs. Take a peek in the tub, if you dare.

So far, so good. Every surprise had been sweet and precious. Jolie's heart thumped as she pulled the shower curtain back.

A gift basket full of soaps, bath mitts, brushes, bath oil, and a loofah was wrapped with a seashell necklace.

All the lotions and oil were hypo-allergenic. Smiling, Jolie pulled the basket from the tub. A coupon for a spa massage for couples was also included.

"Ken, you're too sweet. What am I going to do with you?" Jolie unfolded the notecard.

My bride of life. Don't let all these gifts get to your head. What I want is your loving heart. Now do your part and let's get wed. Text 'yes' to be my wife.

She turned the card over, but there was no further clue. Her pulse thundered and heat flooded her veins. Was this another one of his hinted proposals?

Her heart thundered and her eyes darted around, waiting to see if he'd jump up and yell "surprise," or sweep her into his arms, and assure her this was real, that he wanted her—allergies, OCD, and all.

Silence warred with her hopeful, but ultimately stupid heart. What had Nikki said? That she was too trusting? That she should test men before believing their sweet words?

Men did not propose to women they barely knew.

Especially men who aspired to be actors and worked for an escort agency.

Jolie set the basket on the sink and found her cell phone. All her spidey senses were a jumble, and she definitely was not going to text him to accept a proposal. Whatever happened to the bended knee and the ring?

Not that Warren had done the song or dance. But even he at least had taken her to a jeweler and had her choose her own ring.

She brought up her call log and called Bad Boys for Hire. It was time to get her head out of the clouds and face the truth.

"Bad Boys for Hire," a male voice said. "How may I help you?"

"I left you a message about hiring a beach bum or surfer for my Barbie and Ken beach party. Is there one available?"

"We have one who's a professional surfer, but he's out of town right now."

"Oh, bummer. Would you happen to know when he'll be available?" Jolie's hands tightened into fists. So, Nikki had been lying to her.

"He should be back from Hawaii next week. When's your party?"

"Not for a while. What's his name?"

"We don't give out this information without a contract. If you'd like to stop by, I'll be happy to help you."

"Thanks, but I want to know what I'm getting before signing up," Jolie said as a sickening feeling engulfed her stomach.

"His picture's on our website. Got good reviews, too."

Jolie thanked the man and hung up. Tears dripped down her cheeks. What a fool she'd been.

Ken was bought and paid for, and worst of all, he hadn't told her the truth. Even if his intentions were good, he'd played her emotions, toyed with her heart.

Now she knew what surprise she'd throw on him. She would see whether he truly cared for her or was only in it for the money.

She called the front desk and asked for a room, then texted Ken.

Tomorrow's surprise is on me. Meet me in the lobby at six.

Chapter Twenty

"You're going to love my surprise." Jolie turned the rental car she was driving off the main highway. They'd left Honolulu far behind, and were climbing the switchbacks to a private location beneath the saw-toothed ridges of volcanic peaks, now covered with lush tropical vegetation.

Ken gripped the safety bar, otherwise known as the 'oh shit' handle on the rental, as the little car climbed to higher elevations. Wherever she was taking him, it involved heights.

Last night had been strange. Rather than thanking him for the surprises, Jolie had moved to another room. All she'd said was he hadn't been honest with her, and that he knew what she was referring to.

Could it be his financial situation? After all, he didn't have much in terms of a job. He still had a few sponsorships from surfing, but they would be gone if he didn't get back to the big waves. Or it could be his job with Bad Boys for Hire. All she had to do was browse their website and she'd find out he escorted women to parties and events. Maybe he should let her know sex was not part of the deal. The contracts specifically stated that for both his protection and that of the clients.

"You said, you're up for anything," Jolie reminded him of his overconfident boast a few days ago.

"Sure, no problem." He swallowed a gulp, hoping she couldn't hear the drumming of his heart. "What's out here anyway?"

"It wasn't easy to line up the guides, but it's going to be an experience of a lifetime," she said, turning into a small parking area behind a gate.

"There's no sign of anyone here," Ken said. "You didn't say to bring hiking boots. I'm not sure what we're doing so high up."

Hopefully, they weren't hiking up those ridges. The edges of trails out in the more remote areas were not maintained well, and the drops were sheer.

"I'm not saying anything," she teased. "It's a surprise. I liked all your surprises, so you better love mine."

Ken surveyed the gorgeous jungle surrounding them. This was not a region of gently rolling hills, but one of sharp volcanic ridges sliced with deep canyons. If they weren't hiking, what were they doing here?

He tried to slow his breathing, but his nerves tremored under every inch of his skin. Sweat prickled and he saw dots. Should he tell her he was afraid of heights?

A jeep pulled up next to them, and two men jumped out. They wore belts and harnesses around their shoulders and waists.

"Those are our guides," Jolie said, pulling Ken along. "They have all the equipment we need."

"Welcome to Waterfall Walking Tours." One of the men extended his hand. "I'm Keoni, and this is Alfredo. Have you folks ever rappelled down a waterfall before?"

Ken felt his eyes bugging out. His heart grew weak, flopping like a dying fish, and his mouth dried. Tingles and sweat prickled his palms and his stomach turned.

"Not a waterfall," Jolie said. "But I've done it off a skyscraper. It was so much fun."

Fun? Ken couldn't picture him going close to the edge of a building and looking down. No way was he going off a waterfall.

"This is the same principle, but we're going down a wall of water," Keoni said.

"Won't it be slippery?" Ken asked, panic seizing his heart. A wall of water could wash him from the ropes.

"Not really, you're kicking off against the rock wall, not standing on it," Alfredo explained. "I take it you haven't rappelled before."

"Uh, no, walking off cliffs isn't my thing." Ken darted a glance at Jolie. He wanted to be her hero, and she'd be disappointed if she knew what a wuss he was around heights.

Ken swallowed hard and he could barely keep his heart in his chest. Maybe he could do it if he didn't panic. All he had to do was close his eyes and kick off the wall. Not look down.

He went through the motions of taking instruction from the guides. He was strapped in a harness around his waist and legs. There was something about letting the ropes go and leaning back perpendicular to the wall to keep from falling.

"Let's go to a small wall to practice," Alfredo said. "I'll help Jolie, and Keoni will work with you. Once we're ready, we'll hike to the top of the first waterfall. There's a sixty foot drop, followed by a fifty footer, and for the grand finale, one hundred feet all the way to the bottom of the canyon."

"Come on, Ken, you can do it," Jolie said, smiling sweetly, as the ropes were passed through her clips.

He hung back as they hiked to the edge of an outcrop. It wasn't too high. He could do it. He just wouldn't look down. He'd keep his eyes on the sky. He was in control of the descent. He would go slow.

Jolie disappeared off the edge of the cliff first. How could she trust the anchor? This was crazy. The ropes could break, or the carabiners could slip. The rock wall could crumble, and any tree could be uprooted.

"What's wrong?" Keoni asked Ken when it was his turn.

"I can't do this," he admitted. "I'm afraid of heights."

The other man rubbed his jaw and shook his head. "The things guys do for their honeymoon. Let me give you a hint."

"It doesn't matter. I can't do it. She'll be disappointed, but you guys go ahead. She seems to be enjoying it."

"The hint wasn't for rappelling," the other man said. "You and your wife are young, and you think these differences don't matter, but if you're afraid of heights and she loves climbing, hiking, and high places, you've got some rough roads ahead. They say opposites attract, but opposites don't live together for long."

"Thanks for the advice. I guess I better call a friend and see if they could come get me. I'm assuming you have a car at the bottom of the falls to bring Jolie back up."

"You sure you don't want to go down?" Keoni checked the ropes at the anchor point. "This is just the practice cliff."

"I can't do it." Ken waved him off.

"Sure, let me clean up the ropes then," Keoni said, leaving Ken to his disappointment.

He felt like shit, chickening out, and Jolie would never look at him, all admiring, the way she had on the surfboard.

It had fallen apart last night with the scavenger hunt. She'd left everything, the chocolate, earrings, and spa basket.

She also hadn't texted 'yes.'

It was probably that last poem that had turned her off.

It wasn't his fault that 'wed' rhymed with 'head.' Maybe he should have left the original. *Do your part and let's go to bed.*

She would have liked that better. He shouldn't have gone romantic and carried his groom roleplaying so far. Stupid. Stupid. As if a put together business woman would marry a beach bum doing odd jobs.

He called Carol to see if she and Nikki could pick him up.

"What happened?" Carol asked. "Why did she take you rappelling? I thought I told her you were afraid of heights."

"You told her that?" Ken could strangle his sister sometimes. "Why'd you do that for?"

"To avoid exactly this situation. I can't believe you didn't tell her," Carol said. "After all, she gave you a long list of stipulations and limitations."

"I can't believe she knew full well before setting this up." Fury boiled deep in Ken's belly.

"Pretty much. She asked me for ideas, and I told her no zip lining, hiking steep cliffs, and balloon rides."

"Why did she do this?" Ken paced back and forth in the small parking area. "Is she trying to get rid of me?"

"I don't know," Carol replied. "Maybe she is, or she's not considerate like you are."

"I think it was deliberate," Ken said, recalling how overly joyous Jolie had acted when she went over the cliff. "Tell Nikki this gig is over. I'll pay her back for your plane ticket."

A deep nausea overwhelmed his body and he sat on a lava rock with his head between his legs. Dizziness and cold sweat poured over his head.

Jolie knew he was afraid of heights.

What did it say about her feelings for him?

Chapter Twenty-One

"Woohoo, that was awesome." Jolie kicked herself off the last drop and eased the rope, landing next to her guide, Alfredo.

The practice cliff had been a piece of cake, and as long as she looked skyward and trusted the equipment, she was fine. Usually, she worried about every detail, but for some strange reason, the exhilaration of the controlled fall got her blood flowing and heart pumping in a way that made her feel alive—not restricted by what she couldn't eat or couldn't do.

"Where's Ken?" She peered up at the lip of the cliff. "I don't see him setting up."

"Since he hasn't done this before, Keoni's probably explaining things," Alfredo said. "Shall we go to the next cliff? It has a waterfall and you'll get to see a rainbow."

"Let's wait for Ken to come down. I want to get a picture with him." Jolie unscrewed her water bottle and took a drink.

If Ken truly cared about her, he'd at least do the practice cliff. After all, she'd taken a chance and had gone surfing with him. But if he were only playacting the groom and had no true feelings for her, he would find an excuse and back out.

Just like Warren had backed out of the marriage. There was a reason why Nikki kept guys hanging without letting them know her true feelings. She was testing them to see if they were worthy of her. She'd always told Jolie she had to be bitchier to get a truly devoted guy, instead of one who came and went as he pleased and ended up ditching her on the most important day of her life.

Jolie straightened her spine and put her hand over her eyebrows to shade the sun from her eyes. There didn't appear to be any movement up above.

"He's not coming down, is he?" she asked Alfredo.

"Let me text Keoni and see what the holdup is." Alfredo pulled out his phone.

A minute later, he said, "You're right. Keoni says Ken's waiting for his sister and friend to pick him up. Lucky they were sightseeing in the vicinity."

"Why didn't he text me?" Jolie pressed her lips together, now thoroughly pissed. "He ditched me without even telling me."

She took her phone from her backpack and texted him. *We're waiting for you. What happened?*

Couldn't he see how easy this first drop was? Well, actually, he hadn't even peered over the cliff and waved at her. Wouldn't a guy who cared about a woman at least want to see how she was doing?

Alfredo was also texting. "Keoni says your husband's afraid of heights. How come you didn't know?"

"He's not really my husband." Jolie bunched her fists and stomped her foot. "I was ditched at my wedding, stood up and humiliated, and Ken was hired by my friends to pretend to be my husband so I can have fun on my honeymoon."

Alfredo tossed his head back and blew a long whistle. "I thought I'd heard it all. This one's a doozer. What do you want to do now?"

"Can we go back up? I'm not feeling like doing the rest of the rappelling. I wanted Ken to enjoy something I enjoy, but this isn't fun anymore."

Not to mention she felt like bursting into tears, although why should she care? It wasn't as if he were really her boyfriend, fiancé, groom, or husband.

He was only a Bad Boy for Hire.

Except when he held her in his arms, when he looked at her with those gorgeous blue eyes, when he kissed her and swept her hair from her face, when he made love to her and snuggled with her, it hadn't felt like an act.

It had felt so real and right.

But then, she'd always been a fool—a fool in love, inventing romantic moments with Warren when all he'd rather do was play video games. She'd set out candles and put on romantic music, dimmed the lights, and served him dinner wearing only lingerie.

Had he appreciated any of it? Or was it all a prelude to the few minutes of mounting her before rolling off and snoring?

"Hey, I hate to break it to you," Alfredo said, cutting into her misery. "But if you want to go up, we have a long hike. There's no clear trail from here. We should at least go to the next level down and catch a loop that leads us close to the road. Then we'd have to walk up the switchbacks to the parking lot, or, we might as well finish all the waterfalls and get to where Keoni and I left the car. Your choice."

Jolie wiped her eyes with her forearm. "I'm already sweating too much. Let's keep going down. Doesn't look like my fake groom cared enough to return my text message."

She put her cell phone back in the plastic bag and slipped it inside her zippered pouch.

"You don't need him to have a good time," Alfredo said. "If you'd like to have lunch with me after all this is over, I know a shrimp truck on the North Shore. It's world famous and we can write our names on the panel."

Jolie peered at the tan Hawaiian man who was easy on the eyes. His dark brown eyes held mischief and his smile was crooked with a dimple on one side.

"Sure, why not? You only live once."

She neglected to mention her allergies. She hated ruining everyone's fun with her limitations. Besides, she'd gotten a refilled EpiPen at the ER.

What could go wrong?

# # #

"I don't feel like talking," Ken said to Nikki and Carol when they pulled into the parking area. "But thanks for coming to get me."

"Are you okay?" Carol reached from the backseat and patted his shoulder as he got into the car. "Any dizzy spells or headaches?"

"I was dizzy walking so close to the edge. They called it a practice cliff, but, anyway, I'm fine." He flashed his sister a weak smile. How could he blame her for caring?

"I can't believe she did this," Nikki, said. "She's not even into rock climbing as much as I am. Last time I had to drag her up Half Dome."

"You two went up Half Dome?" Carol's voice held newfound respect. "I did that climb last year."

"How did you two turn out so different?" Nikki asked. She backed out of the parking area and started down the switchbacks.

"My stepdad's afraid of heights, and he took Ken surfing while my mother took me hiking. She loved the clean air up on top of the mountain, but hated the beach."

"They used to fight all the time about vacations and trips," Ken recalled. Now that he thought about it, maybe it was better that Jolie had done this trick on him. It showed that she didn't care about him one bit.

But then, she didn't owe him anything. It had been his idea to play honeymoon honey with her. His heart flailed in his chest and a giant lump blocked his throat.

Had he allowed his feelings to get ahead of the playacting? Sure, he'd thought about Jolie through the years, but it wasn't as if he'd made any effort to find her. Then when he saw her at her reception, he'd made himself a bet.

Now that he wasn't Ken Dog anymore, but reasonably attractive to women, at least from what he could tell of the women who came on to him, he was going to see if he could get Jolie to fall for him.

But they weren't in elementary school anymore, and maybe he'd been wrong to try and horn in on her at such a vulnerable time.

"I don't know what was going on in Jolie's mind," Nikki said. "She's usually so considerate of people. It must be all the stress of the wedding and the non-honeymoon."

"Maybe," Ken conceded. "I want to go home."

"We still have one more day," Carol said. "Nikki and I are going on a jeep tour tomorrow. Do you want to come with us?"

Ken wiped his face with both hands and took a long, deep breath. "I can wait another day, as long as we don't go with Jolie. Maybe she's getting back together with Warren."

"He did like to climb and hike," Nikki said. "That man's fearless. He even went base jumping. Of course, Jolie worried the entire time he was gone."

There. More evidence Jolie wasn't over Warren yet.

He checked his phone and saw a message from Jolie. *We're waiting for you. What happened?*

It sounded so demanding, like he was her servant.

No more.

He turned to Nikki. "You didn't tell Jolie about our arrangement, did you? That you paid for Carol's ticket?"

"No, of course not. She asked if I'd hired you and I said I hadn't."

"Then I'll pay you back for the ticket." He deleted Jolie's message and contact information. "I'm not obligated to spend the last day of her honeymoon with her."

"Why, Ken," Carol said. "You sound hurt. This is more than helping her be happy on her honeymoon, isn't it?"

"It's nothing ..." He sighed and ran his fingers through his hair.

"You sure?" His sister was always more perceptive than he gave her credit for. "You're looking brokenhearted, sighing and pawing your hair."

He glanced at Nikki, but she kept her eyes on the road. Was Carol really going to go into this with Jolie's best friend present?

"Look, we had a few good days, but it's over. Now that Jolie's not around, we can finally eat all the good food this island has to offer." He held up his hand to high five his sister.

She returned the slap. "I've been hankering to try some of that delicious garlic shrimp they have at Big John's Shrimp Truck."

"Me, too," Ken agreed. "I can't wait."

Chapter Twenty-Two

The last waterfall was over one hundred feet of beauty—white mist over slippery black rock, surrounded by the greenest hanging plants growing out of the crevices. Jolie was soaked but she didn't mind at all. Walking backwards, totally trusting the rope and the anchor up top, while surrounded by the roar of water and the bright blue sky above was like being in another world.

True, she shouldn't have sprung this surprise on Ken, knowing that he was afraid of heights, but then, he never said a word, even when she asked if he was okay. Hadn't she admitted her fears to him about being dragged out to sea?

Why hadn't he trusted her?

Duh. He was nothing to her—the hired help. When she returned to Honolulu, she was going to strangle Nikki. She'd bald-faced lied about not hiring Ken.

As for Ken, her heart twinged and she missed a step. Crap. She slipped and her body smashed into the rock wall. Water showered over her.

"Push away and walk up the wall," Alfredo yelled. "You got it."

The dangling was the pits, but Jolie took a deep breath and swung out, then caught the wall with her feet, leaning back. Her heart was pounding, and she shivered from the chill, but this trip was worth it.

Out here, with only the water, the rocks, the jungle, and the sky, she didn't need Ken or Warren or any other man to do the things she wanted.

No more playing second fiddle and waiting for a man to plan her vacation, honeymoon, or life.

Soon, she dropped into the pool right into Alfredo's arms.

"You scared me up there. You okay?" He removed her helmet and examined it. "I have to ask this. Did you hit your head?"

"No, I didn't. My shoulder slammed into the wall."

"Which side?" He rubbed her back.

"Left side, but I'm fine. I didn't pack any dry clothes."

"Hey, this is Hawaii, it doesn't matter." His white teeth gleamed into a broad grin. "Let me get these ropes and harness off you, then we can take off our clothes and dry them on the rocks while we skinny-dip."

"Seriously?" She narrowed her eyes at him.

"Yolo!" He flashed her the shaka or "hang loose" sign.

"Sure, why not?" This wasn't on her list of things to do, but who needed lists when life was full of surprises?

# # #

Ken salivated over all the food he could pack in during his last days in paradise. He and Carol had made a list while Nikki drove, starting with garlic shrimp. Once he was back in Honolulu, he was going to hit another luau-type buffet without the entertainment, so he could pig out on all the goodies he missed.

They drove down Kamehameha Highway, watching the surf pounding the North Shore. The waves were bigger and more brutal than the gentle ones of Waikiki. They called to him with each roaring boom. Out here, at the edge of the sea, was life, energy, meaning, everything.

As soon as the doctor okayed it, Ken was going back to the big waves. Nothing beat the rush of dropping down the face of a fifty-footer. The crashing of the waves and the salt spray combined with speed put him into a trance—the pinpoint of each moment where all that mattered was the surfboard carving through the water.

No wonder he'd never been too interested in the women, booze, and parties that others lived for. His life had always been compressed fully into the present moment—nothing more—no fear and no judgment.

It was him and the wave, not against the wave, but with the wave—never worrying about wiping out and getting hurt.

So why was he so nervous about heights? It, too, should be one step at a time. Except looking down was the worst, dizzying and heart-catching. Yet, Jolie enjoyed it. She'd whooped happily while going down the rock wall. One step at a time. She loved it, and it meant she wasn't for him.

Food trucks were lined up along the roadway, and Nikki rolled around the parking area until she found Big John's Shrimp Truck. The aroma of garlic wafted in the air, and the line wound around the truck. Sure enough, the formerly white truck was covered with writing.

"It smells delicious," Carol said as Ken helped her into her wheelchair.

"Uh oh," Nikki said. "I'm not sure we should stop at this truck. There a couple of other ones we passed."

"Why?" Carol asked. "This is the original Big John's Shrimp Truck. Besides, I want to write my name on it."

"Don't look, but …" Nikki dipped her head to whisper in Carol's ear.

As soon as Nikki said not to look, Ken narrowed his eyes and checked out the people in line. His heart hammered to a stop. Jolie was standing at the front of the line with one of the guides from the waterfall. She was wearing nothing but a hot pink bikini, and her skin was bright red—burnt.

"What is she doing at a shrimp truck?" Ken charged toward Jolie and the guide. They'd obviously finished the waterfall rappelling, and the Hawaiian guy was one who enjoyed the same things she did. He was the one who'd taken her on a thrilling adventure and now, he was her hero.

But he obviously didn't care about Jolie's allergies.

As Ken approached the truck, Jolie ordered a plate of garlic shrimp. Was she crazy? Or showing off for the waterfall guide?

Ken shoved himself in her face. "Hey, are you sure you can eat this?"

Jolie's eyes bulged and her mouth gaped. She glanced back at the man she was with and then at Nikki and Carol.

"Line's back there," the Hawaiian fellow said, jerking his thumb toward the end of the line.

"She's allergic to shrimp," Ken said. "Did she bother to tell you?"

"Seriously?" The man glared at Jolie. "How come you didn't say anything? Is this guy the fake husband you were talking about?"

"Ken!" Jolie screeched. "Keep your nose in your own business."

Ken had no time for this nonsense. He grabbed Jolie by the arm and dragged her from the line. "You're endangering your life. Everything in this truck can cause an allergic reaction."

"I can have the hot dog and rice," she argued.

"You don't eat pork, and the rice has egg in it," he countered. "We need to talk."

"Talk?" Her chameleon eyes changed from blue-green to blue-gray. "What's there to talk about, Mr. Bad Boys for Hire? You faked everything because Nikki paid you to be nice to me. You don't care if I choke or die or anything."

"So, you endanger yourself by eating shrimp?" Ken's blood boiled. Of course he was in the doghouse now that she knew about the plane ticket and how Nikki had convinced him to play honeymooner with her.

"No, I'm tired of my restrictions. I'm tired of what I can't do and how I have to follow plans and schedules." She turned away from him, swiping her eyes. "Before you showed up, Alfredo thought I was a fun girl. Now he's probably glad he got away from me and my problems."

"Good." Ken took Jolie's hand, wrapping his fingers around hers. "Because you and your problems are mine."

She swallowed, her throat bobbling, and blinked, her eyes watery. "Are you being paid to say this?"

"No. It was never about Nikki and the plane tickets or Bad Boys for Hire." Ken palmed her face and led her into the shade of a grove of large leafed trees. "When I saw you and recognized you, I wanted to see if you'd like me now that I'm all grown up. But I'm not sure you do."

"You think I don't?" Two spots of color made her cheeks even redder.

A weight pressed on his chest, and he shook his head slowly. "You don't. That's why you took me on the waterfall trip when Carol warned you about me and heights. I'm still suffering from a concussion and not supposed to get dizzy and risk falling and reinjuring my head. I'm not even surfing big waves right now until the doctor gives the okay. But you didn't care, and I don't blame you."

"I'm sorry," Jolie said. "I don't know what I was thinking."

He tipped his finger over her lips and shushed her. "It's okay, Jolie. I took advantage of your emotions and moved too fast. You need time to get over Warren. You need to find your own comfort zone. You need to accept yourself, and right now, you don't need a guy like me trying to horn in on you and catch you on the rebound."

"I didn't mean to hurt you."

"It doesn't matter. You need time. I'll leave you alone now. Go back to your date, but be truthful about what you want and who you are."

"What about our honeymoon?" She angled her face up at him, blinking hard. "We have one more day."

"Honeymoon's over." He leaned down and kissed her lightly on the lips. "It was all real."

"It was real, for me, too." She gazed into his eyes, her lips trembling.

He could drown in her eyes, in her beauty, her openness, but her emotions were too raw. What she thought was real could be an illusion in her present state of mind.

"Goodbye, Jolie." He forced his voice to stay steady. "Maybe in time, you'll realize we're like Pele and Kamapua'a. Fire and water don't mix, and even though we make a lot of steam, we can't exist together. We're not compatible, and we can't compromise the full embodiment of what life should mean to us, because if we do, we'll end up hating each other. You love the mountains, climbing, and heights, and I'm all about water and the big waves. Let's leave while we're still feeling charitable toward each other."

"We can make it work. I do care about you." She bit that sweet lip of hers, but her words rang hollow.

Opposites may attract, but cannot coexist.

"I'm going now. Don't look back." He kissed her cheeks, tasting the tears trailing down her face. "Instead of goodbye, I say 'aloha.'"

Chapter Twenty-Three

"Trust is built in the smallest moments," Carol said to Jolie once they were back at the hotel. "It's not in the big words and grand gestures, like a wedding, a proposal, or a life or death situation."

Jolie dabbed her eyelids and wet another tissue. "I betrayed him, and he'll never trust me again. I shouldn't have done that nasty surprise. I don't know what I was doing."

Nikki put her hand on Jolie's shoulder, rubbing it. "It's hard for you to trust when you've been betrayed so much. I'm sorry for setting Ken up like this, but the truth is, he didn't want me to pay him other than the airplane ticket for Carol."

"Which I'm going to pay back," Carol said.

"Actually Ken already offered to pay me back." Nikki put her arm around Jolie. "It's my fault. I didn't want you to miss out on everything you planned."

Warmth overwhelmed Jolie's heart at the way her friend cared so much about her, knowing how obsessive she was with the little details of her checklist and things she just had to do— groom or no groom.

She hugged Nikki. "You're a good friend, and I should be mad at you for setting Ken up to make me happy. I should be screaming and throwing a fit, but all I feel is my heart breaking. This isn't about Warren or you, or a perfect wedding or honeymoon. It's about me screwing up the best thing that ever happened to me."

"You really feel that way?" Carol asked. "Then you should go to him and explain. I'm sure he understands about Warren hurting you and how stressed you are."

"No excuses. I was wrong." Jolie strode to the window of the high rise hotel.

The sun was setting over the shimmering waters, painting the sky a brilliant palette of crimson, golds, and purples. She should have been in Ken's room sharing the view with him, instead of wringing her hands with his sister.

"Maybe you should go to him and apologize," Nikki said.

Jolie slowly shook her head, blinking back the ever-present tears. "That would be words only. He'd thank me and that would be that. His heart would still be closed to me."

"You don't know that," Carol maneuvered her wheelchair onto the balcony and stared at the sunset. "My brother's never acted so sweet and caring to any woman before. He's probably already in love with you."

"Then I hurt him even worse." Jolie shielded her eyes from the pinpoint of sun still visible above the horizon. "He doesn't believe we can make things work because we're opposites— fire and water."

"My mom and stepfather made it work," Carol said. "They've traveled the world both together and on separate vacations."

"Is that what you want?" Nikki asked. "To make it work with Ken?"

"Go to him," Carol said. "He's a forgiving guy."

"No." Jolie bit her lip as the sun disappeared into the dark ocean. "I don't want his forgiveness. I want his love."

"You might already have it," Carol said. "That's why he was so eager to come on this trip. He saw the honeymoon project as an opportunity to get you to fall in love with him."

"But how do I know he wasn't acting? That he wasn't doing all this to make me feel better about being dumped? That he was only trying to cheer me up and make me feel like someone loved and cared about me—including all my phobias, food restrictions, and OCD-craziness?"

"Beware of the naked man selling a shirt," Carol said, taking Jolie's hand and patting it. "That's what Ken says to me whenever I wonder if any man would love me in a wheelchair."

"Naked man selling a shirt?" Nikki huffed. "What does that mean?"

"He's selling something he doesn't believe in," Carol said. "If you don't love yourself, how can you believe anyone else could love you? If you don't love your brand of craziness, you'll never believe anyone else could love you. It's hard, and I haven't figured it out yet. Maybe it's because all I focus on is my shirtlessness, the fact that I can't walk, and not all the other qualities I have."

Jolie let the thought sink into her mind and heart. The three women sat in silence staring out at the darkening afterglow as the last of the orange rays reflected over the peaceful sea.

Chapter Twenty-Four

"There's something I have to do before we leave," Jolie said the next morning as she and Nikki got ready to go on the jeep tour of an island ranch.

"Ken took Carol surfing already." Nikki handed Jolie a tube of sunscreen. "You don't have time to catch them before the tour leaves."

"I told you I'm not speaking to Ken, not until I'm ready." Jolie smeared sunscreen over her peeling skin. Her arms and shoulders burned from skinny-dipping the day before.

"Don't wait too long," Nikki said, her eyebrows creasing with exaggerated concern. "If you don't want him, there are plenty of women who would."

Jolie picked up her purse and turned the doorknob of their room. "If he's so easily caught by someone else, then he wasn't meant for me. I'll meet you in the lobby. This won't take but fifteen minutes."

It wasn't that she was afraid to go after Ken, but that she wasn't worthy. Not when she didn't truly believe anyone could love her the way she was. All she'd do would be to beg him to give her another chance and make him feel sorry for her—not the way to win a man's trust or heart. Nope, she had to fix herself first, and the first thing she had to do was to get closure with Warren Wayne, her former groom.

She forced her shoulders back and chin up, then marched down the corridor to the hotel room she was supposed to have shared with Warren.

He opened the door to her sharp knock and his lips stretched in a leer. "I knew you'd come back to me."

"Fifteen minutes." She shoved him aside and entered the room.

"That's more than enough time." Warren flexed his fingers and reached for her. His eyes were bleary and his hair was greasy. A musky stale odor emanated from his body, and he hadn't shaved.

What could she possibly have seen in this man, other than he'd been scheduled at exactly the right time in her life?

"Keep your paws off me. I said fifteen minutes, not fifteen seconds." She reached into her purse and popped out a small box containing her engagement ring. "Better luck next time."

Warren grabbed the ring box and opened it. His face darkened and his bushy brows drew over his stark green eyes. "Oh no, you don't. I'm not paying this off."

"Loan's under your name, buddy, and I just closed the joint account and moved all my money out last night. This is it, Warren. I'm cutting all ties with you." Jolie's pulse was skittering through her veins, but she held her gaze steady. "I cut the credit card, too. Thought it fair warning to let you know you're going to have to cough up the cash to pay when you check out."

Most likely, he'd been watching porn and racking up the pay-per-view. Too bad.

"Hey, wait. We were splitting the honeymoon fifty-fifty." Warren lunged for her, but she stepped aside as he careened into the wall.

Yep, definitely hungover.

"Why did you bother showing up here?" Jolie asked. In order to move on, she had to see Warren for the scum he was, instead of the idealized romantic image she'd imagined him to be—a vigilante investigator, on the side of justice and truth. Maybe he did have some heroic qualities in him, but he was definitely not her perfect husband material.

"I missed you, Jol." He rubbed his palm over his sandpapery stubble. "I wanted to keep the honeymoon the way we planned it. I knew how much it meant to you, everything choreographed. Honestly, it wasn't my fault your friends tied me up. I had plenty of time to make it to the altar, and I was only acting with the stripper."

Jolie plugged her ears and shook her head tightly. "I don't want to hear about it. Just tell me straight up, Warren Wayne, and don't lie. Do you love me or not?"

"I did everything I was supposed to do." Warren's eyes slid to the side, blinking. "I was your perfect boyfriend, your perfect fiancé. I followed your timetable and played by your rules. I even wore a pink tie to the wedding and wore the tux you picked out. I had a pink boutonniere and pink sash. I played the part. I was your dress up doll."

"That wasn't what I wanted," Jolie began, but her stomach lurched and her heart sagged inside her ribcage. That was exactly what she had wanted, and how she'd treated Warren. She'd idealized him—big, bad biker dude with the super secret investigator job. He was brave and foolhardy, jumping off cliffs and doing dangerous stunts.

And oh yes, he was badass enough to impress all her friends and scare her relatives, but charming enough to win over her parents and present himself well—a handsome, studly, hunky blond guy with gorgeous green eyes and bulging biceps.

It was all in the image she'd given him to suit her fantasies, including the pink wedding. Everything had always been her lists, her restrictions, her rules, her fancies, her ideas, her dictation—from their first date to the moment they were supposed to say "I do." Heck, she'd even written the vows for both of them to recite. The only freedom she'd given Warren was the honeymoon, because traditionally, it was the groom's job to plan it.

"What do you want?" Warren lowered his face and stared at the floor. "Because it looks like you don't want me anymore. You have your new man, the perfect Ken doll for you to dress up and primp."

Jolie swallowed a growing lump in her throat and placed her hand on Warren's arm. "I'm sorry. I should have asked myself if I loved you or not. Instead, I wrote the script to our love story, and you played along."

"So, you're dumping me for a better model? A new episode in your life?" His upper lip curled into a snarl. "Did you readjust your schedule? Or did Ken agree to substitute for me, down to the baby you're supposed to conceive during our honeymoon and the minivan we're supposed to need for our growing family?"

"Shhh …" Jolie placed her finger over Warren's lip. "Ken is no longer with me. He saw through me, Warren. He's left."

He captured her hand and caressed her fingers. "So, does that mean we're back together on our honeymoon?"

"No, Warren." She felt a tear dribble down her cheek. "No. It means I'm letting you go. You deserve better than to be a prop in my life, or any woman's life."

"I want to be the one in your life." He wiped the tear from her cheek. "I'm sorry about the stripper and the porn. The luau with the pig and the fishing trip."

"No need to be sorry, dude." She stepped back and surveyed the big guy. He was disheveled and reeked of stale alcohol. "Next time some woman tells you her biological clock's ticking, run. Run far away and fast."

She dug through her purse and found her planner, the one marked with all the milestones she had yet to accomplish, the one with her bucket list and projected schedule of achieving each goal.

She opened it to the page marked "Honeymoon" and ripped it from the planner. Balling it up, she threw it in the wastebasket.

"You were a good sport," she said, her throat tight. "But next time I have a wedding, it's going to be blue."

"Yeah, pink rhymes with stink, but blue rhymes with true. I saw some of those practice rhymes Ken left in the wastebasket. I think he really cares about you, Jol. Don't ruin it."

"I already have," Jolie admitted. "But I'm free now. I see myself clearly and I have a lot of work to do."

"So do I." Warren's voice was husky and he swallowed, his eyes watery. "Is this goodbye?"

She tipped on her toes and gave him a kiss on the cheek. "I prefer farewell."

Chapter Twenty-Five

Ken pushed Carol and her wheelchair through the front door of her apartment and ran to the ringing phone. Their last day in Hawaii was spent tandem surfing—Carol lying prone on the board while Ken steered them over the gentle swelling waves of Waikiki. He'd called her his mermaid and helped her swim by tying her paralyzed legs together so she could control her movements in the water. It had been, all in all, a fun and sweet way to end their Hawaiian vacation.

"Better get that phone," Carol said, maneuvering her wheelchair into the living room. "Maybe it's Jolie calling to ask you to give her another chance."

He grabbed the receiver, but all he got was a dial tone. Too late. "They hung up. I doubt it was her."

"Hmmm …" Carol wheeled herself to the telephone and hit the call log. "Whoever called you has been calling nonstop. Why don't you call them back?"

Ken's heart pulsed in his chest and he licked his dry lips. The number was local, but it was not Jolie's cell phone, unless she had gotten another one. There wasn't a moment that he didn't want to text her, to check up on her, or to hear her voice, but he had to let her be. She was never as into him as he was into her. His feelings were real—she just said it back to him because she felt guilty for the surprise she'd pulled on him.

"Well?" Carol prompted. "I'll go to my room and close the door."

As soon as Carol's door closed, Ken picked up the phone and hit redial. A man answered after three rings. "Hello, this Ken Cassidy?"

"Yep." A weight dropped over Ken's shoulders and he swiped his hand through his hair. "What can I do for you?"

"Tucker Scott, Beach Bommie's Board Sports. I saw you the day before yesterday surfing with a handicapped woman, and I'd like you two to do some modeling for our new line of beach wear and accessories. Who's the young lady, by the way?"

"My sister, Carol. I'll need to check with her though."

"Of course," Tucker said. "We'd also like to get videos of her strapped to your back and surfing something bigger than the ankle biters at Waikiki. You think you're up for the North Shore?"

Ken swallowed and pressed his lips together while Tucker explained that the human interest side of their story would make them more than just sportswear models, but also inspiration for others with disabilities.

He could do this. He hadn't had a headache since returning from Hawaii, and he'd almost forgotten about his head injury. Would Carol, who loved to hike and feared water, be brave enough to surf on his back?

Would he conquer his fear of heights and hike with Carol on his back?

He promised Tucker he'd give the model contract careful consideration, then hung up and knocked on Carol's door.

"It wasn't Jolie," Carol stated rather than asked. She could always read him—too well.

"No, not Jolie. But an opportunity." He explained Tucker's offer to have Carol model with him, both on and off the surfboard.

"He wants me to be strapped onto your back standing up?" Carol's mouth opened wide. "What happens if we have to bail or get worked by a monster wave?"

"We'll hold our breaths and swim right back up." Ken pulled a chair and sat next to his sister. "You enjoyed surfing and swimming in Hawaii."

"Because the water was calm," Carol said. "I don't get why we have to surf bigger waves. It's not like anyone's going to see our clothes. We'll probably have to wear wetsuits."

"It's the human side of the story. It'll be inspirational and I guess sell more clothes. But if you're not comfortable, I won't do it. I can always pick up more gigs with Bad Boys for Hire. Rex says there's a woman wanting to have a Barbie and Ken beach party."

"You should quit that gig." Carol pursed her lips and her nostrils flared. "I know sex isn't part of the job, but if you mess up, you'll never get Jolie back."

"Maybe I don't want her back." He stood abruptly. "I've been too much of a pushover in Hawaii. I tried to show her what it was like to be loved and appreciated, but she humiliated me. Made me look like a wuss."

"So, your ego's hurt?" Carol quirked an eyebrow and gave him a long, piercing look. "I'll make a deal with you. Take me up Half Dome, and I'll surf strapped on your back."

"Half Dome?" Ken's heart thundered in his chest and sweat dampened his forehead. "That's straight up a wall of rock."

"They have cables for you to hold onto near the end. You just have to walk in between them." Carol woke her tablet up and browsed to the website. "I'm trusting you. If you fall, I fall, so the least you can do is trust yourself."

Right, and before he could trust someone else, he had to trust himself.

Chapter Twenty-Six

Jolie dragged her professional makeup kit through the lobby of the hospice care center. Weeks had gone by since her ill-fated honeymoon, and she was losing hope that Ken would ever forgive her.

She'd kept in touch with Carol, but met a brick wall as far as prying about Ken was concerned. Carol would only say that she and Ken were training to climb Half Dome in between trips to Hawaii where they had a modeling gig for surfwear.

Life went on, as it always did, and right now, Jolie wasn't on any schedule as far as dating, marriage, or family went. How could she set a timetable when her heart ached for a man who would never trust her again? Even the Half Dome climb was overcompensation on Ken's part. She'd made him feel two feet tall by rubbing his fears in his face.

She'd ruined her own life, and frankly, the only thing she could do now was to give happiness to others, which was why she was at the hospice center to help a patient celebrate her birthday.

The patient's mother met her at the doorway with a warm hug. "I'm so glad you came. This is a big surprise for Faith. She's never had a professional makeover before. It'll be an even bigger surprise for her husband."

"I've brought a selection of wigs, like you suggested," Jolie said. "She's going to be amazed at the results."

Faith's room was decorated with streamers, balloons, and posters all over her wall of puppies, kittens, and cute babies—everything designed to make her smile. A patchwork quilt rested on her lap, and she was propped up with many colorful pillows.

Jolie greeted the woman, who was in her early forties. She'd lost her hair, eyebrows, and eyelashes, but despite her gauntness, her brown eyes twinkled with mischief when her mother explained who Jolie was and why she was here with a portable makeup studio.

"I can't wait to see the look in Roger's eyes after you're done." Faith clapped her hands. "This old girl's still got some sass left."

"You are going to be runway ready," Jolie reassured. "He's going to wonder where the red carpet is."

"He's going to remember the day you two were married," Faith's mother said, wiping a tear from her eye.

"I want him to remember me that way." Faith blinked and swallowed hard. "I want him to always remember all the ways I love him."

"He will, darling," her mother replied, while Jolie bit her own lip, remembering all the ways Ken had made her feel special. It was all real, he'd whispered that last time they spoke.

For the next hour, Jolie applied eyebrow powder, mascara, foundation, blush, and gave Faith the entire gamut of makeup. She styled the wig and with the help of the health aide, they dressed Faith in an ombré pink to magenta fringed evening gown—not a ruffle in sight.

Faith's husband jumped ten feet when he stepped through the doorway, and her children bounced excitedly at the sight of their mother looking so vibrant and alive.

Jolie couldn't help but be drawn into the love surrounding the family and Faith's courage. She was radiant under all the makeup, and for a few hours that Saturday afternoon, life returned to normal as she celebrated what was no doubt her last birthday on earth.

# # #

Ken kissed the check he'd gotten from Beach Bommie's Board Sports for his cut of the modeling contract. This was more money than he'd earned in surfing competitions and much steadier work. News agencies around the country had picked up on the story of Ken and Carol, the brother who carried his sister on his back on land and on sea.

Climbing Half Dome had been the most terrifying experience in his life, but strangely, more exhilarating than facing the waves at Mavericks.

Water was fluid and unpredictable, but the rock? It didn't move, and climbing was simply putting one foot in front of the other on solid ground. Going down had been a lot harder, of course—it was the looking down that scared the crap out of him, but with Carol whispering encouragement in his ear, and most of all, with her trusting her life to him, Ken learned that trusting was the prelude to love, not the other way around.

Tucking the check into his pocket, Ken wandered through the doors of a jewelry store and was immediately accosted by a salesman. Even though he hadn't heard heads or tails from Jolie, he decided to trust her at her word—that everything that happened in Hawaii had been real for her, too.

More than that, her body language screamed her love and regard for him—from the way she'd looked up to him, to the pinking of her cheeks, and the touching and cuddling up to him. She was always making eye contact with him, and when she looked at him, it was as if the rest of the world ceased to exist.

Besides, she wouldn't have been hurt and worried about it all being an act if she didn't have feelings for him. She wouldn't have tested him with the waterfall rappelling had she not been afraid he'd only been hired to make love to her.

Ken didn't hear half of what the salesman said about clarity, cut, and color. The entire array of diamond solitaires was too dazzling to comprehend, but one thing stuck in his mind. It was a rhyme his mother used to quote. *Married in pink, your marriage will stink. Married in blue, your love will be true.*

"I'll take that blue-green diamond, the one that looks gray when I hold it a certain way."

Chapter Twenty-Seven

Ken stood in front of the mirror in the dressing room of the Evergreen Theater. He straightened the collar of his costume and took a deep, cleansing breath. Tonight was the premiere of *Romeo and Juliet*, and he had the starring role of Romeo. He knew his lines. His throat was relaxed, and his family was in the audience.

The sound of knocking was quickly followed by the door opening.

"Makeup artist," a female voice announced.

Jolie stepped through the door with her makeup kit and a plate of cookies. She looked radiant. Her hair glowed in a multitude of reddish highlights, and her gorgeous chameleon eyes were bluish gray today. She was wearing a lacey white bikini cover up over a hot pink bikini, and flip-flops on her feet, as if she'd come fresh off Waikiki beach.

Ken's heartbeat jumped and his pulse skyrocketed. He hadn't seen her since Hawaii when he'd left her and asked her not to look back. It hadn't been easy to walk away, and he'd thought about her every day, especially with a ring burning a hole in his pocket.

"Jolie?" His throat tightened and his brain turned to mush.

She handed him the cookies. "Allergy Safe Cookies for you. No diary, no eggs, no peanuts, and gluten-free. For after the show, of course."

"I didn't know you'd be doing my makeup," he blabbered. "I don't know what to say."

"Sit." She pressed his shoulder down onto the chair in front of the mirror. "I'll do all the talking, but first let's apply foundation. Are you nervous?"

"Definitely, and now that you're here, I think I'm going to have a heart attack. I probably forgot all my lines by now."

"You'll do great." She tapped the tip of his nose with the foundation brush. "Sit still and let me put on your makeup."

Ken sucked in a cleansing breath and sat stiffly with his heart in his throat. All these weeks, he wondered about Jolie, whether she'd figured out what she wanted from life, how she was doing, and whether she was ready to take the next leap of faith with him.

Her fragrance, warmth, and touch as she brushed foundation over his cheekbones made his hands itch to grab her and kiss the living daylights out of her.

"Why did you give me allergy-free cookies?" he said, only to say something and tamp down his fantasies of making her his Juliet.

"Because they're part of what I am." She smoothed his hair back to get makeup on his forehead all the way to his hairline. "I'm much more than my allergies, fears, and lists. I'm a makeup artist. I'm a daughter, a friend, a business woman, and a girl who loves surprises."

"Surprises?" He raised his eyebrows.

"Stop moving your face, or your makeup's going to be uneven." She brushed the furrows between his eyebrows. "As I was saying, I loved all your surprises, the surfing lesson, the play we went to, the notes you left me, the little gifts, your thoughtfulness, the care you took of me, the kisses, cuddles, and sweet caresses. Now, let's get the concealer out and blend the bags from under your eyes."

"I don't have bags." Ken couldn't help smiling now that she was here, touching him and taking his breath away.

"Don't move your face." She patted his cheek lightly, and brushed under his eyes and up under his brow.

"Yes, boss. You were saying …"

"Guess I should apologize for that nasty trick of taking you to the waterfall." She got out a large powder brush and fluffed powder on his nose. "I did it because I was insecure. I didn't think you actually liked me, so I put you in a no-win situation. That way you'd leave me alone, and I wouldn't have to worry that you'd reject me."

"Sounds convoluted." Ken wrinkled his nose, feeling a sneeze coming on.

"Stop moving your face," she said. "That's my canvas."

"Ahhh-choo." He sneezed, covering his mouth with his hand. "Sorry."

She took a tissue and gave it to him. "I'm the one who's sorry. I threw everything we had away because I didn't believe you'd want someone with my baggage. Maybe you still don't, but while I'm doing your makeup you have to sit here and listen to me."

His heart swelled and he felt a load lifted from his shoulders at hearing her words. It was brave of her to come to him unannounced and tell him the depths of her heart. She'd made herself vulnerable and that meant she wanted him back.

He grabbed her wrist to keep the powder from flying all over his face. "I've missed you, Jolie. And believe me, I want you and all your baggage. I want the complete package."

"I missed you, too." She let the brush drop as he stood and pulled her into his arms. "I've been working on loving myself, accepting everything about me, my limitations, my allergies, my fears and doubts. Even more, I see all the good I do, how I volunteer at the hospital and put makeup on cancer patients, and how I'm always trying to be helpful and show kindness to others, how I have a big heart to forgive Warren for hurting me. Most of all, I forgive myself for all the stupid things I've done, like hurting you. I'm so sorry."

"You weren't hurting me." He curled a strand of her hair around his finger and swept it over her ear. "You were running from me, because you were afraid I'd hurt you. So, are you ready now? To restart what we had?"

A smile broke over her face, and she tugged at her cover up shirt. "I believe I'm worth it. I won't even say despite my limitations and allergies. I'm worth loving because I'm me, Jolie Becker, and I have so much love inside me that I want to share. I was scared to come talk to you, but at the same time, I'm not scared, because whether you want me or not, I still want myself and love myself. Do I sound arrogant?"

"Not arrogant, but brilliant. You're definitely selling a shirt I want to buy." His lips hovered over hers. "I haven't been munching on anything you're allergic to. May I kiss you?"

"I know you'd never endanger me. I trust you, Ken, with my life, my heart, my everything." She pressed her lips against his, opening up to him.

Ken eagerly kissed her, tilting her head and sealing his lips against hers. He wrapped his arms around her and held her tightly, securely, savoring her warmth, the feel of her skin and the softness of her breasts against his chest. Her bikini strings beckoned, but he still had a play to act in, a show that must go on.

"Trust me, too, Ken." She said after they broke the kiss, both breathless and hot.

He laughed and picked up the makeup brush. "I don't think I have a choice, do I?"

"You don't, pig man. I'm going to make you so hideous no other woman will want you." She brushed powder over his eyes.

"Paint me anyway you want, fire goddess." Ken sat back onto the chair. "Because I'll be raining love all over your parade for a long, long time."

Epilogue

Jolie and Ken held hands as they stood at the top of an unmarked waterfall high above a deep canyon in the center of Oahu. The water was a veil of lace spraying over the black volcanic rock covered with lush green ferns.

"How many feet is this again?" She asked Keoni, the guide who attached the anchor point to a large tree trunk.

"You can't get deeper than a five hundred foot drop," he said.

"Sure you have enough rope?" Ken adjusted the GoPro camera on Jolie's helmet and kissed her. The look of love and admiration etched in his eyes added to her thrill of going down the wall of water. "I can't wait to see the video," he said. "You're going to be okay, right?"

"It'll be great. Meet you at the bottom." She kissed him, unable to take her gaze off her delectable husband.

Yes. They were honeymooners—this time for real. The day before, while Ken surfed the giant waves of the North Shore, Jolie had relaxed on the beach with her long lens camera, taking pictures and videos of him.

Today was her day, and Ken would meet her down below at the swimming hole. Even though he'd climbed Half Dome, that had been a hike on solid ground, not dropping off the side of a watery cliff. This time, Jolie wasn't disappointed in Ken. She loved him, all of him, and the fact that he trusted her to do the things she enjoyed without pressuring him to participate.

"We always have more rope than we need and a contingency rigging." Alfredo checked Jolie's harness and the figure-8 descender. "Try not to worry."

"I can't help it." Ken wiped his thumbs over Jolie's cheeks. He dipped his lips to hers again, and they kissed long and passionately.

When Jolie was all rigged up, she gave Ken a thumbs up and dropped down the edge of the cliff. Her heart blossomed at the way he bravely stood at the side, waving to her.

She descended slowly, her eyes locked onto him, as water misted over her head like the gentle rain of his love, refreshing her, and constantly reminding her of the care and concern he showered her with.

Much later, she was naked, swimming in the pool at the bottom of the gulch canyon. The guides had departed, leaving her alone with Ken, who'd driven down the steep, treacherous road to meet her.

They held hands and ducked under the lip of the falls into a private cavern carved out of volcanic rock. The walls glistened like the inside of a cathedral under the roaring rush of water. Vines trailed like a beaded curtain, guarding their privacy with a luxurious coat of leaves.

"How's this for our perfect honeymoon suite?" Ken brushed Jolie's hair from her face and stared into her eyes.

"It's unforgettable. So beautiful and unexpected. Thanks for coming to the top of the waterfall with me." She dabbed a kiss on his lips, knowing how hard it had been for him to look over the edge.

"I didn't want to miss something you love to do so much. Told you I'd meet you down here. Do you want to see the tent I set up?"

"You've been here before?" Jolie's eyes widened and a jolt of joy shot through her chest. "When did you have time to set this up?"

Ken's face split with a sexy grin. "During my supposed bachelor's party while you were having your bachelorette party with all the male strippers and debauchery."

"I'll have you know, I didn't participate." Jolie tapped Ken's chin. "Are you telling me you missed your own bachelor's party?"

Ken pulled her toward a ledge beneath the falls. "Setting up a surprise for you is better than getting drunk over strippers."

Aww … He always thought about her and her feelings first. What a lucky bride she was.

Ken picked up a flashlight and shone it into the lava tube. The light reflected and shimmered off the jagged rock patterns surrounding them.

Jolie followed the light, crouching to get through the rough-edged tunnel to a hidden chamber, where a two-man tent sat on a flat and level area.

"You weren't kidding," Jolie said, giving Ken a kiss.

"Can't beat the view." He chuckled and opened the flap of the tent.

"I love it." She crawled in and sat on a double air mattress which was covered with satin sheets. Sprigs of flowers and colorful petals were scattered over the bedding amongst soft, colorful pillows.

"Aloha, beautiful bride." Ken put a lei around her neck. "Welcome to my chamber of molten love."

"Pure cheese." She giggled before pulling his body over her. "But I love you just the same. You and all your surprises."

"I love you too, Jolie, and I hope every day we're together will be filled with surprises—good ones." He kissed her, long and slow, as he moved his hands down to her breasts.

Her nipples were tender, more than usual, but Jolie held her breath, hoping he wouldn't notice—at least not until she was ready to spring her surprise on him.

"You okay?" He, of course, was always so perceptive.

"A little sore from last night when we got sand all over ourselves." They'd spent the night before in a tent on the beach where Ken had surfed into the evening, and then made love late into the night.

"Watching you go down that cliff made me want you more, if that's even possible." Ken licked a trail down her neck, sucking at her sensitive zones.

Jolie let out a moan as he rolled one nipple with his tongue. Somehow the pain mingled with the shocks of pleasure built the fires inside her to a burning pitch.

He laved at each nipple, driving her to a heat of frenzy before moving his talented lips down the center of her belly, nipping and licking.

"You know heights make me horny?" she uttered as he circled her clit with his tongue. "It must be the same with you and surfing."

His answer was to kiss her clit, wrapping his tongue around her nub and sucking on it. Thunder bolts of sensation zinged through her and she throbbed, feeling engorged inside. Hot lava built up deep inside her chambers and she groaned loudly at the lapping of his tongue and the sweetness of his love raining down on her.

She wanted, no needed, more, harder and faster—like the pulsing of war drums in her inner ear. She jerked herself against him and grabbed him, lifting him to cover her.

"I need you inside, filling me with all of you—everything you have," she muttered, not wanting to come without him.

"Your wish is my command, my fair bride." Ken rubbed his cock against the engorged and wet lips between her legs. He circled her entrance and she bucked up, needing him inside, filling her and making love to that ring of fire within her.

He dove in, groaning as he slid his thick hard shaft into her, all the way to the hilt. Jolie gasped at the moment, gazing into deep blue eyes full of love, care, and concern. Her Ken knew every inch of her body. Would he sense anything different? Notice the tiny bit of resistance in her womb?

His lips came down on hers as he smiled and began moving. Slowly and circular, his cock hitting all the angles she loved so much. But this time was different. Each upstroke was more pleasurable, firmer, and drew full-throated moans from her—primeval and earthy. And the downstrokes? Unyielding and firm, massaging every erotic cell inside to a fiery pitch.

His tongue mirrored the movements of his cock, not thrusting rudely, but stroking and drawing out the heat within her, until she was blazing and teetering on the edge of oblivion.

She wanted, no, needed him to pummel her. To slam into her, to ravish her, so she gripped his ass, digging her nails into him to spur him on.

But to no avail. Ken continued stroking and circling, moving his hand and resting it over her pubic bone. He caressed the womb that was starting to harden and make itself known, and she could feel him smile against her lips.

"You're baking me a little bun, gluten-free." His voice was a low burr of pure satisfaction. "You thought I didn't know? I have to be careful."

It was just like observant Ken to know what was going on with her. Well, then, she wouldn't find out the gender of the baby, but knowing him, he'd guess correctly.

"I can handle it," she protested, wanting him to lose control and pound her like a fifty foot wave, to unleash the power and energy he held coiled in that hard rod between his legs.

"I know you can, but this way is better." He stroked her clit, moving the entire area underneath while his cock caressed the spongy tissue inside. He was driving her insane, zinging her with more pleasure than she imagined possible, and he was in no rush—none at all.

He was killing her control, forcing her to go with the flow, to lose herself and to surprise herself. And showing her how much better it was to trust him—fully.

Closing her eyes, she let go of herself and gave in to the rapture showering over her entire body, loving him and receiving his love.

The passion built like a subterranean volcanic explosion. Her climax snuck up on her, a sensation so strange, like a slow ice bucket spreading from her core to her arms and legs, chilled and hot at the same time—it was one hundred percent sheer ecstasy too hard to comprehend.

She was dimly aware of wrapping her arms and legs around Ken, not sure where she ended and where he began. Her orgasm shimmered over every nerve, surface and deep, as euphoria flooded her with the pumping of her husband's seed deep into her fertile womb.

They held each other through the aftershocks, warm and enveloped in a cocoon of pure love which spread into a mystical glow over their bodies and souls, lingering deep into their dreams.

~ THE END ~

Thank you for reading Ken and Jolie's story, book #2 of my *Bad Boys for Hire Series*, featuring empowered women not looking for, but finding love in the most unexpected places. If you enjoyed this story, please consider leaving a review and recommending this book to your friends.

Nikki Chu is about to find out why Mamas aren't supposed to let their boys grow up to be cowboys when she hires Chad Colson to show her everything Western: how to line dance, ride a mechanical bull, drive an ATV, and prepare her to film a travel feature for a dude ranch aimed at Asian tourists.

Be sure to look for the *Bad Boys for Hire Series* of hot, fun, and uplifting romances where the last person you think is the "One", ends up roping your heart and riding off with you into the sunset of love.

http://rachelleayala.me/books/bad-boys-for-hire-series/

About Rachelle

Rachelle Ayala is a bestselling author of dramatic romantic suspense and humorous contemporary romances. Her heroines are feisty and her heroes big-hearted. She writes sweet and funny stories, and believes in the power of love and hope. She is the winner of multiple awards, including the 2015 Angie Ovation Award for best Multicultural Romance with *Knowing Vera* and the 2015 Readers' Favorite Gold Award for best Christian Romance with *A Father for Christmas*.

Check out her sports romances, romantic suspense, holiday stories, and more. Reader's Guide with series and heat rating at http://rachelleayala.me/reading-guide/

Like Rachelle's Facebook Page:
http://www.facebook.com/RachelleAyalaWriter

Contact Rachelle at:
http://rachelleayala.me/author-bio/contact/

For updates and a surprise free book, sign up for Rachelle's newsletter at
http://bit.ly/RachAyala

To chat and read new works in progress, join her Reader's Club at
http://www.facebook.com/groups/ClubRachelleAyala/

SANDS
OF
SEDUCTION

KATY WALTERS

A passionate love story that roams over two centuries.

Fleeing from a tragic love affair, Clarrissa Culling, a talented rising artist, discovers a medieval town nestling at the foot of Arundel Castle. With a deserted coastline nearby, she is free to explore the towering dunes and paint on deserted beaches. Even if she can never escape the torment, she may heal – in time.

She meets a mysterious stranger, a time traveller, posing as a modern day entrepreneur. Against her will, she is attracted to his rugged dark looks and charming flamboyance. Little does she know, she is of value as an artist to certain aristocratic circles in the Regency era, or that he is in fact Lord Drago, the ninth Earl of Hatherstone. He is determined to take her back to 1812, to a past that offers everything she has ever dreamt of, yet forces gather around, threatening Clary with danger, torture and death. Can Drago save her?

I would like to thank Bee Payne, Kairen Kellard, Jenny Dean and Carol Hitchen from 'Our Beta Reading Group' for all their dedicated hours of proof reading. Thank you guys.

Chapter 1
Present day
Clary's decision.

She took a deep breath; was there ever a good time? She must do it; accept it, not hide away anymore. Right now, she needed a roof over her head and a job far away from the taunts and stares.

Clary heard the letterbox of the front door snap shut. The post was never ending; every day she gathered up over half a dozen envelopes and yet more leaflets, more dead trees. As she slammed the spam into the recycle bin, a glossy photo caught her eye. Her heart leapt, just what she was looking for; a cottage for sale in a picturesque hamlet, nestling at the foot of a forest in the South Downs. It was half way across the country, but the further the better. She frowned reading the message, maybe it was just a general advert, but it seemed personal.

Delighted you are reading this. I invite you to make an appointment as soon as possible. Your dream cottage by the sea is waiting for you; within easy reach of Brighton and London.

Phone or email Cecil Partridge now, don't hesitate.

02890 760723 cpartridge@tellomail.co.uk

After pouring a fresh cup of coffee, she picked up the leaflet, taking it to the small dining room, serving as an office. Sitting at the PC, she bent to stroke the head of her white retriever, gazing up at her with those brown soulful eyes. 'Would you like to live by the beach? Run on the sands, swim in the sea?'

Lila raised her head, with a huge smile, a pink tongue lolling out of her black lips. 'Yes you would wouldn't you. Okay – let's do it. Right now.' Clary googled 'MoveNow', the best website for buying and selling houses or apartments. She tried to swallow the hurt; it seemed so strange searching for property without Theo by her side. It was impossible to ban the memories, the grief. Clenching her teeth, she rubbed away the tears stinging her eyes; dread welled up. Fight it Clary, fight it. Her chest tightened, as she forced herself to search the list of properties for sale. After only a few seconds of scrolling along, she recognized the hamlet. There was more information on the list; it was near a medieval market town with an ancient castle. The tiny village was a picture postcard, composed of cottages either side of a cobbled street, with a village store. The price was low and within her range. It was all she needed or wanted.

For the first time in over a year, Clary felt her heart lift; a ripple of anticipation flushed through her stomach; something she never thought to feel again, as she read the description: a galley kitchen, lounge; two beds; a box room, garden, and to top it all an adjacent studio. It was a shed really, but it would do.

'This could be it, Lila.' she murmured, 'it's not right on the sea, but as near as dammit, with a forest and a beach, you'd love that wouldn't you?' She smiled; Lila was completely happy when her nose was to the ground, her main joy being to push her face into clumps of ferns. 'Okay, so let's see if the estate agents are still open.'

She realized she was holding her breath, as she picked up the phone, tapping in the number for 'White Knights Estate Agents,' the name sounded in keeping with the ancient town. She held her breath, as she enquired if the property was still for sale. She punched the air, yes – yes; it was free, and it was one she could afford. She didn't hesitate, and made an appointment to view for the next day. Why wait? Cecil Partridge sounded pleasant and eager to see her. If she left it, she might get cold feet again. Damn the fear, damn the dread, she would do it, do it now before she started making up excuses. She hadn't realized how much she'd depended on Theo. She knew her mercurial nature, knew it ran off in different directions, with lots of ifs and buts. She gritted her teeth; she had to leave Theo behind.

'Well that's it Lila.' She looked down at her denim jeggings. Tomorrow she'd better wear the cream pair, and team them with a blue silk top. Pulling her chestnut locks into a tousled knot on her head, she ruffled Lila's white curls. 'Let's go and tell Ceci.' She grimaced, wondering how on earth she would tell her sister. She'd tried to move once before, but seeing the hurt look on Ceci's face; she'd shelved it. Now she had to be strong, even though she felt the dread welling up again. She shivered even though it was twenty eight degrees outside. If she kept on trying to talk about it, she would never do anything. It was a heart-wrenching decision, but one she had to fight to keep.

Celia opened the door with a welcoming smile. 'Come in. I'm just having a drink on the patio.' As she stood aside, the retriever dashed through the open door, searching for the usual bowl of treats by the kitchen cupboard.

Clary followed her through the house out to the back garden, praying her sister would understand. But, she had to listen to her inner voice, a voice that up to now lay lost and forsaken.

Perching on the two seater bamboo lounger, she stuttered, but got the words out. 'I … I … don't want to hurt you, but I'm moving to the South Coast.'

'That's drastic.' Celia's voice shook.

'I can't stand it in the house any longer, Theo's always there, whatever room I go in; he's waiting. It's driving me crazy. I can't eat, can hardly sleep, and if I do, I have nightmares. I'm sorry; I must move; I can't face it anymore.'

'But, what about your business?' Celia asked, twisting a lock of russet hair.

'It doesn't matter does it; it's online. However, I thought I'd go ahead and start an art centre there; it will break up this torture. Mum and Dad's faces are always….' She stopped; her voice breaking. She still couldn't talk about them. Theo's eyes loomed in front of her, dear God; however, hard she tried to blank them out, and they haunted her day and night, would it ever stop?

'You've always wanted to do that. But, you need help to get started. Wouldn't it be better—' Celia's voice choked. 'Clary – don't go, I need you; we need each other. You can't just up and go.' Celia wrung her hands, whilst Lila whined, sensing her grief, and padded over to her, placing her large head on her knees.

'Come with me, there's nothing stopping you.'

Choking back tears, Celia ruffled the soft fur. 'I don't know I can ever leave here now, I can't leave … them.'

Clary's stomach twisted in pain. 'I know, but I have to do something Ceci. I know Mum and Dad are still here in spirit may be, but I must … I must go. It's selfish of me, Ceci; I'm torn; I don't want to leave you, but I can't bear it anymore.'

'Selfish, you selfish? Never. You're the one who's really suffering. It wasn't my fiancé who…. Oh why must you move? Can't you just get to grips with it here?'

'I am getting to grips with it; it was to be our home, our dream home and I'm living in it alone because he … he's a …. Oh God don't make me say it. I have to escape. Ceci, there are too many memories, too many people who look the other way when they see me. It hurts Ceci, hurts. I'm moving. I'm sorry, so sorry.' Clary cried, the tears streaming down her cheeks.

Chapter 2.
Arundel 1812

'So a toast to the proud papa.' Drago, the ninth Earl of Hatherstone nonchalantly raised his glass and drained it.

'Hmm, not yet, but soon old chap.' Lord Henry Livingston, Viscount of Torsbury groaned, raking long fingers through wheat gold hair. 'I shan't be sorry to have it all over with. I never knew there would be such a fuss.'

'Come old man, have another brandy. Drago grinned, a lock of black hair falling across a high forehead, his sparkling dark blue eyes narrowing wickedly. He leant over picking up a King Charles spaniel, who immediately showed his teeth at Henry. 'Hey Beelzebub, enough of that, be polite will you? Drago's huge muscled shoulders filled out the superfine navy jacket, as he stroked the dog's long silky ears.

'Friendly little devil, he'd have my throat in a second.' Henry laughed, as the dog snarled at him.

'Well, that's what he's trained for, he's small, but he's got balls, scared off many a huge lout' Drago beamed down at the aristocratic little bundle of fur. 'Small, precious and lethal ain't you?' He frowned, 'Hey, the devil's licking my deerskin pants. Paid a fortune for those; stop it dammit.' He paused looking at Henry. 'Well I'm off; a game of Faro, you coming? It will surely lift the spirits.'

'And empty your pockets.' Adjusting his blue and silver striped waistcoat, Henry grimaced. 'Devil's teeth, why not? I promised Miriam I would steer clear of them, but that was before I was surrounded by a gaggle of women cackling on about babies. One had a fit of hysterics, gushing over the latest layette, cooing and almost frothing from the mouth.'

'Hah, you at least have a sense of humour over it. You're a braver man than I am. I'll just be content watching from the side lines.'

'Fiend's teeth, I sometimes wish Miriam stuck to her painting, far easier to cope with than babies.'

'It was her passion, doesn't she miss it?'

'Hmm now and then, but of course, she can always go back to it. I had a room renovated for her, so I think in time, she will.'

'I find I'm spending more and more time at my clubs. It's not Miriam; it's all the visits, every day, if it isn't the grandmothers, it's the aunts, and if it isn't the aunts, it's the friends and —'

'Devil take it, drink up old chap; we're off to the gaming hells.'

'Mark my words Drago, your time will come, no matter how cunning you think you may be. The Big Season is upon us, and the mamas are on the rampage dragging their fluffy chicks in white satin and feathers to every ball. One of them is going to cast her dewy-eyed beauty over you, blond curls, plump bosoms, and you'll be down on your knees begging.'

'Never, I am content with my succulent mistresses; one for every night of the week.'

'In your dreams. My dearest friend you have no option, what of the estate – your heir and the spare.' He glanced over to see the fleeting desolation in his friend's eyes. He'd suffered loss and rejection too often in his childhood to trust love, let alone marriage.

Downing his brandy, Drago slammed his glass on the table with more force than usual. 'I already have an escape route; my heir is a distant cousin who has dastardly schemes to be rid of me. I have to be on my guard of a night-time, lest he pay some mercenary ruffians to make an end of me.'

'Hmm, it's a fate we all had to face; those distant heirs are always lurking or scheming. I'm lucky I guess, safely ensconced in the arms of Miriam and a young heir on the way.'

Drago chuckled, 'don't count on it; it may well be a filly.'

'Huh, I have seen to that, I paid my solicitor a visit; had the estate entailed to both male and female heirs. I had to do it, Miriam being a modern miss and all; she insisted on it. So tell me, our sweet Blanche is still warming your bed?'

'Deuce; gone these last three weeks. I tired of her whining, every time we neared the bedroom door she insisted on more jewellery or a gown and so on. It became tiresome, but she accepted a healthy annuity, and is now happily installed with Lord Whitemoor.'

'Hah, I'm surprised she entertained that old roué.'

'Well he may be nursing the gout, but his pockets are deep, enough to satisfy our little bird of paradise.'

'You're fairly flush in the pockets old man.'

Drago nodded grimly. 'Well let's say she may well put Venus to shame, but she set her cap at me – told me in uncertain terms, no marriage – no bed, not even a lift to the skirt. My step mother threatened to strangle me with her own garter if she saw me abroad with a light of love. Can't ruin the family name can we?'

'Shame, beautiful girl. Bit of a feather brain though.'

'Her brain? I am not giving her a set of rubies to have a conversation.'

Henry laughed. 'Like I said, one of these days you'll sing a different tune.'

'Never, I have fashioned my life to consist of clubs, racing, horses, and pleasuring my mistresses, what more could an honest man want?'

Henry raised his eyebrows, as a footman in pale blue livery and a powdered wig, appeared at Drago's side, carrying a small roll of parchment on a silver salver.

Drago frowned, looked at the tied red ribbon and seal. 'Hmm, don't like the look of this.' He nodded to the man, giving him a shilling. Pursing his lips, he broke the seal, 'Hmm, it's from old Partridge – Arundel.' His brows beetled as he hissed. 'Seems a possible replacement contacted Partridge, she's going for an interview tomorrow. However, Partridge warns there are some rogues up to no good.'

'Well that's good news and bad news. We've waited long enough.'

'If she takes the bait, the summons could come anytime. We must be prepared, seeing as you're up to your ears in babies and scheming grandmothers, I'll take Daykin with me.'

'Lucky fellow, give him my regards.'

Drago picked up his glass and drained it. 'Dammit, I was going to escort a certain Cyprian to the theatre, private box and night of lust. She is renowned for her low décolletage.' He scowled, ruffling Beelzebub's head, who snarled and nipped him on the finger. 'Huh, you little bastard.' But he laughed, dipping his finger in the brandy, and sucking it clean. 'Behave or I'll leave you behind.' To which Beelzebub growled, as he licked his master's injured finger, enjoying the taste of blood and alcohol.

Henry examined the report. 'Seems from this epistle, she's a lovely girl.'

'What's her name?' Drago gave the little spaniel a biscuit, fondly stroking its bristling back.

'Clarissa Culling.'

Chapter 3
Present day
A journey to dreams

At just after five thirty pm the next day, Clary arrived in Arundel to find the estate agent's office crammed between two old Tudor buildings bowing over the road and listing to one side. A portly gentleman rose from behind his desk, his apple red cheeks shining as brightly as his bald pate. Smiling benignly, he bowed, as he took her hand. 'Hah, Miss Culling, you made it. How was your journey? Pleasant I hope?'

'Yes it was, there was some beautiful scenery on the way down here.' She looked at him, trying not to stare at his elegant cravat and silver striped waistcoat; it smacked of the regency period, indeed he looked like something out of a Jane Austen novel. Suddenly, it all seemed so right for her to be there.

He pushed at his wire-rimmed glasses perched upon the tip of his nose. It seems he had a penchant for antiquated glasses. 'I must say I do enjoy a train journey, far better than being cramped up in a car for so many hours. At least, you can get up and walk about, and the dining carriage often serves delicious food.'

Clary nodded; she'd made do with a sandwich and a bag of crisps for later on. She needed every penny if she was to make this move. 'Yes, I started off at 7.00 am this morning. I had to make a few changes at the stations, but the porters did help.'

Ushering her to a chair, he beckoned to a girl sitting typing at a desk across the small office. 'Miss Timmins will you bring us a tray of tea and biscuits please?'

The girl lifted her head, shaking blond ringlets framing a pretty face of cornflower blue eyes, and peach hued cheeks. She smiled brightly showing small white teeth, 'Yes Mr. Partridge – right away.' She came from around the desk; looking quite stunning in pale blue jeggings and a lacy voile top.

Beaming, he rubbed his hands. 'Now let me show you the details. 'He handed her a glossy paper with a large photograph of the property. Clary's eyes widened; it was like a little slice of heaven; the cottage was newly thatched, with a long front garden bedecked with flowered borders, and a winding path of paving stones leading to what looked like a carved oak door; the windows were latticed, and the walls plastered white.

'Oh goodness, it's lovely, far better than the pamphlet and the website.'

'Yes, one cannot do Squirrel Cottage justice on that piffling website. The photos, they are so small on there, but now you have a better idea of it.' He pushed over more papers. 'Here's some photos of the various rooms and outbuildings.'

'Outbuildings? Really? That would be marvellous, I am looking for a decent sized studio.'

'As every artist should. Forgive me, but I am aware of your fame on the web; I am a fan of two of your websites.' He didn't add he knew everything about her from what she had for breakfast, to her doctor to her hairdresser. He was well aware of the tragedy she survived.

'Umm. Yes.'

Miss Timmins appeared with an antique carved trolley holding porcelain cups and plates with silver cutlery.

'I hope you like confits Miss Culling.'

'Confits?'

'Yes our delicious tea cakes from an old recipe, goes back to the early nineteenth century.'

'Oh really? I am sure I will love them.'

'Miss Timmins please pour for us and serve the cakes.' He turned back to Clary, 'So do you only paint in oils?'

'No, I use a variety of things, acrylic oils, pastels and pen and ink.'

'How wonderful.' His pale blue eyes glittered. 'So who do you prefer Rembrandt? Constable, the Pre-Raphaelites?'

Clary took a breath, this gentleman, was obviously an avid fan of art. 'Well, I do appreciate them all really, but my main love is Regency. There is little known of the female artists of that era, but I am fascinated with them.'

'Hmm, I visited your website, and you did a very good job of the Gainsborough copy, and your regency work shows great sensitivity.' He picked up a delicate porcelain tea cup, taking a sip.

Clary smiled, encouraged by his interest. 'Some of my clients prefer me to paint a Gainsborough scene complete with the family and their pet dog, or horse, and I really enjoy doing it. However, I loved the Regency era from 1811 to 1820 most of all.' Putting down her cup, she picked out a cake.

'Hah, I am delighted to hear it; I am a great fan of Joshua Reynolds, Gainsborough and I too favour the Regency era.' She heard a deeper undertone to his voice, as if she'd just passed some kind of test. She shook her head, was it her imagination?

'How exciting, it looks like heaven has looked down on us.' Mr. Partridge exclaimed.

'Really?' Clary grinned.

'Yes, I will explain later, but now let's return to the property. Here's a fuller description. As you will see, it is more spacious than it looks on the advert.'

Surprised, she eagerly took the papers. To her delight, the rooms were generous, with three elegant bedrooms of average size and a cute box room. 'My goodness, I didn't think it would be so large.'

'Well my dear, it's been in probate for six years, and the beneficiaries are desperate to sell. I would say with respect, you are getting a bargain here.'

Clary almost laughed with delight. She could not believe her luck, or that she would actually feel such joy again. Grinning, Mr. Partridge pushed over the last sheet. 'Now that's the studio attached to the left wall of the cottage. It was once the old stables, and the last owner had it partially renovated as an art studio.'

Clary could not believe her eyes, as she read the dimensions, 'Goodness, two rooms both six metres by four?'

'Yes m'dear, now you understand why I said heaven is looking down on us. Miriam had a flourishing art and craft business; people came from miles around to the hamlet. She had such a fine reputation.'

Clary wanted to ask what happened, but felt it would be imposing. However, Mr. Partridge seemed to sense her unspoken questions. 'Sadly my dear, Miriam just disappeared – disappeared from the face of the earth – a brilliant painter like that. No-one knew why or where she went, just plain disappeared. Of course, we searched for her, but with no success. I must say we were distraught; every member of our little community is important.'

'Oh, so you are part of the community?'

'Oh yes, and proud to be so.'

'But what about her family? Didn't they have any information?'

'No, they passed away some years ago.'

'Really, so how old was she?'

'Just a couple of years older than you. Not yet in her prime.' His lips tightened. 'Ah yes, such a gifted young lady.' He rubbed his hands together. 'It appears you may well be our missing link.'

Clary frowned; it sounded like serendipity. It was almost like one of those deja vu moments. Strange, but she didn't dwell on it.

Chapter 4

1812

An evening at the theatre

Lady Lavinia, a widow of some five years, and now a noted Cyprian of outstanding beauty, clapped her hands beaming down at the stage, 'Did you see that my lord, truly she is a splendid performer.'

Half hidden by the heavy brocade curtain, Drago sat back, insouciantly plucking at the gems encrusted on her bodice. He lifted his lorgnette, and peered down at the actress on the stage passionately, gesticulating at her woebegone lover. 'God's teeth this is bloody boring, how long is it going on for?'

'My Lord, tis only the first act. How can you not love Sarah Siddons; her Euphrasia is out of this world? Tis such a tragedy.'

'Give me clowns any day.' he sighed, 'May I suggest we dine later; I hear there is a new place opened, Claridges, tis also a hotel, fine wines, fine food.'

'I dined there the other day – enjoyed a magnificent meal.' Viscount Griffin Daykin, interjected, his muscles filling out a superb black cutaway tailcoat, over a maroon damask waistcoat. Tight black satin breeches and white stockings enhanced his long toned legs set off with black velvet court shoes. He turned his attention back to the young woman on his lap, his large hand massaging her plump bottom. He had a penchant for what he called a healthy-looking woman.

Tutting, Gertie playfully slapped the side of his head with her fan, disarranging his blond curls. 'My lord, someone will surely see us.'

'What up here, deuce no, the box is heavily curtained; now be a good girl and kiss me.'

Drago laughed. 'We are better entertained in here than the funereal performance.'

Nodding, Daykin handed the girl a glass of sparkling champagne. 'Come sip my dear, put a blush in those pale cheeks.' His hand slid deftly lifted up her skirts, whilst she obeyed, giggling. 'It tickles my nose. And you sir, are tickling my thigh.'

'Hmm,' he leered, stroking her legs. 'So the lady wears silk stockings and garters.'

Lady Lavinia sniffed, raising her chin. 'Hush, have you no manners? You are drowning out her voice.' As she turned to glare at them, there was a slight tap on the door, which opened to admit a footman in red and gold livery. He presented a silver salver to Drago and waited. Frowning, Drago took his hand from Lavinia's bosom, and picked up the sealed letter. 'Hmm methinks tis another message.' Breaking the seal open he perused the contents. 'Seems we will have to forego that meal'. He looked over to Lord Griffin intent on undoing the girl's garter. 'Better read this old chap, seems we've been summoned.' he passed the note over.

'Hmm, it doesn't leave us much time. So my lady, we must continue this sweet episode another time.' Daykin hefted the young light skirt off his lap, then stood brushing down his breeches. Hastily, he checked the front of his fall.

Drago kissed the long swan like neck of Lavinia, murmuring. 'Dearest, I shall be away for some time, but will send for you on my return. Please to stay and enjoy the performance. I will have a carriage waiting for you after the performance.'

Lavinia raised her head, a slight smile hovering over her luscious lips. He detected relief, not regret in those large brown eyes.

'I shall await your pleasure my lord.'

He bent to her, his hand slipping into her low décolletage and tweaking a nipple. She gasped, opening her mouth for his passionate kiss, whereupon he grasped her up in his arms, his tongue dancing long and deep into her honeyed sweetness. Reluctantly, he released her to the velvet cushions, whereupon she fanned her flushed face furiously, before turning away to watch her beloved Sarah Siddons.

~*~*~*~

His valet fussed, as Drago sunk in the copper bath.

'You will catch your death of cold my lord, is it necessary to strip right off?'

'Deuce Hodgson, don't be such a big girl. When going through the time portal, one must be as Mother Nature made us. Someone went through, the other year, took no heed of the warning, and found their shirt sunk into their skin and wrapped around their beating heart. Tragedy really.

'Tragedy?'

Did he die?'

'Well of course, so would you with your shirt beneath your skin, and wrapped around your heart. Tis true, believe me.'

'If you say so my lord, but you could go down with a fever, stuck in that awful place, and what then?'

'Well you'll be with me.'

'Yes as naked as you, and just as likely to be overcome with cold and delirium.'

Drago smiled. 'Come on Hodgson just get on with it.'

'Can't you take a trunk with you; at least have some decent clothes?'

'Certainly not, God knows what would happen if I tried to do that. No, our skins are all we need, besides; they have different fashions in the twenty-first century, you know we have a wardrobe there, full of clothes.'

'But what if no-one is waiting at the other end, what if they forget to bring any robes?'

'Hodgeson if I hear another word, I will dunk your head in here. Now hand me my towelling robe and towel. Hurry man, Lord Daykin and his valet will be waiting for us.'

His burly valet shuddered, 'God protect us, tis a soulless place. I fear tis the abode of the devil himself.' He ran thick fingers through corn coloured hair,

'So Hodgson have you bathed?'

'Bathed, you expect me to bathe? Tis a nonsense, just because that curmudgeon Brummell and his followers do it, doesn't mean we become part of the witless herd. I would not demean myself by bathing. I do splash my face and hands every day and....' He coughed; 'and the intimates at least once a month.'

'Hodgeson, you do tend to give off a ripe odour.'

Drago wrapped himself in the towel and pointed at the tub, the steam still rising 'Get in the tub now.'

'You will send me to my death my lord. I am here to obey, and serve you my lord, but this I refuse.'

'Do it man. You cannot go through the portal with any grime on you. Come we have no time to lose.'

Hodgeson saw that menacing look in his master's eyes and stepped into the tub. 'We are going to our death my lord, our death.'

Chapter 5
Present day
Moving on

Clary rubbed her hands together looking around the bedroom with dark oak beams and white lath and plaster walls. It had taken three months to move, but now she was here at last. She looked at the suitcase then walked over to the chest of drawers. She dreaded opening them, fearing to find they would they would be dusty even grimy but to her astonishment, she opened one to find it covered with a blue flowered sweet-smelling paper. In there was a small note.

'Dear Miss Cullling,

You will see the drawers are ready for your clothes; I had them all thoroughly cleaned and then papered so you do not have to waste time moving in.

With kind regards.
Cecil Partridge.

Clary bit her lip; she had the desire to clean the drawers anyway. She looked around to Celia. 'He's had them cleaned.'

'He sounds really sweet. D'you remember when we moved to our last home? Poor old mum she was mortified. It was so filthy we couldn't eat in the kitchen for ten days.'

'Yes it was awful wasn't it? We had to pull out that cooker. It was disgusting, dripping in old grease and the extractor fan was choked with fat.' Clary smiled inwardly, at least they could talk about their parents without breaking down; the memories still pained them, but it was not so savage.

Celia bent down and smelt the drawer. Mmm, that's really nice; I recognize the air freshener; 'Wild Orchid.' Anyway, I'm glad I came with you, there's so much to do here; you couldn't have done it all on your own. It would have taken weeks.'

'It was good of you to take the time off.'

'My pleasure, I get a break; we've got a new boss, and he's been reorganizing the whole place.'

Clary bent beside her. 'Huh, d'you like him?'

'Hmm, he's okay, full of himself though, it's his first job as a Chief Librarian, treats us like morons.'

'Well there's a partnership in the offing here with me. You just have to say the word.'

'D'you know what Clary, I might just take you up on that, I love the village and the sea on our doorstep, just give me a little time to sort things out.'

'You mean you'll come to live here, with me?'

'Hmm ….' Her face puckered up, and she bit her lip. 'Yes, yes I will. I mean I can't bear to see you on your own and well; I've noticed there's a lovely country library here.'

'Yes it closed at the moment; the librarian retired. You could really make it hum.' Clary frowned, 'I think I'll give this a little wipe over. I know it's clean but—'

'That's your obsessive personality coming through Clary.'

'I know I can't help it. It started with that move to our last house, like you said, it was abominable. I never got over it really, now I have to clean everything myself just to make sure.'

Ceci took the cloth from her hand. 'Look, I'll do that; you go down and check the drawers and cupboards in the kitchen.'

'Okay.' Clary ran nimbly down the stairs, and entered the kitchen. It fairly sparkled in the sunlight. On one of the kitchen tops in front of the window was a note.

'Everything cleaned with Detox, tops, cupboards, drawers, fridge and cooker.'

My compliments
Cecil Partridge.

Clary felt the tears spring to her eyes. Mr. Partridge was so kind. She felt an immediate sense of security, at least she knew she had one caring neighbour. She went to the bottom of the small stair that curled round at the top onto the landing. 'Celia, I'm going to start unpacking the boxes in the kitchen. It's really clean down here. I can smell the Detox.'

'Fine, I'll carry on up here; I'm giving the drawers a wipe, just for your peace of mind okay?'

'Yes, that's great, the kitchen's fine.'

'D'you mean you're not going to wipe them over again?'

'Hmm, no they're good.'

'Wonders will never cease, seems this place is doing you good already.'

Clary returned to the kitchen, and heard a tap on the back door. She opened it to see Miss Timmins on the step holding a covered Pyrex bowl. She smiled in welcome. 'Miss Timmins come in.'

'Denise, please.' She grinned, looking pretty in a spotless white top and pink mini skirt, her blonde curls bouncing around her face.

Putting the bowl on the kitchen top, she took off the cover. Clary's mouth watered to see two pies covered with a crust of golden pastry. 'I hope you like these; one is a beef pie, and the other is mushroom and onions. I didn't know whether you were vegetarian or not.'

'Oh, thank you, I am actually neither, I do eat fish, but this is great. My sister is with me, and she loves beef steak pie, and my favourite is mushroom and onion. Wow, thank you so much.'

Denise laughed, making Clary jump; it sounded like a parrot that stepped on a nail; it was such a contrast to the girl's delicate looks. 'It's so lovely in here; it takes you back in time doesn't it?'

'Oh, I can imagine how it must have been. Mr Partridge said, it was early nineteenth century, 1780 or thereabouts.' Clary heard Celia clattering down the wooden stairs. 'Ah that's my sister; she's helping me move in.'

'Oh really?' Denise beamed as Celia entered the kitchen. 'Hello, I've just brought you some food to tide you over. Just heat it up.' She looked over to the microwave, 'Mr. Partridge made sure it's in working order. I know l can't do without mine. Now I must be going; I don't want to be in your way.'

'That's really nice of you Denise. Actually; I'm famished.' Celia grinned.

'Me too, we can have a feast now; I've brought some wine.' Clary said. Looking at Denise retreating to the door, she said, 'Would you like a glass?'

'That's really nice of you, but I really have to go. Mr. Partridge is waiting to go for his lunch, so I have to be back in the office.'

'You sure?'

'Yes, I don't want to be dancing into the office do I?' Celia almost jumped back, as Denise laughed, the parrot squawk, screeching through the kitchen, at which point Lila with a high-pitched whine, rushed into the kitchen, then lifting her head, howled.

Celia grinned, chuckled, then burst out laughing. Within seconds, the three girls laughed in unison, tears streaming down their faces, to Lila's howls.

Celia watched the girl trip down the path, then wiping the tears from her cheeks, giggled, 'God; she's hilarious.'

Clary nodded. 'Well she didn't actually say anything funny, but it's that laugh; it frightened the life out of me, then had me splitting my sides.'

Chapter 6
1812
Drago's Dressing Room.

Having left the running of the Keep in his steward's capable hands, Drago and Daykin followed by their two valets, made their way buck naked to the dungeons. Two footmen, carrying lit torches walked behind lighting their way. Even though it was the height of summer, down in these deep dark depths, the narrow stone steps leading to the lower levels of the Keep, were icy and treacherous. 'Hold on tightly to the bar now lads, tis a sheer drop on the other side.'

Griffin muttered, 'couldn't you have made a spiral or circular staircase. T'would be far safer old man.'

'Nope, we must maintain the Keep in its original state; otherwise, it could interfere with the portal.

Reaching the earthen floor, they were unaware of two figures with blackened faces, crouched in the narrow tunnel some twenty feet away.

Drago crept quietly along to the farthest dungeon and unlocking the rusted iron barred gate, entered with the others close behind, the marble tiles beneath their feet as cold as ice. The footmen then placed the torches into the sconces on the stone walls and stepped back.

As usual, Drago felt a sense of dread as they crossed the floor towards a dark niche on the far wall where even the flaming torches could not cast any light. He turned to the group. 'I will warn you again, move swiftly through the darkness, do not hesitate or try to turn back, or you will be caught in a time lapse; trapped for an eternity in a darkness so deep not even the stars will lighten your terror. Tis worse than death for we can never rescue you.'

Mutely, he stepped into the blackness of the niche in the stone wall.

The two figures crept from their hiding place hurrying to the dungeon, watching as the group disappeared into the niche.

The taller and burlier of the two, raked stubby fingers through thin ginger hair; straightened his superfine frock coat and adjusted the sapphire pin in his cravat. 'Huh, he'll not have her; she's worth a fortune. They don't have a clue about the tunnel. '

Unaware of any threat to his venture, Drago moved into a heavy space to emerge in exactly the same spot as he left the nineteenth century and entered in twenty-first century England. The dungeon appeared exactly the same, the marble tiles cold beneath his feet, the same rusted iron gate, but before them stood a gentleman, dressed in a different fashion of a tailored jacket and trousers, albeit the waistcoat of silver and white stripes was Regency style. He looked over his shoulder, to see Daykin and the two valets emerge, their faces white and grim. Stepping forward Partridge bowed, his bald pate shining in the dusky light from torches in the iron sconces. 'My Lord tis good to see you once more.'

Drago bowed in return. 'Good to see you too sir. I came as swiftly as possible.'

Partridge turned and beckoned two young men forward carrying clothes over their arms.

Now recovered from the shock of his bath, Hodgeson stepped forward claiming Drago and his clothes. In minutes, they dressed, ready to enter the twenty-first century and followed Partridge out of the dungeon.

'I have prepared the rooms for you and your companions. D'you wish to go straight up to your rooms my lord or would you prefer to take the tunnel to the castle?'

'No, for now let us remain in the Keep. I wish to hear every detail of the threat to our replacement.'

Partridge beamed. 'We are informed the villains plan to travel through the portal.'

'How so? It is guarded day and night.'

'I know my lord, but nevertheless, they may overthrow the guards, or even bribe them. The news is grave; it is a maze of tunnels from here to the hamlet; it is nigh impossible to guard them all. But come; let us discuss it in the confines of the study.'

Once seated in bespoke armchairs and recliners, Drago sipped at his whiskey, 'Hmm, Writer's Tears, a fine whiskey, I must say this is most welcome.'

Partridge downed his own glass, and clasped his hands together on his knee. 'I have two names my lord, the Baron Stennet, and Viscount Rackcape. Damn, nasty pair of buggers, my sources warn me they plan to kidnap little known but talented artists from the twenty-first century and take them back.'

'What is their purpose may I ask?'

'My lord, it is their intention to force these unfortunate artists to paint copies of Gainsborough, Reynolds, Turner and Constable. These copies are being sold on the 1812 market, claiming to be the originals and are much in demand. They are changing hands for thousands of guineas. Also, there is a demand for portraits of family members, trading them off with unskilled and unknown artists painting under the names of leading artists.'

'My dearest Partridge, why not use artists from 1812? Surely it would be a lot easier – hey what?'

'There are precious few of 'em my lord. And as for female artists – only a handful. Besides the artists from 1812 are known to family and friends, whereas the artists abducted from this time, will be isolated and subject to their villainous schemes.'

'Hmm, yes.

 Some of the estates are flung far and wild; they would escape notice.'

Partridge stroked his chin. 'Yes, now they plan to kidnap our artist – our very own replacement; I know not how we can guard every last tunnel under the hamlet; the place is riddled with them let alone the ones to the castle and the Keep.'

'Then we must needs watch her closely. She still does not have enough presence on the net or in the art circles, which suits our purposes. The girl is extremely talented in both in landscape and portraiture, and she has a passion for the Regency style. Her paintings sell for hundreds of pounds, and her popularity is gaining pace, she sold one to an American for over one thousand six hundred pounds.'

'Then we must protect her from these felons.'

'Yes, the girl is perfect for my needs. As you say there are very few female artists, and we have need of her to renovate our faded family portraits and more importantly, paint fresh ones for our expanding families. My portrait gallery is in sore need of her expertise.' Drago said, 'There is a great call for portraits, and as you say she has a fine sensitivity to Regency.'

'Yes, she subscribes to the artist and author websites for Regency, and has just embarked on one of her own, solely addressing the Regency era. As I said, she has already gained a following, but as yet, her disappearance will be of little note. As you know, her parents are dead; her sister is contemplating moving here, so we can induce her to accompany Clarissa if necessary.

Drago hunched his shoulders holding his hands together over elegant knees. 'My plan is first to entice Clary to visit us, she is beautiful, her tragic experience may well be in our favour. Once she has seen the poor state of our galleries, she may well agree to joining us. She has nothing to lose.'

Partridge, nodded. 'It's a wonder she overcame it; I am in awe of her bravery.'

'Yes, and it is that which we need for our project. Her nature as far as I can make out is not subject to bribery, we must lure her, fascinate her with the very thought of the project.'

'Use that seductive charm of yours Drago.'

Griffin laughed, 'Bed her, wed her and—'

'Devil's teeth, bed her yes, but wed her? Never. My Lavinia, more than satisfies my needs.'

Griffin slapped his knee. 'One day, some young woman is going to steal your heart Drago, and you won't even know it, until you are on your knees begging for her sweet hand.'

Chapter 7
Present day
A meeting in the dunes

Clary inspected the two large empty rooms adjacent to the cottage. Mr. Partridge had already engaged a small team of builders and decorators to work on the studio. She looked across to Celia busily examining the curtain samples. 'It's such a lovely day; I think I'll get some painting in.'

'Okay.' Celia picked up the batch. 'I think I'll go along and order the curtains and blinds. You sure you want eyelet curtains and satin steel poles?'

'Yes, they will look really fresh, and the eyelets are so popular now.'

'So, you want the yellow for the workshop, and display area and the blue for the bookshop and coffee lounge?'

'That's right; I don't want any bold colours; it will detract from the paints and paintings. I'll take Lila with me; she can mooch about the dunes, and she'd love that.'

'You going to Climping?'

'Yes, they've got huge stretches of sand dunes with ferns and wild flowers. I went there the other day, and it was heavenly; the soft sands, sea breeze and fresh scent of the flowers.'

Lila picked up her ears at the sound of her name. Panting she rose to her feet and pattered over, rubbing her head against Clary's knee. 'You know what we're saying don't you.'

'Honestly, I think she understands everything we say.'

Smiling, Celia got to her feet. 'Shall we have a takeaway tonight?' 'I'm fed up with salad and salmon.'

'Okay, that'll be good. See you tonight then.

D'you want a lift into town?'

'Please; you going to be long on the beach?'

'Well yes, a few hours, I must start some painting. I'll grab a bite to eat at the beach café."

'Fine, I'll catch the bus back.'

After dropping Celia off in town, Clary drove to the beach. The car park was almost deserted at this hour of the morning, but at least there were a few people around. Lila was such a gentle dog, but a great guard dog if necessary. Once, someone had got too close to her, and Lila immediately pushed in front of him, showing those magnificent fangs. The guy fled. Taking the easel out of the boot, she reached in for an eighteen by twenty-four inch canvas and her boxes of paints, brushes and mediums. It was not often she painted en plein air, preferring to do a rough water colour sketch, together with a photograph, and then paint the scene or portrait in her oil acrylics in the studio. Today, however, was glorious; the dunes and the sea called to her. In this weather, she would spend at least six hours at the easel, with a break for a trip to the café. She was happy to leave her easel as she could keep it in view whilst having a snack.

As Lila roamed the dunes behind her, she sat applying the undercoat in varied warm background colours of ochre, pink and orange. She looked at the sun glittering on the wavelets, as sharp and beautiful as a bevelled mirror. How on earth could she capture such an incredible light? She could give dramatic effects of light and shade, yet no matter how much she played with them; she knew she could not capture the steel glittering brilliance. In the distance, she glimpsed a sailing boat with sails unfurled, gliding towards the horizon. Quickly, she sketched it, leaning back to see the painting taking place; a young woman with long blond hair, standing on a high dune, her white muslin dress falling in soft folds from a high waist to her ankles. She held onto a straw hat, the blue satin ribbon fluttering in a soft breeze. As Clary dipped her brush into yellow hued paint, a dark shadow loomed on the canvas.

'I hope you will excuse me, but I do admire your work.' The voice was rich, and low. She looked up to see a shock of dark curls, a tanned face and the most startling blue eyes framed by double black eyelashes.

She turned in her seat to see him better. 'Why thank you. But, it is only the first impressions.'

'You don't mind me intruding do you? Or am I upsetting the artistic flow?'

'Err, well you are really, but I was ready for a break.'

He knelt before her coming into direct view. Her heart lurched, as she saw the chiselled upper lips, his smile revealing white teeth, and the glint of laughter in his eyes. Her heart thudded, in her mind's eye she immediately captured him on canvas. Shocked with her reaction, she bit her lip, her brush tapping some invisible line.

'If you're stopping for a break, can I tempt you into having a coffee? They do a fine cappuccino in the café over there.'

She cast her eyes back to the canvas feeling rather confused; this guy attracted her. She'd vowed never to get involved with another guy. So, how could this happen? In a split second, she'd met a guy who raided her senses. 'I don't know that—'

'Please, it's not often I have the pleasure of meeting an artist, especially one as beautiful as you.'

'You're embarrassing me. I love art, but I don't pretend to be all that good.'

'D'you sell?'

'Oh yes, much to my surprise.' And to her surprise that she was even talking to him.

'Where? Locally?'

'Well—'

'You know I'll bet you're global.'

Clary didn't answer; the peach flush rising in her pale cheeks.

'There I knew it, come on just a quick coffee, so I can cadge your autograph.'

She jumped, as he took her hand and kissed the knuckles, 'Come on I'm begging you.'

Laughing despite herself, she nodded. 'Oh alright, but I can't stay long as the paint will dry.'

'Oh so it's not oils then?'

'It's a combination of oils and acrylics, so it does dry quite quickly, especially in the sun.'

Holding out a strong bronzed hand, he helped her up from the rickety stool.

'I cannot go too far; I need to be in sight of the easel.'

At that moment, Lila came bounding up. 'Your dog I presume?' He wiped his pants, and then stroked Lila's fluffy head.

'Yes, she will have to come with us, but she's very good; we can sit outside.'

'And her name?'

'Lila.'

'Hah short for Delilah, I hope you're not going to cut off my hair.'

'Well she can hardly wield a pair of scissors.'

He raised his eyebrows. 'I was talking about you, not your dog, but she is gorgeous. They say owners look like their dogs.'

'Really, then I should look like a hearth rug.'

As they laughed together, she felt a long lost sense of comfort. Folding her arm in his, he led her from the dunes on to the soft sands, the heat almost burning her bare feet. 'Blast, I forgot my sandals.'

'The café's on the beach so you don't need them.'

'It's not that, the sand's hot; it's burning my ... oh.'

She gasped, as he swept her up in his arms. 'Then I shall carry you my lady.'

She giggled, as he swung her around. What on earth was happening? She was actually laughing and being carried by some devilishly good looking stranger to a café on the sands. Dark handsome seducers were usually the stuff of romance novels, but he was for real. Her stomach lurched. She shouldn't be feeling like this, guilt swept over her. 'Please, put me down. I can walk.'

Oblivious to her embarrassment, he hefted her higher. 'And burn those delicate feet, never.'

She grasped her hat, as it slid to one side, and gave in to temptation.

Once seated at a table, shaded by an umbrella, she watched him waiting at the counter for the coffees, taking in the tall sturdy figure, the arm muscles bunched and toned, the broad chest tapering down to a slim waist, and tight buttocks, his thick thighs filling the denim washed jeans.

As he set the tray down on the table before her, he grinned. 'Couldn't resist the fresh doughnuts, one jam; one cream.'

Clary raised her eyebrows. 'Now I can't refuse.'

'Then indulge me.' His eyes held hers, the double sided message quite clear in those mischievous sapphire eyes.

Chapter 8
Present day
A café on the beach

He watched her pick up the cream doughnut, a ripple going through to his stomach as she took a bite, her lips moist. So this was his quarry, he'd seen her photograph, but she was far more beautiful in the flesh. Drago's blood surged to his head, as he imagined those luscious lips doing something far more erotic. He was mesmerized with the sparkling jade eyes, the winged brows and delicate features. She was indeed like a Dresden statuette, fragile but with an inner depth that begged recognition. Yet even now, as she glanced fleetingly over to him, he could see the shadows, the hesitation.

He breathed deeply; he must always be aware of his speech and manners, taking care to mimic the twenty-first century, so different from 1812. He'd seen the way her doe eyes flitted over his muscles, eyelashes fluttering as her gaze roamed over his thick muscled thighs, the workouts at the gym were yielding results. Yes, the lady was for the taking; it was now or never; he decided to raise their encounter to a more intimate level. Taking her hand, he felt the bones, as delicate as a bird's wing. 'So tell me, why have I never met you? You are too beautiful to miss.'

'Well, I've only just moved here actually.'

'Hmm, I thought the accent was a little different. Well, that explains it. I would never have forgotten even a glimpse of you. So where are you from?'

'Ullswater, it's in the Lake District, Cumbria and you?'

'Huh, I live at the Keep.'

'Oh, I thought it was a castle.'

'It's part of a castle; it was a getaway for the knights if they were losing a battle. The castle is a ruin now, but we've kept the Keep up?'

'It's beautiful; it must be ancient?'

'Yes, it goes back before the Normans. So tell me, how long have you painted?'

His eyes fascinated her, sparkling, shadowed by those long black eyelashes. She glanced down at his arms, resting on the table, the strong bones of his wrists; the black bristles covering hunky forearms. 'Oh forever. When I was a child, I drew pictures for my younger sister; she was often in hospital with bronchial trouble. In the sixth form I was allowed to choose a specialized subject, and I plumped for art. I've painted ever since.'

'Well I'm over the boughs to meet such a wonderful artist'

She frowned. *Over the boughs?* What part of the country did he come from? 'How can you say that, it's only a draft?'

'Look, if that's a quick sketch, then you are truly talented. And might I say so, very different. I mean, one envisages an artist with Rastafarian cornrows, ripped jeans, face cutlery and loads of black Kohl." He saw her flush, lowering her eyes. She was still in pain, damn that fiancé he'd like to throttle him better still run him through with a sabre – slowly. To ease the situation, he leant over and picked up a lock of her long chestnut hair. 'Now what colour would you say that is?'

''Err – brown – chestnut.'

He shook his head, 'Methinks tis like fire dusted with gold and bronze lights, a fiery maid indeed.'

'Huh, a poet, d'you know you sound like you've just stepped out of the eighteenth or nineteenth century, or are you teasing?'

He flinched, dammit; he'd done it again; he had to remember she was a modern miss. 'Just jesting, you reminded me of my favourite TV dramas, Jane Austen and Tolstoy.'

Oh really – Regency romance? I would have thought you'd like the Paranormal, or the Walking Dead.'

'The Walking Dead? Hmm, 'he racked his brain, trying to place it. Wasn't it something about Zombies? Yes, that was it. 'Well, it's gory; shocking, but—'

'Gory – yes, I don't like it, but I'm hooked. I switch on every week. I'm disappointed when a series finishes; we have to wait months for the next.'

'Hmm quite a feisty ….' He stopped; dammit get the language right. 'Quite a blood thirsty madam then?'

'Not really, I got caught up with it when I was with my….' A deathly pallor painted her face.

He waited, prompting her to tell him the guy's name. But once more, she faltered and fell silent. 'So are you seeing anyone?'

She raised her eyebrows then spoke softly, haltingly. 'I was but … I can't … can't talk about it.'

'I'm sorry; I shouldn't be so bloody nosy.' He held her eyes. 'Forgive me?'

Clary nodded, twisting her fingers together.

He covered her hands with his. 'So the paranormal? You think I'm hiding the fangs then?' he gnashed his teeth and clawed his fingers scratching her throat.

Jumping back, she gave a little playful shriek. 'You'd make a good actor.'

'Hmm, no, I do not have any artistic talent, but I do appreciate beauty when I see it. He looked straight at her, appraising her, those moist succulent lips. He leant nearer, saw her eyelashes sweep down; felt his heart race; his body tighten, as desire ran from his toes to his groin to his head. There was nothing he could do, he kissed her.

To his surprise, she responded, her tender lips pressing on his, felt them part. Recklessly, his tongue penetrated her lips, seeking her mysteries. But then she shuddered, springing back in her chair.

He grasped her hand, feeling the tremor. 'I'm smitten; smitten with your glorious face, body – you.' He sought her eyes, but she turned her face away.

Rising from her seat, she pushed the chair back. 'I think I ought to go.' Her spine tingled, as her stomach clenched. What on earth just happened? Was he some magician? Never before had she kissed on an impulse; for God's sake, she'd just met the man. Again, he confused her, as she felt her core tingling. All over a kiss? He was dynamite; perilous, and she didn't know how to handle him except to walk away. However, she wanted more, wanted to taste his power, sink into her arms. Dangerous, shouted a warning voice in her head, now she couldn't ignore it; he'd seduced her, just by looking at her, kissing her. She couldn't resist him. Rising abruptly, she pushed back her chair. 'I have to go – now.'

He rose as well, walking around the table to put his arm gently about her waist. 'I sense what you're feeling, I feel it too; if we were alone I would kiss you senseless, 'til you swooned in my arms. Instead, I have to sit and make inane conversation, whilst your honey sweetness eludes me. I can't fight this power you have over me, dammit; I've never experienced anything like this before. But, I promise to be good – promise.' He held her gaze this time, his eyes speaking to hers, pulling her into those bright iridescent depths.

She sighed, a wry smile in her eyes. 'Okay, but behave.'

He breathed a sigh of relief, 'Whew that was close. Let's start again; taste this delectable cake.'

She laughed. 'You are incorrigible.'

'Oh and why?'

'You are a seducer of women.'

He raised his eyebrows; he was not however surprised; he was a renowned rakehell in his own time of 1812, yet invariably he got his woman.

Picking up the cream doughnut, Clary took a deep bite. 'Mm, this is delicious.'

He grinned, reaching over to wipe the corner of her mouth with a long finger. Deliberately, he held up a morsel of cream then licked it. She felt her stomach clench, sending sizzling heat to her groin. What on earth was the man doing to her? How could he arouse such erotic feelings? 'You're wicked, you know that? Wicked.'

His laugh was fresh, full of fun, yet his eyes held a gleam that spelt sex and secrets. 'Don't you think we should know each other's names?

Clary sat back startled. They had got to this point, where she felt hot, and he perspired profusely. 'Well my name is Clarissa Culling; Clary for short.'

He beamed, putting those hefty arms back on the table; she longed to stroke the black hairs glistening on the tanned skin. What in heaven's name was happening? She'd gone to the café with him purely for a cup of coffee, and a quick one at that, yet here she was heart pounding, fairly panting for him.

He lounged back in the wooden seat. 'I am Drago, the ninth Earl of Hatherstone.'

Clary laughed. 'You're back to Jane Austen. Well, if you want to play, I am the Queen of Naples.'

'Hmm I thought you were going to say the Queen of navels.'

'Drago, if that is your name, stop it; you are talking to a lady.'

'Exactly, a gorgeous, beautiful, tempting lady.'

'Thank you.' She grinned 'Look I've got to see to Lila now; she's edging further and further away.'

'We have to meet up again. I'll bring my dog.'

Clary hesitated, should she get involved? Or, should she nip it in the bud, or ... she felt her temptation rising. She hadn't laughed in ages, yet today; she'd shrieked at his antics. Her heart flipped, as she nodded. 'I think that would be ... nice.'

Suddenly, her voice was small and tight; he knew how much it took her to say that one small word. This was not going quite as he planned, she fascinated him, pulled strings he never knew he had. Now he felt guilty for keeping so much from her. But, he comforted himself that he could offer her so much more, but at present, she was vulnerable, his plans for her too far-fetched to accept. However, he would wait.

'What's your dog's name?'

He crinkled his eyes. 'Beelzebub.'

'The name of the devil?'

'Yes, he is a little demon; he'll snarl sooner than look at you.'

'But – look I'm sorry; he could hurt Lila.'

'Err no, he is charming around the ladies; it's only the male dogs he wants to take a bite at. Oh no, he'll guard her with his black soul, especially a seductress like Delilah. Now where shall we meet again?'

'Err, I am busy I have so much to do with the cottage and…. Look let me have your phone number, and I'll ring you.'

He beetled his eyebrows, looking fierce and totally heart wrenchingly handsome. 'Is this a turn –off?'

'Oh no, really, I would like to meet up again; it's just I've got a big project on, starting in three days' time.' She didn't want to go into details about the studio and art centre, not yet anyway.

Pushing his chair back, he rose to his feet, towering above her. 'I'll see you in three days from now.'

She frowned, her mercurial temper rising; he could be bloody bossy. 'What? I'm busy like I said, I'll call you. You're too dominant, did you know that?'

He looked up with narrowed eyes, sending a shiver down her spine. 'Don't break my heart, if I don't hear from you in three days, I will come looking for you.'

'Like hell you will,' she hissed. She looked at him for half a second and then turned on her heel.

Drago frowned; he'd forgotten his place here again. In his Regency time, titled and finely reared young ladies were schooled never to upset, cross or refuse a man's valid request, if he offered for her hand, she had to have a damn good excuse not to accept. And even then a lady had to have an adequate reason for the refusal.

'Forgive me sweet Clary, I was carried away. Three days then?' he gave a twisted grin, believing his request was reasonable, at least he hadn't ordered her to oblige.

Tutting, she waved back, he was impossible, impossibly handsome and impossibly dominant.

Watching her go, his eyes narrowed, as he thought of Griffin, had he managed to charm the pants of her sister or would it involve more planning? He rose to his feet; for the first time, he was in trouble with a woman, already she'd invaded his heart – his black heart as Lavinia called it.

Chapter 9
Present Day
Yellow curtains

Celia examined the curtain samples once more, yes the yellow check would look great; give a sunny atmosphere to the showroom. As she turned, she bumped into a tall block of hard muscle.

'Oh, I'm sorry.' She looked up into grey eyes, and looked again. Usually, she preferred blue or dark brown, grey was too indiscriminate. These startled her; his eyes glittered as if flecked with quartz crystals, rather like the quartz stones found in Ireland. The sun bounced off his unruly blond curls as he grinned. 'Don't be, it's not often I get to be bowled over by a gorgeous girl.'

She chuckled, gazing up; admiring the high cheek bones and strong jaw line. As she stepped to one side, he did as well, ending in them both grinning. 'Shall we dance?' He laughed, holding out his arms. Seeing Celia struggle to lift a bolt of yellow check linen, he stepped forward hefting the bolt easily in toned muscled arms. 'Allow me to carry that for you, tis far too heavy for such a delicate young lady.'

Surprised, Celia looked at him; she would not have described herself as delicate, yes she had lost some weight, but size twelve was far on the horizon; she had a way to go yet. He was so well spoken, exuding an olde world charm, even though dressed in a silk sweat shirt and cut frayed jeans – expensive cut jeans by the look of them, whilst his designer trainers looked brand new; maybe he was an actor or something. Celia nodded willingly.

She almost ran to keep up with him as he said, 'Trouble today is, the assistants are slow to help. They take their time tidying shelves or talking and damn the customers.'

'Yes, you'd think one of them would have come running to help you.' He looked around, 'The shop's deserted – strange. They're very trusting aren't they? We could walk out of here with a few bolts under our arms.' He felt quite proud of his little speech seeing as he'd never set foot inside a shop, and his tailors visited him. Indeed, he never even requested samples, his tailor fitted him at the castle, advising and dressing him in the latest cloths and fashion of the first stare.

'Well you might, but I could hardly lift one.'

He grinned. 'Me Tarzan; you Jane.'

She giggled; again he'd used such an old fashioned phrase. However, the more she was with him; the more she fell for that olde worlde charm.

Reaching the counter, he rang the bell. 'I'll wager no-one comes rushing in. Years ago, the shopkeeper and his assistants stood behind the counter eager to please, advising, serving, lifting and packing and carrying it out for you.' He nearly bit his lip, deuce; he'd used the word 'wager' but maybe she wouldn't notice that.

Celia raised her eyebrows; he was far too with it and too young to remember all that, as was she. Yes, he was rather old fashioned, but charming. Maybe he was used to village shops and old fashioned ways. Arundel certainly was full of quaint shops and eating places. Mullioned windows bowed over cobble stone pavements, interiors dark and cosy with low oak beams and fires in the grates, and the tantalizing aroma of cinnamon buns baking in the oven. 'So are you from around here?'

He looked around for an assistant. 'Oh no, just visiting.'

She nodded, that explained it. 'So where are you from?'

'The Lake District, Ullswater.'

'Oh, so am I. Beautiful place, a couple of old castles great to visit, boating, riding, and climbing. You climb?'

'Oh yes – it's my passion. I spend a lot of time in Cumbria, the Peak District and Scotland of course. Boating is another past-time.' He frowned looking around, 'Fiend's teeth, where the hell is everybody?'

'Fiends' teeth? I've never heard that before.' Celia laughed.

He coloured up 'Huh, err … a joke going around at the moment; it's catching.'

'Never heard of it.'

Griffin clenched his own teeth. Dammit he'd nearly given the game away. Trouble was when he, and Drago travelled to this century; they kept their social life to the Keep and the Castle rarely venturing out to the town. However, it was necessary to ensnare her; she would be their leverage if Clary proved difficult. Thing was, on seeing Celia's photograph; he was determined to meet her, she was a looker, and on meeting her here, turned out to be even lovelier, plump and beautiful.

As he went to ring the bell again, a middle-aged woman with flushed cheeks and rounded figure appeared from the back room of the shop, and came panting to the counter. 'So sorry to keep yer waitin' but me assistants have gone off for a birthday lunch. Now how can I help yer?'

Celia stepped forward, 'I have the measurements for some curtains for an Arts Centre. Do you do made to measure?'

'Oh yes. Now let me get out a catalogue.'

'We also want them to be hung on white poles with matching eyelets.'

'Yes, now is it a width and half you want or double?'

'Oh a width and a half; I don't think we'll draw them; they're just for effect. I also want some voile for a couple of windows. You have a bolt of it back there.' She turned pointing to a side counter. 'We'd like them in white please.'

'I see, and the style?'

'Err just gathered on the wire please. I've got the measurements for them, and we'll want double width for those.' Celia said, handing a detailed list of measurements to her. The woman scribbled down the order and looked up beaming. 'Fine. Now I'll work out the cost and send you a quote, could you give me your address? I'll also need your phone number and have you an email address?'

Griffin stiffened, email address, now that would come in handy. He'd found the computer tiresome to learn, but in the end was now hooked on the latest war games, especially Bonaparte's *Peninsula Wars* – fascinating. However, he was sworn to secrecy by the Brotherhood, he couldn't even go back with the latest medication or technology. But that was the price they paid. He grimaced; he would have made an incredible spy for Wellington.

Celia's eyes darted up to Griffin, lounging, muscled arms folded across his magnificent chest. She didn't want to give away her addresses or details, but how could she get him to go without sounding impolite.

Reading the message in her glance, he grinned, raising his hands, 'I'll see you outside okay?'

She nodded, surprised. He'd taken it for granted she wanted to meet him again.

Chapter 10
Present day
Alpha Male

'So d'you think you'll call him?' Celia sipped her tea.

'He's too alpha male for me; I know Theo ... was weak, but I don't want to make another mistake do I?'

Celia nodded. 'Tread carefully then.'

'Trouble is, there's something about him, different you know, but he's so powerful; I could not believe I would end up wanting to kiss him.'

Celia felt her heart lift; she never dreamt Clary would succumb readily on a first meeting; she thought it would take months of guarded courtship. He must be extraordinary to win her over. 'Never mind the parting shots; did you enjoy being with him?'

'Oh God yes.' Clary became quite dewy eyed. 'He has this knack you know; I had no intention of talking to him about the painting, neither did I have any wish to go for coffee, and certainly not wanting to kiss him; I think I know what the word seduction really means now.'

'So you didn't pull away when he kissed your hand?'

'Oh no, quite the opposite, I wanted to kiss him. Honestly Ceci, I've read of that impulse in the romance novels, but never got to grips with the heroine having feelings darting to her stomach and down to her groin. But, this guy's knocked me off my pedestal, I'm not the iron maiden I thought I was, in fact, all I could think of, was his iron rod.'

'Good god Clary, is that you talking? Really? You sexy thing.'

'Hmm – I know I was mad with him, but the feeling hasn't gone away either.'

'So you'll ring him then?'

'Yes, I've cooled down now; I can see he was teasing me. I feel like ringing him, but honestly I don't want him to think I'm a push over, or panting for him. He's so dominant; he'd have my knickers down before I had chance to breathe.'

'Wow he sounds incredible, ring him, go on, ring him – now.'

'No, I have to be strict, make him wait. But, he did say that if I didn't ring him in three days, he'd come looking for me. Mind you, he did beg and tease me, but underneath. I think he really meant it, he will come looking for me.'

'Go on; ring him, maybe he could help out at the Centre.'

'Hmm I'm not sure; he has muscles in all the right places, well at least, I hope he does.'

Celia shrieked, 'Clary, gosh; you've got it bad.'

'I know; I should feel guilty Ceci but all I can think of …. I'm not going to say anymore; I am overheating here.'

'Okay, then let's change the subject.'

'No – no, first you've got to tell me about the guy you met, you promised.'

Celia blushed. 'Well he was tall, with blond curls, in fact, my heart was going nineteen to the dozen; he was an Adonis come to life. His eyes glittered, like quartz stone, if that's the right word for them. He's such a zany character you know; joking, laughing, but he was a wee bit weird.'

'How?'

'Well, he was high fashion you know, like one of those super male models, all muscle, slim hips, smouldering eyes, and yet he was old fashioned in his manner and his speech. There's no other way to describe it, he talked like he'd stepped out of a Jane Austen novel.'

'My God, and I'm not taking the lord's name in vain; I had the same experience; my guy could have been Darcy come to life. You know that scene where he walks out of the lake, his shirt plastered against his skin, showing off his muscles, sexy as hell? Well, my guy was the same, but walking on the beach. He was one tough dude, like you say, old fashioned but hard. It was as if he'd stepped through time – so strange.'

'Yes, but I thought it was … well the only word I can find to describe him, is charming. I think maybe Griffin comes from a little old village, but you know come to think of it, he never did tell me where he came from.'

Clary frowned, 'Same for me; I did think he was on holiday, olde worlde village type, but then he looked too fit for that, you know, designer tee shirt, tight jeans, expensive trainers.'

Ceci nodded 'It seems like we're describing twins, except yours had dark hair and mine had blond.'

'Like made to order mannequins.' Clary chuckled. 'You know the names are so different too; I mean my guy's name was Drago —'

'And mine – Griffin. You don't hear of names like that anymore'

'Not outside of Regency Romance. D'you think they know each other? Maybe there's a group of them on holiday from some obscure village in the wilds of Scotland or Wales.'

Clary bit her lip then said, 'Sounds a bit like the Stepford Wives.'

'Oh no, Drago's untrainable, wild I would say. D'you know he calls his dog Beelzebub.'

'The devil's name.'

'I know, that's what I said, bit sinister don't you think?'

'Yeah, dark; was he menacing?'

'Drago? Not a bit, just bright, cheerful, but as dominant as hell.' She got to her feet. 'I can't finish this tea; I've been drinking it all day, D'you fancy a wine?'

'Yes, I've got some chilli crackers too, want some?'

'Yes, let's treat ourselves.'

'You know, thinking about where they come from, Griffin didn't have an accent.' Ceci sat down with a bag of hot chilli crackers on the small round table beside her.

'No, he spoke kind of … well … posh?' Clary answered, sitting down on the small settee, and tucking her legs up underneath her. Lila came, and sat beside her, looking adoringly at the crackers. Bending over, Clary gave her a small piece. 'Sorry Lila, but you're on a diet.'

'She's looking so much better Clary, how much weight has she lost now?'

'Well she was seven stone two pounds – forty-nine kilos, but she's lost nearly ten kilos. The vet told us she still had a few more to lose.' She looked down at Lila. 'He says we have to resist those big brown eyes. I know; Lila lives for eating, adores food, all sorts of food; she'd eat herself to death if I let her. D'you know she'll even eat cucumber and lettuce. I could not believe I had to join her slimming club. She's had photos taken of before and when she gets down to 35 kilos., they're going to put her picture up on the success panel.'

'How did she take to Drago?'

'Loved him, came up and inspected him, and he passed the test, so she went off snuffling in the sand dunes, leaving us to it.'

'So have you told Drago about the Arts Centre?'

'Not yet, I was so overwhelmed with him; I just couldn't go into it all; he was far too sexy to even think of carpentry and plumbing.'

'There are some very sexy carpenters around and plumbers.'

Clary laughed, taking a gulp of wine.' Hmm, with those muscles I can just see him wearing a leather belt and wielding a hammer. I mean he looked like one mind blowing guy with bulging muscles and an ab slab that pushed against his tee shirt.'

'I think you've just described Griffin too.'

Clary picked out a chilli cracker, biting into it. 'So let's stop talking about them, at the moment I feel like leaping over to the phone. God my stomach's on fire.'

'And other places.' Celia groaned, drinking down the wine and topping up her glass. 'Okay, let's toast the Art's Centre; Mr. Partridge has already engaged a team of builders and decorators, he said they were very competent. Two more days and we start'

'Haven't you met them?'

'No, he said he'd see to all of that. He's knows all the local firms around here. I'm relieved as I wouldn't have known where to start.

Chapter 11

Present day
Tin hats and leather belts.

'You know Griffin, be prepared for Clarissa to kick up when we get there, never known a woman like her. Quick to bite. The chit actually told me to go to hell.'

Griffin guffawed. 'Fiend's teeth, she's the first woman to have you worried, Drago, positively frightened I would say.'

'No, just a prickly little kitten with sharp claws. Nothing I can't handle.'

Griffin grinned hearing the apprehension in his friend's usually confident voice.

~*~*~*~

The studios looked bare; the walls painted a fresh satin white. The shelves, flat pack cupboards, tables and chairs all stood stacked in corners. Clary stood with her back to the door, 'Now we need ample shelving, but we don't want people to have to stand on tiptoe to reach them.

'I plan to have one room entirely for oils and acrylic oils. There'll be shelves for the tubes, bottles and pots; another for brushes, palette knives, rollers for acrylics, then roller dishes. The lower shelves will house the canvasses of various sizes, rolls of canvas and the cheaper canvas paper. I'm making sure they are all at eye level, unless they are stand up show cases.'

'Gosh, you've really done some thinking.'

'Hmm, yes. There'll be another room off the one for oils, the top shelf catering for watercolours, again, tubes, pan and liquids. Like the oils, the rolls of paper and books of sheets will be on the lower shelves. I'll have the easels dotted about with a painting on each of them.'

'That sounds great.' Clary could see Celia was taken up with the ideas.

'We've got to think of all ages. There're lots of middle-aged people who've just found the joy of painting as Bob Ross would have said.' She sighed, 'Loved that guy. I came upon his TV series just by chance and d'you know; he was a far better teacher than my tutors. He knocked their socks off. He taught me a lot you know, taught me how to get right into the canvas with the first brush stroke, not to be scared of it. He just made it such a delight. I mean I was painting not one but a forest of fir trees in my first session of watching his videos. I was ecstatic.'

She turned to see the door opening, then stammered, 'Oh my goodness, look who's just come in.'

Celia swung round and gasped. 'Griffin?'

Clary joined her, as she exclaimed 'Drago?' She looked wide-eyed at the tee-shirt and leather belt swung low on slim hips with various workmen's gadgets jingling. However, it was the tin hat low over his eyes that did it for her. 'What on earth are you doing?'

Drago grinned, striding over to her, an aristocratic King Charles Spaniel at his heels. 'What does it look like, let me introduce myself once more, Drago, manager and my worthy partner Griffin, a master craftsman.'

'This is a joke, and I'm not enjoying it. Please leave.' She tried to look serious, as Lily raced over to immediately sniff the dog's bottom, which he instantly reciprocated by smelling hers. How on earth could she look serious, with Lily and Beelzebub intent on each other's anuses?

Drago laughed, 'Atta boy.'

Whereupon, Clary gritted her teeth.

Flashing an amused glance at Griffin, he muttered, 'told you, didn't I? Feisty miss.' He turned to Clary. 'I promise you; this is no joke; I have a team of men arriving soon.'

'But you never said—'

'Didn't see the need, I was too engrossed with you. I did tell you I'd be seeing you. Just didn't think it was the time or place, but then neither did you. You didn't say one word about the Centre.'

Lila growled; her canine admirer was getting too bold. She swished her long silky tale across the spaniel's face. Whereupon, he jumped up licking her ear, a typical courting gesture.

'Like his master, doesn't take no for an answer.' Clary tried to hide a grin. 'You're right I think we were too caught up to think about doors, and screws.'

He burst out laughing, 'Maybe an inappropriate word my lady?'

Clary flushed, he was at it again, *my lady* indeed.

Celia waited as Griffin came up to her. 'Now dearest girl, where do you want us to start?'

She looked over to Clary. 'She's in charge; it's her Centre.'

He nodded, 'Fair enough.' He went over to Clary, giving an elegant bow, sweeping off his tin hat. 'My apologies my lady, I am at your service.'

Clary grimaced at Drago, her eyes narrowing. 'Have you seen the plans?'

'Of course, but I want to check it all over with you personally. We have already prepared the shelves.' He waved a hand over to the stacked wood.

'I would like one room for oils and acrylics, also my favourite the oil/acrylic paints and the Stand oil for mixing. The top shelf would cater for the tubes of paint, pans and liquid paints and paint mixers. The rolls of paper and books of different size sheets will be on the lower shelves, so I'm thinking about four main shelves in here. I'll have the easels dotted about with a painting on each of them.'

Drago frowned. 'What about your watercolours and pastels?'

Oh yes.' She paused looking at him quizzically. 'You sure you are not an artist?'

He gave a wry smile. 'Well I don't think I am up to your standard, wish I was.'

'But you don't know my standard; you've only seen me do a rough sketch.'

He narrowed his eyes. 'I do know you are an excellent artist, one day I'll explain.'

'Now there's a mystery. I hate mysteries, tell me.'

Drago bit his lip. 'Not now, I'll tell you over a dinner for two.'

She punched him lightly. 'You are incorrigible.' She swung around to Celia, 'Didn't I tell you? He can be infuriating. However, never mind, let's concentrate on this.' She walked over to the table studying the plans. Just as Lily rounded on Beelzebub her fangs on display, whereupon Beelzebub went down on his front paws his head bowed in submission.

'Huh, you could learn some manners from your dog.'

Drago's eyes widened; no woman would have got away with that in his time. She would have been banished to her bedroom. Fiends' teeth, the woman was a witch.

'Madam, may I fetch your broomstick?'

Griffin walked up between them. 'Hang on, we've got a centre to build, let's get to it.'

Scowling now, looking at the plans Drago snarled. 'So this is how you want the reading room?'

'Yes, people can browse through brochures, catalogues and books on arts and artists.'

'Okay.' He took a breath trying to calm down, when all he wished was to put her straight over his knee. This lady needed putting in her place. 'Anything you want to add to it?'

'Well, I need a counter and shelves there as well; I thought of selling box sets of the classic artists' works and biographies from the renaissance, right up to the present day.'

Still furious, Drago leafed through the plans. 'Well I think we've got enough to go on. You've got down here you want tea and coffee facilities, with a place to serve sandwiches and cakes.'

'Yes, I thought we could have that at the far end of the reading room. Oh, I'll also need a shelf for brushes; I'm going to supply, sable, hog and mongoose hair brushes. Then there're the sable brushes, horse hair and synthetic brushes as well as palette knives, and sponges.'

Celia butted in, 'You could do Christmas cards, and calendars too. Honestly, it sounds wonderful, but how on earth will you achieve it?'

'I intend to have two assistants besides myself.'

Feeling calmer now, Drago murmured, 'What about your own art? Sounds like you won't have too much time for that?'

'I'll be painting solidly for the next three weeks. My finished work will be on display as well.'

Drago realized he had to seduce the woman, not get so embroiled. 'That's a lot of work, but I'm sure we can fit in a dinner or two, you've got to eat.' That reminded him, he had to instruct Hodgeson to go back and have some of his clothes ready for when they returned, plus some emergency clothes for Clary and Celia, now they had an idea of their measurements.

Clary felt her stomach clench; those were the words Theo would use to entice her away from the easel. To her consternation, as she thought of her lost love, she did not feel a dagger stabbing her heart; instead, her eyes flitted to Drago. Dominant or not, he fascinated her; she'd never met a man like him, all passion, muscles, dominance and tenderness. One moment she wanted to slap him, and the next cup his balls. Whoops, now where did that thought come from? But now, she realized this man could snatch her from the abyss.

Unaware of her raging hormones, he put the plans in his file. 'Okay ladies, I think we have a good idea of what you want, so leave us to it.'

'But ... can't we help?' Celia said

Griffin shook his head. 'No, there's a team of men arriving soon. There will be saws, hammers, nails and god knows what in here, safer for you two ladies to see to the curtains and table cloths.'

Clary rolled her eyes at Celia, typical arrogant male 'You mean we should go and play with the kittens?'

'Well my dear, you were not made for such manual work, tis bad for that fragile brain.'

Clary gasped, 'Fragile brain? How dare you?'

'I do dare my love; I care about you, no need to worry your pretty little head, or sully those delicate hands; they were made to paint or play a pianoforte.'

'Pretty little heads? Pianoforte? Clary looked at Celia, with wide eyes, now she really wanted to hit him. 'Did you hear that Celia, did you?' She glared ominously at Drago taking a step towards him her teeth bared, but he'd already turned his back, engrossed in the layout of the rooms.

Well, she could wait; he would not get away with that.

Chapter 12
Present day
And so it begins

A couple of days later, Clary decided not to continue the feud; she realized he was not insulting her, but genuinely cared for her in his gross Neanderthal way. During the next two weeks, he frequently referred to the need to care for her fragile brain, to protect her delicate hands and not to overwork her pretty little head. There was no sign of a smirk, or sarcasm in those devastating blue eyes, only genuine concern. Nevertheless, he was a mystery and despite her misgivings, one she didn't want to unravel.

The next few weeks turned into a furore of builders, carpenters and plumbers to name a few, men working shifts, arriving at dawn and leaving at seven or eight in the evening, or as long as the light lasted. The workmen seemed intent on taking over the cottage and the studios. Arriving at dawn, they turned the radio on up loud, then proceeded to sing or whistle along with battling female vocalists, on a radio interview, intent on out-shrieking each other for that blessed top note. Saws scraped, hammers thumped, and drills screamed through plaster and wood. Occasionally, she glimpsed Drago moving amongst them, her heart leaping, as she watched him gesticulating, talking, consulting the plans, tilting that sexy tin hat over that stunning face. Why was she so attracted to him; her knees weakened, when he walked across to consult her? There was nothing she could do about it, no matter how hard she tried to distance herself from him, to appear quite unaffected by the nearness of his virile body almost touching hers. The only thing they had in common was separating the dogs, who were now desperately in love with each other. Thankfully, Lila was spayed, but that didn't stop her flirting and presenting her gorgeous tail of white silk to him. Beelzebub a good foot shorter than her, didn't stand a chance even on his hind legs, but bless him, he did try.

She sighed; it was getting ridiculous; she would lie in bed tossing and turning, imagining Drago there, those burly arms reaching out to him, lifting her close. Maybe she should date one of the men on site. Goodness knows she'd had enough invites, some quite stunning, with muscled long limbs, hair slick with sweat wielding a hammer, smiles that promised passion. The strength they used to break up boards or slam down a hammer took her breath away, if they were that strong, what would they be like in bed? Yet, however hard she tried to dismiss him; she could not control the desire welling up when he appeared.

Occasionally, they met for a cup of tea and chat over the renovations, where she tried to be distant, unaffected by those sparkling sapphire eyes. However, even as she appeared calm and composed and not the slightest interested in his innuendos, he always managed to frustrate her, filling her with longing, dammit; she wanted him in her life, in her bed.

One Tuesday, Clary slipped down to the cellar. The other week she'd discovered half a dozen huge, empty barrels, maybe they could be turned into tub seats; they would certainly give a rustic look in keeping with the cottage and studio. As she bent to examine one, she felt a pair of hands grasp her waist, lifting her off her feet. Gasping, she looked up into those dangerous blue eyes. 'Hah, caught you my beauty.

Clary didn't know whether to wallop him or kiss him, but instead pushed away from that block of amorous muscle. 'What d'you think you're doing, stop it.' Struggling, she hissed, 'let me go now.'

Immediately, he put up his hands in defeat, only for her to fall promptly on her butt. In one swift movement, he bent and picked her up, apologizing. 'Oh look I'm sorry; really, I just couldn't resist those luscious curves.' She tried to step back, as he hurriedly brushed down her jeggings, now covered with moss and grime. His voice was low, 'you're avoiding me aren't you?'

'Avoiding you? How can you ask me that after what you've just done?'

'I did what any admirer would do. Anyway, I need to talk with you.'

'Then talk,' she growled, folding her arms across her chest in defiance.

For once, she saw confusion flash across his eyes; quickly dispatched, but long enough for her to see it. So he did have some weak spots.

'Look, how about having a cuppa in the kitchen? That's innocent enough isn't?'

She bit her lip, nodding. She was lost for words, never having experienced a man like him; she sighed, trying not to look at that magnificent torso, or touch those bristling curls springing from the neck of his tee shirt. She longed to put her hands on the leather belt and pull him to her. Instead, she glowered. 'Oh alright. But just a cup of tea okay?'

'Well I can't possibly do anything else in a kitchen, could I?

Clary could not stop her grin. 'Really?'

Drago grinned back. 'Come my pet, at least we'll have a few minutes alone. She walked in front of him, then shrieked, slipping on the step. 'A mouse – God.'

He caught her in his arms, delighted to feel her arms around his neck. 'Poor little devil; he's terrified.'

'So am, I.' She grabbed his neck tighter, watching it scuttle towards the stone wall disappearing into a crevice.

Grinning, he kissed her soundly on the lips, his tongue seeking hers.

To her confusion, she moaned, as their tongues danced a salsa. Managing to regain control, she pulled away, reluctantly. What strange power did this guy have over her?

As he put her gently on her feet, he beamed. 'Can't miss an opportunity can I?'

She meant to scold him but instead tried to stifle a smile. He utterly confused her. Trying to regain her composure she stammered, 'Err, 'm glad we've met anyway; I wanted to ask you about the barrels in the cellar. I thought they could be made up to look really attractive as tub chairs.'

He raised his eyebrows, his eyes twinkling. 'Hmm – yeah. Good thinking, I'll get the lads to have a look.'

A week later, she received a note delivered in a bouquet of red roses. Surprised, she opened the note to see elegant script writing.

'I pray you will do me the honour of joining me in a picnic in the orchard?' *I hope this menu entices you.*

King Prawns in Rose Marie Sauce,
Lobster Tails in lemon
Brie and Camembert cheeses
Raspberry trifle with fresh cream
One bottle of champagne.
Come alone.
Your ardent admirer.
Drago.

Fragile brain or not, she couldn't help smiling and shocked herself by kissing the letter. She shouldn't go; he'd only try to seduce her or patronize her, and they'd end up having another spat. No, she wasn't going.

Chapter 13

Present day
Kings Prawns and Raspberry Trifle

That morning, she dressed with care, a pair of cream slim fit jeans and a red silk top to match the roses. She'd given in to that mercurial mind of hers,

Her heart beat rapidly, as she made her way through the back garden full of scented country flowers to the orchard; admiring the fresh crop of red apples. She saw him wave and walk towards her. As usual, her knees trembled; maybe she shouldn't have come, maybe she was making a bad mistake.

'Come and sit down, I expect you're hungry.'

'Yes I am actually; I've been working on quite an intricate painting, at first I just couldn't get it to come alive, but now it's working; I had to really get into the couple; they were too hard, rigid.'

'So what is it?'

'Uh, well it's Regency, a man and a woman meeting in a folly at the edge of a forest.'

'A romantic tryst?'

'Hmm could be.'

She made herself comfortable on the blanket, looking over the array of prepared dishes, and a silver ice bucket with what looked like a bottle of champagne. 'Wow this looks delicious. Did you prepare all this yourself?'

'Err no, I had some help.'

'Oh, who from?'

He frowned slightly. 'My chef. I must admit I haven't got a clue about how to prepare anything. In fact, he wrote the menu, and I copied it. Anyway come and sit down, make yourself comfortable. I brought some cushions, so you wouldn't be sitting on hard ground.'

'Err, thank you.' She bit her lip; his own chef, when he wore a tin hat and wielded a hammer?

Leaning over, he handed her a plate, 'Help yourself.' He picked up a bottle from the ice bucket. 'Champagne?' Drago looked at her full lips moist with the juice of the lobster tails. He wanted to reach over and kiss them, but held himself back. He had to take this gently. He hoped the modern-day language lessons he attended with Griffin, would help win her over. He had yet to reveal his true identity, and his aim to entice her back to his time. Engaging a tutor was difficult, as they did not wish to give away any hint of their identity. It paid off, as a struggling language student was more than pleased to help them, their explanation being they hailed from a remote village that still held all its traditions and dialect.

Clary could not resist the prawns in the Marie Rose sauce, and yet as she ate, she noticed something different about him. Whatever it was; she felt more relaxed and confident in his presence. She was enjoying his conversation, and not just his incredible body and mind wrenching eyes. Of course, she loved his humour, and basked in his admiration, but there was now a difference, one that had her puzzled, but enthralled. As she brushed off some crumbs from her jeggings, he grinned and reached over for the basket, 'Dessert. I hope you like raspberry trifle?'

'Oh yes, I love it, but it doesn't love my waistline.'

He grinned, 'You have a lovely figure, and one I would love to caress with your permission.'

She pushed him playfully on the shoulder. 'Keep your mind on the dessert.'

He looked searchingly into her eyes. 'May I ask a favour of you?'

'Well it depends on what it is.' she replied jokingly.

'Umm, we hold an open day at the Keep each year, devoted to Jane Austen. We'd like to celebrate the day of her birth but as it's in December, it's much too cold for an outdoor event, so we hold it in memory of her death, July 1817. Our members and visitors all dress up in

Regency costumes and we have a whale of a time. We sometimes finish off with a masked ball, just a small one, but it's fun.' He was proud of that modern term; he would use it again. He continued. 'You say you're just finishing a Regency style painting, and I wondered if you would demonstrate at the event, maybe give us a short lecture on the period with regard to painting, and female regency artists.' He saw fear mounting in those beautiful eyes, saw her slender figure stiffen, as she took a tight breath.

Clary shuddered inwardly. 'I can't. I'm sorry. I've … I've been through a bad time and—'

'I'm sorry; look is there any way I can help?' He took her hand, feeling the tremble.

'No – I thought I was getting over it. But the thought of facing all those people just fills me with dread.'

Drago shifted nearer, putting an arm around her shoulder. 'Look I'm here, tell me how I can help.'

She shook her head. 'I guess I came off the meds' too soon. I didn't want to keep on taking them; I need a clear head to paint.'

He held her, stroking her back lightly, soothingly.

She stuttered, 'M … Maybe … maybe, if I'm painting, I … I won't have to face too many people, but I can't give a lecture – I'd die.'

'How about just demonstrating then? It could be a good way of you getting back in the saddle, as they say.'

She groaned 'I don't know. I thought I was getting over it, but the very thought of demonstrating and talking to lots of people fills me with dread.' she gritted her teeth, 'But I've got to pluck up the courage; I've got to fight it. The Centre will be ready soon. Oh God, have I taken on too much? I was too optimistic.'

'You could have a try, and if you don't like it, just make an excuse and leave.'

'I can't do that, a panic attack doesn't let you move or speak; it just comes out of nowhere and grips you. You can't breathe hardly; you go as still and silent as a block of ice, whilst your heart is hammering so hard it seems it's going to tear its way out of your chest.'

He remained silent, not trying to push her or coerce her into anything she wasn't prepared to do. Maybe she trusted him enough to unfold to him, but that was a vain hope; she was only just accepting his company. There was no way he could tell her he knew of her tragedy, knew she fought her way back to life.

She picked at the grass. 'I know I appear confident, but it was fine with just you and Griffin; I could be myself and not put on an act, and I didn't have much to do with the workmen, so it was okay. But this – no – it's too big.' She choked back tears, 'I thought I'd beaten it.' She wrenched her hands, 'I – I've got to fight it; I've been alone too long. I mustn't lose heart'

'Well you can have mine; I've fallen in love with you Clary.' He held her tightly in his arms, as if instilling his strength into her, guarding her against the world. In that instant, he knew he loved her, more than anything, he wanted to take away pain, to see her jade eyes glittering with joy and confidence. He realized he'd loved her from the day he saw her painting on the dunes, from the day she told him to go to hell. No woman had ever confronted him before.

He'd been struck with admiration, the love settling beneath his incredulity. He knew she wasn't ready to respond to his declaration, not yet, but he was determined to win her.

Gently tipping up her chin, he kissed her softly on the lips; looking deep into those jade eyes, drowning in sadness. 'You're never alone, such as I am, you've got me. And we're going to find a way sweetheart – find a way.' He shocked himself; he'd hadn't set out that afternoon to declare his love. Oh yes, he was deeply attracted to her, but now he felt a powerful flush of love stinging every nerve and pump every blood vessel in his body; he loved her fiercely. He would do anything to protect her, anything. And he would find a way for her to demonstrate her incredible talent.

Clary bit her lip; she knew she was deeply attracted to him despite their differences and spats; they were drawn to each other, and had been from their very first meeting on the beach. 'I … I need time Drago; it's just….' Her voice trailed away as guilt flooded through her. How could she be so shallow as to declare her love for this incredible, dominant, frustrating man with the shadow of horrific deaths hanging over her?

'Sweetheart, I will wait. I know it's too soon, and I don't want to rush you. However, know this….' He paused, a mischievous grin lightening his face. 'I will win you.'

Chapter 14
Present day
A Regency affair.

Celia arranged the ringlets to fall either side of Clary's delicate features, catching the rest of her thick chestnut hair into tousled curls on the crown of her head. Deftly she pulled down some stray tendrils to whisper down her slender neck. She looked into the mirror at her sister. 'You look lovely Clary. Now all you need is the costume.'

Clary managed a smile, she still hadn't told her sister of Drago's declaration of love. It would arouse too much guilt, and too many memories, memories that tormented them both. She heard a knock on the front door. 'That must be it.' Her heart thudded, 'I hope it's going to fit.'

Carrying the box up to the bedroom, Celia put it on the bed. 'Now let's have a look. It's rather romantic, a man choosing a dress for you, but you should have tried it on before he had it made.'

'He said he wanted it to be a surprise.'

'Well he didn't have much time.'

'Oh the dress was already made; it just needed adjusting here and there. He said it was an authentic one made in 1812.'

Shocked, Celia raised her eyebrows, 'Good grief, that means it's nearly two hundred years old. I'm frightened to open it.'

Clary held her breath as they raised the lid, and took out the tissue paper. Gently retrieving the dress, Clary held it up. 'Oh gosh, it's lovely.'

Celia stood back admiring it. It just so beautiful, satin and net, and the green goes with your eyes. Gingerly Clary put it on, and turned for Celia to button up dozens of tiny buttons.

Stepping back, she went to the mirror. 'Oh no, it's too low; I can't wear it like that.'

'Well they did in those days; the bosom was supposed to be on show. Most women just about hid their nipples.' Celia fished around in the box and pulled out a triangle of lace. 'Hah, I think this is a fischu; they used them to cover up, if that's what the lady wanted; few did though.'

Clary frowned, fumbling around until she had it in place. 'That's better; I don't want to look like a light skirt as they called them. I want to go unnoticed.

'Ladies did wear a very low décolletage Clary believe me. I have read most of the books on Regency fashion in the library, and this one is quite modest.'

'Huh,' Clary twirled around. 'I do like the way the gown falls in folds from the chest – high empire line. The puffed sleeves are pretty, and the lace is lovely.'

'Yes, yes it called Valenciennes and look at the ruffles of lace on the hem, with tiny cream silk roses. But look; there's a gold embroidered panel, you attach it to hang under the bosom from the sides to show off the satin and net dress.'

Clary pulled out some satin slippers holding them up to the light. 'Look at these, they're actually embroidered with green gemstones and sequins.'

Once dressed, Clary took up the elbow length gloves and pulled them on for effect. 'It's all very dressy, but Drago said that people will turn up dressed already for the masquerade ball, as some may not have a change of costume.'

'Good idea,' Celia got out her cell. 'I've got to take a shot of it, its glorious Clary.'

Clary went to the box, and pulled out a brown packet; opening it, she saw a note and a gold laced mask. She read the note out loud. 'This is to be worn to the fete.' She put it on, and turned toward the mirror. 'Gosh, I've never worn a mask; I like it.' She pirouetted around the room, 'It's going to be interesting to paint people in masks.'

'Will you be wearing one?' Celia asked.

'Oh yes, it was Drago's idea, he said it would be such a novel event and entertaining for people to have sketches of them dressed for a masquerade.'

Celia went to the window, 'Griffin said he was sending me an outfit, but it hasn't arrived yet. Like you, he only wanted my size, and said to leave the rest to him.'

'There you are Ceci; he wants to surprise you. He's fallen for you; he can't keep his eyes off you.'

'Oh no, I mean we've only just met.'

Well, we've all been thrown together one way and another for four weeks now, so that's time enough.'

'Yes, I suppose so.' Ceci turned to Clary, her cheeks flushing a bright peach. 'I can't stop thinking about him; he's quite a dish.'

She caught her breath, as Drago met her at the gates of the Keep, he was not wearing a mask, but then neither was she. To her surprise, she felt confident enough to do without, after all she was not doing the lecture. As he walked towards her, she felt her whole body tingle. He looked glorious, so elegant with those wide shoulders and chiselled features, as if he'd stepped out of a drama series. His hair was dressed a la Brutus Regency style, a green emerald pin nestling in his white cravat in a waterfall of folds. His wide shoulders filled out a superfine tailcoat with squared cut away in front, over a silver and gold waistcoat. The black breeches showed off his muscled thighs, and white stockings enhanced the toned calf muscles, finishing off with highly polished buckled shoes.

She saw the love in his eyes, as he said, 'My lady, you light up the day with your dazzling beauty. The dress fits you perfectly, and the green satin shows off the luxuriant chestnut hair, tis fairly blazing in the sun.'

She didn't know quite what to say to such effusive compliments, so she smiled jerkily.

As they gazed down at an herbaceous border of country flowers, he said, 'So how do you feel my love?'

'Err, better, I'm actually looking forward to doing some sketches; the masquerade was such an incredible idea. I feel so much better now.' She felt relaxed, realizing that he would not push her to commit to him.

He hugged her close. 'Uh – uh inappropriate behaviour on a Jane Austen day, in her time, we shouldn't be hugging, unless we are married, tis the height of impropriety. But I may offer you my arm to walk. He proceeded to show her around the magnificent lawns leading down to a lake glittering in the distance. The centre piece of the main garden was a fountain in a circle of carved stones with an occasional statue of a nymph in Greek or Roman style.

Tents were erected housing a second-hand bookshop, and a dress shop exhibiting antique Regency memorabilia for sale, whilst others displayed shoes from the era, with dresses, pelisses, shawls, hats and underwear.

Clary was mesmerized with the whole scene, as people strolled around with lace parasols, dressed in the costumes of the long ago era. Some wore the masks; others went without. She particularly admired some of the bonnets made of silks, velvets, and straw, festooned with tiny rosebuds or silken bows; a few of the older matrons wore lace mob caps or headdresses made of a silk panel from which sprung two or three ostrich feathers.

After an hour, Drago led her to a quiet corner on the edge of the lawns where stood a table and chair, and on which lay her sketch book, pencils, a quill pen and a little crystal inkwell were to hand if she so wished. She looked around to see some people forming a queue.

'Hmm, you've caught their interest.' Drago murmured.

Clary looked up into those haunting blue eyes, the double black eyelashes. She took a breath feeling surge of confident energy fill her being. She really wanted to sketch these people; capture the aura of the bygone era. She beamed up at him, 'D'you know? I'm okay. I'm looking forward to sketching them. It was just the anticipation I suppose.'

It was a day she would remember, the day she fell in love with Drago, his quaintness, his love of Regency and history. She'd heard of a soul mate, but never realised until today, there was such a thing. He gave her love, strength, and compassion, but also his fair share of irritating ways, but all in all, she loved him for his strengths and his weaknesses. But now was not the time or place to tell him. It would keep for a more intimate moment.

Yet her peace did not last long. She turned to greet the next subject only to feel a shudder wrack her body. He was tall, burly, of middling age, with a long bulbous nose and small narrow eyes under bushy red eyebrows, his thin red hair captured under a black tricorn hat. For some reason, she felt threatened, yet she steadied herself. Why let some strange looking individual spoil it? She waited whilst he brushed invisible specks off his clothes then fiddled with his cravat. He must be a man of means, as he sported a large sapphire stick pin. She glanced around for Drago, but he was nowhere to be seen.

Sighing, she politely waved him to a chair and began sketching. His manner was offensive, as he leered at her, his tone patronizing. 'How does a filly like yerself, be gifted with such talent. I am interested ter see what ye make of me lady. I must admit I've seen some of the sketches and am impressed. Little chit like yerself, can't seem possible.'

She nodded, realizing he spoke in the same manner as Drago, maybe they came from the same village wherever that was. Her pencil flew over the thick paper as she sketched him, disliking him more by the moment. However, when she offered the finished work to him, he beamed, showing yellow cracked teeth. 'Well done. I could put you to good use. You would do well by me.' He gave a sweeping bow, flourishing his tricorn hat. Throwing some coins on the table, he swaggered away.

Clary grimaced, *put her to good use?* What on earth was he talking about? There was something menacing about him, she'd have to ask Drago if he knew him.

Chapter 15
Present day
A table for two

Clary checked herself in the mirror, feeling a rush of excitement, tonight was their first date in over ten days, and Drago told her he had a surprise for her, an important surprise. The Centre had taken over their lives; all four of them working body wracking hours to finish the renovations. Funds were running low, and they needed to recoup let alone make any profit.

Drago met her at odd times, in shadowy corners, where he kissed her senseless, his hands over her curves leaving her gasping, her body burning with desire. Celia saw little of Griffin as she was hard at work promoting and advertising the opening day, stapling posters to bill boards, lamp posts, bus shelters, and the village shop and then traveling to Arundel, the medieval castle town, now burgeoning with tourists from every corner of the world. She coaxed shops, pubs, restaurants, even the local library and post office, to show the posters and leaflets, and to her delight, managed to get the galleries on board, after all it was a great way for cross promotion, where both would benefit.

The days stretched into the early hours of the morning, as Clary sat with Celia at their PCs advertising the opening day and running promotions on Facebook, Twitter and their websites and blogs. However, for tonight, they all agreed; it was time to pause, to recover some sanity.

Clary stepped carefully over the cobblestone pavement; she'd taken pains to look attractive, but she'd still understated it. She hadn't worn the false eyelashes, as Celia suggested, using only a violet eye shadow, the lightest touch of pencil outlining her eyes, and a hint of rose blusher over her high cheekbones. She put on a wine-red lipstick and grimaced, wiping it off; a dusky rose would go better with the violet eye shadow. She pulled up the strap of her modest silk white top finished off with tiny seed pearls spilling down the centre panel. Celia talked her into it earlier, insisting that they go shopping. Clary had fallen into wearing cotton tops and jeggings, but as her sister showed her the latest mini-skirt, she shook her head; it would only just cover her bottom, until she bent over of course. How on earth was she supposed to sit or cross her legs without bringing him to the boil? Besides, he'd see the scars on her upper thigh. They'd faded with time, but they were still visible. She obviously couldn't wear knickers; they'd be longer than her skirt, and she couldn't wear a thong that would have been a complete come on. She settled for a clinging skirt to her knees. Unwittingly, she sprayed some exotic perfume between her thighs, something she'd always done for … Theo. She took a breath, Theo? Why? Why did you do it? Why did you destroy our lives? Her thoughts raced to Drago, and the evening ahead. She must think only of that, of Drago and a dinner for two – maybe she would tell him then, tell him she loved him with all her heart.

Waving to a delighted Celia, who almost skipped away to Griffin, Clary saw Drago's hunky figure just outside the mullioned windows of the pub, the old-fashioned glass bulbs giving a satanic sheen to his dark locks. She clutched her sequined purse and then took a step forward, only to go plunging to the pavement, yet even before her head crashed into the pebble stones Drago caught her, lifting her up in his arms.

'Well, well,' he grunted, kissing her on the cheek. 'What a pleasure, an armful of silks and exotic perfume.' He couldn't ignore the skirt riding up long legs, the slim thighs, and the glimpse of a lacy red thong. Panting, trying to look elegant with her skirt riding up her bottom, her legs splayed in the most inelegant way, she squirmed in his arms. 'Put me down – put me down.'

Gently, he let her slip to the pavement through his large hands, skimming over the curve of her bosom, over the seed pearls and down to a slit skirt that had his eyes working overtime. He frowned seeing a rather vicious scar on her upper thigh, but for the fall, he wouldn't have been aware of it, no wonder she always wore jeggings or long skirts. Was it the work of that devilish fiancé? He'd like to throttle him. 'Hmm, six-inch heels, what is it with you women, couldn't you wear something a little less dangerous?'

'I hardly think trainers would go with the outfit.'

'My apologies dear maiden. I did not mean to be rude, it's just I'm used to women wearing silk slippers.'

'Oh really, and what planet have you come from then?'

Drago clenched his fist; he'd done it again; he'd got confused with the regency slippers' worn by women in the Regency era. 'Err what I meant was, you are tall and so slim you could take a short heel. After all, you come up to my chin in flats.'

'What are you gabbling on about?' Clary looked up at him and giggled. She couldn't help it; he looked quite puzzled.

'Umm, just trying to soothe your ruffled feathers, my chick.'

Clary raised her eyebrows; this guy really did come from some antiquated village on the edge of nowhere. 'Look, thank you for catching me, I would have had a nasty fall without you.' She looked at the strong muscles filling out the silver grey leather jacket, his long legs and strong thighs straining the chino jeans. He was a dish, even if he was antiquated. He looked down at her with those sapphire eyes, the long double eyelashes. Her heart filled with feelings threatening to overwhelm her, she must tell him tonight. God he was so handsome.

He stopped just before the door of the pub, and cupped her chin in his strong hand. 'I would never forgive myself if anything happened to you in my company. I'm here to protect you, and that I will do, with my life.'

'Your life?' That's a bit dramatic.'

'How so, I would not think twice about calling out any cur that dishonoured you in any way.'

'Call them out?'

'What d'you mean? Call them out?'

Drago paused, beetling his brows as if searching for the right words. Now his heart was pounding; he'd really put his foot in it.

Chapter 16
Present day
Kill for love

Drago growled, 'give them a bloody good hiding. Like I said, you've got me now and no-one will touch you.'

Clary was lost for words, and yet felt safe with him and strange to say, cherished, something she'd never experienced before, not even from Theo. It was a weird feeling, for Clary realized he would do just that; fight to the death for her. It was as if they'd travelled back to Arthurian times when the knight protected his lady, or the Regency era, where the lord duelled to the death with anyone who slighted his lady. He was so sincere, and in that second, strength surged through her, giving her belief in the good to come. She wanted to grab him, hold him fast, kiss those chiselled lips but instead, she squeezed his hand affectionately.

As they approached the table, he murmured, 'I ordered a private table near the window.'

He must have sensed her hesitation as he said, 'Don't you like that?'

'Not really, I don't like passers-by looking in as I eat.'

'Ah well, that's easily remedied. 'He beckoned the waiter, who came over, smiling obligingly.

'Could you find us a table at the back please; I see there's one over there in the corner.'

'Of course sir, we're not too busy tonight. I'll just prepare the table for you. Would you care to take a drink by the bar; I'll only be a few minutes?"

'That is very sweet of you.' Clary murmured, as they went to the bar.

He beamed, putting his hand on the small of her back 'I am here to serve your every whim.'

'And what of your whims?'

'Well we won't go into that now sweetheart; I think that's more for the midnight hours. But, I am planning to take you back to the dunes, to moonlight and soft hot sands. '

'Oh really?'

'Yes, my intentions are to seduce you. Something I've been planning since I first saw you.'

'You know; I was so surprised to see you come into the Centre that day. You didn't say a word about it at the beach.'

'I was too interested in you and your painting.'

'So you really are interested in art. You said you weren't an artist.'

'It's a hobby of mine; my main interest is in Sweet Mead Keep and the village. It is a beautiful spot, and I like to keep it that way, you know, protect it from the invasion of those brutal renovators. Trouble is they come along, pull down the thatched roofs, get rid of the country gardens and lay a concrete drive for their cars and so on. The days of horse and carriages are long gone, but at least we can keep the authenticity of the village.'

'Right down to the village pump in the square?'

'Oh yes and the church as well. Some bright spark wanted to tear the guts out of that, and modernize it with pine and plastic. They were going to do away with the pews and boxes for the gentry, not that there're any gentry anymore.'

'I'm glad you're taking care to protect the character of the village. I know I fell in love with it as soon as I saw it in the leaflet and even more so when I saw it on Google. Now I never want to leave.'

'Hmm and I fell in love with you, as soon as I saw you.'

Clary blushed, and leaning over kissed him on the cheek.

She felt his eyes on her, then his hand covering hers. 'I meant what I said the other week; I fell in love with you within minutes of meeting you. At first, I was just dazzled, by your beauty, by that straw hat and russet curls, the flimsy white dress, but then I talked with you, and fell in love for the very first time in my life.'

Clary felt her eyes fill up. 'I … I love you too Drago, so much. I wanted to say it at the picnic, but I was overwhelmed.'

'I know sweetheart, but now you've said it, and I am the happiest man on the planet. Hah, there's the waiter beckoning, come on, I'm hungry aren't you?'

'Oh yes.' She wasn't thinking about food; she was hungry for him. She bit her lip and took up the menu. He watched, taking in the silky softness of her pale ivory skin, the swanlike neck and elegant slope of her shoulders, set off by that slip of silk serving as her top, the centrepiece, a tiny cascade of pearls over her full breasts. Her perfume, deep tones of lilies and wine, and a sensuous underlying musk, almost incensed him,

Her full lips invited him, glistening with the juices from the smoked salmon it took him back to the picnic, and his urge to ravish her. He leant over, and filled her glass, the red wine reminding him of her lacy thong. Their talk melted from bantering exchange to the talk of lovers probing for secrets. As the waiter served coffee, Drago peeled the golden paper off the chocolate mint, then popping it onto her tongue, wanted to plunder her mouth. Fascinated, simmering with desire, Drago ordered the coffee and took her hand; he wanted her, her hand, her breast, her most secret parts.

As he took her arm to lead her from the restaurant, she shivered at the touch of his fingers on her skin. 'My car's not far from here, I thought we could go to the beach, embrace the night, look at the moon...' he left the rest hanging.

Clary shivered, was it time for her, time to let go, time to commit to love?

Just as they turned the corner, Drago caught sight of two men sitting at a bar across the road, deep in conversation. Luckily, they hadn't noticed him. He walked on quickly, his face tightening in fury. Clary had to almost run to keep up with him. 'What's wrong?'

Nothing, just thought I saw someone I knew.'

'Who?'

'Someone who needs killing.'

'What? Drago, that's not very nice.'

'Hmm, neither is he.'

So who is he?'

'Nobody you would like to know.' He would have to keep a close eye on her now. He could not warn her, could not tell her she was in danger, not yet, not until he explained everything. And that was going to be damned difficult.

'Oh, so you'd call him out then?'

'Yes. If he comes anywhere near you, I will kill him.'

'So haven't I got a right to know?' She paused frowning. 'You know that reminds me, I saw a guy at the Regency fete; he was awful, threatening. He said the most peculiar thing.'

Drago bristled, 'What? Tell me?'

'Well after I finished his sketch, he said I would be of great value to him.'

The blood pounded in Drago's head; his eyes narrowed, his tone icy. 'Describe him.'

'Well he was tall, large with thin red hair, dressed up of course.'

'Anything else?'

'No, not really except he had an incredible large sapphire pin in his cravat; it looked like the real McCoy.'

Drago tensed; it was Stennet. 'Damn – damn. I wish to God you'd told me.'

Seeing her alarm, he took her hand and kissed her fingers. 'Forgive me, it's just I get bloody angry if I think anyone's upset you.' He glowered then hugged her close, almost lifting her off her feet. He knew as they spoke, Griffin was disclosing all to Celia, if they wanted to tempt Clary to 1812, they had to persuade her. She was their only leverage. 'Right, Griffin's tied up with Celia at the moment, so we'll let them finish their meal.'

'So it's that serious?'

'Yes, but enough, let's enjoy the rest of the night.'

Chapter 17
Present day
Seduction

She felt the goose bumps rising on her arms as his hand came over to stroke her knee. As they drove through the forest to the beach, the trees formed intricately carved arches stretching through charcoal sketched clouds. They reminded her of walking through a cathedral in France. Pulling into a gravelled clearing behind a low stone wall, he took a blanket from the car before walking around to open her door. 'Hah, the delightful, but impossible six-inch heels. You'll ruin them and you can't go barefoot over the gravel, so here goes.' He bent down and dropped the blanket in her lap before scooping her up in his arms. Despite her laughing protests, he lifted her over the wall, and on to the dunes.

As he put her down, her feet slipped on the soft silky sands beneath her feet. Taking her hand, he led her through the secrets of the ancient dunes, until they reached a bower surround with fresh smelling ferns, sweet flowers and the sea. He whipped out a blanket from under his arm. She helped him smooth it down and then turned to gaze at the sea. 'Look, the moon's cast a silver stream across the sea.'

'Enchanting.' He stood beside her, aware of her scent wafting up, the sweetness of lilies and that dusky undertone of musk. Gently, he turned her to him, his lips softly seeking hers. Clary's heart pounded, she wanted him, wanted to respond, but she pulled back. Sensing her need and her fear, he whispered, 'Come lie with me, goddess of the night.'

She closed her eyes. 'You are such a sweet poet.' She allowed him to pull her down onto the softness of the blanket, feeling a fern brush against her legs and then her face. She moved into the warmth of his body releasing her fear, her guilt, feeling only the rapid beat of her heart, desire rippling from her forehead to her toes. He pulled her to him, as he nuzzled her neck, his lips finding hers, his tongue questing, entering, flicking over the inside of her cheek. She arched to him as their tongues danced towards desire. She knew he was seducing her, and she welcomed it. For one painful moment, she thought of Theo and then banished it. He could not hurt her now, not now.

His kisses moved from her neck to her swelling breasts, as he gently slipped the silk strap from her shoulder to find a lacy bra, which he deftly unclipped and threw to one side. At least, he didn't have the bother of laces and whale bones with the twenty-first century woman, or voluminous skirts to manoeuvre, before the woman lost interest. Finding the nipples nestling in large dark pink aureoles, he kissed, sucked then gently pulled the engorged nipple into his mouth, until she moaned, 'Yes, oh … yes,' her legs coming over to his thighs.

He rose up on his elbows gazing down at her lovely face bathed in moonlight, those strings tugging at his heart, 'My love, my sweet love.' His hands massaged her flat stomach, fingers pushing down the slinky skirt, pulling it off and casting it aside. His kiss now went deeper, plundering her mouth, tasting the wine and the honey. As she clung to his shoulders, her nails softly digging, he moved down to that small triangle of chestnut curls, feeling her legs tremble, as he buried his face in her warmth, his fingers pushing apart the velvet petals, revelling in the honeyed wetness, his tongue seeking entrance to the divine. She gasped, and arched her body, lifting her legs high wrapping them around him, as her fingers clutched the dark wavy locks at his neck. Moaning, she raised her head nibbling his shoulders, her hands pulling at his jeans. Pausing, he unclipped his belt and tore down the zip, pushing the jeans from muscled legs and pulling out a condom. She knew now there was no turning back; she wanted him, needed him, and they would not stop. She panted, pushing up at his tee shirt until he rose, swiftly tearing it off. Growling, he collapsed once more on her body, arching to him, his hand now on her wetness, her desire.

As he cupped her mound, cupping her mound, she felt his finger enter, moving rhythmically, then inserting another, pushed deeper and harder until she cried out, fighting for breath, her body tensed. He found her swollen nub massaging and rubbing, until she tensed, her hands fisting, as her body exploded in a thousand lights.

Falling limply back, she breathed deeply, as he rose above her, his rod iron hard, his teeth clenching, as he found her. He paused then plunged, penetrating, filling her, his kisses on her neck and chest, holding her tight and close, as he drummed deeper and faster. She screamed out, as he pumped, driving them over the edge into an oblivion of exquisite ecstasy.

The drive home was a whirl of sensations and future dreams. He looked down at her head on his shoulder, the moon casting a golden sheen on her hair. Until now, love or sex rather was made to order, a superb mistress who obeyed his rules, but this young lady would have none of that, she was a modern woman of the twenty-first century, and by god knew what she wanted from love. He grimaced. He thought he'd seduced her, but now it was she who did the seducing, unwittingly maybe.

He breathed deeply; he decided he had to come clean, to confess all, there was no way he could deceive her into going through the portal with him to 1812. He would have to be as open as she. He looked for a clearing in the forest.

'Clarissa, we have to talk.'

Chapter 18
Present day
Revelations

His words resounded through her head; they sounded ominous. 'We have to talk.' Clary's stomach lurched, was he regretting it? Was he going to tell her it couldn't go on? Mutely, she sat back, her heart pounding. Her self-confidence was so low. She immediately thought the worse. When she first met Theo, she was an optimistic sociable girl, with a bright future beckoning. Now she was a wreck with dashed hopes and broken dreams. She clenched her hands; she didn't want it to end, not now; she'd given herself to him, surely he just couldn't.... She bit back her words; she must be quiet, wait, but she wanted to cry out, ask him, needing to end her fear right now.

He took her hand, and felt it trembling. His throat dried up, making it difficult to swallow. Deuce, he'd do anything for a brandy. 'Clarissa, just remember I love you; I've loved you from the first moment I saw you. You were a vision of loveliness to me, and I knew then; I couldn't let you go.'

Clary gulped back a sob, and bit her knuckles. Seeing her distress, he gathered her into his arms. 'Sweetheart, what's wrong?' Is it me?'

'Oh no, no, it's just I thought ... thought you didn't—'

'Love you?' He held her close, the stubble on his chin scratching against her forehead. 'Never – never think that. I love you with all my heart. I just hope you will love me after I reveal....'

She waited. 'What – tell me; what?'

'Who I am.' He rushed on before she could interrupt. 'Clary, I never thought I'd fall in love, or that you would love me.'

'Why? Why doubt it?'

He bit his lip, 'I wonder how deep love can be, how strong? You don't know me Clary, and now I am going to break my heart and yours.'

She took a juddering breath, 'Why?'

'Clary I am not who you think I am; I'm a stranger, a stranger to your century. I....' he paused 'I come from the past?'

Shaken, Clary stared at him; he wasn't joking, but at least he wasn't breaking her heart. 'What d'you mean, another century?'

'I am from the past.'

'You mean a time – a time traveller?'

'Yes.'

Clary nearly bit through her lip. 'But – oh my God! You can't be.'

'It's true, so is Griffin.' His voice gathered strength, as he realized she was not shutting him out. 'I head a group who strive to preserve the Keep and the hamlet.'

'So you're old?'

'Oh no, the time travel does not age me. I'm actually from the Regency era, my time back there is 1812. For centuries, our family owned the Keep and the estate, so we have sole charge of it. However, over time, it became dilapidated and the hamlet almost deserted, all fell into rack and ruin until they were abandoned. But then, this time travel happened by accident. When I was an infant, my father was having a folly built, a la Greque some eight years ago, when he unearthed a tunnel leading to the Keep, and others branching off. He put some of our agricultural labourers and estate workers to clearing out the tunnels, some of which led to the Keep; he had to deter scoundrels and thieves bent of acquiring the family silver and jewels. As he cleared the tunnel leading to the Keep, he accidentally discovered a time portal.' As he talked, his voice strengthened; she heard the relief in his voice, as he revealed his incredible secret.

'You can imagine the shock when he stepped through a niche and climbed the stairs only to find such strange surroundings, a ruin in fact. As you can imagine he thought he'd gone mad, to say the least. He quickly returned to the dungeon and the niche. It was Partridge's uncle who took over and stepped back into the niche. He reappeared minutes later, and explained that the Keep they'd left was exactly the same, only years later. My father realized they'd stepped into a different world and time. Gradually, he learnt how to control it and formed a group dedicated to the portal and our hamlet. On his demise, I took over.'

'So the hamlet was built before that?'

'Oh yes, it is a medieval hamlet really, rebuilt in 1790 in the same clearing in the forest, as was the way of our ancestors. Originally, it consisted of one long hall within a stockade, with small one room huts scattered around it. It was the last one still intact from our time. We realized we must preserve it.'

'So where do you live then, here or in 1812?'

'I go to and fro, I am telling you all this, because I want you to know me, accept me.'

'So Mr. Partridge, Sonya, they're?'

'Yes, everyone here also lives in 1812, in the hamlet but mostly in the Keep. We vowed to renovate the hamlet and Keep to how it was in the Regency era, mainly because we do not know if we change anything, it could upset the time travel. The people come and go as they please, but they do not venture outside of the Keep or the hamlet unless it is absolutely necessary. Partridge and Miss Timmins do work in Arundel at various intervals, to keep account of anyone wishing to live in the hamlet. As the hamlet is part of my estate, it is not questioned. To safeguard our secret, we do not allow anyone to rent a cottage here, neither do we allow caravans, tents and so on. So now, changing the subject, with regard to your paintings, I have watched you for some time. T'was I, who instructed Partridge to send you the leaflet. If you hadn't responded, we would have visited you, tried to persuade you.'

'And what if I said no?'

'Then it was our loss. We would not have forced you, if that's what you mean.'

Shocked, Clary reached out to take his hand. He prayed to God she would accept the bizarre situation.

'There's more Clary. If you do travel with me, you have to know what kind of scoundrel I've been. People will talk you see. In 1812, gossip is an important factor in peoples' lives, some of the *ton* live for scandal.'

Clary looked at him, her eyes wide, 'Scoundrel? You?'

'Yes, it's just, I've never trusted ... couldn't...I 'm a rake, Clary with a sordid reputation as a rakehell. I've left a trail of broken hearts behind me. I'm not cruel believe me; it's just I never wanted marriage or children – could never trust a woman; they only leave you; they've always left in the end. Best I cut it before someone gets hurt.'

'You – you mean? Tell me Drago, who's hurt you?' Clary felt her heart pounding, still shocked, but ready to take away his pain. She loved him, time traveller or not. She couldn't stop loving him because his life was different. He was still Drago to her, strange, dominant, frustrating and loveable Drago.' His hand gripped hers, 'I feel stupid, a grown man talking like this.'

'Why shouldn't you? Tell me. Who hurt you?'

His jaw clenched, as he gripped her hand. 'I – I lost my mother when I was two years old. I don't really remember her. I have some hazy flashes of a woman's face, a smile, fair curls, a voice so faint I can hardly hear it.' he paused, nervously clearing his throat. 'My father married again; I do have a vague memory of her, dark hair and a smile, always a smile. I remember her singing to me, but she too died giving birth to my step-brother. Then my father brought home another wife....'

'Go on Drago. I'm listening.'

His voice dropped to a whisper, 'she eloped, ran off in the night, now I do remember her; she crept into my room and held me in her arms. She was ... she was crying, sobbing, and told me she loved me, but ... she had to go. Asked me to forgive her. I was too young to understand, so I just held her hand – pleaded with her not to go, to take me with her.' His voice broke, 'She ... she said she would never forget me. I never saw or heard from her again.' He turned to her, the tears brimming and tumbling down that proud, handsome face.

Clary felt her own tears sting her eyes, when he reached over, and took her in his arms, his head lowered to her. She felt the heave of those broad shoulders; he'd been carrying this grief too long, too long for anyone to bear. 'Oh Drago, I love you so much, and I will never leave you, never.' As she stroked his dark wavy hair, she whispered, 'Just remember, whatever happens; I love you and always will.'

The corners of his mouth twitched, hinting at a smile. 'However, I must admit my plan was to seduce you, but instead my love; you seduced me.'

'But how? I never flirted with you?'

'You didn't have to; I knew all about you; one look at you sitting on the sands, and I was smitten.'

Clary felt her body go cold, the goose bumps rising on her arms. 'So – so you know about—'

'Theo? Yes, my love, I know.'

'You – you don't hate me?' She crossed her arms across her chest, hunching over; she looked lost and forlorn.

His heart went out to her. 'How could I ever hate you Clary? I love you'

'He – he shot us – shot my ... her voice broke. 'Shot my dad and ...' she couldn't talk. Gathering her up in his arms, he kissed the top of her head. 'I pray that I can help you.'

She talked, her face pressed into his shoulder; she could smell the male musk, feel his sweat. 'He shot my father, my mother, then ... then me; he missed and shot my leg. I crawled over to them, Mum, was still alive, but struggling to breathe, the blood - blood. But then she lay still. They were both ... I wanted to – go – die with them.' She buried her head in her hands; her words almost cut off. 'I told him I didn't love him –couldn't. He threatened me, said he would go after them. I didn't believe him.' she sobbed her head hung low. 'I killed them didn't I?' she struggled in his arms trying to get away, her delicate hand on the car door. 'Let me go.'

'Never. I'll never let you go.' Drago felt his muscles bunching, as she struggled, she was strong for such a slender girl. Her hair muffled her voice. 'I was a coward – shouldn't have run to my parents.' He was raging, followed me. I shouldn't have told him I wanted to break it off – didn't ... didn't love him. I was selfish. I should have gone away, somewhere he couldn't find me.'

'How could you have known, dearest, don't punish yourself.'

Her breath came in ragged gasps. 'Should have lied ... told him I loved him, lied my head off, but...'

'You didn't know, how could you?'

'He was getting worse, jealous, threats – started to ... hit me. I should have known.' Clary went limp in his arms and cried, her tears dripping through his tee shirt.

He put his lips to her forehead, murmuring, 'It was the drugs, the crack, not you, never you.'

She lay quietly, sobbing in his arms. He glanced through the window to see the outline of black trees against a violet sky, their inky fingers clutching at purple clouds; some seemed to reach past the stars.

He lifted her chin, rubbing away her streaked eyeliner with his thumb. 'Marry me Clary.'

She lifted her head. 'Marry you? You're just sorry—'

'Never sorry, I love you, never loved a woman before; never thought I would; didn't think you'd even look my way, all the women in my life left me.'

'God, you're so handsome Drago, and so nice. Why wouldn't any woman love you?'

'All the ones that mattered, that I loved left me, but you've given me faith Clary. Faith – trust, strange feelings. I pray I can get used to them. I came to this century to find an artist; instead, I found the love of my life, my future wife.'

'But shouldn't we —'

'Wait? Don't do that to me Clary, my ego's fragile enough as it is.'

Clary bit her lip; she'd always seen him as arrogant, bombastic, charming – frustrating.'

'Then yes, Drago, yes, yes, yes. I will marry you.'

He hugged her close, and took a small blue leather box from his pocket. 'The surprise.' He presented it to her. 'You've just made feel a king amongst men, I could rule the world with you at my side.'

Clary's fingers trembled, as she opened it, then bit her lip. 'Oh Drago, a ruby?' the gem glowed in the shafts of moonlight. 'It's beautiful. I love it.'

'It was my great grandmother's, then my grandmother, my mother and now....'

Chapter 19
Present day
Running to the past

Arriving at the cottage, he drew up behind a sleek Peugeot. 'Griffin's here.'

Clary pulled down the vanity mirror, rubbing her eyes; she flicked back a tangle of hair. 'Gosh, I look a mess.'

Drago reached for tissues from a box on the back seat. 'Here take these.'

Clary stepped into the lounge, to Lila's excited barks and to see Griffin and Celia hurriedly pull apart. 'Oh we didn't hear the car.' Celia said, not realizing her top was undone.

Clary signalled behind Drago, whereupon Celia blushed and buttoned it up. Drago didn't bat an eyelid.

'I've explained it all to Celia; there are no secrets here.' Griffin said, hugging her.

Drago nodded, then turned to Clary. 'D'you mind if I have a word with Griffin in the kitchen?'

'No – no, go ahead.' She smiled stroking an ecstatic Lila, now rolling on her back to have her stomach rubbed

Once in the privacy of the kitchen he muttered. 'I saw Baron Stennet and Racknape tonight; they're here old chap. We've got to sort them out. If they lay a finger on Clary, I'll murder them.'

'D'you think they're after her?'

'Definitely and Celia. She's leverage.' Drago paced the floor, 'So first, we get body guards here, tonight. We can't leave the girls alone. Then we go looking. However, now we've got to tell them.'

Walking through the door, he cleared his throat. 'Err would you both like to sit down; I'm afraid there is something we have to tell you. We were going to wait awhile, but now it's serious.'

Startled, Clary sat down on the settee with Ceci.

Drago, gritted his teeth, 'First Ceci, Griffin tells me he's explained it all, so you'll understand.' He paused, 'D'you think we could get a drink? I need one I don't know about you?'

Clary sprang up and went to the drinks' cabinet, getting out glasses, brandy and wine. Ceci handed them around and sat down.

Drago sipped at his brandy, feeling the alcohol almost scorch his throat. 'We planned to invite you back with us to 1812, to work on some old damaged portraits. Portrait artists in our time are rare; Gainsborough, Reynolds and their cronies are fully employed so we're left with the dregs.' He paused, looking at Clary. 'So we scoured this time to find artists we could take back with us. However, now, it's going to be bloody dangerous. Some fraudsters followed us here. '

'Fraudsters; from your century?' Clary gazed at his downcast face, his clenched fists.

'It appears their latest trick is to kidnap talented artists from this time and force them to copy famous paintings of our time; Gainsborough, Reynolds, Lawrence, and some of the female artists.'

Clary gasped. 'But they are geniuses, what artist could copy them and get away with it. They are unique.'

'Maybe, but your work is good Clary; it would muster a pass to untutored eyes. These fraudsters must have got to know about you through us.'

'Who are they then?'

'Baron Stennet and Viscount Racknape. These criminals would also force you to paint private portraits for the aristocracy, there're thousands of pounds involved in this.'

'But I would refuse. I'd ask for help from the estate owners or something.'

'Not if they had Celia as a hostage, that would ensure your silence. Don't forget, the estates of the aristocracy and the rich merchants, were far larger than they are today, there were few trespassers, as the grounds were guarded night and day, and trespassing was a hanging crime anyway. Furthermore, a lot of the estates were in the wilds of Wales, Cornwall and Scotland. News travelled slowly; people disappeared never to be seen again.'

'But, surely you had a police force?'

'There was nothing official. Estate owners paid watchmen or constables to patrol at night. Villains could get away with murder, literally. It's up to us to stop them, and by God, we will. I'll have Beelzebub; he's a nasty piece of work; he'll attack on demand.'

'Yes, Lila once saw someone off who insulted me. I think I told you about that. Take her with you, she's fearsome if crossed.'

'Thank you, now you'll be quite safe; we'll arrange for four guards outside and one downstairs. We have to look for them tonight; we can't waste any time; they're not going to hang around once they know where you are. I'll introduce you to the guards, and then we'll lock up securely.'

'Couldn't you guard the portal?' Clary asked, trying to sound calm.

Drago shook his head, 'There is a maze of tunnels leading to it; no one is sure how many there are. Look I'm off to arrange the guards. Griffin will wait here until I return.' He bent swiftly kissing her fully on the lips. 'Don't' worry dearest, all will be well.'

Chapter 20
Drago – where are you?

Clary awoke shivering and glanced at the clock; 3.00 am. She looked around the room in trepidation, searching the shadows in the corners. Something awoke her, some noise, was it an intruder? She sat up slowly, where were the guards? She saw a dark blur moving fast towards her. She started to scream, only to have it smothered with a cloth. She choked; it was an acrid smell, instantly burning her skin. She looked up into evil eyes, dark, venomous. Gasping, fighting for breath, she struck out punching, kicking, only to fall into blackness.

Celia opened her eyes to muffled sounds coming from Clary's room. Instantly alert, she leapt from the bed running to the window to alert the guards. A pair of heavy arms clamped around her, knocking the breath from her body, cutting off her cries. She gasped, fighting for breath only to find a cloth stuffed into her mouth. Still struggling, still trying to scream, she felt the skin around her mouth stinging; retching at a sickening smell, she fought.

~*~*~*~*~

Arriving back at the cottage, Drago let the dogs out of the boot.
Griffin walked over to the guards. 'Everything alright.'
'Yep, not a sound sir. Sleeping like babes.'
'Okay, get some rest.'
'D'you want us tomorrow night as well guv?'
'I'll see. Have a good sleep. And thank you.'
Putting a key into the lock of the front door, Drago breathed a sigh of relief, letting the dogs in before him. A sour smell met them. 'Devils' teeth, what's that.'
Griffin frowned, 'Where's the damn guard?'
They looked into the lounge, but there was no sign of him. Running, they broke into the kitchen to see the man gagged, and trussed up in a chair.'
'Dammit it to hell, what's happened?' Without waiting for an answer, Drago dashed back into the lounge, to see Lila and Beelzebub's tails disappear into the tiny hall. He looked up the stairs, as the dogs rounded the narrow landing. Taking the stairs at a leap, with Griffin right behind him Drago made for Clary's room.
'It's chloroform Drago – chloroform.' The blood pounded in his head, as Drago kicked open the bedroom door to find slivers of silvery dawn light slipping around the edges of heavy brocade curtains. He peered towards the bed; the duvet lay half flung across the bed and trailing on the floor. 'She's gone.' 'Check Celia's room.' He spoke to thin air; Griffin was already searching for her.
They met on the landing, their faces grim. 'Where the hell have they taken them?'
Griffin grimaced. 'Come with me.' He led him to a cupboard in the corner of the room. 'See, at the back there, a sliding panel. There's another tunnel leading from the cottage, look.'
Drago peered into the narrow cupboard to see the panel pushed to one side, revealing stone steps. He gritted his teeth, another way through to the portal – fiends teeth, if they harm them, I'll kill the buggers.'
Enraged, Drago practically jumped down the stairs. 'Come, we have to be quick. Bring the dogs with you. It'll be quicker by car.' Leaping into the driving seat, he put his foot down hard on the accelerator. Thankfully, as they raced to the Keep the roads were deserted, and the hamlet still asleep, Drago clenched his jaw 'There are so many tunnels; we damn well missed that one.'
As the Keep came into view, Griffin drove down the mile long drive, swerving around on the gravel to the main entrance, making for a side door. Calling to the dogs, they ran to huge double oak doors, braced with iron bars and hinges. Wrenching them open, they sped down spiralled stone steps leading to the dungeons. Reaching the lowest level, they sped off down a low-ceilinged tunnel with a row of barred dungeon doors. Lunging to the last one, they wrenched it open to find nothing.'

'Damn it, they've used a different tunnel.'

Griffin began stripping. 'They've got a few hours on us; they couldn't have got far.'

Wrenching off his jacket, and pulling off his jeans Drago muttered, 'maybe, but where the hell did they go, what direction?'

Finally stripped, Griffin bent down to Lila. 'Better take their bloody collars off, or we won't have any dogs at the other end.'

Drago nodded, unbuckling Beelzebub's, who stood shivering and whimpering.

'What's the matter with him?' Griffin muttered.

'He knows I'm bloody angry, if he could get near the buggers, he'd tear their throats out.'

Griffin turned to Drago, 'You ready?'

Drago nodded, pushing Beelzebub in front of him.

They stepped from the niche, both breathing a sigh of relief. No matter how many times they went through the time portal, they still had a lingering fear that maybe they wouldn't come to the other end, that they would be lost trailing in an eternal darkness.

Chapter 21
The Keep 1812

Wiping brows, grunting vows to kill the abductors, they made their way through several corridors, stairs and floors eventually arriving at Drago's dressing room. Pulling the bell cord, he summoned Hodgeson, 'Good thing I sent him back to get the girls' clothes ready.

Within minutes, the valet arrived to see them both hurriedly dressing; their expressions grim. 'My lord, I did not expect you otherwise I would have —'

'We have an emergency Hodgeson, our artist and her sister have been abducted. I just hope to God, the villains didn't take the closed carriage; they must have taken some of the horses. If it's still here, bring the carriage or another round to the front. Make sure we have Ben driving with Johnny beside him, then I want four footmen as guards in the carriage, and four outriders.'

'So where are we headed my lord?'

'There's only one main coach road, heading either East or West, there must be fresh tracks, so get Johnny to trace which way they went.'

'Maybe they went on horseback?' Hodgeson muttered.

'Wouldn't have thought so, but we'll have to chance that. If they have gone by carriage, we'll catch them up on horseback; Johnny can follow us with a carriage. They must be making for the first or second coaching inn; they'll have to rest or change horses at some point.'

He turned to Griffin, 'I'll go to the gun room; our steward will supply us with all the artillery we need.'

'Make sure the pistols are loaded. I left my guns back in 21st century, but I've got a pistol and my trusty sword. I hope to have the pleasure of gutting Stennet.'

Drago grinned evilly. 'Yes, as for Racknape, a beheading would be too kind; he'll suffer, by God, he'll suffer.'

Chapter 22
West Sussex 1812
Where are you now my love?

Clary awoke to a low oak beamed ceiling, white plastered walls and one of the hardest beds she'd ever slept on. Struggling up, she realized she was naked except for her top and pants. She looked down to see Celia curled up beside her fast asleep. Nudging her, she whispered, 'Ceci, Ceci, wake up. Wake up.'

Groaning, Ceci rubbed her eyes then looked around her. 'What? Where are we?'

'I don't know; I can't remember anything, except someone smothering me with a cloth.'

Ceci looked up at her. 'You've got red marks around your mouth.' She felt her own, 'God it stings.'

Clary slipped from the bed to feel hard boards beneath her feet. Frowning, she went straight to the door with bolts and latches. 'It's bolted from the other side. Oh God.' She knocked loudly, shouting, 'Is there anyone there? Hey, we can't get out. Please, someone? Help.' After a couple of fruitless banging, she turned to Ceci. 'We've got to find a way out of here.' She rushed past a carved oak armoire to a tiny leaded window under the eaves. Looking out she exclaimed, 'Come, come quick.'

Ceci hurried to her side, peering down. 'Carriages – horses. Look at the way they're dressed. Queer top hats, cloaks, and—'

'The women are wearing the same dresses as us at the fete.'

'Must be a party or something, or another fete.' Ceci banged on the window, but made little impact. She reached up to open the small top window, only to find it stuck fast.

Clary clenched her teeth and running over to the bed pulled a pillow slip from the pillow. Bunching it around her fist, she made for the window, furiously punching the tiny diamond glass panes, but to no avail.

'Damn we're three floors up, so they can't even see us.' Ceci muttered,

Clary shook her head, a sense of dread flooding her body, 'Oh no; it can't be.'

'Can't be what Clary? What?'

'I think we're in the nineteenth century, look no cars, nothing but horses, carriages and carts.'

'Don't be silly, we couldn't be. I must be dreaming.'

'Why not? Drago did tell us about the portal. And we ….' Clary broke off, as a woman appeared carrying two pails of water hanging from a large plank of wood across her shoulders. 'That couldn't be fancy dress surely?'

Ceci grimaced, walking over to a carved oak low cupboard. 'What's in here?'

Clary looked over, 'That's an armoire. See if it's got any clothes in it.'

Opening it, Ceci said, 'Look, dresses just like the ones we wore at the Regency fete. 'Damn, it's all so weird. Come on, let's use them anyway, before anyone else comes in. We're practically naked.'

Clary nodded, hurriedly snatching a pale blue muslin gown, putting it against her to judge the length.

Ceci picked out a pale lemon cotton dress, then bent down to open the first of two deep drawers in the armoire. 'Look underwear, well if you can call it that, chemises with laces, the same as we had; no pantaloons though. There's some stockings here and garters.'

Clary muttered, 'they didn't actually wear pants in those days. We'll just have to keep ours on.'

Realizing there was no water or towels, to have a quick wash, they hurriedly donned the clothes. Clary threw the stockings to one side. 'I'm not wearing those stupid things; it's summer so we'll go without.'

Ceci nodded, as she laced Clary up, and then turned for her to return the favour.'

544

Rushed, fearful, and on the verge of tears, they jumped, as the door opened to admit, a short plump woman in a long grey dress with a lacy apron and matching mobcap. Giving a bob of a curtsey she said, 'Beg pardon ma'am here's some water ter wash yer face, and some fresh towels. She stepped in, followed by a short burly man in a rough cotton check shirt and baggy dark trousers. 'This be Tom.'

It looked like he was some kind of bodyguard, as she kept close to him, hardly looking at them.

Ignoring him, Clary pounced on the maid. 'Look you've got to help us, we've been kidnapped – please fetch the police....' She stopped biting her lip, remembering Drago saying they didn't have police in this time.

The maid bit her lip, and looked at Tom. 'Police? I don't know what you're talking about ma'am. I'm just 'ere ter see you be dressed ma'am.'

'Please, listen, we need help, fetch someone who can help us, the Watchman, a constable?'

Ignoring Clary's pleas and Celia's tears they hurried to the door, but Ceci beat them to it, only for the man to snatch her around the waist and drag her back. Screaming, she kicked him, as Clary managed to push the maid aside to dash through, only to be blocked by a tall thick set man.

Looking up, she shouted, 'you – you; you bastard. What the hell d'you think you're doing? Let us go now.'

The man sneered, as he bowed, doffing his hat to reveal thin red hair. 'Sorry to disappoint you my lady, Baron Stennet at your service.'

'I know who you are, you bastard.'

'Come now my little artist, we have great plans for you. Seeing as you are dressed; quite prettily may I say, we are going to the carriage; so I want your promise that you will behave like ladies; make no sound, otherwise I shall be forced to fetter you.'

Clary caught Ceci's eye, there were two of them against him. Surely one of them could escape and run for help, or at least scream to anyone downstairs. She made a rush for him, only to see Tom and a younger man with a dirt marked face, and wild dark hair step through the door.

Stennet sighed, looking to them 'What a pity. Restrain the ladies.'

'Help, anyone, help.' Ceci yelled, as she saw Tom carrying iron collars and manacles.

Ignoring her, the young man grabbed Ceci roughly, whilst Stennet pinned Clary to the bed. Despite her feverish struggles, Tom clamped a heavy wicked looking collar around her neck then locked the manacles on her wrists. Stennet looked at her. 'That's better.'

Clary screamed at him. 'You can't do this; you're evil – evil. Help – anyone – help.'

The Baron thundered. 'Listen to me now. You can scream as much as you like, but I've informed the Innkeeper, and his good lady; we're transporting you both to Bedlam. He smirked, 'I have the papers here, signed and sealed by a magistrate, a good friend of mine.'

'You can't do this – Drago will—'

'Tut – tut my lady. We are in the year 1812, and Bedlam is a place much to be feared. No one will listen to your demented squawks.'

He turned to Tom, 'Now this one.'

Ceci kicked out, as Tom approached her, but to no avail. Once manacled, Clara and Ceci looked in horror, as Stennet held up two iron muzzles.

Clary gasped, what in God's name was he going to do?

He raised his eyebrows. 'Your screams have forced me to use these. They are called Scolds bridles. Contraptions used to punish women who nag their long suffering husbands. For goodness sake if you'd only come quietly, you are a fine artist and there is plenty of work here for you, fame even.'

'You can't make us do this – it's mad, you can't' Clary hissed.

'I see you will not behave yourselves.' Stennet scowled. 'I can't take the risk there may be some bacon-head do-gooder who will leap to your cause, so you will wear these.'

She let out one heartrending cry, as Stennet nodded his head to Tom, who grabbed her. Showing no pity, Stennet pushed the iron vicious bridle on her head and face, forcing open her mouth to place the curb plate with vicious spikes on her tongue. He pointed his finger in warning. 'One word from you, and those spikes will go through your tongue.'

As they struggled, Ceci kicked and bit her captor, but he held her fast.

In silence, they shuffled down the stairs, past curious onlookers, some aghast at the manacles and bridles, others shouting out ribald remarks. Not one came to their aid.

Once in the carriage Clary closed her eyes, the tears streaming, half choking with the strange bit in her mouth. 'Drago, please – please find us.'

Chapter 23
West Sussex 1812
Sabres and tears

Placing the dogs in the carriage, guarded by armed outriders to follow them, Drago spurred his horse on, with Griffin at his side, the four equally armed riders bringing up the rear. 'There's the second coaching inn. They had a few hours lead on us, but if they stopped for vittles or a rest, I can't see them getting any further.'

Griffin grimaced, 'There's a lot of hustle and bustle outside; seems busy. I know the landlord – Wilkins. Hope he's there.' Drago pulled up on the reins, guiding his horse to the tethering posts.

Alighting, he walked over to the guards. 'I'll take a look inside, be ready to move when I say.' They nodded, grim faced.

Griffin had already gone ahead, entering the tap room, as Drago caught up with him.'

The bartender looked over, seeing Drago's stern expression he said, 'so my Lord, what shall it be?'

'I have no time Wilkins. I'm in a hurry. Have you seen Baron Stennet and Lord Racknape by any chance, with two young ladies?'

'The bartender raised his eyebrows. 'Well there's been a right ruckus, here my lord. Sure you won't have a drink to slake yer thirst?'

Drago waved his hand 'Nay, tell me, did you see them?'

'Yes the Baron and his lordship left maybe half an hour ago. They came in the middle of the night; they did. Got me and my good wife up out of bed.'

'I see.' Drago glanced to Griffin. 'So the two young ladies were they alright?'

'Wot them two? Nah my lord, they be headed for Bedlam.'

'Bedlam? Drago bristled, his chin jutting forward. 'What the hell d'you mean, Bedlam? They are two young ladies who—'

The bartender raised his hands in supplication. 'My lord, they were trussed up in irons, and they had those woman scolds on their 'eads. Looked right devils those two. It's a brave man, as would escort them lunatics. Screaming and shouting they were, cursing enough ter bring the walls down, they were. The good wife nearly had a heart attack; she did so.'

Drago's heart leapt to his throat. 'I am talking about two young ladies, no more than their early twenties.'

'Yes, that be right, but those don't be ladies my lord; they be demons. I crossed meself I did, and I don't be no church going man, but me good wife she held up her crucifix to ward off their evil. Proper churchgoing woman she is – me wife. She be abed with the vapours. They had the evil eye they did. Wot say you Harry?'

A surly man with a wide girth and bloated face nodded. 'Had ter knock back a drink of two after that. There're some as have gone home, and that's a fact. Twas like being in hell here; it was so.'

Another scrawny old man joined in, 'Yeah, twas a whippin' they should have; spend a day in the stocks. No … the good Baron, he did handle them like a true gentleman, stood no nonsense mind you, even lifted them into the carriage. Fine gentleman I say – damn fine.'

Drago tried to contain his fury. 'So, you said there was another gentleman?'

'Yeah Lord Rackcape, don't know him too well, he be not from these parts.'

Cursing Drago ran from the bar. Galloping out of the courtyard, he scowled. 'Devil's teeth, I'm going to kill them with my own hands Griffin, tear their bloody heads off. Come, there's no time to lose, those damn scold bridles can tear a woman's mouth apart. The cursed maniac won't live to see the morning.'

Spurring their horses on, they rode in hot pursuit with the four guards following.

As they came to a fork, Drago swore, damn it to hell, which way would they go. He alighted from his horse, and examined the tracks. Unfortunately, at this time of day, there were several carriages and horses on the road. Griffin came to his side, being a master Huntsman, was more astute with tracking than Drago. 'See here – these carriage tracks are lighter than the travel coach which holds a lot more people. I would guess we should take the right hand fork.' Drago nodded, relying on his friend's expertise.

'Let's pray you're right.'

After half an hour of hard riding, they espied a carriage ahead with a coachman, and aide along with four outriders. Drago immediately recognized Stennet and Racknape.

Huh, so let's to it. I think sabres Griffin. Pistols are no use here; we'll need more than one shot, and we can't wait to reload, so sabres it is. He also patted the dagger in his boot, with the shot gun bedded in his belt, if necessary.

Stennet turned to see them, and shouted to the foreman, who immediately lashed the horses to go faster. However, Drago and Griffin were upon them within minutes. Drago shouted to one of his men. 'Stop the wheeler horse.' Nodding, the man leapt from his horse onto the horse at the back, actually pulling the carriage, bringing it to a halt.

Clary looked out of the window to see men fighting with hatchets, sabre and daggers. She shut her eyes, and prayed, not daring to shout out, as she'd already cut her tongue, which bled profusely. Slashing with his sword, Drago fought his way to the carriage and yanked open the door, climbing inside. Horrified, he saw Clary covered in blood, Fiend's teeth she could have choked on her own blood. 'Try not to move, we'll get you out of this.' Rage pounded his head; he felt helpless; he could not unlock the damn contraption. Leaping out of the carriage he screamed at Stennet. 'The keys, where are the keys'

Stennet sneered, as he made to ride away. 'The bitch will bleed to death for all I care.'

Seething, Drago leapt back on his own horse and reaching down to his boot pulled out a dagger, throwing it at the man's back, catching him on the shoulder. Instantly Stennet cried out, 'You bastard.' He made to ride on, but Drago caught up with him, dragging him from the horse. As they both plunged to the ground, Stennet fell on his back screeching, as the dagger dug further into his shoulder. Drago wanted to kill him there and then, but instead turned him over searching for the keys. Seeing Griffin and his men roping up Racknape and his rogues, he ran to the coach, and climbed in. His fingers trembled as he searched for the right key to unlock the bridle. 'Right my darling, I'll soon have you free.' He tried not to flinch as fresh spurts of Clary's blood poured over his hands. He planned to kill Stennet slowly.

With juddering breaths, he managed to unlock the bridle, gently taking the bit from her torn mouth, her tears falling on his fingers. He swore, damn it, dammit; men don't cry, as his own tears stung his eyes. Gently, he undid Ceci's bridle, and took the bit from her mouth. Luckily, she suffered only a slight tear in her inner cheek, yet Clary's mouth looked ravaged.

Wrenching off his jacket, he pulled off his linen shirt, tearing it into strips, then began cleaning some of the blood from her mouth, neck and chest.

Griffin came to the door; his eyes glazed with fear for Ceci. 'Dearest, are you alright?'

Ceci nodded dumbly, as she looked at the blood-soaked Clary. Griffin looked at Drago, his face grim. 'I've trussed the buggers up like pigs. Stennet and Racknape are on their knees. Shall we kill them now?'

Drago's eyes darkened, as he nodded. But then felt Clary's urgent touch on his arm, he turned to see her jade eyes widen, as she tried to shake her head.

'Dearest girl, they need to die; they hurt you both, humiliated you. They would not be spared in a duel; they will hang anyway.'

Clary managed a small shake of her head groaning with pain. She clutched his hand. 'N …no.'

Drago led the carriage back to the Inn where Wilkins bowed obsequiously, obeying his every command. The prisoners were dispatched to a cattle shed, whilst Griffin sent men to alert the magistrate, and bring the watchmen who would escort the prisoners to the local goal.

Shocked and injured, Clary and Ceci needed time to recover. Drago ordered the innkeeper to prepare the main suite of two bedrooms and a small lounge; arrange for servings maids to attend them and send for the physician. He never left Clary's side except when she was blanket bathed, and put to bed. Ceci had the comfort of a warm bath in a copper tub lined with fresh linen. She too was put to bed in the adjoining room.

Once alone, Drago sat on the side of Clary's bed, 'My love, is it difficult to talk?'

She nodded, whispering, 'Yes – can't'

'Then I shall talk for you.'

She managed a small grin. He was back to his usual bombastic self, and she loved it.

Seeing the glint in her eye, he said, 'We cannot marry in your century, as I am already dead. However, we can have a small private ceremony in our chapel on the estate, and we can invite the people from the hamlet.'

She whispered, 'wait.'

'Of course, that's why I will arrange it for six weeks from now – a double wedding. Griffin has agreed.'

Clary tried to laugh but winced instead.

Epilogue
1812 – Sweet Mead Keep.
Roses and Rings

As the bridal wedding march boomed within the small chapel, Ceci nervously arranged Clary's dress. She looked beautiful in a dress of cream silk; the low décolletage decorated with tiny pink rose buds. The sleeves puffed and adorned with pink silk ruched ribbons. Attached at the back was a train some fourteen feet in length, and like the hem of the dress festooned with pink rosebuds and seed pearls, Drago gave her his birth mother's small tiara of seed pearls to wear atop chestnut curls falling down her shapely back.

Ceci took a deep breath, stroking down her white silk dress embroidered with an array of wildflowers in pastel colours, the shimmering folds outlining her slender figure; the bodice and hem adorned with silk flowers to match the embroidery, and a train of some fourteen feet decorated with the finest Valenciennes lace in pale cream, scattered with seed pearls. She wore a crown of fresh flowers from which flowed a fine net veil flowing down her back. Around her neck, she wore a necklace of sapphires, a present from Griffin's mother.

The wedding service flowed in a dream of music, hymns, vows and promises until Drago smiled softly, gently pushing the ring on Clary's finger, as Griffin proudly kissed the ring on Ceci's.

The minister beamed. 'I now pronounce you man and wife; he turned to Drago and repeated the statement.

As the couples, somewhat dazed and supremely happy, walked down the aisle, they were scarcely aware of the sighs, the laughter and clapping hands as they walked into the sun and the rest of their lives. A young woman in a white muslin gown embroidered with daisies ran up to Clary and curtseyed. Breathlessly, she said, 'My lady, please accept this on behalf of my family.'

Another little girl scarcely four years old, looking adorable in a pink satin and frothy net dress, toddled up to Ceci presenting a posy of wildflowers from which dangled a silver key. She managed a wobbly curtsey and lisped, 'Lady – key of love for you.'

Laughing, the Earl and his wife the Countess of Hatherstone made their way to the gold trimmed carriage bearing the Hatherstone heraldic arms, covered in sprays of flowers. Viscount Daykin of Linley helped his Viscountess into an equally adorned carriage.

Clary hardly dared to breathe; it was just so beautiful, such a different story from when she searched for somewhere to hide away from the world.

She just wished her mother and father were there to see her and Ceci married and so happy. She looked over to the Keep, nestling at the foot of the forest, the spacious lawns rolling down to a meadow of wild flowers overlooking the dunes and the sea.

She hoped their future children would be happy in both places; the Keep of the twenty-first century and the Keep of 1812. She was just so glad she fought to find herself; never dreaming it would take her across the country and through time; or that her fear and sadness would be conquered by love.

Now she could look forward to a career here in 1812 painting her romantic portraits, and a career in the twenty-first century with her beloved pop art. She laughed, as Lila and Beelzebub ran up to the carriages, nipping at each other to be the first to greet them.

She smiled, looking at the sands, the sands where Drago seduced her, but maybe it was the other way round.

oOo

About the Author:

Katy lives on the South coast with her husband and a loving hyper friendly dog who likes to greet and lick everyone on sight. She has a BA Hons (Psych), BA Eng.Lit., MA in Religion and Mysticism and a Dr. Science for research into pain control.
She was a psychologist and hypnotherapist before changing direction for full time creative writing and painting. Her main genres in writing are historical romance, crime and science fiction.

https://twitter.com/@katywalters07

http://www.katy-walters.com/

http://katywaltersnewsandviews.com/

https://www.facebook.com/KatyWaltersAuthor

List of Books by Katy Walters.

> **Sands of Seduction**
> **A Lady's Plight**
> **Lady Henrietta's Dilemma**
> **Lady Phillipa's Peril,**
> **Lady Venetia's Vow**
>
> **Return to Rhonan**
> **Possessed at Rhonan**
> **Reunited at Rhonan**
>
> **Where are the Children – Splintered Night**
> **Death Marks**
> **Fractured Night.**
>
> **Cyborg, First Generation.**
>
> Publishing - Four new books.

Protecting Her Pigg

Melissa Keir

I'll huff and I'll puff and I'll burn your house down….

As chief arson investigator of a small town in Ohio, Lily O'Neill has always needed to be strong to survive in a man's world.

Former military man, Lucas Pigg has kept his feelings buried for so long, he's unsure of how to react when flames spark between Lily and him.

Arson and fire may bring them together, but their passion for one another could be more dangerous. What will cause the most damage…the arsonist bent on revenge or their own stubborn ways?

To my father who reads all my books.
Thank you, Dad, for supporting my dreams.

CHAPTER ONE

Flames danced along the wall, creating a surreal painting of reds and oranges. The beauty of my work filled my chest with pride. Maniacal laughter echoed in my ears. I recognized my own hilarity and covered my mouth to stop the sound from escaping. Inhaling the scent of gasoline, I pulled off the gloves and tossed them into the flames.

"I'll huff and I'll puff and I'll blow your house down."

The sounds of sirens resonated in the distance. Running toward the gathering crowd, I stood to watch over my latest creation. Glee filled my heart as I ached to proclaim my masterpiece. Pulling the baseball cap lower over my eyes to hide my elation, I stood watch, hoping my adversary would arrive in time to see magnum opus.

***

When the call came, I pulled my long hair into a ponytail and quickly left for the crime scene. I'd constantly felt I needed to be tougher and better than everyone else, especially as a girl in a man's world. I didn't want any person to second-guess why I'd been given the job. No one could accuse me of nepotism.

Arriving on the scene, the smell of smoke with the tang of gasoline assaulted my lungs. The building was a total loss. It bothered me to see something once so beautiful destroyed.

"Sir, you can't be here," the officer I'd assigned to the perimeter yelled.

Turning toward the commotion, I witnessed a tall, dark-haired man storming toward me with violence in his approach. Sizing up the advancing danger, I threw my shoulders back and met the man halfway.

"This is my building. Who are you, and what do you know so far?" His gravel voice caused goose bumps to form on my skin.

"I'm sorry, Mr...?" Up close, the man took my breath away. His features weren't "pretty boy" beautiful, but striking. Chiseled chin, full lips, slightly curved nose. Must have been broken at one time.

"Pigg, Lucas Pigg. And you are?"

Caught staring at his lips, I almost missed the question. "I'm Lily O'Neill, chief arson investigator. We don't know much so far. I've only begun my investigation. This wasn't an accident. It was set with gasoline as the accelerant. The smell is noticeable. I have some questions for you. I'd like to meet you in my office to talk." No matter how good-looking, Mr. Pigg was my first suspect.

"You can't think I did this." Anger tinged his voice.

Even with my small stature, I wasn't about to back down. Stepping closer, our gazes met and tempers flared.

"Look, Mr. Pigg." My own voice grew louder, like a barking dog defending its territory. "Everyone's a suspect until they're eliminated. I'm looking forward to asking you some questions. You may want to bring your lawyer."

His eyes narrowed. "Fine. I'll meet you in your office."

With his declaration, I turned toward the scene and sought out the fire chief. *No man's going to stop me from doing my job.*

***

Hiding behind the crowd, I watched him arrive on the scene. Giggles strained to escape my lips as his face clouded over with anger and frustration. I'd needed to see his eyes when he witnessed my greatest work to date. The building stood as a beautiful piece of burnt wood and charred metal.

"The game is on. You can't catch me...not by the hair of my chinny chin chin."

Stepping away, I disappeared into the crowded city street.

***

The smell of stale bodies streamed into my office in the police precinct. The dreary puke-green paint and metal furniture reminded me of the setting of old Barney Miller television show. But Barney's office was in a big city, while mine was in 'small town Ohio'.

Pacing in my tiny office, I recalled Lucas Pigg's dominating presence. With a scruffy beard and his piercing gaze, Lucas's rugged good-looks shouted dangerous. *Yeah, dangerous to a girl's heart.* He seemed like a guy used to getting what he wanted. However, Lucas was a suspect and therefore off limits, no matter what my hormones said. Arson had definitely caused the fire, but if he wasn't the one who'd set it, then who? Finding out was the most important thing.

A knock sounded. My ankle boots clicked across the linoleum as I strode toward the door. I opened it and forgot to breathe. Lucas Pigg stood in front of me, alongside two other uber-sexy men. Together, they made a five-course meal of gorgeous.

"Come in, gentlemen. Please take a seat. I'm Lily O'Neill. I know Mr. Pigg," I said, keeping my voice professional.

The tallest man with a quirky smile on his face pushed his hand into mine. "I'm Marcus Pigg, Lucas's older brother. Lucas didn't tell us how beautiful you are."

A blush heated my face. *Darn my fair skin.*

Glaring at his brother, Lucas sat down and slouched in the metal chair across from my desk. The third man pulled on Marcus's shoulders, forcing him to release my hand. "I'm Detective Jonah Pigg and the oldest of these ruffians. Thank you for meeting with us."

Wow. God did something right when he made these men. Charming and professional, but with an air of danger.

"Please be seated, gentlemen." I indicated to the other chairs, walked behind my desk, and sat down to calm my wobbly knees. "Detective Pigg, I've heard of you. Congratulations on your recent bust of the drug dealer who was transporting narcotics through his trucking company. I watched in the audience when you received your commendation."

"Thank you. The police department is at your disposal as you find the criminal who destroyed our building." The detective imparted.

"At this moment, we're gathering evidence. While we have to look at all of you as a suspect, I believe we can rule it out with a little help."

Jonah spoke with authority and appeared to be taking charge for the group. "Since Lucas was the first on the scene, I'd like him to be your liaison and work with you. He can help you gather information, and, with his background, he'll be an asset to your investigation."

Hiding my frustration, I spoke through gritted teeth. "I appreciate your offer, Jonah, but you know I can't have a civilian on my case, especially someone involved in this investigation."

The chair legs screeched on the floor as Lucas stood, his brow drawn tight over his eyes and mouth set in a grim line, a haze of anger radiating off his body. "I'm helping you whether you like it or not. You can either decide to work with me, or I'll find the lowlife on my own. And you won't like it when I do."

What did I get myself into? "Mr. Pigg…Lucas, I want this person caught as much as you do. However, we have to do it legally or they'll get off on a technicality. I *know* you don't want them to go free." I tried to play on his empathy and need for justice.

"I'll run my own investigation. And may the best person win." He focused on my face, daring me to look away. I hadn't been in a staring match since third grade, but I never passed up a challenge.

"Don't obstruct my investigation or I'll have you in my jail, waiting on bail." I raised my eyebrow and threw down the gauntlet. I'd learned long ago in this man's world, women needed balls, too. *Game on, Lucas Pigg, and may the best investigator win.*

Jonah walked between us, breaking our stares. "I don't want any problems. Lucas, you'll behave. I'm not bailing your ass out of jail because you got in the middle of something you shouldn't. Miss O'Neill, if you need anything, please don't hesitate to contact one of us. Let's get out of here so Miss O'Neill can do her job." He signaled with his head, indicating they should leave.

Marcus walked toward me. He took my hand in his and kissed it. "I'm here for you, should you need anything."

I glanced over his shoulder and caught Lucas's gaze. A scowl marred his sexy face. Licking my lips, I fantasized about *his* lips on my palm. Moisture pooled in my underwear. Funny how Marcus's kiss didn't move me in the way Lucas's deep, penetrating gaze did.

The Pigg brothers left my office. My legs turned to Jell-O, and I sat down, picked up a piece of paper, and fanned myself. Lucas Pigg's sensual image seared my brain. *Yep, I'm certainly in trouble with a capital T.*

CHAPTER TWO

Unable to get Lucas Pigg off my mind, I'd tossed and turned all night. Fantasies of naked limbs intertwined among my sheets filled steamy dreams. The lack of sleep made me grumpy, so I stopped at the local coffee shop for a pick-me-up. White wainscoting and dark-gray walls gave the café an upscale ambiance. The small white tables and chairs provided quiet areas for work or conversation. I'd spent many hours slumped over those tables, avoiding the din of the precinct.

"Hey, Detective, long time no see. Will you have the usual?" Jessi Johnson worked for A Coffee Perk for years. She'd become the closest thing I had to a friend. "You're looking a little wore out. I heard about the arson the other night. It's all anyone in the neighborhood talks about."

I grabbed the caramel iced coffee and leaned against the black granite counter. "The whole incident stinks of revenge. The place flamed way too quick to be an amateur. I've been running the names of career arsonists, but most are out of commission."

"I heard you met the Piggs. Those are three men I'd love to play cops and robbers with." Jessi winked then wiggled her eyebrows.

Ignoring her comment about the Piggs, I changed the subject. Since we'd been friends for the last five years, she'd see right through any lie I told about how sexy they were. "So, what's the rumor mill saying about this fire?"

"Well…word on the street is you brought the Piggs in for questioning. They couldn't have done it. They wouldn't have torched their own building." Jessi shook her head.

"Many people have for the insurance money." I raised my brow. People had done a lot more for a lot less.

"But not them. They own this building." She waved her hand in the air, indicating her shop. "Sweet guys. When their parents died, those boys practically raised themselves. Jonah took on the parent role. His job as a detective and his strong moral code wouldn't allow him to do anything nefarious." Jessi rubbed down the counter. A smile crossed her face. "As a matter of fact, he recently married the woman he'd set out to protect, when the dealers targeted her."

"I've met him a few times in the line of duty. It's not that I think they did it, but I have to check every angle." I pursed my lips.

"Those guys are so clean they squeak. I know Lucas hides his feelings and Marcus is the biggest flirt. Honestly though, they'd never harm someone for money. When their parents died, they came into a large settlement." She glanced toward the front of the café. "Oh look. Speak of the devil."

The door of the coffee shop opened with a jangle of bells. The man who'd kept me up all night with wicked dreams sauntered inside. "Hello, Jessi." A scowl marred his gorgeous face. "Ms. O'Neill. How's the investigation going?"

"Everything's going well. If you think of anything which will add to my investigation, like who might want to target you, please contact me." I handed him my business card. A spark zinged across my hand when our fingers brushed. "Thanks for the pick-me-up, Jessi. We'll talk soon." I waved my cup at her and headed toward the door.

"Here, let me get this." I hadn't seen him move, yet there he was, holding the door and standing close enough the heat from his body engulfed me. My breath hitched.

"Thank you." I offered him a tentative smile. My mom would be proud I used my manners.

"You don't look like you got much sleep last night. Is this investigation getting to you?" A twinkle flashed through his gaze.

"Wow, charming. Insulting a girl and telling her she doesn't look good. I'd hate to see you really try to win someone over." Sarcasm filled my voice. His comments stung, especially since thoughts of his hot body had kept me up all night. And here he looked well rested and so damn sexy. I frowned.

"Whoa." Lucas raised his hands in mock surrender. "I'm sorry. I hate seeing a beautiful lady upset."

"You think I'm beautiful?" A doubt entered my mind. Was this actually Lucas? The flirting seemed more Marcus's style. "Okay, who are you and what did you do with Lucas Pigg? He'd never be so nice." I narrowed my eyes and stared at him. "What do you want?"

His deep throaty laugh filled the air and made my pussy clench. *Great, now I'm going to have another night of restless sleep.*

"My mom taught me how to behave. She also told me I'd get more flies with honey than with vinegar. I thought it over and decided to help rather than fight you. The day of the fire, you caught me at my worst. Usually, I'm not so grumpy, but seeing your business go up in flames has a way of ruining your good mood." He reached out toward me. "Let's start over. I'm Lucas Pigg. Pleasure to meet you."

Tentatively, I clasped his hand, his grip strong and manly as if he worked with them each day. The rough texture made me wonder how his fingers would feel on my naked body. "Nice to meet you, too."

His shoulders shook as we touched. Could he feel the same energy passing between us? I licked my lips to dampen them. His gaze followed the trail of my tongue. I thought I heard panting coming from him.

"Do you have plans for lunch? I'd love to spend some time with you. We can make it a working lunch if it'd make you more comfortable." He leaned toward me. "You can grill me about my building and who'd want to hurt my family."

Even knowing I shouldn't get involved with a suspect in an ongoing investigation, I couldn't help myself. This side of Lucas Pigg intrigued me. Justifying the lunch as business, I agreed. "Sure. Where do you have in mind?"

"Why don't we meet here around noon? Jessi makes the best sandwiches."

"Sounds good. I can't share confidential information with you about the investigation, but I'd love your take on what you think's going on. Besides"—I winked at him—"with Jessi here, I know you'll behave if Mr. Grumpy comes back."

A grin broke out on his face, showing a dimple in his chin. He should smile more. "I'd better return to the precinct. See you at noon."

As I left the building, I noticed a shadow and whirled toward it. *Is someone there?* At a second glance, it had disappeared. *Was I imagining things?* I shook my head. *Now I'm seeing shadows everywhere.* Remembering Lucas's dimples, I walked to my office with a big goofy grin on my face.

The noise of the precinct felt like home. Phones rang. Voices rose in discussions. I sidestepped around a perp in cuffs sitting on the bench waiting to be processed.

"Hey, O'Neill, what's the grin for?" Mark Leary yelled across the room. Mark's sense of humor always left much to be desired. "You solved your arson already, or are you getting laid?"

"Hey, Leary. I'll solve my case before you solve yours. With all your talk about getting laid, I wonder if you're getting any yourself." I sneered at his smirk. Being a part of the all-boy's network meant I had to put up with some good-natured teasing, but I'd learned to give as good as I got.

"No complaints from my lady. However, I'm happy to show you how it's done."

Chuckles echoed through the room.

"No thanks. I'm not interested in sloppy seconds."

The laughter grew.

Mark strolled toward me and pulled me into a hug, planting a wet kiss on my cheek. "There's your seconds."

My laughter joined the rest of the occupants. I ran my hand over my cheek and rubbed it on Mark's shirt. "You know, we're quite the comedy show. Maybe we should give up this glamorous life"—I motioned around the room—"and go on tour."

"Enough." He took a deep breath. "Any leads on your arson? We opened the tip lines, but, so far, only crazies are calling in. We've had a few people call to tell us they saw wolves lighting the fire."

"No leads. I've pretty much ruled out the Piggs. They don't need the money, and the building was their baby. They'd fixed it up recently, renovating everything. No one would spend the money to torch it."

"I'll fill you in if anything else comes of the tips. Want to grab a bite for lunch?"

My face grew warm. Sure I was blushing, I couldn't meet Mark's gaze. "I have plans. Maybe another time."

"Alright. Your loss. Stay safe, O'Neill. I don't want to have to break in a new partner." Mark turned and marched toward his desk.

The noise level still set my nerves on edge, so I strode to my office and closed the door. Falling into my desk chair, I pulled up the information on my computer I'd gathered on the Piggs. Still nothing showing they'd done it. *I wonder who they pissed off.*

CHAPTER THREE

The smell of gasoline became a sweet perfume. It had been nothing to knock the woman unconscious. Knowing she lay just inside, a flicker of madness escaped my lips. "I'll huff and I'll puff and I'll blow your house down."

Overhearing Lucas Pigg meeting the arson detective here had fueled my obsession. Dousing the outer wall and rear door, I stood in the alley and gazed at my work. I rubbed my hands together, anxious to begin. Soon, the dance of flames would mix with the gas, creating a beautiful piece of art.

Flicking my lighter, I watched the colors swirl—red, yellow, blue along the base. I reached out to stroke the colors, to caress their beauty. Even the flames can't hurt me. They can't burn me. Maybe they'll burn the lady inside, but they sway for me.

Crouching down I set my masterpiece on fire. "You can't catch me. I'm the big bad wolf." I walked away before Lucas arrived. I longed to see his face, to see the pain in his eyes. My body shook with need to show off my masterpiece to the man I'd set out to destroy. But, I had another appointment to keep.

***

My stomach rumbled. Glancing up from the pile of recent arson investigations, I rubbed my eyes. "There's no match yet." When my stomach grumbled again, I looked at the clock. "Crap. I'm supposed to meet Lucas in five minutes."

I snagged my purse and practically vaulted over the desk. Slamming my office door, I rushed past the bullpen with a shout and booked out the door like my butt was blazing.

"Hey, where's the fire?" With the sound of the familiar voice, my foot stumbled on the step and my world shifted on its axis. My arms flailed as I reached out, but his arms enveloped me as I righted myself.

"Wow, close call! Glad I was here." His smile reminded me of a shark since it never reached his eyes.

I pulled out of his embrace, uncomfortable being this close to him. There was a face I'd hoped to never see again. "Hello, Grim. What brings you to the 302? Slumming?" I couldn't keep the sarcasm out of my voice.

"I've been transferred. I'm your new boss." His predatory gaze gave me a chill. I rubbed my hands on my arms to force the cold from my veins.

"Congratulations." I hope I sounded sincere. I didn't want to alienate him. Fears about working with Nathan flooded my brain. "I wish I could stand and chat, but I have a meeting I'm late for. Congrats again."

Luckily, A Coffee Perk was just a couple of blocks from the precinct. It did a steady business being close to the station. What they said about cops, coffee, and doughnuts being true. Jessi brought in a nice amount each week, often remarking, "She does have the best coffee and pastries. My hips will attest to that."

The bells jingled as I opened the door. The interior appeared deserted. No one sat at any of the tables. *At least I beat Lucas here.* I didn't want him to think I was rushing to see him or anything. I ran a hand over my hair and bet I looked a mess. I headed to the bathroom to check and felt a tingle of unease over the quietness. Unable to let it go, I left the bathroom and headed toward the kitchen.

Strange. Jessi usually has music going or kitchen noises. It's too quiet.

At the door to the kitchen, smoke assaulted my nose. My training kicked in. Dialing 911, I call it in. Checking the swinging door for heat, I ran my hand up and down the length then, pulling my scarf over my nose, opened the door with caution. The haze of smoke darkened the room. However, I couldn't see a fire or flames. Going to my hands and knees, I entered the kitchen, intent on making sure no one was inside. As I moved closer to the rear of the building, the smoke doubled. Suddenly, I noticed Jessi lying on the floor in front of the rear delivery door.

I crawled to her, fear raging in my brain. "Jessi." I shook her. "Jessi, are you okay?" She looked like a crumpled piece of trash. Running my hands up her body, I felt her chest rise and released the breath I'd been holding since I saw her. "Thank God."

"Ooohhh. What happened?" She tried to sit up. Coughs wracked her body, and she reached out blindly before collapsing onto the floor. "What's going on? Why are you here?"

"There's a fire. Did you leave the oven on? Are you able to move?"

"I never leave the oven on. My head hurts." She winced when she touched the back of her head. Her fingers came away red. "I think my head is bleeding."

A noise behind Jessi caught my attention. A pop and then a whoosh. Flames engulfed the rear door to the alley. Frantic, I pulled Jessi toward me and the outer door. "Come on. Let me help you. We need to get out."

Her body felt like dead weight as she tried to stand. She fell to the ground and moaned. "I can't walk. I'm nauseous."

The kitchen door slammed open. In shadow, a tall man strode in, looking like a hero from my favorite romance novel. My heart sped up.

"Anyone in here? The building's on fire!" Thank God Lucas had arrived.

"We're here. Jessi's hurt."

He must have followed the sound of my voice because, a moment later, he stood in front of me and then scooped Jessi up in his arms. "Put your hand on the belt on my waist. Follow me. The kitchen wall is in flames, and the smoke's too dense for breathing."

Reaching out, I threaded my fingers into his belt, glad for the help with Jessi and knowing, somehow, he'd make sure we'd get out.

***

The sounds of voices and sirens loomed as we walked out of the front door. I didn't want to let go of the safety of his belt but squared my shoulders and put on my "fire investigator" face, observing the broken front glass on the restaurant, the open door, and the crowd standing witness outside.

"Over here. I've got an injury." Lucas signaled the EMT's standing by their vehicle. He set Jessi's body gently on the stretcher as the two professionals began to examine her injuries. I wanted to run and make sure she was safe but knew she'd be in good hands, so I turned toward the building. It's best for me to do what I've been trained to do.

"What do you think you're doing?" Lucas's voice came from behind me. When I didn't turn, his hand grasped my shoulder.

"What? Keep your hands off me." I met his gaze and noticed the disquiet in it. Why was he concerned about me? "I'm doing my job. The fire's suspicious, and I need to take a preliminary glance around."

"You were inside. There's smoke in your lungs. You need to get checked out, too." His body invaded my personal space. But I wasn't going to give him the satisfaction of stepping away.

"I'm fine." I looked him in the eyes and ground my teeth so as not to say more. What I really wanted was to fall into his strong arms and thank him for saving us. Yet, I couldn't. Another suspicious fire and Lucas around again.

"Humor me." A smile flittered across his face but never reached his eyes.

"Listen, I'm a big girl. Besides, why do you care so much?" I angled my head and raised an eyebrow, determined to win the staring contest.

"I don't care." *Ouch. Those words stung.* "But this was my building, and I'll be damned if you've been hurt in it and don't get proper attention." He brushed his thumb along my jawline. "You've got soot on your face."

His touch made my legs turn to jelly. Breaking eye contact, I glanced at the dimple on his chin before raising my gaze to his once more. "Jessi told me you were the owner. Now let me get my job done so I can give you a report."

"You could have said 'thank you', you know."

I'm glad he doesn't realize how much I want him. Just his touch sizzled my nerves.

"Thanks." Turning, I walked away before I let my emotions win against the argument in my head.

The firemen did their job while I checked on Jessi. I spoke with her briefly, but she couldn't give me much information. Her head injury wasn't serious, but the EMTs took her to the hospital for observation, just in case of a concussion. She'd inhaled more smoke than I did, having been inside for longer. She was lucky I'd arrived when I did; otherwise, she might have been much worse. And we have Lucas to thank for getting us both out. Grinding my teeth, I tensed my jaw. I hate being indebted to him, especially since he's still a potential suspect, not to mention the man in my nightly sex dreams.

When the fire was out, I scoured the alley, looking for evidence. Gasoline permeated the air just like the other arson scene. No gas can remained behind as evidence, though. Sure wish it had been as easy to solve—fingerprints on a can or maybe a signed note from the arsonist. I rubbed my lower lumbar which ached from fatigue. Examining the building's alley wall, I noticed the door appeared to be the primary location of the gasoline. It's like the arsonist wanted to make sure Jessi and no one else could get out.

"Hey, O'Neill. Looks like someone had a hot date." Mark stood at the end of the alley. His rumpled tan jacket stood in stark contrast to the darkened bricks, his hair stood up as if he'd been hit by lightning, and the biggest grin filled his face. His laughter echoed in the tight space but grounded me.

"You know it. Glad to see you. Now get over here. I want to show you something." Leary had been my partner when I first started in the squad. His sarcastic sense of humor made me laugh. All too often, he ran interference with my father who demanded the best of his rookie daughter.

"Always glad to help. You know you owe me." A twinkle flashed in his eyes, which added to the charm of his rugged good looks.

"Leary, remember the investigation of '13? You owed me for that one. Besides, at your great age comes wisdom…or so I've been told." Our banter was legendary around the squad room.

"Hey, I'm only seven years older than you!" He walked over, squatting beside me among the damp debris.

"What do you think of this pattern of the accelerant?" I pointed to the wall surrounding the door.

"The concentration was here." He moved closer then tilted his head. "But if you look up from this angle, you can see an image. Can you see it?"

Squinting, I angled my head to see. "I'm not sure."

"Look." He used his finger to trace the image. "Are you blind? It looks like an animal."

His finger moved again, and, at last, I began to see the shape. "Not just an animal, but a dog head? Or wolf? It's weird." I closed my eyes as I tried to imprint the image on my mind.

"Maybe it's a pattern. Have you ever seen this design before?"

I tried to think about the fire at the Pigg Detective Agency to see if there'd been something similar, but I couldn't remember. "I'll have to put it into our database. We could get a hit. Can you get me some paper to draw the image?"

Leary pulled a small notebook and pencil from his back pocket. "Where'd your purse go? You always have paper."

"Let me get this down, and I'll show you." A quick sketch and the sign of the wolf stood on the page. "Around front. This way."

"Let me, my lady." Leary put his arm in mine and we left the alley for the front of A Coffee Perk.

Leary and I walked the scene inside the shop as soon as the fire marshal gave us the all clear. Chairs and tables littered the floor in the eating area. The bright-white paint now dingy and blackened in places. The smell of delicious baked pastries blended with the smoke, causing my nose to itch. Burnt coffee wasn't a smell I'd soon forget. Puddles of water squished under my ankle boots.

The door had been locked, which was strange. I knew for a fact Jessi wouldn't have locked the door while the place was open. And I'd come in the same locked door, just after the fire was set. It was another piece of the puzzle.

"Hey, there's your purse. It's like a storm blew through here." Trust Leary to try to make a joke. But the room did appear as if a whirlwind had hit. The chairs were knocked over and tables were pushed to the side, as if someone had rushed through the room.

"Oh!" Awareness clicked in my brain. "It was hurricane Lucas. The room wasn't a mess when I walked in. It looked like Jessi had just opened. My purse was on the floor, though. I threw it down there by the door when I smelled the smoke."

"Smart thing to do, especially knowing how you women like to load up those purses. Yours would have needed its own rescue." Pain shown in Leary's eyes. We lived with death every day on this job—the loss of family treasures, the loss of home, and the loss of lives. If our places had been switched and he'd been this close to danger, I'd have been scared.

I reached over and hugged him tight. Tears filled my eyes. For the first time, I realized just how close I'd come to dying.

"Man, make a comment about a woman's purse and she gets all weepy. You really are a girl, you know O'Neill?" Jokes often masked our true feelings. It was another way of dealing with the pain and fear. But as I pulled away, I saw the moistness mirrored in his eyes.

We entered the kitchen where the damage was concentrated. Soot trails climbed the walls. Puddles still saturated the floor. Luckily, the fire hadn't been able to do too much damage to the structure. A few pieces of cabinetry were totaled, and the kitchen wall had sections missing. Smoke was far deadlier than the fire, and there had been more than enough to kill Jessi and me. Taking a deep breath to push away the morbid thoughts, I inspected the evidence.

"What do you see, Leary? I need fresh eyes."

"The fire was started on the back wall, but the brick outside wall contained much of the flames and damage. The metal alley door is warped from the heat, which shows the accelerant increased the temperature quite high. The smell of gasoline still permeates the air. It looks like, though, the unknown subject or unsub didn't want to burn the building down but make a message or use the smoke as his weapon. This fits with the pattern of the wolf. This guy is doing this for attention and fun."

I nodded. "Agreed. We need to scan the witnesses. Unsubs who like attention are usually watchers. They want to see their work."

"Too bad we didn't canvas the last fire to see if anyone had been at both scenes. I wonder if there are any city cameras which would have captured either event. We should check."

I turned and motioned to Leary then nodded toward the door. "Let's take a stroll outside and see who's interested in what's going on."

I paused next to my purse on the floor near the front window. As I reached down to touch it, Leary coughed. "You do know your purse is a part of evidence and you can't take it home for a bit. What are you going to do without your lipstick, O'Neill? What about the driver's license? You know the law. You can't drive around without it." A smirk filled his face, lighting his eyes up.

My shoulders dropped as the tension slid off me. *Yep, we're joking again. Everything's normal.*

We exited the front door, and I ran into a brick wall. Tilting my head back, I stared into the smoldering eyes of Lucas Pigg.

"What's this about your lipstick?" His gaze dipped to my lips. "I don't know why you women think you need it."

Breathless, yet not wanting to show how he'd affected me, I took a step back. "Don't you know, Pigg, women want attention drawn to ourselves?" I tried to keep the teasing in my voice. *Treat him just like one of the guys. Talk like you would to Leary.*

"Without the makeup, women would be like this…." Leary tugged on his face, making it a hideous caricature of a Botox patient. Both men laughed.

"I can't see Lily looking hideous without makeup. Maybe this way." Lucas yanked on his eyes and lips, making another face.

The boys were joining in male bonding. A little twinge of anger flew into my stomach. But I realized it was just boys being boys. And if you can't beat them, join 'em.

"I'd hate to see you in the morning. I bet you have a horrible morning mien. Your hair is like this…." I pushed my hair up over my face, making it like a rat's nest.

"Wouldn't you like to know?" A twinkle filled his eyes. But his words triggered a reaction deep inside me. The thought of waking up next to Lucas after a long night of sex…uh, it had been way too long if I was letting him get to me.

"All kidding aside, did you find out anything new?" His mood returned to serious in a second.

Leary jumped in to save me. "We really can't tell you anything. You *are* still a suspect. But I can assure you…one, we have leads. Two, we need to talk to you more about who has it in for your family because these weren't accidental fires. You and your brothers are the target. And three, O'Neill doesn't wake up appearing like a crazy lady."

A gleam look crossed Lucas's face. I couldn't tell what it meant. *Was it anger? Why am I worried about it?* "As far as people who are out to get us, I can make a list. My brother recently brought down a drug ring with the help of his fiancée. But as P.I.s, we make a lot of people mad. Be ready for a long list." Lucas cocked his head and glanced at me before continuing, "Lily is fresh as a flower in the morning, then?"

Leary's eyes twinkled with mischief. "Stakeout buddy. We've been up all night, and, other than some creative snoring, she's good in the morning."

"Hey! I don't snore!" I put my hands on my hips and tried to appear mad. Obviously by the smirks on their faces, it didn't work. "Let's get back to business. If you can have the list to us right away, we can start checking people off. Leary, we need to take care of that business." I gave him a pointed stare to remind him about the unsub possibly watching us.

"Sure. Anything you say, boss lady." Leary shook hands with Lucas. "It's been fun chatting. We'll see you soon with the list. And really, O'Neill's the best. She'll get to the bottom of this. Trained her myself."

We headed toward the police officer in charge of securing the scene. I could sense Lucas's gaze on me. Each time I saw him, my heart beat faster, and I couldn't get the images of him in bed out of my head. Fanning my face again, I scanned the crowd. Unlike the television shows, the bad guy doesn't have a tell which shows when we scrutinize him. He seems like a normal person. He could be a neighbor or coworker.

"Hey, O'Neill, heard you had a close call." Grim's honeyed voice over my shoulder startled me.

"Hello, Grim. What brings you by?" I tried to smile but knew my smile was coached. I couldn't warm up to him. Too many whispers about problems…too many innuendos.

"I heard about the incident on the radio. Thought I should check on things." His gaze traveled the length of my body. "You okay?"

His concern was nice but didn't sound genuine. My stomach lurched. I nodded.

"Do you have any suspects yet?" His brows rose with his question.

"Not yet. We have some leads. We're looking things over. Thanks for stopping by. I should return to work." Where was Leary? This would be the perfect time for him to rescue me.

"You're the legend," he carried on. "I'd figure you'd have it solved by now. What's taking so long?" Conversations from the firefighters, questions from the crowd, boots on pavement, and metal clanging against metal, I'd tuned out the various sounds to focus on the whiny voice of my captain. Panic set in, I needed an escape. I sensed someone approaching, so I turned. Well, it wasn't Leary, but even better…. *Lucas.*

"Ms. O'Neill, I have started the list and wanted to know how far back I should go." His voice poured over me like hot chocolate. My toes curled. *What is it about this guy? He oozes sex.*

Since manners dictated, I introduced the two and stalled Lucas's question. "Captain, this is Lucas Pigg. Lucas, this is Captain Nathan Grim. He stopped by to make sure things were under control."

Lucas reached out his hand. "Hello, Captain. You seem familiar. Have you worked in the department long?" His brow furrowed as if he was trying to place the captain.

Nathan shook hands with Lucas without the usual macho posturing and tough-guy need to prove strength. "Hello, Mr. Pigg. I was recently transferred, but I've been on the force for a while. Maybe we met at an event with your brother, Jonah."

"That's probably it." Lucas turned toward me. "Ms. O'Neill, a minute of your time, please?"

"Sure." I rotated, looking at Grim. "We'll talk later, Captain."

Lucas and I walked toward the building. "To answer your question, go back two years from now. This guy just recently started targeting your family. I'm sure something new was the instigating factor." I smiled up at him, thankful he'd saved me from having to talk longer to Grim.

He brushed his fingertip across the top of my hand. "I've racked my brain about who'd target us. But the real reason I came over was because you didn't look comfortable with your boss. I was worried about you."

I sighed then bit my lip. "Thank you. I appreciate it. He's my boss, but there's something about him which makes me uncomfortable. He's come on to me a few times but nothing I couldn't handle."

Lucas put his hands up. "Your body language was screaming 'get him away from me,' so I thought to help." He pushed his hand through his hair. "You've always got to be in charge? Can't you accept help?"

Frustration filled my chest. I didn't want to get into a fight. I laid my hand on his arm. Those zings of desire ran from my fingers to my toes. "I'm sorry, Lucas. I've needed to be a big girl in this man's world. I am grateful you butted in. We never did get lunch. We should reschedule."

Lucas placed his hand over mine. Desire pooled in my pussy, soaking my undies. "What are you doing for dinner tonight?" His voice deepened as he spoke, causing shivers to climb my spine. "How much longer will you be?"

"I should be able to leave in a half hour. What do you have in mind?" My voice sounded breathless as if I'd run a mile.

"There's this steak place. Maybe you've heard of it. You cook your steak at your table on a sizzling hot stone. I've wanted to try it but never had someone I wanted to go with. I figured you'd enjoy burning some meat at the table." He licked his lips.

There were two ways to take his comment. I didn't know if I should be flattered he wanted to take me to this place over everyone else, or if I should be upset he thought I wanted to burn something. "I've heard of the restaurant. Haven't been there either. Let me head home and change or I will smell like smoke all night. Do you want to meet there at 6:30?"

"Naw, let me pick you up. No sense in both of us driving. This time, his smile lit up his face. It was like the sun had come out from behind the clouds on a rainy day. I could get used to his smiles.

"Okay. Then hand me your phone and I'll enter my address and cell number. Luckily, my cell was the one thing which wasn't in my purse." After I entered my information, Lucas walked away. A hand waved in front of my face.

"Earth to O'Neill. You in there?" Leary had the strangest timing. My face heated, and I worried he'd caught me ogling Lucas.

"Anything new, Leary?" I turned and peered at him, hoping my blush wasn't evident.

"Officer Johnson who secured the scene didn't notice anyone in particular standing around watching. But I did find out the bank on the corner has security cams, and I'll make sure to get the video feeds. Also the gas station on the next block has cameras. We can study them to see if anything…." Leary paused. "You look like death warmed over. Why don't you head home? I can take it from here. Besides, we've done all we can." He patted my shoulder then gave it a squeeze. It was our way of showing friendship. The guys' club didn't allow us to hug and get all emotional. Knowing this close call affected him as well, I put my hand on his and gave it a squeeze in return.

"Thanks. You're a good friend. I'll see you tomorrow, and we can go over the videos." I headed toward my car, reaching into my pocket for my keys. License or not. I was driving home. Luckily, for me, I'd kept those in my pocket, too. Otherwise, I'd be walking.

CHAPTER FOUR

Stepping into the hot shower, I felt the warmth flowing over me, caressing my skin. I squirted some rose body wash into my hands and lathered my arms, stomach, and legs. My nipples hardened as my hands passed over my breasts. I thought about Lucas touching me and kissing me, and my legs almost gave way. Leaning on the shower wall, I touched my fingers to my pussy lips. They felt swollen. Just one soft touch sent spasms through my body.

I closed my eyes and imagined Lucas in the shower with me. My hands became his hands as they caressed my folds and then teased my clit. My breathing sped up as I brought myself to orgasm. Sitting down on the floor of the shower, I let the aftershocks float through me. I wished Lucas had been in the shower with me. There was something so sensual about him. The full lips which hardly ever smiled. The deep penetrating eyes that seemed to see into my soul. The large callused hands of a man who wasn't afraid to work hard. All those things were my weakness. It didn't matter Lucas was a part of a case. I couldn't change my desire. I only hoped I could keep my feelings out of this. Let it be sex…not one piece more.

Slipping on black slacks, a green blouse, and my leather jacket, I sat on the ottoman to tug my black boots on and tucked my small pistol into the ankle holster. I wore my kick-ass outfit, which I wore when I needed to push a suspect for information. The leather became a shield for my feelings as well. No way was I going to let Lucas into my heart.

The doorbell rang, and my heart skipped a beat. *Lucas.* Sauntering to the door, I pulled it open, a smile pasted on my face to combat the butterflies doing the tango in my stomach. "Hi, Lucas. Any problem finding the place?" I retreated into the foyer.

He stepped inside. His glance swept over my home then flew back to me. The heat from his gaze slid up my body. I raised my brow.

He bent over and kissed my cheek. "You look beautiful, spectacular." His breath caressed my neck as he spoke.

Pulling my coat close around my body like a shield, I grabbed the keys off the side table. "I'm starving and ready to go. I can't wait to see how this 'steak on a stone' works." I turned and checked to make sure my door was locked. I felt his hand clasp my elbow.

"I'm starving, too." He licked his lips and wiggled his eyebrows at me.

"Better behave. You're playing with fire, and I know how hot it burns."

His laughter echoed in the dark night as we climbed into his car.

***

At last, they left. I'd been observing her place for hours, imagining her naked body at my mercy. Then *he* showed up. Why must he spoil everything?

Racing the stairs to her apartment, I thought about how she'd considered him. Just another reason for him to be punished. She'd always been mine. He was not going to take her, too.

Outside her door, I looked around before picking the lock. Smiling and waving as I entered her space, no one would think I wasn't the close friend I dream I was.

Her bedroom beckoned me. Just inside the room, I paused, closed my eyes, and inhaled her scent. I sauntered toward her bed as if she'd lay there anticipating me. Grabbing her pillow, I rubbed my face in the smell of her shampoo. Harder than I'd ever been in my life, I wanted nothing more than to mark her bed with my cum. But it'd leave evidence—traceable evidence—and it wasn't time for her to know I stalked her…yet. Dropping the pillow on the mattress, frustration crawled up my spine. I imagined her in bed with *him*, opening herself, letting his hands caress her curves. Fury spotted my vision.

Pulling the can of red spray paint from my pack, I slashed the word "whore" onto her sheets, "slut" onto the wall, and across her dresser. The spray mimicked my sexual release. Now panting from the pleasure, I stuffed the can into my sack. Hopefully, she'd heed my warning. If not….

***

Steaks and Stones' cozy interior and secluded booths screamed "date joint", which made me uncomfortable. While I'd ruled Lucas out as the arsonist, mixing fire business and romance was like mixing hydrogen and flame…unstable, explosive, and bad news. Yet, trying to explain all this to my ovaries was like trying to explain quantum physics to a toddler. My hormones were throwing a huge hissy fit, screaming "want Lucas, want Lucas" each time I got near him. No matter how rational my brain acted, in this battle, the ovaries were winning.

I scooched into the burgundy leather booth the hostess had indicated. Smiling, I grabbed the menu and perused the choices, all the while secretly studying the handsome man sitting across from me. His dark hair brushed the collar of the blue button-down shirt. My hands ached to find out if his hair was as soft as it looked.

"See anything good…on the menu?" His gaze met mine.

My face heated. I'd been caught.

Luck was on my side as the waiter appeared. "Hello, my name is John. The special tonight is the addition of shrimp or scallops to our 10 oz. Steak on a Stone. Our vegetable is asparagus and the soup is clam chowder. Is there anything I can get you to drink while you're deciding on dinner?"

"I'll have a glass of Honey Jack if you have it, and ice water." I nodded toward the waiter.

"Scotch neat, house brand, for me."

"I'll grab your drinks and return to take your order." The waiter wrote the drinks down on a pad then strode away.

"I'll repeat…did you see anything you liked?" His lips curved into a smirk, which I longed to wipe off his face had he not caught me red-handed.

"You're handsome. You know it." I laid my menu down. "I'm sure you have women falling all over you. But no matter how sexy you are, I like more…substance in my men."

He reached his arm out and ran a finger over the back of my hand. His gaze, though, never left mine. "You said handsome and sexy, so I guess you do like me."

"Did you stop listening after you heard what you wanted?" I playfully swatted him away.

"No." He grabbed my hand and turned it over. This time, he ran his finger over my palm, sometimes firm and sometimes soft, drawing patterns, writing words. "My grandmother was a Romanian Gypsy. She taught me how to read palms. Would you like me to show you what it says?"

I nodded.

"You hide so much of yourself behind a shell, I'm not quite sure of where I stand around you. At first, you made me angry. Feisty little redhead dictating what I could do. Slowly, I began to see more, like how you fight twice as hard for everything just because you're a woman. Your need to be taken seriously for your knowledge and skills rather than your looks. And how you trust so few…Leary being a part of the few…your family."

"You got all that from my palm? You should take your show to Vegas." I leaned in. Anger tinged my voice. "You think you have me pegged, huh?" I raised my left eyebrow and smirked, irritated he'd seen right through my walls.

"I'd like to think, as a PI, I have some skills for noticing things." He tossed his fiercest weapon at me—his dimples—and I crumbled.

My smile turned genuine. "You better move your head or you might get a drink on your lap."

He whipped his head around, almost colliding with the waiter and our drinks.

"Observant, huh?"

Lucas's face reddened, yet he still held tight to my hand.

The waiter placed our drinks in front of us then wrote down our order. "The food will be out right out."

"Hard to see anything when I'm staring at the most beautiful woman in the room." He tugged my fingers to his lips.

His tongue touched my fingertips. A shot of fire trailed down my spine. I crossed my legs to stop the tingling in my panties. *This man's mouth should be labeled as a dangerous weapon.* Shifting again, I struggled to follow the conversation as the waiter set our salad plates in front of us. Now it was my turn to blush. "Such a charmer. I bet you say those sweet nothings to all the women."

"No. Only the ones who are beautiful. Would you believe my brothers tease me because I'm the serious one? Marcus is the ladies' man, never me. Somehow, you've brought this side out in me. You intrigue me with your wary attitude but keen understanding of crime." Those treacherous dimples showed on his face once again. He looked like a fallen angel and tempted me like one.

Our dinner conversation turned toward mundane things like family, our favorite movies, and our food. I was relieved to avoid talking shop. Even while he wasn't a suspect anymore, it wasn't policy to share details with anyone outside the department. The steak was tasty and tender, but none of it really whet my appetite. Tonight felt more like a date rather than two friends having dinner, and I found myself relaxing and enjoying his company. The surly man I met at the first arson scene had turned into a kitty cat...a sexy beast for sure. I imagined how he'd taste. *Would his kisses burn as the fire had the building?*

Lucas's hand waved in front of my eyes. I realized he'd been talking, and I had missed something. Heat flooded my face. "What?"

He smirked. "Wool-gathering?" He reached out and caressed my hand. Tingles sizzled up my arm.

"Thinking about the case," I lied.

I took my bottom lip between my teeth. His gaze lingered on my mouth. He licked his own lips. I forgot to breathe. My lungs froze as he brushed his fingertip across my lips. Gently, I touched my tongue to his finger. He slapped his credit card down on the table like a man possessed as the waiter arrived with the bill.

"Thank you, sir, and madam. Will there be anything else?" Clearly, the waiter couldn't take a hint.

"No. Just ring me out, now." Lucas's eyes never left my face. I shivered from the intensity of his gaze, or maybe the anticipation of being alone with him in the car.

The waiter dashed away only to return in seconds. "Sign, please. Thank you again for coming to Steaks and Stones. It's been our pleasure." He laid the tin on the table along with a pen.

Lucas sighed as he signed the check and pocketed his credit card. Standing, he held his hand out for me. As his larger fingers enveloped mine, I stood then was pulled into his arms. We stood toe to toe and nose to neck. I had to look up to see his face. His hard body melded to mine, and I was enveloped in his warmth.

A busboy bumped into us with his cart, forcing us to jump apart.

"Let's get you home." Lucas's voice deepened. He led me with one arm around my waist to his car.

The chill in the night air cooled my feverish body and cleared my mind. *Should I be doing this? Oh, I know I want it, but is it a good idea?* My mind and sex argued over my decision. Each one had a strong case.

He opened the door to his car and helped me into the soft leather interior. Resting my head against the seat, I allowed the argument in my body to continue, knowing whatever they decided would be fine with me.

CHAPTER FIVE

The sexual tension in the car had me crossing and uncrossing my legs. Both of us were silent during the drive to my house, yet our heavy breathing kept fogging up the windshield. Thinking about what I was about to do and the fifty million reasons I shouldn't, thoughts ran through my head like deer with a bobcat on their heels. Nervously, I bit my lip and said a little prayer I'd have no regrets in the morning.

Lucas parked his car in my driveway, shut off the engine, and turned toward me. He placed his hand on my thigh, and I twitched. "Are you sure you...?"

I pulled him in close and kissed him, deeply with passion, keeping him from probing my doubts. And while I wasn't 100 percent sure boinking Lucas would be a good idea, my hormones had won this round. I wasn't going to back down now.

Breaking our kiss, he opened the car door, walked around, released mine, and tugged me out. Drawing me in tight to his body, he ran his hands over my shoulders and caressed my ass, pulling me closer so I didn't need to guess if there was a roll of quarters in his pocket.

"Let's get inside where it's comfortable." Tucked under his arm, we strolled toward my door. On the porch, I pulled my keys from my pocket. As I pushed the key into the lock, the door swung open. Instantly alert, I drew my gun from my boot. "Stay back," I whispered harshly as I pushed Lucas aside. "I've got this. Call 911." But when I glanced at him to make sure he'd followed my directions, he held his gun in his hand, too. Scowling at him, I spat, "Just don't get shot."

"Been there, done that. It doesn't hurt much." His smirk melted my heart. I'd forgotten Lucas's military training. Having him as a partner wouldn't be so bad.

I shoved the door open so it hit the wall and positioned myself, ready to shoot at anything in the room. However, the living room was empty. Motioning with my head for Lucas to cover me, I started in, stepping to the side, my back along the wall, checking for anyone who might be in the house. Systematically working together, Lucas and I cleared the kitchen, living room, guest room, and bathroom. Nothing had been disturbed. Nothing taken. As we approached my bedroom, I'd begun to think I'd left the door open on accident.

The last ajar door beckoned. I glanced at Lucas who stood behind me, protecting my back through the search. He raised his brow as if to question then nodded. I kicked the door open. It hit the wall, sending a bang reverberating throughout my body. Scanning the room, I slid along the door. The room was silent. Empty.

"What the hell?" Lucas's voice echoed in my ears.

I holstered my gun and surveyed the message on my sheets. The red dripping down the wall, destroying my dresser. Rage emanated off each word. Chills slid down my spine. My home, my sanctuary had been violated. I dropped to my knees. Lucas wrapped me in his embrace and rubbed my shoulders until I stopped shaking.

When I got myself under control, he withdrew, pulled his phone from his pants' pocket, and called 911. He relayed the information while I wandered in my room. The violation people talked about had me feeling dirty, as if someone had touched my body and rummaged through my mind. I shivered.

My drawers had been ransacked and the bed trashed. Red paint marred the sheets where I'd slept peacefully just this morning. Hugging my arms around my middle I marched to the living room and slumped down on the couch. My house had become a crime scene, so I didn't touch anything.

Lucas sat next to me, placing his hand on my leg. "It'll be okay. I'm not going to let this sicko get away with this. First targeting me and now you. It's obvious he knows about us." His voice held a quiet whisper of steel and anger.

"Us? We had a dinner. I think you're jumping to conclusions that this"—I swept my arm toward the rear of the house—"was the work of our arsonist. More likely, a jealous ex of yours." I tried to hold my anger in check, but frustration forced me to lash out.

Sirens blared outside. A knock sounded as I strode to open the door. Two men in blue uniforms stood in front of me.

"I'm Officer Tucker and this is Officer Woodlawn," the taller man introduced his partner. "I understand there was a break-in."

"Thank you, sir. Yes. I'm the homeowner, Lily O'Neill. I work with the department in the arson investigation division." I retreated from the doorway and motioned for the officers to enter. "Come in."

Their all-business faces lit up when they noticed Lucas standing by the sofa. "Hey, Lucas. What's going on?"

"Hey, Mike. Hi, Joseph." Lucas reached out and shook hands with both men before patting them on the shoulder. "Miss O'Neill and I were out having dinner then found this when I brought her home."

Another knock sounded and I returned to the door, opening it. "Hello, Jonah." I smiled at Lucas's brother. "I didn't know break-ins needed a detective."

He followed me into my home. "Not usually until we've determined the crime was committed, but since you're almost family...." He turned and shoved his brother. "Should have known. Trouble follows you, Lukey." A smile belayed his words.

I grinned for the first time since returning from dinner, my mood lightening. Seeing the brothers tease each other made me wish for a sister. "So you admit, Jonah, one of Lucas's ex's is behind this?"

"Let me take a look." He strode into my bedroom, the two officers behind.

As I started to follow, Lucas tugged at my arm. "Let them do their job. My brother's here as a favor to me. You know he'll take care of this."

I leaned my head onto his chest, desperate to share the burden of my anxiety. "Do you really think this is tied to our arsonist?" I mumbled.

His hands caressed my back, soothing. Even as his words sent another chill down my spine. "I do."

A noise from the hall had us jumping apart like two teens caught necking on the porch. Running my fingers through my hair, I took a deep calming breath. *I hope it'll work, but anytime I'm close to Lucas, my ovaries have me acting like a sex-starved virgin.*

Jonah returned to the living room with Officer Tucker. "Lucas, give your statement to Officer Tucker while I take Lily's. I know they are the same, but I want to do this by the book, so when we catch this guy...*and we will*...I'll put him away for a long time."

Tucker and Lucas headed off to the kitchen to talk, while Jonah waved his hand toward the couch. "Let's talk here."

I joined him on the sofa. He was a little shorter than Lucas, broader with lighter, blonder hair, but I could see a similarity on his face. His nose? His eyes?

Jonah smiled, and his dimples appeared. Yep, the smile—although, Jonah's seemed less predatory and more brotherly. "Your brother picked me up at 6:30. He drove us to Steaks and Stones, we had one drink each, and both ordered the ribeye."

Jonah wrote down my statement. "Did you pay by credit card?"

I nodded. "Lucas paid, and we drove here. The drive was less than 30 minutes. We arrived to find the door ajar. I requested your brother call 911, but he was determined to be my backup. I pulled my revolver from my boot, and we cleared each room, starting in the living room and finishing in my bedroom."

"Were you sure you locked your door?" He glanced at my face.

"I was sure I had, but when I went through my home, I doubted myself until I saw my bed." My voice cracked. "I'm sorry. This is harder than I thought."

"Try watching someone you love dealing with it. I hated not being able to protect my wife, Betsie. Even with all three of us watching out for her. I almost lost her." His voice deepened with emotion.

I pasted a smile on my face. At least I hoped it was a smile and not the grimace I frequently used. "Thanks. I'll continue. After seeing the mess, we never touched a thing, just pocketed our guns and Lucas called for the police. Nothing else looked out of place. I didn't see any scratches on the door, but I'm sure I locked it. I always do." I took another deep breath. "Lucas thinks this is the work of the arsonist who's been targeting your buildings. Do you think it could be?"

Jonah nodded. "Lucas isn't a ladies' man. The women he's been with wouldn't do this. There aren't any angry ex's. Besides, the backside of your pillow has a tiny black stain on it. The substance was microscopic and hard to see, but it appeared the person touched or laid on your pillow. We'll have to take it in for the lab to run tests on it."

"You're sure?" I took a deep breath, fighting not to scream. I shivered, knowing someone had put their head where mine laid.

"Yes. Officer Woodlawn noticed it. He even smelled it but said it didn't have a noticeable odor. I'd rather you find another place to stay at this point."

I shook my head. "No. This is my home."

His teeth clenched as he spoke with determination. "It's now my crime scene, and since I do think the arson and your break-in are related, I don't want to take a chance you'll get hurt. I'd never forgive myself, especially since your dad was my good friend." Jonah's no-nonsense manner and calm voice convinced me he'd do everything he could to find the horrible person who'd invaded my home.

I shifted my shoulders and gritted my teeth. "Fine. Can I at least grab some clothes?"

"Nope. I'm sorry." He patted my leg. "I'll have my brother drive you to a local hotel. I'll give you a call when I have more information or when the scene is cleared for you to return." He stood. "Should just be tonight."

Rising from the couch, I turned toward the kitchen. Lucas and the police officer returned. Their conversation about last Sunday's Bengals game reminded me of how upset my own unit would be about this incident.

Focusing on Jonah, I tapped him on his arm. "Can I at least let my partner know what's going on? I don't want him hearing about this through inter-office politics. It'd crush him."

"Sure. But keep it just with him. Right now, it looks like we are after the same unsub. And I'd rather he didn't learn about things from us."

"Great." I yanked my hair into a ponytail and twisted the band from my wrist around it.

Jonah walked to the officer then turned toward me again. "I'll be in touch."

CHAPTER SIX

With my mind driven on solving the puzzle of the arsonist, I didn't realize the car had stopped until Lucas opened my door.

"Where are we? This isn't the Holiday Inn." I examined the quaint home in front of me. A large front porch with a swing welcomed visitors to stop and visit. The front door had an inlay of beveled glass in the center of the dark wood. A bright glass chandelier shone light on the gray painted porch.

"It's my home."

I turned back to look at Lucas.

"Well, my family home." He shrugged.

"Okay. So, why are we here? I thought Jonah told you to take me to a hotel. If you are thinking about finishing what we started at dinner…." I raised my chin. "I'm not in the mood now."

Lucas's fingers trailed over my lips and along my jawline. "I thought you might want to stay here tonight. It's safe." His heated gaze was at odds with his caring words. "My sister-in-law, Betsie, lives here with Jonah. And Marcus is home this weekend, too. Besides, it's comfy and *home*." His emphasis on the last word showed just how much this place meant to him.

Beginning to understand his thinking, I smiled. "Thanks. I'm sure no one would want to break into the police detective's home. Not with his badass brothers at home."

"I knew even with dead bolts, after the break-in, you wouldn't feel safe. You can even borrow a nightshirt from Betsie." He tugged me up the steps. "Come on, slowpoke." Lucas's smile filled his face. It was refreshing to see this side of him. So far, I'd witnessed brooding, angry, ferocious, tantalizing, and now caring and compassionate.

Before we reached the walnut-stained door, it flew open. A petite blonde woman stood framed in the doorway. The bright light behind her cast her features in shadows. "Lucas. Lily. Come in. Jonah called. He knew you'd come here."

Overwhelmed, I took a step away. Lucas held tight to my arm. I swore he said be brave under his breath.

The small tornado of a woman scooped me into her embrace, hugged me, and patted my back. "I'm Betsie Pigg, Jonah's wife. You poor thing. I can just imagine how scared you are. One time when my boss was after me, I slept with a knife under my pillow. We'll take good care of you."

I glanced at Lucas who rolled his eyes at me. Giving him my fiercest look, the one I'd used on my dad when I needed to borrow the car in high school, I implored Lucas to help.

"Betsie, Lily needs to breathe." He tapped the woman on the shoulder. "Why don't you show her around the house? She can have my room and I'll bunk in with Marcus. It'll be just like old times."

I smiled at her, nodded, and agreed to whatever Lucas had planned. Anything to avoid the touchy-feely stuff by someone I'd met once at a police banquet. "It's very nice of you to put me up here. I'd love to see where I'm crashing. As you can imagine, the whole event's got me on edge."

Betsie ushered me up the staircase, photos lining the wall. I paused to look at the one image of a loving family with three small boys fishing near a stream. I grinned at the image of the Pigg brothers as children. Their carefree smiles and small fists holding up tiny fish as if they were huge prizes. But it was the love evident on their parents' faces which stole my heart. It'd been years since I looked through my own childhood photo albums, but I had no doubt the same love shown on my dad and mom's faces as well.

Following Betsie up to the top landing, I stared at the beautiful workmanship done in this home. While old-fashioned, it had a warm, cozy feel without being cramped or crowded. The landing opened onto four dark-wood doors. She opened the first one on the left.

"This is Jonah's and my room. Let me grab you a nightshirt." She walked into the room and grabbed a shirt out of the top dresser drawer. A large window cast the room in moonlight. She handed me the dark-green material.

I smiled. "Thank you. I appreciate this. You have a beautiful home. How long have you lived here?" I slung the shirt over my shoulder.

"Almost two years. The house belonged to the boys' parents, and when they died, Jonah took over caring for Lucas and Marcus, put them through college, and kept the house," Betsie shared with pride.

"Wow. I knew he'd been their role model, but all the other things, too? He sounds like a saint!" I shook my head and stared down at my boots. "I remember how hard it was to care for a house and look after my dad when my mom passed. I can't imagine raising siblings, too." Raising my head, I beamed. "He's always been a great detective. Now I understand more about his drive and determination."

As we walked into the hall, Betsie pointed to the room across from her room. "Behind that door is Marcus's room. I do minimal cleaning in there. Just a quick dusting and vacuuming once in a while. He's been gone a lot on assignments." She blushed, her cheeks turning a light pink. "Or maybe to give Jonah and me more time alone. Even Lucas is hardly here. But he has...*had* the fancy loft in the building which first caught fire."

Betsie opened the door next to her room. "This is the bathroom. We only have the one on this floor, but it's not a big deal. No one seems to hog it. Although"—she leaned close to me—"I swear those boys sometimes urinate out their windows so they won't make me leave during my bath time. Just let me know if you need to be out the door at a certain time, so we can avoid any issues." She winked at me, which had me doubting if the story was true or not. But then again, knowing Lucas...I could see him writing his name in the snow or trying to trick his brothers into eating the yellow snow.

We approached the last door. A yawn escaped my lips. The incident at my house had plumb tuckered me out. I was ready for sleep.

Betsie pushed the door open then waited, gauging my reaction. The large log bed dominating the forest-themed room took my breath away. My jaw dropped. I wasn't sure what I'd expected. With wide eyes, I scanned the interesting pieces in the room. A hammock chair hung in the corner. Shelves made out of driftwood flanked the bed. Small shells, hand-carved animals, and antique-looking books lined the shelves.

"I'd never have guessed." I shook my head at Betsie. "What a cool room. Has it always been this way?"

She nodded. "The boys decided to keep their rooms the same as when they were kids. Each room is uniquely theirs. Lucas told me his father used to sit on the bed and read him adventure stories. One time he...." She glanced around to see if anyone was listening then lowered her voice. "Thought he was going to become a forest ranger." She straightened. "But that was before his parents' deaths. It changed all the boys. Lucas went into the military and became closed off. He always seemed more the loner, but that was before this arsonist...and you."

My face heated at her words about Lucas and me. "How amazing to have this place to come home to." My eyes teared up when I thought about a young Lucas with his father in this room. After my mom passed, my old family home was bleached of her things, as if seeing her in the home was too painful for my father. But now I longed for just one small part to keep with me. Another yawn escaped my lips. "Thanks for lending me the nightshirt. I'll be up at first light. Still have work in the morning. After all, old habits die hard."

"Good night. I'll see you in the morning, then. Sleep well." Betsie pulled the door closed as I slumped on the edge of the bed and withdrew my pistol from my boot, laying it on the shelf next to the headboard. After kicking off my shoes, I scooted up to the pillow and, at last, succumbed to sleep.

***

Something woke me. *A nightmare? A sound?* The dark unfamiliar room confused me until I remembered the bright-red paint on my white sheets.

Creek. The hammock chair moved. My heart rate sped up as my eyes searched the shadows. Reaching for my weapon, I considered all the escape avenues.

"Lily, put the gun down."

I removed my hand from the weapon. "What the hell? Don't you know not to antagonize a girl with a gun? I could have shot you." I gritted my teeth, picked up the pillow, and tossed it at Lucas. "I should have," I mumbled.

He grabbed the pillow before it hit him, stood, and carried it to the bed. "You may want this." He handed it to me. "I was watching over you. I figured you might be uncomfortable in a strange bed, different house. I didn't want you to wake up scared."

I lifted my brow and eyed him. "It's nice of you. I was tired as you can see. Never made it under the covers. Besides, I'm a big girl. I am fine. Now get out of my room."

"Don't you mean my room?"

I wished I could wipe the smirk off his face. Lucas was so full of himself. A light bulb went off. Two could play this game. I slid off the bed and stood in the shaft of moonlight from the window. Unbuckling my belt, unbuttoning and unzipping my jeans, I slid them down my legs then placed them on the bottom of the bed.

"Mmmm…." A moan escaped his lips. "I thought you wanted me to leave," he teased.

"I do. But since you woke me." With each sentence, I unbuttoned one of the buttons on my green blouse. "I'm going to get comfortable. No sense sleeping in my clothes." I licked my lips and smiled at him then slipped the blouse off my shoulders and laid it on top of my jeans.

I turned my back to him and unhooked my bra, letting it slowly fall off my shoulders. Tossing it onto the bed, I covered my breasts with my hands and turned to find the bedroom door open and me alone in the room.

Giggling, I grabbed Betsie's nightie and slipped it over my head then climbed into the bed under the covers. Pulling the comforter tight against me, I snuggled down into the bed, closed my eyes, and returned asleep, sure the smile on my face would keep any nightmares away.

CHAPTER SEVEN

Thankfully, Lucas missed breakfast. Early appointment? Or had I scared him off with my shenanigans last night? After Jonah announced at breakfast my home had been cleared as a crime scene, I had him drop me off. Relief flooded my heart, but also a little fear. Going home would mean facing the invasion again.

Cleansing my home was my top priority. Too bad I didn't have time before work. Entering my bedroom, I froze. Instead of my old bed, a new log bed and dresser which matched the one in Lucas's home stood sentinel. Crisp clean sheets, blankets, and quilt completed the ensemble. A note lay on the bed.

Dear Lily,
I hope this will help you find your own piece of home and restful sleep. I overheard your conversation with Betsie and knew sleeping here after the break-in would be difficult. You'll have sweet dreams in this new bed...although, I will forever think of you in my own bed.
Yours, Lucas

"Well, this answers where he was instead of at breakfast." I wiped at the tears on my cheeks. I'd never have thought he would be so concerned about my feelings. I sat on the edge of the bed and clutched my chest. My heart ached. What was I feeling? Could this be love? I shook my head. My heart beat out my hormones, but I don't know where he stands...and I won't ask.

At least I have a fresh bed. With one less thing on my checklist, I quickly dressed for work.

I grabbed my keys and backup purse, locked the door, and headed down to the garage. Slipping behind the wheel of my Firebird, I turned the key, revved the engine, and listened to her purr. I cranked up the radio then backed out of my space and headed into work.

I headed into the bullpen. The cacophony of sounds, phones ringing, voices yelling.... It felt like home. The boss's door was closed, the shades drawn. Clearly, the Do Not Disturb sign was out, which is fine by me. Not that I'd ever think of Grim as my boss. A letch or maybe pervert but not boss. Leaders deserved respect, and he'd never done a thing to earn it.

I strode into my office, plopped down at the desk, and booted up my computer. The files on the Pigg arsons had come in. The crime lab found the accelerant was gasoline at both scenes. They were even able to trace it to a local gas station due to the additives in the gasoline. The fire at Jessi's started in the alley and, luckily, hadn't totaled the place. She'd be closed for a while even after she got back on her feet. Feeling safe will be a big concern.

Opening the video files from the surrounding locations, I hesitated, closed the file, and reopened it. No change. I stood and walked toward my office door. Leary sat at his desk, enjoying his morning coffee. I hated to disrupt a man with a high level of bliss on his face. "Hey, Leary. When you're done filling your body with go-go juice, come into my office and look at this file."

He lifted the cup to his lips, swallowed then moaned. I rolled my eyes at him and stomped to my desk.

Mark entered and plopped in the ratty black chair across from my desk. "What's up?"

"If you're done having an erotic experience with your coffee, can you explain what happened to the videos from the nearby businesses during the Pigg building arsons?"

He raised his shoulders and looked lost. "What do you mean?"

"They're not here." I pointed at my computer.

"Not to sound like a parrot but, what do you mean?" He rose from the chair and stalked around my desk. I relinquished my chair, and he sat down. "Did you restart? Look in the other files? Check your recycle bin?" But with each of my nods, his shoulders slumped.

I stood sentinel over his shoulder as he coaxed my computer to give him the files he put there. But all the files of the arson scenes had been wiped clean.

Slapping my hand on the desk, I made my point. "See. They were there and now they aren't. How could this have happened and, more importantly, who did it?"

He never raised a glance at me. "No one should have been able to. This is a department file server which is protected by firewalls and passwords." He continued to punch the keys on the keyboard. "The only way someone could have gotten into this system was from the inside."

I grabbed his shoulder, turning him in my chair and then bent over. Got in his face. Nose to nose. "What do you mean, inside? Are you sure it wasn't a hacker?"

He shook his head. "No hacker. They'd have taken more than just these case files. They were important to us and to the arsonist…or someone working for him or her."

I closed the office door. Running my hand through my hair, I leaned against the door. "So, we have a mole. No wonder my house was trashed."

Leary jumped up and ran toward me. "Are you okay? What happened?" His slack-jawed face exposed his shock.

"Yesterday, someone broke into my house and spray painted my sheets with a 'love' message. Lucas thought it was related to the arson investigation, but I thought it was too personal." I hid my face in my palms.

Mark dropped in to the old office chair. His eyes wide and mouth forming an O. "It's obvious everything is connected. The arsons, the missing files, and your place. Someone doesn't want this case solved."

"Jonah Pigg is the lead detective on my break-in, and he's aware of the arsons and has access to the computer system, but he's got alibis for the arsons. And why would he want to burn his family businesses?" I always thought better on my feet, so I paced the office, my boots making an annoying clacking sound on the linoleum. "We'd pretty much ruled the Piggs out since the money wasn't a motive and they'd never had a problem with the law."

"Now we're at a dead end. Those videos might have given us evidence of who witnessed the arsons." Leary flung his hand toward my desk. "Maybe the person who erased them knew they implicated the arsonist." He shot to his feet. "Since I'm sure the bank and the gas station haven't deleted their videos yet, I'll go grab them again."

My eyes widened. My heart pounded. Things were getting more dangerous. I grasped his shirt sleeve. "This has to stay in this room. Just the two of us."

A knock sounded on my door, causing me to jump. After looking at Leary, who shrugged, I opened the door. "Hi, Grim. Did you need something? Leary and I were going over our files."

The captain brushed past me and stepped into the room. He glanced at Leary who stood next to my desk with a pen in his teeth and paper in his hands. He grabbed my arms and pulled me into a hug then stepped away. "Are you okay? I just heard about the break-in."

Rubbing my palms down my arms, I pasted my plastic smile on my face. "Yes. I'm fine. Stayed at a hotel last night. No worries." I ached to pour bleach on my body to clean it, and throw away the shirt he just touched. But I kept my fake smile in place. "They cleared my home today. Nothing taken."

Grim glanced at Leary. "You'll make sure she gets safely home today, right?"

Leary nodded. Then Grim returned his focus on me. "If you need anything, you know how to reach me." He put his hand in mine and squeezed. "Even if you don't want to be alone. I'd never forgive myself if something happened to you."

Ick, ick, ick! "Thanks, Boss." I turned, strode to my desk then sat down. "Better return to work. Would you mind closing the door on your way out?" Again with the fake smile. I hope my voice sounded sincere.

"Sure. Take care." And the man of my nightmares left.

Leary rounded toward me. "Lil—"

I held up my hand. "It's alright. I'll be fine. We'd better get these files updated." I opened a blank word document on my computer and began typing random words. Leary peered over my shoulder but kept his mouth shut. When I heard the shoes squeak away, I let out the breath I'd been holding.

Leary stared at me as if I had a stain on my face. "What was that?" His face scrunched up. "You and the captain?"

Placing my finger in my mouth, I made choking sounds. "No way. He'd like to think so, but I avoid those close encounters. You know how easy it would be to have a whisper say I slept my way to the top." I shook my head. "I earned this. Worked harder and deserve it. Not because of dating anyone in the office."

"What about suspects?" Leary's voice teased, and I sent him my dirtiest look.

"Lucas and I aren't dating. We've had dinner together once…to discuss the case."

"You know what Shakespeare says…. The lady doth protest too much."

"You read Shakespeare? Will wonders never cease?" I stood and slipped on my black leather jacket. "How about we go grab those tapes and meet at the pizza joint for lunch?"

"Sounds like a plan. I'll visit the gas station and you can hit the bank. Ha ha…hit the bank. Did you get my joke?"

This time I did slap him upside the head. "Let's roll."

***

The aroma of pizza made my stomach growl before I opened the door to the quaint restaurant. Red-checkered tablecloths covered the tabletops. Scenes of farms and wineries decorated the walls. The sound of plates, silverware, and conversations filled the main room. A favorite with the locals for lunch, most tables and the bar were full. Seeing Leary waving at me from a back table, I made my way toward him across the black-and-white checkered floor. A pitcher of soda and a couple of glasses sat ready on the table.

I sat down. "Have you ordered?"

"The usual. One large pepperoni and mushroom. Should be up soon." Leary furtively glanced around the room then leaned in. "Funny thing about the gas station. They had a fire last night."

I raised my eyebrows, surprised at the news. "Arson?"

"Nope." He shook his head. "Gas pump exploded. Took out the whole building."

"Isn't this convenient." I gritted my teeth. "You're going to *love* my news," I replied sarcastically. "I spoke with the bank manager. According to him, another police officer came in and collected the tapes, originals and all."

"So, will he be able to describe the police officer? Did he get a name?" Leary was like a dog with a new chew toy. He looked as if he'd bounce off his seat.

"Funny thing. The officer's name was O'Neill, but it was a dark-haired guy with a mustache and beard. The manager even saw a badge, which I'm sure was mine from my purse which was left at the second scene."

The waitress dropped off the pizza and plates. I poured us each a glass of soda and thought about all we'd learned. My stomach growled loud enough for my partner to hear. He put a slice on my plate and passed it to me.

"Just watch my fingers when you take this. I like having all ten." Here he was, trying to make jokes, and all the while we both knew the truth. Someone was making sure our leads were dead ends.

CHAPTER EIGHT

"Step away from the pizza and no one will be hurt," a deep voice whispered in my ear.

I continued to eat, even as my heart jumped.

"Thought I said, put it down."

Butterflies danced in my stomach—not from the food but the sexy guy whispering to me.

Grabbing another piece, I placed it on my plate then lifted it to my shoulder. "Want to join us?" Smiling, I handed the plate to Lucas without pausing my own lunch.

He took the plate and sat in the chair on my left. "How did you know it was me?" he mumbled as he took a bite.

"First, your voice is unmistakable. Second, Leary here would have shot you if were trying to hurt me." I inclined my head toward my partner. "He's protective."

Lucas nodded at Leary, who shrugged and returned his gun to his shoulder holster. "Suppose it's a good thing I was just after the pizza." Lucas reached over and grabbed another piece. "Don't mind if I help myself. So, what brings you two here?"

Leary stared at me and raised his brow. As partners, we were used to our own silent communication. I nodded. "We found some interesting circumstances. All the videos of the crime scene were erased from the police server and then mysterious circumstances eliminated the original files. A fire at the gas station and an imposter at the bank."

"Looks like someone really wants this case to remain unsolved."

I reached over and grabbed the pizza out of Lucas's hand. "We suspect an inside job. Only someone from the department could have wiped the computer files."

"Pizza thief!" He reached for the piece, but I held it away from him. He paused. "Maybe you should set up a sting. Catch them at their own game."

"Hmm. What do you think, Leary?" When I glanced at my partner, Lucas ripped the pizza out of my hand and devoured it.

Leary's face was thoughtful but his shoulders were tense. "It's your call. I'm not sure who to trust but you anymore."

Lucas chimed in. "The arsonist has already come after Lily once. What's stopping them from doing it again? We got lucky she wasn't home."

My partner leaned over the table and went nose to nose with Lucas. "I'm not willing to take a chance with her life. Are you?"

Lucas pushed his chair back and stood. "No. She'll be with me, where I can keep her safe. You haven't been able to."

The other patrons paused in their meals to stare. I tugged at his hand. "Sit. We need to talk calmly." I turned to Leary. "It's my call, right?" He glared at me as if daring me to disagree. "You two need to play nice. I say we go for it."

With Leary's jaw clenched, he barely kept it together. But he should have known not to dare me. I've always taken on the tough challenges to prove I didn't get my job on my dad's coattails or my gender. Knowing I'd hurt him, I reached over and slipped my hand in his. "I can do this. With you and Lucas on my side, I know I'm safe." I flashed my dazzling smile, hoping he would cave. It'd always worked with my dad.

Leary squeezed my hand and smiled. "I'm not going to lose you."

"Alright." I acquiesced. The three of us bent our heads together. "Let's plan."

***

The office hum had died down when Leary and I returned. Grim's door stood open. I nudged Leary and nodded toward the boss's room as we headed toward my space.

He grasped my hand, gave it a squeeze, and then slammed his fist into the wall. "Look, O'Neill, Pigg's a liar. I don't like you being chummy with him." His loud voice carried, bouncing off the pale-blue walls.

Turning to face him, I narrowed my eyes and gritted my teeth. "No one tells me what to do. Back off."

He clutched my arms and held them tight to my body. "You're not safe. Can't you see?"

"You're not my boss." I yanked my arms free. "I'm meeting him at the coffee shop. We're going to keep looking for evidence. If you don't like it, leave now."

"I'm gone. Don't say I didn't warn you." Leary stomped away, kicking over a chair as he headed out the door.

I stood frozen, my arms wrapped around my waist. All my co-workers stared at me. Unwilling to let the tears fall, I slid into my office and shut the door.

A knock sounded as the office door opened. Grim stood framed in the doorway. A chill slid down my spine as I recalled the strange hug from before. "Hi, Boss. Did you need something?"

"No. I'm only checking to see if you are okay." He moved toward my desk. "Everyone saw the argument. Do you want me to talk to Leary?"

I shook my head. "No. It's his right to disagree." I rubbed at my eyes, wiping at the tears which threatened to fall.

"I don't like discontent in my office. Leary better shape up, or I will talk to him."

As Grim reached for me, I receded. The back of my legs hit the desk, making me jump. "I know it's late, but I'm gonna catch up on some paperwork if you don't mind."

"Sure thing. As I said before, I'm here for you." He left my office, closing the door behind him.

Walking around the desk, I slumped into the chair and placed my head on the desk. After my heartbeat slowed, I slipped my black leather jacket on, checked to make sure my firearm was in my boot, and opened the office door. Unable to meet the glances of my co-workers, I kept my head down and left the building.

The brisk walk to the coffee shop chafed my face, causing it to burn. Yellow police tape crisscrossed the entrance. I pulled it down and pushed the unlocked door open. The musty smell of old smoke and mold flooded my nasal passages. I tipped upright one of the tables and picked up a chair. I brushed off the seat, sat down, and recalled everything Leary said.

Closing my eyes, I inhaled deeply as I listened to the silence. Not even the sound of cars could be heard. Headlights filtered into the dining room between the window blinds. Raising my head, I pulled my small backup revolver from my boot and laid it on the table. My eyes focused on the door, I propped my feet on the table and laid a hand over my pistol. Only thing left to do was wait.

CHAPTER NINE

I woke to the smell of gasoline. It took me a moment to recall where I was. I didn't mean to sleep, but now I was wide awake. Standing, I grabbed my pistol and bolted out of the front door.

Leary ran from behind the building and quickly joined me. "I can't believe the sting worked."

"It's what we hoped for." The gasoline smell was stronger outside. A crowd had gathered. I scanned the group in front of the building. A man wearing a grungy army fatigue jacket lay on the pavement with a bullet wound to the head. Grim stood over him with a smug look on his face and his gun in his hand.

"What happened?" I wheezed, trying to stop my heart from jumping out of my chest.

The captain faced me. "This is our arsonist. He'd sprayed the building and was holding a lighter. I ordered him to put it down. He refused." He held his gun out. "You need to take this in for evidence."

"So, why shoot him? Why didn't you call for backup?" I wrinkled my brow and pursed my lips. Something didn't make sense.

"He'd already doused the building with gas and held a lighter to the can. I couldn't take the chance it might blow, harming others on the street." Grim pointed to the can and lighter which lay near the dead man. "Are you questioning me, your boss?" he snarled.

Leary held up his hands. "No. We're playing devil's advocate here. Pointing out what the police will ask."

"Are the police on their way?" When Grim shook his head, I pulled out my phone and called 911, giving the dispatcher the information. "They're on their way. Leary, get the crowd behind the tape and set a perimeter."

"Alright, back up." Leary's booming voice and broad shoulders forced the spectators across the street.

I felt a hand on my shoulder. Grim came closer. "I knew you were inside. I did this for you."

He knew? How? A chill sprinted down my spine. "Really? Please don't put this on me." I spun away from him. "No one, least of all me, wanted you to kill someone."

"He's the arsonist. He was going to burn you alive. I watched him pour gasoline on the building. I ordered him to stop." He voice level grew with each statement.

I shook my head. "Murder's wrong for any reason." I stomped to Leary and helped with crowd control.

Someone grabbed my arm. "Don't touch me," I yelled and tugged, trying to pull away.

"Lily, it's me. Are you okay?" Lucas's breathless voice almost caused my knees to buckle.

I grasped a hold of his shoulders. "I'm so glad you're here. Grim shot the arsonist."

He dipped his head as his lips caressed mine. "So, the fires are over?"

"We need to find out all the details, but tonight the trap sprung and my boss found the man trying to douse the building, for a second time. The arsonist wouldn't put down the gasoline can, and Grim fired, killing him." I shrugged. "Why did this guy come back here? Why burn the place a second time? Too many questions and only a dead body to talk to." I clenched my hands.

"We may never know why he targeted my family." Lucas tore away from me, striding to stare at the dead man.

I followed, hating to leave him alone to face this. Studying Lucas's face, puzzlement was evident. "Do you know him?"

He shook his head. "I've never seen him before. I hope the police will be able to get some answers."

Sirens echoed through the city streets, coming closer. Two black-and-whites parked at the end of the alley. Detective Pigg climbed out of the second car and headed straight for us.

"Hello, Jonah." I stretched out my hand to shake his. "It appears the captain's solved the arson case for me."

***

Things had been quiet around town for a week. Life moved on. Children attended school. Families went to church, and I went to the office each day to work on new cases. Grim had given his statement, and while the investigation into the shooting hadn't been closed, he'd closed the arson investigation.

I stood in front of the vending machine, trying to feed in a buck. As the bill fell to the ground for the bazillionth time, I slammed my hands on the brightly lit, plastic front. "Damn apparatus. Take the dollar."

"What did the evil contraption do to you, Lily?" Lucas whispered in my ear, forcing me to jump.

I turned and looked into his dark-blue eyes. Butterflies flittered in my stomach. "Stupid machine doesn't want my money. I'm desperate for a pop. Cold caffeine is the solitary caffeine which passes these lips."

His tongue darted out and ran over his top lip. "The only thing to touch your lips?" His gaze had dropped to my mouth, causing those butterflies to do summersaults.

"I'm not witty without the soda." I bent over, grabbed the dollar, and tossed it at him. "Soda first, lips later." I winked.

"Promises, promises." Lucas opened his wallet, stuffed the dollar in, and snatched a different bill out then shoved it into the machine. "What's your poison?"

I pushed the cola button and sighed as the bottle dropped to the bottom. Practically racing, I grasped the bottle, opened it, and took a swig. The bubbles tickled my throat on the way down, settling the butterflies. "Hits the spot. Thanks."

"You're welcome. Let's talk lips…." After putting his wallet away, he snagged my soda and stole a drink.

"What did you have in mind?" I appropriated the soda and swallowed a big gulp.

"Dinner…dancing…." Lucas wiggled his brows.

A giggle escaped my lips. "I'm up for it. Pick me up at six thirty." I slammed my hand against the vending machine then turned and walked away. Stopping, I faced the six feet of sexiness. "Thanks again for the pop."

A smile on my face, I sauntered down the hallway. Suddenly, I ran into someone. "Oomph. Sorry."

"Head in the clouds?" Leary teased.

My face heated. "You know me without the caffeine." I tipped the bottle to him.

"I'm glad you're happy…and Lucas isn't a suspect." He patted my arm.

I tilted my head. "He wasn't a suspect after about five minutes…but let's not fight." I pursed my lips. "Don't you think it is strange how this investigation went down? You know, with the captain catching and killing the suspect?"

Mark frowned. "Right place at the right time?" He scratched his head. "It doesn't add up. With the loss of our evidence, we were so sure it was someone on the inside."

Taking a deep breath, I shook my head. "I'm not convinced. But it's not for me to decide. I'll leave it up to Jonah Pigg and the police department."

I headed back to my office, my step a little less sassy as I pondered the case.

CHAPTER TEN

After a boring day of analyzing accelerants, I jumped at the chance for another dinner with Lucas. This time, we planned on a trip to the nearby big city for a night of jazz music and seafood.

Dressed to the nines in a silky violet sheath dress, I had nowhere to put my sidearm. My small purse had just enough room for some lipstick and cash.

Opening my door, I stepped out onto the porch and waved at Lucas who stood near his car. "Hey, you look yummy. Can I have you for dinner?"

"Ha-ha. You always want to get out of buying me dinner. I don't order much, and I never order the expensive items." I tucked my hair behind my ear and grasped my clutch in my hand as I started down the walkway to the drive.

Lucas met me halfway and took me in his arms. "Mmm…. You smell good enough to eat." The warmth of his body burned through his burgundy dress shirt, causing my breath to catch. He nibbled on my neck. "Certainly, tasty."

My legs weakened and so did my interest in dinner. I pulled his head closer as I tilted my face to the side. Shocks sizzled down my spine, and a warmth settled in my pelvis. "Lucas, I thought we were going out." *Is my voice really that breathless?*

He shook his head as if waking from a dream. His eyes glazed over. *Could I have stirred such passion?*

"Right. Dinner." He stepped away from me and moved robotically toward the car. Opening the door for me, his gaze followed my every move into the passenger seat. The tightness of the dress hugged my curves, causing me to wiggle as I climbed in.

Lucas bent over, reached in, and trailed his fingers along my knee up toward the edge of the dress. As his fingers slipped under the hemline, I shivered. "Lucas," I softly moaned.

He withdrew his hand, eliciting a sigh from me. I watched as he stood tall, a bulge evident in his pants.

While he walked around the car, I yanked on the neckline of my dress, accentuating my breasts, forcing them higher. I licked my lips and tried to calm my racing heart. I pulled my seat belt around my body and took a deep breath. Closing my eyes, I imagined Lucas naked in my bed. *Can I take the step? Even before the arson investigation was wrapped up, he had my heart.*

Lucas slid into the driver's seat, fastened his seat belt, and then started the car. Soft oldies rock music filled the interior. Keeping my face forward, I glanced at him out of the side of my eyes. *Yep, still sexy and rock hard.*

"Do you like seafood?" His hands gripped the steering wheel, forcing his knuckles to stand out. Deciding to live dangerously, I leaned over and ran one finger over his hands. They were tight and pulsing with intensity.

"Yes. I love seafood. Deep-sea scallops are my favorite," I whispered. I trailed my finger up his arm, feeling the muscles jump under my gentle touch.

"Good. You can change the music station if you want."

I moved my hand higher, touching his chest and heading toward the light stubble on his face. "No. The music is fine. Am I bothering you? I hope so. I truly want to tease you."

His eyes briefly opened wide and he swallowed. "You're doing a good job. But aren't you afraid you'll make me crash?"

I ran my finger over his lips, silencing him. "Nope. Turnabout is fair play. You teased me earlier."

Lucas's tongue darted out and lapped at my finger before he put his lips around it and took it into his mouth. His teeth held it in place while his tongue caressed it.

Now I'm the one losing this game…or am I winning? A groan filled the car, and I realized it was mine. I pulled my hand away from his face and planted it in his lap. Lucas was the one moaning. I gripped the hard length of his shaft through his slacks. His unrestrained cock jutted up toward my hand.

"You're going to get burned." Lucas pulled the car over to the side of the highway. He unlatched my seat belt and hauled me onto his lap before I took another breath. His mouth covered mine, and his tongue pushed past my lips to tease and taste my own tongue.

Only able to feel, not able to think. My hands scratched at his back as our kisses deepened. "I don't think we're going to make it to dinner," I whispered between kisses.

"I'd rather have you, anyway. But not here." He straightened the neckline of my dress. Then I climbed to my side. Snapping my seat belt once more, I reached over and laced my hand in his. He put the car in drive, and, once again, we were on our way.

Unable to keep our hands to ourselves, we stopped at the closest hotel. Threading my fingers with Lucas's, we approached. The six-story Chessandra Hotel boasted a four-star rating for its luxurious rooms. Inside, the check-in counter was empty.

"We'd like a room." I unwound my hand from his and turned to examine the lobby. Tall white pillars highlighted the opulent furnishings. Despite the extravagance, the hotel felt warm and inviting. I could see myself sitting in the atrium, reading or even people watching.

"How long will you be staying with us?" the concierge asked.

Heat flooded my face as I waited for Lucas's answer.

"Just for tonight. We've had a long day of driving and need to get on the road again." How easily the little white lie crossed his lips. I reached out and ran my hand along his back. He turned and smiled at me. "Don't worry. We can still get to our folks in time for dinner." With a wink, he turned toward the concierge.

The clerk processed the paperwork and handed the plastic keycard to Lucas. "Your room is on the second floor. Take the hallway to the right. The elevator is at the end of the hall. We have a complimentary breakfast bar in the morning. Thank you for choosing the Chessandra. I hope you enjoy your stay with us."

Our room sat two doors down from the elevator. The canopied king-sized bed dominated the room and beckoned to me. I heard the lock click on the door, and my heart sped up.

Lucas wrapped his arms around me and whispered, "We're going to use every inch of that big bed."

His warm breath tickled my ear, causing my juices to flow.

He slowly unzipped my dress and slipped it from my shoulders. A shiver racked my core—not from cold but from the thought of his hands on my body. Lucas wrapped his arms around me again before he cupped my breasts in his hands. "Mmmm...." His lips trailed over my neck. "You smell like strawberries. One day, we're going to have to see how you taste with whipped cream on your body."

Lucas ran his thumb over the top of my lace bra, and then gently pulled the lace south, exposing my hard nipples. The sensation of his thumbs on my sensitive peaks made my pussy clench. One of his hands trailed from my breast lower toward my stomach. The feeling of his warm hand felt like a branding iron. With his other hand, he squeezed my tips, rolling it between his fingers.

I bit down on my bottom lip to stop the moan from escaping my mouth. He bent his head to take my now-swollen breast in his mouth. He nibbled then sucked on it. I crossed my legs to ease the pressure growing between my thighs.

He trailed kisses and nibbles from my breasts toward my stomach. Unable to wait, I ran my hand over the bulge in his slacks. "You've been holding out on me. I didn't know how armed and dangerous you were."

He chuckled as he scooped me up into his arms and laid me on the bed. "No. You're the one who likes to play with fire. Just remember, Firebaby...it burns both ways."

Lucas unbuttoned his dress shirt then slacks, peeling away his clothes. His penis jutted out from his body like a torpedo.

"Mmmm.... You've got quite the weapon there." I crawled over, mesmerized, unable to not touch his cock. A pearl of pre-cum dotted the tip. I lick my lips, wanting my mouth on him. I crooked my finger and beckoned him closer. "Come over here."

When he reached the side of the bed, I grasped his cock, licking it from balls to tip then filled my mouth. His hands tangled in my hair as we set up a rhythm of in and out. But after a few moments, he stopped.

"Hold on...I want all of you." He pushed me onto the coverlet and kissed his way from my toes to my thighs. His warm breath heated my pussy, and his hands tugged on my panties. He yanked them down and tossed them aside. Kissing his way up my belly, over my breasts, and up to my neck, he removed my bra exposing my breasts to the chilly air.

My nipples beaded and heated up as he sucked on each of them, forcing them into peaks. He stood at the foot of the bed and stared at me. His gaze filled with passion, and he reached down, grabbed his slacks, and pulled a condom from his pants' pocket.

I watched, spellbound, as he sheathed his rod. Gasping with need, I cupped my breasts then ran my hands down between my legs.

"Are you wet for me?" he growled.

I nodded as I teased my clit with my fingertip. Lucas's weight dipped the bed as he climbed on, crawling toward me like a lion stalking his prey. Unable to take my gaze off him, I bit my bottom lip and tried not to beg for him to hurry.

CHAPTER ELEVEN

As Lucas finally reached my body, a sense of calm washed over me. *At last, I'll share my body with the man who already has my heart.*

He spread my legs and knelt between them. He traced his finger over my pussy lips and spread them open, exposing my bud. "You are wet. I've dreamed of you, like this. I've wanted to feast on your body since the first day I met you at the fire."

My hips lifted toward his fingers. I ached to have him fill me. Still, I held my plea.

He flicked my clit with his fingertip, sending a zing of desire shooting up my spine. Determined not to beg, I bit harder on my bottom lip.

"But after getting to know you, I wanted more than a one-night stand." He inserted one finger into my wet folds.

"Ohhh," I moaned.

His gaze captured mine. "I want all of you. Your body and your heart." Lucas slowly withdrew his finger.

The loss forced tears to trickle down the sides of my face and into my hair.

"Are you ready for all of me? My body and soul?" He positioned his cock at my entrance. With one swift plunge, he filled me to my core. A scream tore from my throat. Lucas lay still over me then took my face in his hands. "I love you, Lily. I've only said it to one other woman in my life...my mom."

I grasped his neck and pulled Lucas into a kiss. "I love you, too. Let's finish what we've been dancing around for weeks."

Lucas began moving his cock in and out of my body, increasing in tempo. His kisses teased my mouth, deepening at times, nipping at my lips before diving in with his tongue. His body pressed me down onto the mattress as he pounded into me. Tumbling over the precipice, my orgasm pulsed through me. My body rang with pleasure, delicious shivers crashing over me in wave after wave.

With a final plunge, Lucas's body stiffened, shuddered, and then relaxed with release. He nuzzled my hair. I glided my hands over his back, loving the feeling of him inside and on top of me.

"Mmm...what a trip," I murmured.

"Why did we wait so long?" He kissed my neck then stood and sauntered to the bathroom. I could hear the water running as he cleaned up. His footsteps were light as he returned, carrying a washcloth. "Here." He handed me the rag and sat on the edge of the bed.

"Thanks." My pussy ached and tingled. The cool washcloth soothed the area. I scrunched my nose. "Do you smell smoke?"

"I smell gas." Lucas stood and approached the door. "There's smoke coming in underneath." He ran to the bathroom, grabbed a towel, and then returned to the door. Placing the towel at the bottom of the door, he stopped the smoke. "Get dressed. Throw something on."

The alarm sounded in the hallway. Quickly, we dressed.

"Lucas, I'm going to check to see if we can use the hallway to escape." I ran to the door and put my hands on it. The wood was warm to the touch. Sounds of fighting and screaming from the hallway were muffled but noticeable. Using the peephole, I peered into the hallway, but darkness greeted me. "The door isn't burning hot yet, but I can't see in the hallway. Do we have another exit?"

He sprinted for the windows. "They're sealed shut. But we could break them."

I scampered over. "I'd rather give it a try than take a chance with the hall and stairs."

A loud whoosh and pop had us looking at the door. The towel blazed like the sun as fire spread up the door.

"Gasoline." I nodded toward the burning entrance. "This explains how the fire grew so quickly. And it means we have to escape immediately."

Lucas pointed at the sprinkler head in the ceiling. "Why aren't they going off?"

I rubbed my chin then motioned for him to hurry up. "My guess is, since this fire was set, the person broke the system."

Lucas grabbed the comforter and blanket off the bed and tossed them to me. "Do you think this is our arsonist?"

"Seems too coincidental. Better wrap up in the blanket." He picked up the desk chair and swung it at the window. The impact caused a stress fracture to crack the glass. The spider-web designs were beautiful, but, until the glass broke into smaller pieces, we weren't going anywhere.

The heat from the fire intensified. Sweat broke out on my forehead. Looking up, I stared as it flowed across the ceiling closer to us. "Try it again, Lucas. We don't have much time."

He took a second swing with the chair. The glass shattered. Lucas ran the chair legs around the window frame, knocking out as much of the shards as possible. Though most hotels used tempered glass, cuts still happened. With the window opened, the fire blossomed. The extra air fed it.

Crash. The hotel room doorway fell to the floor. We stared. A man stood silhouetted in the flames.

"Are you here to get us out?" Lucas yelled. The man wore a special fireproof suit. His entrance brought more of the fire into the room. The flames danced around the man, across the carpet, and along the walls.

The man's silence frightened me. With just his eyes showing, I couldn't tell if it was one of my team or a stranger. As he approached, Lucas shoved me behind him.

"Lucas, be safe." I squeezed his hand. He pulled his shirt up over his face.

"Do you know who I am?" the voice boomed out of the suit. "I'm your judge, Lucas Pigg."

"What makes you my judge? You don't even know me," Lucas shouted at the man. Smoke and fire filled the room. Coughing uncontrollably, I fell to my knees.

"You take what isn't yours. You've stepped up on the bodies of others." Each time the man spoke, he came closer. It was a race to see which would reach us first—the man or the fire.

Lucas's hands bunched at his side. A snarl covered his face. "Only a real man would face me and say it."

"I am facing you," the stranger's voice cackled.

"No," Lucas coughed. "You're still hiding. Always in the shadows. Always the weaker man, unable to face the threats on your own. Letting someone else take the chance, to take on the danger," Lucas baited him.

The man's laughter turned maniacal. He was almost on top of us. Wiping at the tears streaming down my face, I realized Lucas still gripped the chair. As he bent over to cough then straightened himself, Lucas swung upward with the chair, connecting with the stranger, sending him falling backward.

"Look who it is! It's Grim." With the man's hood skewed, I saw my boss's face. *What is he doing here?* "Lucas, what was he talking about? Do you know him?"

Grim stood up, tossed the head-covering on the floor. "You don't remember, Pigg. What a joke. The worst event in my life and you don't remember."

I crawled toward Lucas and grabbed a hold of his leg. "Captain, what's going on? What are you talking about?"

"Shut up, slut. You were mine. He shouldn't have touched you." He reached out and grabbed my arm, pulling me to him. "Was she good, Pigg? It'll be the last time you touch her or anyone else."

"Lily isn't a part of this. Let her go. I don't know why you're targeting me. Make me understand." Lucas took a step toward him, only to have Grim put his hands around my throat.

"In Iraq.... You walked away from the car bomb but my brother didn't." Grim's hands tightened on my throat. "Now you both will pay." Black dots swam in my vision as I struggled to breathe. I had to do something, the fire was too close, and I'd pass out soon. Going limp, I collapsed on the floor, dragging Grim with me. I threw my head back and knocked him in the nose, his scream music to my ears.

As he grabbed at his face, Lucas pulled me to safety. "We need to jump now. The fire is too close."

The flames beat behind me, pulsating along with the thumping of my heart. Holding his hand, Lucas and I dashed for the open window. With our hands entwined, we sprinted toward the opening and jumped.

Hitting the moist grass, we rolled. Thank goodness we'd been on the second floor and not higher. But there would be bruises tomorrow.

I looked up at our room. Grim stood silhouetted in the window. Flames danced around him. "Jump, Grim," I screamed as the flames crawled over his body. "Save yourself."

He saluted me then turned and strode into the room. Sirens played in the distance, but the firemen would be too late. The hotel was fully engulfed in flames. I ran toward the building, but Lucas grabbed me.

"What are you doing?" he hollered and pulled me tight against his body.

I strained against his hold. "I have to save him." Tears fell down my cheeks. "Even though he set the fires, no one deserves to die like that."

"It's too late," he spoke in my ear and kissed my cheek.

We watched as small explosions erupted in the building. Lucas pulled me farther away, and we stood with the other survivors. With the arrival of the fire trucks and police, we, like everyone else, stood sentinel as the building burned.

EPILOGUE

Two months later....

I sat at my desk and worked on the latest arson investigation, when I heard a knock at the door. I looked up and my heart skipped a beat. It was amazing how one look at Lucas forced my hormones into overdrive.

"Hi, Captain. Got time for a lunch date with your husband?" Tall, dark, and sexy stood framed in the doorway, wearing tight jeans, a T-shirt, and his leather jacket.

I smiled, stood, and walked toward him. "I always have time for you."

Lucas pulled me into his arms and kissed me. "You know, Betsie is still upset she didn't get to help you plan the big wedding. Just today she complained about how we ran off to Vegas."

I chuckled. "She's lucky we didn't have the formal shindig. She'd have ended up with some hideous bridesmaid dress. After all, I couldn't let my glowing and pregnant sister-in-law show up the bride." I laid my head on his chest. Listening to his heartbeat soothed me.

"Jonah is over the moon. He's planning an addition to the house for a nursery." He shook his head. "Good thing he's the only one of us Piggs with the baby fever."

My face heated. I leaned over to whisper in his ear. "He won't be the only one, Daddy."

The End

PROTECTING HIS WOLFE
(Book one in the Pigg Detective Agency)

Spend some quality time with Detective Jonah Pigg as he protects a murder witness, Betsie Wolfe, from the drug dealers after her. Is their passion only a part of the danger or will they find a happily ever after?

ABOUT THE AUTHOR

For my wedding in Vegas, my books and computer came with me but there wasn't enough room for my wedding shoes. It's all about priorities! As an avid reader, I was probably born with a book in hand. Luckily my mom was also an avid reader, so it was easy to "borrow" her books when my books were finished.

I was reading from an early age about dashing men on horseback riding to the rescue of strong willed and capable women who didn't really need rescuing. I came to expect that women in fairy tales should have fought their own battles. When I was older, I found Margaret Atwood and realized that women could re-tell history in their own way and I experimented with changing those basic fairy tales.

Fortunately for me, my husband allows me the opportunity to be myself (spend my salary on books) and still takes care of the really important things for me like killing spiders and opening jars. As an elementary teacher, teaching children about the many worlds inside of books is a gift that I'm lucky enough to do for a living. Teaching the next generation to love reading is a lot of fun! Reading the right book can make a new world come alive!

Currently living in the suburbs of Ann Arbor, Michigan with my darling husband, way-too-grown-up children and spoiled dogs, I enjoy getting away through a book to escape the harsh winters or summer road construction.

I'd love to hear from you!

www.melissakeir.com
http://www.facebook.com/melissakeir
www.twitter/melissa_keir

Other Books by Melissa Keir

Wilder Sisters Series:

Forever Love

Beach Desires

A Christmas Accident

Charming Chances:

Charming Chances

Second Time's a Charm

Three's a Crowd

Pigg Detective Agency:

Protecting His Wolfe

Protecting Her Pigg

Chalkboard Romance:

Love, Bake, Write (recipe book)

The Way to the Heart (recipe book)

We'd Rather Be Writing (recipe book)

Musings of a Madcap Mind (non-fiction)

Book Bundles:

Cowboy Up

Cowboy Up 2

Crashing into Love

Cowboy, Mine

Cowboys Forever

Pool Boy Wanted:
No Experience Preferred

✄

Summer 1997.
His life would never be the same.

Benji, The Lost Years

Dani Haviland

He'd never known a woman before, and that's just what she wanted.

Dedicated to those who know, or at least hope, that there's a better life out there. Never give up, no matter how glum or desperate your situation appears.

ISBN 978-0692661680
Copyright 2016 Dani Haviland

Pool Boy Wanted: No Experience Preferred
Late Spring 1997
North Carolina

There. That should do it.

The chauffeur penned the quick sign on the plain paper wrapper from the girlie magazine he had just purchased.

"What's a pool boy?" Sept asked, laying his twelve-pack of beer on the convenience store counter.

"He scoops the leaves out of a swimming pool, maybe pushes the brush around a bit, and pours in a few chemicals, if needed."

"Sort of like a gardener for water, aye?"

The chauffeur chuckled. "Yeah, I guess that's one way to look at it. But he has to be young. And buff. You know anyone like that? It would save me the trouble of finding one."

"I have just the lad for you." Sept pushed the box of brews closer to the uniformed older man. "Buy this for me and tell me where to bring him. We can help each other, I'm sure."

Ж

Sept walked out of the store, his free beer tucked under his arm. "Tomorrow morning I got a job for Benji," he told his eldest son as he got into the driver's seat of the bashed and battered utility van. "So, Eight, it's up to you to get some money out of Michael. That runt's just about worthless."

"I'm on it, Pa," Eight said, snagging one of the brews. "I just made some contacts myself."

Ж

"Don't say you'd do anything for food," Michael warned.

Benji nodded his head, thinking of some of the repugnant things he had done in the past: scrounging food from trash bins and stealing from markets and church offering plates. "But some real meat—not this gamey possum flesh—would be nice. And fresh fruit. I'd even eat greens." He shook his head. "How many times did I refuse to eat them when I was a lad..."

"Yeah, me, too," Michael said, and pushed his plastic spoon through the slop, inspecting his turnip and vermin stew for small bones and roaches.

"What? We're not feedin' you well enough?" Sept bellowed as he walked down the rickety basement steps. "Tough! Oh, and I think I found a job for you. I'll take care of collectin' the wages, as always..."

"And if we behave ourselves, ye'll make it worth our while," chorused Benji and Michael.

"Now, don't be sassin' me or you'll be beggin' me for the flat end of the belt rather than the buckle."

Benji grimaced and nodded in obedience. He was now almost two heads taller than Sept, but that didn't matter. The old man had been working his psychological tricks on him for at least five years. He'd lost track of how long, but knew he'd been his hostage since he was twelve. Sept knew that withholding food was more effective than thrashing him with a belt or birch switches. Plus, now that Michael was here, he needed to protect him, too, so rising up or smart mouthing was out of the question.

Wee Michael had involuntarily joined the small group only recently. His parents were rich, according to Sept. It didn't matter how much Michael protested, insisted that he was just an orphan and had never known his father, Sept was certain that he was Michael Fornay, runaway illegitimate son of Armando Reynaldo, millionaire playboy and heir to some cellphone manufacturing corporation he had seen in a magazine.

Michael told him that the only place he had run away from was the homeless shelter where he and his now deceased mother had lived. Sept said that his story was a load of horse crap. The fact that Michael had been living on the streets when he found him—and not even in the right part of the country—and didn't have the assumed father's swarthy coloring and tall stature meant nothing. The slightly built, fair-haired boy had been in

Sept's clutches for six months. His written ransom demands to the company had gone unheeded, his daily phone calls ended with a click. Sept didn't give up on an investment easily, though.

"One more week, Mr. Michael Fornay, and then you're sold. Eight's out there right now, lookin' for the right customer. Or customers. Yeah, your type is much sought after in the right markets…" Sept licked his lips and tilted his head, viewing the young man from a different angle. He might be of value yet.

Ж

A huge green salad, with romaine lettuce and young spinach, tossed with fresh mandarin orange segments and honey-roasted peanuts, sprinkled with Chinese noodles and a savory soy sauce dressing. Benji could feel the crunch and taste the salty sweetness of real food. The scent of fresh baked apples wafted through the air. "Eat your salad first, dear," his mother said. "I've got custard sauce for the apples when you're done."

Umph!

Benji was rudely awakened from his aromatic dream by the thud of a heavy weight landing on top of him.

"Wait. What?" he asked, as he looked around the darkened cellar.

"The man said he'd let us know, but he didn't offer much for your scrawny hide. Said you was too old for his tastes. He's gonna ask around. You gotta be of some value to us, but twenty bucks is too low. You'd be worth more as pie fillin'!"

Michael rolled off of Benji, said, "Excuse me," and winced as he repositioned himself next to his big friend on the pile of straw.

"Are ye all right?"

"He will be if he doesn't try to sit down," Eight said sarcastically. "He probably won't be able to do that for a week!"

Benji sat up straight, fists clenched, his body tensed for a fight. But it was too late. The door was bolted shut before the last word was out of Eight's mouth.

"I'll be all right," Michael said. "Don't worry about me."

"Don't worry about ye?" Benji whispered hoarsely. "Protectin' ye is my job!"

"Too bad it doesn't pay," Michael said, and chuckled. "Come on, let's go to sleep. It's been a long day and I don't feel like talking."

After Michael was captured, he and Benji had quickly learned that shared warmth was better than being conventional or proper. They each had been given a holey blanket, but rather than shiver alone, they covered the ancient straw with one—to help keep the dampness and bugs away—spread the other over top of them, and then snuggled under it together, like puppies in a litter.

Benji lay beside his friend, but slumber wouldn't come. He had suspicions about what had happened, but hoped he was wrong.

A few minutes later, Michael fell asleep.

Then the whimpering and crying began. "Don't! Please! I'll do anything but that. You're too big…"

Suspicions confirmed. He'd strangle Eight if it was the last thing he did. And he didn't care if he died trying.

Nobody was going to hurt his friend again. Ever.

Ж

Sept bellowed his usual good morning to his two hostages: "Wake up, you lazy good fer nuthins'!"

The two young men had been awake for hours, though. The light spilling from the opened door was the only way they could tell if it was day or night. Their cellar was a virtual dungeon. There weren't any devices of torture—other than the strap and array of birch switches the old man was so proud of displaying—but the darkness, cold, and stench of the moldy basement were torture enough.

"I found you a job, Benji, workin' for a woman. The old bag's driver said she didn't care if you had any experience or not. You're gonna be a pool boy. That's kinda like a gardener 'cept for swimming pools. She likes 'em young and buff, he said. I guess that red hair of yours is

592

buff enough. And you may be tall, but that baby face of yours will show her you're a young 'un. If not, maybe you'd rather meet one of Eight's friends. Michael may not have been to their likin', but I hear tell that gingers are gettin' popular."

"Leave Michael be. Let him come up fer some fresh air, do the cookin' maybe, and then I'll do as ye ask. No belt or switch required."

"Now you're learnin', lad. Now you're learnin'."

Ж

"Here's your new pool gardener," Sept said, as he let Benji out in front of the convenience store, the agreed upon drop off spot. "I'll take another twelve pack and payment in advance, if you don't mind."

"Here's the beer," the chauffeur said. "No money until she finds him satisfactory, though."

Sept grunted and grabbed the beer. "Have him back by four. He's got other chores, you know."

"I'm sure he does…"

Benji waited obediently until the driver indicated where to sit. "Ride up here with me. The back is for guests."

There was no conversation, but Benji was still at ease. The morning was warm and the fresh breeze streaming through the open windows was invigorating. The idea of working with green plants and warm, clean earth gave him hope that he'd be able to find a way out of the prison he and Michael were in. He had stopped caring about what happened to himself long ago, but now his new best friend was in danger. He needed an escape plan and a destination.

The chauffeur pulled up to a gleaming white southern plantation-style home "The garden shed is over there. Just mow the front yard and trim the hedges a bit. No need to hurry. She's up there, watching. And take off your shirt."

Benji didn't argue or ask about the pool, but did notice that the lawn was already well-groomed. He pulled his torn and patched shirt off and headed for the shed, a clean and orderly structure four times the size of the cellar he and Michael ate and slept in.

"Not that one," the driver said, as Benji approached the riding lawn mower. "Use the push mower. She doesn't care for the stink of a motor. Besides, pushing it shows off your muscles. That's why you're here. She likes fresh meat."

Benji nodded and pulled the old fashioned grass cutter away from the wall. A wide variety of gardening hand tools were hanging from the pegboard: shears, loppers, pruners, and clippers. These very basic tools would work well for a small yard, but this was a mansion, a huge estate. Power assisted tools were much more efficient. Apparently, efficiency was not what the lady of the manor required, though. Still, if it kept him employed—and Michael away from Eight's sleazy friends—he'd grounds-keep the old fashioned way. It was also job security and a way to get fresh air and sunshine at the same time.

Ж

The bright sun on his fair skin burned, but after being chilled for months, it warmed places he forgot he even had.

After pushing the mower for half an hour, he was covered in sweat, the beads of perspiration rolling off his brow, stinging his eyes. He tried wiping the wetness with his hands, but that only made it worse. Now he had grime everywhere. All he had for a cloth was his dirty and ragged shirt. Still, it was better than fiery eyes.

The chauffeur had made himself scarce, yet Benji still felt as if he were being watched. He glanced up at the windows, looking for his employer. Was he allowed to take a break to wash his face?

Confident that he wasn't doing anything wrong, he headed for the gardener's shed and his shirt.

And then he saw her.

She was holding a tall glass of lemonade in one hand, a towel in the other. "Care for a little refreshment?"

"Thank ye, ma'am," he said, and reached for the cloth.

Her scowl stopped him in mid-grasp. He blinked, thought quickly, then said, "Ach, I am so sorry, miss. The sweat; it's in my eyes. I can see now that yer a lass, not a ma'am."

The woman whose leathery and lined skin had seen many years, and too much sun, gave him a genuine smile of gratitude.

Yes, this young buck would do nicely. Well-formed, articulate, and with a grace that men many years his senior had never attained.

"What is your name?" she asked, and gave him the towel.

"Benji, mmm," he stuttered, almost calling her ma'am again. *Best to leave off any designation!* "I'm called Benji."

"You did a fine job on the lawn. Have you ever cleaned a swimming pool?"

"No, but how hard could that be?"

She laughed brightly, like a teenager. "You're so right there. The pool house has a skimmer and a brush. Not much else is needed. Do you have a suit?"

"A suit? I only have the clothes I came in."

She giggled again. "No, silly. A bathing suit. Never mind. I keep a few in the pool house. Go ahead and find one that fits. I'll be back with a light snack. I don't want you to overexert yourself."

Benji was filthy. He knew he stank, but either the wind was blowing away from him, or she was being gracious. Yes, that was it. She was a gracious lady.

Benji made use of the shower outside the pool house and scrubbed off the first and second layers of filth with his shirt, rinsing it out afterwards. He hadn't been able to wash his clothes in over a month. Maybe he'd have a chance to change into swim trunks and give his jeans a quick scrubbing before she reappeared.

He found them right next to the towels, but these couldn't be what she was referring to. These were bikini bottoms. 'Itsy bitsy, bright yellow, but without any polka dots' bikini bottoms!

Then he saw it. The calendar with muscle-bound men posing in barely-there bathing suits like the ones she had on hand. *Men wore swimming trunks like those?* And then he remembered. The chauffeur said she liked to watch. Hopefully, that's all she wanted to do.

"Those fit just right," she cooed when she saw him. Her hand rose as if to stroke the fabric, then pulled back. "If you don't mind, I'll stay out here and catch some rays while you clean the pool. That wind storm last night really made a mess."

Benji grinned and nodded. There were less than a dozen leaves in the pool. But, if she liked the way he worked, she'd pay Sept. Money always made the old man happy. Maybe then he'd buy real food instead of stewing roadkill and stolen turnips.

Ж

Benji looked for something else to do. He had worked too fast at skimming the leaves. Just as he was reaching for the long-handled brush, the lady asked, "Would you do me a favor? I can't reach my back."

He hadn't noticed her move, but she was now lying face down on the chaise lounge, wearing nothing but a lace and string bikini bottom. She was definitely old—even older than his mother—but had a nice body. Yes. Tanned, fit, and showing more skin than he'd ever seen in real life.

Benji realized his mouth was hanging open. She couldn't see him, though. Or could she? He realized that all the garden decorations had polished surfaces and were actually mirrors. The shiny-bellied Buddha statue reflected her face. She was smiling at him.

Or was it a leer.

He took the lotion from her hand and applied it to her back gently. He closed his eyes. If he hadn't already seen her face, she could have been the blond on that TV series. He'd only seen the show once, was it 'Friends' or 'Neighbors,' but oh, she was so gorgeous...

Gulp. He shouldn't have thought about her. His tiny swimming suit was bulging. The lady was sure to notice.

"Yes, that suit fits you just fine. Would you care to join me in the pool for a bit?"

"But I just put lotion on your back…"

"Don't worry about it. I have a new pool boy and he'll take care of everything. Won't you?"

Benji couldn't answer. She had one hand cupping his man parts, and was leading him to the shallow end of the pool. "I'd really like to get to know you better. Do you think you can return tomorrow? I have a gift I'd like to give you."

Benji nodded. "Aye, I'll tell Sept ye'd like me to c-c-come back…"

"Yes, I'd like you to *come* tomorrow. But for now, I just want to get to know you better."

The lady now had her hand in his Speedo, her thin fingers wrapped around his firm cock. "Do your girlfriends do this for you?"

Benji gasped and shook his head briskly. "Uh-uh. No g-g-girlfriends."

"Oh, really? Are you the type who likes boys?"

"B-b-boys? I have a friend, but he doesn't do that!"

"Would you like me to do more?"

Benji couldn't see her. His eyes had rolled back into his head, her gentle kneading up and down his shaft driving him to a place he'd never been before. And didn't want to leave. "What? What did you say?"

Now her tongue was in his ear. She thrust it inside until he squirmed, then nipped his earlobe before pulling away. She shoved his cock sideways into his swim shorts so it would fit, then sat up straight. "Tomorrow. Return tomorrow at ten. And plan to stay the whole day."

Benji opened his eyes. She was gone. A towel, clean shirt, and a pair of brightly colored flower-print shorts were laid out on the table next to her chaise. He quickly dried off and put the shorts on over the swimsuit, then donned the shirt.

"Are you ready to return home, sir?" the chauffeur asked, handing him a paper lunch sack.

Benji looked around. People came and went so quickly around here.

Ӂ

The Lincoln Town Car pulled to a stop in front of the convenience store. Sept was there, glaring at the driver, his hand out, waiting for payment. Benji quickly wrapped the bag inside his wadded up clothes so Sept and his sons wouldn't take it from him. No roadkill stew for him and Michael tonight.

Benji got to sit in the front of the van this time. Now he wouldn't bounce off the walls when the old man sped around corners and came to sudden stops to intentionally throw those in the back around.

"The driver gave me this," Sept said, and waved a fistful of twenty dollar bills in Benji's face. "He said his boss wants you again tomorrow. She has a big project planned, and your strong back is just what she needs."

Benji remained mum. It wasn't his *back* she was after, and he knew it.

Ӂ

"I've got some real food for us today, Michael. I'm not sure what's packed in here, but I'll wager it doesna have vermin or turnips in it."

Benji sat down and Michael joined him as he investigated the contents of the bag. He felt around and pulled out a baggie. "Let's see, we have a sandwich, nicely cut in two. Here, this one's yours." He took a big bite. "Oh, tuna. Not bad…" Benji wanted to stuff the white bread creation into his mouth all at once before Eight and his little brother Niner came to investigate, but decided he'd chance it. He savored the intended snack that was now the first course of a shared dinner. "See what else is in there."

Michael reached in and pulled out the fruit. "A banana! And it's huge! Can I peel it?"

Benji winced at the phallic symbol, evidently put there as a reminder of what she wanted from him the next day. "Be my guest."

Michael broke the banana in half, then offered the bigger piece to his friend. "Here, you labored for it. What did you have to do? And what's a pool gardener? I think Sept got the name wrong. Pools don't need trimming."

"No, but they do need raking. At least, today I scooped out some leaves and…weel, let's finish dinner first: chips and Twinkies. We can talk later," Benji said, hoping the details of the 'handling' by his boss never came up.

Ж

The next morning, Sept dropped Benji off at the store again. The chauffeur was already waiting, a twelve pack of beer on the hood of his car, his head shaking back and forth.

"No?" Sept asked. "Not even a little advance."

"Nope." He turned to Benji. "Get in, boy."

Benji got in the front seat and let the slight roll off his back. He didn't know what to expect today. If all went well, he would ask Lady for a real job, one that would support him and Michael. He gulped. Better not tell her about him. She might decide she needed two boy toys.

Ж

Chauffeur pulled in front of the house. Lady was waiting on the porch, leaning against one of the marble columns, her broad-brimmed hat canted to one side. "Let's get started right away. You have some training to do."

Lady led the way into a huge parlor. Two big 27" color TVs and at least three VCRs were set into the dark wood shelves.

"That's the biggest TV I've ever seen," Benji said. "And you have a VCR? Three VCRs? What do ye need that many for?"

"It's 1997, Benji, and I'm a rich woman. I can buy anything I want. Everything is for sale. For a price. That's lesson number one."

Benji wasn't sure if the lesson was about her being rich or everything was for sale, but he wasn't going to ask.

"Sit down, make yourself comfortable. Would you like a drink? Maybe a little weed?"

"No, thanks, m.." Benji choked as he started to say ma'am out of habit. "Miss… I'm sorry, I dinna even ken yer name."

"How about if I let you give me a name. Pick one."

The first name that came into his head was the name of his first crush, the eldest daughter in the Brady Bunch.

"Marcia."

"All right, I'm Marcia. I'll let you keep the name Benji. It's so sweet, just like you, I'm sure."

The older woman now called Marcia helped him sit back on the sofa, plumping pillows behind his back. "I have a few tutorials I'd like you to watch before we get started," then clicked the remote, turning on the TV.

Evidently the VCR was already on and playing. A man with an enormous hard on was urging a young brunette to go down on him. Apparently, she thought it was a good idea, too, because she appeared to be enjoying herself.

"You can do that?" Benji asked in an adolescent squeak, his adult voice not fully formed.

"Yes," she purred, then bent over his lap. Lady fumbled with the tie on his shorts and released his already firm cock. "I like it, too." She licked up and down, then opened her mouth and tickled her tonsils with him, nearly choking on his massiveness.

"Are…are ye okay?" he asked, gently patting her on the back.

She raised her head and wiped her mouth. "Oh, yeah. Very okay."

She toyed with him for a moment longer, then pulled away. "Where did you get that accent?" she asked, intentionally distracting him. She didn't want him to come. Yet. "You don't sound like you're from around here, or anywhere else in the South."

"Actually, I was born near Greensboro, but I spent my early years in Scotland. I got the accent from my da and my classmates…" He looked down and saw his pink rod winking at him. *Stop talking, woman, and get back to business. I feel like I'm going to burst!*

"I like your voice," she said. She knew she had brought him to the edge. Teasing was often the most fun. At least, it was with virgins. "Tell me more about yourself. How old are you?"

"I…I'm sorry. It's hard to think when I'm…"

"When you're hard?"

He blushed and nodded in reply. Plus, he didn't want to tell her he didn't know what year it was, so how could he know his age? If it really *was* 1997, he was 17. But with what she was doing, he didn't want her to know he was a minor. She might stop.

"Let's pretend you're 16, maybe even 15. I like them young. And inexperienced. I want to train you myself. You're mighty tall, but there's barely a hair on your chest. I can wax those few whiskers so you'll look 15. Of course, we'll leave these ginger curls down here…" She ran her fingers through his pubic hair, then down and around to cup his balls. "I want to feel them tickling me down here."

Marcia stood up and dropped her panties. He'd never seen her nude on the front side. "Do you like?" she asked, swirling her hips suggestively.

"Uh-huh." She was totally hairless. And hot. He didn't care how old she was. He wanted her and she could tell.

She clicked two remotes and the image on the screen changed. A man had his face in a woman's crotch. "What's he doing down there?" Benji asked. He'd never even heard of such an act, much less seen one.

"He's showing you what I want you to do for me." She leaned back on the couch and spread her legs. "Start by kissing here, on my inner thighs. Work your way to the center…"

Benji bent to the task, glancing one more time at the man who was now sucking intently on a tiny bit of flesh between the folds of the woman's shaved pubis.

"Not quite so rough, Benji. Start soft and slow, lick gently, using the backside of your tongue on that…that… Oh, yeah. You're a natural."

"Marcia, Marcia," he moaned when he came up for air, "You're perfect," then went back for more.

His jaw and tongue were aching, but he didn't stop. Making her squirm was so much fun.

Finally, she squealed, "Oh, oh, oh, yes, yes, yes!"

At first Benji bolted, then returned to sucking and tongue swiping every pink spot he could find. She was making the screams of ecstasy the actresses in the videos had used. He had made her happy. And he didn't feel so bad himself.

Marcia flicked him on the shoulder, telling him without words that he should stop. He'd soon learn her non-verbal cues. And if he didn't, there was always another hungry young boy looking for comfort and housing, not necessarily in that order. But Benji was cleaner than some of the ones her chauffeur had brought from surrounding cities. And taller, too. Young was a must; well-hung, essential; broad shouldered, a nice bonus; but this red-haired find was a quick learner and well-mannered. If he was good in the sack, she'd take all she could before getting rid of him.

Ж

"How about a little wine with lunch. I had a simple fruit and cheese plate put together. You are hungry, aren't you?"

"Aye, I do seem to have worked up a bit of an appetite." Benji reached for an empty plate. *Why did she make me stop? She gets up to give me sliced fruit and runny cheese when she knows I'm ready to pop?*

"Have you ever had brie? Here, sit down and let me feed you."

Marcia took the plate from him, then used a petite silver knife to cut across the powdery white surface of the soft cheese. She lay the creamy slice across a picture-perfect wedge of pear and offered it to him saying, "A repast worthy of a young god."

He wanted to eat it all in one bite, but she pulled it away. "Don't rush." She picked up the crystal flute and brought it to his lips. "Now, swallow."

She's treating me like a bairn! All I'm missing is the bib.

Lady picked up the lace-edged napkin and wiped his mouth. "There, there; we don't want to make a mess, now, do we?"

Suddenly, Benji's head was swimming. "I guess I'm not used to drink. What did ye give me?"

"Champagne, my darling."

Benji slumped forward, out cold.

Marcia pushed him back into the chair. "And a bit of roofie."

Ж

Benji awoke in the back of a van. It wasn't Sept's, though. This one sported a silky sheet-covered mattress and he was lying on it, his mouth dry and head aching.

The side door opened and bright sunlight spilled in. "Out. Now."

The chauffeur handed Benji a brown bag as he stumbled out. "She says she'll see you Monday. She has a party tomorrow. Besides, she doesn't do boys on the weekends."

Ж

Michael ignored the MacLeod clan's grumblings as his friend, clutching his middle, climbed into the back of the old utility van. Maybe he had another bagged lunch hidden? Whatever the MacLeods were saying didn't make much difference anyhow. Sept and Eight's complaints were always the same: no ransom money, the beer was lousy in America, and the younger son, Niner, whining about having to ride in the back with *them*, those good-fer-nothin' hostages.

"I made some new contacts while you were enjoying your morning as a pool gardener, Benji. Your little friend Michael will finally be payin' his way," Eight said.

Sept sped another sharp corner, spilling Niner on top of Benji. "Next time, I'm ridin' in front with you, Pa. I'm tired of these two. The sooner they're out of our lives, the better."

"Not without makin' money off them first," Sept called back. "And mind your manners or I'll be finding a job for you, too."

Ж

By the time they reached the run down former feed store that Sept called his place, Benji's head had almost cleared, but he still felt terrible. He'd been set up and used, then thrown aside like a dirty paper towel.

"I've got great news for you, Benji," Michael whispered as they made their way to the cellar, staying one step ahead of Eight's boot. "I got a real job! Well, Eight got one for me. Of course, he said he'll take care of the money end, and I have to be very polite…but I get to be a camp cook! I guess I'll find out more about it later. They're moving us out of here pronto. Actually, I think they got caught squatting. There was a noisy row this morning—voices I've never heard before—and then Eight and Niner flipped on all the lights and came down here. They swarmed all over the place, grabbing anything worth a nickel, throwing it in boxes. Here, I hid the blankets and your spare clothes. You won't be able to wear those new Hawaiian shorts everywhere, you know."

Benji squirmed. Or be seen in public in the wee swimming briefs he was wearing underneath.

Niner appeared at the top of the stairs, his skinny chest puffed out and voice forcefully lowered to sound bossy. "Bring those boxes up here! Now!"

Michael grabbed the nearest one, then scrambled up the rickety steps. Benji piled the last two on top of each other, then paused and looked around. Good riddance to cockroaches, beetles, and spiders. He shuddered. *Bugs!*

Sept was already behind the wheel of the rusty white van, smacking his hand on the horn that still didn't work. "Hurry up and climb in! If we don't get out of here now, they'll find us."

Ka boom!

Benji and Michael stopped and spun around at the loud noise behind them. Smoke billowed up from the stairwell, then Eight burst through, a shower of tinkling glass raining down around him. Sept's raggedy eldest son laughed at the mayhem, then tossed a gasoline-filled bottle stuffed with a fiery rag through the doorway. "Try and collect rent for that!"

"Get in!" hollered Sept, letting up off the brake, allowing the van to move away slowly.

Eight hopped in, then smacked the dash with his hand. "Yahoo! I feel like I just won the lottery!"

Niner moved up from the back and poked his head between the two other MacLeods. "You won money?"

"Nah. I got jobs for both Michael *and* Benji. Oh, by the way, I popped into a restaurant and used their phone when no one was looking. I thought it might work if I called from another number, but as soon as the secretary heard my voice, she hung up. Still no money for the pipsqueak. I thought it was worth a try, though."

"Good thinking. But you got them both jobs? A second job for Benji?" Sept asked. "Where and how much?"

"Not sure how much, but here, I got directions. Keep heading down this road. It's outside of town a ways. The man wouldn't give me a rate, just said he'd pay them what they was worth. Of course, I told them I was their agent and he was to pay me, not them."

"You're not in charge, Eight, and I'll make sure that miscontraption...misconfusion... I'll tell them I'm the money man and *I'll* be collecting the wages."

Eight groaned, "Yes, sir." *One of these days, I'll be in charge, and it won't be soon enough.*

An hour later, over bumpy, gravelly roads and after several cuss-word colored U-turns, Sept pulled into the run down farm. The main house may have been nice once, but it hadn't been kept up. Broken and boarded windows outnumbered the intact ones. The north side of the house still had a few areas where the whitewash paint was visible, but most of it was bare timber or overgrown with kudzu vines.

A broad shouldered, gray-haired man approached the new arrivals—the man in charge by his swagger and judgmental glare.

"Hello, I'm Atholl Grant MacLeod the Seventh, but you can call me Sept," he said and stuck out his candy bar-sticky hand. "My son here, Eight, said he made arrangements with you for hiring these two strapping young men. I'll be taking care of the wages for them. They're strong, but a little weak in the head, if you know what I mean."

"The new workers get the oldest cabin." The foreman pointed to the last shack in a long row of rickety buildings, intentionally ignoring the offered hand. "You and your sons will either have to sleep in your van or find other accommodations."

"Accomma... ammodations..." Sept stuttered.

"That means you can't stay here unless you're working. Eight did tell me that you and your sons had, *ahem*, conditions that prevented you from strenuous labor, right?"

"Yes, yes. Weak hearts run in the family. We have to save our strength."

The foreman snorted, then turned and walked away. He'd seen lazy sorts before, and these three were classic examples of slavers. The two workers they brought in didn't look like they were related. Probably more homeless boys from the city. It didn't matter to him. As long as the work got done.

Sept walked over to his hostages, trying to match the foreman's swagger and tone. "You and Michael can stay in that fine apartment over there. The boys and I have to go back to town. Benji, I'll be by to pick you up on Monday morning. You're young and strong enough to work both jobs."

Eight and Niner didn't even wait until the lecture was over. "Shotgun!" Niner yelled and pushed his older brother aside, dashing to claim the passenger seat.

"Good riddance," Benji muttered under his breath. "Come on, Michael. Let's check out our new place."

The two picked their way through the maze of tall weeds toward the smallest shack at the back of the complex.

"I dinna ken fer sure, but these look like old slave quarters," Benji said. He pushed aside the tattered canvas door and looked inside. "Whoa. Some of these iron rings still have bits of rope attached to them."

"Maybe they tied up horses or cows in here," Michael suggested.

"No. If they had, there'd be signs. No cow patties or horse nuggets around here."

Michael shook his head, not wanting to think about the previous residents, then looked up at the hole in the roof and the lack of windows. "Hmph. I don't know if this place is any better than the last. Do you think Sept will really come back for us?"

"Aye, our labor is his only source of cash. He can't pay for gas with stolen TVs and stereos, at least, not very often."

"I guess it's not too bad…"

"Ach, this is fine fer now. Fresh air, daylight… and no MacLeods! Oh, and here. I have some food fer us. The driver must have thought I looked malnourished. I dinna get a chance to eat the lunch my boss lady put out fer me."

Michael pulled a wooden bench away from the wall. "We may not have a table yet, but we do have a place other than the floor to sit. Aye, this is better."

Benji unwrapped his clothing and pulled out the paper bag. "It looks like the chips may have been smashed a bit on the ride over, but the sandwich and apple are intact." *And this food was certainly better than runny cheese and spiked wine!*

Ӂ

Clearing brush and stacking it for burn piles wasn't the easiest job, but it was honest work and he got to keep his clothes on. Still, he had a soft spot in his heart—and a hard spot in his pants—for the blond 'Marcia.' *Keep working, Benji, and the weekend will jest slip by. Maybe passing out wasna her fault…*

"Are you okay, Benji? You look like your head is somewhere else."

"Aye, I'll bide fine. I'm jest confused. I'm tryin' to figure a way to get a real job so we can get out from under Sept's control. I'm not sure about our new boss. It might not go well if I try to kick Sept out of the picture so the two of us can get paid directly. Shoot, I dinna even know where we are or where we'd run to if we did leave. Let's jest think of this as a temporary place."

"Ah, don't worry about it. I think Sept will goof up again and make this guy mad. If he does, and we've been doing a good job, the boss will keep us and get rid of the old man himself. At least, I can hope Sept and his sons go bye-bye."

"Not too soon, though. I have another job on Monday. I'm hoping to get ahead there. The lady says I have, um, potential," Benji said, trying to hide his grin.

The foreman suddenly appeared. "Quit your yabbering and get back to work. Hey, you, little guy. Do you really know how to cook? The old man said you could. You're not big enough to get much of anything done out here. Get over to that gray building with the smoke coming out of it. Tell the cook that he's been relieved and you're taking over."

"Yes, sir. See you later, Benji!" Michael said brightly, happy that his new job wouldn't give him blisters or splinters.

Ӂ

Eight shoved the snoozing Benji on the shoulder, knocking him over from his propped-up seated position beneath one of the two dry spots in the hovel. "Get in the van. We're late."

"You, too!" Niner hollered, and smacked Michael on the back of the head.

Benji and Michael scrambled to their feet and followed the brothers to the van where the old man was tapping the steering wheel, chewing his bottom lip. "Now!" he barked. As soon as the rear door of the van slammed shut, he stomped on the gas.

"Wait for me, Pa!" Eight shouted, running alongside the van, clinging to the passenger window frame, trying to jump in.

Sept grunted in frustration, then slammed on the brakes. The sudden stop caused Eight to smack his forehead on the side mirror, but he still managed to climb in.

The van took the sharp corners at top speed, skidding across the dirt road, barely missing a curious deer. Suddenly, pavement appeared, and all of the car's occupants hit the roof, Niner yelling the loudest. "Can't we steal a different vehicle, Pa? I don't want to die in this piece of crap. I don't have a seat belt, much less a seat!"

"Quit yer bitchin' and give Benji a piece of gum. He didn't get a chance to wash up this morning. I want him to at least have fresh breath!"

Benji was grateful for the minty chew, but wished he had been given the opportunity to at least water a tree. His bladder was bursting.

Ӂ

The chauffeur was waiting in front of the mini market, his foot on the dash of a pink '67 Cadillac El Dorado, reading a novel. "You're early," he said, "and you stink. Use the restroom in the back of the store to clean up. I'm a little pickier than she is about who I let near me."

Benji did the best he could with the foamy dispenser soap and wall-mounted blow dryer, but still felt icky. He looked in the mirror. His beard was coming in faster than ever. It had never been so thick. Why now? Was it because he was excited by a woman? Marcia didn't like body hair. He gulped then shifted the front of his shorts. Except down there.

Ж

Marcia was on the front porch, sipping coffee, reading the newspaper when they arrived. "You're early," she said, then grinned and rose slowly. "I don't like it when a man comes early…" She opened the front door for Benji, pointed upstairs, then licked her lips. "You have some more lessons to learn. Oh, and you'll need to be uncovered for them." She sniffed the air and frowned. "Let's start with a shower."

She led the way to the lavish bedroom suite, then ordered brusquely, "Take off your clothes and come in here."

Benji looked around, trying to figure out what he had done wrong. For some reason, she was acting like a schoolmarm whose shoes were two sizes too small.

"Go in the bathroom and wash yourself. And hurry. I have things I want you to do, but not if you stink."

Benji nodded in reply, not feeling brave enough to speak lest he accidentally call her ma'am again. He rushed through his shower, foregoing the second shampoo he was sure he needed after his weekend of hard labor. It wasn't polite to keep a lady waiting. Or a woman waiting. Right now, she wasn't acting much like a lady.

When he came out, she was there. Or a teenaged version of herself was. She had put her hair up into two ponytails and was wearing frilly, short, pink pajamas. He looked closer. Even though she was old, her breasts were ample and perky, her nipples visible through the fabric. This must be what was called a negligée. He had spied a few of them when sneaking peaks at Sept's magazines, but this was different. She was warm and soft and just a few feet away. Then he noticed. The air smelled delicious: musky like the woods, but flowery like his mother's butterfly garden.

Gulp. Don't think about mothers and her at the same time. She was definitely old enough to be his, but she wanted him to think of her as a teenager. It would be easy enough for him to oblige as long as he ignored her crepe paper skin.

Marcia, Marcia, Marcia kept going through his head. Keep thinking of her, not *her* he thought to himself, then smiled at his imagined sweetheart.

Lady came up to him and pouted. "I know I've been a little cranky lately, but I've missed you. And I want to give you something." She wiggled her hips, then pulled up her negligée to show off her split-crotch panties. "You've been wanting this, haven't you?"

"Oh, yes, yes, yes, Marcia. I'll do anything you want."

She chuckled harshly, not at all like the sweet young thing she was imitating. "Well, then. Let's see how you do. Just don't be in a hurry."

Suddenly, the TV was on. 'Another tutorial,' but he pushed the thought aside. She was going to do it her way, no matter what. His loins craved her, or at least part of her, but his brain said 'beware.'

"Get down here and get me moist," she ordered, then changed her tone and giggled like a young girl. "Pretty please."

He sighed without thinking. At least she was trying to make him comfortable.

Marcia, Marcia he repeated in his head, but it wasn't working. He was going through the motions, licking and humming like she had taught him, but she could have been a sour watermelon for what it was doing for him.

"Turn me over," she said softly. "I need a back rub."

He didn't dare tell her that he didn't know how to give one, so just did the best he could, imaging how much pressure he'd want if someone was rubbing him down.

"Lotion," she said, and pointed to the nightstand.

That helped. Her back was bony, but he didn't have to look at her painted face. She was keeping her words short, too.

After a minute, her leathery body faded away, and a young Marcia's appeared. His head was swimming, too. "Is there something in this lotion? I feel sort of giddy."

"Just a little essence of cannabis to heighten the senses and relax certain muscles." She rolled over and checked on his progress, flipping his semi-rigid cock with her index finger. "Just don't get any on your dick. I have plans for it."

Benji didn't know whether to grimace or grin, then decided it was better for him in the long run—and for her—that he smile.

The volume on the TV suddenly got louder, a woman's moaning and a man's grunting filling the room with sexual tension. "Does that help?" she asked, then put down the remote.

Benji shook his head in uncertainty. It probably should help, but his fear of the unknown was overcoming his sexual appetite. But he couldn't tell her that.

As if she read his mind, she asked, "You've never been with a woman, a real woman, have you?"

He got up from the bed and shook his head sheepishly. "Never had the chance. I dinna think I was old enough, either."

She strolled over and stood right in front of him, cupping his balls with one hand. "These are big enough to make this," she began stroking his cock, "work on demand, so what are you waiting for?"

"I guess the right wo…wo…girl," he answered, and kissed her on the top of her ponytailed head.

"Right answer, Benji. But let's start at the beginning. I'll be right back."

Benji sat down hard in the overstuffed chair at the other end of the room. Lady had disappeared into the dressing room and closed the door behind her. His emotions were yo-yoing and she knew it. Shoot, she was doing it on purpose. How could he even pretend to love a woman like her?

Love. His memories were clear on that. His parents said they loved each other all the time. The gentle kiss Da gave Mom on the forehead when she was stressed about burning dinner or losing her purse; the kisses and neck rubs she gave him when he was fretting about money: that was real love. He didn't know if his parents still made love physically—they already had two children and didn't say they wanted more—but sex and making love couldn't be just for creating babies, or it wouldn't be such a big deal. With all the magazines Eight stole and movies that Lady had for her VCR, there had to be a big demand for 'love.'

No. He couldn't think of it as love. It was simply sex.

Sex. That's what Lady wanted. She didn't love him any more than he loved Sept. If it helped him get a real job and a place to stay for him and Michael, he'd put out 'sex.' But he wouldn't—couldn't—love her. He'd save that for someone special.

Benji's inner reflections were interrupted by Lady appearing in full businesswoman attire. A sharp cut blue jacket, cream-colored silk blouse, and matching tight skirt made her look like a female version of the president of something or other.

"In order to get close to a woman, you have to make her feel that way: like a woman. Come here and get close to me."

Benji rose, thinking of her as an opportunity for freedom. She was no more than an overgrown garden that needed to be conquered. Bit by bit, he'd rid her of trash and weeds. Take charge. Clean up any messes. He'd do what it took to brighten her disposition and make her feel the way she wanted.

"Come here, woman," he said, and pulled her close. His lips spoke, "You're mine," but he thought, 'Mine to conquer,' and pressed his lips to hers.

"Now you're getting with the program," she said, responding to his toughness, even though she had plans to lead him another way. *He might be worth keeping around, after all!*

Benji clutched the back of her head as he worked his tongue in her mouth. She started to protest, but he pulled back and said, "My way," and got rougher with his insistence.

He slipped one hand down the front of her jacket, fumbling with the two buttons that closed it. When she tried to help, he mumbled, 'uh-uh,' and continued kissing, this time down the side of her neck.

Despite herself, moans of pleasure sneaked out. She didn't want to think it was the botanically-enhanced loving lotion and incense she had provided. It had never had this effect on her before.

Now his hand was on the zipper at the back of her skirt. She melted momentarily, again, and then quickly reached up and unbuttoned her blouse. The tiny buttons would be awkward to work with his big hands, and she didn't want him to rip it off. Or maybe she did.

"No panties?" he asked, grabbing her bottom roughly.

"N...no," she panted. "Just the bra."

Benji had no idea how a bra attached or how to take it off. Did it have buttons? Snaps? A zipper?

"Let me help with this," she said meekly. "The hooks are sometimes fussy."

Benji put his large hands over hers as she reached back and pushed the hooks from the eye closures. "I'll get it by myself next time," he murmured, then bit her on the ear lobe.

She squealed like the happy teenager she was trying to become again.

He didn't wait for her to do anything else. He was in charge. He had seen enough videos of men and women copulating in the last few days, he was certain he could perform without her 'instructing.'

He lifted the now breathless woman onto the edge of the bed, then pushed her back into the fluffy comforter. His hands slipped under her ass and brought her moist and squirming female parts to his face. He inhaled deeply, then dove into her garden, visualizing each fold of her woman-ness as an area to be conquered and tamed, licked and sucked until she would give him anything he wanted.

He didn't wait for her permission to climb on top, either. He was the master gardener and she was the wildness he was bringing into order.

She reached down to grab his cock. "Mine," he huffed, and pushed her hand away.

It was only a flash, but he saw the rage in her eyes. He had crossed the line. Right now, he didn't care. He wanted to finish what he started. And he was going to do it his way.

How dare him! That hard length of man-meat was hers, and so was the overgrown teenager attached to it. She wouldn't let him forget it, either. But first, she'd let this virgin take her. He could believe he was in charge for a few more minutes, or however long he lasted. Virgins were fun, but they were always too quick to pop. Once he had shot his load, she'd show him who was boss.

Benji was excited, but not about her. He was visualizing his ideal home with a pretty—and young—wife and a few bairns playing in the yard. He'd have his own farm maybe. He'd be as self-sufficient as a man could be in the 20th century.

Benji stopped. He didn't want to stay here. Now. In this time. He wanted to go back to the late 18th century. Yes, if he could manage to get some silver, gold maybe, he'd find a way to travel back to his birth era, to be with his grandparents…

Lady smacked him rapidly on the ass, her lips pulled tight in frustration: get on with it.

Benji didn't explain. He couldn't—wouldn't—let her in on his deepest desires. He put on a façade and approached each section of her body in an emotionally detached manner, his voice and actions mimicking the actors on the videos. "You're so hot and slick," he said seductively.

He glanced up, saw her face, and remembered that this was the evil woman who had drugged him on more than one occasion. He was ready to penetrate her, just inches away. But he was 'giving' her his greatest gift, one he could never get back: his virginity.

His self-disgust made him soften. He pulled away, not wanting her to see what was happening, or give her the opportunity to make fun of his impending failure. Instead, he faked a moan, then went down on her again. He gave her clit a slow, teasing suck, then ran his tongue up her midline, pausing at her belly button to give the fold of skin above it a nip.

She seemed to like that. He did, too. He couldn't literally bite the hand that fed him, but he could get close.

Rubbing his cock against the silkiness of the bed covering worked to get him hard again. He fantasized his ideal home: a cabin in the woods he had built himself, a stone hearth, a field getting ready for harvest.

Fully erect, he ground his hips again, now slipping close to where she wanted him.

He must be doing something right. She was moaning and panting as much—no, more—than the actresses on the videos. "Please, please," she whispered, as if she didn't want to ask aloud, "Get inside me. Now."

Benji chuckled deviously. He had conquered her. He had weeded her field and brought her into submission. It was time to plow.

He had to admit, entering her felt good. He was conflicted, though. It shouldn't be pleasurable because she was an evil woman who had manipulated his emotions and physical parts to do her bidding, robbing him of what he had wanted to save for a wife.

Plow the field! If you don't, you'll never get your home or your wife. This is a sacrifice! She is a vile priestess. Don't whimper. Just do what has to be done and get it over with.

The voices on the video were loud again. He glanced up and saw Lady put the remote down. She was watching the actors, not him.

All right, Benji. You be her actor. Watch the man on the TV, grunt when he does, suck when he does, come when he does. It's not you making love or even having sex with her. You're simply a body double. You're the remotely controlled mouth and dick. Time your ending to that bleach blond actor's. She seems to like him best anyway.

And he can have her, anytime he wants. Maybe she has enough money to buy him. As soon as this is over, I'm out of here!

Change of Plans

"Change of plans. We're not working at that shit hole of a farm," Sept grumbled after they let Benji off.

Niner snorted and asked, "Since when were you working?" then gulped and looked down.

"Getting' a bit sassy there, ain't ya?" Sept reached for his belt—his favorite instrument for attitude adjustment—then remembered he had forgotten to take it down from the rafters before Eight torched the place. "I'll let it slide this time..."

"Yes, Pa."

"Now, as I was saying, *we're* not working there anymore. It looks like that lazy-assed foreman doesn't want pipsqueak Michael there without Benji." He looked back at Michael, glared, then resumed his tirade. "Seems the old cook is still around, not worth a lick in the fields, and is willing to work for half wages if he can have his old job back. Foreman said he only took Michael's scrawny hide because Benji could do the work of two men. Without him... Well, let's just say I'm sure I can find another way to get a few dollars for the runt. At least until that no good father of his pays the ransom. And as far as new housing goes, Eight did some asking around and found us a five-star place to stay."

"What's five-star mean, Pa?" Niner asked, his index finger stuck up his nose, searching for a fresh chew.

Sept rubbed his chin, thought for a moment, then said, "Damned if I know. But he did say it was big enough for all of us. We'll check it out for tonight. We can always sneak out in the morning if its crappy. In the meantime, I have some needs to be taken care of." He subconsciously rubbed his crotch. "I'll drop you three off downtown to find some lunch. And see if you can snag me a burger or fish sandwich while you're at it. I'm feeling a bit peckish."

Ж

Sept knew the best time to troll for hookers was after dark, but the hornies were calling, and self-service hadn't been enough. He needed a pro and needed her now.

Although it was still early, it didn't take too long for him to discover the right—or rather wrong—side of town.

It could have been the beat up van he drove, but every daytime lady of the night he solicited was too expensive. "You're out of your pink and purple-haired mind!" he screeched.

"Hey, how about a senior discount? No? All right, how much for a blow job?" They were all too pricey as far as he was concerned. And none of the hookers were willing to go down on the price of going down.

He had to have some relief, though. "How much for a hand job?" he asked the last one. "Twenty bucks? All right, I can swing that."

Ж

Sept peeled off twenty one-dollar bills. "Damned, she was ugly," he grumbled after his service agent left the van. "Michael's prettier than her."

Hmm. Take the runt to a hairdresser, put him in a fancy dress, and apply a little of that war paint—er—make-up. Set him to work in a dark alley, and no one will know the difference. It's not as if he can run away. As long as he doesn't have Benji to protect him, he'll stay put. Yeah, divide and conquer. Schedule them right and those two will never know where the other one is working.

Ж

It wasn't a five-star—or any kind of—hotel that Eight had arranged. It was simply a gathering of forlorn folks around a fire pit in a wide spot in the woods. The homeless camp was quiet, though, just the occasional whoosh of tires as trucks wheeled down the two lane highway towards town.

Michael joined the half dozen established residents hovered around the low glow of burning trash and twigs. A green bottle of cheap wine was passed around, but it was empty by the time it got to him. Not that Michael drank; he just wanted to be a part of something. He checked out his fellow 'five-star folks.' They were a rainbow of colors, ethnicities, and genders. The one aspect they all had in common—besides the stomach-turning tang of unwashed bodies—was the blank stare. Certainly they had different eye colors, but they all looked the same dull, slate gray.

He shook his head. This couldn't be his destiny, could it? If he bolted from Sept and sons, was this his fate? The job as a cook at the camp had been decent enough, but his self-worth had taken another blow: they didn't want him without Benji. And Benji was nowhere to be seen, totally off the radar, spending all his time with his new job and girlfriend.

Sept and his boys showed up, and the grousing and arguing began, fracturing the peacefulness of the new old neighborhood. Michael rushed over to his pile of brush and rag-wool bedding, lay down, relaxed his shoulders, and closed his eyes, pretending to nap.

He had perfected the act of appearing to be sound asleep years ago and it paid off. Again. Even with hushed whispers, he could hear their plot.

"Who needs a pretty girl to put on the streets? All I have to do is doll Michael up and be his pimp."

"You can do that, Pa? I mean, won't a guy know the difference?" Niner asked.

"They're called johns, you idiot. And Michael can keep his skirt on for the blowing and hand jobs. If one of you can sneak in there at the right time, you might be able to pick a wallet or two. Eight said those movie guys weren't interested in him as a male whore. So, what? Do you two have a better idea on how to make a few bucks?"

"No, Pa," Eight and Niner chorused.

"Sounds great," Niner added. "As long as I don't have to help get him gussied up. Eight can do that."

"Nah. I got something else planned…"

Michael tuned them out. How could Sept and his sons be so manipulative, so disgusting? All they wanted was someone to use, a blood-pumping source of income that wouldn't require any of them to perspire.

He glanced at a broken wine bottle and dismissed the thought almost as soon as it entered his head. He wasn't going to scar up his face just so he'd be unappealing to others. This was the face God gave him and he'd keep it. But he'd start looking for a way to leave the MacLeods and find gainful employment right away, with or without Benji at his side. He loved the big lug like the brother he never had, but becoming a prostitute—offering *any* part of his body to strangers—wasn't an option he'd allow. Surely, Benji would feel the same way if their places were switched. Still, it would be nice if Benji was around so they could talk about it.

"Hey, wake up you lazy good for nothin'…nothin'!" Sept said, booting Michael in the ribs.

"Yeah, Pa wants to take you into town for a make-over." Niner giggled. "Nothin' nothin'!"

Ж

Sept pushed open the glass door. "Hey. You. Are you the one I talk to about getting some fancy hair work done?"

"Yes, I'm a hair stylist. Did you need to make an appointment?"

"Me? Hell, I mean, heck no. I'm good-lookin' enough. This here boy needs some major work done. He's, um, going to be in one of those theater productions, like in the movies. He's supposed to look like a girl. A nice, fancy lady-type. Can you fix him up?"

Alisha looked down at her schedule book. Something smelled fishy beyond the old man's unkempt, dirty clothes and lack of personal hygiene. She glanced at the petite young man sitting near the window. He was definitely not in favor of this. He was practically in tears. If she didn't intercede, the bully would hit all the salons until he found one that would take his money. She sighed deeply. She'd work through lunch. Again. But she'd make the creep pay.

"I had a cancellation," she said, grimacing at the out-and-out lie. "I can do a complete make-over. It will take at least two hours, maybe more. $150 ought to cover it."

"What?" shouted Sept. "That's highway robbery."

"That does include make up…"

"Nah, still too much. Someone up the road will be cheaper, I'm sure."

606

"I'll tell you what, I'll do it for $100 and throw in a dress, panty hose, and a good pair of used heels. That will save you the hassle of taking him shopping. I'm sure your time is worth a lot, too."

"Hmm. Now that you mention it, I forgot how much clothes would cost."

Sept had planned on stealing clothes from some unfortunate's clothesline, but he hadn't seen laundry hanging outside in these neighborhoods. They were all over the place in Scotland. Maybe she was right.

He reached into his pocket, peeled off the hundred-dollar bill from his roll of ones, and slapped it on the table. "Here. Fix him up nice. I'll be back by four. Or not. Depends on whether someone's buying rounds."

Alisha ignored the remark and walked up to the pensive young man. "This way, sir."

Sept looked back at the two as he headed out the door. "Don't give her any trouble or you know what'll happen." He chuckled, then said softly, "Pretty boy."

Alisha reached over and patted her new client on the shoulder. "What's your name?"

"Michael. Michael Callahan."

"Hi, I'm Alisha. Now, I may be mistaken, but you don't want to look like a girl, do you?"

"No, ma'am. I don't dare say more, but if I had my druthers—and a few bucks—I'd be out of here in a heartbeat."

"Where are you staying?"

"Right now, with him. That's Atholl Grant MacLeod the Seventh, or Sept as he wants to be called. He and his two sons—Eight and Niner—kidnapped me and my friend, Benji. We're stuck. No money and nowhere to go."

"Well, now you have money." She put the hundred-dollar bill in his hand, then tenderly wrapped his fingers around it. "This should help."

"Wow! I mean, yes, it will definitely help." He looked up into her warm brown eyes and his broad smile faded. "I still don't have anywhere to go, though. And I don't want to take off without my friend." He shook his head. "I don't know where he is. Sept drops him off somewhere, then someone else picks him up and takes him to work. Sept says he's a pool gardener, but he mangles words and names all the time."

"The old man said he'd be back around 4:00. That gives us lots of time to figure out a plan. Would you care for a shampoo and style while we think? On the house. Oh, and I promise, it will *not* be a ladies' style."

Michael's dimpled grin returned as he looked up at the caramel-colored young woman who was at least six inches taller than him. "That would be wonderful."

By the time the shampoo, shave, and blow dry were done, the two had a rough outline of a plan. Alisha shared with him that she was ready to start her own salon. She and Michael could lay low for a while, locate the right place to set up a shop, find where Benji was, and 'kidnap' him back. Michael would help her in the new salon, and Benji could find work wherever.

"He's very talented and has a strong back," Michael bragged. "Now, where in the heck has he been disappearing to?"

Ж

Just before three o'clock, Sept strolled into the salon and screeched as if he'd been pinched with pliers. "What did you do to his hair? I told you I wanted him to look like a girl!"

Alisha gulped back her squeal of surprise. She hadn't had time to sneak Michael out the back door. She had to think fast. "Oh, don't worry. I'll make him look like a beauty queen. The hair will work with either gender. I didn't know you wanted me to keep it long. You should have said something."

"Give me my money back. And where's the dress you said you'd get for him?"

"He's not my size. I'll have to take him shopping. I want to match the makeup to the outfit, too. I don't think we have time to do that now, so have him here tomorrow at ten."

Michael grimaced at her words. He thought he was going to stay with her; that she liked him. Yes, the haircut and shampoo were great, but she was going to give him back to that creep? He sighed loudly and walked toward the door. "Later," he grumbled, and intentionally elbowed Sept on the way out.

"Don't worry about a thing, Michael," Alisha called out.

Sept showing up early really screwed things up. Now Michael had to go back with that monster for the night. And she never had the chance to tell the sweet young man how much she wanted to be with him.

Ж

Sept, Eight, Niner, and Michael waited outside the convenience store for Benji. It seemed like hours, but was only 15 minutes by the dashboard clock. The long town car pulled up and Benji got out, strong, silent, and confident, as if he'd just discovered how to turn lead into gold.

"Just a minute, lad," Sept said, and walked to the other side of the car. Grimy hand outstretched, he waited impatiently while the exasperated driver counted out twenties into his hand. "Tomorrow?" he asked.

The chauffeur nodded, mumbled, "Be here by nine," and then took off in a cloud of dust, wheels spinning on the dry, gravelly parking lot.

Benji's glow of accomplishment faded. Crap! He thought he was done with her, but Lady expected him back. He looked over and saw the dour look on Michael's face. Something was wrong. Well, whatever it was, he'd help him through it. He'd suffer one more day with the wrinkled witch of the south. Then he and Michael would vanish together, one way or another.

Benji pulled his shoulders back and reclaimed his earlier sense of control.

"What got into you?" Sept asked.

"Just got a lot accomplished today. I thought the job was done, but I just overheard the chauffeur tell you that the boss lady wants me at her place early. I must have impressed her," he said and swallowed a groan.

"Yeah, I'll bet," Eight said sarcastically.

"Yeah, I'll bet," Niner mimicked.

"Don't you worry about Benji," Sept warned and headed back to the van.

Eight pulled his father aside, out of earshot of the others. "Hey, what about Michael? I thought he was going to get all gussied up like a girl for those suckers in the city?"

"Not your concern, boy. I have it under control. Besides, he's not finished with his outfit yet."

Ж

The vagrant camp almost looked homey compared to where he'd lived in the past, but Michael couldn't help but fear what was in store for him. He'd have to find a way to get out from under the MacLeod's control soon. He didn't want to leave for good without Benji, though.

"I thought I was going to be able to tell you about my new *girlfriend*," Benji said with an eye roll when the two of them were alone. "But…you wouldn't believe it," and shook his head in disbelief.

Michael cut him off before he could finish the thought. "Well, I thought I'd have one to tell you about, too, but I guess I was wrong about her."

Benji suddenly felt protective of his 'little' brother from another mother. He tousled his hair affectionately. "Ach, give her a while. She'll grow to love ye in no time, jest like me. Hey, where'd ye get the haircut? Looks right nice. And ye smell better, too."

"My almost girlfriend gave it to me. Sept told her to make me look like a girl. I guess he's going to have me stand on the street corners, dressed up like a hooker, and then Eight or Niner will roll the guys when they try to get some. Or afterwards, whatever he means by that." He shuddered. "As long as he doesn't want me to have sex with them. There's nothing wrong with being gay, but men just don't appeal to me. Then again, neither does wearing a dress. Different strokes for different folks, if you know what I mean."

"But that's not what you want to do, is it?"

"Hell, no. I'm not a prostitute! But until one of us finds a way out of here and a place to stay, I guess we'll have to bow to Sept's crazy plans. I just hope they get the john's money before I'm discovered…or have to pretend to be a girl."

608

"Weel, maybe I have a way out. My boss is kinda sweet on me. She's a bit older…a mighty bit older…and so, so, ergh!" He snorted, trying to erase the memory of her and his forced compliance. "But I think I've figured out a plan. If I can just… Let's just say I need to stay on her good side for at least one more day."

Michael looked down his nose, shook his head, and said, "I don't think I want to know details."

Benji grinned and shrugged his shoulder in embarrassment. "Don't worry. I willna kiss and tell. But I'm hopin' she stays sweet on me so she'll give me a job." He blushed for no apparent reason and corrected himself. "Give me a *real* job. I guess she has a large crop growing and processing operation and…"

"If you don't mind, I'd like to be alone for a bit. I thought it was a good day, but it seems it's about as bad as it can get."

Alisha

The van, now spray painted lime green, pulled up to the mini market. "Out you go to earn your keep, Benji," Sept said, then sped off to town to see Michael's new beauty coordinator.

Ж

"Now, I paid you handsomely yesterday," Sept told Alisha, his index finger wagging in admonishment. "And I want him pretty as a picture of a four-dollar whore on a three-dollar bill."

"Wait, what?" Alisha shook her head at his lame attempt at a joke. "No, never mind. I get the idea." Out of the corner of her eye she saw Michael peeking around the back of the van. "Come on, we have a big day ahead of us." She turned at Sept, "How about you pick him up around six. And don't worry. I won't charge you overtime."

"You'd better not! You should be giving me a refund, taking two days to do a two-hour job." Sept wiped his nose with the back of his hand, then added, "Time is money. My money. The longer he's outta work, the less money he's making me."

Eight shoved Michael from behind the van towards Alisha. "You might want to give him a bath, too. He stinks!" He held his nose between thumb and finger, then laughed aloud. "Prettier than a four-dollar whore."

Alisha wrapper her arm around the much shorter Michael. "Don't worry about a thing," she said softly. "Play along with me until those jerks leave."

Michael's back straightened up in hope, then sagged again as he returned to his beaten man persona.

The van sped away, nearly running into a postal truck as it merged into traffic. "Asshole!" Sept, Eight, and Niner chorused.

"Asshole is right," Michael said. "Rather assholes. I hope I never see them again for the rest of my life."

"Well, if I have my way, that's exactly what's going to happen. Now, since I already gave my notice two weeks ago and no longer work here, would you care to come to my place? I have some details I'd like to go over with you. And, if you're still willing to go on with the plan..." She bowed her head, and looked into his eyes, silently asking, 'forgive me?'

He nodded and smiled a silent, 'yes.'

"...then you'd be a big help to me in my new business. You seem like a sharp man and I need a partner. Or, to start with, a receptionist, cashier, shampooer and clean up person rolled into one."

"I'm pretty short. I think I can roll all those tasks into one. That is, if you think I'm up to it."

"I'm a great judge of character, Michael Callahan. I'm sorry if I didn't give you a heads-up yesterday. My mind was going a hundred different directions at the same time, planning how I could put my new business plan together with you as my vice-president, and also how to get you away from that horrid Sept and sons. In the big picture, having you with me makes it much easier. I can't do everything myself, and I don't know anyone I can trust."

"Well, you're a little bit wrong, but mostly right," he said, and gave her a mischievous grin.

Alisha's mouth twitched, not knowing whether to smile or frown. "Explain, please."

"You can trust me, for sure, and I'll work harder than you can imagine, but I can't be the vice-president."

"Why not?"

"Because companies, at least corporations, need to have a president and a secretary. You, madam president, are looking at the man who would love to be your secretary. But please, don't make me wear a skirt."

"No worries there. Now, how about we go to my apartment and I'll test your skills as a shampooer?"

"As long as you don't mind if I take a shower first. Oh, and I may have to wear a towel until I can wash these clothes. They're the only ones I have."

"The only ones right now. I have a few bucks held back. We are going to have the most kick-butt salon in the state with the most awesome attire. No dull and usual uniforms for us!"

Ж

"It's small, but efficient," Alisha said, as she opened the door to the studio apartment. "I took it because I was saving at least two hundred dollars a month in rent over a one-bedroom. I've had some pretty healthy tippers lately, and I've saved every cent. Lots of folks have given me their phone numbers, too, and told me to call them if I ever opened up my own salon. So, I kinda, sorta have a clientele already. At least, I will when we find a place."

Michael couldn't help but grin. There was only one bed in the micro apartment: a futon couch. He sucked back his smile and asked, "You did say I could stay here with you, right?"

"Yup," she answered and chuckled. "You get the bathtub."

"Oh. Okay. I guess…"

"Oops! I forgot. I don't have a bathtub. This place only has a shower. It's a big shower, but not big enough to sleep in. You'll have to sleep with me, I suppose…"

His smile returned. "How about we check out that big shower first."

"You read my mind, Michael Callahan. I can feel the ick from just being in the same room as Sept. If you wash my back, I'll wash yours."

"I do like your plans, Alisha. Especially the ones you tell me about."

"Oh, sorry about that. Will you forgive me?"

"Already did. Hey, before we get too far ahead, do you have a bag I can put these clothes in? I don't want them to smell up the car on the way to the laundromat. And I think I'd better take a pre-shower before you come in for a back scrub."

Alisha handed him a trash bag. "Fill 'er up, then put it outside the bathroom door. I'll take it to the dumpster then join you."

"But, but…"

"Don't worry. I have some sweats you can wear. Later."

Ж

What did you do to deserve such a good-looking, sweet woman, Michael Callahan? All those years of living on the edge of starvation and danger, and then she pops into your life. They say if something seems too good to be true, it is, but I hope that isn't the case here.

Michael looked down through the suds and saw his cock waving hello, glad to be happy. He laughed softly. *Yeah, just you and me and Alisha makes three, buddy. No men allowed.*

"Are you ready for me to come in?" Alisha called.

"Um, yeah, I suppose…" Michael forced his hand down over his erection, but that didn't work. "Ah, hell. Come on in!"

Alisha laid the towels on top of the toilet seat. "I'm sure glad this has a handicapped shower. I can sit on the shower bench while you wash my hair. But let's not get too far ahead. Here," and handed him a washcloth. "You can wash my back first, and then I'll get yours."

She didn't look down, but knew he was insecure about something. She turned around and felt his embarrassment poke her. She glanced back. He definitely should be proud of that sword, not bashful. *'Big man, big dick,' Mama used to say. 'Little man, all dick,' was right!*

"God, you're beautiful," Michael said without thinking. "Um, did I just say that out loud."

"Yes, you did, and thank you. You know, it isn't easy being tall. And being of mixed blood—well, I never felt like I fit in with the black community, and the white folks were okay sometimes, but uppity others. Shoot, I was either too white or too black for just about anything but basketball. Then, both groups wanted to claim me."

"Yeah, well, I had the shorty syndrome."

Alisha chuckled, and reached back. "If they only knew…"

Michael laughed along with her. "Well, I didn't do anything to earn that, or my stature." He worked up a lather on her shoulders. "Man, your skin tone is so absolutely beautiful."

"And I didn't do anything to earn that, either. But you know, when I first met you, I swear I saw your soul. It was right there, bright and scared, and said, 'Here I am. You've been looking for me for years, and now I'm here.'"

Michael wiped broad circles across her back, then worked lower. Pensive. Scared. Excited. "I wanted you so bad," he admitted. "Yes, I was scared, but I saw that you could see right through Sept. When you took that money from him, well, I wasn't sure if I was glad or sad. I hoped you were going to help me. Nah, I knew you wouldn't hurt me. Even when he showed up early and you sent me away with him, I *knew* you weren't selling me into prostitution, even if the words sounded like it."

Alisha shook her head and sucked in her bottom lip, but said nothing. The apology needn't be repeated and he wasn't looking for it. "Here, let me wash your back."

Michael turned around, then stepped away from the shower bench. "Here, it might be easier if you sat down to wash me."

"Yes, it would. But don't feel weird about it. I'd say we were a very unconventional couple, me being tall and all." Alisha gasped. "Did I just say that?"

"You mean about being a couple? Yup, you did. But we both know it's right. Right?"

"I've never been so sure of anything in my life. And I'm a pretty determined woman."

"Pretty *and* determined." Michael turned around, leaned down, and kissed her forehead. "And there are lots of ways we can accommodate our size difference."

She reached out and grabbed his cock. "I don't know… that's a lot of size for me to accommodate. And I don't have any of that slicker stuff, er, lube."

"I'm sure we can think of something. The shower feels pretty wet to me."

"In here?" Alisha reached out and grabbed the safety bar. "Hmm. Looks like this place is already tricked out. As long as the hot water lasts, we should be fine. Oh, and just to be sure, you aren't a minor, are you?"

Michael chuckled. "I'm twenty-three. Everyone thinks I'm younger. As long as it helps keep me out of trouble, I'll let them think it. But I promise you, I'm definitely legal."

Alisha wrapped her hands around his cock. "I am, too, but what I want to do with this is illegal in a few states." She wrapped her mouth around the head and teased it in and out a couple of times. "My secretary. Yum."

Determined and Bound

"She told me to tell you that she's waiting upstairs for you," the chauffeur said when he pulled up in front of the house. "Just don't make her wait too long. She can get real grumpy. You won't like her when she's grumpy."

Benji's eyes widened. This was the most the driver had ever said to him. And it almost sounded like a warning. It also sounded as if he spoke from experience.

"Aye, thanks."

Benji raced up the stairs, two at a time. She was sure to be able to tell by his footfalls that he was eager to do her bidding. Hopefully, he hadn't left a sour taste in her mouth. He groaned softly. *Don't think about tastes in your mouth now.*

She was dressed in hot-pink short shorts and a halter top, her sly smile accentuated by the lipstick that matched her attire. "Take off your clothes and lie down here for a moment. I want to try these bracelets on you."

No hi, hello, or glad to see ye? Well, he'd show her he had manners.

"Good mornin' to ye," he said, making sure his accent was as thick as he pleased. She did say she liked it. He definitely wanted to get on her good side today if he was going to ask for a *real* job.

"Bracelets? Ye dinna need to get me jewelry…" He kicked off his tattered tennis shoes, stripped, then lay down on the king-sized bed. As soon as his feet hit the new comforter, he realized something was wrong. He sat up quickly. "Wait, what are those? Those aren't bracelets; they're handcuffs!"

"Hold still," she said gruffly, and grabbed for his wrist.

Benji obediently, but reluctantly, put out his hand. Once again, the sweet young thing in the old woman's body was gone, and a grouchy prison guard—rivaling Sept or Eight—had taken her place. Her provocative smile was replaced by a scowl that made the crow's feet and double lines between her eyebrows stand out, as if someone had darkened them with a black marker.

"The other hand now."

Benji complied and closed his eyes. *What a wicked witch!* He breathed in deeply and slowly. How was he going to get out of this mess?

His train of thought was interrupted by her grasping his ankle, tugging it toward the end of the bed. Then he noticed them. What he thought were decorative rings on the bedposts were hitching rings for the handcuffs and leg irons. This was a first for him. And a last. Imprisonment he'd dealt with for years; emotional bondage, bad enough. But at least he had a respite from those when he was asleep. The loss of control over his body parts was something he'd never let happen again. Ever. But first he'd have to suffer through this.

Ж

There must have been something in the lemonade she gave him after she had her way with him. The last thing he recalled was her apologizing for being so rough with her riding crop. However, as compensation, she had offered him the foreman position for her southern grow site. How many acres did she have under cultivation, and what was she growing? He didn't ask, but had never seen any fields.

The breeze pushed open the lightweight cotton curtain, allowing a bright ray of sunshine to wash across his face. His nose twitched as he stifled a sneeze, then he stopped. Even that small movement made his head throb. Either his brain had swelled or his skull had shrunk. Or he had been drugged again. He eased one eye open to see where he was, then reached up to shield his eyes from the brightness.

Or tried to.

His hands were free, but his wrists weren't. He tried to untie the frilly cloth that secured him, but it was no use. It was a tight knot. She had swapped the handcuffs for a more feminine version of restraint while he was out.

Lady sashayed into the room wearing a floor-length gown, glittering with golden sequins and crystals, a martini glass in her hand. "Comfy, darling?"

"Ye've no right to truss me up like this. I dinna do anythin' wrong. Everything ye've asked of me, I've done. And then some."

"Now, don't get sassy with me. I own a lot of acreage. I could have someone bag you up and bury you alongside the other boys out there. No one would ever know."

He inhaled deeply and held his breath. Shoot! Even Sept didn't know where he was. To the old man, he was no more than a rolled up newspaper, dropped off and picked up for further delivery, to be used or abused as his paying client saw fit. Or bagged, buried, and forgotten!

"Aye, I'll be fine," he said, and transitioned into video actor mode. He smiled as if he wanted her again and said seductively, "It's jest my neck. I'd appreciate it if ye'd fluff my pillow for me," and pursed his lips.

She came up beside him and added a throw pillow behind his head. "Now, be a good boy while you're hanging there... and start thinking about *your* Marcia." She picked up his limp dick with her whip. "We have to show the girls how big this gets when it's angry, ready for a good time."

The Bidding

The guests had arrived. The tea service and hors d'oeuvres were laid out on her finest linen. It was time to turn a profit.

"Girls, I have a treat for you. I know we don't always share secrets, but I've found the most delicious young boy. If you'll help me out with a bit of business, I'll share. He's young and hung. Oh, and well-learned in the fine art of pleasuring a woman. I should know. I trained him myself. A virgin is fun only once and then, well, he's not a virgin anymore. But the awkwardness has worn off, and he's polished and ready to serve. Now, who'll start the bidding."

"What? You're going to sell him?"

"Of course not. What I'm selling are kilos of North Carolina's finest cash crop. The more you buy, the more time you get with young Benji."

"Are you giving out samples?" the dowager with the cane asked.

"Of which?" Lady answered.

"Either one, although I'd like a sampling of your young man. My new hip cost me a fortune, but the doctor said I'll be ready for anything after some physical therapy."

Ж

He started working the knot on the other wrist. It was easy, so in no time, his hands and feet were unbound. He guzzled water from the bathroom faucet, washed his face, got dressed, and headed downstairs.

It appeared Lady was hosting a party. At least two dozen women were there. All nicely dressed. All colors and body types, but all about the same age as the whip-wielding bondage queen.

"Oh, excuse me. I thought you were alone," Benji said, and looked toward the kitchen, hoping he could make an escape out the back door.

"No, no," she said. "You're fine. Come down and meet some of my friends. I was going to have them come up to see you one at a time, but this will work, too."

Dowager waved her cane in the air. "I'll take *him* for my physical therapist. I'll buy as much product as it takes."

The chauffeur, now dressed as a butler, entered the room. "Would you like me to bring out the other 'refreshments,' my lady?" he asked with a wink and a nod, referring to Benji.

"Yes, please do. Ladies, my man will bring out samples of our excellent green product. I don't suggest you imbibe, but you can check the aroma and bud size. I think you'll be favorably impressed. I have a list of the varieties on the table with the particular attributes of each one. One bud makes you relaxed, another more creative, another," she did a little bump and grind, and nodded to Benji, still standing halfway up the stairs. "Another enhances your pleasures."

The murmurs of the women in the room rose, a few chuckles slipped out, but all eyes were on Benji.

"But before we begin the bidding, Benji, take off your shirt. Oh, and I hope you're still wearing your swimming 'trunks.'"

Benji's stomach was in turmoil. 'Bagged and buried' kept going through his mind. The only way he was going to get through this would be to change personas. Again. He pulled his shoulders back, pasted on his best imitation of the bleached-blond actor's grin, and descended down the last few steps. He looked the women in the eyes, slowly unbuttoned his shirt, dipped one shoulder then the other, and slipped it off.

"More, more," the women encouraged.

He responded, but only because he didn't have an option. He stuck his thumbs in the front of the Hawaiian-print board shorts and swiveled his hips, bringing the shorts down just a bit. He glanced up and saw the chauffeur trying to get his attention. Benji shifted his focus to the woman next to him, but knew the driver could tell he was watching him, too. His new friend's eyes looked toward the kitchen, telling him to make haste and get out of there.

Benji teased the women with another flirtatious grin, grabbed himself by the crotch, but didn't lower his pants. "Not yet, ladies," he said. "I'll be back in a moment."

Lady wasn't sure what to do, but knew that this was the optimal time to get the bidding started. They were hot and bothered, and wanted to see what this sexy, tall and young red head had to offer. "Let the bidding begin!"

Benji strutted toward the kitchen like a runway model, then looked back over his shoulder and winked, as if he was willing—no, wanting—to stay around for the rest of the proceedings.

"What's up?" he asked Chauffeur when they were alone.

"I've got the car started and ready for us to leave."

Benji's eyes widened, but he didn't say a word.

"Hey, bud, I don't like this crazy broad any more than you do. Before she was into boys, she was into… Well, let's just say I'm as eager to get out of here as you are. I've taken what's mine. If you don't leave now, with me, it might be a while before you get another chance, if ever. I can almost guarantee, though, that whatever is in your future with her is worse than the unknown out there."

"I'm ready. There's nothing here I'm taking," Benji said, "except for this." He grabbed one of the foot-long sub sandwiches from the counter. "It doesn't have anything 'funny' in it that will make me pass out or anything, does it?"

"Nah, it's virgin. But let's make tracks!"

Benji and Chauffeur took off in a black '57 Mercury Cruiser. "My name's Ben, as in Benjamin," the driver said.

"Another Benji?"

"Maybe that's why I was fond of you. I really tried not to like you. I had to distance myself from the boys she brought in. It hurt me too bad when they disappeared. Oh, and by the way, I didn't have anything to do with that. She has some goon from the Midwest come in and off the boys when she's tired of them. I had to pick up the guy from the airport today, so I knew your time was short. I'm not supposed to bring him back from the hotel until tomorrow noon. That would mean you have a life expectancy of less than 24 hours if you stick around there."

"Wow. And thank ye! Is there anything I can do for ye?"

"I'd like you to call the cops and report her for taking advantage of underage males, but I don't know if that would work unless you're willing to testify. Here, this is her card with all her contact information on it. On the back, I put down first names and the dates her former *boys* disappeared. I never knew any last names. I don't know where her disposal site is, but she did mention something about not developing any of her southern acreage. I'd tell the cops to look for fresh tilled earth there."

Benji turned the card over. There were eight names on it, two of them Ben. He took in a deep breath and let it out slowly. That was a close one.

"Where to?" the former chauffeur asked.

"Same place: the convenience store. I need to get my friend."

"I know there's something fishy going on with you and that old man who collects for you, but you'll be fine. Here's a few bucks." He handed him two one-hundred dollar bills. "I'm sure you'll get out from underneath his claws soon. You're resourceful. And, from what I saw this afternoon, a great actor, too."

"Thanks. Now all I need is the right stage."

Ж

"I think I have a plan," Michael said, as he sat up on the couch he and his new mate had shared as a bed.

Alisha rubbed the sleep from her eyes. She hadn't planned on falling asleep, but had been totally relaxed for the first time in ages. The first round of making love had invigorated both of them, but the second time, kneeling in front of the futon, knocked both of them out. "Plan for what?"

"A plan to get Benji back."

"Okay, I'm all ears."

"Not hardly. I'd point out your other parts, but I don't want to get distracted. I don't have all the details worked out yet, but I can go back with Sept tonight. You can follow him to the mini market pick up and drop off spot, then we can snag Benji from there."

"You want to go back to Sept?"

"Hell, no! But I do want Benji. I can't think of another way to do it. It would be one thing if I knew where that convenience store was, but I always had to ride in the back of the van. I don't even know what town it's in."

Alisha looked up at the clock. "It's still early enough. Sept was going to pick you up at the salon in half an hour. If we hurry, we can make it."

"I just hope Benji isn't spending the night with his boss lady." Michael shook his head. "I feel bad. There was a lot he wasn't telling me last night. I think he needed to unload, but I was too depressed to listen."

"Don't worry about it. We can't change the past. You can be there for him from now on, though. We both will."

Ж

Alisha let Michael out at the salon, but went back to her car to wait. She couldn't bear to see him with that creep. Besides, it would be impossible for the two of them to hide how they felt about each other, even in front of Sept.

Michael stood in front of the salon, shifting from foot to foot, trying to figure out how he'd tell Sept that he wasn't going to be able to play bait for his 'roll the johns' plan.

Sept and the boys pulled up in the green van that now had 'for hire' scribbled on the side with a fat black marker.

"Hey! You don't look like a girl! Pa, looks like you got ripped off again."

"Shut up, Niner," Sept said. "Where's that little hussy, Michael?"

"Um, she said she was going to hand deliver a ransom note to my father for me. She said the reason you weren't getting paid is because I hadn't signed it. She helped me write it, said it would get you more money than dressing me up as a girl for a theater production..."

Sept nodded in agreement. "She doesn't want any of the reward, does she?"

Michael shook his head. "Nope. She said she was going to ask for a finder's fee from, um, my old man." Michael brightened up as his creative juices started flowing. "She's going to Vegas after she gets it. She's going to be a showgirl!"

Sept snorted in disagreement about her career choice. "When's the money coming?"

"She, um, asked for it to be delivered to that convenience store you always go to for beer and girlie magazines."

As soon as he said it, Michael cringed inside. He didn't know where it was, but did Sept know that he didn't know?

"Smart girl. Let's go there now. I expect Benji will be there soon. Hey! Maybe I'll have a double payday today!"

Ж

Alisha parked her vintage yellow Civic behind the mini market. She looked over at the passenger seat. Empty. But only for a while. She had someone in her life now. Someone she knew would be there for her—and with her—forever.

Hmm. Michael said Benji was tall, much taller than she was. She looked in the back seat. Not much leg room there with both front seats scooted all the way back. Maybe she should get out and push the passenger seat forward? It was either that or have Michael ride in the back. Nope. She didn't want that. He was going to be by her side. Forever.

She heard Michael call, "Come on, let's get out of here!"

Alisha looked up and saw the red-haired youth was nearly a head taller than her. "Whoa! He is big. He'll have to ride in front."

"Benji, Alisha. Alisha, Benji," Michael said, as he crawled into the back seat. "Now, let's get out of here. And wherever you're going, take the long way around. He's sure to get lost."

Alisha took several side streets before coming back to the highway and flipping a U-turn.

"I think you lost them already, Alisha," Michael said. "How about stopping off at a diner. I'll treat." He winked and flashed the hundred-dollar bill.

"Where'd ye get that?" Benji asked. "Ye didn't, um, go out on the streets, and um…"

"Hell, no! But this *is* from Sept. It's the money he gave Alisha to make me look like a girl. She gave it to me."

"And your haircut was free," she added. "So, yes, let's eat. I'm hungry. Between running away from bad guys, and, um, other things, I've really worked up an appetite."

She and Michael looked at each other and blushed.

"I dinna care to hear how ye worked up yer appetites, but it does look like ye shared the experience and enjoyed it. That's what's important, aye? Having someone to share good times with?"

"You got that right. Benji," Michael said. "I'm certain you'll find your Mrs. Right."

"No, she'll be a miss. But I'll make her a missus as soon as I make sure she's the right one for me."

"We're here guys," Alisha said, pulling into an unlit parking spot near the dumpster. "I'll be back in a flash. I just need to use the ladies room."

The two men sat down in a booth in the darkest part of the diner, out of sight, just in case Sept did find them. "Weel, Michael, it looks as if ye know where yer going and who yer going with."

"That's for sure. What are you going to do?"

"I've been wanting to talk to ye about that. Ye know how I told ye I was born in the 18th century, that I always wanted to go back to see my grandparents?"

"Yes…"

"I have a few bucks now. The driver gave me two hundred-dollar bills before he dropped me off. He sorta felt sorry for me, I guess. Well, after I talk to the cops about the operation my former boss has going, and the young boys she's responsible for making disappear, I'm going back to the 18th century! I remember my da talking about a time portal somewhere near Greensboro…"

"Benji, don't do this. You're delusional. Those were just dreams, a fantasy you created when your parents died."

Benji took a deep breath and looked away. He had never said his parents were dead, but he had led Michael to believe that they were. He had to tell him. "My parents are not dead. But I can't go see them. Especially after what jest happened."

"What? What just happened? Oh, hi, Alisha. You look as beautiful as ever."

"Thank you. A woman never tires of being flattered. I'm sorry, you two seem to be in the middle of a deep discussion. I don't want to interrupt. I can go see what's on the jukebox."

"No, I think we're done," Benji said.

He looked at Michael. He was definitely in love, getting lost in his new sweetheart's smile. His friend had other concerns now and didn't need to be involved in his. Besides, he had told him about his early years before and knew that no matter how much he tried to convince him, Michael would never believe the truth. It might be best to let him think that he had just been fantasizing, that he knew he really wasn't from the 18th century.

That didn't mean he wouldn't stop trying to go back in time, though. That's where he belonged.

"Here." Alisha handed Benji a business card. "That's my cousin's phone number and address in Ashland. He's always complaining about not being able to find anyone who's willing to work. Or learn. He's a mechanic. I wrote you a quick character reference on the back. Stick with him, and you'll learn everything about anything with wheels, tracks, or wings. You may have to bust tires or sweep floors to start with, but he'll be good to you, I promise."

"As long as I don't have to sweep pools," Benji said and chuckled. He turned the card over.

'Hire the big kid—Alisha'

"Thanks. After I get with the cops about *her*, I'll use this," he rubbed his two hundred-dollar bills between thumb and fingers, "for a bus ticket west. Aye, let's hope "Go West, young man" works for me."

ЖЖЖ

The End

POOL BOY WANTED:
No Experience Preferred

Pool Boy Wanted: No Experience Preferred is the first book in the new series *Benji, The Lost Years*. These stories aren't being released in chronological order, but rather as the lead character reveals his history to me. (No defined number of books in the series as of yet.)

SUMMER LOVIN'

JACQUIE BIGGAR

Can two mismatched lovers find a way past their mistakes, or will they keep their lonely hearts forever guarded?

Jacquie Biggar has a wonderful gift for writing hot and extremely likable military men! ~~Jacqui Nelson~~

I have so many people I'd like to thank. First and foremost my husband, Robert John. Without you I wouldn't have had the courage to pursue my dreams. Thank you.

My mom, who has always been my guiding light and allows me to toss ideas with her. Thank you.

My daughter, Brandy; you are my inspiration to never give up.

To my critique buddies, you know who you are. Without you pushing me to better myself, this book might never have happened.

To my beta readers for their tremendous input, and the reviewers who are key to a writer's success, thank you.

Copyright © 2016 Jacquie Biggar
ISBN No. 978-1-988126-01-2

This book marks the fifth in the Wounded Hearts series centered on the citizens of Tidal Falls, Washington. The characters have grown and taken on a life of their own and I've had great fun getting to know them.

I hope you enjoy Mitch and Rebecca's story.

Jacquie

FOREWARD

Mitch Taylor and Rebecca Sorenson share a secret.

Rebecca's job is rewarding as secretary of Cascade Elementary—the same school she attended as a child. She has a great group of friends, even though many of whom are married now. And if sometimes she wished she was up there in that sparkling white dress…

Except, wait—she did get to wear bridal white. Granted, it was a slinky party dress and the justice of the peace was Elvis in a gold lame jacket, but still, the deed was done.

She'd tied the knot.

Mitch Taylor doesn't do regrets. It would be a waste of energy bemoaning the mistakes he'd made in his life. The end of his promising football career taught him nothing in life was a guarantee.

Like love.

What were the chances two people from the same po-dunk town in Washington would end up together in a nightclub in Las Vegas? A few too many drinks later, a hasty ceremony performed by the king of rock 'n' roll, and they'd been hitched. The night that followed lived on in his dreams, but when he'd woken the next morning she was gone.

Can these two mismatched lovers find a way past their mistakes, or will they keep their lonely hearts guarded forever?

CHAPTER ONE

Would this day never end? Rebecca Sorenson shuffled the papers on her desk and glanced up at the school clock for the tenth time in so many minutes. She had plans, big plans and couldn't wait to get a start on the weekend.

Tonight was the big night for her best friend, Annie's, bachelorette celebration. Which is why—Rebecca glanced at the clock again just as the bell rang signaling classes were done—she needed to get going. There was still a ton of last minute preparations before the party.

She hurried to log off the computer, finished stacking her secretarial files, and reached into the bottom drawer for her hobo styled handbag and striped sun hat. Annie made fun of the fact she had to give up two paychecks to afford her purse with its straw look and leather straps, but hello, *Jimmy Choo*. She wouldn't call herself vain exactly, but she definitely preferred good quality whenever she could afford it.

The elementary kids poured out of their classrooms, laughing and talking, not a worry on their sweet minds. Rebecca envied them their youth. Life had a way of bleeding that exuberance away.

Okay, enough with the maudlin shit.

She pasted a smile on her lips and rounded the end of the counter to join the melee heading for the front entrance.

"Bye, Miss Sorenson," little Jessica Reed sang as she rushed past with a couple of friends in tow.

Becky's heart pinched. She loved each and every one of the precious little rug-rats. Outside parents stood in friendly groups chatting, some with strollers or fussy preschoolers tugging on their hands. The moment they caught sight of their children, welcoming smiles broke out and arms opened wide to hug them close. The gentlest of breezes, just enough to take the heat out of the early summer sunshine, teased the girls' dresses and flirted with the boys' jackets. It was like a Hallmark movie.

She lifted the strap of her purse higher, plunked her hat on her head, and dodged families as she made her way across the playground, intent on reaching the bike rack where her prized baby blue Schwinn waited with a sturdy padlock.

A boy, maybe grade three going by his size, was crouched near the back tire of a beat-up black bike covered in superhero decals. He looked near tears as he fought to free the bike from its lock. Rebecca hesitated, anxious to get going, but the kid's obvious turmoil tugged at her heart.

"Hi," she said brightly. "Looks like you have a problem there. Can I help?"

The boy looked up at her through the thickest set of dark lashes and puppy dog eyes. She moved closer and his grubby fingers covered the combination while his gaze became even more fearful.

Rebecca stopped and raised her hands. "It's okay, kiddo, I work here." She pointed at the school behind them. "In the office. I'm Miss Sorenson. What's your name?"

He looked down, wiped his nose with the sleeve of his jacket, and mumbled, "Tommy."

Becky crouched and set her purse beside her on the tarmac. She knew most of the children attending Cascade Elementary, but not this little guy.

"What class are you in, Tommy?"

He flushed and looked toward the kids romping on the playground. When he turned back his face was belligerent. "I don't go to this dumb school."

Well, that explained why she didn't recognize him. She started to rise, saw the hint of desperation in his gaze, and stilled.

She nodded toward the bicycle. "That's a pretty terrific bike you have there. Do you want me to try and get that lock for you?" She hoped he wasn't trying to steal the machine. It looked as though his life might already be rough enough without adding theft to the mix.

He shook his head once, then reluctantly changed it to a nod. When he got up to give her room she noticed his threadbare sneakers. She gave him a reassuring smile and picked up the rusty lock. That was no doubt half the problem; the mechanism needed oiling. She was relieved to see that he'd used the right combination though. An experimental tug or two later proved her theory. Becky reached into her open bag and searched until she found the small tube of Vaseline she kept for chapped lips. Tommy looked anxious and confused when she handed him the ointment.

"Buddy, I need your help." She wiggled the lock. "I need you to rub some of that lotion onto the lock as I pull. Hopefully we'll get a little bit inside and it'll loosen the mechanism, how does that sound?"

Becky waited while he considered her idea. He finally nodded hesitantly.

"Don't worry," she smiled. "We'll get this." She positioned the lock between them. "Okay, partner, now."

He opened the tube and carefully squeezed it over the lock.

"That's great, Tommy. Now rub it in for me." She kept up a push-pull on either side of the lock until gradually it loosened and finally popped open.

His eyes widened with delight. "You did it," he said, his voice filled with awe.

Rebecca grinned, impressed it actually worked. "No, *we* did it," she said and impulsively leaned over to give him a hug.

He held himself stiff for a moment, then his arms wrapped her middle and squeezed the heck out of her. Warmed by a sudden burst of affection, she dropped a light peck on the top of his head.

A rough tug yanked the boy out of her arms.

"I told you to get yer damn bike and git yerself back home, boy."

Rebecca gasped, startled. A brutish man stood, legs astride, in front of them aiming a malevolent glare toward Tommy. His bullish face sported a bulbous nose lined with ugly red veins and lank, greasy hair. It didn't take much to guess that he spent a good portion of his time on the end of a bottle.

His hand twisted in the scruff of Tommy's jacket, and he gave it a shake. Instant tears sprang to the poor kid's eyes.

"There's no need to be rough," she snapped and reached down to lift her bag from the ground. "I asked him to help me out for a couple of minutes." She studiously ignored his start of surprise. "Is that a problem, Mr.?" She damn sure wanted this joker's name. Jack would be interested to hear how he was treating a little boy.

The guy snorted. "You think I'm an idiot, lady?"

He shoved Tommy toward his bike, almost knocking him off his feet. "Git goin', I'll be right behind ya."

Tommy gave her a helpless glance then yanked his bike out of the rack, threw a leg over the cracked seat, and peddled away as though his life depended on it.

The man moved into her personal space. Rebecca held her ground but her heart was thrashing its way up her throat.

He lifted cigarette stained fingertips and ran them up and down the strap of her purse. "You don't want to mess with me, lady. Just forget today ever happened, you got it?"

Becky swayed, more scared than she'd ever been in her life. She opened her mouth to answer she didn't know what, when a familiar, and at the moment welcoming, voice spoke from over her shoulder.

"Hey, Becky, there you are." Mitch's big body cast a looming shadow over the man in front of her. He took a hasty step back.

Mitch wrapped a muscular arm in a short-sleeved shirt around her waist and tugged her close. Rebecca glanced up to tell him to lay off and cringed at the stony expression at odds with his jovial tone.

"You have a problem with my *wife*, mister, you take it up with me." He stared the other man down, totally ignoring her gasp of outrage. "Got it?" His choice of words made it clear he'd heard at least the end of the conversation.

The man swore and spat on the ground between them—*ew*—then turned and stomped off to a faded red pickup sitting near the school fence.

The engine roared, sending up a blast of blue smoke. He left behind the stench of burnt gas and an uncomfortable silence.

She twisted out of Mitch's hold and fisted her hands on her hips.

"Husband? You're about five years too late to be making that claim, Mitchell Taylor."

CHAPTER TWO

Mitch tracked the departing truck until it disappeared from sight. There was something familiar about that guy...

"Did you hear me?" Becky demanded.

His lips quirked at her impatient tone. Damn, it was easy to get her dander up. He thought how much fun it would be to get her all worked up just so they could have make-up sex. His body hardened, on board with the idea in two seconds flat. *Pathetic, man, you're so pathetic.*

A floppy garden hat shaded her face and matched the hobo handbag she was digging through. She glanced up and her eyes matched the sky for their crystalline brilliance.

Mitch cocked his head toward the road. "What was that about?"

She followed his gaze, visibly shuddered, then squared her shoulders. "Nothing I can't handle." She lifted her chin and he wanted to kiss her. "I'm good at taking care of myself."

Yeah, he knew that.

"I never doubted you could, sweetheart."

A slim hand rose to hold him off. "Stop it," she demanded.

She hesitated, then slipped past him to get her bike. "I have to go. I need to stop by the sheriff's office."

Jealousy flared. Mitch cursed under his breath.

She glanced back. "Pardon me?"

He bit the inside of his lip, warning himself to keep it cool. "I just asked if you wanted me to see Jack so you could go ahead with your day."

A group of pint-sized kids rushed past, pushing and shoving each other in fun.

"See you next week, Miss Sorenson," they called.

She smiled and tugged her bike free of the rack. "Have a good weekend," she answered to their backs. "Did you remember your homework?"

"Yes," they shouted, laughing amongst themselves.

Rebecca placed her purse in the front basket decorated with a large plastic daisy and lifted a shapely leg over the center bar before turning her gaze on him.

"Thanks, but I wanted to speak to Jack for a moment anyway, I'll go." Her butt slid onto the seat, tightening the material of her skirt along her thigh.

He swallowed back the harsh words that threatened to escape, instead answering with a simple nod.

"You never told me why you were here," she said.

No, he hadn't. He nodded over his shoulder, his gaze on her. "Just meeting a friend."

Something flickered behind her eyes. She searched the grounds behind him, then gave him the saddest imitation of a smile he'd ever seen.

"I better go. It was good seeing you, Mitch." She didn't wait for his reply, but pushed off and peddled down the lane until she was out of sight.

"Yeah, you too," he murmured.

~o~

Rebecca kept a steady pace even though everything inside screamed to get away as fast as she could. Her heart beat like a captured bird frantic to escape the walls of her chest. She could barely keep a grip on the handlebars her hands were so sweaty.

Seeing Mitch again had overshadowed the unpleasant encounter with the stranger and her worry for little Tommy. It was months since she'd run into him, ever since Katy had been attacked last fall behind Grace's diner.

He looked good.

His hair was a little longer, but still the same rich gingerbread color she'd loved. His athlete's body had filled out, was more mature now. He'd lost the awkwardness of youth and become a virile, handsome man.

Too handsome for her peace of mind.

A horn honked, scaring the heck out of her. The woman drove past, shaking her head at Becky's stupidity for crossing over the bike lane line.

A timely warning.

Her life was on track, she didn't need to go screwing it up again. Especially over Mitch Taylor.

She signaled a left turn, checked over her shoulder for traffic, and swung onto Elm Street. A couple more blocks and she reached her destination. The sheriff's office looked inviting with the sun warming its red brick façade. Laurel's car still sat in its spot in the receptionist's stall. Rebecca sighed, relieved she hadn't missed her ride. She parked her bike, locked it up, and hurried inside.

Laurel glanced up and broke into a welcoming smile.

"You made it, I was starting to worry." She stood to open the pass-through countertop and let Becky in, wrapping her in a rose-scented hug.

"Sorry, I'm late." Becky met her friend's curious gaze. "I'll tell you all about it on the way there, but first I need to talk to that sexy new husband of yours."

Laurel's cheeks flushed and her eyes sparkled with love. Becky was happy for her. And just think, if her mother hadn't decided to take that long overdue holiday Laurel wouldn't have moved here, taken the job, and been swept off her feet by Jack Garrett.

Sometimes fate worked in mysterious ways.

"Sure, c'mon, he's in his office." Laurel swiveled on four-inch heels—Becky had serious shoe envy—and led the way across the bull-pen. Rebecca smiled and nodded at the men she knew. Deputy Randolph, whose wife was a good friend of her mother's. Sid Carmichael, a longtime veteran of the force. And lastly, Norm Walters.

"Rebecca." Norm hurried to stand, his chair banging against the desk behind him with a loud clang. He cleared his throat and doffed his hat. "How've you been?"

This isn't awkward or anything.

"I'm good, Norm, thanks. How are you doing?" As soon as the words were out, she winced. *Nice job, Einstein.*

She'd gone out with him a few times and had a lot of fun until he started to get serious and she had to call it quits with the ol' 'it's not you, it's me' line, which was just lame even if it was the truth. There had to be something wrong with a woman who had an attractive, nice guy interested and then shut him down just because of a lunch with her no-good ex-husband who she could not get out of her mind.

Norm swept a hand through his wavy dark hair, the muscles in his arms bulging under his uniform.

"Look, Rebecca..."

A door opened a few feet away and Jack stepped out, his face softening when he caught sight of Laurel.

Relieved, Becky laughed, cringing at the higher than normal tone, and smirked at her friend. "You'd think you guys were still newly-weds, when you've already been married what... three months?"

Laurel tapped Becky's shoulder, her gaze fixed on her approaching spouse. "Two months and ten days, as you well know."

That she did. Between Katy and Laurel, and now, Annie, she'd amassed a nice collection of bridesmaid's gowns.

Jack gave Becky a passing glance then settled on his wife. He leaned down, gave Laurel a lingering kiss and whispered something naughty in her ear, going by the hot flush that stained her cheeks.

"Jack, we're not alone," she warned, even as she stepped into his open arms.

He shared an amused glance with Norm before eyeing Becky. "I noticed, my love. What can we do for you, Rebecca?"

Now that she had an audience, Becky wasn't sure how to start.

"I had a problem at the school today." She nervously plucked at the strap of her handbag. "There was this boy, maybe eight or nine years old. I ran into him at the bike rack. He was attempting to unlock an old bike."

"You're thinking he was trying to steal it?" Norm asked.

She shook her head and stuffed a stray lock of hair behind her ear. "No, I don't believe so. He knew the right combination, the lock was just giving him trouble."

"Okay," Jack said, "well, thanks for letting us know." He looked at Norm who shrugged.

Becky sighed. Great, now they thought she was a nitwit. "There's more. A man showed up and told the boy to get home but he wasn't very nice about it. I'm worried. If Mitch Taylor hadn't been there…"

Norm stiffened while Laurel shot her an *I want the details* grin.

Great. Mitch wasn't even in the building and he was causing complications.

CHAPTER THREE

Tommy cried all the way home. Not great hiccupping sobs like he'd done in the past when they'd first arrived at his uncle's house and realized they were worse off now than when their parents died. No, these tears were silent. A steady stream that ran down his face and dripped unheeded off his chin. Tears of despair, of a childhood lost, of faded dreams.

Just for a moment today with that pretty schoolteacher he'd felt something close to peace. Her scent when she'd held him in her arms reminded him of his mom and he hadn't wanted to let go. But then his uncle had shown up.

He reached the edge of town and looked for the overgrown drive. A broken down gray wooden fence and a lopsided *Keep Out* sign pointed the way to the old cabin hidden amongst tall spruce trees. The dirt lane was rutted so bad it tossed his bike from side to side but he refused to walk; his uncle had warned them there were snakes in the grass just waiting for little boys. Tommy wasn't taking any chances.

He pulled up next to the sagging porch and slowly laid his bike on its side, listening for his brother. A soft humming led him to the corner of the building. Jasper sat in the dirt, his scrawny bare back bent over a little toy truck he was using to make roads with in the sand. Tommy sighed his relief, no new marks that he could see. He'd gotten here in time then.

"Hey, brother, whatcha doin'?" He let Jasper know he was there before moving forward.

Jasper jumped up, ready to flee, then realized who'd spoken and cracked a mile wide smile. "Tommy, Tommy you're back." He ran and wrapped his arms around his brother and Tommy frowned at how thin they were.

"Did you eat the food I hid for you?" he demanded.

Jasper shrugged, his chin digging a hole in Tommy's chest. "I wasn't very hungry," he mumbled.

Tommy frowned and set him back so he could look him in the eye. "Jas, you gotta eat. We ain't ever gonna get outta here if you ain't strong enough to run."

Jasper's eyes lit with hope. "Can we go now? Can we, huh?"

Tommy cursed his big mouth. Why'd he go and say anything? "No. We can't go until we have a plan." Jasper's lips wobbled and Tommy changed the subject. "Show me the roads you've been building."

It worked, for now. Jasper trotted over and sprawled out on his belly, reaching for the little blue car he'd been playing with. "Wait 'til you see this. I made a hill and my car flies," he said, his voice filled with excitement.

Tommy followed more slowly, his mind on that nice teacher. Why couldn't someone like her have taken them in? He missed his mom so bad and yet sometimes he got scared because he couldn't quite picture her in his head anymore. The teacher reminded him of her though. She smelled good too and had a pretty dress. His mom always wore nice clothes; she said she liked to look pretty for her boys. Man, he missed her. She'd know what to do right now because he sure didn't. The only thing he did know for certain was that he'd promised to take care of his brother and he darn sure was going to.

The rumble of a vehicle coming up the drive had both boys scrambling for cover. A ratty blue tarp hanging over a pile of scrap metal nearby did the job, though it was a tight fit. Their uncle had warned them often enough to keep outta sight of strangers.

"Who is it?" Jasper asked, his voice squeaky with a mix of fear and excitement.

"Shh, we'll know soon enough," Tommy whispered. "Just keep quiet, okay?"

The rattle as the engine shut down told him who it was even before the tinny door slammed shut and his uncle stomped around the corner looking like the axeman from Snow White.

"Where the hell are you hiding, you stupid little shits?" he roared. His heavy work boots kicked up tufts of dust as he circled the yard in search of them. He glanced at Jasper's toy car, reached down, picked it up, and sent it flying into the bushes.

Jasper whimpered but thankfully held silent, his body vibrating so hard the tarp rattled. Tommy jerked him away, pulling him up against his own shaking body. He was so scared he needed to pee.

"You come on out of there or your stupid ass brother is going to pay the price." The edge of the tarp lifted and a hand reached in and latched onto Tommy's arm in a death grip. Jasper's eyes grew big as pie plates and welled up with tears. Tommy cried out in pain but shook his head viciously at his brother, warning him to keep quiet and stay still.

And then he was yanked out and thrown to the ground. Uncle Pete stood over him as he lay in the dirt, lips twisted in a snarl that sent shards of fear through Tommy's gut.

"You better explain yourself, boy." He nudged Tommy with his boot. "What did you think you were doing at the schoolhouse today?"

Tommy thought fast. There was no way he was going to tell this man the real reason. He had to come up with something to defuse the anger brewing in his uncle's eyes. He reached into his pocket and reluctantly withdrew the gold chain he'd taken from the teacher lady's purse.

"I was getting you some money, Uncle." A beefy hand reached out and swiped the necklace from his hand. His uncle eyed him suspiciously for a moment before lifting the cross on the chain to the light.

"You aware this is stealing, boy?" He gave the chain a little shake and the cross glinted so bright it practically blinded Tommy.

"I did it just the way you showed me, sir." Tommy lifted himself to his elbows. "She won't know who it was."

Uncle Pete frowned, his brows like bats wings over his eyes. "You better hope the hell not, kid. Your brother doesn't like when you screw up." He laughed, his belly jiggling under the dirty plaid shirt. He turned and strode toward the shack, hollering over his shoulder, "Git in here and make me some grub, I'm hungry after chasing you all over creation."

Tommy waited a few minutes, knowing full well that it was his uncle's routine to go into the house, grab a bottle of booze and flop down on the ugly green sofa for the night. He had time to make sure his brother was okay now.

He pulled back the tarp to let Jasper out, then went searching for the toy car, the last thing Jas had from their mom. A few moments later he found it under the edge of a blackberry bush. Careful to avoid the painful spikes, he managed to retrieve it with only a couple of minor scratches.

"Here you go, buddy, I found it." He turned and offered it to Jasper but his attention was on the house. "Don't worry, I won't let him touch you again." And when his brother looked at him with eyes that knew more than any five-year-old kid outta know about pain, Tommy's gut tightened with a white-hot rage.

He fingered the wallet in his pocket he'd also stolen from the teacher. Soon. Soon he'd have enough to get them far away from here. And they weren't never coming back.

CHAPTER FOUR

Rebecca sighed and turned to Jack, the noise of the busy station fading to the background. "Look, I know you think I'm wasting your time but there was something off about that guy, Jack." She met Laurel's sympathetic gaze and attempted a smile but it fell flat. "I'm worried about Tommy."

Jack gave Laurel a peck on the lips before letting his arms drop away. "Okay, let's get a statement and then we'll take it from there, fair enough?"

Rebecca nodded, relieved.

He waved her toward his office. She squeezed Laurel's hand and then slipped between the men, aware that Norm was less than pleased that Jack was going to handle this himself.

She took a place on the edge of a wooden chair and waited for the sheriff to close the door and join her across the man-sized desk. Jack's chair creaked beneath his weight as he rolled it forward and reached for a neat stack of forms beside a geriatric computer.

"Shouldn't you upgrade that thing one day?" Laurel had told her about his reluctance to join the twenty-first century but Becky hadn't taken her seriously.

He patted the clunky top of the monitor affectionately. "Why fix it, if it ain't broke?" He pulled a pink pen from his pocket, and grimaced when she smirked. "Laurel gave me this as a reminder of the first time we met."

Oh, she'd heard. Laurel liked to share with almost anyone who'd listen how smitten she'd been the first time she laid eyes on the handsome sheriff—and how he'd almost stolen her favorite pen.

"What can you tell me about the kid?" He waited, pen poised over legal looking papers and Rebecca suddenly realized she might be jumping to conclusions and causing unnecessary difficulty for the boy.

"Well, he seemed kind of shy, at least to start with." She reached into her bag, searching for the chain she always fingered when she was nervous or upset. It wasn't in the side pocket where she normally kept it for safety. What the heck? Giving up on subtlety she ducked her head and began to paw through the bag and that's when she noticed something else missing— her wallet.

"What's wrong?" Jack tapped his pen on the desk and stared at her curiously.

Becky glanced up, met his narrowed gaze, and returned to combing through her purse. *Please, be there. Please, please...*

It wasn't, and if she confessed the loss, Tommy would be in a lot of trouble. She didn't have the heart to do that to a kid who already had two strikes against him. Faking a nonchalance she was far from feeling, Becky withdrew a lipstick and tried to touch up her lips without trembling noticeably. The wallet was bad, but at least those items could be replaced— the chain on the other hand...

Jack leaned back in his seat and frowned. "What's this really about, Rebecca?"

She rotated the bottom of the tube until the lipstick disappeared, carefully capped the top and stowed it away before meeting Jack's gaze.

"I've met men like that guy who bothered Tommy before. They aren't nice men, Jack." She tucked a strand of hair behind her ear and fingered the scar on her neck. "They take pleasure in abusing those weaker than themselves."

Jack contemplated the ceiling for a long moment, then sat up, and the sympathy lighting his dark brown eyes warmed her heart even as it embarrassed her.

"Okay, let's say you're right. We can start an investigation on him and see who he is and what he's been up to. How's that sound?"

Becky sighed her relief. "Thanks, Jack."

~o~

631

Mitch couldn't get his mind off his ex-wife. He needed to get moving and catch up to Kyle Fowler, who was at the school waiting to pick up a kid as a favor to his twin sister, Katy. She was planning a bachelorette party for the child's mother, while Kyle and the new groom-to-be, Jared Martin, were in charge of the kidlets.

Kyle was only in town for a short visit so Mitch had to meet him when he could, even if that meant hanging out in an elementary school yard. And running into the one woman he wanted to avoid. Rebecca Sorenson Taylor. That's still how he thought of her, though the ink hadn't even dried on the separation papers before she'd changed her name back.

Normally it wasn't a problem to stay out of her way, they didn't exactly move in the same social orbit. He was steel-toed boots and beer at Duke's Bar while she was pretty dresses and fancy meals at La Lune—the two didn't match. He still wasn't quite sure how they'd ended up hitched in the first place.

Okay, that was a lie.

He'd taken a trip to Vegas to try and forget about the fact that his career as a football star was in the toilet and his life was running a close second. He'd been working on getting drunk in a bar off the strip when she'd strolled into the lounge wearing a little black dress designed to drive a man crazy. Mitch knew who she was right away, he remembered her from school, so he'd waved her over and found out she was in town for a teacher's convention and, bless his luck, had lost track of her group. They'd ended up spending the most amazing night of his life together. By the time he got up the next morning he'd been married and she'd been gone.

He'd wasted his last hours in the city trying to find her, then hopped an early flight home. A few days later the separation papers arrived and he'd known it was just a dream. Love didn't happen at first sight. Lust, hell, yeah. But love… that was something poets wrote about, it wasn't reality.

Since then they'd made a career out of avoiding each other, and in a town of only seven thousand people that wasn't always easy. He'd run into her more than once when one or the other of them were out on a date with someone else. Talk about your soap opera moments. They should just file for divorce and end this insanity, but he couldn't bring himself to make it final.

"You turning on the old Taylor charm again, bro?" Kyle joined him near the bike rack, a little boy with reddish hair and a freckled face lagging close behind.

Mitch forced a laugh and smiled down at the kid. "You must be Chris. I've been friends with your dad for a long time."

Chris considered him from serious green eyes. "Are you from the navy too?"

Mitch shook his head and crouched to meet Chris's gaze. "No. Your dad was pretty brave to do what he did, like Uncle Kyle here." He glanced up to see if Kyle was listening. He was. "They both did their duty, but now it's time they enjoy their lives. Your dad told me how excited he is to make you guys part of his family."

Chris looked up at Kyle and then nodded his understanding. "Yes, sir, my mom's real happy too."

Mitch's heart gave a painful tug. This could easily be his story, getting to know a son he had no knowledge of until years later. Kudos to Jared and Annie for solving their issues to give this little boy the family he deserved. He rose and shrugged off the envy he felt. At least Jared wasn't alone anymore.

"How about some ice cream?" There weren't very many problems that couldn't be solved over a heaping dish of vanilla ice cream covered in chocolate sauce and sprinkles.

Chris and Kyle both wore identical grins and after a resounding high-five they were off, Mitch in his welding truck, while Kyle drove a shiny black jeep. They pulled up at The Soda Shoppe and strolled to the front door behind a group of chattering teen girls whose laughter suited the warm and sunny weather.

Mitch held the door and smiled at a familiar looking girl as she passed through the opening. He was surprised when Chris ran ahead and tugged on her hand.

"Tina," he shouted. "I'm getting some ice cream."

The girl stopped and smiled down at the boy. "Hey, Chris, I didn't see you. Are you here with your mom?" She searched the room, briefly meeting Mitch's gaze before glancing away.

"No." Chris waved his hand at them. "I'm with my dad's friends. My mom's going to a party." The touch of pride in his voice when he mentioned his dad put a lump in Mitch's throat.

"I'm going to get in line," Kyle said. "You got him?"

Mitch nodded. He strode over to introduce himself and realized why she seemed familiar; she was Jack's daughter.

There'd been a time when he and Jack Garrett had done damn near everything from hockey practice, homework, and hanging out, to chasing women, drinking, and football, together. And then April Montgomery came into their lives and nothing was ever the same. Tina had her face and the promise of her mother's killer body, but it was Jack's friendly brown eyes smiling innocently at him right now.

"Hi, Mr. Taylor. My dad's told me a lot about you," she said, her gaze curious as it rested on him.

So Jack talked about him, did he? Interesting.

"Your father and I go way back," he said, and frowned when some boys jostled her as they hurried past to grab a table. "I better let you go, this place looks pretty busy."

Her smile shy, she nodded and ruffled Chris's hair. "I'll see you at the shop, sport." And then she was gone in a cloud of sweet-smelling perfume and long blonde hair. Jack was going to have his hands full in a couple more years.

"She works for my mom," Chris offered in the silence, his gaze pensive as he watched her flirting with the boys.

Mitch well remembered his first crush so he diverted the kid's attention. "Looks like Kyle's ordering without us, we better get up there." He turned to usher the kid ahead of him and came face to face with Jack.

Kyle better be getting him a double scoop.

CHAPTER FIVE

Mitch nodded a passing acknowledgement, and placed his hand on Chris's shoulder to guide him along. There had been too much water under the bridge for either him or Jack to ever be comfortable in one another's company. And sadly, it was all due to a stupid misunderstanding.

"Mitch, I need a word." Jack halted him in his tracks. "You got a minute?"

Mitch wasn't sure what this was about but he didn't plan on being the afternoon's entertainment either. They were already drawing attention.

"Yeah, sure, Chief. Just let me get my buddy here settled and I'll meet you out front."

Jack nodded and turned away to greet his daughter. His big body dwarfed hers even though she was fairly tall for her age. Mitch placed her at around fifteen or sixteen. Funny, how much time had passed by without him realizing it. She'd been around young Chris's age when her mother left town. Dark days those were. That woman had done her level best to destroy anyone in her path. Even though it cost him his career and his best friend, Mitch celebrated the day April Montgomery left Tidal Falls.

Chris's squirming body under his hand reminded him of what he was supposed to be doing. A quick search found Kyle surrounded by a group of too-young-for-him girls all vying for his attention. And he was soaking it up, a come-to-papa smile on his lips.

"There he is, kid. Let's go catch up to our ice cream before he gives it away."

Kyle shrugged when they drew near, laughter turning his eyes a clover green. "'Bout time. I thought you said you were buying."

Mitch pretended to check his pocket. "Sorry, mate, next time." He grinned, unrepentant, and snagged the smallest and the biggest dishes from the counter. "Here you go, kid."

Chris's eyes grew wide at the sight of his treat topped with chocolate and candy pieces. "Wow, my mom never lets me have this much."

Kyle's brows lowered. He reached for the bowl but Chris yanked it away. "Hey."

"Well, if you're going to get into trouble…"

Chris shoved a heaping spoonful into his mouth and the girls giggled.

"He's cute."

"Aw."

"My brother's just like that."

"Hey look, there's Tony Secora." A young teen with a mouth full of braces, pointed excitedly toward some newcomers. And just like that Kyle became yesterday's news as they took off in hope of catching the jock's attention.

"You know you're old when…" Mitch joked.

"A bunch of simpering girls gives you a headache," Kyle finished, and both men grinned.

"What's so funny?" Chris wanted to know, glancing back and forth between them, ice cream dripping down his chin.

Mitch grabbed a napkin and gave him a swipe. "You'll know when you get to be dinosaurs like us, kid. Now we're all roar and no action."

"Speak for yourself, *Dino*," Kyle mumbled around a scoop of banana and whipped cream. He lifted a maraschino cherry by its stem and deposited it on the lopsided mountain in Chris's bowl.

Mitch noticed Jack leaving and his mood sank. What the hell did the sheriff want, unless this had something to do with the school incident earlier today?

His mouth tightened. If Becky was in trouble he wanted to know about it. The ice cream felt like it was curdling in his gut and he pushed the half-full bowl away.

Kyle eyed it and then him. "Not your flavor, or what?"

Mitch snorted. "How can you go wrong with vanilla?" He pressed away from the counter. "I'm just going to step outside for a minute—be right back."

Kyle's gaze followed Jack's departing back. He frowned. "You sure, man?"

Mitch shrugged. "He wants to talk."

Kyle cursed under his breath. Chris's head swiveled back and forth like a bobble-head as he tried to keep up with the conversation.

"I'm here if you need me, dude, but don't hurt his pretty face. He's family now," Kyle warned.

Mitch gave Chris a fist bump and started back through the ever-growing crowd. Now that school was out it seemed as though every teen in town was here. Kyle didn't need to worry, he and Jack had come to an understanding long ago. If the two of them were going to remain in Tidal Falls—and they were—it was necessary. They'd even sat at the same table for Kyle's twin sister's wedding to Jack's brother, Ty, last fall. And if the occasional barb passed between the two men, it was still very civilized. No spilled drinks or anything. He figured he'd done pretty fricken good considering Jack's date for the night was none other than Rebecca. His Becky.

The door slammed open with more force than he intended, banging against the stopper and rattling the glass. Great, might as well announce his antagonism to the world and get it over with.

Jack stood a few feet away, his face impassive. His arms were crossed over his chest and his hat was tipped back on his head in a show of two-buds-havin'-a-chat. Nothing to see here.

"Tough day?"

Mitch hated that cool exterior, and itched to ruffle the man's composure. Instead, he shrugged and dug a toothpick out of his pocket. The sharp bite of the peppermint-flavored stick calmed his temper before he got himself in shit. He needed to remember this was the sheriff, not his nemesis.

"It was alright. What's up, Sheriff?"

Jack nodded toward the parking lot where his vintage flat black 'stang sat at the far end, away from possible fender-benders. "Let's go over there where we won't be overheard."

Those words did nothing to ease Mitch's anxiety, but he played nice and strolled through the mixture of four-by's and cruisers kids preferred to drive these days. He came to a stop near the Mustang's back fender.

"Okay, we're here. What's going on?"

Jack took his hat off and rubbed a hand through his short nut-brown hair before replacing the ivory Stetson on his head.

"I heard you were at Cascade Elementary today."

Mitch stiffened. "Yeah. Is it against the law?"

Jack kicked at a few loose rocks, sending them skittering across the top of the pavement. "Don't be an ass, Taylor. I only mentioned it because Rebecca Sorenson dropped by the office today and she was understandably upset over an incident I believe you were a witness to, am I right?"

Mitch propped a hip on the back fender and ignored Jack's lowered brows. "Yeah, I was there. She tried to help a kid and ended up getting reamed out by some old drunk for her trouble."

"Did you get a good look at either one?" Jack tapped his shirt pocket and pulled out a coiled notepad and a girly looking pink pen.

Mitch smirked. "Nice pen." Then he straightened and got serious. "The kid had dark wavy hair, brown eyes, about four foot tall, and wore threadbare clothes on a too-skinny frame." He waited for Jack to jot down the information. "The guy acted like a guardian or something. He stunk of booze and B.O., and drove a faded red pickup that's seen better days." Again he waited for Jack to finish writing before he dropped his bombshell.

"I've been thinking about it all afternoon and I think I know who that guy is."

"Well?" Jack asked pink pen poised.

"I'm almost positive it's your brother-in-law, Jack."

CHAPTER SIX

The entire time Rebecca, Laurel, and Katy were setting up for the evening's events, Becky couldn't get the afternoon out of her mind. She laughed and joked with the caterers and teased Laurel on her obsession with a certain burly sheriff, but continually replayed the abject fear on Tommy's face when he'd been manhandled by that creep. She should have done something more to control the situation. It worried her what might have happened after Tommy got home. The signs of abuse, at least mental if not physical, had been there and she'd let him go. But it had happened so fast there'd been no real response time until it was too late.

She sighed and rearranged the cutlery for at least the tenth time. Hopefully Jack would do as he said and look into the child's homecare condition for her.

"You're going to wear the silver right off that knife soon," Laurel said from behind her shoulder.

Becky smiled and set the piece down before turning to her friend. "Oh, you look gorgeous." Laurel had switched from her workday clothes to a shell pink sequined party dress that should have clashed wildly with her red-gold hair and fair complexion. Instead, it brought her to vivid, runway model perfection.

Laurel blushed and ran nervous pink-tipped nails down her hips. "Do you think it's too much? I know this is Annie's night, but I saw this dress and fell in love."

Rebecca shook her head and grabbed her friend's hands. "You look amazing. Jack's not going to know what hit him." The two shared a smile. "Don't worry about Annie. If I know her, she's going to show up in something incredible and knock Jared flat on his butt."

Laurel laughed and Becky was pleased to see the doubt vanish from her eyes. They'd clicked right from the moment they met in college. Laurel had come to town just before Christmas for a temporary job and ended up engaged to the sheriff. Becky was happy for them. No one deserved a second chance more than Jack did. He was everything a father should be for Tina. The whole town had stood behind him after the accident and the subsequent loss of his football career.

"Where's Katy?" Laurel glanced around the newly decorated backroom of Duke's Bar.

"She just went to check on the kitchen."

It was a huge stress-reliever to arrange flowers and lay out tablecloths after the day from hell she'd just endured. Duke had offered the space to them pro bono and it worked out perfectly for their plans. The attached Rendezvous Hotel hosted a well-organized kitchen willing to cater the event, there were even rooms available for those who over-imbibed. The decorating had gone smoothly and Duke agreed to supply the alcohol and entertainment.

Becky glanced down at her own black velvet dress. Mitch would have liked it; he was a very tactile man. The mink-like texture would appeal to him. A ghostly sensation of calloused fingers feathered across her torso and made her shiver. Damn him. Five years later and he still occupied way too many of her thoughts. After this wedding chaos with Annie was finished she needed to find a lawyer and quietly end their marriage. It was time to move on.

She took a big gulp of the white Zinfandel she'd been sipping on for the past couple hours and promptly choked. Coughing and sputtering, she felt like an idiot as she waved away Laurel's concerned attempt to pat her back. By the time it settled her eyes were teary and her face burned with embarrassment.

"Classy, hey?" She used a mauve monogrammed napkin to dry her lips leaving a blot of bright red lipstick behind.

Katy entered from the far set of doors before Laurel could comment, her lemon slip dress glowing under the track lighting. "Okay, the kitchen's ready. I think we have us a party, girlfriends." When she drew closer she noticed the tears and her brow creased with concern. "What's going on? What did I miss?"

"Just me not able to hold my liquor, no worries." Becky hurried to assure her best friend. Tonight was about having a good time, dammit, and no six-foot pain in the ass was going to ruin it for her.

Katy smiled, relieved, and lifted her flute in a toast. "To love, ladies."

They clinked glasses and took a sip just as the first guests began to arrive. To love, wherever it may be.

~o~

Mitch straightened his tie for what felt like the hundredth time and gazed around the crowd of partygoers. He wasn't sure what drove him to come here tonight. His plan had been to hang with Kyle and the kids, but when asked he'd jumped on Jared's invitation like a dirty shirt. Speaking of which… He looked down and made sure his tie covered the small grease stain on his dress shirt.

This so wasn't his kind of thing.

He should just go. It wasn't like he'd be welcomed anyway. These were Jack's friends, Jack's family. And besides, this night was for Jared and Annie. They didn't need him around causing dissent.

He'd just turned to make his way back to the bar when a hand clapped him on the back.

"Mitch Taylor, it's been a long, long time, son."

Mitch swallowed hard and swung around. Jack's grandfather stood before him, older, stooped, but with the same kind eyes and warm smile he'd always had for his grandkid's friends.

"Mr. Garrett. It's great to see you, sir." He stuck out a hand and was instead engulfed in a surprisingly strong man-hug.

"No need to stand on formality with me, young man. I've known you too damn long for that." Mr. Garrett leaned back but kept hold of his shoulders in a firm grip. "Neil, call me Neil." He waited until Mitch nodded before letting him go. "Now, what say you and I head over to the bar and get ourselves a drink?" He winked and nodded behind him to the server surrounded by guests in the corner of the room.

Without waiting for a reply, the elder Garrett began to make his way through the crush of people. Mitch sighed. He couldn't leave now, someone might plow the old man over by accident. He had to follow.

"Mitch, glad you could make it." Neil's sister, Tess Garrett smiled as she leaned in and kissed her brother's cheek. "Neil, don't forget you owe me a dance."

Neil grumbled but it was easy to see the affection between the siblings. As if on cue, the overhead lights dimmed and a four-piece band that had been setting up on stage strummed a few preliminary chords.

All eyes turned to the dance floor, the spotlight picking out a vision in gold lame as Annie glided onto the floor. But Mitch couldn't take his gaze off the stunning beauty holding her hand. Rebecca wore a heart-stopping, thigh-hugging, breath-stealing dress that made him want to rip out every guy's eyes from their skulls. And that was before she laughingly turned to dance with her friend and made his mouth run dry. There must have been a shortage of velvet material because there was no damn back on that thing. He could almost see down to the top of her ass for crying out loud. How the hell did it stay up?

He was on the move before the opening notes died away, peeling his dinner jacket off his shoulders as he went. His temperature rose with every step. What was she thinking? A dress like that meant one thing only. If she wanted sex then it was damn well going to be with him and no one else. She was his wife. Maybe it was about time he reminded her of that fact.

Annie looked startled when she caught sight of him stomping towards them. Then her eyes lit with satisfaction and she performed a twirl worthy of a score of ten to bring Becky's gaze around to him. She stumbled to a halt, a hand going defensively to her breast.

"Mitch, what are you doing here?" she hissed.

More than aware he was making a spectacle of himself, he stepped forward and threw his coat around her shoulders. Holding the ends together under her chin, he tipped her wide-eyed gaze to his and stole Tess's line. "I think you owe me a dance."

Her cornflower blue eyes flickered with anger and something else—despair? Before he had time to ponder the significance she turned away and apologized to Annie. "Do you mind?"

Annie shot him a *you-better-treat-her-right* warning glare over Becky's head before giving a reassuring smile to her friend. "Of course not. You go ahead. Besides," she nodded to the handsome man pushing his way through the crowd, "I think our party is officially crashed." She didn't seem too upset by that as Jared swept her up in a searing kiss that turned up the temperature in the room by several degrees.

With a last wistful look at the happy couple, Becky turned to Mitch and the contrast in her expression was like a slam to the gut.

"Shall we?" she said, her tone anything but welcoming.

Some perverse demon riding his shoulder prodded him to force her into admitting their relationship to her friends. The peace-making angel on the other side whispered dire warnings in his ear. He'd only make things worse. She'd never forgive him. He'd lose her forever.

Mitch brushed them both away and forged his own path. He nudged a stray black curl behind her ear, satisfaction curling like warm smoke between them as he registered her involuntary reaction.

"Oh yes, sweetheart, we shall." And they both knew he wasn't talking about the dancing.

CHAPTER SEVEN

Rebecca was in Hell.

What other explanation could there be for the reappearance of Mitch in her life when she'd worked so diligently to avoid him for the best part of eighteen hundred and eighteen days—not that she was counting.

The divorce papers sitting on the desk at home were burning a hole through her brain, making her ache with things she dared not admit.

He looked amazing, by far the handsomest man in a room full of fine-looking men. His white dress shirt emphasized the breadth of those impossibly wide shoulders, honed to steel by years of honest manual labor. But then she'd always admired that about him. When his football career had come to an abrupt end he could have turned to a bottle and no one would have faulted him for it. Instead he picked himself up, went to a community college, got his welding ticket, and opened a business. Now his work was often sought after from all over the state and his shop had grown from a backyard garage to a fully equipped warehouse on a prime piece of Tidal Falls land. Mitch Taylor was a local success story.

He grasped her hand and she reluctantly followed his lead across a floor now packed with swaying bodies. He didn't stop until they reached a shadowed alcove off to one side of the stage. When he turned and held out his arms she stepped forward like a lamb, letting his jacket drop onto a nearby chair. The moment his arms wrapped around her and his calloused fingers found the bare skin of her lower back, Becky knew she was in trouble.

Her startled gaze rushed upward and tangled in the molten heat of his amber eyes. The light and shadows created by their surroundings turned his face lean and mysterious and oh-so-hypnotic. Someone bumped into them but she barely noticed, she was so caught up in his aura. It had been like this before—in Las Vegas.

Rebecca tried to pull away, her heart beating double time, an out-of-sync counterpoint to the drums playing on stage. Mitch simply tugged so that she had to grasp the front of his shirt to keep from falling—not that he would have let her. There were many things about Mitch Taylor that bothered her, but she never doubted his kindness.

He bowed his head and rested his cheek against her temple and his voice rumbled through her soul. "It's just a dance, sweetheart. What are you afraid of?"

Everything.

Him.

Herself.

She gave in and let him win this round. Besides, her body had already betrayed her and snuggled into the protective warmth of his chest.

They were barely moving. Her hips brushing against his hardened thighs left her breathless and aching, not helped by his fingers exploring each curve and valley of her spine like braille.

Her own hands were busy documenting the changes since they'd last known the ridges and planes of a man's chest. They may have been separated but she'd never once given thought to sleeping with anyone else, even if her marriage was little more than a joke.

Disturbed from her sensual fog, Rebecca lifted her head with the intention of ending this farce. But before she could string two words together Mitch's lips lowered to hers. All the lights and sounds became a sparkling kaleidoscope and mixed with the sheer perfection of his mouth.

Oh my…

She could die happy right now, in this moment. That wicked, delicious tongue knew where every nerve was located and how to parry and thrust until Becky was utterly lost. She hung on for dear life, eyes sealed shut to keep the world at bay. Every sense was on fire. Her skin prickled, desperate to know the mastery of his touch. He held her so close she could feel his arousal.

Somehow, that helped. Knowing he was as affected by what was happening as she was made her feel less helpless, more in control.

Her arms roped his neck, keeping his head where she wanted him while her pelvis ground shamelessly against his erection, desperate for some kind of release... until the nearby laughter from a couple of women nearby ripped the blindfold away.

What was she doing?

They'd practically been having sex in the middle of the dance floor for crying out loud. Frantic, she tried to push away, her gaze searching for witnesses, and only minimally relaxing when she realized the room was half dark and no one was looking at them. Mitch refused to let her go, and she growled, "Get your hands off of me."

Slow on the uptake, it took him a moment to switch focus and realize she wasn't on the same page anymore. Hell, she didn't even want to be in the same book.

He loosened his grip and took a step back, hands raised in surrender. "Calm down. What's your problem?"

Seriously?

"You, Mitch Taylor. You're my fricken problem. But not for much longer."

She turned, and with as much dignity as a woman on the edge could summon, she walked off the dance floor and into the blessed darkness.

CHAPTER EIGHT

Mitch listened to the clanging of the band—or was that his brain?—for a few seconds then started off the dance floor in search of his estranged wife. Enough with this bullshit. He was sick and tired of her walking out on him. They needed to hash this thing between them out one way or the other.

He only hesitated long enough to grab his jacket and take a deep calming breath. Rebecca was driving him crazy. Maybe it would be best if he let her do as she so obviously wanted and divorce him. Then they could continue on with their lives, instead of living in this limbo. The problem was he couldn't picture letting her go. She'd wormed her way under his skin that night in Vegas and he couldn't seem to extricate her.

Mitch punched a hole through the crowd, anxious to find her. He headed in the same general direction she'd taken but stopped when Ty slapped him on the back.

"Hey, glad you could make it."

He shook his friend's hand while searching the crowded room. No sign of her. Where did she disappear to so quickly?

Sighing, he focused on Ty and his new wife, Katy. "How's the theatre working out?" He'd been grateful for the opportunity to update the old Twilight Theatre last fall for Katy and her family. The building was a town landmark and the job had been a bonus for his business.

She beamed up at him, a ray of sunshine with her shiny blonde hair and yellow dress. "It's perfect. Ty and I can't thank you enough. We're getting bookings from as far away as Seattle. They heard of the new multi-level stage and want to try it out. Isn't that great?"

Mitch swallowed his envy as she gazed adoringly at her husband. He craved someone like that to share his successes with. He was damn tired of going back to an empty house at night.

He smiled at Katy's enthusiasm. "You can thank your husband. Those plans of his kicked butt."

"I have more where they came from. We should talk," Ty said, sliding an arm around his wife's trim waist.

Mitch had enjoyed the challenge of making Ty's dream a reality. If he had more ideas of that caliber... "I'm interested. Meet me at the office tomorrow."

"Meet for what?" The unmistakable rumble came from behind and Mitch tensed before twisting to meet Jack's ever-so-friendly scowl. Laurel stood at his side, ravishing as always, her pale pink nails wrapped around his arm.

"Just talking business, bro, no worries." Ty grinned, not in the least intimidated by his older brother. "Good thing I'm a happily married man or I'd be thinking of stealing your wife away tonight. You look amazing, Laurel."

Laurel smiled good-naturedly. "You Garretts are all the same, natural born flirts."

Mitch smirked. Ignoring Jack, he leaned over and bussed first Laurel's cheek, then Katy's. "Fun as this is turning out to be, I need to get going. I'm trying to catch up to someone."

That caught the women's attention.

Damn. Women's intuition was a scary thing.

"She ducked out the back door," Katy said, and grasped his arm. "Don't go unless you mean it, Mitch Taylor. Someone scared her off men a long time ago. She doesn't need you if you're not serious."

He appreciated the warning; they were only trying to protect their friend. Actually Mitch was relieved Rebecca had a strong support network. There was nothing worse than feeling alone in this world. He should know.

"Honey, they have to work out whatever it is for themselves," Ty said, and gave Mitch an awkward shrug.

Mitch smiled and patted Katy's hand. "Don't worry, I promise not to hurt her. I only want what's best for Becky." And if that included him, so much the better.

~o~

Rebecca pushed open the steel exit door and reveled in the cool caress of night air on her flushed body. She'd like to attribute her warmth to the crowded party but knew it had more to do with Mitch and her momentary loss of control. Thank goodness none of her friends had seen them necking like a couple of teenagers or she'd never live it down.

Becky prided herself in being the levelheaded member of their group. She was the one others came to for advice. Ironic really, since she didn't have the foggiest idea what to do with her own love life.

"Well, what do we have here?"

She inhaled a startled gasp as two men came out from the shadows of the building and scared the crap out of her.

The tall, skinny one sneered. "Hello, pretty lady. Did you make a wrong turn?"

She backed up against the door, her head shouting to get the hell out of there.

"I don't want any… any trouble." She pushed, but the door wouldn't budge.

"Hey, ain't you that teacher we saw this afternoon?" The other man moved closer to stare at her through blurry eyes and Becky's heart crammed into her throat. It was Tommy's guardian, or whoever he was. This wasn't good, not good at all.

"Look, you guys can go back to whatever you were doing." She really didn't want to know. "I have a friend joining me right away. He wouldn't like it if you bothered me."

"Ooh, tough talk, teach. Except I don't see anybody out here except us chickens," Tommy's guardian cackled. Then the smile slowly faded and something much darker took its place. "I think maybe I should be the one to school you a lesson. One on how to mind your own good goddamn business." He grasped her arm and yanked her away from the door so hard she fell against his sour-smelling body. "What do you think of that, Teach?"

Rebecca let out a yelp just before his lips mashed against her teeth. His tongue poked out and tried to force an entry. Becky bit down hard and he jerked back. The next thing she knew she was seeing stars as his fist exploded against the side of her face. She tasted blood and gagged, not sure if it was his or hers. He let go and she fell to her hands and knees, barely registering the scrape of cement breaking skin.

Stunned, she panted through the pain then tried to scramble away but the skinny guy grabbed her hair, tipping her head back while he fought with his zipper. "We're going to have us some fun tonight," he crowed.

Petrified, Becky reached up and frantically tried to free herself from his grip, her breath see-sawing so hard it burned her chest.

A muted clang and then a roar sounded in the distance followed by the sudden release of her hair. Rebecca sank to the ground, the pavement cool against her aching face, and let the tears flow.

CHAPTER NINE

Mitch pushed the steel bar to open the exit doors and peered to see through the rays of light streaming from the hallway. They could use some better illumination back here. Rebecca wouldn't be foolish enough to wander around in the dark, would she?

Something turned his gaze to the far side of the alley and his heart stopped. Time warped. Becky was on the ground with two dark, hulking figures standing over her. One of them had her hair twisted in his fist, yanking her head back viciously.

Mitch saw red.

A growl rose from his chest and he charged them, the urge to kill taking over logical thought. They noticed him at the last moment and attempted to run, casting Rebecca aside like a piece of trash.

That was their first mistake.

The second was assuming he'd let them go.

He caught the guy who had hurt her with a roundhouse jab to the chin, snapping his head backward with a resounding crack. He dropped like a felled tree.

Mitch crouched to make sure Becky was okay. Her sobs twisted his insides into a knot of helpless rage. He brushed a gentle hand down her back to let her know she was safe, and cursed when she recoiled.

Anger rode him hard.

His focus shifted to the asshole cowering against a stack of garbage cans. He pulled his cell from his pocket, rose and stalked the scum, more than ready to pounce if he even breathed wrong.

"Tidal Falls County Sheriff's Office," a competent female voice chirped in his ear.

"I need help. There's been an assault." Mitch hesitated, "You'd better send an ambulance."

"Okay, sir, slow down." The dispatcher became all business. "I need your name and where you are so we can send someone to assist. Are you in any danger?"

Mitch turned to check on the fallen man who had started to groan. "No, but…"

Something slammed his head with the force of a sledgehammer. The blow drove Mitch to his knees. Squinting through a haze of pain he watched the blurry form step carefully around him, throwing the two-by-four aside and hefting his partner to his feet before the pair of them loped off down the alley.

Fuck.

Talk about your rookie mistake. He deserved the splitting headache no doubt heading his way. He felt around on the ground until his hand connected with the cracked body of his cellphone. *Great.*

Giving up on the phone he rose and stumbled back to Rebecca. She lifted her head as he knelt beside her and Mitch swore a blue streak. Her right eye and cheek had already turned several shades of purple and her lip was split and sore looking.

"Oh, baby," he murmured. He laid a gentle hand against the injury, wishing like hell he could draw the pain into his body.

Rebecca raised her shaking hand in turn and touched his aching forehead with cool fingertips. "You're bleeding."

Mitch ignored that, more interested in making sure they hadn't done anything worse before he arrived on scene. "Did those bastards lay a hand on you?"

Her eyes overflowed. She shook her head. Mitch sighed his relief. He flopped down on his ass and wrapped his arms around her, tucking her up tight against his heart while sirens wailed in the distance.

The exit doors slammed back on their hinges. First Jack—who'd probably received a call from the station—then Ty, Jared, and half the damn town spilled into the alley.

"What the hell, Taylor?" Jack demanded, towering over their prone bodies.

Mitch didn't bother to raise his head from its safe haven against Rebecca's tousled hair, it hurt too damn much. "Hey, chief."

"Give them some room," he yelled, and Mitch scowled as the words reverberated in his brain. "C'mon, back it up." Then he crouched beside them and Mitch would've smirked at the crack from Jack's knees if he didn't hurt so bad. "What happened, Mitch? Is Rebecca hurt?"

No shit, Dick Tracy.

"Nah, we just decided to take a break. Out here…" He glared at Jack. "In. The. Freaking. Alley." His tone rose with each syllable, but he couldn't help it. The adrenaline had ebbed, leaving him shaking and about to go bonkers. What if he hadn't followed her? Who the fuck were they? Where was that ambulance?

Rebecca lifted her head and the men around them collectively swore.

"Holy shit."

"What the hell happened?"

"Calm down," Becky lisped, her poor lip swollen and discolored. "I'm fine. Mitch showed up before anything worse could happen." She turned her gaze on him. "I guess I owe you. Again."

Mitch's brows lowered. He didn't need her feeling beholden to him. It was sheer good luck that he happened to be in the right place at the right time. First with that kid's guardian, then… hey, wait a minute. Why hadn't he noticed before?

"It was him, wasn't it? The same asshole that bothered you this afternoon at school." He turned to Jack. "Why haven't you caught him yet? If you did your job, this never would've happened."

Ty stepped forward. "Hey, man, cool it. Whatever it is you're talking about, you know Jack's doing everything he possibly can."

Jack glanced at his brother over his shoulder. "It's okay, Ty. He has reason to be pissed. I'd feel the same way." The deputy's car turned into the alley with the ambulance hot on its tail. The emergency lights flashing on the walls created a surreal image of the scene.

Jack rose and went to meet the car, leaving an uneasy silence in his wake. Mitch nodded to Jared, who reached down and helped Rebecca to her feet. Ty held out a hand to Mitch. He contemplated ignoring him but thought better of it and grabbed on, squeezing his eyes shut against the resulting pain and dizziness at the change in elevation. *Whoa,* might have a bit of a concussion going on. Getting hit in the head with a chunk of wood could do that to a guy.

The ambulance attendants rushed over with medical bags and proceeded to twenty question Becky who was looking worse by the minute. Mitch waved away the one who turned to him. His only concern was to see that Rebecca got the care she needed. A few minutes and a thorough exam later a gurney was brought out against her wishes and she was headed for the hospital.

Mitch followed to the back of the ambulance and watched them load her inside. The female attendant turned to him, her hand on the door, "Are you a family member of the patient?"

How was he supposed to answer that one? Screw it, he intended to ride to the hospital with her and there was only one sure-fire way to make that happen.

"I'm her husband."

CHAPTER TEN

Peter Montgomery was sick and fricken tired of do-gooders getting into his business. It wasn't like they were going to hurt that teacher-lady. They was just havin' a bit of fun with her, that's all. He cursed and yanked Davey into a recessed doorway as a cop car raced past. Just what he needed, the fucking cops on his tail. It didn't matter that his stupid sister's ex was the sheriff. There'd be no help from that quarter.

"Where's that bottle o' whiskey I told you to hold on to?" He held out a shaky hand and frowned, grasping his wrist to hold it steady.

Davey backed up another step and almost tripped over a cement stair. "I dropped it when we ran."

Pete cursed and lunged forward.

"It slipped." Davey covered his head and cowered. "I didn't mean to. C'mon man, take it easy." He felt around in his jacket pockets and pulled out a silver pint flask. "Here, have some of this, it's better anyway. One-eighty proof. I made it myself."

Pete snapped it out of his hand almost before the idiot quit yammering. He twisted the cap off, gave the top a swipe with his coat sleeve, and took an appreciative sniff. Yep, Davey knew how to make some damn fine hooch, that's for sure. The first sip burned its way down his gut like a dragon's breath and he let out a little gasp.

Davey reached for the flask and Pete batted his hands away, glaring. Then he lifted the half-full container to his lips and drank deep, letting it wash the anger and frustration away.

"Hooyah," he wheezed when the carafe was finally drained. He stumbled and lost his balance for a minute, smacking up against the tin-sided building.

"Shh," he said, and then laughed.

Davey stood him up and retrieved his now empty flask, stuffing it into his jacket. "Thanks for sharing, man. C'mon, we better get movin' before the cops show up." He shoved a shoulder under Pete's arm, almost reefing the thing out of its socket.

"Take it easy. I use that once in awhile you know." He guffawed at his own crude joke.

"Yah, man, you're a riot. Let's go." Davey helped him get his feet moving in the right direction. "I have more 'shine where that came from."

See? Things were looking up already.

~o~

Rebecca lay in embarrassed silence as the ambulance drove them to the hospital. Wonder how good her chances were that no one heard Mitch's little announcement? A glance at the smiling EMT gave her her answer. Damn it.

What was he thinking? They'd carried this secret around for so many years. Nobody was going to understand. Her friends were going to freak out. And what about her mom?

Oh, my God.

"Your heart rate is climbing. Are you in pain?" the paramedic asked, placing two fingers to her wrist and checking her watch.

"No. I really don't need to go to the hospital. You could let me out at the corner. I can walk." She started to sit up but the EMT put a hand to her shoulder, pressing her back down.

"Just let them do their job, honey," Mitch said, humor warming his voice.

Rebecca glared at him. "You're not helping here."

He met her look, unrepentant. Then his gaze roamed her face and the amusement died. His jaw clenched and he nodded toward the injuries. "She going to need stitches?"

The EMT leaned over to check Mitch's forehead. "No, but they'll want to hold her to check for possible concussion."

He hissed and pulled away from her touch.

"You too."

"Just take care of Becky, I'm fine."

The paramedic hesitated, then shrugged and sank onto her seat. She picked up a clipboard and started filling in the info. "So, have you two been married long?"

"We're not married," Rebecca answered.

"Five years," Mitch said.

The EMT looked from one to the other of them, eyebrow reaching for her hairline.

Rebecca shot him a shut-up-or-die glare. "We're separated. It's been so long I'd forgotten."

The paramedic eyed them skeptically, then made a note on the clipboard. "Yep. Check for concussions."

CHAPTER ELEVEN

Rebecca was actually glad they had to spend the night in the hospital. The whole episode in the alley had shaken her up more than she'd let anyone know.

Especially Mitch.

He'd resembled an avenging angel bursting out that door and racing to the rescue. Her heart beat a little harder. Thank God they didn't have weapons. As it was, he had a lump the size of a tennis ball on his forehead. By the time the ambulance delivered them to the hospital she'd been worried about his pallor, but none of the nurses who cared for her could fill her in on how he was doing.

By morning she was seriously frazzled. And sore. And she had the headache from hell. Right now nothing sounded better than a hot cup of coffee, some breakfast from Grace's diner, and a long soak in a bubble bath. But first she had to know about Mitch.

She'd just levered herself gingerly up in bed and dropped her legs over the side when the door swung open and he stepped in, charging the room with his presence.

He hesitated when he saw her, a flash of relief turning his lips into a near smile.

"You're up."

He let the door slide closed, sealing them in together, and moved to her side.

"You look like shit." He accompanied the words with a tender kiss to her forehead.

Flustered, she yanked the blanket over her bared legs and used her free hand to try and pat down her bedhead before meeting his gaze. Her eyes widened as she took in the purple coloring that spread upward from his left eye to an impressive sized goose egg.

"Oh, Mitch." Helpless tears formed. She feathered his cheekbone with her fingertips. "I'm so sorry."

He captured her hand and brought it to his lips, releasing her with a gentle squeeze. "You have nothing to be sorry for. I'm just glad I decided to follow you."

Yeah, she was too. Chills broke out when she thought of what could have happened. She shivered.

Mitch glanced around until he spotted a throw blanket folded neatly on a nearby chair. He picked it up and wrapped her shoulders. "You totally rock that hospital green." He grinned.

Grateful for the added warmth, Becky smiled back and struck something of a pose. "You think?"

Mitch's gaze dropped to the gaping V in front. His attention heated her more than any blanket could do. "Oh, yeah."

Uncomfortable, she changed the subject. "Did you get a good look at the guy who hit you?"

Mitch shook his head, wincing a little. "No, but I think I know who it was."

"The same man from the school yesterday." She twisted her hands in her lap. "He recognized me right away."

Mitch swore. "Shit, I knew that guy was bad news. Did you tell the deputies when they came to get our statements last night?"

"It was Jack, and yeah, I told him," she answered. "He said he's working on it."

"Damn rights, since the guy is practically his family." Mitch paced the room.

Rebecca frowned. What was that supposed to mean?

"I think you better explain."

Mitch stopped in front of her and lifted her abused hand in his. "I thought he seemed familiar. It took me a while to figure it out, but then I remembered." He met her confused gaze. "Did you know Jack's first wife, April Montgomery?"

A picture of a beautiful blonde came to mind. She'd been a senior to Rebecca's junior, but still in the same school. They hadn't been friends.

"Yeah, I remember her. She was part of the "*I am*" crowd."

Mitch looked at her quizzically.

"You know. *I am* the prettiest. *I am* a cheerleader." Becky flipped her hair in an imitation of a ditzy chick. "*I am* too good for you."

Mitch smirked. "Yeah, that's the one. She has an older brother. Guess who?"

Rebecca's eyes widened.

Mitch nodded. "That's him. Peter Montgomery, asshole, jackass, and all round dipshit. I guess he hasn't changed."

A young nurse entered the room and strode over wearing squeaky white shoes. "How are we feeling today?" she asked, her eyes going to Mitch for a flirtatious second before she focused on the monitors.

"The doctor should be in soon, then we can remove this…" She lifted Rebecca's hand with the IV attached, "and get you on your way. Sound good?"

Relieved, Becky gave her a friendly smile. "Better than good. No offense, but your coffee doesn't hold a candle to Grits and Grace's."

The nurse laughed. "No offense taken. I go there all the time myself." She glanced at Mitch again, cleared her throat. "Okay, well… I'm just going to check on my other patients. Give me a shout if you need anything." She wrote a quick note on the chart, opened the curtains to let in a stream of light, and left the door open a few inches on her way out.

Rebecca grinned. "She liked you."

Now it was his turn to look uncomfortable. "I never noticed."

Rebecca decided to let him off the hook and returned to their previous subject. "What do you think the connection is between Peter Montgomery and Tommy?"

Mitch shrugged. "Father? Uncle maybe?"

"He didn't really act like a father. More like a guardian or something." Becky thought about how scared Tommy had been. "Whatever the case, I hope Jack can help Tommy. I hate to think of him with that man."

"Jack and I don't always see eye-to-eye, but he's a solid guy. There's no way he'll let a child get injured on his watch." Mitch squeezed her hand. "We'll get this jerk, honey. Don't worry."

Rebecca hoped he was right. There'd been something about those two last night, that even now froze the blood in her veins.

CHAPTER TWELVE

Tommy glanced to the right, made sure the coast was clear, and waved at his brother to hurry up. Jasper grinned. No doubt this was all a high adventure in his mind. Tommy rolled his hand at him to get a move on. Jasper nodded and stood on tiptoes to reach the shiny red apples in the bin.

Laughter rippled nearby.

Tommy's heart jumped into his throat. He turned and peeked around the next aisle; two teenagers stood in front of a row of magazines giggling over the muscled men on the front cover.

Girls.

A thunderous boom behind made him duck until he realized the noise came from the row where his brother should be. Afraid to look, Tommy peered around the corner and his eyes almost bugged out of his head.

Jasper sat on the floor looking stunned, surrounded by a sea of red. The apple bin lay smashed on its side nearby. The two girls raced past, kicking the fruit aside until they could kneel beside him.

The one with blonde hair leaned over and gave Jasper a quick hug. "Don't cry, little guy. Accidents happen. Mr. Lee is really nice. He won't be mad as long as we clean it all up."

She turned and caught Tommy's eye. "You just going to watch or are you going to help us here?"

He straightened as though he had a broomstick shoved up his spine. Who did she think she was? He'd been taking care of his little brother all the years she was probably playing Barbie.

Embarrassed, he stomped over, picked up an apple, and took a big bite out of it; even though his stomach churned so bad he thought he might puke.

"Quit your cryin', Jasper. It ain't gonna help." He avoided his brother's wide-eyed gaze and wiped the back of his hand across his mouth. "Git up now and give me a hand. I's told ya not to play around them bins."

"But…" Jasper started to protest until he caught his brother's glare and subsided into silence. He climbed sullenly to his feet and began to gather apples into a tumbling pile.

"You don't need to be mean to him. He's just little," the teen scolded.

"And cute," her friend added.

A shuffling step interrupted their happy little group. "What's a happen here?" Mr. Lee, the store owner, came trundling down the aisle, a scowl creasing his already ancient-looking face.

Jasper dropped the fruit he'd been holding and edged behind his brother. Tommy stood taller and attempted to widen his shoulders. He hid the bitten apple behind his back and tried to look innocent. If the old guy called their uncle, they'd be dead for sure.

The blonde girl stood and moved between him and the storeowner, her ponytail swishing back and forth like a horse's tail. "I'm sorry, Mr. Lee. I grabbed an apple from the bottom and it avalanched. I should have known better."

Tommy's mouth dropped open. She'd covered for him.

Mr. Lee tsk, tsked and shuffled by to straighten the bin. He wasn't much taller than Tommy and grunted trying to force it upright. Tommy pushed the apple into his brother's hand and hurried forward, brushing by the flowery smelling girls. Mr. Lee gave him a grateful glance—and didn't that feel great considering he'd just been attempting to steal from the man—and they both put their shoulders to the heavy wooden crate. It crashed down and rocked for a breath-stealing second before settling into place.

"You good boy," Mr. Lee huffed and gave him a toothy grin. He bent with more agility than Tommy expected and tossed him an apple. "You too skinny. Eat."

Tommy caught the fruit and tried to swallow past the hard lump in his throat. He turned away from the teen's soft brown gaze and surreptitiously wiped the moisture from his eyes. He put the apple away in his pocket for later and began gathering the fallen fruit and placing them gently in the righted bin. Jasper joined him first, then the girls.

Blondie met his gaze and smiled. "Hi, I'm Tina."

His face turned hot. He ducked his chin. "I'm Tommy, and this here is Jasper."

"You guys new to town? I haven't seen you around." She dropped an apple in the bin, dusted off her hands, and waited for an answer.

Jasper looked at him nervously and Tommy gave his head a slight shake. "Yeah, we just moved here." He answered, and hoped she'd let it go. Of course she didn't.

"Where are you living? I been here my whole life so I know most areas of town."

"Tommy," Jasper said.

"You're kinda nosy." Tommy tried to change the subject.

Tina giggled. "I've heard that once or twice," she said good-naturedly.

"Tommy," Jasper whined.

"What?" Tommy snapped, turning to glare at his brother. Jasper pointed, and Tommy's stomach plunged down to his toes. A man built like the Hulk stood beside Mr. Lee, and he had a gun.

CHAPTER THIRTEEN

When Jack Garrett entered the Pine Bluff Corner Store on his way home from work, the last thing he expected to see was his daughter in the midst of what seemed to have been an apple free-for-all.

Just once couldn't his day be normal?

Sighing, he stepped forward to offer a hand and that's when he noticed the two young boys. The youngest was chomping his way through an apple twice the size of his grubby hands, reddish-blond hair sticking straight up in the back. The other kid looked to be a couple years older with bedraggled clothes and dirty brown hair. He was grinning at something Tina must have said as he carefully set a couple pieces of fruit in the bin.

She smiled back, and Jack's stomach dropped into his shoes. They wore the exact same expression. These were April's kids. Mitch was right.

The older one turned just then and got an eyeball full of Jack and his holstered weapon. The shock would have been comical except for the fact he could relate. He was feeling a little—okay, a lot—flummoxed himself.

Tina noticed him and ran forward. "Hi, Daddy."

At the same second, Jack saw the kid perform a set of hand signals worthy of a pro baseball catcher. The younger one nodded and disappeared around the bottom of the aisle.

Shit.

"Hey, hold up there," he called, and took a step, only to almost land on his ass when an apple rolled under his foot.

The older kid, seeing his chance, turned and dived around the end of the bin.

"Stop," Jack yelled, arms flailing as he tried to regain his balance.

"Daddy," Tina cried, screeching to a halt looking dazed and bewildered.

Join the crowd.

Mr. Lee was chanting some kind of Chinese mumbo-jumbo, his frail arms crossed and head bobbing up and down.

"Dad, wait."

Jack grabbed his cell and dialed the station. "Not now, Tina. I'll explain later."

Much later, if he had his way.

"You read my mind," Laurel purred. "Grab some strawberries and whipped cream on your way home, honey. I have plans."

Oh, yeah.

"Do you always answer the phone that way?" He smiled, momentarily lulled by the image she'd placed in his head. "What if it wasn't your husband?"

"Oops. Jack, is that you?" she teased.

He laughed outright, then got reluctantly back to business. "We'll talk about your insubordination later. Right now I need you to send a car to the Corner Store, stat."

"Oh, Jack. Are you okay?"

"I'm fine, just walked in on a bit of a disturbance." He picked his way more carefully through the little red landmines waiting to trip him up. "I need someone to help take statements, that's all."

He'd have to tell Laurel and his daughter the whole story at some point, but he wasn't sure how to go about it. *Hey, Tina, guess what? You have a couple of step-brothers.*

Color him excited.

He caught a glimpse of blond hair near the paper product aisle and snuck down the cat food row to catch him on the other end. Except he must have made more noise than he thought, because when he rounded the corner he was met by a hailstorm of TP.

What the...?

A roll bounced off the top of his head and tumbled down his shoulder, leaving a trail of white tissue in its wake. His eyes narrowed. This was getting out of hand. The culprits stood about five feet away doing an impressive job of holding him back—for the moment.

He raised his arm as a shield and forged ahead, refusing to be outdone by a snot-nosed brat. And that's where he made his mistake.

~o~

Mitch opened the door to the grocery store and couldn't believe his eyes. It looked as though a bomb had gone off. Apples lay all over the produce section and Mr. Lee rocked back and forth yelling something in Mandarin that made no sense at all. Something about guns and kids and toilet paper?

It was like a scene from *The Twilight Zone.*

He glanced out the glass door and made sure Becky was still in the truck. Last thing he needed was her getting hurt again. Her gaze was on something in her lap—cell phone probably—so he headed straight for Tina who was wringing her hands and staring toward the back of the store.

"What's going on?" he asked, nodding toward the mess.

She turned a distraught puppy-dog gaze on him that about melted his heart.

"My dad thinks two boys did this deliberately, but they didn't." Her tone said her dad was an idiot sometimes. Mitch couldn't argue the point. "He chased after them, even though I tried to tell him."

He knew he should have stopped at the supermarket instead. *Dammit.*

"I'll see if he needs a hand. You take care of Mr. Lee, okay? And if you see Miss Sorenson come in, keep her here." He waited for her to nod her understanding then hurried in the direction of war-whoops and crashing shelves, not sure what to expect.

It sure wasn't finding Jack on his ass, a shelving unit across his legs, and unraveled toilet paper decorating his head and shoulders.

Mitch skidded to a halt, a slow grin lighting his lips. Jack looked up from where he'd been trying to extricate himself from the mess and swore.

"Hey, big guy. Life got you down in the dumps? Just try a roll of this, it's guaranteed to cushion your fall."

"Oh, you're a barrel of laughs," Jack growled. "Help me up."

Mitch pulled his phone out and snapped a couple quick shots first.

Never know when they might come in handy.

CHAPTER FOURTEEN

Rebecca finished checking her newsfeeds, moved on to texting her mom that she was okay, and no she didn't need to cancel her trip, and still, Mitch hadn't returned from the store. What was he doing, buying the place out? She wanted to get home and have a long, hot shower in the worst way.

Lowering the visor, she inspected the bruising on her face, relieved that most of the swelling had gone down and she didn't resemble the train wreck her body felt like it had been through. Funny how a few chance events can change the course of one's life. If anyone had told her a few days ago that she would be sitting in her ex-husband's vehicle anxiously waiting for his return, she'd have asked them if they'd taken a recent trip into la-la land.

Where is he?

She opened the door and slid out of the cab. What is it with guys and big trucks? She yanked her skirt down where it had ridden up, grimacing at the picture she must make. Flyaway hair, a beat-up face, and last night's party clothes—now dirty and wrinkled—not exactly haute couture.

Shrugging away her vanity, Rebecca marched toward the store, but halted when she heard pounding feet coming from the far side of the building. A tow-headed boy appeared, running like the hounds of hell were after him, but his attention was on something behind him and he didn't see the low parking barricade he was about to run into.

"Look out," Becky called.

He glanced back, startled, but it was too late. His foot caught the meridian and he went flying over the top, landing in a heap on the other side.

Rebecca gasped, picked up her long skirts, and ran.

Another boy appeared and zipped across the lot to the fallen kid. When she arrived and crouched to help the crying child, Tommy's familiar fear-filled brown eyes greeted her. His gaze widened on her bruised face, then he eyed the little guy's rapidly swelling ankle and tears formed.

"Please, Miss, that's my brother. You gotta help him," Tommy begged, rocking back and forth on his heels. "Don't cry, Jasper. It's gonna be okay, just please don't cry."

Rebecca smiled reassuringly, though she could see that it was most likely a break. Poor guy. Her heart squeezed in sympathy. "I'm afraid he might have a broken leg. Let me see your hands, buddy. Did they get hurt too?" She lifted the hand he was cradling in his lap and cringed. The skin was scraped, with little pebbles poking out of the lacerations. It looked very painful.

Tommy blanched and then the tears did fall. "I'm sorry, Jasper. I should've left you at home."

Jasper used the least damaged hand to pat his brother's shoulder. "It's not your fault, Tommy. I shoulda been looking where I was runnin'. I messed up, didn't I? *He's* gonna be mad."

An instant vision of the previous night's assault pebbled Becky's skin with revulsion. If these kids had to put up with even an ounce of what she had...

"Who is he talking about?" She leaned forward and grasped Tommy's knee. "I want to help you and your brother, but you have to trust me. Can you do that?" Shivers racked his narrow frame and Becky ached to take them both in her arms, but she respected their reserve. How could anyone treat little children the way she suspected these two had been handled? It made her blood boil to think of it.

Tommy eyed her for a long moment then seemed to come to a decision, his shoulders bowing from untold months of stress. "He's our uncle. Momma... she ain't alive no more, and the child welfare people made us come live here with *him*."

He looked up and hatred shone from eyes that held a wealth of horrible experiences. It broke her heart.

"Oh, honey." She gave in and tugged him close, even though it was like holding a steel pole. "Don't you worry, you aren't ever going to have to stay there again. I promise." She gave Jasper a watery smile and set Tommy back. "Okay, let's get your brother some help, shall we?"

Just then Jack and Mitch came tumbling out the back door and Tommy scrambled to his feet, his eyes desperate.

"Tommy, don't leave me," Jasper cried, clearly scared.

Tommy mouth turned down. "As if I would," he said, squaring his shoulders and stepping in front of his brother. "You better leave us alone," he shouted at the men.

Rebecca saw when Mitch caught sight of her sitting on the ground. He shook his head, ignored the warning, and strode to her side, dropping down on his haunches. "You couldn't just wait in the truck, huh?" he teased, and ran a light finger down her cheek.

Becky's skin zinged, the sparks zapping between them.

Mitch's gaze zeroed in on her lips and darkened. "You and me—later. I'm tired of waiting. It's time we settled our past so we can move forward with our lives." He leaned in and gave her a quick, hard kiss, their breath co-mingling and tasting of the coffee he'd stopped and bought for her.

Rebecca sighed and gave herself up to the moment, though in the back of her mind his words nipped and stung, warning her that it was going to hurt when he left. How did this happen? When did Mitch Taylor become necessary to her happiness?

God. She was in love with him.

Her mouth slackened. Mitch sat back and looked at her quizzically for a moment, then he turned away to help young Jasper, and she tried to pay attention, she really did. But, all the time he was asking Tommy what happened, and running gentle fingers over the injury, and she was smiling and murmuring reassurance, her heart was breaking into a million tiny pieces.

CHAPTER FIFTEEN

When had his life become so difficult? Mitch kept sneaking glances at Becky while trying to determine the kid's injuries and not get stabbed in the back by the older boy. And what the hell was Jack doing? He stood a few feet away with a cell phone plastered to his ear and brows drawn in a forbidding line. No wonder the kid had freaked out. Jack didn't have the friendliest looking mug at the best of times, never mind when he figured someone was messing with his precious town.

The boy cried out when he touched a particularly tender area and his cornflower blue eyes filled with tears. Becky tut-tutted and sent Mitch a reproachful look before sliding her hand over the kid's.

"Shh, he didn't mean to, honey. The sheriff is probably calling for help right now. We'll get you fixed up and on your feet again in no time."

Tommy shook his head. "He cain't go to no doctor. We's got no money." He made rabbit ears of his pockets to prove his point.

Mitch smiled to ease the boy's mind. "Don't worry about the bill. The sheriff will handle it," he said, noticing Jack had moved closer to the group.

Jack let out a loud harrumph, and ignored him to look at Rebecca, his face softening with empathy. "How are you doing? Sorry we didn't make it up to the hospital, Laurel wasn't feeling too good this morning. She was some upset when she heard about what happened." He slid a glance at the kids. "You find out anything?"

She gave a slight nod. "I'll explain later. Is help on the way? He's being so brave." The boy's attention wavered between them.

Jack shifted and Tommy cringed, backing up a step and damn near landing on his brother. Mitch reached out and steadied him before letting go. He shot Jack a warning glance. These kids were gun-shy. For some reason they had decided to trust Becky, and by default himself, but that's as far as they were willing to go. Going by last night's little misadventure, he couldn't blame them. It pissed him off all over again thinking about those assholes hurting either child.

Jack looked hurt, concern turning his face into a grim mask. He loved his daughter so much; everyone knew it, so Mitch had no doubt that it was painful the children were leery with him. It was kind of odd that they were okay around him, he'd never had anything to do with kids. Not many around his line of work. Which led him back to Rebecca. Her life revolved around children; secretary at the elementary school, her friends and their kids. He had no place in that life.

She deserved someone who could give her the moon, all he could offer was a slice of cheese. The best thing he could do was sign the divorce papers and step back, let her go. Even if it Broke. His. Goddamn. Heart.

And it would. Mitch had no doubt of that now. He'd managed to stuff his feelings down deep inside, but the truth was, from the moment he'd laid eyes on her all those years ago, he'd known. She was The One.

He'd never really moved on since. There'd been a few women—he was a normal, healthy male—but none that connected on the same wavelength as Rebecca. She was his missing piece.

And because of that he wanted what was best for her, which didn't include a dumb tradesman like himself.

"Here comes the ambulance now," Jack said, and waved them over when they turned into the lot.

"I'm scared," Jasper whispered, his face shades lighter than the pavement he was laying on.

Tommy knelt on the ground and gave his brother a fierce hug. "It's going to be okay, Jas. Just think, we get to ride in an ambulance."

Mitch swallowed around the lump in his throat. Tommy wasn't much older than his kid brother, but had taken on the role of provider just the same. Mitch planned on making it his business that useless piece of skin they had the misfortune to call an uncle never came near any of them again. He glanced at Jack and caught the exact same emotion shining out of his eyes. Their gazes met in a rare moment of solidarity and the lump grew to mammoth proportions.

"Can I ride with you guys?" Rebecca asked the boys. "I love ambulances. Maybe they'll even flash their lights for us."

Mitch gave her an incredulous look, though he shouldn't be surprised. Of course she'd set aside her own comfort if it meant helping kids. His heart pinched. He loved her so damn much it hurt.

He cleared his throat and stood out of the way as the EMTs took over. Jasper kept a death grip on Becky's hand the entire time they splinted his leg then loaded him onto a stretcher and wheeled it to the back of the vehicle, Tommy dogging their heels.

She glanced back, and something like regret chased shadows across her face, then they were gone with a squeal of tires and the requested blare of sirens.

The parking lot seemed dull and dismal after she left. The thought of losing the right to call her his wife ripped a hole in his gut.

"You comin'?" Jack asked.

Mitch shrugged off the black mood and nodded. "Where we headed?"

"That was Sid, my deputy. He has a lead on the location of our perp. Thought I'd take a drive and check it out."

Anticipation zipped through Mitch's veins. Damn right he wanted to catch up to the creeps. "I'm in, let's go." He started toward the front of the store where his truck was parked.

"Hey, Mitch," Jack called.

Mitch turned, impatient to get a move on and maybe release some of his inner tension on a face or two.

"Look, about before," Jack said. "You know, with April." He glanced down, then looked Mitch square in the eye. "It's been a long time, man. Let's put it behind us, agreed?"

Mitch hesitated. If he kept his mouth shut, the whole episode could be put to rest. Forgiven if not forgotten. It wasn't enough though. He needed to clean the slate. Until April pulled her little stunt, the men had been as close as those two brothers they'd just placed in the ambulance. It was long past due that they cleared the air between them.

"April Montgomery was a beautiful woman," he started, then hurried on when Jack stiffened. "But, she was *your* woman, Jack. I know you figured we had something going on, and hell, I wouldn't put it past her to foster that impression, but I swear to you we didn't."

He kicked a rock and listened to it ping off the garbage dumpster. "Listen, I know you loved her and all, but there was something seriously wrong with her. She thrived on making you jealous. You have to see that, right?"

Jack stood as though frozen in time, and maybe he was. April had single-handedly destroyed not only their friendship, but also two promising careers. Not to mention abandoning a child. She would never rate for any mother of the year awards, that's for damn sure.

"So all this time, while I've been wondering if Tina was mine," Jack growled, but before he could finish what he was going to say they heard a gasping cry from behind.

Tina stood near the open back door, hands over her mouth and tears streaming down her white face.

"Tina," Jack croaked.

She turned and blindly stumbled toward the door.

"Honey, wait."

But, it was too late. She was gone.

CHAPTER SIXTEEN

Pete woke up to the strident ringing of the telephone. His face was plastered to the floor and it felt like a ten-piece band was rehearsing in his skull. *Ugh.* His mouth tasted like somethin' crawled up and died in there. It took him two tries to lift his head and focus bleary eyes on Davey passed out at the kitchen table, a half-full glass of rotgut still in his hand.

Sunlight seeped through the gaps around the front door and fought with the dirty windowpanes to stream into the room and push away the gloom. He'd told that fricken kid to keep them curtains closed, dammit. A surge of bile rose and he forced himself to his feet, barely managing to bounce off the hall walls and make it to the can in time. Grimacing, he bent under the tap and rinsed with lukewarm water, then sluiced it over his head, hoping for some clarity. The red-rimmed gaze that met him in the veined mirror wasn't encouraging.

It was those kids' fucking fault. If they hadn't stressed him out... He ignored the fact that he'd been drinking like this long before they came on the scene. What the hell did he know about kids? Why his sister named him their guardian, he'd never know. The only good thing to come out of this mess was the money. April had done good for herself—a fuck of a lot better than she had in this shithole. If not for the accident, she'd promised to take care of him, maybe even bring him out there to L.A. to live with her and that high-falutin' dentist husband of hers. Now that dream was gone.

But not the money.

As the only living relative, he'd been appointed trustee of the kids' inheritance. It wasn't his fault it took a lot to live these days. Speaking of which... where the hell were they? Usually the youngest one was driving him up the bend by now with the noise he made. He'd had to lay down the law a couple of times already. Pete rubbed his bristly jaw and thought about the welts he'd caused on the kid's back. Remorse rode the waves of discomfort rolling in his gut. He hadn't meant to, he weren't no molester. It's just the noise about drove him nuts. The kid would learn. He'd better. They were a team now; they had to figure out how to get along.

He staggered back down the hall, his legs still unsteady, and gave Davey a shove, frowning when the hooch sloshed over the rim of the glass. He snagged it as the other man moaned and groaned the stupor away.

"What the hell, man?" Davey whispered, his voice hoarse.

"Get up. You gotta help me find those brats."

Davey wiped the drool off his face. "Fuck, man, they're probably out in the yard. What's the big deal?"

Pete sucked back the booze, closing his eyes to relish the shiver that worked its way down his spine. "The deal is that I said it's time to git up." He kicked the leg of the chair. "Now move."

Davey shot him a death wish glare laced with uncertainty—guy was smarter than he looked—and lurched to his feet. "Whatever, man."

Satisfied, Pete threw open the door and growled as the light pierced his eyeballs. Shit, that hurt.

When he thought he could move without his head exploding, he pitched down the stairs and into the dirt yard. Nothing stirred. What the hell? He waved Davey around the other side and then went left himself, heading for the kid's homemade sandpit. Nothing but a damn Tonka toy. He picked it up and hurled it into the trees just as Davey showed up shaking his head.

He was gonna kill those little fucks.

CHAPTER SEVENTEEN

By the time Rebecca arrived home from the hospital she was tired and sore, but relieved Jasper's ankle had turned out to be a bad sprain, instead of broken. The kids were in her living room now, eating grilled cheese sandwiches with giant glasses of milk, and watching superhero cartoons while she... she was finally having that hot bath she'd been dreaming about.

And *boy*, did it feel good.

She leaned back in the clawfoot tub and closed her eyes, relaxing for the first time in days. Aching muscles sang *hallelujah* as the warm water and soapy bubbles did their job. Her lips twitched at the muted sound of the television and childish laughter coming from the other room. Ever since her mom bought a condo in the new senior's subdivision, Rebecca had been alone in the house. She thought she liked it that way, but this was... nice.

Jack had cleared it with Social Services so the boys could come home with her. Eventually more permanent arrangements would have to be made, but for now at least, they were safe. Unfortunately, cases like this happened all too often. Working within the school system, teachers and staff were often the first line of defense for children like Tommy and Jasper. It wasn't right, and it wasn't fair, it just was.

She ran a finger along the scar under her ear and remembered a time when she'd been grateful for a teacher's intervention. If it were up to her no child would ever go hungry or be afraid in their own home. Tommy was too young to have to take on the responsibility of his brother. He'd done the best that he could.

Mr. Lee called the hospital while they were there and reassured her there would be no charges, but he wanted Tommy to come and help at the store to make up for what he'd done. Tommy had been stunned when she'd relayed the message. Obviously, he was used to a more substantial punishment. Not any more. Not if she had any say in the matter.

Rebecca woke sometime later, chilled. She sat up, sloshing water against the sides of the deep bathtub. Her hair had slipped its topknot and now lay suctioned against her goose-pimply arms and chest. Shoot, some caregiver she was.

The television still blared, though she couldn't hear the kids any more. Maybe they'd followed her example and fallen asleep on the sofa.

She looked down and grimaced. Half-dry soap bubbles covered her upper body. She hurried to sluice off, shivering as the cool washcloth passed over her skin. Catching the chain with her toe, she pulled the plug, then stood and stepped out onto a plush white bathmat. Reaching over to the hook on the door, she grabbed the navy blue bathtowel and hurried to dry herself before slipping into her cotton candy pink robe and snuggling into its enveloping warmth.

The bang of the back door and a child's cry halted the combing of her damp hair. She opened the door and padded in bare feet down the carpeted corridor. She peeked into the living room on the right. *Spiderman* was climbing the outside of a building on the TV, but no one was watching him. The kids' plates sat empty where she'd left them on the coffee table, the milk half drunk.

Concerned, she turned and hurried the rest of the way down the hall to the kitchen. Maybe they were still hungry and had gone looking for food. She hoped Tommy had the sense not to use the stove to make more grilled sandwiches.

Rounding the corner, she shrieked. Two men sat at her kitchen table wolfing down what seemed like the entire contents of her fridge. Tommy and Jasper were on the floor near the back door. Tommy had an arm around his brother's shoulders. Tears had left tracks down both boys' cheeks. All four looked up when she entered the room and her hands fluttered up to the edges of her robe.

"Well, if it ain't the teach." The heavier-set man—Tommy's uncle, she was sure—plucked at his yellowed teeth with a toothpick. "We were wondering where you were. Not very nice leavin' kids by themselves. No tellin' how much trouble they'll git into."

"I told ya I'd go git her," the other guy said. His smarmy gaze made her feel as though she were naked even though the robe covered her from head to toe.

"What are you doing here?" she demanded. The unwashed stench of sweat and alcohol permeating the room from their bodies was awful. It also warned her as nothing else could that these were desperate men with nothing left to lose.

"They…" Tommy started to rise, but a warning glare from his uncle had him sinking down again, sullen and angry.

Rebecca gave her head the slightest shake. *Please don't do anything stupid.*

"Shut your trap, boy. You're lucky I didn't beat your ass for taking off like that." He took a long chug of milk—right out of the carton—then focused on Becky. "What did you do to my littlest boy, Teach? That how you treat kids in that fancy school of yours? Imagine my surprise to hear a message from the hospital saying you'd been givin' permission to bring them home—prior to an investigation."

Rebecca gasped. He was trying to blame Jasper's accident on her? "If you had food for them to eat, they wouldn't have been trying to steal some."

The moment the words left her lips she knew it was the wrong thing to say. Pete turned his attention to Tommy who cowered into the corner. Jasper started sobbing and covered his head with his arm, bandaged leg sticking vulnerably at an angle from his body.

Pete stood, the chair scraping on the ceramic tiles. His fist clenched around the carton, and milk gushed over the top of his hand. Swearing, he threw the container and it splattered on the wall above the boys' heads.

Incensed, Becky screeched and ran toward him, fists raised to pound some sense into the idiot. She never got the chance.

The other man came at her from the side and knocked her to her knees, his weight driving her facedown onto the floor. Panicking, she bucked and twisted, desperate to get him off her, but he only laughed and dug his bony hand into the center of her back to hold her still.

"I knew you'd like it rough," he said. "You and I have unfinished business, Teach."

"You let her go," Tommy cried.

Becky turned her head in time to see him jump to his feet and try to lunge across the distance between them, but his uncle grabbed him by the back of his shirt and stopped his momentum.

He gave the kid a little shake and sent him stumbling back to his brother. "You heard the kid, Davey. We didn't come here for none of that crap. She'll just get us into a world of trouble. Let's go, man. We got what we came for."

Davey swore and Becky could feel him shake his head above her. "Nah, you want to wuss out, go ahead. I'm good right where I am." He rubbed his hand along her hip and helpless tears sprang into Becky's eyes.

There was a moment's silence when all she could hear was her terrified breaths and Jasper's sobs, then Pete gave a harsh laugh and said, "Whatever, man. It's your funeral."

Black work boots with undone laces shuffled into her line of vision. "You sure, Dave? This is a felony. You could do jail time, man."

Davey shifted, his weight squeezing all the air out of her lungs. Or maybe that was the fear.

"They gotta catch me first," Davey answered, his hand petting her hair like she was some sort of dog. "Don't worry, I'll catch up with you later and tell ya all about it over a drink or two." Rough laughter erupted, then the boots moved away and her heart intensified its already staccato beat.

She filled her head with visions of Mitch. The prospect of his warm smile and strong arms wrapping her in safety and love. The taste of his kisses and the goal of a future together would be her reason for succeeding. That, and the fact that she refused to go down without a fight. How was she going to get out of this? He was too strong to overpower. She needed a weapon…

Her comb.

It was in the pocket of her robe. If she could just get her hands on it, she might have a slim chance. Possibly, her only chance

CHAPTER EIGHTEEN

Mitch glanced over at Jack's clenched hands on the steering wheel and the grim line of his jaw. He wished there was something he could say. If only Tina had waited for an explanation.

"Jack, I'm sorry I brought all that shit up. This should never have happened." He turned his gaze to the front, hoping against hope to catch a glimpse of the girl. "We'll find her, she couldn't have gone far."

"And then what?" Jack growled. "I tell her her mother was a whore who'd split her legs for anyone willing to pay?" He slapped the steering wheel. "I can't believe I said that back there. Of course she's my daughter, blood or no blood. I don't really give a fuck. She's been mine since the day she was born."

He rolled down the windows and the smell of fresh-cut grass swept into the car. There was nothing except the sound of the Mustang's powerful engine for a couple of blocks, then Jack sighed. "I never blamed you, you know." He glanced at Mitch. "I knew what April was like, but she had her hooks in me good. And then, when things fell apart, I needed a scapegoat. After all, it couldn't be my fault we failed, right?" His laugh was cynical.

Mitch frowned. That damn woman had a lot to answer for.

They turned the corner and motored down Becky's street. He glanced out the window to see if she'd made it home from the hospital yet.

"Stop." His breath backed up his throat. "There, in the alley. See that?" He pointed to the half-hidden nose of a dusty red truck. "I think that's Pete Montgomery's pick-up. What the hell is he doing here?"

Jack drove past and parked a couple of houses down the street. He threw his arm over the seat and gazed through the back window while Mitch stared out his side mirror, his hand on the door handle.

"Hold on," Jack warned. "We don't want to go rushing in there and make things worse. You stay here, and I'll go have a look around. Call for back-up."

Mitch opened his door and was out of the car before Jack could stop him. "Like that's gonna happen."

Jack climbed out and glared over the roof. "Fine. Then we do this my way. We don't want to give away our position until we know what we're dealing with, so you go around the far side and check the windows—carefully—and I'll do this side. We'll meet in the back yard. Good?"

Mitch hesitated. His instincts were shouting at him to get to his woman, but he could see the validity of Jack's plan. They had to make sure she was safe first. But God wouldn't be able to help the son-of-a-bitch if he'd done anything to hurt her.

Mitch reluctantly nodded, waiting impatiently while Jack called it in, and then they were on the move.

The first two sets of windows had drawn curtains, ramping his anxiety levels into the stratosphere. The next one was her office, dark except for the glowing computer. He had to negotiate his way through a rhododendron to get to the next window, the living room. The blinds were pulled but there was just enough room for him to see it too was empty, though the television was on, so someone was definitely home.

Where was she? Maybe he was wrong and that was just a neighbor's truck, but something told him it was more. His heart throbbed in time with the words running through his head, *hurry, hurry before it's too late.*

He pushed his way out of the bushes, careful to make as little noise as possible, and rounded the corner into the back yard. Jack stood, hands raised in front of him, in the middle of the yard. What the…?

Mitch faded into the old house's shadow and tried to get a handle on what was happening. At first he couldn't see anything, but then the kid, Tommy, stumbled into view with an arm around his brother's waist, acting as a crutch. They started a hobbling run, but froze when someone yelled at them from the house.

"You kids stop right there or you won't be sitting down for a week once we get home. You're lucky I haven't punished you already."

Mitch swore long and fluidly under his breath. He'd been right, Tommy's uncle was here. Where was Rebecca?

"Let them go, Montgomery. My men are on the way." Jack turned his hands over in a pleading gesture. "Please, Pete. She doesn't have anything to do with this." The raw emotion pouring from his friend's voice told Mitch what was going on before he even saw the blonde head forced back against Montgomery's shoulder, his hand wrapped around her neck.

Fuck. What was Tina doing in the middle of this mess?

"Does *she* know we're kin, Jack?" Pete's laugh was harsh. He jerked his head to the left and the boys slowly made their way toward the pick-up. "Yeah, I thought not. Stay back and I'll let 'er go. Get in my way and you won't like the consequences."

"Daddy…" Tina's cry was agonizing.

Mitch's hands clenched. He edged along the wall, waiting for an opportunity to jump the bastard without hurting Jack's daughter. A fleeting glance showed Jack doing the same, his face a grim mask. Suddenly, Tina tripped and gave Jack the time he needed to sack Pete in an impressive interception worthy of *Heisman* consideration.

The two rolled on the ground until Jack got the upper-hand with a clip to the jaw that put the other man down. He pulled his cuffs and yelled, "Go."

He didn't need to be told twice.

With a quick check to make sure Tina was okay, Mitch jumped the porch stairs and threw himself against the half-closed door. It slammed back on its hinges and revealed a scene right out of his worst nightmares.

Becky lay sprawled out on the kitchen floor, her housecoat up around her thighs as she fought to unseat the man on her back. He had her hair wrapped around his fist, and when Mitch entered the room, he gave it a vicious twist, causing her to cry out in pain.

He looked up and grinned, his blackened teeth turning Mitch's stomach. "Seems like we been here before, don't it?" The smile faded and something dark and ugly took its place. "You want to see her live, I suggest you back your ass right out that there door. It'd be a shame if her neck *accidently* snapped."

Mitch froze, except for the muscle in his cheek jumping uncontrollably.

"I'm going to rip you apart." He gritted through clenched teeth. It was an oath. One he intended to keep.

Rebecca tried to meet his gaze and the fucker slammed her head onto the floor.

Mitch exploded.

He copied Jack's move, albeit not as gracefully, and plowed headfirst into the asshole's chest. The momentum sent them flying backward against the far wall. Mitch shook his head, dazed. The other guy lifted his knee and nailed him in the sack.

Fuuuck, that hurt.

Stunned, Mitch rolled to the side, his body going fetal as sparks jumped behind his eyelids. A booted foot kicked him in the ribs repeatedly until he managed to lash out and knock the prick off his feet.

He inhaled a pained breath, turned to finish the fight… and sat up in shock.

Rebecca perched on the guy's chest, a Valkyrie come to life. She'd pounced and had a rat tail comb poised near his jugular. Her hair resembled a porcupine having a bad day, and her cheeks were flushed as pink as her god-awful robe. She wore the biggest victory smirk he'd ever witnessed. He'd never seen anything more beautiful.

"I guess you got your man," he said, his voice hoarse.

She met his gaze and the love shining out of those impossibly blue eyes made him feel like he'd taken a trip to heaven.

"Yes," she said. "I think I have."

CHAPTER NINETEEN

Rebecca sipped her coffee and smiled absently to Susan's chatter, until she mentioned how lucky she was, and how her mom would have a conniption fit if she knew what happened.

"Don't call her, Susan, please." She met the worried gaze of her mom's best friend and reached out to grasp her hand. "I'm fine. Mom's having the holiday she always dreamed of. I don't want her to cut it short because of me."

Susan set the coffee pot on the café tabletop and leaned over to give her a swift hug. "Okay, sugar, but don't you go scarin' me like that again, you hear?"

Becky laughed. "Not if I can help it."

She was just grateful Jack's deputies had arrived in time to assist in the arrest of Tommy and Jasper's uncle and his asshole friend.

Someone hollered down the way, and Susan grimaced "Hold yer horses, Phil, I'm coming."

She picked up the pot, winked at Becky, and was gone, a bright ray of sunshine with her bleached blonde hair highlighted by a neon green streak running down the side, and her crazy assortment of jewelry. Today she wore Elvis Presley earrings from his Vegas show, the cape and belt glowing with rhinestones.

The bell tinkling above the door drew Rebecca's attention. Her heart stuttered as Mitch walked in, his arms loaded with the biggest bouquet of daisies she'd ever seen. The room grew quiet as he drew closer, but Becky barely noticed. This man was her husband. Why did it take a near catastrophe for her to realize how very important he was to her existence?

"Hi," he murmured, handing the flowers over.

She buried her face in them until she could get her thoughts together. She'd mentioned how much she loved daisies way back when they'd spent that evening in Las Vegas getting to know each other.

And he'd remembered.

His big body slid onto the bench beside her and his arm went around her waist before she felt able to lift her head without bursting into tears.

"They're beautiful," she whispered, her gaze on his dear face.

"So... are you ready to give us a shot now?" he asked, his expression vulnerable.

Happy beyond words, she nodded and threw herself into the haven of his arms.

"Yay, the teacher said yes," Tommy cried.

Becky looked up, surprised, and noticed their friends surrounding the table. From a grinning Jack, his arms wrapped around Laurel and Tina, who hadn't been harmed in the incident, thank God. Becky would never forget her fear when Pete opened the kitchen door and Tina was there. She'd fought with her dad and come searching for the boys after finding out the shocking news that they were her stepbrothers. It would take some time but Jack was a great father—he'd work it out.

Next, Becky's teary gaze moved on to Ty and Katy, Katy's baby bump pronounced in the summer dress she was wearing.

Mitch's buddy, Jared, stood off to the side, a knowing smirk on his lips, his wife-to-be, Annie, tucked in front of him. Grace stepped forward, a gorgeous wedding cake in her hands.

Becky turned a bemused gaze on Mitch. "They know?"

He turned faintly red. "I wasn't going to give you a chance to run away this time."

Rebecca didn't know what to say.

"Miss Sorenson." Tommy stood at her elbow, his hand held out to show a fragile gold chain.

Tears leaked down Becky's face as she reached out and lifted the locket from his palm.

"You found it."

She ran a finger over the filigree workmanship and gave Tommy a watery smile before glancing shyly at Mitch. "Do you remember this?"

A look of wonder turned his eyes almost the same shade of gold. "I bought you that for a wedding gift. You kept it," he said with a quiet satisfaction.

"Of course," she answered. "When the man you love buys you a gift, you hang on to it."

Mitch leaned down and placed his lips to hers.

"Forever," he said.

"Forever," she agreed.

OTHER BOOKS BY THIS AUTHOR

Summer Lovin' is the fifth novel in The Wounded Hearts series. The people of Tidal Falls have grown into much-loved extended families that endure life's difficulties with grace, charm, and humor. I hope you'll welcome these stories into your home.

Tidal Falls
The Rebel's Redemption
Twilight's Encore
The Sheriff Meets His Match
Summer Lovin'

Jacquie lives in paradise along the west coast of Canada with her family. She loves reading, writing, flower gardening, and swears she can't function without coffee.

Learn about upcoming news, contests, recipes, and more from my newsletter **http://eepurl.com/2MFvX**

You can follow me on:
   http://jacqbiggar.com
   http://Facebook.com/jacqbiggar
   http://Twitter.com/jacqbiggar

Thank you for letting my story into your world for a few hours. Reviews are the lifeblood of any successful author. Without you, we can't be heard.

If you enjoy the story, please consider sharing on your favorite social media sites, as well as GoodReads and from wherever you've bought the book.

Best Wishes,

Jacquie

DARK WOLF:

A Shifters of Dundaire Novella

Angelique Armae

When Highland wolf Callen MacHendrie catches intern Miranda Kendrick stealing his prized sword, the term wild romp takes on a whole new meaning.

"…extremely talented…" – Sherrilyn Kenyon, #1 NY Times Bestselling Author

Chapter ONE

New Orleans, Louisiana.

Weddings were not his thing.

Callen MacHendrie, heir to Scotland's oldest shapeshifter clan, stood on the balcony of his uncle's St. Charles Avenue mansion and thanked his lucky stars for having fled the ballroom in time. A second longer spent with guests and that high-as-a-kite D.J. would have ushered him onto the dance floor along with all the other unmated shifters. Talk about being clueless. Even omegas knew you didna crowd horny wolves and vamps into a pint-sized space. Music alone could turn the deadest of the undead into a wanton creature. Toss into the mix a few shit-faced, feral shifters, and you'd soon have an all-out howl fest on your hands.

He shook his head and tried to get the perverse images out of his mind. At least he wouldna have to deal with that crap tonight as he'd be half-way to Dundaire before whatever racket was to come, broke loose. He was never so grateful for his pilot suggesting a redeye to Glasglow as he was this very second. Leaving early turned out to be the smartest move he'd made all week.

He leaned on his cane and took a step forward, put a bit more distance between him and the rowdy wedding guests. The steady beat of music drummed at his ears as the odor of musk coupled with sweat tempted his nose.

Damn D.J.

He closed his eyes and tried to remember what was like to dance. To get close enough to a female where only the layer of clothes separated his body from hers. To be so near a woman she was willing to grind against his crotch for the sheer pleasure of it, rather than being paid or having been forced into it by a clan elder who only wanted to marry her off solely for the status of being a future-alpha's in-law.

He hadn't danced in centuries. And today's moves were light years away from the ones he'd been taught back in Medieval Scotland.

Emptiness filled his soul.

To hell with his injury.

A damn dance might do him some good.

Callen opened his eyes and turned back toward the ballroom.

As he pivoted, his foot slipped, forced his leg to give out.

His cane went flying.

The star-filled sky above flipped and fell out of view.

He landed on his ass.

Anger rose in his soul. *Another frickin' fall.* The pity he'd garnered this morning with the whole tripping at the altar fiasco was more than enough shame for one day.

Stretching for his cane, he grabbed the silver stick and then pushed himself up. He brushed off his jacket. A rip marred the tuxedo's left cuff. *Bloody bum leg.* No way was one of those hot little numbers in the ballroom going to want to dance with him now.

Gathering his senses, he retreated in the other direction. He limped forward, his right thigh throbbing. The curse festering in his leg always grew worse at night and summer's sticky heat only escalated the discomfort. Not that it took much to intensify. These periodic flare-ups were a bitch.

Taking a deep breath, he willed his mind to focus elsewhere, but that only made him reflect on the bastard at the core of his agony. And thinking of that good-for-nothing Viking witch forced his fingers to ball.

He flexed his hand.

He'd give anything to meet up with the vile creature who had cursed him, left him to live in torment for a thousand years. But his sources were always one step behind the bastard. If he ever crossed paths with that wicked Jarle again, he'd tear the man to shreds. Something he should have done the first time they'd met.

A warm breeze carried across the moonlit balcony.

Callen headed toward the balustrade. He leaned heavy on his cane, forced his palm down on the snarling wolf head topping the silver walking stick. The beast roared to life, its sharp teeth nipping at his flesh.

Down boy.

The normally inanimate ornament stilled.

He might not have a wolf pack that wanted him as leader, but he'd always have his trusted sword and its magick-infused scabbard-turned-cane. Even cursed, the weapon was still part of him.

Callen stopped mid-stride.

Lifting the cane, he gave the head a good nudge, made sure it wasn't about to come loose and set free the cursed blade housed inside. Unleashing the sword's tainted magick on an unsuspecting world would cause total chaos.

Content with his findings, he continued his trek across the balcony.

At the row of marble spindles, he rested, sucked in a gulp of warm, humid air. Heat filled his lungs.

How in hell any vampire could stand living in a hot, muggy climate was beyond him. But his uncle Mortimer had come to favor this city and that meant as the man's nephew, he too, would be spending a lot of time in New Orleans. Not that he didn't like the place. In truth, the city fascinated him, its centuries-old vibe of magick offered his soul an odd feel he couldn't quite explain. But the summer heat stifled him, irked the wolf in his soul, and for that reason alone he would never trade his beloved Highlands for the sunbaked metropolis. But he did have to stick it out a few more hours for Mortimer's sake. The man had gone above and beyond caring for him and his brothers after their mother had died. No other vampire, despite being half-wolf, would have taken in a pack of pups and their widower wolf father. But his mother's brother did so without question. And for that, he owed the man.

Another stab of pain filtered through his right thigh.

He huffed and leaned on his cane.

"You really need to have that looked at." His uncle Mortimer's voice called from the other side of the balcony.

"And curse another being? Never."

The vampire appeared next to him. "It's not about managing the damn curse, Cal. It's about living. And I haven't seen you live in centuries."

A lecture wasn't what he needed now. "I'm fine. I haven't aged since the day I turned twenty-eight. And other than the leg hampering me a bit, I can do anything I did back then."

"You need a healer."

"We've had this conversation before and it's not going to change." The second a supernatural doctor touched his leg, the energy created from that contact would disperse into the person working on his leg and they'd share his curse. "I will not have another soul suffer this pain."

"We don't know for sure if that will happen."

His uncle's words were not convincing enough. "Jarle warned me himself that if manipulated, the curse can spread. It's the one time I believe the Viking spoke the truth. But even if he lied, it's too risky to toy with another person's life. I can live with the pain."

"But you might be able to be free of it."

"Might. And that's not good enough. Besides, I canna just think of myself. What if the curse is capable of spreading to another soul? What if it attacks my brothers, my nephews? My father? I canna let that happen."

Mortimer remained silent. He leaned on the balustrade and folded his hands, looked out at the lawn below.

Now would be a good time to tell his uncle about going home to Dundaire. "I'm taking the redeye back to Scotland tonight."

"Why?"

"Rhys called earlier and said another batch of artifacts arrived at Wolfsden this morning. Apparently, the excavations at your ruined castle are moving faster than either of us expected. And I need to get those items sorted. The sooner the better."

Mortimer pushed off the marble railing and placed his hand on Callen's shoulder. "That's fine. Let me know if your mother's locket is found. I'd love to see it again."

"Of course." He paused. He hadn't told his father he was returning to Dundaire yet. "Can you do me a favor?"

"What?"

"Tell my dad to stay here. He needs time away from Wolfsden and I don't want him to be combing through the items if they contain my mother's belongings. He's a sentimental old dog and I know it will be hard for him to see her things just tossed about. I want them cleaned up and organized in a meaningful way that's more than just a pile of stuff, before he takes a look at them."

The vampire nodded. "Don't worry about your father. I'll see to it he stays here a few more days." Mortimer patted Callen's shoulder, then vanished.

His family had been through so much over the centuries, at least this trip to New Orleans ended with a celebration and not another disaster.

He checked his watch. He better get his ass in gear and off to the airport or he'll have one pissed off his pilot to deal with. Getting back to Dundaire, to Wolfsden Keep, would do him good.

Home was where he belonged.

Home was free of preternatural women who didna want to have anything to do with him.

Home was free of the pack that didna want a cursed, wounded future-alpha who cudna lead them.

Home was safe.

And safe was exactly how he intended to spend his summer.

~~o0o~~

Inverness, Scotland

Miranda Kendrick studied the open silver locket resting on the table's metal surface. It belonged to a broken heart, probably female, probably human. Why that mattered to her, she didn't know, but her coven master, Jarle, had many slaves across the globe and the one who's heart aura was encased in this locket must have owed the witch a huge debt. Binding a heart twice wasn't the norm.

Jarle looked up from blending a batch of herbs. "Is it still beating?"

"Yes." The pulsing aura filling the walnut-sized cavity emitted a low hum each time it thumped. The vibration tingled her fingers.

"Finish the deed before the twelfth beat or we'll lose the chance to double bind it. Once lost, you can't reclaim a heart."

She dropped a pea-sized piece of obsidian inside the locket, then added a few purple buds of French lavender.

"You're doing it all wrong." Jarle snatched the metal trinket and dragged it toward him. "You can't bind a heart with obsidian. The stone blocks negativity." He scowled. "Are you trying to betray me, slave?"

"Of course not."

He glared at her, his eyes turning black as coal. "If I find out someone is paying you to break the spell on their heart, I'll triple the one on yours."

She reached for the locket draped around her neck and rubbed its ornate, raised pattern. The scent of tarnished silver reached her nose. Being bound to Jarle, even in the slightest way, was suffocating. Tripling those ties to him would no doubt choke whatever life she had left, out of her.

"You better brush up on your magick, slave, or I'll show you what it truly means to anger me. Is that clear?"

She nodded.

He flew across the table and grabbed her cheeks, dug his bony fingers into her flesh. "I didn't hear you."

"Yes." The word came out mumbled, thanks to the bastard's tight grip.

The witch released her. "You're going north tomorrow." He reached across the table, grabbed the locket she'd been working on, and threw it back at her.

She scrambled to catch the thing before it bounced to the floor. "Where to?"

"Dundaire. It isn't on any map, so you probably haven't heard of it. I'm sending you to Wolfsden Keep as an intern to help an old enemy of mine. He has something I want. And you're going to get it for me."

She didn't like doing Jarle's dirty work. "I've already paid my debt to you."

"Your debt will be erased when I say so."

"But I've been with you for two years. Surely that's long enough."

Jarle's nostrils flared, made her think of a raging bull honing in on a target who had nowhere to run.

She hated when he turned angry, especially when she was said target.

But the mythical bull wasn't her only concern. Remnants of dark magick in the form of gray matter, released from the Viking's aura and swarmed the room like angry bees whose hive had just been disturbed.

The thin, front braids of his hair stood out as if charged by electricity.

Miranda stepped back.

Silver beads from Jarle's braids slid down his hair and bounced to the floor. "I took you off that filthy New York street. Gave you a bed. Fed you. Cultivated your magick. How can you put a price on what I've done for you?"

She couldn't believe her ears. "What are you implying?"

"It's simple really. I own you, Miranda. And until I no longer have use for you, you'll do as I say or your dirty little secret will be made public."

"That's blackmail."

"That's survival."

She couldn't have the details of that night Jarle had found her, getting out. Just thinking about the horrid state she was in brought bile to her throat. From her malformed hands and feet that looked no different than a dog's paws, to the tail she swore she felt at her spine, to the high-pitched screech ringing in her ears. Never mind the pool of her own urine she'd been sitting in. Whatever the hell those scientists had done to her at the lab, it had been bad. No man had a right to do that to another human being. At least Jarle fixed her limbs, brought them back to normal looking. The man's team of plastic surgeons were geniuses. Even the screech in her ears had stopped.

"I can always send you back, Miranda. I'm sure those scientists would love to have their little experiment returned to them."

Her stomach knotted. "What do I need to do in Dundaire?"

The swirling gray emitting from Jarle's aura, retreated back into this body. "You're a quick learner, slave." He smirked. "I want you to retrieve a sword."

"Give me specifics."

The man rounded the table and pulled up a stool next to her. The smell of garlic fanned her face as he let out a deep breath. "It's nothing fancy. Thinner and much lighter than a claymore. And it might or might not have a hilt."

"So it may be just a blade?"

"Correct."

"Any identifying marks?"

"A curse is inscribed along its edge."

Great. Another vexed artifact. The last one had a living soul inside and she hadn't a clue about that fact until she was half way back to Dover from Calais. Trying to conceal a wailing, shouting, tormented soul while on a ferry in the middle of the English Channel was not an easy job. Water attracts spirits. And on that day a whole pile load followed the one she was transporting. "Are they expecting me at this Wolfsden Keep?"

"Yes."

"What's my cover?"

"You'll be posing as a grad student. Wolfsden put the word out at several universities that they had a position open that involved cataloguing recently discovered artifacts from a dig site the family owns. You've proven good with Celtic artifacts in the past, hence the reason I'm sending you on this job. I want you back in a week."

That didn't give her much time.

Jarle rose from the stool and headed for the door.

She wiped her sweaty palm across her thigh, the denim of her jeans scratching against her skin. "When I return, can we please discuss the terms of our agreement?"

The witch paused. "Bring me the blade and I'll guarantee you'll be free of me."

"I'll get my passport back, too?"

"Why? Planning on going somewhere, slave?"

She wasn't sure. Jarle had taken her many places, from London to Paris to Stockholm and now to Inverness. But she wanted to go far away from the man and start new. "It's all I have to my identity."

"But we made it up."

"I still want it." It didn't matter she had no clue about who she was or where she really came from. Her memory was so shot with holes it made Swiss Cheese look solid. But Miranda Kendrick came to be a person she liked. And she wasn't giving up the new her for anyone. Not even Jarle.

"When you bring me the sword, I'll no longer have use for your passport." With those words, the Viking witch left the room.

She prayed her master wouldn't renege. But just in case, she slid the small piece of obsidian discarded from the cursed heart, off the table, and squeezed it between the latch of her locket. She also retrieved the silver hair beads from the floor and slipped them into her jeans pocket. Having something of the Viking on her person could help her lessen his powers if need be. At least temporarily with the right spell. If, when she returned from Dundaire she had to fight Jarle for her freedom, she'd be able to repel some of his darkness. And that might give her something to bargain with.

Chapter TWO
Wolfsden Keep, Dundaire, Scotland

The plane ride home had vexed Callen's leg with a pain so wicked, he found it nearly unbearable to walk yesterday. At least this morning he made it downstairs. Another day in the States and he would have been bedridden for at least a week.

He lowered himself into the library's sole overstuffed chair and rested his walking stick against its arm. The cane's custom-made wolf head slid into a small tear, its open mouth biting down on a chunk of MacHendrie-blue tartan. If only his destiny was as easy to grab hold of.

His gaze traveled to the coffee table. A tattered, leather-bound French copy of Sun-Tzu's *The Art of War* sat in the center, a stack of political thrillers piled to its left.

His butler Rhys knew him well.

If it weren't for books, he'd have no escape from the reality of being an Alpha-in-waiting with no mate and no warriors. Even his brothers had gone on to new lives, setting up homes scattered across the estate. Not that he'd begrudged his siblings their freedom, for they each had enough pups to form their own packs, and he loved his devilish nephews to the point he'd give his life to save theirs. But family cudna erase the loneliness that settled into his world thanks to Jarle's curse. And until he found a way to lift the damn hex without harming anyone else, he'd have no chance at fulfilling the role he was born to take.

The muscles in his thigh cramped.

Stretching his legs, he pushed the coffee table out for more space, making a mess of Rhys' meticulously grouped furniture arrangement. Did the man really think a six-foot-four wolf could fit his legs into a one-foot gap? Even bent his limbs cudna find comfort in that pigeonhole.

The room's double doors creaked open.

Rhys entered. His lemon yellow Bermuda shorts and lime green, floral printed shirt nearly shot blinding rays from their brightness.

"What in heaven's name do you have on?"

The butler glanced down at his clothes. "A gift from Mortimer and Katya. One of their vampiric fledglings flashed over this morning and dropped it off. Apparently their honeymoon has afforded them excellent shopping opportunities."

Excellent was not the word he would have chosen to describe Rhys' outfit, but a happy butler made for a happy wolf. And this wolf was not in the mood to be put out today.

"Up for a dram, sir?" Rhys asked. The clanking of glass echoed from the liquor cabinet as the butler shuffled two decanters.

He'd kill for a good Scotch, but the pain killers had him in a daze as it was. "I'll pass. But thanks."

He rubbed his thigh, the friction from his kneading fingers seeping through his jeans. The massage offered little relief from the weeks-old pain hammering his leg, but at least it was something.

"Finbar isn't usually this late." He eyed the green and blue Rococo clock centered on the marble mantle. Marie Antoinette's gift was never off, not even by a second.

"I'm afraid Ms. Finbar won't be returning to Wolfsden."

He quirked a brow. "Why not?"

"While you were on holiday, the woman came by to retrieve a hat she'd left behind on her last visit."

"And?"

Rhys hesitated. "I was roaming the grounds, au naturel."

Damn. He knew Rhys hadn't been wolf for long, but after fifty years the man should have learned to guard his animal form. "How many times have I told you not to wander the estate, as wolf, in broad daylight? That's the third intern I've lost this year, thanks to you scaring them off. Never mind that sweet little grad-student who came all the way up from Edinburgh."

"Do not fret, sir. I cleared up the mishap by explaining to the university how Wolfsden has a wild life preserve and one of the wolves had escaped its pen, but that the incident will not repeat itself."

"And yet, Finbar will not be returning."

"I'm afraid not. Apparently she doesn't favor wolves."

At the moment he didn't favor a particular wolf either. "We'll need to find a replacement."

"I notified several universities that we were in need of a new intern. A replacement was found almost immediately. She'll be here within the hour."

"Did you offer enough money to make it worth the trip?"

"Of course."

Paying a hefty sum afforded him some degree of no questions asked when it came to the artifacts he needed catalogued. For the right price, there was always someone willing to trek up to Dundaire.

He let out a deep breath. "Maybe I will have that Scotch." *Drugs be damned.* At least as an immortal shifter, he didna have to worry about killing himself by mixing alcohol and pills. He'd get a slight buzz, maybe a bit of a hazy brain, but he'd survive.

Rhys approached with the drink, dropped a coaster onto the table, and handed Cal the glass.

A prism of color glinted off the cut crystal.

Taking a swig of the caramel-colored malt, warmth coated his throat. Nothing relaxed him more than did a good gulp of his favorite liquor.

His thoughts returned to the intern. Starting over with a new student meant facing a slew of questions, as humans were excessively inquisitive. They always needed to know about the castle's history, why there were so many wolf symbols built into the structure, how long had his family lived here, and so on. And for what? Over the years, he had answered a crapload of questions, hired the top interns and scholars, and still he was no closer to learning how to get rid of his damn curse without putting others in harm. He'd have thought by now, that at least one of the artifacts uncovered from the sight of his battle with Jarle would have given him a direct link to the bastard which could have been used as a shield to block the curse from going into another soul. Maybe he could even reverse the hex, send it back to Jarle. And it didn't even have to be a large item to do so, one of those silver beads the man had worn in his hair would have been enough. He specifically remembered pulling on the Viking's braids and ripping free several of the small silver pieces when they were fighting. But to date none not a single artifact belonging to the Viking witch had been unearthed.

And now he'd have to start again. He did his best to keep his responses as close to the truth as possible, omitting only the details about him being an immortal wolf shifter. And he had to rehash the same centuries-old lie about injuring his leg in a freak accident while renovating the keep's armory because eventually each person he'd hired ended up asking about his limp. The last intern had no desire to press the issue. He liked her. The ones who lacked sympathy and were concerned only with doing their job and getting paid, were his kind of people. The more distance between him and humans, the better chance his inner wolf remained concealed.

"Have you given any more thought to hiring a preternatural physician, sir?"

"I have. And like I told my uncle Mortimer, I'm still against it."

Rhys frowned. "They'd know how to treat you properly."

He leaned forward and placed his glass on the table, its edge teetered off the coaster with a clink. No sense moving the darn thing since his chance of getting it right was less than slim thanks to his foggy brain. He sat back and rubbed his thigh again. "First, I will not put another soul in danger of absorbing the curse. And second, an immortal canna be trusted in this case. I dinna need someone who might have a connection to Jarle, poking around my leg. That bastard still lives and he is not getting anywhere near Wolfsden unless it's on my terms. And for that, I need to find him before he finds me. I will not risk my family."

The doorbell rang, prompting Rhys to leave the library without commenting further.

Thanks be to God. His trusted butler never failed to have an opinion and while he was thankful for the man's concern, Rhys didna have the same responsibilities as an Alpha-in-waiting.

He rose and grabbed his wolf-headed walking stick before limping into the main hallway. He glanced down, once, checked his white shirt for signs of spilled Scotch since the painkillers had him in a bit of a daze, but no stains marred the garment. He was good to go.

He took a single step and his ears pricked.

The hairs at his nape stood on end.

Raising his gaze to the front door, his eyes met the back of Rhys' loud shirt. The man's broad body blocked all views of their new helper.

This cudna be good. Humans didna usually put him on edge.

He continued to stare at Rhys' back.

What the hell was the man waiting for? Didna he know not to waste time with niceties when it came to mortals who were not part of their inner circle? The student didna need to feel welcome at Wolfsden. She just needed to be comfortable enough to do her job.

He limped toward the chatting butler, his wolf sense still uncertain about the woman at the door.

Rhys stepped aside.

Cal's breath caught. He'd never seen hair as vibrant, coppery red as on the woman who'd just entered his home.

"Miss Miranda Kendrick," Rhys said, turning to face Cal.

And she had the most brilliant sky blue eyes. He gaped, of that he was certain for he didna feel his mouth close after it had dropped open.

"Excuse me," Rhys said to Miss Kendrick. He stepped away, approached Cal and leaned in. "'Tis just a woman, sir. Humans do come in that sex."

He huffed. Sarcasm always brought him back to reality. "Forgive my lack of manners." He pushed the snarky Rhys out of the way. "The leg pain sometimes gets the best of me."

Liar.

Stay out of my head Rhys or you'll be sleeping with the dogs tonight rather than in your tricked-out wolf pad. And I do mean the real dogs.

The butler nodded, then walked over to shut the door.

"Miranda," the woman said.

Cal offered Miss Kendrick his hand. "Callen MacHendrie. But please call me Cal. All my friends do."

I thought making friends was off limits.

I thought you didna like sleeping in the kennel.

Rhys snickered.

Cal smirked and then focused on Miranda. "Please," he said, shifting his lips into what he had hoped was the most flattering smile ever. "The first crates of artifacts are across the hall, but if you need to do paperwork before hand or have questions, we can start in the library."

"Everything I need is right here." Miranda patted her black tote bag dangling from her right hand. She retrieved a blue folder from inside. "My professor filled me in on the details. He said you have swords and jewelry that need cataloguing."

"There are a few other items, but yes, the majority of this lot is made up of weapons and jewels." Miss Kendrick seemed to have a genuine interest in the job. He liked that. Maybe this one would stick around and help with the next batch of goods found at the dig. "I guess we should get to work, then." He turned and headed toward the room at the far end of the hall, that he'd been using as an interim storage facility.

"My original intern had planned on two weeks to catalogue this batch. Can you stay that long?" He was curious about Miranda's schedule as Rhys hadn't mentioned any details.

"I can give you a week, it's what you paid for. Anything more and I'll have to check with my professor."

"No, a week will do. Just plan on working long hours."

"Not a problem."

"I'm glad of it." He was curious about her accent. "Where are you from?"

"New York, but I'm interning in Inverness this summer."

"Are you enjoying Scotland?"

She nodded. "It's different from what I'm used to. Especially up here in Dundaire."

"Tourists say this is a magickal place. To me, it's just home."

Something caught the bottom of his walking stick. Lifting the wolf-headed cane, Cal noticed a model car tire jammed into the skid resistant base. *Blasted toys*. When would he learn to stop buying his nephews playthings with small parts? Jiggling the tire free, he also loosened the cane's rubber-tipped foot. A good slam against the hall's marble-tiled floor pushed it back.

A thud sounded behind him.

Spinning around, he found Miranda flat on her face, the files from her folder scattered about her splayed body.

He limped to her aid and crouched. "Are you hurt?"

"I'm fine. Thank you."

He offered her his hand.

A zing of electricity shot up his arm as her fingers touched his.

Miranda appeared unaffected. She stood and straightened her green shirt and brushed off her jeans. "How mortifying, I must have tripped over my own foot."

He glanced around to check for additional toy parts, but found none. "Please, no need to feel embarrassed. You're talking to the king of tripping for no reason. I've landed on my ass more times than I can count and some days I canna even stand straight." He gathered the documents and handed them, along with the blue folder, back to Miranda.

She grabbed the papers and shoved the pile into her bag.

Her eyes flashed neon blue.

Cal blinked.

Miranda stared at him, a puzzled look on her face. Her eyes were back to their previous coloring. "Is something wrong?"

He hesitated. "Um…no. Just another twinge of pain in my leg, that's all. The artifacts are this way." He headed once again toward the storage room.

What the hell was happening to him? He hadn't hallucinated in centuries. Maybe mixing drugs and alcohol was not as harmless to his wolf as he'd thought.

Or…

Maybe Miss Kendrick was not the innocent human he had believed her to be.

This one needed watching.

~~o0o~~

She was so screwed.

Her eyes hadn't changed color since she'd made that disastrous mistake of thinking one of Jarle's warriors was cute. Turned out the guy was a total jerk, but that was beside the point. The experience taught her something new about the magickal side of her soul, revealed one more clue about who she really was that she didn't know before. She prayed to God Callen didn't notice the color shift. If he did, she was going to have to explain herself and that wouldn't be easy. Especially when she really didn't have a full explanation herself.

Walking forward, she blew a stray strand of hair away from her forehead.

It would be a miracle if she made it out of Wolfsden Keep alive. This MacHendrie dude was not the typical badass like the usual deviants Jarle counted among his associates. The slam of his cane against the floor actually made the marble tiles give out under her feet. And from what little she knew about magick, only the most powerful of souls could make the ground move. And talk about being hot. The heat radiating from his touch nearly melted the flesh off her arm. Usually she wanted to run from her targets, get as far away from them as was possible, and not just because she didn't want to get caught holding stolen goods, but the creeps Jarle sought revenge on were usually lower than low. Callen MacHendrie didn't fit in with that trash. He also had the slightest, yet sexiest brogue. This was a man she wanted to run *to*, not from. Staying in his embrace until the tingling warmth of his touch filled her from head to toe was a definite possibility.

She fanned her face. Jarle was so going to have her ass for this.

A zap licked the small of her back.

She froze.

Cal's hand pushed gently against her spine as he opened the storage room door. "After you."

God, but the feel of his palm against her back felt good.

She stepped forward and entered the room. One glance around the place and her heart skipped a beat. There were swords and daggers galore. And enough pearls and rubies to fill a pirate's chest. The horde was endless. And magnificent. Every last item gave off a soft glow, an aura that screamed each one had been touched by magick, somewhere along its history. No wonder Jarle wanted her up here.

"We'll start with the jewelry," Callen said. "I've had Rhys file everything according to stone and metal but we didn't go through it all with a fine-tooth comb. Some items might need to be better inspected. I've found a few pieces stuck together that needed separating." He pulled out a green, padded chair and motioned for her to sit.

The guy was a modern-day version of a chivalrous medieval knight. Not to mention he was a handsome dude and as sexy as all sin. From his jet-black hair to his dark brown, gold-flecked eyes, everything about Cal MacHendrie screamed sex.

If she could conjure up a perfect mate, it would be this Scot.

Taking her seat, she dropped her tote to the floor.

Callen placed a notebook and mechanical pencil in front of her on the table. "I like to do things old school first time around, with entries getting logged into the computer later."

Old school. She wondered what else he did differently than today's average guy. He didn't wear an earpiece, or even have a cell phone glued to his palm. In fact, she didn't notice any bulges in his jeans save for the one in front and that had nothing to do a damn phone. Living in an ancient castle must have given him a different perspective on things. Made him take things a bit slower than most people did today. Maybe he took his time with everything that he did and not just with his work concerning ancient artifacts.

She wondered what it would be like to spend a night with a man who wasn't texting, checking the scoreboard, or engaging in one of those dumb multi-player games on his phone every five seconds.

Visions of a four poster draped in velvet curtains clouded her thoughts. And of course it wasn't the image of an empty bed that had to fill her mind, but rather one that boasted a sprawled out Callen MacHendrie, his well-muscled chest fully exposed, his lower body barely covered by a strategically placed silk sheet. A sheet she would have no problem getting under and....

She moaned.

"Miss Kendrick?"

She was beyond humiliated. "Sorry. Something was stuck in my throat." Did she really just say that? Oh. My. God. *You are such a little ho, Miranda.*

A smirk crossed Callen's lips.

Lips that were made for kissing. Not too thin, not too plump. Manly lips that she had no doubt knew how to explore a woman's body.

That smirk remained on his face. On odd feeling settled in her bones. Was it possible Callen knew what she was thinking? "Is something wrong, Mr. MacHendrie?"

He lowered his gaze to the table. A curl of black hair fell across his brow. "I think we should concentrate on our work. Don't you agree?"

She *was* concentrating on her work. Callen MacHendrie was her assignment. Well, stealing from him was her exact job, but she couldn't take something she hadn't yet found. In the meantime, she needed to feel him out. And that was what she was doing. "I'll get started with the silver pieces."

"Good decision."

Callen pulled a plastic shoebox crammed with sealed plastic lunch bags containing individual pieces of jewelry. He slid the container her way. "Aside from item name and number that's on the bag, I'd like as detailed a description as possible recorded in the notebook. It will make it easier to retrieve things later."

"Got it." She reached for the first bag and snatched it from the box. A silver ring in the shape of a wolf's head rested inside. "Are wolves significant to your family?"

Callen looked up. "They're part of the MacHendrie coat of arms."

"So that's why they're all over the place."

"Yes. The family has a long history of using the animal as their emblem." He balanced the handle of his cane on the table and then turned around to grab a nearby chair. "Have you worked on other medieval collections?"

"A few," Miranda said. "But none this large. I've also never worked at an actual dig site. Everything I've done to date has been within the confines of museums or private collections." She omitted the detail about her stealing said items.

"Do you enjoy your work?"

She couldn't answer truthfully. She hated stealing from people, but Jarle would kill her if she didn't do what he asked of her. "I do like Celtic artifacts. I find their designs beautiful." At least that was not a lie.

"As do I. In fact, I love everything about Wolfsden Keep and about my heritage. It is who I am."

If only she knew who she really was, maybe she could have a place to love, too.

Rhys entered the room and brought tall glasses of iced tea. "I thought refreshments might be needed." As he set one drink in front of Miranda, he bumped Callen's cane. The stick inched in her direction, came to a stop after it collided with the side of her pinky.

"Would you care for a sandwich, Miss Kendrick?"

"No, thank you, Mr. Rhys. I ate before coming here."

The butler's gaze shifted to his boss. "And for you, sir?"

"I'm good for now."

"If either of you change your mind, don't hesitate to ring." Rhys gave a slight bow, then sauntered from the room.

A low buzz echoed at Miranda's ears. She scanned the area, but noticed nothing out of the ordinary coming from the bagged jewelry.

Something nipped her finger.

Her gaze flew to her hand, to the wolf-head topping the Cal's cane. The animal's snarling mouth was biting down on her pinky.

The image of an inscribed blade popped into her head.

Jarle's sword. The weapon had to be encased inside the walking stick.

She eyed Callen to make sure he wasn't watching her and much to her relief he appeared quite focused on an emerald pendant hanging from a strand of pearls.

She carefully nudged her foot toward the cane and dislodged the walking stick from the table.

Callen looked up, a confused look crossing his face.

"Sorry." *Liar.* She hoped he believed her feign of innocence. Reaching out, she grabbed the cane before it fell to the floor.

A bolt of energy hammered her arm. It entered her fingers as a bright, white pulse, and proceeded to shoot up to her shoulder.

She gasped.

Callen was on her in a flash. "Let it go."

"Never."

"It will kill you."

"It'll save me."

He grabbed for her hand.

A second dose of electricity zapped her.

She slid off the chair and landed on the tile floor.
Callen ended up on top of her, his chin level with her breasts.

CHAPTER THREE

No one was going to steal his sword. Least of all a human who hadn't a clue as to what powers the blade possessed. It was as cursed as was his leg. "I said, let it go."

Miranda shook her head. Her wavy, copper-colored hair shimmied around her face, framed her features with varying glints of red that lit up like sparks with each move.

She reminded him of a spitfire. A bit too hot to handle on the outside, yet overly tamed on the inside. Just the type of woman he'd want in his bed. A mate who was willing to embrace the wolf in his soul while surrendering to the man in his heart. Too bad she was a thief.

Her eyes went neon again.

"What are you?"

"A woman. But I thought that was obvious with these." She arched her breasts closer to his face.

A verra bad move. He swallowed, his mouth becoming moist. The sound of his frantic heartbeat pulsed at his ears. He knew he should look away, but didn't. "I was referring to your animal side."

"Are you for real? Do I look like an animal?" She squirmed under him. The second button on her blouse popped, revealed more of her ample breasts as they pushed through her shirt, her creamy flesh spilling out from under the bands of a lime green satin bra. He couldn't help but stare. And his eyes weren't the only part of him that wanted a piece of her, his hands were itching to cop a feel, as well. But letting go of Miranda's wrists was not a risk he was willing to take. Yet. "Humans canna change eye color at will."

"You think I'm doing that by choice?"

So she *was* aware of her abilities. The revelation piqued his interest in her even more. "You're not human."

A look of fear crossed her beautiful face. "You're a frickin' nut. You know that?"

"I didna say it to frighten you."

"I'm not scared."

He doubted that. The scent of her panic enveloped their space like the stench of road tar on a hot summer day. In the wild, she'd have been tracked by even the least capable of shifters. "Relinquish my cane."

"I can't."

"You must."

"Not going to happen."

He wondered what would have made her interested in a simple walking stick. To the average human it had no value. "Why not?"

"I'm being paid to steal it."

So she needed the money. "I'll give you double the amount to let go."

"It's more complicated than that. And I can't discuss it."

The woman could steal from him, but couldn't tell him why. "That's a bit unfair, don't you think?"

"You have a room full of swords. Why not just let me have this one?"

Her disclosure shocked him. Miss Kendrick knew the truth about his wolf-headed walking stick and that was not a good thing. "Who told you it's a sword?"

She swallowed. Then squirmed.

He tightened his grip on her wrists.

She released a deep breath.

An intoxicating perfume filled the air. It smelled of orange, honeysuckle, and a trace of clove.

The revelation sacked him in the gut.

His thoughts propelled back a thousand years.

"*Smell the air, Callen,*" his grandmother said. "*The scent of your mate is unique. No other soul will give off the same smell and no other wolf will be able to detect it. The scent is specific between you and her. Even if she is not wolf.*"

He closed his eyes. The aroma of a fresh cut orange teased his nose. So did the scent of honeysuckle and a pinch of clove.

Miranda wiggled beneath him, the movements of her body sending his wolf's desire of her skyrocketing.

His mind came hurling back to the present.

Crap. He didna need this now. The Wolfsden pack would never accept a thief as their future alpha's mate. As his mate.

"Get off me," Miranda said.

He stared her in the eyes.

She stilled. A soft moan escaped her luscious lips.

He leaned forward, sniffed her neck, brought his tongue to her flesh and licked her skin.

Miranda sighed.

Callen leaned closer. He trailed his lips up to her ear, nibbled on her lobe.

"Oh…"

He went in for the kill. An all-out kiss that filled his mouth with the unique taste of a sugary sweet nectar that was exclusive to Miss Miranda Kendrick. He sucked hard on her skin.

Her body eased beneath him.

The crotch of his jeans grew tight. He shifted. He should not be doing this, playing into Miranda's naïve state. She hadn't a clue as to what she was and neither did he. But he intended to find out. And fast.

Callen lifted his head.

Miranda frowned.

"Disappointed?"

She didn't answer.

Against his better judgement, he lowered his head once more and brushed his lips against hers.

She parted for him, welcomed his tongue without protest.

The flavor of honey filled Callen's mouth. He released his hand from Miranda's right wrist and glided his fingers under her shirt, over her waist and then up to her right breast.

His palm collided with her plump nipple, the protruding bud straining against the satin fabric of her bra.

He groaned. The feel of her aroused nipple under his hand made his cock rigid.

A slight moan escaped Miranda's throat. Arching her hips, she bumped against his crotch.

Callen pulled away. "Don't do that."

"What? This?" She shifted against him a second time.

"Yes. That. Now stop it." A flash of silver caught his eye. He brought his hand to Miranda's neck and pulled free a decorative locket on a sterling chain.

"Let it go," she said.

The object was cursed; of that he was certain. "You shouldn't be wearing this." A drumming vibration pulsed against his palm. *The aura of a living heart.* The locket reminded him of the one found in his mother's jewelry box at Mortimer's castle before Vikings sacked the structure. He wrapped his fingers around the piece and held tight.

She used her free hand to slam his chest.

"Don't fight me, wumman." He tried to keep her left hand braced against the floor while fending off the punches. It didn't work.

Miranda squirmed, broke free just enough to send her knee into his wounded thigh.

Stars clouded his vision. He rolled off his sexy little thief and stifled a howl. He cudna let her see him as wolf. Not yet.

Miranda was out of the room in seconds.

Rhys appeared in the doorway and ran to Callen's aid. "What the hell happened in here?"

"I'll explain later."

"We should be going after Miss Kendrick." The butler offered Callen his hand. "She's taken your sword."

"She'll be back. I have her heart."

"Perhaps you're being a bit too presumptive, sir?"

Callen rose. "No. I mean literally." He lifted his hand and revealed the swinging locket. "I have her heart. Well, I have the aura of it, which magickally is the same. Miranda won't make it two feet past the front door without this." He steadied himself by leaning on the edge of the work table.

"I'll go get her," Rhys said.

"No. I think it best be me. We need to have a chat, the two of us."

The pain from being kneed in the leg started to ease. Callen headed out of the storage room and straight for the front door.

~~o0o~~

Miranda's heartbeat accelerated.

Wolfsden Keep afforded no place to hide, its grounds being made up of open, rolling hills that seemed to go on forever, their vibrant green color appearing almost surreal. But beautiful countryside wasn't going to save her from Callen MacHendrie and for some odd reason, she was suddenly too tired to move. Running away was not going to be possible.

A row of privy hedges lining the front of the castle caught her attention. She rounded the green bushes and slumped to the ground. As she leaned back, the castle's stone façade cooled her rising temperature. A trickle of sweat dripped down her cheek. Of all the years for Scotland to have a warm summer, it had to be this one.

She wiped her face with the back of her hand. Callen's cane remained gripped in her fingers, the silver wolf at its head watching her, its mouth twisting in a snarl.

Jarle had a penchant for guarding her every move. A second hawk wasn't what she needed. With a gentle roll, she turned the wolf away.

A warm wind blew across the lawns.

She caught her breath, sucked in a deep gulp of air. The scent of roses danced under her nose. On the drive over, she hadn't taken in the beauty of the castle's immense grounds, but sitting here now, with the hills fanning out for as far as the eye could see, the landscape at Wolfsden was breathtaking.

All she remembered of her past, with the exception of a few distinct memories of her childhood, was that dark, dank street where Jarle had found her living no better than a rabid dog. Dundaire offered so much more than any crowded city could give. No wonder Callen MacHendrie was in love with his castle and the magnificent finds it kept revealing from its archeological digs. She'd become engrossed with Wolfsden Keep, too, if it were her home.

Plucking the top of her shirt to peel it off her sweaty chest, Miranda detected the spicy scent of bergamot mixed with clove. The perfume clung to her clothes, teased her nose.

Callen.

The man even smelled good. He was a hot Scot, to say the least. From his jet-black hair, to his muscled chest and arms, the man was blatant perfection. And his kissing abilities were off the chart. In fact, her lips and neck still stung from the heat of his touch.

Visions of that velvet-draped bed returned to her head.

Don't even go there, girl. Cal MacHendrie was not part of her future. He couldn't be. She came to steal from him and that little blemish did not make for good girlfriend material.

Her eyelids grew heavy. She hadn't felt this tired in ages and all she did was run a few feet. What the heck was happening? A fit twenty-something who ran eight miles on a daily basis should be able to run marathons around this place and not peter-out.

Miranda lowered her head. She inched forward and ran her free hand over the cool grass.

A pair of brown, tasseled loafers appeared in front of her.

Cal.

Her gaze raked up his legs, over his chins and thighs, settled for a brief second at his crotch.

680

He cleared his throat. "Up here."

She knew damn well heat flushed her face, she felt her cheeks warm. Raising her stare, she met Callen in the eye. He towered over her, standing like a mythic god ready to pounce. Her sliver locket dangled from his hand.

She gasped and relinquished the cane, bringing her hands to her neck. "My heart."

CHAPTER FOUR

The moment Miranda's fingers slipped off the cane, Callen extended his hand, palm side up, and commanded the object to come to him.

It flew from the ground. "Never let your guard down, Miss Kendrick."

She didn't appear to be overly concerned about losing the item she'd just pinched from him. Her gaze remained fixed on the locket. "My heart's in there. Give it back."

"In time."

"It's not yours."

"And I don't want it. But I think it's in your best interest not to wear it right now."

She didn't look pleased. "I need it."

He crouched and eyed his sexy thief head on. The scent of honeysuckle filled his nose. "Who are you?"

"Miranda Kendrick."

She was a verra good liar. "I mean your real name."

"I don't know."

That could be the truth or it could be another lie. He wasn't sure. "Why did you come to Wolfsden? And don't tell me you're here as a student working to steal artifacts for a private collector or for your professor. The student gig died when you went after my sword. No intern would have known what was hidden in my cane."

Miranda let out a deep breath and lowered her gaze. "I work for a sleazy two-bit gangster who steals things. Priceless things. From people he claims are his enemies."

"Why do you do it?"

She hesitated. "I owe him. Besides, he's a witch. Has powers that can change a person."

So his beautiful mate believed in magick. He wondered if she'd believe in him being a shifter. "Are you a witch?"

"I'm not sure as I don't remember my past. But I do believe people have abilities to do things, like how you just commanded your sword. Yet not everyone can move inanimate objects. That level of magick can only come naturally and most of us lose those abilities as we age because we get too caught up in the material world. But some of us do retain a portion of those powers. At least I know I do, though I don't have proper command of them."

"How did you know about the sword?"

"The witch told me. Though he didn't know it was hiding in a walking stick. That I sensed on my own and with a little help from the biting wolf-head." She checked her pinky as if looking for a mark.

Sensing his sword was a damn powerful talent. Miranda Kendrick was no typical witch. "So, you accept magick."

"To a degree, yes. I believe in prophetic dreams, spells, mind over matter. That sort of stuff. My boss has taught me a lot, exposed me to all sorts of unimaginable things."

"I see. And does this miscreant have a name?"

"Why is it so important to you? You have your damn sword...cane...whatever the heck it is...back. Give me my locket and I'll be out of your hair."

He smirked. She was not going to get off that easy. "You're not leaving Wolfsden until I say so."

"Great. Another wicked witch. Tell me, do you make a habit out of belittling women? Ordering them to do what you want or else?"

"First, I'm no witch. Second, I'm doing this for your own good."

She shook her head as if she didna believe him.

"Now, back to this miscreant. Does he have a name?"

Miranda nodded, brought her stare level to his. "Jarle."

He felt his stomach drop. His mate was working for the man who had been his bane for a thousand years. It cudna be possible.

Callen rose and stepped away from Miranda. He paced. The woman was obviously one of Jarle's slaves, the bound heart proof of the witch's claim over her. But her not knowing the reason behind her changing eye color or even not knowing her real name, if that statement was true, nagged at him. She also didn't seem to realize just how powerful a witch she was.

Leaning on his cane, he scanned the area. Searched for any of Jarle's minions in the vicinity, but thankfully none were nearby. "We're going inside."

"No we're not," Miranda said. "My ass is staying right here until you return my locket."

He spun around, bent forward and grabbed her arm. "If you think I'd have my mate be put in danger, you're sorely mistaken. Now get."

She was on her feet in a heartbeat. "Listen dude, I can accept the whole loving the castle lifestyle, I can even dismiss the wolf-at-every-turn design thing, but I am so not your mate."

He walked her to the front door.

"I'd be insane to shack up with a guy like you."

He froze. "Why? What's wrong with a guy like me?"

"For starters, ordering a woman to do your bidding does not make a dude date material."

She might have a point there. "Go on."

"Second, you don't bring up marriage…being your mate…on the first date."

"I wasn't aware we were on a date."

"Even worse. We haven't gotten that far and already you're telling me I'm yours."

She did make the whole thing sound a bit desperate. But he was wolf. And MacHendrie wolves knew their mates the moment they smelled their scent. They also protected them from that point forward. He didn't see the point of all that sissy courting stuff. He was a man who believed time was precious and playing the dating game was only a waste. Mates were meant to be together whether they courted or not. But he had to admit, taking time to get to know Miranda did appeal to the human side of his soul. Being trapped between man and wolf was not always easy.

A click echoed from inside the front hall.

Miranda swung her head toward the open door. "Whoa. That is some serious ammunition."

If he could have died that verra moment, he would have. "What in God's name are you doing, Rhys?"

"Protecting you, sir."

"With a machine gun and enough silver bullets to fend off an entire pack of wolves?"

"She stole your sword and we all know only one witch would be interested in that cursed blade."

"You can put the gun down," Callen said. "Miss Kendrick poses no threat."

Miranda agreed. "Yeah, Rambo. What he said."

It took a moment, but Rhys eventually relented. The firearm, along with the excessive cache of bullets, vanished.

"Miss Kendrick and I will be in the library." He entered the castle and headed across the hall, his grip still strong on Miranda's arm. The woman needed protecting from that bastard Jarle and he was going to find a way to free her from the witch, even if it killed him to do so. His mate was not going to be bound to another soul. Eventually he was going to make Miranda realize they were meant for each other.

Rhys followed him across the entrance hall. "I notified your uncle."

Callen stopped midstride. "Now why would you do that?"

"I feared for your life."

"Call him back and tell him there's no need to worry."

"Are you sure, sir?"

"Verra."

The butler turned away, but not before snarling at Miranda.

"I think I've made him mad," she said.

"He'll get over it." The scent of honeysuckle and orange filled his space again, stirred his senses like no fragrance ever did in the past. If he didna find a way to convince Miss Kendrick they were eternal mates, he'd go mad. Of that he was certain.

In the library Callen let go of Miranda's arm.

"I feel like I've just run a marathon," she said. "And I have no frickin' clue why."

He was going to have to explain about the whole bound heart thing. "Sit and I'll get you some water." The scent of her perfume wafted away as he left her side and headed for the bar.

"I've never seen so many books in one room. Have you read them all?"

"No," he answered. "But some I've read multiple times. The collection belongs mainly to my father." From the bar he watched Miranda maneuver about the room. As she checked out the bookshelves, she maneuvered her fingers along the spines of the leather bound volumes, running her hands over the gold lettering, going from one book to the next. "This is a magnificent collection. If I had books like these I'd never leave the room."

If he had a wumman like her, he'd never leave his bed. Her moves made him crave her touch, crave the feel of her fingers against his skin, the kiss of her lips against his mouth. God, but he was hopeless. And to think just a few days ago he thought he'd never mind a mate. Of course convincing her of the fact was a different matter.

She strolled over to his chair and dropped down. "Could this chair be any bigger? I think I can get lost in here."

He laughed. "All MacHendrie men are tall. You should see our beds."

Miranda's cheeks went red.

Damn. "That probably was not first date material, was it?"

She shook her head. "You are so screwed, dude."

Rhys returned. Eyeing Miranda in the MacHendrie tartan chair, he gasped.

"What?" she asked.

"You're in the Alpha's seat. And no one sits in the Alpha's seat except for Bane of Wolfsden or his eldest son."

She started to get up.

"Stay," Cal said. "You're fine right where you are." He turned his focus on Rhys. "Is there a purpose to your presence right now?"

"Mortimer wasn't exactly sure you should be left alone up here."

He didna like the sound of that. "And?"

Rhys fidgeted with the hem of his brightly colored shirt. "Vidar is on his way."

For the love of heaven. He did not need his uncle's brother-in-law staying at Wolfsden Keep. The Viking was the most brooding wolf he'd ever come across, never mind the fact he and Vidar were barely on speaking terms. "When he gets here, take him to a guest room. I don't want him disturbing my discussion with Miss Kendrick."

"Will do, sir." Rhys glared at Miranda, but didn't linger.

Grabbing a bottle of cold water, Callen walked over to the chair and sat down on the edge of the coffee table, so he could face his sexy thief. He handed her the drink and then set his cane on the sofa.

"I take it your father is Bane of Wolfsden?" Miranda asked.

"He is. And yes, I am the oldest son, heir to his...legacy." Explaining about the wolf pack just yet didn't seem right.

Miranda yawned. "I am really exhausted. I think something is wrong with me."

"You're feeling tired because you're not wearing your locket. How long have you had it?"

"Since Jarle found me. He swore it wasn't bound, just there to protect me. I saw him perform the protection spell before he gave it to me."

"He lied. These lockets are magickal and are used strictly to bind one's heart. Do you mind if I open it?"

She shook her head.

Callen worked the silver latch and popped the oval in two. Inside sat a pulsing aura. A sprig of knotweed lay on top. "Here's the cause of your heart being bound." He pointed to the herb.

Miranda leaned forward and studied the locket. "Take it out."

"If I remove it, Jarle will know since he's the one who worked the spell. And while it's connected to him in only a faint way, it's enough that he'll sense it's been tampered with if we remove the knotweed. I say leave it be for now but keep the locket off you neck."

She reached for his arm. "Can he tell if I'm not wearing it?"

"Keep it near you, but not on you and you'll be fine." He handed the item back to her.

"If I don't get the sword Jarle sent me to retrieve, he'll kill me. Of that I'm sure. He has a violent temper and I know for fact others in my situation have gone missing, never to be seen again."

"I won't let harm come to you. I promise."

Miranda sat back. "He found me on the street. I was in a terrible state. So bad, I don't even like to talk about it. But Jarle helped me. His surgeons fixed my hands and feet."

Surgeons? That was a new one for the Viking witch. Sources at Wolfsden might not have been able track the bastard's every move, but they had always managed to know what the witch was up to last, even if it were after the fact. And surgeons were never mentioned. "What was wrong with you?"

She lowered her head.

"Miranda, I walk with a limp. You have nothing to fear from me. I would never judge you."

"This is going to sound ridiculous."

"You have no idea the things I've heard and seen." He took her hand in his. "You're safe with me. Your secrets are safe with me."

"I don't really remember much. It's all bits and pieces but my hands, they were like…like paws."

Now the change of eye color made sense. His sexy thief was more than just a witch, she also a wolf shifter. Cal let out a deep breath. He let go of Miranda's hands and ran his palms over his face. "He lied to you. Jarle lied about all of it. He has no surgeons and your hands did not need fixing."

A look of fear veiled the woman's face. "What do you mean?"

He was going to have to tell her about being wolf and that might scare the hell out of her. She obviously never remembered shifting, with the exception of that one memory about her hands and feet. Who knew how she'd take the news? Her wolf was being suppressed for some reason and he needed to find out why. If it was by her own doing, it would take time for her to learn to set it free. If it was by Jarle's doing, releasing her wolf now could kill her. The matter needed to be discussed with care. "Do you remember anything else?"

"Sometimes I recall scenes where I'm surrounded by doctors. Jarle said they were experimenting on me, but I'm not so sure. I never felt like anyone did anything to me, but rather the other way around. I know it sounds totally bizarre."

Not to him. "You have nothing to worry about with me. And you're safe at Wolfsden Keep, trust me on that. But I think we've talked enough for now. We can discuss more after dinner or in the morning, if you'd prefer. I'll take you up to your room and then fetch some food from Cook."

"What about the artifacts?"

The items from the dig were the least of his worries at the moment. "They can wait."

She toyed with the small hole in the chair's plaid fabric. "I'll have to check in with Jarle but not until mid-week. I can't tell him I've confided in you."

"Of course not. We'll think of something for you to say before the call needs to be made."

Miranda stood. "Can you really free me from the beast?"

He certainly hoped so. If not he'd die trying. "I promise I'll do everything in my power to see to it you're not bound to that bastard."

If he couldn't fight Jarle, he could always barter with his sword and his own soul. The Viking would probably be more than glad to add a Highland wolf to his horde of slaves. And for his mate, even if Miranda never wanted him, Callen was willing to give up all.

CHAPTER FIVE

Vidar arrived in his usual brooding mood and refused to wait in a guest room. Callen found him sitting on a pile of four camouflage-patterned duffle bags stacked next to the bottom of Wolfsden Keep's main staircase, as he was coming down from the second floor after having settled Miranda in a guest room. The scent of soap and crisp air lingered in the hall.

"Vidar."

"Highlander."

At least the man acknowledged him, which was more than he'd expected. "I'm sorry Mortimer asked you to come all the way out here. There really was no need."

The Viking stood. "I may not understand what my sister sees in your uncle, but Katya is all I have. And for her, I am here. No other reason. Besides, I had just arrived in Copenhagen last night, so it was not a far trip. Inconvenient, yes. Long, no." Reaching into his shirt pocket, Vidar retrieved a thin strip of leather and used it to pull back his blond hair into a low ponytail.

Callen eyed the bags. "I take it you'll be staying a while?"

Vidar's brow furrowed. "Why would think that?"

He nudged his chin toward the stack of duffle bags.

"Those do not contain clothes, but weapons." Vidar reached behind the bags and pulled out an overstuffed backpack, then raised it high. "This carries clothes."

"I doubt we'll be going to war, Viking."

"So say you. That bastard Jarle will have a different view. He may be a Norseman, but he is no kin of mine. I detest the man."

At least they were on the same side in this incident. Encountering Vidar as an enemy had to be brutal. "I trust my uncle told you everything that Rhys told him?"

"About Miss Kendrick grabbing your sword, yes."

Vidar made the whole thing sound a bit dirty, which it wasn't. Though he did get quite an eyeful tackling Miranda afterward and he had to admit if he had his choice, he'd like to have the woman in his bed. But now was not the time to be thinking about Miss Kendrick's assets. He cleared his head of all images of her lovely breasts. "I'll need you to use your connections to find out what Jarle is planning to do with Miranda."

"The witch's slave?"

"Yes. But she won't be for long. I have her heart and I intend to free her."

A slow grin crept across Vidar's lips. "You are a sly one, Highlander."

"Excuse me?"

"You like this woman."

He was not giving the Viking details. "She's an enemy of my enemy. Nothing more."

Vidar walked up to him and slapped him on the shoulder. "Maybe you and I are not so different."

He was nothing like Vidar. "We're worlds apart."

"You're wrong. We are two of a kind, you and I. You have no pack because of the curse Jarle placed on you when he injured your leg. And I have no woman because of the curse placed on my wolf when my heart was mistaken for a vampire's and staked."

He'd never known the story behind Vidar's moodiness. "I had no idea you were staked."

Vidar dropped his hand from Cal's shoulder. "We will not speak of this again. Yes?"

"Understood."

"Now, about Jarle. What do you need me to do?"

Callen led Vidar in to the library. "I know you have vast connections with the Viking shifters. I need you to find out everything you can about Miranda Kendrick. She thinks she's from New York and possibly had something to do with the medical field."

"That is not much to go on." Vidar helped himself to a beer at the bar. The man apparently had no problem making himself right at home.

"She's also wolf."

The Viking froze. "Now that I think of it, there was talk about two years ago, of a wolf captured by Jarle. But my men could not find proof of the story." Vidar sauntered over to the sofa, sat down and then propped his boot-covered feet on to the coffee table. With a single twist of his bare hand, he popped the cap on the beer bottle and tossed it into the ashtray on the end table.

"Maybe Miranda is that wolf." Callen took a seat on the opposite sofa.

"If she is, then she would be the first female wolf Jarle ever captured. He usually prefers vampires and other night creatures. I wonder what makes your Miranda so different?"

He'd like to know that himself. "She's not my Miranda."

"But she will be. I see it in your eyes. She's your mate and you know it. You've smelled her scent, yes?" Vidar raised the beer to his lips and gulped.

"Has Jarle employed a group of doctors lately?"

A pensive look crossed the Viking's rugged face as he lowered the bottle. He shook his head. "Not that I'm aware of. My sources keep fairly good tabs on the witch, though they don't always know where he's hiding, which is a major problem. But a medical staff would have been something we'd have found out about."

He wondered why Jarle had lied to Miranda. As his slave, he could have just had her do his bidding without covering up her background. "There must be something about Miss Kendrick that Jarle knows and needs. I don't think he took her in simply to capture a wolf. As you said, he's never taken one of our kind in the past."

"No. He prefers to kill us, not jail us."

And yet Miranda had been kept alive for two years. He definitely needed to know why. "I hope you don't mind, but I'm going to leave you to have dinner with Rhys while I spend time with Miranda. I think with a bit of talk she might remember something more from her past."

"I tolerate you, Highlander. But not so much the other skirt-wearing man. Maybe I will eat alone tonight."

Callen stood. "Rhys is good company. And it's called a kilt, not a skirt."

"They are the same."

"Oh, no they're not. Also, if worn properly, they make tupping a hell of a lot easier."

"Tupping?"

Callen huffed. "Sex."

It took Vidar a moment. "Oh. I see. Less clothes to remove if you wear nothing underneath. I will have to remember that, Highlander. Maybe I need a skirt myself."

The image of the Viking sitting on his sofa going commando in a kilt was not something Callen cared to think about. "You know where the dining room is and you've stayed in Katya's room before, so you know your way around upstairs. Will you need anything else?"

"I'm good. Go be with your woman."

Miranda was not officially his woman, but repeating the fact to Vidar would be mute. "I'll see you in the morning."

He headed upstairs.

~~o0o~~

Miranda sat on the end of the bed, her mind reeling with questions. What if that night in New York didn't actually happen? Did Jarle trick her into remembering something that never took place? That never was? The Viking witch was a master of persuasion. She'd witnessed him using his charms on countless victims over the last two years. And if he could stoop that low with her, he must have had good reason. The witch only did things to benefit himself. Which meant he was holding her captive for some purpose other than her owing him.

The notion sickened her.

Closing her eyes, Miranda thought back to the night Jarle said he'd found her on the street. The sterile smell of a laboratory teased her nose, but no matter how hard she tried to remember anything visual, other than being on the sidewalk with paw-like hands and feet, her mind went blank.

She took a deep breath and attempted to relax.

The fleeting image of her moving her hands over the body of a dog…maybe a wolf…flickered through her mind. Then the darkness returned.

Just like that, the small bit of memory faded.

She opened her eyes and huffed.

On her own, she would never be able to break free from Jarle. She probably could fight him, wound him, maybe even weaken his magjck a bit. But in the end, he would win out. She couldn't control her powers and she'd have to be able to do so in order to defeat the likes of her Viking captor. Jarle's magickal powers were so beyond that of an ordinary witch's, it wasn't even funny.

Callen MacHendrie was her only hope.

But how could she expect the man to help her after she tried to steal his most prized possession? It didn't matter that he had offered. Taking his help would be wrong. Guilt was starting to seep into her bones and she only had herself to blame. That sword seemed to mean a lot to Cal and she didn't think it had anything to do with his penchant for collecting ancient weapons. Investigating the matter further was a must.

Leaning back, she toyed with the tasseled edge of one of the yellow pillows propped on the bed. So much for her imagined four poster draped in velvet. This room was totally modern, from its plain, painted yellow walls, to its super-thin flat screen television. Not a single hint of medieval anything, anywhere.

Maybe Callen wasn't the man of her dreams. Just because he was handsome, rugged, sexy, and kissed like no dude should ever have the right to, didn't mean he was her perfect match. In fact, now that she thought about, she didn't like that he'd taken advantage of her.

Her mind wandered back to the kiss she'd shared with Cal in the storage room.

Well, maybe she liked it a bit.

Possibly even more than a bit.

Oh, who was she kidding? She thoroughly enjoyed the lip smacking. Even wished it would happen again. Callen MacHendrie was the hottest guy she'd met in the last two years, which since she had almost no memory of her life prior to Jarle, Cal was the hottest guy she'd ever met. Even if he did have an out-of-the-ordinary attachment to wolves. At least it wasn't alligators or snakes. Wolves she could live with, reptiles, definitely not.

And talk about wielding magick. The way he commanded that sword to fly off the ground was more than incredible. She could never even hope to achieve supernatural talent on such a high level. Cal was the genuine thing. And he seemed like a nice guy to boot.

If she learned anything over the last two years, it was that her ability to judge people was rarely wrong. Of course Jarle was her one mistake. Not that she didn't think him vile and disgusting, but she never saw him as having been a liar when it came to telling her the details of the night he'd found her. Now she was starting to believe otherwise.

A knock sounded at the door.

"Come."

The door opened and Callen popped his head in. "Am I disturbing you?"

"Heck no. I was just sitting here trying to decide what to watch on television." Admitting she was thinking about his magickal abilities and the way he'd kissed her didn't seem appropriate.

"I've brought dinner," Cal said, entering the room while carrying a silver tray in his hands. His cane dangled from his wrist. "Nothing fancy. Just sandwiches, salad and a house wine. Cook also added a berry custard. Of course, if you'd like something different, I can go back to the kitchen."

"Sandwiches are fine." She rose from the bed and went over to the table in the corner of the room and plucked her tote bag off the top and placed it on the floor.

Cal set the food down, then balanced his cane against the wall. "My uncle's brother-in-law, Vidar, arrived a short while ago, delaying dinner. I hope you didn't mind waiting."

"Not at all."

He pulled out the chair for her.

"Maybe there is hope for you yet," Miranda said.

"Hope?"

"On becoming date material."

"Oh. Right." He gave a slight grin. "I know we just met, Miranda. But believe me when I say I'm attracted to you."

"Love at first, ha?"

"It's a bit more complicated than that." He sat down in the chair across from her and shook out a cloth napkin before placing it over his lap.

She could get used to a man like Callen MacHendrie. "I think you were right about Jarle lying to me."

"Do you remember more from the night he said he found you?" Cal reached for a ham sandwich and placed it on his plate.

"I'm not sure. I tried to think back, but I only get flickering images. At least nothing I can really verify. I vaguely remember helping an animal, once. Possibly a dog or wolf. But I can't say for sure. And I do remember a few earlier memories, but just things from my childhood, like being a little girl and playing with herbs. Mixing leaves with a mortar and pestle. Nothing related to Jarle."

Callen reached across the table and poured Miranda a glass of wine from the bottle he brought with the food. "Vidar will have his men look into the matter. I gave him whatever information you told me and he'll see if his guys can dig up information on your true identity."

"Do you think they can despite Jarle being in the way? He moves around a lot, never stays in one place for long. And when he leaves he destroys all traces of him having been in a place."

He laughed. "Trust me, Vidar's goons are good."

She prayed Callen was right. If not, she'd eventually have to go back to Jarle and if she returned without the sword she'd come to Dundaire to steal, she'd be going home to her grave.

~~o0o~~

Callen watched Miranda eat. The way she broke off a small piece of sandwich and brought it to her mouth, the way she toyed with the stemmed wine glass. Everything his mate did, he found interesting. And yet they were the simplest of movements. The most base things a person could do, and still he found them intriguing. Miranda was right, he was so screwed.

He reached for his wine and raised it to his lips.

"You said you are the oldest of your father's children. How many brothers and sisters do you have?"

He put down his glass. "Five brothers, no sisters."

"Are you close to them?"

"Verra. They all live on the grounds of Wolfsden, but in their own homes."

"And your father?"

"My dad lives here, at the main castle, but he's away at the moment."

"I can't imagine anyone wanting to leave this place. It's so beautiful and serene. I can actually hear myself think up here, unlike in the city. You must really enjoy it."

He took a moment to answer, not sure how to explain that the keep was the castle belonging to the pack's Alpha and that when his father was in residence, so too were a horde of rowdy wolves. Most nights, getting more than an hour of sound sleep was near impossible. "It's quiet now because I'm the only one, save for a few members of the castle's staff, here. When my dad comes back, this place will take on a whole other atmosphere."

Miranda pushed her plate away. "That sandwich hit the spot, even the salad was good." She wiped her hands on the napkin and then placed it on the table.

"You still have to eat Cook's berry custard." Callen nudged a small crock off the tray.

"I couldn't."

She certainly didn't eat like a wolf. And if Miranda Kendrick was ever going to fit in at Wolfsden Keep, Callen was going to have to change her eating habits. "At least have a taste." He grabbed a spoon and scooped out the custard along with two blueberries from the top of the dish. Reaching across the table, he fed Miranda the dessert.

690

She took the treat and moaned. A second later she smiled. "That is the most delicious custard I have ever had. I'll take the rest of it."

Callen laughed as he slid the crock to her side of the table. "It's addictive, I know. We keep it as a staple here at the castle as my dad really likes it and has fits if it's not available."

"It must be nice having a family." Sadness veiled Miranda's blue eyes.

He wanted to reach out, tell her she had him, his family. But he'd already seemed desperate and didna want to push his luck. "Do you remember anything about your parents or possible siblings?"

"Nothing. The few memories I have of me being a child are of me alone. But I am mixing herbs in the visions, so someone had to have taught me what to do."

Miranda could have come from mixed lineage—one parent a wolf, the other a witch. His own mother had vampiric blood and was only half wolf. Mixing of breeds was common among some packs. "What do you do for Jarle. Other than steal artifacts?"

"Most days I practice my spell casting. The rest of the time I tend to the coven's herbs, oils and ointments. I also, on occasion, work directly with Jarle…" She paused and started rolling the edge of the cloth napkin on the table. "I'm not proud of what I do, but I don't have a choice."

He reached for her hand. "What does the bastard make you do, Miranda?"

"I help him bind souls, bind hearts to him. But only those that need to have their tether to him reinforced. Sometimes, Jarle's slaves find a way to weaken his hold on them. That's when he makes me adjust the binding spells. Other times it's for a soul who has passed on, but he's not willing to let it rest in peace."

"I wasn't aware he could bind a dead person's heart."

She nodded. "But I try, every chance I get, to weaken the spells if Jarle isn't in the room or isn't watching me. I do it because I hope that some of those souls can break free of him. If he ever knew, he'd kill me."

Under his watch, Miranda Kendrick was not going to have to worry about that bastard Viking. "While you're here, you have nothing to worry about. Jarle canna touch you on my father's property. You're welcome to stay for as long as you like."

"He'll come for me if I did go back."

"He'll have to face an army of…" He paused. Keeping his wolf secret was becoming increasingly difficult. "My father has good security. Trust me."

Miranda pulled her hand away from his. "But can any of them best Jarle's spell casting?"

"Believe me, my family has many witches among them. As a whole, we'll protect you."

She offered him a slight smile, but nothing enough to convince him that she believed his words.

And that pained him more than anything.

CHAPTER SIX

Cal left shortly after they had dinner, Rhys calling him to say Vidar had already received information from his men and insisted they discuss it tonight. The progress should have made Miranda feel better, but instead she was in bed, tossing and turning, and unable to sleep.

Visions of Jarle filled her head.

On the nightstand, her cellphone buzzed.

She reached over and grabbed it, the smooth rubber casing cool against her skin.

Jarle's number appeared in black on the lit up screen.

Damn. She wasn't supposed to check in until mid-week. What the heck was she going to tell the man? Certainly not the truth.

She flipped the phone open. "Hello?"

"You didn't call."

"You told me I didn't have to until Wednesday."

"Plans have changed. Did you get the sword?"

She hesitated.

"Miranda?"

"Not yet."

Jarle's heavy breath echoed over the phone. "Why not? Did you fuck up or is your failure due to another cause?"

"MacHendrie hasn't started cataloguing any weapons yet. The moment he does, I'll have access to all the swords in the castle. He's assured me of it."

Silence greeted her excuse. She prayed to God, Jarle would believe her lie.

"You need more protection. I'm increasing the charge to your locket."

She did not need more of Jarle's powers binding her soul. "What makes you think I'm in danger?"

"You should be appreciative of my concern, slave. I've invested a lot in your horrible excuse of a life and I want to keep what is mine safe. Is that clear?"

"Of course. But I've been very careful to stick with our plan, with my role as student. MacHendrie doesn't suspect a thing and there hasn't been anyone here that I'd suspect as a threat against me. I don't see the need for increased protection."

A growl vibrated against her ear. "Someone is looking into your past and I don't want your secrets getting out. Do you?"

She was starting to think she didn't have secrets, but letting Jarle in on that little tidbit wouldn't do her any good. Keeping a calm demeanor was best, though she'd really like to give the bastard a piece of her mind right about now. "Of course not." It was all she could think to say.

"What are you hiding from me, Miranda?"

Panic struck her nerves. "Nothing."

"If you don't bring me the sword, not only will you die, but Callen MacHendrie will suffer a loss so great, it will be unlike any pain he's endured over the last thousand years."

Thousand years? Cal? Impossible.

"Are you still there, slave?"

"Yes, Jarle."

"I'm adding to your assignment."

The Viking witch never veered off his original course when it came to stealing what he wanted. Miranda wondered what heck the guy was up to. "Go on."

"Besides the sword, there is a locket. It looks similar to yours, but is much older and contains a ruby at the latch. Bring it along with the blade."

"And what do I get in return?"

"I'll terminate our agreement."

"But you already agreed to that in exchange for the sword. I want extra payment if I have to bring you the locket, too."

Jarle hesitated, took a deep breath. The noise came across like a barrage of static.

Miranda slid the phone away from her ear until she heard the witch speak again.

"And what compensation do you desire for a fucking locket, slave?"

"Leave MacHendrie alone."

"What has he done to you, Miranda? Filled your head with nonsense that he can save you from me? Do you know his uncle killed my wife?"

No. She did not know that fact.

"Or that he himself once attempted to kill me too?"

"I don't believe you. MacHendrie does not seem the type to have a temper, let alone be capable of attempted murder."

Jarle paused.

Her throat grew dry. A prickling sensation stirred her every nerve. "I'll be careful around him." She hoped those words would appease her captor.

"If you want proof, check the locket. It bears an inscription of my wife's name, Kenna, entwined with mine. Find it and you'll know the truth. MacHendrie is a deceiver."

Now she didn't know who to believe. Jarle was a vile, wicked soul, but she knew what to expect from him. Callen was almost a stranger.

"I'll bring you the sword."

"And the locket?"

"Yes, and the locket. But this is the last job I'm doing for you, Jarle. It ends here."

"Believe me, I will have no trouble severing our agreement."

The phone went dead on the other end.

Miranda tossed the darn gadget onto the nightstand and then flopped back into the pile of bed pillows. Callen never mentioned his uncle's killing of Jarle's wife. And what were the MacHendrie's doing with the woman's locket? Maybe her master had reason for being the bitter soul that he was.

Or maybe it was all just another trick. A deception she couldn't see through.

Either way, she wanted out. Risking her life just wasn't worth it.

~~o0o~~

Callen studied the documents spread across his desk and couldn't believe what he was reading. Vidar's men had done incredible work in such a short time. The Viking's connections had to be beyond vast. "Are you certain all this information is true?"

"Everything has been verified," Vidar said. "Miranda Kendrick is your woman's real name. We just can't establish the whereabouts of her New York clinic because she was very good at keeping the business underground. Preternatural physicians are rare, even in the city."

Miranda was right about thinking she had helped animals. As a doctor who tended to shifters she would have come across many of their kind. "She'll be happy to know some of the few memories she has left of her life before Jarle are real."

The Viking shook his head. "What that man has done to Dr. Kendrick is despicable."

He couldn't agree more.

"Miranda is a rare breed," Vidar said. "She helped many shifters who otherwise would not have gotten the medical care they needed. But her work didn't stop at just healing their bodies, she also offered a safe environment, kept their identities confidential."

His mate was a healer. No wonder the pain in his leg had eased after she kneed him in the thigh. He imagined she could do even better if she took a serious look at his wound. "How did she end up bound to Jarle?"

Vidar pushed a file across the desk. "She was tending to one of the witch's slaves. A big cat. She tried to help the shifter by arranging for a safe house and making plans to get the female to safety. The witch found out and then took Miranda. He had to have had inside help, but my men have not been able to find out who turned on Dr. Kendrick. We believe Jarle killed or mesmerized everyone who was connected to Miranda's clinic. Pulling a few mind tricks on humans who would have questioned the act, would be easy for someone with his powers."

"Jarle gives witches a bad name."

"I agree," Vidar said. "My mother was half-witch. I take offense to slime like that rotten bastard."

Callen paused. He closed the file and pushed it away. "What about her family? Is there no one looking for her?"

Vidar shook his head. "She is an immortal wolf, but a new wolf, born only twenty-seven years ago. She was orphaned at a young age, taken in by her grandmother who taught her the skills of a witch. But the woman died when Miranda was in college. She's been on her own ever since and has no other relatives that my men could find."

"With no one concerned for her, Jarle could do anything and never have to pay for it. No one probably even knows she's missing. Miranda's locket must be destroyed."

Vidar gave him a serious stare. "Be very careful, my friend. If you don't break the binding spell first, the person whose heart aura rests inside the locket, will die."

He hadn't thought about complications. "I appreciate the help, Vidar. You have no idea how much this means to me."

"Well, we are family now. And Katya would kill me if I didn't help. So, I make the best of the situation."

"Maybe I can repay the favor one day."

The Viking smiled. "If I can think of anything, I will let you know."

Callen couldn't wait to tell Miranda what Vidar's men had discovered about her past. He hoped she'd be pleased. But even if she couldn't come to terms with who she really was and what had happened to her, he still had to find a way to free her from Jarle. And with only a few days left before Miranda had to go back to the witch, time was running short.

CHAPTER SEVEN

Miranda added another entry into the log, this one detailing the number and description of a gold Celtic brooch that had survived in good condition, its three amber stones still intact. When finished, she moved the piece aside and went for a silver wolf-shaped pin. Masking tape from the pin's baggie snagged her tee-shirt and stuck to the cotton front.

She'd hoped by starting early, and working alone, she'd get a chance to search the bins for Jarle's mysterious locket, but the item remained elusive.

"You didn't come down to breakfast," Callen said.

She looked up and saw him standing in the doorway, his black hair having that slightly messy, just out of bed, tussled appearance. A gray cotton shirt and worn jeans added to his ruggedness. No man had a right to look that sexy. "I wanted to get a head start on cataloguing, since we didn't get much work done yesterday."

"I would have thought you'd prefer to discuss the report Vidar's men sent over."

She did, but with Jarle on her case, finding out who she was no longer mattered. "I owe you a week, that's what you paid for and that's what I'm going to give you. I don't want anything in return."

Leaning on his cane, Cal entered the room and approached the table. "Something's wrong. And don't lie to me because I can sense your anxiety." Telling him about the phone call from Jarle would do neither of them any good. "Last night I had time to think and I just want to do my job and then leave."

"You won't be able to escape the Viking on your own."

"I can try. And don't worry, I have no plans on stealing your sword."

"It's not about the damn sword, Miranda." He rested his cane against the back of a nearby chair and then reached for her hands. "We need to talk about what Vidar told me last night."

She wanted to talk about what Jarle had told her, but knew better. Callen MacHendrie might appear to be a tame man on the surface, but she didn't know him. And even if Jarle had lied, and Callen and his family were innocent of the crimes the Viking had accused them of, she had the distinct feeling the Highlander would not take the news lightly. And garnering more trouble from Jarle was not something she needed. "Fine. We can talk now. Here."

Cal frowned, but agreed. He let go of her hands, backtracked across the room and then closed the door.

Miranda noticed he'd left his cane behind and that his limp didn't seem as pronounced as it had been yesterday. "How is your leg?"

"Surprisingly, the pain has eased. It's barely a twinge now."

"I'm glad my knee didn't aggravate it more."

"I think it might have helped, actually, but we'll get to that later."

She moved the artifacts out of the way and rested her elbows on the table top. "I'm all ears."

Callen sat down in the chair next to her. "First you have to understand that some of what I'm about to tell you might not seem logical. But it is all true."

"Okay…I guess."

"Second, whatever you do, don't panic."

She quirked her lips. "You do realize you're sounding a bit…touched in the head." She twirled her finger at her right temple and whistled.

"I'd rather have you think me crazy, then never know the truth."

She wondered if he'd feel the same if she told him what Jarle had accused him of last night. "Go ahead, I'm ready to hear whatever you have to say."

He shifted in the chair. "Miranda Kendrick is your real name. And you are a New Yorker, born and bred."

The news came as a relief. At least not everything about her past was lost. "If I really am Miranda Kendrick, we have a name to go by. Which means I must have some sort of paper or digital imprint that can get us more information."

"To a degree, yes. But apparently you're very good about covering your tracks."

She didn't understand. "Okay. Now you're starting to freak me out. Am I like a mass-murder or something?"

He gave up a soft laugh, revealed his perfectly straight, white teeth. "No. Quite the opposite in fact. You're a doctor. A veterinarian to be precise."

"That's why I remembered the dogs." She plucked the strip of tape off her tee-shirt and rolled it into a ball before sticking it on the table's metal surface.

Leaning forward, Callen offered her a serious stare, the gold flecks in his brown eyes seeming to grow brighter. "Dogs weren't your only patients. You were helping one of Jarle's slaves. The woman wanted to escape the witch but couldn't do it on her own. In the process someone turned on you, told Jarle what you were trying to do and that is how you came to be bound to him."

"But you said I was a vet. Why would I be helping a woman?"

Cal swallowed. "This is going to be hard to accept, but you need to know."

"I can take it. Trust me. You have no idea the crap I've seen working for that madman."

"The woman was a shapeshifter. A feline shifter."

She believed in magick and witchcraft, but people turning into animals? That was insane. "That's not possible."

"I'm going to show you something and I don't want you to freak out." Callen slid off the chair. "Whatever I do, know I will not harm you. Don't panic at what you're about to see." He stepped away from the table and closed his eyes, seemed to be concentrating on something very serious.

Miranda folded her arms. MacHendrie might have a good heart, and a hot bod, but the guy was definitely missing a few marbles upstairs.

Cal hunched. His hands shifted form, changed into paws. His entire body morphed. In a matter of mere seconds her sexy Scot had shifted into…a wolf. A real live, fur-covered wolf. His clothes were nowhere to be found, vanished just as had Callen's human form.

Her heart skipped a bit. And not in a good way.

She inched off the chair.

"Don't fear me, Miranda. I won't bite."

Oh. My. God. "How did you do that?"

"It's called morphing"

"No, not the physical thing, the getting into my head part."

"I just changed from human form into wolf and all you want to know is how can I get into your head? Aren't you curious about the wolf part or anything else?"

"I would like to know how old you are."

"I'm immortal. I've lived for more than a thousand years."

"You don't look a day over twenty-eight, twenty-nine."

"It's just the way things work with us."

She took a few steps forward and held out her hand, ran the tips of her fingers over Cal's now gray-haired head.

He nipped at her wrist. "Hey, you said you didn't bite."

"No. I said I wouldna bite. There's a difference. And that was a nip, not a bite."

She inched back and thought about what she'd just witnessed. If she could believe Jarle capable of capturing her heart's aura in a locket, why not believe Callen MacHendrie could shift form? "The memory of me having paws for hands and feet. Do you think that was real or was Jarle just messing with my mind on that one?"

"You're my mate, Miranda. I know it for fact. You're as much wolf as am I, but I believe you are also half-witch. Your grandmother was a witch."

It was nice to know something of her roots. But this whole wolf business intrigued her more for the moment. "Are we humans who can take wolf form or the other way around? And how old do you think I am? As old as you? Am I immortal, too?"

"Humans who can shift into wolf. But the other kind do exist. As for your age, Vidar says you're a new wolf. You've only been here for twenty-seven years. But yes, you're immortal."

The thrill of excitement thrummed through her body. She could never go back to Jarle now. She wanted to know about the MacHendrie wolves and their magickal world of shifting. "Teach me to take wolf form."

"Morphing canna be taught. It must be brought about from the core of your soul."

"Oh." She frowned. "There's no way I'll ever be able to do it. I just can't wrap my head around the dynamics, despite now believing it possible."

"I'm sure you've done it before. Before Jarle came into your world. You'll do it again, when you're ready."

Her gaze traveled to his hind right leg. A nasty pink scar ran down the length of it and no fur grew around it. "Is that scar the reason you use a cane?"

"It is. Jarle struck me with my own sword and then cursed both my wound and the weapon. It's why I conceal the sword in the cane, so no one can touch its tainted magick."

She reached over and trailed her fingers down the furless stretch of leg. "Jarle is a bastard. How could he have done this to you?" Now she knew why MacHendrie must have tried to kill the Viking witch. She'd have gone after Jarle too, if he'd jammed a sword into her leg. The pain Callen endured had to have been horrific.

A whine escaped Cal's mouth.

"Sorry. Didn't mean to hurt you."

"It's okay. Just a bit tender to the touch. Though I must admit, the feel of your hand warms the scar and that's never happened before."

"Maybe we can work on it. I've formulated numerous salves in Jarle's potting shed, several specifically for soothing sore muscles. If Rhys can get the ingredients, I can recreate them here."

"I'll talk to him." Callen turned around and padded across the room, his wolf body disappearing behind the table.

"Where are you going?"

"To shift back."

"Why are you hiding?"

He gave a low growl.

"Callen?"

"This was not a planned morph, Miranda. I will be naked when I change back."

She rounded the table.

"A bit of privacy, please."

"This coming from the same man who didn't seem to mind taking in a good view of my breasts yesterday. Where was the privacy there?"

"Touché. But this is different. I will be fully naked."

"And your point being?"

Callen growled again, a low guttural noise that sounded more annoyed than angry. *"There is a kilt in the wardrobe on the far wall, in a box on the top shelf. Please bring it to me."*

"A polite wolf. Now that's something I would have never expected."

"Just bring the kilt, wumman."

Miranda headed for the wardrobe. "You're also a testy little dog."

"Do not call me a dog."

"You certainly bark orders like one. I hope you don't expect me to cook dinner every night because that won't be happening. I'm more a microwave chick."

"Planning on sticking around, are you?"

"Crap. I didn't mean to say that out loud."

"Too late."

She returned, kilt in hand, and froze. "What am I supposed to do now? I think it might be too heavy to drape over you."

"You think me that weak?"

"No, but..."

"Just leave it on the floor."

She placed the blue plaid garment at Cal's feet.

"Now turn around. Please."

"You are such a prude. I really didn't expect that from you."

Callen remained silent on the matter.

A few seconds later she felt the touch of his hand on her shoulder. She spun around. Her sexy Scot was back.

Miranda licked her lips, her gaze taking in the whole of Cal's naked torso, from his ripped chest to his bulking biceps. The man was more gorgeous without clothes than she had imagined. "You really need to get a velvet-draped, four-poster bed."

"Need? I already have one?"

"Get, out." She slapped him on the chest. A playful little pat.

He pulled her close.

The aroma of bergamot filled her space, a note of clove topping it off. She ran her hand over his chest, brought her head to rest against his shoulder. "You smell incredible."

"It's my wolf scent and only you can detect it." Callen lifted her chin with his finger. Lowering his head, he brushed his lips against hers.

Heat warmed Miranda's body. The taste of fresh lime lingered on her tongue, coated her mouth as Cal's tongue danced with hers. Callen MacHendrie was a man she could easily fall into bed with, maybe even love.

Cal deepened the kiss.

She moaned and wrapped her arms around his neck.

He grabbed the hem of her shirt and slipped his large hand underneath, seeking her breasts.

Her bra's front clasp popped.

Callen didn't waste a second. He had her shirt over her head and on the floor in a flash. The bra went flying as well.

He lifted her and sat her on the table before dipping his head to her right nipple. His tongue darted out, caressed her swollen bud with vicious licks, brought it to a full peak.

Pain mixed with pleasure as the tip of her breast grew taught.

Miranda reached for the open side of Cal's kilt and slipped her hand under the fabric. Her fingers glided over his hard penis.

He gasped.

His cock twitched in her hand. She liked knowing she had some hold over him, that his body welcomed her touch.

"If we do this, Miranda, there will be no going back."

"I want to be yours, Callen."

He leaned his forehead against hers. "You'll have to accept my pack, even if they don't accept me. Do you understand that? It won't be easy."

"Why wouldn't they accept you."

He let out a deep breath. "With my leg, I am not capable of leading them the way a true Alpha should. I have been alone for a long time because of my wound."

She wanted to be his regardless of what the MacHendrie wolves thought of him. "You said I'm your mate."

"Aye. And we mate for life."

"Then I will be yours for life." She pulled his head down and kissed him.

A groan escaped Callen's throat. He slid his hand to her waist and undid the zipper of her jeans, then tugged them off her legs.

She shimmied out of her lace panties and spread wide for him. Her desire to be taken by Callen was something she couldn't explain, but it was overwhelming, controlling her every inch. Maybe it was the wolf in her soul, the wolf that had been suppressed.

"I should take you in my bed. This is not proper, claiming you on a table."

"There's no time, Cal. I want you to take me here. Now." The strong desire to be claimed by him, to allow him to show his pack he had a mate, consumed her. "The pack must know I'm yours."

"You truly are my mate, Miranda. Any other female would not be doing what you're agreeing to now."

He positioned himself between her thighs and ran his hand over her inner leg.

Heat radiated from his fingers, warmed her flesh and shot up to her clit. She clenched.

Callen reached for her mound, rubbed his thumb over the sensitive prize.

Miranda leaned back. She spread her legs wider. As she enjoyed the flick of Cal's finger against her clit, she worked his cock with her hand. Wrapping around the hard rod, she then pumped up and down, noting that her fingers barely contained him, his girth so thick.

Cal went back to teasing her nipple with his masterful tongue. First he toyed with the right one, then he teased the left one. In seconds both her peaks were protruding to the point of pain, but it was a pleasure she enjoyed.

She thrust her breasts closer to his mouth.

A bead of liquid touched her palm as she caressed the tip of Cal's penis.

He pushed her hand away, and then lifted his kilt and brought his cock to her slit. One finger dipped inside her. "Christ, Miranda, you are so wet. And tight."

"Love me, Callen."

"I cudna refuse, even if I wanted to." He slid his penis inside her, just enough to tease her sensitive walls.

She moaned. "Don't stop there. Please."

A chuckle escaped his lips. "You're a wonton little wolf."

"I can't help it. I've never felt like this before."

"It's the animal in your soul, Miranda. It's still there and that's a good thing."

Callen inched his cock deeper into her.

Like a million little pings of pleasure, a sweet pulse rippled through her privates. She clenched, held tight to Cal's long, hard penis.

He pulled out with a moan.

A soft groan rose in her throat.

Callen slid back inside, this time with a fiercer thrust, a pound that hammered her and sent the sound of slapping flesh echoing through the room.

She gripped the table's edge and met Cal's every move.

He grunted, his breath coming in deep pants as he rammed into her over and over.

Pleasure exploded inside her. Miranda let out a cry and leaned forward, wrapped her arms around Callen's neck and rode out the exquisite sensation until she could move no more.

Cal held her steady, then pumped one last time, spilling his seed into her tight slit. A low howl came from his core.

Mating with her Alpha wolf was a pleasure she would have never imagined, even in her wildest dreams.

~~o0o~~~o0o~~

After they made love, Callen helped Miranda back into her clothes. Knowing he had a mate, was a feeling he could not explain. It lingered somewhere between elation and concern, because even though he wanted to protect her the moment he realized Miranda was indeed his destiny, the desire to protect her now was tenfold.

"You said you would explain more about your leg feeling better." Miranda said.

"I think you're a healing witch."

She adjusted her tee-shirt and then stared at his kilt. "Can I see your wound, in human form now?"

He frowned. "I don't know if that is a good idea."

"We just banged our brains out, I think looking at your thigh would not be considered taboo."

"No. I don't mean it in that way. I'm concerned for your safety. In order for the curse to be lifted from my leg, it will either have to be destroyed or be absorbed by someone else. I don't want to put you at risk. Yesterday's aid happened by chance. And until I know you won't be put in danger by working directly on my wound, I won't have you touching it."

"Maybe a salve would help. I can make one and you can apply it yourself."

He nodded. "That would be acceptable."

She reached her hand for his chin. "You're an agreeable wolf. I thought Alphas were tough."

"You like me now, but wait until my father comes home and brings the pack with him. They are a rowdy bunch and the single wolves tend to camp out here a lot. Better get your sleep while you can."

The door opened and Vidar walked in. He glanced at Callen's kilt. "Sorry to intrude on the tupping." He inched back.

Miranda quirked an eyebrow. "I am familiar with the term and you are not intruding, sir."

"He's no sir," Callen said. "Trust me on that. He's Vidar, the Viking. My uncle's brother-in-law."

Vidar remained at the door. "I will come back, later."

"Don't leave yet. Did you have more information?"

The hulking man glanced from Callen, then to Miranda and back to Callen.

"I think I'll go find Rhys," Miranda said. She headed for the door. "It was nice to meet you Vidar. Thank your men for helping me."

The Viking nodded, then stepped aside to allow her to pass.

Once Miranda was out of ear shot, Callen motioned for Vidar to take a seat. "What did you learn?"

"Jarle is on the warpath. He knows my men have been looking into Miss Kendrick's background. He'll be coming for her soon. Of this I am certain."

The news was not what he wanted to hear. "Can you get reinforcements here in time?"

"They are already on the way, my friend."

He was never so glad for Vidar in all his life. "Good, then we will be ready."

"There is more."

This cudna be good. "Spill it."

"He wants your mother's locket."

What did his mother's locket have to do with Jarle? "We don't even know where it is. And why would Jarle want it. It's not a heart locket."

"No, but it could be used as one to bind her soul in the afterlife."

Jarle had no right. Anger infused Callen's veins. "I will not let that bastard harm my mother's peace."

"My men overheard him talking to someone saying that Mortimer killed his wife. I think he wants revenge. You mother was Mortimer's sister, the only female in her family. By binding her soul, it would avenge his wife's death."

Callen fisted his hands. "Katya could be in danger as well."

Vidar shook his head. "My sister cannot be bound to Jarle. She uses a spell my grandmother taught her, to protect her soul and the bastard can't break it."

That left only his mother. The only other female linked to Mortimer. "I will not have that bastard curse my mother's soul."

"Find the locket and she'll remain at peace."

Thank goodness he had Miranda here. He was going to need her help if he had any chance of going through the entire horde of jewelry before Jarle arrived.

CHAPTER EIGHT

After showering and then having lunch, Miranda was back in the storage room and going through a box of jewelry she retrieved from a crate on the far wall. Callen had explained how he needed to find his mother's locket and she was eager to help. She also wanted desperately to tell him about Jarle's call and how the witch claimed the same item as having belonged to his wife. But what if Cal's mother had secrets of her own? After living without knowing anything about her past for the last two years, she knew how powerful finding the truth could be. And just in case Callen's mother was not the woman he believed her to be, she didn't want Cal to suffer. She'd find the truth first, then tell him about the call from Jarle.

"The locket has a ruby clasp," Callen said. His back was to her as he was bent over a crate, searching through unsorted artifacts. Pieces of straw fell from his hands as he removed items from the large bin.

Thoughts of her mating with Callen weighed heavy on her mind. And for that she was glad to be working from crates and not at the table. Every time she looked at the piece of furniture she couldn't help but think of what they had done on it.

"That's not a bad thing."

"You can do that in human form, too?"

He looked up from the crate. "Yes. But I try not to."

She glanced at the table. Then frowned.

"I'll have it put in storage, if you'd like."

"I just don't think I will ever be able to get work done on it again. And I'm sure you have lots of things yet to be catalogued."

A grin spread across his lips. "We have other tables. I'm sure you'll find one to your liking and we can swap it out. And I promise, next time I'll bring you to our bed."

Our bed. The words made her feel all tingly inside. Two years of being under Jarle's command, belonging to no family, no friends, had been lonely. Being with Callen, even though they had just met, felt right. The wolf in her soul could not be denied. "So much has happened since yesterday. My world has changed drastically."

"Life can take sudden changes for MacHendrie wolves. It's been our way for as far back as we've existed."

"Did all your brothers take mates quickly?"

He gave a pensive stare as if thinking the matter over. "All but Ulrich. He mated with a human who does not descend from wolf blood."

"Is that permitted?"

"She was his mate, his destiny. It's just the way it turned out."

There was a lot she was going to have to learn about the wolves of Wolfsden Keep.

Rhys knocked on the doorjamb.

Callen turned to face the butler. "Yes?"

"Vidar's men have arrived and I don't know where to put them."

Callen huffed. "I'll go find the Viking. We should have room for his troops in one of the other buildings. They'll probably prefer it out there anyway as I'm sure they will want to explore the grounds and stake out the place." He turned back to Miranda. "Do you mind if I leave for a bit? I hate to have you go through this stuff on your own, but Vidar's men are not the sort to leave unattended. They can get into a lot of trouble if left without any guidance."

She gave up a slight chuckle and waved her hand. "Go. I'll be fine here."

"Sure you don't mind?"

"Positive."

Callen grabbed his cane from the back of a nearby chair and then motioned for Rhys to follow him into the entrance hall.

Miranda returned to searching through the box of silver jewelry.

A cold breath blew at her ear. She cupped her lobe.

Wisps of gray energy swirled around her body, starting at her feet and traveling up to her shoulders. A single tether of the gossamer mist licked her cheek.

"I come in the name of Jarle," the mist said. "Our master wants his locket or the wolf will die."

"You have no right being here." She scolded in a low voice. "This is protected territory. How did you even get in?"

The mist circled her. "I came with the Viking warriors. They have many witches among them and their energy was permitted, which cleared the way for me since I piggy-backed it."

"You had no right. Now leave."

"Jarle wants his locket."

Her heartbeat picked up speed. "Tell him he'll get the damn thing when I find it."

"Don't betray him, Miranda. Or the wolf dies." The gray swirls faded from her sight.

Miranda took a deep breath and prayed to God, Vidar's men could stop Jarle. The thought of that bastard destroying the MacHendrie strong hold sickened her. She had to do something. She had to keep Callen and his family safe.

A plastic bag slipped from a stack on top of a half-open crate in the corner. The slight noise jarred her thoughts.

She brought her hands to her chest and tried to calm her nerves.

Her heartrate slowed.

A red glint caught her eye.

Miranda walked over to the bag that had slipped off the crate and plucked it from the floor. It hadn't been labeled. No name, no number, no description.

She undid the slide and reached her fingers inside.

Cool silver caressed her skin as her hand touched a ruby cabochon topping the item's side clasp.

The locket.

Lifting the item out of the bag, Miranda scrutinized it. She turned it on its side and popped it open. A piece of red velvet lined the interior cavity but the space contained no pulse or herbs. Not that she had expected something this old to have its original content intact, but she didn't sense that it had ever been used in the same manner as had her own locket.

Her fingers glided over the soft fabric lining. A piece snagged her nail and lifted.

Miranda peeled it back.

Ornate scroll work decorated the smooth interior surface. Looking closer, she detected two names etched in a fancy script—Kenna and Jarle.

The witch had been telling the truth, at least about the two names having been inscribed inside the locket. Yet she still didn't believe the bastard. Maybe there was more to the story than what Jarle had told her.

She turned toward the window and watched as Callen appeared to be explaining something about the property to Vidar's men. He looked regal out there, pointing to different parts of the estate, exuding command over his territory. He would one day make a fine Alpha. Of that she had no doubt.

The locket warmed her hand. Miranda slipped the silver item into her jeans pocket and went back to searching through the crated artifacts, acting as if she hadn't found anything yet. Maybe Vidar could help her sort out the locket's secrets. If his men really were that good at getting to the truth, no matter how much Jarle tried to cover it up, then perhaps they could help her learn the meaning behind the two names inscribed in the locket's interior.

Until she knew the truth, Callen didn't need to worry.

~~o0o~~

Callen stood on the side lawn of Wolfsden Keep and marveled at the proficiency of Vidar's men. These were not the same troops he remembered from childhood. His acquaintances had grown up since he'd last worked with them directly and he was glad of it.

"They will protect your land, friend." Vidar came to stand at his side. "Jarle will not harm your woman."

"The witch has great forces. If he does attempt to breech our barricades, I fear for your clan."

"Please. They are men. Immortal Viking wolves, witches and vampires. They live for war and for dying. If any of them passes from this life with a battleax in his hand, then he has fulfilled his destiny."

That might be true, but he still didn't wish them to die under his watch. All lives were precious.

A warrior came running up the hill. "A wolf has been injured, Vidar. A pup."

His nephews were all in New Orleans. "It can't be one of mine. It must be a stray."

"Do you have many strays in the area?" Vidar's eyes turned cold.

"I've only come across one once before."

The Viking huffed. "This is not good, friend. I fear we have trouble among us, the pup might be a ploy."

Callen glanced back at the castle. "Jarle means to engage us in battle. I should be with Miranda to keep her safe."

An arrow sped passed his head.

Vidar pushed him to the ground. "There is no time to go back, now. We must fight." He pulled a dagger out from the inside of his boot and handed it to Callen. "I'm going to my men. Do what you must, but remember if we can't stop Jarle before he steps foot on your land, then we will not be able to stop him at all."

He agreed with the Viking. Miranda was safer in the castle, with Rhys to guard her, while he fought to keep the enemy from coming near his home.

Callen took a deep breath and pushed himself up.

He followed Vidar down the hill.

CHAPTER NINE

"What the hell is he doing?" Miranda eyed Callen limping down the hill, his leg seeming to bother him more now than it had before.

Rhys stood at her left, his hand gripped to the window sill. "I believe he is going to fight alongside the Vikings."

"The man is insane."

"Jarle's army must be approaching. I'll go get my silver bullets."

She turned and watched Rhys flash from the room, only to come back a second later, bullets strapped to his chest, gun in hand.

"I had no idea a wolf could move so fast," she said.

"We can do a lot of things, when necessary."

"This is all my fault."

Rhys tsked. "You cannot blame yourself. Jarle would have come here eventually, he's had it out for Callen since they first battled at his uncle Mortimer's castle."

"But he's here now, after he sent me to intrude in Callen's life." She wondered why the witch had picked her.

"You should go upstairs, Miss Kendrick. Lock the door. Under the bed in your room you'll find a magickally charged sword. Use it to defend yourself against Jarle, if he makes it this far. I'll guard the castle from down here. And pray you have no need of the weapon upstairs."

She wasn't going to leave Rhys alone. "I'm staying put."

"Callen will have my head for this. Please. Go. Upstairs."

The man did not look pleased at her. "Okay, fine. But if I hear you firing that gun, I'm coming back down and fighting at your side."

"Fair enough, Miss Kendrick."

Miranda left the fully armed butler in the storage room and headed for the main staircase. Halfway up, she stopped. She had the locket Jarle wanted and she had her own life. Maybe Jarle would settle his anger with Callen if she gave him Kenna's jewelry and agreed to serve him for eternity. At least it was worth a try. And she knew the moment Jarle saw her, he'd think she had what he wanted and that could halt the fighting temporarily.

She turned around and took the stairs two at a time. With a glance at the storage room, she saw Rhys still glued to the window. This was her chance to leave.

Making a beeline for the front door, Miranda was out of the house in an instant. She scooted around back. And froze.

Jarle stood against the castle's stone façade, his arms folded. "It's about time, slave. I thought you'd never come out of that damn hellhole."

Wolfsden was not a hellhole. "How did you make it past Vidar's men?"

The bastard reached for her neck. He ran a gnarly finger over her flesh. "The moment you removed your locket, the powers I had over it shifted to wherever you left it."

The damn thing was sitting on the nightstand in the guest room.

"That's right, slave. I am now free to roam this land as I wish. I own it like I owned you. And Callen MacHendrie cannot stop me. He is powerless over me at the moment and it is all thanks to you."

"You used me."

Jarle's eyes grew dark. "I use all of my slaves."

She inched back. "Why did you chose me?"

The witch huffed, a deep breath that blew out like a warm, summer wind. A hint of dark magick danced on the air. "You are a rare breed of healer, Miranda. You may be wolf, but your talents go beyond healing your kind. You are the sole shifter who can remove my hexes."

She had no frickin' clue. "I can heal Callen."

"At one time, yes. But not now."

"Why? What's changed?" Anger rose in her soul.

"You won't make it to him in time. My men will destroy Vidar's horde of warriors, and Callen will fall with them."

Her mate was not going to die. "Take me instead."

"I sent you here to get the man's sword and you want me to leave it be and take your life instead? The life I already own? That's a shitty bargain, Miranda. Even a lowly wolf-witch like yourself should agree on that point."

"I have the locket." She reached into her jeans pocket and retrieved the silver article. "Take me, for all eternity. And take the locket. In exchange, free Callen."

Jarle sucked his bottom lip. Brought one of his bony fingers to his chin and tapped. "All eternity? Is that what you are agreeing to?"

She nodded.

"And you'll turn over Kenna's locket?"

She wasn't sure that was the best thing to do, but if it did truly belong to Callen's mother, the woman's soul would surely want to protect her son's life. She prayed she was doing the right thing. "Yes."

"Then mote it be."

In a flash the world faded to black. When the darkness dissipated, she was back at Jarle's work room in Inverness.

~~oOo~~

Jarle's warriors faded from his sight. Callen stared at the land in front of him and wondered where the hell the vile creatures had disappeared to.

"They are gone," Vidar said.

"This canna be good." Callen paused. He searched the landscape for as far as he could see, and not a single one of Jarle's men remained. "It must be a trick."

One of Vidar's warriors approached. "The witch has retreated to Inverness."

"Are you certain?" Callen didn't trust Jarle to just pick up and leave without finishing the fight.

"It has been confirmed by our sources in the city," the warrior said.

Callen turned back toward the keep. "I don't trust the witch."

"Nor do I," Vidar said. "I will go to Inverness myself, but leave my men here for added protection until we know what the bastard is up to."

He appreciated the Viking's willingness to keep tabs on Jarle. "I'm going to check on Miranda."

Heading up the hill, Callen limped back to the castle. The pain in his leg escalated to the point of sheer agony by the time he made it to Wolfsden's front door.

Inside the castle he found Rhys bolting down the stairs. "She's gone, sir."

"What do you mean, gone?"

"Miranda is not in the castle."

"But I instructed you to keep her safe."

The butler lowered his gaze. "I did as you said, sir. I sent her upstairs, told her about the sword under the bed. But she is not there now."

"Is the sword still in its place?"

Rhys nodded.

"Damn it, man. Miranda never went upstairs."

"I know she left the storage room. But I do admit, I was focusing on defending the castle, watching out the window to guard for approaching troops."

His money was on Jarle. "I'm going to Inverness. Vidar's men believe the witch is there. I believe Miranda is with him."

"She would never betray you, sir. I'm sure of it."

He was too, which meant Miranda had probably gone and done something very stupid, like convincing Jarle to leave Wolfsden Keep alone. "I'm going to find her. And bring her back."

"But the witch will kill you if he's given the chance. You're in no condition to fight him, not with the hex still imbedded in your leg."

705

"I'll take my chances." He was not going to let Miranda die. She was his mate. And he would give his life to spare hers.

CHAPTER TEN

Miranda stood in the center of Jarle's Inverness office and waited for the witch to reprimand her. He might have agreed to her terms to leave Callen alone, but she knew he wasn't going to let her get away with betraying him.

Jarle entered the office. The metal door at the entrance closed behind him with a thud. "I'm giving you a new locket, Miss Kendrick. One that you will not be able to remove. It will bind you to me for life. This one and the next."

She swallowed. Living with Jarle for all eternity was going to be the pits. But at least Callen would be spared. "I want you to remove the hex from MacHendrie's leg."

"I'm allowing him to live. That is more than generous on my part."

"My life for his. The locket for his sword, which means the hex should be lifted because the weapon will no longer be bound to you."

A dark gaze filled Jarle's eyes. He sat down at his desk and tapped his fingers against the blotter. "I will agree only if our arrangement includes you using your healing powers to do whatever I ask."

She thought that would be automatically included in the bargain. Apparently, not. Maybe she was more powerful than she had previously thought. But at this stage, her magickal abilities no longer counted for anything. Jarle was going to use her to do evil. With any luck, her powers would eventually fade. "Fine."

"Let's start with the locket." The Viking witch wiggled his fingers, commanded her to display the silver piece of jewelry.

Miranda obeyed. She plucked the item from her jeans pocket and dangled it from her hand. "Before I turn this over to you, I want you to verbally free MacHendrie."

Jarle leaned back in his chair and growled. He then nodded. "I, Jarle, witch and warrior, release the MacHendrie from my control."

The office door slammed opened. "Not so fast, Viking." Callen stood at the threshold, his sword raised high. "Get out of the room, Miranda."

"She stays put," Jarle said, rising from his chair. "The woman is mine."

"Like my mother?"

"That wolf never knew her place. Your father complicated matters for me."

Callen stepped into the room. "Yours and Rorrick's war with Mortimer should never have been. Your ally fought my uncle under false pretenses. He owed you nothing. Took nothing from you, either. If you lost members of your family during that battle, you have only yourself to blame."

The witch did not appear pleased.

A sword materialized in Jarle's hand. "I have agreed to free you, Highlander. Now go and leave the woman to me."

"Never."

He eyed Miranda. "Get out of that chair and step away from the desk."

She was on her feet in a heartbeat. "I've already made the agreement, Callen. This is your chance to be free of pain. You deserve to live life without being in agony every moment."

"I said, step away from the desk."

"No."

"Now is not the time to be stubborn, wumman."

She wasn't going to let him give up his one chance at freedom. "I'm staying with Jarle."

Callen glared at the witch. "Take my sword and take me. In exchange, my mother's locket is returned to Wolfsden and Miranda is freed."

The witch smirked. "An eye for an eye. I think that is fair."

Cal motioned for Miranda to come to him.

Tears clouded her eyes. "I won't let you do this."

"You must go. Now."

Her feet moved forward, but not by her own command. The scent of bergamot and clove caressed her nose. She pulled out the silver beads she'd been keeping in her pocket and slipped them to Callen at the door.

"What are these?"

"They came from Jarle's hair. Use them to help deflect some of his energy."

Callen reached for her and then pushed her from the room and slammed the door shut.

~~o0o~~

Jarle walked up to him and grabbed him by the hair, forced his head back. "I am not content to own you, Highlander. Wolves have only presented problems for me and have done so for more than a thousand years. I say we fight today. Put an end to our war, winner take all. Loser dies."

He had no problem killing the Viking bastard. "Agreed."

"Toss the sword."

"I thought you'd want the fight to be balanced, witch. Or your victory would not be a true one."

Jarle flung his sword across the room. He dropped his hand from Callen's hair and then moved his arm, commanding all the furnishings in the office to vanish.

A second later they were in an open field.

"Drop your weapon, wolf."

He did as was asked.

"Good, dog. Now I will choke the life out of you. I've waited so long for this moment." The witch punched him in the thigh.

Callen fell to his knees.

A new sword materialized in Jarle's hand.

Memories of their first fight came flooding back to Callen. How he was running down the tunnel under Mortimer's castle. How he shifted to wolf form and charged the Viking witch. He should have shredded the beast back then. The wolf in him would have delighted in putting an end to Jarle's evil soul.

"Take your last breath, dog," Jarle said.

Nobody called him a dog.

Callen shifted, brought his wolf to the surface of his soul. In animal form, he snarled.

Jarle raised his sword.

Callen rolled away.

The witch went after him. "I bested you once, I will do so again."

"You won't win this time, Viking."

"I have the advantage. I have the only weapon on the field."

But he had teeth. Razor sharp teeth.

Callen leapt forward. As his body shifted, he tossed the silver beads at the Viking witch.

They did no good. All these years he'd searched for them and it was all for nothing.

Jarle swung his sword.

The blade sliced Callen's midsection. Blood gushed from his body as he flew through the air, then landed on the ground.

Pain hammered his every muscle.

Jarle laughed above him. "Now I will finish you off. Kill you like I should have done when we first met."

He was not going to let the bastard get away with this. Concentrating on his wolf soul, Callen garnered every last bit of strength he had left in his wounded body and took one more go at the witch.

Jarle inched backward. His feet slipped and went out from under him, sending him to his knees.

The beads. Thanks be to heaven, they did work.

Leaping from the ground he went for the Viking's neck. He tore into the bastard's flesh, then his bone, and finally snapped his spinal cord.

Jarle fell to forward, all life drained from his body.

It was finally over. His hex lifted and Miranda was safe. He thought of the many other slaves Jarle had owned. They were now all free souls, too. The world was already a better place.

A warm breeze blew across the grass.

The field vanished, replaced by the empty office. Callen looked down at his wound. No wolf could survive that much blood loss, but at least he would go to his grave knowing Miranda was safe. He had saved his mate, and for that he was grateful.

Metal slamming against wood echoed through the room.

"For the love of Thor, Highlander. What have ye done to yourself?" Vidar ran to his side.

Callen shifted form. "It's over, friend."

"Like hell it is. I will not be known for letting a Highland wolf die on my watch. And I certainly will not let you go to Valhalla while I am left on this earth. You will tell bad tales of me there."

He gave up a laugh, but it hurt like hell. "Take care of Miranda."

"I will not take an American wolf as a ward." He slapped a handful of something moist on Callen's side.

Heat flared against his skin. "What in heaven's name did you put on me?"

"A salve. Compliments of your woman."

The pain subsided. "Bury me at Wolfsden."

"If I bring your corpse back to your father's land, he will kill me. Now get on your feet."

He tried to push himself up, but it was no use. He hadn't the energy. "I canna move."

"Then I guess I will have to carry you. But not without your skirt."

Vidar produced a kilt and covered him. "Now we can go to Wolfsden."

He was going home to his mate. To his pack. Callen's destiny was now free for him to one day fulfill. Life as wolf could not be any better.

EPILOGUE

He'd spent two weeks in bed. And couldn't take another minute of not doing a damn thing.

Miranda walked into the room and reached for the pillow behind his head.

"Hey, I was comfortable with that one."

She fluffed it and then put it back. "Your father will be here in a few hours."

He was not looking forward to telling his Alpha what went down with Jarle. "He is not going to be pleased that I let that Viking witch on his land."

"You can blame me. After all, it was my locket that allowed Jarle access to Wolfsden."

She joined him on the bed.

He pulled her down next to him and nipped at her ear.

"I don't think you've healed enough for sex yet," she said.

"It's been two weeks, wumman. I don't even have a scar anymore." He reached for Miranda's skimpy nightshirt and had it off her in seconds.

"That salve was never tested before I used it on you. I won't take any chances with it not having healed you completely."

He flipped her onto her back and settled between her thighs. "Trust me. If we don't do this now, we won't get the chance to do it in peace for a while. The pack travels with my father and they lodge at Wolfsden. Privacy will be non-existent once they get here. Which means this place is going to become something akin to a fraternity house in a few hours."

"I can't believe it will be that bad. You're exaggerating."

The poor wumman hadn't a clue what was to come. But for now he could make her feel pretty damn good. Callen leaned forward and ran his tongue along Miranda's neck.

His hands cupped her breasts. The sight of her rosy, pink nipples protruding from the peak of her creamy globes, made him hard.

Miranda's red hair spilled over the pillows. He loved seeing her in his bed, comfortable with him.

Dipping his head, he took one swollen bud into his mouth and sucked. Hard.

She moaned. "Whatever you do, don't stop that."

He nipped at her nipple.

"Oh...Callen..."

With his free hand, he trailed his fingers down her side, over her thigh and up to her clit. The musky scent of her arousal forced a growl from his throat.

~~oOo~~

Nothing felt as good as the weight of Callen's body on top of hers. Gliding her hands down her mate's back, she settled her fingers on his firm backside and pulled him closer to her.

He obliged by sliding his cock into her slit.

The thick girth of him stretched her, filled her to the core. She couldn't imagine life without Callen MacHendrie at her side.

She loved her wolf.

"*Marry me, Miranda.*"

"*If you think you're going to get away with not going down on one knee, you are sorely mistaken.*"

"*But I'm asking in a velvet-draped, four-poster medieval bed.*"

"I should have never told you about my bed fantasy."

He pulled his mouth from her nipple, stretching the taut bud before releasing it. "I promise to get down on one knee as soon as I can. But in the meantime, are you really going to keep me waiting for your answer?"

She bucked her hips against his.

"Don't do that, wumman."

"Don't talk, Highlander."

He groaned.

She gyrated a second time, loving the feel of him inside her.

Callen got the message and thrust forward. He drove himself deep, filled her to the point where she didn't think she could take more.

As he pulled out and then repeated the thrust, a glorious spasm rocked Miranda's body.

Life with her wolf was good.

~~o0o~~

About this Series

The Shifters of Dundaire Series is about a family of hot, sexy Scottish and Viking wolf shifters who are on the prowl searching for their eternal mates. These guys love hard and they love forever.

DARK WOLF

VIKING WOLF

HIGHLAND WOLF

BLOOD WOLF

National bestselling author Angelique Armae / J. C. Makk is a native New Yorker who loves all things royal, can trace her Irish roots back to the Scottish Highlands, is half Italian, and is owned by a long-haired Tuxedo feline. She spends most days writing, unless her cat deems otherwise. Miss Armae is represented by Holly Root of the Waxman Leavell Literary Agency.

Newsletter: **http://eepurl.com/bSGTPD**

Twitter: **https://twitter.com/AArmae**

Facebook**: https://www.facebook.com/AngeliqueArmaeFans**

Website: **http://www.angeliquearmae.com**

Thanks for reading Summer Heat – Love on Fire

Contact information for each of the individual authors is at the end of her story.

Please visit her sites or check out her other stories at your favorite book buying source.

And the best thank you an author can get is an honest review. Those glittering stars and words of praise (and even criticism) are fuel to our writing fire.

Dani Haviland, author and publisher

www.ingramcontent.com/pod-product-compliance
Lightning Source LLC
Chambersburg PA
CBHW081137020726
47504CB00009B/1898